COST ACCOUNTING

COST ACCOUNTING

Third Edition

Edward B. Deakin
The University of Texas at Austin

Michael W. Maher
The University of California at Davis

IRWIN

Homewood, IL 60430
Boston, MA 02116

The diagram on the cover is a symbolic representation of the three major parts of cost accounting covered in this book.

The computer terminal symbolizes *cost accounting systems,* which are discussed in Chapters 3–9.

The decision symbol denotes *differential costs for decision making,* which is covered in Chapters 10–16.

The performance chart symbolizes *cost data for performance evaluation,* which is covered in Chapters 17–23.

Material from the Uniform CPA Examination Questions and Unofficial Answers, copyright © 1972, 1974, 1975, 1976, 1977, 1978, 1979, 1981, 1985, and 1987 by the American Institute of Certified Public Accountants, Inc., is reprinted (or adapted) with permission.

Material from the Certificate in Management Accounting Examinations, copyright © 1978, 1979, 1980, 1981, 1982, 1983, 1985, 1986, and 1987 by the National Association of Accountants, is reprinted and/or adapted with permission.

Sponsoring editor: Ron M. Regis
Developmental editor: Cheryl D. Wilson
Project editor: Waivah Clement
Production manager: Ann Cassady
Designer: Maureen McCutcheon
Cover Illustrator: Valerie Sinclair
Artist: Benoit Design
Compositor: Better Graphics, Inc.
Typeface: 10/12 Times Roman
Printer: Von Hoffmann Press, Inc.

Library of Congress Cataloging-in-Publication Data

Deakin, Edward B.
    Cost accounting / Edward B. Deakin, Michael W. Maher.—3rd ed.
        p.   cm.
    Includes bibliographical references (p.   ) and index.
    ISBN 0-256-06919-0
    1. Cost accounting.   I. Maher, Michael, date.   II. Title.
HF5686.C8D24   1991
657'.42—dc20   90–4645

Printed in the United States of America
1 2 3 4 5 6 7 8 9 0 VH 7 6 5 4 3 2 1 0

PREFACE

OUR PHILOSOPHY

We continue to see dramatic changes in accounting. For example, international competition makes it imperative that production systems be efficient, and cost accounting is key to this effort. Automated production methods in both service and manufacturing industries have made labor-intensive applications of cost accounting obsolete in many cases. Airlines, banks, and government agencies, among others, have developed a new interest in cost accounting. For students to understand fundamental cost accounting concepts, we believe it is important for them to see how those concepts are applied in practice and to see them adapted to nonmanufacturing operations and new production technologies.

For example, the chapters on cost systems discuss the use of costs for computing inventory values and cost of goods sold on financial statements, but they also apply these ideas to product costing for managerial purposes in service and merchandising companies. The job costing chapter includes a section on job costing in service organizations. The cost allocation chapters demonstrate potential product cost distortions if costs in automated plants are assigned to products using traditional labor-based application methods. The chapter on inventory management includes an expanded discussion of just-in-time production and inventory systems.

The use of computer-based models has increased the importance of avoiding "garbage-in, garbage-out" when using cost data in companies. The emphasis in this book is on the accountant's role in providing data and interpreting output from the models. For example, the discussion of linear programming in Chapter 13 shows how accounting data are used in formulating the problem, and it shows the student how to interpret the output. Further, it shows how the results of product choice decisions can be affected by misapplication of full-absorption cost data in the multiple-product model.

Developments in such related disciplines as economics, behavioral sciences, statistics, and operations research have also had a major impact on cost accounting. These disciplines regard cost data as given and focus on the concepts and methods of their respective disciplines. Cost accounting is the "mirror image." We do not "rehash" the material in these other fields but focus on the *use* of cost data in decision models. We emphasize *accounting* issues and the *comparative advantage of accountants* on the management team.

THIS BOOK'S UNIQUE FEATURES

Real World Applications

We have short inserts, titled "Real World Application," in most chapters, which describe real cost accounting applications. For example, Chapter 7 has a real world application that describes how job costing helped an advertising agency improve planning and decision making. We have included examples from 3M, Hewlett-Packard, American National Bank, a hospital, the Wayne Gretzky trade from the Edmonton Oilers to the Los Angeles Kings, oil production from Alaska, and many others.

We have also integrated numerous real world examples throughout the text and in problem materials to demonstrate particular concepts. For example, to help explain why companies allocate costs, we indicate why K mart allocates corporate headquarters' costs to stores.

Cost Accounting in the New Manufacturing Environment

We have integrated the role of cost accounting in the new manufacturing environment throughout the text because these issues apply to many cost accounting topics. We believe these issues are too important and pervasive to place in a "special topics" chapter. We introduce the reader to cost accounting in a high-tech environment in Chapter 1. Chapter 2 shows how cost drivers are developed to derive product costs using *activity-based costing*. By developing activity-based costing this early, and by applying it to an interesting example, we enable instructors to refer to this new topic and apply it at any time during the course. Developing the concept this early also emphasizes its importance.

Chapters 4 through 8 present cost allocation and product costing using the two-stage allocation model as a conceptual framework. Chapter 4 discusses numerous issues and problems in cost allocation, including problems with labor-based allocation bases and incentive problems with cost-plus contracts. Chapter 4 identifies the cost of complexity as a particular problem in the new manufacturing environment and discusses ways to identify cost drivers to measure complexity effects.

Chapter 14 features just-in-time inventory. Chapter 20 shows how to account for standard costs in a "demand-pull" environment. The real world applications in Chapters 15 and 22 discuss problems in providing incentives to invest in innovative production methods.

These new topics are presented so students learn concepts, not technical details or jargon.

Overview of Production Methods

Many cost accounting students are not familiar with production methods. We believe it is important that students understand how products flow through various stages of "work in process," arrive at finished goods, and are shipped to customers to understand how to accumulate and allocate costs for these production stages. Consequently, we describe the process of producing stone-washed jeans (adapted from a real company) and tie it to our discussion of cost accumulation in Chapter 3. Chapter 7 introduces job costing by showing how alternative costing systems are used in alternative production environments (for example, job shops, repetitive manufacturing, continuous flow processing).

Logical Organization of Text, with Flexibility

The chapters in this book are grouped into cost accounting's three major topic areas: cost accounting systems, differential costing for decision making, and costing for planning and performance evaluation. This enables instructors to assign chapters in a logical order, and it addresses negative reactions from students who are adverse to skipping around the text.

It is also important that a text provides instructors flexibility in assigning topics to fit their preferences or the needs of their curricula. We have done this by making all chapters self-contained, so that chapters can be rearranged as needed. This preface has a section called "Organization and Use of the Book" that describes how the book may be used. The *Instructor's Lecture Guide* that accompanies this book provides detailed alternative course outlines.

Service Sector Applications

The service sector not only increases in importance, but increasing competition in airlines, banking, and health care, among others, have also made service organizations more concerned about product costing and cost control.

We have integrated applications to the service sector throughout this book. For example, Chapter 3 contains a section on cost accumulation in service organizations, Chapter 7 discusses job costing in service organizations, Chapter 9 applies variable costing to airlines, Chapter 15 discusses capital budgeting in service organizations with particular emphasis on not-for-profit organizations, Chapter 17 discusses budgeting in service (and not-for-profit) organizations, and many other chapters apply cost concepts to service organizations. Many real world applications apply cost accounting methods to service organizations, as do numerous end-of-chapter exercises and problems.

We believe this book has integrated more applications to service organizations than any other cost accounting text.

Variety of End-of-Chapter Materials, Including Spreadsheet Problems

We have included a variety of end-of-chapter materials so this book can be used in a variety of courses and by students with different backgrounds, interests, and skills. Each chapter contains self-study problems with detailed solutions, short questions designed to help discuss concepts and issues, short numerical exercises to demonstrate the chapter's key points, longer problems that integrate concepts from the chapter, and longer integrative cases that integrate material from several parts of the book.

Exercises are particularly appropriate for undergraduates who have little or no background in managerial accounting. Longer problems and integrative cases are better for more advanced undergraduate and graduate students. In response to reviewers and users of previous editions, we have modified and edited many of the longer problems to make them shorter and more straightforward.

This edition also has 70 exercises and problems designed for spreadsheet solution on a new software package which is available free to adopters.

Exercises Tied to Learning Objectives

Each chapter has two to five learning objectives, one for each of the major chapter points. There are several exercises keyed to each learning objective, so instructors can easily assign exercises to cover all key points, or they can emphasize particular points. This also makes it easier to assign alternative exercises to cover the same key point in different course offerings.

Readable Writing Style

Previous users and reviewers have told us that students find this text readable and understandable. This is important. We believe this edition is even more readable because we have thoroughly reviewed and revised each part of each chapter to make this a better book. We have selected more interesting examples in the chapters to keep students interested in the material. For example, to demonstrate cost accumulation in Chapter 3 we describe how costs are accumulated in making stone-washed blue jeans. We have revised many of the exercises and problems to use more interesting goods, services, and company names.

Definitions of Key Concepts in Margins

Key concepts are defined both in the text and in chapter margins. This enables students to easily identify and review key concepts. The book also has a complete glossary.

Ethical Issues in Cost Accounting

There is increasing concern that students be equipped to deal with ethical issues in their careers. Chapter 1 includes a section on ethics, and there are two ethics-related appendixes at the end of the book. Appendix A features the creed of Johnson & Johnson, and Appendix B contains the AICPA Code of Professional Conduct.

Outstanding Supplements

This text is part of a complete learning package that includes the best supplementary material available for cost accounting textbooks. For example, in addition to the *Solutions Manual*, the package contains an *Instructor's Lecture Guide* with more than 200 pages of lecture transparency masters, examples to use in the classroom, alternative problem assignments, ideas for assignments, self-tests with solutions, and many other features. This lecture guide is an excellent resource for anyone teaching cost accounting and is certain to enhance the classroom experience. We are grateful to Mark Nigrini for his creative work and effort to make this resource available to cost accounting instructors.

The *Test Bank* now contains more than 1,900 test items, including short problem, true-false, and multiple-choice items. Robert Gruber (University of Wisconsin—Whitewater) and Mark Nigrini (University of Cincinnati) have thoroughly reviewed and significantly revised this test bank.

The *Study Guide* helps students become more self-sufficient in learning cost accounting. We have received considerable positive feedback that the *Study Guide* achieves this objective. Students who find accounting difficult have found this study guide particularly helpful.

Other supplements include a new computer software package (free to adopters), check figures, and transparencies for all exercises, problems, and cases.

NEW IN THIS EDITION

▼ More coverage of contemporary topics in cost accounting.
▼ New section on activity-based costing and cost drivers in Chapter 2.
▼ Expanded discussion of just-in-time inventory in Chapter 14.
▼ New section on finding cost drivers for the cost of complexity in high-tech companies in Chapter 4.
▼ More real world applications of cost accounting practices, including many nonmanufacturing examples. (For example, United Bank and the Gretzky trade from Edmonton Oilers to Los Angeles.)

▼ Revised order of product costing chapters so the three cost allocations chapters are grouped together and now precede the job and process costing chapters.

▼ More adaptations of cost accounting to "high-tech" production methods, particularly in Chapters 1, 2, 4, 14, and 20.

▼ Expanded number of learning objectives. Exercises are now keyed to each chapter's learning objectives.

▼ Definitions of key concepts in the margins.

▼ More variety in assignment material, ranging from questions, to basic exercises, to problems, to integrative cases.

▼ More emphasis on basic concepts in exercises.

▼ More mid-level problems.

▼ Expanded test bank with more than 1900 test items.

▼ Expanded instructor's lecture guide with cross-references between the second and third editions for exercises, problems, and cases categorized according to level of difficulty; self-tests with solutions; alternative problem assignments; lecture notes, including additional classroom discussion points and problems; and 219 transparency masters.

▼ New computer software package with LOTUS 1-2-3 diskette featuring 70 selected exercises and problems is free to adopters.

ORGANIZATION AND USE OF THE BOOK

Cost accounting covers three major topic areas: cost accounting systems (e.g., process costing, job costing), costing for nonroutine decision making (e.g., multiple product decisions, capital investment decisions), and the use of cost data in planning and performance evaluation (e.g., budgeting, variance analysis). The chapters in this book are grouped into these three major topic modules as follows:

Part One of the text, Chapters 3 to 9, contains a comprehensive discussion of *cost accounting systems,* including the flow of costs, job and process costing, cost allocation, and variable product costing.

Part Two of the text, Chapters 10 to 16, addresses the use of *differential costs for decision making.* Here the focus is on the role of the accountant as a supplier of cost data for use in making decisions. This part includes cost estimation, cost-volume-profit analysis, differential costing for short- and long-run decisions, and capital investment analysis. This approach shows why differential cost concepts are important, how to identify costs that are differential, and how to use those differential costs in decisions.

Part Three, Chapters 17 to 23, addresses the use of *cost data for performance evaluation and control.* In this section, the budget as the operating plan is presented. We also analyze budget versus actual results, flexible budgets, variance analysis, and standard costs. Performance evaluation in decentralized organizations is also discussed in this part of the text.

Chapters 1 and 2 introduce the book and provide the background needed to proceed to *any* part of the book. Chapters 24 to 26, **Part Four,** deal with cost issues under conditions of uncertainty.

An advantage of grouping topics into these categories is that it overcomes students' negative reactions to the lack of cohesion if similar topics are scattered throughout the book. It also allows instructors to cover topics in a logical sequence without skipping around the book.

At the same time, it is important that instructors have the flexibility to adapt the text to their particular curriculum, students, and personal preferences. We have built flexibility into this text in two ways. First, some instructors prefer to cover major topic areas in a different sequence than presented in this book. For example, some instructors prefer to cover decision-making topics or planning and control topics before covering cost accounting systems. This book is designed so that any major part, or "module," can be covered after Chapter 2, which presents all of the background concepts necessary for continuing to any of the three major topic modules. Adopters have used the book in class with each of the following sequences of the three major modules:

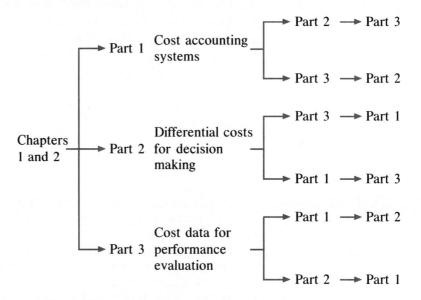

Second, chapter is self-contained. Therefore, instructors can skip chapters or rearrange the sequence of chapters. Adopters of the first two editions were able to skip chapters or change the sequence as appropriate. We have put special emphasis on making this easier in the present edition. End-of-chapter materials that cover topics from more than one chapter (e.g., integrative cases) are clearly labeled to facilitate flexibility.

COMPLETE LEARNING PACKAGE

The text and related materials are integrated into a complete, accurate, and clear learning package. The total learning package contains numerous items to help the student and instructor.

1. The text uses examples and illustrations to make the concepts understandable. Each chapter has learning objectives, a summary of important concepts, key terms, and extensive end-of-chapter materials. Several chapters have appendexes to facilitate flexibility in covering topics in more detail or at a more advanced level. The glossary at the end of the book has definitions for all key terms and concepts.

2. The *Solutions Manual* presents solutions in large, easy-to-read type to facilitate the creation of quality overhead transparencies for classroom use.

3. The *Instructor's Lecture Guide*, prepared by Mark Nigrini (University of Cincinnati), provides extensive materials for the instructor, including the following:
   a. Sample course outlines.
   b. Assignment charts showing topic coverage and degree of difficulty for exercises and problems.
   c. Chapter-by-chapter discussions of chapter objectives, overview, and topic outlines.
   d. Lecture transparency masters, 219 in all, for each chapter with detailed lecture notes.
   e. Self-tests with solutions.

4. The *Test Bank* has more than 1,900 true-false, multiple-choice, and short problem items with detailed solutions. Prepared by Robert Gruber (University of Wisconsin—Whitewater) and Mark Nigrini (University of Cincinnati).

5. *CompuTest 3* is an advanced-featured test generator that allows the instructor to add and edit questions, save and reload tests, create up to 99 different versions of each test, attach graphics to questions, import and export ASCII files, and select questions based on type, level of difficulty, or keyword. The program allows password protection of saved tests and question databases and is networkable.

6. The *Study Guide* is designed to help students learn the material in the text. Each chapter contains:
   a. Chapter overview and outline to review major points in the chapter. The outline encourages students to ''get back into the text'' with frequent references to illustrations and examples.
   b. A set of questions that matches key terms and concepts with definitions and tests student's basic knowledge of the concepts discussed in the chapter.
   c. Numerical exercises and problems with fully worked out solutions. These help the student see how to work exercises and problems in the text.

7. *Solution Transparencies* for all exercises, problems, and cases.

8. *Computer-assisted student learning.* For the third edition, software has been developed which contains 70 selected exercises and problems from the text prepared by Minta Berry (Berry Publication Services). These problems and exercises are identified in the text by a spreadsheet symbol.

9. A *Check list of key figures* is available free in quantity to adopting instructors.

END-OF-CHAPTER MATERIALS

Cost accounting is best learned by applying the concepts and methods to exercises, problems, and cases. The end-of-chapter material in this book is extensive, covering various levels of difficulty. It is organized into five parts.

1. *Self-study problems.* There are two or three self-study problems, with fully worked out solutions, that test students' understanding of the material in the chapter.

2. *Questions*. Questions review the major concepts and issues in the chapter.

3. *Exercises*. Each exercise deals with a single concept in the chapter. They are in sequential order to show how topics build on each other. Exercises give students an opportunity to get feedback on points developed in the chapter, and they are helpful during classroom demonstration.

4. *Problems*. Problems are more challenging than exercises, are longer, and integrate more than one concept from the chapter. For example, exercises in the process costing chapter (Chapter 8) ask the student to compute specific parts of a production cost report, such as equivalent units, whereas problems ask the student to prepare and use the entire report. There is a variety of types of problems. Some problems are comprehensive but straightforward applications of several concepts in the chapter; others are challenging problems that ask students to find missing data or solve for unknowns. (The *Instructor's Lecture Guide* categorizes problems according to their level of difficulty.)

5. *Integrative cases*. The cases integrate material from several parts of the book, are usually longer than problems, and often require some tolerance for multiple solutions and interpretations. These cases are usually based on factual situations in real organizations.

The variety and quantity of end-of-chapter materials allow the book to be used in various levels of courses. If students are undergraduates with little or no background in managerial accounting, instructors can rely more on the exercises than they will in the advanced and graduate classes. The integrative cases, on the other hand, are particularly useful for classroom discussion in advanced and graduate classes. Instructors have informed us that this useful feature enables them to use this text across a variety of courses ranging from basic introductory courses to the master's level.

STUDENT BACKGROUND

This book is intended to be used in a cost or managerial accounting course in which students have had a course in accounting principles or financial accounting. This prerequisite assures that students understand basic accounting terminology and the financial reporting system. *It is not necessary that students have a previous course in managerial or cost accounting.*

Users of the book should have a knowledge of elementary algebra. Although previous coursework in statistics, operations research, computer sciences, and other similar disciplines is not required, such work can enrich the student's experience with this book.

There is ample material in the text to challenge students who have had a previous course in managerial accounting. The material in chapter appendixes, the longer problems and integrative cases, and the last three chapters in the book are designed to challenge students who have had at least one course in managerial accounting.

This book can be used in either undergraduate or graduate courses. Most instructors emphasize exercises and short problems in basic undergraduate cost courses; longer problems and cases are more widely used in MBA programs.

ACKNOWLEDGMENTS We are indebted to many people for their assistance and ideas. Robert N. Anthony was instrumental in developing this book. He provided helpful guidance and support on each of several drafts. He and Professor James S. Reece graciously permitted us to use several of their cases copyrighted by Osceola Institute.

We wish to thank the following reviewers for their valuable comments and insightful recommendations. They have made a tremendous contribution to the third edition.

Donald R. Simons
University of Wisconsin—Oshkosh

Frances McNair
Mississippi State University

Patrick McKenzie
Arizona State University

Melkote Shivaswamy
Ball State University

Kenneth Sinclair
Lehigh University

Lynn Rans
California State University—Los Angeles

Arnold Schneider
Georgia Institute of Technology

Richard J. Murdock
Ohio State University

Leo Ruggle
Mankato State University

Thomas Hrubec
Northern Illinois University

James Emig
Villanova University

Kenneth Danko
San Francisco State University

Jacob Wambsganss
Emporia State University

Ted Compton
Ohio University

Robert A. Gruber
University of Wisconsin—Whitewater

Harold B. Cook
Central Michigan University

Special thanks goes to Mark Nigrini for his excellent suggestions. He has prepared an outstanding *Instructor's Lecture Guide* to accompany the text.

We are grateful to numerous colleagues for their comments and reviews of this and earlier editions.

Rich Antle
Yale University

David Brecht
California State University—Sacramento

Wayne Bremser
Villanova University

Ray Brown
California State University—Sacramento

Stephen Butler
University of Oklahoma

Robert Colson
Case-Western Reserve University

Eugene Comiskey
Georgia Tech University

Frank Daroca
Loyola Marymount University

Andrew DeMotses
Fairfield University

M. Laurentius Marais
University of Chicago

Joseph Razek
University of New Orleans

Alfred Nanni
Boston University

Harry Newman
University of Illinois—Chicago

C. Douglas Poe
University of Kentucky

Kasi Ramanathan
University of Washington

James Reece
University of Michigan

Avi Rushinek
University of Miami

Carl S. Smith
West Chester State College

Thomas Stober
Indiana University

Joel Demski
Yale University

Ron Dye
Northwestern University

John Fellingham
Yale University

James M. Fremgen
Naval Postgraduate School

Robert Kaplan
Harvard University

Lawrence Klein
Bentley University

Eugene Laughlin
Kansas State University

James Mackey
California State University—
Sacramento

Curtis Stanley
California State University—
Sacramento

Peter Tiessen
University of Alberta

John Tracy
University of Colorado

Neil Wilner
University of North Texas

Harry Wolk
Drake University

Rick Young
Ohio State University

Numerous students and associates have read the manuscript, worked problems, checked solutions, and otherwise helped us to write a teachable, error-free manuscript. We are grateful to Steven Elconin, Malcolm MacDonald, Steve McBrearty, Patricia Kardash, David Mest, Vanessa Smith, Karen Sorenson, Betsy Maclean, Martin Chew, Tom Terpstra, Dorothy Brady, and particularly Elliot Maltz and Shawn Elias, and numerous students who class tested this material. We acknowledge the helpful feedback from users of the previous editions.

We wish to express our appreciation to the many people and organizations who allowed us to use their problems and cases. These include the Certificate in Management Accounting Examinations by the Institute of Management Accounting of the National Association of Accountants; the Uniform CPA Examinations by the American Institute of Certified Public Accountants; the President and Fellows of Harvard College; the Osceola Institute; Professor David Solomons; and l'Institut pour l'Etute des Methodes de Direction de l'Entreprise (IMEDE).

We are grateful to all the people at Irwin for their outstanding support. In particular we thank Ron Regis, sponsoring editor; Cheryl Wilson, development editor; Elizabeth Storey, marketing manager; Waivah Clement, project editor; Maureen McCutcheon, designer; and Ann Cassady, production manager.

We extend special thanks to our families and colleagues who have supported us in this endeavor.

Ideas from users for text revision and problem materials have been particularly helpful in making this the best possible textbook for teaching cost accounting. We welcome ideas from the people who face the day-to-day challenge of teaching, and we look forward to receiving more.

Edward B. Deakin

Michael W. Maher

CONTENTS IN BRIEF

CONTENTS

PART 1

COST ACCOUNTING: AN OVERVIEW

OUTLINE

COST ACCOUNTING: ITS NATURE AND USEFULNESS

LEARNING OBJECTIVES

1. To see how accounting is used to help manage organizations.
2. To understand the place of accountants in organizational structures.

This book deals with the use of accounting to help people manage organizations. In recent years, we have seen a dramatic increase in managerial interest in cost accounting because more and more managers are concerned about their costs of doing business. Meanwhile, cost accounting systems are undergoing major change because people are becoming increasingly sophisticated in using computers.

Cost accounting is especially important to organizations facing increases in competition. We find increasing competition in most industries such as:

Airlines, utilities: Facing a less regulated environment, these industries are focusing on ways to better estimate costs and to increase profits from the services they offer.

Hospitals, defense contractors: Operating in a new environment where their major customers are interested in changing from cost-plus to competitive bids, these companies are interested in better cost data to squeeze maximum outputs and profits from a contract.

Automobiles, electronics: These industries used to be dominated by U.S. manufacturers. They did not focus on costs because they were operating in an environment of high profit margins. Because of increased pressures from foreign manufacturers, profit margins have been reduced, and better information on how to control costs and to deliver competitively priced quality products is crucial to survival.

For example, during a recent visit to a leading electronics company, the authors were told by management, "In the early 1980s we sold a particular calculator for $120 each. We knew each cost somewhere between $15 and $50 to make, but we didn't care about more precise estimates because costs did not affect our decisions. Because of increased competition, the price of the calculator has dropped to $35. Now our cost estimates must be more precise; otherwise, we won't know whether it is profitable to produce these calculators."

The increased competition has made better estimates of cost crucial to the decision-making process. Management now needs to know which products are profitable and where costs should be controlled.

WHAT IS COST ACCOUNTING?

Cost Accounting The field of accounting that records, measures, and reports information about costs.

Cost A sacrifice of resources.

This chapter presents an overview of cost accounting and previews the rest of the book. We examine the nature of cost accounting, who uses it, why they use it, and how recent changes in industry affect cost accounting. We also discuss how cost accounting relates to other fields such as financial accounting and economics.

Cost accounting is the field of accounting that measures, records, and reports information about costs. A cost is a sacrifice of resources. Costs are represented in the accounting systems by outlays of cash, promises to pay cash in the future, and the expiration of the value of an asset. These include the cost of inventory, the costs of increasing sales volume, and the costs saved from energy-efficient equipment.

We deal with the primary uses of cost information: decision making and performance evaluation, as shown in Illustration 1–1. These functions are

Illustration 1-1   **Relationship of Cost Accounting Systems to Uses of Cost Information**

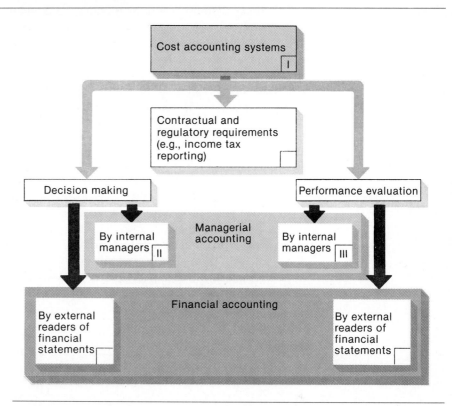

Note: I, II, and III refer to parts of the book in which each topic is discussed.

sometimes referred to as planning and control, respectively. Notice that the cost accounting system provides data for both managerial and financial accounting.

When costs are used inside the organization by managers to evaluate the performance of operations or personnel, or as a basis for decision making, we say the costs are used for **managerial accounting** purposes. When costs are used by outsiders, such as shareholders or creditors, to evaluate the performance of top management and make decisions about the organization, we say costs are used for **financial accounting** purposes. Further, cost accounting systems provide data for cost-based contracts, such as those used by many contractors to the federal government, and for tax purposes. In short, cost accounting systems provide data for many important purposes.

This book focuses on cost accounting systems and on managerial uses of cost data for decision making and performance evaluation. That is, we explain the accounting data used to fulfill the roles identified as boxes I, II, and III as shown in Illustration 1-1.

Managerial Accounting The preparation of cost and related data for managers to use in performance evaluation or decision making.

Financial Accounting The preparation of financial statements and data for outsiders.

COST DATA FOR MANAGERIAL PURPOSES

Managers must often choose between two or more alternatives. Their decision is usually based on each action's financial consequences. Choosing among alternative actions is an important management activity in all organizations—large and small; profit making and nonprofit; traditional and high tech; manufacturing, merchandising, and service. Their calculations range from simple "back-of-the-envelope" figuring to complex computer simulation; but regardless of the complexity, calculating the financial consequences of alternative actions is an important part of managing every organization. Managers also use cost data to help evaluate performance and control operations. Because these activities are so important for the success of a venture, it is important to understand how costs can be used (and misused).

Costs for Decision Making

One of the most difficult tasks in calculating such financial consequences is to estimate how costs (or revenues or assets) will *differ* among the alternatives. For example, suppose the management of a department store is considering expanding its operations and store size to include several new product lines. As an alternative, the store could open a new outlet in a different location. The key is to determine which would be most profitable: remain the same size, expand operations in the current location, or open a

---

REAL WORLD APPLICATION

Note to readers: We have included "real world applications" of cost accounting in this and many later chapters. Our purpose is to describe some of the many cost accounting issues that occur in the real world. These brief applications are based on articles by practitioners who describe their experiences, or on research into real world problems by academics. We hope you will find these applications enjoyable and informative.

A classic example of the problems that arise from failure to monitor costs properly is the case of Bethlehem Steel Corp. The company operated in a market characterized by government import restrictions and few domestic producers. The net effect was limited competition and an environment where prices could be set to cover any cost structure. Like other domestic steelmakers, Bethlehem failed to invest in more efficient basic oxygen furnaces because to do so would increase initial cash outlays even though long-

run costs would be reduced. As a result, Bethlehem lost its ability to produce steel at as low a cost as foreign producers. Export markets for U.S. steel dried up. Imports rose as fast as possible under control regulations. Moreover, because Bethlehem and other U.S. steel producers charged excessive prices to compensate for their excessive costs, substitute materials like fiberglass, prestressed concrete, aluminum, and plastics took over a substantial portion of the market for steel products.

The U.S. steel industry declined from near total domination of world steel markets in the 1950s to being a marginally profitable minor presence in world steel by 1990. Steel was not the first nor will it probably be the last industry to ignore costs at its own peril. With increased world competition, the steel industry has begun to pay closer attention to costs. Whether the industry can stage a comeback is an open question.*

* For a comprehensive discussion of the causes of the decline in U.S. competitiveness and the recent steps taken to restore U.S. industry, see H. Segal, *Corporate Makeover: The Reshaping of the American Economy* (New York: Viking Press, 1989).

Differential Costs Costs that change in response to a particular course of action.

new outlet. Using cost accounting techniques, the store can estimate **differential costs,** that is, how costs will differ for each alternative.

For example, suppose Jennifer's Sandwiche Shoppe has been open for lunch only, Monday through Friday, from 11 A.M. to 2 P.M. The owner-manager, Jennifer, is considering expanding her hours by opening Monday through Friday evenings from 5 P.M. to 8 P.M. Jennifer figures her revenues, food costs, labor, and utilities would increase 50 percent, rent will remain the same, and other costs will increase by 25 percent if she opens in the evening. Jennifer's present and estimated future costs, revenues, and profits are shown in columns 1 and 2 of Illustration 1–2. The differential costs, revenues, and profits, shown in column 3, are the differences between the amounts in columns 1 and 2.

The analysis shows an increase in operating profits of $145 if the shop is opened in the evening. All other things being equal, Jennifer would therefore probably expand her hours. Note that only differential costs and revenues figure in the decision. For example, rent does not change, so it is irrelevant to the decision.

Costs for Planning and Performance Evaluation

Responsibility Center A specific unit of an organization assigned to a manager who is held accountable for its operations and resources.

An organization usually divides reponsibility for specific functions among its employees. A maintenance group, for example, is responsible for maintaining a particular area of an office building, a Kmart store manager is responsible for most operations of a particular store, while the president of a company is responsible for the entire company. A **responsibility center** is a specific unit of an organization assigned to a manager who is held accountable for its operations and resources.

Consider the case of Jennifer's Sandwiche Shoppe. When Jennifer first opened her shop, she managed the entire operation herself. As the enterprise became more successful, she added a catering service. She then hired two

Illustration 1–2   **Differential Costs, Revenues, and Profits for One Week**

JENNIFER'S SANDWICHE SHOPPE
Projected Income Statements
For One Week

	(1) Status Quo Open 11 A.M.–2 P.M.	(2) Alternative Open 11 A.M.–2 P.M. and 5 P.M.–8 P.M.	(3) Difference (2) − (1)
Sales revenue	$1,100	$1,650[a]	$550
Costs:			
Food	500	750[a]	250
Labor	200	300[a]	100
Utilities	80	120[a]	40
Rent	250	250	—
Other	60	75[b]	15
Total costs	$1,090	$1,495	$405
Operating profits	$ 10	$ 155	$145

[a] Fifty percent higher than status quo.

[b] Twenty-five percent higher than status quo.

managers: Sam to manage the shop and Carol to manage the catering service. Jennifer, as general manager, oversaw the entire operation.

Each manager is responsible for the revenues and costs of his or her department. Jennifer's salary, rent, utilities, and other costs are shared by both departments. Jennifer is directly responsible for these shared costs; the department managers are not.

Jennifer's organization has three responsibility centers as follows:

Responsibility Center	Manager Responsible	Responsible for
Entire organization	Jennifer, general manager	All of the organization's operations and resources, revenues, and costs
Sandwich Department	Sam, manager	Sandwich Department operations and resources (see Illustration 1–3 for revenues and costs)
Catering	Carol, manager	Catering operations and resources (see Illustration 1–3 for revenues and costs)

Departmental income statements are shown in Illustration 1–3. Note that some costs—utilities, rent, other, and general manager's salary—are not considered departmental costs.

Budgeting

Managers in all organizations set financial goals for return on investment, cash balances, costs, earnings, and other performance indicators. Each responsibility center usually has a **budget** which is a financial plan of the resources needed to carry out the center's tasks and meet financial goals. Estimates, as stated in budgets, help managers to decide if their goals can be achieved and, if not, what modifications will be necessary.

At regular intervals of time, resources actually used are compared with the amount budgeted to assess the center's and the manager's performance. By comparing actual results with the budget plans, it is possible to identify the probable causes of variances from planned costs, profits, cash flows, and other financial targets. Managers can then take action to change their activities or revise their goals and plans. This process of planning and performance evaluation for responsibility centers is sometimes called *responsibility accounting*.

As part of the planning and control process, managers prepare budgets which contain expectations about revenues and costs for the coming period. At the end of the period, actual results are compared with the budget to see what, if any, changes can be made for improving operations in the future. Illustration 1–4 illustrates the type of statement that might be used to compare actual results with the planning budget for Jennifer's Sandwich Department.

By analyzing the figures in Illustration 1–4, Sam, the department manager, can immediately see which, if any, costs need to be controlled and how the budget may need to be revised to assist in planning for future months.

For instance, Sam observes that the Sandwich Department sold 4,100 sandwiches as budgeted, but actual costs were higher than budgeted. Costs that appear to need follow-up are the cost of fish and meat and the cost of counter labor. Should Sam inquire whether there was waste in using fish or

Budget A financial plan of resources needed to carry out tasks and meet financial goals.

Illustration 1-3   **Responsibility Centers, Departmental Costs, and Revenues**

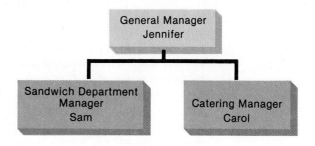

JENNIFER'S, INC.
Income Statement
Month Ending October 31

	Sandwich Department	Catering	Total
Sales revenue	$17,000	$11,000	$28,000
Department costs:			
Food	7,000	3,000	10,000
Labor[a]	3,000	5,000	8,000
Total department costs	10,000	8,000	18,000
Department margin[b]	$ 7,000	$ 3,000	$10,000
Nondepartment costs:			
Utilities			$ 1,500
Rent			2,500
Other			900
General manager's salary (Jennifer)			4,000
Total nondepartment costs			8,900
Operating profit			$ 1,100

[a] Includes department managers' salaries but excludes Jennifer's salary.
[b] The difference between revenues and costs attributable to a department.

Illustration 1-4   **Department Costs**

JENNIFER'S SANDWICH DEPARTMENT
Department Budget versus Actual
Month Ending October 31

Department	Budget	Actual
Food:		
Bakery	$1,100	$ 1,050
Meat	2,500	2,700
Fish	1,500	1,750
Dairy	1,500	1,500
Total food	6,600	7,000
Labor:		
Kitchen	1,000	1,000
Counter	800	1,000
Manager	1,000	1,000
Total labor	2,800	3,000
Total sandwich costs	$9,400	$10,000
Number of sandwiches sold	4,100	4,100

meat? Did the cost per pound rise unexpectedly? Were customers given larger portions than expected? Was there unexpected overtime for the counter staff? These are just a few of the questions that would be prompted by the information in Illustration 1–4.

We should also note that budgeting is difficult, and differences between actual costs and budget could also be due to budgets set too low or too high. Finally, differences between budget and actual costs are information signals that things are not as we expected; they do not necessarily imply that something is wrong.

Different Needs Require Different Data

Each time you are faced with an accounting problem, you should first ascertain whether the data will be used for managerial or financial purposes. Is the goal to value inventories in financial reports to shareholders? Is it to provide data for performance evaluation? Or, are the data to be used for decision making? The answers to these questions will guide your selection of the most appropriate accounting data.

HISTORICAL PERSPECTIVE

Although even the early Babylonians and Egyptians practiced cost accounting, the roots of modern cost accounting developed between 1880 and 1920.[1] During this period, companies began integrating production cost records with financial accounts, and standardized cost systems emerged.

The 1920s and 1930s were especially eventful. Accounting for financial reports became subject to the regulations of the Securities and Exchange Commission (SEC) in 1934 and the Committee on Accounting Procedure of the American Institute of Certified Public Accountants (AICPA) in 1938. In addition, budgets became important tools for planning, cost control, and performance evaluation. Estimating and measuring costs for managerial decisions about alternative actions also became increasingly common. In his 1923 book, *The Economics of Overhead Costs,* J. M. Clark established the principle of different costs for different purposes, which is widely recognized and implemented by managerial accountants today.

The content of cost accounting textbooks has reflected accounting changes over the years. In the early 1950s, cost accounting textbooks focused on procedures for measuring, recording, and reporting actual product costs for external purposes. The scope of cost accounting has broadened to include application of mathematical and statistical techniques to cost analysis; consideration of how accounting affects managerial decision models used in finance, economics, and operations management; and examination of the motivational impact of accounting.

This broad view of cost accounting is not clearly distinct from managerial accounting. In most organizations, people who are called cost accountants, managerial accountants, and/or financial analysts have the responsibility of operating the internal accounting system.

---

[1] See David Solomons, "The Historical Development of Costing," in *Studies in Cost Analysis,* ed. David Solomons (Homewood, Ill.: Richard D. Irwin, 1968); and Robert Kaplan and Thomas Johnson, *Relevence Lost: The Rise and Fall of Management Accounting* (Boston: Harvard Business School Press, 1987).

While the traditional role of cost accounting to record full product cost data for external reporting and pricing remains important, cost accounting for decision making and performance evaluation has gained importance in recent decades. Consequently, cost accountants must actively work with management to determine what accounting information is needed.

Management Accounting and GAAP

Generally Accepted Accounting Principles (GAAP) The rules, standards, and conventions that guide the preparation of financial accounting statements.

In contrast to cost data for financial reporting to shareholders, cost data for managerial use (that is, within the organization) need not comply with **generally accepted accounting principles (GAAP).** Management is quite free to set its own definitions for cost information. Indeed, the accounting data used for external reporting may need to be modified to provide appropriate information for managerial decision making. For example, managerial decisions deal with the future, so estimates of future costs may be more valuable for decision making than the historical and current costs that are reported externally.

RECENT DEVELOPMENTS IN COST ACCOUNTING

Cost accounting is experiencing dramatic changes. Developments in computer systems have reduced manual bookkeeping. Changing production methods have made traditional applications of cost accounting obsolete in some cases. There is an increasing emphasis on cost control in hospitals, in industries facing stiff foreign competition and in many organizations that have traditionally not focused on cost control. No longer restricted to manufacturing companies, cost accounting has become a necessity in virtually every organization including, banks, fast-food outlets, professional organizations, hospitals, and government agencies.

The traditional role of cost accounting to record full product cost data for external reporting remains important. However, cost accounting for decision making and performance evaluation has gained importance in recent years. Cost accountants must be prepared to actively work with management to determine what data is needed to make informed, intelligent decisions.

Cost Accounting in High-Tech Companies

Recently, many companies have installed computer assisted methods of manufacturing products, merchandising products, or providing services. These new technologies have had a major impact on cost accounting. We discuss throughout this book the impact of these new developments.

For example, robots and computer assisted manufacturing methods have replaced humans for some jobs. Labor costs have shrunk from 20–40 percent of product costs in traditional manufacturing settings to less than 5 percent in many highly automated settings. Cost accounting in traditional settings required much more work to keep track of labor costs than is necessary in current systems. On the other hand, in highly automated environments, cost accountants have had to become more sophisticated at determining the causes of manufacturing costs because those costs are no longer driven by labor.

Just-in-Time Method In production or purchasing, each unit is purchased or produced just in time for its use.

The development of **just-in-time (JIT) production and purchasing** methods also affects cost accounting systems. Using just-in-time methods, inventories are kept to a minimum. If inventories are low, accountants can spend less time on inventory valuation for external reporting. For example, a Hewlett-Packard plant eliminated 100,000 journal entries per month after installing just-in-time production methods and adapting the cost accounting system to this new production method. This freed up two additional staff people to assist managers in running the business.[2]

ORGANIZATIONAL ENVIRONMENT

In most corporations, the controller is the chief accounting officer and a senior member of the management team. In some firms, the controller has the rank of corporate vice president and reports directly to the company president. In others, the controller and the treasurer both report to a financial vice president who is responsible for both accounting and financial affairs. The cost accounting function is typically the responsibility of the controller.

Illustration 1–5 shows an abbreviated version of the du Pont Company's organization chart. The board of directors establishes policy. Officers of the company carry out that policy. Either the board chairman or the president is designated chief executive officer. The *chief executive officer* (CEO) is responsible for supervising all officers of the corporation and thus is the top-ranking manager. Vice presidents are assigned responsibility over individual divisions. They will usually appoint managers to supervise specified activities within their divisions.

The Office of Controller

As the chief accounting officer, the controller is responsible for both external and internal accounting reports. External reports include published financial statements and reports to taxing authorities like the Internal Revenue Service and regulatory bodies like the Securities and Exchange Commission (SEC).

Internally, the controller is responsible for supplying management with accounting data for planning, performance evaluation, and decision making and for overseeing the company's internal control system. In addition, the controller maintains all cost and other accounting records, including inventories, receivables, payables, and fixed asset accounts. Most of these duties require the use of electronic data processing. In some cases, the controller supervises data processing operations, but frequently, data processing is an independent department reporting to the financial vice president or another staff vice president.

In many organizations, the *internal audit department* provides a variety of auditing and consulting services, including auditing internal controls, auditing cost data for managerial use, and assisting outside auditors in their examination of external financial reports.

The internal audit manager sometimes reports directly to the controller. However, because the controller's recordkeeping role may conflict with the audit function, the audit manager may report directly to the controller's superior (as at Du Pont) and is often given authority to communicate to the audit committee of the board of directors.

---

[2] Rick Hunt, Linda Garrett, and C. Mike Merz, "Direct Labor Cost Not Always Relevant at H-P," *Management Accounting,* February 1985, pp. 58–62.

Illustration 1–5   **Partial Organization Chart, E. I. du Pont de Nemours & Company**

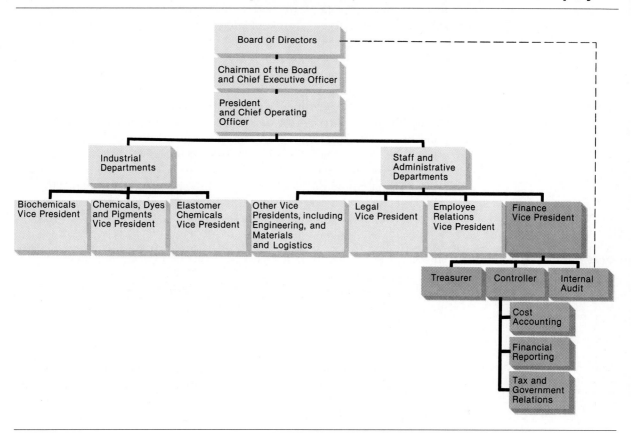

The Office of Treasurer   The corporate treasurer is primarily responsible for managing liquid assets (cash and short-term investments) and handling credit reviews and collection of receivables. The treasurer usually conducts business with banks and other financial sources and oversees public issues of stock and debt. In most cases, the treasurer focuses on financial problems, while the controller concentrates on operating problems.

**PROFESSIONAL
ENVIRONMENT**   The accounting profession includes many kinds of accountants—external auditors, consultants, controllers, internal auditors, tax experts, and so forth. Because accounting positions carry great responsibility, accountants must be highly trained and well informed about new developments in their field. As a result, special organizations and certification programs have been established to serve accountants' needs and the public interest.

Organizations   Numerous organizations have arisen to keep accounting professionals aware of current issues. Most of these organizations have journals that help keep professional accountants up to date. Some of these organizations are listed below.

The *Financial Executive Institute* is an organization of financial executives such as controllers, treasurers, and financial vice presidents. It publishes a monthly periodical, *Financial Executive,* and a number of studies on accounting issues.

The *National Association of Accountants* is open to anyone who works in management accounting. It publishes the journal *Management Accounting* and numerous policy statements and research studies on accounting issues. It also sponsors the Certified Management Accounting (CMA) program.

The *Institute of Internal Auditors* is an organization of internal auditors. It publishes a periodical called the *Internal Auditor* and numerous research studies on internal auditing. It also sponsors the Certificate in Internal Auditing program.

The *Association of Government Accountants* is an organization of federal, state, and local government accountants. It publishes the *Government Accountant's Journal.*

Certifications

Anyone who wishes to be licensed as a certified public accountant (CPA) must pass an examination that includes questions on cost accounting as well as other questions on accounting practice, theory, law, and auditing. We have included samples of CPA examination cost accounting questions in this book.

Certified Management Accounting A program established to recognize educational achievement and professional competence in management accounting.

The **Certified Management Accounting (CMA)** program recognizes educational achievement and professional accomplishment in the field of managerial accounting. The examination, education, and experience requirements for the CMA are similar to those for CPA certification, but they are primarily for professionals in management and cost accounting. We have included a large number of problems from CMA examinations in this book.

In Canada, the Society of Management Accountants gives the professional examination and certification for the certified management accountant (CMA) certificate.

Cost Accounting Standards Board

The **Cost Accounting Standards Board (CASB)** was set up by the U.S. Congress in 1970 to establish cost accounting standards for U.S. defense contractors. The CASB's primary purpose was to avert disputes between the U.S. government and defense contractors about the allocation of costs in cost-based government contracts. Its rules and standards are still used in numerous federal government purchases.[3]

Ethical Issues

Accountants report information that can have a substantial impact on the careers of managers. Managers are generally held accountable for achieving financial performance targets; failure to achieve these targets can have serious negative consequences for them. If a division or company is having trouble achieving financial performance targets, accountants may find

---

[3] For more details about the Cost Accounting Standards Board, see Gary F. Bulmash and Louis I. Rose, "The Cost Accounting Standards Board," in *The Managerial and Cost Accountant's Handbook,* ed. Homer A. Black and James Don Edwards (Homewood, Ill.: Dow Jones-Irwin, 1979), pp. 1231–60.

themselves under pressure by management to make accounting choices that will improve performance reports.

For example, companies have been known to record sales before the revenue was earned.[4] This early revenue recognition would occur just before the end of the reporting period, say, in late December for a company using a December 31 year-end. Management might rationalize the early revenue recognition on the grounds that the sale would probably be made in January anyway; this practice just moved next year's sale (and profits) into this year.

REAL WORLD APPLICATION

The Accountant as a Communicator*

Although accounting is often called the language of business, it is a *foreign* language to most people in business. According to Joseph Barra, a division controller at Lever Brothers Co., the solution may lie with accountants. "I have encountered many very good accountants who were excellent technical people and who really knew their field but could not communicate with management and get the message across. They could not present basic accounting information in a simplified way."

What financial issues are poorly understood by nonfinancial managers? Mr. Barra lists four areas at Lever Brothers that require extra communication effort.

1. The effects of little or no depreciation expense because assets are old. Purchase of new assets may increase depreciation expense and reduce reported profits for a product line.
2. The effects of inflation, particularly on asset replacement and the cost of capital.
3. The role of overhead costs in profit analysis.
4. The coordination of the entire planning and control process—Mr. Barra must be able to coordinate marketing and purchasing and work with the president of his business unit.

Communication with nonaccountants is particularly important because of the interaction that takes place between accountants and users of information. According to Mr. Barra, marketing people at Lever Brothers look to the accountants for information about distribution costs for established products. If management decides to change a product, the accountants work with people in purchasing to obtain new materials and packaging cost information. If the company is considering a new product, "the analysis and estimation of the cost is controlled by the controller right from the beginning. . . . Ideally, this process results in a combination of the disciplines. The marketing people make the estimates of what they think sales will be and also calculate what happens if the estimates are missed."

What is required for effective communication with nonfinancial people? Mr. Barra lists four basic ground rules:

1. Keep examples simple.
2. Avoid technical jargon.
3. Show an understanding of marketing and production issues.
4. Avoid lessons in bookkeeping

Good communication is self-serving. By making nonfinancial managers aware of the financial implications of their proposals, accountants will find their services in greater demand.

* Source: Joseph A. Barra, "Marketing the Financial Facts of Life," *Management Accounting,* March 1983, p. 29.

---

[4] For example, see M. Maher, "Divisional Performance Incentives and Financial Fraud" (working paper, Graduate School of Management, University of California, Davis, August 1990).

In its Standards of Ethical Conduct for Management Accountants, the National Association of Accountants (NAA) states that management accountants have an obligation to maintain the highest levels of ethical conduct by maintaining professional competency, refraining from disclosing confidential information, and maintaining integrity and objectivity in their work.[5] The standards recommended that accountants faced with ethical conflicts follow the established policies that deal with such conflicts. If the policies do not resolve the conflict, accountants should consider discussing the matter with superiors, potentially as high as the audit committee of the board of directors. In extreme cases, the accountant may have no alternative but to resign.

COSTS AND BENEFITS OF ACCOUNTING

Cost-Benefit Requirements The criterion that an alternative will be chosen if and only if the benefits from it exceed the costs. This criterion is one basis for evaluating cost systems.

How much accounting information will suffice? Managers often complain that they never have all the facts they need. More data could usually be provided to decision makers, but at a cost. For example, a company recently installed a cost system that cost several million dollars. Management could justify the expenditure for more accounting because it believed the system would help control costs and increase the efficiency of operations, thereby saving the company much more than it cost.

The question of how much accounting information will suffice can be resolved by evaluating costs and benefits of accounting information. In practice, it is especially difficult to measure the benefits of accounting systems. Future benefits and costs can never be known with certainty. Nonetheless, accounting for managerial uses must, in principle, meet **cost-benefit requirements.**

The analysis of costs and benefits requires considerable cooperation between the users of accounting information and accountants. Users are more familiar with the benefits of the data, and accountants are more familiar with the costs. Such cooperation is shown in Illustration 1–6, where users identify their decision-making needs and demand data from accountants, who develop information systems to supply the data when it is cost-benefit justified. In practice, the process sometimes works in reverse. Accountants sometimes report data that users do not use. But if accountants and users interact, they eventually settle on a cost-benefit-justified supply of accounting data that meets users' needs.

Accounting theoreticians are working on solutions to the difficult problem of determining the optimal cost-benefit-justified accounting data system. We present some of these developments in Chapter 26, "Information Economics." Throughout this book, we assume that both users and accountants assess the costs and benefits of information in deciding whether to change an accounting system, whether to prepare a special report, and so forth.

---

[5] See *Standards of Ethical Conduct for Management Accountants* (Montvale, N.J.: National Association of Accountants, June 1, 1983).

Illustration 1-6   **Interaction between Users and Accountants**

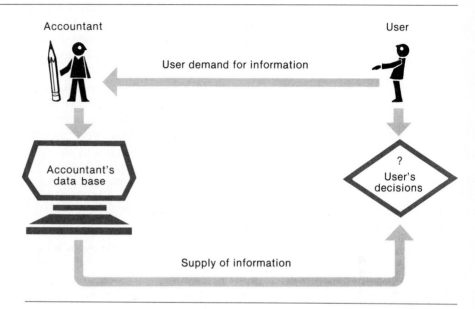

HOW DOES COST ACCOUNTING RELATE TO OTHER FIELDS?

Cost accounting interfaces with many other fields of study. Consequently, you will discover concepts in this book that are discussed in other books also. One of the primary uses of cost accounting—valuing inventory and cost of goods sold for external reporting to shareholders—is part of financial accounting. Cost accounting is closely related to microeconomics. Some think of differential cost analysis, in particular, as a form of applied microeconomics. Cost accounting provides data for use in decision models for finance, operations management, and marketing. Cost accounting also relates to motivation and behavior because it is used in planning and performance evaluation. Finally, tools from statistics, mathematics, and computer sciences are used to perform cost analysis.

ORGANIZATION OF BOOK

Chapter 2 describes fundamental concepts on which the rest of the book is based, including discussion of activity-based costing, which is growing in use. The remaining chapters are organized around the four major subject areas in the book: (1) cost accounting systems, (2) costs for managerial decision making, (3) costs for managerial performance evaluations, and (4) cost accounting in an uncertain environment.

1. Cost accounting systems. Chapters 3 through 9 describe the design of cost systems in a variety of organizations, including service, merchandising, and manufacturing. These chapters show how costs are recorded and reported in these organizations. They discuss cost allocation, which is fundamental to most decisions about usefulness for decision makers. Recognizing recent developments in cost accounting, these chapters not only discuss the use of cost data for external financial reporting but particularly emphasize the design of cost systems for managerial purposes. The emphasis in these chapters is on designing multipurpose cost accounting systems, whereas the emphasis in later chapters is on using the data that come out of these systems for particular types of decisions.

2. Costs for managerial decision making. Chapters 10 through 14 are concerned with the estimated impact of managerial decisions on costs and, conversely, the impact of decisions on estimated costs. The focus is on short-term operating decisions. For example, how will costs (as well as revenues and profits) be affected by an increase in volume? By closing a store? By developing a new product line?

Chapters 15 and 16 cover the use of cost accounting in long-term capital investment decisions. We discuss cash flow estimation and include tax effects of capital investment decisions.

3. Costs for managerial performance evaluation. Chapters 17 through 21 discuss how managers use cost accounting to plan and budget their activities and to evaluate performance. Chapters 22 and 23 discuss the use of cost accounting in managing decentralized organizations.

4. Cost accounting in an uncertain environment. Chapters 24 through 26 cover advanced topics, including decision making under uncertainty, variance investigation models, and economics of information.

SUMMARY

This chapter provides an overview of cost accounting, which is the field of accounting that records, measures, and reports information about costs.

This book discusses cost accounting systems and the use of cost accounting in its two primary managerial uses: decision making and performance evaluation. In decision making, cost accounting is used by managers to assess financial consequences of alternative actions. In performance evaluation, accounting is used by managers to assign responsibility for costs and to measure employee performance.

Cost accounting has changed from an emphasis on inventory and cost of goods sold valuation for external financial reporting to an emphasis on cost uses for managerial purposes in recent years. While cost accounting still provides data essential for external financial reporting, it has recently achieved an increasingly important role in management.

Like any other service, product, or system in an organization, cost accounting is subject to economic cost-benefit evaluation. Perfectly accurate and complete accounting information, even if possible to obtain, would almost certainly be too costly to justify. The benefits of cost accounting information are usually derived by the managers who use it. Determination of the costs and benefits of accounting information requires cooperation between the users of information and the accountants who supply it.

TERMS AND CONCEPTS

The following terms and concepts should be familiar to you after reading this chapter:

Budget

Certified Management Accounting (CMA)

Cost

Cost Accounting

Cost Accounting Standards Board (CASB)

Cost-Benefit Requirements

Differential Costs

Financial Accounting

Generally Accepted Accounting Principles (GAAP)

Just-in-Time (JIT) Production and Purchasing

Managerial Accounting

Responsibility Center

SUPPLEMENTARY READINGS

Atkinson, Anthony A. "Choosing a Future Role for Management Accounting." *CMA—The Management Accounting Magazine*, July–August 1987, p. 29.

Brown, Victor H. "The Tension between Management Accounting and Financial Reporting." *Management Accounting*, May 1987, p. 39.

Deakin, Edward B. "Cost Accounting in a Capital-Intensive Economy." *Today's CPA*, April–May 1987, pp. 18–22.

Deakin, Edward B.; Michael W. Maher; and James J. Cappel. *Contemporary Literature in Cost Accounting*, Homewood, Ill.: Richard D. Irwin, 1988.

Demski, J. S.; James R. Emore; and James Cress. "On Teaching Management Accountants." *Management Accounting*, February 1987, pp. 44, 60.

Ferguson, Daniel C. "A CEO's View of the Controller." *Management Accounting*, February 1987, p. 21.

Klemstine, Charles F., and Michael W. Maher. *Management Accounting Research: A Review and Annotated Bibliography*, New York: Garland, 1984.

Mihalek, Paul H.; Anne J. Rich; and Carl S. Smith. "Ethics and Management Accountants." *Management Accounting*, December 1987, pp. 34–36.

QUESTIONS

1–1. Column 1 lists three decision categories. Column 2 lists three accounting costs and a corresponding letter. Place the letter of the appropriate accounting cost in the blank next to each decision category.

Column 1	Column 2
_____ Analysis of divisional performance	A. Costs for inventory valuation
_____ Costing for income tax purposes	B. Costs for decision making
_____ Determining how many units to produce in the coming week	C. Costs for performance evaluation

1–2. A manager once remarked, "All I need are the differential costs for decision making—don't bother me with information about any other costs. They aren't relevant." Give examples of other costs useful to management. Comment on this remark.

1-3. You are considering sharing your living quarters with another person. What costs would you include if you decide to split costs. What costs would differ if another person were to move in with you? Discuss the agreement options available to you.

1-4. Would you support a proposal to develop a set of ''generally accepted'' accounting standards for performance evaluation? Why or why not?

1-5. A telephone company established discounts for off-peak use of telephone services. A discount of 35 percent is offered for calls placed in the evenings during the week, and a discount of 60 percent is offered for late-night and weekend calls. Since the telephone company would probably not be profitable if these discounts were offered all the time, explain what cost considerations may have entered into management's decision to offer the discounts.

1-6. A critic of the expansion of the role of the accountant has stated, ''The controller should have enough work filling out tax forms and the paperwork required by the bureaucracy without trying to interfere with management decision making. Leave that role to those more familiar with management decisions.'' Comment.

1-7. You are considering whether to purchase a new car to replace your present car. Being strictly rational in an economic sense, which of the following costs would you include in making your decision?

   a. Cost of the present car.
   b. Trade-in value of your present car.
   c. Maintenance costs on the present car.
   d. Maintenance costs on the new car.
   e. Fuel consumption on the present car.
   f. Fuel consumption on the new car.
   g. Cost of parking permits, garage rental, and similar storage costs.
   h. Liability insurance on the present car.
   i. Liability insurance on the new car.
   j. Property and collision insurance on the present car.
   k. Property and collision insurance on the new car.
   l. Changes in the relative frequency of your friends saying, ''Let's use your car since it's newer,'' and the related costs of using the new car.
   m. Annual time depreciation on the present car.
   n. Annual time depreciation on the new car.
   o. Financing costs of the present car.
   p. Financing costs for the new car.

   You should be able to give reasons why each element should or should not be included in your analysis. (Hint: Which costs will be differential, that is, will be different if the new car is purchased?)

1-8. Why would the controller have an interest in the structure of an organization and in knowing the distinction between line management and staff functions?

1-9. It is common practice for the internal auditor to report to the same person who is responsible for preparation of the accounting reports and the maintenance of accounting records. What are some advantages of such a supervisory relationship? What conflicts might exist, and what procedures might be installed to minimize the extent of conflict?

1-10. For a corporation organized according to the organization chart in Illustration 1-5, what potential conflicts might arise between production managers and the controller's staff? How might these potential conflicts be resolved with a minimum of interference from the chief executive officer?

1-11. What certifications are available to a person in an accounting career?

1-12. One of your colleagues commented, ''I want to be a CPA. Why should I take cost accounting?'' Indeed, why should a potential CPA study cost accounting?

1-13. What are the differences between the duties and responsibilities of the controller and the treasurer?

EXERCISES

1-14. Cost Data for Managerial Purposes
(L.O.1)[6]

In your first day as a member of the controller's staff, you are asked to report on a contemplated change in the equipment layout in the plant. The new layout is expected to result in a 10 percent reduction in labor costs but no changes in any other costs. Last year, labor costs were $7 per unit produced. Other costs were $9 per unit produced. The company can sell as many units as it can manufacture. The company's union contract contains a provision for a 6 percent increase in labor costs for the coming year. In addition, analysis of other costs indicates that these costs may be expected to increase by 4 percent in the coming year.

Required:

a. Identify the differential costs for the decision to rearrange the plant.

b. Describe how management would use the information in *a.*, and any other appropriate information, to decide whether to proceed with the contemplated rearrangement.

1-15. Cost Data for Managerial Purposes
(L.O.1)

Management of the Calculator Division of Huey Packard wants to know whether to continue operations in the division. The division has been operating at a loss for the past several years as indicated in the accompanying divisional income statement. If the division is eliminated, corporate administration is not expected to change, nor are any other changes expected in the operations or costs of other divisions.

Required:

What costs are probably differential for the decision to discontinue this division's operations?

HUEY PACKARD CALCULATOR DIVISION
Divisional Income Statement
For the Year Ending December 31

Sales revenue	$850,000
Costs:	
Advertising	35,000
Cost of goods sold	420,000
Divisional administrative salaries	59,000
Selling costs	82,000
Divisional share of building occupancy costs	181,000
Share of corporate administration	96,000
Total costs	873,000
Net loss before income tax benefit	(23,000)
Tax benefit at 40% rate	9,200
Net loss	$ (13,800)

[6] Each exercise in this book is keyed to one or more learning objectives. The key L.O.1 refers to the First Learning Objective on the title page of the chapter.

1–16. The Role of Accounting in Organizations
(L.O.2)

Roger Farley has just been named chief executive officer of a high-technology company. Roger started in the budgeting section of the controller's office and has risen rapidly through the ranks of the organization. He has been so impressed with the importance of budgeting that he proposed creating a new vice president for budgeting since, as Roger noted, it was often difficult for a mere "supervisor" to obtain the complete cooperation of other division managers in the budgeting function.

Required:

Comment on the proposed new position and suggest other ways that Roger might accomplish his objectives.

1–17. The Role of Accounting in Organizations
(L.O.2)

Marlene McHarris was recently appointed chief executive officer of a diversified corporate organization. The company has been organized along functional lines similar to Illustration 1–5. This company has three separate manufacturing divisions, each dealing with different products and markets. Each manufacturing division is headed by an assistant vice president, with a vice president for manufacturing heading up all manufacturing operations. One vice president proposed that the organization would be more efficient if the company set up each manufacturing division as a decentralized unit. As the vice president pointed out, "Each of these manufacturing divisions is sufficiently dissimilar that they would operate better on their own. If each division had its own engineering and accounting staffs, there would be less need to cross division lines each time an engineering study or an accounting report is required. Moreover, the accounting sections could adapt their decision-making and performance-evaluation functions to the needs of the specific manufacturing divisions rather than treat them all alike."

Required:

Prepare comments on the advantages and disadvantages of the proposal. Your supervisor is the controller, who coordinates accounting activities for all three divisions.

1–18. The Role of Accounting in Organizations
(L.O.2)

Terri Burns has just been hired as the new controller for Cardinal Glassworks Inc., a manufacturer of high quality glassware. The vice president of finance reports directly to the president of the company. The finance area has three offices—controller, treasurer, and internal audit. Other departments who have vice presidents reporting directly to the president are Marketing and Production.

The controller's office consists of three departmental supervisors who each supervise three employees. The three departments are Cost Accounting, Financial Reporting, and Tax.

Required:

a. Construct an organizational chart for Cardinal Glassworks.
b. What duties would you expect the Controller and her staff to perform?

1–19. The Role of Accounting in Organizations
(L.O.2)

Joe Garcia, corporate vice president for MegaProduct, a large multinational corporation, made a request for a review of the corporate human resource management system. The review was assigned to Jennifer Jones, a senior internal auditor.

The human resource management system was introduced eight years ago and has been modified and enhanced periodically. Josh Simmons, director of human resources planning and management, designed the original system and currently manages it.

Required:

Suggest ways that Jones can clearly communicate the results of her audit to Garcia and Simmons. (Hint: See the second Real World Application in the chapter.)

(CMA adapted)

PROBLEMS

1-20. Cost Data for Managerial Purposes

Lamar Corporation entered into an agreement to sell 20,000 units of a product to a government agency this year at "cost plus 20 percent."

Lamar operates a manufacturing plant that can produce 60,000 units per year. The company normally produces 40,000 units per year. The costs to produce 40,000 units are as follows:

	Total	Per Unit
Materials	$ 480,000	$12
Labor	760,000	19
Supplies and other indirect costs that will vary with production	320,000	8
Indirect costs that will not vary with production	440,000	11
Variable marketing costs	80,000	2
Administrative costs (all fixed)	160,000	4
Totals	$2,240,000	$56

Based on the above data, company management expects to receive cash equal to $67.20 (that is, $56 × 120 percent) per unit for the units sold on this contract. After completing 5,000 units, the company sent a bill (invoice) to the government for $336,000 (that is, 5,000 units at $67.20 per unit).

The president of the company received a call from the contracting agent for the government. The agent stated that the per unit cost should be:

Materials	$12
Labor	19
Supplies, etc.	8
Total	$39

Therefore, the price per unit should be $46.80 (that is, $39 × 120 percent). The agent ignored marketing costs because the contract bypassed the usual selling channels.

Required:

What price would you recommend? Why? (Note: You need not limit yourself to the costs selected by the company or by the government agent.)

1-21. Cost Data for Managerial Purposes

Amos Division is a division of a large corporation. It normally sells to outside customers but, on occasion, will sell to another division of the corporation. When it does, corporate policy states that the price will be cost plus 10 percent. Amos received an order from the Field Division, which is also a division of the corporation, for 10,000 units. Amos Division's planned output for the year had been 50,000 units. The costs for producing those 50,000 units are:

	Total	Per Unit
Materials	$ 20,000	$ .40
Direct labor	100,000	2.00
Other costs varying with output	10,000	.20
Fixed costs	90,000	1.80
Total costs	$220,000	$4.40

Based on these data, the Amos Division controller, who was new to the corporation, calculated that the unit price for the Field Division order should be $4.84 ($4.40 × 110 percent). After producing and shipping the 10,000 units, Amos Division sent an invoice for $48,400. Shortly thereafter, Amos received a note from the buyer at Field Division that stated this invoice was not in accordance with company policy. The unit cost should have been:

	Per Unit
Materials	$ .40
Direct labor	2.00
Other costs varying with output	.20
Total	$2.60

The price would be $2.86 ($2.60 × 110 percent) per unit.

Required:

If the corporation asked you to review this intercompany policy, what policy would you recommend? Why? (Note: You need not limit yourself to the Field Division calculation or current policy.)

1–22. Cost Data for Managerial Purposes

Coffee & Cream, Inc., operates a small coffee shop in the downtown area. Profits have been declining in the past, and the management is planning to expand and add ice cream to the menu. The annual ice cream sales are expected to increase revenue by $20,000. The cost of purchasing ice cream from the manufacturer is $10,000. The coffee shop and the ice cream shop will be supervised by the present manager. However, due to expansion, the labor costs and utilities would increase by 50 percent and other costs by 20 percent.

COFFEE & CREAM, INC.
Annual Income Statement
Before Expansion

Sales revenue	$35,000
Costs:	
Food	15,000
Labor	8,000
Utilities	2,000
Rent	4,000
Other costs	2,000
Supervisor's salary	6,000
Total costs	37,000
Operating pofit (loss)	$ (2,000)

Required:

a. Identify the costs that are different for the decision to open the ice cream shop.
b. Should the management open the ice cream shop?

1–23. Cost Data for Managerial Purposes

Denver Data Corp. writes software for computer applications. Recently, one of the company's officers was approached by a representative of a scientific research firm who was seeking some specialized programs. Denver Data Corp. reported the following costs and revenues during the past year:

Denver Data Corp.
Annual Income Statement

Sales revenue	$600,000
Costs:	
Programmer labor	285,000
Equipment lease	42,000
Rent	36,000
Supplies	27,000
Officers' salaries	175,000
Other costs	19,000
Total costs	584,000
Operating profit	$ 16,000

If the company decides to take the contract to produce scientific programs, it will need to hire a full-time programmer at $60,000. Equipment lease would increase by 20 percent because of the need to buy certain computer equipment. Supplies would increase by an estimated 10 percent and other costs would increase by 20 percent. The existing building has space for the new programmer. In addition, management believes that no new officers will be necessary for this work.

Required:

a. What are the differential costs that would be incurred as a result of taking the contract?

b. If the contract will pay $75,000 in the first year, should Denver Data take the contract?

c. What considerations, other than costs, would be necessary before making this decision?

1–24. Analyze Costs for Decision Alternatives

Blinko Copies is a chain of copy centers offering general duplication services near major universities. Decisions about what equipment to use are made by central management. Blinko's management is currently evaluating three different types of machines. Operating and cost data for these machines are as follows:

	Model Number		
	IX360	JX380	KX400
Capacity (sheets per minute)	108	112	120
Annual fixed costs*	$5,620	$6,020	$7,100
Variable cost per sheet	.0265	.023	.022
Machine life	7 years	7 years	8 years
Cost of machine	$16,250	$18,870	$24,425
Salvage value	2,400	3,800	4,250

* Includes depreciation.

Required:

a. Assuming each of the three machines could be used interchangeably at any Blinko outlet, what types of cost information would be relevant for this decision?

b. If a machine operates for 200,000 minutes per year, what is the average total unit cost for each type of machine?

(Contributed by Leo Ruggles)

COST CONCEPTS AND BEHAVIOR

LEARNING OBJECTIVES

1. Understanding the basic concept of *cost* as it is used in accounting.

2. Knowing how costs are presented in financial statements.

3. Ability to identify basic cost behavior patterns.

4. Knowledge of the components of full cost.

5. Familiarity with new developments in cost analysis: Activity based costing.

This chapter introduces the fundamental concepts of cost accounting. You will discover that the term *cost* is ambiguous unless it is used in a specific context. The adjectives that modify the term *cost* describe the specific context.

This chapter is organized as follows. We begin with general concepts of the nature of cost. Then we discuss definitions of those costs that are commonly used in describing cost accounting systems. Finally, we discuss additional cost concepts used in decision making and performance evaluation. Illustration 2–14 at the end of this chapter summarizes the major cost definitions. It should be helpful to refer to Illustration 2–14 as you read the chapter.

THE CONCEPT OF COST

Outlay Cost A past, present, or future cash outflow.

A cost is a sacrifice of resources. In going about our daily affairs, we buy many different things—clothing, food, books, perhaps an automobile, a desk lamp, and so on. Each item has a price that measures the sacrifice we must make to acquire it. Whether we pay immediately or agree to pay at some later date, the cost is actually established by that price.

There are two major categories of costs: outlay costs and opportunity costs. An **outlay cost** is a past, present, or future cash outflow. Consider the cost of a college education. Clearly, the cash outflow for tuition, books, and fees are outlay costs for college. For many college students, cash is not all that is sacrificed. Students also sacrifice their time to get a college education.

Opportunity Cost The lost return an alternative course of action could provide.

While there is no cash outlay because of this time sacrifice, there is an opportunity cost. **Opportunity cost** is the *return* that could be realized from the *best foregone alternative use* of a resource. For example, many students give up other jobs to earn a college degree. Their foregone income is part of the cost of getting a college degree. This foregone income is the return that could be realized from an alternative use of the scarce resource—time. Similarly, the opportunity cost of funds invested in a government bond is the foregone interest that could be earned on a bank certificate of deposit, assuming both securities were equal in risk and liquidity. The opportunity cost of using a factory to produce a particular product is the sacrifice of profits that could be made by producing other products or by renting the factory to someone else. In each case, we assume that the foregone alternative use was the *best* comparable use of the resource given up.

Of course, no one can ever know all the possible opportunities available at any moment. Hence, some opportunity costs will undoubtedly not be considered. Accounting systems typically record outlay costs but not opportunity costs. Hence, opportunity costs are sometimes incorrectly ignored in decision making.

Cost and Expenses

Expense A cost that is charged against revenue in an accounting period.

It is important to distinguish *cost* from *expense*. As previously discussed, a cost is a sacrifice of resources. An **expense** is a cost that is charged against revenue in an accounting period; hence, expenses are deducted from revenue in that accounting period. We use the term expense only when speaking of external financial reports.

The focus of cost accounting is on *costs*, not expenses. Generally accepted accounting principles (GAAP) and regulations such as the income tax laws specify when costs are to be treated as expenses. In practice, the terms *costs* and *expenses* are sometimes used synonymously. We use the term *cost* in this book unless we are dealing with expense as an income measurement issue under GAAP.

We shall relate much of our analysis and discussion to income statements. This makes it easier to see where the specific object of our analysis fits into an organization's total performance. Unless otherwise stated, we assume these income statements are prepared for *internal* management use, not for external reporting. We focus on **operating profit,** which for internal reporting purposes is the excess of operating revenues over the operating costs incurred to generate those revenues. This figure differs from **net income,** which is operating profit adjusted for interest, income taxes, extraordinary items, and other adjustments required to comply with GAAP and other regulations.

Cost accounting provides cost data for external reporting, and also provides data for managerial accounting. To distinguish the amounts that might be reported internally from those reported externally, we reserve the term *net income* for external reporting.

Operating Profit   The excess of operating revenues over the operating costs necessary to generate those revenues.

Period Costs versus Product Costs

Product Costs   Those costs that can be attributed to a product; costs that are part of inventory.

Period Costs   Costs that can be attributed to time intervals.

Cost accounting often divides costs into product or period categories. **Product costs** are costs more easily attributed to products, while **period costs** are more easily attributed to time intervals. The annual rent of an office building and the salary of a company executive are period costs. The costs of merchandise purchased for resale or related transportation-in costs are examples of product costs.

As shown in Illustration 2–1, marketing and administrative costs are not product costs in either merchandising or manufacturing companies. Merchandising companies inventory merchandise purchases and their related costs while manufacturing companies inventory the materials, labor, and overhead that go into making a product.

COSTS IN FINANCIAL STATEMENTS

We now discuss product costing for measuring the value of inventory. The product costs assigned to inventory are carried in the accounts as assets. When the goods are sold, the costs flow from inventory to cost of goods sold. At that time, these previously inventoried costs become period costs or expenses.

Cost of a Product Sold in Merchandising

Consider the cost of items offered for sale in a merchandising organization like a supermarket, clothing store, or furniture store. In such companies, no manufacturing activity takes place; the items purchased are sold in the same condition they are received. Merchants do not incur additional costs to alter the form or nature of the products they acquire.

Even in such a basic cost accounting situation, the cost of the merchandise acquired for sale may include a number of individual costs. Besides the cost of the merchandise itself, the buyer may pay to transport the merchandise to the selling outlet, and insure it while it is in route.

Illustration 2-1   **Comparison of Product and Period Cost**

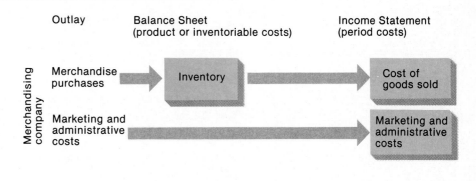

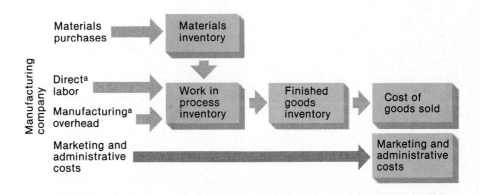

a These costs are part of product costs under *full-absorption costing*. Under *variable costing*, only the variable portions of manufacturing costs, such as materials purchases and direct labor, are product costs; the fixed manufacturing costs, such as manufacturing overhead, are period costs under variable costing.

For example, Masthead Clothing Stores had a beginning inventory of $125,000 on January 1. They purchased $687,000 during the year and had transportation-in costs of $26,000. During the year, they sold goods costing $662,000, which included transportation-in costs. Sales revenue for the year was $1 million; marketing and administrative costs were $200,000. Masthead had an ending inventory of $176,000 on December 31.

An income statement and a cost of goods sold statement are shown in Illustration 2–2. The term **cost of goods sold** is self-descriptive. It includes only the actual costs of the goods that were sold. It does not include the costs of selling the goods, such as the salaries of sales and delivery people. Nor does it include the cost of the facilities in which the sales are made. These are other costs of doing business. They are deducted from sales revenue as a period cost when they are incurred.

Cost of Goods Sold   The cost assigned to products sold during a period.

Cost of a Manufactured Product

Now consider a manufacturing operation. The cost of a manufactured product includes all the costs of making it. The manufacturer purchases materials (for example, unassembled parts), hires workers to work on the material to

Illustration 2-2

MASTHEAD CLOTHING STORES
Income Statement
For the Year Ended December 31

Sales revenue	$1,000,000
Cost of goods sold (see statement below)	662,000
Gross margin	338,000
Marketing and administrative costs	200,000
Operating profit	$ 138,000

Cost of Goods Sold Statement
For the Year Ended December 31

Beginning inventory	$ 125,000[a]
Cost of goods purchased:	
Merchandise cost	687,000
Transportation-in	26,000
Total cost of goods purchased	713,000
Cost of goods available for sale	838,000
Less cost of goods in ending inventory	176,000[a]
Cost of goods sold	$ 662,000

convert it to a finished good, then offers the product for sale. For cost accounting purposes, three cateogries of manufacturing costs receive attention:

Direct Materials Those materials that can feasibly be identified directly with the product.

1. **Direct materials** from which the product is made. (To the manufacturer, purchased parts, including transportation-in, are included in direct materials.) Direct materials are also called *raw materials*.

2. **Direct labor** of workers who transform the materials into a finished product.

Direct Labor The cost of workers who actually transform materials into finished products during the production process.

3. All other costs of transforming the materials to a finished product, often referred to in total as **manufacturing overhead.** Some examples of manufacturing overhead are:

   a. *Indirect labor* the cost of workers who do not work directly on the product yet are required for the factory to operate, such as supervisors, maintenance workers, and inventory storekeepers.

Manufacturing Overhead All production costs except direct labor and direct materials.

   b. *Indirect materials*, such as lubricants for the machinery, polishing and cleaning materials, repair parts, and light bulbs, which are not a part of the finished product but are necessary to manufacture the product.

   c. *Other manufacturing costs*, such as depreciation of the factory building and equipment, taxes on the factory assets, insurance on the factory building and equipment, heat, light, power, and similar expenses incurred to keep the factory operating.

Although we use the term *manufacturing overhead* in this book, other common synonyms used in practice are factory burden, factory overhead, burden, factory expense, and the unmodified word *overhead*.

STAGES OF PRODUCTION

There are three stages in which materials might exist in a manufacturing company at any time. The company may have *direct materials* that have not yet been put into production. There is also likely to be uncompleted work on the production line, which accountants refer to as **work in process.** And there may be **finished goods** that have been completely processed and are ready for sale. Because material in each of these stages has incurred costs, a cost accounting system will include three different inventory accounts: Direct Materials Inventory, Work in Process Inventory, and Finished Goods Inventory.

Each inventory account is likely to have a beginning inventory amount, additions (debits) and withdrawals (credits) during the period, and an ending inventory based on the units still on hand. Those costs which are initially charged to inventory accounts are called **inventoriable costs.**

An example of the accounting for manufacturing costs is provided by the following case. WonderWheels, Inc., is a bicycle manufacturer. A review of last year's operating results provides the following information.

The company's direct materials inventory on hand January 1 was $200,000, purchases during the year were $800,000, ending inventory on December 31 was $150,000, and cost of direct materials put into production during the year was $850,000. A schedule of the cost of direct materials put into production appears as follows:

Beginning direct materials inventory, January 1	$ 200,000
Add purchases during the year	800,000
Direct materials available during the year	1,000,000
Less ending direct materials inventory, December 31	150,000
Cost of direct materials put into production	$ 850,000

The Work in Process Inventory account had a beginning balance on January 1 of $350,000. As shown in the schedule below, costs incurred during the year were $850,000 in direct materials from the schedule of direct materials costs; $700,000 in direct labor costs; and $1,850,000 in manufacturing overhead. The sum of materials, labor, and manufacturing overhead costs incurred, $3,400,000, is the total manufacturing costs incurred during the year.

Adding the beginning work in process inventory, $350,000, to the $3,400,000 gives $3,750,000, the total cost of work in process for the year. At year-end, the inventory is found to have a cost of $400,000. This $400,000 is subtracted to arrive at $3,350,000, the cost of goods manufactured. These events are summarized in the following cost of goods manufactured schedule which is part of the comprehensive statement appearing in Illustration 2–3.

Beginning work in process inventory, January 1		$ 350,000
Manufacturing costs during the year:		
Direct materials	$ 850,000	
Direct labor	700,000	
Manufacturing overhead	1,850,000	
Total manufacturing costs incurred during the year		3,400,000
Total cost of work in process during the year		3,750,000
Less ending work in process inventory, December 31		400,000
Cost of goods manufactured during the year		$3,350,000

Finished Goods Inventory

The work finished during the period is transferred from the production department to the finished goods storage area and is added to the beginning inventory of **finished goods** as items available for sale. The beginning and ending finished goods inventory balances were $920,000 and $1,460,000, respectively. Cost of goods manufactured, or finished, by production and transferred out of work in process inventory was $3,350,000. Cost of goods sold was $2,810,000 as computed in the following schedule:

Beginning finished goods inventory, January 1	$ 920,000
Cost of goods manufactured (finished) during the year	3,350,000
Cost of goods available for sale during the year	4,270,000
Less ending finished goods inventory, December 31	1,460,000
Cost of goods sold	$2,810,000

Cost of Goods Manufactured and Sold Statement

As part of its internal reporting system, WonderWheels prepares a **cost of goods manufactured and sold statement.** This statement is shown in Illustration 2–3. It incorporates and summarizes information from the previous schedules.

If you compare Illustration 2–2 with Illustrations 2–3 and 2–4, you will see that product costing in a manufacturing setting is more complex than product costing in merchandising. As a result, we devote a substantial amount of discussion to cost flows and product costing in a manufacturing setting in later chapters. Many of the product costing concepts used in manufacturing can be applied to merchandising and service organizations, too.

The cost of goods manufactured and sold statement in Illustration 2–3 is composed of three building blocks. The gray shaded area is the schedule of the cost of direct materials. Direct materials costs are combined with direct labor and manufacturing overhead which collectively form the charges to work in process. The shaded blue area of Illustration 2–3 reflects the Work in Process account with its beginning balance, charges, and ending balance. The last item in the blue shaded area is the credit to work in process which reflects the transfer to finished goods. The unshaded area of the statement is

Illustration 2-3

WONDERWHEELS
Cost of Goods Manufactured and Sold Statement
For the Year Ending December 31

Beginning work in process inventory, January 1			$ 350,000
Manufacturing costs during the year:			
Direct materials:			
Beginning inventory, January 1	$ 200,000		
Add purchases	800,000		
Direct materials available	$1,000,000		
Less ending inventory	150,000		
Direct materials put into production		$ 850,000	
Direct labor		700,000	
Manufacturing overhead		1,850,000	
Total manufacturing costs incurred during the year			3,400,000
Total cost of work in process during the year			3,750,000
Less ending work in process inventory, December 31			400,000
Cost of goods manufactured during the year			3,350,000
Beginning finished goods inventory, January 1			920,000
Finished goods inventory available for sale			4,270,000
Less ending finished goods inventory, December 31			1,460,000
Cost of goods manufactured and sold			$2,810,000

Illustration 2-4

WONDERWHEELS
Income Statement
For the Year Ending December 31

Sales revenue	$4,500,000
Cost of goods sold (see Illustration 2-3)	2,810,000
Gross margin	1,690,000
Less: marketing and administrative costs	1,440,000
Operating profit before taxes	$ 250,000

the adjustment to reflect differences between the beginning and ending finished goods inventory. The final line item is, of course, cost of goods manufactured and sold.

Income Statement

In addition to the manufacturing costs noted above, WonderWheels incurred marketing and administrative costs of $1,440,000 and generated sales revenue of $4,500,000. These period costs, together with revenues and the cost of goods manufactured and sold are presented in the income statement. The income statement is shown in Illustration 2-4.

Differential Costs

Differential Costs   Costs that change in response to a particular course of action.

Fixed versus Variable Costs

Variable Costs   Costs that change with a change in volume of activity.

Fixed Costs   Costs that are unchanged as volume changes within the relevant range of activity.

Mixed Cost   A cost that has both fixed and variable components.

Decision making involves estimating costs of alternative actions. **Differential costs** are costs that change in response to a particular course of action. To estimate differential costs, the accountant determines which costs will be affected by an action and how much they will change.

Suppose the contemplated action is a change in the volume of activity. Management might ask questions like:

▼ How much will our costs decrease if the volume of production is cut by 1,000 automobiles per month?

▼ How much will our costs increase if we serve 200 more meals per day?

▼ Between 1979 and 1982, Chrysler Corporation reduced its break-even point (where revenues equal costs) from 2.2 million units to 1.2 million units. What cost reduction occurred to accomplish this?

To answer questions like these, we need to know which costs are **variable costs** that will change proportionally with the volume of activity and which costs are **fixed costs** that will not change. Estimating the behavior of costs—which are fixed and which are variable—is very important for managerial purposes.

Variable manufacturing costs typically include direct materials, direct labor, and some manufacturing overhead (for example, indirect materials, materials-handling labor, energy costs). Also, such nonmanufacturing costs as distribution costs and sales commissions are variable. Much of manufacturing overhead and many nonmanufacturing costs are usually fixed costs.

Direct labor has traditionally been considered a variable cost. Today at many firms, the production process is very capital intensive. In a setting where a certain amount of labor is needed to keep machines operating, and the amount of labor varies very little with the amount produced, direct labor is probably best considered as a fixed cost.

In merchandising, variable costs include the cost of the product and some marketing and administrative costs. In merchandising, all of a merchant's product costs are variable; in manufacturing, a portion of the product cost is fixed.

In service organizations (for example, consulting and auto repair), variable costs typically include direct labor, materials used to perform the service, and some overhead costs.

Two aspects of cost behavior complicate the task of classifying costs into fixed and variable categories. First, not all costs are strictly fixed or strictly variable. For example, electric utility costs may be based on a fixed minimum monthly charge plus a variable cost for each kilowatt-hour in excess of the specified minimum usage. Such a **mixed cost** has both fixed and variable components.

Second, the distinction between fixed and variable costs is only valid within specified volume limits. Capacity limits are usually maximum and minimum outputs that can be produced without altering the physical plant. If the capacity of operations is increased or decreased beyond the specified limits, a new estimate of cost behavior is required. For example, if the manager of a restaurant considers increasing the volume of meals from 300 per day to 2,000 per day, expanded facilities would be needed. Rent costs, utilities, and many other costs would then increase. Although these costs are usually thought of as fixed, they change when activity moves beyond a certain range. This range within which the fixed costs do not change is referred to as the **relevant range.**

Relevant Range The activity levels within which a given fixed cost will be unchanged even through volume changes.

We now return to the WonderWheels example. After reviewing the previous year's results the marketing vice-president told the other members of the team that the bicycle market was experiencing a major slowdown. Sales could not be increased without lowering prices substantially, and there were no apparent additional efficiencies that could be derived to lower costs further.

The marketing VP noted that there was additional room in the factory to build another product and presented a plan to build a new product, skateboards. The marketing VP estimated annual sales of 10,000 skateboards to be sold wholesale for $40 each. The necessary manufacturing equipment could be leased.

The controller suggested that the team develop an estimate of product costs. Fixed costs per year would be divided by 10,000 units to obtain a unit cost. However, it would be understood that the unit fixed cost number would be correct only at a volume of 10,000 units. The controller developed the numbers that appear in Illustration 2–5. The following conversation took

Illustration 2-5   **WonderWheels—Unit Cost Buildup**

	Cost per Unit
Variable manufacturing costs:	
Direct materials	$ 9
Direct labor	6
Variable manufacturing overhead	5
Total variable manufacturing cost per unit	20
Variable marketing and administrative costs:	
Commission (5% of selling price)	2
Distribution costs	1
Total variable marketing and administrative cost per unit	3
Fixed manufacturing costs:	
Manager ($30,000 ÷ 10,000 units)	3
Equipment ($20,000 ÷ 10,000 units)	2
Total fixed manufacturing cost per unit	5
Fixed marketing and administrative costs	2
Total costs	$30

Summary Based on 10,000 Units per Year

	Per Unit		Per Year	
Variable costs	$23	($20 + 3)	$230,000	($23 × 10,000)
Fixed costs	7	($5 + 2)	70,000	($7 × 10,000)
Total costs	$30		$300,000	

Illustration 2-6   **WonderWheels—Differential Cost Analysis for Year One**

	(1) Status Quo[a]	(2) Alternative[b]	(3) Difference (2) − (1)
Sales revenue	$4,500,000	$4,900,000	$400,000
Total costs	4,250,000	4,550,000	300,000
Operating profit	$ 250,000	$ 350,000	$100,000

[a] Amounts based on Illustration 2–4.

[b] Column 1 amounts plus $400,000 revenue ($40 × 10,000 skateboards) and $300,000 costs from Illustration 2–5.

place among officers of the company concerning the plan to manufacture and sell skateboards.

VP Production: "Since I don't have a lot of experience with skateboards, I went to one of my friends in another factory and asked how much time it took to assemble one. I then used that figure and multiplied it times our regular wage rate, including benefits, to determine our direct labor cost per unit. Direct materials cost is based on quotes from our suppliers. Variable overhead is based on my estimate of energy costs, indirect materials such as cleaning solutions needed to keep workstations in good shape, and other variable manufacturing overhead costs.

Controller: Whether we produce one skateboard or 10,000, we have to hire a manager and lease additional equipment.

VP Production: That's right. My estimate is $30,000 per year for the manager and $20,000 per year for the equipment.

VP Marketing: I estimate that we'll need to hire additional marketing and administrative staff and incur other fixed costs amounting to $20,000.

Controller: That gives a total cost per unit of $30. [See Illustration 2–5.] Next we use differential analysis to see what impact adding the skateboard line would have on profits. I used last year's results as the status quo and added the skateboard numbers to the status quo to see what new profit numbers would be. [See columns 1 and 2 of Illustration 2–6.] As shown in column 3, we anticipate a $100,000 increase in operating profits. Now I think it's time to make a recommendation to the president.

Cost-Volume-Profit Analysis

It is often convenient to express fixed and variable costs in mathematical form and to develop graphs to show cost and revenue relationships visually. Two equations are used to express cost-volume-profit relationships, the cost equation and the profit equation.

Equation 1: Cost Equation

$$\text{Total costs} = \text{Fixed costs} + (\text{Variable costs} \times \text{Volume})$$
$$TC = F + VX$$

Where:

TC = Total costs
F = Fixed costs per period
V = Variable costs per unit
X = Volume of activity for the period

Equation 2: Profit Equation

Operating profit = Total revenue − Total variable costs − Fixed costs
$$\pi = PX - VX - F$$

Where:

π = Operating profit
PX = Total revenue, where P = Average sales price
VX = Total variable costs
F = Fixed costs per period

These equations would be applied to the WonderWheels example as follows:

$$TC = F + VX$$
$$TC = \$70,000 + \$23X$$

Where:

F = \$70,000 (fixed manufacturing cost of \$50,000 + fixed marketing and administrative costs of \$20,000)
V = \$23 (variable manufacturing costs of \$20 + marketing and administrative costs of \$3)

If we add the estimated selling price of \$40 to the equation, we get the profit equation:

Operating profit = Total revenue − Variable costs − Fixed costs
$$\pi = PX - VX - FC$$
$$\pi = \$40X - \$23X - \$70,000$$

The profit for 10,000 skateboards is:

$$\pi = (\$40 \times 10,000) - (\$23 \times 10,000) - \$70,000$$
$$= \$400,000 - \$230,000 - \$70,000$$
$$= \$100,000$$

Another useful form of the profit equation is:

$$\pi = (P - V)X - F$$
$$= (\$40 - \$23)X - \$70,000$$
$$= \$17X - \$70,000$$

Contribution Margin The difference between revenues and variable costs.

where the term $(P - V)$ is the unit contribution margin. The **contribution margin** is the amount each unit contributes towards (*a*) covering fixed costs and (*b*) providing a profit. For our example $(P - V)$ = \$17. This analysis indicates that each skateboard contributes \$17 toward covering fixed costs and providing a profit.

Illustration 2–7 presents the fixed and variable costs graphically. Total fixed costs remain constant over some range of activity, while total variable costs increase proportionally with increases in activity levels. Although the graph runs from zero to infinity, we know these cost relationships are only valid within the relevant range.

Illustration 2–8 shows the cost-volume-profit relationship and the profit at 10,000 skateboards. The slope of the revenue line is the average selling price per unit, \$40. The total cost line is taken from Illustration 2–7. This simple

Illustration 2-7   **WonderWheels—Fixed and Variable Costs**

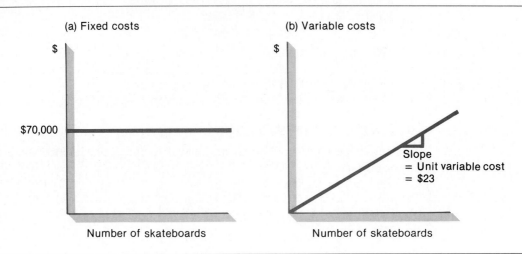

(a) Fixed costs   (b) Variable costs

Illustration 2-8   **WonderWheels—Cost-Volume-Profit Relationships**

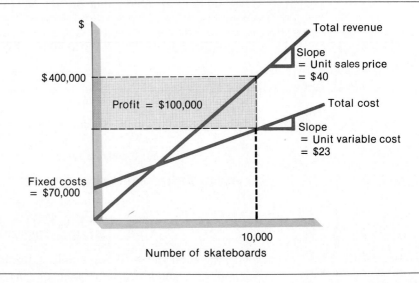

graphic display can be a useful way to present an overview of basic relationships.

Sunk Costs

Sunk Cost An expenditure made in the past that cannot be changed by present or future decisions.

A **sunk cost** is an expenditure made in the past that *cannot be changed*. Sunk costs in and of themselves are not differential costs even though people sometimes act as if the sunk costs were relevant. For example, a clothing store has 15 pairs of slacks that cost the retailer $20. No slacks have been sold at the regular price of $39.95, and they cannot be returned to the manufacturer. The manager of the store knows that he can sell the slacks at

$15 per pair, but he refuses to take a loss on them. The manager states, "I've got $20 apiece in these slacks. How can I afford the loss?" The $20 expenditure per pair of slacks is a sunk cost. It is not affected by the sale of the product. Consequently, the $20 is not relevant to the pricing decision. The store manager should ignore the sunk cost. The "loss" occurred when the market value of the slacks fell below the cost. The manager must act in the best way possible given the present and expected future conditions. If the expected future price is less than $15, the best the manager can do is take the loss now.

Most past expenditures are sunk costs. However, this does not mean that information about past expenditures is irrelevant. The store manager should ignore the cost of the slacks *now owned*, but information about the difficulty of selling the slacks for more than their cost is relevant for future decisions about buying that kind of merchandise. Also, the past cost is relevant for deriving the tax and book gain or loss on the eventual sale of the slacks.

COMPONENTS OF FULL COST

Prime Costs and Conversion Costs

Prime Cost The sum of direct materials and direct labor.

Conversion Costs The sum of direct labor and manufacturing overhead.

The sum of direct materials and direct labor is called **prime cost.** We think of manufacturing as the conversion of raw materials into a finished product. Direct labor and manufacturing overhead are required to accomplish this conversion. Therefore, the total of direct labor and manufacturing overhead is called **conversion cost.**

Illustration 2–9 summarizes the relationship between conversion costs and the three elements of manufactured production cost—direct materials, direct labor, and manufacturing overhead.

REAL WORLD APPLICATION

Analyzing Fixed and Variable Costs in a Hospital

The analysis of cost behavior is found in all organizations. For example, as hospitals have become increasingly concerned about cost control in recent years, they have been increasing their use of financial models relying on fixed and variable cost analyses. The Leonard Morse Hospital in Massachusetts recently acquired a hospital financial planning model from a Big 8 public accounting firm. One of the first steps in implementing the model was to identify which costs were variable and which were fixed.

For example, in the dietary department, the cost of food was variable. However, the hospital had a contract with an outside company to provide labor services, which was fixed. In other cases, the fixed costs were found to be constant for small changes in activity, but they changed in steps over larger changes in activity. For example, the hospital "may be able to service up to 10 operations per day with one anesthesiologist; however, once volume exceeds 10 operations per day, a second anesthesiologist may be required. For 10 or fewer operations per day, the hospital has one level of fixed cost; above 10 operations per day, it has a higher level of fixed cost."

The information that was collected for this financial planning model was used to provide forecasts and to prepare reports about past financial and operating activities.

Source: Swan A. Larracey, "Hospital Planning for Cost-Effectiveness," *Management Accounting*, July 1982, p. 47.

Illustration 2-9   **Components of Manufactured Product Cost**

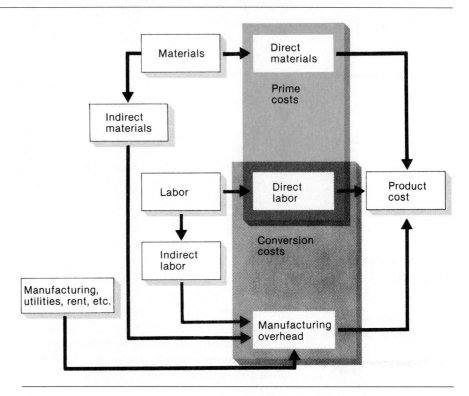

Nonmanufacturing Costs

Nonmanufacturing costs are composed of two elements: marketing costs and administrative costs. **Marketing costs** are the costs required to obtain customer orders and provide customers with finished products. These include advertising, sales commissions, shipping, and marketing departments' building occupancy costs, among others. **Administrative costs** are the costs required to manage the organization and provide staff support. They include executive and clerical salaries; costs such as legal, finance, data processing, and accounting services; and building occupancy for administrative personnel.

Nonmanufacturing costs are expensed in the period incurred for financial accounting, so they are considered *period* expenses for *financial* accounting purposes.

It is sometimes difficult to distinguish between manufacturing costs and non-manufacturing costs. For example, are the salaries of accountants who handle factory payrolls manufacturing or nonmanufacturing costs? What about the rent for offices for the manufacturing vice president? There are no clear-cut classifications, so companies usually set their own guidelines and follow them consistently.

Direct versus Indirect Costs

Earlier we distinguished between *direct* and *indirect* labor costs. *Direct* labor costs are the costs of the workers who transform direct materials into

Cost Object Any end to which a cost is assigned. Examples include a product, a department, or a product line.

finished products, while *indirect* labor costs are the costs of workers who are needed to operate the factory but do not work directly on a product.

Any cost that can be directly related to a **cost object** is a direct cost of that cost object. Those that cannot are indirect costs. A cost object is any end to which a cost is assigned—for example, a unit of inventory, a department or a product line.

Accountants use the terms *direct cost* and *indirect cost* much as a non-accountant might expect. The only difficulty is that a cost may be direct to one cost object and indirect to another. For example, the salary of a super-visor in a manufacturing department is a direct cost of the department but an indirect cost of the individual items produced by the department. So when-ever someone refers to a cost as either direct or indirect, you should immediately ask, "Direct or indirect with respect to what cost object? Units produced? A department? A division?" (When we use the terms *direct* and *indirect* to describe *direct labor, direct materials, indirect materials,* and *indirect labor,* the cost object is the unit being produced.)

Indirect costs are sometimes referred to as *common costs.* When indirect costs result from the sharing of facilities (buildings, equipment) or services (data processing, maintenance staff) by several departments, some method must frequently be devised for assigning a share of those costs to each user. The process of assignment is referred to as **cost allocation.** The allocation of costs pervades cost accounting. We discuss implications of allocating costs throughout this book.

Cost Allocation The process of assigning indirect costs to cost objects.

By now you realize that there are numerous definitions and concepts of costs. In practice, graphic displays clarify cost relationships. We have found the buildup of unit costs presented in Illustration 2–10 helps to clarify such distinctions as **full cost** per unit versus **full manufacturing cost** per unit and variable cost per unit versus variable manufacturing cost per unit. The numbers in this illustration as well as those used in Illustrations 2–11 and 2–12 are taken from the WonderWheels example.

Full Cost The sum of fixed and variable costs of manufacturing and selling a unit of product.

Full Manufacturing Cost The cost used to compute a product's inventory value under generally accepted accounting principles.

Illustrations 2–11 and 2–12 are diagrams designed to clarify distinctions between profit margin, gross margin, and contribution margin. Note that for each unit, the margin equals unit selling price minus a particular unit cost:

$$Profit\ margin\ =\ Sales\ price\ -\ Full\ cost$$
$$Gross\ margin\ =\ Sales\ price\ -\ Full\ manufacturing\ cost$$
$$Contribution\ margin\ =\ Sales\ price\ -\ Variable\ costs$$

ACTIVITY BASED COSTING

Activity Based Costing A cost-ing method that derives product costs as the sum of the cost of the activities that occur to make the product.

Since rising competition makes accurate cost information more important, managers are demanding that costs be related to activities on a causal basis. This has led to the development of **activity based costing** (also known as transactions based costing).

Activity based costing provides a more detailed analysis of what causes costs than conventional costing methods do. Conventional costing methods divide the total cost incurred in a responsibility center by the units produced in the center to derive a cost per unit. In contrast, activity based costing starts with the detailed activities required to produce a good or service and computes a product's cost in the following three steps.

Illustration 2-10   **WonderWheels—Unit Cost Buildup**

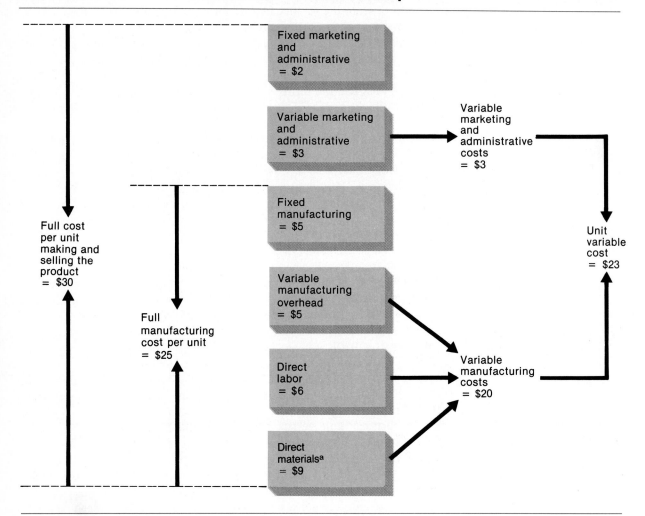

ᵃ Direct labor and direct materials are assumed to be variable costs for this illustration. Direct labor is classified as a fixed manufacturing cost in some settings—particularly in highly automated settings.

Cost Drivers Activities or transactions that cause costs to occur.

1. Identify the activities or transactions that cause costs to be incurred. These are called **cost drivers.**
2. Assign a cost to each activity.
3. Sum the costs of the activities that occur to make the product.

For example, Susan Healy, the manager of Outdoor Adventures, a company specializing in wilderness excursions, was concerned that the company was losing money on river-rafting trips. To deal with this problem, she went through the following activity based costing analysis to find the causes of costs and to understand better how to price various types of trips.

Step 1. Identify activities that cause costs. The manager of Outdoor Adventures broke down each trip into the following activities:

Illustration 2-11   **WonderWheels—Gross Margin**

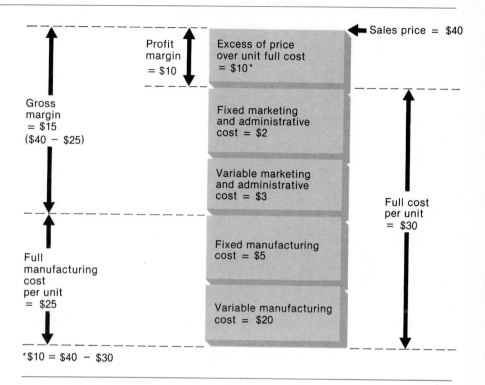

*$10 = $40 − $30

Illustration 2-12   **WonderWheels—Contribution Margin**

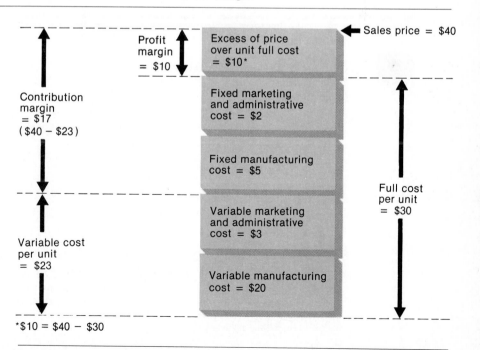

*$10 = $40 − $30

Advertise trip, which is done on a per trip basis.

Obtain permit to use river.

Determine cost of equipment use, including repair and wear and tear.

Obtain insurance.

Employ guides.

Feed customers and guides.

Step 2. Assign costs to activities. Using information available in the accounting records and making estimates where necessary, the manager assigned the costs shown in the top of Illustration 2–13 for two categories of trips: float trips and white-water trips.

Step 3. Derive the costs for the product or service. The manager of Outdoor Adventures analyzed the costs for four different expeditions: a three-day float trip with one raft which holds six customers and a guide; a three-day float trip with two rafts; a three-day trip with one raft on a difficult "white-water" river; and a three-day two-raft trip down a difficult white-water river. The results of her calculations are shown on the bottom of Illustration 2–13.

Illustration 2-13   **Outdoor Adventures—Activity Based Costing**

Identify activities that cause costs (Step 1)	Assign costs to activities (Step 2)	
	Float Trips (3-Day)	**White-Water Trips (3-Day)**
Advertise trips	$200 per trip	$200 per trip
Permit to use the river	30 per trip	50 per trip
Equipment use	20 per trip plus $5 per person	40 per trip plus $8 per person
Insurance	75 per trip	125 per trip
Paying guides	300 per trip per guide	400 per trip per guide
Food	60 per person	60 per person

Compute product costs (Step 3)

	Float Trips		White-Water Trips	
	7 Person (One Guide)	**14 Person (Two Guides)**	**7 Person (One Guide)**	**14 Person (Two Guides)**
Advertise trips	$ 200.00	$ 200.00	$ 200.00	$ 200.00
Permit	30.00	30.00	50.00	50.00
Equipment	55.00	90.00	96.00	152.00
Insurance	75.00	75.00	125.00	125.00
Guides	300.00	600.00	400.00	800.00
Food	420.00	840.00	420.00	840.00
Total cost	$1,080.00	$1,835.00	$1,291.00	$2,167.00
Cost per customer[a]	$ 180.00	$ 152.92	$ 215.17	$ 180.58
Current price per customer[b]	$ 175.00	$ 175.00	$ 250.00	$ 250.00

[a] Amounts equal total cost divided by 6 for 7-person trips (each raft has one guide who is not a customer) and total cost divided by 12 for 14–person trips.

[b] Given in the text.

By analyzing costs through activity based costing, the manager of Outdoor Adventures has discovered what each trip costs her company. This allows her to price her services. In addition, she has become more familiar with what drives costs and how they affect each of the products. This will allow her to make decisions on which products to push the hardest and which costs to control.

For example, the manager knows that the market price per person on float trips is about $175 for a three-day trip. She now knows that if she is going to offset her costs, she must run at least two rafts on all float trips. If she only runs one raft, her cost is $180 per customer, as shown in Illustration 2–13.

On the other hand, Ms. Healy knows she can charge $250 per person on a three-day white-water trip. As can be seen from Illustration 2–13, she can run one or two rafts per white-water trip and still be profitable. Activity based costing has also shown her that two raft trips are much more profitable than single raft trips.

It is interesting to note that using conventional accounting methods, Ms. Healey would just add up all the costs incurred each month and divide by the number of customers to determine her cost per customer.

For example, in a recent month, Outdoor Adventures calculated the costs to run eight river trips with 72 total customers. Total costs for the month were $12,318. Using conventional accounting methods, the following information was reported:

Cost per trip = $1,539.75 ($12,318 ÷ 8 trips)
Cost per customer = $171.08 ($12,318 ÷ 72 customers)

Activity based costing methods would not only have given the cost per trip and per customer, but also the cost per type of trip and a better understanding of which trips were profitable.

The amount of time and effort that goes into activity based costing methods makes them more costly than conventional accounting methods. Managers and accountants would normally want to ascertain whether the benefits of more detailed information justifies the additional costs in time and funds. One case in which activity based costing was viewed to have benefits exceeding costs was the Roseville Networks Division of Hewlett-Packard in Roseville, California. Activity based costing replaced a traditional overhead cost allocation based primarily on labor with a system using several cost drivers.[1]

SUMMARY

The term *cost* is ambiguous when used alone; it has meaning only in a specific context. The adjectives used to modify the term *cost* describe that context. Illustration 2–14 summarizes alternative uses of the term. Each cost concept can be applied to specific managerial problems. For example, most managerial economic decisions rely on the concept of differential costs.

---

[1] Source: Debbie Berlant; Reese Browning; and George Foster, "How Hewlett-Packard Gets Numbers It Can Trust." *Harvard Business Review,* January–February 1990, pp. 178–83.

Illustration 2-14   **Summary of Definitions**

Concept	Definition
	Nature of Cost
Cost	A *sacrifice* of resources.
Opportunity cost	The return that could be realized from the best foregone alternative use of a resource.
Outlay cost	Past, present, or near-future cash outflow.
Expense	The cost charged against revenue in a particular accounting period. We use the term *expense* only when speaking of external financial reports.
	Cost Concepts for Cost Accounting Systems
Product costs	Costs that can be more easily attributed to products; costs that are part of inventory.
Period costs	Costs that can be more easily attributed to time intervals.
Full manufacturing costs	Costs used to compute a product's inventory value for external reporting.
Direct costs	Costs that can be directly related to a cost object.
Indirect costs	Costs that cannot be directly related to a cost object.
	Additional Cost Concepts Used in Decision Making
Variable costs	Costs that vary with the volume of activity.
Fixed costs	Costs that do not vary with volume of activity.
Differential costs	Costs that change in response to a particular course of action.
Sunk costs	Costs that result from an expenditure made in the past and cannot be changed by present or future decisions.

Product costing and inventory valuation use concepts related to full manufacturing costs.

It is important to consider how use of these terms in cost accounting differs from common usage. For example, in common usage, a variable cost may vary with anything (geography, temperature, and so forth); in cost accounting, variable cost depends solely on volume.

TERMS AND CONCEPTS

The following terms and concepts should be familiar to you after reading this chapter:

Activity Based Costing	**Differential Costs**
Administrative Costs	**Direct Labor**
Contribution Margin	**Direct Materials**
Conversion Costs	**Expense**
Cost Allocation	**Finished Goods**
Cost Drivers	**Fixed Costs**
Cost Object	**Full Cost**
Cost of Goods Sold	**Full Manufacturing Cost**
Cost of Goods Manufactured and Sold Statement	**Inventoriable Costs**
	Manufacturing Overhead

Marketing Costs　　　　**Prime Cost**
Mixed Cost　　　　　　**Product Costs**
Net Income　　　　　　**Relevent Range**
Operating Profit　　　　**Sunk Cost**
Opportunity Cost　　　　**Variable Costs**
Outlay Cost　　　　　　**Work in Process**
Period Costs

SUPPLEMENTARY READINGS

Cooper, Robin, and Robert S. Kaplan. "How Cost Accounting Distorts Product Costs." *Management Accounting*, April 1988, pp. 20–27.

Cornick, Michael; William D. Cooper; and Susan B. Wilson. "How Do Companies Analyze Their Overhead?" *Management Accounting*, June 1988, pp. 41–43.

Dilts, David M., and Grant W. Russell. "Accounting for the Factory of the Future." *Management Accounting*, April 1985, pp. 34–40.

Dorwood, N. "The Mythology of Constant Marginal Costs." *Accountancy*, April 1986, pp. 98–99 (published in Great Britain).

Edwards, J. B., and J. A. Heard. "Is Cost Accounting the No. One Enemy of Productivity?" *Management Accounting*, June 1984, pp. 44–49.

Eiler, R. G.; W. G. Goeltz; and Daniel P. Keegan. "Is Your Cost Accounting up to Date?" *Harvard Business Review*, July–August 1982, pp. 133–139.

Gordon, Paul N., and Ian Cook. "Managing Costs: How to Make Informed Cost Management Decisions." *Corporate Accounting*, Summer 1986, pp. 73–75.

Hargraves, Robert F. "Controlling Expenses in a Large, Changing Company." *Corporate Accounting*, Fall 1985, pp. 59–65.

Jayson, Susan. "Goldratt and Fox: Revolutionizing the Factory Floor." *Management Accounting*, May 1987, pp. 18–22.

Mackey, James T. "Eleven Key Issues in Manufacturing Accounting." *Management Accounting,* January 1987, p. 32.

Morse, Wayne J., and Harold P. Roth. "Why Quality Costs Are Important." *Management Accounting*, November 1987, pp. 42–43.

Patell, James M. "Cost Accounting, Process Control and Product Design: A Case Study of the H-P Personal Computer Division." *Accounting Review*, October 1987, p. 808.

Richardson, Peter R. "Adopting a Strategic Approach to Costs." *Canadian Business Review*, Spring 1986, pp. 27–31.

Schiff, Jonathan B. "Developing Concepts for Management Accounting: A Challenge." *Management Accounting*, August 1987, p. 57.

SELF-STUDY PROBLEM NO. 1

The following items appeared in the records of Shoreline Products, Inc., for a current year:

Administrative costs	$ 304,000
Depreciation—manufacturing	103,000
Direct labor	482,000
Finished goods inventory, January 1	160,000
Finished goods inventory, December 31	147,000
Heat, light, and power—plant	39,000
Insurance—manufacturing plant	48,000
Marketing costs	272,000
Miscellaneous manufacturing costs	12,000
Plant maintenance and repairs	40,000
Property taxes—manufacturing	34,000
Direct materials purchases	313,000
Direct materials inventory, January 1	102,000
Direct materials inventory, December 31	81,000
Sales revenue	2,036,000
Supervisory and indirect labor	127,000
Supplies and indirect materials	14,000
Work in process inventory, January 1	135,000
Work in process inventory, December 31	142,000

Required:

Prepare an income statement with a supporting cost of goods manufactured and sold statement. (Refer to Illustrations 2–3 and 2–4).

SOLUTION TO SELF-STUDY PROBLEM NO. 1

SHORELINE PRODUCTS, INC.
Income Statement
For the Year Ended December 31

Sales revenue	$2,036,000
Cost of goods sold (see statement below)	1,239,000
Gross margin	797,000
Less:	
Marketing costs	272,000
Administrative costs	304,000
Operating profit	$ 221,000

Cost of Goods Manufactured and Sold Statement
For the Year Ended December 31

Beginning work in process inventory, January 1			$ 135,000
Manufacturing costs during the year:			
Direct materials:			
Beginning inventory, January 1	$102,000		
Add purchases	313,000		
Direct materials available	415,000		
Less ending inventory, December 31	81,000		
Direct materials put into production		$334,000	
Direct labor		482,000	
Manufacturing overhead:			
Supervisory and indirect labor	127,000		
Supplies and indirect materials	14,000		
Heat, light, and power—plant	39,000		
Plant maintenance and repairs	40,000		
Depreciation—manufacturing	103,000		
Property taxes—manufacturing	34,000		
Insurance—manufacturing plant	48,000		
Miscellaneous manufacturing costs	12,000		
Total manufacturing overhead		417,000	
Total manufacturing costs incurred during the year			1,233,000
Total costs of work in process during the year			1,368,000
Less ending work in process inventory, December 31			142,000
Cost of goods manufactured during the year			1,226,000
Beginning finished goods inventory, January 1			160,000
Finished goods inventory available for sale			1,386,000
Less ending finished goods inventory, December 31			147,000
Cost of goods manufactured and sold			$1,239,000

SELF-STUDY PROBLEM NO. 2

Your boss is upset. "I keep hearing our people refer to costs without carefully defining terms! Can you help us by presenting a simple example that shows the relationship among these various costs? Here are some basic facts you can use."

Price per unit	$ 100
Fixed costs:	
Marketing and administrative	12,000 per period
Manufacturing overhead	20,000 per period
Variable marketing and administrative	5 per unit
Direct materials	30 per unit
Direct labor	15 per unit
Variable manufacturing overhead	10 per unit
Units produced and sold	1,000 units per period

Required:

Using these data as an example, put amounts beside each label in Illustrations 2–10, 2–11 and 2–12 in the text.

SOLUTION TO   **Unit Cost Buildup (from Illustratiion 2–10)**
SELF-STUDY
PROBLEM NO. 2

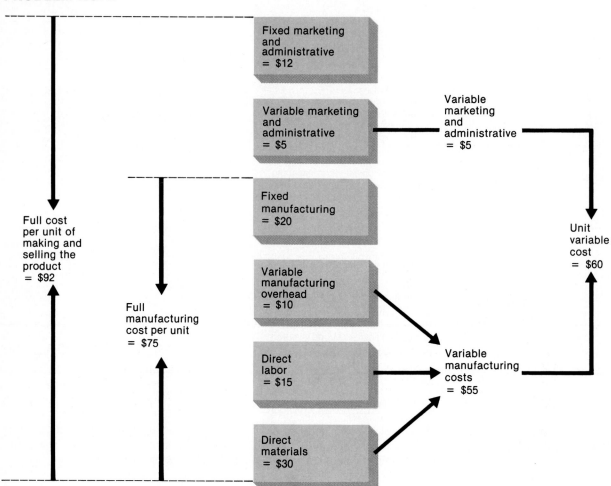

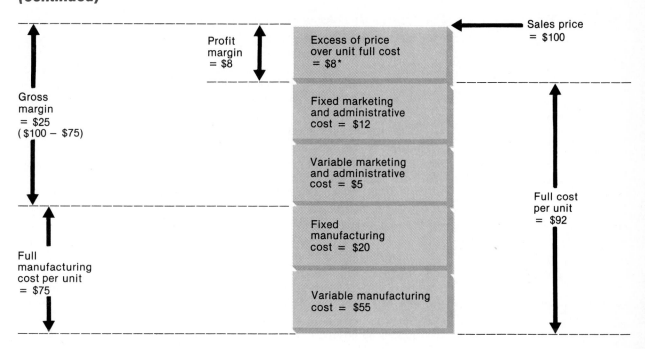

Gross
margin
= $25
($100 − $75)

Full
manufacturing
cost per unit
= $75

Profit
margin
= $8

Excess of price
over unit full cost
= $8*

Fixed marketing
and administrative
cost = $12

Variable marketing
and administrative
cost = $5

Fixed
manufacturing
cost = $20

Variable manufacturing
cost = $55

Sales price
= $100

Full cost
per unit
= $92

*$8 = $100 − $92

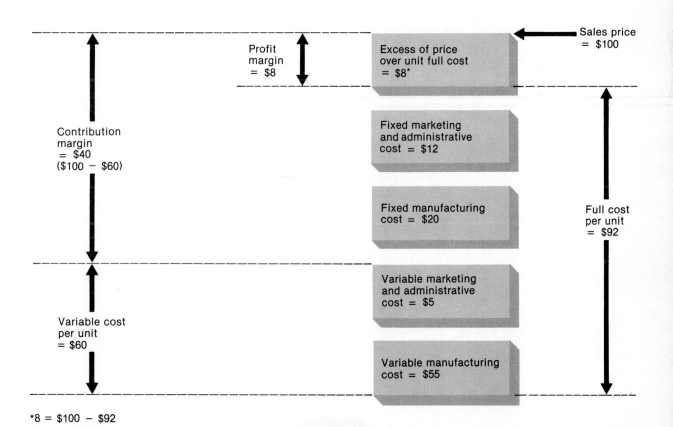

Contribution
margin
= $40
($100 − $60)

Variable cost
per unit
= $60

Profit
margin
= $8

Excess of price
over unit full cost
= $8*

Fixed marketing
and administrative
cost = $12

Fixed manufacturing
cost = $20

Variable marketing
and administrative
cost = $5

Variable manufacturing
cost = $55

Sales price
= $100

Full cost
per unit
= $92

*8 = $100 − $92

QUESTIONS

2–1. Contrast the meanings of the terms *cost* and *expense*.

2–2. Identify the difference between product costs and period costs.

2–3. Is cost of goods manufactured and sold an expense?

2–4. Identify the similarities between the Direct Materials Inventory account of the manufacturer and the Merchandise Inventory account of the merchandiser. Are there any differences between the two accounts? If so, what are they?

2–5. What are the three elements of product cost in a manufacturing operation? Describe each element briefly.

2–6. ''Prime costs are always direct costs, and overhead costs are always indirect.'' Comment on this statement.

2–7. Unit costs represent the average cost of all units produced. If you want to know the cost to produce an extra quantity of product, why not just multiply the unit average cost by the extra quantity you want?

2–8. Compare the accounting for marketing and administrative costs in a manufacturing organization with the way those costs are treated in a merchandising organization.

2–9. Must a manufacturing company use generally accepted accounting principles (GAAP) for its internal reporting? Why or why not?

2–10. Since historical costs are sunk (and, hence, not directly useful for decision-making purposes), why are accounting systems and reports based on historical costs?

EXERCISES

2–11 Basic Concepts
(L.O.1)

For each of the following costs incurred in a manufacturing operation, indicate whether the costs would be fixed or variable (F or V) and whether they would be period costs or product costs (P or R, respectively) under full manufacturing cost.

a. Transportation-in costs on materials purchased. *Product*

b. Assembly-line workers' wages. *Product*

c. Property taxes on office buildings for sales staff. *Period*

d. Salaries of top executives in the company. *Period*

e. Overtime premium for assembly workers. *Product*

f. Sales commissions. ~~Product~~ *Period*

g. Sales personnel office rental. *Period*

h. Production supervisory salaries. *Product*

i. Controller's office supplies. *Period*

j. Executive office heat and air conditioning. *Period*

2–12. Basic Concepts
(L.O.1)

For each of the following costs incurred in a manufacturing operation, indicate whether the costs would be fixed or variable (F or V) and whether they would be period costs or product costs (P or R, respectively) under full manufacturing cost.

a. Executive office security personnel.

b. Supplies used in assembly work.

c. Factory heat and air conditioning.

d. Power to operate factory equipment.

e. Depreciation on furniture for sales staff.

2–13. Prepare Statements for a Merchandising Company
(L.O.2)

Microsort sells personal computers and software. On January 1 last year, it had a beginning merchandise inventory of $250,000 including transportation-in costs. It purchased $1,300,000 of merchandise, had $120,000 of transportation-in costs, and had marketing and administrative costs of $800,000 during the year. The ending inventory of merchandise on December 31 was $160,000, including transportation-in costs. Revenue was $2,600,000 for the year.

Required:

Prepare an income statement with a supporting cost of goods sold statement.

2–14. Prepare Statements for a Manufacturing Company
(L.O.2)

The following information appears in Henry's Company's records for last year:

Administrative costs	$ 44,100
Manufacturing building depreciation	27,000
Indirect materials and supplies	6,300
Sales commissions	15,200
Direct materials inventory, January 1	18,400
Direct labor	34,600
Direct materials inventory, December 31	19,000
Finished goods inventory, January 1	10,900
Finished goods inventory, December 31	9,100
Materials purchases	22,300
Work in process inventory, December 31	13,100
Supervisory and indirect labor	14,400
Property taxes, manufacturing plant	8,400
Plant utilities and power	23,500
Work in process inventory, January 1	15,200
Sales revenue	212,400

Required:

Prepare an income statement with a supporting cost of goods manufactured and sold statement.

2–15. Prepare Statements for a Manufacturing Company
(L.O.2)

The following information appears in Molly's Muffins' records for last year:

Administrative costs	$ 42,100
Manufacturing building depreciation	25,000
Indirect materials and supplies	4,300
Sales commissions	13,200
Direct materials inventory, January 1	16,400
Direct labor	32,600
Direct materials inventory, December 31	17,000
Finished goods inventory, January 1	8,900
Finished goods inventory, December 31	7,100
Materials purchases	20,300
Work in process inventory, December 31	11,100
Supervisory and indirect labor	12,400
Property taxes, manufacturing plant	6,400
Plant utilities and power	21,500
Work in process inventory, January 1	13,200
Sales revenue	193,400

Required:

Prepare an income statement with a supporting cost of goods manufactured and sold statement.

2–16. Prepare Statements for a Manufacturing Company
(L.O.2)

The following balances appeared in the accounts of J. B. Manufacturing during a current year.

	January 1	December 31
Direct materials inventory	$16,400	$ 18,300
Work in process inventory	19,100	17,700
Finished goods inventory	7,300	8,500
Direct materials used	–0–	86,600
Cost of goods sold	–0–	301,000

Required:

Reconstruct a cost of goods manufactured and sold statement and fill in the following missing data:

a. Cost of goods manufactured during the year.
b. Manufacturing costs incurred during the year.
c. Direct materials purchases during the year.

2–17. Prepare Statements for a Manufacturing Company
(L.O.2)

The following information appears in Gaskey's Tool and Dye's records for last year:

Sales revenue	$252,300
Work in process, January 1	15,400
Work in process, December 31	12,420
Direct materials inventory, January 1	17,200
Direct materials inventory, December 31	16,100
Finished goods inventory, January 1	7,100
Finished goods inventory, December 31	8,900
Direct materials transportation-in	2,300
Direct materials put into process	25,520
Direct labor	39,700
Supervisory and indirect labor—plant	21,900
Administrative salaries	35,000
Supplies and indirect materials—plant	2,900
Heat, light, and power (77.6 percent for plant)	25,000
Depreciation (80 percent for plant)	30,000
Property taxes (75 percent for plant)	8,400
Cost of goods manufactured during the year	142,700
Other administrative costs	7,700
Marketing costs	31,700

Required:

Prepare an income statement with a supporting cost of goods manufactured and sold statement.

2–18. Cost Behavior
(L.O.3)

CanDynamics Corporation manufactured 1,000 units of product last year and identified the following costs associated with the manufacturing activity (variable costs are indicated with V; fixed costs, with F):

Direct materials used (V)	$25,200
Direct labor (V)	46,500
Supervisory salaries (F)	11,100
Indirect materials and supplies (V)	8,000
Plant utilities (other than power to run plant equipment) (F)	9,600
Power to run plant equipment (V)	7,100
Depreciation on plant and equipment (straight-line, time basis) (F)	4,800
Property taxes on building (F)	6,500

Unit variable costs and total fixed costs are expected to remain unchanged next year.

Required:

Calculate the unit cost and the total cost if 1,200 units are produced next year.

2–19. Cost Behavior
(L.O.3)

Refer to the information in exercise 2–18. Based on that information and assuming the unit sales price is $150 per unit, construct graphs of total revenue and total costs illustrating the relationship between fixed and variable costs.

2–20. Components of Full Costs
(L.O.4)

Illustrations 2–10 to 2–12 in the text show basic relationships among costs and margins. Given the following facts, complete the requirements below:

Sales price	$200 per unit
Fixed costs:	
Marketing and administrative	24,000 per period
Manufacturing overhead	30,000 per period
Variable costs:	
Marketing and administrative	6 per unit
Manufacturing overhead	9 per unit
Direct labor	30 per unit
Direct materials	60 per unit
Units produced and sold	1,200 per period

Required:

a. How much are each of the following unit costs (see Illustration 2–10)?
   1. Variable manufacturing cost.
   2. Variable cost.
   3. Full manufacturing cost.
   4. Full cost.

2–21. Cost Behavior
(L.O.3)

Given the data in exercise 2–20, graph total revenue and total cost lines (as in Illustration 2–8).

2–22. Components of Full Costs
(L.O.4)

For external financial reporting, all costs of manufacturing the product are product costs (that is, they are inventoriable). (See Illustration 2–1.)

Required:

Using the data from exercise 2–20, what are the following:
a. Product cost per *unit*.
b. Period costs for the *period*.

2–23. Components of Full Costs
(L.O.4)

The following cost, price, and volume data apply to Springs & Teen Company for a particular month:

Sales price per unit	$ 1,000 per unit
Fixed costs:	
Marketing and administrative	130,000 per period
Manufacturing overhead	150,000 per period
Variable costs:	
Marketing and administrative	80 per unit
Manufacturing overhead	100 per unit
Direct labor	200 per unit
Direct materials	250 per unit
Units produced and sold	1,000 per period

Required:

a. How much are each of the following *unit* costs (see Illustration 2–10)?
    1. Variable manufacturing cost.
    2. Variable cost.
    3. Full manufacturing cost.
    4. Full cost.
b. How much are each of the following unit margins (see Illustrations 2–11 and 2–12)?
    1. Profit margin.
    2. Gross margin.
    3. Contribution margin.

2–24. Cost Behavior
(L.O.3)

Given the data in exercise 2–23, graph total revenue and total cost lines (as in Illustration 2–8).

2–25. Components of Full Costs
(L.O.4)

Swifty Cleaners provides janitorial services to various organizations. For a particular month, it had the following costs and revenues:

Hours worked and billed to customers	10,000 hours
Price charged per hour	$30
Variable costs per hour	20
Fixed costs for the month	$50,000

Required:

a. What is the full cost *per unit* of providing the service?
b. What are the following *unit* margins?
    1. Profit margin.
    2. Contribution margin.

2–26. Activity Based Costing
(L.O.5)

Refer to the discussion of activity based costing in the chapter and the numbers that appear in Illustration 2–13.

Required:

Compute the cost of the following products:
a. A 28-person float trip with four rafts and four guides.
b. A 28-person white-water trip with four rafts and four guides.

2–27. Activity Based Costing
(L.O.5)

Refer to the discussion of activity based costing in the chapter and the numbers that appear in Illustration 2–13. Assume that the manager of Outdoor Adventures discovered that she had omitted one activity from her analysis, namely, transportation to and from the river, which cost $50 per raft per trip for regular float trips and $80 per raft per trip for white-water trips. All other costs remain as reported in Illustration 2–13.

Required:

Recompute the cost of each of the four products (that is, types of trips) shown in Illustration 2–13. Recompute the cost per customer.

2–28. Activity Based Costing
(L.O.5)

Assume you belong to a club that wants to offer a trip to its members. (You pick the trip. It could be to a ski slope, the beach, or wherever you want!) Your club will pay all costs of the trip, including meals, transportation, and lodging, and will ask the travelers to pay a flat fee to the club. List all of the activities that would cause costs to be incurred. Start with a brochure that advertises the trip and continue listing activities until your travelers are home (safely, we hope). Although the club pays all costs of the trip, you may exclude personal items (for example, ski rentals, telephone calls). Be sure to state what items you are explicitly excluding from the calculation. (Good luck!)

PROBLEMS

2–29. Find the Unknown Account Balances

Each column below is independent. The data refers to one year for each example. Use the data given to find the unknown account balances.

Account	Example 1	2	3	4	5
Direct materials inventory, January 1	(a) ✓	$ 3,500	$ 16,000	$ 4,000	$ 22,500
Direct materials inventory, December 31	$ 3,600	2,900	14,100	6,200	(i)
Work in process inventory, January 1	2,700	6,720	82,400	6,280	(j)
Work in process inventory, December 31	3,800	3,100	76,730	6,280	42,600
Finished goods inventory, January 1	1,900	(d)	17,200	1,400	167,240
Finished goods inventory, December 31	300	4,400	28,400	2,300	Unknown
Purchases of direct materials	16,100	12,000	64,200	(h)	124,200
Cost of goods manufactured during this year	(b)	27,220	313,770	29,000	759,110
Total Manufacturing costs	55,550	23,600	308,100	29,000	763,400
Cost of goods sold	56,050	27,200	302,570	28,100	(k)
Gross margin	(c)	16,400	641,280	6,700	937,300
Direct labor	26,450	3,800	124,700	11,600	(l)
Direct materials used	15,300	(e)	66,100	7,500	117,100
Manufacturing overhead	13,800	7,200	(g)	9,900	215,300
Sales revenue	103,300	(f)	943,850	34,800	1,679,950

2–30. Differential Cost Analysis for Decision Making

Rob Roberts has been working a summer job that pays $1,100 a month. His employer has offered to convert the job into a full-time position at $1,500 per month. Take-home pay is 70 percent of these amounts. In view of this offer, Rob is tempted not to return to school for the coming year. His friend Alice is trying to convince him to return to school. Rob remarks, "I've been talking to other friends, and no matter how you figure it, school is extremely expensive. Tuition is about $2,200 per year net of scholarship assistance. Books and supplies are another $600. Room and board will cost $3,700 a year even if I share a room. It costs $2,400 a year to keep up my car and clothing, and other incidentals amount to about $3,000 per year. I figure school will cost me the total of all these costs, which is $11,900 plus my lost salary of $18,000 per year. At $29,900 a year, who can justify higher education?

If you were Alice, how would you respond to Rob's remarks?

2–31. Cost Analysis in a Service Organization

Pat MacDonald, an independent engineer, has been invited to bid on a contract engineering project. Pat is not the only bidder on the project and wants the bid only if it will return an adequate profit for the time and effort involved. The contract calls for 250 hours of Pat's time. The following cost data have been extracted from Pat's records and are not expected to change for the contract period.

	Per Hour
Normal consulting rate	$100
Office costs, secretary, etc.	(38)
Travel, other variable costs	(22)
Normal "profit" per hour	$ 40
Billable hours (typical week)	30

The hourly rate for the office costs, secretary, etc. is based on a fixed cost of $1,140 per week divided by the 30 billable hours per typical week. Billable hours represent the time which Pat can charge to clients. However, these costs are fixed regardless of the number of hours Pat works per week. Under the contract, the travel and other expenses will be the same as for normal consulting.

Required:

What is the relevant "cost" for Pat's bid under each of the following independent situations? Support your chosen cost basis.

a. Pat will work on the contract during hours that would otherwise not be billable to other clients.

b. Pat will give up work for other clients to meet the time requirements under the contract. No ill will would be generated as a result of accepting the contract.

c. Pat believes that the contract would be the start of a long-term business relationship that could take up most of Pat's time. The initial bid would have to be close to the amount charged on subsequent projects. While Pat has the time now to take the project without giving up clients, eventually Pat would have to give up some other clients.

2-32. Reconstruct Financial Statements

The following data appeared in Pacific Northwest's records on December 31 of last year:

Direct materials inventory, December 31	$ 85,000
Direct materials purchased during the year	360,000
Finished goods inventory, December 31	90,000
Indirect labor	32,000
Direct labor	400,000
Plant heat, light, and power	37,200
Building depreciation (⅞ is for manufacturing)	81,000
Administrative salaries	51,400
Miscellaneous factory cost	31,900
Marketing costs	37,000
Overtime premium on factory labor	12,100
Insurance on factory equipment	19,000
Transportation-out	1,600
Taxes on manufacturing property	13,100
Legal fees on customer complaint	8,200
Direct materials used	382,100
Work in process inventory, December 31	24,600

On January 1, at the beginning of last year, the Finished Goods Inventory account had a balance of $80,000, and the Work in Process Inventory account had a balance of $25,900. Sales revenue during the year was $1,625,000.

Required:

Prepare a cost of goods manufactured and sold statement and an income statement.

2-33. Prepare Projected Statements Based on Past Data

Assume that the statements of Shoreline Products, Inc. (self-study problem no. 1) were based on sales for 4,000 units. Next year, the following changes are expected:

1. Sales will increase to 4,800 units with a 5 percent increase in selling price per unit.

2. No additional property or equipment will be required to meet increased demand.

3. Labor wage rates will increase by 10 percent, and materials costs will increase by 15 percent before considering the increased volume.

4. Production will increase 20 percent (from 4,000 to 4,800 units) to meet the added demand.

5. Direct labor, direct materials, supplies, and indirect materials are variable costs. All other costs are fixed; that is, they do not change because of a change in production activity. (However, they may change because of price changes.)

6. Heat, light, power, and maintenance and repairs costs are expected to increase by 50 percent, regardless of volume. All other costs will remain unchanged.

Required:

Prepare a report showing the total costs to be incurred in manufacturing activity during the coming year. (Round numbers to nearest whole dollar.)

2-34. Cost Behavior: Estimate Most Profitable Operating Level[2]

The following production and sales data are for a company division with a capacity of 13,000 units and an unchangeable unit sales price of $4.50. The company is required by a sales contract to keep the division operating and wants to operate at the optimal level given these conditions. The manufacturing vice president suggested: "We should operate at 13,000 units since that gives us the lowest unit cost."

	Production Volume			
	10,000	**11,000**	**12,000**	**13,000**
Variable manufacturing cost	$37,000	$40,800	$44,600	$48,400
Fixed manufacturing cost	9,000	9,000	9,000	9,000
Marketing costs	6,000	6,600	7,200	7,800
Administrative costs	6,000	6,000	6,200	6,400
Total costs	$58,000	$62,400	$67,000	$71,600
Unit cost	$5.80	$5.67	$5.58	$5.51

Required:

What is the optimal level of output if production must take place at one of the levels indicated in this schedule?

2-35. Analyze the Costs at Different Demand Levels[3]

To increase production beyond the current level of 10,000 units, Melville Corporation must lease additional equipment and pay overtime premiums to its employees. At the present level of operations of 10,000 units, fixed costs total $50,000 and variable costs are $3 per unit. If Melville incurs an additional $20,000 in fixed costs, they can produce and sell an additional 10,000 units at a variable cost of $5 each. Management policy forbids expanding capacity unless unit profit remains the same as at present. Thus, average cost must remain constant.

Required:

Prepare a schedule showing average costs with the expansion as well as under present activity levels.

2-36. Activity Based Costing

Eye Shop is a small optometry practice run by a Doctor Shrewd. The optometrist employs one receptionist and one assistant.

The receptionist schedules appointments, checks patients in, and handles the billing. The average time per patient for scheduling of an appointment is two minutes, and the average time per check-in and seating is also two minutes. Average time spent per billing is five minutes. The receptionist is paid $10 an hour.

The assistant conducts the preliminary eye test, shows styles of frames available, and fits frames to the customer. The average time for preliminary tests is 15 minutes;

---

[2] Adapted from W. J. Vatter, "Tailor-Making Cost Data for Specific Uses," *National Association of (Cost) Accountants Bulletin (1954 Conference Proceedings).*

[3] Adapted from C. Purdy, R. K. Zimmer, and J. H. Grenell, "Costs in Relation to Pricing Products and Services," in *The Managerial and Cost Accountant's Handbook,* eds. Homer A. Black and James Don Edwards (Homewood, Ill.: Dow Jones-Irwin, 1979).

the average time for showing and fitting frames is 20 minutes. The assistant is paid $20 per hour.

Dr. Shrewd takes care of all fittings of new prescriptions for both regular lenses and contacts. As part of the normal checkup, he conducts a glaucoma test and a test to ensure that the current prescription is correct and interviews each patient to discuss any specific problems the patient may be experiencing. Fitting for a new prescription for glasses averages 30 minutes. Fitting for contacts requires one hour on the initial visit plus two follow-up visits, each lasting 30 minutes. Glaucoma tests take 5 minutes. The test to ensure that the current prescription is correct averages 15 minutes, and the individual interview on specific problems averages 10 minutes. Dr. Shrewd costs his time at $50 per hour.

Average costs for materials are as follows: frames—$15; lenses—$25; contact lenses including start-up kit—$20.

Required:

a. Identify the activities that cause costs and assign costs to each activity.
b. How much would it cost to conduct a normal checkup?
c. How much does it cost to conduct a preliminary examination and prescribe and fit regular glasses? Contacts?

2–37. Activity Based Costing

Refer to problem 2–36. Calculate the costs for the following situations.

a. After a preliminary examination, a customer finds she needs vision correction and chooses glasses.
b. A regular customer comes in and tells the doctor everything is fine, but she is leaving the country for six months and requests a glaucoma test and a second pair of glasses for the trip.
c. A new customer comes in and has his contact lens prescription with him but needs a new pair of lenses.

INTEGRATIVE CASES

2–38. Analyze the Impact of a Decision on Income Statements

You have been appointed manager of an operating division of HI-TECH, Inc., a manufacturer of products using the latest developments in microprocessor technology. Your division manufactures the chip assembly, ZP-1. On January 1 of this year, you invested $1 million in automated processing equipment for chip assembly. At that time, your expected income statement was as follows:

Sales revenues	$3,200,000
Operating costs:	
Variable (cash expenditures)	400,000
Fixed (cash expenditures)	1,500,000
Equipment depreciation	300,000
Other depreciation	250,000
Total operating costs	2,450,000
Operating profits (before taxes)	$ 750,000

On October 25 of this year, you are approached by a sales representative for the Mammoth Machine Company. Mammoth wants to rent to your division a new assembly machine which would be installed on December 31. The new equipment has an annual rental charge of $460,000. The new equipment would enable you to increase your division annual revenue by 10 percent. Fixed cash expenditures would decrease by 5 percent per year due to the more efficient machine. You will have to write off the cost of the old machine this year because it has no salvage value. Equipment depreciation in the income statement above is for the old machine.

Your bonus is determined as a percentage of your division's operating profits before taxes. Equipment losses are included in the bonus and operating profit computation.

Ignore taxes and any effects on operations on the day of installation of the new machine. Assume the data given in your expected income statement is the same for this year and next year if the current equipment is kept.

Required:

a. What is the difference in this year's divisional operating profit if the new machine is rented and installed on December 31 of this year?

b. What would be the effect on next year's divisional operating profit if the new machine is rented and installed on December 31 of this year?

c. Would you rent the new equipment? Why or why not?

2–39. Chris Collins's Use of Costs in Decision Making[4]

Chris Collins supervised an assembly department in Dexter Electronics Company. Recently, Collins became convinced that a certain component, number S-36, could be produced more efficiently by changing assembly methods. Collins described this proposal to Dexter's industrial engineer, who quickly dismissed Collins's idea—mainly, Collins thought, because the engineer had not thought of the idea first.

Collins felt that producing the S-36 component at a lower cost might provide Collins the opportunity to start a new business. Dexter's purchasing agent assured Collins that Dexter would buy S-36s from Collins if the price were 10 to 15 percent below Dexter's current cost of $1.65 per unit. Working at home, Collins experimented with the new assembly method. This experimentation seemed successful, so Collins prepared estimates for large scale S-36 production. Collins determined the following:

1. A local toolmaker would make the required assembly workstations for $800 each. One workstation would be needed for each assembly worker.

2. Assembly workers were readily available, on either a full-time or part-time basis, at a wage of $3.75 per hour. Another 20 percent of wages would be necessary for fringe benefits. Collins estimated that on average (including rest breaks), a worker could assemble, test, and pack 15 S-36s per hour.

3. Purchased components for the S-36 would cost $.85 per unit. Shipping materials and delivery costs would cost $.05 per unit.

4. Suitable space was available for assembly operations at a rental of $600 per month.

5. Collins would receive a salary of $2,000 per month.

6. An office manager was required and would cost $900 per month in salary.

7. Miscellaneous costs, including maintenance, supplies, and utilities, will average about $325 per month (all fixed costs).

8. Dexter Electronics would purchase between 400,000 and 525,000 units of S-36 a year, with 450,000 being Dexter's purchasing agent's "best guess." Collins would have to commit to a price of $1.40 per unit for the next 12 months even though the exact volume would not be known.

Collins showed these estimates to a cost analyst in another electronics firm. This analyst said that the estimates appeared reasonable, but the analyst advised buying enough workstations to enable producing the maximum estimated volume (525,000

---

[4] Source: Copyright © Osceola Institute, 1979, with the permission of Professors Robert N. Anthony and James S. Reece.

units per year) on a one-shift basis (assuming 2,000 labor-hours per assembler per year). Collins thought this was good advice.

a. What are Collins's expected variable costs per unit? Fixed costs per month? What would be the total costs per year of Collins's business if volume was 400,000 units? 450,000 units? (Limit yourself to cash costs; ignore depreciation of workstation equipment. Also, disregard any interest costs Collins might incur on borrowed funds.)

b. What is the average cost per unit of S-36 at each of these three volumes (400,000, 450,000, and 525,000 units)?

c. Re-answer requirements (a) and (b) assuming that (1) Collins wanted to guarantee each assembly worker 2,000 hours of pay per year; (2) enough workers would be hired to assemble 450,000 units a year; (3) these workers could work overtime at a cost (including fringes) of $6.75 per hour; and (4) no additional fixed costs would be incurred if overtime were needed. (Do not use these assumptions for requirement [d].)

d. Re-answer requirements (a) and (b), now including depreciation as a cost. Assume the workstation equipment has a useful life of six years and no salvage value. Straight-line depreciation will be used.

e. Would you encourage Chris Collins to resign from Dexter Electronics and form the proposed enterprise? Assume Chris would need to invest $70,000 for working capital plus whatever is needed for the assembly workstations. Support your answer.

ACCOUNTING FOR COST FLOWS: COST ACCUMULATION

LEARNING OBJECTIVES

1. Knowledge of basic cost flow model.

2. How costs are accumulated in merchandising organizations.

3. How costs are accumulated in manufacturing organizations.

4. How costs are accumulated in service organizations.

In this chapter we provide an overview of cost flows by showing how costs are accumulated in the accounting systems of merchandising, manufacturing, and service organizations. For now, we emphasize a broad perspective and reserve some of the more technical aspects of cost accumulation and allocation for later chapters.

Anyone who uses cost accounting information must understand the system that provides the data. Even people who are not cost accounting experts need to understand how the accounting system works if they are to use the information wisely and help design accounting systems that provide the data they need.

OVERVIEW

The essential purpose of any organization is to transform inputs into outputs. The activity for merchandising, manufacturing, and service organizations is shown in Illustration 3–1. These organizations share many *similarities*. All require labor and capital as inputs, and all transform them into a product or service for the market.

These organizations also differ from one another in many respects. The *differences* between these organizations are reflected in their accounting systems. A **merchandising organization** starts with a finished product and markets it. Because inventory is acquired in finished form, its cost is easily ascertained.

Merchandising Organization
An organization characterized by marketing goods or services.

Illustration 3–1   **Transformation of Inputs to Outputs**

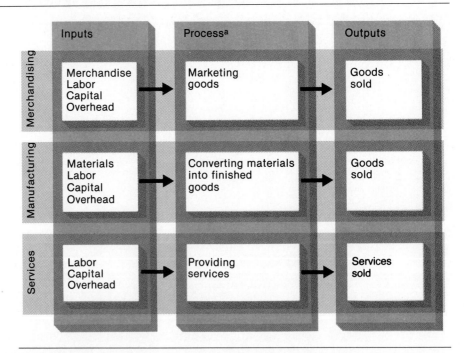

a The process refers to the major activity of the organization. Manufacturing and service organizations have marketing activities in addition to their major production activities.

Manufacturing Organization
An organization characterized by the conversion of raw materials into some other output products.

Service Organization An organization whose output is the result of the performance of some activity.

The accounting system for a **manufacturing organization** is more complex because direct materials are first acquired and then converted to finished products. A manufacturer's accounting system focuses on work in process, which is the account that reflects the costs involved in transforming input materials into finished goods.

Service organizations are different from manufacturers and merchandisers because they have no inventory of goods for sale. Costs are charged to responsibility centers for performance evaluation. In a public accounting firm, for example, costs are charged to the audit department, the tax department, and so forth. Costs are also charged to jobs. Here is how a breakdown of professional service costs might look:

	Department	
Job	**Audit**	**Tax**
Mary Jones, tax return		$ 84
Dunkin Dozens, tax return and audit	$1,347	262
Gonzalez Manufacturing, Inc., audit	8,179	

This assignment of costs to jobs and departments helps managers control costs. It also facilitates performance evaluation. The manager of each department is held responsible for the costs of the department; the manager of each job is held responsible for the cost of that job.

Of the three kinds of operations, manufacturers require the most complex and comprehensive cost accounting system. All three need cost information for decision making and performance evaluation. But in addition, manufacturers need product costing for inventory valuation and to measure cost of goods sold reported on external financial statements. Many manufacturers also have service and merchandising activities whose costs must also be recorded.

THE BASIC COST FLOW MODEL

The **basic cost flow model** is used to summarize the flow of costs in accounting systems. This model is:

$$\begin{array}{ccccc} \text{Beginning} & \text{Transfers-} & & \text{Transfers-} & \text{Ending} \\ \text{balance} & + & \text{in} & = & \text{out} & + & \text{balance} \\ (BB) & & (TI) & & (TO) & & (EB) \end{array}$$

Rearranging terms slightly, we have:

$$BB + TI - EB = TO$$

which shows in summary form the basis for the flow of costs in the Work in Process Inventory and Finished Goods Inventory accounts. The interaction between these accounts is shown below:

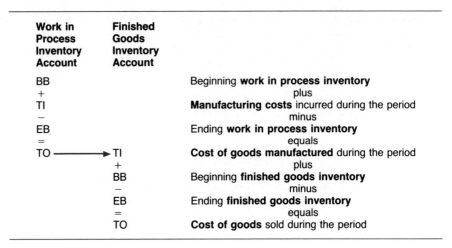

Work in Process Inventory Account	Finished Goods Inventory Account	
BB		Beginning **work in process inventory**
+		plus
TI		**Manufacturing costs** incurred during the period
−		minus
EB		Ending **work in process inventory**
=		equals
TO ⟶	TI	**Cost of goods manufactured** during the period
	+	plus
	BB	Beginning **finished goods inventory**
	−	minus
	EB	Ending **finished goods inventory**
	=	equals
	TO	**Cost of goods** sold during the period

This basic cost flow model will help you to understand the flow of costs through various inventory accounts, such as Direct Materials Inventory, Work in Process Inventory, and Finished Goods Inventory. Each of the next several sections in this chapter has examples applying the basic cost flow model.

COST ACCUMULATION: MERCHANDISING ORGANIZATIONS

Merchandise Inventory In a merchandising organization, the cost of goods acquired but not yet sold.

Transportation-in Costs The costs incurred by the buyer of goods to ship the goods from place of sale to the place the buyer can use the goods.

First-in, First-out (FIFO) Costing The first-in, first-out inventory method whereby the first goods received are the first goods charged out when sold or transferred.

The major activities of a merchandising organization are the buying and marketing of goods. They typically do not have the facilities to produce their own products. They generally purchase these products from manufacturers.

The flow of costs through the accounts in a merchandising operation is shown in Illustration 3–2. The top portion of the illustration deals with the purchase and sale of **merchandise inventory**. These accounts are of particular concern to buyers, whose performance often is judged on total sales of the goods they purchase from manufacturers and the gross margin that is attained on those sales. You will remember from Chapter 2 that gross margin is the difference between sales revenue and product costs. In the case of merchandising organizations, the product cost is the acquisition cost, the price the buyer negotiates to purchase the goods from the manufacturer, plus the **transportation-in costs** (also called freight-in costs).

The Merchandise Inventory account shows the product costs for which buyers are responsible. The cost of units sold during the period is transferred to Cost of Goods Sold account. For financial reporting, assumptions about inventory flow [for example, **first-in, first-out (FIFO)** versus **last-in, first-out (LIFO)**] and valuation decisions (for example, current cost versus historical costs) are needed to value inventory.

Perpetual and Periodic Inventories

The **perpetual inventory** method requires an ongoing record of transfers-in and transfers-out. In a supermarket, specific goods and quantities are recorded for each sale. In a perpetual inventory system, an ongoing record of

Illustration 3-2   **Flow of Costs: Merchandising**

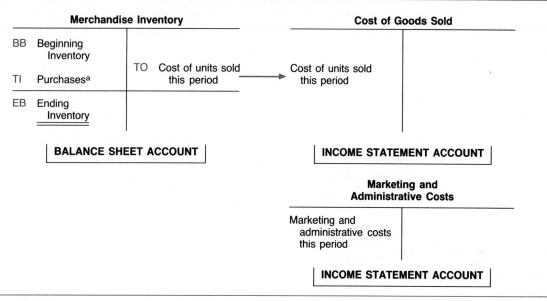

a Includes transportation-in costs.

Note: BB = Beginning balance; TI = Transfers-in; EB = Ending balance; TO = Transfers-out.

Perpetual Inventory   A method of accounting whereby inventory records are maintained on a continuously updated basis.

Periodic Inventory   A method of inventory accounting whereby inventory balances are determined on specific dates (such as quarterly) by physical counts rather than on a continuous basis.

credits is made to the inventory account. The **periodic** (or *physical*) **inventory** technique does not require an ongoing record of inventory transfers-out. Instead, the total transfers-out are derived from knowledge of beginning and ending inventories and transfers-in. Hence, any time management needs to know the cost of goods sold, a physical inventory must be taken.

For example, consider the sale of Brand XX tennis racquets at Martha's Sport Shop in March. Beginning inventory was 10 racquets, and ending inventory was 15 racquets, and 40 racquets were purchased by the store. The racquets are valued at $10 each. From the basic cost flow model:

$$BB + TI = TO + EB$$

we solve for the unknown cost of goods sold, or TO,

$$TO = BB + TI - EB$$

Beginning inventory (10 racquets at $10)	$100
Ending inventory (15 racquets at $10)	150
Purchases (40 racquets at $10)	400

$$TO = \$100 + \$400 - \$150$$
$$TO = \underline{\$350}$$

A perpetual inventory provides more data than a periodic inventory. For example, with a perpetual system, up-to-date inventory balances and cost of goods sold are always available. But with a periodic system, these data are only available after making a physical inventory count. Perpetual inventory is useful for control purposes, too, because the clerical record of transfers-out can be compared with a physical count to check for theft, spoilage, and other problems. However, the perpetual method requires more expensive data maintenance systems.

With the expanded use of bar codes and other computerized inventory systems nearly all large organizations use perpetual inventories. Periodically—say, every six months—they may take a physical inventory to check for shortages, theft, and clerical accuracy and to satisfy internal or external auditors. They use the periodic methods for such things as office supplies and small merchandise.

Just-in-Time Inventory in Merchandising

Just-in-time (JIT) inventory is being applied in many merchandising organizations. Using computerized inventory reports, buyers work with their manufacturers to ensure that reorders arrive at their stores just as they are running out of stock. This is becoming increasingly common in clothing stores carrying items that are reordered on a continual basis, such as underwear and hosiery.

For example, Levi Strauss, the large manufacturer of blue jeans, has been working with their major customers to have computer-generated reorders sent automatically to its warehouse. Shipments of the needed size and style are then automatically sent to the merchandisers placing the order. This allows the merchandiser to have the right style and size on hand while minimizing the amount of money tied up in inventory.

Cost Flows

The Marketing and Administrative Costs account in the lower portion of Illustration 3–2 shows all the period costs required to run the company and sell the merchandise. These costs can be thought of as value added in merchandising. A merchandising company adds value by acquiring products and distributing them to customers in an efficient manner. Marketing and administrative costs are not added to the value of inventory but are expensed in the period in which they are incurred.

The following example shows how costs would flow through the accounts in a merchandising operation. The journal and T-account entries present a standard model for accumulating costs in merchandising.

The Denim Shop sells one product: denim slacks. In April, The Denim Shop purchased 2,000 pairs of slacks at $9 each and sold 1,200 for $20 each. Transportation-in costs were $1 per pair. The Denim Shop had 100 pairs on hand on April 1 that had cost $7 per pair plus transportation-in of $1 per pair. No other merchandise was bought or sold during the month. The company uses the FIFO basis for inventory costing. Marketing and administrative costs were $5,000. All transactions were on account.

The following entries were made to record these transactions:

(1)	Merchandise Inventory		18,000	
	Accounts Payable			18,000
	To record the purchase of 2,000 pairs of slacks.			
(2)	Merchandise Inventory		2,000	
	Accounts Payable			2,000
	To record transportation-in of $1 per pair of 2,000 pairs of slacks.			
(3a)	Accounts Receivable		24,000	
	Sales Revenue			24,000
	To record the sales of 1,200 pairs of slacks at $20 per pair.			
(3b)	Cost of Goods Sold		11,800	
	Merchandise Inventory			11,800
	To record the FIFO cost of goods sold at 100 pairs of slacks from beginning inventory at $8 per pair (merchandise cost of $7 plus transportation-in of $1) and 1,100 pairs from current month purchases at $10 per pair (merchandise cost of $9 plus transportation-in of $1).			
(4)	Marketing and Administrative Costs		5,000	
	Accounts Payable			5,000
	To record marketing and administrative costs for April.			

The flow of costs is shown in Illustration 3–3 and the income statement in Illustration 3–4. The numbers in parentheses in Illustration 3–3 correspond to the numbers of the journal entries above.

In merchandising, performance evaluation and cost control are based on revenues and costs, usually accounted for by product line and department. For example, in a retail department store, costs are accumulated and reported for each major product line and department—sportswear, housewares, furniture, and so forth. Accounts like those in Illustration 3–3 would be provided for each department in a merchandising company.

Illustration 3–3   **Merchandise Cost Flow**

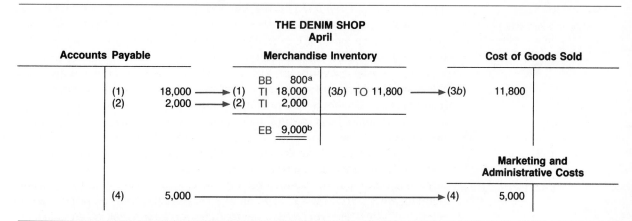

Note: BB = Beginning balance; EB = Ending balance; TI = Transfers-in; and TO = Transfers-out.
[a] Beginning inventory consists of 100 units at $8 ($7 purchase price plus $1 transportation-in).
[b] Ending inventory consists of 900 units at $10 each.
 The 900 units is equal to the 100 units in beginning inventory plus the 2,000 units purchased and less the 1,200 units sold.
 The $10 price per unit is the $9 purchase price plus $1 transportation-in.

Illustration 3–4

THE DENIM SHOP
Income Statement
For the Month Ended April 30

Sales revenue	$24,000
Cost of goods sold	11,800
Gross margin	12,200
Marketing and administrative costs	5,000
Operating profit	$ 7,200

Cost of Goods Sold Statement
For the Month Ended April 30

Beginning merchandise inventory		$ 800
Cost of goods purchased:		
Merchandise cost		18,000
Transportation-in		2,000
Cost of goods available for sale		20,800
Less cost of goods in ending inventory		9,000
Cost of goods sold		$11,800

COST ACCUMULATION: MANUFACTURING ORGANIZATIONS

Cost Accumulation The process of assigning costs to a cost object, such as a job, department, or inventory account.

Just like merchandising organizations, manufacturers face issues concerning inventory cost flow assumptions (FIFO, LIFO, etc.). Manufacturers also can employ perpetual or periodic methods and make use of contemporary systems like JIT. The major difference is that manufacturers need to accumulate and distribute the costs necessary to acquire and transform materials into goods for sale. This calls for a somewhat more complex flow of costs.

The flow of costs in the transformation of direct materials into finished goods is shown in Illustration 3–5. The focal point is the Work in Process Inventory account. This account both *describes* the transformation of inputs into outputs and *accounts* for the costs incurred in the process. Manufacturing costs are *accumulated* in the left (debit) side of the Work in Process Inventory account. (This is referred to as **cost accumulation**.) When units are completed, their costs are credited to Work in Process Inventory and debited to Finished Goods Inventory.

When a unit passes through Work in Process Inventory, it is charged with the costs of manufacturing it: direct materials, direct labor, and manufacturing overhead. This total cost of manufacturing the unit is its inventory value for external financial reporting under generally accepted accounting principles.

When the unit is sold, this cost is expensed against revenue as cost of goods sold for financial and tax-accounting purposes. These costs are also often used as input to product pricing, in contracts that call for cost-plus reimbursement, for long-range planning, in contracts based on prices, and in regulated industries where an organization's revenue is based on costs.

Costing for Performance Evaluation

Most companies have a separate Work in Process Inventory account for each department (for example, the assembly department, the finishing de-

Illustration 3-5   **Flow of Costs: Manufacturing**

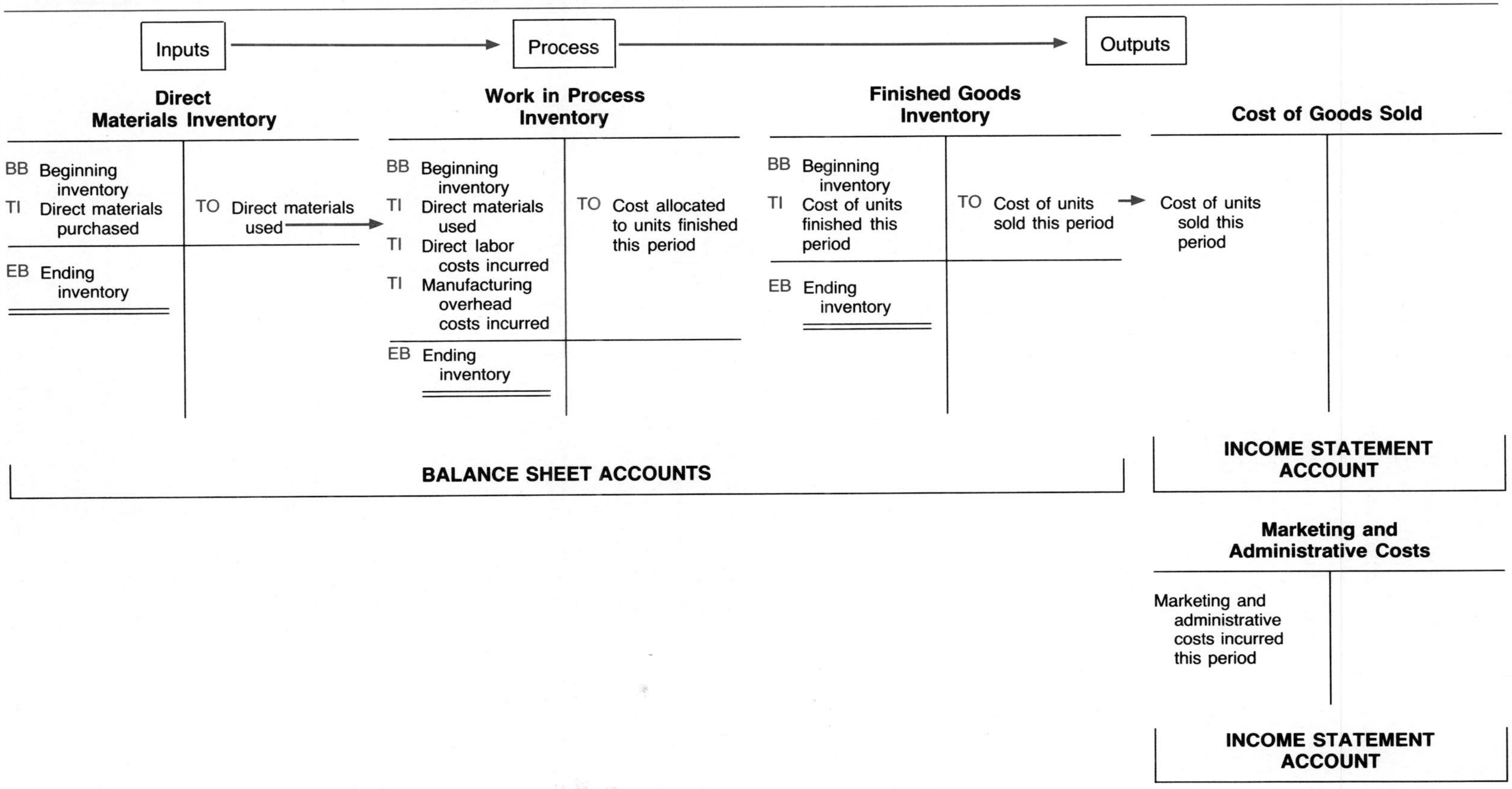

Inputs	→	Process	→	Outputs

Direct Materials Inventory

BB Beginning inventory	
TI Direct materials purchased	TO Direct materials used
EB Ending inventory	

Work in Process Inventory

BB Beginning inventory	
TI Direct materials used	TO Cost allocated to units finished this period
TI Direct labor costs incurred	
TI Manufacturing overhead costs incurred	
EB Ending inventory	

Finished Goods Inventory

BB Beginning inventory	
TI Cost of units finished this period	TO Cost of units sold this period
EB Ending inventory	

Cost of Goods Sold

Cost of units sold this period

INCOME STATEMENT ACCOUNT

Marketing and Administrative Costs

Marketing and administrative costs incurred this period

INCOME STATEMENT ACCOUNT

BALANCE SHEET ACCOUNTS

partment) and for each product line. Department managers are held responsible for the costs incurred in their departments. The information also can aid department managers in their efforts to control costs.

Companies often have little direct control over prices paid for direct materials or prices received for finished goods, particularly if they operate in purely competitive markets. A key factor for the success of such companies is how well they can control their conversion costs—direct labor and manufacturing overhead. Thus, companies monitor those costs closely in Work in Process Inventory.

The Direct Materials Inventory account is also useful for cost accountability. The purchasing department is responsible for obtaining materials at a good price. A comparison of the actual cost of materials purchased (shown on the left/debit side of Direct Materials Inventory) with budgeted costs provides a measure of the purchasing department's performance in purchasing materials at a good price.

In short, accounting for costs in Work in Process Inventory is very important for manufacturing companies. The costs data collected in that process can provide important information for many management purposes, and it is absolutely necessary for financial accounting. In the next section, we illustrate the process of product costing in manufacturing by showing a comprehensive example of costs flows through the accounts.

The Manufacturing Process

Cost accumulation in a manufacturing environment can be better understood if one can picture the manufacturing process. With this in mind, we will now present a simplified version of the manufacturing process of a firm that makes jeans, Unique Denims.

Unique Denims has two departments that manufacture the jeans: Cut, Make and Trim (CMT) which is responsible for creating a garment that meets customer specifications for fit, trim, and size distribution; and Finishing, which is responsible for meeting customer specifications for washing and final inspection. Unique also has two other departments: Direct Materials Warehousing, which is responsible for bringing in shipments and stocking raw materials used in the making of the garment; and Finished Goods Packaging which is responsible for getting finished goods packed for shipment to the customer. For a complete listing of departmental responsibilities see Illustration 3–6.

When Unique Denims receives an order, a manager estimates how much denim is required, orders the fabric, and sends a copy of the order to Direct Materials Warehousing.

When the denim shipment arrives at the factory, the Direct Materials Warehousing Department checks the quantity shipped against the quantity ordered and inspects the denim for flaws. After passing inspection, the fabric is placed in direct materials inventory.

When the manufacturing process is ready to begin, CMT requisitions the fabric and trim from Direct Materials Warehousing. The fabric goes on long tables where the denim is cut into individual pieces of jeans (e.g., legs, waistbands). The trim is taken to the sewing stations where it will be sewn into the jeans. After cutting, the pieces of jeans go to the sewing stations where the individual pieces are sewn together, trim is incorporated, and a

Illustration 3-6   **Unique Denims—Departmental Responsibilities**

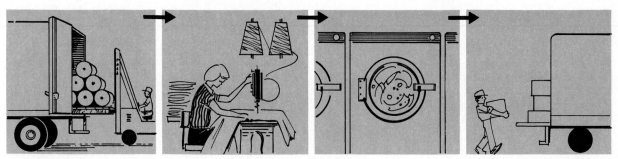

Direct Materials Warehousing

Receive raw materials.
Ensure that correct amount
is received.
Inspect materials.
Store raw materials inventory.
Release materials to
manufacturing as needed.

Cut Make and Trim (CMT)

Make pattern to conform
with customer specifica –
tions for fit and size
distribution.
Cut denim into individual
parts for sewing.
Sew garments.
Apply buttons, zippers and
labels.

Finishing

Wash garments to
customer specifications.
Inspect garments for fabric
or sewing flaws.

Finished Goods Packaging

Pack finished garments to
customer specifications
for size and style.

pair of rough-sewn jeans is produced. The rough-sewn jeans are then taken to the Finishing Department. The Finishing Department washes the jeans to customer specifications for hand feel and appearance. Finally, the Finishing Department inspects each garment to ensure there are no fabric or sewing flaws. Garments that pass this inspection are considered first-quality finished garments and are sent on to Finished Goods Warehousing. The Finished Goods Department packs garments in boxes as they arrive from the Finishing Department. The garments are held in the finished goods warehouse inventory until the entire order is complete. When the order is completely filled, the garments are loaded on trucks and shipped to the customer.

Unique received an order for 40,000 pairs of a particular style of jeans to be delivered before April 1. This was the only product for the month ending March 31. The manager placed an order for the required amount of denim to be delivered on March 1. During March, the 40,000 pairs of jeans were produced. The costs of manufacturing and selling those jeans and the revenue from the sales were as follows:

Units produced	40,000
Units sold	40,000
Manufacturing costs:	
Direct materials purchased and used	$120,000
Direct labor	80,000
Manufacturing overhead	240,000
Total manufacturing costs	$440,000
Marketing and administrative costs	$100,000
Sales revenue (40,000 units at $20)	800,000

Illustration 3-7 **Manufacturing Cost Flows**

Unique Denims Inc.
Ending March 31

Direct Materials Inventory

(1)	120,000	(2) 120,000 →	

Work in Process Inventory—CMT

(2)	120,000	(6) 376,000 →	
(3)	64,000		
(5)	192,000		

Work in Process Inventory—Finishing

(6)	376,000	(7) 440,000 →	
(3)	16,000		
(5)	48,000		

Finished Goods Inventory

(7)	440,000	(8b) 440,000 →	

Cost of Goods Sold

(8b) 440,000	

Manufacturing Overhead

(4)	240,000	(5) 240,000	

Wages and Accounts Payable

	(1) 120,000
	(3) 80,000
	(4) 240,000
	(9) 100,000

Marketing and Administrative Costs

(9) 100,000	

Accounts Receivable

(8a) 800,000	

Sales Revenue

	(8a) 800,000

BALANCE SHEET ACCOUNTS

INCOME STATEMENT ACCOUNTS

Note: Numbers in parentheses are journal entries in the text. Arrows show the flow of product from direct materials to cost of goods

We assume for this example that all costs and revenues are on account. To illustrate the flow of costs through departments, we now follow the production of jeans through Unique Denims' two manufacturing departments: Cut, Make and Trim (CMT) and Finishing. The manufacturing costs charged to the two production departments are as follows:

	CMT	Finishing	Source Documents
Direct materials	$120,000	—0—	Materials requisition request
Direct labor costs	64,000	$16,000	Assignment of time between depart- ments on time cards
Manufacturing overhead	192,000	48,000	Many sources, in- cluding invoices and time cards.
Totals	$376,000	$64,000	

The following journal entries describe Unique Denims' flow of costs. These entries correspond to the T-accounts in Illustration 3–7. Tracing the entries through the T-accounts will help you visualize the flow of resources through the company. Each entry summarizes the transactions for the month. (In practice, weekly or daily entries would be made.)

(1) Direct Materials Inventory	120,000	
Accounts Payable		120,000

To record the purchase of direct materials. This entry is made as materials are purchased.

(2) Work in Process Inventory—CMT	120,000	
Direct Materials Inventory		120,000

To record the requisition of direct materials for the production of 40,000 pairs of jeans. This entry is made when materials are sent to manufacturing.

(3) Work in Process—CMT	64,000	
Work in Process—Finishing	16,000	
Wages Payable (or Accrued Factory Payroll)		80,000

To record costs of direct labor work in each manufacturing department. This entry is made when the payroll is computed—usually weekly.

(4) Manufacturing Overhead	240,000	
Accounts Payable		240,000

To record manufacturing overhead costs. These costs are recorded as incurred.

(5) Work in Process Inventory—CMT	192,000	
Work in Process Inventory—Finishing	48,000	
Manufacturing Overhead		240,000

To assign manufacturing overhead to each manufacturing department. This assignment is based on the actual costs incurred during the period. It usually takes place after all costs for the period have been recorded. (It is possible for entry (4) and entry (5) to be combined if the overhead costs are assigned to each manufacturing department when the costs are incurred.)

(6)	Work in Process—Finishing	376,000	
	Work in Process—CMT		376,000
	To record the transfer of assembled units to the finishing department when units are transferred.		
(7)	Finished Goods Inventory	440,000	
	Work in Process Inventory—Finishing		440,000
	To record the transfer of finished units to the finished goods storage area. ($376,000 costs incurred in assembly and $64,000 added in finishing.)		
(8a)	Accounts Receivable	800,000	
	Sales Revenue		800,000
	To record the sale of goods.		
(8b)	Cost of Goods Sold	440,000	
	Finished Goods Inventory		440,000
	To record the costs of 40,000 pairs of jeans sold during the month.		
(9)	Marketing and Administrative Costs	100,000	
	Accounts Payable		100,000
	To record marketing and administrative costs when incurred.		

These entries describe the flow of costs from the acquisition of inputs through the sale of the jeans. They represent the basic model of accounting for resource flows in manufacturing companies.

The data are taken from the accounts to prepare internal statements. For example, the income statement for March is shown in Illustration 3–8.

Cost Flows with Inventory Balances

The following example demonstrates the flow of costs when there are inventory balances. Assume the following facts apply to Unique Denims for July when the company manufactured 40,000 pairs of jeans and sold 38,000.

Production:	
Units produced	40,000
Direct materials purchased	$135,000
Direct materials used	125,000
Direct labor used:	
CMT department	64,000
Finishing department	16,000
Manufacturing overhead:	
CMT department	192,000
Finishing department	48,000
Inventories:	
Beginning direct materials	10,000
Ending direct materials	20,000
Beginning work in process (all in CMT)	15,000
Ending work in process (all in CMT)	20,000
Beginning finished goods	30,000
Ending finished goods	52,000
Marketing and administrative costs	100,000
Sales:	
Units sold	38,000
Sales revenue ($20 per pair of jeans)	$720,000

As previously, we assume that all transactions were on account.

Illustration 3-8

Unique Denims
Income Statement
For the Month Ended March 31

Sales revenue	$800,000
Costs of goods sold[a]	440,000
Gross margin	360,000
Marketing and administrative costs	100,000
Operating profit	$260,000

[a] As there were no beginning and ending inventories, the cost of goods sold is simply the sum of direct materials, direct labor, and manufacturing overhead costs for the month.

The flow of costs is shown in Illustration 3–9. (A good self-study technique is to make journal entries and demonstrate the flow of costs through T-accounts based on the above facts; then look at Illustration 3–9 to check your work.) Although some of the July amounts differ from those for the month ended March 31 in the previous example, the basic structure of the entries is the same.

Overview

We have presented an overview of cost flows in manufacturing organizations in this section. The analysis presented here is the foundation of much of our work in subsequent chapters. In later chapters, for example, we build on the cost flow entries and T-accounts presented here for manufacturing companies. It is important to understand the cost flow analysis presented here before proceeding to subsequent chapters. This overview will keep you in touch with the "big picture" when we develop the cost flow analysis in more detail.

COST ACCUMULATION: SERVICE ORGANIZATIONS

Service organizations do not have input materials like manufacturers or merchandise inventory like merchandisers. Thus, service businesses, unlike manufacturers and merchandisers, do not need to account for inventories of finished goods.

However, most service organizations maintain a Work in Process Inventory account for internal use. Entered in this account is the cost of services performed for a customer but not yet billed. Labor and overhead are accumulated for each job, or "unit," much as they would be in a manufacturing company.

The flow of costs in service organizations is similar to the flow in manufacturing, as shown in Illustration 3–10. Input costs include the labor and overhead that are part of the service provided. Costs are usually collected by departments for performance evaluation purposes. In public accounting, consulting, and similar service organizations, costs are then charged to jobs or clients. As in manufacturing job shops, costs are collected by job for performance evaluation, to provide information for cost control, and to compare actual costs with past estimated costs for pricing of future jobs.

Illustration 3-9   **Flow of Costs when There Are Inventory Balances**

Unique Denims
July

	Direct Materials Inventory			Work in Process Inventory—CMT			Work in Process Inventory—Finishing			Finished Goods Inventory			Cost of Goods Sold	
BB	10,000		BB	15,000		BB	–0–		BB	30,000		(8b)	418,000	
(1)	135,000	(2) 125,000 →	(2)	125,000	(6) 376,000 →	(6)	376,000	(7) 440,000 →	(7)	440,000	(8b) 418,000 →			
			(3)	64,000		(3)	16,000							
			(5)	192,000		(5)	48,000							
EB	20,000		EB	20,000		EB	–0–		EB	52,000				

	Manufacturing Overhead			Marketing and Administrative Costs	
(4)	240,000	(5) 240,000	(9)	100,000	

	Wages and Accounts Payable			Sales Revenue	
		(1) 135,000			(8a) 720,000
		(3) 80,000			
		(4) 240,000			
		(9) 100,000			

	Accounts Receivable	
(8a)	720,000	

INCOME STATEMENT ACCOUNTS

BALANCE SHEET ACCOUNTS

Illustration 3-10   **Flow of Costs—Service Organization**

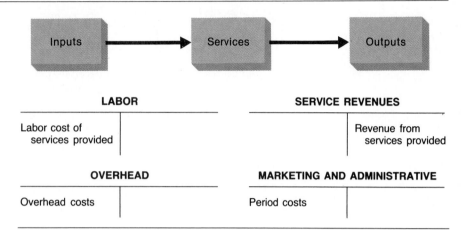

LABOR		SERVICE REVENUES	
Labor cost of services provided			Revenue from services provided

OVERHEAD		MARKETING AND ADMINISTRATIVE	
Overhead costs		Period costs	

For example, consider the cost flows of a public accounting firm, Arthur Ross & Company. For the month of September, Arthur Ross & Company worked 200 hours for Client A and 700 hours for Client B. Ross bills clients at the rate of $80 per hour, while the labor cost for its audit staff is $30 per hour. The total number of hours worked in September was 1,000 (100 hours were not billable to clients), and overhead costs were $10,000. (Examples of unbillable hours are hours spent in professional training and meetings unrelated to particular clients.) Overhead is assigned to clients based proportionally on direct labor-hours; so Client A is assigned $2,000, Client B is assigned $7,000, and $1,000 remains unassigned. In addition, Arthur Ross & Company had $5,000 in marketing and administrative costs. All transactions are on account. Entries to record these transactions are as follows:

(1)	Direct Labor—Client A		6,000	
	Direct Labor—Client B		21,000	
	Direct Labor—Unbillable		3,000	
	Wages Payable			30,000
	To record labor costs for September and to assign direct labor costs to Client A (200 hours @ $30 = $6,000), Client B (700 hours @ $30 = $21,000), and unbilled (100 hours @ $30 = $3,000).			
(2)	Unassigned Overhead		10,000	
	Accounts Payable			10,000
	To record or accumulate overhead before it is assigned to clients.			
(3)	Overhead—Client A		2,000	
	Overhead—Client B		7,000	
	Unassigned Overhead			9,000
	To assign overhead costs for September to clients (that is, jobs).			
(4)	Marketing and Administrative Costs		5,000	
	Accounts Payable			5,000
	To record marketing and administrative costs for September.			

(5)	Accounts Receivable	72,000	
	Revenue—Client A		16,000
	Revenue—Client B		56,000

To record billings for services in September to Client A
(200 hours @ $80 = $16,000) and to Client B (700 hours
@ $80 = $56,000).

Illustration 3–11 demonstrates cost flows through T-accounts. The September income statement is presented in Illustration 3–12.

REAL WORLD APPLICATION

The Impact of New Technology on Cost Accumulation*

After installing a new production process, a Hewlett-Packard plant that makes printed circuit boards found that (1) inventory levels were almost zero, (2) direct labor was only 3 to 5 percent of total product costs, and (3) most labor and overhead costs were fixed. The accountants realized that this change in production technology could have dramatic effects on cost accumulation methods. First, direct labor was such a small part of total product cost that it was no longer accounted for as a separate category; instead, it was lumped together with overhead.

Second, lower inventory levels and reduced time between production and delivery of finished product meant that virtually all of the overhead and direct labor incurred in a month was expensed in the same month.

> Tracking overhead through work in process and finished goods inventory (for each job) provided no useful information. Management decided, therefore, to treat manufacturing overhead as an expense charged directly to cost of goods sold. Overhead remaining in work in process and finished goods is maintained with end-of-month adjusting entries.†

The new method at the Hewlett-Packard plant is compared with a conventional system in the accompanying diagram. Only materials are recorded in inventory accounts; labor and overhead are expensed when incurred. An estimated 100,000 journal entries per month were eliminated by simplifying the accounting system because labor and overhead were no longer allocated to each product going through work in process.

The net result of these changes is that Hewlett-Packard realized significant savings in staff time and costs without any significant changes in costs reported in their financial statements, costs used in planning and controlling production, or costs analyzed for pricing and make-or-buy decisions. Production line managers can now understand the simpler reports provided by the accounting department and actually use the information in those reports. Accountants can now "focus on solving tomorrow's problems instead of unraveling yesterday's errors," one of the goals of H-P's accounting staff.‡

* R. Hunt, L. Garrett, and C. M. Merz, "Direct Labor Cost Not Always Relevant at H-P," *Management Accounting*, February 1985, pp. 58–62. See also J. M. Patell, "Adapting a Cost System to Just-in-Time Inventory," in *Accounting and Management in Organizations: A Field Study Perspective*, ed. W. Bruns and R. Kaplan (Boston: Harvard Business School, 1987).

† Hunt, Garrett, and Merz, p. 61.

‡ Ibid.

SUMMARY

In this chapter, we discussed methods of recording and reporting cost flows in merchandising, manufacturing, and service organizations. The business of every organization is to transform inputs into outputs. Part of the accounting function for both external and internal reporting purposes is to trace the flow of resources and account for them.

In *merchandising*, product costs are the purchase price of the merchandise plus the direct costs of obtaining it (for example, transportation-in costs) and making it ready for sale. This amount is used to value inventory for financial accounting and for decision making. For performance evaluation, costs are assigned to merchandising responsibility centers (for example, sporting goods, shoes, housewares).

REAL WORLD APPLICATION

(concluded)

Comparing Cost Flows: H-P's Simplified System and a Conventional System

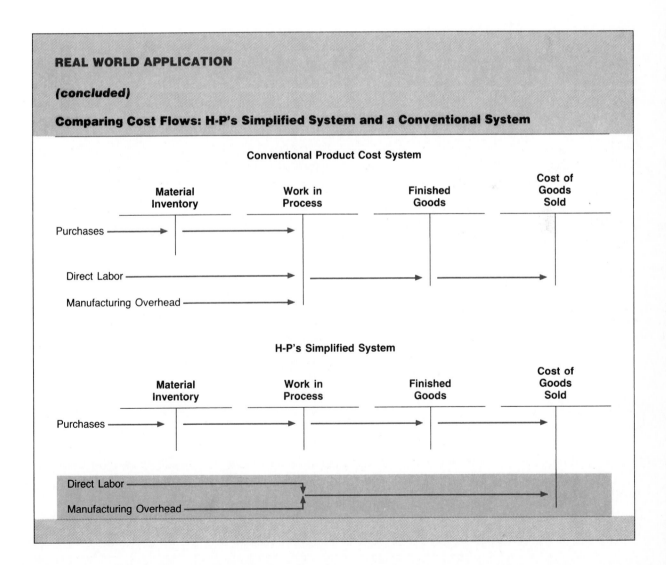

Illustration 3-11   **Service Cost Flow**

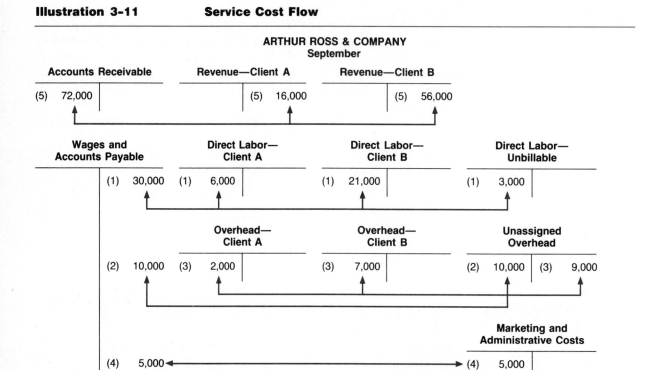

Illustration 3-12

ARTHUR ROSS & COMPANY		
Income Statement		
For the Month Ended September 30		
Revenue from service for clients		$72,000
Less costs of service to clients:		
Labor	$27,000	
Overhead	9,000	
Total costs of service to clients		36,000
Gross margin		36,000
Less other costs:		
Labor	3,000	
Overhead	1,000	
Marketing and administrative costs	5,000	
Total other costs		9,000
Operating profit		$27,000

In *manufacturing*, costs of inputs are accumulated in manufacturing (work in process) departments as production occurs. These departments are the basic responsibility centers in manufacturing, so the costs collected in these departments provide important information for performance evaluation and cost control. The information is also needed for full product costing. Thus, work in process inventory accounts are the focal point of accounting in manufacturing organizations.

There are two methods of accounting for inventories: perpetual and periodic. The perpetual method requires an ongoing record of transfers-out and inventory balances. The periodic method requires only a periodic (often monthly) count and valuation of inventory.

The costing systems of service organizations are similar to those of manufacturing with one important difference—there are usually no inventories of finished products. Like manufacturing, there are labor and overhead inputs. Many costing methods for manufacturing can be applied to service organizations if direct materials are omitted.

TERMS AND CONCEPTS

The following terms and concepts should be familiar to you after reading this chapter:

Basic Cost Flow Model

Cost Accumulation

First-in, First-out (FIFO)

Last-in, First-out (LIFO)

Manufacturing Organization

Merchandise Inventory

Merchandising Organization

Periodic Inventory

Perpetual Inventory

Service Organization

Transportation-in Costs

SUPPLEMENTARY READINGS

Brimson, James A. "How Advanced Manufacturing Technologies Are Reshaping Cost Management." *Management Accounting*, March 1986, pp. 25–29.

Clifford, Loretta A., and Marilyn P. Plomann. "Cost and Quality: Two Sides of the Coin in Cost Containment." *Healthcare Financial Management*, September 1985, pp. 30–32.

"Evaluating a Client's Cost Accounting System." *CPA Journal*, March 1986, pp. 79–80.

Godfrey, James T., and William R. Pasework. "Controlling Quality Costs." *Management Accounting*, March 1988, pp. 45–51.

Howell, Robert A., and Stephen R. Soucy. "Cost Accounting in the New Manufacturing Environment." *Management Accounting*, August 1987, pp. 42–48.

Kaplan, Robert S. "One Cost System Isn't Enough." *Harvard Business Review*, January–February 1988, pp. 61–66.

Lammert, T. B., and R. Ehrsam. "The Human Element: The Real Challenge in Modernizing Cost Accounting Systems." *Management Accounting*, July 1987, pp. 32–37.

Mackey, Jim. "Eleven Key Issues in Manufacturing Accounting." *Management Accounting*, January 1987, pp. 32–37.

Roth, Harold. "New Rules for Inventory Costing." *Management Accounting*, March 1987, pp. 32–6, 45.

Schonberger, Richard J. "Frugal Manufacturing." *Harvard Business Review*, September–October 1987, pp. 95–100.

On January 1 of a current year, Blazer Building Products has a beginning inventory of direct materials of $80,000. Work in process inventory at the start of the period amounts to $32,000, and finished goods inventory equals $75,000. The balance in cost of goods sold is zero. T-accounts showing these balances appear as follows:

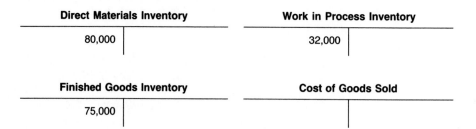

Direct Materials Inventory		Work in Process Inventory	
80,000		32,000	

Finished Goods Inventory		Cost of Goods Sold	
75,000			

During the year, $22,000 of direct materials are purchased, and $18,000 are transferred to the production area of the plant.

Direct labor costs of $17,500 are incurred, and $30,000 of overhead is incurred. All of the overhead costs are on account. Goods with a cost of $81,000 are completed and transferred to the finished goods warehouse. Additionally, goods costing $92,000 are sold at a price of $170,000. Marketing and administrative costs of $73,000 are incurred.

Required:

a. Prepare journal entries to show these events.

b. Prepare T-accounts to show the flow of costs.

c. Prepare an income statement and cost of goods manufactured and sold statement.

SOLUTION TO SELF-STUDY PROBLEM

a. In journal entry form, these events are recorded as follows:

(1) Direct Materials Inventory   22,000
     Accounts Payable   22,000
    To record the purchase of materials.

(2) Work in Process Inventory   18,000
     Direct Materials Inventory   18,000
    To record the transfer of materials to the
    production area.

(3) Work in Process Inventory   17,500
     Wages Payable (or Accrued Factory Payroll)   17,500
    To record the distribution of payroll costs of
    direct labor.

(4) Manufacturing Overhead   30,000
     Accounts Payable   30,000
    To record manufacturing overhead costs incurred.

(5) Work in Process Inventory   30,000
     Manufacturing Overhead   30,000
    To assign manufacturing overhead to work in
    process inventory.

(6) Finished Goods Inventory   81,000
     Work in Process Inventory   81,000
    To transfer the costs of goods completed to
    finished goods inventory.

(7) Cost of Goods Sold   92,000
     Finished Goods Inventory   92,000
    To recognize as a period cost the costs of the
    goods sold during the period.

(8) Marketing and Administrative Costs   73,000
     Accounts Payable   73,000
    To record marketing and administrative costs
    incurred during the period.

(9) Accounts Receivable   170,000
     Sales Revenue   170,000
    To record sales on account.

b. T-accounts to show the flow of costs:

BLAZER BUILDING PRODUCTS

Direct Materials Inventory

BB	80,000	(2)	18,000
(1)	22,000		
EB	84,000		

Work in Process Inventory

BB	32,000	(6)	81,000
(2)	18,000		
(3)	17,500		
(5)	30,000		
EB	16,500		

Finished Goods Inventory

BB	75,000	(7)	92,000
(6)	81,000		
EB	64,000		

Cost of Goods Sold

(7)	92,000

Wages and Accounts Payable

	(1)	22,000
	(3)	17,500
	(4)	30,000
	(8)	73,000

Manufacturing Overhead

(4)	30,000	(5)	30,000

Marketing and Administrative Costs

(8)	73,000

Accounts Receivable

(9)	170,000

Sales Revenue

	(9)	170,000

c. Statements:

BLAZER BUILDING PRODUCTS
Income Statement
For the Year Ended December 31

Sales revenue	$170,000
Cost of goods sold (see statement below)	92,000
Gross margin	78,000
Marketing and administrative costs	73,000
Operating profit	$ 5,000

BLAZER BUILDING PRODUCTS
Cost of Goods Manufactured and Sold Statement
For the Year Ended December 31

Beginning work in process inventory, January 1			$ 32,000
Manufacturing costs during the year:			
Direct materials:			
Beginning inventory, January 1	$ 80,000		
Add purchases	22,000		
Direct materials available	102,000		
Less ending inventory, December 31	84,000[a]		
Direct materials put into process		$18,000	
Direct labor		17,500	
Manufacturing overhead		30,000	
Total manufacturing costs incurred during year			65,500
Total costs of work in process during year			97,500
Less ending work in process inventory, December 31			16,500[b]
Cost of goods manufactured during the year			81,000
Beginning finished goods inventory, January 1			75,000
Finished goods inventory available for sale			156,000
Less ending finished goods inventory, December 31			64,000[c]
Cost of goods manufactured and sold			$ 92,000

[a]$84,000 = $102,000 − $18,000.
[b]$16,500 = $97,500 − $81,000.
[c]$64,000 = $156,000 − $92,000.

QUESTIONS

3–1. Differentiate between the processes used in a manufacturing operation and the processes used in a merchandising operation.

3–2. Why are there no inventories in a service organization?

3–3. Describe the three primary inventory accounts used by a manufacturer.

3–4. A merchandiser comments, "I perform services that add to the value of the products that I sell. My marketing staff facilitates economic efficiency by purchasing the right product, informing the consuming public of its availability, and distributing it in an efficient manner. Why shouldn't I be allowed to include my marketing and administrative costs as part of the book value of my inventory?" Reply to this comment.

3–5.   What do we mean when we say, "After a unit has passed through work in process inventory it has been charged with the 'full costs' of manufacturing"?

3–6.   For what purposes would full manufacturing cost data be used?

3–7.   Why is the Work in Process Inventory account often considered the heart of the cost accounting system?

3–8.   For each of the following accounts, indicate whether a balance in the account would appear on the balance sheet or on the income statement:

Marketing Costs	Manufacturing Overhead
Direct Materials Inventory	Cost of Goods Sold
Accounts Receivable	Accumulated Depreciation
Work in Process Inventory	Sales Revenue
Finished Goods Inventory	

3–9.   For each of the following accounts indicate whether the account would be on the books of a service company, merchandiser, or manufacturer. Some accounts may appear on more than one organization type's books. Use "M" for a manufacturer, "R" for a merchandiser, and "S" for a service organization.

Cost of Goods Sold	Merchandise Inventory
Work in Process Inventory	Marketing Costs
Client Receivables	Finished Goods Inventory
Accounts Payable	

3–10.   What is the basic cost flow model? Explain each term.

EXERCISES

3–11. Basic Cost Flow Model
(L.O.1)

Video Productions Inc. experienced the following events during the current year:

1. Incurred marketing costs of $197,000.
2. Purchased $971,000 of merchandise.
3. Paid $26,000 for transportation-in costs.
4. Incurred $400,000 of administrative costs.
5. Took a periodic inventory on December 31 and learned that goods with a cost of $297,000 were on hand. This compared with a beginning inventory of $314,000 on January 1.
6. Sales revenue during the year was $1,850,000.

All costs incurred were debited to the appropriate account and credited to Accounts Payable. All sales were on credit.

Required:

Identify the following:

a. Beginning Balance (BB) Merchandise Inventory account.
b. Transfers-in (TI) Merchandise Inventory account.
c. Ending Balance (EB) Merchandise Inventory account.
d. Transfer-out (TO) Merchandise Inventory account.

3-12. Cost Accumulation: Merchandising
(L.O.2)

Refer to the data for Video Productions Inc. (exercise 3-11).

Required:

Use T-accounts to show the flow of costs for these data.

3-13. Cost Accumulation: Merchandising
(L.O.2)

Refer to the data for Video Productions Inc. (exercise 3-11).

Required:

a. Prepare journal entries to reflect these transactions.
b. Prepare an income statement.

3-14. Basic Cost Flow Model
(L.O.1)

The following events took place at the Fleetfoot Shoe Corp. for the current year.

1. Purchased $80,000 in direct materials.
2. Incurred direct labor costs of $42,000.
3. Purchased manufacturing equipment for $67,200.
4. Other manufacturing overhead was $92,000.
5. Transferred 70 percent of the materials purchased to work in process.
6. Completed work on 60 percent of the goods in process. Costs are assigned equally across all work in process.
7. Sold 90 percent of the completed goods.

There were no beginning balances in the inventory accounts. All costs incurred were debited to the appropriate account and credited to Accounts Payable.

Required:

Identify the following

a. Beginning balance (BB) in Work in Process account.
b. Transfers-in (TI) to Work in Process account.
c. Transfers-out (TO) of Work in Process account.
d. Ending balance (EB) in Work in Process account.

3-15. Cost Accumulation: Manufacturing
(L.O.3)

Refer to the data for Fleetfoot Shoe Corp. (exercise 3-14).

Required:

Use T-accounts to show the flow of cost for these data.

3-16. Cost Accumulation: Manufacturing
(L.O.3)

Refer to the data for Fleetfoot Shoe Corp. (exercise 3-14).

Required:

a. Prepare journal entries to reflect these transactions.
b. Prepare a cost of goods manufactured and sold statement.

3-17. Basic Cost Flow Model
(L.O.1)

Fill in the missing item for the following inventories:

	(A)	**(B)**	**(C)**
Beginning balance	$40,000	?	$35,000
Ending balance	32,000	$16,000	27,000
Transferred in	?	9,000	8,000
Transferred out	61,000	11,000	?

3–18. Basic Cost Flow Model
(L.O.1)

Fill in the missing item for the following inventories:

	(A)	(B)	(C)
Beginning balance	$29,000	$17,000	$ 4,100
Ending balance	32,000	?	6,200
Transferred in	70,000	26,000	?
Transferred out	?	19,000	12,000

3–19. Basic Cost Flow Model
(L.O.1)

The following T-accounts represent data from Leopold Lighting's accounting records. Find the missing items represented by the letters. (Hint: Rearrange accounts to conform with flow of costs.)

Cost of Goods Sold

82,000	

Direct Materials Inventory

BB	a		
Purchases	18,000	Transferred out	21,000
EB	7,500		

Finished Goods Inventory

BB	46,400	d	
	c		
EB	f		

Work in Process Inventory

BB	6,000		
Materials	b		
Labor	17,000		58,600
overhead	e		
EB	9,700		

3–20. Cost Accumulation: Merchandising
(L.O.2)

Pasta to Go is a fast food outlet that caters to busy professionals who don't have time to cook dinner every night. It prepares various styles of pasta dishes that can be picked up and heated at home. It experienced the following events during the current year (all transactions were on account):

1. Incurred marketing costs of $98,500.
2. Purchased $485,500 of merchandise.
3. Paid $13,000 for transportation-in costs.
4. Incurred $200,000 in administrative costs.
5. Took a periodic inventory on December 31 and learned that goods with a cost of $148,500 were on hand. This compared with a beginning inventory of $157,000 on January 1.
6. Sales revenue during the year was $925,000.

Required:

a. Prepare appropriate journal entries to record these transactions.
b. Prepare an income statement based on the data.

3–21. Cost Accumulation: Manufacturing
(L.O.3)

The following events took place at the Crater Manufacturing Corporation for the current year:

1. Incurred direct labor costs of $72,000.
2. Purchased manufacturing equipment for $63,200.
3. Purchased $101,000 in direct materials.
4. Manufacturing overhead was $116,900.

5. Transferred 60 percent of the direct materials to work in process.
6. Completed work on 80 percent of the work in process and transferred the finished goods to finished goods inventory. Costs are assigned equally across all work in process.
7. Sold 70 percent of the finished goods.
8. Marketing and administrative costs were $70,000.
9. Revenues were $240,000.

There were no beginning balances in any of the inventory accounts. All costs incurred were debited to the appropriate account and credited to Accounts Payable. All revenues were on account.

Required:
a. Prepare journal entries to reflect these events.
b. Show corresponding T-accounts.

3–22. Cost Accumulation: Manufacturing
(L.O.3)

Refer to the data in exercise 3–21.

Required:
Prepare a cost of goods manufactured and sold statement and an income statement from the data.

3–23. Cost Accumulation: Service
(L.O.4)

For the month of March, Conehead Consulting Group (CCG) worked 400 hours for Big Manufacturing, 100 hours for Little Manufacturing, and 200 hours for Retailers, Inc. CCG bills clients at the rate of $100 per hour, while labor cost is $40 per hour. A total of 800 hours were worked in March, with 100 hours not billable to clients. Overhead costs of $12,000 were incurred. Overhead was assigned to jobs (that is, clients) on the basis of direct labor-hours. Since 100 hours were not billable, some overhead was not assigned to jobs. CCG had $6,000 marketing and administrative costs. All transactions are on account.

Required:
Prepare T-accounts and journal entries to reflect these events.

3-24. Cost Accumulation: Service
(L.O.4)

Refer to the data in exercise 3-23. Prepare an income statement for CCG for the month ending March 31.

PROBLEMS

Following are data for the Shasta Ski Company:

3–25. Basic Cost Flow Model

	Balance, March 1	Balance, March 31
Direct materials inventory	?	$ 40,000
Work in process inventory	?	280,000
Finished goods	$100,000	80,000
Other information:		
Direct labor costs		240,000
Manufacturing overhead		112,000
Material purchases		180,000
Direct materials put into process		200,000
Cost of goods sold		360,000
Marketing costs		100,000
Administrative costs		80,000
Sales on account		600,000

Required:

Use T-accounts to show the flow of costs for March for the Shasta Ski Company and then prepare an income statement for the month of March. All transactions are on account.

3-26. Basic Cash Flow Model

Partially completed T-accounts and additional information for Redwood Landscaping for the month of March are presented below:

Direct Materials Inventory			
BB 3/1	1,000		
	4,000	3,200	

Work in Process Inventory		
BB 3/1	2,000	
Direct labor	2,400	
Manufacturing overhead	2,200	

Finished Goods Inventory		
BB 3/1	3,000	
	6,000	4,000

Cost of Goods Sold	

During the month, sales were $8,000, and marketing and administrative costs were $1,600.

Required:

a. What was the cost of direct material issued to production during March?

b. What was the cost of goods manufactured during March?

c. What was the balance of the Work in Process Inventory account at the end of March?

d. What was the operating profit for March?

3–27 Basic Cost Flow Model

A hysterical Ima Dunce corners you in the hallway 30 minutes before her accounting class. "Help me, help me!" Ima pleads. "I woke up this morning and discovered that Fifo and Lifo (two pet German Shepherds) ate my homework, and these shredded pieces are all that I have left!" Being a kind and generous soul, you willingly declare, "There is no need to fear! I am a real whiz at accounting and will be glad to help you." A relieved Ima Dunce hands you the following torn homework remnants.

Page 1

Direct labor-hours used	375
Direct labor rate - $5 per hour	
Direct materials purchased	$5,250
Direct materials beginning inventory	$1,400

Page 2

Actual manufacturing overhead	$ 750
Beginning work in process inventory	1,500
Cost of goods manufactured	8,000
Ending finished goods inventory	3,000

Page 3

Job remaining in ending work in process inventory:	
Labor	$ 500
Direct materials	1,300
Overhead	200
Ending work in process inventory	$ 2,000
Total revenue	$13,500
Gross margin	4,000
Marketing and administrative costs	
Operating profit	1,000

Required:

a. Prepare T-accounts to show the flow of cost and determine each of the following:
   1. Marketing and administrative costs.
   2. Cost of goods sold.
   3. Beginning finished goods inventory.
   4. Direct materials used.
   5. Ending direct materials inventory.

b. Prepare an income statement.

3–28. Basic Cost Flow Model

After a dispute concerning wages, Steve W. Ozniak contaminated the computerized accounting system at Sparkle Company with a virus that destroyed most of the company records. The computer experts at the company could only recover a few fragments of the company's factory ledger, as shown below:

Direct Materials Inventory		Manufacturing Overhead	
BB 4/1 15,000			

Work in Process Inventory		Accounts Payable	
BB 4/1 4,500			
			EB 4/30 9,000

Finished Goods Inventory		Cost of Goods Sold	
EB 4/30 11,000			

Additional investigation and reconstruction from other sources yielded the following additional information.

1. The controller remembers clearly that actual manufacturing overhead costs are recorded at $3 per direct labor-hour.
2. The production superintendent's cost sheets showed only one job in work in process inventory on April 30. Materials of $2,600 had been added to the job, and 300 direct labor-hours had been expanded at $6 per hour.
3. The accounts payable are for direct materials purchases only, according to the accounts payable clerk. He clearly remembers that the balance in the account was $6,000 on April 1. An analysis of canceled checks (kept in the treasurer's office) shows that payments of $42,000 were made to suppliers duuring the month.
4. The payroll ledger shows that 5,200 direct labor-hours were recorded for the month. The employment department has verified that there are no variations in pay rates among employees (this infuriated Steve, who felt his services were underpaid).
5. Records maintained in the finished goods warehouse indicate that the finished goods inventory totaled $18,000 on April 1.
6. The cost of goods manufactured for April was $89,000.

Required:

Determine the following amounts:

a. Work in process inventory, April 30.
b. Direct materials purchased during April.
c. Manufacturing overhead incurred during April.
d. Cost of goods sold for April.

3–29. Cost Accumulation: Merchandising

The Niagara Dress Shop uses the periodic inventory method and closes its books monthly. Below find the transactions for May.

1. Purchased dresses costing $90,000 on account. Niagara has a special arrangement with its supplier to pay a set rate for all purchases each month. The cost this month is $10 per dress.
2. Paid $9,000 in transportation-in charges.
3. Sales commission of $84,000 was incurred in cash.
4. The receiving department found defective dresses valued at $3,400, which were returned to the supplier.
5. Administration expenses totaled $38,000 and were paid in cash.
6. Cash sales were $248,000 and credit sales were $162,000. They sold 12,000 dresses.
7. Niagara purchased $4,000 in newspaper advertising on account.

Other information: Beginning inventory was $500,000. Each dress in beginning inventory was $20.00. The company used a first-in, first-out (FIFO) accounting system.

Required:

a. Prepare journal entries to record the transactions.
b. Prepare an income statement and a cost of goods sold statement. (Hint: Treat the $3,400 returned dresses as a decrease in cost of goods available for sale.)

3–30. Cost Accumulation: Manufacturing

The income statement and the cost of goods manufactured and sold statement for the Live Oak Manufacturing Company are reproduced as follows:

LIVE OAK MANUFACTURING COMPANY
Income Statement
For the Year Ended December 31

Sales revenue	$37,200
Cost of goods sold (see statement below)	25,700
Gross margin	11,500
Marketing costs	3,100
Administrative costs	2,700
Operating profit	$ 5,700

Cost of Goods Manufactured and Sold Statement
For the Year Ended December 31

Beginning work in process inventory, January 1			$ 1,200
Manufacturing costs during the year:			
Direct materials:			
Beginning inventory, January 1	$1,300		
Add purchases	6,500		
Direct materials available	7,800		
Less ending inventory, December 31:	1,700		
Direct materials put into process		$ 6,100	
Direct labor		12,400	
Manufacturing overhead		8,600	
Total manufacturing costs incurred during year			27,100
Total costs of work in process during the year			28,300
Less ending work in process inventory, December 31			1,800
Cost of goods manufactured during the year			26,500
Beginning finished goods inventory, January 1			5,200
Finished goods inventory available for sale			31,700
Less ending finished goods inventory, December 31			6,000
Cost of goods manufactured and sold			$25,700

Required:

Prepare T-accounts to show the flow of costs for the company. Assume that all dollar exchanges are on account.

3–31. Cost Accumulation: Manufacturing

Using the statements for Live Oak Manufacturing Company, problem 3–30, construct journal entries that would summarize the events disclosed in the statements.

3–32. Cost Accumulation: Manufacturing

Sonya's Software Company has the following information in its records on December 31 of the current year:

Materials inventory, December 31	$ 85,000
Materials purchased during the year	360,000
Finished goods inventory, December 31	90,000
Indirect labor	32,000
Direct labor	400,000
Indirect materials and supplies	
(taken from materials inventory)	14,000
Factory heat, light, and power	37,200
Building depreciation (all manufacturing)	81,000
Administrative salaries	51,400
Miscellaneous factory costs	17,900
Marketing costs	37,000
Factory supervision	12,100
Insurance on factory equipment	19,000
Transportation-in on materials	1,600
Taxes on manufacturing property	13,100
Legal fees on customer complaint	8,200
Direct materials used	382,100
Work in process inventory, December 31	24,600

On January 1, the Finished Goods account had a balance of $80,000, and the Work in Process Inventory account had a balance of $25,900. All transactions are on account (except depreciation, which is recorded with a debit to Manufacturing Overhead and a credit to Accumulated Depreciation). Sales equaled $1,625,000.

  a. Prepare T-accounts to show these events and the flow of costs for the company.

  b. Give the beginning direct materials inventory balance.

3–33. Cost Accumulation: Manufacturing

Using the data for Sonya's Software in problem 3–32, prepare journal entries to summarize events.

3–34. Cost Accumulation: Service

White and Brite Dry Cleaners has five employees and a president, Hexter Strength. Hexter and one of the five employees manage all the marketing and administrative duties. The remaining four employees work directly on operations. White and Brite has four service departments: dry cleaning, coin washing and drying, special cleaning, and repairs. A time card is marked, and records are kept to monitor the time each employee spends working in each department. When business is slow, there is idle time, which is marked on the time card. (It is necessary to have some idle time because White and Brite promises 60-minute service, and it is necessary to have direct labor-hours available to accommodate fluctuating peak-demand periods throughout the day and the week.)

Some of November operating data are as follows:

	Idle Time	Dry Cleaning	Coin Washing and Drying	Special Cleaning	Repairs
Sales revenue		$2,625	$5,250	$2,000	$625
Direct labor (in hours)	25	320	80	125	90
Direct overhead traceable to departments:					
Cleaning compounds		$ 500	$ 250	$ 400	–0–
Supplies		125	200	175	$140
Electric usage		250	625	100	25
Rent		200	500	90	10

Other data:

1. The four employees working in the operating departments all make $4 per hour.
2. The fifth employee, who helps manage marketing and administrative duties, earns $1,000 per month; and Hexter earns $1,500 per month.
3. Indirect overhead amounted to $512 and is assigned to departments based on direct labor-hours used. Since there are idle hours, some overhead will not be assigned to a department.
4. In addition to salaries paid, marketing costs for such items as advertising and special promotions totaled $400.
5. In addition to salaries, other administrative costs were $150.
6. All revenue transactions are cash, and all others are on account.

  a. Use T-accounts to show the flow of costs.

  b. Prepare an income statement for White and Brite for the month of November. No inventories were kept.

Prepared by K. McGarvey

3–35. Cost Accumulation: Service

Prepare journal entries for the November transactions in problem 3–34.

3–36. Cost Accumulation: Service

For the month of August, Correctall Accountants worked 500 hours for Misfit Manufacturing, 150 hours for Hang Ten Surf Shop, and 250 hours for Mandarin Restaurants. Correctall bills clients at $80 an hour, and labor costs are $30 an hour. A total of 1,000 hours were worked in May with 100 hours not billable to clients. Overhead costs of $15,000 were incurred. Overhead was assigned to clients on the basis of direct labor-hours. Since 100 hours were not billable, some overhead was not assigned to jobs. Correctall had $10,000 in marketing and administrative costs. All transactions were on account.

Required:

a. Show the flow of costs through T-accounts.

b. Prepare journal entries for the transactions shown above.

c. Prepare an income statement for the month of May.

COST ALLOCATION CONCEPTS

LEARNING OBJECTIVES

1. To understand why costs are allocated.

2. To know how to select from alternative allocation bases.

3. To be able to use single as well as dual/multiple allocation bases.

4. To see how complexity can be factored into allocations.

In this chapter, we discuss concepts for assigning costs to jobs, departments, products, and other cost objects when the cost affects two or more cost centers. This cost assignment process is called *cost allocation*. Allocated costs are indirect and, hence, common to two or more cost objects. If management wants to assign these costs to the individual cost objects, some method must be established to share the common costs. In this chapter, we present general principles for allocating costs, and we examine reasons for making cost allocations. Since cost allocations have been subject to a great deal of controversy, we discuss how cost allocations can potentially mislead users of accounting information and how to minimize such misleading effects.

HOW ARE COSTS ALLOCATED?

Cost Object Any end to which a cost is assigned.

A cost allocation is a proportional assignment of a cost to **cost objects**. For example, if two divisions share a facility that costs $15,000, that shared cost is referred to as a **common cost**. If we decide that the cost should be shared

REAL WORLD APPLICATION

Bellcore is the central research and engineering organization for the seven regional holding companies that were previously part of the Bell system of companies. Bellcore charges its client companies for its services based on cost. In 1983, the company developed a system of internal cost allocations so that it could determine the cost of each research or engineering job performed. By 1987, management noticed that its technical staff was typing its own letters and preparing its own graphics even though the company had word processing and graphics support available. Technical staff pay rates are way too high to justify their use as typists, yet this was what was happening at Bellcore.

Upon further investigation, Bellcore learned that word processing was charging $50 per page of document. This charge was fully justified by the calculated costs. Similar high costs were reported for other "people-intensive" cost centers. We focus on word processing in this illustration.

Management established a task force to investigate the situation and to consider options. A comparison with outside word processing companies showed that Bellcore was incurring excessively high building occupancy costs for its word processing group. Bellcore allocated building costs based on area occupied. Although this method is widely used, in Bellcore's case the allocation base did not recognize that a substantial amount of billing space was specially constructed for laboratories. Lab space was three times as expensive as the type of office space used for word processing, yet all space was allocated on the same basis. The result was a substantial overcharge to word processing, which increased the costs that word processing had to recover through page charges.

Costs of the library and travel support were allocated based on number of employees in departments. Further investigation revealed that only technical personnel used the library or took trips. Word processing was being charged for a share of the library and travel support costs out of all proportion to their benefits from these costs. Again, these costs were passed through in the form of higher charges per page of output.

Bellcore carefully evaluated all of the cost centers and found that significant fine-tuning of its allocating system was in order. After implementing the task force's recommended revisions to the cost allocation system, word processing costs fell to the point where use increased and technical staff found it more economical to work on research and engineering projects rather than to type letters. By adjusting the cost allocation system, the company was able to induce economically optimal behavior.

Source: Adapted from Edward J. Kovac and Henry P. Troy, *Harvard Business Review*, September–October, 1989, pp. 148–154.

Common Costs Costs of shared facilities, products, or services.

based on, say, the number of employees in each division, then the number of employees is the allocation base and the divisions are the cost objects. Carrying this one step further, if 40 percent of the employees are in the first division, then that division is charged with 40 percent of the $15,000 cost, or $6,000. This $6,000 is the cost allocated to the first division. The remaining 60 percent, or $9,000, is allocated to the second division. All of the common costs are allocated to the divisions based on their proportional use of the allocation base. Hence, the full $15,000 has been allocated to the divisions based on the relative number of employees in each division.

WHY ARE COSTS ALLOCATED?

There are numerous examples of cost allocation in organizations. Manufacturing overhead is a common cost that is usually allocated to each unit produced by a manufacturer. This allocation is required for financial reporting.

Multiunit organizations often allocate headquarters' costs to individual branches. For example, an executive of K mart, a retail company with over 2,500 stores, told us: "Allocating corporate headquarters' costs to stores makes each store manager aware that these costs exist and must be covered by the individual stores for the company as a whole to be profitable." This allocation was used as an attention-getting device by management.

Certain corporate overhead must also be allocated to inventories for tax purposes. The allocation method chosen can affect a company's tax liability.

Depreciation of long-term assets is another form of cost allocation required for financial reporting. The purpose of depreciation is to allocate the original cost of the asset over the time periods that the asset helps generate revenues.

In short, allocations are required for a variety of reasons. Because of the cash flow and behavioral effects of allocations, the approach taken must be carefully considered. The usual approach is to relate indirect costs to cost objects using an allocation method that reflects a cause-and-effect association.

ALLOCATING COSTS TO A DIVISION

To describe how cost allocation works, consider the following example. Computerworld, Inc., sells microcomputers in two different markets: business and personal. Because the two markets have different requirements, each company has set up two divisions for handling the markets. Each division has its own separate sales staff and a separate area in the company store. However, because most hardware may be used for either business or personal applications, the company has a common showroom. This common showroom reduces the company's investment in computer systems for display.

Computerworld, Inc., evaluates each division using "divisional operating profits" as a performance measure. A bonus is assigned to each division based on the relative amount of operating profits earned by each division. This bonus is then shared by the division employees. The greater the profits in any division, the greater the bonus for the division. The greater the division bonus, the greater the bonus for each employee in the division.

The following information is available concerning last month's activities by the company:

	Business Division	Personal Division	Total
Sales revenue	$266,000	$121,800	$387,800
Cost of goods sold	159,600	73,080	232,680
Other costs traced directly to divisions	87,900	38,500	126,400
Division "Operating profits" before showroom costs	$ 18,500	$ 10,220	$ 28,720
Number of units sold	28	42	70

Showroom costs, which amounted to $9,000 during the month, were common to both divisions. Company management needed to decide how to allocate the showroom costs to the two divisions. The manager of the business division said, "The showroom is used to display *units* of hardware. Therefore, the number of units sold should be used as the allocation base."

Following this argument, costs were allocated on the basis of units sold. The Business Division was charged with 28/70 times $9,000, or $3,600, for its share of the common costs. The Personal Division was charged with 42/70 times $9,000, or $5,400. Division operating profits, after the allocation of showroom costs, were:

Business Division: $14,900 = $18,500 − $3,600
Personal Division: $ 4,820 = $10,220 − $5,400

Any bonus would be split with 75.6 percent going to the Business Division

$\left(.756 = \dfrac{\$14,900}{\$14,900 + \$4,820} \right)$ and 24.4 percent to the Personal Division

$\left(.244 = \dfrac{\$4,820}{\$14,900 + \$4,820} \right)$. This example is a typical cost allocation

problem. In practice, you will find that managers are very concerned about the choice of cost allocation methods because this choice can affect the costs allocated to their organizational units. In turn, this can affect their job performance evaluation.

THE ARBITRARY NATURE OF COST ALLOCATION

By definition, costs that are common to two or more cost *objects* are likely to be allocated to those cost objects on a somewhat arbitrary basis. This arbitrariness has led critics of cost allocation to claim that arbitrary cost allocations may result in misleading financial reports and poor decisions. Despite these asserted problems, a recent study of corporate cost allocation found 84 percent of companies participating in the survey reported allocating common headquarters costs to divisions.[1] The study indicated that the primary managerial reason for cost allocation was to *remind responsibility*

[1] See J. M. Fremgen and S. S. Liao, *The Allocation of Corporate Indirect Costs* (New York: National Association of Accountants, 1981).

center managers that common costs exist and had to be recovered by division profits.

Cost allocation is an important topic in both financial and managerial accounting. Few accounting topics have evoked as much literature and debate.[2] No matter what career you choose, you will encounter the use of allocations. They may be used to compute the performance measures by which you and your division are evaluated. Or they may be used to determine costs in a contract between you or your employer and some other party. The method of allocation and its basis may be significant determinants of the value of the performance measure or the amount of the contract settlement.

The inherent arbitrariness of cost allocation implies that if there is no single method that is "absolutely right," then different people with interests in the outcome of an accounting measurement may prefer one allocation method over another. Returning to the Computerworld example, the initial allocation of income for bonus sharing might be expected to lead to some questions by the Personal Division.

Indeed, the manager of the Personal Division suggested that the Business Division manager's allocation was inappropriate. The Personal Division manager stated: "The Business Division people take a lot more time demonstrating each machine they sell. Indeed, I think everyone uses the showroom facilities in roughly the same proportion as the dollar sales, not the number of units sold.

If the costs are allocated on a sales basis, then the Business Division should be charged with $266,000/$387,800 times the $9,000 common showroom cost, which comes to a charge of $6,173. We should be charged with the remaining $2,827. This is equal to our proportional share of sales, which is $121,800/$387,800 times $9,000."

Using the Personal Division manager's recommended cost allocation, the income for each division is:

Business Division: $18,500 − $6,173 = $12,327
Personal Division: $10,220 − $2,827 = $ 7,393

The Personal Division would receive 37.5 percent of the bonus, which equals $\frac{\$7{,}393}{\$12{,}327\ +\ \$7{,}393}$. The Business Division would then receive the remaining 62.5 percent.

Upon hearing the debate between the two division managers, the company president stated: "Since there is no agreeable way to allocate showroom costs, we shall avoid the problem by *not allocating showroom costs.*" Unfortunately, that did not resolve the debate about sharing the bonus. Omitting the allocation of showroom cost would result in splitting the bonus based on the division operating profit before showroom costs. Then the

---

[2] Extensive discussions of cost allocation are presented in A. L. Thomas, *The Allocation Problem in Financial Accounting,* Studies in Accounting Research No. 3 (Sarasota, Fla.: American Accounting Association, 1969); A. L. Thomas, *The Allocation Problem: Part Two,* Studies in Accounting Research No. 9 (Sarasota, Fla.: American Accounting Association, 1974); and S. Moriarity, ed., *Joint Cost Allocations* (Norman: Center for Economic and Management Research, University of Oklahoma, 1981).

Business Division would receive $\dfrac{\$18,500}{\$10,220 + \$18,500}$, or 64.4 percent of the bonus. The Personal Division would have a 35.6 percent share computed as $\dfrac{\$10,220}{\$10,220 + \$18,500}$.

The shares of the bonus under each alternative are summarized as follows:

Allocation Method and Base	Business Division Share	Personal Division Share
Number of units	75.6%	24.4%
Sales revenue	62.5	37.5
No allocation	64.4	35.6

As the Computerworld example demonstrates, the cost allocation method, or lack thereof, can have a significant direct effect on the amounts paid to employees. Even when employee bonuses are not directly tied to operating profits, the profit performance of a division is a very important factor in determining pay and bonus amounts. This helps explain why cost allocation is frequently a controversial "hot" topic among managers in many organizations. The next section of the chapter describes the general methods of cost allocation used in many organizations.

COST ALLOCATION METHODS

The cost allocation process is composed of two stages. The first stage allocates costs to responsibility centers; the second stage allocates responsibility center costs to units. There are three activities in stage 1.

STAGE 1: ALLOCATING COSTS TO RESPONSIBILITY CENTERS

1. Identifying the cost objects or recipients of the allocated costs (for example, a department).
2. Accumulating the costs incurred by the organization as discussed in Chapter 3.
3. Selecting an allocation method for relating the costs that were accumulated to the cost objects. This is known as selecting an *allocation base*.

The third activity is the most challenging and controversial because common costs cannot be directly associated with a single unit or department. The accountant must therefore find an allocation base that will be a meaningful link between costs and cost objects, knowing that there is no perfect way to allocate costs.

Selecting Allocation Bases

Consider, for example, the salary of the supervisor of Contractors, Inc., a house construction company. During the month of June, five different jobs were started, and two were completed. There were no jobs in process at the beginning of the month. Each job benefited from the supervisor's planning and management, so his salary was a common cost to all five jobs. The company decided to allocate the supervisor's costs to the jobs for inventory valuation purposes at the end of June.[3] What is the appropriate allocation method? The company considered the following alternatives:

1. Allocate the salary equally to each job.
2. Charge the entire salary to any one job (because as long as the supervisor works on at least one job, he must be paid a month's wages).
3. Allocate the salary in proportion to the cost of direct materials used on each job.
4. Allocate the salary on the basis of the direct labor-hours (or costs) on each job.
5. Require the supervisor to keep time records by job and allocate on the basis of the time spent on the job.

An argument could be made to support each of these allocation bases. Contractors, Inc., decided that alternative 4 was best. Alternative 4 was preferable to alternative 5 because it was an almost costless procedure. It was preferable to alternatives 1, 2, and 3 because most of the supervisor's time was spent supervising direct labor. Therefore, Contractors, Inc., believed that alternative 4 related the indirect costs to the cost object in a manner that reflected a cause-and-effect relationship. This is typical of the reasoning that takes place when accountants select allocation bases.

Typical Allocation Bases

Most common costs can be categorized into one of four groups. Certain bases of allocation are commonly associated with each. Presumably, the bases reflect a cause-and-effect association. The allocation bases reflect, presumably, factors which drive the common costs. For any common cost, one or more **cost drivers** may be used.

1. *Labor-related common costs.* Labor-related common costs are usually allocated on the basis of number of employees, labor-hours, wages paid, or similar labor-related criteria. (See items 1 and 2 in Illustration 4–1.)
2. *Machine-related common costs.* Machine-related common costs are usually allocated on the basis of machine-hours, current value of machinery and equipment, number of machines, or similar machine-related criteria. (See items 3 through 6 in Illustration 4–1.)
3. *Space-related common costs.* Space-related common costs are usually allocated on the basis of area occupied, volume occupied, or similar space-related criteria. (See items 7 through 11 in Illustration 4–1.)
4. *Service-related common costs.* Service-related common costs may be allocated on the basis of quantity, value, time, and similar service-related criteria. (See items 12 through 16 in Illustration 4–1.)

These allocation bases are examples only. Common costs should be analyzed case by case to determine the most suitable allocation base.

---

[3] Indeed, under the 1986 Tax Act, this allocation is required for tax purposes. See Edward B. Deakin, "Cost Allocation Concepts under the 1986 Tax Act," *Journal of Petroleum Accounting*, Spring 1988.

Illustration 4-1   **Typical Allocation Bases for Common Costs**

	Common Cost	Typical Allocation Base
Labor Related	1. Supervision 2. Personnel services	Number of employees Payroll dollars or labor-hours Number of employees
Machine Related	3. Insurance on equipment 4. Taxes on equipment 5. Equipment depreciation 6. Equipment maintenance	Value of equipment Value of equipment Machine-hours, equipment value Number of machines, machine-hours
Space Related	7. Building rental 8. Building insurance 9. Heat and air conditioning 10. Concession rental 11. Interior building maintenance	Space occupied Space occupied Space occupied, volume occupied Space occupied and desirability of location Space occupied
Service Related	12. Materials handling 13. Laundry 14. Billing and accounting 15. Indirect materials 16. Dietary	Quantity or value of materials Weight of laundry processed Number of documents Value of direct materials Number of meals

Dual Allocation Rates

Dual Rate Method   A method of cost allocation that separates a common cost into fixed and variable components and then allocates each component using a different allocation base.

When two different cost behavior relationships exist between a common cost and a cost object, two bases may be used to allocate common costs. Such an allocation is called a **dual rate method**. For example, All-Tech purchased computer equipment based on projected demand for services. In addition to costs of purchasing or renting the computer, costs are incurred when the equipment is used. (These are mostly supplies and labor costs for computer operators.) Thus, there are two different relationships between the computer costs and the user departments: (1) capacity available to the user department and (2) current time usage.

Assume that the costs of renting the computer and other capacity costs are fixed costs, while the costs incurred for time usage are variable. The following equation could be used to allocate costs:

$$\frac{\text{Rate per unit}}{\text{of time charged}} = \frac{\text{Variable cost}}{\text{per unit of time}} + \frac{\text{Fixed capacity costs}}{\text{Units of time}}$$

Hence, user departments will be charged for an "average" use of both time and capacity. Further, user departments who use a lot of time but do not need much capacity subsidize user departments who need more capacity but do not use as much time.

An alternative method is to divide the computer costs into two separate components:

1. The fixed or capacity costs that are allocated on the basis of *capacity* demanded.

2. The variable costs that are allocated on the basis of *time* used.

With this alternative, the costs assigned to individual departments reflect as closely as possible the relationship between the cost allocated and the factors that caused the company to incur the cost.

For example, All-Tech, Inc., rents a specialty computer for $55,000 per month. This fee is based on the capacity of the equipment and has no relationship to actual usage. It costs $250 per hour to operate the computer. Department A requested that it have access to 500 units of capacity, while department B requested that it have access to 300 units of capacity. During the past month, department A used 200 hours of computer time while department B used 400 hours. Assuming these are the only two departments using the computer, how should the computer costs be allocated?

The firm first considered allocating costs on the basis of *time usage* alone. The cost allocation on the basis of time usage was:

Department A: $\dfrac{\text{200 department hours used}}{\text{600 total hours used}} \times \$205,000^{a} = \$\ 68,333$

Department B: $\dfrac{\text{400 department hours used}}{\text{600 total hours used}} \times \$205,000^{a} = \underline{\ 136,667}$

Total cost of the computer center $\underline{\underline{\$205,000^{a}}}$

[a] $205,000 = \$55,000 + (200 \text{ hours} + 400 \text{ hours}) \times \$250.$

When this method was proposed, the manager of department B argued, "My department is being charged for the monthly fixed rental fee on the basis of computer time used, but that monthly fee might have been lower if department A had not demanded so much capacity!"

To deal with this argument, the firm next allocated solely on the basis of *capacity demanded*. The resulting allocation was:

Department A: $\dfrac{\begin{array}{c}\text{500 department units of}\\\text{capacity requested}\end{array}}{\begin{array}{c}\text{800 total units of}\\\text{capacity requested}\end{array}} \times \$205,000 = \$128,125$

Department B: $\dfrac{\begin{array}{c}\text{300 department units of}\\\text{capacity requested}\end{array}}{\begin{array}{c}\text{800 total units of}\\\text{capacity requested}\end{array}} \times \$205,000 = \underline{\ 76,875}$

Total cost of the computer center $\underline{\underline{\$205,000}}$

When this method was proposed, the department B manager was happy, but the department A manager argued, "My department is being penalized because of our demand for capacity. We believe more costs should be allocated to department B because they used 400 hours of computer time while we only used 200 hours."

Instead of using either method alone, the firm used a dual rate based on both capacity demanded and time usage. The resulting allocation is shown in Illustration 4–2.

Illustration 4–2 **Dual Rates for Cost Allocation**

$$
\begin{array}{llll}
\text{Department A:} & \text{Capacity:} \dfrac{5}{8} \times \$55,000 & = & \$\ 34,375 \\
& \text{Time: } 200 \text{ hours} \times \$250 \text{ per hour} = & & \underline{\ 50,000} \\
\text{Total Department A} & & & \underline{\underline{\$\ 84,375}} \\
\\
\text{Department B:} & \text{Capacity:} \dfrac{3}{8} \times \$55,000 & = & 20,625 \\
& \text{Time: } 400 \text{ hours} \times \$250 \text{ per hour} = & & \underline{\ 100,000} \\
\text{Total Department B} & & & \$120,625 \\
\text{Total cost of the computer center} & & & \underline{\underline{\$205,000}}
\end{array}
$$

Multiple-Factor Method

The dual basis method can be extended to include multiple factors. The multiple-factor method is often used when there are many cause-and-effect relationships between common costs and cost objects.

Suppose, for example, that a company wants to allocate corporate headquarters' costs to each of its two divisions. Some people might assert that these costs are related to the size of the payroll; others might argue that these costs are related to the volume of business. Still others might argue that administrative costs are related to investment in assets. Actually, all three suggested bases may be valid. In such cases, a company may use a **multiple-factor formula** that incorporates all of the factors in the allocation base. In this case, the percentage of the common cost to be allocated to a plant may be the arithmetic average of the following three percentages:

Multiple-Factor Formula
An allocation formula that uses multiple bases for allocating overhead.

1. Percentage of payroll dollars in each division to the total payroll dollars for all divisions.
2. Percentage of volume in each division to the total volume in all divisions.
3. Percentage of the average gross book value of tangible assets of each division to the total gross book value of tangible assets in all divisions.

Assume the company has $282,000 in corporate headquarters' costs to apportion to the two divisions. An analysis of company records provides the following information:

Division	Payroll Dollars		Volume of Business		Gross Book Value of Tangible Assets	
	Amount	Percent	Amount	Percent	Amount	Percent
1	$1,300	65	$6,750	75	$ 5,600	40
2	700	35	2,250	25	8,400	60
Totals	$2,000	100	$9,000	100	$14,000	100

The multiple-factor allocation to each division would be computed as shown in Illustration 4–3.

Illustration 4–3.   **Multiple-Factor Method**

Division	Fraction	Allocated Cost
1	$\frac{65\% + 75\% + 40\%}{3} = 60\%$	60% × \$282,000 = \$169,200
2	$\frac{35\% + 25\% + 60\%}{3} = 40\%$	40% × \$282,000 = 112,800
	Total allocated costs	\$282,000

In recent years, many state taxing authorities have used this "three-factor" formula approach to assign the income of a multistate business to the individual state for state income tax purposes. For example, the State of Illinois Income Tax Return has the following section. (We have included penciled amounts to make the form easier to follow.)

Business Income Apportionment Formula

		1 Total Everywhere	2 Inside Illinois	3 Column 2 ÷ Column 1	
1 Property factor	1	1,000,000	100,000	.10	
2 Payroll factor	2	200,000	30,000	.15	
3 Sales factor	3	800,000	160,000	.20	
4 Total-add lines 1 through 3				4	.45
5 Average					5 .15

The amount in line 5 is multiplied by total business taxable income to compute the amount of taxable income for the state of Illinois.

States that use these factors assume the measures of property or assets, sales, and payrolls reflect the income generated in the states where the company operates.

So far, we have focused on Stage 1 of the cost allocation process; namely, the allocation of costs to departments. Most organizations also want to know the costs of products, in which case they have a second stage which allocates department costs to products. Manufacturing companies allocate costs to products not only to know how much products cost for managerial purposes but also to place a value on inventory for external financial reporting. We now turn to cost allocation—Stage 2.

STAGE 2: ALLOCATING RESPONSIBILITY CENTER COSTS TO UNITS

Some common bases for allocating manufacturing overhead to products are direct material costs, direct labor costs, direct labor-hours, machine-hours, and units of output.

Direct materials costs may be an appropriate basis when overhead costs are closely related to the volume of materials handled. In an assembly area

Typical Allocation Bases for Stage 2

where many of the costs correspond to the quantity of materials used, it may be appropriate to assign overhead on the basis of direct materials costs.

Direct labor costs are used as an allocation base when they are related to overhead costs. When skilled workers use costly machinery and unskilled workers perform tasks that do not require similar capital investments, the use of rates based on direct labor costs may be appropriate. Such an allocation base would reflect the relationship between the higher overhead costs associated with skilled labor and the lower overhead costs associated with unskilled labor. Jobs that require more skilled labor would be charged a proportionately greater share of overhead.

Direct labor-hours are an appropriate allocation base when overhead costs do not vary among different wage classes of labor or when labor rates are influenced more by seniority or other factors that are unrelated to job skills. Direct labor costs and hours are frequently used bases in service organizations.

Machine-hours are particularly appropriate when the manufacturing operations is capital-intensive and overhead is machine related (for example, the costs of power to run machines, or maintenance costs). In practice, we find the use of machine-hours as an allocation basis is increasing as manufacturing becomes more automated.

Units of output are used when the manufacturing operation is homogeneous for all products and the output of each department is easily defined.

Applying Overhead Costs to Products

The Terminals Division of All-Tech makes two products: personal terminals and office terminals. The personal terminal has a small screen and is usable on most personal computer products. The office terminal has a much larger screen and more complicated hardware. It is designed to be used in the office environment for more complicated applications. Total manufacturing overhead charged to terminals for the month was $50,000.

The production facility at the Terminals Division made 2,000 personal terminals in one month, using 15,000 direct machine-hours. It made 10 office terminals using 5,000 direct machine-hours. Because terminal manufacturing is very capital-intensive, management has decided to use machine-hours as its allocation base. The overhead per unit is computed as follows:

Step 1: Compute manufacturing overhead rate per machine-hour:

$$\text{Rate} = \$50,000 \div (5,000 \text{ hours} + 15,000 \text{ hours})$$
$$= \$2.50 \text{ per hour}$$

Step 2: Multiply rate times allocation base (machine-hours in this case)

$$
\begin{array}{llr}
\text{Personal:} & \$2.50 \times 15,000 & = \$37,500 \\
\text{Office:} & \$2.50 \times 5,000 & = \$12,500
\end{array}
$$

This gives the overhead allocated to each product line but not to each unit. This is done in step 3.

Step 3: Divide total manufacturing overhead by units produced:

Personal: $37,500 ÷ 2,000 units = $18.75 per unit of personal terminals

Office: $12,500 ÷ 10 units = $1,250 per unit of office terminals

This concludes the two-stage process of allocating units: *first* to responsibility centers and *second* to units. Next, we consider a potential misinterpretation that arises when fixed manufacturing overhead is allocated to units.

Unit Fixed Costs Can Be Misleading for Decision Making

When fixed costs are allocated to each unit, accounting records often make the cost appear as though it is a variable cost. For example, allocating some of factory rent to each unit of product would result in including the rent as part of the "unit cost" even though the total rent does not change with the manufacture of another unit of product. Cost data that includes allocated common costs may, therefore, be misleading if used incorrectly. The following example demonstrates the problem.

Superstar Inc., manufactures ski boots which have a unit production cost of $80, made up of the following per unit costs (each pair of boots is one unit):

Direct materials (variable cost)	$20
Direct labor (variable cost)	25
Variable manufacturing overhead	5
Total variable costs per unit	$50

Fixed manufacturing overhead costs allocated to units:

$$\text{Unit cost} = \frac{\text{Fixed manufacturing cost per month}}{\text{Units produced per month}}$$

$$= \frac{\$600,000}{20,000 \text{ units}} \qquad = \underline{30}$$

Total unit cost used as the inventory value for external financial reporting	$80

Superstar received a special order for 1,000 pairs of ski boots at $75 each. These units can be produced with capacity that is currently idle. Marketing, administrative costs, and the total fixed manufacturing costs of $600,000 would not be affected by accepting the order. Accepting this special order would not affect the regular market for this product.

Marketing managers believed the special order should be accepted as long as the unit price of $75 exceeded the cost of manufacturing each unit. When the marketing managers learned from accounting reports that the inventory value was $80 per unit, their initial reaction was to reject the order because, as one manager stated, "We are not going to be very profitable if it costs us more to make than our selling price!"

Fortunately, some additional investigation revealed the variable manufacturing cost to be only $50 per unit, and marketing management accepted the special order, which had the following impact on the company's operating profit:

Revenue from special order (1,000 units × $75)	$75,000
Variable costs of making special order (1,000 units × $50)	50,000
Contribution of special order to operating profit	$25,000

The moral of this example is that it is easy to interpret unit costs incorrectly and make incorrect decisions. In the example above, fixed manufacturing overhead costs had been allocated to units, most likely to value inventory for external financial reporting and tax purposes, which made the resulting unit cost of $80 appear to be the cost of producing a unit. Of course, only $50 was a variable cost of producing a unit, while the fixed costs of $600,000 per month would not be affected by the decision to accept the special order.

EFFECTS OF USING LABOR-BASED ALLOCATIONS IN AUTOMATED MANUFACTURING

Accountants have been concerned about the effect that the choice of an allocation base can have on the assignment of costs to different cost objects. Recently this concern was highlighted by some rather unusual cost allocations that gave rise to very high priced purchases under U.S. defense contracts. Critics of cost accounting have also argued that cost accounting is inappropriately applied in highly automated manufacturing plants. Although people may have used an inappropriate basis for cost allocation, the fundamental accounting principles are unchanged: the basis chosen should reflect a cause-and-effect association between the cost to be allocated and the cost object. If this association does not hold, the results may be quite misleading.

As an example, the Mountain Grown Coffee Pot Manufacturing Co. produces two types of coffee pots: (1) domestic and (2) commercial. The pots are identical except for certain trim items and the company logo inscribed on the pots. Materials used in the pots cost $7 regardless of the type of pot. The company produces 250,000 pots per year. The company's manufacturing operations are highly automated. Annual manufacturing overhead costs $1 million. The labor involved in the process is limited to monitoring the production machinery at the start of operations and checking occasionally to make sure the equipment is operating properly. Manufacturing labor costs for the year are estimated at $160,000. Overhead has been allocated to products on the basis of these labor costs for the past 30 years. This allocation base is still used by the company.

Yesterday, the company started the production line for manufacture of domestic pots. Labor costs of $400 were incurred for this production run. After producing 1,000 domestic pots, the company received a rush order for 10 commercial pots. The manager decided to produce those pots at the end of the day. Labor costs of $300 were incurred to reset the equipment and monitor this run. Ten pots were produced. Cost data for the day are summarized as follows:

	Domestic	Commercial
Units produced	1,000	10
Direct materials	$7,000.00	$ 70.00
Labor	400.00	300.00
Overhead	2,500.00	1,875.00
Total production costs	$9,900.00	$2,245.00
Cost per pot	$9.90	$224.50

Overhead is allocated based on a formula which takes the annual overhead ($1 million) and divides by annual labor costs ($160,000) to obtain a rate of 625 percent. Therefore, the $2,500 overhead assigned to the domestic pots is 625 percent of the $400 labor costs and the $1,875 assigned to commercial pots is 625 percent of $300.

Considering that the units are virtually identical, the wide difference in per unit prices is questionable. The problem is that the overhead for the company is not a function of this type of labor but, rather, is related more closely to units produced (or direct materials used). Using labor as a basis for allocation of the overhead results in distorted costs. If units produced were used for allocation purposes, the costs would be as follows:

	Domestic	Commercial
Units produced	1,000	10
Direct materials	$ 7,000.00	$ 70.00
Labor	400.00	300.00
Overhead	4,000.00	40.00
Total production costs	$11,400.00	$410.00
Cost per pot	$11.40	$41.00

Using units as the allocation base, overhead is allocated across all units based on factors related to overall production.

The recent criticism of cost allocation methods arises because the allocation base does not reflect the cause-and-effect relationship called for in cost accounting. The problem is usually highlighted when companies use labor-based allocation methods when their operations are highly automated. In these settings, a review of the specific situation could suggest an allocation base that avoids these distortions.

COST ALLOCATIONS IN COST-PLUS CONTRACTS

Many organizations sell products on a "cost-plus" basis, where the "plus" is a profit. Defense contractors, for example, traditionally have sold products to national governments on a cost-plus basis. Hospitals and nursing homes traditionally provided medical services and were reimbursed on a cost-plus basis for their costs from government agencies for particular types of patients.

Cost-plus contracts give incentives to the supplier of the good or service to seek as much reimbursement as possible and therefore to allocate as much cost as possible to the product for which reimbursement is possible. For example, suppose McBoheed Aircraft Co. is deciding how to allocate $120 million of overhead between two major lines of business: commercial and governmental. This overhead is common to the two lines of business and cannot be directly traced to either. Commercial products are sold at a price set in the market, but governmental products are sold for cost plus a fixed profit. Thus, every dollar of overhead that can be allocated to the governmental product line results in an additional dollar of revenue by way of cost reimbursement.

Suppose McBoheed is choosing between labor-hours and machine-hours as the two possible allocation bases. The relative use of labor- and machine-hours and the resulting allocation of overhead follows:

	Lines of Business	
	Commercial	**Governmental**
Percent of labor-hours used	30%	70%
Percent of machine-hours used	60	40

Naturally, McBoheed would prefer to allocate the $120 million using labor-hours because it could seek reimbursement from the government for $84 million (i.e., 70 percent × $120 million), whereas it could seek reimbursement for only $48 million using machine-hours.

McBoheed would be $36 million better off if it could use labor-hours as the allocation base. Of course, the government would argue for machine-hours. Since the allocable costs cannot, by definition, be directly attributed to a contract, allocation debates abound in cost-plus contracting.

In cases like these, it is important to specify in the contract precisely how costs will be defined and how allocations will be made. Facing numerous disputes over cost reimbursements, the U.S. government established the Cost Accounting Standards Board, which existed from 1971 to 1980, to establish cost accounting standards that would serve to reduce disputes between defense contractors and government agencies. This board developed uniform cost allocation principles for defense contractors that are still in use.

COST ALLOCATION IN HIGH-TECH COMPANIES: THE COST OF COMPLEXITY

The allocation bases previously discussed (e.g., direct labor-hours and machine-hours) were primarily volume based. Recently, the *complexity* of production activities has been recognized as an important determinant of overhead costs. This is particularly the case in high-tech companies in which computer-driven production methods enable the production of a great variety of products.

Consider the following example. Terminals, Inc., has two plants that each produce 10,000 computer terminal screens per year. Plant A makes only one kind of screen; namely, a standard monochrome screen. Plant B makes 10 different types of terminal screens of various sizes and colors. Plant A stocks parts for only one type of screen, trains its people how to construct only one type of product, and needs to change equipment settings only when there is a change in model. Plant B has to order and stock parts for 10 different types of screens, trains its people to produce 10 different products, and makes frequent changes in equipment settings as it begins to produce each different product. Although both plants produce the same total volume of computer terminal screens, the overhead costs for Plant B are higher because the production process is more complex.

If complexity causes costs, then various measures of complexity may be relevant to use as allocation bases. Two typical measures of complexity are

(1) the number of different products made in a plant or department and (2) the length of production runs. The following discussion describes how these measures could be used to allocate overhead costs at Terminals, Inc.

1. *Number of different products.* The more products made by a department or plant, the more complex the production process. Increasing the number of different products increases the number of different types of material that must be ordered and stored which increases purchasing, recordkeeping, and storage costs. The number of products also affects the number of different product specifications that must be developed and updated. For Terminals, Inc., the screens produced in Plant B would cost more *per unit* than those produced in Plant A because Plant B produces more types of screens.

2. *Length of production run.* The shorter the production run, the more times machines have to be adjusted or set up to make a new product. Since Plant A makes only one product, for example, it would not have to change its machines as long as it produced the monochrome screen. Since Plant B makes 10 different products, it would have to shut down its production facilities to change its equipment each time it changed products. If management of Plant B wants to make all 10 types of terminals during a 20-work-day period, it would change machines every two days, on average. This would affect, for example, indirect labor used to handle the materials and equipment used in making the change.

Assume Plants A and B of Terminals, Inc., share certain common overhead costs, such as purchasing and energy to operate machines. Management of Terminals, Inc., had previously allocated $1 million of manufacturing overhead that was common to the two plants on the basis of machine-hours worked in each plant, which was 50,000 hours per plant. Consequently, one half of its $1 million common manufacturing overhead cost was allocated to each plant, as shown in the top panel of Illustration 4–4.

Management then decided to reallocate these costs on the basis of both complexity and volume measures. First, the $1 million costs were divided into three categories: (1) costs related to the number of different products, such as purchasing and recordkeeping of materials; (2) costs related to the length of production run (where the shorter the production run, the greater the costs), such as the cost of setting up machines for a new production run; and (3) volume-related costs such as energy costs for machine operation. The following allocation bases were used to allocate each type of cost:

Cost	**Allocation Base**
(1) Costs related to number of different products (for example, purchasing)	(1) Number of different products produced during the year
(2) Costs related to the length of production run (for example, the cost of setting up machines for a new production run)	(2) Number of setups made during the year
(3) Costs related to the volume of production (for example, costs of energy to operate machines)	(3) Machine-hours worked during the year

Illustration 4-4   **Allocating Costs in Complex Operations**

Allocation Base	Costs to Be Allocated	Costs Allocated to	
		Plant A	Plant B
Allocation based only on volume:			
Machine-hours	$1,000,000	$\frac{50,000 \text{ hrs.}^a}{100,000 \text{ hrs.}} \times \$1,000,000$ $= \$\ 500,000$	$\frac{50,000 \text{ hrs.}^a}{100,000 \text{ hrs.}} \times \$1,000,000$ $= \$\ 500,000$
Allocation based on complexity and volume:			
1. Number of different products	$ 220,000	$\frac{1}{11}^b \times \$220,000 = \$20,000$	$\frac{10}{11}^b \times \$220,000 = \$200,000$
2. Number of setups	242,000	$\frac{1}{121}^c \times \$242,000 = \$\ 2,000$	$\frac{120}{121}^c \times \$242,000 = \$240,000$
3. Volume of machine-hours	538,000	$\frac{50,000 \text{ hrs.}^a}{100,000 \text{ hrs.}} \times \$538,000$ $= \$269,000$	$\frac{50,000 \text{ hrs.}^a}{100,000 \text{ hrs.}} \times \$538,000$ $= \$269,000$
Total costs:	$1,000,000	$291,000	$709,000

[a] 50,000 machine-hours worked in each plant.
[b] One product in plant A, 10 different products in plant B.
[c] One setup in plant A, 120 different setups in plant B.

Next, the $1 million common manufacturing overhead cost was divided into these three cost categories, and the following items were counted for each plant: (1) number of different products produced, (2) number of setups, and (3) volume of machine-hours. This investigation resulted in the following data:

Category	Allocation Bases	Cost to Be Allocated	Plant A	Plant B	Total
(1)	Number of different products	$ 220,000	1	10	11
(2)	Number of setups	242,000	1	120	121
(3)	Machine-hours worked	538,000	50,000	50,000	100,000
	Total cost to be allocated	$1,000,000			

Computations for the new allocation bases appear in the bottom panel of Illustration 4-4. As shown in Illustration 4-4, the costs allocated to plant B increase from $500,000 to $709,000 under the new allocation method because of the complexity of operations in plant B.

There are many different types of complexity. Distribution complexity, for example, is caused by distribution processes involving many different customers and channels for distributing products which affect marketing costs. Administrative complexity, caused by complex organizations, affects administration costs. It is important to remember that, all else equal, goods and services produced in complex settings are more costly than those produced in simple settings.

SUMMARY

Cost allocation is the process of assigning common costs to two or more cost objects. Manufacturing overhead is common to units produced, for example, and is allocated to them to place a value on inventory and cost of goods sold for external financial reporting. Allocations of common costs to cost objects are often made on a somewhat arbitrary basis. The general goal is to let the allocation reflect a cause-and-effect association between the costs and the objects to which they are allocated.

Cost allocation procedures are costly because they consume the time of accountants and decision makers. Thus, costs should not be allocated unless there is cost-benefit justification. A common reason for allocating costs is to satisfy external reporting or tax requirements (for example, to value inventory on external financial reports). Cost allocations are rarely required for managerial purposes; however, under certain conditions, they can be useful. Cost-plus contracts and cost-based rate regulations require allocations of common costs.

The first stage of the cost allocation process is to allocate costs to responsibility centers. This involves (1) identifying cost objects, (2) accumulating costs to be allocated, and (3) selecting a basis for relating costs to cost objects. Some common costs and related bases are:

1. Labor-related common costs—number of employees, labor-hours, wages paid, or other labor-related criteria.
2. Machine-related common costs—machine-hours, current value of machinery, number of machines, or other machine-related criteria.
3. Space-related common costs—area occupied, volume occupied, or other space-related criteria.
4. Service-related common costs—computer usage, service personnel time, or other service-related criteria.

Dual and multiple bases are often used for cost allocation when there is more than one relationship between a common cost and a cost object. Complexity measures may also be incorporated into allocation systems when a simple allocation base fails to capture the cause-and-effect criterion.

A second stage of the process in many companies is to allocate manufacturing overhead costs to units produced typically using direct labor-hours, direct labor costs, machine-hours, or units of output.

Cost allocation can be misleading, particularly if costs allocated for one purpose are used for another. For example, fixed manufacturing overhead is allocated to units to place a value on inventory for external financial reporting and tax purposes. It is very easy for decision makers to assume incorrectly that those unit values are the variable costs of manufacturing units.

Costs are accumulated as transactions occur. The accumulated costs are then allocated to cost objects inside the organization. Costs accumulate due to transactions with outsiders. Cost allocations are internal assignments of costs.

TERMS AND CONCEPTS

The following terms and concepts should be familiar to you after reading this chapter.

Allocation Base	**Cost Objects**
Common Cost	**Dual Rate Method**
Complexity	**Multiple-Factor Formula**
Cost Allocation	

SUPPLEMENTARY READINGS

Allen, Brandt. "Make Information Services Pay Its Own Way." *Harvard Business Review,* January–February 1987, pp. 57–63.

Atkinson, Anthony. *Intrafirm Cost and Resource Allocations: Theory and Practice.* Society of Management Accountants of Canada and Canadian Academic Accounting Association Research Monograph, 1987.

Blanchard, Garth A., and Chee W. Chow. "Allocating Indirect Costs for Improved Management Performance." *Management Accounting,* March 1983, pp. 38–41.

Cardullo, J. Patrick, and Richard A. Mollenberndt. "The Cost Allocation Problem in a Telecommunications Company." *Management Accounting,* September 1987, pp. 39–44.

Ericksen, Naomi, and David H. Herskovits. "Accounting for Software Costs: Cracking the Code." *Journal of Accountancy,* November 1985, pp. 81–96.

Fremgen, J., and S. S. Liao. *The Allocation of Corporate Indirect Costs.* New York: National Association of Accountants, 1981.

Hakala, Gregory. "Measuring Costs with Machine-Hours." *Management Accounting,* October 1985, pp. 57–61.

Martin, Pamela De Mars, and Frank J. Boyer. "Developing a Consistent Method for Costing Hospital Services." *Healthcare Financial Management,* February 1985, pp. 30–37.

Mackey, J. T. "Allocating Opportunity Costs." *Management Accounting,* March 1983, pp. 33–37.

Reinstein, A. "Improving Cost Allocations for Auto Dealers." *Management Accounting,* June 1982, pp. 52–57.

Schneider, Arnold. "Indirect Cost Allocations and Cost-Plus Pricing Formulas." *Journal of Cost Analysis,* Fall 1986, pp. 47–57.

Thomas, A. "The Allocation Problem: Part Two." *Studies in Accounting Research No. 9.* Sarasota, Fla.: American Accounting Association, 1974.

Verrecchia, R. E. "An Analysis of Two Cost Allocation Cases." *Accounting Review,* July 1982, pp. 579–93.

Zimmerman, J. L. "The Costs and Benefits of Cost Allocations." *Accounting Review,* July 1979, pp. 504–521.

SELF-STUDY PROBLEM NO. 1

Dual Division Corporation operates its Uno and Duo divisions as separate cost objects. To determine the costs of each division, the company allocates common costs to the divisions. During the past month, the following common costs were incurred:

Computer services (80% fixed)	$254,000
Building occupancy	615,000
Personnel	104,000

The following information is available concerning various activity measures and service usages by each of the divisions:

	Uno	Duo
Area occupied	15,000 sq. ft.	40,000 sq. ft.
Payroll	$380,000	$170,000
Computer time	200 hrs.	140 hrs.
Computer storage	25 mbytes	35 mbytes
Equipment value	$175,000	$220,000
Operating profit—before allocations	$439,000	$522,000

Required:

a. Allocate the common costs to the two departments using the most appropriate of the above allocation bases. For computer services, use computer time only.

b. Allocate the common costs to the two departments using dual rates for the computer services.

SOLUTION TO SELF-STUDY PROBLEM NO. 1

a.

Cost	Allocation Base	Allocated to Uno	Allocated to Duo
Computer services	Computer time	$\dfrac{200}{200 + 140} \times \$254{,}000$	$\dfrac{140}{200 + 140} \times \$254{,}000$
		$= \$149{,}412$	$= \$104{,}588$
Building occupancy	Area occupied	$\dfrac{15{,}000}{15{,}000 + 40{,}000} \times \$615{,}000$	$\dfrac{40{,}000}{15{,}000 + 40{,}000} \times \$615{,}000$
		$= \$167{,}727$	$= \$447{,}273$
Personnel	Payroll	$\dfrac{\$380{,}000}{\$380{,}000 + \$170{,}000} \times \$104{,}000$	$\dfrac{\$170{,}000}{\$380{,}000 + \$170{,}000} \times \$104{,}000$
		$= \$\ 71{,}855$	$= \$\ 32{,}145$
Totals		$\$388{,}994$	$\$584{,}006$

Check: $254,000 + $615,000 + $104,000 = $388,994 + $584,006 = $973,000.

b.

Computer variable costs	Computer time	$\dfrac{200}{200 + 140} \times 254{,}000 \times 20\%$	$\dfrac{140}{200 + 140} \times \$254{,}000 \times 20\%$
		$= \$\ 29{,}882$	$= \$\ 20{,}918$
Computer fixed costs	Computer storage	$\dfrac{25}{25 + 35} \times \$254{,}000 \times 80\%$	$\dfrac{35}{25 + 35} \times \$254{,}000 \times 80\%$
		$= \$\ 84{,}667$	$= \$118{,}533$
Building occupancy— per *(a)*		$\$167{,}727$	$\$447{,}273$
Personnel—per *(a)*		$\$\ 71{,}855$	$\$\ 32{,}145$
Totals		$\$354{,}131$	$\$618{,}869$

Check: $254,000 + $615,000 + $104,000 = $354,131 + $618,869 = $973,000.

SELF-STUDY PROBLEM NO. 2

Merrill's Machine Tools Company has two plants and allocates the headquarters' costs to the plants based on a three-factor formula using plant payroll, plant volume, and gross book value of plant tangible assets. The allocation percentage is an arithmetic average of three percentages:

1. Percentage of payroll dollars in each plant to the total payroll dollars for both plants.
2. Percentage of volume, in dollars, in each plant to the total volume in both plants.
3. Percentage of the average gross book value of tangible assets of each plant to the total book value of tangible assets for both plants.

The company has $480,000 in headquarters' costs to be allocated. The relevant factors for each plant are:

	Payroll	**Volume**	**Assets**
Michigan plant	$120,000	$ 600,000	$ 400,000
Texas plant	180,000	1,000,000	800,000
Total	$300,000	$1,600,000	$1,200,000

Required:

Determine the amount of headquarters' costs to be allocated to each plant using the multiple-factor allocation method.

SOLUTION TO SELF-STUDY PROBLEM NO. 2:

	Michigan Plant	**Texas Plant**	**Total**
Percentage factors:			
Payroll	$\frac{\$120,000}{\$300,000} = 40.0\%$	$\frac{\$180,000}{300,000} = 60.0\%$	100%
Volume	$\frac{\$600,000}{\$1,600,000} = 37.5\%$	$\frac{\$1,000,000}{\$1,600,000} = 62.5\%$	100%
Assets	$\frac{\$400,000}{\$1,200,000} = 33.3\%$	$\frac{\$800,000}{\$1,200,000} = 66.7\%$	100%

Average:

Michigan $\frac{(40.0\% + 37.5\% + 33.3\%)}{3} = 36.9\%$

Texas $\frac{(60.0\% + 62.5\% + 66.7\%)}{3} = \underline{63.1\%}$

Allocation of headquarters' costs:
Michigan $480,000 × 36.9% = $177,120
Texas $480,000 × 63.1% = $302,880
                            $480,000

QUESTIONS

4–1. If cost allocations are arbitrary and potentially misleading, should we assume that management is foolish for using information based on allocated costs?

4–2. What are some of the costs of cost allocation?

4–3. What are some of the benefits of cost allocation?

4–4. What principle is used to decide whether to allocate costs to cost objects?

4–5. One critic of cost allocation noted: "You can avoid the problem of arbitrary cost allocations by simply not allocating any common costs to other cost objects." What are your thoughts on this suggestion?

4–6. What are some management uses of information based on allocated costs?

4–7. List the two major stages in the cost allocation process. What are the three activities in stage 1?

4–8. Is there a reasonable criterion for selecting the basis that is used to allocate costs? Explain your answer.

4–9. List the four broad categories of common costs and the usual basis for allocation of costs in each category. The basis may be expressed as an example or in broad terms.

4–10. A cost such as company headquarters' cost does not fit into any one of the broad categories of common costs. A cost such as this may be a result of a number of different causal factors. Is there a way to allocate such a cost? Describe the approach.

EXERCISES

4–11. Why Costs Are Allocated
(L.O.1)

The Hatfields and the McCoys own two adjacent tracts of land. Each tract has a surface area of 5,000 acres. During a recent shoot-out, crude oil came bubbling to the surface where a bullet had entered the ground. A petroleum geologist determined that there was an underground rock formation which contained a substantial amount of oil and which extended under both tracts of land. The formation was estimated at 600,000 acre feet of volume, of which 200,000 acre feet was under the McCoy's tract of land.

The Hatfields and the McCoys received an offer to buy the mineral rights for $4.5 million provided that they can agree on how much of the purchase price should be allocated to each family.

Required:

a. As a Hatfield, what basis would you recommend for allocating the purchase price? What arguments would you use to support your claim?

b. As a McCoy, what basis would you recommend for allocating the purchase price? What arguments would you use to support your claim?

4–12. Alternative Allocation Bases
(L.O.2)

For each of the types of common cost in the first column, select the most appropriate allocation base from the second column:

Common Cost	Allocation Base
Building utilities	Value of inventories
Payroll accounting	Number of units produced
Property taxes on inventories	Number of employees
Equipment repair	Space occupied
Quality control inspection	Number of service calls

4–13. Alternative Allocation Bases
(L.O.2)

Nautical Novelties produces two types of bathtub toys: rubber ducks and ships. Both are produced in the same plant on the same assembly line, and the company wants to know how to allocate the manufacturing overhead to the products. The relevant data for the possible allocation bases are as follows:

Allocation Base	Ships	Ducks
Materials used	$20,000	$10,000
Direct labor-hours	10,000	15,000
Direct labor costs	$50,000	$70,000
Machine-hours	3,000	2,000
Output	10,000	15,000

The company has $30,000 in manufacturing overhead to be allocated to these two products.

Required:

For each of the five possible allocation bases, calculate the manufacturing overhead that would be allocated to each unit of output.

4–14. Alternative Allocation Bases

(L.O.2)

Refer to your results in exercise 4–13. Your supervisor would like you to compare total production costs for each toy with each allocation base. Be sure to include materials, labor, and overhead.

Required:

a. Prepare a comparison chart of production costs for each toy.

b. Explain why you have presented five different cost numbers for each product and clarify whether the total manufacturing costs would change with each allocation overhead base.

4–15. Alternative Ailocation Bases

(L.O.2)

Wayne's Western Co. produces two styles of cowboy boots: standard and deluxe. The difference between the two is in the amount of handcrafting that is done. The deluxe boot uses more skilled labor because additional cutting and trimming is done by hand, which is not done for the standard boot. The relevant figures for the year just completed are given below.

Allocation Base	Standard	Deluxe
Materials used	$200,000	$ 100,000
Direct labor-hours	100,000	150,000
Direct labor costs	$700,000	$1,800,000
Machine-hours	40,000	10,000
Output, in pairs	80,000	15,000

The company has $750,000 in manufacturing overhead costs to allocate to these two product lines.

Required:

For each of the five potential allocation bases, determine the amount of manufacturing overhead that would be allocated to each unit of output.

4–16. Alternative Allocation Bases

(L.O.2)

Refer to your calculations for exercise 4–15. Your supervisor wants to know how much it costs to make a pair of standard boots and a pair of deluxe boots, including the cost of materials, labor and manufacturing overhead.

Required:

a. Give your supervisor five different answers, for each type of boot, to the question: "How much does it cost to make?"

b. Explain to your supervisor why there are five different cost numbers for each product. Also indicate whether total manufacturing costs are the same for Wayne's Western Co. regardless of the overhead allocation base used.

4–17. Alternative Allocation Bases—Service

(L.O.2)

WKRP Enterprises has a TV and a radio station that share the common costs of the company's AP wire service, which is $48,500 a year. You have the following information about the AP wire and the two stations:

Station	Wire Service-Hours Used This Period	Hours of News Broadcasts
TV	460	120
Radio	316	480

Required:

a. What is the AP wire service cost charged to each station if wire service-hours is used as an allocation basis?

b. What is the AP wire service cost charged to each station using hours of news broadcast as a basis for allocation?

c. Which method allocates more costs to TV? Which method allocates more costs to Radio?

4–18. Single versus Dual Rates

(L.O.3)

Refer to data for the company in exercise 4–17.

Determine the cost allocation if $26,000 of the wire service costs are fixed and allocated on the basis of hours of news; and the remaining costs, which are variable, are allocated on the basis of wire service-hours used.

4–19. Alternative Allocation Bases

(L.O.2)

Affiliated Retailers operates a department store in Enola, Pennsylvania. The store has 120,000 square feet. Each department in the store is charged with a share of the cost of the building. The following information is available concerning two of the departments in the store:

	Department	
	Fashion Clothing	Furniture
Sales revenues	$700,000	$800,000
Cost of goods sold	370,000	380,000
Sales commissions, salaries, other direct expenses	210,000	240,000
Allocated administrative expenses	60,000	65,000
Operating profit before building occupancy costs	$ 60,000	$115,000
Area occupied	10,000 sq. ft.	30,000 sq. ft.

Other departments use the other 80,000 square feet. The total building occupancy costs are $600,000 per year.

Required:

a. If area occupied is the basis for allocation of building occupancy costs, what is the operating profit or loss for each of these two departments?

b. Would you change your answer to (*a*) if you learned that the fashion clothing department is located in an upstairs back corner of the store? Discuss why you would (or would not) change your answer.

4–20.   Alternative Allocation Bases
(L.O.2)

General Hospital has two departments that share the common costs of the hospital's respiratory equipment which is $485,000. You have the following information about the two user departments:

User Department	Service-Hours Used This Period in Each User Department	Value of Equipment (in thousands)
A	460	$121,250
B	316	480,000

Required:

a.   What is the respiratory equipment cost charged to Departments A and B if service-hours is used as an allocation basis?

b.   What is the respiratory equipment cost charged to Departments A and B using value of equipment as a basis for allocation?

c.   Which method allocates more costs to Department A? Why? Which method allocates more costs to Department B? Why?

4–21.   Single versus Dual Rates
(L.O.3)

Refer to the data in exercise 4–20.

Determine the cost allocation if $260,000 of the respiratory equipment costs are fixed and allocated on the basis of value of equipment and the remaining costs, which are variable, are allocated on the basis of service-hours used this period. (See Illustration 4–2 for example.)

4–22.   Single versus Dual Rates
(L.O.3)

Compare your answers to exercises 4–20 and 4–21.

From General Hospital's point of view, does it matter whether service-hours, equipment value, or the dual rate is used? Does it matter to the managers of Departments A and B which method is used?

4–23.   Single versus Dual Rates
(L.O.3)

A CPA firm has two departments, audit and tax, and word processing that is common to both departments. The cost of word processing is $200,000. The following information is given concerning the support staff and the two departments.

	Pages of Word Processing Used by Department	Payroll of Department
Audit	2,000	$200,000
Tax	6,000	150,000

Required:

a.   What is the support staff cost charged to each department if pages of word processing is the allocation basis?

b.   What is the support staff cost charged to each department if departmental payroll is the allocation basis?

4–24.   Single versus Dual Rates
(L.O.3)

Using the data for the CPA firm in exercise 4–23, what is the cost allocation if there are fixed support staff department costs of $90,000 that are allocated on the basis of department payroll, and the remaining costs (all variable) are allocated on the basis of pages of word processing used by the department?

4–25. Multiple Factor Allocations

(L.O.3)

Mozart Musik operates four record stores and allocates headquarters' costs based on the arithmetical average of three factors:

1. Percentage of payroll dollars in each store to the total payroll dollars for all stores.

2. Percentage of sales dollars in each store to the total volume in all stores.

3. Percentage of the average gross book value of tangible assets of each store to the total book value of tangible assets for all stores.

The company has headquarters' costs of $150,000. The relevant factors for the stores are:

	Stores				
	Akron	**Boston**	**Columbus**	**Detroit**	**Total**
Payroll	$ 60,000	$ 85,000	$ 70,000	$ 35,000	$ 250,000
Sales	1,000,000	1,200,000	1,100,000	700,000	4,000,000
Assets	140,000	250,000	210,000	200,000	800,000

Required:

Determine the amount of headquarters' costs allocated to each store.

4–26. Multiple Factor Allocations

(L.O.3)

MoIllCal, Inc., operates in three states: Missouri, Illinois, and California. The following information is available concerning the activities and taxing bases for each of the three states:

	Missouri	**Illinois**	**California**
Income tax rate	—0—	5%	7%
Basis for allocating income	—	Illinois sales over total sales	California sales, payroll and property three-factor formula
Company sales occurring by state	—	$2.4 million	$1.8 million
Company payrolls by state	$2.6 million	.8	.6
Company property by state	1.2	.3	.5

Company headquarters are located in Missouri. Total company profits were $750,000 before state taxes.

Required:

What is the income tax liability due to each state?

4–27. Multiple Factor Allocations—Complexity

(L.O.4)

Refer to the facts presented in Illustration 4–4. Assume the costs to be allocated and the allocation bases are as follows:

Category	Cost to Be Allocated	Allocation Base	Plant A	Plant B	Total
1	$230,000	Number of different products	1	10	11
2	484,000	Number of setups	1	120	121
3	286,000	Machine-hours worked	50,000	50,000	100,000

| Required: | What would be the new allocation of costs to Plants A and B? Why would it differ from the allocation in the bottom panel of Illustration 4–4? |

4–28. Multiple Factor Allocations—Complexity
(L.O.4)

Refer to the facts presented in Illustration 4–4. Assume the management of Terminals, Inc., shifted production of five products from Plant B to Plant A because "Plant A had lower costs than Plant B." Afterwards, the costs and allocation bases were as follows:

Category	Cost to Be Allocated	Allocation Base	Plant A	Plant B	Total
1	$220,000	Number of different products	6	5	11
2	242,000	Number of setups	61	60	121
3	538,000	Machine-hours worked	75,000	25,000	100,000

Required:

What would be the new allocation to Plants A and B? Why would this allocation differ from the allocation in Illustration 4–4?

PROBLEMS

4–29. Choosing an Appropriate Allocation Base in a High-Tech Environment

Silicon Valley Corp. manufactures two types of computer chips. The ROM-A chip is a commonly used chip for personal computer systems. The RAM-B chip is used for specialized scientific applications. Direct materials costs for the ROM-A chip are 25 cents per unit and for the RAM-B are 28 cents per unit. The company's annual output is 32 million chips. At this level of output, manufacturing overhead amounts to $2.4 million, and direct labor costs total $625,000.

The company's assembly process is highly automated. As a result, the primary function for direct labor is to set up a production run and to check equipment settings on a periodic basis.

Yesterday the equipment was set up to run 800 RAM-B units. When that run was completed, equipment settings were changed, and 100,000 RAM-A units were produced. Part of the daily cost report is as follows:

	ROM-A	RAM-B
Units Produced	**100,000**	**800**
Direct materials	$25,000	$224
Direct labor	1,000	600

Required:

a. For yesterday's production run, what is the total manufacturing cost per unit for ROM-A and RAM-B if direct labor costs are used to allocate manufacturing overhead?

b. For yesterday's production run, what is the total manufacturing cost per unit for ROM-A and RAM-B if units produced is the basis used to allocate manufacturing overhead?

4–30. Choosing an Appropriate Allocation Base in an Automated Environment

Birmingham Fabrication Corp. produces fence materials. One division manufactures fence rails and fence posts. As a general rule, more fence rails are produced than posts. For example, during the past week, 900 rails and 30 posts were manufactured.

Direct materials costs are $3.10 per rail and $3.00 per post. Direct labor of $200 was attributed to the rail manufacturing operation, and $250 was attributed to posts during the past week. Most of the direct labor costs are incurred in setting up the automated equipment. In the manufacturing process, it takes about the same amount of time for the equipment to produce one rail as it does to produce one post.

This division has $550,000 in annual manufacturing overhead which is allocated based on direct labor costs. The annual direct labor costs are estimated at $44,000. The company produces 250,000 units per year.

Required:

a. Prepare a schedule to show the cost assigned to each rail and each post using direct labor as the basis for allocating overhead.

b. Prepare a schedule computing the unit costs of rails and posts using units of production as a basis for allocating overhead costs.

c. In light of the information provided, which method of overhead allocation appears more reasonable? Why?

4–31. Cost Allocation for Rate-Making Purposes

Failsafe Insurance, Inc., asked the regulatory board for an increase in the allowed premiums from its insurance operations. Insurance premium rates in the jurisdiction in which Failsafe operates are designed to cover the operating costs and insurance claims. As a part of Failsafe's expenses, its agents earn commissions based on premium revenues. Premium revenues are also used to pay claims and to invest in securities. Administrative expenses include costs to manage the company's investments. All administrative costs are charged against premium revenue. Failsafe claims that its insurance operations "just broke even" last year and that a rate increase is necessary. The following income statement (in millions) was submitted to support Failsafe's request:

Insurance income:	
Premium revenue	$400
Operating costs:	
Claims	250
Administrative	70
Sales commissions	80
Total operating costs	400
Insurance profit (loss)	–0–
Investment income	30
Profits after investment income	$ 30

Further investigation reveals that approximately 20 percent of the sales commissions may be considered related to investment activities. In addition, 10 percent of the administrative costs are incurred by the investment management division. The state insurance commission (which sets insurance rates) believes that Failsafe's insurance activities should earn about 5 percent on its premium revenues.

Required:

a. If you were a consumer group, how would you present Failsafe's income statement? (For example, how would you allocate administrative costs and sales commissions between the "insurance income" category and the "investment income" category?)

b. If you were Failsafe's management, what arguments would you present in support of the cost allocations included in the above income statement?

4–32. Cost Allocation for Travel Reimbursement

Your company has a travel policy that reimburses employees for the "ordinary and necessary" costs of business travel. Quite often employees will mix a business trip with pleasure either by extending the time at the destination or by traveling from the business destination to a nearby resort or other personal destination. When this happens, an allocation must be made between the business and personal portions of the trip. However, the travel policy is unclear on the allocation method to follow.

Consider the following example:

An employee obtained an excursion ticket for $660 and traveled the following itinerary:

From	To	Mileage	Regular Fare	Purpose
Washington, D.C.	Salt Lake City	1,839	$350	Business
Salt Lake City	Los Angeles	590	150	Personal
Los Angeles	Washington, D.C.	2,288	400	Return

Required:

Compute the business portion of the air fair and state the basis for the indicated allocation that would be appropriate according to each of the following independent scenarios:

a. Based on the maximum reimbursement for the employee.

b. Based on the minimum cost to the company.

c. What do you recommend?

4–33. Cost Allocations Using Multiple Factors

The Cost Accounting Standards Board has concluded that certain indirect costs that cannot be related to a government contract by any other manner are to be charged to the contract based on a three-factor formula. The three factors are property, payrolls, and "all other costs" charged to the contract. These factors are entered into three fractions. The three fractions are summed and the sum divided by three. The result of this operation is the portion of these costs that are chargeable to the contract.

Stealthy Products, Inc., has a secret government contract. The company also engages in other activities. During the past year, it incurred $650,000 in costs chargeable to the government contract other than costs that must be allocated based on the three-factor formula. The company incurred a total of $812,500 in this "all other cost" category of costs.

In addition, Stealthy used $2 million of its $3 million in property for the government contract. Payrolls of employees engaged in the government contract amounted to $390,000 out of total payrolls of $468,000.

Stealthy's costs subject to the three-factor formula are $122,000.

Required:

How much of the $122,000 is chargeable to the government contract using the three-factor formula? (See Illustration 4–3 for an example.)

4–34. Cost Allocations in Contracting

Idiograms, Inc., entered into a contract to produce certain units on a cost-plus basis. During the contract period, Idiograms had 280 of its 520 employees working on the contract exclusively. Idiograms paid $340,000 in wages to the contract-related employees. During the same time, it paid $480,000 in wages to its noncontract-related employees. Its labor-related overhead costs amounted to $275,000. Idiograms submitted the following invoice to the purchaser:

Materials costs	$ 645,306
Labor costs	340,000
Other overhead	260,000
Labor-related overhead (not included elsewhere)	148,077
Total costs	1,393,383
Agreed profit (20%)	278.677
Contract balance due	$1,672,060

Upon receipt of the invoice, the purchaser questioned the allocation of labor-related overhead, noting that the costs seemed "out of line."

Required:

a. What basis did Idiograms use for the allocation of labor-related overhead costs?

b. What would be the effect on the contract balance due if Idiograms used the alternative basis suggested in the problem?

c. Is it possible to conclude which basis is more appropriate?

4–35. Interaction of State Taxes and Contract Costs

ArkFla, Inc., has two operating divisions. Fla Division operates entirely in Florida and is engaged exclusively in the manufacture and sale of commercial products. Ark Division operates exclusively in Arkansas and is engaged in the manufacture of military equipment. Prior to receiving a new defense contract, ArkFla, Inc., had the following distribution of property, payrolls, and sales between the two states:

	Arkansas	**Florida**
Property	$4.9 million	$ 5.6 million
Payrolls	1.2	1.6
Sales	7.4	11.7

Total income was $3 million. ArkFla received a government contract that required the addition of $1 million in property in Arkansas. Payroll in Arkansas was increased by $.9 million, and sales increased by $3.1 million. The contract added $300,000 to income.

Florida levies its 6 percent state income tax using the property, payrolls, and sales factors. No other elements in the factors for either state changed.

Required:

What effect, if any, did the defense contract have on the Florida tax liability?

4–36. Cost Allocations in Cost-Plus Pricing

Global Airlines is considering offering Business Class service on its transpacific routes. The problem Global faces is that it wants the Business Class service to provide an equivalent return to that which it obtains from its Economy Service. The Business Class fare must be set in such a way that it will provide the same margin per seat as the Economy Class fare. Management has some question as to the appropriate way to assure that this objective will be met.

The published economy class fare is $800 one way. However, as noted by the revenue accounting manager, discount fares result in an average Economy Class fare of $500 one way.

Business Class service would incur a meal cost estimated at $45 per passenger. This compares with the Economy Class meal service cost of $25 per passenger.

One and a half Economy Class seats would fit into the space used for each seat in Business Class. Baggage handling, reservations, and similar incidental costs are estimated at $10 per passenger for the variable portion of those costs for either class.

Fixed costs per flight (crew salaries, fuel, landing fees, etc.) are allocated at $275 per passenger for either class.

Required:

What fare for Business Class would meet management's objectives?

4–37. Allocated Costs and Incentive Contracts

Volume Sales Company has a highly competitive organization. Division managers (and division employees) receive a bonus if the division reports "above-average" returns for a year. Profits are determined using allocated common costs. Returns are measured by dividing profits by the book value of assets in each division.

The following profit and performance reports were prepared for the managers of the Fashion and Style divisions, two of many divisions in the company (dollar figures are in thousands):

	Fashion	Style
Sales revenue	$450	$600
Costs:		
Direct costs	200	300
Allocated costs	200	160
Division profit	$ 50	$140
Division assets	$200	$560
Division return (profit ÷ assets)	25%	25%

The average return for the company was also 25 percent.

The manager of the Fashion Division notes that allocated costs were distributed to each division on the basis of number of employees. She suggests that costs should be allocated on the basis of assets because the allocated costs are headquarters' costs. In her view, the primary role of headquarters is to provide assets for the use of operating divisions. Had the costs been allocated on the basis of division assets, she calculated that the Fashion Division would have been allocated with costs of $140 and the Style Division with costs of $390.

The manager of the Style Division argues that central management is really concerned with maintaining employee relations. The advantage to a large organization such as this one is that employees identify with the company, not just with a division. He further asserts that the greater an employee's pay, the more the employee requires services of corporate headquarters. He therefore suggests that payroll costs be used as the basis for allocation of the common costs. If payroll costs were used, he calculated that the Fashion Division would be allocated with $220 of allocated costs and the Style Division with $135.

Required:

What would be each division's return using each manager's proposal? What suggestions do you have for the solution to the incentive compensation problem for Volume Sales Company?

4–38. Cost Allocation for Regulated Utility Pricing

Regulated utilities are generally permitted to charge users with the costs to service the specific class of users. Cost allocations are required to share common costs. For example, for an electric utility, common costs include costs of generating and distribution facilities. Variable costs, such as fuel costs, are normally considered direct.

Common costs are distributed on the basis of the capacity demanded by each class of users. Capacity may be measured in terms of peak use in a day or peak seasonal use. An alternative measure is to use average demand for allocating capacity charges.

Average demand is the same as the actual use of electricity and, hence, is the basis for charging direct costs to users.

For example, Progressive Electric Company serves a three-county area. The area has two classes of users: (1) residential and (2) manufacturing. During the past year, the following data were generated:

User Class	Daily Peak Use	Seasonal Peak Use	Average Demand
Residential	50 million kwhr.	35 million kwhr.	15 million kwhr.
Manufacturing	25	20	18

The following costs were reported during the same period:

Common costs	$3 million
Direct costs	2 million

Required:

a. Calculate the portion of direct costs allocated to each user class (residential and manufacturing).

b. The $3 million in common costs can be allocated to each user class (residential and manufacturing) by selecting one of three alternative capacity measures (daily peak use, seasonal peak use, or average demand) as the allocation base. Calculate each of the three possible common cost allocations for each user class.

c. What are the three sets of rates per kilowatt-hour (common plus direct costs) charged to each user class under the three alternative allocation bases?

INTEGRATIVE CASES

4–39. Distortions Caused by Inappropriate Overhead Allocation Base*

Steve Stanley, Inc. (SSI) manufactures creamy deluxe chocolate candy bars. The firm has developed three distinct products, Almond Dream, Krispy Krackle, and Creamy Crunch.

While SSI is profitable, Steve Stanley is quite concerned over the profitability of each product and the product-costing methods currently employed. In particular, Steve questions whether the overhead allocation base of direct labor-hours accurately reflects the costs incurred during the production process of each product.

In reviewing cost reports with the marketing manager, Steve notices that Creamy Crunch appears exceptionally profitable, while Almond Dream appears to be produced at a loss. This surprises both Steve and the manager, and after much discussion, they are convinced the cost accounting system is at fault and that Almond Dream is performing very well at the current market price.

Steve Stanley decides to hire Jean Sharpe, a management consultant, to study the firm's cost system over the next month and present her findings and recommendations to senior management. Her objective is to identify and demonstrate how the cost accounting system might be distorting the firm's product costs.

Jean Sharpe begins her study by gathering information and documenting the existing cost accounting system. The system is rather simplistic, using a single overhead allocation base, direct labor-hours, to calculate and apply overhead rates to all products. The rate is calculated by summing variable and fixed overhead costs and then dividing the result by the number of direct labor-hours. The product cost is

---

* Copyright © Michael W. Maher, 1990.

determined by multiplying the number of direct labor-hours required to manufacture the product by the overhead rate and adding this amount to the direct labor and direct material costs.

SSI engages in two distinct production processes for each product. Process 1 is labor-intensive, using a high proportion of direct materials and labor. Process 2 uses special packing equipment which wraps each individual candy bar and then packs them into boxes of 24 bars. The boxes are then packaged into cases containing six boxes. The special packing equipment is used on all three products and has a monthly capacity of 3,000 boxes, each containing 144 candy bars.

To illustrate the source of the distortions to senior management, Sharpe collects the cost data for the three products—Almond Dream, Krispy Krackle, and Creamy Crunch (see Exhibit A).

SSI recently adopted a general policy of discontinuing all products whose gross profit margin [(gross margin/selling price) × 100] percentages were less than 10 percent. By comparing the selling prices to the firm's costs and then calculating the gross margin percentages, Sharpe could determine which products, under the current cost system, should be dropped. The current selling prices of Almond Dream, Krispy Krackle, and Creamy Crunch were $85, $55, and $35 per case, respectively.

Required:

a. Complete the following schedule (Exhibit A) under the current cost system and determine which product(s), if any, would be dropped.

b. What characteristic of the product that would be dropped makes it appear relatively unprofitable?

c. Calculate the gross profit margin percentage for the remaining products. Assume SSI can sell all products it manufactures and that it will use the excess capacity from dropping a product to produce more of the most profitable product. If SSI maintains its current rule about dropping products, which additional products, if any, would SSI drop under the existing cost system? Overhead would remain $69,500 per month under all alternatives.

Exhibit A (4-39)

	Almond Dream	Krispy Krackle	Creamy Crunch
Product costs:			
Labor hours per unit	7	3	1
Total units produced	1,000	1,000	1,000
Material cost per unit	$ 8.00	$ 2.00	$ 9.00
Direct labor per unit	42.00	18.00	6.00
Labor-hours per product	7,000	3,000	1,000

Total overhead = $69,500
Total labor-hours = 11,000
Direct labor costs per hour = $6.00
Allocation rate per labor-hour =   (a)

	Almond Dream	Krispy Krackle	Creamy Crunch
Costs of products:			
Material cost per unit	$ 8.00	$ 2.00	$9.00
Direct labor cost per unit	42.00	18.00	6.00
Allocated overhead per unit (to be computed)	(b)	(c)	(d)
Product cost	(e)	(f)	(g)

d. Recalculate the gross profit margin percentage for the remaining product(s) and ascertain whether any additional product(s) would be dropped.

e. Discuss the outcome and any recommendations you might make to management regarding the current cost system and decision policies.

4–40. Multiple Allocation Bases*

Refer to integrative case 4–39.

Jean Sharpe decides to gather additional data to identify the cause of overhead costs and figure out which products are most profitable.

Jean Sharpe notices that $30,000 of the overhead originated from the equipment used. She decides to incorporate machine-hours into the overhead allocation base to see its effect on product profitability. Almond Dream requires two hours of machine time, Krispy Krackle requires seven hours and Creamy Crunch requires six hours. Additionally, Jean notices that the $15,000 per month spent on the rental of 10,000 square feet of factory space accounts for almost 22 percent of the overhead. Almond Dream is assigned 1,000 square feet, Krispy Krackle is assigned 4,000 square feet, and Creamy Crunch is assigned 5,000 square feet. Jean decides to incorporate this into the allocation base for the rental costs.

Since labor-hours is an important element of overhead, Jean decides she should use labor-hours to allocate the remaining $24,500.

SSI still plans to produce 1,000 cases each of Almond Dream, Krispy Krackle, and Creamy Crunch. Assume SSI can sell all products it manufactures and that it will use excess capacity, if it drops any products, to produce additional units of the most profitable product. Overhead will remain $69,500 per month under all alternatives.

Required:

a. Based on the additional data, determine the product cost and gross profit margin percentages of each product using the three allocation bases to determine the allocation assigned to each product.

b. Would management recommend dropping any of the products based on the criteria of dropping products with less than 10 percent gross profit margin?

c. Based on the recommendation you make in (*b*), recalculate the allocations and profit margins to determine whether any of the remaining products should be dropped from the product line. If any additional products are dropped, substantiate the profitability of remaining products.

4–41. Impact of Using Machine-Hours versus Labor-Hours for Allocating Overhead

Herbert Manufacturing Company manufactures custom-designed restaurant furniture. Actual overhead costs incurred during the month are applied to the products on the basis of actual direct labor-hours required to produce the products. Overhead consists primarily of supervision, employee benefits, maintenance costs, property taxes, and depreciation.

Herbert Manufacturing recently won a contract to manufacture the furniture for a new fast-food chain. To produce this new line, Herbert Manufacturing must purchase more molded plastic parts for the furniture than for its current line. An efficient manufacturing process for this new furniture has been developed that requires only a minimum capital investment.

At the end of October, the start-up month for the new line, the controller prepared a separate income statement for the new product line. The profitability for the new line was less than expected. The president of the corporation is concerned that stockholders will criticize the decision to add this lower quality product line at a time when profitability appeared to be increasing with the regular product line.

The results as published for the first nine months, for October, and for November are (in thousands):

	New Fast-Food Furniture	Regular Custom Furniture	Total
Nine months year to date:			
Gross sales	—	$8,100	$8,100
Direct material	—	2,025	2,025
Direct labor		2,630	2,630
Overhead	—	1,779	1,779
Cost of sales	—	6,434	6,434
Gross margin	—	$1,666	$1,666
Gross margin percentage	—	20.6%	20.6%
October:			
Gross sales	$400	$ 900	$1,300
Direct material	200	225	425
Direct labor	90	284	374
Overhead	60	180	240
Cost of sales	350	689	1,039
Gross margin	$ 50	$ 211	$ 261
Gross margin percentage:	12.5%	23.4%	20.1%
November:			
Gross sales	$800	$ 800	$1,600
Direct material	400	200	600
Direct labor	159	250	409
Overhead	98	147	245
Cost of sales	657	597	1,254
Gross margin	$143	$ 203	$ 346
Gross margin percentage	17.9%	25.4%	21.6%

Ms. Jameson, cost accounting manager, stated that on the basis of a recently completed study of company overhead, she feels that only the supervision and employee benefits should be allocated on the basis of direct labor-hours. The balance of the overhead should be allocated on a machine-hour basis. In Jameson's judgment, the increase in the profitability of the custom-designed furniture is due to a misallocation of overhead.

Actual direct labor-hours and machine-hours for the past two months are shown below.

	Fast-Food Furniture	Custom Furniture
Machine-hours:		
October	1,320	18,480
November	2,560	17,040
Direct labor-hours:		
October	10,000	30,000
November	17,500	26,250

Actual overhead costs for the past two months were:

	October	November
Supervision	$ 13,000	$ 13,000
Employee benefits	95,000	109,500
Maintenance	50,000	48,000
Depreciation	42,000	42,000
Property taxes	8,000	8,000
All other	32,000	24,500
Total	$240,000	$245,000

Required:

a. Reallocate the overhead for October and November using direct labor-hours as the allocation base for supervision and employee benefits. Use machine-hours as the base for the remaining overhead costs.

b. Support or criticize the conclusion that the increase in custom-design profitability is due to a misallocation of overhead. Use the data developed in requirement (a) to support your analysis.

(CMA adapted)

4–42. Eastern Refineries, Ltd. (Cost Allocations in Contract Dispute)*

In 1980, American Oil Corporation and United Petroleum (two large, integrated petroleum companies) entered into an agreement to construct and operate a petroleum fuels refinery in the Far East. A corporation named Eastern Refineries Limited was formed to operate the refinery. At the time the agreement was drawn up, American provided 70 percent of the capital, while United provided 30 percent.

The sponsoring companies received capital stock in Eastern in proportion to the capital provided by them.

The refinery

The refinery processes crude oil through various heat, pressure, and chemical operations to extract as much gasoline from the crude as possible. Other products such as sulphur, kerosene, distillate fuels, and asphalt are produced as by-products. A certain quantity of fuel extracted from the crude is used to provide the heat necessary to operate the refinery as well as to provide heat and power for the refinery administrative and service support functions.

The original Eastern fuels refinery consisted of five principal processing units as diagrammed in Exhibit A. Crude oil was shipped to the refinery and piped to the crude splitter. This unit separates the crude oil into two products: (1) "overheads," which consist of the lighter fractions from the crude, and (2) "bottoms," which contain the heavier fractions. Bottoms have relatively little energy content and are sold as asphalt with very little further processing.

Overheads contain naphtha, a very light fraction; fuel oil, an intermediate product; and sulphur. The sulphur must be removed before the overheads can be processed into finished products. A desulphurization unit extracts the sulphur from the overheads. The remaining overhead flow is then distilled in the fractionator. The products with the lower boiling point (that is, the lighter fractions) vaporize as the temperature in the fractionator equals the boiling point of the respective fraction. The vaporized fractions are then cooled and return to their liquid state.

Naphtha, one of the lighter fractions, is used to make gasoline. With the use of heat and pressure in the reformer unit, naphtha is converted into gasoline. The remaining fractions are then directed to the catalytic cracker. This unit employs

---

* CIPT Co. 1989.

Exhibit A (4-42)   **Flow of Product through the Eastern Fuels Refinery**

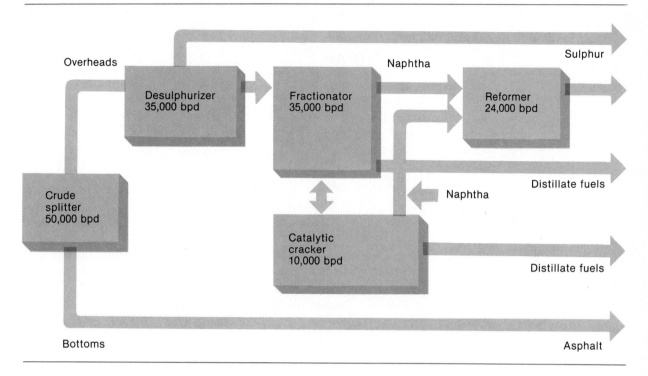

chemical and heat processes to convert some of the heavier materials from the fractionator into the more valuable naphthas. The naphthas from the catalytic cracker are then processed through the reformer in the same manner as the naphthas from the fractionator. The remaining output from the catalytic cracker is sold as distillate fuel products (such as kerosene, jet fuel, and heating oil).

Refinery investment costs. The costs to construct the initial refinery totaled $60 million. These initial costs were related to different units and support functions as follows (in thousands):

Unit	Investment Cost
Crude splitter	$10,000
Desulphurizer	6,000
Fractionator	13,000
Catalytic cracker	15,000
Reformer	9,000
Administrative, support and other	7,000
Total	$60,000

The sponsoring companies entered into a contract for the processing of crude oil through the refinery. Each sponsor was permitted to utilize the refinery capacity to process crude oil in the same ratio as their equity investment. Thus, American was

Exhibit B (4-42)   **Summary Operating and Cost Data (in thousands)**

	1985	1986
Crude processed (barrels):		
American	12,700	12,775
United	4,100	4,050
Total	16,800	16,825
Variable costs:		
American	$ 3,061	$ 2,965
United	1,008	954
Total	$ 4,069	$ 3,919
Fixed costs:		
American	$ 6,510	$ 6,447
United	2,790	2,763
Total	$ 9,300	$ 9,210
Products delivered:		
American:		
Gasoline (barrels)	6,126	6,103
Distillate fuels (barrels)	2,780	2,759
Sulphur (tons)	16	16
Asphalt (barrels)	417	408
United:		
Gasoline (barrels)	2,362	2,376
Distillate fuels (barrels)	591	597
Sulphur (tons)	7	8
Asphalt (barrels)	134	136

permitted to process 35,000 barrels per day (70 percent of 50,000 bpd capacity). The refinery acts as a processing service that receives the crude, processes it, and delivers the end products to each processor. To recover its costs, the refinery charges a processing fee to each of the sponsors. The processing fee consists of a variable charge based on the crude oil actually processed during a period plus a fixed charge based on the sponsor's share of refinery capacity.

Certain operating and cost data related to refinery processing during the years 1985 and 1986 are shown in Exhibit B.

Expansion proposal

American had been utilizing close to its share of capacity for several years. Indeed, to supply all of its customers in the market area served by this refinery, it was necessary to import finished distillate fuels from other, distant refining facilities. On occasion, to supply its customers, American was required to purchase distillate fuels on the spot market.

As a result of market conditions, American's management proposed that parts of the Eastern refinery be expanded. The expansion would provide additional distillate fuels for American's local needs and, in addition, would provide naphthas that could be transported to another American refinery for further processing. There would be a net reduction in the company's transportation costs from savings in distillate fuels transportation. As a result of this, and by eliminating the need to make spot market purchases, American management estimated it could obtain net after-tax cash savings of $2.5 million in each of the estimated 20 years' life of the refinery expansion. The return on investment for the project was quite high because the project could utilize the tankage, wharf, and piping systems already in place at the refinery site.

According to the agreement between the sponsors of Eastern, any sponsor could request that the refinery company construct an expansion or modification to increase the maximum capacity of the refinery. If one of the sponsors proposed an expansion, it had to advise the other sponsor of the nature of the project and the estimated investment costs of the project together with an estimate of the fixed costs that would arise from the expansion. The other sponsor could elect to join in the project or could decline. If this sponsor declined participation, the expansion could still be conducted, but all of the investment costs would then be charged to the sponsor that proposed the expansion.

The agreement between the sponsors further provided that any such expansion would become a part of the refinery but that the sponsor who financed the expansion would receive the exclusive right to use the expansion. In addition, appropriate adjustments were to be made to the accounting procedures to reflect the existence of the expansion and to make certain that neither party was adversely affected by the expansion. The definition of "appropriate adjustments" was not specified in the agreement.

In 1985, American submitted a proposal to expand the crude splitter, desulphurizer, and fractionator. Summary data concerning the estimated differential costs, investment required, and capacity expansions for the units are shown in Exhibit C. Information concerning American's estimated cash savings from the project were not disclosed because those data are proprietary.

After reviewing the proposal, United notified Eastern that it did not wish to participate. United objected to Eastern's construction of the proposed expansion on the grounds that they would suffer a reduced ability to compete with American should American obtain the proposed additional ability to produce distillate fuels.

American agreed to finance all of the costs of the expansion. The expansion was constructed for the investment costs shown in Exhibit C. The new units were placed in service at the start of 1987.

At the end of 1987, a report of operating and cost data was prepared. This report is reproduced in Exhibit D. The fixed costs included $9.5 million attributed to the original refinery plus $560,000 considered related to the expansion.

Upon receipt of this statement, United immediately objected to the allocation of fixed costs. In a memorandum to the board of directors of the refinery, United management stated:

> As you know, we objected to the expansion of this refinery because we believed such an expansion was not in the best interest of the refinery and would be harmful to our competitive position in the local market.
>
> Our agreement calls for the allocation of fixed costs on the basis of the maximum capacity of the Eastern refinery. Whereas we previously had 30 percent

Exhibit C (4–42)   **Proposal for Expansion (dollars in thousands)**

Units to be expanded:
  Crude splitter
  Desulphurizer
  Fractionator

	Unit		
	Crude Splitter	**Desulphurizer**	**Fractionator**
Incremental capacity	30,000 bpd	10,000 bpd	10,000 bpd
Projected costs of investment	$4,000	$800	$2,200
Projected incremental fixed costs (per year)	$300	$100	$150

Exhibit D (4-42)   **Summary Operating and Cost Data (in thousands)**

	1987
Crude processed (barrels):	
American	23,750
United	3,840
Total	27,590
Variable costs:	
American	$ 5,556
United	1,150
Total	$ 6,706
Fixed costs:	
American	$ 7,210
United	2,850
Total	$10,060
Products delivered:	
American:	
Gasoline (barrels)	6,128
Distillate (barrels)	6,320
Sulphur (tons)	25
Asphalt (barrels)	830
Naphthas (barrels)	3,975
United:	
Gasoline (barrels)	2,337
Distillate (barrels)	610
Sulphur (tons)	7
Asphalt (barrels)	133

of that maximum capacity and paid 30 percent of the fixed costs, we now only have 18.75 percent of that capacity. However, you have charged us 28.3 percent of the total fixed costs. Our share of the fixed costs should not exceed 18.75 percent, and we request an immediate adjustment to our account.

We note that under your allocation scheme our fixed costs per barrel amounted to $.74 this year, but the fixed costs allocated to American only amounted to $.30. This disparity clearly demonstrates that your method of allocation is incorrect.

Finally, it is apparent that the wharf and related facilities, which we helped construct, are being utilized to a much greater extent now that American is processing a greater share of the refinery throughput. We believe that American should be required to reimburse us for the difference between our 30 percent investment in the wharf and our usage, which this year only amounted to 13.9 percent.

We trust this matter can be resolved promptly at the next meeting of the board.

The chairman of the board of Eastern has directed this memorandum to the controller's office with the following comment:

The points raised in this letter will be discussed at next week's meeting of the board. It is imperative that we straighten this out at once. The points appear logical, and I hope that any error in your office can be corrected.

What is the amount by which they appear to have been overcharged? How would their method affect the economic viability of the expansion? What accounting principles did you use in arriving at your method of allocation?

Required: The controller asked you to prepare a draft of a response to the chairman of the board together with any supporting schedules or documents that would be required. Your response would address each of the points raised in the letter from United.

ALLOCATING SERVICE DEPARTMENT COSTS

LEARNING OBJECTIVES

1. To learn how to use the direct method of allocating service department costs.

2. To be able to calculate the step method of allocating service department costs.

3. To understand the simultaneous solution method of allocating service department costs.

4. To know the difference between plantwide and departmental rates.

Previous chapters have discussed the two stages of allocating costs to products: (1) The allocation of service department costs to production departments and (2) the allocation of production department costs to units produced.

In this chapter, we expand the discussion of service department cost allocation. We present three methods of allocating service department costs to production departments.

NATURE OF SERVICE DEPARTMENTS

Service organizations, merchandising organizations, and manufacturing organizations all have production or marketing departments *and* service departments. The former are directly involved in producing or marketing a service (for example, the intensive care unit in a hospital); the latter are support departments (such as the hospital laundry). Examples of production or marketing and service departments are:

Service Department   An organizational subunit whose main job is to provide service to other subunits in the organization.

Manufacturing   Term used to describe production departments in organizations that manufacture goods such as an assembly department.

Final Cost Center   A cost center, such as a production or marketing department, from which costs are not allocated to another cost center.

Intermediate Cost Center   A cost center whose costs are charged to other departments in the organization.

User Department   Organizational subunit that uses services of service departments.

Organization	Service Department	Production or Marketing Department
Manufacturing plant	Maintenance	Assembly
Retail store	Data processing	Sportswear
Hospital	Laundry	Intensive care unit
City government	Motor pool	Patrol units of the police department

The terms **manufacturing** and **production** are not synonymous—production is broader than manufacturing. In this book, when we refer to *manufacturing* departments, we specifically mean *production* departments in organizations that manufacture goods, such as an assembly department. An example of a production department in a service organization would be the tax department of a public accounting firm.

Service departments are sometimes called **intermediate cost centers**, while production or marketing departments would be the **final cost centers**.

We refer to any department that provides a service to another department as a **service department** and any department that uses the services of a service department as a **user department**. Service departments include centralized computer services, legal and accounting departments, and cost centers such as building occupancy, which include building maintenance and repairs as well as other shared occupancy costs. User departments include (1) *production or marketing* departments or (2) other *service* departments as shown in Illustration 5–1.

RATIONALE FOR CHARGING THE COST OF SERVICE DEPARTMENTS TO USERS

Why do companies allocate service department costs to user departments? One reason in manufacturing companies is to allocate the cost of manufacturing service departments to units produced. This is required under generally accepted accounting principles (GAAP) for external financial reporting. Another reason is to make the user department managers aware of the cost of services they are using.

For example, suppose a company has one service department that provides services to two user departments that manufacture the company's two

Illustration 5–1   **Service and User Departments**

Service department provides service to the final user department.

Service department A provides service to service department B, which provides service to the final user department.

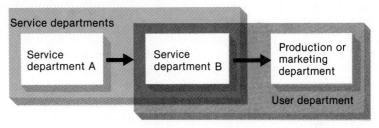

Illustration 5–2   **Allocation of Service Department Costs to Production Departments and to Units**

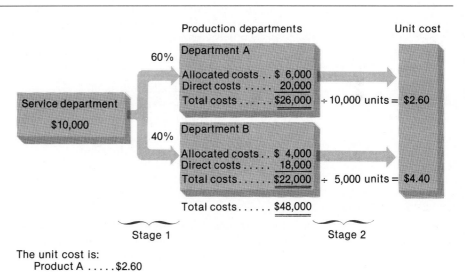

The unit cost is:
    Product A $2.60
    Product B $4.40

products: product A and product B. The service department's costs are $10,000 for the month of November. These costs are allocated 60 percent to production department A and 40 percent to production department B. (Methods of deriving allocation percentages are discussed later in this chapter; for now, assume the percentages are given.) Production department A has direct costs of $20,000. It manufactured 10,000 units of product A in

November. Production department B had direct costs of $18,000. It manufactured 5,000 units of product B in November. As shown in Illustration 5–2, service department costs are first allocated to the production departments using the services. (In previous chapters, we simply called these costs manufacturing overhead without regard to which service department was responsible for them.) This phase of allocation is referred to as stage 1. Then, direct plus allocated costs of those production departments are assigned to units produced. This phase is referred to as stage 2.

METHODS OF ALLOCATING SERVICE DEPARTMENT COSTS

In this section, we describe three methods of allocating service department costs: the direct method, the step method, and the simultaneous solution method. To make each method easier to understand, we use a comprehensive example. While our example is of a manufacturing company, keep in mind that the same methods can be used in nonmanufacturing organizations.

Assume All-Tech Manufacturing has three service departments: product engineering (S1), building occupancy (S2), and factory supervision (S3). Costs are accumulated in these departments and allocated to two manufacturing departments and one marketing department: networks (P1), terminals (P2), and the marketing department (P3). All six departments share the same building.

All-Tech Manufacturing allocates costs to networks and terminals for two purposes: (1) to value inventory for external financial reporting and (2) to encourage department managers to monitor each other's costs; that is, *cross-department monitoring*. These are the manufacturing overhead costs for All-Tech Manufacturing. Costs are allocated to marketing only to encourage cross-department monitoring because marketing does not produce inventory.

Each service department is an *intermediate cost center* where costs are accumulated as incurred and then distributed to other cost centers. At All-Tech Manufacturing, product engineering (S1) costs are distributed on the basis of engineering staff time required by the user department. Building occupancy (S2) costs are distributed on the basis of area occupied by the user department. And factory supervision (S3) costs are distributed on the basis of the user department's payroll dollars.

Allocation Bases

Illustration 5–3 shows the basis of allocating costs for each service department and the proportions of costs allocated to user departments. For example, product engineering costs are allocated on the basis of engineering labor-hours worked for each user department. During the period, product engineering worked 14,000 hours for networks and 56,000 hours for terminals. Thus, 20 percent of product engineering costs are allocated to networks

$$\left(20 \text{ percent} = \frac{14{,}000 \text{ hours}}{14{,}000 + 56{,}000 \text{ hours}} \right)$$

and 80 percent to terminals. Identical methods are used to derive the percentages for allocating building occupancy and factory supervision costs. (Percentages are shown in Illustration 5–3.)

Methods of allocating costs are discussed next.

Illustration 5-3   **Bases for Service Department Cost Allocations**

ALL-TECH MANUFACTURING

Product Engineering (S1)

Allocation base: Product engineering labor-hours worked in each user department.

User Department	Product Engineering Labor-Hours Used	Proportion of Total
Networks (P1)	14,000	.20
Terminals (P2)	56,000	.80
Marketing (P3)	–0–	–0–
Totals	70,000	1.00

Building Occupancy (S2)

Allocation base: Area (square footage) in each user department.

User Department	Square Footage	Proportion of Total
Networks (P1)	80,000	.32
Terminals (P2)	60,000	.24
Marketing (P3)	60,000	.24
Product engineering (S1)	20,000	.08
Factory supervision (S3)	30,000	.12
Totals	250,000	1.00

Factory Supervision (S3)

Allocation base: Annual payroll dollars of user departments.

User Department	Payroll Dollars	Proportion of Total
Networks (P1)	$360,000	.45
Terminals (P2)	240,000	.30
Marketing (P3)	–0–	–0–
Product engineering (S1)	120,000	.15
Building occupancy (S2)	80,000	.10
Totals	$800,000	1.00

The Direct Method

Direct Method A method of cost allocation that charges costs of service departments to user departments and ignores any services used by other service departments.

The **direct method** allocates costs directly to the final user of a service, ignoring intermediate users. Illustration 5–4 shows the flow of costs and the allocations to be recognized for the departments when the direct method is used. The direct costs of departments are first accumulated in service departments. These are shown in parentheses on the debit side of the service department accounts. Then, service department costs are allocated to the user departments. If manufacturing overhead is transferred to work in process inventory, that would be the next step in the manufacturing departments. If predetermined rates are used, then these actual overhead costs are compared with those applied to work in process using normal costing, as discussed in Chapter 7.

There are no allocations between service departments. Thus, the building occupancy costs and the factory supervision costs that are attributable to the product engineering department are not allocated to product engineering. Likewise, the factory supervision costs that are related to the building

Illustration 5-4   **Flow of Cost Allocations—Direct Method**

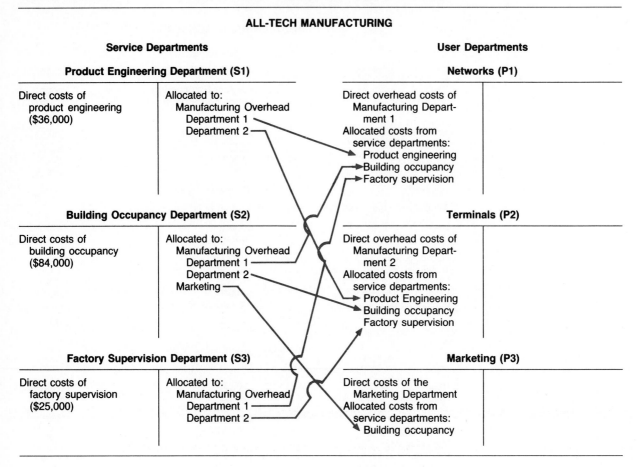

ALL-TECH MANUFACTURING

occupancy function and the costs of the building space occupied by the factory supervision activity are not allocated to their respective service departments.

The use of the direct method of cost allocation at All-Tech Manufacturing is discussed below and shown in Illustration 5–5. Assume the accounting records show that costs of $36,000, $84,000, and $25,000 are accumulated in each service department, S1, S2, and S3, respectively. Costs are allocated directly to Networks (P1), Terminals (P2), and Marketing (P3)—hence the name *direct* method.

Allocate Product Engineering Department Costs

Product engineering department costs of $36,000 are allocated to P1, P2, and P3 based on the product engineering labor-hours used by P1, P2, and P3. According to the facts given in Illustration 5–3, P1 used 20 percent and P2 used 80 percent of the total product engineering labor-hours. The marketing department did not use any product engineering labor-hours. Hence, the allocation of product engineering department costs is simply:

P1	20% × $36,000 =	$ 7,200
P2	80 × 36,000 =	28,800
Total	100%	$36,000

Allocate Building Occupancy Department Costs

Building occupancy department costs are distributed to P1, P2, and P3 in the same ratio as the proportions of the square footage occupied by those departments alone. That is, the square footage proportions for P1, P2, and P3, based on data given in Illustration 5–3, are:

P1		.32
P2		.24
P3		.24
	Total	.80

When these are scaled to 100 percent, we have:

P1	40%	= .32/.80
P2	30	= .24/.80
P3	30	= .24/.80
	Total	100%

Illustration 5-5   **Cost Allocation Computations—Direct Method**

Service Department	This Month's Department Costs	Proportion Chargeable to:		
		Networks (P1)	Terminals (P2)	Marketing (P3)
Product engineering (S1)	$36,000	.2	.8	–0–
Building occupancy (S2)	84,000	.4	.3	.3
Factory supervision (S3)	25,000	.6	.4	–0–

Direct Method Cost Allocation:

From		To		
Service Department	Amount	Networks (P1)	Terminals (P2)	Marketing (P3)
Product engineering (S1)	$ 36,000	$ 7,200	$28,800	–0–
Building occupancy (S2)	84,000	33,600	25,200	$25,200
Factory supervision (S3)	25,000	15,000	10,000	–0–
Total allocated	$145,000	$55,800	$64,000	$25,200

Additional computations:
Product engineering:	$ 7,200 = .2 × $36,000 (P1)
	$28,800 = .8 × $36,000 (P2)
Building occupancy:	$33,600 = .4 × $84,000 (P1)
	$25,200 = .3 × $84,000 (P2) and (P3)
Factory supervision:	$15,000 = .6 × $25,000 (P1)
	$10,000 = .4 × $25,000 (P2)

These proportions are used to allocate building occupancy department costs as shown in Illustration 5–5.

Allocate Factory Supervision Department Costs

Similar calculations are made for factory supervision department costs that are allocated on the basis of labor-dollars. The labor-dollars proportions for P1, P2, and P3 are (see Illustration 5–3):

P1		.45
P2		.30
P3		.00
	Total	.75

When these are scaled to 100 percent, we have:

P1	60%	= .45/.75
P2	40	= .30/.75
P3	0	= –0–/.75
	Total	100%

These proportions are used to allocate factory supervision department costs as shown in Illustration 5–5.

Once these proportions are computed, the allocation proceeds with the cost distribution shown in Illustration 5–5. The $36,000 product engineering costs are allocated $7,200 (or 20 percent) to manufacturing overhead—Networks, and $28,800 (or 80 percent) to manufacturing overhead—Terminals. The total allocated ($7,200 + $28,800) equals the total costs in the product engineering intermediate cost center ($36,000). (The step of scaling to 100 percent assures this result.)

Similar allocations are made for the other two service cost centers. As a result of these allocations, the total service department costs charged to Networks are $55,800; to Terminals, $64,000; and to marketing, $25,200.

Limitations of the Direct Method

The direct method has been criticized because it ignores services provided by one service department to another. If one purpose of cost allocation is to encourage cross-department monitoring, then the direct method falls short because it ignores the costs that service departments themselves incur when they use other service departments. An attempt to remedy this problem has resulted in the *step method* of allocating service department costs.

The Step Method

Step Method The method of service department cost allocation that recognizes some interservice department services.

The **step method** recognizes services provided to other service departments. Allocations usually begin from the service department that has provided the greatest proportion of its total services to other service departments or that services the greatest *number* of other departments. Once an allocation is made *from* a service department, no further allocations are made back *to* that department. Hence, a service department that provides services to another service department and also receives services from that department will have only one of these two reciprocal relationships recognized. By choosing the allocation order suggested, we minimize the number of relationships that are ignored in the step allocation process. For example, when the step method is used at All-Tech, costs are allocated from the factory supervision department to building occupancy department, but not vice versa as discussed below.

An analysis of service usage among service departments of All-Tech indicates that factory supervision supplies 25 percent of its services to other service departments, while building occupancy supplies 20 percent of its services to other service departments. (See Illustration 5–3.) Product engineering provides no services to other service departments. Hence, assume the rank ordering for step allocation is:

Order	Service Department
1	Factory supervision (S3)
2	Building occupancy (S2)
3	Product engineering (S1)

Allocating Factory Supervision Department Costs

Factory supervision costs would be allocated to all service departments that made use of factory supervision's services, whereas building occupancy's costs would be allocated only to the service department that ranks below it in the allocation order. Recall that under the step method, once a service department's costs have been allocated to other departments, no costs can be allocated back to it. The computation of service department costs allocated to other service departments at All-Tech is shown in Illustration 5–6.

Factory supervision department costs are charged to user departments based on the total labor dollars recorded for each. The distribution results in 15 percent of the $25,000 in factory supervision department costs being charged to product engineering, 10 percent to building occupancy, 45 percent to Networks, and the remaining 30 percent to Terminals (based on Illustration 5–3).

Allocating Building Occupancy Department Costs

In calculating the allocation of building occupancy department costs (second in the allocation order), the step method ignores the area occupied by the factory supervision department because costs have already been allocated from that department. As a result, the portion of building occupancy department costs to be allocated to product engineering is determined by taking the 20,000 square feet used by product engineering (as shown in Illustration 5–3) and dividing by the 220,000 square-foot basis (250,000 total square feet less the 30,000 occupied by factory supervision). The result is approximately 9 percent.

The total costs to be allocated from building occupancy is the sum of the direct costs ($84,000) plus the allocated costs ($2,500 from factory supervision). Therefore, the transfer to product engineering is 9 percent of $86,500, which equals $7,785. Similar computations are made for the other departments as shown in Illustration 5–6.

Illustration 5-6   **Cost Allocation Computations—Step Method**

ALL-TECH MANUFACTURING

Service Department	This Month's Department Costs	Proportion Chargeable to:					
		S3	S2	S1	P1	P2	P3
Factory supervision (S3)	$ 25,000	–0–	.10	.15	.45	.30	–0–
Building occupancy (S2)	84,000	–0–	–0–	.09[a]	.37[a]	.27[a]	.27[a]
Product engineering (S1)	36,000	–0–	–0–	–0–	.20[b]	.80[b]	–0–
	$145,000						

Step Method Allocation:

From:	Cost Allocation to:					
	S3	S2	S1	P1	P2	P3
Direct service department costs	$ 25,000	$ 84,000	$ 36,000			
Factory supervision (S3)[c]	$(25,000)	2,500	3,750	$11,250	$ 7,500	–0–
Building occupancy (S2)[d]		$(86,500)	7,785	32,005	23,355	$23,355
Product engineering (S1)[e]			$(47,535)	9,507	38,028	–0–
Total costs allocated				$52,762	$68,883	$23,355

[a] Allocation of building occupancy to departments on a square footage basis. Total square feet are 220,000, which equals 250,000 total minus 30,000 used by factory supervision, according to Illustration 5–3:
  .09 = 20,000 ÷ 220,000 square feet (rounded).
Similarly,
  .37 = 80,000 ÷ 220,000 square feet (rounded)
and
  .27 = 60,000 ÷ 220,000 square feet (rounded).
[b] Percentages from Illustration 5–3.
[c] Factory supervision (S3):
  $2,500 = .10 × $25,000; $3,750 = .15 × $25,000; etc.
[d] Buillding occupancy (S2):
  $86,500 = $84,000 + $2,500 (allocated costs from S3)
  $7,785 = .09 × $86,500; $32,005 = .37 × $86,500; etc.
[e] Product engineering (S1):
  $47,535 = $36,000 + $3,750 + $7,785 (allocated costs from S2)
  $9,507 = .20 × $47,535; $38,028 = .80 × $47,535.
  Proof:
  $25,000 + $84,000 + $36,000 = $52,762 + $68,883 + $23,355.

Allocating Product Engineering Costs

Product engineering was used 20 percent by Networks and 80 percent by Terminals, according to Illustration 5–3. These services are not used by any other service department, so they are allocated directly to the user departments (20 percent to P1 and 80 percent to P2).

The flow of costs under the step method is diagrammed in Illustration 5–7. Notice that Illustration 5–7 differs from Illustration 5–4, which showed cost flows using the direct method, because some costs flow from one service department to another. In addition, the costs allocated *from* service departments include not only the direct costs of the service departments but costs allocated *to* the service departments as well.

The step method may result in more reasonable allocations than the direct method because it recognizes that some service departments are users of other service departments. However, it does not recognize reciprocal services—for example, that building occupancy and factory supervision both

Illustration 5-7   **Flow of Cost Allocations—Step Method**

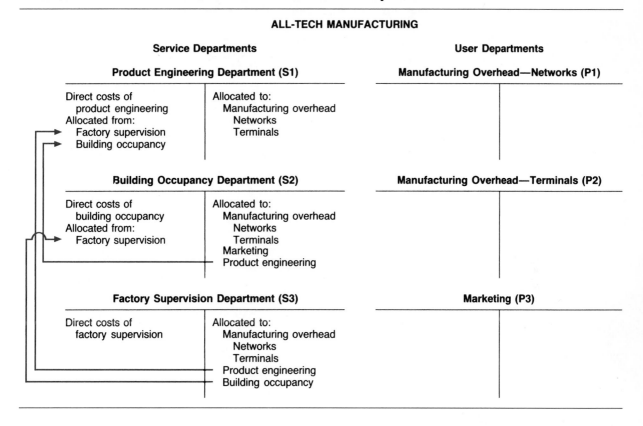

ALL-TECH MANUFACTURING

provide and use each other's services. The simultaneous solution method of service department cost allocation deals with this problem. The step method is *not necessarily* better than the direct method when both the costs and benefits of using cost allocation are taken into account. A company that already uses the direct method may find it uneconomical to switch methods, especially if the only purpose of cost allocation is to value inventory for external financial reporting.

The Simultaneous Solution Method

Simultaneous Solution Method The method of service department cost allocation that recognizes all services provided by any service department, including services provided to other service departments.

With the **simultaneous solution method,** the costs of each production, marketing, and service department are written in equation form:

$$\text{Total costs} = \frac{\text{Direct costs of}}{\text{the service department}} + \frac{\text{Costs to be allocated}}{\text{to the service department}}$$

The system of equations is then solved simultaneously using matrix algebra.[1] By solving all of the equations simultaneously, we provide for all interservice department allocations. This method is sometimes called the *reciprocal services method* because it accounts for cost flows in both directions among service departments that provide services to one another.

---

[1] The use of matrix algebra in accounting is explained in detail in J. K. Shank, *Matrix Methods in Accounting* (Reading, Mass.:Addison-Wesley Publishing, 1972).

The key difference between the step and simultaneous solution methods is shown in Illustration 5–8. Note that the simultaneous solution method accounts for the reciprocal services between the building occupancy and factory supervision departments. The step method accounted for only one direction of services—from factory supervision to building occupancy, but not vice versa.

Simultaneous Solution Method Using Matrix Algebra when There Are Three or More Service Departments

The mathematical details of the simultaneous solution method when there are three (or more) service departments are presented in the appendix to this chapter. Generally, a computer is used to solve this allocation problem. (Illustration 5–10 presents the costs allocated to the production and marketing departments using each of the three methods for All-Tech Manufacturing.)

Simultaneous Solution Method Using Linear Algebra when There Are Only Two Service Departments

When there are only two service departments, linear algebra can be used to solve the allocation problem. To show how this works, we present a simpler example than the one previously used in this chapter.

Illustration 5–8 **Flow of Cost Allocations—Simultaneous Solution Method**

ALL-TECH MANUFACTURING

Service Departments	User Departments

Product Engineering Department (S1) **Manufacturing Overhead—Networks (P1)**

Direct costs of
  product engineering
Allocated from:
  Factory supervision
  Building occupancy

Allocated to:
  Manufacturing overhead
    Networks
    Terminals

Building Occupancy Department (S2) **Manufacturing Overhead—Terminals (P2)**

Direct costs of
  building occupancy
Allocated from:
  Factory supervision

Allocated to:
  Manufacturing overhead
    Networks
    Terminals
  Marketing
  Product engineering
— Factory supervision

Factory Supervision Department (S3) **Marketing (P3)**

Direct costs of
  factory supervision
Allocated from:
  Building occupancy

Allocated to:
  Manufacturing overhead
    Networks
    Terminals
  Product engineering
— Building occupancy

Assume a company has two service departments, S1 and S2, and three production departments, P1, P2, and P3, with the following direct costs and allocation percentages:

				Percent of Costs Allocated to:		
Department	**Direct Costs**	**S1**	**S2**	**P1**	**P2**	**P3**
S1	$ 79,000	—	30%	30%	30%	10%
S2	26,000	10%	—	15	15	60
	$105,000					

The two service departments' costs may be expressed in equation form as:

$$\frac{\text{Total}}{\text{costs}} = \frac{\text{Direct costs of the}}{\text{service department}} + \frac{\text{Costs to be allocated}}{\text{to the service department}}$$

$$S1 = \$79{,}000 + .1\ S2 \quad \text{Equation (1)}$$
$$S2 = \$26{,}000 + .3\ S1 \quad \text{Equation (2)}$$

These yield two equations with two unknowns that can be solved by substitution.

Substituting Equation (2) into Equation (1) gives:

$$S1 = \$79{,}000 + .1(\$26{,}000 + .3\ S1)$$
$$S1 = \$79{,}000 + \$2{,}600 + .03\ S1$$

Collecting terms and solving:

$$.97\ S1 = \$81{,}600$$
$$S1 = \underline{84{,}124}$$

Now substituting this value for S1 back into Equation (2) gives:

$$S2 = \$26{,}000 + .3(\$84{,}124)$$
$$S2 = \$26{,}000 + \$25{,}237$$
$$S2 = \underline{\$51{,}237}$$

Thus, costs are simultaneously allocated between the two service departments. The values for S1 ($84,124) and S2 ($51,237) are then used as the total costs of the service departments that are to be allocated to the production departments. The allocations are:

		Allocated to:					
		P1		**P2**		**P3**	
From:	**Total Cost**	**Dollars**	**Percent**	**Dollars**	**Percent**	**Dollars**	**Percent**
S1	$84,124	$25,237	30%	$25,237	30%	$ 8,412	10%
S2	51,237	7,686	15	7,686	15	30,742	60
Totals		$32,923		$32,923		$39,154	

Computations:

	For P1 and P2	For P3
S1:	$25,237 = .3 × $84,124	$8,412 = .1 × $84,124
S2:	$7,686 = .15 × $51,237	$30,742 = .6 × $51,237

The total cost allocated to the production departments amounts to $105,000 (= $32,923 + $32,923 + $39,154), which equals the costs to be allocated from the service departments ($79,000 + $26,000 = $105,000).

Comparison of Methods

There are two ways to compare these three service department allocation methods. The first is to examine how each allocates costs to departments receiving services. Returning to the All-Tech example, as shown in Illustration 5–9, only the simultaneous solution method allocates costs to all departments receiving services from other departments.

The second way to compare these three methods is to examine the costs each ultimately allocates to manufacturing and marketing departments, as shown in Illustration 5–10. (Computation of the simultaneous solution method costs is given in the appendix to this chapter.) Each method allocates the same total cost for All-Tech—$145,000. The difference is in the amounts allocated to particular manufacturing and marketing departments.

The major factor affecting these allocations is the distribution of building occupancy costs. Under the direct method, the use of the building by other service departments is ignored. This results in a higher cost allocation to the marketing department (and less cost allocated to manufacturing) because that department makes no use of the other service departments. As the utilization of the building by other service departments is recognized, the allocation to marketing decreases.

If these departments managers' performance evaluation is based on their ability to keep costs down, then which cost allocation method would they prefer? Answer: According to Illustration 5–10, Marketing would prefer the

Illustration 5-9

Comparison of Services Provided with Departments Receiving Costs for Each Cost Allocation Method

ALL-TECH MANUFACTURING

Departments Receiving Costs under Each Method

Service Department	Services Provided to:	Direct Method	Step Method	Simultaneous Solution Method[b]
Product engineering (S1)	P1	$ 7,200	$ 9,507	P1
	P2	28,800	38,028	P2
Building occupancy (S2)	S1	None[a]	7,785	S1
	S3	None[a]	None[a]	S3
	P1	33,600	32,005	P1
	P2	25,200	23,355	P2
	P3	25,200	23,355	P3
Factory supervision (S3)	S1	None[a]	3,750	S1
	S2	None[a]	2,500	S2
	P1	15,000	11,250	P1
	P2	10,000	7,500	P2

[a] These are user departments receiving services, but costs are not allocated to them under the indicated method.

[b] These amounts are not calculated separately.

Illustration 5-10

Comparison of Dollar Amounts Allocated under Each Cost Allocation Method

ALL-TECH MANUFACTURING

Allocated Service Costs

Department	Direct Method	Step Method	Simultaneous Solution[a]
Networks (P1)	$ 55,800	$ 52,762	$ 53,661
Terminals (P2)	64,000	68,883	70,328
Marketing (P3)	25,200	23,355	21,011
Totals	$145,000	$145,000	$145,000

[a] These costs are computed in the appendix to this chapter.

simultaneous solution method; Networks would prefer the step method; and Terminals would prefer the direct method!

As a general rule, when there are interservice department activities to which costs can be assigned, the allocations to manufacturing and marketing departments will differ under each method. If there are no interservice department activities, then all three methods will give identical results.

APPLYING OVERHEAD FROM SERVICE DEPARTMENTS TO PRODUCTS

Allocating service department costs to products in manufacturing and service organizations is a two-stage process. The first stage is to allocate service department costs to production departments, which has been the focus of our discussion so far in this chapter. The second stage is to allocate production department costs to units and jobs produced. We now describe that stage.

Service department costs are added to overhead costs that can be directly traced to departments, as shown earlier in Illustrations 5-4, 5-7, and 5-8. Overhead is then allocated in the second stage to products using one or more allocation bases, such as direct labor-hours or machine-hours. This brings up a fundamental question about allocation to products: Should a single rate be used for all production activities or should separate rates be determined for each production activity? This is often called the *plantwide versus department overhead rate choice,* where the plantwide refers to a single rate for all activities and the department rate refers to multiple rates, one for each production activity. These names may suggest that this is primarily a manufacturing problem, but the issue comes up in all organizations that produce a good or service.

Plantwide versus Department Rates

Plantwide Rate A single rate used to allocate overhead to all departments in the company.

To demonstrate the choice of **plantwide** versus **department rates,** assume the service department costs have been assigned to two production activities represented by All-Tech's two manufacturing departments: Networks and Terminals. In addition to these costs allocated to the departments, assume that certain overhead costs can be directly traced to Networks and Terminals; that is, they are costs directly traceable to the department but not to the

Department Rate   The rate used to allocate overhead to an individual cost center within a firm.

products. These costs are shown in the top of Illustration 5–11. Assume Networks is a capital-intensive department that uses a lot of machine time on jobs passing through it but very little direct labor. Terminals is just the opposite; it is very labor-intensive but uses little machine time.

Assume that just two jobs go through these departments: Job L, which is primarily worked on in Terminals because it requires a lot of labor work, and Job M, which is primarily worked on in Networks because it requires a lot of machine work. Illustration 5–11 shows the amount of labor and machine time that each job requires in each department. We would expect both jobs to be allocated the same amount of costs because both use an equal proportion of time in the departments (that is; Job L uses 90 percent of the labor time in Terminals; Job M uses 90 percent of the machine time in Networks) and the overhead costs in the two departments are equal.

Using a Plantwide Rate

Now, suppose a plantwide rate is used. Pick labor-hours as a starting point. Job M uses relatively few labor-hours, so it would be allocated relatively few costs, as shown in Illustration 5–11. On the other hand, Job M looks relatively costlier if machine-hours are used to allocate costs because it requires relatively more machine-hours. It is not clear from this example that either rate is preferred over the other; however, it is clear that the choice of rates has an effect on job costs.

Further, the choice of one particular rate, say, labor-hours, makes it more costly for job managers to have labor-intensive jobs, such as Job L, than to have machine-intensive jobs. (If machine-hours were used as the base, then it would be more costly to have machine-intensive jobs like Job M.) Top management should be aware of these incentives because they could easily lead to lower managers making choices about jobs primarily because of the allocation basis that is used.

Advantages of Department Rates

The costs allocated to jobs using department rates are shown at the bottom of Illustration 5–11. The amount of costs allocated to Job M is the same as the costs allocated to Job L when department rates are used (in this case).

Different departments cause different costs. The use of departmental rates allows managers to recognize these different causes of costs. Department rates also help address the incentive and costing problems that occur with a single plant-wide rate. Note that this approach could be carried still further. For example, in Networks, some of the $90,000 overhead costs are likely to be labor-related overhead and some machine related. We could divide the $90,000 into labor-related costs and machine-related costs and allocate labor-related overhead in Networks on the basis of labor-hours and machine-related overhead in Networks on the basis of machine-hours.

American business has been criticized for its inability to compete on a cost basis in the international marketplace. Many people believe the Japanese can build a small automobile for $2,000 less than U.S. manufacturers can, for example. Managers in many companies do not know how much it costs to make goods and provide services because the use of single overhead

Illustration 5–11   Department versus Plantwide Overhead Rates

	Networks (Machine-intensive Production Department)	Terminals (Labor-intensive Production Department)	Total
Department Overhead Costs:			
Stage 1: Allocate S1 and S2 costs to P1 and P2 (See Illustration 5–10. Assume the direct method was used.)	$55,800	$64,000	$119,800
Trace other overhead costs directly to the production departments. Assume these direct department overhead costs are:	34,200	26,000	60,200
Total manufacturing overhead	$90,000	$90,000	$180,000
Stage 2: Allocate department overhead costs to jobs Assume there are two jobs that use the following machine-hours and labor-hours in the two production departments:			
Job L: Labor-hours	200 hrs.	1,800 hrs.	2,000 hrs.
Machine-hours	200 hrs.	200 hrs.	400 hrs.
Job M: Labor-hours	200 hrs.	200 hrs.	400 hrs.
Machine-hours	1,800 hrs.	200 hrs.	2,000 hrs.

Plantwide Rate:
a. Using labor-hours:
    1. Rate per hour

$$= \frac{\text{Total overhead for both departments}}{\text{Total labor-hours for both jobs}}$$

$$= \frac{\$180,000}{2,400 \text{ labor-hours}} = \$75$$

    2. Overhead cost per job:
        Job L: $75 × 2,000 = $150,000

        Job M: $75 × 400   = $30,000

b. Using machine-hours:
    1. Rate $= \dfrac{\$180,000}{2,400 \text{ machine-hours}} = \$75$

    2. Overhead cost per job:
        Job L: $75 × 400   = $30,000

        Job M: $75 × 2,000 = $150,000

Department Rate:
1. Rate per department:

    Rate $= \dfrac{\$90,000}{2,000 \text{ machine-hours}}$ worked in the Networks department $= \$45$ per machine-hour

    Rate $= \dfrac{\$90,000}{2,000 \text{ labor-hours}}$ worked in the Terminals department $= \$45$ per labor-hour

2. Costs assigned to jobs:

Job L:	$45 × 200 m.h. = $ 9,000	$45 × 1,800 l.h. = $81,000	$90,000
Job M:	$45 × 1,800 m.h. = $81,000	$45 × 200 l.h. = $ 9,000	$90,000

rates does not reflect the relation between the work that is done and the amount of overhead costs associated with that work.[2]

A single overhead rate is usually adequate for valuing inventories and computing cost of goods sold on external financial statements; however, management may benefit from having a more detailed analysis of overhead costs. This is particularly so if overhead is a large proportion of total product costs, such as in most service organizations and in capital-intensive manufacturing companies. Performing more detailed analyses of overhead costs is a time-consuming activity, however. In how much detail should these overhead cost analyses be done? That depends on the costs and benefits to the company.

ISSUES IN ALLOCATING SERVICE DEPARTMENT COSTS

It is usually advisable to allocate costs on a cause-and-effect basis. If this is not practical, the most reasonable basis possible should be found. By establishing a cause-and-effect relationship for the allocation of costs, service department managers can trace costs to their cause. Moreover, managers of user departments have an incentive to limit their use if the costs of the service center are allocated on a cause-and-effect basis. For example, in the early days of data processing, companies often charged a rate per unit of time for computer usage. No charge was made for support services such as programming. This encouraged users to request programming time because it carried no cost. The programmers were kept very busy and frequently engaged in programming activities that offered only marginal benefits. This represented a substantial cost to the computer services department that it was unable to pass on to user departments except through increases in the time-based rates. These rates then became so high that departments found it uneconomical to use the programs they had commissioned.

Thus, when the basis of cost allocations does not reflect cause and effect, cost control becomes difficult because departments tend to make excessive demands for underpriced services. Moreover, evaluation of the computer services department is difficult because its output is measured in terms of computer hours while its costs are a function of both computer hours and programmer hours. Identifying the effect of each factor on total costs is made more difficult by a cost allocation system that ignores programmer hours.

In this case, more detailed cost allocations are needed, but in other cases, more detail does not provide more benefit. When costs cannot be directly related to production activities, production managers have no control over them and need relatively little information about them. Hence, an aggregate allocation both reduces the cost of allocating costs and reduces the time spent by production managers in sifting through excessive and unnecessary detail.

For example, many companies own or lease a building that houses both manufacturing and nonmanufacturing activities. The costs of the building

---

[2] For an extensive discussion of these and related issues, see Robert S. Kaplan, "Measuring Manufacturing Performance: A New Challenge for Management Accounting Research," *The Accounting Review,* 58, no. 4 (October 1983), pp. 686–705.

lease or depreciation, property taxes, heat, air conditioning, light, water, repairs, security, maintenance and similar costs occur as part of the overall building operation and cannot be directly associated with any particular activity within the building. The activities in individual cost centers have so little effect on overall building costs that their managers do not need item-by-item details of the building occupancy costs charged to their departments. A single item, "Building occupancy costs," is usually sufficient. Better control may be obtained by accumulating the total building costs in a centralized cost center, so the building supervisor can be apprised of the detailed cost item and held responsible for controlling them.

The determination of how detailed a cost allocation should be is like other managerial decisions—it should be made on a cost-benefit basis. Cost allocation is, in itself, a costly procedure. If the benefits from increasing the detail of cost allocation are minimal, then more detailed cost allocations are probably not economically wise.

Allocating Fixed Service Department Costs

Although the allocation of variable service department costs can be useful for charging user departments, the allocation of fixed costs can have unintended effects. For example, the top administrators of Southwest University observed that faculty and staff were using the university's WATS (Wide Area Telephone Service) so much that the lines were seldom free during the day.[3] WATS allowed the university unlimited toll-free service within the United States. The fixed cost of WATS was $10,000 per month; variable cost per call was zero.

The top administrators learned that there was an average usage of 50,000 minutes per month on the WATS line, so they initially allocated the $10,000 monthly charge to callers (that is, departments) at a rate of 20 cents per minute ($10,000 ÷ 50,000 minutes). Now that they were being charged for the use of WATS, department heads discouraged their faculty and staff from using the telephone. Hence, the number of minutes used on WATS dropped to 25,000 per month, which increased the rate to 40 cents per minute ($10,000 ÷ 25,000). This continued until the internal cost allocation per minute exceeded the normal long-distance rates, and the use of WATS dropped almost to zero. Southwest University's total telephone bill increased dramatically.[4] The top administrators subsequently compromised by charging a nominal fee of 10 cents per minute. According to the University's chief financial officer, "The 10 cents per minute charge made us aware that there was a cost to the WATS service, albeit a fixed cost. The charge was sufficiently low, however, so as not to discourage bona fide use of WATS."

---

[3] This example is based on one given by Jerold L. Zimmerman, "The Costs and Benefits of Cost Allocations," *The Accounting Review,* July 1979, pp. 510–511.

[4] The solution to this problem is not necessarily zero. According to Zimmerman (1979), the correct price to charge users is "the cost imposed by forcing others who want to use the WATS line to either wait or place a regular call . . . this cost varies between zero (if no one is delayed) to, at most, the cost of a regular toll call if a user cannot use the WATS line" (p. 510). The necessary procedure to implement such a pricing system is very difficult and costly. Zimmerman suggests that fixed allocations could be a simplified way of approximating the results of the more complicated, theoretically correct pricing systems.

Moral

The moral of the cost allocation story is as follows: Service department costs allocations are common in all types of organizations. Costs are allocated for a variety of reasons—for example, to satisfy regulatory and external financial reporting requirements; to meet contract requirements (for example, in cost-reimbursement defense contracts); to encourage cross-department monitoring of costs; to make user department personnel aware of costs incurred by service departments; and to compute product costs for decision making. Costs allocated for one purpose usually have unexpected side effects. Hence, cost allocations should be made much like doctors prescribe medicine—"with an eye on the side effects."

SUMMARY

Costs are accumulated in a department largely for performance evaluation purposes—that is, to make the department manager (and other personnel) responsible for controlling department costs. When a department provides services and support to other departments rather than producing or marketing the organization's output, its costs are often allocated to the departments it services. Hence, the service department is *directly* responsible for its own costs, and user departments are *indirectly* responsible for service department costs. This makes user department personnel aware of service department costs, and it can give them incentives to help control service department costs.

Service department costs are allocated to production departments to measure the cost of goods or services for decision making.

Finally, manufacturing service department costs are allocated to production departments for external financial reporting and other contractual and regulatory purposes to value inventory and measure cost of goods sold.

In the first stage of cost allocation, service department costs are allocated to user departments as follows:

1. Departments that provide and use each other's services are identified. At All-Tech Manufacturing, for example, Networks used the services of all three service departments.
2. Allocation bases are established. (Production engineering's costs were allocated to user departments based on the engineering labor-hours worked in each user department.)
3. One of three methods of allocating service department costs is selected:
   a. Direct method.
   b. Step method.
   c. Simultaneous solution method.

The direct method allocates costs directly to production and marketing departments. Only production and marketing departments are recognized as user departments—other service departments are not.

The step method recognizes some, but not all, service departments as user departments. Costs are allocated in steps, usually beginning with an allocation from the service department that provides the greatest portion of its services to other service departments, and continuing until all costs are allocated to production and marketing departments. Once an allocation is made *from* a service department, no more costs can be allocated *to* it.

The simultaneous solution method simultaneously allocates costs to all departments that receive services. Unlike the step and direct methods, all interservice department allocations are recognized. Previously, this method has not been widely used because the mathematics were perceived as difficult, and the procedure as very time-consuming if done manually. However, with the widespread use of computers, use of the simultaneous solution method has increased.

In the second stage of cost allocation, costs are allocated from production departments to units or jobs. In this stage, the choice of plantwide or departmental rates could have a significant effect on product costs.

Cost allocations are often made for multiple reasons. Sometimes an allocation made for one purpose will have unexpected effects elsewhere. Consequently, it is wise to consider all of the effects of cost allocation.

TERMS AND CONCEPTS

The following terms and concepts should be familiar to you after reading this chapter.

Departmental Rate   **Plantwide Rate**
Direct Method   **Service Department**
Final Cost Center   **Simultaneous Solution Method**
Intermediate Cost Center   **Step Method**
Manufacturing   **User Department**

SUPPLEMENTARY READINGS

Cappettini, R., and G. Salamon. "Internal versus External Acquisition of Services when Reciprocal Services Exist." *Accounting Review,* July 1977.

Hoshower, Leon B., and Robert P. Crum. "Controlling Service Center Costs." *Management Accounting,* November 1987, pp. 44–48.

Jacobs, Frederick H., and Ronald M. Marshall. "A Reciprocal Service Cost Approximation." *Accounting Review,* January 1987, pp. 67–78.

Jensen, D. "Variable and Self-Service Costs in Reciprocal Allocation Models." *Accounting Review,* October 1973.

———. "The Role of Cost in Pricing Joint Products: A Case of Production in Fixed Proportions." *Accounting Review,* July 1974, pp. 465–76.

———. "A Class of Mutually Satisfactory Allocations." *Accounting Review,* October 1977, pp. 842–56.

Kaplan, R. G., and G. L. Thompson. "Overhead Allocation via Mathematical Programming Models." *Accounting Review,* April 1971.

Manes, R. P.; S. H. Park; and R. Jensen. "Relevent Costs of Intermediate Goods and Services." *Accounting Review,* July 1982, pp. 594–606.

Rogers, Mike. "Paying for Central Services." *Public Finance and Accountancy,* May 1985, pp. 15–16.

Solomon, Lanny, and Jeffrey Tsay. "Pricing of Computing Services: A Survey of Industry Practices." *Cost and Management,* March–April 1985, pp. 5–9 (published in Canada).

Williams, T. H., and C. H. Griffin. "Matrix Theory and Cost Allocation." *Accounting Review,* July 1964, pp. 671–78.

SELF-STUDY PROBLEM

T. Schurt & Company manufactures and sells T-shirts for advertising and promotional purposes and wholesales T-shirts with various designs for general sale. The company has two manufacturing operations: shirtmaking and printing. When an order for T-shirts is received, the shirtmaking department obtains the materials and colors requested and has the shirts made in the desired mix of sizes. The completed shirts are then sent to the printing department where the custom labels or designs are prepared and embossed on the shirts.

To support the manufacturing activity, the company has a building that houses the two manufacturing departments as well as the sales department. A payroll department has been established to handle the details of recordkeeping for employee wages and salaries as well as for issuing payroll checks. Finally, a design and patterns staff has been hired to develop shirt patterns, label designs, and, on occasion, to draw illustrations for the company's advertising. To aid in cost control, the company accumulates the costs of these support functions in separate service cost centers: (1) building occupancy, (2) payroll accounting, and (3) design and patterns.

During the current period, the direct costs incurred in each of the departments are as follows:

Shirtmaking (P1)	$210,000
Printing (P2)	140,000
Selling (P3)	80,000
Building occupancy (S1)	45,000
Payroll accounting (S2)	20,000
Design and patterns (S3)	10,000

Building occupancy costs are allocated on the basis of the number of square feet of each user department. Payroll accounting costs are allocated on the basis of the number of employees. The design and pattern costs are charged to departments on the basis of the number of designs requested by each department. For the current period, the following table summarizes the usage of services by other service cost centers and other departments:

	S1	S2	S3	P1	P2	P3
Building occupancy (S1) (square feet)	—	8,100	3,900	27,000	36,000	6,000
Payroll accounting (S2) (employees)	3	—	6	30	15	6
Design and patterns (S3) (designs)	—	—	—	15	40	5

Required:

a. Determine the total costs in each of the three "producing" departments using the direct method for service cost allocations.

b. Compute the cost allocations and total costs in each producing department using the step method.

SOLUTION TO SELF-STUDY PROBLEM

To facilitate solution, express the usage of services in percentage terms:

Service Center	Used by					
	S1	S2	S3	P1	P2	P3
S1	—	.100	.049	.333	.444	.074
S2	.050	—	.100	.500	.250	.100
S3	—	—	—	.250	.667	.083

a. Direct method:
Usage of services by producing departments only:

Service Center	Used by		
	P1	P2	S3
S1	.391[a]	.522	.087
S2	.588[b]	.294	.118
S3	.250	.667	.083

[a] .391 = .333 ÷ (.333 + .444 + .074); .522 = .444 ÷ (.333 + .444 + .074); etc.
[b] .588 = .500 ÷ (.500 + .250 + .100), etc.

Allocation		To		
From	Amount	P1	P2	P3
S1	$45,000	$ 17,595[a]	$ 23,490	$ 3,915
S2	$20,000	11,760[b]	5,880	2,360
S3	$10,000	2,500[c]	6,670	830
Allocated costs		31,855	36,040	7,105
Direct costs		210,000	140,000	80,000
Total costs		$241,855	$176,040	$87,105

[a] $17,595 = $45,000 × .391; $23,490 = $45,000 × .522; $3,915 = $45,000 × .087
[b] $11,760 = $20,000 × .588; $5,880 = $20,000 × .294; $2,360 = $20,000 × .118.
[c] $2,500 = $10,000 × .25; $6,670 = $10,000 × .667; $830 = $10,000 × .083.

b. Step method:
Order of allocation: S2, S1, S3.
Usage of services by producing departments and service cost centers excluding reciprocal allocations:

Service Center	Used by:				
	S1	S3	P1	P2	P3
S2	.050	.100	.500	.250	.100
S1	—	.054[a]	.370[a]	.494[a]	.082[a]
S3	—	—	.250	.667	.083

[a] .054 = .049 ÷ (.049 + .333 + .444 + .074) = .049 ÷ .900; .370 = .333 ÷ .900;
.494 = .444 ÷ .900 (rounded); .082 = .074 ÷ .90.

Allocation:

			To			
From	**S2**	**S1**	**S3**	**P1**	**P2**	**P3**
Direct dept. costs	$20,000	$45,000	$10,000			
S2	(20,000)	1,000[a]	2,000[a]	$ 10,000	$ 5,000	$ 2,000
S1		(46,000)[b]	2,484[b]	17,020[b]	22,724	3,772
S3			(14,484)[c]	3,621[c]	9,661	1,202
Total allocated costs				30,641	37,385	6,974
Direct costs of P1, P2 and P3				210,000	140,000	80,000
Total costs				$240,641	$177,385	$86,974

[a] $1,000 = $20,000 × .05; $2,000 = $20,000 × .10; etc.

[b] $46,000 = $45,000 direct costs + $1,000 allocated from S2; $2,484 = $46,000 × .054; $17,020 = $46,000 × .37; etc.

[c] $14,484 = $10,000 direct costs + $4,484 allocated from S1 and S2; $3,621 = $14,484 × .25; etc.

APPENDIX: The Simultaneous Solution Method Using Matrix Algebra[5]

The simultaneous solution method requires that cost relationships be written in equation form. The method then solves the equations for the total costs to be allocated to each department. The direct costs of each department are typically included in the solution. Thus, for any department, we can state the equation:

$$\text{Total costs} = \text{Direct costs} + \text{Allocated costs}$$

The total costs are the unknowns that we attempt to derive.

For example, let's assume the direct overhead costs of the departments at All-Tech Manufacturing are:

Product engineering (S1)	$ 36,000
Building occupancy (S2)	84,000
Factory supervision (S3)	25,000
Networks (P1)	500,000
Terminals (P2)	270,000
Marketing (P3)	185,000

Using the information in Illustration 5–3, the total costs of Networks (P1) may be expressed as:

$$\text{Total costs} = \text{Direct costs} + \text{Allocated costs}$$
$$P1 = \$500,000 + 20\% \text{ S1} + 32\% \text{ S2} + 45\% \text{ S3}$$

Similar equations are constructed for each of the other production departments:

$$P2 = \$270,000 + 80\% \text{ S1} + 24\% \text{ S2} + 30\% \text{ S3}$$
$$P3 = \$185,000 + \quad 0 \quad \text{ S1} + 24\% \text{ S2} + \quad 0 \quad \text{ S3}$$

---

[5] For a more detailed discussion of matrix algebra, see J. K. Shank, *Matrix Methods in Accounting* (Reading, Mass.: Addison-Wesley Publishing, 1972).

And for the service departments, the equations are:

$$S1 = \$36,000 + 8\% \ S2 + 15\% \ S3$$
$$S2 = \$84,000 \qquad\qquad + 10\% \ S3$$
$$S3 = \$25,000 + 12\% \ S2$$

Now we have a set of equations that express the total cost of each department as a function of direct costs and allocated costs.

Setting the Equations in Matrix Form

To set the equations up in matrix form for solution, the terms are rearranged so that direct costs are on the right-hand side of the equation and all unknowns are on the left side. Each equation is expanded to include all the departments in the system.

For example, the cost equation of Networks (P1) is rearranged as:

$$1 \ P1 + 0 \ P2 + 0 \ P3 = .20 \ S1 + .32 \ S2 + .45 \ S3 + \$500,000$$
$$1 \ P1 + 0 \ P2 + 0 \ P3 - .20 \ S1 - .32 \ S2 - .45 \ S3 = \$500,000$$

This is repeated for all production and service departments. The results are:

$$1 \ P1 + 0 \ P2 + 0 \ P3 - .20 \ S1 - .32 \ S2 - .45 \ S3 = \$500,000$$
$$0 \ P1 + 1 \ P2 + 0 \ P3 - .80 \ S1 - .24 \ S2 - .30 \ S3 = 270,000$$
$$0 \ P1 + 0 \ P2 + 1 \ P3 - 0 \ S1 - .24 \ S2 - 0 \ S3 = 185,000$$
$$0 \ P1 + 0 \ P2 + 0 \ P3 + 1 \ S1 - .08 \ S2 - .15 \ S3 = 36,000$$
$$0 \ P1 + 0 \ P2 + 0 \ P3 - 0 \ S1 + 1 \ S2 - .10 \ S3 = 84,000$$
$$0 \ P1 + 0 \ P2 + 0 \ P3 - 0 \ S1 - .12 \ S2 + 1 \ S3 = 25,000$$

Each equation may be interpreted as follows: The costs in any department before allocation (the right-hand side) equals the costs after allocation (the P terms) less the allocations that are to be charged to the service departments (the S terms with negative coefficients).

Reforming the system of equations in matrix notation saves repetition of all of the symbols for the unknowns and results in the following system of matrices and vectors:

$$
\begin{bmatrix}
1 & 0 & 0 & -.20 & -.32 & -.45 \\
0 & 1 & 0 & -.80 & -.24 & -.30 \\
0 & 0 & 1 & 0 & -.24 & 0 \\
0 & 0 & 0 & 1 & -.08 & -.15 \\
0 & 0 & 0 & 0 & 1 & -.10 \\
0 & 0 & 0 & 0 & -.12 & 1
\end{bmatrix}
\times
\begin{bmatrix}
P1 \\ P2 \\ P3 \\ S1 \\ S2 \\ S3
\end{bmatrix}
=
\begin{bmatrix}
\$500,000 \\ 270,000 \\ 185,000 \\ 36,000 \\ 84,000 \\ 25,000
\end{bmatrix}
$$

To solve for the vector of unknowns (that is, the Ps and Ss), matrix algebra is used. If the matrix is labeled A, the vector of unknowns X, and the vector of direct costs B, the matrix form of the equation may be summarized as:

$$AX = B$$

To solve for X, we multiply both sides by the inverse of A, which is noted A^{-1}. This gives:

$$X = A^{-1}B$$

Computing the inverse of a matrix is tedious without the use of a computer.

Solving the Equations   Spreadsheet programs with built-in matrix capabilities may be used to solve this system of equations. One approach is to enter the coefficients matrix (A) beginning in the upper left corner of the spreadsheet.

Using Lotus 123™, these coefficients are entered in Cells A1 through F6 of the spreadsheet. Then use the /**DMI** (Data Matrix Invert) command to perform the matrix inversion. The data range is A1 through F6. The inverse may be output anywhere, but telling the program that the output range begins in Cell A9 allows the entire program and solution to appear on the screen. The computer then computes the matrix inverse and displays it in the range A9 through F14.

Next, enter the vector of direct costs (B) in Cells G9 through G14. To multiply A^{-1} by B, use the /**DMM** command. The first data range is the A matrix inverse, which is A9 through F14. The second data range is G9 through G14. The output range can be anywhere, but if you use H9, the results appear on the same screen. The output vector is the total cost assigned to each of the producing departments in the same order as included in the vector of unknowns (X).

The inverse of A as it appears on the screen is as follows:[6]

$$\begin{bmatrix} 1 & 0 & 0 & 0.20 & 0.3984 & 0.5198 \\ 0 & 1 & 0 & 0.80 & 0.3587 & 0.4559 \\ 0 & 0 & 1 & 0 & 0.2429 & 0.0243 \\ 0 & 0 & 0 & 1 & 0.0992 & 0.1599 \\ 0 & 0 & 0 & 0 & 1.0121 & 0.1012 \\ 0 & 0 & 0 & 0 & 0.1215 & 1.0121 \end{bmatrix}$$

The product of $A^{-1}B$, which is the solutions vector, is as follows:

$$\begin{bmatrix} 553{,}661 \\ 340{,}328 \\ 206{,}012 \\ 48{,}330 \\ 87{,}546 \\ 35{,}509 \end{bmatrix}$$

The amount $553,661 is the total of the direct and allocated costs for Department P1; $340,328 is the total direct and allocated cost for Department P2; and $206,012 is the total direct and allocated cost for Department P3.

The service costs allocated to Department P1 are $53,661, which is the solution vector element $553,661 minus the direct costs of Department P1 ($500,000). Likewise, for Department P2, the allocated costs are $70,328, which is $340,328 less $270,000. Similarly, for Department P3, the allocated

---

[6] Brackets have been added for ease of presentation.

costs are $21,012, which is the difference between the solution vector of $206,012 and the direct costs of $185,000.

Computational Hints

Let NP be the number of producing departments and NS the number of service departments. The coefficients matrix (A) should be square with NP + NS rows and NP + NS columns. All of the diagonal elements of the matrix should be 1's. In the first NP columns, the off-diagonal elements should all equal 0. In the rightmost NS columns, the off-diagonal elements are all negative. The sum of the rightmost NS columns should equal 0, within rounding.

You can check to see that the total of the costs charged to the producing departments equals the sum of the direct costs by using the @SUM command for H9 through H11 and comparing that total to the sum of G9 through G14. The check total is $1,100,000.

If these computational notes are followed, chances are quite high that the resulting cost allocation will be computationally correct.

These results may be tabled as follows:

Department	Allocated Cost		Total Cost		Direct Cost
Networks	$ 53,661	=	$553,661	−	$500,000
Terminals	70,328	=	340,328	−	270,000
Marketing	21,012	=	206,012	−	185,000
Total allocated cost	$145,000 (rounded)				

As a result of the allocation, a total of $145,000 has been allocated from the service departments to the operating departments. All of the interrelationships among service departments have been taken into account in this allocation.

APPENDIX SELF-STUDY PROBLEM

Using the data provided in the T. Schurt & Company example, which is the self-study problem at the end of the chapter, compute the cost allocation and total costs for each producing department using the simultaneous solution method.

SOLUTION TO APPENDIX SELF-STUDY PROBLEM

Simultaneous solution method:

Step 1. Construct the cost equations.

$$P1 = \$210,000 + .333\ S1 + .500\ S2 + .250\ S3$$
$$P2 = \$140,000 + .444\ S1 + .250\ S2 + .667\ S3$$
$$P3 = \$80,000\ + .074\ S1 + .100\ S2 + .083\ S3$$
$$S1 = \$45,000\ \qquad\qquad + .050\ S2$$
$$S2 = \$20,000\ + .100\ S1$$
$$S3 = \$10,000\ + .049\ S1 + .100\ S2$$

Step 2. Arrange the cost equations to place the coefficients in one section and the direct costs on the right-hand side of the equation.

$$
\begin{aligned}
1\, P1 + 0\, P2 + 0\, P3 - .333\, S1 - .500\, S2 - .250\, S3 &= \$210{,}000 \\
0\, P1 + 1\, P2 + 0\, P3 - .444\, S1 - .250\, S2 - .667\, S3 &= 140{,}000 \\
0\, P1 + 0\, P2 + 1\, P3 - .074\, S1 - .100\, S2 - .083\, S3 &= 80{,}000 \\
0\, P1 + 0\, P2 + 0\, P3 + 1.000\, S1 - .050\, S2 - .000\, S3 &= 45{,}000 \\
0\, P1 + 0\, P2 + 0\, P3 - .100\, S1 + 1.000\, S2 - .000\, S3 &= 20{,}000 \\
0\, P1 + 0\, P2 + 0\, P3 - .049\, S1 - .100\, S2 + 1.000\, S3 &= 10{,}000
\end{aligned}
$$

Step 3. Use the information in step 2 to construct a matrix of coefficients, a vector of unknowns, and a vector of direct costs.

$$
\begin{bmatrix}
1 & 0 & 0 & -.333 & -.500 & -.250 \\
0 & 1 & 0 & -.444 & -.250 & -.667 \\
0 & 0 & 1 & -.074 & -.100 & -.083 \\
0 & 0 & 0 & 1 & -.050 & 0 \\
0 & 0 & 0 & -.100 & 1 & 0 \\
0 & 0 & 0 & -.049 & -.100 & 1
\end{bmatrix}
\times
\begin{bmatrix}
P1 \\ P2 \\ P3 \\ S1 \\ S2 \\ S3
\end{bmatrix}
=
\begin{bmatrix}
\$210{,}000 \\ 140{,}000 \\ 80{,}000 \\ 45{,}000 \\ 20{,}000 \\ 10{,}000
\end{bmatrix}
$$

Step 4. Invert the matrix A using a spreadsheet program such as Lotus™ beginning at the upper left of the spreadsheet. Use the **/DMI** command to invert the matrix. The data range should be cells A1 through F6. Place the results in a range beginning with cell A9. The inverse should appear on the screen as follows:

$$
\begin{bmatrix}
1 & 0 & 0 & .3997 & .5450 & .2500 \\
0 & 1 & 0 & .5109 & .3422 & .6670 \\
0 & 0 & 1 & .0894 & .1128 & .0830 \\
0 & 0 & 0 & 1.0050 & .0503 & 0 \\
0 & 0 & 0 & .1005 & 1.0050 & 0 \\
0 & 0 & 0 & .0593 & .1030 & 1
\end{bmatrix}
$$

Step 5. Enter the direct costs in the range G9 to G14 and multiply the A matrix inverse by the direct costs vector using the **/DMM** command. The first data range is A9 through F14. The second data range is G9 through G14. Set the output range as H9. The results which appear in the output range should be as follows:

$$
\begin{bmatrix}
241{,}388 \\
176{,}506 \\
87{,}106 \\
46{,}231 \\
24{,}623 \\
14{,}728
\end{bmatrix}
$$

Check to see that the total of the costs charged to the producing departments equals the sum of the direct costs by using the **@SUM** command for H9 through H11 and comparing that total to the sum of G9 through G14. The check total is $505,000.

The costs allocated to P1 are obtained by taking the difference between the total costs from the solutions vector ($241,388) less the direct costs of $210,000. This difference is $31,388. For P2, the allocated costs are $36,506, which is the difference between the total costs of $176,506 and the direct costs of $140,000. Finally, for P3, the allocated costs are $7,106, which is the difference between the total costs of $87,106 and the direct costs of $80,000.

QUESTIONS

5-1. "Direct materials" are considered direct with respect to both the manufacturing department using the materials and to the product. However, "indirect materials" cannot be associated directly with a specific job or product but may be related directly to the manufacturing department where the indirect materials are used. Explain the concepts *direct* and *indirect* in this setting.

5-2. What are the reasons for establishing service departments as intermediate cost objectives?

5-3. Why would the manager of an operating department not need reports that include the details of the cost items that comprise the operating department's share of the cost of building occupancy?

5-4. What argument(s) could be given in support of the simultaneous solution method as the preferred method for distributing the costs of service departments?

5-5. Under what conditions would the results obtained from using the direct method of allocations be the same as the results from using either other method? Why?

5-6. Consider a company with two producing departments and one service department. The service department distributes its costs to the producing departments on the basis of number of employees in each department. If the costs in the service department are fixed, what effect would the addition of employees in one department have on the costs allocated to the other department? Comment on the reasonableness of the situation.

5-7. Compare and contrast the direct method, the step method, and the simultaneous solution method of allocating costs.

5-8. The manager of an operating department just received a cost report and has made the following comment with respect to the costs allocated from one of the service departments: "This charge to my division does not seem right. The service center installed equipment with more capacity than our division requires. Most of the service department costs are fixed, but we seem to be allocated more costs when other departments use less. We are paying for excess capacity of other departments when other departments cut their usage levels." How might this manager's problem be solved?

5-9. What criterion should be used to determine the order of allocation from service departments when the step method is used? Explain why.

5-10. (Appendix.) The inverse of the matrix *A* in the cost allocation example can be subdivided into four submatrices in the following form:

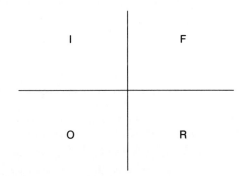

The partitions are established by drawing a line below the last row of coefficients that are related to producing departments (that is, row three in the appendix example) and a vertical line to the right of the last column of coefficients for producing departments (that is, between the third and fourth columns in the appendix example). Examine the elements of each of these submatrices and consider how the elements are used in the matrix multiplication to determine the allocation of costs. Give an explanation of the functions of each of these submatrices.

EXERCISES

5–11. Cost Allocations—Direct Method
(L.O.1)

Thermal Corporation has two producing departments and two service departments labeled P1, P2, S1, and S2, respectively. Direct costs for each department and the proportion of service costs used by the various departments are as follows:

Cost Center	Direct Costs	Proportion of Services Used by:			
		S1	S2	P1	P2
P1	$90,000				
P2	60,000				
S1	20,000	—	.80	.10	.10
S2	30,000	.20	—	.50	.30

Required:

Compute the allocation of service department costs to operating departments, using the direct method.

5–12. Cost Allocations—Step Method
(L.O.2)

Refer to the data for the Thermal Corporation (exercise 5–11). Use the step method to allocate the service costs, using:

a. The order of allocation recommended in the text.

b. The allocations made in the reverse of the recommended order.

5–13. Allocating Service Department Costs First to Production Departments, Then to Jobs
(L.O.1)

Refer to the facts in exercise 5–11. Assume P1 and P2 each work on two jobs: Job 10 and Job 11. Costs are allocated to jobs based on labor-hours in P1 and based on machine-hours in P2. The labor- and machine-hours worked in each department are as follows:

		P1	P2
Job 10:	Labor-hours	80	10
	Machine-hours	10	20
Job 11:	Labor-hours	10	10
	Machine-hours	10	90

Required:

How much of the service department costs allocated to P1 and P2 in the direct method would be allocated to Job 10? How much to Job 11?

5–14. Plantwide versus Departmental Rates
(L.O.4)

Refer to the facts in exercises 5–11 and 5–13.

Required:

a. Assume the company uses just one basis for applying overhead to jobs going through both P1 and P2: *labor-hours.* How much of the service department costs would be allocated to Job 10 and to Job 11? Why is this different than the amount applied to each job that was computed in exercise 5–13?

b. How would your answer to requirement *(a)* change if the company had used *only machine-hours* in allocating costs to Job 10 and Job 11?

5–15. (Appendix) Cost Allocations—Simultaneous Solution
(L.O.3)

Refer to the data for the Thermal Corporation (exercise 5–11). Use the simultaneous solution method to allocate the service costs.

5–16. Cost Allocations—Simultaneous Solution Method—Two Service Departments
(L.O.3)

A company wants to know if eliminating a service department and replacing services with an outside supplier would be feasible. The center under consideration for elimination is labeled S1.

During the past month, the following costs were incurred in the three operating departments and two service departments in the company:

P1	$230,000
P2	615,000
P3	790,000
S1	124,000
S2	109,000

Use of services by other departments is as follows:

Service Cost Center	User Department				
	S1	S2	P1	P2	P3
S1	—	.40	.30	.20	.10
S2	.10	—	.20	.15	.55

Required:

Allocate service department costs to P1, P2, and P3 using the simultaneous solution method.

5–17. Cost Allocations—Direct Method
(L.O.1)

Meridian Box Company has two service departments (maintenance and general factory administration) and two operating departments (cutting and assembly). Management has decided to allocate maintenance costs on the basis of the area in each department and general factory administration costs on the basis of labor-hours worked by the employees in each of their respective departments.

The following data appear in the company records for the current period:

	General Factory Administration	Maintenance	Cutting	Assembly
Area occupied (square feet)	1,000	—	1,000	3,000
Labor-hours	—	100	100	400
Direct labor costs (operating departments only)			$1,500	$4,000
Service department direct costs	$12,000	$20,000		

Required:

Use the direct method to allocate these service department costs to the operating departments.

5-18. Cost Allocation—Step Method
(L.O.2)

Refer to the data for the Meridian Box Company in exercise 5–17. Allocate the service department costs using the step method. What effect does using this method have on the allocation of costs?

5-19. Cost Allocation—Simultaneous Solution Method
(L.O.3)

Refer to the data for the Meridian Box Company in exercise 5–17. Allocate the service department costs using the simultaneous solution method. (Matrix algebra is not required because there are only two service departments.)

5-20. Evaluate Cost Allocation Methods
(L.O.1, L.O.2, L.O.3)

Refer to the solutions to exercises 5–17, 5–18, and 5–19. Which method do you think is best? How much would it be worth to the company to use the best method over the worst of the three methods? (Numbers not required in this answer.)

PROBLEMS

5-21. Step Method with Three Service Departments

Oakland Corporation operates two producing departments—painting and polishing—in its automotive refinishing operations. The company has three service departments for its plant: building occupancy, payroll accounting, and equipment maintenance. The accumulated costs in the three service departments were $180,000, $250,000, and $132,000, respectively. The company decided that building occupancy costs should be distributed on the basis of square footage used by each production and service department. The payroll accounting costs are allocated on the basis of number of employees, while equipment maintenance costs are allocated on the basis of the dollar value of the equipment in each department. The use of each basis by all departments during the current period is as follows:

Allocation Base	Used by:				
	Building Occupancy	Payroll Accounting	Equipment Maintenance	Painting	Polishing
Building area	5,000	15,000	10,000	180,000	45,000
Employees	9	5	6	35	50
Equipment value (in thousands)	$12	$240	$35	$624	$324

Direct costs of the painting department included $475,000 in direct materials, $650,000 in direct labor, and $225,000 in overhead. In the polishing department, direct costs consisted of $820,000 in direct labor and $145,000 in overhead.

Required:

a. Using the step method, determine the allocated costs and the total costs in each of the two producing departments.

b. Assume 1,000 units were processed through these two departments. What is the unit cost: For painting? For polishing? Total?

5-22. Solve for Unknowns

Pronto's Pizza has a commissary that supplies food and other products to its pizza restaurants. It has two service departments, computer services (S1) and administration and maintenance (S2), which support two operating departments, food products (P1) and supplies (P2). As an internal auditor, you are checking the company's procedures for cost allocation. You find the following cost allocation results for June:

Costs allocated to P1:
$20,000 from S1
? from S2

Costs allocated to P2:
$11,250 from S2
? from S1

Total costs for the two service departments:
$50,000

S2's services are provided as follows:
20 percent to S1
50 percent to P1
30 percent to P2

The direct method of allocating costs is used.

Required:

a. What are the total service department costs (S1 + S2) allocated to P2?

b. Complete the following:

	To:	
From:	**P1**	**P2**
S1	$20,000	_____
S2	_____	$11,250

c. What were the proportions of S1's costs allocated to P1 and P2?

5–23. Cost Allocations: Comparison of Dual and Single Rates

High Skies Airlines operates a centralized computer center for the data processing needs of its reservation, scheduling, maintenance, and accounting divisions. Costs associated with use of the computer are charged to the individual departments on the basis of time usage. Due to recent increased competition in the airline industry, the company has decided it is necessary to more accurately allocate its costs so it can price its services competitively and profitably. During the current period, the use of data processing services and the storage capacity required for each of the divisions were as follows (in thousands):

Division	Time Usage	Storage Capacity
Reservations	2,500	15,000
Scheduling	1,700	6,000
Maintenance	6,300	2,100
Accounting	5,000	1,900

During this period, the costs of the computer center amounted to $3,525,000 for time usage and $2,500,000 for storage-related costs.

Required:

Determine the allocation to each of the divisions using:

a. A single rate based on time used.

b. Dual rates based on time used and capacity used.

You may round all decimals to three places.

5–24. Allocation for Economic Decisions and Motivation

Bonn Company recently reorganized its computer and data processing activities. The small installations located within the accounting departments at its plants and subsidiaries have been replaced with a single data processing department at corporate headquarters responsible for the operations of a newly acquired large-scale computer system. The new department has been in operation for two years and has been regularly producing reliable and timely data for the past 12 months.

Because the department has focused on its activities on converting applications to the new system and producing reports for the plant and subsidiary managements, little attention has been devoted to the costs of the department. Now that the department's activities are operating relatively smoothly, company management has requested that the departmental manager recommend a cost accumulation system to facilitate cost control and the development of suitable rates to charge users for service.

For the past two years, the departmental costs have been recorded in one account. The costs have then been allocated to user departments on the basis of computer time used. The following schedule reports the costs and charging rate for last year.

DATA PROCESSING DEPARTMENT
Costs for the Year Ended December 31

1.	Salaries and benefits	$ 622,600
2.	Supplies	40,000
3.	Equipment maintenance contract	15,000
4.	Insurance	25,000
5.	Heat and air conditioning	36,000
6.	Electricity	50,000
7.	Equipment and furniture depreciation	285,400
8.	Building improvements depreciation	10,000
9.	Building occupancy and security	39,300
10.	Corporate administrative charges	52,700
	Total costs	$1,176,000
	Computer hours for user processing*	2,750
	Hourly rate ($1,176,000 ÷ 2,750)	$428

*Use of available computer hours:

Testing and debugging programs	250
Set-up of jobs	500
Processing jobs	2,750
Downtime for maintenance	750
Idle time	742
	4,992

The department manager recommends that costs be accumulated by five activity centers within the department: systems analysis, programming, data preparation, computer operations (processing), and administration. He then suggests that costs of administration activity should be allocated to the other four activity centers before a separate rate for charging users is developed for each of the first four activities.

The manager made the following observations regarding the charges to the several subsidiary accounts within the department after reviewing the details of the accounts:

1. Salaries and benefits—records the salary and benefit costs of all employees in the department.

2. Supplies—records disk costs, paper costs for printers, and a small amount for miscellaneous other costs.

3. Equipment maintenance contracts—records charges for maintenance contracts; all equipment is covered by maintenance contracts.

4. Insurance—records cost of insurance covering the equipment and the furniture.

5. Heat and air conditioning—records a charge from the corporate heating and air conditioning department estimated to be the incremental costs to meet the special needs of the computer department.

6. Electricity—records the charge for electricity based upon a separate meter within the department.

7. Equipment and furniture depreciation—records the depreciation charges for all owned equipment and furniture within the department.

8. Building improvements—records the amortization charges for the building changes required to provide proper environmental control and electrical service for the computer equipment.

9. Building occupancy and security—records the computer department's share of the depreciation, maintenance, heat, and security costs of the building; these costs are allocated to the department on the basis of square feet occupied.

10. Corporate administrative charges—records the computer department's share of the corporate administrative costs. They are allocated to the department on the basis of number of employees in the department.

   a. For each of the 10 cost items, state whether or not it should be distributed to the five activity centers. For each cost item that should be distributed, recommend the basis upon which it should be distributed. Justify your conclusion in each case.

   b. Assume the costs of the computer operations (processing) activity will be charged to the user departments on the basis of computer-hours. Using the analysis of computer utilization shown as a footnote to the department cost schedule presented in the problem, determine the total number of hours that should be employed to determine the charging rate for computer operations (processing). Justify your answer.

(CMA adapted)

5–25. Cost Allocation: Step Method with Analysis and Decision Making

O-Hi-O Corporation is reviewing its operations to see what additional energy-saving projects might be carried out. The company's Intermac plant has its own electric generating facilities. The electric generating plant is powered by the production of some natural gas wells that the company owns and that are located on the same property as the plant. A summary of the use of service department service by other service departments as well as by the two producing departments at the plant is summarized as follows:

		Services Used by				
		Electric Generating			Production Department	
Service Department	Natural Gas Production	Fixed Costs	Variable Costs	Equipment Maintenance	No. 1	No. 2
Natural gas production	—	—	.40	—	.10	.50
Electric generating:						
Fixed costs	.10	—	—	.10	.30	.50
Variable costs	.10	—	—	.05	.55	.30
Equipment maintenance	.20	.10	.05	—	.50	.15

Direct costs (in thousands) in the various departments and the labels used to abbreviate the departments in the calculations are as follows:

Department	Direct Costs	Label
Natural gas production	$ 35	S1
Electric generation:		
Fixed costs	15	S2
Variable costs	40	S3
Equipment maintenance	24	S4
Production maintenance:		
No. 1	300	P1
No. 2	220	P2

The company currently allocates costs of service departments to production departments using the step method. The local power company indicates that the power company would charge $80,000 per year for the electricity now being generated by the company internally. Management rejected switching to the public utility on the grounds that its rates would cost more than the $55,000 ($15,000 + 40,000) costs of the present company-owned system.

a. What costs of electric service did management use to prepare the basis for its decision to continue generating power internally?

b. Prepare an analysis for management to indicate the costs of the company's own electric generating operations. (Use the step method.)

c. Would your answer in *(b)* change if the company could realize $29,000 per year from the sale of the natural gas now used for electric generating? (Assume no selling costs.)

5–26. Cost Allocations Simultaneous Solution (computer required)

If O-Hi-O Corporation, problem 5–25, above, used the simultaneous solution method for cost allocation, what would the company's estimated cost savings (or loss) be if it were to acquire electricity from the outside and sell natural gas for a net realization from the gas sales of $29,000 per year? Use a spreadsheet program to solve the system of simultaneous linear equations.

5–27. Job Costing with Service Department Cost Allocations

WX Service Company operates a job shop with two producing departments: Department A and Department B. Jobs are started in Department A and then moved to Department B. When the work is finished in Department B, the jobs are immediately sold. The company also has two service Departments, W and X, which perform support services for the producing departments. In addition, Departments W and X perform services for each other.

Overhead in Department A is applied to jobs on the basis of prime costs (that is, total direct materials and direct labor). Overhead in Department B is applied on the basis of machine-hours. For this period, the estimated overhead and estimated activity levels for applying overhead were as follows:

Department A:	Estimated overhead	$66,000
	Estimated prime costs	44,000
Department B:	Estimated overhead	33,000
	Estimated machine-hours	30,000

During the month, direct materials and direct labor costs were incurred on jobs as follows:

	Job No. 22	Job No. 28	Job No. 36
Department A:			
Prime costs	$26,000	$13,200	$8,200
Department B:			
Direct materials	16,350	7,100	900
Direct labor	16,000	18,000	-0-
Machine-hours	12,000	18,000	-0-

The balances of other departmental costs in the accounts for the service and producing departments (before allocation of service department costs) are as follows:

Department W	$11,300
Department X	14,000
Department A	46,300
Department B	21,500

The use of services by other departments was as follows:

	Used by:			
Services of:	W	X	A	B
W	—	20%	30%	50%
X	40%	—	45	15

The company uses the step method for service cost allocation. Jobs No. 22 and No. 28 were completed during the period and were sold. Job No. 36 is in department B.

a. What was the current period cost on Job Nos. 22 and 28 that was transferred to cost of goods sold?

b. If actual overhead had been charged to Job No. 28, what amount of current period costs would have been transferred to cost of goods sold for that job?

5–28. Cost Allocation and Decision Making

The promotion department of the Doxolby Company is reponsible for the design and development of all marketing campaign materials and related literature, pamphlets, and brochures. Management is reviewing the effectiveness of the promotion department to determine if the department's services could be acquired more economically from an outside promotion agency. Management has asked for a summary of the promotion department's costs for the most recent year. The following cost summary was supplied:

PROMOTION DEPARTMENT
Costs for the Year Ended November 30

Direct department costs	$257,500
Charges from other departments	44,700
Allocated share of general administrative overhead	22,250
Total costs	$324,450

Direct department costs are those that can be traced directly to the activities of the promotion department, such as staff and clerical salaries, including related employee benefits, supplies, etc. Charges from other departments represent the costs of services that are provided by other departments of Doxolby at the request of the promotion department. The company has developed a charging system for such interdepartmental uses of services. For instance, the in-house printing department charges the promotion department for the promotional literature printed. All such services provided to the promotion department by other departments of Doxolby are included in the "Charges from Other Departments." General administrative overhead is composed of such costs as executive salaries and benefits, depreciation, heat, insurance, property taxes, etc. These costs are allocated to all departments in proportion to the number of employees in each department.

Required:

Discuss the usefulness of the cost figures as presented for the promotion department of Doxolby, Inc., as a basis for comparison with a bid from an outside agency to provide the same type of activities as Doxolby's own promotion department.

(CMA adapted)

5–29. Allocate Service Department Costs—Direct and Step Methods

Parker Manufacturing Company has three service departments (general factory administration, factory maintenance, and factory cafeteria), and two production departments (fabrication and assembly). A summary of costs and other data for each department prior to allocation of service department costs for the year ended June 30 are as follows:

	General Factory Administration	Factory Maintenance	Factory Cafeteria	Fabrication	Assembly
Direct material costs	–0–	$ 65,000	$ 91,000	$3,130,000	$ 950,000
Direct labor costs	$ 90,000	82,100	87,000	1,950,000	2,050,000
Manufacturing overhead costs	70,000	56,100	62,000	1,650,000	1,850,000
	$160,000	$203,200	$240,000	$6,730,000	$4,850,000
Direct labor-hours	31,000	27,000	42,000	562,500	437,500
Number of employees	12	8	20	280	200
Square footage occupied	1,750	2,000	4,800	88,000	72,000

The costs of the service departments are allocated on the following bases: general factory administration department, direct labor-hours; factory maintenance department, square footage occupied; and factory cafeteria, number of employees.

Required:

Round all final calculations to the nearest dollar.

a. Assume that Parker elects to distribute service department costs directly to production departments using the direct method. The amount of factory maintenance department costs allocated to the fabrication department would be:
1. $0.
2. $111,760.
3. $106,091.
4. $91,440.
5. None of the above.

b. Assume the same method of allocation as in (a). The amount of general factory administration department costs allocated to the assembly department would be:
1. $0.
2. $63,636.
3. $70,000.
4. $90,000.
5. None of the above.

c. Assume that Parker elects to distribute service department costs to other departments using the step method (starting with factory cafeteria, then factory maintenance), the amount of factory cafeteria department costs allocated to the factory maintenance department would be:
1. $0.
2. $96,000.
3. $3,840.
4. $6,124.
5. None of the above.

d. Assume the same method of allocation as in (c). The amount of factory maintenance department costs allocated to the factory cafeteria would be:
1. $0.
2. $5,787.
3. $5,856.
4. $148,910.
5. None of the above.

(CPA adapted)

5–30. Plantwide versus Departmental Overhead Rates

MumsDay Corporation manufactures a complete line of fiberglass attache cases and suitcases. MumsDay has three manufacturing departments—molding, component, and assembly—and two service departments—power and maintenance.

The sides of the cases are manufactured in the molding department. The frames, hinges, locks, etc., are manufactured in the component department. The cases are completed in the assembly department. Varying amounts of materials, time, and effort are required for each of the various cases. The power department and maintenance department provide services to the three manufacturing departments.

MumsDay has always used a plantwide overhead rate. Direct labor-hours are used to assign the overhead to its product. The predetermined rate is calculated by dividing the company's total estimated overhead by the total estimated direct labor-hours to be worked in the three manufacturing departments.

Whit Portlock, manager of Cost Accounting, has recommended that MumsDay use departmental overhead rates. The planned operating costs and expected levels of activity for the coming year have been developed by Portlock and are presented by department in the following schedules (000 omitted).

	Manufacturing Departments		
	Molding	**Component**	**Assembly**
Departmental activity measures:			
Direct labor-hours	500	2,000	1,500
Machine-hours	875	125	–0–
Departmental costs:			
Raw materials	$12,400	$30,000	$ 1,250
Direct labor	3,500	20,000	12,000
Variable overhead	3,500	10,000	16,500
Fixed overhead	17,500	6,200	6,100
Total departmental costs	$36,900	$66,200	$35,850
Use of service departments:			
Maintenance:			
Estimated usage in labor-hours for coming year	90	25	10
Power (in kilowatt-hours):			
Estimated usage for coming year	360	320	120
Maximum allotted capacity	500	350	150

	Service Departments	
	Power	**Maintenance**
Departmental activity measures:		
Maximum capacity	1,000 kwhr.	Adjustable
Estimated usage in coming year	800 kwhr.	125 hours
Departmental costs:		
Materials and supplies	$ 5,000	$1,500
Variable labor	1,400	2,250
Fixed overhead	12,000	250
Total service department costs	$18,400	$4,000

Required:

a. Calculate the plantwide overhead rate for MumsDay Corporation for the coming year, using the same method as used in the past.

b. Whit Portlock has been asked to develop departmental overhead rates for comparison with the plantwide rate. The following steps are to be followed in developing the departmental rates.

1. The maintenance department costs should be allocated to the three manufacturing departments, using the direct method.

2. The power department costs should be allocated to the three manufacturing departments as follows: the fixed costs allocated according to long-term capacity and the variable costs according to planned usage.

3. Calculate departmental overhead rates for the three manufacturing departments using a machine-hour base for the molding department and a direct labor-hour base for the component and assembly departments.

c. Should MumsDay Corporation use a plantwide rate or departmental rates to assign overhead to its products? Explain your answer.

(CMA adapted)

5–31. Allocate Service Department Costs Using Direct and Simultaneous Solution Methods

(Note: Matrix algebra is not required for this problem. An algebraic equation can be set up for the costs of each of the two service departments and solved by substitution.)

Barrylou Corporation is developing departmental overhead rates based upon direct labor-hours for its two production departments—molding and assembly. The molding department employs 20 people, and the assembly department employs 80 people. Each person in these two departments works 2,000 hours per year. The production-related overhead costs for the molding department are budgeted at $200,000, and the assembly department costs are budgeted at $320,000. Two service departments—repair and power—directly support the two production departments and have budgeted costs of $48,000 and $250,000, respectively. The production departments' overhead rates cannot be determined until the service departments' costs are properly allocated. The following schedule reflects the use of the repair department's and power department's output by the various departments.

	Department			
	Repair	**Power**	**Molding**	**Assembly**
Repair hours	0	1,000	1,000	8,000
Kilowatt-hours	240,000	0	840,000	120,000

Required:

a. Calculate the overhead rates per direct labor-hour for the molding department and the assembly department using the direct allocation method to charge the production departments for service department costs.

b. Calculate the overhead rates per direct labor-hour for the molding department and the assembly department using the simultaneous solution method to charge service department costs to each other and to the production departments.

(CMA adapted)

5–32. Simultaneous Solution (computer required)

Tonto Electronics manufactures circuit boards through a four-step process. In the first department, the boards are washed in a chemical bath to prepare them for the etching department. After etching, the boards are dried and inspected in a third department. Completed boards that meet standards are sent to the packing department where automated equipment prepares them for shipment. Service activities are carried out in three departments: Power, Computer Support, and Engineering.

A schedule of the current period costs together with the use of different service units by all departments is as follows:

Item	Power	Computer Support	Engineering	
Direct costs	$582,400	$135,600	$391,650	
Service usage:				
Kwhr. of power	0	2,500	1,500	
Computer units	120	0	580	
Engineer's time	160	650	0	
Item	**Washing**	**Etching**	**Drying**	**Packing**
Direct costs	$795,000	$1,286,500	$935,800	$645,000
Service usage:				
Kwhr. of power	35,000	80,000	145,200	68,000
Computer units	1,700	12,600	980	2,390
Engineer's time	220	800	310	180

Power costs are allocated using kwhr. of power consumed. Computer services are allocated based on units of computer usage. Engineering department costs are charged using engineers' time spent in each activity.

Required:

Use a spreadsheet program to compute the total costs of each producing department using the simultaneous solution method for cost allocation.

5–33. Sensitivity to Cost Allocations (computer required)

The Packing Department of Tonto Electronics (Problem 5–32, above) discovered that it could purchase a new computer to control its operations. If it acquires this computer, the direct costs of the Computer Service Department will decrease by 10 percent. The Packing Department will incur a period cost of $10,000 for the new system. No other service usages or total costs will change.

Required:

a. What is the reduction in costs charged to the Packing Department if the new computer is acquired?

b. Are there any other changes in costs charged to other producing departments as a result of the Packing Department's acquisition of the new computer?

c. If there are changes in costs charged to other producing departments, how would you explain these changes since the problem specified that no other costs would change?

5–34. Cost Allocations (computer required)

Save the Students, Inc., is an international foundation organized to help students survive final exams through study support, tutorial services, and around-the-clock food and coffee services. These student services are viewed as production departments for cost allocation purposes. The foundation needs to determine the costs of each service to provide information for its new fund-raising drive. The manager of the foundation believes that the service costs should include not only the direct costs of services but the costs of the necessary supporting activities.

The foundation has an administration, fund raising, and communications network which acts as service departments. These service departments provide services to each other as well as to the "producing" departments.

A schedule of the direct costs of each activity together with relevant information for allocation purposes gives the following information:

Item	Study Support	Tutorial Services	Food and Coffee
Direct costs	$2,480,000	$1,525,000	$2,090,700
Service usage:			
Labor-hours	38,400	52,600	21,960
Office salaries	2,210	3,150	1,130

Item	Administration	Fund Raising	Communications
Direct costs	$576,100	$1,421,400	$285,100
Service usage:			
Labor-hours	17,300	38,750	5,840
Office salaries	6,440	2,970	1,860

Administration costs are allocated based on labor-hours. Fund raising costs are allocated based on the direct costs of each department. Communications costs are incurred to support office personnel in each department, so the office salaries are used for allocation of those costs.

Required:

What are the costs of each of the student support services provided by STSF using the simultaneous solution method for allocation of service department costs?

INTEGRATIVE CASES

5-35. Issues in Cost Allocations: What Price Progress[7]

In discussing the cost of operations, the analogy was drawn of the restaurateur who adds a rack of peanuts to the counter, intending to pick up a little additional profit in the usual course of business. His accountant-efficiency expert has some unpleasant news for him.

Expert: Joe, you said you put in these peanuts because some people ask for them, but do you realize what this rack of peanuts is *costing* you?

Joe: It's not going to cost! It's going to be a profit. Sure, I had to pay $100 for a fancy rack to hold the bags, but the peanuts cost 24 cents a bag and I sell 'em for 40 cents. Suppose I sell 50 bags a week to start. It'll take 12½ weeks to cover the cost of the rack. After that I have a clear profit of 16 cents a bag. The more I sell, the more I make.

Expert: That is an antiquated and completely unrealistic approach, Joe. Fortunately, modern accounting procedures permit a more accurate picture, which reveals the complexities involved.

Joe: Huh?

Expert: To be precise, those peanuts must be integrated into your entire operation and be allocated their appropriate share of business overhead. They must share a proportionate part of your expenditures for rent, heat, light, equipment depreciation, decorating, salaries for your waitresses, cook, . . .

Joe: The *cook?* What's he got to do with the peanuts? He doesn't even know I have them.

Expert: Look, Joe, the cook is in the kitchen, the kitchen prepares the food, the food is what brings people in here, and the people ask to buy peanuts. *That's* why you must charge a portion of the cook's wages, as well as a part of your own salary, to peanut sales. This sheet contains a carefully calculated cost analysis, which indicates the peanut operation should pay exactly $2,278 per year toward these general overhead costs.

Joe: The peanuts? $2,278 a year for overhead? Nuts!

Expert: It's really a little more than that. You also spend money each week to have the windows washed, to have the place swept out in the mornings, to keep soap in the washroom, and to provide free cokes to the police. That raises the total to $3,313 per year.

Joe: [*Thoughtfully*] But the peanuts salesman said I'd make money—put 'em on the end of the counter, he said—and get 16 cents a bag profit.

Expert: [*With a sniff*] He's not an accountant. Do you actually know what the portion of the counter occupied by the peanut rack is worth to you?

Joe: Nothing. No stool there—just a dead spot at the end.

Expert: The modern cost picture permits no dead spots. Your counter contains 60 square feet, and your counter business grosses $60,000 a year. Consequently, the square foot of space occupied by the peanut rack is worth $1,000 per year. Since you have taken that area away from general counter use, you must charge the value of the space to the occupant.

Joe: You mean I have to add *$1,000 a year more to the peanuts?*

Expert: Right. That raises their share of the general operating costs to a grand total of $4,313 per year. Now then, if you sell 50 bags of peanuts per week, these allocated costs will amount to $1.65 per bag.

Joe: WHAT?

---

[7] This piece appeared in a publication by Coopers and Lybrand as a reprint. The author is unknown to us.

Expert: Obviously, to that must be added your purchase price of 24 cents per bag, which brings the total to $1.89 cents. So you see, by selling peanuts at 40 cents per bag, you are losing $1.49 cents on every sale.

Joe: Something's crazy!

Expert: Not at all! Here are the *figures.* They *prove* your peanut operation cannot stand on its own feet.

Joe: [*Brightening*] Suppose I sell *lots* of peanuts—1,000 bags a week instead of 50?

Expert: [*Tolerantly*] Joe, you don't understand the problem. If the volume of peanut sales increases, your operating costs will go up—you'll have to handle more bags, with more time, more depreciation, more everything. The basic principle of accounting is firm on that subject: *The bigger the operation, the more general overhead costs that must be allocated.* No, increasing the volume of sales won't help.

Joe: Okay. You're so smart, *you* tell *me* what I have to do!

Expert: [*Condescendingly*] Well—you could first reduce operating expenses.

Joe: How?

Expert: Move to a building with cheaper rent. Cut salaries. Wash the windows biweekly. Have the floor swept only on Thursday. Remove the soap from the washrooms. Decrease the square-foot value of your counter. For example, if you can cut your expenses 50 percent, that will reduce the amount allocated to peanuts from $4,313 down to $2,157 per year, reducing the cost to $1.07 per bag.

Joe: [*Slowly*] That's better?

Expert: Much, much better. However, even then you would lose 67 cents per bag if you charge only 40 cents. Therefore, you must also raise your selling price. If you want a net profit of 16 cents per bag, you would have to charge $1.23.

Joe: [*Flabbergasted*] You mean even after I cut operating costs 50 percent, I still have to charge $1.23 for a 40-cent bag of peanuts? Nobody's that nuts about nuts! Who'd buy them?

Expert: That's a secondary consideration. The point is, at $1.23 you'd be selling at a price based on a true and proper evaluation of your then-reduced costs.

Joe: [*Eagerly*] Look! I have a better idea. Why don't I just throw the nuts out—put them in a trash can?

Expert: Can you afford it?

Joe: Sure. All I have is about 50 bags of peanuts—cost about 12 bucks—so I lose $100 on the rack, but I'm out of this nutsy business and no more grief.

Expert: [*Shaking head*] Joe, it isn't quite that simple. You are *in* the peanut business! The minute you throw those peanuts out, you are adding $4,313 of annual overhead to the *rest* of your operation. Joe—be realistic—*can you afford to do that?*

Joe: [*Completely crushed*] It's unbelievable! Last week I was making money. Now I'm in trouble—just because I believe 50 bags of peanuts a week is easy.

Expert: [*With raised eyebrow*] That is the object of modern cost studies, Joe—to dispel those false illusions.

Required:

What should Joe do?

5–36. (Appendix) Cost Allocation and Analysis of Applied Overhead

White Paper Packaging Corporation prepares cardboard cartons according to customer orders. The company uses a job cost system because the orders are sufficiently different from one customer to another. The company has two producing departments: printing and folding. Box cardboard is received in the printing department. There it is cut to the appropriate size and imprinted with the customer's specified advertising or other information. Printed cardboard is transported to the folding department where special equipment folds and glues the boxes. When the boxes are completed, they are delivered to the warehouse for shipment to customers. Normally, boxes are considered finished when they are ready for shipment to the customer.

The producing departments are serviced by three service areas: materials handling, payroll accounting, and building occupancy. Materials-handling costs are allocated based on direct materials used by each department. Payroll accounting costs are allocated based on total employees in each department, while dual allocation rates are used for building occupancy costs. The fixed building costs are allocated on the basis of department area, while the variable costs are allocated on the basis of labor costs.

During the current month, the following information is available concerning the direct costs and the use of various allocation bases by each of the departments.

Department	Direct Costs	Building Area	Labor Costs	Number of Employees
Materials handling (S1)	$245,000	.25	.10	.08
Payroll accounting (S4)	90,000	.10	.07	—
Building occupancy:				
Fixed costs (S2)	128,000	—	.05	.07
Variable costs (S3)	49,000	.05	—	.03
Printing (P1):				
Direct materials	975,000			
Direct labor	430,000			
Overhead	650,000	.25	.35	.37
Folding (P2):				
Direct materials	65,000			
Direct labor	480,000	.35	.43	.45
Overhead	615,000			

Overhead is applied to production on the basis of 200 percent of direct labor costs in the departments. In printing, 30 percent of the direct overhead was fixed, while in folding, 80 percent of the direct overhead was fixed. Materials-handling costs are considered variable, and payroll accounting costs are considered fixed for analytic purposes.

Estimated labor costs for the period were $575,000 in printing and $450,000 in folding. While the allocated fixed costs were as anticipated, budgeted fixed costs in the printing department were $195,000, and in folding the costs were budgeted at $396,000.

Required:

Determine the applied overhead in each of the producing departments. The first two rows of the matrix A^{-1} are as follows:

	P1	P2	S1	S2	S3	S4
	1	0	.938	.560	.507	.499
	0	1	.062	.440	.493	.501

5–37. Patient's Hospital (Cost Allocation, Step Method)[8]

The annual costs of hospital care under the medicare program amount to $20 billion per year. In the medicare legislation, Congress mandated that reimbursement to hospitals be limited to the costs of treating medicare patients. Ideally, neither nonmedicare patients nor hospitals would bear the costs of medicare patients nor

---

[8] © 1982 by CIPT Co.

would the government bear costs of nonmedicare patients. Given the large sums involved, it is not surprising that cost reimbursement specialists, computer programs, publications, and other products and services have arisen to provide hospital administrators with the assistance needed to obtain an appropriate reimbursement for medicare patient services.

Hospital departments may be divided into two categories: (1) revenue-producing departments and (2) nonrevenue-producing departments. This classification is simple but useful. The traditional accounting concepts associated with "service department cost allocation," while appropriate to this context, lead to a great deal of confusion in terminology since all of the hospital's departments are considered to be rendering services.

Costs of revenue-producing departments are charged to medicare and nonmedicare patients on the basis of actual use of the departments. These costs are relatively simple to apportion. Costs of nonrevenue-producing departments are somewhat more difficult to apportion. The approach to finding the appropriate distribution of these costs begins with the establishment of a reasonable basis for allocating nonrevenue-producing department costs to revenue-producing departments. Statistical measures of the relationships between departments must be ascertained. The cost allocation bases listed in Exhibit A were established as acceptable for cost reimbursement purposes. The regulated order of allocation must be used for medicare reimbursement.

A hospital may then use either a simultaneous solution method to the cost allocation problem, or they may use the step method. If the step method is used, the order of departments for allocation is the same order as that by which the departments are listed in Exhibit A. Thus, depreciation of buildings is allocated before depreciation of movable equipment. Cost centers must be established for each of these nonrevenue-producing costs that are relevant to a particular hospital's operations.

Exhibit A 5-37   **Bases for Allocating Nonrevenue Department Costs to Revenue-Producing Departments**

Nonrevenue Cost Center	Basis for Allocation
Depreciation—buildings	Square feet in each department
Depreciation—movable equipment	Dollar value of equipment in each department
Employee health and welfare	Gross salaries in each department
Administrative and general	Accumulated costs by department
Maintenance and repairs	Square feet in each department
Operation of plant	Square feet in each department
Laundry and linen service	Pounds used in each department
Housekeeping	Hours of service to each department
Dietary	Meals served in each department
Maintenance of personnel	Number of departmental employees housed
Nursing administration	Hours of supervision in each department
Central supply	Costs of requisitions processed
Pharmacy	Costs of drug orders processed
Medical records	Hours worked for each department
Social service	Hours worked for each department
Nursing school	Assigned time by department
Intern/resident service	Assigned time by department

In the past year, the hospital reported the following departmental costs:

Nonrevenue-producing:	
Laundry and linen	$ 250,000
Depreciation—buildings	830,000
Employee health and welfare	375,000
Maintenance of personnel	210,000
Central supply	745,000
Revenue-producing:	
Operating room	1,450,000
Radiology	160,000
Laboratory	125,000
Patient rooms	2,800,000

Percentage usage of services by one department from another department were as follows:

From	Laundry and Linen	Depre-ciation—Buildings	Employee Health and Welfare	Mainte-nance of Personnel	Central Supply
Laundry and linen	—	.05	.10	—	—
Depreciation—buildings	.10	—	—	.10	—
Employee health and welfare	.15	—	—	.05	.03
Maintenance of personnel	—	—	—	—	.12
Central supply	.10	—	—	.08	—

	Operating Rooms	Radiology	Laboratory	Patient Rooms
Laundry and linen	.30	.10	.05	.40
Depreciation—buildings	.05	.02	.02	.71
Employee health and welfare	.25	.05	.04	.43
Maintenance of personnel	.36	.10	.08	.34
Central supply	.09	.04	.03	.66

The proportional use of revenue-producing department services by medicare and other patients was as follows:

	Medicare	Other
Operating rooms	25%	75%
Radiology	20	80
Laboratory	28	72
Patient rooms	36	64

Required:

What is the amount of the reimbursement claim for medicare services, using the step method of allocation?

5–38. (Appendix) Patient's Hospital—Simultaneous Solution Method (computer required)

Refer to the facts in case 5–37. What is the claim for medicare services, using the simultaneous solution method?

ALLOCATING JOINT COSTS

LEARNING OBJECTIVES

1. Ability to allocate joint costs based on the net realizable method of joint cost allocation.

2. Knowing the physical quantities method of joint cost allocation.

3. Being able to account for by-products.

4. Seeing how cost data are used in the sell-or-process-further decision.

5. Understanding the replacement method of joint cost allocation. (Appendix)

Joint Cost A cost of a manufacturing process in which two or more outputs come from the process.

Joint Products Outputs from a common input and common production process.

Split-Off Point Stage of processing where two or more products are separated.

A **joint cost** occurs when a single process contributes to the production of several different outputs. For example, logs may produce lumber and chipboard. The cost of the logs is a joint cost of these two **joint products**. The problem in such cases is whether and how to allocate the joint cost of the input (for example, the logs) to the multiple outputs (for example, lumber and chipboard).

For example, Illustration 6–1 diagrams the flow of costs incurred to process logs by the Sacramento-Sierra Company. These costs include direct materials, direct labor, and manufacturing overhead. As the logs are processed, two products emerge: lumber and chipboard. The stage of processing where the two products are separated is called the **split-off point**. Costs incurred in processing prior to the split-off point are called joint costs. This chapter shows how those joint costs can be allocated to products.

WHY ALLOCATE JOINT COSTS?

Joint costs are allocated for many reasons. A major reason in manufacturing companies is that joint costs must be allocated to value inventory and compute the costs of goods for external financial reporting under generally accepted accounting principles (GAAP). But there are many other reasons, too.

Joint cost allocations are useful in valuing inventory for insurance purposes. Should a casualty loss occur, the insurance company and the insured must agree on the value of the lost goods. One factor to be considered in arriving at a settlement is the cost of the material destroyed. If joint products are destroyed, material and process costs must be divided between the goods destroyed and those not destroyed.

Cost allocations can also be helpful in pricing cost of goods sold for measuring executive performance. Many companies compensate executives and other employees, at least partly, on the basis of departmental or division earnings for the year. When a single raw material is converted into products sold by two or more departments, the cost of the raw material must be allocated to the products concerned.

When companies are subject to rate regulation, the allocation of joint costs can be a significant factor in determining the regulated rates. Crude oil and natural gas are usually produced out of a common well. In recent years,

Illustration 6-1   **Diagram of Joint Cost Flows**

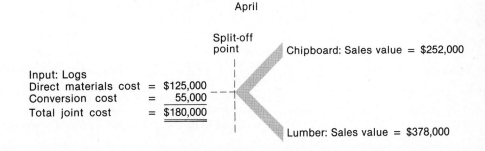

SACRAMENTO-SIERRA COMPANY

April

Input: Logs
Direct materials cost = $125,000
Conversion cost   =   55,000
Total joint cost   = $180,000

Split-off point

Chipboard: Sales value = $252,000

Lumber: Sales value = $378,000

energy price policies and gas utility rates were based in part on the allocation of the joint costs of crude oil and natural gas.

In each of these cases, opposing interests are involved. For example, neither the insurance company nor the insured wishes to pay more or receive less than is fair. Executives and employees will object to a cost of goods sold figure that they feel is overstated against them and understated for another department. Buyers and sellers of regulated products or services are both affected by pricing, and neither wishes to give the other an advantage. When the allocation of costs can impinge on the financial fortunes of opposing parties, both sides review the allocation method critically.

Of course, any cost allocation method contains an element of arbitrariness. No allocation method can be beyond dispute. Consequently, methods of allocation must be clearly stated before they are implemented.

JOINT COST ALLOCATION METHODS

There are two major methods of allocating joint costs: (1) the **net realizable value method** and (2) the **physical quantities method**. A third method, the **replacement method**, is discussed in the appendix to the chapter.

Net Realizable Value Method

Net Realizable Value Method Joint cost allocation based on the proportional values of the joint products at the split-off point.

Using the **net realizable value method** (also known as the *relative sales value method*), joint costs are allocated based on the net realizable value of each product at the split-off point. The net realizable value is the estimated sales value of each product at the split-off point. If the joint products can be sold at the split-off point, the market value or sales price may be used for this allocation. However, if the products require further processing before they are marketable, then it is necessary to estimate the net realizable value at the split-off point. This approach is sometimes referred to as the netback or workback method. Normally, when a market value is available at the split-off point, it is preferable to use that value rather than the netback method. The *net realizable value* at the split-off point is estimated by taking the sales value after further processing and deducting those added processing costs. Joint costs are then allocated to the products in proportion to their net realizable values at the split-off point.

Illustration 6-2   **Gross Margin Computations Using Net Realizable Value Method**

SACRAMENTO-SIERRA COMPANY
April

Item	Chipboard	Lumber	Total
Sales value	$252,000	$378,000	$630,000
Less allocated joint costs	72,000	108,000	180,000
Gross margin	$180,000	$270,000	$450,000
Gross margin as a percent of sales	71.43[a]	71.43[a]	71.43[a]

[a] 71.43 = $180,000 ÷ $252,000 = $270,000 ÷ $378,000 = $450,000 ÷ 630,000

For example, the Sacramento-Sierra Company produces lumber and chipboards. Direct materials (that is, logs) cost $125,000, and conversion costs are $55,000, for a total of $180,000 in April. Lumber and chipboard have a total sales value of $630,000 at the split-off point. Chipboard has sales value of $252,000 or 40 percent of the total, while lumber's value is $378,000, or 60 percent of the total. (We assume there is no additional processing required after the split-off point to make lumber and chipboard for purposes of this example.)

The cost allocation would follow the proportional distribution of net realizable values:

To chipboard:
$$\left[\frac{\$252,000}{\$630,000}\right] \times \$180,000 = \$\ 72,000$$

To lumber:
$$\left[\frac{\$378,000}{\$630,000}\right] \times \$180,000 = \underline{\ \ 108,000}$$
$$\underline{\underline{\$180,000}}$$

A condensed statement of margins at the split-off point is shown in Illustration 6–2.

Note that the margins as a percentage of sales are 71.43 percent for *both* products. This demonstrates an important concept of the net realizable value method—namely, that revenue dollars from any joint product are assumed to make the same percentage contribution at the split-off point as the revenue dollars from any other joint product. This approach implies a matching of input costs with revenues generated by each output.

Illustration 6–3 shows the flow of these allocated costs through T-accounts. Note that logs are materials held in direct materials inventory until they are allocated to work in process inventory.

Illustration 6-3   **Flow of Costs Using Net Realizable Value Method**

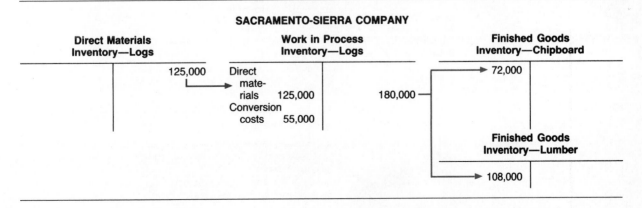

Estimating Net Realizable Value when Further Processing Is Required

Estimated Net Realizable Value Sales price of final product minus additional processing costs necessary to prepare a product for sale.

Not all joint products can be sold at the split-off point. Further processing may be required before the product is marketable. When no sales values exist for the outputs at the split-off point, the *net realizable values* must be estimated by taking the sales value of each product at the first point at which it can be marketed and deducting the processing costs that must be incurred to get there from the split-off point. This process is often referred to as "working back" to a value at a point in a process. The resulting **estimated net realizable value** is used for joint cost allocation in the same way as an actual market value at the split-off point.

Suppose the management of Sacramento-Sierra finds the market for chipboard has changed such that it can no longer sell plain chipboard, but it can sell laminated chipboard. Additional processing to laminate the chipboard costs $98,000 before it can be marketed for (only) $260,000. Lumber can still be marketed at the split-off point for $378,000. Illustration 6–4 diagrams the process.

Illustration 6–5 shows the allocation of the $180,000 joint cost to laminated chipboard and lumber if the laminated chipboard is manufactured.

Physical Quantities Method

The **physical quantities method** is often used when output product prices are highly volatile, when much processing occurs between the split-off point and the first point of marketability, or when product prices are not available. This latter situation may arise in regulated pricing situations or in cost-based contract situations.

Illustration 6–4   **Flow of Costs—Further Processing beyond Split-Off Point**

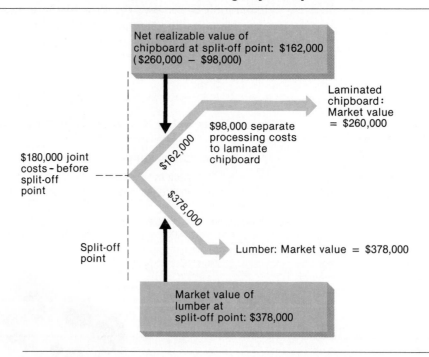

Illustration 6-5   **Net Realizable Value Method Using Estimated Net Realizable Value for Laminated Chipboard**

SACRAMENTO-SIERRA COMPANY

Item	Laminated Chipboard	Lumber	Total
Sales value	$260,000	$378,000	$638,000
Less additional process costs to point of marketability	98,000	–0–	98,000
Estimated net realizable value at split-off point	162,000	378,000	540,000
Allocation of joint costs:			
$\left[\dfrac{\$162,000}{\$540,000}\right] \times \$180,000$	54,000		
			180,000
$\left[\dfrac{\$378,000}{\$540,000}\right] \times \$180,000$		126,000	
Margin	$108,000	$252,000	$360,000
Margin as a percent of estimated net realizable value at split-off	66.67	66.67	66.67

Illustration 6-6   **Physical Quantities Method**

SACRAMENTO-SIERRA COMPANY
April

Item	Chipboard	Lumber	Total
Output quantities	1,400 units	1,960 units	3,360 units
Joint allocation:			
$\left[\dfrac{1,400}{3,360}\right] \times \$180,000$	$75,000		
$\left[\dfrac{1,960}{3,360}\right] \times \$180,000$		$105,000	$180,000

Physical Quantities Method   Joint cost allocation based on measurement of the volume, weight, or other physical measure of the joint products at the split-off point.

With the physical quantities method, joint costs assigned to products are based on a physical measure. This might be volume, weight, or any other common measure of physical characterisitics. Many companies allocate joint costs incurred in producing oil and gas on the basis of energy equivalent (BTU content). They use this method because, while oil and gas are often produced simultaneously from the same well, the products are typically measured in different physical units [gas by thousand cubic feet (mcf.), oil by barrel]. Moreover, the price of most gas is regulated so that relative market vaues are artificial. However, the common measure of quantity and the perceived value of the products is the relative energy content.

For example, assume that relative market values at the split-off point are not available at Sacramento-Sierra Company and that for every $180,000 of joint costs in processing logs we obtain 1,400 units of chipboard and 1,960 units of lumber. The allocation of joint costs using these physical quantity measures is shown in Illustration 6-6.

As long as the physical measures reflect economic values, this method of assigning costs may provide a reasonable basis for joint cost allocation.

However, there are many cases where an allocation based on physical quantities would not accurately reflect economic values. For example, gold is often found in copper deposits. The physical quantities of gold may be small, yet their value may be significant. If the joint costs of mining the ore that contains the gold and copper were to be allocated to the output products on the basis of weight, the resulting product costs would not reflect a matching of costs with economic values.

Comments on Joint Cost Allocation Methods

Due to the nature of joint production processes, it is not possible to separate the portion of joint costs attributable to one product or another on any direct-charge basis. As a result, if allocated joint costs are used for decision-making purposes, they should be used only with full recognition of their limitations. As long as the method used for allocation reasonably reflects the relative economic benefits obtained from the jointly produced outputs, the method is usually considered acceptable for financial reporting purposes, for cost-based regulation, and for contracts based on costs (for example, to compute executive bonuses).

SELL-OR-PROCESS-FURTHER DECISIONS

Many companies have opportunities to sell partly processed products at various stages of production. Management must decide whether it is more profitable to sell the output at an intermediate stage or to process it further. In such a sell-or-process-further decision, the relevant data to be considered are (1) the additional revenue after further processing and (2) the additional costs of processing further.

Suppose Sacramento-Sierra Company can sell chipboard for $252,000 at the split-off point or process it further to make a new product, reinforced chipboard. The additional processing costs are $20,000, and the revenue from reinforced chipboard would be $290,000. Should the company sell chipboard or process it further? As indicated in earlier examples, the revenue from lumber is $378,000, and the joint cost of processing logs is $180,000.

Illustration 6-7   **Income Statements for Sell-or-Process-Further Decisions**

Item	Sell	Process Further	Additional Revenue and Costs from Processing Further
Revenues:			
From chipboard	$252,000	$290,000	$38,000
From lumber	378,000	378,000	—
Total revenues	630,000	668,000	38,000
Less costs:			
Joint costs	(180,000)	(180,000)	—
Separate processing of chipboard	–0–	(20,000)	(20,000)
Margin	$450,000	$468,000	$18,000 net gain from processing further

As shown in Illustration 6–7, the profit will be greater by $18,000 if chipboard is processed further. It is important to note that the allocation of the joint costs between chipboard and lumber is irrelevant. The $38,000 additional revenue from processing beyond the split-off point justified the expenditure of $20,000 for additional processing, regardless of the way joint costs are allocated. *The only costs and revenues that are relevant to the decision are those that are changed by it.* These are examples of differential costs and revenues.

ACCOUNTING FOR BY-PRODUCTS

By-Products Outputs of joint production processes that are relatively minor in quantity or value.

By-products are outputs from a joint production process that are relatively minor in quantity and/or value when compared to the main products. For example, sawdust and wood chips are by-products of lumber production, and kerosene is a by-product of gasoline production. You may have seen advertisements for carpet and cloth mill ends at low prices. These are often by-products of textile production.

The usual objective of by-product accounting is to reflect the economic relationship between the by-products and the main products with a minimum of record keeping for inventory valuation purposes. Two common methods of accounting for by-products are:

Method 1:   The net realizable value from sale of the by-products is deducted from the cost of the main product.

Method 2:   The proceeds from sale of the by-product are treated as other income.

Assume that By-Product Company has a production process that yields output C as the main product and output D as the by-product, all of which

Illustration 6–8   **Accounting for By-Products**

BY-PRODUCT COMPANY

	Acounting Method[a]	
	(1)	**(2)**
Sales revenue from output C	$200,000	$200,000
Other income	–0–	800[b]
Total revenue	200,000	200,800
Cost of sales: Total production costs	80,000	80,000
Less by-product: Net realizable value	800[b]	–0–
Adjusted cost of sales	79,200	80,000
Gross margin	$120,800	$120,800

[a] Description of accounting methods:
  1. The net realizable value of the by-product is deducted from the cost of the main product.
  2. The net realizable value from the sale of the by-product is treated as other income.

[b] $800 is the net realizable value of the by-product ($1,100 selling price minus $300 separate costs to process the by-product).

Illustration 6-9   Accounting for By-Products

BY-PRODUCT COMPANY
Flow of costs[a]

Work in Process Inventory

Joint costs of processing (1)	80,000	(5)	79,200
		(4)	800

Separable By-Product Costs

(2)	300	(4)	300

Finished Goods Inventory

(5)	79,200	(6)	79,200

Cost of Goods Sold

(6)	79,200

By-Product Revenue

(4)	1,100	(3)	1,100

[a] Cost flows are shown using method 1 in the text. According to this method, the net realizable value of the by-product is deducted from the product costs of the main product.

Journal entries:

(1)	Work in Process Inventory	80,000	
	Direct Materials Inventory*		
	Wages Payable: Direct Labor*		80,000
	Manufacturing Overhead*		
	* Credit to these accounts assumed for illustrative purposes.		
(2)	Separable By-Product Costs	300	
	Direct Labor*		
	Manufacturing Overhead*		300
	* Credit to these accounts assumed for illustrative purposes.		
(3)	Accounts Receivable*	1,100	
	By-Product Revenue		1,100
	* Debit to this account assumed for illustrative purposes.		
(4)	By-Product Revenue	1,100	
	Separable By-Product Costs		300
	Work in Process Inventory		800
	To deduct the net realizable value of the by-product from the cost of the main product		
(5)	Finished Goods Inventory	79,200	
	Work in Process Inventory		79,200
(6)	Cost of Goods Sold	79,200	
	Finished Goods Inventory		79,200
(7)	Accounts Receivable*	200,000	
	Sales Revenue (from main product)		200,000
	* Debit to this account assumed for illustrative purposes.		

are sold this period. Sales of C total $200,000, while the sales of D total $1,100. Processing costs up to the split-off point are $80,000. These costs are like joint costs, but they are not allocated between output C and output D—they are *all* allocated to output C, the main product.

Also assume output D requires $300 additional costs of processing to make it salable; hence, output D's net realizable value is $800 ($1,100 − $300). The two methods of accounting for the by-product, output D are shown in Illustration 6–8. The flow of costs through T-accounts using method 1 is shown in Illustration 6–9.

Whereas we have indicated two methods of accounting for by-products, there are many variations of these methods used in practice. By-products are relatively minor products, by definition; hence, alternative methods of accounting for by-products are not likely to have a material effect on the financial statements for either internal or external reporting.

Scrap

Our discussion so far has assumed that the secondary or by-product output has a positive net realizable value—that is, its sales value exceeds the costs of further processing and marketing. If an output's net realizable value is negative, it is usually considered *scrap*, and it is disposed of at minimum cost. The cost of scrapping an output is usually debited to manufacturing overhead.

SUMMARY

Joint cost allocations arise from the need to assign common costs to two or more products manufactured from a common input. The usual objective of joint cost allocation is to relate the economic sacrifice (costs) of the inputs to the economic benefits received. Since there is no direct way to do this for joint products, approximations are necessary. The two methods of joint cost allocation distribute joint costs based on net realizable value (or estimated net realizable value) or the physical quantities method. While these methods are acceptable for financial reporting purposes, care must be exercised before attempting to use the data for decision policy-making purposes because of the inherent arbitrariness in joint cost allocations.

The net realizable value method allocates joint costs to products in proportion to their relative sales values. If additional processing is required beyond the split-off point before the product can be sold, an estimate of the net realizable value can be derived at the split-off point by subtracting the additional processing costs from the sales value that is known.

The physical quantities method allocates joint costs to products in proportion to a physical measure (for example, volume or weight).

Management must often decide whether to sell products at split-off points or process them further. Joint cost allocations are usually irrelevant for these decisions.

By-products are relatively minor outputs from a joint production process. The two methods most commonly used to account for by-products are (1) to reduce the cost of the main product by the net realizable value (sales value minus by-product processing cost) of the by-product or (2) to treat the net realizable value of the by-product as other income.

**TERMS AND
CONCEPTS**

The following terms and concepts should be familiar to you after reading this chapter:

By-Products	**Net Realizable Value Method**
Estimated Net Realizable Value	**Physical Quantities Method**
Joint Costs	**Split-Off Point**
Joint Products	

**SUPPLEMENTARY
READINGS**

Barton, M. Frank, and J. David Spiceland. "Practical Alternative to Joint Cost Allocation." *Woman CPA,* July 1985, pp. 24–26.

Biddle, Gary C. "Allocation of Joint and Common Costs." *Journal of Accounting Literature,* Spring 1984, pp. 1–45.

Hamlen, S. S.; W. A. Hamlen; and J. T. Tschirhart. "The Use of Core Theory in Evaluating Joint Cost Allocation Schemes." *Accounting Review,* July 1977, pp. 616–27.

Lowenthat, Franklin. "Multiple Split-Off Points." *Issues in Accounting Education,* Fall 1986, pp. 302–8.

McLaughlin, John K., and Anne Farley. "Resolved: Joint Costs Should Be Allocated (Sometimes)." *CPA Journal,* January 1988, p. 46.

Moriarity, S., ed. "Joint Cost Allocation." *Proceedings of the University of Oklahoma Conference on Cost Allocation.* Norman, Okla.: Center for Economic and Management Research, 1981.

Munter, Paul, and Don W. Finn. "Industry Joint-Product Cost Allocations." *On Oil and Gas Accounting, 20th,* Southwestern Legal Foundation, 1984.

Robinson, Daniel D., and Herbert K. Folpe. "Joint Costs in Voluntary Health and Welfare Organizations." *CPA Journal,* April 1984, pp. 32, 34. 36–39.

Schneider, Arnold. "Simultaneous Determination of Cost Allocations and Cost-Plus Prices for Joint Products." *Journal of Business and Finance and Accounting,* Summer 1986, pp. 187–95 (published in Great Britain).

Steinwurtzel, Samuel L. "Current Developments on Joint Costs of Not-for-Profit Organizations." *CPA Journal,* March 1986, pp. 65–67.

**SELF-STUDY
PROBLEM**

Ferguson Confections Company purchases cocoa beans and processes them into cocoa butter, cocoa powder, and cocoa shells. The standard yield from each 100-pound sack of unprocessed cocoa beans is 20 pounds of butter, 45 pounds of powder, and 35 pounds of shells. The butter must be molded and packed before it can be sold. The further processing costs $.15 per pound, but the resulting processed butter can be sold for $1.25 per pound. The powder can be sold for $.90 per pound at the split-off point. The shells, which are considered a by-product, sell for $.04 per pound. The company estimates net realizable values at the split-off point if no market price is available at that point.

The costs of the cocoa beans is $15 per hundred pounds. It costs $37 in labor and overhead to process each 100 pounds of beans up to the split-off point.

Required:

a. Assuming that the shells are recorded as other income at the time they are sold, compute the allocated joint cost of the butter and powder produced from 100 pounds of cocoa beans, using the net realizable value method.

b. Assuming that the shells are recorded as other income at the time they are sold, compute the allocated joint cost of the butter and powder produced from each 100 pounds of cocoa beans, using the physical quantities (pounds) method.

c. If the net realizable value of the shells is entered as a credit to the primary manufacturing costs at the time the shells are recovered and if the net realizable value method is used for joint cost allocation, what would be the allocation of the joint costs to the main products?

d. Suppose that powder could be processed further at a cost of $.70 per pound and the resulting product sold as instant cocoa for $1.50 per pound. Should the company sell the powder or process it further into instant cocoa?

SOLUTION TO SELF-STUDY PROBLEM

a. The joint costs to be allocated amount to $52—the total of the $15 in direct materials costs and the $37 in conversion costs.

Since the butter must be processed further, the sales value at split-off is approximated by deducting the additional processing costs ($.15 per pound) from the sales value at the first point of marketability (which is $1.25 per pound). The resulting sales value for butter is $1.10 per pound (computed at $1.25 less $.15) multiplied by the 20 pounds obtained per 100 pounds of beans. The total sales value for butter, then, is $22 (which is $1.10 per pound times 20 pounds).

The net realizable value of the powder is $40.50, which is the product of the selling price of $.90 per pound times the standard yield of 45 pounds per hundred pounds of input.

The allocation follows:

To cocoa butter:

$$\frac{\$22}{\$22 + \$40.50} \times \$52 = \underline{\underline{\$18.304}}$$

To cocoa powder:

$$\frac{\$40.50}{\$22 + \$40.50} \times \$52 = \underline{\underline{\$33.696}}$$

This results in an allocation of the total cost of $52 (which is $18.304 + $33.696) to the two products

b. Since there is a total of 65 pounds of output of major products (20 pounds of beans and 45 pounds of butter) at the split-off point, the allocation is:

To cocoa butter:

$$\frac{20}{20 + 45} \times \$52 = \underline{\underline{\$16.00}}$$

To cocoa powder:

$$\frac{45}{20 + 45} \times \$52 = \underline{\underline{\$36.00}}$$

resulting in an allocation of the total $52 to the two products.

c. If the net realizable value of the shells is considered a reduction in the costs to be allocated, then the allocation would proceed as in part (a), but using $50.60 (which is $52.00 less $1.40) as the cost to be allocated. This results in the following allocation:

To cocoa butter:

$$\frac{\$22}{\$22 + \$40.50} \times \$50.60 = \underline{\underline{\$17.8112}}$$

To cocoa powder:

$$\frac{\$40.50}{\$22 + \$40.50} \times \$50.60 = \underline{\underline{\$32.7888}}$$

As with the other methods, this, too, results in a full allocation of the $50.60 (that is, $17.8112 + $32.7888 = $50.60).

d. The company should sell the powder without further processing. Each pound processed further provides incremental revenue of $.60 (=$1.50 − $.90), but incremental processing costs are $.70 per pound.

**APPENDIX:
The Replacement
Method**

The replacement method for joint cost allocation is widely used in industries where management can change output proportions. In petroleum refining and chemical processing, for example, the same input can be converted into numerous mixes of output. The replacement method is used when an output proportion is changed from a previously established mix.

For example, assume that Sacramento-Sierra Company had used the physical quantities method to allocate the $180,000 joint cost of log processing as follows:

$$\text{Chipboard, 1,400 units: } \frac{1,400}{1,400 + 1,960} \times \$180,000 = \$75,000$$

$$\text{Lumber, 1,960 units: } \frac{1,960}{1,400 + 1,960} \times \$180,000 = \$105,000$$

One day, management decides to change this output mix to produce more chipboard. They find chipboard can be increased by 100 units if lumber is reduced by 80 units. They find it is also necessary to change the processing method in a way that adds $2,470 to the joint costs of processing logs.

Before the change in output mix, the unit cost of chipboard was $53.57 ($75,000 ÷ 1,400 units), and the unit cost of lumber was $53.57 ($105,000 ÷ 1,960). The cost of the 80 units of lumber that would be given up to produce the additional 100 units of chipboard would be $4,286 ($53.57 × 80 units). This amount would be added to the costs of chipboard together with the additional $2,470 processing costs. The costs of lumber would be credited with the $4,286. This would result in the cost allocation shown in Exhibit A. Exhibit B diagrams these cost flows in the accounts.

Exhibit A   **Replacement Method**

SACRAMENTO-SIERRA COMPANY

	(1)	(2)	(3)
			Cost
Product	Units	Cost	per Unit[a]
Chipboard (initial allocation)	1,400	$ 75,000	$53.57
Replacement cost of lumber used to produce chipboard	100	4,286	
Additional processing costs		2,470	
Totals	1,500	$ 81,756	54.50
Lumber (initial allocation)	1,960	$105,000	53.57
Replacement cost of lumber used to produce chipboard	(80)	(4,286)	53.57
Totals	1,880	$100,714	53.57

[a] Rounded to two decimal places. Column (3) = Column (2) ÷ Column (1).

Exhibit B   **Replacement Method**

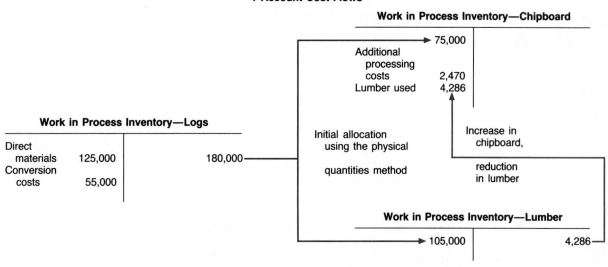

SACRAMENTO-SIERRA COMPANY
T-Account Cost Flows

Note that the unit cost of lumber remains $53.57, but the unit cost of chipboard increases from $53.57 to $54.50. Thus, the product that increases in volume is charged with the additional cost. The unit cost is left unchanged, however, for the product whose volume is decreased.

In summary:

1. The replacement method is used *after* joint costs are allocated to output products using another method (for example, the physical quantities method or the relative sales value method).

2. The replacement method is used when management decides to change a previously determined product mix.
   a. For the output that is *decreased,* product costs are reduced (that is, credited to work in process inventory) by the number of units decreased times the unit cost of those units.
   b. For the output that is *increased,* product costs are increased (debited to work in process inventory) by the sum of the amount of costs removed from the product that was decreased and additional processing costs that are required to change the output mix.

3. The replacement method is used only when a previously established product mix is changed so that one output is increased and another is decreased.

4. The cost of the input is assumed to be the same both before and after the change in product mix.

QUESTIONS   6–1. What is the objective of joint cost allocation?

6–2. Why would a number of accountants express a preference for the net realizable value method of joint cost allocation over the physical quantities method?

6-3. When would one prefer a physical quantities method for allocation?

6-4. Explain the basic difference between the method of accounting for joint products and that for by-products.

6-5. State the conditions under which an item should be treated as a by-product rather than as a joint product.

6-6. Explain the two principal methods of assigning joint costs to joint products. State circumstances under which each would be appropriate.

6-7. Why are joint costs irrelevant in the sell-or-process-further decision?

6-8. The chapter indicated that joint costing is used mostly for financial reporting, inventory valuation, and regulatory purposes. Under what conditions might the method of joint cost allocation have an impact on other decisions?

6-9. What is the difference between joint products, by-products, and scrap?

6-10. How is joint cost allocation like service department cost allocation?

6-11. For external financial reporting, is it possible to avoid joint cost allocations? If so, how?

EXERCISES

6–12. Net Realizable Value Method
(L.O.1)

A company processes Chemical DX-1 through a pressure treatment operation. After the process is complete, there are two outputs: L and T. The monthly costs of processing DX-1 are $45,000 for materials and $160,000 for conversion costs. This processing results in outputs that sell for a total of $455,000. The sales revenue from L amounts to $273,000 of the total.

Required:

Compute the costs to be assigned to L and T in a typical month, using the net realizable value method.

6–13. Net Realizable Value Method
(L.O.1)

Brazos Corporation operates an ore processing plant. A typical batch of ore run through the plant will yield three refined products: lead, copper, and manganese. At the split-off point, the intermediate products cannot be sold without further processing. The lead from a typical batch will sell for $20,000 after incurring additional processing costs of $8,000. The copper is sold for $40,000 after additional processing costs of $1,000. The manganese yield sells for $30,000 but requires additional processing costs of $6,000. The costs of processing the raw ore, including the ore costs, amount to $55,000 per batch.

Required:

Use the net realizable value method to allocate the joint processing costs.

6–14. Net Realizable Value Method to Solve for Unknowns
(L.O.1)

O'Connor Company manufactures leprechauns and shamrocks from a joint process on a product called Green. For leprechauns, 4,000 units were produced having a sales value at the split-off point of $15,000. If leprechauns were processed further, the additional costs would be $3,000 and the sales value would be $20,000. For shamrocks, 2,000 units were produced having a sales value at split-off of $10,000. If shamrocks were processed further, the additional costs would be $1,000 and the sales value would be $12,000. Using the net realizable value method, the portion of the total joint product costs allocated to leprechauns was $9,000.

Required:

Compute the total joint product costs.

(CPA adapted)

6–15. Net Realizable Value Method—Multiple Choice
(L.O.1)

a. Net realizable value at split-off is used to:
   (1) Allocate separable costs.
   (2) Determine relevant costs.
   (3) Determine break-even in sales dollars.
   (4) Allocate joint costs.

b. Net realizable value at split-off is used to allocate:

	Cost beyond Split-Off	Joint Costs
(1)	Yes	Yes
(2)	Yes	No
(3)	No	Yes
(4)	No	No

c. For purposes of allocating joint costs to joint products, the net realizable value at split-off is equal to:
   (1) Sales price less a normal profit margin at point of sale.
   (2) Final sales price reduced by cost to complete after split-off.
   (3) Total sales value less joint costs at point of split-off.
   (4) Separable product cost plus a normal profit margin.

d. The method of accounting for joint product costs that will produce the same gross margin for all products is the:
   (1) Net realizable value method.
   (2) Physical quantities method.
   (3) Both methods.
   (4) Neither method.

6–16. Net Realizable Value Method—Multiple Choice
(L.O.1)

Each of the three multiple-choice exercises should be considered independent of each other.

a. The Rote Company manufactures products C and R from a joint process. The total joint costs are $60,000. The sales value at split-off was $75,000 for 8,000 units of product C and $25,000 for 2,000 units of product R. Assuming that total joint costs are allocated using the net realizable value at split-off approach, what were the joint costs allocated to product C?
   (1) $15,000.
   (2) $30,000.
   (3) $45,000.
   (4) $48,000.

b. Superior Company manufactures products A and B from a joint process, which also yields a by-product, X. Superior accounts for the revenues from its by-product sales as other income. Additional information is as follows:

	A	B	X	Total
Units produced	15,000	9,000	6,000	30,000
Joint costs	?	?	?	$264,000
Sales value at split-off	$290,000	$150,000	$10,000	$450,000

Assuming that joint product costs are allocated using the net realizable value at split-off approach, what was the joint cost allocated to product B?
   (1) $79,200.
   (2) $88,000.
   (3) $90,000.
   (4) $99,000.

c. Helen Corp. manufactures products W, X, Y, and Z from a joint process. Additional information is as follows:

Product	Units Produced	Sales Value at Split-off	If Processed Further Additional Costs	If Processed Further Sales Values
W	6,000	$ 80,000	$ 7,500	$ 90,000
X	5,000	60,000	6,000	70,000
Y	4,000	40,000	4,000	50,000
Z	3,000	20,000	2,500	30,000
	18,000	$200,000	$20,000	$240,000

Assuming that joint total costs of $160,000 were allocated using the net realizable value method, what joint costs were allocated to each product?

	W	X	Y	Z
(1)	$40,000	$40,000	$40,000	$40,000
(2)	$53,333	$44,444	$35,556	$26,667
(3)	$60,000	$46,667	$33,333	$20,000
(4)	$64,000	$48,000	$32,000	$16,000

6–17. Physical Quantities Method
(L.O.2)

Questions (a) and (b) are based on Vreeland, Inc., which manufactures products X, Y, and Z from a joint process. Joint product costs were $60,000. Additional information is provided below.

Product	Units Produced	Sales Value at Split-off	If Processed Further Sales Values	If Processed Further Additional Costs
X	6,000	$40,000	$55,000	$9,000
Y	4,000	$35,000	$45,000	$7,000
Z	2,000	$25,000	$30,000	$5,000

a. Assuming that joint product costs are allocated using the physical quantities (units produced) method, what were the total costs of product X (including $9,000 if processed further)?
   (1) $27,000.
   (2) $29,000.
   (3) $33,000.
   (4) $39,000.

b. Assuming that joint product costs are allocated using the net realizable value method, what were the total costs of product Y (including the $7,000 if processed further)?
   (1) $27,000.
   (2) $28,000.
   (3) $28,350.
   (4) $32,200.

(CPA adapted)

6–18. Physical Quantities Method
(L.O.2)

Riverside Plant Protein Corporation uses organic materials to produce fertilizers for home gardens. Through its production processes, the company manufactures a high-nitrogen fertilizer (with the trade name Hi-Nite) and a high phosphorus fertilizer (with the trade name Hi-Bloom). A by-product of the process is methane, which is used to generate power for the company's operations. The fertilizers are sold either in bulk to nurseries or in individual packages for home consumers. The company chooses to allocate the costs on the basis of the physical quantities method.

Last month, 500,000 units of input were processed at a total cost of $120,000. The output of the process consisted of 100,000 units of Hi-Nite, 200,000 units of Hi-Bloom, and 300,000 cubic feet of methane. The by-product methane would have cost $1,200 had it been purchased from the local gas utility. This is considered to be its net realizable value, which is deducted from the processing costs of the main products.

Required:

What is the share of the joint costs to be assigned to each of the main products?

6–19. By-Products
(L.O.3)

Health Age Foods Company engages in a manufacturing process that uses soy flour to produce three outputs (cereal, milk, whey). Cereal and milk are considered main products. Whey is a by-product. During a recent month, the following events occurred.

1. Produced and sold 200 units of cereal and 100 units of milk. Produced 25 units of whey.
2. Recorded sales revenue of $35,000 from sales of cereal and milk. The cost of sales before accounting for the by-product was $18,000.
3. Incurred $125 to process the 25 units of whey to completion. These costs are charged as they are incurred against any by-products' sales. (None of these by-product costs are kept in inventory at the end of the period.)
4. Received $570 in revenue from the sale of 10 units of whey.

Required:

Prepare a statement showing, in parallel columns (as in Illustration 6–8), the sales revenue, other income, cost of goods sold, separate costs to process by-products, and gross margin that would be reported for each of the two methods of by-product accounting described in the text.

6–20. By-Products— Multiple Choice
(L.O.3)

The following questions are based on Eloise Corporation, which manufactures a product that gives rise to a by-product called Zet. The only costs associated with Zet are additional processing costs of $1 for each unit. Eloise accounts for Zet sales first by deducting its separable costs from such sales and then by deducting this net amount from the cost of sales of the major product. (This is method 1 discussed in the text. See Illustration 6–8, for example.) This year, 1,000 units of Zet were produced. They were all sold at $4 each.

Required:

a. Sales revenue and cost of goods sold from the main product were $400,000 and $200,000, respectively, for the year. What was the gross margin after considering the by-product sales and costs (that is, the "gross margin" in Illustration 6–8)?
   (1) $200,000.
   (2) $203,000.
   (3) $196,000.
   (4) $197,000.

b. If Eloise changes its method of accounting for Zet sales by showing the net amount as "other income," Eloise's *gross margin* would:
   (1) Be unaffected.
   (2) Increase by $3,000.
   (3) Decrease by $3,000.
   (4) Decrease by $4,000.

    c. If Eloise changes its method of accounting as indicated in *(b)* above, what would be the effects of the change on the company's profits?
        (1) No effect.
        (2) Increase by $3,000.
        (3) Decrease by $3,000.
        (4) Decrease by $4,000.

(CPA adapted)

6–21. Sell or Process Further
(L.O.4)

Deep Forest Mills, Inc., operates a sawmill facility. The company accounts for the bark chips that result from the primary sawing operation as a by-product. The chips are sold to another company at a price of $5 per hundred cubic feet. Normally, sales revenue from this bark is $450,000 per month. The bark is charged to inventory at $2.20 per hundred cubic feet, although there is no direct cost of processing bark chips.

As an alternative, the company can rent equipment that will size the chips and bag them for sale as horticultural bark. Approximately 20 percent of the bark will be graded "large" and will sell for $15 per hundred cubic feet. About 65 percent will be graded "medium" and will sell for $8 per hundred cubic feet. The remainder will be called mulch and will sell for $1 per hundred cubic feet.

Costs of the grading equipment and the personnel to operate the equipment are $260,000 per month and are fixed regardless of the quantities of bark processed.

Required:

Should the company sell the bark for $5 per hundred cubic feet or process it further (assuming a typical month)?

6–22. (Appendix) Replacement Method
(L.O.5)

Valley Cane Company processes sugar cane into various output products. The outputs from the first stage of the process consist of two grades of sugar: refined and turbinado. In a typical month, $218,000 in sugar cane are processed and $325,000 in labor and overhead are incurred. A standard output mix consists of 40 percent refined sugar and 60 percent turbinado. Engineering studies assign 55 percent of the joint processing costs to the refined sugar.

If the processing temperature is increased, the yield of refined sugar can be increased by 20 percent (that is, from 40 percent of the initial output to an amount equal to 48 percent of the initial output). However, processing costs are increased 7.5 percent when this is done, and 15 percent of the original yield of turbinado is lost. The replacement cost is to be estimated on the basis of actual costs, not net realizable values.

Required:

Compute the costs that would be assigned to the additional refined sugar, using the replacement method.

PROBLEMS

6–23. Net Realizable Value of Joint Products—Multiple Choice

Miller Manufacturing Company buys zeon for $.80 a gallon. At the end of distilling in department 1, zeon splits off into three products: argon, xon and neon. Argon is sold at the split-off point, with no further processing; xon and neon require further processing before they can be sold. Xon is used in department 2, and neon is solidified in department 3. Following is a summary of costs and other related data for the year ended December 31.

	Department		
	Distilling	**Fusing**	**Solidifying**
Cost of zeon	$96,000	—	—
Direct labor	14,000	$45,000	$65,000
Manufacturing overhead	10,000	21,000	49,000

	Products		
	Argon	**Xon**	**Neon**
Gallons sold	20,000	30,000	45,000
Gallons on hand at Year end	10,000	—	15,000
Sales in dollars	$30,000	$96,000	$141,750

There were no beginning inventories on hand at January 1, and there was no zeon on hand at the end of the year on December 31. All gallons on hand on December 31 were complete as to processing. Miller uses the net realizable value method of allocating joint costs.

Required:

a. For allocating joint costs, the net realizable value of argon for the year ended December 31 would be:
   (1) $30,000.
   (2) $45,000.
   (3) $21,000.
   (4) $6,000.

b. The joint costs for the year ended December 31 to be allocated are:
   (1) $300,000.
   (2) $95,000.
   (3) $120,000.
   (4) $96,000.

c. The cost of xon sold for the year ended December 31 is:
   (1) $90,000.
   (2) $66,000.
   (3) $88,857.
   (4) $96,000.

d. The value of the ending inventory for argon is:
   (1) $24,000.
   (2) $12,000.
   (3) $8,000.
   (4) $13,333.

(CPA adapted)

6-24. Net Realizable Value

The Harumby Manufacturing Company produces three products by a joint production process. Raw materials are put into production in department A, and at the end of processing in this department, three products appear. Product X is immediately sold at the split-off point, with no further processing. Products Y and Z require further processing before they are sold. Product Y is processed in department B, and product Z is processed in department C. The company uses the net realizable value method of allocating joint production costs. Following is a summary of costs and other data for the quarter ended September 30.

There were no inventories on hand at the beginning of the quarter, or July 1. There was no raw material on hand at September 30. All the units on hand at the end of the quarter were fully complete as to processing.

| | Products | | |
	X	Y	Z
Pounds sold	20,000	60,000	80,000
Pounds on hand at September 30	40,000	-0-	40,000
Sales revenues	$30,000	$162,000	$283,500

| | Departments | | |
	A	B	C
Raw material cost	$112,000	-0-	-0-
Direct labor cost	48,000	80,900	202,000
Manufacturing overhead	20,000	21,100	73,250

Required:

a. Determine the following amounts for each product: (1) estimated net realizable value as used for allocating joint costs, (2) joint costs allocated, (3) cost of goods sold, and (4) finished-goods inventory costs, September 30.

b. Assume that the entire output of product X could be processed further at an additional cost of $2.00 per pound and then sold at a price of $4.30 per pound. What is the effect on operating income if all the product X output for the quarter had been processed further and sold, rather than all being sold at the split-off point?

6–25. Finding Missing Data— Net Realizable Value

Air Extracts, Inc., manufactures nitrogen, oxygen and hydrogen from a joint process. Each gas can be liquified and sold for more. Data on the process are as follows:

| | Product | | | |
	Nitrogen	Oxygen	Hydrogen	Total
Units produced	8,000	4,000	2,000	14,000
Joint costs	$ 72,000	*a*	*b*	$120,000
Sales value at split-off	*c*	*d*	$30,000	200,000
Additional costs to liquify	14,000	$10,000	6,000	30,000
Sales value if liquified	140,000	60,000	40,000	240,000

Required:

Determine the values for the lettered spaces.

(CPA adapted)

6–26. Joint Cost Allocations

The Roving Eye Cosmetics Company buys bulk flowers and processes them into perfumes in a two-stage process. Their highest-grade perfume, Seduction, and a residue that is processed into a medium-grade perfume called Romance, come from a certain mix of petals. In July, the company used 25,000 pounds of petals. Costs involved in the first stage—which is a joint process, known as reduction, reducing the petals to Seduction and the residue—were as follows:

▼ $200,000 direct materials.

▼ $110,000 direct labor.

▼ $90,000 overhead and other costs.

The additional costs of producing Romance via the second pressing were as follows:

▼ $22,000 direct materials.

▼ $50,000 direct labor.

▼ $40,000 overhead and other costs.

At the end of the month, total completed production equaled 5,000 ounces of Seduction and 28,000 ounces of Romance. In addition, 2,500 ounces of Seduction and 12,500 ounces of Romance had just completed reduction. There was no beginning inventory on July 1. There are no uncompleted units in the second pressing stage.

Packaging costs incurred for each product as completed were $40,000 for Seduction and $161,000 for Romance. The sales price of Seduction is $90 an ounce; Romance sells for $31.50 per ounce.

a. Allocate joint costs using the estimated net realizable value method.

b. Allocate the joint costs using the physical units method. Round all percentages to one decimal place.

c. Are there any problems in using the physical units method in this case?

d. Assume that Roving Eye can sell the squeezed petals from the reduction process to greenhouses for use as fertilizer. In July, there were 12,000 pounds of squeezed petals left over that sold for $.75 per pound. The squeezed petals are a by-product of reduction. With this new information, answer parts *a* and *b*.

6–27.   Joint Costing in a Process Costing Context —Net Realizable Value Method

Harrison Corporation produces three products: alpha, beta, and gamma. Alpha and gamma are main products, while beta is a by-product of alpha. Information on the past month's production processes are given as follows:

1.   In department I, 110,000 units of raw material rho are processed at a total cost of $120,000. After processing in department I, 60 percent of the units are transferred to department II, and 40 percent of the units (now unprocessed gamma) are transferred to department III.

2.   In department II, the materials received from department I are processed at a total additional cost of $38,000. Seventy percent of the units become alpha and are transferred to department IV. The remaining 30 percent emerge as beta and are sold at $2.10 per unit. The additional processing costs to make beta salable are $8,100.

3.   In department III, gamma is processed at an additional cost of $165,000. A normal loss of units of gamma occurs in this department. The loss is equal to 10 percent of the units of good ouput. The remaining good output is then sold for $12 per unit.

4.   In department IV, alpha is processed at an additional cost of $23,660. After this processing, the alpha can be sold for $5 per unit.

Required:

Prepare a schedule showing the allocation of the $120,000 joint cost between alpha and gamma, using the net realizable value approach. Revenue from sales of by-products should be credited to the manufacturing costs of the related main product (method 1 in the text).

(CPA adapted)

6–28.   Find Maximum Input Price—Net Realizable Value Method

Rambling Rose Corporation produces two joint products from its manufacturing operation. Product J sells for $37.50 per unit, while product M sells for $15.80 per unit. In a typical month, 19,000 input units are processed. Four thousand of these units become product J after an additional $37,500 of processing costs are incurred.

The remaining units are processed at a cost of $20,000. After processing these latter units, shrinkage amounting to 20 percent of the good output occurs. The good output is product M. Product M could be sold before this further processing at a price of $12 per unit.

The joint process has only variable costs; no fixed costs. In a typical month, the conversion costs amount to $114,075. Materials prices are volatile, and if prices are too high, the company will stop production.

Required:

What is the maximum price the company should pay for the materials?

6–29. Effect of By-Product versus Joint Cost Accounting

Ninja Turtle Company processes input Leonardo into three outputs: Michaelangelo, Raphael, and Donatello. Michaelangelo accounts for 70 percent of the net realizable value at the split-off point, while Raphael accounts for 25 percent. The balance is accounted for by Donatello. The joint costs total $159,050. If Donatello is accounted for as a by-product, its net realizable value at split-off of $9,900 would be credited to the joint manufacturing costs using method 1 described in the text (see Illustration 6–8).

Required:

What are the allocated joint costs for the three outputs:

a. If Donatello is accounted for as a joint product?
b. If Donatello is accounted for as a by-product?

6–30. Joint Cost Allocation and Product Profitability

Prednose Refining Company receives silicon crystals which it processes into purified wafers and chips. Silicon crystals cost $30,000 per tank-car load. The process is such that the crystals are heated for 12 hours, at the end of which time there are 40,000 purified wafers, with a market value of $10,000, and 20,000 chips, with a market value of $65,000. The cost of the heat process is $7,200.

Required:

a. If the crystal costs and the heat process costs are to be allocated on the basis of units of output, what cost would be assigned to each product?
b. If the crystal costs and the heat process costs are allocated on the basis of the net realizable value, what cost would be assigned to each product?
c. Can you determine which product is more profitable? Explain why or why not.

6–31. Find Missing Data— Net Realizable Value Method

A clerk at the Hargis Corporation prepared a diagram showing the flow of materials and costs through the company's processing operation. However, certain pieces of data are missing from the diagram. You learn some additional information as follows:

1. Each of the three output products can only be sold at the end of all processing.
2. Joint costs are allocated estimating the net realizable value at split-off.
3. Costs of processing in each branch of the diagram are noted directly above the horizontal line for that branch.
4. Allocated joint costs are shown in parentheses on the diagonal line for the related branch of the process.
5. Sales values at split-off are shown on the diagonal line for the related branch of the process.
6. Letters represent missing data. If the letters are in parentheses, the missing item is a cost. If the letter is not in parentheses, the missing item is a sales value.
7. Total joint costs for the first process are $99. These are allocated to (b) and (c).

The diagram appears as follows:

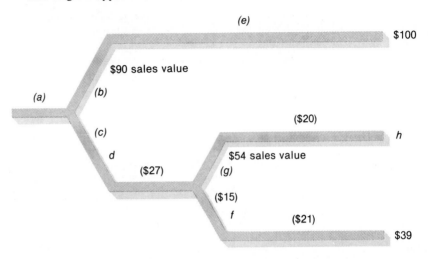

Required: Provide amounts for each letter. (Hint: Start with *a*, then solve for *f*, then for *d*.)

INTEGRATIVE CASES

6-32. Effect of Cost Allocation on Pricing and Internal versus External Buy Decisions

Indio Agresearch is a large farm cooperative with a number of agriculture-related manufacturing and service divisions. As a cooperative, the company pays no federal income taxes. The company owns a fertilizer plant, which processes and mixes petrochemical compounds into three brands of agricultural fertilizer: Greenup, Maintane, and Winterizer. The three brands differ with respect to selling price and with respect to the proportional content of basic chemicals.

The fertilizer manufacturing division transfers the completed product to the cooperative's retail sales division at a price based on the costs of each type of fertilizer plus a markup.

The manufacturing division is completely automated so that the only costs incurred are costs of the petrochemical feedstocks plus overhead that is all considered fixed. The primary feedstock costs $2 per pound. Each 100 pounds of feedstock can produce either of the following mixtures of fertilizer:

| | Output Schedules (in pounds) | |
	A	B
Greenup	50	60
Maintane	30	10
Winterizer	20	30

Production is limited to the 900,000 kilowatt-hours monthly capacity of the dehydrator. Due to different chemical makeup, each brand of fertilizer requires different dehydrator use. Dehydrator usage in kilowatt-hours per pound of product is:

Product	Kilowatt-Hour Usage per Pound
Greenup	32
Maintane	20
Winterizer	40

Monthly fixed costs are $75,000. Now the company is producing according to output schedule A. Joint production costs including fixed overhead are allocated to each product on the basis of weight.

The fertilizer is packed into 100-pound bags for sale in the cooperative's retail stores. The manufacturing division charges the retail stores the allocated costs plus a 50 percent markup. The sales price for each product charged by the cooperative's retail sales division is as follows:

	Sales Price per Pound
Greenup	$10.50
Maintane	9.00
Winterizer	10.40

Selling expenses are 20 percent of the sales price.

Identical chemical fertilizers may be acquired by the retail division from other manufacturers and wholesalers at the following prices per pound:

Greenup	$7.50
Maintane	5.80
Winterizer	7.70

The manager of the retail division has complained that the price charged for Maintane is excessive and that he would prefer to purchase Maintane from another supplier.

The manager of the manufacturing division argues that the processing mix was determined based on a careful analysis of the costs of each product compared to the prices charged by the retail division. As was noted previously, a certain amount of Maintane must be produced. The manufacturing manager stated, "It is not reasonable to allow the retail division to purchase from the outside because the manufacturing division would then be left with Maintane on hand that would have to be sold to outsiders. After selling and delivery expenses, the manufacturing division would only realize $5.30 per pound, which is less than cost."

Required:

a. Assume joint production costs including fixed overhead are allocated to each product on the basis of weight. What is the allocated cost per pound of each product, given the current production schedule?

b. Assume joint production costs including fixed overhead are allocated to each product on the basis of net realizable value. What is the allocated cost per pound of each product, given the current production schedule?

c. Assume joint production costs including fixed overhead are allocated to each product on the basis of weight. Which of the two production schedules produces the higher operating profit to the firm as a whole? What is the maximum monthly operating profit that can be obtained by the firm?

d. Would your answer to part *(c)* be different if joint production costs including fixed overhead are allocated to each product on the basis of net realizable value? If so, by how much?

6–33. (Appendix) Joint Costing—Replacement Method

In refining crude oil, three primary classes of products are obtained: (1) gasolines; (2) distillates such as jet fuel, heating oil, and diesel fuel; and (3) residual fuel. Due to marketing considerations, a primary objective of the refining process is to obtain as much gasoline from the oil as possible. While some gasoline can be obtained with relatively little processing, obtaining greater yields of gasoline requires the use of catalytic processes under high pressures and temperatures. In addition to the characteristics of the refining process, a major determinant of the quantity of gasoline obtainable from a barrel of crude oil is the initial gravity of the oil. Certain heavy oils, while plentiful and relatively inexpensive, have yielded fairly low quantities of gasoline.

Great Lands Refining Company developed a new process for obtaining more gasoline from heavy crude oils. Without the new process, the typical yield from heavy crudes is 60 percent gasoline, 22 percent distillates, and 18 percent residual. With the new process, the yield of gasoline rises to 65 percent, distillates decrease to 20 percent, and residual decreases to 15 percent.

To obtain the increased yields, the variable costs of processing a barrel of crude oil increase by $1 from $2. The refinery that would process this crude has a daily capacity of 50,000 barrels. The capacity would be unchanged by the process, but the fixed costs of the refinery would increase from $200,000 per day to $240,000 per day. The cost of a barrel of heavy crude is $24.

Joint processing costs are first allocated using engineering estimates of the "refining effort" to obtain the standard mix of each product. Under the present system, 60 percent of the refining effort is considered applicable to gasoline, 22 percent to distillates, and 18 percent to residual fuels. Any change in the product output would be charged into the accounts using the replacement method.

A standard barrel of oil contains 42 U.S. gallons. The refiner's gasoline price is $1.10 per gallon, while the price of distillates is $1 per gallon and the price of residual fuels is $.82 per gallon.

All figures can be reported in terms of the cash and income flows from one day's operations. For simplicity, assume there is no loss of mass in refining and the refinery operates at 100 percent capacity.

Required:

Use the replacement method to determine the cost of the increased gasoline production on a per barrel basis.

JOB COSTING

1. To understand the accounting systems designed for different production methods.

2. To see how to assign costs in a job cost system.

3. To know how to assign overhead using predetermined rates.

4. To apply product costing methods in a service environment.

5. To learn the causes and accounting treatment for differences between actual and applied overhead (Appendix).

This is the first of two chapters that present methods of accumulating and applying costs to products. Chapter 4 presented an overview of the two stages of cost allocation: (1) allocating common costs to user departments and (2) allocating production department costs to units produced. Chapters 7 and 8 focus on the details of second stage cost allocation—allocating production department costs to units. In this chapter, the units produced are called **jobs.** Jobs are units or batches of units that are easily distinguishable from other units or batches of units.

Jobs Units or batches of units that are easily distinguishable from other units or batches.

PRODUCTION METHODS AND ACCOUNTING SYSTEMS

Job Costing An accounting system that traces costs to individual units of output or to specific contracts, batches of goods, or jobs.

Project A complex job that often takes months or years to complete and requires the work of many different departments or divisions or subcontractors.

As shown in Illustration 7–1, production methods vary across organizations, depending on the type of output produced. The accounting system varies with the different type of production method. Print shops, custom home builders, defense contractors, and custom machine manufacturers use **job costing** to account for the cost of each job. Certain service organizations such as public accounting firms and consulting firms also use job costing to determine the cost of each job performed for a client. Hospitals use job costing to determine the cost of care for each patient.

Job costing methods are also used for **projects.** A project is a complex job that often takes months or years to complete and requires the work of many different departments or divisions or subcontractors (for example, bridges, shopping centers, complex lawsuits). Projects are unique and nonrepetitive, have more uncertainties, and involve more skills and specialties than jobs.

The accounting task in job costing is to measure the costs of producing each job. These costs are used for setting prices, bidding, controlling costs,

Illustration 7–1   **Production Activities**

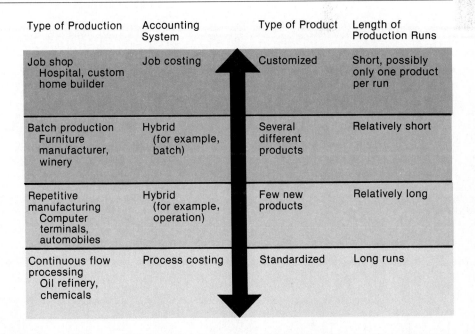

Type of Production	Accounting System	Type of Product	Length of Production Runs
Job shop Hospital, custom home builder	Job costing	Customized	Short, possibly only one product per run
Batch production Furniture manufacturer, winery	Hybrid (for example, batch)	Several different products	Relatively short
Repetitive manufacturing Computer terminals, automobiles	Hybrid (for example, operation)	Few new products	Relatively long
Continuous flow processing Oil refinery, chemicals	Process costing	Standardized	Long runs

Source: Adapted from Joseph G. Monks, *Operations Management: Theory and Problems* (New York: McGraw-Hill, 1987).

and evaluating performance. Prospective customers always ask for estimates in advance, and they frequently award jobs on a competitive basis. Consequently, suppliers must be able to estimate costs accurately if they are to compete and make a profit.

For example, management of Public Consultants, a firm that customizes accounting systems for government agencies, recently completed jobs for two municipalities. The job for Gotham City, a large metropolis, required 7,000 hours of staff time and several sophisticated computer applications. The job for Smallville, a modest farming community, required 70 hours of staff time and one very simple computer application. To charge each municipality the same price by averaging the estimated total costs for the two jobs would obviously be incorrect. Job costing allowed Public Consultants to accurately estimate the costs for each job separately. Thus, they were able to submit a competitive bid and still make a reasonable profit on each job.

REAL WORLD APPLICATION

Developing Job Costs in an Advertising Agency

JKL, Inc. (a fictitious name) is a New York-based advertising agency that was very successful in the 1970s. Management was so busy keeping up with day-to-day business demands that they had no time to develop a job costing system. In 1981, the company suffered a major loss, and management tried to determine why.

One of the reasons for the loss was the company's inadequate cost control. "Some [advertising] accounts were highly profitable and others extremely unprofitable, but top management had no idea which were which."* To deal with this problem, JKL set up a cost system that would show forecasts of revenues and costs for each advertising account. (Each advertising account is a job.) The key to the system was the analysis of employee costs, which are the only major variable costs. Rent, lights, and administration costs cannot be changed on a short-term basis. An important advantage of measuring costs for each account is that it alerts management that a particular account may be unprofitable before the fact. "Prior to the development of the forecasting system, a loss situation was discovered *after* the fact, rather than before it."†

The second part of the system was to develop a reporting system that compared each account (i.e., job) forecast with actual results. This required some additional effort and time because employees were now required to keep track of their time spent on each job. Management stressed the importance of accurate time reporting, and "there would be no punishment for working too much or too little on any account."

This new system has several benefits. Keeping track of costs for each account provides feedback about the accuracy of the forecasts. It also provides information to account managers to help them manage their jobs efficiently. "For example, an account manager noticed a large amount of supervisory creative time was being spent on her account and decided to investigate further. It turned out that the supervisors were doing the actual creative work (rather than the creative department). She pointed this out to her superiors, and a junior creative team was appointed to her account, saving a great deal of money." ‡

Since developing the new cost system, management knows better which accounts are profitable, which accounts are not, and why.

* William B. Mills, "Drawing up a Budgeting System for an Ad Agency." *Management Accounting*, December 1983, p. 47.
† Ibid., p. 49.
‡ Ibid., p. 59.

Batch Orders consisting of identical units that go through the exact same production process.

Batch Production Manufacturing process characterized by the production of product families that require some of the same production techniques but are varied so that frequent production line changes are required.

Repetitive Manufacturing Production process characterized by long production runs, few products, and infrequent production line changes.

Operation A standardized method or technique that is repetitively performed.

Operation Costing A hybrid-costing system often used in manufacturing of goods that have some common characteristics plus some individual characteristics.

Hybrid A costing system that incorporates both job and process costing concepts.

Continuous Flow Processing Systems that generally mass-produce a single, homogeneous output in a continuing process.

Process Costing An accounting system used when identical units are produced through a series of uniform production steps.

Some companies process large orders of identical units as a group through the same production sequence. Each of these orders is called a **batch.** In **batch production,** costs are allocated to each batch. Whenever a change in the production line is required to continue production, a new batch is created. A furniture manufacturer may produce a batch of chairs, then a batch of tables, then a batch of chests, and so forth. Generally, job costing concepts are used to account for batch production, and each batch is treated as a job for costing purposes.

Repetitive manufacturing lends itself to the use of automated equipment which minimizes the amount of manual material handling. Automobile assembly plants, foods processing plants, and computer terminal assembly plants are examples of repetitive manufacturing.

An **operation** can be defined as a standardized method or technique that is repetitively performed regardless of the distinguishing features of the finished product. **Operation costing** is a **hybrid** costing system often used in repetitive manufacturing where finished products have some common characteristics plus some individual characteristics. A television assembly plant which produces a basic chassis and component system but which varies options such as remote control and cabinetry would be a logical user of operation costing.

Continuous flow processing is at the opposite end of the spectrum from job shops. Process systems generally mass-produce a single, homogeneous product in a continuing process. Process systems are used in manufacturing chemicals, grinding flour, and refining oil. **Process costing** is used when identical units are produced through an *ongoing series of uniform production steps.* Because individual units are not readily identifiable, process costing systems differ from job costing systems. We discuss specific methods of accounting for process systems in Chapter 8.

Many organizations use job systems for some work and process systems for others. A home builder might use process costing for standardized homes with a particular floor plan. The same builder might use job costing when building a custom-designed home for a single customer. Honeywell, Inc., a high-tech company, uses process costing for most of their furnace thermostats, but job costing for specialized defense and space contracting work. Some organizations use hybrid systems that incorporate both job costing and process costing concepts (for example, operation costing and project costing).

If you understand the concepts presented in Chapters 7 and 8, you will be able to understand how costs are applied to products in any accounting system you encounter.

ASSIGNING COSTS TO JOBS

Source Document A basic record in accounting that initiates the entry of an activity into the accounting system.

In job operations, managers estimate and control costs by keeping separate records of costs for each job. The **source document** is some type of job cost record, called a job cost *sheet, card,* or *file.* Job cost files are used when accounting data are collected and stored by computer. Job cost sheets or cards are used when data are collected manually.

An example of a job cost record is shown in Illustration 7–2. This is a printout for Job No. 102 for Custom Manufacturing Company, which was started and finished in January. Note that this record shows detailed calcula-

Illustration 7-2   **Job Cost Record**

Job number: 102   Customer: D. Bell
Date started: Jan 8   Date finished: Jan 26
Description: Manufacture custom equipment
              according to blueprint No. 48-102.

                          Assembly Department

Direct materials			Direct labor			Manufacturing overhead	
Date	Requisition number	Cost	Date	Employee number	Cost	Date	Cost
Jan 8	102-A1	$23,000	Jan 8-14	88	$980	Jan 31	$52,000[a]
Jan 13	102-A2	4,000	Jan 12-18	67	720		
Jan 24	(return to storeroom)	(3,000)					

(Many more employees were added to this list. In total, $40,000 direct labor cost was incurred).

                          Total costs
              Direct materials $24,000
              Direct labor   40,000
              Manufacturing overhead   52,000[a] $116,000

        Transferred to finished goods inventory on   Jan 26

Total job costs:	Actual	Estimate
Direct materials	$24,000	$26,000
Direct labor	40,000	36,000
Manufacturing overhead	52,000[a]	46,800[a]
Total	$116,000	$108,800

Explain any unusual items below:

Note: Data and comments are assumed for purposes of this illustration.
Manufacturing overhead was applied, as discussed later in the chapter.

tions for the direct materials, direct labor, and manufacturing overhead charged to the job.

As noted on the job cost record, the actual costs accumulated for the job are compared with estimated costs to evaluate employee performance in controlling costs and to provide information for negotiating for a price increase with the customer. The comparison of actual and estimated job costs also provides feedback on the accuracy of the cost estimation, which can be very important. In most job shops, the accuracy of job cost estimates can be the difference between a profitable organization and one that is bankrupt.

Recording Job Costs in the Accounts

This section discusses methods of (1) obtaining materials, labor, and other items needed for production and (2) accounting for the costs of production in job operations. Most companies with job operations follow these basic steps in accounting for job costs. We show the journal entries to record cost flows using Custom Manufacturing Company as an example. The account, Work in Process Inventory, is a control account. Each individual job is a subaccount within Work in Process Inventory.

Custom Manufacturing had one job in process on January 1—Job No. 101. After some minor work on Job No. 101, it was completed and shipped to a customer in January. The costs for the second job of Custom Manufacturing, Job No. 102, were presented on the **job cost record** in Illustration 7–2. Job No. 102 was started in January and moved to finished goods inventory on January 26. At January 31, it awaited shipment to a customer. The third job, Job No. 103, was started in January and is still in process on January 31.

Job Cost Record The source document for entering costs under job costing. This is sometimes referred to as a job cost sheet, job cost file, or job card.

Beginning Inventories

Materials inventory on hand January 1 was $10,000. Beginning work in process inventory on January 1 was comprised of Job No. 101, which was in process on January 1.

The following costs had been incurred for Job No. 101 prior to January 1:

Direct materials	$14,000
Direct labor	22,000
Manufacturing overhead	25,000
Total	$61,000

Hence, the work in process inventory balance on January 1 was $61,000. There was no beginning finished goods inventory. These beginning balances are shown in Illustration 7–3.

Accounting for Materials

A company typically purchases, in advance, the materials that it commonly uses and stores them in materials inventory. Companies may keep one inventory account for all types of materials, or they may keep separate accounts. Assume that in January, Custom Manufacturing purchased

Illustration 7-3   Cost Flows through T-Accounts—Materials

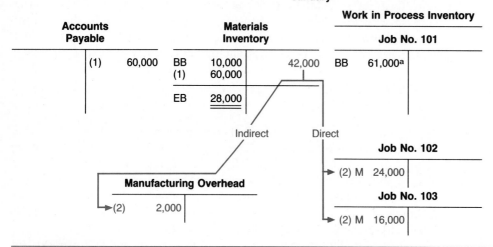

CUSTOM MANUFACTURING COMPANY
January

Note: BB = Beginning balance; EB = Ending balance; and M = Materials. Numbers in parentheses correspond to journal entries presented in text.

[a] Beginning inventory is composed of:

Direct material	$14,000
Direct labor	22,000
Manufacturing overhead	25,000
Total	$61,000

$60,000 of direct and indirect materials and accumulated the costs in one account. This purchase was recorded as follows:

(1) Materials Inventory	60,000	
Accounts Payable		60,000

When the supplier sends an invoice or bill for the shipment, the payable is recorded as shown earlier. Payment is recorded with a debit to Accounts Payable and a credit to Cash.

When materials are needed for a job or contract, the job supervisor or other authority requisitions them. The requested materials are removed from materials inventory and taken to the department where the job is being produced. The **materials requisition** form is next sent to the accounting department where it is the source document for the entry transferring materials from materials inventory to the job.

No materials were requisitioned for Job No. 101 in January. Job No. 102 had requisitions for materials totaling $27,000 and a return of $3,000 excess materials to materials inventory (see Illustration 7–2). The entries to record these transfers of direct materials are as follows:

(2a) Work in Process Inventory—Job No. 102	27,000	
Materials Inventory		27,000
Per requisitions 102–A1 and 102–A2 (see Illustration 7–2).		

Materials Requisition A form used to obtain materials from a storeroom.

Materials inventory	3,000	
Work in Process Inventory—Job No. 102		3,000
Return of materials to materials inventory (see Illustration 7–2).		

Direct materials of $16,000 were requisitioned for Job No. 103, and recorded in entry (2*b*) below. The flow of costs is shown in Illustration 7–3. Each job is a subaccount for work in process inventory.

Indirect materials. Materials inventory is also used for indirect materials and supplies that are not assigned to specific jobs but are charged to the Manufacturing Overhead account. For Custom Manufacturing, indirect materials requisitioned amounted to $2,000 in January and were recorded in entry (2*b*) below.

(2*b*)	Work in Process Inventory—Job No. 103	16,000	
	Manufacturing Overhead	2,000	
	Materials Inventory		18,000
	To record direct materials costs of $16,000 assigned to Job No. 103 and indirect materials costs of $2,000 charged to manufacturing overhead.		

Note that Illustration 7–3 presents the ending materials inventory balance, which can be found from the facts given above by solving the basic cost flow equation:

$$
\begin{array}{ccccccc}
\text{Beginning} & + & \text{Transfers-} & = & \text{Transfers-} & + & \text{Ending} \\
\text{balance} & & \text{in} & & \text{out} & & \text{balance} \\
BB & + & TI & = & TO & + & EB \\
\$10{,}000 & + & \$60{,}000 & = & \$42{,}000 & + & EB \\
\$10{,}000 & + & \$60{,}000 & - & \$42{,}000 & = & EB \\
& & & & EB & = & \$28{,}000
\end{array}
$$

Accounting for Labor

Production workers are usually paid an hourly rate and account for their time each day on time cards, time sheets, or other records. The time record provides space for them to account for the hours spent on the job during the day. This time record is the basis for the company's payroll.

The total cost to the company includes gross pay plus the employer's share of social security taxes and employment taxes, employer's contribution to pension and insurance plans, and any other benefits that are paid for the employee by the company. In general, these costs range from about 15 percent to about 70 percent of the wage rate, depending on the fringe-benefit plans in effect at a company. It is common for companies to add their fringe-benefit costs to the wage rate to assign costs to jobs. For example, if a particular employee has a wage rate of $15 per hour and the additional costs to the employer for fringe benefits and payroll taxes are 30 percent of wages, then the cost of the employee's time to the company will be $19.50 per hour [$15 + (.30 × $15)]. When we refer to a labor rate per hour in this book, we are referring to the cost to the company including an allowance for the employer's costs for fringe benefits and payroll taxes.

For example, the payroll department of Custom Manufacturing Company recorded accumulated costs of $110,000 for manufacturing employees. Of the $110,000 total, $80,000 was attributed to direct labor costs, including employee benefits and taxes. The $80,000 is charged (that is, debited) to Work in Process Inventory and posted to the specific jobs worked on during the period. Based on time cards, Job No. 101 was charged with $10,000 in January, Job No. 102 was charged with $40,000 as presented in the job cost record in Illustration 7–2, and Job No. 103 with $30,000. The remaining $30,000 is *indirect labor* and charged to Manufacturing Overhead. This indirect labor includes the costs of supervisory, janitorial, maintenance, security, and timekeeping personnel, as well as idle time by direct labor employees and overtime premiums paid to direct laborers. The following entry was made to record labor costs in January.

(3)	Work in Process Inventory—Job No. 101	10,000	
	Work in Process Inventory—Job No. 102	40,000	
	Work in Process Inventory—Job No. 103	30,000	
	Manufacturing Overhead	30,000	
	Wages Payable (or Accrued Factory Payroll)		110,000

To record direct labor costs of $80,000 assigned to jobs and indirect labor costs of $30,000 charged to Manufacturing Overhead.

The flow of labor costs through the T-accounts is shown in Illustration 7–4.

Accounting for Manufacturing Overhead

Indirect manufacturing costs, including indirect materials and indirect labor, are usually accumulated in the Manufacturing Overhead account. Each department usually has its own Manufacturing Overhead Summary account

Illustration 7-4   **Cost Flows through T-Accounts—Labor Costs**

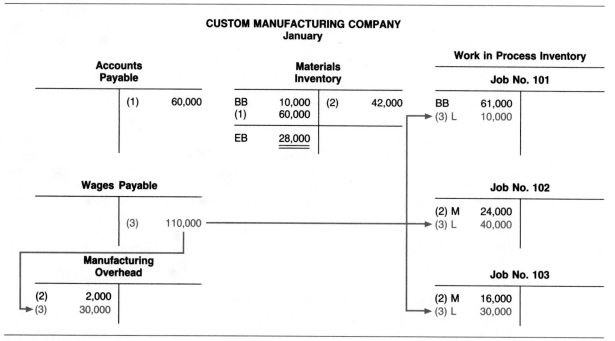

Note: M = Materials; L = Labor.

so each department manager can be held accountable for departmental overhead costs. This helps top management evaluate how well department managers control costs. This first stage of cost allocation is to allocate costs from the accounts in which they were initially entered to responsibility centers. In this case, the responsibility centers are departments.

For example, in January, Custom Manufacturing has indirect materials costs of $2,000 and indirect labor costs of $30,000 charged to the Manufacturing Overhead account as shown in entries (2) and (3). Utilities and other costs credited to accounts payable were $46,000. An amortization of $7,000 representing the portion of prepaid taxes and insurance applicable to the period is included in the actual overhead, as is depreciation of $19,000. These items total $104,000 and represent the actual overhead incurred during the period. These are called **actual costs.** Some of these costs are allocated to the department. For example, depreciation is the cost of an asset allocated over time, and utilities at Custom are allocated between manufacturing and nonmanufacturing.

Actual Costs Amounts determined on the basis of actual (historical) costs incurred.

The journal entry to record manufacturing overhead was:

(4)	Manufacturing Overhead	72,000	
	Accounts Payable		46,000
	Prepaid Expenses		7,000
	Accumulated Depreciation		19,000
	To record actual manufacturing overhead costs other than indirect labor and indirect materials.		

This entry is labeled (4) in the T-account diagram in Illustration 7–5.

Stage 2 allocation takes place at the end of the month. Custom Manufacturing totals the actual manufacturing overhead costs incurred and applies them to jobs on the basis of machine-hours used on each job. For January, the total manufacturing overhead costs incurred were $104,000, made up of $2,000 indirect materials, $30,000 indirect labor, and $72,000 overhead costs shown in entry (4). Custom used 800 machine-hours (mh.) for the month of January, so the overhead application rate was $130 per machine-hour.

$$\frac{\text{Actual manufacturing overhead costs}}{\text{Machine-hours used}} = \frac{\$104,000}{800 \text{ mh}} = \$130 \text{ per mh.}$$

The manufacturing overhead applied to each job in January was:

	Machine-Hours Used		Actual Overhead Rate		Manufacturing Overhead Applied
Job No. 101	100	×	$130	=	$ 13,000
Job No. 102	400	×	$130	=	52,000
Job No. 103	300	×	$130	=	39,000
Total	800				$104,000

The entry to record this allocation of overhead to jobs is shown below.

(5)	Work in Process Inventory—Job No. 101	13,000	
	Work in Process Inventory—Job No. 102	52,000	
	Work in Process Inventory—Job No. 103	39,000	
	Manufacturing Overhead		104,000
	To record application of manufacturing overhead to jobs.		

Illustration 7–5   **Cost Flows through T-Accounts—Manufacturing Overhead Costs**

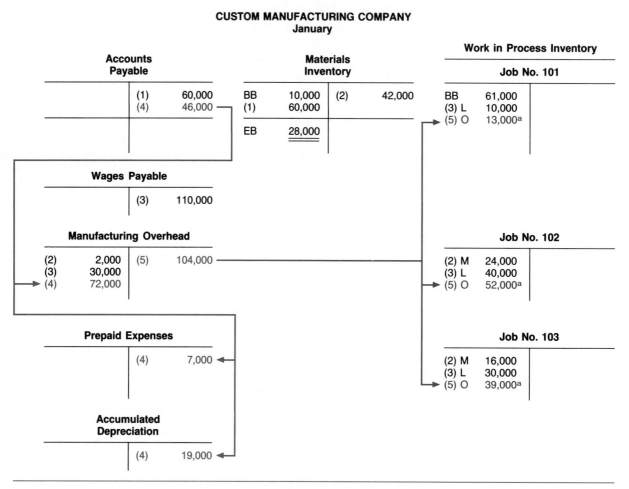

CUSTOM MANUFACTURING COMPANY
January

Note: M = Direct materials; L = Direct labor; O = Manufacturing overhead.

[a] Overhead application rate = $130 per machine-hour = $\dfrac{\text{Total Overhead}}{\text{Total mh}} = \dfrac{\$104,000}{800 \text{ mh}}$

The flow of these costs through T-accounts is illustrated in Illustration 7–5.

Overhead is allocated to jobs if management wants to know whether a specific job was profitable. Overhead may also need to be allocated to jobs for determining inventory values for financial reporting purposes.

Transfers to Finished Goods Inventory

When jobs are transferred out of production to the finished goods storage area, an entry is made transferring the costs of the jobs from the various work in process inventory accounts to the Finished Goods Inventory account. For example, Custom Manufacturing completed Job Nos. 101 and 102 in January and transferred them to the Finished Goods Inventory account. The journal entry is:

(6)	Finished Goods Inventory	200,000	
	Work in Process Inventory—Job No. 101		84,000
	Work in Process Inventory—Job No. 102		116,000
	To transfer completed jobs to the finished goods storage area.		

Note that the amount transferred includes costs incurred in both the current period and in previous periods. For example, the transfer for Job No. 101 includes both $61,000 from beginning work in process inventory and $23,000 of costs incurred in January to complete the job.

Transfer to Cost of Goods Sold

When the goods are sold, they are transferred from the Finished Goods Inventory account to the Cost of Goods Sold account. For example, Custom Manufacturing sold Job No. 101 in January for $120,000 on account. When the job was sold, the journal entry to record the cost of goods sold was:

(7)	Cost of Goods Sold	84,000	
	Finished Goods Inventory		84,000
	Accounts Receivable	120,000	
	Sales Revenue		120,000

The flow of all manufacturing costs, from the acquisition of materials to the final sale, are summarized in Illustration 7–6.

Marketing and Administrative Costs

Marketing and administrative costs do not flow through Work in Process Inventory accounts. These costs are recorded in temporary accounts that are closed at the end of the accounting period. For example, Custom Manufacturing's marketing and administrative costs (all on account) were $10,000 in January. The entry to record these costs is:

Marketing and Administrative Costs	10,000	
Accounts Payable		10,000
To record marketing and administrative costs incurred in January.		

Completion of the Operating Cycle

Custom Manufacturing's income statement for January is shown in Illustration 7–7. The income statement and T-account flows can be related by cross-referencing many of the manufacturing costs from Illustration 7–6.

JOB COSTING IN SERVICE ORGANIZATIONS

Job operations are also found in service organizations, such as engineering, consulting, and accounting firms. The job costing procedure is basically the same in both service and manufacturing organizations, except that service firms use no direct materials.

Example. Custom Engineering Company is an engineering consulting firm. Custom *Engineering* has the same cost data for January as Custom *Manufacturing,* but Custom Engineering *has no direct materials*. In addition, Custom Engineering has $2,000 in supplies in place of the $2,000 in indirect materials that Custom Manufacturing had. These supplies are purchased on account and shown on the debit side of the Service Overhead account.

CUSTOM MANUFACTURING COMPANY
January

Work in Process Inventory

Job No. 101

BB	61,000	(6)	84,000
(3) L	10,000		
(5) O	13,000		
	–0–		

Job No. 102

(2) M	24,000	(6)	116,000
(3) L	40,000		
(5) O	52,000		
	–0–		

Job No. 103

(2) M	16,000		
(3) L	30,000		
(5) O	39,000		
EB	85,000		

Finished Goods Inventory

BB	–0–	(7)	84,000
(6)	200,000		
EB	116,000		

Cost of Goods Sold

84,000	

Materials Inventory

BB	10,000	(2)	42,000
(1)	60,000		
EB	28,000		

Accounts Payable

	(1)	60,000
	(4)	46,000

Wages Payable

	(3)	110,000

Manufacturing Overhead

(2)	2,000	(5)	104,000
(3)	30,000		
(4)	72,000		

Prepaid Expenses

	(4)	7,000

Accumulated Depreciation

	(4)	19,000

Illustration 7-7

CUSTOM MANUFACTURING COMPANY
Income Statement
For the Month Ended January 31

Sales revenue	$120,000
Costs of goods sold (see statement below)	84,000
Gross margin	36,000
Less marketing and administrative costs	10,000
Operating profit	$ 26,000

Cost of Goods Manufactured and Sold Statement
For the Month Ended January 31

Beginning work in process inventory, January 1			$ 61,000
Manufacturing costs during the month:			
Direct materials:			
Beginning inventory, January 1	$10,000		
Add purchases:	60,000		
Materials available	70,000		
Less ending inventory, January 31	28,000		
Total materials used	42,000		
Less: Indirect materials used:	2,000		
Direct materials put into process		$ 40,000	
Direct labor		80,000	
Manufacturing overhead		104,000	
Total manufacturing costs incurred during the month			224,000 [a]
Total costs of work in process during the month			285,000
Less work in process inventory, January 31			85,000
Cost of goods manufactured during the period			200,000 [b]
Beginning finished goods inventory, January 1			–0–
Less ending finished goods inventory, January 31			116,000
Cost of goods manufactured and sold			$ 84,000 [c]

[a] This amount equals the total debits made to Work in Process Inventory in January (not counting the beginning balance).
[b] This amount equals the total debits to Finished Goods Inventory in January.
[c] This amount equals the total credits to Finished Goods Inventory in January.

Illustration 7–8 illustrates job costing in a service organization. It parallels Illustration 7–6, which shows cost flows for a manufacturing organization, except that direct materials costs have been deleted, there is no "finished goods inventory," and some minor changes have been made in account titles. Also, we assume that the January 1 cost balance for Job No. 101 was $22,000 in direct labor and $25,000 in service overhead, for a total of $47,000. Job No. 102, which was completed in January, is assumed to have been billed in January.

USE OF PREDETERMINED OVERHEAD RATES

In the Custom Manufacturing Company example, actual manufacturing overhead was applied to jobs after the end of the month; therefore, there was no difference between actual and applied overhead.

Illustration 7-8 **Cost Flows through T-Accounts—Completed Work**

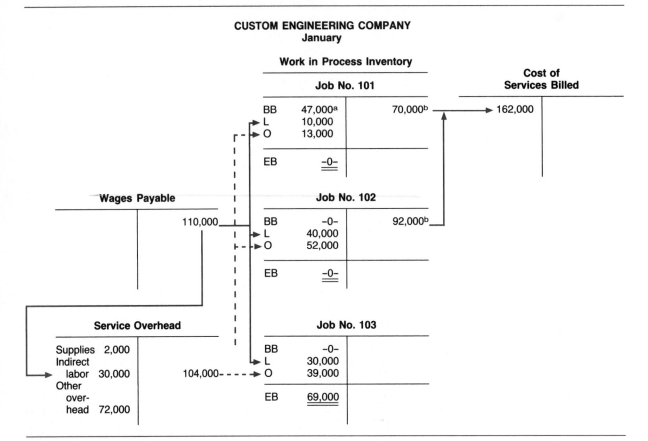

CUSTOM ENGINEERING COMPANY
January

[a] Beginning balance represents contract work in process but not billed. It is composed of $22,000 for direct labor and $25,000 for service overhead incurred in previous periods on Job No. 101.

[b] Job Nos. 101 and 102 were completed and billed in January.

Predetermined Overhead Rate An amount obtained by dividing total estimated overhead for the coming period by the total estimated overhead allocation base for the coming period.

Normal Costing A system of accounting whereby direct materials and direct labor are charged to objects at actual costs, and manufacturing overhead is applied.

Actual Costing A system of accounting whereby overhead is assigned based on actual overhead costs incurred.

In reality, manufacturing overhead is often applied to jobs *before* the actual overhead is known. When this is done, a **predetermined overhead rate** is used to apply manufacturing overhead to jobs. This rate is usually established before the year in which it is to be used, and it is used for the entire year. This normalizes the application of manufacturing overhead to jobs; hence, the resulting product costs are called normal costs. The following chart shows that the only difference between **normal costing** and **actual costing,** which is the method used in the Custom Manufacturing example, is the rate used to apply overhead to jobs and other products.

	Product Costing Method	
	Actual	**Normal**
Direct materials	Actual cost	Actual cost
Direct labor	Actual cost	Actual cost
Manufacturing overhead	**Actual rate** times actual allocation base	**Predetermined rate** times actual allocation base

Example. Deluxe Manufacturing Company is exactly like Custom Manufacturing Company in every respect, except Deluxe Manufacturing uses an annual predetermined rate for applying manufacturing overhead to jobs. The predetermined rate is based on estimated machine-hours. These are based on the estimated volume of activity, sometimes called the *normal volume* of activity. The activity is usually estimated for one year. However, cyclical businesses may use estimates for periods longer than one year.

$$\text{Predetermined rate} = \frac{\text{Estimated manufacturing overhead for the year}}{\text{Estimated machine-hours for the year}}$$

$$= \frac{\$1,200,000}{10,000 \text{ mh.}}$$

$$= \$120 \text{ per machine-hour}$$

Here is how Deluxe Manufacturing used its predetermined rate to charge manufacturing overhead to individual jobs. (Compare these amounts applied to jobs with the actual manufacturing overhead charged to jobs at Custom Manufacturing in Illustration 7–6.)

	Actual Machine-Hours Used		Predetermined Overhead Rate		Manufacturing Overhead Applied
Job No. 101	100	×	120 per mh	=	$12,000
Job No. 102	400	×	120	=	48,000
Job No. 103	300	×	120	=	36,000
Total	800	×	120	=	$96,000

By using a predetermined rate, Deluxe Manufacturing normalizes the overhead applied to jobs. Over the course of time, manufacturing overhead costs can be quite erratic. Preventive maintenance costs are often higher in months when activity is low. Utility costs in cold climates are higher in winter than in summer, and the opposite is true in warm climates. If Deluxe Manufacturing used actual costing, a job in some months would be assigned more overhead than an identical job in other months.

In addition, a company might not know its actual overhead costs until after the close of a fiscal year. Use of normal costing enables management to prepare financial statements and use product-cost data for managerial purposes based on a good estimate of product costs in the interim.

Illustration 7–9 compares the flow of costs when manufacturing overhead is applied using actual costing and normal costing. Two accounts may be used to separate actual and applied overhead so that all entries in one account refer to *actual* overhead, while all those in the other account refer to **applied overhead.** We title the account that records actual overhead, ''Manufacturing Overhead'' (as we did for Custom Manufacturing) and call the new account that records applied overhead, ''Manufacturing Overhead Applied.''[1]

Applied Overhead Overhead applied to a cost object using a predetermined overhead rate.

---

[1] Companies can combine the overhead into one variance account. In such a setting, the left side of the account is basically overhead ''incurred'' and the right side is overhead ''applied.'' The balance is the overhead variance.

Illustration 7-9   **Comparison of Manufacturing Overhead Cost Flows Using Actual and Normal Costing Methods**

Overhead: Actual costing (Custom Manufacturing Company)

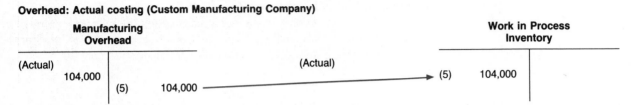

Overhead: Normal costing (Deluxe Manufacturing Company)

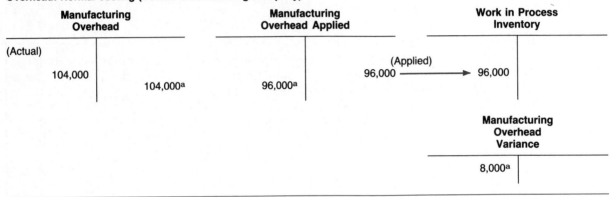

a Refers to closing entry.

At the end of an accounting period, the actual and applied accounts are closed. Usually this is not done until the end of the year when the books are closed. For illustrative purposes, however, we assume that Custom Manufacturing and Deluxe Manufacturing close their books for the month of January. The actual account is left with a zero balance under actual costing because all of the actual overhead is debited to Work in Process Inventory and credited to the Manufacturing Overhead account.

Under normal costing, however, the amount debited to the actual account (the actual manufacturing overhead) is unlikely to equal the amount applied. The reasons for this are discussed in the appendix to this chapter. The difference between the actual and applied manufacturing overhead is called an **overhead variance** and is debited or credited to Work in Process, Finished Goods, and/or Cost of Goods Sold through the proration procedure discussed below. Temporarily we use a *Manufacturing Overhead* account. For example, assume $96,000 was debited to Work in Process Inventory and credited to Manufacturing Overhead Applied, as shown in Illustration 7–9. Now, the entry to close actual against applied overhead for Deluxe Manufacturing is:

Overhead Variance The difference between actual and applied overhead.

Manufacturing Overhead Applied	96,000	
Manufacturing Overhead Variance	8,000	
Manufacturing Overhead		104,000

Underapplied Overhead The excess of actual overhead over applied overhead in a period.

Underapplied overhead *occurs when actual overhead exceeds applied overhead* as for Deluxe Manufacturing. Underapplied overhead is shown as

Overapplied Overhead The excess of applied overhead over actual overhead incurred during a period.

a *debit* to the Manufacturing Overhead Variance account. **Overapplied overhead** *occurs when actual overhead is less than applied overhead.* Overapplied overhead is shown as a *credit* to the Manufacturing Overhead Variance account.

Disposition of the Manufacturing Overhead Variance

At year end, the manufacturing overhead variance is either (1) prorated to Work in Process Inventory, Finished Goods Inventory, and Costs of Goods Sold; or (2) assigned in total to Cost of Goods Sold. Illustration 7–10 recaps the costs of jobs before proration at Deluxe Manufacturing.

Method 1: Prorate the Overhead Variance

If the variance is prorated to Work in Process Inventory, Finished Goods Inventory, and Cost of Goods Sold, then the cost of each job is adjusted to approximate actual cost. For Deluxe Manufacturing, the status and cost of each job *before* prorating the overhead variance is shown in Illustration 7–11. The variance will be prorated so that each account and job bears a share of the $8,000 manufacturing overhead variance. This share will be proportional to the overhead applied to the account during the month as shown in Illustration 7–11.

The following entry is made to prorate the variance:

Cost of Goods Sold	1,000	
Finished Goods Inventory	4,000	
Work in Process Inventory	3,000	
Manufacturing Overhead Variance		8,000

The adjusted balances of the Work in Process Inventory, Finished Goods Inventory, and Cost of Goods Sold accounts are exactly the same as if the actual costing method were used. (Note that Deluxe's adjusted account balances are the same as those for Custom Manufacturing shown in Illustration 7–6.)

Method 2: Assign the Adjustment to Cost of Goods Sold

Many companies do not prorate the manufacturing overhead variance to inventories and Cost of Goods Sold; instead they transfer the entire variance

Illustration 7–10

DELUXE MANUFACTURING COMPANY
Costs of Jobs before Prorating the Manufacturing Overhead Variance

Job No.	Beginning Inventory	Direct Materials	Direct Labor	Manufacturing Overhead Applied in January	Total Costs Charged to Jobs	Status of Job at End of Month
101	$61,000	–0–	$10,000	$12,000	$ 83,000	Cost of Goods Sold
102	–0–	$24,000	40,000	48,000	112,000	Finished Goods Inventory
103	–0–	16,000	30,000	36,000	82,000	Work in Process Inventory
	$61,000	$40,000	$80,000	$96,000	$277,000	

Illustration 7-11

DELUXE MANUFACTURING
Manufacturing Overhead Variance

Job	Account	Manufacturing Overhead Applied in January[a]	Percent of Total Overhead Applied in January[b]	Prorated Variance[c]	Costs Charged to Job before Overhead Variance[d]	Total Costs Assigned to Jobs after Prorating Overhead Variance[e]
101	Costs of Goods Sold	$12,000	12.5	$1,000	$ 83,000	$ 84,000
102	Finished Goods Inventory	48,000	50.0	4,000	112,000	116,000
103	Work in Process Inventory	36,000	37.5	3,000	82,000	85,000
		$96,000	100.0	$8,000	$277,000	$285,000

[a] $120 per machine-hour
[b] 12.5% = $12,000 ÷ $96,000; 50.0% = $48,000 ÷ $96,000; 37.5% = $36,000 ÷ $96,000
[c] Multiply the adjustment which is $8,000 times the appropriate percent for each account. For example $1,000 = 12.5% × $8,000.
[d] From Illustration 7-10.
[e] Add the amount to the amount before the overhead variance.

to Cost of Goods Sold for both internal and external reporting using the following journal entry:

Cost of Goods Sold	8,000	
Manufacturing Overhead Variance		8,000

In a company with many kinds of products and inventories, proration can be complicated. If the amounts to be prorated are immaterial relative to inventory values and net income for external reporting, it may not be necessary to prorate for external reporting. For internal, managerial purposes, the overhead variance is usually not prorated because management focuses on actual manufacturing costs incurred rather than on the amounts applied. Knowledge about the causes of differences between actual costs and the costs that were applied to jobs may, in some circumstances, suggest that management may need to revise overhead rates, impose new cost-control procedures, or take other actions.

Prorating the overhead variance to inventories and Cost of Goods Sold does not necessarily make the inventory values more "accurate." Furthermore, any difference between actual and applied overhead will eventually be expensed (or credited to expense), even if a company prorates. Prorating the overhead variance merely defers expensing the portion allocated to inventories until those inventories are sold.

For external reporting, therefore, the difference between prorating the variance and assigning it in total to Cost of Goods Sold is a matter of timing. For managerial purposes, one must ask how useful it is to revalue work in process and finished goods inventories to actual cost. A large overhead adjustment may affect some cost control, performance evaluation, pricing, and other decisions, but if the adjustments are small, proration is probably not worthwhile.

Interim Reporting

When normal costing is used and the overhead accounts are not closed monthly, there are two ways of reporting the balance in the Manufacturing Overhead Variance account on financial statements. It can either be (1) reported on the income statement, for example, as an adjustment to Cost of Goods Sold or (2) carried on the balance sheet as an adjustment to inventory or as a deferred debit or credit. The first option treats the adjustment as a period cost; the second, as a product cost. Management and accountants select the option they prefer and use it continuously for interim reporting consistency. When the accounts are formally closed, the Manufacturing Overhead Variance account is prorated (Method 1, above) or closed to Cost of Goods Sold (Method 2, above).

SUMMARY

Most methods of producing goods and services can be classified into two general categories: job and process. Each requires a different costing system. Job costing concepts are used when products are easily identifiable as individual units or batches of identical units. In job costing, costs are traced to each unit or job. Construction contractors, print shops, and consulting firms are likely to use job costing methods.

Many service organizations use job costing. Their methods are similar to those used in manufacturing, except service organizations do not have direct materials costs.

Process costing is used by organizations that produce identical units through an ongoing series of uniform production steps. Oil refineries and chemical companies would use process costing methods. In process costing, costs for an accounting period are accumulated by department and spread evenly (or averaged) over all units produced in the period.

Job costing may require more recordkeeping than process costing, which may make it more expensive to use. But many organizations find that benefits of knowing the cost of each job justify the added cost of operating a job costing system. Job costing data can be used in bidding and pricing, controlling costs, and evaluating performance.

Our discussion of cost flows in the chapter is summarized by the flow of cost diagrams in Illustrations 7–6 and 7–8.

The source document for job costing is the job cost record (also called a job cost sheet or card). Each job has a separate record on which its costs are accumulated. These records are used to value inventory for external financial reporting, for feedback on the accuracy of job cost estimations, and for evaluating how well costs were controlled on each job.

Manufacturing overhead is often applied to jobs before the actual overhead is known. A predetermined overhead rate is used instead of the actual overhead rate. This is known as normal costing.

When predetermined overhead rates are used, actual overhead rarely equals applied overhead. The difference is a variance. This manufacturing overhead variance may be debited or credited in total to Cost of Goods Sold or prorated to goods in inventory and goods sold.

TERMS AND CONCEPTS

The following terms and concepts should be familiar to you after reading this chapter. Terms followed by an asterisk are found in this chapter's appendix.

Actual Costs	**Operation**
Actual Costing	**Operation Costing**
Applied Overhead	**Overapplied Overhead**
Batch	**Overhead Variance**
Batch Production	**Predetermined Overhead Rate**
Continuous Flow Processing	**Process Costing**
Denominator Reason*	**Process Systems**
Favorable Variance*	**Production Volume Variance***
Hybrid	**Project**
Job Costing	**Repetitive Manufacturing**
Job Cost Record	**Source Document**
Jobs	**Spending Variance***
Materials Requisition	**Underapplied Overhead**
Normal Costing	**Unfavorable Variance***
Numerator Reason*	

SUPPLEMENTARY READINGS

Gulledge, Thomas R.; Norman K. Womer; and M. Murat Tarimcilar. "Discrete Dynamic Optimization Model for Made-to-Order Cost Analysis." *Decision Sciences*, Winter 1985, pp. 73–90.

Sena, James A. and Lawrence Murphy Smith. "Designing and Implementing an Integrated Job Cost Accounting System." *Journal of Information Systems*, Fall 1986, pp. 102–12.

Williams, H. James. "Job Order Cost Accounting Information Systems." *Journal of Small Business Management*, April 1985, p. 17.

SELF-STUDY PROBLEM NO. 1

Information on the Farawell Industrial Equipment Company, a job order company specializing in custom-built industrial equipment, has been somewhat sketchy. Management wishes to determine various unknown balances and has hired you for assistance. The following data are available for last year:

Account Balances	Beginning of Year (January 1)	End of Year (December 31)
Materials inventory	$205,000	$?
Work in process inventory	68,550	?
Finished goods inventory	31,000	65,000[a]
Manufacturing overhead (actual)	–0–	247,000
Accounts payable—production materials	16,000	24,000
Costs of goods sold	–0–	769,650[a]

[a] Before prorating the overhead adjustment.

Accounts payable are for production materials only. The Work in Process Inventory account balances are supported by data in job cost records, which relate to jobs in process at the balance sheet dates. At the beginning of last year, January 1, there were two jobs in process, as follows:

Job Number	Direct Materials	Direct Labor
206	$14,200	$ 8,400
217	6,500	9,000
	$20,700	$17,400

At the end of last year, December 31, there was only one job in process, Job No. 372. However, the only available information on the job was the accumulated direct labor costs of $12,000 and direct materials of $21,900. Overhead is applied to jobs as a predetermined percentage of direct labor costs. The following additional information is available to you about events last year:

Payments made to suppliers last year	$342,000
Indirect materials issued from inventory	14,000
Direct labor costs incurred	140,000
Direct materials costs transferred from work in process to finished goods inventory during last year	403,800
Current period applied overhead in the ending finished goods inventory on December 31 of last year	30,000

Required:

Determine the following:

a. T-accounts for the flow of costs detailed in this problem.

b. Materials purchased.

c. Direct materials issued to work in process inventory. (Hint: Consider how much was transferred out of work in process to finished goods.)

d. Materials inventory ending account balance, December 31.

e. Overhead application rate.

f. Overhead applied to the Work in Process Inventory account during the year.

g. Over- or underapplied overhead.

h. Cost of the goods transferred to the Finished Goods Inventory account during the year.

i. Work in Process Inventory ending account balance, December 31.

j. Applied overhead in the ending Work in Process Inventory account on December 31.

SOLUTION TO SELF-STUDY PROBLEM NO. 1

a. We recommend setting up T-accounts before solving the problem, then recording the amounts in the accounts as you solve for each of the items below. Completed T-accounts are shown in Exhibit A.

For each of the items below, we use the basic inventory cost flow model:

$$\text{Beginning balance} + \text{Transfers-in} = \text{Transfers-out} + \text{Ending balance}$$
$$BB \quad + \quad TI \quad = \quad TO \quad + \quad EB$$

Note: Data given in the problem are indicated with an asterisk (*).

Exhibit A   **Self-Study Problem No. 1—T-Accounts**

Materials Inventory

BB 1/1	205,000*		14,000*
(b)	350,000	(c)	405,000
(d) EB 12/31	136,000		

Work in Process Inventory

BB 1/1	68,550*	(h)	803,650
(c)	405,000		
Given	140,000*		
(f)	245,000		
(i) EB 12/31	54,900		

Finished Goods Inventory

BB 1/1	31,000*		769,650*
(h)	803,650		
EB 12/31	65,000*		

Cost of Goods Sold

769,650*	

Accounts Payable

	342,000*	BB 1/1	16,000*
		(b)	350,000
		EB 12/31	24,000*

Manufacturing Overhead

EB 12/31	247,000*	247,000c

Manufacturing Overhead Applied

	245,000c	(f)	245,000

Manufacturing Overhead Variance

2,000c	

* Given in the problem.
Note: The symbol for closing entry is c.

b. To find materials purchased, use the Accounts Payable account:

$$BB + TI \text{ (increases in}$$
$$\text{accounts payable are} = TO + EB$$
$$\text{materials purchased)}$$
$$TI = TO + EB - BB$$

Materials purchased (*TI*) = Payments to suppliers (*TO*) + Accounts payable,
December 31 (*EB*) − Accounts payable, January 1 (*BB*)

= \$342,000* + \$24,000* − \$16,000*

= \$350,000

c. The Materials Inventory account has two unknowns; so to find direct materials issued, find the amount of direct materials transferred out of work in process inventory plus the amount in ending work in process inventory (issued this period) minus the amount in beginning work in process inventory (issued in a previous period).

Direct materials issued = Direct materials costs transferred to finished goods inventory
+ Direct materials in ending work in process inventory
− Direct materials in beginning work in process inventory

= \$403,800* + \$21,900* − \$20,700*

= \$405,000

d. To find the Materials Inventory account balance on December 31, use the following formula:

$$BB + TI = TO + EB$$
$$BB + TI - TO = EB$$

Materials inventory, December 31 (*EB*) = Materials inventory, January 1 (*BB*)
+ Purchases *(TI)*
− Direct materials issued *(TO)*
− Indirect materials issued *(TO)*

= \$205,000* + \$350,000 (*b*) above
− \$405,000 (*c*) above
− \$14,000*

= \$136,000

e. Overhead application rate:

Work in process inventory, January 1 = Direct materials + Direct labor
+ Overhead applied

\$68,550* = \$20,700* + \$17,400*
+ Overhead applied

Overhead applied = \$68,550 − \$20,700 − \$17,400

= \$30,450

Overhead application rate = Overhead applied ÷ Direct labor

= \$30,450 ÷ \$17,400*

= 175%

f.

$$\text{Overhead applied to work in process inventory} = \text{Direct labor costs incurred} \times \text{Overhead application rate}$$

$$= \$140,000^* \times 175\%$$
$$= \underline{\$245,000}$$

g.

$$\text{Over- or underapplied overhead} = \text{Overhead applied—Actual manufacturing overhead}$$

$$= \$245,000 - \$247,000^*$$
$$= \underline{-\$2,000} \quad \underline{\text{(underapplied)}}$$

h. To find the cost of goods transferred to the Finished Goods Inventory account, find *TI* to finished goods inventory:

$$BB + TI = TO + EB$$
$$TI = TO + EB - BB$$

$$\text{Cost of goods transferred to finished goods inventory } (TI) = \text{Cost of goods sold } (TO) + \text{Finished goods, December 31 } (EB) - \text{Finished goods, January 1 } (BB)$$

$$= 769,650^* + \$65,000^* - \$31,000^*$$
$$= \underline{803,650}$$

i. To find the ending work in process inventory balance, use the Work in Process Inventory account:

$$BB + TI = TO + EB$$
$$BB + TI - TO = EB$$

$$\text{Work in process inventory, December 31 } (EB) = \text{Work in process inventory, January 1 } (BB) + \text{Direct materials } (TI) + \text{Direct labor } (TI) + \text{Overhead applied } (TI) - \text{Cost of goods transferred to finished goods inventory } (TO)$$

$$= \$68,550^* + \$405,000 + \$140,000^* + \$245,000 - \$803,650$$
$$= \underline{\$54,900}$$

j.

$$\text{Applied overhead in ending work in process inventory} = \text{Direct labor in ending work in process inventory} \times 175\%$$

$$= \$12,000 \times 175\%$$
$$= \underline{\$21,000}$$

APPENDIX
Spending and
Production
Volume Variances

Actual and applied manufacturing overhead are usually unequal when the normal costing method is used because normal costing uses *predetermined* instead of actual overhead rates. There are two basic reasons why actual and applied rates may not be equal: the **numerator reason**, which causes the

Numerator Reason The overhead variance caused by differences between estimated and actual overhead costs for the period.

Spending Variance A variance caused by a difference between actual and estimated manufacturing costs.

Denominator Reason Overhead variance caused by differences between actual activity and the estimated activity used to compute the predetermined rate.

Production Volume Variance A variance caused by a difference between actual and estimated volume.

spending variance; and the denominator reason, which causes the production volume variance. These two variances combine to make up the total manufacturing overhead variance.

The *production volume variance* is caused by the difference between estimated and actual volumes of activity. The actual volume of activity may turn out to be higher or lower than originally estimated. The *spending variance* is the difference between the actual manufacturing overhead cost and the amount estimated to be spent at the actual activity level. The following example demonstrates how to derive these variances. It is helpful to separate what happens before the period when the estimates are made from what happens during and after the period.

Before the Period

Assume the predetermined overhead rate for a company was based on the assumption that manufacturing overhead would be $TC = F + VX = \$6,000 + (\$.40 \text{ per machine-hour} \times \text{machine-hours})$.

If Activity Level Is	Then Manufacturing Overhead Is Expected to Be:		
Activity Level	Fixed	Variable	Total
(1) 3,000 machine-hours	$6,000	$.40 × 3,000 = $1,200	$7,200
(2) 5,000 machine-hours	6,000	.40 × 5,000 = 2,000	8,000
(3) 7,000 machine-hours	6,000	.40 × 7,000 = 2,800	8,800

Now, assume that the company *expects* machine-hours to be 5,000. It would compute the predetermined overhead *rate* as follows:

$$\text{Predetermined rate} = \frac{\text{Estimated manufacturing overhead}}{\text{Estimated machine-hours}}$$

$$= \frac{\$6,000 + (\$.40 \times \text{Machine-hours})}{\text{Machine-hours}}$$

$$= \frac{\$6,000 + (\$.40 \times 5,000)}{5,000}$$

$$= \frac{\$8,000}{5,000}$$

$$= \$1.60 \text{ per machine-hour.}$$

Note that this is the predetermined rate for activity level (2): $5,000. The predetermined rate would be different than $1.60 per machine hour if some other activity level had been estimated.

During and after the Period

Assume the *actual* machine-hours worked are 3,000 [that is, activity (1)] and the *actual* manufacturing overhead costs are $7,900. Now the amount applied equals the predetermined rate ($1.60) times the actual volume of activity (3,000 machine-hours); that is, $4,800 ($1.60 × 3,000 hours). The actual and applied amounts are shown below:

Manufacturing Overhead		Manufacturing Overhead Applied	
(Actual) 7,900			(Applied) 4,800

Comparing the amount applied to the actual cost shows the amount underapplied = $3,100 ($7,900 − 4,800). How much of this $3,100 is due to the lower-than-expected activity level? Did the company spend more than it expected for manufacturing overhead at this level of activity?

Compute Spending and Production Volume Variances

To answer these questions, we compute the *spending* and *production volume variances* as follows:

$$\text{Spending variance} = \begin{array}{c}\text{Actual}\\\text{manufacturing}\\\text{overhead}\end{array} - \begin{array}{c}\text{Manufacturing overhead}\\\text{expected to be incurred}\\\text{at the actual activity level.}\end{array}$$

For this example:

$$\text{Spending variance} = \text{Actual} - \begin{array}{c}\text{Budgeted overhead}\\\text{at activity level (1)}\end{array}$$
$$\$700 = \$7,900 - \$7,200$$

Note that the manufacturing overhead expected to be incurred is based on *the level of activity that actually occurred,* not on the estimated activity level. The company spent less on overhead than the $8,000 originally estimated, but then they *should* have spent less because activity was lower than originally esimated. *The variable overhead is expected to be lower if activity levels are lower,* so the actual overhead is compared with the "revised estimate" for activity level (1), not the original estimate for activity level (2).

The predetermined rate was based on the original estimate, of course, because it was derived before the period—before the actual activity became known.

The *production volume variance* is computed as follows:

$$\begin{array}{c}\text{Production}\\\text{volume}\\\text{variance}\end{array} = \begin{array}{c}\text{Manufacturing overhead}\\\text{expected to be incurred}\\\text{at the actual activity level}\end{array} - \begin{array}{c}\text{Manufacturing}\\\text{overhead}\\\text{applied}\end{array}$$

$$\begin{array}{c}\text{Production volume}\\\text{variance}\\\$2,400\end{array} = \begin{array}{c}\text{Overhead amount expected}\\\text{at activity level (1)}\\\$7,200\end{array} \begin{array}{c}\text{Amount}\\- \text{ applied}\\- \$4,800\end{array}$$

The amount of the underapplied overhead attributable to a lower-than-expected activity level is $2,400. The breakdown of the total underapplied manufacturing overhead into *spending* and *production volume* components is shown in Illustrations 7–12 and 7–13.

Favorable and Unfavorable Variance

The terms *favorable* and *unfavorable* are often used in practice to indicate whether these amounts are underapplied or overapplied, where *unfavorable means overhead was underapplied* and *favorable means overhead was over-*

Illustration 7-12   **Components of Over- or Underapplied Overhead: Spending Variance and Production Volume Variance**

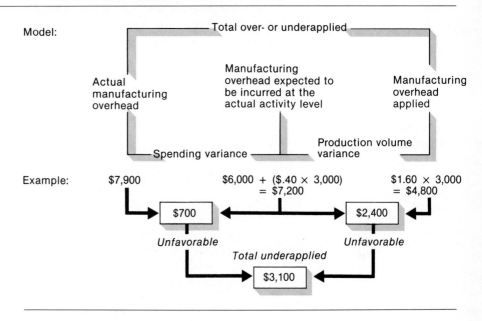

Illustration 7-13   **Graphic Presentation of Spending and Production Volume Variances**

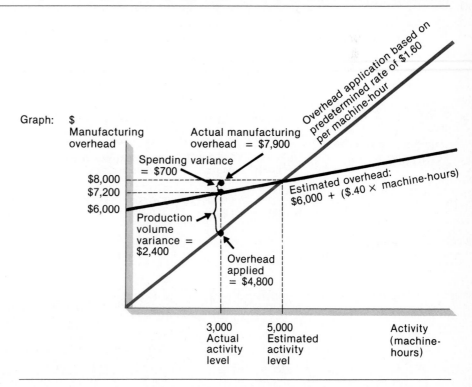

applied. The terms *favorable* and *unfavorable* are *not* intended to indicate whether a variance is good or bad.

In later chapters we shall see how these variances between actual and applied overhead may provide information useful for evaluating how well an organization and its people are performing.

SELF-STUDY PROBLEM NO. 2 (Appendix)

Assume the following facts:

$$\text{Estimated manufacturing overhead for Year 1} = \$20{,}000 + (\$5 \times \text{Direct labor-hours}).$$

Manufacturing overhead is applied on a direct labor-hour basis.
Estimated direct labor hours for Year 1 = 1,000 hours.

Required:

a. Compute the predetermined overhead rate for each of the following possible levels of activity:
1. 800 direct labor-hours.
2. 1,000 direct labor-hours.
3. 1,200 direct labor-hours.

b. During Year 1, the company works 700 direct labor-hours on Job A-01 and 500 direct labor-hours on Job B-01. The actual manufacturing overhead was $27,000. What is the amount of overhead applied to each job if the predetermined rate was $25 because the company had estimated 1,000 hours would be worked?

c. Refer to the facts in b. What is the:
1. Total under- or overapplied overhead?
2. Spending variance?
3. Production volume variance?

d. Graph the relationship between overhead costs and direct labor-hours like the graph shown in Illustration 7–13.

SOLUTION TO SELF-STUDY PROBLEM NO. 2 (Appendix)

a.

Level	Estimated Hours	Expected Total Manufacturing Overhead Costs	Predetermined Rate per Hour
(1)	800	$20,000 + ($5 × 800) = $24,000	$24,000 ÷ 800 = $30
(2)	1,000	$20,000 + ($5 × 1,000) = $25,000	$25,000 ÷ 1,000 = $25
(3)	1,200	$20,000 + ($5 × 1,200) = $26,000	$26,000 ÷ 1,200 = $21.67

b.

	Manufacturing Overhead Applied	
Job 1	**Job 2**	**Total**
$25 × 700 hours = $17,500	$25 × 500 hours = $12,500	$30,000

c.

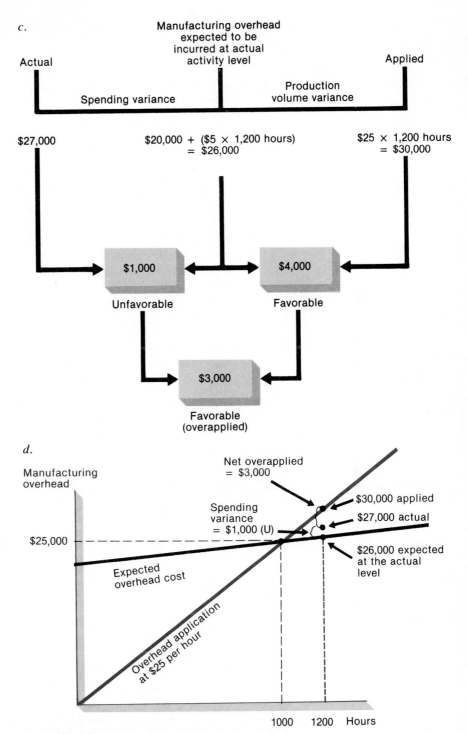

Manufacturing overhead
expected to be
incurred at actual
activity level

Actual   Applied

Spending variance | Production volume variance

$27,000 $20,000 + ($5 × 1,200 hours) $25 × 1,200 hours
                        = $26,000   = $30,000

$1,000 $4,000

Unfavorable   Favorable

$3,000

Favorable
(overapplied)

d.

Manufacturing
overhead

Net overapplied
= $3,000

Spending
variance
= $1,000 (U)

$30,000 applied

$27,000 actual

$25,000

$26,000 expected
at the actual
level

Expected
overhead cost

Overhead application
at $25 per hour

1000   1200   Hours

Production volume variance is the difference between
$30,000 applied and $26,000 expected at the
actual activity level = $4,000 F.

U = Unfavorable variances
F = Favorable variances

QUESTIONS

7-1. What are the characteristics of companies that are likely to be using a job order cost system?

7-2. What is the function of the *job cost record?*

7-3. What is the difference between the *Manufacturing Overhead* account and the *Manufacturing Overhead Applied* account?

7-4. On the first day of the job, a member of the management training program remarked: "The whole procedure of applying overhead and then spending a lot of time adjusting the Inventory and Cost of Goods Sold accounts back to the actual numbers looks like a complex solution to a simple problem. Why not simply charge the actual overhead to production and be done with it?" How would you reply to this comment?

7-5. The assignment of costs to departments and then to jobs is carried out partly for control purposes. Explain.

7-6. What methods, documents, and approvals are used to control materials inventories?

7-7. Why is control of materials important from a *managerial-planning* perspective?

7-8. Labor fringe benefits and similar costs associated with the direct labor may be considered part of direct labor or part of manufacturing overhead. What are the justifications for each alternative treatment?

7-9. How is job costing in service organizations (for example, consulting firms) different from job costing in manufacturing organizations?

7-10. What are the *normal costs* of a product?

7-11. Why might differences between actual and applied manufacturing overhead not be prorated to inventories?

EXERCISES

7-12. Assigning Costs to Jobs

(L.O.2)

On January 1, there were two jobs in process at the Bondview Printing Company. Details of the jobs are:

Job No.	Direct Materials	Direct Labor
J-1	$90	$70
J-2	20	40

Materials inventory at January 1 totaled $460, and $60 in materials were purchased during the month. A requisition for $10 in indirect materials was filled. On January 1, finished goods inventory consisted of two jobs: Job No. D-15 costing $200 and Job No. D-25 with a cost of $80. Both these jobs were sold during the month.

Also during January, Job Nos. J-1 and J-2 were completed. Completing Job No. J-1 required an additional $30 in direct labor. The completion costs for Job No. J-2 included $50 in direct materials and $100 in direct labor.

Job No. A-40 was started during the period but was not finished. A total of $160 of direct materials were brought from the storeroom for all jobs during the period, and total direct labor costs during the month amounted to $200. Actual overhead was applied at 150 percent of direct labor costs to all of the jobs in this exercise, including those in beginning inventory.

Required:

Determine costs for Job Nos. J-1 and J-2 and balances in the January 31 inventory accounts.

7–13. Assigning Costs to Jobs
(L.O.2)

Refer to the information in exercise 7–12. Prepare journal entries representing the transactions discussed in the exercise.

7–14. Assigning Costs to Jobs
(L.O.2)

The following transactions occurred at the March Production Company, a job order custom manufacturer:

1. Purchased $40,000 in materials.
2. Issued $2,000 in supplies from the materials inventory.
3. Purchased materials costing $30,000.
4. Paid for the materials purchased in transaction 1.
5. Issued $34,000 in materials to the production department.
6. Incurred direct labor costs of $50,000, which were credited to Payroll Payable.
7. Paid $80,000 cash for utilities, power, equipment maintenance, and other miscellaneous items for the manufacturing plant.
8. Applied overhead on the basis of 175 percent of $50,000 direct labor costs.
9. Recognized depreciation on manufacturing property, plant, and equipment of $21,000.

Required:

Prepare journal entries to record the above transactions.

7–15. Assigning Costs to Jobs
(L.O.2)

Refer to the data in exercise 7–14. The following balances appeared in the accounts of March Company:

	Beginning	**Ending**
Materials Inventory	$74,100	
Work in Process Inventory	16,500	
Finished Goods Inventory	83,000	$ 66,400
Cost of Goods Sold		131,700

Required:

Prepare T-accounts to show the flow of costs during the period.

7–16. Assigning Costs to Jobs
(L.O.2)

Partially completed T-accounts and additional information for the XYZ Company for the month of March are presented below:

Materials Inventory		**Work in Process Inventory**	
BB 3/1 1,000		BB 3/1 2,000	
4,000	3,200	Direct labor 2,400	

Finished Goods Inventory		**Cost of Goods Sold**	
BB 3/1 3,000			
6,000	4,000		

Manufacturing Overhead		**Manufacturing Overhead Applied**	
2,200			

Additional information:

1. Labor wage rate was $12 per hour.
2. Manufacturing overhead is applied at $8 per direct labor-hour.
3. During the month, sales revenue was $8,000, and selling and administrative costs were $1,600.
4. The accounting period is one month long.

Required:

a. What was the amount of direct materials issued to production during March?

b. What was the amount of manufacturing overhead applied to products during March?

c. What was the cost of products completed during March?

d. What was the balance of the Work in Process Inventory account at the end of March?

e. What was the manufacturing overhead variance during March?

f. What was the operating profit for March?

7–17. Job Costing in a Service Organization
(L.O.4)

For the month of September, Touche Andersen & Company worked 200 hours for client A and 700 hours for client B. Touche Andersen bills clients at the rate of $80 per hour, whereas the labor cost for its audit staff is $30 per hour. The total number of hours worked in September was 1,000 (100 hours were not billable to clients), and overhead costs were $10,000. (Examples of unbillable hours are hours spent in professional training and meetings unrelated to particular clients.) Overhead is assigned to clients based proportionally on direct labor-hours, so client A was assigned $2,000, client B was assigned $7,000, and $1,000 remained unassigned. In addition, Touche Anderson & Company had $5,000 in marketing and administrative costs. All transactions are on account.

Required:

a. Using T-accounts, trace manufacturing costs and revenue flows.

b. Prepare a full absorption income statement for the company for September.

7–18. Assigning Costs to Jobs
(L.O.2)

The Helper Corporation manufactures one product and accounts for costs by a job order cost system. You have obtained the following information for the year ended December 31 of last year from the corporation's books and records:

1. Total manufacturing cost added during last year (called "cost to manufacture") was $1 million based on actual direct material, actual direct labor, and applied manufacturing overhead on the basis of actual direct labor-dollars.

2. Cost of goods manufactured was $970,000, also based on actual direct material, actual direct labor, and applied manufacturing overhead.

3. Manufacturing overhead was applied to work in process at 75 percent of direct labor-dollars. Applied manufacturing overhead for the year was 27 percent of the total manufacturing cost added during last year.

4. Beginning work in process inventory, January 1, was 80 percent of ending work in process inventory, December 31.

Required:

Prepare a cost of goods manufactured statement for last year (year ending December 31) for Helper Corporation. Show actual direct material used, actual direct labor, and applied manufacturing overhead.

(CPA adapted)

7–19. Predetermined Overhead Rates
(L.O.3)

Leomard Company estimates its manufacturing overhead to be $20,000 and its direct labor costs to be $40,000 for Year 1. The actual direct labor costs were $10,000 for Job 1; $15,000 for Job 2; and $20,000 for Job 3 during Year 1. The actual manufacturing overhead was $24,000 during Year 1.

Required:

a. How much overhead was assigned to each job during Year 1?

b. What was the manufacturing overhead variance for Year 1?

7–20. Prorate Under- or Overapplied Overhead
(L.O.3)

Refer to the information in exercise 7–14 to answer the following questions:

a. What is the amount of the manufacturing overhead variance?

b. Regardless of your computations for exercises 7–14 or 7–15, assume that the current applied overhead in each of the inventory accounts and the Cost of Goods Sold account is as follows:

Work in Process Inventory	10%
Finished Goods Inventory	25%
Cost of Goods Sold	65%

Prepare a schedule to show the proration of the manufacturing overhead variance.

7–21. Apply Overhead Using a Predetermined Rate (Multiple Choice)

(L.O.3)

Bowen Company uses a job order accounting system for its production costs. A predetermined overhead rate based on direct-labor hours is used to apply overhead to individual jobs. An estimate of overhead costs at different volumes was prepared for the current year as follows:

Direct labor-hours	100,000	120,000	140,000
Variable overhead costs	$325,000	$390,000	$455,000
Fixed overhead costs	216,000	216,000	216,000
Total overhead	$541,000	$606,000	$671,000

The expected volume is 120,000 direct labor-hours for the entire year. The following information is for November. Jobs 50 and 51 were completed during November.

Inventories, November 1:	
Raw materials and supplies	$ 10,500
Work in process (Job 50)	54,000
Finished goods	112,500
Purchases of raw materials and supplies:	
Raw materials	135,000
Supplies	15,000
Materials and supplies requisitioned for production:	
Job 50	45,000
Job 51	37,500
Job 52	25,500
Supplies	12,000
	$120,000
Factory direct labor-hours:	
Job 50	3,500 DLH
Job 51	3,000 DLH
Job 52	2,000 DLH
Labor costs:	
Direct labor wages	$ 51,000
Indirect labor wages (4,000 hours)	15,000
Supervisory salaries	6,000
Building occupancy costs (heat, light, depreciation, etc.):	
Factory facilities	6,500
Sales and administrative offices	2,500
	$ 9,000

Factory equipment costs:	
Power	$ 4,000
Repairs and maintenance	1,500
Other	2,500
	$ 8,000

Required:

Answer the following multiple-choice questions.

1. The predetermined overhead rate (combined fixed and variable) to be used to apply overhead to individual jobs during the year is:
   a. $3.25 per DLH.
   b. $4.69 per DLH.
   c. $5.05 per DLH.
   d. $5.41 per DLH.
   e. None of these.

   Note: Without prejudice to your answer to requirement 1, assume that the predetermined overhead rate is $4.50 per direct labor-hour. Use this amount in answering requirements 2 through 5.

2. The total cost of job 50 when it is finished is:
   a. $81,750.
   b. $135,750.
   c. $142,750.
   d. $146,750.
   e. None of these.

3. The factory overhead costs applied to job 52 during November were:
   a. $9,000.
   b. $47,500.
   c. $46,500.
   d. $8,000.
   e. None of these.

4. The total amount of overhead applied to jobs during November was:
   a. $29,250.
   b. $38,250.
   c. $47,250.
   d. $56,250.
   e. None of these.

5. Actual factory overhead incurred during November was:
   a. $38,000.
   b. $41,500.
   c. $47,500.
   d. $50,500.
   e. None of these.

6. At the end of the year, Bowen Company had the following account balances:

Overapplied Overhead	$ 1,000
Cost of Goods Sold	980,000
Work in Process Inventory	38,000
Finished Goods Inventory	82,000

What would be the most common treatment of the overapplied overhead?

a. Prorate it between work in process inventory and finished goods inventory.
b. Prorate it between work in process inventory, finished goods inventory, and cost of goods sold.
c. Carry it as a credit on the balance sheet.
d. Carry it as miscellaneous operating revenue on the income statement.
e. Credit it to cost of goods sold.

(CMA adapted)

7–22. Compute Job Costs for a Service Organization
(L.O.4)

At the beginning of the month, Renhor Architects had two jobs in process that had the following costs assigned from previous months:

Job No.	Direct Labor	Applied Overhead
X-10	$640	?
Y-12	420	?

During the month, Jobs X-10 and Y-12 were completed but were not billed to customers. The completion costs for X-10 required $700 in direct labor. For Y-12, $2,000 in labor were used.

During the month, a new job, Z-14, was started but not finished. No new jobs were started. Total direct labor costs for all jobs amounted to $4,120 for the month. Overhead in this company refers to the cost of doing architectural work that is not directly traced to particular jobs. Examples of such costs are copying, printing, and travel costs for meetings with clients. Overhead is applied at a rate of 160 percent of direct labor costs for this and previous periods. Actual overhead for the month was $6,500.

Required:

a. What are the costs of Jobs X-10 and Y-12 at the beginning and the end of the month?
b. What is the cost of Job Z-14 at the end of the month?
c. How much was the manufacturing overhead variance for the month?

7–23. Analyze the Over- or Underapplied Overhead
(L.O.5)

Refer to the data for exercise 7–19. Assume all manufacturing overhead costs were fixed costs.

Required:

How much of the under- or overapplied overhead was a spending variance, and how much was a production volume variance?

7–24. Analyze the Overhead Variance (Appendix)
(L.O.5)

Martinez Company estimates manufacturing overhead to be $80,000 + (.60 × Direct labor costs). Direct labor costs are estimated to be $100,000 for Year 1. The actual manufacturing overhead costs for Year 1 were $150,000. The actual direct labor costs were $120,000.

Required:

a. What is the expected total overhead for each of the following activity levels:
   1. $80,000?
   2. $100,000?
   3. $120,000?
b. How much is the under- or overapplied overhead for Year 1?
c. How much is the spending variance? The production volume variance?

7–25. Analyze the Over- or Underapplied Overhead (Appendix)
(L.O.5)

Assume the following facts:

$$\text{Estimated manufacturing overhead for Year 1} = \$30,000 + (\$10 \times \text{Direct labor-hours}).$$

Estimated direct labor-hours for Year 1 = 1,000 hours.

Required:

a. Compute the predetermined overhead rate.
b. What is the expected manufacturing overhead for each of the following levels of activity:
   1. 800 direct labor-hours?
   2. 1,000 direct labor-hours?
   3. 1,200 direct labor-hours?
c. During Year 1, the company works 800 direct labor-hours on Job 21 and 400 direct labor-hours on Job 22. The actual manufacturing overhead was $37,000. What is the amount of overhead applied to each job?
d. What is the:
   1. Total under- or overapplied overhead?
   2. Spending variance?
   3. Production volume variance?

7–26. Analyze Over- or Underapplied Overhead (Appendix)
(L.O.5)

Based on the information in exercise 7–25, graph the relationships between overhead costs and direct labor-hours like the graph shown in Illustration 7–13.

PROBLEMS

7–27. Estimate Hours Worked from Overhead Data

Terne Corporation had projected its fixed overhead costs to be $240,000. Direct labor was estimated to total 30,000 hours during the year, and the direct labor-hours would be used as a basis for the application of overhead. During the year, all overhead costs were exactly as planned ($240,000). There was $8,000 in overapplied overhead, but no spending variance.

Required:

How many direct labor-hours were worked during the period? Show computations.

7–28. Assigning Costs— Missing Data

Materials Inventory

BB 10/1	8,000		
	(a)	4,300	
EB 10/31	9,700	(b)	

Finished Goods Inventory

BB 10/1	14,200		
	(e)		(f)
EB 10/31	(g)		

Work in Process Inventory

BB 10/1	22,300		
	180,500		
	121,000		
	94,000		
EB 10/31	17,700	(e)	

Cost of Goods Sold

402,800	

Manufacturing Overhead Applied

	(d)

Wages Payable

		BB 10/1	124,300
162,000			(c)
			36,200
		EB 10/31	119,500

Manufacturing Overhead

121,000	
4,300	
36,200	
31,600	
3,200	

Accounts Payable—Materials Suppliers

	100,000

Accumulated Depreciation—Manufacturing Property, Plant, and Equipment

	BB 10/1	204,100
		(h)
	EB 10/31	235,700

Prepaid Insurance

BB 10/1	24,300	
EB 10/31	21,100	*(i)*

Required:

Compute the missing amounts indicated by the letters *(a)* through *(i)*.

7–29. Assigning Costs— Missing Data

The following T-accounts are to be completed with the missing information. Additional data appear after the accounts.

Materials Inventory

EB 9/30	28,200	

Work in Process Inventory

BB 9/1	16,300	
Direct Materials	43,100	

Finished Goods Inventory

EB 9/30	50,500	

Cost of Goods Sold

Manufacturing Overhead

(Actual)		

Manufacturing Overhead Applied

	132,000

Wages Payable

Sales Revenue

	362,700

1. Materials of $56,800 were purchased during the month, and the balance in the inventory account increased by $5,500.
2. Overhead is applied at the rate of 150 percent of direct labor cost.
3. Sales are billed at 80 percent over the normal cost of the jobs to which the sales relate.
4. The balance in finished goods inventory decreased by $14,300 during the month.
5. Total credits to the Wages Payable account amounted to $101,000. All credits in this account are related to the manufacturing plant.
6. Factory depreciation totaled $24,100.
7. Overhead was underapplied by $12,540. All other charges for overhead incurred required payment in cash. Underapplied overhead is to be prorated.
8. The company has decided to allocate 25 percent of underapplied overhead to work in process inventory, 15 percent to finished goods inventory, and the balance to cost of goods sold. Balances shown in T-accounts are before proration.

Required: Complete the T-accounts.

7–30. Tracing Costs in a Job Company

On June 1, two jobs were in process at the Springer Landscaping Company. Details of the jobs are as follows:

Job No.	Direct Materials	Direct Labor
A-15	$87	$32
A-38	16	42

Materials inventory (for example, plants and shrubs) on June 1 totaled $460, and $58 in materials were purchased during the month. Indirect materials of $8 were withdrawn from materials inventory. On June 1, finished goods inventory consisted of two jobs, Job No. A-07, costing $196 and Job No. A-21, with a cost of $79. Both of these jobs were transferred to cost of goods sold during the month.

Also during June, Jobs No. A-15 and A-38 were completed. To complete Job No. A-15 required an additional $34 in direct labor. The completion costs for Job No. A-38 included $54 in direct materials and $100 in direct labor.

Job No. A-40 was started during the period but was not finished. A total of $157 of direct materials was used (excluding the $8 indirect materials) during the period, and total direct labor costs during the month amounted to $204. Overhead has been estimated at 150 percent of direct labor costs, and this relation has been the same for the past few years.

Required:

Compute costs of Jobs No. A-15 and A-38 and balances in the June 30 inventory accounts.

7–31. Tracing Costs in a Job Company

The following transactions occurred at Super Dynamics, Inc., a defense contractor that uses job costing:

1. Purchased $40,000 in materials.
2. Issued $2,000 in supplies from the materials inventory.
3. Received materials with a cost of $31,600 at the storeroom.
4. Paid for the materials purchased in (1).
5. Issued $34,000 in materials to the production department.
6. Incurred wage costs of $56,000, which were debited to a temporary account called Payroll. Of this amount, $18,000 was withheld for payroll taxes and other similar liabilities. The remainder was paid in cash to the employees. [See transactions (7) and (8) for additional information about Payroll.]
7. Recognized $28,000 in fringe benefit costs, which were incurred as a result of the wages paid in (6). This $28,000 was debited to the temporary account called Payroll.
8. Analyzed the Payroll account and determined that 60 percent was direct labor, 30 percent was indirect manufacturing labor, and 10 percent represented administrative and marketing costs.
9. Paid for utilities, power, equipment maintenance, and other miscellaneous items for the manufacturing plant. The total amount was $43,200.
10. Paid $53,500 for new equipment.
11. Applied overhead on the basis of 175 percent of *direct* labor costs, including fringe benefits recorded in (6) and (7) above.
12. Recognized depreciation on manufacturing property, plant, and equipment of $21,000.

Required:

a. Prepare journal entries to record these transactions.

b. The following balances appeared in the accounts of Super Dynamics, Inc.:

	Beginning	**Ending**
Materials Inventory	$74,100	—
Work in Process Inventory	16,500	—
Finished Goods Inventory	83,000	$ 66,400
Cost of Goods Sold	—	131,700

Prepare T-accounts to show the flow of costs during the period.

7–32. Cost Flows through Accounts

Donegal Woolens employed 20 full-time knitters at $5 per hour. Since beginning operations last year, they had priced the various jobs by applying a markup of 20 percent on direct labor and direct material costs. However, despite operating at capacity, last year's performance was a great disappointment to the managers. In total, 10 jobs were taken and completed, incurring the following total costs:

Direct materials	$ 51,770
Direct labor	200,000
Manufacturing overhead	52,000

Thirty percent of the $52,000 manufacturing overhead was variable overhead; 70 percent was fixed.

This year Donegal Woolens expected to operate at the same activity level as last year, and overhead costs and the wage rate were not expected to change.

For the first quarter of this year, Donegal Woolens had just completed two jobs and was beginning on the third. The costs incurred were as follows:

Jobs	Direct Materials	Direct Labor Costs
111	$6,860	$24,500
112	4,650	15,620
113	4,700	9,880
Total factory overhead		$13,560
Total marketing and administrative costs		5,600

You are a consultant associated with Vesting Concerns Management Consultants, the firm Donegal Woolens has approached. The senior partner of your firm has examined Donegal Woolens' books and has decided to divide actual factory overhead by job into fixed and variable portions as follows:

	Actual Factory Overhead	
Jobs	Variable	Fixed
111	$1,495	$ 5,200
112	1,375	4,410
113	230	850
	$3,100	$10,460

In the first quarter of this year, 40 percent of marketing and administrative costs were variable and 60 percent were fixed. You are told that Jobs 111 and 112 were sold for $42,500 and $27,500, respectively. All over- or underapplied overhead for the quarter is expensed on the income statement.

Required:

a. Present in T-accounts the full absorption, actual manufacturing cost flows for the three jobs in the first quarter of this year.

b. Using last year's overhead costs and direct labor hours, calculate a predetermined overhead rate per direct labor-hour for variable and fixed overhead.

c. Present in T-accounts the full absorption, normal manufacturing cost flows for the three jobs in the first quarter of this year. Use the overhead rates derived in part (b).

d. Prepare income statements for the first quarter of this year under the following costing systems:
(1) Full absorption, actual.
(2) Full absorption, normal.

7–33. Prorate Overhead Variances

Fermi Processing Corporation has a special-order coating process that operates in two departments: surface preparation and application. Jobs enter the surface preparation department where chemical treatments clean the surface and prepare it chemically for the application of coatings. The coating takes place in the application department under carefully controlled conditions. The following cost and activity amounts were prepared for this year:

	Surface Preparation	Application
Overhead costs	$190,000	$350,032
Direct materials	24,000	785,000
Direct labor	58,900	56,000
Machine-hours	16,000	40,000

During the year, work was performed on a number of jobs. Overhead in the surface preparation department was applied on the basis of $11.875 per machine-hour, while overhead in the application department was applied at the rate of 44.59 percent of direct materials costs.

At the end of the year, the following balances appeared in the inventory accounts and Cost of Goods Sold account:

Work in Process Inventory—Surface Preparation	
Direct materials	$ 3,720
Direct labor	2,945
Overhead applied	2,375
Work in Process Inventory—Application:	
Direct materials	28,000
Direct labor	2,800
Overhead applied	12,485
Finished Goods Inventory:	
Direct materials—surface preparation	2,800
—application	61,250
Direct labor—surface preparation	6,479
—application	11,760
Overhead applied—surface preparation	20,900
—application	27,311

Cost of Goods Sold:	
From last year's production	139,263
Direct materials—surface preparation	17,480
—application	695,750
Direct labor—surface preparation	49,476
—application	41,440
Overhead applied and prorated—surface preparation	150,100
—application	321,450

The overhead applied and prorated in the Cost of Goods Sold account represents the applied overhead plus a debit or credit for any under- or overapplied overhead for the period. That is, all of the overhead variance has been charged or credited to Cost of Goods Sold.

Required:

Determine the entry that would be required to prorate the over- or underapplied overhead for surface preparation and application. (Round amounts to the nearest dollar.)

7–34. Show Flow of Costs to Jobs

Pulsar Light Equipment Company assembles light and sound equipment for installation in various entertainment facilities. An inventory of materials and equipment is on hand at all times so that installation may be started as quickly as possible. Special equipment is ordered as required. On September 1, the Materials and Equipment Inventory account had a balance of $48,000. A Work in Process Inventory account is maintained to record costs of installation work not yet complete. There were two such jobs on September 1, with the following costs:

	Job No. 46 Wheels and Spokes Country Music Hall	Job No. 51 Stars Theater
Materials and equipment	$32,000	$95,000
Technician labor	6,500	9,700
Overhead (applied)	4,800	14,250

Overhead has been applied at 15 percent of the costs of materials and equipment installed.

During September, two new installations were begun. Additional work was carried out on Job Nos. 46 and 51, with the latter job completed and billed to the Stars Theater. Details on the costs incurred on jobs during September are as follows:

	Job No. 46	Job No. 51	Job No. 55	Job No. 56
Materials and equipment	$3,200	$14,200	$17,000	$6,200
Technician labor (on account)	1,800	1,200	3,100	900

In addition to these costs, other events of the period included:

1. $25,000 payment received on Job No. 55 delivered to customer.
2. Purchased materials and equipment for $18,700.
3. Billed Stars Theater $175,000 and received payment for $100,000 of that amount.
4. Payroll for indirect labor personnel totaled $1,300.

5. Issued supplies and incidental installation materials for current jobs. The cost of these items was $310.

6. Recorded overhead and advertising costs for the installation operation as follows (all cash except equipment depreciation):

Property taxes	$1,100
Showroom and storage area rental	1,350
Truck and delivery cost	640
Advertising and promotion campaign	1,200
Electrical inspections	400
Telephone and other miscellaneous	650
Equipment depreciation	900

Required:

a. Journal entries to record the flow of costs for the installation operation during September.

b. Amount of over- or underapplied overhead for the month. This amount is debited or credited to Cost of Goods Sold.

c. Inventory balances for Materials and Equipment Inventory and Work in Process Inventory.

7–35. Reconstruct Missing Data

Disaster struck the only manufacturing plant of the Complete Transaction Equipment Corporation on December 1. All the work in process inventory was destroyed. A few records were salvaged from the wreckage and from the company's headquarters. The insurance company has stated that it will pay the cost of the lost inventory if adequate documentation can be supplied. The insurable value of work in process inventory is made up of direct materials, direct labor, and applied overhead.

The following information about the plant appears on the October financial statements at the company's headquarters:

Materials inventory, October 31	$ 49,000
Work in process inventory, October 31	86,200
Finished goods inventory, October 31	32,000
Cost of goods sold through October 31	348,600
Accounts payable, materials suppliers on October 31	21,600
Manufacturing overhead through October 31	184,900
Payroll payable on October 31	–0–
Withholding and other payroll liabilities on October 31	9,700
Overhead applied through October 31	179,600

A count of the inventories on hand November 30 shows:

Materials inventory	$43,000
Work in process inventory	?
Finished goods inventory	37,500

The accounts payable clerk tells you that there are outstanding bills to suppliers of $50,100 and that cash payments of $37,900 have been made during the month to these suppliers.

The payroll clerk informs you that the payroll costs last month included $82,400 for the manufacturing section and that $14,700 of this was indirect labor.

At the end of November, the following balances were available from the main office.

Manufacturing overhead through November 30	$217,000
Cost of goods sold through November 30	396,600

You recall that each month there is only one requisition for indirect materials. Among the fragments of paper, you located the following pieces:

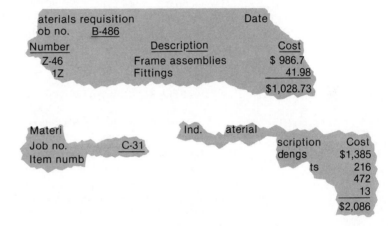

You also learn that the overhead during the month was overapplied by $1,200.

Required:

Determine the cost of the work in process inventory lost in the disaster.

INTEGRATIVE CASES

7–36. Deriving Overhead Rates

Tastee-Treat Company prepares, packages, and distributes six frozen vegetables in two different sized containers. The different vegetables and different sizes are prepared in large batches. The company uses a normal costing job order costing system. Manufacturing overhead is assigned to batches by a predetermined rate on the basis of machine-hours. The manufacturing overhead costs incurred by the company during two recent years (adjusted for changes using current prices and wage rates) are as follows:

	Year 1	Year 2
Machine-hours worked	2,760,000	2,160,000
Manufacturing overhead costs incurred:		
Indirect labor	$11,040,000	$ 8,640,000
Employee benefits	4,140,000	3,240,000
Supplies	2,760,000	2,160,000
Power	2,208,000	1,728,000
Heat and light	552,000	552,000
Supervision	2,865,000	2,625,000
Depreciation	7,930,000	7,930,000
Property taxes and insurance	3,005,000	3,005,000
Total overhead costs	$34,500,000	$29,880,000

Required:

Tastee-Treat Company expects to operate at a 2.3 million machine-hour level of activity in Year 4. Using the data from the two recent years, calculate fixed and variable overhead rates to assign manufacturing overhead to its products. (Hint: The variable rate can be found by comparing the change in costs to the change in hours.)

(CMA adapted)

7–37. Incomplete Data—Job Costing

The Quik Copy Publishing Company is a rapidly growing company that has not been profitable despite its increases in sales. You have been called in as a consultant to find ways of improving the situation. You believe the problem results from poor cost control and inaccurate cost estimation on jobs. To gather data for your investigation, you turn to the accounting system, and find it almost nonexistent. However, you piece together the following information for April:

1. Production:
   a. Completed Job No. 101.
   b. Started and completed Job No. 102.
   c. Started Job No. 103.

2. Inventory values:
   a. Work in process inventory:

      March 31:   Job No. 101—direct materials $1,000
                            —labor   480 hours @ $10 = $4,800
      April 30:   Job No. 103—direct materials $800
                            —labor   520 hours @ $10 = $5,200

   b. Each job in work in process inventory was exactly one half done in labor-hours; however, *all* of the direct materials necessary to do the entire job were charged to each job as soon as the job was started.
   c. There were no direct materials inventories or finished goods inventories at either March 31 or April 30.

3. Actual manufacturing overhead, $10,000.

4. Cost of goods sold (before adjustment for over- or underapplied overhead):

Job No. 101:	
Materials	$ 1,000
Labor	?
Overhead	?
Total	$15,400
Job No. 102:	
Materials	?
Labor	?
Overhead	?
Total	?

5. Overhead was applied to jobs using a predetermined rate per labor-dollar. The same rate had been used since the company began operations. Over- or underapplied overhead is written off each month as a separate expense or contraexpense (not debited or credited to Cost of Goods Sold).

6. All direct materials were purchased for cash and charged directly to Work in Process Inventory when purchased. Direct materials purchased in April amounted to $2,300.

7. Direct labor costs charged to jobs in April were $16,000. All labor costs were the same per hour for April for all laborers.

Required:

Trace the flow of costs through the system, highlighting the following figures:

a. The cost elements (that is, material, labor, and overhead) of cost of goods sold *before* adjustment for over- or underapplied overhead, for *each job sold*.

b. The value of each cost element (that is, material, labor, and overhead) for each job in Work in Process Inventory at April 30.

c. Over- or underapplied overhead for April.

PROCESS COSTING

LEARNING OBJECTIVES

1. To know how to compute equivalent units.

2. Understanding how to allocate costs to units using FIFO.

3. Being able to prepare a production cost report.

4. Understanding how to allocate costs to units using weighted average.

5. Knowing how to account for spoiled goods.

Chapter 7 presented a continuum of production methods and accounting systems. (See Illustration 7–1.) Chapter 7 also presented methods useful in applying costs to products in accounting systems designed primarily around job costing concepts. In this chapter, we continue our discussion of product costing by focusing on process costing methods. We also discuss ways of accounting for spoilage.

Process costing is used in companies with *process systems;* that is, when identical units are produced through an *ongoing series of uniform production steps.*

Companies that manufacture products in a continuous process, such as petroleum and steel making, and companies that make products in large batches, like small appliances and bicycles, use process costing. They find it necessary to identify costs per unit for inventory valuation, cost estimation, and performance evaluation purposes. However, when items are produced through continuous processing, it is impossible to separate each unit of output into individual jobs. In job operations, costs are accumulated for two cost objects: *departments* and specific *jobs.* In process costing, costs are accumulated by department and then allocated evenly to units produced. (See Illustration 8–1.)

Many firms incorporate both job and process costing concepts into their accounting systems. If you understand the concepts presented in Chapters 7 and 8, you will be able to understand how costs are applied to products in any accounting system you encounter.

THE ESSENTIAL DIFFERENCE BETWEEN JOB AND PROCESS COSTING

What is the distinction between job and process costing? Both require accumulating the costs of goods and services. But a key difference occurs in computing *unit* costs. The unit cost of a product results from dividing an accumulated cost number by a measure of volume. The basic distinction between job and process systems is the size of the denominator. In job costing, the denominator is small; for example, one consulting job or one office building. In process costing, the denominator is large; for example, thousands of barrels of oil.

THE EQUIVALENT UNIT CONCEPT

Equivalent Unit The amount of work actually performed on products with varying degrees of completion, translated to that work required to complete an equal number of whole units.

The **equivalent unit** concept is one of the keys to process costing. Under this concept, if two units were started at the beginning of a month and each was 50 percent finished at the end of the month, the cumulative work done on the two partial units would be considered as equivalent to the work done on one whole unit. Thus, for process costing purposes, the two half-finished units would be one equivalent unit. The equivalent unit concept is diagrammed in Illustration 8–2. This concept is not limited to manufacturing. For example, university administrators often count the number of students in a department in terms of "full-time equivalents." Two half-time students are considered to be one full-time equivalent.

The mathematical basis for equivalent unit computations is the basic cost flow model. The basic cost flow model for equivalent unit computations is:

$$\begin{array}{c}\text{Equivalent units}\\\text{in beginning}\\\text{inventory}\end{array} + \begin{array}{c}\text{Equivalent units}\\\text{of work done}\\\text{this period}\end{array} = \begin{array}{c}\text{Equivalent units}\\\text{transferred out}\end{array} + \begin{array}{c}\text{Equivalent units}\\\text{in ending}\\\text{inventory}\end{array}$$

Illustration 8-1   **Comparison of Job and Process Costing**

Job Costing

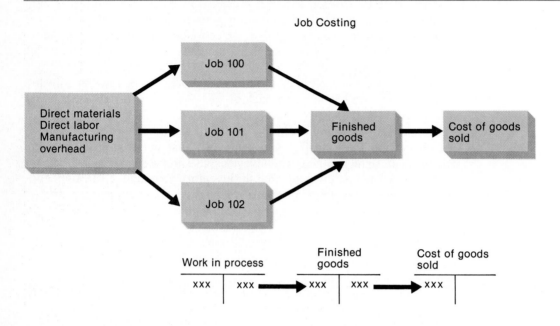

Process Costing

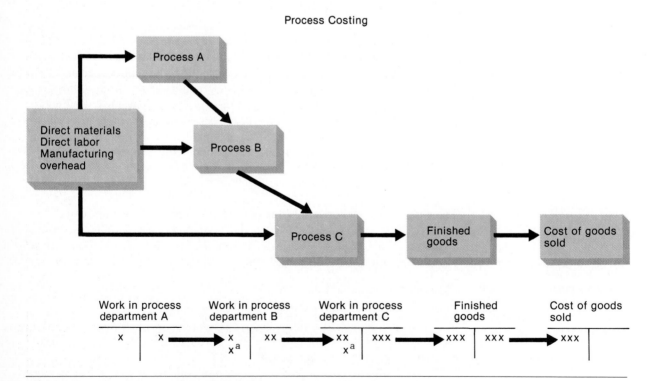

a Direct materials, labor, and manufacturing overhead added in production in the department.

Illustration 8-2   **Equivalent Unit Concept**

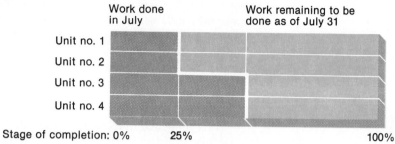

Units 1 and 2, each 25% completed, and units 3 and 4, each 50% completed in July
is equivalent to one and one-half units produced in July.

We demonstrate how this model is applied in the following discussion. At
first, we will assume that there is only one department and that all costs
enter the production process at the same rate. This enables us to show the
basic equivalent unit calculations and the method for assigning costs. As
each of our assumptions is relaxed, *the basic method is unchanged.* More
calculations are, however, required.[1]

**Equivalent Unit
Computations**

We present an application of the equivalent unit concept with an example for
ComChem Inc., a company that produces chemicals for commercial uses.
Assume that the Blending Department of ComChem Inc. had no beginning
or ending inventory in August. Every unit it produced was started and
completed during the month. If the Blending Department started and completed 8,000 units in August, we would say the amount of work it produced
was 8,000 equivalent units. The equivalent units of work done could also be
derived using the basic cost flow model:

$$\begin{array}{c}\text{Equivalent units} \\ \text{of work done} \\ \text{this period}\end{array} = \begin{array}{c}\text{Equivalent units} \\ \text{transferred out}\end{array} + \begin{array}{c}\text{Equivalent units} \\ \text{in ending} \\ \text{inventory}\end{array} - \begin{array}{c}\text{Equivalent units} \\ \text{in beginning} \\ \text{inventory}\end{array}$$

$$= \quad 8{,}000 \quad + \quad 0 \quad - \quad 0$$

$$= 8{,}000 \text{ equivalent units of work done in October}$$

**First-in, First-out (FIFO)
Costing** The first-in, first-out
inventory method whereby the
first goods received are charged
out when sold or transferred.

During August, $14,000 in costs were incurred in the Blending Depart-
ment. To determine the cost per unit using **FIFO,** we divide the cost incurred
in August by the equivalent units produced in August.

$$\text{Unit cost} = \frac{\text{Cost incurred this period (August)}}{\text{Equivalent units produced this period (August)}}$$

$$= \frac{\$14{,}000}{8{,}000 \text{ equivalent units (E.U.)}}$$

$$= \underline{\$1.75 \text{ per unit.}}$$

---

[1] Since there is no inventory in this example, the cost flow assumption does not matter.
However, the assumption becomes relevant as the example unfolds.

Incomplete Units in Beginning Inventory

In October, assume that the blending department had beginning inventory but no ending inventory. On October 1, the blending department had 1,000 units on hand, which the department manager estimated were 80 percent complete. During the month, 10,000 units were completed. There was no ending inventory on October 31.

The 10,000 completed units are composed of two groups:

1. Beginning inventory of 1,000 units that were 80 percent complete at the beginning of October.

2. Nine thousand units started and finished in October.

The 1,000 units in beginning inventory were already 80 percent finished. Therefore, they required the equivalent of only 200 units of work to reach completion (1,000 × .2 = 200). Thus, the total equivalent units produced in the blending department in October would be as follows:

Work necessary to complete beginning inventory (1,000 × .2 =)	200
Work necessary to start and finish 9,000 units	9,000
Equivalent units of work done	9,200

The equivalent units of work done could also be derived using the basic cost flow model:

$$\begin{matrix} \text{Equivalent units} \\ \text{of work done} \\ \text{this period} \end{matrix} = \begin{matrix} \text{Equivalent units} \\ \text{transferred out} \end{matrix} + \begin{matrix} \text{Equivalent units} \\ \text{in ending} \\ \text{inventory} \end{matrix} - \begin{matrix} \text{Equivalent units} \\ \text{in beginning} \\ \text{inventory} \end{matrix}$$

$$= \quad 10,000 \quad + \quad 0 \quad - \quad (1,000 \times .8)$$
$$= \quad 10,000 \quad + \quad 0 \quad - \quad 800$$
$$= 9,200 \text{ equivalent units of work done in October.}$$

If the costs incurred in the blending department were $13,800, the unit cost using FIFO, would be:

$$\text{Unit cost} = \frac{\text{Cost incurred this period (October)}}{\text{Equivalent units produced this period (October)}}$$

$$= \frac{\$13,800}{9,200 \text{ equivalent units (E.U.)}}$$

$$= \underline{\$1.50 \text{ per unit.}}$$

Incomplete Units in Beginning and Ending Inventories

In December, assume the blending department had both beginning and ending inventory. On December 1, there were 1,000 units in beginning inventory that were 80 percent complete, costing $1,200. 12,000 units were started; 10,000 units were completed during the month including the 1,000 units in beginning inventory. Therefore, 9,000 units were started and 100 percent completed during the period, 3,000 units remained in work in process on December 31. The department manager estimated that these units were 60 percent complete. Total costs for the period were $22,000.

The equivalent units computations are shown in Illustration 8–3. The equivalent units for December using FIFO are the total of the work necessary to complete beginning inventory (200 E.U.) plus the work necessary to start and finish 9,000 units (9,000 E.U.) plus the work performed on the ending work in process inventory (1,800 E.U.). Equivalent units for December are 11,000. The middle panel of Illustration 8–3 shows how to derive equivalent units using the basic cost flow model. The bottom of Illustration 8–3 shows the unit cost for December using FIFO.

If the costs incurred in the blending department were $22,000, the unit cost using FIFO, would be:

$$\text{Unit cost} = \frac{\text{Cost incurred this period (December)}}{\text{Equivalent units produced this period (December)}}$$

$$= \frac{\$22,000}{11,000 \text{ equivalent units (E.U.)}}$$

$$= \underline{\underline{\$2.00 \text{ per unit.}}}$$

Illustration 8-3

COMCHEM INC.
Blending Operation
Month Ending December 31

Equivalent Units—FIFO

Work necessary to complete beginning inventory (1,000 × .2[a])	200
Work necessary to start and finish 9,000 units (9,000 × 1.0[b])	9,000
Work performed on ending inventory of 3,000 units (3,000 × .6[c])	1,800
Equivalent units of work done	11,000

Equivalent Units—The Basic Cost Flow Model

$$\begin{matrix} \text{Equivalent units} \\ \text{of work done} \\ \text{this period} \end{matrix} = \begin{matrix} \text{Equivalent units} \\ \text{transferred out} \end{matrix} + \begin{matrix} \text{Equivalent units} \\ \text{in ending} \\ \text{inventory} \end{matrix} - \begin{matrix} \text{Equivalent units} \\ \text{in beginning} \\ \text{inventory} \end{matrix}$$

$$= 10,000 + (3,000 \times .6) - (1,000 \times .8)$$
$$= 10,000 + 1,800 - 800$$
$$= 11,000 \text{ equivalent units of work done in December.}$$

Unit Costs—FIFO

If the costs incurred in the blending department were $22,000, the unit cost using FIFO, would be:

$$\text{Unit cost} = \frac{\text{Cost incurred this period (December)}}{\text{Equivalent units produced this period (December)}}$$

$$= \frac{\$22,000}{11,000 \text{ equivalent units (E.U.)}}$$

$$= \underline{\underline{\$2.00 \text{ per unit.}}}$$

[a] Since beginning inventory was 80 percent complete, only 20 percent of the work needs to be done to complete the units.

[b] Each unit started and completed requires 1 equivalent unit of work.

[c] Units in ending inventory are only 60 percent complete.

ALLOCATING COSTS TO UNITS USING FIFO

The previous section presented how to account for equivalent units using FIFO inventory methods. The data we know from the previous section are recapped in Illustration 8–4. Note the question marks in the illustration. The problem is to allocate costs from beginning inventory and current period costs to goods transferred out and ending inventory. This section will provide a method for solving this problem.

Costs Assigned to Goods Transferred out

Illustration 8–5 presents the cost flows for the blending operation of Com-Chem Inc. in December. Note the question marks in the T-accounts which indicate that we are attempting to derive the cost of goods transferred out and the cost of goods in ending inventory. The costs of goods transferred out are broken down into three components: (1) costs already in beginning inventory, (2) costs to complete units in beginning inventory, and (3) costs of units started and completed in December. These costs can be calculated from the information contained in Illustration 8–4.

Illustration 8–4   **Data for Blending Operation**

COMCHEM INC.
Blending Operation
Month Ending December 31

	Units	Percent Complete	Costs
Beginning work in process inventory, December 1	1,000	80%	$ 1,200
Costs incurred in December			$22,000
Transfers out of blending	10,000	100%	?
Ending work in process, inventory, December 31	3,000	60%	?

Unit cost for December using FIFO = $2.00 (See Illustration 8–3).

Diagram of Unit Flows

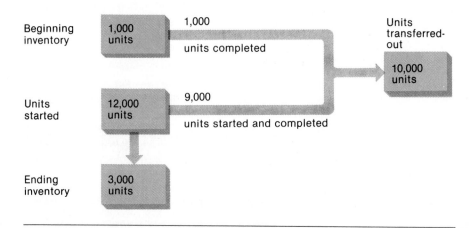

1. Costs already in beginning inventory are given in Illustration 8–4 as $1,200.
2. Costs to complete units in beginning inventory are calculated in Illustration 8–6. Since units in beginning inventory are 80 percent complete, 20 percent of the work must be done to complete the 1,000 units in beginning inventory: 200 equivalent units times $2.00, the unit cost for work done in December, equals $400.
3. Costs of units started and completed are also computed in Illustration 8–6. Since 9,000 units were started and completed in December, we take the unit cost for December, $2.00 times 9,000 equals $18,000, the costs of units started and completed.

As shown in Illustration 8–6, the total cost of goods transferred out is $19,600 ($1,200 + $400 + $18,000).

Costs Assigned to Ending Work in Process Inventory

Next, we compute the costs assigned to ending work in process inventory. Again we use the information from Illustration 8–4. The computation for costs allocated to ending work in process is shown in Illustration 8–7. The ending units are multiplied by 60 percent to compute equivalent units because they are only 60 percent complete. The equivalent units are then multiplied by the unit cost for December.

Illustration 8–8 shows the completed cost flows. Notice that the total cost of goods transferred out of the blending department consists of three components: costs in beginning inventory, costs to complete beginning inventory, and costs of units started and completed in the period.

The ending inventory is calculated using the equivalent unit concept. It could also be calculated using the basic cost flow model:

$$
\begin{aligned}
\text{Ending balance} &= \text{Beginning balance} + \text{Transfers in} - \text{Transfers out} \\
&= \quad \$1,200 \quad\quad + \quad \$22,000 \quad - \quad \$19,600 \\
&= \quad \$3,600
\end{aligned}
$$

Illustration 8–5   **Diagram of Cost-Flows—FIFO**

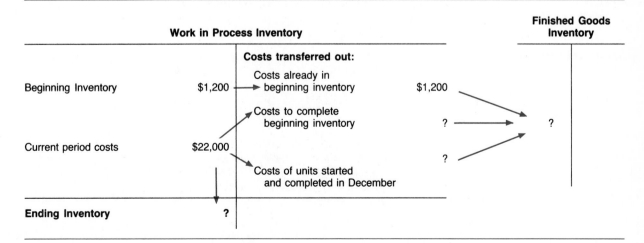

Illustration 8-6

COMCHEM INC.
Blending Department
Costs Assigned to Goods Transferred Out

1. Cost in beginning inventory = $1,200[a]

2.

$$\text{Costs to complete beginning inventory} = \frac{\text{Equivalent units to complete beginning inventory}}{} \times \text{Unit cost}$$

$$= (1,000^a \times .2^b) \times \$2.00^a$$
$$= 200 \text{ E.U.} \times \$2.00$$
$$= \underline{\$400}$$

3.

$$\text{Costs of units started and completed in December} = \text{started and completed in December} \times \text{Unit cost}$$

$$= (9,000^a \times 1.0^c) \times \$2.00^a$$
$$= 9,000 \text{ E.U.} \times \$2.00$$
$$= \underline{\$18,000}$$

Total costs assigned to goods transferred out:

From beginning inventory	$ 1,200
Current costs to complete beginning inventory	400
Costs of units started and completed this period	18,000
Total	$19,600

---

[a] Given in Illustration 8–4.

[b] Since product in beginning inventory was 80 percent complete, 20 percent of the work must be done to complete these units.

[c] Since these units were started and completed, the full unit cost must be applied to each unit.

PRODUCTION COST REPORT

Production Cost Report A report which summarizes production and cost results for a period. This report is generally used by managers to monitor production and cost flows.

A key report for managers of production facilities is the **production cost report.** The report is used to summarize production and process cost results for a period.

The production cost report for the blending department at ComChem Inc. is shown in Illustration 8–9. The report has five sections that are organized into two major categories. The top part of the report contains sections 1 and 2 and summarizes the flow of physical units. The bottom part of the report accounts for costs.

Managing the Flow of Physical Units

Section 1 is presented in two parts, *units to account for* and *units accounted for*. Units to account for includes the units in beginning work in process and

Illustration 8-7

COMCHEM INC.
Blending Department
Costs of Ending Work in Process Inventory

$$\text{Ending work in process inventory} = \frac{\text{Equivalent units in ending inventory}}{} \times \text{Unit cost}$$

$$= (3,000 \times .60) \times \$2.00$$
$$= 1,800 \text{ E.U.} \times \$2.00$$
$$= \underline{\$3,600}$$

Illustration 8-8

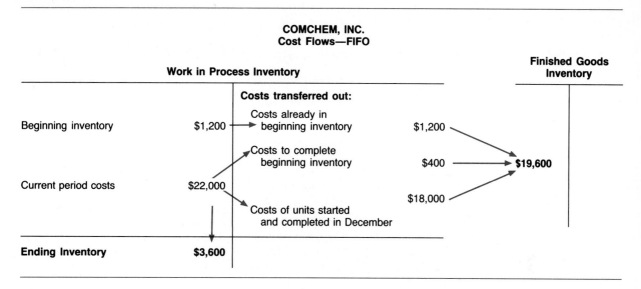

COMCHEM, INC.
Cost Flows—FIFO

units started during the period. As shown in Illustration 8–4, the blending department had 1,000 physical units in beginning inventory and started 12,000 units in December. Computations for this section are shown below.

(1) Physical Units

Units to account for = Units in beginning WIP + Units started in the period
                     =   1,000 units   + 12,000 units
                     = 13,000 units

Units accounted for is composed of units completed and transferred out and units in ending WIP. These figures can also be obtained from Illustration 8–4.

Units accounted for = Units transferred out + Units in ending WIP
                    = 10,000 units   + 3,000 units
                    = 13,000 units

Managers of production facilities know that physical units to account for should equal physical units accounted for on the production cost report. When they are not equal, it is an indication that the flow of physical units is not being adequately controlled.

Section 1 shows *physical units,* not *equivalent unit* production. The blending department worked on 13,000 physical units in December, but only 11,000 equivalent units were produced. The second section of the production cost report converts physical units to equivalent units. Recall that only 200 equivalent units were required to complete the 1,000 physical units in beginning inventory. The computations to obtain equivalent units are below. Note that in FIFO, equivalent unit computations are only required for the physical units included in the "units accounted for" portion of the report.

(2) Equivalent Units

	Physical Units ×	Percent of Work	= Equivalent Units
Units completed and transferred out:			
From beginning inventory	1,000	× 20%	= 200 E.U.
Started and completed currently	9,000	× 100%	= 9,000 E.U.
Units in ending WIP	3,000	× 60%	= 1,800 E.U.
Total equivalent units this period			11,000 E.U.

Reporting Cost Flows

The second part of the production cost report summarizes the flow of costs for the period. This part of the report is divided into three sections: (3) costs to be accounted for; (4) cost per equivalent units; (5) costs accounted for. Costs to be accounted for include the costs in beginning WIP and current period costs. These costs are shown in Illustration 8–4 and are recapped below.

(3) Costs to Be Accounted For

Costs to be accounted for = Costs in beginning WIP + Current period costs
= $1,200   + $22,000
= $23,200

Cost per equivalent unit using FIFO is computed by dividing current period costs by equivalent units for the period:

(4) Cost per Equivalent Unit

$$\text{Cost per equivalent unit} = \text{Current period costs} \div \frac{\text{Current period}}{\text{equivalent units}}$$

= $22,000   ÷ 11,000
= $2.00

Costs accounted for consists of two components: total costs transferred out and total cost in ending WIP. These costs are shown in Illustration 8–9.

(5) Costs Accounted for

Costs in beginning inventory	$ 1,200
Costs to complete beginning inventory	400
Costs of units started and completed in December	18,000
Total costs of goods transferred out	19,600
Total costs of ending WIP inventory	3,600
Total costs accounted for	$23,200

Notice costs to be accounted for equals total costs accounted for.

Illustration 8-9

COMCHEM INC.
Production Cost Report—FIFO
Blending Department—December

Flow of Production Units:

	Section 1 Physical Units	Section 2 Equivalent Units
Units to account for:		
Beginning work in process inventory	1,000	
Units started this period	12,000	
Total units to account for	13,000	
Units accounted for:		
Units completed and transferred out:		
From beginning inventory	1,000	200[a]
Started and completed currently	9,000	9,000
Total	10,000	9,200
Units in ending work in process inventory:	3,000	1,800[b]
Total units accounted for	13,000	11,000

Flow of Costs:

	Total Costs
Costs to be accounted for (Section 3):	
Costs in beginning WIP	$ 1,200
Current period costs	22,000
Total costs to be accounted for	$23,200
Cost per equivalent unit (Section 4):	
($22,000 ÷ 11,000)	$ 2.00
Costs accounted for (Section 5):	
Costs assigned to units transferred out:	
Costs from beginning WIP inventory	$ 1,200
Current costs added to complete	
beginning WIP inventory (200 × $2.00)	400
Total costs from beginning inventory	1,600
Current costs of units started and	
completed:	
(9,000 × $2.00)	18,000
Total costs transferred out	19,600
Total cost of ending WIP inventory	
(1,800 × $2.00)	3,600
Total costs accounted for	$23,200

[a] 20 percent of costs must be added to complete beginning inventory.

[b] Ending inventory is 60 percent complete.

The completed production cost report for the blending department of ComChem Inc. is shown in Illustration 8-9.

Summary of FIFO process costing. FIFO process costing separates current period costs from previous period costs carried forward in beginning work in process inventory. Equivalent units computed under FIFO relate only to the current period costs incurred in a department. When costs are divided between costs to be transferred to a subsequent department (or to finished goods inventory) and costs to be charged to ending inventory, the costs of the beginning inventory are transferred out first. Current period costs are then assigned to the finished units transferred out and to the units in ending inventory.

Even though the FIFO process costing system is more complex, it is widely used in practice because it provides a measure of the work done in a given period. That is, the equivalent units computed using FIFO process costing reflects current period work only. FIFO equivalent units can be compared to costs incurred in the period to see if costs are in line with the amount of equivalent activity produced. No other inventory flow assumption provides this data.

WEIGHTED-AVERAGE COSTING

Weighted-Average Costing The inventory method that combines costs and equivalent units of a period with the costs and the equivalent units in beginning inventory for product costing purposes.

The weighted-average method is somewhat easier to apply than FIFO because with weighted average, one does not keep separate track of the costs of beginning inventory. To illustrate the difference between FIFO and **weighted-average costing** we return to the blending department at ComChem Inc. On December 1, the blending department had 1,000 units in beginning inventory that were 80 percent complete. 10,000 units were completed during the month including the 1,000 units in beginning inventory. 3,000 units remained in work in process on December 31. The manager of the department estimated that these units were 60 percent complete. A recap of the data taken from Illustration 8–4 is shown below:

	Units	Percent Complete	Costs
Beginning work in process inventory, December 1	1,000	80%	$ 1,200
Costs incurred in December			22,000
Transfers out of blending	10,000	100	?
Ending work in process, inventory, December 31	3,000	60	?

Equivalent Units Using Weighted Average

With weighted-average costing, equivalent whole units are the equivalent whole units in beginning inventory plus the equivalent units of work done this period. The formula for weighted-average equivalent units is:

$$\text{Weighted-average equivalent units} = \text{E.U. already in beginning inventory} + \text{E.U. to complete beginning inventory} + \text{Units started and completed} + \text{E.U. in ending inventory}$$

Note that the last three terms on the right hand side of this equation equal FIFO equivalent units.

The total weighted-average equivalent units can be calculated as follows:

$$
\begin{array}{l}
\text{Weighted-average} \\
\text{equivalent units}
\end{array}
=
\begin{array}{l}
\text{E.U. already} \\
\text{in beginning} \\
\text{inventory}
\end{array}
+
\begin{array}{l}
\text{E.U. to} \\
\text{complete} \\
\text{beginning} \\
\text{inventory}
\end{array}
+
\begin{array}{l}
\text{Units} \\
\text{started} \\
\text{and} \\
\text{completed}
\end{array}
+
\begin{array}{l}
\text{E.U. in} \\
\text{ending} \\
\text{inventory}
\end{array}
$$

$$
\begin{aligned}
&= 800 \text{ E.U.} \quad + 200 \text{ E.U.} + 9{,}000 \text{ E.U.} + 1{,}800 \text{ E.U.} \\
&= 11{,}800 \text{ E.U.}
\end{aligned}
$$

A shortcut method can also be used to compute weighted-average equivalent units.

$$
\begin{array}{l}
\text{Weighted-average} \\
\text{equivalent units}
\end{array}
=
\begin{array}{l}
\text{Total units} \\
\text{transferred} \\
\text{out}
\end{array}
+
\begin{array}{l}
\text{Equivalent} \\
\text{units in the} \\
\text{ending} \\
\text{inventory}
\end{array}
$$

The shortcut method is used below. We start with the full formula we used above and show how terms can be combined to derive a simpler approach. The numbers below the terms are the equivalent units for the blending department to show how this shortcut method works.

Long method (used above to compute 11,800 E.U.):

$$
\begin{array}{l}
\text{Weighted-average} \\
\text{equivalent units} \\
\text{(E.U.)}
\end{array}
=
\begin{array}{l}
\text{E.U. already} \\
\text{in beginning} \\
\text{inventory}
\end{array}
+
\begin{array}{l}
\text{E.U. to} \\
\text{complete} \\
\text{beginning} \\
\text{inventory}
\end{array}
+
\begin{array}{l}
\text{Units} \\
\text{started} \\
\text{and} \\
\text{completed}
\end{array}
+
\begin{array}{l}
\text{E.U. in} \\
\text{ending} \\
\text{inventory}
\end{array}
$$

$$
11{,}800 \quad = \quad 800 \quad + \quad 200 \quad + \quad 9{,}000 \quad + \quad 1{,}800
$$

Intermediate method:

$$
\begin{array}{l}
\text{Weighted-average} \\
\text{E.U.}
\end{array}
=
\begin{array}{l}
\text{Units of beginning} \\
\text{inventory transferred out}
\end{array}
+
\begin{array}{l}
\text{Units} \\
\text{started} \\
\text{and} \\
\text{completed}
\end{array}
+
\begin{array}{l}
\text{E.U. in} \\
\text{ending} \\
\text{inventory}
\end{array}
$$

$$
11{,}800 \quad = \quad 1{,}000 \quad + \quad 9{,}000 \quad + \quad 1{,}800
$$

Shortcut method:

$$
\begin{array}{l}
\text{Weighted-average} \\
\text{E.U.}
\end{array}
= \text{Total units transferred out} +
\begin{array}{l}
\text{E.U. in} \\
\text{ending} \\
\text{inventory}
\end{array}
$$

$$
11{,}800 \quad = \quad 10{,}000 \quad\quad 1{,}800
$$

Weighted-Average Unit Cost

The formula for weighted-average unit cost is different than the FIFO formula:

$$
\text{FIFO unit cost} = \frac{\text{Cost incurred this period (December)}}{\text{Equivalent units produced this period (December)}}
$$

$$
= \$2.00 \text{ (see Illustration 8–3 for computations)}
$$

$$\text{Weighted-average unit cost} = \frac{\text{Costs in beginning inventory} + \begin{array}{c}\text{Costs incurred this}\\\text{period (December)}\end{array}}{\begin{array}{c}\text{Equivalent units (E.U.)}\\\text{in beginning inventory}\end{array} + \begin{array}{c}\text{E.U. produced}\\\text{this period}\end{array}}$$

$$= \frac{\$1,200 + \$22,000}{800 + 11,000}$$

$$= \$23,200 \div 11,800$$

$$= \$1.9661 \text{ per unit}$$

As you can see, the weighted-average unit cost in this case is lower than the FIFO unit cost. We have carried out the cost to four decimal places to better illustrate how this difference affects cost of goods transferred out and cost of goods in ending WIP inventory. In practice, cost data will be carried out to computer-rounding limits.

Note that the numerator of each formula (FIFO and weighted average) contains all of the costs that are related to the equivalent units in the denominator. For example, the weighted-average numerator includes beginning inventory costs plus the costs of all work done this period. The denominator includes the equivalent units in the beginning inventory plus the equivalent units for all work done this period.

Costs Assigned to Goods Transferred out—Weighted Average

The costs assigned to goods transferred out is calculated by multiplying units transferred out times the weighted-average unit cost. The weighted-average unit cost, as shown above, is 1.9661. The units transferred out as shown in Illustration 8–4 is 10,000 units.

$$\begin{aligned}\text{Costs of goods transferred out} &= \text{Units transferred out} \times \text{Unit cost}\\ &= 10,000 \text{ units} \times \$1.9661\\ &= \underline{\$19,661}\end{aligned}$$

Costs Assigned to Ending Work in Process Inventory

Next, we compute the costs assigned to ending work in process inventory. Again we use the information from Illustration 8–4. The cost of units in ending inventory equals equivalent units in ending inventory times the weighted-average unit cost.

$$\begin{aligned}\text{Total costs assigned to ending WIP inventory} &= \text{Equivalent units in WIP} \times \text{Unit cost}\\ &= 1,800 \times \$1.9661\\ &= \$3,539\end{aligned}$$

Illustration 8–10 shows a comparison of the production cost report using weighted average as opposed to FIFO. The major differences between the two methods are highlighted in this illustration.

1. The weighted-average method includes the costs and equivalent units from beginning inventory in computing unit costs. Thus, equivalent units used for computations are 11,800 versus the 11,000 equivalent units used in FIFO.

Illustration 8-10

COMCHEM INC.
Production Cost Report—Weighted Average versus FIFO
Blending Department—December

Flow of Production Units:

	Section (1) Physical Units (same for FIFO and weighted average)	Section (2) Equivalent Units	
		Weighted Average (beginning inventory + current period)	FIFO (current period only)
Units to account for:			
Beginning work in process inventory	1,000	800[a]	
Units started this period	12,000		
Total units to account for	13,000		
Units accounted for:			
Units completed and transferred out:			
From beginning inventory	1,000	200[b]	200
Started and completed currently	9,000	9,000	9,000
Total	10,000	9,200	9,200
Units in ending work in process inventory:	3,000	1,800[c]	1,800
Total units accounted for	13,000	11,800	11,000

Flow of Costs:

	Total Costs	
	Weighted Average	FIFO
Costs to be accounted for (Section 3):		
Costs in beginning WIP	$ 1,200	$ 1,200
Current period costs	22,000	22,000
Total costs to be accounted for	$23,200	$23,200
Cost per equivalent unit (Section 4):	($23,200 ÷ 11,800) $1.9661	(22,000 ÷ 11,000) $2.00
Costs accounted for (Section 5):		
Costs assigned to units transferred out	(10,000 × $1.9661) $19,661	(see Illustration 8–9) $19,600
Total cost of ending WIP inventory	(1,800 × 1.9661) 3,539	(1,800 × $2.00) 3,600
Total costs accounted for	$23,200	$23,200

[a] Units in beginning inventory were 80 percent complete.
[b] Twenty percent of costs must be added to complete beginning inventory.
[c] Ending inventory is 60 percent complete.

2. The unit cost using weighted average is $1.9661. In FIFO, the unit cost, which is based on current period costs and equivalent units, is $2.00.

3. The costs assigned to units tranferred out and ending WIP inventory vary depending on the method used. *You should note, however, that total costs accounted for do not change. They still equal total costs to be accounted for—$23,200.*

Illustration 8–11 shows the completed cost flows. Note that the ending WIP inventory could also have been calculated using the basic cost flow model.

Illustration 8-11   **Cost Flows Using Weighted-Average Costing**

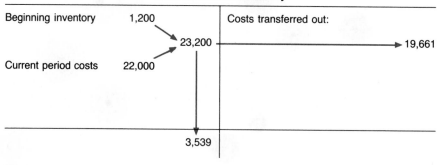

COMCHEM INC.
Blending Operation
Month Ending December 31

$$\text{Ending balance} = \text{Beginning balance} + \text{Transfers in} - \text{Transfers out}$$
$$= \quad \$1,200 \quad + \quad \$22,000 \quad - \quad \$19,661$$
$$= \quad \$3,539$$

Comparison of Weighted-Average and FIFO Costing

Weighted-average costing does not separate beginning inventory from current period activity. Unit costs are a weighted average of the two, whereas under FIFO costing, units costs are based on current period activity only.

Illustration 8–10 compares the unit costs, costs transferred out, and ending inventory values under the two methods for ComChem Inc. Note that in this example costs per unit are lower under weighted average than under FIFO because the unit costs in beginning inventory are lower than current period unit costs. Thus, the lower unit costs in beginning inventory decrease the weighted-average unit cost.

While either weighted-average or FIFO cost is acceptable for assigning costs to inventories and cost of goods sold for external reporting, the weighted-average method has been criticized for masking current period costs. Thus, using weighted-average costing, the unit costs reported for December are based not only on December's costs but also on previous periods' costs that were in December's beginning inventory as well. Whether this obscuring of current period costs is important depends on the extent to which managers' decisions require knowledge of unit costs. If computational and recordkeeping costs are about the same under both FIFO and weighted average, which we believe is generally the case when accounts are computerized, then FIFO costing has a slight advantage.

STEPS FOR ASSIGNING PROCESS COSTS TO UNITS

Illustration 8–12 summarizes the steps to assigning costs to units in process costing. Notice how the steps closely correspond to the production cost report used by management to monitor production unit and cost flows.

Illustration 8-12   **Summary of Steps for Assigning Process Costs to Units**

Step 1: **Summarize the flow of physical units.**

Step 2: **Compute the equivalent units produced.**
Using FIFO, this means adding the equivalent units of work done to:
a. Complete units in beginning inventory.
b. Start and complete units.
c. Work on units still in ending inventory.
Using FIFO, this gives the equivalent units of work done in the current period.
Using weighted average, this means adding the equivalent units of work done in the current period to the equivalent units of work already done in the beginning inventory from the previous period.

Step 3: **Summarize the total costs to be accounted for.**
The total costs to be accounted for are the costs in the beginning work in process inventory and current period costs charged (that is, debited) to Work in Process inventory.

Step 4: **Compute costs per equivalent unit.**
Using FIFO:

$$\frac{\text{Unit cost of}}{\text{current work done}} = \frac{\text{Current period costs}}{\text{Equivalent units of current work done}}$$

Using weighted average:

$$\frac{\text{Weighted average}}{\text{unit cost}} = \frac{\text{Costs in beginning inventory} + \text{Current period cost}}{\text{Equivalent units in beg. inv.} + \text{Equivalent units of current work done.}}$$

Step 5: **Compute the cost of goods transferred out and the cost of ending inventory.**
This is the step where the costs in step 3 are accounted for, either as the cost of goods transferred out or the cost of goods in ending inventory.
Using FIFO, the cost of goods transferred out equals the sum of the following three items:
a. The costs already in beginning inventory at the beginning of the period.
b. The current period cost to complete beginning inventory, which equals the equivalent units to complete beginning inventory from step 2, part a, times the current period unit cost computed for FIFO in step 4.
c. The costs to start and complete units, calculated by multiplying the number of units from step 2, part b, times the current cost computed for FIFO in step 4.
Using FIFO, the cost of goods in ending inventory equals the equivalent units in ending inventory from step 2, part c, times the unit current cost computed for FIFO in step 4.
Using weighted average, the cost of goods transferred out equals the total units transferred out times the weighted-average unit cost computed in step 4.
Using weighted average, the cost of goods in ending inventory equals the equivalent units in ending inventory times the weighted-average unit cost computed in step 4.

DIRECT MATERIALS AND CONVERSION COSTS

In some processes, direct materials are not introduced to the product at the same rate as the work performed on the product. For example, all the direct materials may be introduced at the beginning of the production process and conversion costs (direct labor + manufacturing overhead) may occur throughout the production process, as illustrated in the diagram below. The conversion costs would be allocated like the illustrated blending department costs.

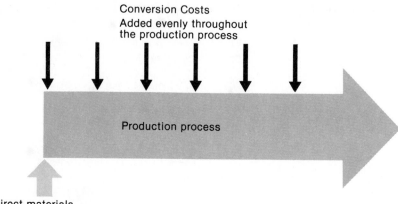

Conversion Costs
Added evenly throughout
the production process

Production process

Direct materials
Added entirely at the
beginning of the
production process

To illustrate this situation, we look at Cures-R-Us, a pharmaceutical company with a production department called pharmacology. The relevant data for April is shown in Illustration 8–13.

On April 1, there were 3,000 units in beginning work in process. All direct materials are added at the beginning of the production process, so materials for units in work in process are 100 percent complete. Direct materials costs in beginning inventory were $3,000. The beginning inventory was 30 percent complete with respect to conversion costs. Conversion costs in the beginning inventory were $7,400. Twenty-seven thousand units were started and completed during the period, and 9,000 units were in ending work in process inventory on April 30. Direct materials cost for the current period were $45,000. Current period conversion costs were $256,470. The units in ending inventory were 100 percent complete with respect to direct materials and 20 percent complete with respect to conversion costs.

The computations for calculating equivalent units and cost flows using FIFO are shown at the bottom of Illustration 8–13. Equivalent units to complete beginning inventory are 0, since the beginning inventory is 100 percent complete with respect to direct materials. Since units started and completed and units in ending inventory are both 100 percent complete, total materials equivalent units for the current period are 36,000 (27,000 + 9,000).

$$\begin{aligned} \text{Materials cost per} \atop \text{equivalent unit} &= \frac{\text{Current period}}{\text{materials costs}} \div \frac{\text{Current period equivalent}}{\text{units for materials}} \\ &= 45,000 \div 36,000 \\ &= \$1.25 \end{aligned}$$

$$\begin{aligned} \text{Materials costs} \atop \text{transferred out} &= \frac{\text{Materials costs}}{\text{from beginning}} + \frac{\text{Current materials}}{\text{costs added to}} + \frac{\text{Materials costs}}{\text{of units started}} \\ &\quad\ \text{WIP inventory} \quad\quad \text{completed WIP} \quad\quad \text{and completed} \\ &= \$\ 3,000 \quad\quad\ + \$0 \quad\quad\quad\ + (27,000 \times \$1.25) \\ &= \$\ 3,000 \quad\quad\ + \$0 \quad\quad\quad\ + \$33,750 \\ &= \$36,750 \end{aligned}$$

Illustration 8-13   **Cures-R-Us Cost of Production Report**

CURES-R-US
Pharmacology Department
Production Cost Report—FIFO
Month Ending April 30

Flow of Production Units:

		Section (2) Equivalent Units for Current Period	
	Section (1) Physical Units	Direct Materials Costs	Conversion Costs
Units to account for:			
Beginning work in process inventory	3,000		
Units started this period	36,000		
Total units to account for	39,000		
Units accounted for:			
Completed and transferred out from beginning inventory	3,000	0	2,100
Started and completed currently	27,000	27,000	27,000
Total	30,000	27,000	29,100
In ending inventory	9,000	9,000	1,800
Total units accounted for	39,000	36,000	30,900

Flow of Costs:

	Total Costs	Direct Materials Costs	Conversion Costs
Costs to be accounted for (Section 3):			
Costs in beginning WIP	$ 10,400	$ 3,000	$ 7,400
Current period costs	301,470	45,000	256,470
Total costs to be accounted for	$311,870	$48,000	$263,870
Cost per equivalent unit (Section 4):		$1.25 ($45,000 ÷ 36,000)	$8.30 ($256,470 ÷ 30,900)
Costs accounted for (Section 5):			
Costs assigned to units transferred out:			
Costs from beginning inventory	$ 10,400	$ 3,000	$ 7,400
Current costs added to complete beginning inventory	17,430	0	17,430[a]
Current costs of units started and completed	257,850	33,750[b]	224,100[c]
Total costs transferred out	$285,680	$36,750	$248,930
Cost of ending inventory	26,190	11,250[d]	14,940[e]
Total costs accounted for	$311,870	$48,000	$263,870

[a] $17,430 = $8.30 × 2,100.
[b] $33,750 = $1.25 × 27,000.
[c] $224,100 = $8.30 × 27,000.
[d] $11,250 = $1.25 × 9,000.
[e] $14,940 = $8.30 × 1,800.

Total cost of ending work in process inventory with regards to direct materials equals equivalent units of direct materials in ending work in process inventory times the current period direct materials unit cost—$11,250 (9,000 × $1.25). Note that costs to be accounted for, $48,000, are the same as costs accounted for.

The ending inventory could also be derived using the basic cost flow model:

$$\text{Ending materials balance} = \text{Beginning materials balance} + \text{Transfers in} - \text{Transfers out}$$
$$= \$\ 3{,}000 \qquad\qquad\quad + \$45{,}000 \qquad - \$36{,}750$$
$$= \$11{,}250$$

Similar calculations are made for conversion costs. For Cures-R-Us, equivalent units with respect to conversion costs are different from the equivalent units with respect to direct materials. The equivalent units are shown in Illustration 8–13 based on the following calculations:

Needed to complete beginning inventory	3,000 × 70% = 2,100
Started and completed	27,000
Started for ending inventory	9,000 × 20% = 1,800

For a total of 30,900 equivalent units with respect to conversion costs.

The conversion costs per equivalent unit are calculated based on the current period conversion costs and the equivalent units for conversion costs as follows:

$$\text{Cost per equivalent unit} = \text{Current period costs} \div \text{Current period equivalent units}$$
$$= \$256{,}470 \div 30{,}900$$
$$= \$8.30 \text{ per equivalent unit}$$

Once the cost per equivalent unit is obtained, it is possible to calculate the costs transferred out and the costs assigned to ending inventory. Remember, under FIFO, all beginning inventory costs are assumed transferred out as long as current period production exceeds the number of units in beginning inventory. The beginning inventory costs of $7,400 are transferred out.

Current period costs are apportioned between transferred out and ending inventory. This period, 2,100 equivalent units of work were required to complete the beginning inventory, so 2,100 times $8.30, which is $17,430, is transferred out. Likewise, the cost of the 27,000 units at $8.30 (or $224,100) is transferred out. The total conversion costs transferred out, then, is $248,930, which is the sum of $7,400 plus $17,430 plus $224,100. All of these figures are shown in Illustration 8–13, Section (5).

Then, we determine the conversion costs in the ending inventory. They equal $14,940, which is the 1,800 equivalent units with respect to conversion costs in the ending inventory times $8.30. The total of the costs transferred out ($248,930) and the ending inventory costs ($14,940) is $263,870, which is the same as the total costs to be accounted for with respect to conversion costs.

The direct materials and conversion cost numbers are usually summed to provide information on the total manufacturing costs in the department. Thus, the first column of the flow of costs section of the production cost report shows a beginning inventory value of $10,400, which is the direct materials of $3,000 and the conversion costs of $7,400. Similarly, totals are prepared for current period costs, costs to be accounted for, costs transferred out, and the cost of the ending inventory.

ACCOUNTING FOR PRIOR DEPARTMENT COSTS

Prior Department Costs
Manufacturing costs incurred in some other department and charged to a subsequent department in the manufacturing process.

Our discussion so far has assumed a single department. Usually products pass through a series of departments, however. As the product passes from one department to another, its costs must follow.

In principle, the units transferred out of one department and into another are essentially the same as any other direct material for the receiving department. The costs of those units, which are called **prior department costs,** or transferred-in costs, are similar to the costs of direct materials put into process at the start of production in that department. Prior department costs are entered as a separate item on the receiving department's production cost report. Equivalent whole units are 100 percent complete in terms of prior department costs, so cost computations for prior department costs is relatively easy.

Assume that on April 1, the Biologicals Department of Cures-R-Us had 4,100 physical units in its beginning inventory with prior department costs of $36,900 attributable to the beginning inventory. Moreover, the units were 40 percent complete with respect to conversion and materials costs. Conversion and direct materials costs totaled $10,168 for the beginning inventory. Materials and conversion costs occur evenly throughout the process in the Biologicals Department.

During the month of April, the units that had been completed in the Pharmacology Department were transferred to the Biologicals Department. The cost of $285,680 for the 30,000 units transferred is a *prior department cost* for the Biologicals Department. The Biologicals Department is not interested in the components of the $285,680, only in the total amount which has been charged to them.

During the month, 24,500 units are started and completed with 5,500 units remaining in ending inventory. The ending inventory is 65 percent complete with respect to conversion costs. The Biologicals Department incurred $183,210 in direct materials and conversion costs.

A FIFO cost of production report which summarize these data is given in Illustration 8–14. As you review this report, you should notice that the prior department costs are treated exactly as direct materials added at the beginning of a production process. Illustration 8–15 shows the flow of costs through the Biologicals Department of Cures-R-Us using FIFO. You should be able to relate the costs in the production cost report to the T-accounts.

Responsibility for Prior Department Costs

An important issue for performance evaluation is: Should a department manager be held accountable for *all* costs charged to the department? The answer is usually no. A department and its people are usually evaluated on the basis of costs *added by* the department relative to the good output from the department. Prior department costs are often excluded when comparing actual department costs with a standard or budget. We discuss this point

Illustration 8-14   Cures-R-Us Production Cost Report

CURES-R-US
Biologicals Department
Production Cost Report—FIFO
Month Ending April 30

		Section (2) Equivalent Units for Current Period	
Flow of Production Units:	Section (1) Physical Units	Prior Department Costs	Materials and Conversion Costs
Units to account for:			
Beginning work in process inventory	4,100		
Units started this period	30,000		
Total units to account for	34,100		
Units accounted for:			
Completed and transferred out			
From beginning inventory	4,100	0	2,460[a]
Started and completed currently	24,500	24,500	24,500
Total	28,600	24,500	26,960
In ending inventory	5,500	5,500	3,575[b]
Total units accounted for	34,100	30,000	30,535

Flow of Costs:	Total Costs	Prior Department Costs	Materials and Conversion Costs
Costs to be accounted for (Section 3):			
Costs in beginning WIP	$ 47,068	$ 36,900	$ 10,168
Current period costs	468,890	285,680	183,210
Total costs to be accounted for	$515,958	$322,580	$193,378
Cost per equivalent unit (Section 4):		$9.5227 (rounded) ($285,680 ÷ 30,000)	$6.00 ($183,210 ÷ 30,535)
Costs accounted for (Section 5):			
Costs assigned to units transferred out:			
Costs from beginning inventory	$ 47,068	$ 36,900	$ 10,168
Current costs added to complete beginning inventory	14,760	0	14,760[c]
Units started and completed	380,305	233,305[d]	147,000[e]
Total costs transferred out	$442,133	$270,205	$171,928
Cost of ending inventory	73,825	52,375[f]	21,450[g]
Total costs accounted for	$515,958	$322,580	$193,378

[a] 2,460 = (1.0 − .4 complete) × 4,100 units.

[b] 3,575 = .65 complete × 5,500 units.

[c] $14,760 = $6.00 × 2,460.

[d] $233,305 = $9.5227 (rounded) × 24,500.

[e] $147,000 = $6.00 × 24,500.

[f] $52,360 = $9.5227 × 5,500.

[g] $21,450 = $6.00 × 3,575.

more extensively in later chapters on performance evaluation, but we raise it here to emphasize that different information is needed for different purposes. Assigning costs to units for inventory valuation requires that prior department costs be *included* in department product cost calculations. However, assigning costs to departments for performance evaluation usually requires that prior department costs be *excluded* from departmental costs.

Illustration 8-15   **Cost Flows with Prior Department Costs—FIFO Method**

Work in Process			Finished Goods	
Beginning inventory: Prior department costs	36,900			
Beginning inventory: Materials and conversion	10,168	Transferred out: from beginning inventory 47,068[a]		
Current costs: Prior department	285,680	Current costs: Prior department 233,305	From WIP: Biologicals	442,133
Materials and conversion	183,210	Materials and conversion 161,760[b]		
Ending inventory: Prior department costs	52,375			
Materials and conversion	21,450			

[a] $47,068 = $36,900 + $10,168.

[b] $161,760 = $14,760 + $147,000.

SPOILAGE

Spoilage   Goods that are damaged, do not meet specifications, or are otherwise not suitable for further processing or sale as good output.

Good Output   Units that are expected to be completed and suitable for further processing or for sale at the end of a production process.

Spoilage refers to the loss of goods during production. If the loss is a normal part of the production operation (such as that due to evaporation, chemical reactions, normal waste, or expected defective items), the reported number of units of product put into process may be adjusted to reflect the normal loss. Thus, units of product started is expressed in terms of expected or actual units of **good output.** The computation results in an increased cost per finished unit that has the effect of averaging the normal losses over the good units.

For example, suppose a department with no beginning inventory started 3,000 units. These units cost $24,000 for materials and conversion costs. It produced only 2,500 units of good output and lost 500 units. Thus, it would record 2,500 units produced at a cost of $9.60 per unit ($24,000 ÷ 2,500 good units = $9.60).

A second method is to record the 3,000 units at their cost of $8 per unit ($24,000 ÷ 3,000 units). At the end of the period, the $4,000 cost of the 500 lost units would be assigned to work in process inventory, finished goods inventory, or cost of goods sold, depending on where the good units are. For example, if 1,000 of the good units are in ending finished goods inventory and the remaining 1,500 good units were sold, the entry would be:

Finished Goods Inventory—Lost Unit Costs	$1,600 \left(= \frac{1,000}{2,500} \times \$4,000 \right)$
Cost of Goods Sold—Lost Unit Costs	$2,400 \left(= \frac{1,500}{2,500} \times \$4,000 \right)$
Work in Process Inventory—Lost Unit Costs	4,000

Assuming there were no beginning inventories and these were the only costs incurred, both methods result in the same value of finished goods inventory and cost of goods sold. However, the second method, which explicitly assigns costs to spoiled units, provides managers with data they would not get from the first method; namely, the cost of spoilage. The flow of costs for both methods is diagrammed in Illustration 8–16. A summary of the computations for both methods is shown below:

Two Methods of Assigning Spoilage to Units	
First method: Assign spoilage costs to good units:	
Costs to be accounted for	$24,000
Equivalent units (E.U.)	÷2,500
Cost per E.U.	=$9.60
Cost assignment to units transferred out	
($9.60 × 2,500 units)	$24,000
Second method: Compute the cost of spoiled units:	
Costs to be accounted for	$24,000
Equivalent units:	
Started and completed	2,500
Spoilage	500
Total equivalent units	3,000
Unit cost ($24,000 ÷ 3,000)	$ 8
Cost assignment:	
Transferred out (2,500 × $8)	$20,000
Spoiled units (500 × $8)	4,000
Total costs accounted for	$24,000

Spoilage Occurs during the Process

What if spoilage occurs and is detected during the process? Then the amount of spoilage under the second method discussed above would be to compute the spoilage based on the equivalent units of the goods produced. For example, starting with the facts from the previous example, assume the following additional facts:

Materials, all added at the beginning of the process	$ 9,000
Conversion costs, added evenly throughout the process	15,000

Spoilage of 500 units occurs and is detected when the process is 40 percent complete (but after all materials have been added).

The cost of spoiled units would be derived as follows:

1. Compute the cost per unit for materials and conversion costs (this is section 4 in the production cost report):

    Materials: $9,000 ÷ 3,000 equivalent units = $\underline{\$3}$ per equivalent unit

    $$\begin{aligned} \text{Conversion costs: } \$15,000 &\div [2,500 + (.4 \times 500)] \\ &= 15,000 \div 2,700 \text{ equivalent units} \\ &= \underline{\$5.556} \text{ (rounded) per equivalent unit} \end{aligned}$$

2. Compute the cost of spoiled units by multiplying the cost per equivalent unit times the number of units spoiled:

    Materials: 500 equivalent units × $3   = $1,500

    Conversion costs: 200 equivalent units × $5.556 = $1,111

    Total cost of units spoiled $\underline{\underline{\$2,611}}$

Illustration 8–16 **Cost Flows for Normal Lost Units**

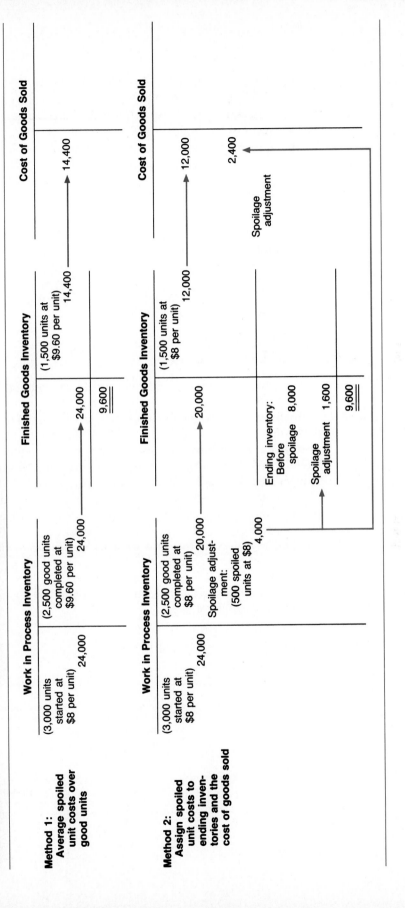

The equivalent units of goods spoiled for *conversion costs* is only 200 (40 percent × 500 units spoiled) because spoilage occurred and was detected at the 40 percent stage. Consequently, the total equivalent units produced, including equivalent units of goods spoiled, equals 2,700, *not* 3,000.

Spoilage occurred after *all materials were added,* however, so the equivalent units spoiled for materials costs equals 500 units; the total equivalent units produced, including spoiled goods, equals 3,000.

Abnormal Spoilage

Lost Units   Goods that evaporate or otherwise disappear during a production process.

Normal Spoilage   Spoiled goods that are a result of the regular operation of the production process.

Abnormal Spoilage   Spoilage due to reasons other than the usual course of operations of a process.

If units are lost for unusual or abnormal reasons, the debit in the journal entry is made to an account such as Abnormal Spoilage Costs, which writes off the costs for the period. Whereas *normal* **lost units** or **normal spoilage** is usually treated as a product cost, abnormal lost units or **abnormal spoilage** is treated as a period cost. For example, if the 500 lost units were lost due to abnormal reasons, the journal entry to record the transfer of costs out of Work in Process Inventory would be:

Finished Goods Inventory	20,000	
Abnormal Spoilage	4,000	
Work in Process Inventory		24,000

The Abnormal Spoilage account would be a period expense and would appear in the income statement.

Companies that employ a production system based on the philosophy that there should be zero defects treat all spoilage as abnormal. For these companies, the Abnormal Spoilage account is monitored closely with the intention of identifying the causes for the spoilage and finding ways to prevent such spoilage from occurring in the future.

When abnormal spoilage is charged to expense, cost of goods sold is stated at the per unit cost excluding the abnormal lost unit costs. Thus, for this example, the cost of goods sold would be $12,000 or $8 per unit. T-accounts to represent this flow of costs are shown in Illustration 8–17.

A comprehensive problem that includes spoilage is presented at the end of this chapter. Illustration 8–21 shows a production cost report for this problem that includes spoilage. (Also, see self-study problems 1 and 2 for additional examples of spoilage.)

Illustration 8-17

SYSTEMS CHOICE: JOB COSTING VERSUS PROCESS COSTING

In job costing, costs are collected for each unit produced, as discussed in Chapter 7. For example, a print shop collects costs for each order, a defense contractor collects costs for each contract, and a custom home builder collects costs for each house. In process costing, costs are accumulated in a department for an accounting period (for example, a month), then spread evenly, or averaged, over all units produced that month. Process costing assumes each unit produced is relatively uniform. A comparison of cost flows under each method is demonstrated by the following example.

Assume Marmaduke Manufacturing Company makes a customized product. In June, three jobs were started and completed (there were no beginning inventories). The manufacturing cost of each job was:

Job No. 10	$16,000
Job No. 11	12,000
Job No. 12	14,000
Total	$42,000

Job No. 10 was sold; hence, the cost of goods sold in June would be the cost of Job No. 10—$16,000. This flow of costs is shown in the top part of Illustration 8–18.

Suppose Marmaduke Manufacturing Company had used process costing. For convenience, assume each job is defined to be a single unit of product. Total manufacturing costs were $42,000, so each unit would be assigned a cost of $14,000. One unit was sold; hence, the cost of goods sold under process costing would be the *average cost* of all three jobs—$14,000. This flow of costs is shown in the bottom part of Illustration 8–18.

Note that with process costing, Marmaduke Manufacturing Company does not maintain a record of the cost of each unit produced. Process costing has less detailed recordkeeping; hence, if a company was choosing between job and process costing, it would generally find that recordkeeping costs are lower under process costing. Of course, process costing does not provide as much information as job costing because records of the cost of each unit produced are not kept using process costing. The choice of process versus job costing systems involves a comparison of the costs and benefits of each system.

A Cost-Benefit Comparison of Job and Process Costing

Consider a house builder. Under job order costing, the costs must be accumulated for each house. If lumber is sent on a truck for delivery to several houses, it is not sufficient to record the total lumber issued—records must be kept of the amount delivered to, and subsequently returned from, each house. If laborers work on several houses, they must keep track of the time spent on *each* house. Process costing, however, simply requires recording the total costs incurred on all jobs. For the home builder, process costing records the average cost of all houses built. A custom home builder would probably use job order costing. A developer might consider each development a job, but use process costing for houses within each development.

Under process costing, the actual cost incurred for a particular unit is not reported. If all units are homogeneous, this loss of information is probably minimal. Is it important for Motorola to know whether the cost of the 10,001st microprocessor chip is different from the 10,002nd? Probably not—particularly if the unit cost is calculated primarily to value inventory for external financial reporting. Cost control and performance evaluation will take place by department, not by unit produced, in process systems. For companies making relatively small, homogeneous units, the additional benefits of job costing would not justify the additional recordkeeping costs.

What if recordkeeping costs were equal under job and process systems for the units in a product line? Then we would say that job systems are better because they provide all of the data that process systems do, plus more. As a general rule, job systems are usually more costly than process systems, however. Thus, managers and accountants must decide whether there are

---

Illustration 8-18　　　　**Comparative Flow of Costs: Job and Process Costing**

MARMADUKE MANUFACTURING COMPANY
June
JOB COSTING

	Work in Process Inventory—Job No. 10		Finished Goods Inventory		Cost of Goods Sold
	→ 16,000	16,000 →	→ 16,000	16,000 →	→ 16,000
			→ 12,000		
			→ 14,000		

	Work in Process Inventory—Job No. 11	
Direct materials direct labor, and manufacturing overhead	→ 12,000	12,000 →

	Work in Process Inventory—Job No. 12	
	→ 14,000	14,000 →

PROCESS COSTING

	Work in Process Inventory		Finished Goods Inventory		Cost of Goods Sold
Direct materials direct labor, and manufacturing overhead	→ 42,000	42,000 →	→ 42,000	14,000[a] →	→ 14,000

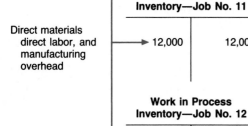

$$^a\ 14,000 = \frac{1\ job}{3\ jobs} \times \$42,000.$$

enough additional benefits (for example, from better decisions) from knowing the actual cost of each unit, which is available in a job costing system, to justify additional recordkeeping costs. For companies producing relatively large, heterogeneous items, the additional benefits of job costing usually justify the additional recordkeeping costs.

COMPREHENSIVE EXAMPLE, INCLUDING FIFO, WEIGHTED AVERAGE, PRIOR DEPARTMENT COSTS, AND SPOILAGE

This section presents a comprehensive process costing example.[2] Dexter Production Company manufactures a single product through a two-department manufacturing process—machining and finishing. In the production process, materials are added to the product in both departments. Normal spoilage occurs in the finishing department, and the spoiled units are not detected until units are completed and inspected. Dexter allocates production costs to spoiled units. These costs are then charged to finished goods inventory because all units finished during the period are in finished goods inventory. The information given in Illustration 8–19 is taken from the company's records for October's activity.

Illustration 8-19   **Comprehensive Example—Facts**

	Machining Department	Finishing Department
Physical flow of units:		
Beginning inventory	–0–	20,000
Transferred in	–0–	60,000
Started in production	80,000	–0–
Transferred out	60,000	60,000
Ending inventory	20,000	18,000
Spoiled units	–0–	2,000

	Machining Department	Finishing Department	
	Ending Inventory	Beginning Inventory	Ending Inventory
Percentage completion:			
Direct materials	100%	100%	100%
Conversion costs	25	50	70
Prior department costs	Not applicable	100	100

	Machining Department	Finishing Department
Beginning inventory costs:		
Direct materials	–0–	$ 28,000
Conversion costs	–0–	27,500
Prior department costs	–0–	118,000
Current costs:		
Direct materials	$320,000	90,000
Conversion costs	130,000	193,800

---

[2] This example was adapted from a CPA examination.

First-in, First-out Method

The production cost report for the machining department, using FIFO, is shown in Illustration 8–20. Preparation of the production cost report for the machining department is relatively straightforward because there is no beginning inventory and no spoilage. For the computation of FIFO equivalent units, there are 60,000 units started and completed and 20,000 units that are

Illustration 8–20

DEXTER PRODUCTION COMPANY
Comprehensive Production Cost Report—FIFO
Machining Department

Flow of Production Units:	(Section 1) Physical Units	(Section 2) Equivalent Units Direct Materials	Conversion Costs
Units to account fo.			
Beginning work in process inventory	–0–		
Units started this period	80,000		
Total units to account for	80,000		
Units accounted for:			
Units completed and transferred out:			
From beginning inventory	–0–	–0–	–0–
Started and completed, currently	60,000	60,000	60,000
Units in ending WIP inventory	20,000	20,000	5,000
Total units accounted for	80,000	80,000	65,000

Flow of Costs:	Total Costs	Direct Materials	Conversion Costs
Costs to be accounted for (Section 3):			
Costs in beginning WIP inventory	–0–	–0–	–0–
Current period costs	$450,000	$320,000	$130,000
Total costs to be accounted for	**$450,000**	**$320,000**	**$130,000**

Cost per equivalent unit: (Section 4):			
Direct materials ($320,000 ÷ 80,000)		$ 4.00	
Direct labor (130,000 ÷ 65,000)			$ 2.00

Costs accounted for (Section 5):			
Costs assigned to units transferred out:			
Costs from beginning WIP inventory	–0–	–0–	–0–
Costs of units started and completed:			
Direct materials (60,000 × $4)	$240,000	$240,000	
Conversion costs (60,000 × $2)	120,000		$120,000
Total costs transferred out (60,000 × $6)	360,000		
Costs assigned to ending WIP inventory:			
Direct materials (20,000 × $4)	80,000	80,000	
Conversion costs (5,000 × $2)	10,000		10,000
Total cost of ending WIP inventory	90,000		
Total costs accounted for	**$450,000**	**$320,000**	**$130,000**

in ending inventory. Ending inventory is 100 percent complete for materials (20,000 E.U.) and 25 percent complete for conversion costs (5,000 E.U.) The sum of the 60,000 units started and completed plus the equivalent units in ending inventory gives the following equivalent units of work done this period (also shown in the top portion of Illustration 8–20):

Materials	80,000 equivalent units
Conversion costs	65,000 equivalent units

Sections 3 through 5 are shown in the middle and bottom portions of Illustration 8–20. Note that 60,000 units are transferred to the finishing department with the following costs:

Direct materials	$240,000
Conversion costs	120,000
Total	$360,000

These costs transferred out of the machining department become the prior department costs transferred into the finishing department. (Find the $360,000 prior department costs transferred into the finishing department in Section 3 of Illustration 8–21.

Preparation of the production cost report for the finishing department is slightly more complicated. Both beginning inventory and spoilage have to be considered to compute equivalent units. Under FIFO, the equivalent units computation starts with the equivalent units needed to complete beginning inventory. The 20,000 partially completed units in beginning inventory are 100 percent complete for prior department costs, 100 percent complete for materials, and 50 percent complete for conversion costs. Therefore, 10,000 equivalent units for conversion costs are required to complete beginning inventory. (See Section 2 in Illustration 8–21.) Based on the facts given in Illustration 8–19, 60,000 units were transferred out of the finishing department. Of these 60,000 units, 20,000 were from beginning inventory and 40,000 units were started and completed. There are 2,000 units that are spoiled, which are 100 percent complete. In ending inventory, there are 18,000 units; prior department costs and materials are both 100 percent complete, but the conversion costs are only 70 percent complete. So, there are 18,000 equivalent units for both prior department costs and materials, and 12,600 equivalent units (.70 × 18,000) for conversion costs. As shown in Section 2 of Illustration 8–21, total equivalent units are 60,000 for prior department costs: 60,000 for materials; and 64,600 for conversion costs.

Sections 3 through 5 are shown in the middle and bottom portions of Illustration 8–21. According to Illustration 8–19, 2,000 units were found to be defective at the inspection point. Note that there is $21,000 of spoilage costs for the 2,000 defective units that were detected at the end of the production process in the finishing department. Because they were detected at the *end* of the process, 100 percent of the costs of making those 2,000 units are

Illustration 8–21

DEXTER PRODUCTION COMPANY
Comprehensive Production Cost Report—FIFO
Finishing Department

Flow of Production Units:	(Section 1) Physical Units	(Section 2) Equivalent Units		
		Prior Department Costs	Direct Materials	Conversion Costs
Units to account for:				
Beginning work in process inventory	20,000			
Units started this period	60,000			
Total units to account for	80,000			
Units accounted for:				
Units completed and transferred out:				
From beginning inventory	20,000	–0–[a]	–0–[a]	10,000[a] (50%)[b]
Started and completed, currently	40,000	40,000	40,000	40,000
Units spoiled	2,000	2,000	2,000	2,000
Units in ending WIP inventory	18,000	18,000	18,000 (100%)[c]	12,600 (70%)[c]
Total units accounted for	80,000	60,000	60,000	64,600

Flow of Costs:	Total Costs	Prior Department Costs	Direct Materials	Conversion Costs
Costs to be accounted for (Section 3):				
Costs in beginning WIP inventory	$173,000	$118,000	$ 28,000	$ 27,500
Current period costs	643,800	360,000[d]	90,000	193,800
Total costs to be accounted for	**$817,300**	**$478,000**	**$118,000**	**$221,300**

Costs per equivalent units (Section 4):			
Prior department costs ($360,000 ÷ 60,000)	$6.00		
Materials ($90,000 ÷ 60,000)		$1.50	
Conversion costs ($193,800 ÷ 64,600)			$3.00

treated as spoilage costs. The $21,000 assigned to these 2,000 defective units are made up of the following costs:

Prior department costs	$12,000 (2,000 units × $6)
Materials	3,000 (2,000 units × $1.50)
Conversion costs	6,000 (2,000 units × $3.00)
Total	$21,000

Illustration 8–23 shows the flow of costs through work in process T-accounts using FIFO for the machining and finishing departments. This is a good summary of the costs assigned to ending inventory and to goods transferred out. The $21,000 costs of spoiled units is transferred out of the

Illustration 8-21   *(concluded)*

	Total Costs	Prior Department Costs	Direct Materials	Conversion Costs
Costs accounted for (Section 5):				
Costs assigned to units transferred out:				
Costs from beginning WIP inventory	$173,500	$118,000	$ 28,000	$ 27,500
Current costs added to complete beginning WIP inventory:				
Prior department costs	-0-	-0-		
Materials	-0-		-0-	
Conversion costs (10,000 × $3.00)	30,000			30,000
Total costs from beginning inventory	203,500			
Costs of units started and completed:				
Prior department costs (40,000 × $6)	240,000	240,000		
Materials (40,000 × $1.50)	60,000		60,000	
Conversion costs (40,000 × $3)	120,000			120,000
Total	420,000			
Total costs transferred out	623,500			
Costs assigned to spoiled units:				
Prior department costs (2,000 × $6.00)	12,000	12,000		
Materials (2,000 × $1.50)	3,000		3,000	
Conversion costs (2,000 × $3)	6,000			6,000
Total	21,000			
Costs assigned to ending WIP inventory:				
Prior department costs (18,000 × $6)	$108,000	108,000		
Materials (18,000 × $1.50)	27,000		27,000	
Conversion costs (12,600 × $3)	37,800			37,800
Total	172,800			
Total costs accounted for	**$817,300**	**$478,000**	**$118,000**	**$221,300**

a Equivalent units required to complete beginning inventory.

b Percent required to complete beginning inventory.

c Stage of completion.

d Costs of units transferred out of the machining department, per illustration 8-20, and into this department.

finishing department to the Finished Goods Inventory account using the following journal entry:

Finished Goods Inventory—Spoilage Costs	21,000	
Work in Process Inventory—Finishing Department (prior department costs)		12,000
Work in Process Inventory—Finishing Department (direct materials)		3,000
Work in Process Inventory—Finishing Department (conversion costs)		6,000

These spoilage costs will be expensed with a debit to the Cost of Goods Sold and a credit to Finished Goods Inventory accounts when the good units that were finished this period are sold.

Illustration 8-22   **Cost Flows through T-Accounts (FIFO method)**

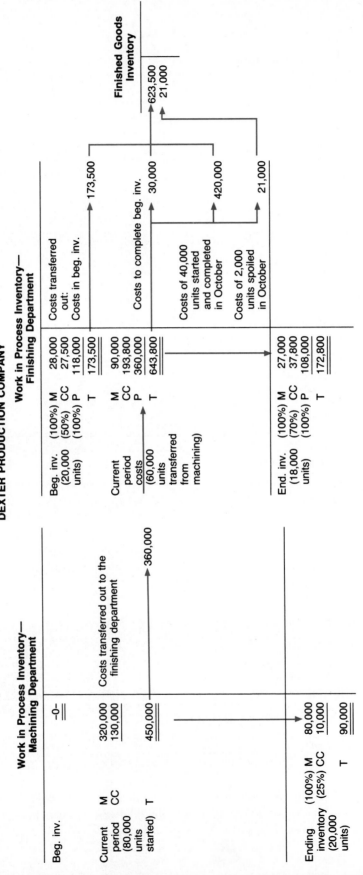

Note: M = Direct materials; CC = Conversion costs; P = Prior department costs; T = Total costs. Percentages in parentheses are stages of completion.

Illustration 8-23

DEXTER PRODUCTION COMPANY
Production Cost Report—Weighted Average
Finishing Department

Flow of Units:	(Section 1) Physical Units	(Section 2) Equivalent Units		
		Prior Department Costs	Materials	Conversion Costs
Units to account for:				
Beginning work in process inventory	20,000	20,000	20,000	10,000 (50%)[a]
Units started this period	60,000			
Total units to account for	80,000			
Units accounted for:				
Units completed and transferred out:				
From beginning inventory	20,000	–0–	–0–	10,000[b] (50%)[c]
Started and completed, currently	40,000	40,000	40,000	40,000
Units spoiled	2,000	2,000	2,000	2,000
Units in ending WIP inventory	18,000	18,000	18,000	12,600 (70%)[a]
Total units accounted for	80,000	80,000	80,000	74,600

Flow of Costs:	Total Costs	Prior Department Costs	Materials	Conversion Costs
Costs to be accounted for (Section 3):				
Costs in beginning WIP inventory	$173,500	$118,000	$ 28,000	$ 27,500
Current period costs	643,800	360,000	90,000	193,800
Total costs to be accounted for	**$817,300**	**$478,000**	**$118,000**	**$221,300**

Cost per equivalent unit (Section 4):				
Prior department costs ($478,000 ÷ 80,000)		$5.9750		
Materials ($118,000 ÷ 80,000)			$1.4750	
Conversion costs ($221,300 ÷ 74,600)				$2.9665

Costs accounted for (Section 5):				
Costs assigned to units transferred out:				
Prior department costs (60,000 × $5.975)	$358,500	358,500		
Materials (60,000 × $1.4750)	88,500		88,500	
Conversion costs (60,000 × $2.9665)	177,990			177,990
Total cost of units transferred out	624,990			
Costs assigned to units spoiled:				
Prior department costs (2,000 × $5.975)	11,950	11,950		
Materials (2,000 × $1.4750)	2,950		2,950	
Conversion costs (2,000 × $2.9665)	5,933			5,933
Total costs assigned to spoiled units	20,833			
Costs assigned to ending WIP inventory:				
Prior department costs (18,000 × $5.975)	$107,550	107,550		
Materials (18,000 × $1.4750)	26,550		26,550	
Conversion costs (12,600 × $2.9665)	37,378			37,378
Total cost of ending WIP inventory	171,478			
Total costs accounted for	**$817,301[d]**	**$478,000**	**$118,000**	**$221,301[d]**

[a] Stage of completion.

[b] Equivalent units required to complete beginning inventory.

[c] Percent required to complete beginning inventory.

[d] Different than total costs to be accounted for because of rounding.

Weighted-Average Method

The production cost report would be the same for the machining department using either FIFO or the weighted-average method. Why? *There are no beginning inventories* in the machining department so the equivalent unit computations and the allocation of costs to units transferred out and to ending inventory are identical whether FIFO or weighted average is used. (Recall that these methods are different only because the weighted-average method computes unit costs using a weighted average of beginning inventory and current period amounts. If there is no beginning inventory, then the "weighted-average" amounts are just the current period amounts.) The production cost report in Illustration 8–20 is appropriate for both FIFO and weighted average because there are no beginning inventories in the machining department.

The weighted-average production cost report for the finishing department is shown in Illustration 8–23. The FIFO and weighted-average reports are different in this case because there are beginning inventories (which have different unit costs than the current period unit costs).

Using weighted average, the equivalent units in beginning inventory are combined with the equivalent units produced during the period. There are 20,000 units in beginning inventory, which are 100 percent complete except for conversion costs, which are 50 percent complete. Therefore, there are 20,000 equivalent units for both prior department costs and materials and 10,000 equivalent units for conversion costs, which are added to the equivalents derived using FIFO to compute equivalent units using weighted average, as shown in section 2 of Illustration 8–23.

The costs to be accounted for (section 3 in Illustration 8–23) are *assumed* to be the same for both FIFO and weighted average. Sections 4 and 5 show the computation of unit costs and the assignment of costs to good units transferred out, to spoiled units, and to ending inventory. If you compare sections 4 and 5 in Illustration 8–23 (using weighted average) to sections 4 and 5 in Illustration 8–21 (using FIFO), you will find that the total costs accounted for are the same in both cases. The differences are in computing unit costs and assigning total costs to good units transferred out, to spoiled units, and to ending inventory.

SUMMARY

Process costing is used when it is not possible or practical to identify costs with specific lots or batches of product. The two most common methods of process costing are first-in, first-out (FIFO) costing and weighted-average costing. FIFO costing separates current period costs from the beginning inventory costs. The weighted-average method makes no distinction between beginning inventory and current period costs. As a result, weighted-average computations are simpler. However, the FIFO method is potentially more informative because it keeps separate track of current and previous period costs.

Refer to Illustration 8–12 for a summary of the steps required to allocate costs to units. In comparing the weighted-average and FIFO methods, note the importance of matching costs with units. Weighted-average costing includes beginning inventory (that is, work done in a previous period) in computing both equivalent units and unit costs, while FIFO costing *excludes* beginning inventory in computing equivalent units and unit costs.

Costs are usually applied to products at different times in the production process. Costs applied at the same time are usually grouped together for computational purposes. For example, if direct labor and manufacturing overhead are applied at the same time, they are combined into one category—conversion costs. Companies typically have three distinct categories of costs: direct materials, conversion costs, and prior department costs. The latter are costs transferred in from previous departments (which, conceptually, are a type of direct materials to the receiving department).

Sometimes inputs and outputs are measured differently. When this is the case, the input units are typically redefined into the way output units are measured.

When units are spoiled in production, a common practice is to spread all costs, including costs incurred on the spoiled units, over the *good units* produced. An alternative is to remove the spoiled units from work in process (that is, credit Work in Process Inventory) and charge them to inventories and cost of goods sold. If the spoilage or lost units are not a normal part of production, then they are typically written off as a period expense for external financial reporting purposes.

Process costing systems accumulate costs for each production department; however, they do not maintain separate records of costs for each unit produced. Thus, when comparing job costing and process costing systems, companies generally find that job costing provides more data but has greater recordkeeping costs. Managers and accountants must decide whether the additional data available under job costing justifies the higher recordkeeping costs. For companies in which relatively homogeneous units are produced in a continuous process, cost-benefit analysis generally favors process costing.

TERMS AND CONCEPTS

The following terms and concepts should be familiar to you after reading this chapter.

Abnormal Spoilage	Prior Department Costs
Equivalent Unit	Process Costing
First-in, First-out (FIFO) Costing	Production Cost Report
Lost Units	Spoilage
Normal Spoilage	Weighted-Average Costing

SUPPLEMENTARY READINGS

Dinius, Sara H. "Matrix Solution to Process Cost Problems." *Issues in Accounting Education*, Spring 1987, pp. 44–56.

Falhaber Thomas A.; Fred A. Coad; and Thomas J. Little. "Building a Process Cost Management System from the Bottom Up." *Management Accounting*, May 1988, pp. 58–62.

Filimon, R., et al. "Spoilage with a Production Function." *Accounting Business Research*, Autumn 1987, pp. 337–48.

Lovata, Linda M. "Experiential Process Costing Project." *Issues in Accounting Education*, Spring 1986, pp. 148–52.

Mensah, Yaw M., and Gulprit S. Cahatwal. "Accounting for Shrinkage in Continuous Flow Industries: An Expository Note." *Abacus,* March 1987, pp. 31–42 (published in Australia).

Mong, Han Kang. "Control Theory Approach to Process Costing." *Accounting and Business Research,* Spring 1985, pp. 129–33 (published in Great Britain).

Siegel, Joel G., and Michael Stevens. "Reporting and Appraisal of Process Cost Data." *Accountants Record,* March–April 1984, pp. 103–19 (published in Great Britain).

SELF-STUDY PROBLEM NO. 1

FlyingFast, Inc., manufactures racquetball racquets. The process requires two manufacturing departments: frames and strings. Racquets are formed in the frames department using aluminum tubing, handle materials, and frame decorations. The completed frames are sent to the strings department where the racquets are strung and packaged for shipment to sporting goods stores. Six thousand frames were transferred to the strings department this month.

Because the racquets are manufactured in such large numbers, the company uses a process costing accounting system to assign costs to racquets. The following information is available for FlyingFast manufacturing activities in the strings department during the past month:

STRINGS DEPARTMENT

	Units	Prior Department Costs	Direct Materials	Conversion Costs
Physical flow:				
Beginning inventory	1,000	100% complete	60% complete	75% complete
Ending inventory	2,700	100% complete	80% complete	45% complete
Transferred in	6,000			
Costs incurred:				
Beginning inventory		$ 7,100	$ 600	$ 420
Current costs		43,200	2,500	6,475

Required:

Assume no units were lost or spoiled until you get to requirements *(e)* and *(f)*.

a. Prepare a production cost report for the strings department using FIFO.

b. Use a T-account to show the cost flows in the strings department using FIFO.

c. Prepare a production cost report for the strings department using weighted average.

d. Use a T-account to show cost flows in the strings department using weighted average.

e. Now, assume that at the end of the stringing process, normal spoilage occurred. This was due to bending of the frames by tension produced at the end of the stringing process. Normal spoilage amounted to 100 units, and consequently, the number of good units in ending inventory is 2,600, which are 80 percent complete for materials and 45 percent complete for conversion costs. Prepare a production cost report using FIFO. Compare it with the report prepared for *(a)* above. What is different? Prepare a journal entry that removes the units from Work in Process Inventory and debits two thirds of their costs to Finished Goods Inventory and one third to Cost of Goods Sold.

f. Now, assume that the spoilage in *(e)* is abnormal spoilage and debited to Abnormal Spoilage expense. Prepare the journal entry to remove spoilage from Work in Process Inventory.

SOLUTION TO SELF-STUDY PROBLEM NO. 1

a. Production Cost Report—FIFO:

FLYINGFAST, INC.
Strings Dept.

Flow of Production Units:	(Section 1) Physical Units	(Section 2) Equivalent Units		
		Prior Department Costs	Materials	Conversion Costs
Units to account for:				
Beginning work in process inventory	1,000			
Units started this period	6,000			
Total units to account for	7,000			
Units accounted for:				
Units completed and transferred out:				
From beginning inventory	1,000	–0–[a]	400[a](40%)[b]	250[a](25%)[b]
Started and completed, currently	3,300[d]	3,300	3,300	3,300
Units in ending WIP inventory	2,700	2,700	2,160 (80%)[c]	1,215 (45%)[c]
Total units accounted for	7,000	6,000	5,860	4,765

Flow of Costs:	Total Costs	Prior Department Costs	Materials	Conversion Costs
Costs to be accounted for (Section 3):				
Costs in beginning WIP inventory	$ 8,120	$ 7,100	$ 600	$ 420
Current period costs	52,175	43,200	2,500	6,475
Total costs to be accounted for	**$60,295**	**$50,300**	**$3,100**	**$ 6,895**

Cost per equivalent unit (Section 4):			
Prior department costs ($43,200 ÷ 6,000)	$7.2000		
Materials ($2,500 ÷ 5,860)		$.4266	
Conversion costs ($6,475 ÷ 4,765)			$1.3589

SOLUTION TO
SELF-STUDY
PROBLEM NO. 1
(continued)

Flow of Costs:	Total Costs	Prior Department Costs	Materials	Conversion Costs
Costs accounted for (Section 5):				
Costs assigned to units transferred out:				
Costs from beginning WIP inventory	$ 8,120	$ 7,100	$ 600	$ 420
Current costs added to complete beginning WIP inventory:				
Prior department costs	–0–	–0–		
Materials (400 × $.4266)	$ 171		171	
Conversion costs (250 × $1.3589)	340			340
Total costs from beginning inventory	8,631			
Costs of units started and completed:				
Prior department costs (3,300 × $7.20)	23,760	23,760		
Materials (3,300 × $.4266)	1,408		1,408	
Conversion costs (3,300 × $1.3589)	4,484			4,484
Total costs of units started and completed	29,652			
Total costs transferred out	38,283			
Costs assigned to ending WIP inventory:				
Prior department costs (2,700 × $7.20)	19,440	19,440		
Materials (2,160 × $.4266)	921		921	
Conversion costs (1,215 × $1.3589)	1,651			1,651
Total cost of ending WIP inventory	22,012			
Total costs accounted for	**$60,295**	**$50,300**	**$3,100**	**$ 6,895**

[a] Equivalent units required to complete beginning inventory.

[b] Percent required to complete beginning inventory.

[c] Stage of completion.

[d] Units in beginning inventory + Units started and completed + Units in ending inventory = Total units accounted for. So: 1,000 + X + 2,700 = 7,000; X = 7,000 − 2,700 − 1,000 = 3,300.

b. Cost flows—FIFO:

Work in Process Inventory— Strings Department			**Finished Goods Inventory**	
Beginning inventory 8,120[a]	To Finished Goods Inventory:			
This period's costs:	From beginning			
Prior department costs included in units transferred into this department this period 43,200[a]	inventory costs 8,120[b]			
	From this period's costs 30,163	→ 38,283[b]		
Materials used this period 2,500[a]				
Conversion costs incurred this period 6,475[a]				
Ending inventory $22,012[b]				

[a] See step 3 in the production cost report.

[b] See step 5 in the production cost report.

SOLUTION TO SELF-STUDY PROBLEM NO. 1
(continued)

c. Production cost report—weighted average:

Flow of Production Units:	(Section 1) Physical Units	(Section 2) Compute Equivalent Units		
		Prior Department Costs	Materials	Conversion Costs
Units to account for:				
Beginning work in process inventory	1,000	1,000	600 (60%)[a]	750 (75%)[a]
Units started this period	6,000			
Total units to account for	7,000			
Units accounted for:				
Units completed and transferred out:				
From beginning inventory	1,000	–0–	400[b] (40%)	250[b] (25%)
Started and completed, currently	3,300[c]	3,300	3,300	3,300
Total	4,300			
Units in ending WIP inventory	2,700	2,700	2,160 (80%)[a]	1,215 (45%)[a]
Total units accounted for	7,000	7,000	6,460	5,515

Flow of Costs:	Total Costs	Prior Department Costs	Materials	Conversion Costs
Costs to be accounted for (Section 3):				
Costs in beginning WIP inventory	$ 8,120	$ 7,100	$ 600	$ 420
Current period costs	52,175	43,200	2,500	6,475
Total costs to be accounted for	$60,295	$50,300	$3,100	$ 6,895
Cost per equivalent unit (Section 4):				
Prior department costs ($50,300 ÷ 7,000)		$7.1857		
Materials ($3,100 ÷ 6,460)			$.4799	
Conversion costs ($6,895 ÷ 5,515)				$1.2502
Costs accounted for (Section 5):				
Costs assigned to units transferred out:				
Prior department costs (4,300 × $7.1857	$30,899	30,899		
Materials (4,300 × $.4799)	2,063		2,063[d]	
Conversion costs (4,300 × $1.2502)	5,376			5,376
Total costs transferred out	38,338			
Costs assigned to ending WIP inventory:				
Prior department costs (2,700 × $7.1857)	19,401	19,401		
Materials (2,160 × $.4799)	1,037		1,037	
Conversion costs (1,215 × $1.2502)	1,519			1,519
Total cost of ending WIP inventory	21,957			
Total costs accounted for	$60,295	$50,300	$3,100	$ 6,895

[a] Stage of completion.
[b] Equivalent units required to complete beginning inventory.
[c] See FIFO production cost report, footnote d.
[d] Rounded down.

**SOLUTION TO
SELF-STUDY
PROBLEM NO. 1
(continued)**

d. Cost flows—weighted average:

Work in Process Inventory—Strings Department

Beginning inventory	8,120[a]	Costs transferred to	
Prior dept. costs	43,200[a]	Finished Goods	
Materials	2,500[a]	Inventory	38,338[b]
Conversion costs	6,475[a]		
Ending inventory	$21,957[b]		

[a] See step 3 in the production cost report.
[b] See step 5 in the production cost report.

e. Production cost report—FIFO (with spoilage):

Flow of production units:	(Section 1) Physical Units	(Section 2) Equivalent Units Prior Department Costs	Materials	Conversion Costs
Units to account for:				
Beginning work in process inventory	1,000			
Units started this period	6,000			
Total units to account for	7,000			
Units accounted for:				
Units completed and transferred out:				
From beginning inventory	1,000	–0–[b]	400[b](40%)	250[b](25%)
Started and completed, currently	3,300[c]	3,300	3,300	3,300
Units spoiled	100	100	100	100
Units in ending WIP inventory	2,600	2,600	2,080 (80%)[a]	1,170 (45%)[a]
Total units accounted for	7,000	6,000	5,880	4,820

Flow of Costs:	Total Costs	Prior Department Costs	Materials	Conversion Costs
Costs to be accounted for (Section 3):				
Costs in beginning WIP inventory	$ 8,120	$ 7,100	$ 600	$ 420
Current period costs	52,175	43,200	2,500	6,475
Total costs to be accounted for	**$60,295**	**$50,300**	**$3,100**	**$6,895**
Cost per equivalent unit (Section 4):				
Prior department costs ($43,200 ÷ 6,000)		$7.2000		
Materials ($2,500 ÷ 5,880)			$.4252	
Conversion costs ($6,475 ÷ 4,820)				$1.3434

**SOLUTION TO
SELF-STUDY
PROBLEM NO. 1**
(continued)

Flow of Costs:

	Total Costs	Prior Department Costs	Materials	Conversion Costs
Costs accounted for (Section 5):				
Costs assigned to units transferred out:				
Costs from beginning WIP inventory	$ 8,120	$ 7,100	$ 600	$ 420
Current costs added to complete beginning WIP inventory:				
Prior department costs	-0-	-0-		
Materials (400 × $.4252)	170		170	
Conversion costs (250 × $1.3434)	336			336
Total costs from beginning inventory	8,626			
Costs of units started and completed:				
Prior department costs (3,300 × $7.20)	23,760	23,760		
Materials (3,300 × $.4252)	1,403		1,403	
Conversion costs (3,300 × $1.3434)	4,433			4,433
Total costs of units started and completed	29,596			
Total cost of good units transferred out	38,222			
Costs assigned to units spoiled:				
Prior department costs (100 × $7.20)	720	720		
Materials (100 × $.4252)	43		43	
Conversion costs (100 × $1.3434)	134			134
Total costs assigned to units spoiled	897			
Costs assigned to ending WIP inventory:				
Prior department costs (2,600 × $7.20)	18,720	18,720		
Materials (2,080 × $.4252)	884		884	
Conversion costs (1,170 × $1.3434)	1,572			1,572
Total cost of ending WIP inventory	21,176			
Total costs accounted for	**$60,295**	**$50,300**	**$3,100**	**$6,895**

[a] Stage of completion.

[b] Equivalent units required to complete beginning inventory.

[c] See footnote d of production cost report for requirement *(a)*.

Journal entry—FIFO:

Finished Goods Inventory	598	
Cost of Goods Sold	299	
Work in Process Inventory—Strings Department:		
Prior departmental costs		720
Direct materials		43
Conversion costs		134

Total spoilage = $879.

Amount assigned to Finished Goods Inventory per problem requirement is $598 (⅔ × $897). The remaining $299 (⅓ × $897) is assigned to Cost of Goods Sold.

SOLUTION TO SELF-STUDY PROBLEM NO. 1 (concluded)

f. **Journal entry—FIFO:**

Abnormal Spoilage	897	
Work in Process Inventory—Strings Department:		
Prior departmental costs		720
Direct materials costs		43
Conversion costs		134

SELF-STUDY PROBLEM NO. 2

Compute Cost of Spoiled Units When Spoilage Occurs during the Process

A company using the weighted-average costing method maintains a Spoilage Expense account for spoiled goods. This account is charged with the cost of units spoiled in process. Each unit spoiled is considered 80 percent complete with respect to conversion costs and 100 percent complete with respect to materials at the time of spoilage.

The accounting records show the following information for the activities in the Work in Process Inventory account:

Beginning inventory:	
Direct materials	$14,800
Conversion costs	21,650
Current period:	
Direct materials	43,100
Conversion costs	79,220
Units transferred out	18,200
Units spoiled	2,300
Ending inventory:	
Physical count	6,400
Percent of completion:	
Direct materials	40%
Conversion costs	25%

Required:

Compute the costs to be assigned to the spoiled units.

SOLUTION TO SELF-STUDY PROBLEM NO. 2

First, compute the equivalent units:

	Direct Materials	Conversion Costs
Transferred out	18,200	18,200
Spoiled 2,300 units	2,300 (100%)	1,840 (80%)
Ending inventory, 6,400 units	2,560 (40%)	1,600 (25%)
Totals	23,060 E.U.	21,640 E.U.

Next, compute the total costs to be accounted for:

	Direct Materials	Conversion Costs
Beginning inventory	$14,800	$ 21,650
Current costs	43,100	79,220
Total costs	$57,900	$100,870

Next, compute costs per equivalent unit:

$$\$\ 57{,}900 \div 23{,}060 \text{ E.U.} = \$2.5108 \text{ per E.U.}$$
$$\$100{,}870 \div 21{,}640 \text{ E.U.} = \$4.6613 \text{ per E.U.}$$

Then, multiply by the equivalent units spoiled:

$$\text{Direct materials:} \quad \$2.5108 \times 2{,}300 \text{ E.U.} = \$5{,}775$$
$$\text{Conversion costs:} \quad 4.6613 \times 1{,}840 \text{ E.U.} = \$8{,}577$$

The total spoiled unit cost is $14,352 (= $5,775 + $8,577).

QUESTIONS

8-1. A manufacturing company has records of its current activity in work in process inventory and of its ending work in process inventory. However, the record of its beginning inventory has been lost. Express in equation form the data that would be needed to compute the beginning inventory.

8-2. If costs change from one period to another, costs that are transferred out of one department under FIFO costing will include units with two different costs. Why?

8-3. Management of a company that manufactures small appliances is trying to decide whether to install a job order or process costing system. The manufacturing vice president has stated that job order costing gives them the best control because it is possible to assign costs to specific lots of goods. The controller, however, has stated that job order costing would require too much recordkeeping. Is there another costing system that might meet the manufacturing vice president's control objectives? Explain.

8-4. Why are equivalent units computed for process costing? What is the distinction between equivalent units under FIFO and equivalent units under the weighted average method?

8-5. Farleigh O. Tuvit is a new member of the controller's staff in the same company as you. Farleigh has just completed a report that urges the company to adopt the LIFO method for inventory accounting. The controller is concerned about the recommendation because the cost records are maintained on a FIFO basis. Indeed, the controller has not even heard of using LIFO for process cost accounting. Can you suggest how the controller might resolve the problem?

8–6. It has been said that prior department costs behave similarly to direct materials costs. Under what conditions are the costs similar? What differences arise that require the costs to be treated separately?

8–7. Write a formula to show how the basic inventory formula can help you solve for equivalent units produced in the current period.

8–8. A company wants to use weighted-average costing because it is simple to apply. However, the company also wishes to be able to monitor its costs. Is it possible to monitor cost trends using weighted average?

8-9. Describe methods for handling lost units in a process that expects certain losses due to shrinkage, evaporation, or other inherent characteristics of the process.

8-10. Select the best answer for each of the following multiple-choice questions.

a. Under which of the following conditions will the first-in, first-out method of process costing produce the same cost of goods manufactured amount as the weighted-average method?
   (1) When goods produced are homogeneous.
   (2) When there is no beginning inventory.
   (3) When there is no ending inventory.
   (4) When beginning and ending inventories are each 50 percent complete.

b. An error was made in the computation of the percentage of completion of the current year's ending work in process inventory. The error resulted in assigning a lower percentage of completion to each component of the inventory than actually was the case. Assume there was no beginning inventory. What is the effect of this error upon:
   (1) The computation of total equivalent units?
   (2) The computation of costs per equivalent unit?
   (3) Costs assigned to cost of goods transferred out for the period?

	1	2	3
(a)	Understate	Overstate	Overstate
(b)	Understate	Understate	Overstate
(c)	Overstate	Understate	Understate
(d)	Overstate	Overstate	Understate

c. In computing the cost per equivalent unit, the weighted-average method considers:
   (1) Current costs only.
   (2) Current costs plus cost of beginning work in process inventory.
   (3) Current costs plus cost of ending work in process inventory.
   (4) Current costs less cost of beginning work in process inventory.

d. When using the FIFO method of process costing, total equivalent units produced for a given period are equal to the number of units:
   (1) Started and completed during the period, plus the number of units in beginning WIP, plus the number of units in ending work in process.
   (2) In beginning WIP plus the number of units started during the period, plus the number of units remaining in ending WIP times the percent of work necessary to complete the items.
   (3) In beginning WIP times the percent of work necessary to complete the items, plus the number of units started and completed during the period, plus the number of units started this period and remaining in

ending WIP times the percent of work necessary to complete the items.

(4) Transferred out during the period plus the number of units remaining in ending WIP times the percent of work necessary to complete the items.

(5) None of these.

(CPA adapted)

EXERCISES

8–11. Compute Equivalent Units—FIFO Method
(L.O.1)

A company's records show the following information concerning the work in process in a chemical plant:

1. Beginning inventory—12,000 units (materials are 20 percent complete; conversion costs are 30 percent complete).
2. Transferred out—34,000 units.
3. Ending inventory—(materials are 10 percent complete; conversion costs are 15 percent complete).
4. Started this month—42,000 units.

Required:

a. Compute the equivalent units for materials using FIFO.
b. Compute the equivalent units for conversion costs using FIFO.

8–12. Compute Equivalent Units—FIFO Method
(L.O.1)

A company's records show the following information concerning the work in process at an assembly plant:

1. Beginning inventory (materials are 15 percent complete; conversion costs are 25 percent complete).
2. Transferred out—30,000 units.
3. Ending inventory—10,000 units (materials are 20 percent complete; conversion costs are 30 percent complete).
4. Started this month—35,000 units.

Required:

a. Compute the equivalent units for materials using FIFO.
b. Compute the equivalent units for conversion costs for using FIFO.

8–13. Compute Costs per Equivalent Unit—FIFO
(L.O.1)

A company uses the FIFO method to account for its work in process inventories. The accounting records show the following information:

Beginning work in process inventory:	
Direct materials	$ 360
Conversion costs	108
	$ 468
Debits to work in process inventory this period:	
Direct materials	$3,714
Conversion costs	2,258

Quantity information is obtained from the manufacturing records and includes the following:

Beginning inventory	300 units
Percent of completion:	
Direct materials	60%
Conversion costs	30%
Current period units started	2,000 units
Ending inventory	600 units
Percent of completion:	
Direct materials	40%
Conversion costs	20%

Required:

Compute the cost per equivalent unit for direct materials and for conversion costs.

8–14. Assign Costs to Goods Transferred Out and Ending Inventory—FIFO Method
(L.O.2)

Refer to the data in exercise 8–13. Compute the cost of goods transferred out and the ending inventory, using the FIFO method.

8–15. Compute Costs per Equivalent Unit—FIFO Method
(L.O.2)

The beginning work in process inventory showed a balance of $48,240. Of this amount, $16,440 is the cost of direct materials, and $31,800 are conversion costs. There were 8,000 units in the beginning inventory that were 30 percent complete with respect to both direct materials and conversion costs.

During the period, 17,000 units were transferred out and 5,000 remained in the ending inventory. The units in the ending inventory were 80 percent complete with respect to direct materials and 40 percent complete with respect to conversion costs.

Costs incurred during the period amounted to $126,852 for direct materials and $219,120 for converison. The FIFO method is used for inventory accounting purposes.

Required:

Compute the cost per equivalent unit for direct materials and for conversion costs.

8–16. Assign Costs to Goods Transferred out and to Ending Inventory—FIFO Method
(L.O.2)

Refer to the data in exercise 8–15. Compute the cost of goods transferred out and the cost of ending inventory, using the FIFO method.

8–17. Prepare Production Cost Report—FIFO Method
(L.O.3)

The following information appears in the records of the Furlong Production Company:

Work in process inventory—Department No. 2:		
Beginning inventory:		
Prior department costs	$ 4,800	3,000 units (100 percent complete)
Department No. 2 costs	1,080	20 percent complete
Current work:		
Prior department costs	10,850	7,000 units (100 percent complete)
Department No. 2 costs	18,585	

The ending inventory has 1,000 units, which are 45 percent complete with respect to Department No. 2 costs and 100 percent complete for prior department costs. Prepare a production cost report, using FIFO. (For an example, see Illustration 8–9.)

8–18. Prepare Production Cost Report—Weighted-Average Method (L.O.3)

Refer to the information in exercise 8–17.

a. Prepare a production cost report, using the weighted-average method. (For an example, see Illustration 8–10.)

b. Is the ending inventory higher using FIFO or weighted average? Why?

8–19. Compute Equivalent Units—Weighted-Average Method (L.O.4)

Using the data in exercise 8–11, compute the equivalent units for materials and conversion costs using the weighted-average method.

8–20. Compute Equivalent Units—Weighted-Average Method (L.O.4)

Using the data in exercise 8–12, compute the equivalent units for materials and conversion costs using the weighted-average method.

8–21. Compute Costs per Equivalent Unit—Weighted-Average Method (L.O.4)

Refer to the data in exercise 8–15. Compute the cost per equivalent unit for direct materials and for conversion costs using the weighted-average method. Are these unit costs under weighted average higher or lower than the unit costs under FIFO? Why?

8–22. Assign Costs to Goods Transferred out and to Ending Inventory—Weighted-Average Method (L.O.4)

Refer to the data in exercise 8–15 and assume the beginning inventory is the same using either FIFO or weighted average. Compute the cost of goods transferred out and the ending inventory using the weighted-average method. Is the ending inventory higher or lower using weighted average compared to using FIFO? Why?

8–23. Compute Costs per Equivalent Unit—Weighted-Average Method (L.O.4)

Refer to the data in exercise 8–13. Compute the cost per equivalent unit for direct materials and conversion costs using the weighted-average method. Are the unit costs higher using FIFO or are they higher using weighted average? Why?

8–24. Assign Costs to Goods Transferred out and to Ending Inventory—Weighted-Average Method (L.O.4)

Refer to the data in exercise 8-13. Compute the cost of goods transferred out and the ending inventory using the weighted-average method.

8–25. Compute Costs of Spoiled Goods—FIFO Method (L.O.5)

Refer to the data in exercise 8–15. Assume that there are 5,000 units in ending inventory, that there was normal spoilage of 1,700 units, and 15,300 good units were transferred out. Spoilage occurs at the end of the process after all materials and conversion costs have been added. All other information is the same as in exercise 8–15.

Required:
a. Using the FIFO method, how much cost would be assigned to spoiled units, to good units transferred out, and to good units in ending inventory? (The company assigns costs to spoiled units; that is, the second method discussed in the text.)
b. If the spoilage had been considered *abnormal spoilage,* would that affect your computations in *(a)* above?

8–26. Compute Costs of Spoiled Goods—Weighted-Average Method
(L.O.5)

Refer to the data in exercises 8–15 and 8–25. Assume the company uses the weighted-average method. Using the weighted-average method, how much cost would be assigned to spoiled units, to units transferred out, and to ending inventory?

8–27. Compute Equivalent Units—Multiple-Choice
(L.O.1)

Each of the following multiple-choice questions is independent. Select the best answer.

Required:

a. Spaulding Corporation's production cycle starts in the First Department. The following information is available for May:

	Units
Work in process, April 1 (50 percent complete)	40,000
Started in April	240,000
Work in process, April 30 (60 percent complete)	25,000

Materials are added at the beginning of the process in the First Department. Using the weighted-average method, what are the equivalent units of production for the month of May?

	Materials	Conversion
(1)	240,000	250,000
(2)	255,000	255,000
(3)	270,000	280,000
(4)	280,000	270,000
(5)	None of the above.	

b. The Second Department is the second stage of Johnson Company's production cycle. On May 1, the beginning work in process (WIP) contained 25,000 units, which were 60 percent complete as to conversion costs. During May, 100,000 units were transferred in from the first stage of the production cycle. On May 31, ending work in process contained 20,000 units, which were 80 percent complete as to conversion costs. Materials are added at the end of the process. Using the weighted-average method, the E.U. produced on May 31 were:

	Prior Department Costs	Materials	Conversion Costs
(1)	100,000	125,000	100,000
(2)	125,000	105,000	105,000
(3)	125,000	105,000	121,000
(4)	125,000	125,000	121,000
(5)	None of the above.		

c. Department A is the first stage of ABC Company's production cycle. The following information is available for conversion costs for the month of April:

	Units
Beginning WIP (60 percent complete)	20,000
Started in April	340,000
Completed in April and transferred to Department B	320,000
Ending WIP (40 percent complete)	40,000

Using the FIFO method, the equivalent units for the conversion cost calculation are:
(1) 320,000.
(2) 324,000.
(3) 336,000.
(4) 360,000.

d. Materials are added at the start of the process in Oak Company's blending department, the first stage of the production cycle. The following information is available for July:

	Units
Work in process, July 1 (60 percent complete as to conversion costs)	60,000
Started in July	150,000
Transferred to the next department	110,000
Lost in production	30,000
Work in process, July 31 (50 percent complete as to conversion costs)	70,000

Using Oak's cost accounting system, the costs incurred on the lost units are absorbed by the remaining good units. Using the weighted-average method, what are the equivalent units for the materials unit cost calculation?
(1) 120,000.
(2) 145,000.
(3) 180,000.
(4) 210,000.
(5) None of the above.

e. The Beta Company computed the physical flow of units for Department A for the month of April as follows:

Units completed:	
From WIP on April 1	10,000
From April production	30,000
Total	40,000

Materials are added at the beginning of the process. Units of WIP at April 30 were 8,000. The WIP at April 1 was 80 percent complete as to conversion costs, and the WIP at April 30 was 60 percent complete as to conversion costs. What are the E.U. produced for the month of April using the FIFO method?

	Materials	Conversion Costs
(1)	38,000	36,800
(2)	38,000	38,000
(3)	48,000	44,800
(4)	48,000	48,000
(5)	None of the above.	

(CPA adapted)

8–28. Multiple-Choice—FIFO Method
(L.O.2)

The following questions are based on the Refining Department. Conversion costs for this department were 80 percent complete as to beginning work in process (WIP) and 50 percent complete as to ending WIP. Information about conversion costs for January is as follows:

	Units	Conversion Costs
WIP at January 1 (80 percent complete)	25,000	$ 22,000
Units started and costs incurred during January	135,000	$143,000
Units completed and transferred to next department during January	100,000	——

The company uses FIFO in the Refining Department.

Required:

a. What was the conversion cost of WIP in the Refining Department at Jan. 31?
   (1) $33,000.
   (2) $38,100.
   (3) $39,000.
   (4) $45,000.

b. What were the conversion costs per E.U. produced last period and this period, respectively?
   (1) $1.10 and $1.30.
   (2) $1.10 and $1.43.
   (3) $1.30 and $1.30.
   (4) $1.30 and $1.43.

c. What is the per unit conversion cost of goods started last period and completed this period?
   (1) $0.88.
   (2) $1.10.
   (3) $1.14.
   (4) $1.30.

d. What is the per unit conversion cost of goods started this period and completed this period?
   (1) $0.88.
   (2) $1.10.
   (3) $1.14.
   (4) $1.30.   (CPA adapted)

PROBLEMS

8-29. Prepare Production Cost Report—Weighted-Average Method

Lakeview Corporation is a manufacturer that uses the weighted-average process cost method to account for costs of production. Lakeview manufactures a product that is produced in three separate departments: molding, assembling, and finishing. The following information was obtained for the assembling department for the month of June.

Work in process, June 1—2,000 units made up of the following:

	Amount	Degree of Completion
Prior department costs transferred in from the molding department	$32,000	100%
Costs added by the assembling department:		
Direct materials	$20,000	100
Direct labor	7,200	60
Manufacturing overhead	5,500	50
	32,700	
Work in process, June 1	$64,700	

The following activity occurred during the month of June: 10,000 units were transferred in from the molding department at a prior department cost of $160,000. The assembling department added the following $150,000 of costs.

Direct materials	$ 96,000
Direct labor	36,000
Manufacturing overhead	18,000
	$150,000

Eight thousand units were completed and transferred to the finishing department.
   At June 30, 4,000 units were still in work in process. The degree of completion of work in process at June 30, was as follows:

Direct materials	90%
Direct labor	70
Manufacturing overhead	35

Required:	Prepare a production cost report, using the weighted-average method. (For an example, see Illustration 8–10.)

(CPA adapted)

8–30. Prepare Production Cost Report—FIFO Method

Refer to the facts in problem 8–29.

Required:

Prepare a production cost report, using FIFO.

8–31. Journal Entries and Cost Flows—FIFO

Refer to the information in problem 8–30. Assume (1) the goods are transferred out to WIP—Finishing, and they were transferred into Assembly from WIP—Molding; (2) materials used this period are credited to direct materials inventory; and (3) conversion costs for the current period are credited to "Various Payables."

Required:

Prepare journal entries and show the flow of costs through T-accounts for all costs flowing through WIP—Assembly.

8–32. Prepare a Production Cost Report and Adjust Inventory Balances— Weighted-Average Method

Spirit Processing Corporation's unaudited records show the following ending inventory balances which must be adjusted to actual costs:

	Units	Unaudited Costs
Work in process inventory	300,000	$ 660,960
Finished goods inventory	200,000	1,009,800

As the auditor, you have learned the following information. Ending work in process inventory is 50 percent complete with respect to conversion costs. Materials are added at the beginning of the manufacturing process, and overhead is applied at the rate of 60 percent of the direct labor costs. There was no finished goods inventory at the start of the period. The following additonal information is also available:

		Costs	
	Units	**Direct Materials**	**Direct Labor**
Beginning inventory (80 percent complete as to labor)	200,000	$ 200,000	$ 315,000
Units started	1,000,000		
Current costs		1,300,000	1,995,000
Units completed and transferred to finished goods inventory	900,000		

Required:

a. Prepare a production cost report for Spirit Processing Corporation using weighted average.

b. Show the adjusting journal entry required to reconcile the difference between the unaudited records and actual ending balances of Work in Process Inventory and Finished Goods Inventory. Adjust Cost of Goods Sold for any difference.

c. If the adjustment in (b) above had not been made, would the company's income and inventories have been overstated or understated?

(CPA adapted)

8-33. Show Cost Flows—FIFO Method

Malcolm Company uses continuous processing of cereals and uses FIFO process costing to account for its manufacturing costs. FIFO is used because costs are quite volatile due to the price volatility of commodities. The cereals are processed through one department. Overhead is applied on the basis of direct labor costs. The application rate has not changed over the period covered by the problem. The Work in Process Inventory account showed the following balances at the start of the current period:

Direct materials	$32,750
Direct labor	65,000
Overhead applied	81,250

These costs were related to 26,000 units that were in the process at the start of the period.

During the period, 30,000 units were transferred to finished goods inventory. Of the units finished this period, 70 percent were sold. After units have been transferred to finished goods inventory, no distinction is made between the costs to complete beginning work in process inventory and the costs of goods started and completed in work in process this period.

The equivalent units this period for materials was 25,000 (using FIFO). Of these units, there were 5,000 equivalent units with respect to materials in the ending work in process inventory. Materials costs incurred during the period totaled $75,100.

Conversion costs of $321,750 were incurred this period, and there were 31,250 equivalent units for conversion costs (using FIFO). The ending inventory consisted of 11,000 equivalent units of conversion costs.

The actual manufacturing overhead for the period was $165,000.

Required:

Prepare T-accounts to show the flow of costs in the system. Any difference between actual and applied overhead of the period should be debited or credited to Cost of Goods Sold.

8-34. Process Costing with Spoilage

West Corporation makes a product called Aggregate in one department of the California Division.

Direct materials are added at the beginning of the process. Labor and overhead are added continuously throughout the process. Spoilage occurs at the beginning of the process just after materials have been added but before any conversion costs have been incurred. In the California Division, all departmental overhead is charged to the departments, and divisional overhead is allocated to the departments on the basis of direct labor-hours. The divisional overhead rate is $2 per direct labor-hour.

The following information relates to production during November:

1. Work in process inventory, November 1 (4,000 pounds—75 percent complete):

Direct materials	$22,800
Direct labor at $5 per hour	24,650
Departmental overhead	12,000
Divisional overhead	9,860

2. Direct materials:

Inventory, November 1—2,000 pounds	$10,000
Purchases, November 3—10,000 pounds	51,000
Purchases, November 18—10,000 pounds	51,500
Sent to production during November—16,000 pounds	

3. Direct labor costs at $5 per hour, $103,350.
4. Direct departmental overhead costs, $52,000.
5. Transferred out, 15,000 pounds.
6. Work in process inventory, November 30, 3,000 pounds, 33⅓ percent complete.

The *FIFO method* is used for *materials inventory* valuation, and the *weighted-average method* is used for *work in process inventories*.

Required:

Prepare a production cost report for this department of California Division for November. Include the costs assigned to spoiled units (the "second method" in the text).

(CMA adapted)

8–35. Prepare Production Cost Report and Show Cost Flows through Accounts—FIFO Method

Mercantile Recovery Corporation has devised a process for converting garbage into liquid fuel. While the direct materials costs are zero, the operation requires the use of direct labor and overhead. The company uses a process costing system and keeps track of the production and costs of each period. At the start of the current period, there were 1,000 units in the work in process inventory. These units were 40 percent complete and were carried at a cost of $420.

During the month, costs of $18,000 were incurred. There were 9,000 units started during the period, and there were 500 units still in process at the end of the period. The ending units were 20 percent complete.

Required:

a. Prepare a production cost report, using FIFO.

b. Show the flow of costs through T-accounts. Assume current period conversion costs are credited to "Various Payables."

8–36. Multiple Departments and Changes in Output Unit Measurements

(Requires solution of problem 8–35). Mercantile Recovery Corporation (from problem 8–35) has a second department that blends the liquid fuel from the first department with ethanol to generate a liquid fuel with a higher octane content. Due to evaporation during the process, the input quantities will equal 105 percent of the output quantities. The company expresses all input units in terms of the equivalent output that can be obtained after allowing for the evaporation losses. Consequently, all beginning and ending inventory figures are stated in units of expected good output.

At the start of the month, there were 800 units in process that were 50 percent complete with respect to the addition of ethanol and 75 percent complete with respect to conversion costs. The costs of the beginning inventory are itemized as follows:

Prior department costs	$926
Ethanol	76
Conversion costs	150

During the period, the units received from the first department were put into production. Costs of $3,000 were incurred for ethanol, and costs of $5,000 were incurred for conversion. The ending inventory consisted of 900 units that were 20 percent complete with respect to the addition of ethanol and 30 percent complete with respect to conversion costs.

Required:

a. Prepare a production cost report, using FIFO.

b. Show the flow of costs through T-accounts.

8–37. Solving for Unknowns—FIFO Method

For each of the following independent cases, determine the information requested, using FIFO costing.

a. Beginning inventory amounted to 1,000 units. There were 4,500 units started and completed this period. At the end of the period, there were 3,000 units in inventory that were 30 percent complete. Using FIFO costing, the equivalent production for the period was 5,600 units. What was the percentage of completion of the beginning inventory?

b. The ending inventory included $8,700 for conversion costs. During the period, 4,200 equivalent units were required to complete the beginning inventory, and 6,000 units were started and completed. The ending inventory represented 1,000 equivalent units of work this period. FIFO costing is used. What was the total conversion cost incurred this period?

c. There were 500 units in the beginning inventory that were 40 percent complete with respect to materials. During the period, 4,000 units were transferred out. Ending inventory consisted of 700 units that were 70 percent complete with respect to materials. How many units were started and completed during the period?

d. At the start of the period, there were 4,000 units in the work in process inventory. There were 3,000 units in the ending inventory, and during the period, 9,500 units were transferred out to the next department. Materials and conversion costs are added evenly throughout the production process. FIFO costing is used. How many units were started this period?

8–38. Solving for Unknowns—Weighted-Average Costing

For each of the following independent cases, determine the units or equivalent units requested (assume weighted-average):

a. There were 8,200 units in the beginning inventory that were 40 percent complete with respect to conversion costs. During the period, 7,000 units were started. There were 6,500 units in the ending inventory that were 20 percent complete with respect to conversion costs. How many units were transferred out?

b. The beginning inventory consisted of 2,000 units with a direct materials cost of $14,200. The equivalent work represented by all of the direct materials costs in the Work in Process Inventory account amounted to 9,000 units. There were

3,000 units in ending inventory that were 20 percent complete with respect to materials. The ending inventory had a direct materials cost assigned of $4,500. What was the total materials cost incurred this period?

c. The Work in Process Inventory account had a beginning balance of $1,900 for conversion costs on items in process. During the period, $18,100 in conversion costs were charged to the account. Also during the period, $19,200 in costs were transferred out. There were 400 units in the beginning inventory, and 4,800 units were transferred out during the period. How many equivalent units are in the ending inventory?

d. There were 2,100 units transferred in to the department during the period. The 3,200 units transferred out were charged to the next department at an amount that included $3,360 for direct materials costs. The ending inventory was 25 percent complete with respect to direct materials and had a cost of $630 assigned to it. How many units are in the ending inventory?

INTEGRATIVE CASES

8–39. FIFO Process Costing, Overhead Allocation

Zeus Company has two production departments (fabricating and finishing). In the fabricating department, polyplast is prepared from miracle mix and bypro. In the finishing department, each unit of polyplast is converted into six tetraplexes and three uniplexes.

Both production departments use process costing systems. All inventories are costed on a FIFO basis. The following data were taken from the fabricating department's records for the current month:

Quantities of polyplast:	
On hand at start of month	3,000
Started during the month	25,000
Transferred to finishing	19,000
Spoiled units (normal)	3,000
Costs of work in process:	
Beginning inventory:	
Direct materials	$ 13,000
Conversion costs	39,000
Current period costs:	
Direct labor	154,000
Direct production overhead	132,000

Spoiled units are discovered at the end of the process.

The direct production overhead above does not include any allocation of the following overhead costs:

Building occupancy	$45,000
Timekeeping and personnel	27,500
Other	39,000

These costs are allocated to production departments using the following bases:

	Building Occupancy: Space Occupied	Timekeeping and Personnel: Number of Employees	Other
Fabricating	75,000	135	50%
Finishing	37,500	90	50
Totals	112,500	225	

Additional inventory data for the fabricating department are:

Percentage of completion:		
Beginning of month	66⅔% materials	50% conversion
End of month	100% materials	75% conversion

Materials inventory:

	Miracle Mix		Bypro	
	Quantity	Amount	Quantity	Amount
Beginning inventory	62,000	$62,000	265,000	$18,550
Purchases:				
12th of the month	39,500	49,375		
20th of the month	28,500	34,200		
Fabricating usage	83,200		50,000	

Required:

a. Prepare a production cost report for the fabricating department for the month. Include the supporting schedules necessary to explain your computations.

b. Show the flow of costs through T-accounts.

(CPA adapted)

8-40. Comprehensive Job Costing with Equivalent Units

The Custer Manufacturing Corporation, which uses a job order cost system, produces various plastic parts for the aircraft industry. On October 9, Year 1, production was started on Job No. 487 for 100 front bubbles (windshields) for commercial helicopters.

Production of the bubbles begins in the fabricating department where sheets of plastic (purchased as raw material) are melted down and poured into molds. The molds are then placed in a special temperature and humidity room to harden the plastic. The hardened plastic bubbles are then removed from the molds and hand-worked to remove imperfections.

After fabrication, the bubbles are transferred to the testing department where each bubble must meet rigid specifications. Bubbles that fail the tests are scrapped, and there is no salvage value.

Bubbles passing the tests are transferred to the assembly department where they are inserted into metal frames. The frames, purchased from vendors, require no work prior to installing the bubbles.

The assembled unit is then transferred to the shipping department for crating and shipment. Crating material is relatively expensive, and most of the work is done by hand.

The following information concerning Job No. 487 is available as of December 31, Year 1 (the information is correct as stated):

1. Direct materials charged to the job:
   a. One thousand square feet of plastic at $12.75 per square foot was charged to the fabricating department. This amount was to meet all plastic material requirements of the job assuming no spoilage.
   b. Seventy-four metal frames at $408.52 each were charged to the assembly department.
   c. Packing material for 40 units at $75 per unit was charged to the shipping department.
2. Direct labor charges through December 31 were as follows:

	Total	Per Unit
Fabricating department	$1,424	$16
Testing department	444	6
Assembly department	612	12
Shipping department	256	8
	$2,736	

3. There were no differences between actual and applied manufacturing overhead for the year ended December 31, Year 1. Manufacturing overhead is charged to the four production departments by various allocation methods, all of which you approve.

   Manufacturing overhead charged to the fabricating department is allocated to jobs based on heat-room-hours; the other production departments allocate manufacturing overhead to jobs on the basis of direct labor-dollars charged to each job within the department. The following reflects the manufacturing overhead rates for the year ended December 31, Year 1.

	Rate per Unit
Fabricating department	$.45 per hour
Testing department	.68 per direct labor-dollar
Assembly department	.38 per direct labor-dollar
Shipping department	.25 per direct labor-hour

4. Job No. 487 used 855 heat-room-hours during the year ended December 31.
5. Following is the physical inventory for Job No. 487 as of December 31:
   Fabricating department:

a. Fifty square feet of plastic sheet.

b. Eight hardened bubbles, one fourth complete as to direct labor.

c. Four complete bubbles.

Testing department:

a. Fifteen bubbles that failed testing when two fifths of testing was complete. No others failed.

b. Seven bubbles complete as to testing.

Assembly department:

a. Thirteen frames with no direct labor.

b. Fifteen bubbles and frames, one third complete as to direct labor.

c. Three complete bubbles and frames.

Shipping department:

a. Nine complete units, two thirds complete as to packing material, one third complete as to direct labor.

b. Ten complete units; 100 percent complete as to packing material; 50 percent complete as to direct labor.

c. One unit complete for shipping was dropped off the loading docks. There is no salvage.

d. Twenty-three units have been shipped prior to December 31.

e. There was no inventory of packing materials in the shipping department at December 31.

6. Following is a schedule of equivalent units in production by department for Job No. 487 as of December 31.

CUSTER MANUFACTURING CORPORATION
Schedule of Equivalent Units in
Production for Job No. 487
December 31

		Fabricating Department		
	Plastic (Sq. Ft.)	Bubbles (units)		
		Materials	Labor	Overhead
Transferred in from direct materials	1,000	—	—	—
Production to date	(950)	95	89	95
Transferred out to other departments	—	(83)	(83)	(83)
Spoilage	—	—	—	—
Balance at December 31	50	12	6	12

CUSTER MANUFACTURING CORPORATION
Schedule of Equivalent Units in
Production for Job No. 487
December 31

	Testing Department (units)		
	Bubbles		
	Transferred In	Labor	Overhead
Transferred in from other departments	83	—	—
Production to date	—	74	74
Transferred out to other departments	(61)	(61)	(61)
Spoilage	(15)	(6)	(6)
Balance at December 31	7	7	7

	Assembly Department (units)			
	Transferred In	Frames	Labor	Overhead
Transferred in from direct materials	—	74	—	—
Transferred in from other departments	61	—	—	—
Production to date	—	—	51	51
Transferred out to other departments	(43)	(43)	(43)	(43)
Balance at December 31	18	31	8	8

	Shipping Department (units)			
	Transferred In	Packing Material	Labor	Overhead
Transferred in from direct materials	—	40	—	—
Transferred in from other departments	43	—	—	—
Production to date	—	—	32	32
Shipped	(23)	(23)	(23)	(23)
Spoilage	(1)	(1)	(1)	(1)
Balance at December 31	19	16	8	8

Required:

Prepare a schedule for Job No. 487 of ending inventory costs for *(a)* direct materials by department, *(b)* work in process by department, and *(c)* cost of goods shipped. All spoilage costs are charged to cost of goods shipped.

(CPA adapted)

VARIABLE COSTING

LEARNING OBJECTIVES

1. To understand the difference between variable costing and full-absorption costing.

2. To appreciate the different uses of the information derived from these two types of cost systems.

Our discussion of inventory valuation methods thus far has been based on the external reporting requirement that inventory in manufacturing companies be valued using *full-absorption costing* (also called *absorption costing*). In this chapter, we introduce an alternative method, *variable costing* (also called *direct costing*). Under **full-absorption costing,** all manufacturing costs—fixed and variable—are assigned to units produced. Under **variable costing,** only variable manufacturing costs are assigned to units produced. Fixed manufacturing costs are considered to be period expenses.[1]

In this chapter, we compare full-absorption and variable costing. We examine the differences between the two methods that arise in cost flows through T-accounts and income statements. We also discuss the uses for which the two methods are appropriate.

Full-Absorption Costing
A system of accounting for costs in which both fixed and variable manufacturing costs are considered product costs.

Variable Costing (or Direct Costing) A system of accounting that only assigns products with the variable cost of manufacturing.

VARIABLE COSTING IN SERVICE COMPANIES

The airline industry recognizes the difference between variable costs and full-absorption costs and uses the concepts presented in this chapter to price airline seats differentially to maximize revenues from each airline flight. As a result, the air fares between Austin and San Francisco vary from a discounted fare of $248 to a full coach fare of $1,100. How can the same product (space on an airplane seat between two cities) vary by such a substantial amount? The answer lies in the cost structure of the airlines and the way fixed and variable costs are treated for pricing purposes.

Once an air carrier decides to offer a flight between two cities, over 90 percent of the costs of that flight are fixed. Given a specific model of aircraft on the route, the flight will cost the airline almost the same amount to operate regardless of whether the plane is carrying 5 passengers or 300. Airlines can maximize revenues by setting a base fare that is high enough so that the revenues from travelers who need to take a specific flight will cover the fixed costs of that flight plus their variable costs. Lower fares can be used to induce others to take additional seats on that particular flight. These lower fares need only be slightly in excess of the variable costs of the flight for the airline to make a profit from the added discount passengers. As a practical matter, the discount fares add substantially to airline operating profits.

For example, suppose the costs of flying a 150-seat plane from Chicago to Boston are $20,000 fixed plus $15 per passenger variable. From past experience, an airline estimates that on the particular flight we are studying, approximately 80 passengers willl take the flight regardless of cost. To cover the fixed and variable costs, the fare must amount to:

$$\frac{\$20,000}{80} + \$15$$

---

[1] Recall from Chapter 2 that variable manufacturing costs vary with the volume of production, while fixed costs remain the same despite changes in production volume within a relevant range of activity. We explore the distinction between fixed and variable costs in more depth in Chapters 10 and 11.

which equals $265. If the airline sets its full fare at $300, its operating profits from the flight will be:

Revenues ($300 × 80)	$24,000
Costs:	
Fixed costs	20,000
Variable costs	1,200
Total costs	21,200
Operating profits	$ 2,800

However, there are 70 empty seats on that flight if only full fare seats are sold. Suppose the airline offers a discount fare of 60 percent off the regular fare to fill up some of the empty seats. This fare adds 40 more passengers to the flight. Operating profits are now:

Revenues:	
Full fare ($300 × 80)	$24,000
Discount ($120 × 40)	4,800
Total revenues	28,800
Costs:	
Fixed costs	20,000
Variable costs	
($15 × 120)	1,800
Total costs	21,800
Operating profits	$ 7,000

Profits from the flight have increased by 250 percent despite offering seats at a 60 percent discount.

Of course, this solution assumes that none of the full fare passengers will buy discount tickets. Moreover, it assumes that larger planes will not be needed to accommodate the added passenger load. To avoid losing full fare passengers to discounting, airlines put restrictions on the discount tickets. The other issues involved in fare setting to maximize profits for varying cost structures are complex. Major airlines have revenue management departments charged with the responsbility of setting fares to maximize profits. Revenue managers need to know the full cost of operating a flight to set the full fares. They need to know the variable costs to set discount fares. In addition, they need to know what the competition is doing so that they are not priced out of markets that they wish to serve. In this chapter, we look at full and variable costing principles which form the foundation for this type of analysis. The analysis itself is called differential costing and is covered in Chapter 12.

VARIABLE VERSUS FULL-ABSORPTION COSTING

This section presents a numerical comparison of variable and full-absorption costing. Assume the facts shown for Stonewall Manufacturing for the months of January and February shown in the chart below.

	January	February
Units:		
Beginning inventory	–0–	100
Production	1,000	1,000
Sales	900	1,100
Ending inventory (all units are finished at the end of the period—there is no work in process inventory)	100	–0–
Costs:		
Variable manufacturing costs (per unit produced):		
Direct materials	$ 10	$ 10
Direct labor	5	5
Variable manufacturing overhead	3	3
Fixed manufacturing costs (per month)	8,000	8,000
Variable marketing costs (per unit sold)	2	2
Fixed marketing and administrative costs (per month)	12,000	12,000
Price per unit sold	45	45

Illustration 9–1 presents the flow of manufacturing costs through T-accounts in January for both full-absorption and variable costing. For now, we use **actual costing;** that is, actual direct materials, direct labor, and

manufacturing overhead costs are debited to Work in Process Inventory. (Later in the chapter, we use **normal costing**, which is like actual costing except that manufacturing overhead is debited to Work in Process Inventory using a predetermined rate.)

Note that while total actual costs incurred are the same under both full-absorption and variable costing, fixed manufacturing costs are debited to Work in Process Inventory under full-absorption costing but not under variable costing. As a consequence, the amounts in Work in Process Inventory and Finished Goods Inventory are higher under full-absorption costing.

Under full-absorption costing, the inventory value is:

$$\begin{array}{l} \text{Number} \\ \text{of units} \end{array} \times \left(\begin{array}{l} \text{Variable manufacturing} \\ \text{cost per unit} \end{array} + \begin{array}{l} \text{Fixed manufacturing} \\ \text{cost per unit} \end{array} \right)$$

$$= 100 \text{ units} \times \left(\$18 + \frac{\$8,000 \text{ fixed manufacturing costs}}{1,000 \text{ units}} \right)$$

$$= 100 \times (\$18 + \$8)$$

$$= \underline{\$2,600}$$

Under variable costing, the inventory value is:

$$\begin{array}{l} \text{Number} \\ \text{of units} \end{array} \times \begin{array}{l} \text{Variable manufacturing} \\ \text{cost per unit} \end{array}$$

$$100 \text{ units} \times \$18 = \underline{\$1,800}$$

Fixed manufacturing costs are treated as **product costs** and therefore assigned to each unit under full-absorption costing. Under variable costing, they are treated as **period costs** and thus are expensed in the period incurred.

Note that *all* manufacturing costs must be either expensed or inventoried for both methods. The fundamental concept is:

$$\text{Costs incurred} - \text{Inventory increase} + \text{Inventory decrease} = \text{Cost expensed}$$

Using full-absorption, finished goods and work in process inventory increases and decreases are more than they are using variable costing because these inventories include fixed manufacturing costs using full-absorption. For example, note the relation between manufacturing costs incurred and those expensed under the two systems shown in Illustration 9–2.

Note the source of difference between the two methods. *Variable* manufacturing costs are treated as product costs under both methods, and marketing and administrative costs are treated as period expenses under both methods. The source of the difference is the treatment of fixed manufacturing costs. *Fixed manufacturing costs are treated as product costs under full-absorption costing and as period expenses under variable costing.*

Effect on Profits

As shown in Illustration 9–3, the $800 higher profit in January under full-absorption costing is exactly the same as the difference in the amount of costs inventoried under the two methods. Full-absorption inventories $800 of fixed manufacturing costs that are expensed under variable costing. Hence, under full-absorption, costs expensed are $800 lower and operating profits are $800 higher than under variable costing. Under full-absorption,

Illustration 9-1 **Variable and Full-Absorption Costing Comparison: Flow of Manufacturing Costs**

STONEWALL MANUFACTURING
January

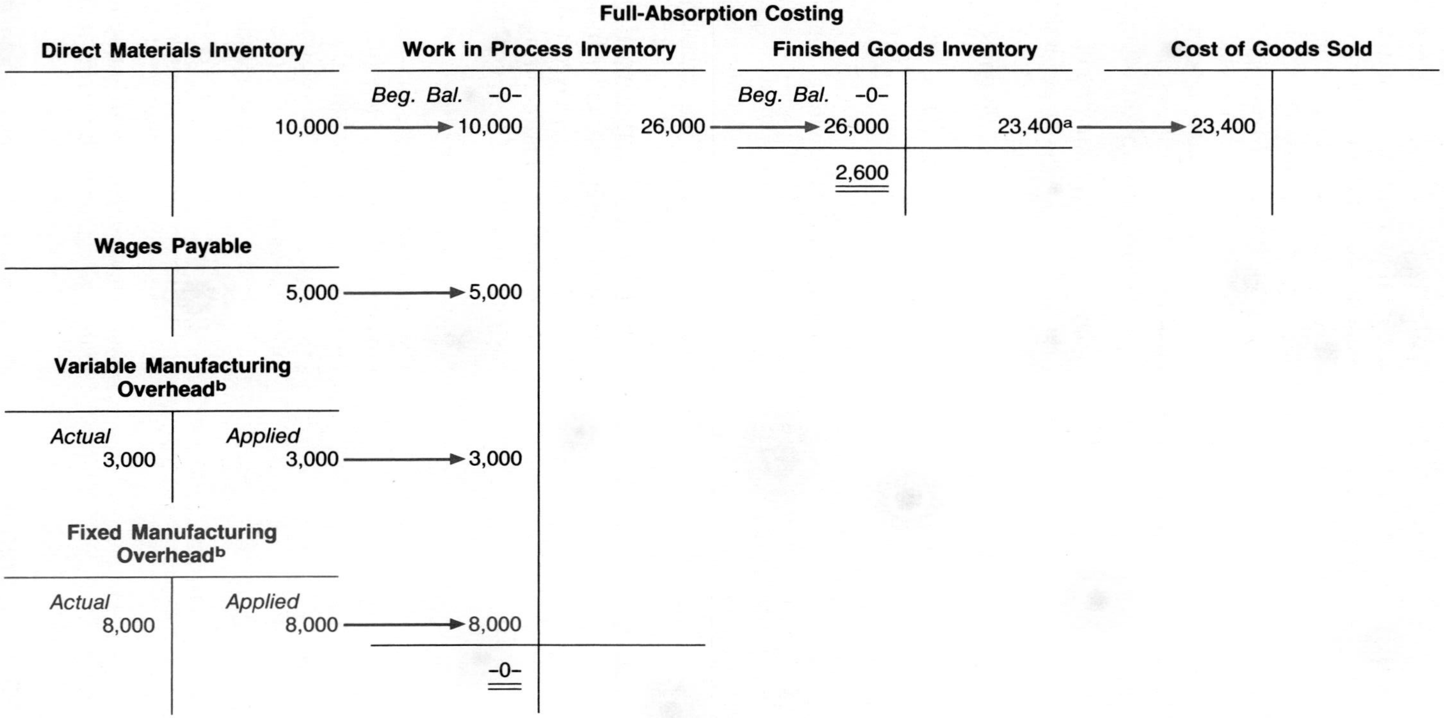

Full-Absorption Costing

Direct Materials Inventory	Work in Process Inventory	Finished Goods Inventory	Cost of Goods Sold
	Beg. Bal. –0–	Beg. Bal. –0–	
10,000 → 10,000	26,000 → 26,000	26,000 → 23,400[a] → 23,400	
		2,600	

Wages Payable

5,000 → 5,000

Variable Manufacturing Overhead[b]

Actual	Applied
3,000	3,000 → 3,000

Fixed Manufacturing Overhead[b]

Actual	Applied
8,000	8,000 → 8,000
	–0–

Variable Costing

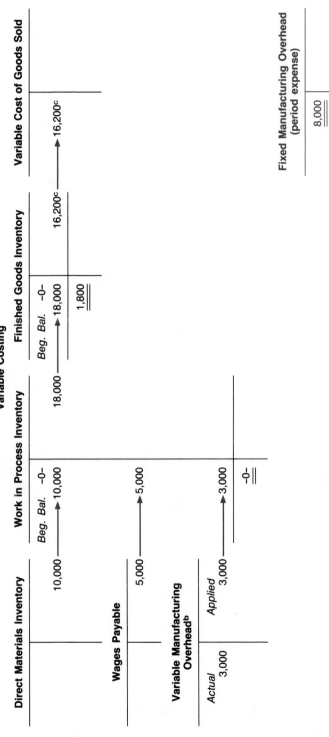

Direct Materials Inventory

10,000	10,000

Work in Process Inventory

Beg. Bal. –0–	
10,000 → 10,000	18,000 → 18,000
5,000 → 5,000	
3,000 → 3,000	
–0–	

Wages Payable

| | 5,000 |

Variable Manufacturing Overhead[b]

Actual	Applied
3,000	3,000

Finished Goods Inventory

Beg. Bal. –0–	
18,000 → 18,000	16,200[c] → 16,200[c]
1,800	

Variable Cost of Goods Sold

| | |
| 16,200[c] | |

Fixed Manufacturing Overhead (period expense)

| 8,000 | |

---

[a] $23,400 = \left[\dfrac{900}{1,000}\right] \times \$26,000 = 900 \times (\$8 + 18) = 900 \times \$26.$

[b] We have placed actual and applied overhead in the same account with actual costs as debits and applied costs as credits. This was done for convenience in presentation. An alternative is to place actual overhead in one account and applied overhead in another account. Both methods are used in practice.

[c] Variable costing cost of goods sold = $18 per unit (= direct materials, direct labor, and variable manufacturing overhead) times 900 units sold = $16,200.

Illustration 9-2 **Manufacturing Costs Incurred and Expensed when Production Volume Exceeds Sales Volume**

STONEWALL MANUFACTURING
January

	Manufacturing Costs Incurred	Minus Increase in Inventory	Equals Manufacturing Costs Expensed
Full-absorption costing:			
Variable manufacturing costs	$18,000	$1,800[b]	$16,200[a]
Fixed manufacturing costs	8,000	800[d]	7,200[c]
Total	$26,000	$2,600	$23,400
Variable costing:			
Variable manufacturing costs	$18,000	$1,800[b]	$16,200[a]
Fixed manufacturing costs	8,000	–0–	8,000
Total	$26,000	$1,800	$24,200

Computations:

[a] $16,200 = 900 units sold × $18 variable cost per unit.

[b] $ 1,800 = 100 units inventoried × $18 per unit.

[c] $ 7,200 = 900 units sold × $\frac{\$8,000 \text{ fixed manufacturing cost}}{1,000 \text{ units produced}}$

= 900 units × $8.

[d] $ 800 = 100 units inventoried × $8 per unit.

Illustration 9-3 **Variable and Full-Absorption Costing Comparison: Income Statements**

STONEWALL MANUFACTURING
January

Full-Absorption Costing

Sales revenue	$40,500[a]
Cost of goods sold	23,400
Gross margin	17,100
Marketing and administrative costs	13,800[b]
Operating profit	$ 3,300

Variable Costing

Sales revenue	$40,500[a]
Less:	
Variable cost of goods sold	16,200
Variable marketing and administrative costs	1,800[c]
Contribution margin	22,500
Less:	
Fixed manufacturing costs	8,000
Fixed marketing and administrative costs	12,000
Operating profit	$ 2,500

[a] $45 × 900 units sold = $40,500.

[b] Fixed costs + Variable costs = $12,000 + ($2 × 900 units sold) = $13,800.

[c] $2 × 900 units sold = $1,800.

the expensing of $800 of fixed manufacturing costs is deferred until the period when the units are sold.

As a general rule, under full-absorption costing, *when units produced exceed units sold* in a period, a portion of the period's fixed manufacturing costs are not expensed in that period. Under variable costing, however, all of the period's fixed manufacturing costs are expensed. Thus, when production exceeds sales, fewer fixed manufacturing costs are expensed, and *operating profits are higher* under full-absorption than under variable costing.

On the other hand, if units sold exceed units produced, then more fixed manufacturing costs are expensed under full-absorption costing, so operating profits are lower under full-absorption than under variable costing. We show this case in Illustration 9–4, which presents Stonewall Manufacturing's cost flows for February. The company produced 1,000 units in February and sold 1,100 units, including 100 units from inventory. In this case, full-absorption costing (FAC) expenses more fixed manufacturing costs than does variable costing (VC), because full-absorption now expenses the fixed manufacturing costs that were deferred from January.

A summary of our analysis of manufacturing costs is shown in Illustration 9–5. Note that manufacturing costs expensed equal costs incurred *plus the decrease in inventory*. In Illustration 9–2, note that in January, manufacturing costs expensed equaled costs incurred *minus the increase in inventory*.

Illustration 9–6 compares full-absorption costing (FAC) and variable costing (VC) at Stonewall Manufacturing for January and February. It presents some important results.

First, operating profits for the two-month period is the same under both methods—$10,000. This occurs because the company had no units in inventory at either the beginning or end of the period in question. Operating profits were higher under full-absorption costing in January, however, because units produced exceeded units sold. The reverse was true in February.

Second, the difference in operating profits between the two costing methods (FAC > VC by $800 in January, VC > FAC by $800 in February) equals the differences in the changes in the Finished Goods Inventory account. (FAC inventory increased by $2,600, while VC inventory increased by $1,800 in January; FAC inventory decreased by $2,600, while VC inventory decreased by $1,800 in February.)

Third, the difference in operating profits in each period equals the difference in fixed manufacturing costs expensed under the two systems.

In general, if there are no inventories, operating profits are the same under both methods. If production volume equals sales volume, the profit figures will differ only if the fixed manufacturing costs per unit differ in beginning and ending inventory.

Important Assumptions

There are three important assumptions to note before leaving this discussion. First, our example assumes that a portion of manufacturing overhead is the only cost that is fixed. In fact, some or all of direct labor might be fixed as well. This occurs when direct labor costs are neither reduced when production volume decreases nor increased when production volume in-

Illustration 9–4   **Variable and Full-Absorption Costing Comparison: Flow of Manufacturing Costs**

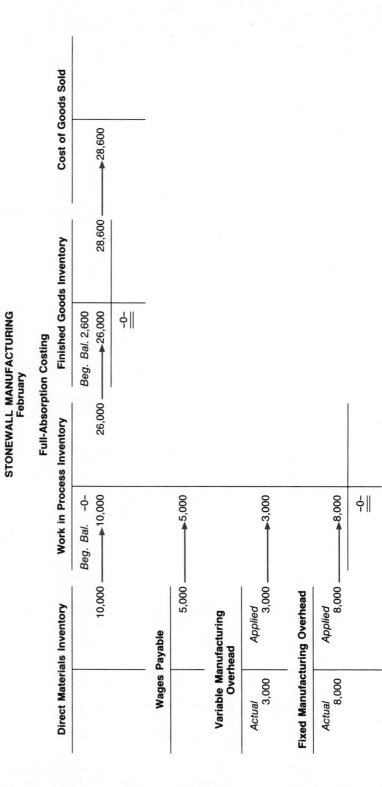

STONEWALL MANUFACTURING
February

Full-Absorption Costing

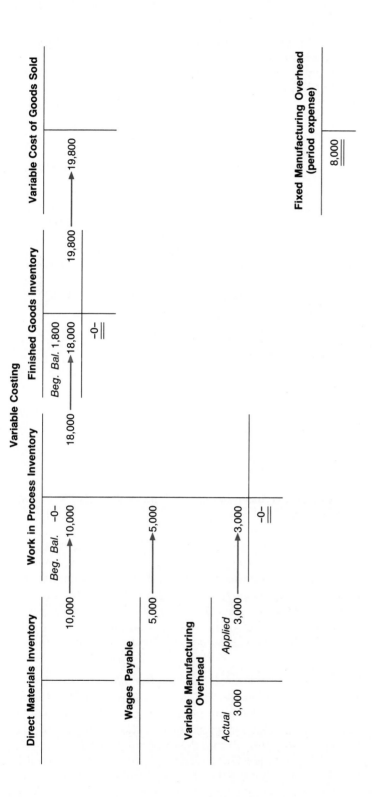

Variable Costing

Direct Materials Inventory

10,000 → 10,000

Work in Process Inventory

Beg. Bal. -0-
10,000 → 18,000

5,000 → 5,000

3,000 → 3,000

-0-

Finished Goods Inventory

Beg. Bal. 1,800
18,000 → 19,800

-0-

Variable Cost of Goods Sold

19,800

Wages Payable

5,000

Variable Manufacturing Overhead

Actual   Applied
3,000   3,000

Fixed Manufacturing Overhead (period expense)

8,000

Illustration 9-5   **Manufacturing Costs Incurred and Expensed when Sales Volume Exceeds Production Volume**

STONEWALL MANUFACTURING
February

	Manufacturing Costs Incurred	Plus Decrease in Inventory	Equals Manufacturing Costs Expensed
Full-absorption costing:			
Variable manufacturing costs	$18,000	$1,800[b]	$19,800[a]
Fixed manufacturing costs	8,000	800[d]	8,800[c]
Total	$26,000	$2,600	$28,600
Variable costing:			
Variable manufacturing costs	$18,000	$1,800[b]	$19,800[a]
Fixed manufacturing costs	8,000	–0–	8,000
Total	$26,000	$1,800	$27,800

Calculations:

[a] $19,800 = 1,100 units sold × $18 variable cost per unit.

[b] $ 1,800 = 100 units from inventory × $18 variable cost per unit.

[c] $ 8,800 = 1,100 units sold × $\dfrac{\$8,000}{1,000 \text{ units produced}}$

= 1,100 × $8

[d] $ 800 = 100 units from inventory × $8 fixed cost per unit.

creases. If direct labor is fixed, it is treated as a *product* cost under full-absorption costing and a *period* cost under variable costing, just like fixed manufacturing overhead in our example.

Second, while our example has assumed that finished goods are the only inventories, the results hold for work in process inventory, too. That is, fixed manufacturing costs would be part of work in process inventory under full-absorption costing, but they would not be under variable costing.

Third, this entire discussion refers only to manufacturing costs, which are the only costs inventoried. It does *not* refer to marketing and administrative costs, which are not part of inventory.

Fourth, we find that companies usually use FIFO for internal reporting purposes. Financial reports usually are based on an adjustment to FIFO data. All problems in this chapter assume FIFO to be consistent with practice.

Effect of Normal Costing and Manufacturing Overhead Variances

In the previous example, we compared full-absorption costing with variable costing when there are no manufacturing cost variances. When manufacturing cost variances exist, as under normal costing, the mechanics of comparison become a little more difficult, but the effects of the different costing methods on calculated profits remain the same as previously discussed.

For example, assume Stonewall Manufacturing decided to use predetermined manufacturing overhead rates of $1.75 per actual direct labor-hour for variable manufacturing overhead and $3.50 per direct labor-hour for fixed manufacturing overhead. In both January and February, each unit required

Illustration 9–6   **Variable and Full-Absorption Costing Comparison:**
Comparative Income Statements

STONEWALL MANUFACTURING
January and February

Full-Absorption Costing

	January	February	Total
Sales revenue	$40,500	$49,500	$90,000
Cost of goods sold	23,400	28,600	52,000
Gross margin	17,100	20,900	38,000
Marketing and administrative costs	13,800[a]	14,200[b]	28,000
Operating profits	$ 3,300	$ 6,700	$10,000
Change in finished goods inventory	+$ 2,600[c]	−$ 2,600	–0–

Variable Costing

	January	February	Total
Sales revenue	$40,500	$49,500	$90,000
Less:			
Variable cost of goods sold	16,200	19,800	36,000
Variable marketing and administrative costs	1,800	2,200	4,000
Contribution margin	22,500	27,500	50,000
Less:			
Fixed manufacturing costs	8,000	8,000	16,000
Fixed marketing and administrative costs	12,000	12,000	24,000
Operating profits	$ 2,500	$ 7,500	$10,000
Change in finished goods inventory	+$ 1,800[c]	−$ 1,800	–0–

Calculations:
  [a] $12,000 + ($2 × 900 units sold) = $13,800.
  [b] $12,000 + ($2 × 1,100 units sold) = $14,200.
  [c] From Illustration 9–2.

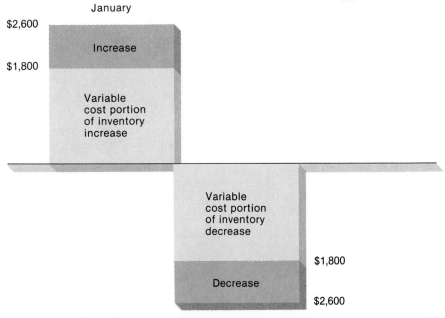

Illustration 9-7   **Variable and Full-Absorption Costing Comparison: Flow of Manufacturing Costs with Overhead Variances**

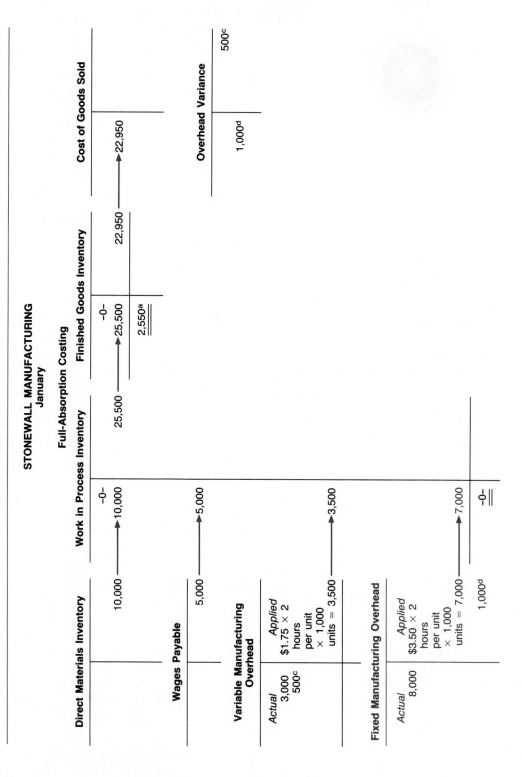

Variable Costing

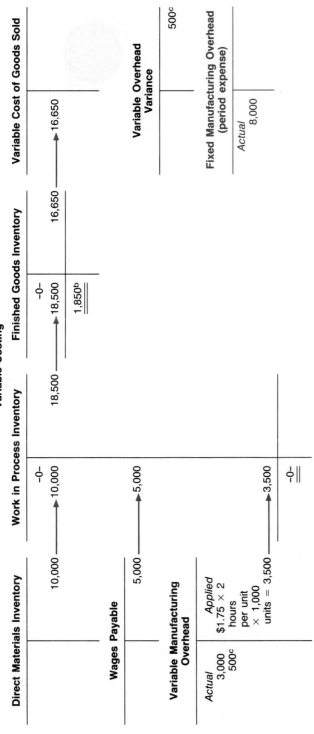

Direct Materials Inventory	Work in Process Inventory	Finished Goods Inventory	Variable Cost of Goods Sold

Direct Materials Inventory
10,000

Work in Process Inventory
-0-
10,000 → 18,500
5,000
units = 3,500
-0-

Finished Goods Inventory
-0-
18,500 → 16,650
1,850[b]

Variable Cost of Goods Sold
16,650

Wages Payable
5,000

Variable Manufacturing Overhead

Actual   Applied
3,000 $1.75 × 2
500[c]   hours
per unit
× 1,000
units = 3,500

Variable Overhead Variance
500[c]

Fixed Manufacturing Overhead (period expense)
Actual
8,000

Calculations:

[a] $2,550 = 100 units left in inventory × $\dfrac{\$25,500}{1,000 \text{ units produced}}$.

[b] $1,850 = 100 units left in inventory × $\dfrac{\$18,500}{1,000 \text{ units produced}}$.

[c] This entry closes the Variable Manufacturing Overhead account.

[d] This entry closes the Fixed Manufacturing Overhead account.

an average of two direct labor-hours to make; hence, you can also think of overhead as applied at the rate of $3.50 per unit produced for *variable* manufacturing overhead and $7 per unit produced for *fixed* manufacturing overhead. These rates were used for both January and February.

Illustration 9–7 shows the flow of manufacturing costs for January under both variable and full-absorption costing. (Recall that 1,000 units were produced; 900 were sold in January.) By comparing Illustration 9–7 with Illustration 9–1, you will see that actual and applied manufacturing overhead are no longer equal; there is $500 overapplied variable overhead and $1,000 underapplied fixed overhead. We assume that the overhead variance is written off as a period cost, not prorated to inventories and cost of goods sold.

Illustration 9–8 compares full-absorption and variable costing when there is an overhead variance.

The use of predetermined overhead rates instead of actual costs usually does not have much effect on the relationship between full-absorption and variable costing. For example, a comparison of Illustration 9–6 (no overhead variance) with Illustration 9–8 (with an overhead variance) shows two key similarities:

1. The conceptual difference between full-absorption costing and variable costing is the same whether or not there is an overhead variance. Differences in operating profits occur because fixed manufacturing costs are inventoried under full-absorption costing but not under variable costing.

2. When all inventory is sold at the end of a period, total operating profits are the same under all methods. For example, in Illustrations 9–6 and 9–8, operating profits for the entire period—January and February—are $10,000, whether or not there is an overhead variance and whether full-absorption or variable costing are used.

DEBATE OVER VARIABLE VERSUS FULL-ABSORPTION COSTING

Debates about the desirability of full-absorption costing versus variable costing have gone on for decades.[2] For the most part, differences of opinion stem from the search for a "conceptually superior" method of valuing inventory and measuring income in external financial statements. Our perspective is much different. *We are not as concerned about selecting a "true" measure of inventory value or net income as we are with selecting the cost measure that is most appropriate for decision making,* after taking into account the costs and benefits of alternative costing methods. The most appropriate cost measure will usually be situation specific—it will depend on the nature of the decision, the nature of costs, the tastes of decision makers, and many other factors. As the airline industry and others have learned, full costs may be appropriate for some decisions and variable costs for others. The accountant's objective is to provide the information that is most useful in a given setting. The appropriate method will depend on the decision at hand. The following discussions present advantages of each

[2] For example, see C. Horngren and G. Sorter, "Direct Costing for External Reporting," *The Accounting Review,* January 1961; and J. Fremgen, "The Direct Costing Controversy—An Identification of Issues," *The Accounting Review,* January 1964.

Illustration 9-8   **Variable and Full-Absorption Costing:**
                              Comparative Income Statements

STONEWALL MANUFACTURING
January and February

Full-Absorption Costing

	January	February	Total
Sales revenue	$40,500	$49,500	$90,000
Less:			
Cost of goods sold	22,950[a]	28,050[c]	51,000
Underapplied overhead	500[b]	500[d]	1,000
Gross margin	17,050	20,950	38,000
Less: Marketing and administrative costs	13,800	14,200	28,000
Operating profits	$ 3,250	$ 6,750	$10,000
Change in finished goods inventory	+$ 2,550	−$ 2,550	−0−

Variable Costing

	January	February	Total
Sales revenue	$40,500	$49,500	$90,000
Less: Variable cost of goods sold	16,650[e]	20,350[f]	37,000
Add: Overapplied variable overhead	500	500[g]	1,000
Less: Variable marketing and			
administrative costs	1,800	2,200	4,000
Contribution margin	22,550	27,450	50,000
Less:			
Fixed manufacturing costs	8,000	8,000	16,000
Fixed marketing and administrative costs	12,000	12,000	24,000
Operating profits	$ 2,550	$ 7,450	$10,000
Change in finished goods inventory	+$ 1,850	−$ 1,850	−0−

Calculations:

[a] $22,950 = 900 units sold × $25.50 cost per unit.

[b] The $500 underapplied overhead is the net result of $1,000 underapplied fixed manufacturing overhead and $500 overapplied variable manufacturing overhead. (See Illustration 9-7.)

[c] $28,050 = 1,100 units sold × $25.50 cost per unit. It also equals the cost of producing 1,000 units, or $25,500, plus the $2,550 cost of the 100 units sold from beginning finished goods inventory.

[d] The underapplied overhead is the same in February as in January because all production quantities and costs are the same in February as in January.

[e] $16,650 = 900 units sold × $18.50 cost per unit.

[f] $20,350 = 1,100 units sold × $18.50 cost per unit. It also equals the variable cost of producing 1,000 units, or $18,500, plus the $1,850 cost of the 100 units sold from beginning finished goods inventory.

[g] Overapplied variable overhead is the same in February as in January because all production quantities and costs are the same in both months.

costing method—variable costing and full-absorption costing—for different uses by decision makers.

Advantages of Variable Costing; Disadvantages of Full-Absorption Costing

Variable Costing Requires Breakdown of Manufacturing Costs into Fixed and Variable Components

Many managerial decisions require a breakdown of costs into variable and fixed components. The variable costing method is consistent with this breakdown. The full-absorption costing method is not; it treats fixed manufacturing costs as if they were unit (that is, variable) costs. Also, note that more data are presented under variable costing than under full-absorption in Illustration 9–6. Variable costing presents fixed and variable cost breakdowns and contribution margins.

Managers usually prefer to plan and control variable costs on a unit basis and fixed costs on a period basis. For example, managers plan and control the amount of direct materials and direct labor required to make a unit of output or the number of hours required to perform a job. Building rent, property taxes, and other fixed costs are planned and controlled per week, month, or year. It seldom makes much managerial sense to refer to rent costs as an amount per *unit* produced. Rather, rent would be referred to as an amount per *month*.

Criticism of Unit Fixed Cost under Full-Absorption Costing

Treating fixed costs as unit costs can be misleading. A unit fixed cost is a function of not only the amount of fixed costs but also the volume of activity. Any given unit fixed cost is only valid when production equals the number of units used to calculate the fixed cost per unit.

For example, a plant manager observed that maintenance costs, which were fixed, had decreased from $12 per unit of output in May to $10 per unit in August. She was on her way to congratulate the maintenance department manager for the cost reduction when she stopped in the plant controller's office. There she learned that maintenance costs had *increased* from $12,000 in May to $18,000 in August. Meanwhile volume had increased from 1,000 units in May to 1,800 units in August. This explained the decrease in unit costs from $12 ($12,000 ÷ 1,000 units) to $10 ($18,000 ÷ 1,800 units).

The plant manager knew maintenance costs were supposed to be fixed. They should not have increased when volume increased. When she investigated further, she found that the maintenance department manager had hired several temporary employees to cover for a major absenteeism problem that occurred in August.

The moral of this story is that the conversion of fixed manufacturing costs to unit costs, which is done under full-absorption costing, can be misleading. Managers frequently find it necessary to convert the "unitized" fixed manufacturing cost (that is, the $12 and $10 per unit in the previous example) back to the original total for performance evaluation and decision-making purposes.

Variable Costing Removes the Effects of Inventory Changes from Income Measurement

Another advantage of variable costing is that it removes the effects of inventory changes from income measurement. For example, under full-absorption costing, a company could increase its reported profits by building up inventory or decrease them by reducing inventory.

For example, Full Products, Inc., uses full-absorption costing to value inventory. After seeing the period 1 financial statements shown in the bottom part of Illustration 9–9, the board of directors fired the president and hired a new one, stating, "Whatever else you do, increase profits in period 2."

The new president promptly stepped up production from 100,000 units to 200,000 units, as shown in column 2 of Illustration 9–9. Operating profits

Illustration 9-9   **Profit Improvement Program**

FULL PRODUCTS, INC.

Facts

	Period 1	Period 2
Sales units	100,000	100,000
Production units	100,000	200,000
Selling price per unit	$ 10	$ 10
Variable manufacturing cost per unit	5	5
Fixed manufacturing costs per period	400,000	400,000
Fixed manufacturing costs per unit produced	4	2
Marketing and administrative costs per period	100,000	100,000

Income Statements
(full-absorption costing methods)

	(1) Period 1	(2) Period 2
Sales	$1,000,000	$1,000,000
Cost of goods sold	900,000[a]	700,000[b]
Gross margin	100,000	300,000
Marketing and administrative costs	100,000	100,000
Operating profits	–0–	$ 200,000

[a] $900,000 = 100,000 units sold × ($5 + $4) manufacturing costs per unit.
[b] $700,000 = 100,000 units sold × ($5 + $2) manufacturing costs per unit.

increased from $0 in period 1 to $200,000 in period 2, and the new president collected a generous bonus.

Was Full Products, Inc., more profitable in period 2? No; in fact, the company had 100,000 additional units in inventory to carry and sell. The apparent increase in profits is solely due to the deferral of fixed manufacturing cost under full-absorption costing by increasing ending inventory. Variable costing would expense the entire $400,000 of fixed manufacturing costs in period 2 despite the increase in inventory. Thus, the period 2 operating profits would have been zero under variable costing—the same as in period 1.

In short, variable costing tends to fit managerial decision models better than full-absorption costing does. In subsequent chapters in this book, when we discuss uses of accounting information for managerial decision making, planning, and performance evaluation, we assume the company uses variable costing for internal purposes unless otherwise stated.

Advantages of Full-Absorption Costing; Disadvantages of Variable Costing

Neither the Financial Accounting Standards Board (FASB) nor the Internal Revenue Service (IRS) has recognized variable costing as *generally acceptable* in valuing inventory for external reports and tax purposes. The Internal Revenue Service defines inventory cost to include: (1) direct materials and supplies entering into or consumed in connection with the product, (2) expenditures for direct labor, and (3) indirect expenses incident to and necessary for the production of the particular item. Indirect expenses necessary for production would include fixed manufacturing costs. Thus, the most obvious advantage of full-absorption costing is that it complies with FASB pronouncements and tax laws.

Proponents of full-absorption costing contend that this method recognizes the importance of fixed manufacturing costs. They hold that all manufacturing costs are costs of the product. Further, they argue, companies that build up inventories in anticipation of further increases in sales are penalized under variable costing—they should be allowed to defer fixed manufacturing costs until the goods are sold, just as they defer variable manufacturing costs.

In practice, companies may prepare *both* variable and full-absorption costing income statements depending on how such information is used. Variable costing reports can be used for internal purposes, while full-absorption reports are prepared for external use. Preparation of many kinds of reports based on alternative accounting methods is possible at rapid speed and low cost with appropriately programmed computer equipment.

Another advantage of full-absorption costing is that it may be less costly to implement since it does not require a breakdown of manufacturing costs into fixed and variable components. While some manufacturing costs may fall neatly into fixed or variable categories, others do not. Supervision, indirect labor, and utilities, for example, are seldom either entirely fixed or entirely variable. Hence, variable costing may be more costly to implement than full-absorption costing. Like other accounting system choices, the costs and benefits of each method should dictate the best course of action in specific situations.

COMPARATIVE INCOME STATEMENT FORMATS

Contribution Margin Format The outline of a financial statement which shows the contribution margin as an intermediate step in the computation of operating profits or income.

Traditional income statement formats do not lend themselves to variable costing beause fixed and variable costs are not separated. The format used with variable costing is known as the **contribution margin format**. The variable costing income statements in this chapter use the variable costing format. For comparative purposes, the two formats are shown in Illustration 9–10. These two statements are based on the January–February totals from Illustration 9–6.

If income statements are used to make decisions involving changes in volume, the contribution margin format can be very helpful. Managers can often understand relationships between prices, costs, and volume better with the contribution margin format than with the traditional approach. Further, the contribution margin format presents more information—namely, the breakdown of costs into fixed and variable portions.

Note the difference between the *contribution margin* and the *gross margin* in Illustration 9–10. The total contribution margin is $50,000 and represents the net revenue available to meet fixed costs and provide operating profits. The contribution margin ratio represents the fraction of each revenue dollar that is contributed toward fixed costs and profits. For the illustration, this amount would be 55.6 percent, which is $\frac{\$50,000}{\$90,000}$.

On the other hand, the gross margin is the difference between revenues and manufacturing costs, regardless of whether those manufacturing costs are fixed or variable. The gross margin represents the amount that remains

Illustration 9–10   **Income Statement Comparison: Traditional and Contribution Margin Format**

STONEWALL MANUFACTURING

Traditional Format		Contribution Margin Format	
	January–February Total		January–February Total
Sales revenue	$90,000	Sales revenue	$90,000
Cost of goods sold	52,000	Less:	
Gross margin	38,000	Variable cost of goods sold	36,000
Marketing and administrative costs	28,000	Variable marketing and administrative costs	4,000
Operating profit	$10,000	Contribution margin	50,000
		Less:	
		Fixed manufacturing costs	16,000
		Fixed marketing and administrative costs	24,000
		Operating profit	$10,000

after the deduction of manufacturing costs. The gross margin ratio does not indicate what would happen if revenues were to increase due to sales volume increases with a corresponding increase in production.

The terms *contribution margin* and *gross margin* are often used interchangeably, but they are not the same. Virtually, the only time they would be mathematically equal is when all cost of goods sold are variable costs and marketing and administrative costs are fixed. We know very few such examples.

SUMMARY

This chapter compares full-absorption costing with variable costing. Manufacturing companies use full-absorption costing for external reporting to comply with generally accepted accounting principles (GAAP) and income tax laws, both of which require that product costs include fixed and variable manufacturing costs. Our previous discussion of full product costing in Chapters 3 through 8 assumed work in process and finished goods inventories were valued using full-absorption costing.

With variable costing, only variable manufacturing costs are inventoriable, while fixed manufacturing costs are treated as period costs. Many manufacturing companies use variable costing for internal reporting because it is consistent with the cost-behavior assumptions used in managerial decision making.

In the remaining chapters in this book, we focus on cost analysis for decision making. Hence, we assume variable costing is used for internal managerial purposes, while full-absorption costing is used for external financial reporting.

The key difference between the two methods is the treatment of fixed manufacturing costs—full-absorption costing "unitizes" them and treats them as product costs, while variable costing treats them as period costs.

Illustration 9–11   **Summary Comparison of Full-Absorption Costing (FAC) and Variable Costing (VC)**

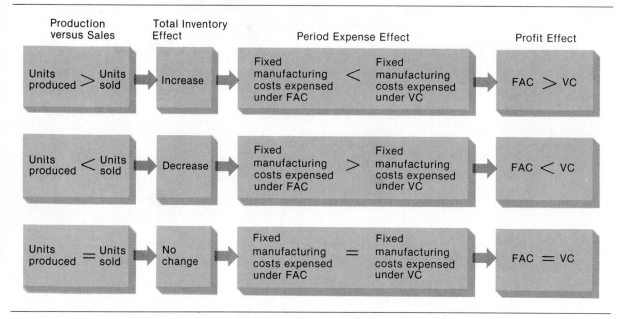

Note: These relationships assume the unit costs of inventory do not change from period to period.

Illustration 9–12   **Treatment of Overhead in Four Costing Methods: Full-Absorption, Variable, Actual, and Normal**

| | | Treatment of Fixed Manufacturing Costs | |
		Product Cost	Period Cost
Treatment of Manufacturing Overhead	**Actual overhead assigned to units**	Actual, full-absorption	Actual, variable
	Predetermined overhead rates	Normal, full-absorption	Normal, variable

Thus, operating profits will differ under each method if units produced and sold are not the same, as shown in Illustration 9–11.

The use of predetermined manufacturing overhead rates (that is, *normal* costing) may give a different unit cost to inventory than does actual costing. Consequently, operating profits may be different under the two systems. But the *conceptual* differences between full-absorption costing and variable costing are the same regardless of the form of overhead rate—namely, fixed manufacturing costs are inventoried under full-absorption costing but not under variable costing. Illustration 9–12 reviews the conceptual differences among the four methods. Self-study problem no. 1 at the end of the chapter presents a numerical application of these differences.

TERMS AND CONCEPTS	The following terms and concepts should be familiar to you after reading this chapter:

Actual Costing	**Period Costs**
Contribution Margin Format	**Predetermined Overhead Rates**
Full-Absorption Costing	**Product Costs**
Normal Costing	**Variable Costing (or Direct Costing)**

SUPPLEMENTARY READINGS

Ajinkya, Bipan; Rowland Atiase; and Linda Smith Bamber. "Absorption versus Direct Costing: Income Reconciliation and Cost-Volume-Profit Analysis." *Issues in Accounting Education,* Fall 1986, pp. 268–81.

Carver, George V. "Condominium Development—Absorption, Absorption, Absorption." *Valuation,* February 1987, pp. 30–34.

Chen, Kung H., and S. J. Lambert, "Impurity of Variable Factory Overhead Variances." *Journal of Accounting Education,* Spring 1985, pp. 189–196.

DeCoster, D., and K. Ramanathan. "An Algebraic Aid in Teaching Differences in Direct Costing and Full-Absorption Costing Models. *Accounting Review,* October 1973, pp. 800–801.

Pearce, Laurence. "Whatever Happened to Gross Profit?" *Management Accounting,* May 1984, pp. 28–29 (published in Great Britain).

Ruedo, Edmundo J. "Cost Accounting: Contribution Margin Analysis Takes Ratio Analysis One Step Further." *Executive,* Fall 1986, pp. 30–34.

Schiff, Michael. "Variable Costing: A Closer Look." *Management Accounting,* February 1987, pp. 36–39.

SELF-STUDY PROBLEM NO. 1

Unit Costs under Various Costing Methods: Actual, Normal, Variable, and Full-Absorption

Dunn Enterprises produced 84,000 units last year and sold 76,000 units. Costs incurred that year were:

Direct materials	$462,000
Direct labor	315,000
Variable manufacturing overhead	105,000
Fixed manufacturing overhead	399,000
Variable marketing and administrative costs	50,400
Fixed marketing and administrative costs	200,600

If normal costing is used, Dunn Enterprises applies variable manufacturing overhead at $.40 per direct labor-dollar and fixed manufacturing overhead at $1.20 per direct labor-dollar. There were no beginning inventories.

Required:

Calculate the amount added to the finished goods inventory, using:

a. Actual/variable costing.

b. Actual/full-absorption costing.

c. Normal/variable costing.

d. Normal/full-absorption costing.

SOLUTION TO SELF-STUDY PROBLEM NO. 1

	Actual	Normal
Unit costs:		
Full-absorption costing:		
Direct materials	$ 5.50[a]	$ 5.50[a]
Direct labor	3.75[a]	3.75[a]
Variable manufacturing overhead	1.25[a]	1.50 (= .40 × $3.75)
Fixed manufacturing overhead	4.75[a]	4.50 (= 1.20 × $3.75)
Total	$15.25	$15.25
Variable costing:		
Direct materials	$ 5.50	$ 5.50
Direct labor	3.75	3.75
Variable manufacturing overhead	1.25	1.50
Total	$10.50	$10.75

Ending inventory:
a. $10.50 × 8,000 = $84,000
b. $15.25 × 8,000 = $122,000
c. $10.75 × 8,000 = $86,000
d. $15.25 × 8,000 = $122,000

[a] Actual cost given above divided by 84,000 units produced.

SELF-STUDY PROBLEM NO. 2

Cash Flows through T-Accounts and Income Statement Preparation

Barton Chemicals produces a line of extra-strength paint remover. The company produced 8,000 barrels and sold 7,500 barrels at a price of $60 per barrel. The costs incurred were as follows:

Direct materials	$ 24,000
Direct labor	80,000
Variable manufacturing overhead	19,200
Variable marketing and administrative costs	24,800
Fixed manufacturing overhead	120,000
Fixed marketing and administrative costs	110,000

There were no beginning inventories. Actual costing is used.

Required:

a. Using T-accounts, trace the manufacturing cost flows under variable costing.

b. Using T-accounts, trace the manufacturing cost flows under full-absorption costing.

c. Prepare an income statement for this period, using the variable costing approach.

d. Prepare an income statement for this period, using the full-absorption costing approach.

**SOLUTION TO
SELF-STUDY
PROBLEM NO. 2**   *a.*   BARTON CHEMICALS

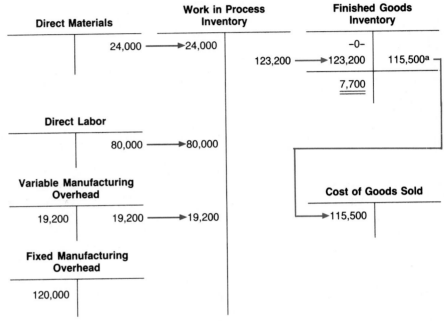

b.

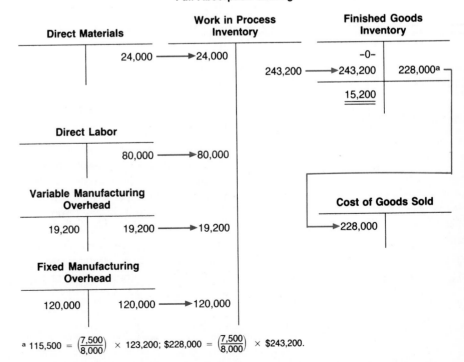

^{a} $115{,}500 = \left(\dfrac{7{,}500}{8{,}000}\right) \times 123{,}200$; $\$228{,}000 = \left(\dfrac{7{,}500}{8{,}000}\right) \times \$243{,}200.$

**SOLUTION TO
SELF-STUDY
PROBLEM NO. 2
(concluded)**

c.

Sales revenue	$450,000
Less:	
Variable cost of goods sold	115,500
Variable marketing and administrative costs	24,800
Contribution margin	309,700
Less:	
Fixed manufacturing overhead	120,000
Fixed marketing and administrative costs	110,000
Operating profit	$ 79,700

d.

Sales revenue	$450,000
Cost of goods sold	228,000
Gross margin	222,000
Less:	
Variable marketing and administrative costs	24,800
Fixed marketing and administrative costs	110,000
Operating profit	$ 87,200

**APPENDIX:
Algebraic
Comparison of
Variable and Full-
Absorption Costing[3]**

This section presents an algebraic comparison of full-absorption and variable costing. The basic concepts are the same as those presented earlier in this chapter; but instead of comparing full-absorption and variable costing using income statements and T-accounts, we demonstrate the difference between methods using algebra.

Basic Models

The algebraic definition of operating profit under full-absorption (actual) and variable costing (actual) follows the notation shown below. The numbers for each equation are based on our previous example—Stonewall Manufacturing—for January.

Notation

X^s = Actual volume sold—superscript *s* designates *sales* volume (900 units for Stonewall Manufacturing in January).

X^p = Actual volume produced—superscript *p* designates *production* volume (1,000 units for Stonewall Manufacturing in January).

P = Actual unit selling prices ($45)

VM = Actual *unit* variable *manufacturing* costs ($18 = $10 direct materials + $5 direct labor + $3 variable manufacturing overhead).

FM = Actual *total* fixed *manufacturing* costs per *month* ($8,000).

VK = Actual *unit* variable *marketing* costs ($2).

---

[3] This section was inspired by D. DeCoster and K. Ramanathan, "An Algebraic Aid in Teaching Differences between Direct Costing and Full-Absorption Costing Models," *The Accounting Review* 48, no. 4 (October 1973), pp. 800–801.

FK = Actual *total* fixed *marketing* and *administrative* costs per month ($12,000).

π_{fa} = Operating profit under full-absorption costing.

π_v = Operating profit under variable costing.

Recall that there is no beginning inventory in this example.

Variable Costing Profit Equation

$$\begin{aligned}
\pi_v &= PX^s - VMX^s - VKX^s \\
&\quad - FM - FK \\
&= (\$45 \times 900 \text{ units}) - (\$18 \times 900 \text{ units}) - (\$2 \times 900 \text{ units}) \\
&\quad - \$8,000 - \$12,000 \\
&= \$2,500
\end{aligned}$$

which is the same as the variable costing operating profit shown in Illustration 9–6.

Full-Absorption Costing Profit Equation

$$\begin{aligned}
\pi_{fa} &= PX^s - \left(VM + \frac{FM}{X^p} \right) X^s - VKX^s - FK \\
&= (\$45 \times 900 \text{ units}) - \left[\left(\$18 + \frac{\$8,000}{1,000 \text{ units}} \right) \times 900 \text{ units} \right] \\
&\quad - (\$2 \times 900 \text{ units}) - \$12,000 \\
&= \$3,300
\end{aligned}$$

which is the same as the full-absorption costing operating profit shown in Illustration 9–6.

Source of the Difference in Operating Profits

Note that the only difference between the two equations above is the treatment of fixed manufacturing overhead. Under variable costing, FM is deducted to arrive at operating profit, while under full-absorption costing, $\left(\dfrac{FM}{X^p} \right) X^s$ is deducted. Hence, the difference in profits between the two methods is:

$$\begin{aligned}
FM - \left(\frac{FM}{X^p} \right) X^s &= \$8,000 - \left(\frac{\$8,000}{1,000 \text{ units}} \times 900 \text{ units} \right) \\
&= \$8,000 - (\$8 \times 900 \text{ units}) = \$800
\end{aligned}$$

That is, variable costing deducts $800 more in deriving operating profits, hence its operating profits are $800 lower in January. It is important to note that if $X^p = X^s$, the fixed manufacturing costs deducted would be the same under both methods.

A similar analysis can be made in February. For variable costing:

$$\begin{aligned}
\pi_v &= PX^s - VMX^s - VKX^s - FM - FK \\
&= (\$45 \times 1,100 \text{ units}) - (\$18 \times 1,100 \text{ units}) - (\$2 \times 1,100 \text{ units}) \\
&\quad - \$8,000 - \$12,000 \\
&= \$7,500
\end{aligned}$$

which is also shown in Illustration 9–6.

For full-absorption costing:

$$\pi_{fa} = \text{Sales revenue} - \text{Cost of goods sold for units produced in January} -$$
$$\text{Cost of goods sold for units produced in February} - \text{Marketing and}$$
$$\text{administrative costs}$$

$$= (\$45)(1{,}100 \text{ units}) - \underbrace{\left(\$18 + \frac{\$8{,}000}{1{,}000}\right)100 \text{ units}}_{\substack{\text{Cost of goods sold for} \\ \text{units produced in} \\ \text{January}}}$$

$$- \underbrace{\left(\$18 + \frac{\$8{,}000}{1{,}000}\right)1{,}000 \text{ units}}_{\substack{\text{Cost of goods sold} \\ \text{for units produced} \\ \text{in February}}} - (\$2 \times 1{,}100 \text{ units})$$
$$- \$12{,}000$$
$$= \$6{,}700$$

which is also shown in Illustration 9–6.

QUESTIONS

9–1. Describe the key difference between full-absorption costing and variable costing.

9–2. How are marketing and administrative costs treated under variable costing? Under full-absorption costing?

9–3. Under what circumstances do you find operating profits under variable costing equal to full-absorption costing profits? When are variable costing profits smaller? When are they greater?

9–4. What are the advantages of variable costing? What are some of the criticisms advanced against it?

9–5. How can a company using full-absorption costing manipulate profits without changing sales volume?

9–6. Describe comparative inventory changes under both variable costing and full-absorption costing when—
  a. Sales volume exceeds production volume.
  b. Production volume exceeds sales volume.

9–7. Multiple choice:
  a. The basic assumption made in a variable costing system with respect to fixed manufacturing costs is that fixed manufacturing costs are:
    (1) A sunk cost.
    (2) A product cost.
    (3) A part of inventory.
    (4) A period cost.
  b. Which costs are included in inventory under variable costing?
    (1) Only prime costs.
    (2) Only variable manufacturing costs.
    (3) All variable costs.
    (4) All variable and fixed manufacturing costs.

    c. Inventory under the variable costing method includes:
      (1) Direct materials cost and direct labor cost, but no factory overhead cost.
      (2) Direct materials cost, direct labor cost, and variable factory overhead cost.
      (3) Prime cost but not conversion cost.
      (4) Prime cost and all conversion cost.
    d. Which of the following must be known about a production process in order to institute a variable costing system?
      (1) The variable and fixed components of all costs related to production.
      (2) The controllable and noncontrollable components of all costs related to production.
      (3) Standard production rates and times for all elements of production.
      (4) Contribution margin and break-even point for all goods in production.

                                           (CPA adapted)

EXERCISES

9–8 Variable Costing versus Full Absorption Costing: Comparison of Operating Profit
(L.O.1)

Milton, Inc., produces a single product, which sells for $14.40. Milton produced 80,000 units and sold 72,000 units last year. There were no beginning or ending work in process inventories last year.

    Manufacturing costs and marketing and administrative costs for last year were as follows:

	Variable	Fixed
Direct materials	$280,000	—
Direct labor	200,000	—
Manufacturing overhead	80,000	$180,000
Marketing and administrative costs	69,120	120,000

Required:

    a. Compute the unit product (manufacturing) cost, using variable costing.
    b. What would Milton's operating profit be using variable costing?
    c. What would operating profit be using full-absorption costing?

9–9. Comparison of Cost Flows under Full-Absorption and Variable Costing
(L.O.1)

Wyandotte Product incurred the following costs for its line of swimming pool pumps:

	Variable	Fixed
Direct materials	$500,000	—
Labor	475,000	$100,000
Supplies	80,000	—
Depreciation	—	70,000
Repairs and maintenance	40,000	120,000
Other manufacturing	30,000	40,000
Marketing and administrative costs	40,000	110,000

100,000 units were produced, and 80,000 units were sold.

Required:

    a. Using T-accounts, trace the manufacturing cost flows under variable costing.
    b. Using T-accounts, trace the manufacturing cost flows under full-absorption costing.

9–10. Comparison of Full-Absorption and Variable Costing on Income Statements
(L.O.2)

Refer to exercise 9–9. Assume the selling price of pumps is $20 each.

Required:

a. Present the income statement using variable costing.
b. Present the income statement using full-absorption costing.
c. Explain the difference in the operating profits.

9–11. Comparison of Full-Absorption and Variable Cost Flows with Overhead Variances
(L.O.1)

Okanagan Products manufactures Ogo Pogos, a line of stuffed toys. Variable manufacturing overhead is applied at the rate of $1.20 per labor-hour, and fixed manufacturing overhead at a rate of $1.80 per labor-hour. Actual costs were as follows:

Direct materials	$ 50,000
Direct labor (at $4.20 per hour)	126,000
Actual variable manufacturing overhead	40,000
Variable marketing and administrative costs	45,000
Actual fixed manufacturing overhead	52,000
Fixed marketing and administrative costs	28,000

During the period, 25,000 units were produced, and 23,800 units were sold at a selling price of $20 each.

Required:

a. Use T-accounts to trace the cost flows using variable costing.
b. Use T-accounts to trace the cost flows using full-absorption costing.

9–12. Comparison of Full-Absorption and Variable Cost Income Statements with Overhead Variances
(L.O.1)

Refer to exercise 9–11 and assume that Okanagan Products debits or credits over- or underapplied overhead to Cost of Goods Sold:

Required:

a. Prepare an income statement for the period, using variable costing.
b. Prepare an income statement for the period, using full-absorption costing.

9–13. Comparison of Variable and Full-Absorption Costing: Analyzing Profit Performance
(L.O.2)

Eaton's Enterprises released the following figures from its records for Year 1 and Year 2:

	Year 1	Year 2
Sales units	240,000	240,000
Production units	240,000	400,000
Selling price per unit	$20	$20
Variable manufacturing cost per unit	$12	$12
Annual fixed manufacturing cost	$1,200,000	$1,200,000
Variable marketing and administrative costs		
per unit sold	$1.25	$1.25
Fixed marketing and administrative costs	$420,000	$420,000

Required:

a. Prepare income statements for both years, using full-absorption costing.
b. Prepare income statements for both years, using variable costing.
c. Comment on the different operating profit figures.

9–14. Comparison of Full-Absorption and Variable Costing—Income Statement Formats

(L.O.2)

Consider the following facts:

	Year 1	Year 2
Sales volume	50,000 units	150,000 units
Production volume	100,000 units	100,000 units
Selling price	$8 per unit	$8 per unit
Variable manufacturing costs	$5 per unit	$5 per unit
Fixed manufacturing costs	$100,000	$100,000
Nonmanufacturing costs (all fixed)	$ 50,000	$ 50,000

Required:

Prepare comparative income statements, using the contribution margin format for the variable costing and the traditional format using full-absorption costing. Show the total results for Years 1 and 2 combined in addition to the results for each year individually.

9–15. Comparison of Variable and Full-Absorption Costing—Multiple-Choice

(L.O.2)

The following questions are based on JV Company, which produces a single product selling for $7 per unit. One hundred thousand units were produced, and 80,000 units were sold during the year.

	Fixed Costs	Variable Costs
Direct materials	–0–	$1.50 per unit produced
Direct labor	–0–	1.00 per unit produced
Factory overhead	$150,000	.50 per unit produced
Marketing and administrative	80,000	.50 per unit sold

JV had no inventory at the beginning of the year.

Required:

a. In presenting inventory on the balance sheet at December 31, the unit cost under full-absorption costing is:
   (1) $2.50.
   (2) $3.00.
   (3) $3.50.
   (4) $4.50.

b. In presenting inventory on a variable costing balance sheet, the unit cost would be:
   (1) $2.50.
   (2) $3.00.
   (3) $3.50.
   (4) $4.50.

c. What is the operating profit using variable costing?
   (1) $50,000.
   (2) $80,000.
   (3) $90,000.
   (4) $120,000.

d. What is the operating profit using full-absorption costing?
   (1) $50,000.
   (2) $80,000.
   (3) $90,000.
   (4) $120,000.

e. What is the ending inventory using full-absorption costing?
  (1) $60,000.
  (2) $90,000.
  (3) $120,000.
  (4) $150,000.
f. What is the ending inventory under variable costing?
  (1) $60,000.
  (2) $90,000.
  (3) $120,000.
  (4) $150,000.

(CPA adapted)

9–16. Find Income Statement Amounts
(L.O.2)

Vagabond Products uses the following unit costs for one of the products it manufactures:

Direct materials	$78.00
Direct labor	49.40
Manufacturing overhead:	
Variable	15.60
Fixed (based on 5,000 units per year)	13.00
Marketing and administrative costs:	
Variable	10.40
Fixed (based on 5,000 units per year)	7.28

This year, there were 1,000 units in beginning finished goods inventory; 5,500 units were produced; and 6,500 units were sold at $200 per unit. There was no beginning or ending work in process inventory. Actual costs were as estimated. Under- or overapplied overhead is debited or credited to Cost of Goods Sold.

Required:

a. Prepare an income statement for the year, using variable costing.
b. Would reported operating profits be more, less, or the same if full-absorption costing was used? Support your conclusions with an income statement using full-absorption costing.

9–17. (Appendix) Comparison of Full-Absorption and Variable Costing, Using the Algebraic Method—Part I
(L.O.3)

Assume the following data about actual prices, costs, and volume for Derivation Company for the first quarter:

Selling price	$5 per unit
Variable manufacturing costs	$3 per unit
Fixed manufacturing costs	$100,000 for the quarter
Marketing and administrative costs	
(fixed and variable combined)	$30,000 for the quarter
Sales volume	100,000 units for the quarter
Production volume	120,000 units for the quarter

There were no beginning inventories.

Required:

a. Using the algebraic method, derive the difference in operating profits between variable costing and full-absorption costing.
b. What is the inventory value at the end of the first quarter under (1) full-absorption costing and (2) variable costing?

9–18. (Appendix) Comparison of Full-Absorption and Variable Costing, Using the Algebraic Method—Part II
(L.O.3)

Refer to the information given in exercise 9–17. Assume it is now the second quarter of the same year. Volumes in the second quarter are as follows:

Sales volume	100,000 units
Production volume	100,000 units

Costs and prices remain the same in the second quarter as in the first quarter.

Required:

Using the algebraic method, show the difference, if any, in operating profit between variable costing and full-absorption costing. (You may assume either LIFO or FIFO inventory flows.)

9–19. (Appendix) Comparison of Full-Absorption and Variable Costing, Using the Algebraic Method—Part III
(L.O.3)

Refer to the information given in exercise 9–17. Assume it is now the third quarter of the same year, and the volumes in the third quarter are as follows:

Sales volume	100,000 units
Production volume	80,000 units

Variable costs and selling price per unit remain the same in the third quarter as in the first quarter, as do quarterly fixed costs.

Required:

Using the algebraic method, show the difference in operating profits between variable costing and full-absorption costing. (You may assume either a FIFO or LIFO inventory flow.)

PROBLEMS

9–20. Comprehensive Full-Absorption and Variable Costing Comparison

Kensington Company manufactures a single product with the following costs:

Selling price	$	5.00 per unit
Variable manufacturing costs (direct materials and direct labor)		3.00 per unit
Fixed manufacturing costs, based on a normal production volume		
of 100,000 units per month (all manufacturing overhead is fixed)		1.00 per unit
Marketing and administrative costs (all fixed)		50,000 per month

Beginning inventory is valued at $4 per unit under full-absorption costing, and at $3 per unit under variable costing. Unit costs have been the same since inception of the company. If sales are greater than production, assume that there is sufficient inventory at normal production cost to take up the slack. Any over- or underapplied overhead is charged to cost of goods sold for this period.

    The president of Kensington wants an analysis on the effect of variations in sales and production units. To help you he has included a chart for you to complete (all numbers in thousands).

Required:

a. Complete the chart.
b. Comment on the results.

		Sales = Production			Sales exceeds Production			Production exceeds Sales		
Units	Sales	100	80	110	100	80	110	80	60	100
	Production	100	80	110	80	60	80	100	80	110
	Sales revenue									
Full-Absorption Costing	Variable cost of goods sold									
	Fixed cost of goods sold									
	Marketing and administrative									
	Operating profit									

Variable Costing	Cost of goods sold (variable)									
	Fixed manufacturing costs									
	Fixed marketing and administrative									
	Operating profit									

9–21. Conversion of Variable to Full-Absorption Costing

The S. T. Shire Company uses variable costing for internal management purposes and full-absorption costing for external reporting purposes. Thus, at the end of each year, financial information must be converted from variable costing to full-absorption costing for external reports.

At the end of last year, management anticipated that sales would rise 20 percent this year. Therefore, production was increased from 20,000 units to 24,000 units. However, economic conditons kept sales volume at 20,000 units for both years.

The following data pertain to the two years.

	Last Year	This Year
Selling price per unit	$ 30	$ 30
Sales (units)	20,000	20,000
Beginning inventory (units)	2,000	2,000
Production (units)	20,000	24,000
Ending inventory (units)	2,000	6,000
Underapplied variable overhead	$ 5,000	$ 4,000

Variable cost per unit for both years was composed of:

Labor	$ 7.50
Materials	4.50
Variable overhead	3.00
	$15.00

Budgeted and actual fixed costs for each year were:

Production	$ 90,000
Selling and administrative	100,000
	$190,000

The overhead rate under full-absorption costing is based on estimated volume of 30,000 units per year. Under- or overapplied overhead is taken to cost of goods sold.

Required:

Using these data:

a. Present the income statement based on variable costing for this year.

b. Present the income statement based on full-absorption costing for this year.

c. Explain the difference, if any, in the operating profit figures.

(CMA adapted)

9–22. Variable Costing Operating Profit and Reconciliation with Full-Absorption

The Sierra Corporation employs a full-absorption costing system for its external reporting as well as for internal management purposes. The latest annual income statement appears as follows:

Sales revenue		$415,000
Cost of goods sold:		
Beginning finished goods inventory	$ 22,000	
Cost of goods manufactured	315,000	
Ending finished goods inventory	(86,000)	
Cost of goods sold		251,000
Gross margin		164,000
Marketing costs		83,000
Administrative costs		49,800
Operating profit before taxes		$ 31,200

Management is somewhat concerned that although they are showing adequate income, there has been a shortage of cash to meet operating costs. The following information has been provided to assist management with its evaluation of the situation:

Statement of Cost of Goods Manufactured

Direct materials:		
Beginning inventory	$ 16,000	
Purchases	62,000	
Ending inventory	(22,000)	$ 56,000
Direct labor		125,100
Manufacturing overhead:		
Variable		39,400
Fixed (including depreciation of $30,000)		94,500
Cost of goods manufactured		$315,000

There are no work in process inventories. Management reports it is pleased that this year manufacturing costs are 70 percent variable compared to last year, when these costs were only 45 percent variable. While 80 percent of the marketing costs are variable, only 40 percent of the administrative costs are considered variable.

Required:

a. Prepare a variable costing income statement for the year.

b. Reconcile the difference between the full-absorption costing operating profit given in the problem to the variable costing operating profit in part *(a)*.

9–23. Full-Absorption versus Variable Costing

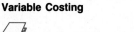

You have been given the following information concerning the All Fixed Company.

1. Sales: 10,000 units per year at a price of $46 per unit.
2. Production: 15,000 units in 1987; 5,000 units in 1988.
3. There was no beginning inventory in 1987.
4. Annual production costs are all fixed and equal $225,000 per year.
5. Ending finished goods inventory in 1987 was one third of that year's current production.
6. Annual marketing and administrative costs are $140,000 per year.

Required:

a. Prepare full-absorption costing income statements for 1987 and 1988, and for the two years taken together.

b. Prepare variable costing income statements for 1987 and 1988, and for the two years taken together.

c. Prepare a reconciliation of full-absorption operating profit to variable costing operating profit for 1987 and 1988.

9–24. Effect of Changes in Production and Costing Method on Operating Profit ("I Enjoy Challenges")

(This is a classic problem based on an actual company's experience.) The X. B. Company uses an actual cost system to apply all production costs to units produced. While the plant has a maximum production capacity of 40 million units, only 10 million units were produced and sold during Year 1. There were no beginning or ending inventories.

The X. B. Company income statement for Year 1 is as follows:

X. B. COMPANY
Income Statement
For the Year Ending December 31, Year 1

Sales (10,000,000 units at $3)		$30,000,000
Cost of goods sold:		
Variable (10,000,000 at $1)	$10,000,000	
Fixed	24,000,000	34,000,000
Gross margin		(4,000,000)
Marketing and administrative costs		5,000,000
Operating profit (loss)		$ (9,000,000)

The board of directors is concerned about this loss. A consultant approached the board with the following offer: "I agree to become president for no fixed salary. But I insist on a year-end bonus of 10 percent of operating profit (before considering the bonus)." The board of directors agreed to these terms, and the consultant was hired.

The new president promptly stepped up production to an annual rate of 30 million units. Sales for Year 2 remained at 10 million units.

The resulting X. B. Company income statement for Year 2 follows.

X. B. COMPANY
Income Statement
For the Year Ending December 31, Year 2

Sales (10,000,000 units at $3)			$30,000,000
Cost of goods sold:			
Cost of goods manufactured:			
Variable (30,000,000 at $1)		$30,000,000	
Fixed		24,000,000	
Total cost of goods manufactured		54,000,000	
Less ending inventory:			
Variable (20,000,000 at $1)		20,000,000	
Fixed $\left(\dfrac{20}{30} \times 24,000,000\right)$		16,000,000	
Total inventory		36,000,000	
Cost of goods sold			18,000,000
Gross margin			12,000,000
Marketing and administrative costs			5,000,000
Operating profit before bonus			7,000,000
Bonus			700,000
Operating profit after bonus			$ 6,300,000

The day after the statement was verified, the president took his check for $700,000 and resigned to take a job with another corporation. He remarked, "I enjoy challenges. Now that X. B. Company is in the black, I'd prefer tackling another challenging situation." (His contract with his new employer is similar to the one he had with X. B. Company.)

Required:

a. What is your evaluation of the Year 2 performance?

b. Using variable costing, what would operating profit be for Year 1? For Year 2? What are the inventory values? (Assume all marketing and administrative costs are fixed.) Compare those results with the full-absorption statements shown above.

9–25. "I Enjoy Challenges"—Normal Costing

Refer to the facts for problem 9–24. What would Year 2 operating profit (loss) be if X. B. Company used full-absorption normal costing with a fixed manufacturing overhead rate of $2.40 $\left(\dfrac{\$24,000,000 \text{ fixed manufacturing costs}}{10,000,000 \text{ estimated unit sales}}\right)$? Prepare an income statement and a T-account diagram of cost flows.

9–26. Comparative Income Statements, with Variances

A client requested your help to analyze the operations of one of her divisions, the Wheeler Division. "I don't understand this! I received this income statement yesterday from the Wheeler Division managers (see Exhibit A), but one of our internal auditors came across this other one (see Exhibit B). The second statement shows a lower net income! I think something strange is going on here. It looks like the division managers are sending me this first statement (in Exhibit A), which makes them look good, while they're hiding the second statement (in Exhibit B), which shows what's really going on. I want you to look into this for me."

Required:

a. How many units were sold in August?

b. What was the *expected* and *actual* production (units) in August?

Exhibit A (9–26)

Wheeler Division
Income Statement
August

Sales revenue	$1,200,000
Cost of goods sold	800,000
Overapplied overhead	50,000
Gross margin	450,000
Selling and administrative costs	200,000
Operating profit	$ 250,000

Notes:
(1) Fixed manufacturing costs applied at predetermined rate of $2 per unit.
(2) No under- or overapplied overhead is prorated to inventories.
(3) Ending inventory is $640,000.

Exhibit B (9–26)

Wheeler Division
Income Statement
August

Sales revenue	$1,200,000
Variable cost of goods sold	600,000
Fixed manufacturing costs	300,000
Gross margin	300,000
Selling and administrative costs	200,000
Operating profit	$ 100,000

    c. What was the *beginning* and *ending* inventory (units) in August?

    d. (1) What were the actual fixed costs incurred in August?

        (2) What were the total amount of fixed costs expensed on the income statement under full-absorption costing?

9–27. Comparison of Full-Absorption and Variable Normal Costing in a Process Operation

After a dispute with the company president, the controller of the Lance Company resigned. At that time, his office was converting the internal reporting system from full-absorption to variable costing. You have been called in to prepare financial reports for last year. A considerable amount of data are missing, but you piece together the following information.

1. The company manufactures valves, which pass through one department. All materials are added at the beginning of production, and processing is applied evenly throughout the department. There is no spoilage. FIFO costing is used.

2. From the marketing department, you learn that 90,000 units were sold at a price of $20 each during last year.

3. From various sources, you determine that variable manufacturing overhead was $330,000 and fixed manufacturing overhead was $210,000 for last year. Non-manufacturing costs (all fixed) were $580,000.

4. In one of the former controller's desk drawers, you discover the draft of a report with the following information:

a. "The present accounting system uses the normal costing approach for both internal and external reporting. We write off over- or underapplied overhead as part of cost of goods sold rather than allocate it to inventories."

b. "Equivalent unit costs during the year and in beginning inventories were: $4 per unit for materials costs and $2 per unit for direct labor. Variable overhead is applied at $3 per unit and fixed overhead at $2 per unit."

c. "110,000 units were transferred from work in process inventory to finished goods inventory. 120,000 units of materials were purchased and 115,000 units requisitioned to work in process inventory."

d. Inventory summary (in units):

	Beginning Inventories, January 1	Ending Inventories, December 31
Work in process inventory	10,000 (40% complete)	15,000 (20% complete)
Finished goods inventory	No records	30,000
Direct materials	No records	10,000

Required:

a. Show the flow of whole units, including units started in work in process inventory, transferred to finished goods, and sold. Be sure to include both beginning and ending inventories.

b. Show the flow of manufacturing costs during the year, including beginning and ending inventories, using full-absorption normal costing.

c. Prepare income statements using:
(1) Full-absorption normal costing.
(2) Variable normal costing.

9–28. Comparison of Full-Absorption to Variable Costing with Product Mix

Classic Brew Corporation operates a processing plant in West Covina, California, that manufacturers two types of a popular soft drink: Classy and Contempo. Classy sells for $26 per quart, while Contempo sells for $14 per quart. A dispute broke out among management concerning the sales effort that should be devoted to each product. Some managers felt that greater emphasis should be placed on Classy because it offers a greater profit per quart. Other managers voted to increase sales of Contempo because it required less labor to manufacture, and labor was in short supply. You have been hired to advise on the appropriate selling emphasis.

The following information is extracted from the accounting records:

	Classy	Contempo
Unit costs:		
Direct materials	$2	$1
Direct labor	4	2
Variable manufacturing overhead	3	3
Fixed manufacturing overhead	1	4
Variable marketing and administrative costs	7	2
Fixed marketing and administrative costs	4	3
Inventories and production data:		
Beginning inventory	1,000 qts.	2,000 qts.
Ending inventory	3,000 qts.	1,000 qts.
Sales this past month	7,000 qts.	12,000 qts.
Normal production	8,000 qts.	10,000 qts.
Minimum production	5,000 qts.	5,000 qts.

Minimum production requirements are established by equipment specifications and cannot be changed. There have been no cost changes in the past few years. FIFO inventory flows are assumed.

Required:

a. Prepare a variable costing income statement for last month.
b. Prepare a full-absorption costing income statement for last month.
c. For Contempo only, prepare a reconciliation between the operating profits in (a) and (b).

9–29. Comprehensive Problem on Process Costing, Variable Costing, and Full-Absorption Costing

(This problem requires knowing how to compute equivalent units.) Whitaker Corporation manufactures Jink, which is sold for $20 per unit. Harsh (a direct material) is added before processing starts, and labor and overhead are added evenly during the manufacturing process. Actual costs per unit of Jink this year are:

Harsh, 2 pounds	$3.00
Labor	6.00
Variable manufacturing overhead	1.00
Fixed manufacturing overhead	1.10

These costs have remained the same for several periods. Inventory data for this year follows:

	Units	
	Beginning: January 1	**Ending: December 31**
Harsh (pounds)	50,000	40,000
Work in process inventory	10,000 (½ processed)	15,000 (⅓ processed)
Finished goods inventory	17,000	12,000

During the year, 220,000 pounds of Harsh were purchased, and 230,000 pounds were transferred to work in process inventory. Also, 110,000 units of Jink were transferred to finished goods inventory. Actual fixed manufacturing overhead during the year was $121,000. FIFO is used for inventory flows. Marketing and administrative costs were $145,000 for the year.

Required:

a. Determine the number of equivalent units produced for both materials (Harsh) and conversion costs.
b. Determine the work in process and finished goods inventories (in dollars) under (1) full-absorption costing and (2) variable costing on January 1 and December 31.
c. Prepare comparative income statements for the year, using full-absorption and variable costing.
d. Prepare a reconciliation of full-absorption to variable costing that compares the fixed manufacturing costs deducted from revenue (that is, expensed) under each method.

(CPA adapted)

9–30. Incomplete Records

On December 31 of last year, a fire destroyed the bulk of the accounting records of Malox Company, a small, one-product manufacturing firm. In addition, the chief accountant mysteriously disappeared. You have the task of reconstructing the records for last year. The general manager has said that the accountant had been experimenting with both full-absorption costing and variable costing on a actual costing basis.

The records are a mess, but you have gathered the following data for last year:

1.	Sales	$450,000
2.	Actual fixed manufacturing costs incurred	66,000
3.	Actual variable manufacturing costs per unit for last year and for units in beginning finished goods inventory on January 1 of last year	3
4.	Operating profit, full-absorption costing basis	60,000
5.	Notes receivable from chief accountant	14,000
6.	Contribution margin	180,000
7.	Direct material purchases	175,000
8.	Actual marketing and administrative costs (all fixed)	21,000
9.	Gross margin	81,000

The company had no beginning or ending work in process inventories. You also learn that full-absorption costs per unit in last year's beginning finished goods inventory is the same as the full-absorption cost per unit for units produced during last year.

Required:

a. Prepare a comparative income statement on a full-absorption and variable costing basis.

b. At a meeting with the board of directors, the following questions were raised.
   (1) "How many units did we sell last year?"
   (2) "How many units did we produce last year?"
   (3) "What were the unit production costs last year under both full-absorption and variable costing?"
   How would you respond?

c. Reconcile the operating profit under variable costing with that under full costing, showing the exact source of the difference.

9–31. Comparative Income Statements

Management of the 2,000 Company uses the following unit costs for the one product it manufactures:

	Projected Cost per Unit
Direct material (all variable)	$30.00
Direct labor (all variable)	19.00
Manufacturing overhead:	
Variable cost	6.00
Fixed cost (based on 10,000 units per month)	5.00
Nonmanufacturing:	
Variable cost	4.00
Fixed cost (based on 10,000 units per month)	2.80

The projected selling price is $80 per unit. The fixed costs remain fixed within the range of 4,000 to 16,000 units of production.

Management has also projected the following data for the month of June:

	Units
Beginning inventory	2,000
Production	9,000
Available	11,000
Sales	7,500
Ending inventory	3,500

Required:

Prepare a projected income statement for June for management purposes under *each* of the following product-costing methods. Be sure to show supporting schedules that calculate the inventoriable production costs per unit for each product-costing method. Ignore income taxes.

a. Full-absorption costing. Under- or overapplied fixed overhead should be debited or credited to cost of goods sold.

b. Variable costing.

(CPA adapted)

9–32. Evaluate Full-Absorption and Variable Costing

The vice president for sales of Huber Corporation received the following income statement for November. The statement has been prepared using variable costing, which the firm has just adopted for internal reporting purposes.

HUBER CORPORATION
Income Statement
For the Month of November
(in thousands)

Sales revenue	$2,400
Less variable cost of goods sold	1,200
Contribution margin	1,200
Less fixed manufacturing costs at budget	600
Gross margin	600
Less fixed nonmanufacturing costs	400
Operating profits before taxes	$ 200

The controller attached the following notes to the statements.

1. The unit sales price for November averaged $24.

2. The unit manufacturing costs for the month were:

Variable cost	$12
Fixed cost	4
Total cost	$16

The unit rate for fixed manufacturing costs is a predetermined rate based upon a normal monthly production of 150,000 units.

3. Production for November was 45,000 units in excess of sales.

4. The inventory at November 30 consisted of 80,000 units.

Required:

a. The vice president for sales is not comfortable with the variable cost basis and wonders what the operating profit would have been under the full-absorption cost basis.
   (1) Present the November income statement on a full-absorption cost basis.
   (2) Reconcile and explain the difference between the variable costing and the full-absorption costing operating profit figures.

b. Explain the features associated with variable cost profit measurement that should be attractive to the vice president for sales.

(CMA adapted)

9-33. Full and Variable Costing Importing Decisions

Far Eastern Couture imports designer clothing which it has manufactured by subcontractors in Taiwan. Clothing is a seasonal product. The goods must be ready for sale prior to the start of the season. Any goods left over at the end of the season must usually be sold at steep discounts. The company prepares a dress design and selects fabrics approximately six months before a given season. These goods are received and distributed at the start of the season. Based on past experience, the company estimates that 60 percent of a particular lot of dresses will be unsold at the end of the season. These dresses are marked down to one half of the initial retail price. Even with the markdown, a substantial number of dresses remain unsold. These remaining dresses are returned to Far Eastern Couture and destroyed. Even though it is known that a large number of dresses must be discounted or destroyed, the company needs to place a minimum order of 1,000 dresses to have a sufficient selection of styles and sizes for marketing the design.

Recently, the company placed an order for 1,000 dresses of a particular design. The cost of the order was $25,000. In addition, the company pays import duties of $5,000. The company pays a commission of $7 for each dress which is actually sold at retail, regardless of whether it is sold at the regular price or at the markdown price. There is a cost of $3 for return mailing and disposing of each dress that is unsold after the end of the markdown period.

Required:

a. Use full-absorption costing to compute the inventoriable cost of each dress in this lot of dresses.

b. Suppose the company sells 30 percent of the dresses in this lot at a price of $75 each during the first accounting period. Using full-absorption costing, what is the value of the ending inventory and what is the operating profit or loss for the period assuming there are no other transactions and that the season has not ended so that the number of dresses subject to markdown or to be returned is unknown?

c. During the second period, 10 percent of the 1,000 dresses were sold at full price and 30 percent were sold at the half-price markdown. The remaining dresses were returned and disposed of. Using full-absorption costing, what is the operating profit or loss for the period assuming there are no other transactions?

d. Suggest a method of accounting for these dresses that would more closely relate revenues and costs.

INTEGRATIVE CASE

9-34. Comprehensive Case on Choosing Full-Absorption or Variable (Normal) Costing— Landau Company[4]

In early August, Terry Silver, the new marketing vice president of Landau Company, was studying the July income statement. Silver found the statement puzzling: July's sales increased significantly over June's, yet income was lower in July than in June. Silver was certain that margins on Landau's products had not narrowed in July and therefore felt that there must be some mistake in the July statement.

When Silver asked the company's chief accountant, Meredith Wilcox, for an explanation, Wilcox stated that production in July was well below standard volume because of employee vacations. This had caused overhead to be underapplied, and a large unfavorable volume variance had been generated, which more than offset the added gross margin from the sales increase. It was company policy to charge all over- or underapplied overhead variances to the monthly income statement, and these production volume variances would all wash out by year's end, Wilcox had said.

---

[4] © Osceola Institute, 1979.

Silver, who admittedly knew little about accounting, found this explanation to be "Incomprehensible. With all the people in your department, I don't understand why you can't produce an income statement that reflects the economics of our business. In the company that I left to come here, if sales went up, profits went up. I don't see why that shouldn't be the case here, too."

As Wilcox left Silver's office, a presentation at a recent National Association of Accountants meeting came to mind. At that meeting, the controller of Winjum Manufacturing Company had described that firm's variable costing system, which charged fixed overhead to income as a period expense and treated only variable production costs as inventoriable product costs. Winjum's controller had stressed that, other things being equal, variable costing caused income to move with sales only rather than being affected by both sales and production volume, as was the case with full-absorption costing systems.

Wilcox decided to recast the June and July income statements and balance sheets using variable costing. (Both the original and the revised income statements and related impact on inventories are shown in Exhibit A.) Wilcox then showed these statements to Terry Silver, who responded, "Now that's more like it! I *knew* July was a better month for us than June, and your new 'variable costing' statements reflect that. Tell your boss [Landau's controller] that at the next meeting of the executive committee I'm going to suggest we change to this new method."

Exhibit A (9–34)   **Effects of Variable Costing**

LANDAU COMPANY
Income Statements
June and July

	June		July	
	Full-Absorption Costing (original statement)	Variable Costing (revised statement)	Full-Absorption Costing (original statement)	Variable Costing (revised statement)
Sales revenue	$865,428	$865,428	$931,710	$931,710
Cost of goods sold (normal)	484,640	337,517	521,758	363,367
Production cost variances[a]:				
Overhead volume	1,730	—	(63,779)	—
Overhead spending	(239)	(239)	(10)	(10)
Gross margin	382,279	527,672	346,163	568,333
Fixed production overhead	—	192,883	—	192,883
Marketing and administrative	301,250	301,250	310,351	310,351
Income before taxes	81,029	33,539	35,812	65,099
Provision for income taxes	38,894	16,099	17,190	31,248
Net income	$ 42,135	$ 17,440	$ 18,622	$ 33,851

Impact on Inventory

	As of June 30		As of July 31	
	Full-Absorption Costing	Variable Costing	Full-Absorption Costing	Variable Costing
Inventories	$1,680,291	$1,170,203	$1,583,817	$1,103,016

[a] Parentheses denote unfavorable (debit) variances.

At the next executive committee meeting, Silver proposed adoption of variable costing for Landau's monthly internal income statements. The controller also supported this change, saying that it would eliminate the time-consuming efforts of allocating fixed overhead to individual products. These allocations had only led to arguments between operating managers and the accounting staff. The controller added that since variable costing segregated the costs of materials, direct labor, and variable overhead from fixed overhead costs, management's cost control efforts would be enhanced.

Silver also felt that the margin figures provided by the new approach would be more useful than the present ones for comparing the profitability of individual products. To illustrate the point, Silver had worked out an example. With full-absorption costing, two products in Landau's line, numbers 129 and 243, would appear as follows:

Product	Production Cost	Selling Price	Unit Margin	Margin Percent
129	$2.54	$4.34	$1.80	41.5%
243	3.05	5.89	2.84	48.2

Thus, Product 243 would appear to be the more desirable one to sell. But on the proposed basis, the numbers were as follows:

Product	Production Cost	Selling Price	Unit Margin	Margin Percent
129	$1.38	$4.34	$2.96	68.2%
243	2.37	5.89	3.52	59.8

According to Silver, these numbers made it clear that Product 129 was the more profitable of the two.

At this point, the treasurer spoke up. "If we use this new approach, the next thing we know, you marketing types will be selling at your usual markup over *variable* costs. How are we going to pay the fixed costs *then?* Besides, in my 38 years of experience, it's the lack of control over fixed costs that can bankrupt a company. I'm opposed to any proposal that causes us to take a myopic view of costs."

The president also had some concerns about the proposal. "In the first place, if I add together the June and July profit under each of these methods, I get almost $61,000 with the full-absorption method, but only $51,000 under the variable costing method. While I'd be happy to lower our reported profits from the standpoints of relations with our employee union and income taxes, I don't think it's a good idea as far as our owners and bankers are concerned. And I share Sam's [the treasurer's] concern about controlling fixed costs. I think we should defer a decision on this matter until we fully understand all of the implications."

Required:

a. Critique the various pros and cons of the variable costing proposal that were presented in the meeting. What arguments would you add?

b. Do you think Landau should adopt variable costing for its monthly income statements?

PART

II

DIFFERENTIAL COSTS FOR DECISION MAKING

OUTLINE

COST ESTIMATION

LEARNING OBJECTIVES

1. Understanding the primary methods used to estimate costs.
2. To know how to interpret regression results.
3. Seeing how to estimate costs with learning curves.

Accounting systems are designed primarily to record and report costs that have been incurred in the past. However, it is important that management also be able to estimate future cost behavior. For example, in deciding among alternative actions, management needs to know the costs that are likely to be incurred for each alternative. Data from the accounting records are often used to help make those estimates about the future.

Among the most frequently asked questions that require cost estimates are:

▼ What will happen to total costs if we increase activity by 10 percent over the present level?

▼ How will costs change if specific labor- or energy-saving devices are installed?

▼ What bid should we enter on this contract?

▼ What profit can we expect if we sell the projected number of units this period?

This chapter discusses methods of estimating costs to answer questions like these.

METHODS OF ESTIMATING COSTS

The basic idea in cost estimation is to estimate the relation between costs and the variables affecting costs. In this chapter, we focus on the relation between costs and one important variable that affects costs—activity levels. You are already familiar with the term *variable costs,* and you know that variable costs are those that change proportionately with activity levels. The formula that we estimate is the familiar cost equation:

$$TC = F + VX$$

where TC refers to total costs, F refers to fixed costs that do not vary with activity levels, V refers to variable costs per unit, and X refers to the volume of activity. In practice, we usually have data about the amount of total costs that are incurred at each of various activity levels, but we do not have a breakdown of costs into fixed and variable components. Yet, knowing which costs are fixed and how costs change as the volume of activity changes is important for most financial decisions made in companies.

This chapter discusses four methods of estimating the relation between cost behavior and activity levels that are commonly used in practice:

1. Account analysis.
2. Engineering estimates.
3. Scattergraph and high-low estimates.
4. Statistical methods (usually employing regression analysis).

Results are likely to differ from method to method. Consequently, more than one approach is often applied so that results can be compared. Because line managers bear ultimate responsibility for all cost estimates, they frequently apply their own best judgment as a final step in the estimation process, modifying the estimates submitted by the controller's staff. These methods, therefore, should be seen as ways of helping management to arrive at the best estimates possible. Their weaknesses as well as their strengths require attention.

We discuss each of the four estimation methods in this chapter. The discussion of regression methods centers on practical applications rather than on the underlying statistical theory. A brief overview of the theory and some important considerations for its application are discussed in the appendix to this chapter.

Account Analysis

Account Analysis The method of cost estimation that calls for a review of each account making up the total cost being analyzed.

The **account analysis** approach calls for a review of each cost account used to record the costs that are of interest. Each cost is identified as either fixed or variable, depending on the relationship between the cost and some activity.

The relationship between the activity and the cost is extremely important. For example, in estimating the production costs for a specified number of units within the range of present manufacturing capacity, direct materials and direct labor costs would be considered variable, while building occupancy costs would be considered fixed.

Illustration 10–1 shows a typical schedule of estimated manufacturing overhead costs prepared for a particular production level by Estimators, Inc. The production process is assumed to produce 40 units per machine-hour. Management has initially considered a production level of 4,600 units. To attain this production level, 115 machine-hours (4,600 units ÷ 40 units per hour) are required. The variable manufacturing overhead may be expressed as a cost per machine-hour or as a cost per unit, depending upon management's preference.

Following this approach, each major class of manufacturing overhead costs is itemized. Each cost is then divided into its estimated variable and fixed components. Management considers building occupancy costs, for example, to be entirely fixed and classifies the costs of quality inspections as entirely variable. The other costs are mixed—they have some fixed and some variable elements. The fixed and variable components of each cost item may be determined on the basis of the experience and judgment of

Illustration 10–1   **Cost Estimation Using Account Analysis, Estimators, Inc.**

Account	Costs at 4,600 Units of Output (115 machine-hours)		
	Total	Variable Cost	Fixed Cost
Indirect labor	$ 321	$ 103	$ 218
Indirect materials	422	307	115
Building occupancy	615		615
Property taxes and insurance	51	40	11
Power	589	535	54
Equipment repairs and maintenance	218	119	99
Data processing	113	88	25
Quality inspections	187	187	
Personnel services	115	47	68
Totals	$2,631	$1,426	$1,205

accounting or other personnel. Additionally, other cost-estimation methods discussed later in this chapter might be used to divide costs into fixed and variable components.

The total costs for the coming period are the sum of the estimated total variable and total fixed costs. For Estimators, Inc., assume that accounting personnel have relied on judgments of a number of people in the company and estimated fixed costs to be $1,205 and the total variable costs to be $1,426, as shown in Illustration 10–1.

Since the variable costs are directly related to the quantity of expected production, the variable manufacturing overhead per unit may be stated as $.31 ($1,426 ÷ 4,600 units). The general cost equation may be expressed as:

$$TC = F + VX$$

Manufacturing overhead costs = $1,205 per period + $.31 per unit times the number of units of output

For 4,600 units:

Manufacturing overhead costs = $1,205 + ($.31 × 4,600)
= $1,205 + $1,426
= $2,631

Now, if management wanted to estimate the costs at a production level of 4,800 units, it would substitute that figure for the 4,600 units in the previous equation. This results in:

Manufacturing overhead costs = $1,205 + ($.31 × 4,800)
= $1,205 + $1,488
= $2,693

This is simpler than re-estimating all of the manufacturing overhead cost elements listed in Illustration 10–1 for the different activity levels that management might wish to consider. Moreover, management's attention is drawn to the variable cost amount as the cost that changes with each increment in unit volume.

The variable costs could also be expressed in terms of costs per machine-hour. Since 115 machine-hours are required to produce 4,600 units (at the 40 units per hour assumed in the illustration), the variable cost per machine-hour would be:

$1,426 ÷ 115 hours = $12.40 per machine-hour

Account analysis is a useful way of estimating costs. It makes use of the experience and judgment of managers and accountants who are familiar with company operations and the way costs react to changes in activity levels. Account analysis relies heavily on personal judgment. This may be an advantage or disadvantage depending on the bias of the person making the estimate. Decisions based on cost estimates often have major economic consequences for the people making the estimates. Thus, these individuals may not be entirely objective. More objective methods are often used in conjunction with account analysis so that the advantages of multiple methods are obtained.

Engineering Estimates

Engineering Estimates Cost estimates based on measurement and pricing of the work involved in a task.

Engineering estimates of costs are usually made by measuring the work involved in a task. A detailed step-by-step analysis of each phase of each manufacturing process, together with the kinds of work performed and the costs involved, is prepared. (This is sometimes part of a *time-and-motion* study.) The time it should take to perform each step is then estimated. These times are often available from widely published manuals and trade association documents.

The times required for each step in the process are summed to obtain an estimate of the total time involved, including an allowance for unproductive time. This serves as a basis for estimating direct labor costs. Engineering estimates of the materials required for each unit of production are usually obtainable from drawings and specifications sheets.

Other costs are estimated in a similar manner. For example, the size and cost of a building needed to house the manufacturing operation can be estimated based on area construction costs and space requirements. An estimate of the needed number of supervisors and support personnel can be based on an estimate of direct labor time.

One advantage to the engineering approach is that it can detail each step required to perform an operation. This permits comparison with other settings where similar operations are performed. It enables a company to review its manufacturing productivity and identify specific strengths and weaknesses. Another advantage is that it does not require data from prior activities in the organization. Hence, it can be used to estimate costs for totally new activities.

A company that uses engineering estimates can often identify where "slack" exists in its operations. For example, if an engineering estimate indicates that 80,000 square feet of floor area are required for an assembly process but the company has been using 125,000 square feet, the company may find it beneficial to rearrange the plant to make floor space available for other uses.

A difficulty with the engineering approach is that it can be quite expensive to use because each activity is using engineering norms. Another consideration is that engineering estimates are often based on optimal conditions. Therefore, when evaluating performance, bidding on a contract, planning for expected costs, or estimating costs for any other purpose, it is wise to consider that the actual work conditions will be less than optimal.

Scattergraph and High-Low Estimates

One way to overcome some of the shortcomings of account analysis and engineering estimates is to observe past cost behavior in relation to a specified activity measure. If a company's operations have followed a discernible pattern in the past and are expected to continue that pattern in the future, it may be possible to use the relationship between past costs and activity to estimate future costs. Of course, if the relationship changes, it may be necessary to adjust the estimated costs accordingly.

Analysts must be careful when predicting future costs from past data. In many cases, the cost-activity relationship changes. Technological innovation, increased use of robots, more mechanized processes, and the like may make the past cost-activity relationships inappropriate for predictive purposes.

In other cases, the costs themselves change so dramatically that old cost data are almost worthless predictors of future costs. Manufacturers using copper and silver in recent years have found that past cost data are not very helpful for predicting future costs. While adjustments to the data may be made, the resulting cost estimates tend to lose their objectivity as the number of adjustments increases.

Relevant Range of Activity

When attempting to extrapolate from past observations, one must consider the relevance of past activity levels to anticipated future activity levels. Extrapolations beyond the upper and lower bounds of past observations are highly subjective. If, for example, the highest activity level observed in the past was 4,100 units per month and we wished to predict cost to manufacture 4,600 units per month, an estimate based on past data may be highly inaccurate, because the past data do not reflect experience with output over 4,100 units.

The limits within which a cost projection may be valid is the *relevant range* for that estimate. The relevant range would include only those activity levels for which the assumed cost relationships used in the estimate are considered to hold. Thus, when past data are used, the relevant range for the projection is usually between the upper and lower limits of the past activity levels for which data are available.

Although the use of past data for future cost estimation has limitations, there are many cases in which it works quite well. In many estimates, past data, even if outside the relevant range, are adequate representations of the cost relationships that are likely to hold in the future. Moreover, reliance on past data is relatively inexpensive. It may be the only readily available, cost effective basis for estimating costs.

Past data do show the relationships that held in prior periods and, at the least, may be a meaningful starting point for estimating future costs as long as their limitations are recognized. In the remainder of this chapter, we discuss specific methods of using past data to estimate future costs.

Preparing a Scattergraph

Plotting past costs against past activity levels is often a useful way of visually depicting cost-activity relationships. Such a plot, called a **scattergraph,** will also indicate any significant change in the relationship between costs and activity at different activity levels.

Scattergraph   A plot of costs against past activity levels.

To prepare such a plot, we first obtain the relevant data. For example, if estimates of manufacturing overhead costs are to be based on direct labor-hours, we must obtain information about past manufacturing overhead costs and related past direct labor-hours.

Number of Observations.   The number of observations to include depends on the availability of the data, the variability within the data, and the relative costs and benefits of obtaining reliable data. A rule of thumb is to use three years of monthly data if the physical processes have not changed significantly within that time. If the company's operations have recently changed significantly, however, data that predate the change may not be useful. If cost and activity levels are highly stable, then a relatively short period (12 months or so) may be adequate.

Data for the past 15 months were collected for Estimators, Inc., to estimate variable and fixed manufacturing overhead. These data are presented and plotted on the scattergraph in Illustration 10–2. Once all the data points were plotted, a line was drawn to fit the points as closely as possible. The line was extended to the vertical axis on the scattergraph.

The slope of the line represents the estimated variable costs, and the intercept with the vertical axis represents an estimate of fixed costs. The slope is referred to as the variable cost because it represents the change in costs that occurs as a result of changes in activity. The intercept is referred to as the fixed cost because it represents the costs that would be incurred at a zero activity level given existing capacity *if the relationship plotted is valid from the data points back to the origin.* Note there are no observations of cost behavior around the zero activity level in this example, so the data do not indicate the costs that would occur when the activity level was zero. Rather, they provide an estimating equation useful within the relevant range. The slope and intercept may be measured using a ruler. However, preparing an estimate on this basis is subject to a good deal of error, especially if the points are scattered widely. Determination of the best fit is often a matter of "eyeball judgment." Consequently, scattergraphs are usually not used as the sole basis for cost estimates. Rather, they are used to illustrate the relationships between costs and activity levels and to point out any past data items that might be significantly out of line.

High-Low Cost Estimation

High-Low Cost Estimation A method of estimating costs based on two cost observations, usually costs at the highest activity level and costs at the lowest activity level.

If the cost relationships can be described by a straight line, any two points on a scattergraph may be used to prepare a cost-estimating equation. Typically, the *highest and the lowest activity points* are chosen—hence the name **high-low cost estimation.** Activity may be defined in terms of units of production, hours of work, or any other measure that makes sense for the problem at hand.

The slope of the total cost line, which estimates the increase of variable costs associated with an increase of one unit of activity, may be estimated by the equation:

$$\text{Variable cost } (V) = \frac{\text{Cost at highest activity} - \text{Cost at lowest activity}}{\text{Highest activity} - \text{Lowest activity}}$$

The intercept is estimated by taking the total cost at either activity level and subtracting the estimated variable cost for that activity level.

$$\text{Fixed cost } (F) = \frac{\text{Total cost at}}{\text{highest activity}} - [\text{Variable cost} \times \text{Highest activity}]$$

or

$$\text{Fixed cost} = \frac{\text{Total cost at}}{\text{lowest activity}} - [\text{Variable cost} \times \text{Lowest activity}]$$

Illustration 10–2   **Data and Scattergraph for Cost Estimation, Estimators, Inc.**

Time Period	Overhead Costs	Machine-Hours (MH)
1	$2,107	62
2	2,040	62
3	2,916	120
4	2,322	71
5	1,896	50
6	2,471	95
7	3,105	142
8	2,316	86
9	2,555	112
10	2,780	136
11	2,061	85
12	2,910	103
13	2,835	96
14	2,715	101
15	1,986	53

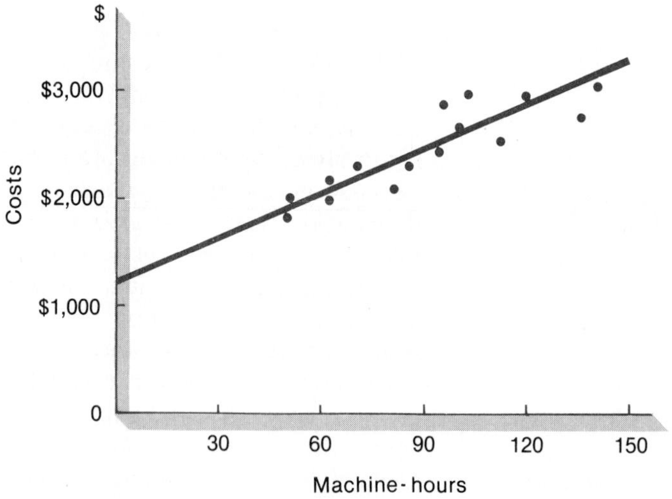

Based on the data for Estimators, Inc., in Illustration 10–2, the highest activity level is 142 machine-hours (MH). At this activity level, total manufacturing overhead costs are $3,105. The lowest activity level is 50 hours, with manufacturing overhead costs of $1,896. Substituting these data in the equation for variable cost yields:

$$\text{Variable cost per MH} = \frac{\$3,105 - \$1,896}{142 \text{ MH} - 50 \text{ MH}}$$

$$= \frac{\$1,209}{92 \text{ MH}}$$

$$= \underline{\underline{\$13.141 \text{ per MH}}}$$

To obtain the fixed cost estimate, either the highest or lowest activity level and costs may be used. Assuming the highest activity is used:

$$Fixed\ cost = \$3,105 - (\$13.141 \times 142\ MH)$$
$$= \$3,105 - \$1,866$$
$$= \underline{\underline{\$1,239}}$$

An estimate for the costs at any given activity level can be computed using the equation:

$$TC = F + VX$$
$$Total\ cost = \$1,239 + (\$13.141 \times specified\ MH)$$

For the 115 hours required to produce 4,600 units, the total cost is:

$$Total\ cost = \$1,239 + (\$13.141 \times 115\ MH)$$
$$= \$1,239 + \$1,511$$
$$= \underline{\underline{\$2,750}}$$

While the high-low method is easy to apply, care must be taken to assure that the two points used to prepare the estimates are representative of cost and activity relationships over the range of activity for which the prediction is made. The highest and lowest points could, however, represent unusual circumstances. When this happens, one should choose the highest and lowest points within the normal range of activity.

The scattergraph can be used graphically to illustrate cost-activity relationships based on past experience. Whenever costs and activity levels can be plotted in two-dimensional space, the scattergraph is a useful visual display. We recommend using it in conjunction with other cost-estimation methods.

Statistical Cost Estimation (Regression)

Regression Statistical procedure to determine the relationship between variables.

Regression techniques are designed to generate a line that best fits a set of data points. Because the regression procedure uses all data points, the resulting estimates have a broader base than estimates based only on high-low points.

In addition, regression techniques generate a number of additional statistics that under certain assumptions enable a manager to determine how well the estimated regression equation describes the relationship between costs and activities. The regression process also permits inclusion of more than one predictor. This latter feature may be useful when more than one activity affects costs. For example, variable manufacturing overhead may be a function of both direct labor-hours and the quantities of direct materials processed.

A comprehensive discussion of regression is not possible within the scope of this text. Many moderately priced hand calculators have regression capabilities, and most computers used in business and academia are equipped with regression programs. Although it is possible to calculate regressions by hand, for practical reasons business applications of regression are computed electronically. Therefore, we leave descriptions of the computational details to statistics and computer courses. Instead, we deal with regression techniques from the standpoint of accountants and managers as users of regression estimates already made for them.

A limited description of the use of regression programs for cost estimation follows. The appendix to this chapter discusses some of the more technical considerations that may interest users of such programs.

Obtaining Regression Estimates

Independent Variables The X-terms, or predictors, on the right-hand side of a regression equation.

Dependent Variable The Y term or the left-hand side in regression.

The most important step in obtaining regression estimates for cost estimation is to establish the existence of a logical relationship between activities that affect costs and the cost to be estimated. These activities are referred to as predictors, *X terms,* **independent variables,** or the *right-hand side (RHS)* of a regression equation. The cost to be estimated may be called the **dependent variable,** the *Y term,* or the *left-hand side (LHS)* of the regression equation.

Although regression programs will accept any data for the Y and X terms, entering numbers that have no logical relationship may result in misleading estimates. The accountant has the important responsibility of making sure that the activities are logically related to costs.

Assume, for example, that a logical relationship exists between machine-hours and manufacturing overhead costs for Estimators, Inc. Assume that a logical relationship also exists between direct materials costs and overhead costs. This latter assumption would be reasonable if the manufacturing process employed a substantial amount of materials and overhead costs included materials handling and storage. The data on manufacturing overhead costs, machine-hours, and direct materials costs for this process are presented in Illustration 10–3.

Estimators, Inc., first estimates costs using simple regression—or only one independent variable—to predict manufacturing overhead costs. They choose machine-hours, so past data on machine-hours would be entered as the X, or independent, variable. Past data on manufacturing overhead costs would be entered as the Y, or dependent, variable. The computer output giving the estimated relationship between machine-hours and manufacturing overhead for this situation is as follows:

$$\text{Total manufacturing overhead} = \$1{,}334 + \$12.373 \text{ per MH}$$

For cost-estimation purposes, when reading the output of a regression program, the **intercept** term, $1,334$, is an estimate of fixed costs. Of course, it should be used with caution because the intercept is outside of the relevant range of observations. The coefficient of the X term (in this example, 12.373 per machine-hour) is an estimate of the variable cost per machine-hour. This is the **slope of the cost line.** The coefficients are often labeled b on

Illustration 10-3   **Data for Regression Estimation, Estimators, Inc.**

Overhead Costs	Machine-Hours	Direct Materials Costs
$2,107	62	$1,964
2,040	62	1,851
2,916	120	3,615
2,322	71	2,902
1,896	50	1,136
2,471	95	2,315
3,105	142	5,013
2,316	86	2,751
2,555	112	2,816
2,780	136	3,461
2,061	85	1,702
2,910	103	3,819
2,835	96	3,940
2,715	101	3,613
1,986	53	1,741

the program output. Thus, the cost-estimation equation based on the regression results above would be:

$$\text{Total costs} = \text{Intercept} + b \text{ times MH}$$

Substituting 115 MH into the equation yields:

$$\text{Total costs} = \$1,334 + (\$12.373 \times 115 \text{ MH})$$
$$= \$1,334 + \$1,423$$
$$= \underline{\underline{\$2,757}}$$

This estimate of cost behavior is shown graphically in Illustration 10–4.

Correlation Coefficients

In addition to the cost-estimating equation, the regression program provides other useful statistics. The **correlation coefficient** (R) is a measure of the proximity of the data points to the regression line. The closer R is to 1.0, the closer the data points are to the regression line. Conversely, the closer R is to zero, the poorer the fit of the regression line.

The square of R is called R-square or the coefficient of determination. R-square is interpreted as the proportion of the variation in Y explained by the right-hand side of the regression equation; that is, by the X predictors.

The **adjusted R-square** is the correlation coefficient squared and adjusted for the number of independent variables used to make the estimate. This adjustment to R-square recognizes that as the number of independent variables increases, R-square (unadjusted) increases. For example, if there are as many independent variables as there are observations, R-square (unadjusted) would be 1.0. Statisticians believe that adjusted R-square is a better measure of the association between X and Y when there is more than one X than the unadjusted R-squared value.

Correlation Coefficient A measure of the linear relationship between two or more variables, such as cost and some activity measure.

Illustration 10-4   **Scattergraph with Regression-Estimated Cost Line, Estimators, Inc.**

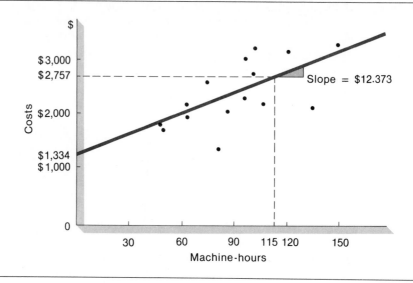

For Estimators, Inc., the correlation coefficients, *R*-square and adjusted *R*-square, are:

Correlation coefficient *(R)*	.896
R-square	.802
Adjusted *R*-square	.787

Since the adjusted *R*-square is .787, it can be said that 78.7 percent of the changes in overhead costs can be explained by changes in machine-hours. For data drawn from accounting records, an adjusted *R*-square of .787 would be considered an exceptionally good fit.

The most commonly used regression technique is called *ordinary least squares regression*. With this technique, the regression line is computed so that the sum of the squares of the vertical distances from each point on the scattergraph to the regression line is minimized. Thus, as a practical consideration, it is important to beware of including data points that vary significantly from the usual. Because the regression program seeks to minimize squared differences, the inclusion of these extreme outliers may significantly affect the results. Consequently, organizations often exclude data for periods of such unusual occurrences as strikes, extreme weather conditions, and shutdowns for equipment retooling. A scattergraph often reveals such outliers so they can then be easily identified and omitted.

Regression with Multiple Predictors: Activity Based Costing

While the prediction of overhead costs in the previous example, with its adjusted *R*-square of .787, was considered good, management may wish to see if a better estimate might be obtained using additional predictor variables as in activity based costing (discussed in Chapter 2). In such a case, they examine the nature of the operation to determine which additional predictors might be useful in deriving a cost-estimation equation.

Assume Estimators, Inc., has determined that direct materials costs may also affect manufacturing overhead. The results of using both machine-hours (X_1) and direct materials costs (X_2) as *predictors* of overhead (Y) were obtained using a computer program. The computer output from the program using machine-hours and direct materials costs yields the prediction equation:

$$\text{Manufacturing overhead costs} = \text{Intercept} + b_1X_1 + b_2X_2$$
$$= \$1{,}334 + \$4.359X_1 + .258X_2$$

REAL WORLD APPLICATION

Estimating Cost Behavior in a Hospital

In an article titled "Management Accounting in Hospitals: A Case Study," Professor Robert Kaplan described some work that a research team made up of faculty and students was doing to help a hospital improve its cost accounting system.* They initially found costs were being reported without regard to the volume of activity in the department. For example, it was impossible to determine whether high nursing costs had been incurred because of inefficiency or because the number of patients was large. The researchers attempted to estimate a cost model, $TC = F + VX$, where X refers to a measure of activity such as number of patient-days or number of procedures performed in the radiology department.

After running the analysis, Kaplan and his students discovered that the "costs" of materials (for example, medical supplies) reported in the records were actually cash expenditures recorded as "costs" when the materials were acquired. A large purchase of materials in one month could show up in the records as a large cost in that month, followed by almost no cost in the following month because materials were not acquired. The hospital administrators had no aversion to putting the cost system on an accrual basis, but such a step would require considerable time and effort.

The researchers then turned to the analysis of personnel costs, which made up a substantial portion of the hospital's total operating costs. One problem in analyzing labor costs over time is that costs increase with increases in wage rates. The researchers dealt with this problem by using hours worked as the dependent variable and various measures of activity as the independent variables. Using this approach, the researchers were able to identify relationships between activity levels and hours worked. For example, one estimate was that RN-hours varied with patient-days such that each additional patient-day required about two extra RN-hours. If the cost of RN time is expected to be, say, $20 per hour, including fringe benefits, then the unit variable cost for RN costs would be $40 per patient-day.

The researchers found that "what seemed like a simple task at first turned out to be much more difficult to do correctly. One constantly had to question the process generating the data being used. . . . However, we have gained a lot of insight into the current operating procedures of the hospital."† The researchers also found that the statistical analysis was useful in suggesting questions and subsequent recommendations to hospital administrators.

* Robert S. Kaplan, "Management Accounting in Hospitals: A Case Study," in *Accounting for Social Goals* (New York: Harper & Row, 1974), pp. 131–48.

† Ibid., p. 147.

where X_1 refers to machine-hours and X_2 refers to direct materials costs. (The intercepts in the simple and multiple regressions round to the same whole number by coincidence.) The statistics supplied with the output are:

Correlation coefficient (multiple R)	.976
Multiple R-squared	.952
Adjusted multiple R-squared	.944

The correlation coefficient (now expressed as *multiple R* because it is related to more than one predictor variable) for this regression is .976, and the adjusted multiple R-squared is .944. Both of these are an improvement over the results obtained when the regression equation included only machine-hours. Improved results may be expected because some overhead costs may be related to direct materials costs but not to machine-hours (for example, storeroom maintenance).

To prepare a cost estimate using this multiple regression equation requires not only the estimated machine-hours for the coming period but the direct materials costs as well. The additional data requirements for multiple regression models may limit their usefulness in many applications. Of course, in planning for the next period's production activity, companies will usually have already estimated direct materials costs and machine-hours, and in such a situation the added costs of obtaining data may be quite low.

For example, Estimators, Inc., estimates its direct materials cost to be $.80 per output unit based on engineering estimates of materials needed and accounting estimates of direct materials costs. Production is estimated at 4,600 units, so direct materials costs of $3,680 (4,600 units × $.80 per unit) are expected in the coming period.

Substituting the 115 machine-hours and the $3,680 direct materials costs in the regression equation results in the following overhead estimate:

$$\text{Overhead} = \$1,334 + (\$4.359 \times 115) + (.258 \times \$3,680)$$
$$= \$1,334 + \$501 + \$949$$
$$= \underline{\underline{\$2,784}}$$

This estimate has the advantage of being based on two factors (machine time and direct materials) that appear to be jointly affecting overhead costs. The correlation coefficient is higher for this equation than for the single predictor equation. An increase in R, alone, should not be the sole criterion for selecting a regression model; however, it is important that the independent variables have a logical relation to the dependent variable.

Using the *bs* as Variable Cost Estimates

When using a simple linear regression, the intercept is often considered analogous to fixed costs and the slope, to variable cost. Indeed, in many companies, regression estimates are used for estimating the fixed and variable components of manufacturing overhead for overhead application and analysis. Care should be exercised when doing this, however. For example, it is possible to have negative intercepts in empirical estimates, but it is highly unlikely that a company would have negative fixed costs.

If more than one predictor variable is used, as in Estimators, Inc.'s multiple regression above, the interpretation of the bs as variable costs is somewhat more hazardous. The assignment of coefficient values under regression is unstable if the predictor variables are correlated with one another. For the multiple regression of Estimators, Inc., the following correlation matrix was part of the computer output. It shows that the machine-hours and direct material dollars are highly correlated with one another (that is, a correlation of .832).

Variable	**b**	
Machine-hours	4.359	
Direct materials cost	.258	
CORRELATION MATRIX:		
	DLH	DMC
DLH	1.00	.832
DMC	.832	1.00

Multicollinearity Correlation between two or more independent variables in a multiple regression equation.

This means that there is overlapping explanatory power among the two predictors. This problem is referred to as **multicollinearity**. It does not affect the Y estimate, but rather, it affects the interpretation of the contribution that each of the Xs (that is, direct material dollars and machine-hours) is making to the prediction of Y.

Regression Must Be Used with Caution. A regression estimate is still only an estimate. Computerized statistical techniques sometimes have an aura of truth about them that is undeserved. In fact, a regression estimate may be little better than an eyeball estimate based on a scattergraph. Regression has advantages, however. It is objective; it provides a number of statistics not available from other methods; and it may be the only feasible method when more than one predictor is used.

Regression is so accessible that it can be used indiscriminately with unfortunate results. We recommend that users of regression (1) fully understand the methodology and its limitations (2) specify the model, that is, the hypothesized relationship between costs and cost predictors; (3) know the characteristics of the data being used; and (4) examine a plot of the data.

Comparison of Cost Estimates

Each cost-estimation method may yield a different estimate of the costs that are likely to result from a particular management decision. This underscores the advantages of using two or more methods to arrive at a final estimate. The different estimates of manufacturing overhead that resulted from the use of four different estimation methods for Estimators, Inc., are summarized in Illustration 10–5.

The figures are relatively close, but there are differences. While it is impossible to state which one is best, management may find that having all four alternatives gives the best indication of the likely range within which

Illustration 10-5　　　**Summary of Cost Estimates, Estimators, Inc.**

Method	Total Estimated Costs	Fixed Estimated Costs	Estimated Variable Cost
Account analysis	$2,631	$1,205	$12.40 per MH[a]
High-low	2,750	1,239	$13.141 per MH
Simple regression (MH)	2,757	1,334	$12.373 per MH
Multiple regression (MH + DMC[b])	2,784	1,334	$ 4.359 per MH +$ .258 per DMC

[a] MH = Machine-hours.

[b] DMC = Direct material costs.

actual costs will fall. Moreover, by observing the range of cost estimates, management may be better able to determine whether more data need to be gathered. If decisions are the same for all four cost estimates, then management may conclude that further information gathering is not warranted.

LEARNING CURVES

The relationship between costs and independent variables is not always linear. A systematic nonlinear relationship has been found when employees gain experience performing a particular task. As their experience increases, their productivity improves and costs per unit decrease. Experience, or learning, obviously affects direct labor costs, but it also affects costs that are related to direct labor, like supervision and many others. In some cases, materials costs may be affected due to reductions in spoilage and waste.

Learning Phenomenon A systematic relationship between the amount of experience in performing a task and the time required to carry out the task.

The **learning phenomenon** often occurs when new production methods are introduced, when new products (either goods or services) are made, and when new employees are hired. For example, the effect of learning on the cost of aircraft manufacturing is well known. Manufacturers of products for the defense industry often develop and produce goods with cost-based contracts. These contracts may recognize the effect of learning by establishing a lower cost for the second item of an order than for the first, a lower cost for the fourth than for the second, and so forth.

For example, National Electronics, Inc., makes an electronic navigational guidance system that is used for spacecraft, aircraft, and submarines. The direct labor to make the system is subject to an 80 percent *cumulative* **learning curve.** This means that the unit *average* time required for two units is 80 percent of the time required for one unit; the unit *average* time for four units is 80 percent of the *average* time required per unit for two units; and so forth.

Learning Curve The mathematical or graphic representation of the learning phenomenon.

The first unit of a production batch, or run, of guidance systems is estimated to require 1,250 direct labor-hours. If the 80 percent cumulative learning curve is used, then the *average* for two units is estimated to be 1,000 hours (.80 × 1,250 hours), a total of 2,000 hours for both units. Thus, the second unit takes 750 hours to produce (750 = 2,000 − 1,250). Four units would take an average of 800 hours each (.80 × 1,000 hours), or a total of 3,200 hours. This means that a total of 1,200 hours (3,200 − 2,000) must be expended to produce the third and fourth units. As the labor-hours change, so do the costs that are affected by labor-hours.

Mathematically, the learning curve effect can be expressed as:[1]

$$Y = aX^b$$

where

Y = *Average* number of labor-hours required for the first X units.
a = Number of labor-hours required for the first unit.
X = Cumulative number of units produced.
b = Index of learning equal to the log of the learning rate divided by the log of 2; for the example with an 80 percent cumulative learning rate, b = −.322.

Thus, the number of labor-hours from the National Electronics example could be derived as follows:

	Number of Labor-Hours			
X	**Average (Y)**	**Total**	**Marginal**	**Computations**
1	1,250	1,250	1,250	
2	1,000	2,000[a]	750[b]	$Y = 1{,}250 \times (2^{-.322}) = 1{,}000$
3	878	2,634[a]	634[b]	$Y = 1{,}250 \times (3^{-.322}) = 878$
4	800	3,200	566	$Y = 1{,}250 \times (4^{-.322}) = 800$
.	.	.	.	.
.	.	.	.	.
.	.	.	.	.
8	640	5,120		$Y = 1{,}250 \times (8^{-.322}) = 640$

[a] 2,000 = 2 units × 1,000 hours,
2,634 = 3 units × 878 hours,
and so on.
[b] 750 = 2,000 hours − 1,250 hours,
634 = 2,634 hours − 2,000 hours,
and so on.

Illustration 10–6 presents the total and average labor-hours required for National Electronics, Inc. The curvilinear nature of the relationship between activity volume and labor-hours shows that the learning effects are large initially but become increasingly smaller as employees learn more about how to make the product.

The function

$$Y = aX^b$$

is curvilinear, as shown in Illustration 10–6. The function is linear when expressed in logs because

$$\log Y = \log a + b \log X$$

---

[1] For more detail on accounting applications of learning curves, see F. P. Kollaritsch and R. B. Jordan, "The Learning Curve: Concepts and Applications," in *The Managerial and Cost Accountant's Handbook*, eds. H. A. Black and J. D. Edwards (Homewood, Ill.: Dow Jones-Irwin, 1979), pp. 971–1017; and W. J. Morse, "Reporting Production Costs that Follow the Learning Curve Phenomenon," *The Accounting Review*, October 1972, pp. 761–73.

Illustration 10-6   **Labor-Hours and Volume Graphs, National Electronics, Inc.**

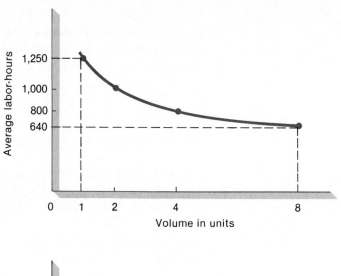

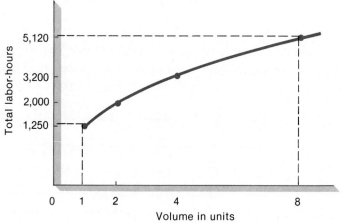

Illustration 10-7   **Labor-Hours and Volume—Log-Log Relationship**

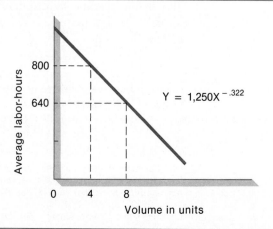

$$Y = 1{,}250X^{-.322}$$

so the function is linear when plotted on log-log paper as shown in Illustration 10–7. A good approximation of the average labor-hours required for X units can be obtained from a plot on log-log paper.

Assume that National Electronics, Inc., estimates the variable cost of producing each unit as follows:

Direct materials cost	$40,000 per unit
Direct labor	$20 per hour
Variable manufacturing overhead	$1,000 per unit plus 60 percent of direct labor costs

So, the variable manufacturing cost per unit is estimated to be:

Unit No.	Direct Materials	Direct Labor	Variable Manufacturing Overhead	Total Variable Manufacturing Cost of the Unit
1	$40,000	$20 × 1,250 hours = $25,000	$1,000 + (.6 × $25,000) = $16,000	$81,000
2	40,000	$20 × 750 hours = $15,000	$1,000 + (.6 × $15,000) = $10,000	65,000
3	40,000	$20 × 634 hours = $12,680	$1,000 + (.6 × $12,680) = $8,608	61,288
4	40,000	$20 × 566 hours = $11,320	$1,000 + (.6 × $11,320) = $7,792	59,112

Applications of Learning Curves to Accounting

The learning phenomenon applies to time, thus it could affect any costs that are a function of time. Hourly labor costs per unit would be affected, while straight piecework pay per unit would not. Any overhead costs that are affected by labor time would also be affected. For example, if indirect labor is a variable cost, reductions in worker time could result in a reduction in indirect labor.

Whenever costs are estimated, the potential impact of learning should be considered. The learning phenomenon can affect costs used in inventory valuation, costs used in decision making, and costs used in performance evaluation. However, learning curves usually apply only to the early phases of production. After the steady state is achieved, costs tend to stabilize.

Inventory Valuation. Failing to recognize learning effects can have some unexpected consequences, as shown in this example. Suppose production of a new product starts in January and continues through the year. The direct materials cost is $10 per unit throughout the year. Because of learning, the labor-hours (cost) per unit drops from 1 hour, at $16 per hour, in January to .25 hour in December. Manufacturing overhead, which is all fixed, is $8,000. The accountants estimate that 1,000 units will be produced in January, requiring 1,000 direct labor-hours, so they apply this overhead to units at the rate of $8 per hour for inventory valuation. This same rate is (mistakenly) used throughout the year. In December of the same year, 1,000 units were produced, requiring only 250 direct labor-hours. Fixed manufacturing over-

Illustration 10-8   **Effect of Learning on Inventory Valuation**

		Unit Inventory Value	
		December	
	January	**Is**	**Should Be**
Direct materials	$10	$10	$10
Direct labor	16 (= 1 hour × $16)	4 (= .25 hour × $16)	4
Manufacturing overhead applied	8 (= 1 hour × $8)	2 (= .25 hour × $8)	8
	$34	$16	$22

head was $8,000. As shown in Illustration 10–8, the overhead was applied at $8 per hour, which turned out to be only $2 per unit. The amount of overhead applied per unit should have been $8 per unit, like it was in January.

Decision Making. AAA Company is considering producing a new product. Fixed costs would be unaffected by the product. The variable cost of making and selling the first unit of the product is $40 per unit, while the selling price is $38. At first glance, the product appears unprofitable because it doesn't even cover variable costs. However, because of learning, the variable cost will drop from $40 to $20 by the end of the first year of production, making it much more profitable.

Performance Evaluation. First National Bank has developed labor time and cost standards for some of its clerical activities. These activities were subject to the learning curve phenomenon. The bank management observed that time spent on these activities systematically exceeded the standard. Upon investigating the problem, management found high personnel turnover, which meant the activities were carried out by inexperienced people. After changes were made in personnel policy, personnel turnover was reduced and the jobs were staffed with more experienced people. Hence, the time spent on clerical activities no longer exceeded standards.

SUMMARY   Accurate cost estimation helps management to make informed decisions concerning the incurrence of future costs and how future costs may vary if conditions change. This chapter discusses four methods of cost estimation: (1) account analysis, (2) engineering estimates, (3) scattergraph and high-low estimates, and (4) statistical methods (usually employing regression analysis). Different methods of estimation are likely to produce different estimates of costs. Consequently, it is often desirable to use more than one approach and to permit management to apply its own best estimate to those arrived at by the controller's staff.

Account analysis calls for the identification of costs and judgment determination of whether a cost is fixed or variable in relation to the activity concerning which a decision is being made. Knowledge of the decision context and of the way an organization's costs relate to cost objects is very important. Once the fixed and variable portions are estimated, the total cost can be estimated by adding the fixed portion to the product of the variable portion per activity level and the activity level. The advantages of the method are its relative ease of application and its use of managerial experience and judgment. The disadvantage is that heavy reliance on judgmental decisions may cause estimates to be biased toward the decision makers' personal biases or perceptions. Classification of cost behavior can be incorporated into the chart of accounts coding scheme to help facilitate future preparation of cost estimates.

Engineering estimates involve careful measurement of the actual cost-causing process. An engineer breaks the process into parts and compares what he observes to standards, specifications, and established scientific relationships. Based on these comparisons, the engineer is able to forecast what costs may be in the future given certain conditions. One form of the engineering approach to cost estimation is the time-and-motion study. The advantage of the engineering approach is that it can detail each step required to perform an operation. This provides a useful means of reviewing a company's total manufacturing process. Disadvantages are that the engineering approach is often quite expensive and that engineering estimates are often based on particular past conditions that may not occur in the future.

Scattergraphs and high-low estimates use past cost behaviors and their relation to some activity measure to estimate future costs given a specific activity level. This approach (and any other approach that uses past data) is limited to future estimates that are made within the relevant range of past activity levels. A scattergraph is a plotting of past costs along the vertical axis and of some activity measure along the horizontal axis. If the points fall into a roughly linear pattern, a line can be estimated to fit these points.

One method of determining the line is the high-low method. The high-low method takes the cost difference between the highest and lowest activity levels and divides it by the difference in activity levels. This gives the slope of the line connecting the cost point at the highest activity level with the cost point at the lowest activity level. The slope represents the estimated variable cost per unit. Estimated fixed cost is determined by taking the total cost at either the highest or lowest activity level and subtracting from it the variable cost at that level. This approach is useful as an easy-to-apply method to derive cost estimates and to illustrate graphically cost behavior at different activity levels. It has the advantage of overcoming the subjectivity of the account analysis approach and the complexity of the engineering approach while still being simple to apply. Disadvantages include a tendency to project costs beyond the relevant range and the possibility of the highest and lowest points being unrepresentative of typical operating conditions.

The primary statistical method is called ordinary least squares regression. Like the scattergraph approach, past data are used, but unlike the high-low approach to estimating costs, all of the data points are used to estimate future variable and fixed costs at expected activity levels. In addition to cost estimates, regression is able to provide a number of additional statistics that aid in the estimate.

The focus of the regression portion of the chapter is on obtaining a basic understanding of the approach and the initial cost estimation from regression output provided by computers or calculators. Data are plotted on a scattergraph, and a mathematically determined line of best fit (minimal variation) is formed. Care must be used to find any unrepresentative outliers and to restrict cost estimates to the relevant range. It is also important to understand how independent variables (predictors) are used and how their relationship to the dependent variable (the cost to be estimated) helps to arrive at a regression equation. The correlation coefficient (R) and the adjusted R-square help to indicate the amount of the cost variation that is explained by the predictors. Simple regression uses only one predictor, while multiple regression uses more than one predictor to help explain a particular cost.

A common nonlinear relationship between costs and activity is the systematic relation between labor time and experience. This learning curve phenomenon implies that unit costs go down as more and more units are made (up to a point) because labor time per unit decreases. The potential impact of the phenomenon should be considered whenever costs are estimated.

TERMS AND CONCEPTS

The following terms and concepts should be familiar to you after reading this chapter.

Account Analysis	Intercept and Slope of Cost Line
Adjusted *R*-square	Learning Curve
Correlation Coefficient	Learning Phenomenon
Dependent Variable	Multicollinearity
Engineering Estimates	*R*-square
Estimate	Regression
High-Low Cost Estimation	Relevant Range
Independent Variable	Scattergraph

Note: The self-study problem for this chapter follows the appendix.

SUPPLEMENTARY READINGS

Belkaoui, Ahmed. *Learning Curve: A Management Accounting Tool.* Westport, Conn.: Quorum Books, 1986.

Crocker, William W. "Underestimating the Costs of Major Weapon Systems: Are Reforms on the Way?" *GAO Review,* Spring 1986, pp. 14–17, 55–56.

Evans, John H., III; Barry L. Lewis; and James M. Patton. "An Economic Modeling Approach to Contingency Theory and Management Control." *Accounting, Organizations, and Society,* December 1986, p. 483.

Kaplan, R. S. "Management Accounting in Hospitals: A Case Study." *Accounting for Social Goals: Budgeting and Analysis of Non-Market Projects.*

LeBrone, H. "The Learning Curve: A Case Study." *Management Accounting,* February 1978.

Rankin, Larry J. and Robert J. Campbell. "Regression Analysis in Planning and Testing." *CPA Journal,* May 1986, pp. 50–58.

Roser, Sherman R., and Lawrence C. Sundby. "Learning Curves and Inflation." *Cost and Management,* July–August 1985, pp. 30–34 (published in Canada).

Russell, Grant W., and David M. Dilts. "Costing the Unknown Product." *CMA—The Management Accounting Magazine,* March–April 1986, p. 38.

Van Alstyne, Byron. "Regression Analysis Helps Stockroom Capacity Planning." *Production and Inventory Management Review,* July 1986, pp. 28, 31, 44.

Washburn, Stewart A. "Establishing Strategy and Determining Costs in the Pricing Decision." *Business Marketing,* July 1985, pp. 64–78.

APPENDIX: Technical Notes on Regression	This appendix discusses some of the practical implementation and technical problems that often arise when regression analysis is used.
Practical Implementation Problems	Computers and hand-held calculators have greatly simplified regression analysis and made it available to more people. Consequently, this method has been increasingly used and potentially misused. In particular, people may be tempted to enter many variables into a regression model without careful thought to their validity. The results can be disastrous.

Some of the more common problems with using regression estimates include: (1) attempting to fit a linear equation to nonlinear data, (2) failing to exclude outliers, and (3) including predictors with apparent but spurious relationships.

Effect of Nonlinear Relationships

The effect of attempting to fit a linear model to nonlinear data is likely to be seen when a company is operating close to capacity limits. Close to maximum capacity, costs accelerate more rapidly than activity due to shift differentials and overtime premiums paid to employees, increased maintenance and repair costs for equipment, and similar factors. The linear cost estimate understates the slope of the cost line in the ranges close to capacity. This situation is shown in Illustration 10–9.

One way to overcome the problem would be to define a relevant range of activity up to, say, 80 percent capacity and use the range for one set of cost-estimating regression equations. Another equation could be derived for the 81 percent to 100 percent capacity levels.

Another approach is to use nonlinear regression techniques to estimate the curve directly. However, nonlinear regression does not provide a constant variable cost estimate—the estimate is different at each level.

Effect of Outliers

Because regression seeks to minimize the sum of the squared deviations from the regression line, observations that lie a significant distance away from the line may have an overwhelming effect on the regression estimates. Illustration 10–10 shows a case in which most of the data points lie close to a straight line, but due to the effect of one significant outlier, the computed regression line is a significant distance from most of the points.

This kind of problem can easily arise in accounting settings. Suppose a year's worth of supplies was purchased and expensed entirely in one month,

Illustration 10-9   **Effect of Fitting a Linear Model to Nonlinear Data**

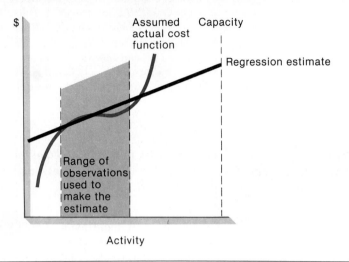

Illustration 10-10   **Effect of Failure to Exclude Outliers**

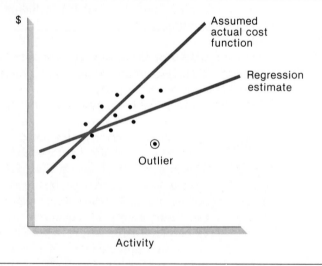

or a large adjustment was made for underaccruing payroll taxes. The accounting records in such cases are clearly abnormal with respect to the activity measure. An inspection of a plot of the data can sometimes reveal this problem.

When an extreme outlier appears in a data set, scrutiny of the output from the regression equation will rarely identify it. Instead, a plot of the regression line on the data points is usually needed. If multiple predictors are used, an outlier will be even more difficult to find. The best way to avoid this problem is to examine the data in advance and eliminate highly unusual observations *before* running the regression.

Spurious Relationships

It is sometimes tempting to feed the computer a lot of data and let the regression program "find" relationships among variables. This can lead to spurious relationships. For example, there may appear to be a relationship between Variable 1 and Variable 2, when, in fact, Variable 3, which was left out of the equation, explains the situation. Early medical studies that found an apparent relationship between cholesterol and heart disease were criticized because the relationship may have been spurious. Numerous other variables that may have been correlated with both cholesterol and heart disease, such as age and diet, were left out. Moreover, later studies found there were two types of cholesterol, each with opposite effects on heart disease.

It is important to have a good model for constructing regression equations. A cause-and-effect relation should exist between the predictor variable and the dependent variable. If such a relation does not exist, it is still possible to obtain a good fit and a regression estimate that, on the surface, appears significant. However, there is no assurance that the relation will continue into the future.

For example, there may be a good *statistical* relation between indirect labor costs and energy costs. One might create a regression equation using such a relation and find that the regression explains much of the change in indirect labor costs. However, there is no *logical* relation between the two costs. Both indirect labor and energy costs may, in part, be driven by inflationary factors, but there is no cause-and-effect relationship between them.

Confidence Intervals for Cost Estimates

When making predictions about future costs, it is almost impossible to develop an estimate that will be exactly equal to the costs that are finally incurred. While it is not possible to eliminate all estimation error, it is possible to place bounds on an estimate so that a decision maker can know the range of likely costs. These bounds are usually expressed in the form of a *prediction interval,* sometimes called a *confidence interval.*

A prediction interval represents a range within which the actual cost is expected to fall a specified percentage of the time. Thus, a 95 percent prediction interval would represent a range within which the actual costs are expected to fall 95 percent of the time. The boundaries of a prediction interval are based on the assumption that the residuals from a regression are normally distributed. If this assumption holds, then the boundaries are equal to the predicted Y value plus or minus the standard error of the estimate of Y times the t-statistic for the specified prediction level. This may be expressed mathematically as:

$$Y \pm t \times SE_Y$$

The t-statistic would be obtained from a table of Student's t, which can be found in statistics textbooks or in most applications from a computer output. The wider the desired prediction interval, the larger the value of t, all other things equal.

The standard error of estimate (SE_Y) for a simple regression is:

$$SE_Y = SE \sqrt{1 + \frac{1}{n} + \frac{(X' - \overline{X})^2}{\Sigma(X_i - \overline{X})^2}}$$

where

SE = Standard error of the regression.
n = Number of observations.
X' = Value of X for which the estimate is desired.
$\overline{X}$ = Mean of the X values in the data set.
X_i = Value of each X in the data set.

The more distant the specified X value is from the mean, the wider the prediction interval.

For example, assume management of Estimators, Inc., had estimated the overhead costs for 115 machine-hours as follows:

$$\begin{aligned} Y &= \$1,334 + \$12.373 \text{ per MH} \\ &= \$1,334 + \$12.373 \times 115 \text{ MH} \\ &= \underline{\underline{\$2,757}} \end{aligned}$$

The computer output for the regression indicated a standard error for the regression of \$182. The standard error of estimate for a Y based on 115 machine-hours is \$192, computed as follows:

$$\begin{aligned} SE_Y &= \$182 \times \sqrt{1 + \frac{1}{15} + \frac{(115 - 91.6)^2}{11,455.6}} \\ &= \$182 \times \sqrt{1 + .06667 + .04780} \\ &= \$182 \times 1.05568 \\ &= \underline{\underline{\$192}} \end{aligned}$$

The computer would provide the information necessary to construct the prediction interval and, in many cases, would compute the interval itself. In this example, we obtain the following output from the computer (or from a statistics book for the t-statistic):

Standard error of the regression	\$182
Standard error of estimate (115 hours)	\$192
t-statistic for 95% confidence interval, $n = 15$; $n - 2 = 13$	2.160

The prediction interval is computed as:

$$\$2,757 \pm (\$192 \times 2.160) = \$2,757 \pm \$415$$

The upper limit of the prediction interval is:

$$\$3,172 = \$2,757 + \$415$$

and the lower limit is:

$$\$2,342 = \$2,757 - \$415$$

which means that we are 95 percent confident that the overhead will be between \$2,342 and \$3,172 when an activity level of 115 machine-hours is attained.

Assumptions About the Residuals

The differences between the *estimated* Y values (found on the regression line) and the actual Ys are called *residuals*. If a residual is random, its expected value is zero for any observation. There are three important assumptions about the residuals: (1) the residuals are independent of each other; (2) the variance of the residuals is constant over the range of independent variables; and (3) the residuals are normally distributed. Violation of these assumptions makes certain inferences about confidence intervals and the significance levels of *b*-estimates questionable.

If the residuals are not normally distributed, the residual for any observation may be statistically related to the residual for another observation. The expected value for the residual is not zero. One such condition in which residuals are related to each other because observations are related to each other over time is known as *serial correlation* or *autocorrelation*. When the residuals are related to each other, the correlation coefficients and the presence of autocorrelation may be tested by using the Durbin-Watson statistic, which is usually provided on the output when regression is run on a computer. Another approach is to obtain a plot of the residuals over time from the regression program. If there is a pattern in the plotted residuals, then an autocorrelation problem exists.

Heteroscedasticity

The variance in cost data may not be constant over all levels of costs. This condition is known as *heteroscedasticity*.

To determine if heteroscedasticity is present, a plot of the residuals over different values of Y is needed. If the scatter of residuals is not constant over these Y values, the assumption of constant variance may be rejected. The problem may be cured by transforming the variables (Xs and Ys) to their logarithms or square roots, or by constructing a regression with a new set of variables. Alternatively, one might adjust the confidence intervals at different activity levels.

We mention these assumptions because they are often violated in cost data. Consequently, we should be careful about the inferences that we draw from regressions. You should consult statistics books for more information about how to deal with violations of these assumptions.

Prediction Intervals for the *b*s

In many cases, it may be desirable to determine if the *b*s are significantly different from zero. The *t*-statistic is used to test for the significance of *b*s.

To test whether the computed *b* is statistically different from zero, a *t*-statistic is computed. This *t* is simply the value of *b* divided by its standard error (SE_b). For the data used in the simple regression for Estimators, Inc., the *t*-statistic for the coefficient is:

$$t = \frac{b}{SE_b}$$
$$= \frac{12.373}{1.703}$$
$$= 7.265$$

where the SE_b of 1.703 is given by the computer output. As a rule of thumb, a t of 2.0 or better may usually be considered significant. We reject the hypothesis that the regression results are due to chance and that the true value of b is zero.

To construct a 95 percent confidence interval around b, we would take the computed b and add or subtract the appropriate t value for the 95 percent confidence interval times the standard error of b. The confidence interval is:

$$b \pm t \times SE_b$$

The computer output for this example gives $SE_b = 1.703$.

The value of t for a 95 percent confidence interval may be obtained from a table of t values in a statistics book.

$$t_{SEb} = 2.160$$

Hence, the confidence intervals are:

$$b \pm 2.160 \times 1.703$$
$$= b \pm 3.678$$

With b equal to $12.373, the upper limit would be:

$$\$16.051 \text{ (that is, } \$12.373 + \$3.678)$$

while the lower confidence limit would be:

$$\$8.695 \text{ (that is, } \$12.373 - \$3.678)$$

We would be 95 percent confident that the variable cost coefficient is between $8.695 and $16.051. These limits are quite wide. To narrow the limits, it is necessary to construct a better-fitting regression.

SELF-STUDY PROBLEM: PROPYLON TEXTILES[2]

Propylon, the wonder fabric of the 1990s, was the brain child of Henry Carr, scion of an old banking family. Pursuing this special interest in polymers as a chemistry graduate student, Carr had created a synthetic compound whose polymer threads were far superior to any of the synthetics in the textile industry. The fabric was crease resistant, wrinkle free, and it simulated the appearance and feel of natural fiber fabrics. Propylon took the world by storm when production began three years ago. In addition to its versatility, propylon is extremely strong and durable, heat resistant, and "breathes" like natural fibers.

By the second year, Propylon Textiles had reached its current production level with 10 product lines. Now, after the third year of production, Natalie Martin, the controller, decided that the company had enough data to merit a detailed analysis of its overhead cost behavior.

The following monthly overhead costs were recorded for the previous two years:

---

[2] © Michael W. Maher, 1990. Prepared by Jean M. Lim under the supervision of Michael W. Maher.

Cost Data for Propylon Textiles (in thousands)

Month, First Year

	J	F	M	A	M	J	J	A	S	O	N	D	Two-Year Totals
Indirect materials	$ 22	$20	$ 23	$ 24	$ 22	$21	$20	$19	$19	$18	$18	$20	$ 503
Indirect labor	40	30	40	40	40	30	20	10	10	10	10	20	630
Lease	12	12	12	12	12	12	12	12	12	12	12	12	288
Utilities	9	9	8	8	8	7	8	7	8	8	9	9	206
Power	5	4	5	6	6	5	3	3	3	2	2	4	104
Insurance	1	1	1	1	1	1	1	1	1	1	1	1	24
Maintenance	20	6	6	6	6	6	20	6	6	6	6	6	200
Depreciation	2	2	2	2	2	2	2	2	2	2	2	2	72
Research and development	7	8	10	9	8	10	6	6	7	4	5	8	171
Total overhead	$118	$92	$107	$108	$105	$94	$92	$66	$68	$63	$65	$82	$2,198
Direct labor-hours	36.0	34.2	37.4	37.8	36.4	35.0	33.2	30.8	30.9	29.4	30.0	33.4	815.8 hours
Direct labor costs	$216.0	$205.2	$224.4	$226.8	$218.4	$210.0	$199.2	$184.8	$185.4	$176.4	$180.0	$200.4	$4,997.4
Machine-hours	45.0	42.6	45.0	47.0	45.2	43.6	41.2	40.0	39.4	37.2	36.5	42.0	1,022.7 hours
Units produced	8.9	8.6	9.2	9.5	8.9	8.6	8.0	7.8	7.6	7.4	7.2	8.1	202.5 units

Month, Second Year

	J	F	M	A	M	J	J	A	S	O	N	D
Indirect materials	$21	$21	$ 23	$ 24	$24	$ 21	$ 22	$20	$19	$19	$21	$22
Indirect labor	20	30	40	50	30	30	30	20	10	10	30	30
Lease	12	12	12	12	12	12	12	12	12	12	12	12
Utilities	10	10	9	9	8	8	8	8	9	9	10	10
Power	5	5	6	7	6	4	5	5	2	5	5	5
Insurance	1	1	1	1	1	1	1	1	1	1	1	1
Maintenance	20	6	6	6	6	6	20	6	6	6	6	6
Depreciation	4	4	4	4	4	4	4	4	4	4	6	4
Research and development	6	8	1	9	8	8	7	7	7	5	8	9
Total overhead	$99	$97	$102	$122	$99	$94	$109	$82	$70	$68	$97	$99
Direct labor-hours	33.2	34.2	36.9	39.6	35.2	34.0	35.2	32.4	30.2	30.4	34.2	35.8
Direct labor costs	$207.5	$213.7	$230.6	$247.5	$220.0	$212.5	$220.0	$202.5	$188.7	$190.0	$213.7	$223.7
Machine-hours	43.4	43.2	46.4	50.0	44.2	42.6	43.2	41.2	38.2	37.6	43.8	44.2
Units produced	8.4	8.6	9.1	9.8	8.9	8.4	8.7	8.1	7.7	7.5	8.6	8.9

Exhibit A **(SSP 1)**

SUBPROBLEM NO. 1:

Dependent Variable = Overhead

Independent variables: DL-hrs., DL cost, M-hrs., units produced

R-square = .8935 R-square adjusted = .8710

Standard error of the regression[a] = 6.2190

Variable Name	No.	Estimated-Coefficient	Standard Error[a]	T-Ratio[a] 19 DF
DL-hrs.	1	3.1337	2.7705	1.1311
DL cost	2	.30600	.32961	.92839
M-hrs.	3	.79964	2.0756	.38526
Units produced	4	−.09679	12.539	.00772
Intercept		−111.91	17.246	−6.4892

24 observations

Correlation matrix of coefficients:

Variable				
1	.94063			
2	.93340	.96964		
3	.92895	.97321	.96158	
4	.93276	.98177	.97041	.97951
	1 DL-hrs.	2 DL cost	3 M-hrs.	4 units produced

SUBPROBLEM NO. 2:

Dependent variable = Overhead

Independent variable: DL-hrs.

R-square = .8848 R-square adjusted = .8796

Standard error of the regression[a] = 6.0101

Variable Name	No.	Estimated Coefficient	Standard Error[a]	T-Ratio[a] 22 DF
DL-hrs.	1	5.9676	.45910	12.999
Intercept		−111.27	15.654	−7.1079

24 observations

SUBPROBLEM NO. 3:

Dependent variable = Overhead

Independent variable: DL cost

R-square = .8712 R-square adjusted = .8654

Standard error of the regression[a] = 6.3538

Variable Name	No.	Estimated Coefficient	Standard Error[a]	T-Ratio[a] 22 DF
DL cost	2	.91426	.07493	12.201
Intercept		−98.789	15.657	−6.3096

24 observations

SUBPROBLEM NO. 4:

Dependent variable = Overhead

Independent variable: M-hrs.

R-square = .8630 R-square adjusted = .8567

Standard error of the regression[a] = 6.5551

Variable Name	No.	Estimated Coefficient	Standard Error[a]	T-Ratio[a] 22 DF
M-hrs.	3	4.9015	.41645	11.770
Intercept		−117.28	17.796	−6.5902

24 observations

Exhibit A (concluded)

SUBPROBLEM NO. 5:
Dependent variable = Overhead
Independent variable: Units produced
R-square = .8700   R-square adjusted = .8641
Standard error of the regression[a] = 6.3834

Variable Name	No.	Estimated Coefficient	Standard Error[a]	T-Ratio[a] 22 DF
Units produced	4	23.799	1.9610	12.136
Intercept		−109.22	16.597	−6.5805
24 observations				

[a] Discussed in the chapter appendix.

You are a financial analyst at Propylon Textiles and have been asked by the controller to prepare a report on the firm's overhead cost behavior.

Exhibit A presents some computer output to help you with the analysis.

Required:

a. Using the account analysis method, calculate the monthly average for fixed costs and the variable cost rate per
   (1) Direct labor-hour.
   (2) Machine-hour.
   (3) Unit of output.

To help you, the controller has classified the various accounts as follows:

Account	Cost Behavior
Indirect Materials	Variable
Indirect Labor	Variable
Lease	Fixed
Utilities	Fixed
Power	Variable
Insurance	Fixed
Maintenance	Fixed
Depreciation	Fixed
Research and Development	Fixed

b. Plot direct labor costs against total overhead. Are there any outliers? If so, determine possible causes.

c. Using the high-low method, identify the fixed and variable components for the following activity bases:
   (1) Direct labor-hours.
   (2) Direct labor costs.
   (3) Machine-hours.
   (4) Units of output.

Explain the apparent negative fixed costs.

d. (Appendix) Subproblem 1 in the computer output (Exhibit A) is a multiple linear regression with overhead as the dependent variable; and direct labor-hours, direct labor costs, machine-hours, and units of output as independent variables. Explain the paradox between the high adjusted R^2 value and low t-statistics (labeled T-Ratio in the output).

e. Subproblems 2, 3, 4, and 5 in the computer output (Exhibit A) are simple linear regressions with overhead as the dependent variable and independent variables of direct labor-hours, direct labor costs, machine-hours, and units of output, respectively. Select the most appropriate activity base for overhead cost and explain your choice.

f. Plot indirect labor costs against direct labor-hours. What kind of cost behavior pattern do you observe?

g. Using the activity base selected in *(e)*, sketch the overhead cost function. What does this overhead cost function tell you about the relationship between current production levels and capacity?

h. Verify the computer output in Exhibit A for subproblems 1, 2, 3, 4, and 5 by entering the data in a computer or calculator.

SUGGESTED SOLUTION TO SELF-STUDY PROBLEM

a.

Indirect materials	$ 503,000
Indirect labor	630,000
Power	104,000
Total variable costs	$1,237,000

Lease	$ 288,000
Utilities	206,000
Insurance	24,000
Maintenance	200,000
Depreciation	72,000
Research and Development	171,000
Total fixed costs	$ 961,000

$$\text{Monthly fixed costs} = \frac{\$961,000}{24} = \$40,042$$

$$\text{Variable cost per DLH} = \frac{\$1,237,000}{815,800} = \$1.516$$

$$\text{Variable cost per machine-hour} = \frac{\$1,237,000}{1,022,700} = \$1.210$$

$$\text{Variable cost per unit produced} = \frac{\$1,237,000}{202,500} = \$6.109$$

b.

The first observation ($216,000; $118,000) might be an outlier. The most probable cause for the higher overhead cost is the relatively higher amount spent on maintenance that month. (Only 23 points are shown because 2 points are the same—namely, February and November of the second year.)

c. (1) Direct labor-hours:

$$V = \frac{\$122,000 - \$63,000}{39,600 - 29,400} = \underline{\underline{\$5.784}}$$
$$F = \$63,000 - \$5.784(29,400) = \underline{\underline{-\$107,050}}$$

(2) Direct labor costs:

$$V = \frac{\$122,000 - \$63,000}{247,500 - 176,400} = \underline{\underline{\$.830}}$$
$$F = \$63,000 - \$.830(176,400) = \underline{\underline{-\$83,412}}$$

(3) Machine-hours:

$$V = \frac{\$122,000 - \$65,000}{50,000 - 36,500} = \underline{\underline{\$4.222}}$$
$$F = \$65,000 - \$4.222(36,500) = \underline{\underline{-\$89,105}}$$

(4) Units of output:

$$V = \frac{\$122,000 - \$65,000}{9,800 - 7,200} = \underline{\underline{\$21.923}}$$
$$F = \$65,000 - \$21.923(7,200) = \underline{\underline{-\$92,846}}$$

The fixed costs appear to be negative because the estimate is made outside the relevant range. The implicit assumption of the above calculations is that unit variable costs are unchanged for all levels of production.

d. (Appendix) The independent variables are correlated to one another, giving rise to the problem of multicollinearity. This causes large standard errors resulting in low *t*-statistics. Nevertheless, most of the variance in the dependent variable is explained by the fitted line, and hence the high adjusted *R*-square.

e. Based on the highest adjusted *R*-square and *t*-statistic, direct labor-hours would be the most appropriate activity base. Machine-hours may not be appropriate if processes for the various product lines are radically different. Since there are 10 product lines, unit of output would not be a good activity base. In any event, statistical analysis alone is not sufficient for picking the activity base.

f.

The costs are semifixed or step costs. Note that this is inconsistent with the controller's classification of these costs as "variable costs." Not all 24 data points are presented because some points are the same in different months; February of the first year is the same as February of the second year, for example.)

g.

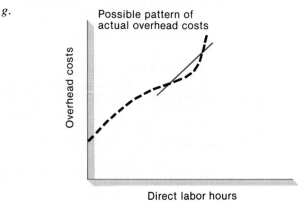

The steepness of the overhead function seems to imply that the firm is currently operating at capacity and is facing increasing marginal costs. In the long run, the company should seriously consider capacity expansion.

h. See output in Exhibit A.

QUESTIONS

10–1. Which method of cost estimation is not usually based on company records?

10–2. The following costs are labeled fixed or variable according to a typical designation in accounting. Identify the circumstances under which any of these costs would behave in a manner opposite to that listed:

a. Direct labor—variable.

b. Equipment depreciation—fixed.

c. Utilities (with a minimum charge)—variable.

      d. Supervisory salaries—fixed.

      e. Indirect materials purchased in given sizes that become spoiled within a few days—variable.

10–3. What is the connection between the relevant range and the range of observations included in a data set for cost-estimation purposes?

10–4. Why would a long-time executive prefer account analysis to statistical cost-estimation methods?

10–5. If one simply wishes to prepare a cost estimate using regression analysis and enters data into a program to compute regression estimates, what problems might be encountered?

10–6. When preparing cost estimates for account analysis purposes, should the costs be extracted from the historical accounting records?

10–7. How can one compensate for the effects of price instability when preparing cost estimates using high-low or regression techniques?

10–8. Under what conditions would engineering-based cost estimates be preferred to other estimation techniques?

10–9. When using cost-estimation methods based on past data, what are the trade-offs between gathering more data and gathering less?

10–10. The scatter diagram and the regression methods seem to go hand in hand. Why?

10–11. (Appendix) What considerations need to be included when constructing a confidence interval for a specific cost estimate (Y)?

10–12. What problems might arise when multiple independent variables are used?

10–13. (Appendix) A decision maker is interested in obtaining a cost estimate based on a regression equation. There are no problems with changes in prices, costs, technology, or relationships between activity and cost. Only one variable is to be used. What caveats might be in order if a regression is prepared for this purpose?

10–14. When using past data to predict a cost that has fixed and variable components, it is possible to have an equation with a negative intercept. Does this mean that at a zero production level the company will make money on its fixed costs? Explain.

EXERCISES

10–15. Methods of Estimating Costs—Account Analysis
(L.O.1)

The accounting records of a company report the following manufacturing costs for the past year:

Direct materials	$210,000
Direct labor	241,500
Manufacturing overhead	372,800

Production was 70,000 units. Fixed manufacturing overhead was $240,000.

For the coming year, the direct materials costs are expected to increase by 20 percent, excluding any effects of volume changes. Direct labor rates are scheduled to increase by 10 percent. Fixed manufacturing overhead is expected to increase 7.5 percent, and variable manufacturing overhead per unit is expected to remain the same.

Required:

a. Prepare a cost estimate for an activity level of 80,000 units of product this year.

b. Determine the costs per unit for last year and for this year.

10–16. Methods of Estimating Costs—Account Analysis
(L.O.1)

The accounting records of a company indicate the following manufacturing costs were incurred in Year 1:

Direct materials	$575,000
Direct labor	479,000
Manufacturing overhead	726,000

These costs were incurred to produce 50,000 units of product. Fixed manufacturing overhead amounts to $475,000.

For Year 2, direct materials costs are expected to increase by 10 percent per unit. Direct labor costs are due to increase by 15 percent per unit. Variable manufacturing costs are expected to remain constant per unit, while fixed manufacturing overhead for Year 2 is expected to increase by 5 percent.

Required:

a. Year 2 production is estimated to be 65,000 units. What are the estimated direct materials, direct labor, variable overhead, and fixed overhead costs for Year 2.

b. Determine the total manufacturing costs per unit for Year 1 and Year 2.

10–17. Methods of Estimating Costs—High-Low Cost
(L.O.1)

During the past five years, operations at a company have remained relatively stable. Over this time, the following data are available from the accounting records:

Item	Highest Amount	Lowest Amount
Marketing costs	$ 213,600	$ 129,300
Dollar sales	4,103,200	2,130,400

Required:

a. Use the high-low method to estimate the fixed and variable portion of the company's marketing costs.

b. Estimate the marketing costs for sales of $3,750,000.

c. Using the cost estimates computed in requirement (a), how much would you expect marketing costs to increase for every one dollar increase in sales?

10–18. Methods of Estimating Costs—High-Low
(L.O.1)

The National Airlines Company provides you with the following cost data for maintenance work on its fleet of airplanes:

Hours Operated per Month	Maintenance Cost ($ millions)
5,000	$1.2
7,000	1.4
9,000	1.6

Required:

a. Use the high-low method to estimate the fixed cost per month and the variable cost per hour.

b. What would be National's estimated costs if they operate 8,000 hours this month? 10,000 hours?

10–19. Methods of Estimating Costs—High-Low
(L.O.1)

Racy Motors Company makes motorcycles. Management wants to estimate overhead costs to plan its operations. A recent trade publication revealed that overhead costs tend to vary with machine-hours and/or materials costs. To check this, they collected the following data for the past 12 months:

Month No.	Machine-Hours	Materials Cost	Overhead Costs
1	175	$4,750	$4,500
2	170	4,600	4,225
3	160	4,200	3,780
4	190	5,900	5,250
5	175	4,600	4,800
6	200	5,250	5,100
7	160	4,350	4,450
8	150	4,350	4,200
9	210	6,000	5,475
10	180	4,950	4,760
11	170	4,450	4,325
12	145	3,800	3,975

Required:

a. Use the high-low method to estimate the fixed and variable portions of overhead costs based on machine-hours.

b. If the plant is planning to operate at a level of 200 machine-hours next period, what would be the estimated overhead costs? (Assume no inflation.)

10–20. Methods of Estimating Costs—Scattergraph
(L.O.1)

Prepare a scattergraph based on the overhead and direct machine-hour data in exercise 10–19.

10–21. Methods of Estimating Costs—Scattergraph
(L.O.1)

Prepare a scattergraph based on the overhead and materials cost data in exercise 10–19.

10–22. Interpreting Regression Results—Simple Regression
(L.O.2)

Simple regression results from the data of Racy Motors Company (exercise 10–19) are as follows:

Equation:
  Overhead = $348.17 + ($24.298 × machine-hours)

Statistical data:
  Correlation coefficient   .904
  R-squared   .818

Required:

Prepare an estimate of overhead if the company expects to use 200 machine-hours for the next period and costs are stable.

10–23. Interpreting Regression Results—Multiple Regression
(L.O.2)

Multiple regression results from the data of Racy Motors Company (exercise 10–19) are as follows:

Equation:
  Overhead = $694.24 + $9.1840 × machine-hours + .47833 × materials cost

Statistical data:
  Correlation coefficient   .935
  R-squared   .874

Assume that management predicts the materials cost to be $5,150 and machine-hours to be 200 for the coming period.

Required:

Use the multiple regression results to prepare an estimate of overhead costs for the coming period.

10–24. Interpreting Regression Results—Multiple-Choice

Alpha Company is making plans for the introduction of a new product that it will sell for $6 a unit. The following estimates have been made for manufacturing costs on 100,000 units to be produced the first year:

Direct materials $50,000
Direct labor $40,000 (the labor rate is $4 an hour × 10,000 hours)

Manufacturing overhead costs have not yet been estimated for the new product, but monthly data on total production and overhead costs for the past 24 months have been analyzed using simple linear regression. The following results were derived from the simple regression and will provide the basis for overhead cost estimates for the new product.

Simple Regression Analysis Results

Dependent variable—Factory overhead costs
Independent variable—Direct labor-hours

Computed values:
  Intercept $40,000
  Coefficient of independent variable $ 2.10
  Coefficient of correlation   .953
  R^2 .908

Required:

a. What percentage of the variation in overhead costs is explained by the independent variable?
  (1) 90.8 percent.
  (2) 42 percent.
  (3) 48.8 percent.
  (4) 95.3 percent.
  (5) Some other amount.

b. The total overhead cost for an estimated activity level of 20,000 direct labor-hours would be:
  (1) $42,000.
  (2) $82,000.
  (3) $122,000.
  (4) $222,000.
  (5) Some other amount.

c. What is the expected contribution margin per *unit* to be earned during the first year on 100,000 units of the new product? (Assume all marketing and administrative costs are fixed.)
   (1) $4.49.
   (2) $4.89.
   (3) $0.30.
   (4) $5.10.
   (5) Some other amount.

d. How much is the variable manufacturing cost per *unit,* using the variable overhead estimated by the regression (and assuming direct materials and direct labor are variable costs)?
   (1) $.90.
   (2) $1.11.
   (3) $1.50.
   (4) $3.
   (5) Some other amount.

e. What is the manufacturing cost equation implied by these results, where x refers to *units* produced?
   (1) TC = $40,000 + 1.11x$.
   (2) TC = $40,000 + 3.00x$.
   (3) TC = $130,000 + 2.10x$.
   (4) Some other equation.

(CMA adapted)

10–25. Interpreting Regression Results
(L.O.2)

The advertising manager of Ninja Sales Company wants to know if the company's advertising program is successful. The manager used a pocket calculator to estimate the relation between advertising expenditures (the independent variable) and sales dollars. Monthly data for the past two years were entered into the calculator. The regression results indicated the following equation:

$$\text{Sales dollars} = \$845,000 - \$520 \times \text{Advertising}$$
$$\text{Correlation coefficient} = -.902$$

These results might imply that the advertising was reducing sales. The manager was about to conclude that statistical methods were so much nonsense when you walked into the room.

Required:

Help the manager. What might cause the negative relationship between advertising expenditures and sales?

10–26. Interpreting Regression Results—Simple Regression
(L.O.2)

A fast-food restaurant, McGlurgs, is estimating overhead based on food cost. Data were gathered for the past 24 months and entered into a regression program. The following output was obtained:

Equation:	
Intercept	$21,405
Slope	1.150
Statistical data:	
Correlation coefficient	.872
R-square	.760
Adjusted R-square	.731

The company is planning to operate at a level of $24,000 of food costs per month for the coming year.

Required:

a. Use the regression output to write the overhead cost equation.

b. Based on the cost equation, compute the estimated overhead cost per month for the coming year.

10–27. Interpreting Regression Data (Appendix)
(L.O.2)

Staplehare Airport Authority needs to forecast its personnel department costs. The following output was obtained from a regression program used to estimate personnel department costs as a function of the number of airport employees:

Equation:
    Personnel costs = $5,310 + $408 × Employees

Statistical data:	
Correlation coefficient	.923
R-squared	.852
Adjusted *R*-square	.834
Standard error of slope	34.250
t-statistic for slope	11.912

Monthly data for the past two years were used to construct these estimates. Cost relationships are expected to be the same for the coming period.

Required:

a. What are the estimated personnel costs for 2,800 employees.

b. Construct a 95 percent confidence interval for this cost prediction. The standard error of estimate is $582.30. (Use $t = 2.074$).

c. Construct a 95 percent confidence interval for the slope coefficient. (Use $t = 2.074$.)

10–28. Learning Curves
(L.O.3)

General Affairs manufactures high-technology instruments for spacecraft. The company recorded the following costs subject to a 75 percent cumulative learning effect.

Cumulative Number of Units Produced, X	Average Manufacturing Costs per Unit
1	$1,333
2	1,000
4	?
8	?
16	?

Required:

Complete the chart by filling in the cost amounts for volumes of 4, 8, and 16 units.

10–29. Learning Curves
(L.O.3)

European Electronics estimates the variable cost of producing each unit of a product as follows:

Materials	$2,000 per unit
Direct labor	$30 per hour
Variable overhead	$500 per unit plus 80 percent of direct labor costs

The first unit requires 100 hours to make. Labor time is subject to an 80 percent cumulative learning curve, therefore, $Y = aX^{-.322}$.

Required:

Compute the variable costs of making two units, three units, and four units.

PROBLEMS

10–30. Methods of Estimating Costs—High-Low, Scattergraph, and Regression

The Franklin Plant of the Ramon Company manufactures electrical components. Plant management has experienced difficulties with fluctuating monthly overhead costs. Management wants to be able to estimate overhead costs accurately to plan its operations and its financial needs. A trade association publication reports that for companies manufacturing electrical components, overhead tends to vary with machine-hours.

A member of the controller's staff proposed that the behavior pattern of these overhead costs be determined to improve cost estimation.

Another staff member suggested that a good starting place for determining cost behavior patterns would be to analyze historical data.

Following this suggestion, monthly data were gathered on machine-hours and overhead costs for the past two years. There were no major changes in operations over this period of time. The raw data are as follows:

Month Number	Machine-Hours	Overhead Costs
1	20,000	$84,000
2	25,000	99,000
3	22,000	89,500
4	23,000	90,000
5	20,000	81,500
6	19,000	75,500
7	14,000	70,500
8	10,000	64,500
9	12,000	69,000
10	17,000	75,000
11	16,000	71,500
12	19,000	78,000
13	21,000	86,000
14	24,000	93,000
15	23,000	93,000
16	22,000	87,000
17	20,000	80,000
18	18,000	76,500
19	12,000	67,500
20	13,000	71,000
21	15,000	73,500
22	17,000	72,500
23	15,000	71,000
24	18,000	75,000

These data were entered into a computer regression program. The following output was obtained:

Coefficient of correlation	.9544
R-square	.9109
Coefficients of the equation:	
Intercept	39,859.000
Independent variable (slope)	2.1549

Required:

a. Use the high-low method to estimate the Franklin Plant overhead costs.

b. Prepare a scattergraph showing the overhead costs plotted against machine-hours.

c. Use the results of the regression analysis to prepare the cost-estimation equation and to prepare a cost estimate for 22,500 machine-hours.

(CMA adapted)

10–31. Methods of Cost Estimation—Account Analysis, Simple and Multiple Regression

Mountain View Outdoor Products Corporation has prepared a schedule of estimated overhead costs for the coming year. This schedule was prepared on the assumption that production would equal 80,000 units. Costs have been classified as fixed or variable according to the judgment of the controller.

The following overhead items and the classification as fixed or variable form the basis for the overhead cost schedule:

Item	Total Cost
Indirect materials	$ 37,500 (all variable)
Indirect labor	194,200 ($171,000 fixed)
Building occupancy	236,420 (all fixed)
Power	27,210 (all variable)
Equipment depreciation	181,000 (all fixed)
Equipment maintenance	24,330 ($8,500 fixed)
Personal property taxes	14,100 ($6,350 fixed)
Data processing	11,220 ($9,470 fixed)
Technical support	16,940 (all fixed)
Total estimated overhead	$742,920

In the past, the overhead costs have been related to production levels. However, price instability has led management to suggest that explicit consideration be given to including an appropriate price index in the cost equation. While management realizes that to estimate future costs using a regression model that includes both production and a price index as independent variables requires predicting a future value not only for production but for the price index as well, at least some recognition would be given to the dramatic price changes that have been experienced in the past few years. For cost-estimation purposes, it is assumed that the next value of the index will be the same as the last period value of the index.

Following management instructions, data were gathered on past costs, production levels, and an appropriate price index. These data are:

Overhead Costs	Production (units)	Price Index
$718,480	62,800	89
735,110	72,800	90
768,310	93,400	93
717,670	56,900	95
715,960	58,800	98
726,880	69,000	100
753,420	87,000	101
777,640	98,000	103
720,410	59,200	103
718,100	62,600	106
736,800	73,100	108
714,220	60,400	113

There have been no significant changes in operations over the period covered by these data nor are there any significant changes expected in the coming period.

When the data above were entered into a regression program using only the production level as the independent variable, the following results were obtained:

Equation:
    Overhead = $626,547 + $1.504 × Production (units)

Statistical data:
    Correlation coefficient   .988
    R-squared   .976
    Adjusted R-square   .974

When both predictors were entered in the regression program, the following results were obtained:

MULTIPLE REGRESSION RESULTS:

Equation:
    Overhead = $632,640 + ($1.501 × Production) − ($59.067 × Index)

Statistical data:
    Correlation coefficient (multiple R)   .988
    R-square   .976
    Adjusted R-square   .972

Correlation matrix:

	Production	Index
Production	1.00	−.087
Index	−.087	1.00

Required:

a. Prepare a cost-estimation equation using the account analysis approach.

b. Use the high-low method to prepare a cost estimate for the activity expected in the coming period.

c. Prepare a cost estimate using simple linear regression.

d. Use the multiple regression results to prepare an estimate of overhead costs for the coming period.

e. Comment on which method you think is more appropriate under the circumstances.

10–32. Interpreting Regression Results—Simple Regression

Your company is preparing an estimate of its production costs for the coming period. The controller estimates that direct materials costs are $7.35 per unit and that direct labor costs are $15.40 per hour. Overhead is applied on the basis of direct labor costs. However, estimating total overhead is difficult.

The controller's office estimated overhead costs at $300 for fixed costs and $12 per unit for variable costs. Your nemesis on the staff, Farleigh O. Tuvvit, suggested that the company use the regression approach. Farleigh has already done the analysis on a home computer and reports that the "correct" cost equation is:

$$\text{Overhead} = \$883 + \$10.70 \text{ per unit}$$

Farleigh further reports that the correlation coefficient for the regression is .82 and says, "With 82 percent of the variation in overhead explained by the equation, it certainly should be adopted as the best basis for estimating costs."

When asked for the data used to generate the regression. Farleigh produces the following list:

Month	Overhead	Unit Production
1	$4,762	381
2	5,063	406
3	6,420	522
4	4,701	375
5	6,783	426
6	6,021	491
7	5,321	417
8	6,133	502
9	6,481	515
10	5,004	399
11	5,136	421
12	6,160	510
13	6,104	486

The company controller is somewhat surprised that the cost estimates would be so different. You have, therefore, been given the task of checking out Farleigh's equation.

Required:

Analyze Farleigh's results and state your reasons for supporting or rejecting Farleigh's cost equation.

10–33. Interpreting Regression Results—Multiple Regression (Appendix)

Malibu Products Corporation molds fiberglass into automobile bodies that are replicas of antique cars. A major component of the company's overhead is the costs of handling materials used in the molding process. It was suggested at a recent meeting of the controller and the production vice president that past data be reviewed to see if a relationship could be found between the materials-handling costs and some predictor variable. The production vice president suggested that the quantity of materials be used. The controller suggested that the dollar value of the materials be used since the dollar value would explicitly include the effects of price fluctuations. It was also noted in the discussion that some of the materials-handling costs seem to vary with the number of shipments received in a month.

Data were gathered on materials-handling costs, weight of materials received, dollar value of receipts, and number of shipments. The data were gathered for the past 18 months. Eighteen months ago, the semiautomated materials-handling equipment in use today was installed. Prior to that time, a manual system was in use.

The data appear as follows:

Materials-Handling Costs	Weight of Materials	Dollar Value of Materials	Number of Shipments
$606,000	2,425	$3,031,000	6
491,000	1,790	2,238,000	14
621,000	2,613	3,266,000	21
602,000	2,419	3,084,000	32
561,000	2,110	2,701,000	7
684,000	2,732	3,688,000	9
630,000	2,504	3,305,000	12
681,000	2,915	3,717,000	6
599,000	2,004	2,725,000	15
518,000	1,610	2,222,000	13
539,000	1,824	2,517,000	10
581,000	1,996	2,730,000	8
611,000	2,103	2,934,000	11
713,000	2,741	3,826,000	7
737,000	2,602	3,851,000	14
622,000	2,191	3,111,000	9
681,000	2,508	3,674,000	12
599,000	1,941	2,788,000	7

Based on these data, the following regressions are obtained:

REGRESSION 1: Materials-handling costs and weight of materials

Equation:
  Materials-handling costs = $271,610 + $150.80 × Weight

Statistical data:

Correlation coefficient	.863
R-square	.745
Standard error of slope	22.054
t-statistic for slope coefficient	6.838

REGRESSION 2: Materials-handling costs and value of materials

Equation:
  Materials-handling costs = $236,790 + .123 × Value

Statistical data:

Correlation coefficient	.975
R-square	.950
Standard error of slope	.007
t-statistic for slope coefficient	17.438

REGRESSION 3: Materials-handling costs and shipments

Equation:
  Materials-handling costs = $628,680 − $1,127.8 × Shipments

Statistical data:

Correlation coefficient	.109
R-square	.012
Standard error of slope	2,578.4
t-statistic for slope coefficient	−.437

After reviewing the above regressions, it was decided that a multiple regression including the dollar value of materials and the weight of materials might be more useful. The results of that regression were:

REGRESSION 4

Equation:
  Materials-handling cost = \$251,760 + (.176 × Value) − (\$78.50 × Weight)

Statistical data:

Correlation coefficient	.987	
R-square	.973	
Standard error of coefficients:		
Value	0.154	t-statistic 11.412
Weight	21.385	t-statistic −3.671

Correlation matrix

	Weight	Value
Weight	1.00	.94
Value	.94	1.00

Required:

a. Prepare the cost estimate for handling 2,600 units of weight with a value of \$4,005,000, using each relevant regression.

b. Which regression would you recommend, if any? Why?

10–34. Interpreting Regression Results—Multiple-Choice (Appendix)

Armer Company is accumulating data to prepare its annual profit plan for the coming year. The behavior pattern of the maintenance costs must be determined. The accounting staff has suggested that regression be employed to derive an equation in the form of $y = a + bx$ for maintenance costs. Data regarding maintenance-hours and costs for last year and the results of the regression analysis are as follows:

	Hours of Activity	Maintenance Costs
January	480	\$ 4,200
February	320	3,000
March	400	3,600
April	300	2,820
May	500	4,350
June	310	2,960
July	320	3,030
August	520	4,470
September	490	4,260
October	470	4,050
November	350	3,300
December	340	3,160
Sum	4,800	43,200
Average	400	3,600

Average cost per hour (43,200 ÷ 4,800) = \$9

Intercept	684.65
b coefficient	7.2884
Standard error of the intercept	49.515
Standard error of the b coefficient	.12126
Standard error of the regression	34.469
R-squared	.99724
t-value intercept	13.827
t-value b	60.105

Required:

a. In the standard regression equation of $y = a + bx$, the letter b is best described as the:
   (1) Independent variable.
   (2) Dependent variable.
   (3) Constant coefficient.
   (4) Variable cost coefficient.
   (5) Coefficient of determination.

b. The letter y in the standard regression equation is best described as the:
   (1) Independent variable.
   (2) Dependent variable.
   (3) Constant coefficient.
   (4) Variable coefficient.
   (5) Coefficient of determination

c. The letter x in the standard regression equation is best described as the:
   (1) Independent variable.
   (2) Dependent variable.
   (3) Constant coefficient.
   (4) Variable coefficient.
   (5) Coefficient of determination.

d. If the Armer Company uses the high-low method of analysis, the equation for the relationship between hours of activity and maintenance cost would be:
   (1) $y = 400 + 9.0x$.
   (2) $y = 570 + 7.5x$.
   (3) $y = 3,600 + 400x$.
   (4) $y = 570 + 9.0x$.
   (5) Some other equation.

e. Based upon the data derived from the regression analysis, 420 maintenance-hours in a month would mean the maintenance would be budgeted at:
   (1) $3,780.
   (2) $3,461.
   (3) $3,797.
   (4) $3,746.
   (5) Some other amount.

f. The coefficient of correlation for the regression equation for the maintenance activities is:
   (1) $34.469 \div 49.515$.
   (2) .99724.
   (3) $\sqrt{.99724}$.
   (4) $(.99724)^2$.
   (5) Some other amount.

g. The percent of the total variance that can be explained by the regression equation is:
   (1) 99.724%.
   (2) 69.613%
   (3) 80.982%.
   (4) 99.862%.
   (5) Some other amount.

h. (Appendix) What is the range of values for the marginal maintenance cost such that Armer can be 95 percent confident that the true value of the marginal maintenance cost will be within this range? (Use $t = 2.23$.)
   (1) $7.02–$7.56.
   (2) $7.17–$7.41.

(3) $7.07–$7.51.

(4) $6.29–$8.29.

(5) Some other range.

(CMA adapted)

10–35. Learning Curves

Kelly Company plans to manufacture a product called Electrocal, which requires a substantial amount of direct labor on each unit. Based on the company's experience with other products that required similar amounts of direct labor, management believes that there is a learning factor in the production process used to manufacture Electrocal.

Each unit of Electrocal requires 50 square feet of direct material at a cost of $30 per square foot, for a total material cost of $1,500. The standard direct labor rate is $25 per direct labor-hour. Variable manufacturing overhead is assigned to products at a rate of $40 per direct labor-hour. The company adds a markup of 30 percent on variable manufacturing costs in determining an initial bid price for all products.

Data on the production of the first two lots (16 units) of Electrocal is as follows:

1. The first lot of eight units required a total of 3,200 direct labor-hours.

2. The second lot of eight units required a total of 2,240 direct labor-hours.

Based on prior production experience, Kelly anticipates that there will be no significant improvement in production time after the first 32 units. Therefore, a standard for direct labor-hours will be established based on the average hours per unit for units 17–32.

Required:

a. What is the basic premise of the learning curve?

b. Based upon the data presented for the first 16 units, what learning rate appears to be applicable to the direct labor required to produce Electrocal? Support your answer with appropriate calculations.

c. Calculate the standard for direct labor-hours that Kelly Company should establish for each unit of Electrocal.

d. After the first 32 units have been manufactured, Kelly Company was asked to submit a bid on an additional 96 units. What price should Kelly bid on this order of 96 units? Explain your answer.

e. Knowledge of the learning curve phenomenon can be a valuable management tool. Explain how management can apply the learning curve in the planning and controlling of business operations.

(CMA adapted)

10–36. Learning Curves

Xyon Company has purchased 80,000 pumps annually from Kobec, Inc. The price has increased each year, and it reached $68 per unit last year. Because the purchase price has increased significantly, Xyon management has asked that an estimate be made of the cost to manufacture pumps in its own facilities. Xyon's products consist of stampings and castings. The company has little experience with products requiring assembly.

The engineering, manufacturing, and accounting departments have prepared a report for management that included the estimate shown below for an assembly run of 10,000 units. Additional production employees would be hired to manufacture the subassembly. However, no additional equipment, space, or supervision would be needed.

The report states that total costs for 10,000 units are estimated at $957,000 or $95.70 a unit. The current purchase price is $68 a unit, so the report recommends a continued purchase of the product.

Components (outside purchases)	$120,000
Assembly labor[a]	300,000
Factory overhead[b]	450,000
General and administrative overhead[c]	87,000
Total costs	$957,000
Fixed overhead	50% of direct labor-dollars
Variable overhead	100% of direct labor-dollars
Factory overhead rate	150% of direct labor-dollars

[a] Assembly labor consists of hourly production workers.

[b] Factory overhead is applied to products on a direct labor-dollar basis. Variable overhead costs vary closely with direct labor-dollars.

[c] General and administrative overhead is applied at 10 percent of the total cost of materials (or components), assembly labor, and factory overhead.

Required:

a. Was the analysis prepared by the engineering, manufacturing, and accounting departments of Xyon Company and the recommendation to continue purchasing the pumps, which followed from the analysis, correct? Explain your answer and include any supportive calculations you consider necessary.

b. Assume Xyon Company could experience labor cost improvements on the pump assembly consistent with an 80 percent learning curve. An assembly run of 10,000 units represents the initial lot or batch for measurement purposes. Should Xyon produce the 80,000 pumps in this situation? Explain your answer.

(CMA adapted)

INTEGRATIVE CASES

10–37. Interpreting Regression Results—Process Costing

(Knowledge of equivalent units is required for this problem.) Management of Waverly Processing, Inc., wants to obtain better cost estimates to evaluate the company's operations more satisfactorily. As a new management trainee, you recall some of the cost-estimation techniques discussed in cost accounting and suggest that these techniques may be useful in this situation.

The following data are given to you for analysis purposes:

Month	Equivalent Production	Overhead
1	1,425	$12,185
2	950	9,875
3	1,130	10,450
4	1,690	15,280
5	1,006	9,915
6	834	9,150
7	982	10,133
8	1,259	11,981
9	1,385	12,045
10	1,420	13,180
11	1,125	11,910
12	980	10,431

Last month, the beginning work in process inventory contained 1,000 units that were 65 percent complete with respect to conversion costs. The manufacturing department transferred out 1,500 units last month. There were 1,200 units in ending inventory, and these units were 30 percent complete with respect to conversion costs.

Using the above information, you go to the regression program in your computer and obtain the following output:

Equation:	
Intercept	$3,709.000
Slope	6.487
Statistical data:	
Correlation coefficient (R)	.956
Adjusted R-square	.904

Required:

a. Use the high-low method to estimate the overhead cost function.

b. Use the regression method to estimate the overhead cost function.

c. Compute the equivalent units of production with respect to conversion costs for last month.

d. Use the regression results to estimate the overhead costs for last month.

10–38. Methods of Estimating Costs—Account Analysis and Regression Methods—Bayview Manufacturing Company[3]

(Computer required.) Bayview Manufacturing Company is preparing cost estimates for the coming year. The controller's staff prepared a preliminary income statement for the coming year based on an analysis of the various cost accounts and on a study of orders received. The projected income statement appeared as follows:

Sales revenue		$3,000,000
Cost of sales:		
Direct materials	$1,182,000	
Direct labor	310,000	
Factory overhead	775,000	
Total cost of sales		2,267,000
Gross profit		733,000
Marketing costs		450,000
Projected operating profit		$ 283,000

Bayview produces three products: A, B, and C. A profit per unit for each product has been prepared by management and appears as follows:

	A	B	C
Sale price	$20.00	$10.00	$30.00
Less:			
Direct materials	7.00	3.75	16.60
Direct labor	2.00	1.00	3.50
Factory overhead	5.00	2.50	8.75
Marketing	3.00	1.50	4.50
Net unit profit	$ 3.00	$ 1.25	$ (3.35)

[3] Adapted from a problem in "Report of the Committee on the Measurement Methods Content of the Accounting Curriculum," *Supplement to Volume XLVI of The Accounting Review.*

On the basis of this information, the company planning committee decided that as few Cs should be produced as possible. Moreover, the committee recommended that the company emphasize the production of A and perhaps start a promotional campaign to increase sales of A.

Before a final recommendation on the plan, the management planning committee asked the controller's office to make certain that these profit numbers were correct.

A review of the controller's recommendations indicated that the controller estimated that 20 percent of the overhead was variable and that 50 percent of the marketing costs were also variable.

Some additional data have been gathered from the accounting records.

First, the units are produced in two departments (molding and finishing). The following production rates indicate the times required to produce each unit in each department:

	A	**B**	**C**
Molding	2 per hour	4 per hour	3 per hour
Finishing	4 per hour	8 per hour	4/3 per hour

Direct labor cost and overhead incurred in each department and for the company as a whole over the past 10 years is as follows:

Direct Labor Cost (in thousands)			**Overhead Cost (in thousands)**		
Molding	**Finishing**	**Total**	**Molding**	**Finishing**	**Total**
$140	$170	$310	$341	$434	$775
135	150	285	340	421	761
140	160	300	342	428	770
130	150	280	339	422	761
130	155	285	338	425	763
125	140	265	337	414	751
120	150	270	335	420	755
115	140	255	334	413	747
120	140	260	336	414	750
115	135	250	335	410	745

Production cost relationships have not changed over this period. Information on marketing costs for the past 10 years and on the sales of products A, B, and C for the same period was obtained also. These data are:

Sales (in thousands)				**Marketing Costs (in thousands)**
Product A	**Product B**	**Product C**	**Total**	
$2,000	$400	$600	$3,000	$450
1,940	430	610	2,980	445
1,950	380	630	2,960	445
1,860	460	620	2,940	438
1,820	390	640	2,850	433
1,860	440	580	2,880	437
1,880	420	570	2,870	438
1,850	380	580	2,810	434
1,810	390	580	2,780	430
1,770	290	610	2,670	425

Required:

a. Comment on the use of the per unit profit measures for planning purposes.

b. Use regression estimates to determine if the estimates of fixed and variable overhead are reasonable.

c. Would you recommend the use of plantwide or departmental overhead rates? Why?

d. Prepare regression estimates of the fixed and variable components of marketing costs.

10–39. Methods of Estimating Costs—Cost of Prediction Error

(Computer required.) The manager of the chemical processing division of Diamond Products Corporation, a small petrochemical company, is preparing a fixed price bid to process up to 800 units per month of certain feedstocks for a large farm cooperative. All of Diamond's customers have processing agreements that specify the allowed production and processing fee Diamond can charge. Diamond receives the feedstocks, processes them, and then delivers the finished products to the contracting company.

Diamond incurs conversion costs in the process. Diamond's plant has a maximum capacity of 9,000 units per month. In a typical month, usage is less than the full capacity and is expected to run at 7,300 units per month over the period of the contract with the cooperative. The manager knows that the cooperative can obtain similar processing elsewhere for a fee of $3.51 per unit. Any bid of $3.50 per unit or less will be accepted by the cooperative. A schedule of past production and processing costs is:

Month	Conversion Costs	Production (units per month)
1	$23,840	7,300
2	25,714	7,615
3	21,375	6,410
4	24,163	7,130
5	27,332	8,120
6	21,163	6,110
7	23,143	7,040
8	27,582	8,340
9	23,913	7,280
10	23,708	7,045
11	25,315	7,610
12	26,862	8,030
13	27,439	8,150
14	23,840	7,115
15	24,988	7,580
16	23,100	6,960
17	24,189	7,320
18	24,631	7,540
19	25,917	7,880
20	23,711	7,210
21	22,324	6,510
22	23,684	7,130
23	28,790	8,410
24	25,446	7,830

The manager turns to the computer terminal and enters these data to obtain regression estimates of fixed and variable costs. The following results appear on the screen:

Equation:	
Y = \$868.433 + \$3.216X	
Statistical data:	
Correlation coefficient	.980
R-square	.960
Adjusted R-square	.958
t-statistic for slope coefficient	22.847

After looking at the results, the manager prepares a bid of \$3.50 for the processing. The manager's bid is forwarded to the controller's office for review and approval.

The controller notes the bid and cost estimates. The controller expresses concern with the regression results because fixed costs are lower than expected. The controller pulls out the cost report for the division and notes the following items, which are believed to be fixed costs:

Building occupancy	\$1,200
Utilities	450
Equipment depreciation	1,100

In addition, the controller notes that there are a number of "mixed" costs in the chemical processing operation. Since the controller's estimate of fixed costs substantially exceeds the fixed cost estimate in the manager's regression equation, the controller asks the manager to explain the difference in the estimates.

The manager states that because the fixed costs will not change as a result of the contract, they can be excluded from consideration.

Required:

a. Without the use of a computer, prepare an estimate of the fixed and variable costs that can be used to confirm or reject the manager's regression results.

b. (Computer required.) Prepare your own regression estimate of fixed and variable costs.

c. Assuming the manager submits a bid of \$3.50 per unit for the 800 units per month, how much better or worse off would the company be each month compared to not submitting a bid? (That is, what is the cost of prediction error?)

10–40. Interpreting Regression Results—Loss Prediction (Appendix)

Johnstar Company makes an expensive chemical product. The costs average about \$1,000 per unit of weight, and the material sells for \$2,500 per unit of weight. Materials storage is extremely hazardous; therefore, a batch is made each day to fill customers' needs for the day. Failure to deliver the required quantity results in a shutdown for the customers, with a corresponding cost penalty assessed against Johnstar. However, excess chemicals on hand at the end of the day must be disposed of in costly, secure facilities.

The chemical increases in weight during processing, but the exact increase varies depending on temperature and pressure conditions as well as on the impurities present in the input materials. It is important for the company to know the final weight from any batch as soon as possible so that a new batch can be started should the expected final weight be smaller than required for customer needs.

A consultant was hired to advise the company on how to estimate the final weight of the product. The consultant recommended that the product be weighed after three hours and that the weight after three hours be used to predict the weight at the end of processing. Based on 20 processed batches, the following observations were made:

Batch Number	Weight at Three Hours	Final Weight	Batch Number	Weight at Three Hours	Final Weight
1	55 units	90 units	11	60 units	80 units
2	45	75	12	35	60
3	40	80	13	35	80
4	60	80	14	55	60
5	40	45	15	35	75
6	60	80	16	50	90
7	50	80	17	30	60
8	55	95	18	60	105
9	50	100	19	50	60
10	35	75	20	20	30

Data obtained from the regression analysis included the following:

R-square	.4127
Coefficient of correlation	.6424
Coefficients of the regression:	
Constant	28.6
Slope	1.008
Standard error of slope coefficient	.2834
t-statistic for slope	3.5559
Standard error of estimate	14.20 (for 70–72 units)

Required:

a. Use the results of the regression to calculate the estimate of the final weight of today's batch, which at the end of three hours weighs 42 units.

b. (Knowledge of statistics required.) Customer orders for today total 68 units. The smallest batch that can be started must weigh at least 20 units at the end of three hours. What factors should be considered in deciding whether to start a new batch?

(CMA adapted)

CHAPTER

11

COST-VOLUME-PROFIT ANALYSIS

LEARNING OBJECTIVES

1. Seeing how costs, volume, and profit relate to each other.

2. Knowing how to use cost-volume-profit (CVP) analysis as planning and decision-making aids.

3. Understanding extensions to the basic CVP model.

4. Learning how to apply CVP analysis to multiple products.

Cost-Volume-Profit (CVP) Analysis The study of the interrelationships between costs and volume and how they impact profit.

In this chapter, we discuss the use of **cost-volume-profit (CVP) analysis** for managerial decision making. Managers must understand the interrelationship of cost, volume, and profit for planning and decision making. They rely on their cost accounting departments to supply the information and analyses that aid them to anticipate and make sound decisions involving any of these three items.

During a gasoline shortage that hit the American automobile industry particulary hard, executives of one automobile company announced a price increase to reduce losses. Many observers were surprised that the company would raise prices when car sales were slumping and argued that the decision would further reduce the company's sales. The observers were correct in forecasting a decrease in the quantity of cars demanded at the higher price. But the auto executives had carried the analysis several steps further and determined that increased prices would have a positive impact on the company's operating profits.

In making their decision, the executives needed to understand relationships between selling prices, sales, volume, and costs. They also needed to understand which costs would vary with changes in volume and which costs would stay the same. Without this kind of analysis, they could not accurately determine the effect of price, volume, or cost changes on the company's operating profits.

Although their decision to raise prices in the face of decreasing demand struck some people as odd, these managers believed that the increase in price, coupled with an expected decrease in volume, would have little impact on total revenue. However, the total variable costs would be reduced with lower volume, so operating profits would be higher.

THE PROFIT EQUATION

A simple relation exists between total revenues (TR), total costs (TC), and operating profit (π).

$$\text{Operating profit} = \text{Total revenues} - \text{Total costs}$$
$$\pi = TR - TC$$

Profit Equation Operating profits equals total contribution margin less fixed costs.

Both total revenues and total costs are likely to be affected by changes in the quantity of output.[1] A statement of the **profit equation** that takes quantity of output into account adds useful information for examining the effects of revenue, costs, and volume on operating profits. Total revenue (TR) equals average selling price per unit (P) times the units of output (X):

$$TR = PX$$

The total costs (TC) may be divided into a fixed component that does not vary with changes in output levels and a variable component that does vary. The fixed component is made up of total fixed costs (F) per period, while the variable component is the product of the average variable cost per unit (V) times the quantity of output (X). Therefore, the cost function is:

$$TC = VX + F$$

---

[1] Unless otherwide stated, we adopt the simplifying assumption that production volume equals sales volume so that changes in inventories may be ignored.

Substituting the expanded expressions in the profit equation yields a more useful form, as follows:

$$\pi = TR - TC$$
$$\pi = PX - (VX + F)$$

Collecting terms, we have

$$\pi = (P - V)X - F$$

Contribution Margin The difference between revenues and variable costs.

The **contribution margin,** $(P - V)$, shown in this version of the profit equation is the amount each unit sold *contributes* toward (1) covering fixed costs and (2) providing operating profits.

Note that V is the sum of unit *manufacturing costs* and unit *marketing and administrative costs;* F is the sum of total fixed *manufacturing costs,* fixed *marketing costs,* and fixed *administrative costs* for the period; and X refers to the number of units produced and sold during the period.

This model assumes *all* fixed costs are costs of the *period;* fixed manufacturing costs are not allocated to products and "unitized." Thus, the CVP model is consistent with variable costing but inconsistent with full-absorption costing.

For example, Sport Autos is an automobile dealership that carries one line of sports cars. During the month of February, Sport Autos purchased 20 sports cars and sold them at an average price of $15,000 each. Here is how the average variable cost of each car was determined.

Cost of each automobile to Sport Autos	$12,300
Dealer preparation costs	100
Sales commission	600
Average variable cost per car	$13,000

The fixed costs of operating the dealership for a typical month are $30,000.

REAL WORLD APPLICATION

Breaking Even at Chrysler

For some companies, break-even is more than a point on the profit-volume graph: it's a goal to achieve. This was certainly the case at Chrysler Corporation in the early 1980s. For several years, Chrysler operated at a loss. Company executives endured considerable criticism for receiving a U.S. government loan guarantee for a "failing" company. Finally, in 1982, the headlines read, "'We're in Black,' Iacocca Chortles."*

The turnaround came primarily because cost-cutting measures reduced the break-even from 2.2 million units in 1979 to 1.2 million units in 1982. The company received concessions from the United Auto Workers that reduced annual increases in labor costs. The company also reduced variable costs by increasing efficiency in production and reduced fixed costs, in part by laying off many white-collar workers.

* *Detroit Free Press,* June 6, 1982.

Using the profit equation, the results for February are:

$$\pi = (P - V)X - F$$
$$= (\$15,000 - \$13,000)20 \text{ cars} - \$30,000$$
$$= \underline{\$10,000}$$

Although the $10,000 operating profit was derived algebraically, it could also be determined from the company's income statement for the month, as shown in Illustration 11–1.

THE IMPACT OF COST-VOLUME-PROFIT (CVP) RELATIONSHIPS

The following example demonstrates how the profit equation can be used to find CVP relationships. Assume in the earlier example the manager of Sport Autos foresees a downturn in sales volume in March but hopes for improvement in April. In fact, the manager hopes just to break even in March with an operating profit of $0. He hopes for $50,000 in operating profits for April, however. What volumes of sales will provide the expected operating profits? We start with the following profit equation:

$$\pi = TR - TC$$
$$= (P - V)X - F$$
$$= (\$15,000 - \$13,000)X - \$30,000$$
$$= \$2,000X - \$30,000$$

where $2,000 is the contribution margin per unit and $30,000 is the fixed cost per month.

The manager sets operating profit equal to zero for March and to $50,000 for April to find the required volumes:

For March

$$\pi = (P - V)X - F$$
$$\text{If } \pi = \$0$$

$$\$0 = (\$15,000 - \$13,000)X - \$30,000$$
$$\$30,000 = \$2,000X$$
$$\frac{\$30,000}{\$2,000} = X$$
$$X = \underline{\underline{15 \text{ cars}}}$$

Illustration 11–1   **Income Statement**

SPORT AUTOS
Income Statement
February

Sales (20 cars at $15,000)	$300,000
Variable cost of goods sold	248,000
Variable selling costs	12,000
Contribution margin	40,000
Fixed costs	30,000
Operating profit	$ 10,000

For April:

$$\$50,000 = (\$15,000 - \$13,000)X - \$30,000$$
$$\$50,000 + \$30,000 = \$2,000X$$
$$\frac{\$80,000}{\$2,000} = X$$
$$X = \underline{\underline{40 \text{ cars}}}$$

Now the manager knows that Sport Autos must sell 15 cars in March to break even and 40 cars in April to make the targeted operating profit of $50,000.

Equation for Finding Target Volumes

In general, the equation for finding target volumes is:

$$\text{Target volume (in units)} = \frac{\text{Fixed costs} + \text{Target profit}}{\text{Contribution margin per unit}}$$
$$X = \frac{F + \pi}{P - V}$$

For April, in the above example:

$$X = \frac{F + \pi}{P - V}$$
$$= \frac{\$30,000 + \$50,000}{\$15,000 - \$13,000}$$
$$= \frac{\$80,000}{2,000}$$
$$= \underline{\underline{40 \text{ cars}}}$$

Break-Even Point

Break-Even Point The volume level where profits equal zero.

The **break-even point** is a special case of the above equation where π is set equal to zero:

$$X = \frac{F}{P - V}$$

For March, in the above example:

$$X = \frac{F}{P - V}$$
$$= \frac{\$30,000}{\$15,000 - \$13,000}$$
$$= \underline{\underline{15 \text{ cars}}}$$

Illustration 11–2 presents these relationships in graphic form, and explains the elements in the graph.

Profit-Volume Model

Profit-Volume Analysis A version of CVP analysis using a single profit line.

For convenience, the cost and revenue lines are often collapsed into a single profit line. This summary version of CVP analysis is called **profit-volume analysis.**

A graphic comparison of profit-volume and CVP relationships is shown in Illustration 11–3. Note that the slope of the profit-volume line equals the

Illustration 11-2   **CVP Graph, Sport Autos**

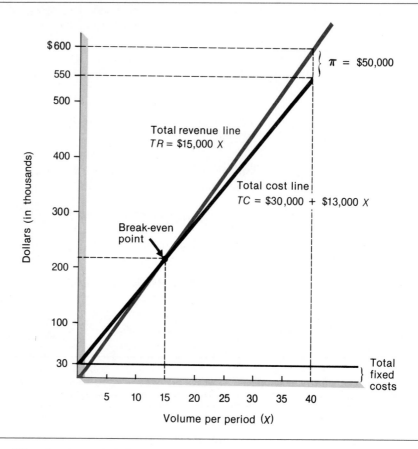

*Note that the vertical distance between *TR* and *TC* at $X = 40$ is the target π for April: $50,000.

The *vertical axis* presents dollars (for example, revenue-dollars, cost-dollars).

The *horizontal axis* presents the volume of activity for a time period (for example, number of cars sold per month).

The *total revenue (TR)* line relates total revenue to volume (for example, if Sport Autos sells 40 cars in a month, its total revenue would be $600,000, according to the graph). The slope of *TR* is the price per unit, *P* (for example, $15,000 per car for Sport Autos.)

The *total cost (TC)* line shows the total cost for each volume (for example, the total cost for a volume of 40 cars is $550,000 = [40 × $13,000] + $30,000). The intercept of the total cost line is the fixed cost for the period, *F* (for example, $30,000 for the month), and the slope is the variable cost per unit, *V* (for example, $13,000 per car).

The *break-even point* is the volume at which *TR* = *TC* (that is, the *TR* and *TC* lines intersect). Volumes lower than break-even result in an operating loss because *TR* < *TC*, volumes higher than break-even result in an operating profit because *TR* > *TC*. For Sport Autos, the break-even volume is 15 cars.

The amount of operating profit or loss can be read from the graph by measuring the vertical distance between *TR* and *TC*. For example, the vertical distance between *TR* and *TC* when *X* = 40 indicates $\pi = 50,000$.

Illustration 11-3   **Comparison of CVP and Profit-Volume Graphs, Sport Autos**

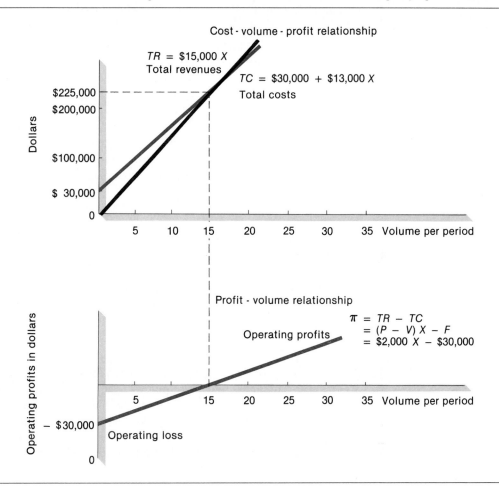

average unit contribution margin; the intercept equals the loss at zero volume, which equals fixed costs; and the vertical axis measures operating profit or loss.

Solving for Unknowns   A major application of the CVP model is solving for unknowns. For example, suppose that after examining the figures just presented, Sport Autos' manager pointed out, "We cannot obtain 40 cars from the manufacturer to sell in April. If we can only get 30 cars to sell, can we still make $50,000 in April?" An answer can be obtained by holding outputs at 30 units and operating profits at $50,000, and solving for each of the other terms in the following profit equation:

$$\$50,000 = (P - V)30 \text{ cars} - F$$

1. Solve for Contribution Margin

Find the average contribution margin per unit required to cover Sport Autos' $30,000 fixed costs and provide operating profits of $50,000:

$$\$50,000 = (P - V)30 - \$30,000$$
$$\$80,000 = (P - V)30$$
$$(P - V) = \frac{\$80,000}{30}$$
$$= \underline{\underline{\$2,667}}$$

Thus, the average contribution margin per car must be $2,667 if Sport Autos is to make $50,000. The increase in the contribution margin from $2,000 to $2,667 must come from a price increase, a decrease in variable costs per unit, or a combination of the two.

2. Solve for Fixed Cost

Holding the contribution margin per unit constant at $2,000, find the decrease in fixed costs that provides operating profits of $50,000 if 30 cars are sold:

$$\$50,000 = (\$15,000 - \$13,000)30 \text{ cars} - F$$
$$\$50,000 = \$60,000 - F$$
$$F = \underline{\underline{\$10,000}}$$

For Sport Autos to sell 30 cars while holding the unit contribution margin at $2,000 and to make operating profits of $50,000, a reduction in fixed costs from $30,000 to $10,000 would be required.

Managers can thus use CVP analysis to determine how to achieve profit goals by changing particular variables in the CVP equation. (This is a particularly useful application of computerized spreadsheet analysis.)

CVP analysis provides a valuable tool for determining the impact of prices, costs, and volume on operating profits. An important part of management's job is to manage each factor that affects operating profits to improve profitability.

Margin of Safety

Margin of Safety The excess of projected or actual sales over the break-even volume.

The **margin of safety** is the excess of projected (or actual) sales over the break-even sales level. This tells managers the margin between current sales and the break-even point. In a sense, margin of safety indicates the risk that a company faces of losing money. That is, the margin by which sales can fall before the company is in the loss area. The margin of safety formula is:

Sales volume − Break-even sales volume = Margin of safety

If Sport Autos sells 20 cars and its break-even volume is 15 cars, then its margin of safety is:

Sales − Break-even = 20 − 15
= 5 cars

Sales volume could drop by five cars per month before a loss is incurred, all other things held constant, as shown in Illustration 11–4.

Illustration 11-4   **Margin of Safety**

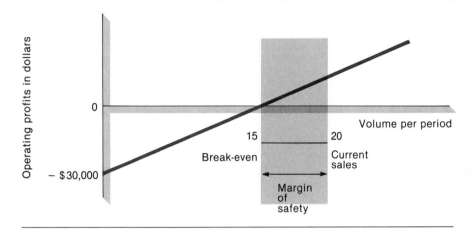

EXTENSIONS OF THE BASIC MODEL

CVP: Cash Flow Analysis

Sometimes decision makers may be more interested in the impact of the volume of activity on cash or working capital than on accrual profits. They often want to know if it is possible to operate at a loss and still generate positive cash flows. This type of analysis may be particularly relevant in adverse economic times or when a company is phasing out part of its operations. So long as there are sufficient cash flows, it may be optimal to continue the operation, even though there is an accounting loss.

Both revenues and costs include noncash items. But the most significant noncash item tends to be depreciation, which is usually included in fixed costs. This classification is common because depreciation generally represents the allocation of the acquisition cost of plant and equipment (capacity) over time based on an estimate of their useful lives.

To see how noncash items can affect CVP analysis, suppose that the fixed costs of Sport Autos include depreciation of equipment and other assets of $4,000 per month and that this is the only noncash revenue or expense.

Illustration 11–5 compares cash flow and accrual profit-volume relationships. By substituting appropriate numbers into the profit equation, you can demonstrate that if Sport Autos operates at an accrual profit break-even volume each month, it will generate monthly net cash flows of $4,000. This is a short-run phenomenon only, of course. When the time comes to replace the depreciable assets, the need for a large cash outflow must be faced.

Depreciation also may be included in *variable costs* if it is based on the *units of production* of some asset and thus related to volume. A common example is the depreciation of a machine based on its usage. Also, the costs of oil or gas wells are usually depreciated over the number of units of oil or gas produced since the economic life of a wasting asset is dependent on the number of units of the resource rather than the age of the well.

Income Taxes

Assuming that operating profits before taxes and taxable income are the same, income taxes may be incorporated into the basic model as follows:

Illustration 11–5   **Comparison of Short-Run Cash and Accrual Profit-Volume Relationships for Sport Autos**

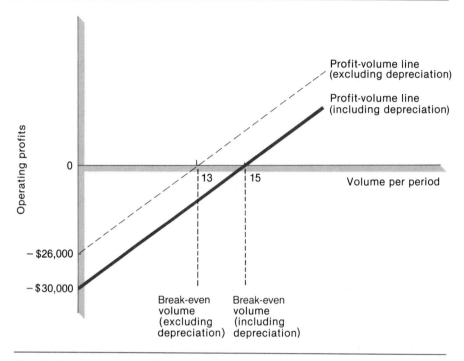

Note: The "cash break-even point" is found as follows:

$$X = \frac{\text{Fixed cash costs}}{\text{Cash contribution margin per unit}}$$

$$= \frac{\$30,000 - \$4,000 \text{ depreciation}}{\$15,000 - \$13,000} = \frac{\$26,000}{\$2,000} = 13 \text{ cars}$$

After-tax operating profit = (Before-tax operating profit)(1 − Tax rate)

If we let π_a designate after-tax operating profits, π_b designate before-tax operating profits, and t designate the tax rate (which is held constant for our purposes), then we have:

$$\pi_a = \pi_b(1 - t)$$

Substituting our earlier definition of operating profit, we obtain

$$\pi_a = [(P - V)X - F](1 - t)$$

Suppose that the manager of Sport Autos is interested in determining what volume is required to provide \$50,000 in operating profit *after taxes* in April, and $P = \$15,000$; $V = \$13,000$; $F = \$30,000$; and $t = .4$ (that is, an average tax rate for April of 40 percent). To find the required X that provides π_a of \$50,000:

$$\pi_a = [(P - V)X - F](1 - t)$$
$$\$50,000 = [(\$15,000 - \$13,000)X - \$30,000](1 - .4)$$
$$\$50,000 = (\$2,000X - \$30,000)(.6)$$

$$\$50,000 = \$1,200X - \$18,000$$
$$\$68,000 = \$1,200X$$
$$\frac{\$68,000}{\$1,200} = X = 56\tfrac{2}{3} \text{ units}$$

It is common for "fixed costs" to behave in a step fashion as follows:

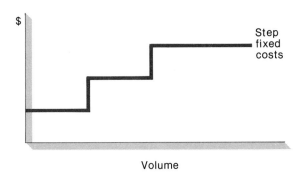

Suppose the managers of a manufacturing company are considering extending a factory's hours of operations to the evening hours. Assume the price, volumes, and costs would be as follows:

	Monthly Production and Sales	Total Fixed Costs	Variable Cost	Price
Regular shift	0–10,000 units	$200,000	$15 per unit	$40 per unit
Evening shift	10,001–18,000 units	300,000	15 per unit	40 per unit

The CVP lines would be as shown in Illustration 11–6.

As indicated on the graph, if the company operates only one shift, its capacity is limited to 10,000 units. Adding the second shift increases the capacity to 18,000 units. Profits will increase if enough additional units can be sold.

The company would have two break-even points—one within each level of activity:

$$X = \frac{F}{P - V}$$

$$\text{Break-even } X \text{ (regular shift)} = \frac{\$200,000}{\$40 - \$15} = \underline{\underline{8,000 \text{ units}}}$$

$$\text{Break-even } X \text{ (evening shift)} = \frac{\$300,000}{\$40 - \$15} = \underline{\underline{12,000 \text{ units}}}$$

Should the company open the second shift, assuming all other things are the same except for the increase in each period's fixed costs and the increase in volume noted above? From the calculations shown below, and assuming the company can sell everything it makes, it is more profitable to operate with two shifts than with one.

Illustration 11-6   **CVP Analysis with Semifixed Costs**

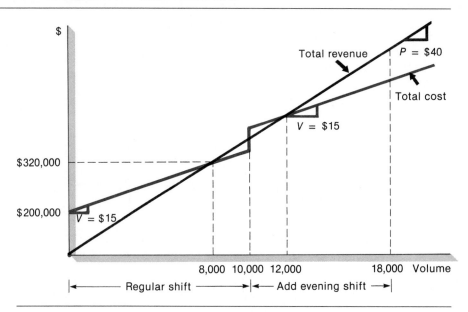

	Regular Shift Only	**Add Evening Shift**
Volume in units	10,000	18,000
Sales revenue	$400,000 (=$40 × 10,000)	$720,000 (=$40 × 18,000)
Variable costs	150,000 (=$15 × 10,000)	270,000 (=$15 × 18,000)
Total contribution	250,000	450,000
Fixed costs	200,000	300,000
Operating profit	$ 50,000	$150,000

MULTIPRODUCT CVP ANALYSIS

We assumed that Sport Autos buys and sells only one line of sports cars. Many companies, of course, produce and/or sell many products from the same asset base.

Dual Autos sells two car models: Regular and Deluxe. The prices and costs of the two are:

	Regular	**Deluxe**
Average sales price	$12,000	$20,000
Less average variable costs:		
Automobile cost to dealer	(9,600)	(14,600)
Supplies used to prepare car for sale	(200)	(400)
Sales commission	(1,200)	(2,000)
Average contribution margin per car	$ 1,000	$ 3,000

Average monthly fixed costs are $36,000.

Illustration 11-7   **Combinations of Break-Even Volumes for Dual Autos**

| Regular Model | | Deluxe Model | | Total Contribution for Both Models |
Quantity	Total Contribution	Quantity	Total Contribution	
36	$36,000	0	$ -0-	$36,000
33	33,000	1	3,000	36,000
30	30,000	2	6,000	36,000
.	.	.	.	.
.	.	.	.	.
.	.	.	.	.
6	6,000	10	30,000	36,000
3	3,000	11	33,000	36,000
0	-0-	12	36,000	36,000

The profit equation presented earlier must now be expanded to consider the contribution of each product:

$$\pi = [(P_r - V_r)X_r] + [(P_d - V_d)X_d] - F$$

where subscript r designates the Regular model and subscript d designates the Deluxe model. Thus, the company's profit equation is:

$$\pi = (\$1,000X_r) + (\$3,000X_d) - \$36,000$$

The manager of Dual Autos has been listening to a debate between two of the sales personnel about the break-even point for the company. According to one, they have to sell 36 cars a month to break even. But the other claims that 12 cars a month would be sufficient. Who is right? The claim that 36 cars must be sold to break even is correct if *only* the *Regular* model is sold, while the claim that 12 cars need to be sold to break even is correct if *only* the *Deluxe* model is sold. In fact, there are many break-even points. This is evident from Dual Auto's profit equation, which has two unknown variables. All possible break-even points for Dual Autos are listed in Illustration 11-7 (assuming, of course, that only *whole* autos can be sold).

Illustration 11-8 is a graphic presentation of the possible break-even volumes for Dual Autos. The break-even line in Illustration 11-8 is one of a family of lines known as **isoprofit lines.** Profits are the same at any point on an isoprofit line. (Think of "iso" as "equal.") So operating profits are the same for any combination of volumes at any point on that line. The dashed line parallel to the break-even line shows the isoprofit line for the various combinations of volumes that would provide $3,000 in operating profit.

Isoprofit Lines Family of constant profit lines where operating profits are the same for any combination of volumes on each of those lines.

Note in Illustration 11-8 that any combination of products to the right of the break-even line provides profits, while any combination to the left results in losses.

In general, the multiproduct CVP equation for n different products is:

$$\pi = (P_1 - V_1)X_1 + (P_2 - V_2)X_2 + \ldots + (P_n - V_n)X_n - F$$

CVP analysis of multiple products is *much* more complex than is analysis of a single product. As indicated in the Dual Autos example, even for a two-product company, the number of possible solutions is large because there

Illustration 11–8   **Illustration of Possible Break-Even Volumes for Dual Autos**

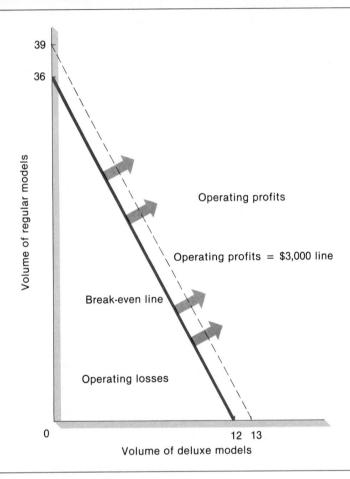

are many combinations of product volumes that will yield a given profit. You can imagine the complications when hundreds of products are involved.

Simplifying Multiproduct CVP

To simplify matters, managers often assume a particular product mix and compute break-even or target volumes using either of the following two methods.

Assume a Fixed Product Mix

Using this method, managers define a "package" of products in the typical product mix, then compute the break-even or target volume for the package.

For example, suppose the manager of Dual Autos would be willing to assume that the Regular and Deluxe models would be sold in a six-to-four ratio; that is, out of every 10 cars sold, 6 would be Regular models and 4 would be Deluxe models. Defining X as a "package" of 6 Regulars and

4 Deluxes, the contribution from this package is:

$$
\begin{aligned}
\text{Regular } 6 \times \$1,000 &= \$\ 6,000 \\
\text{Deluxe } 4 \times \$3,000 &= \underline{\$12,000} \\
\text{Total} &\quad \underline{\underline{\$18,000}}
\end{aligned}
$$

Now the break-even point is computed as follows:

$$
\begin{aligned}
X^* &= \frac{\text{Fixed costs}}{\text{Volume}} \\
&= \frac{\$36,000}{\$18,000} \\
&= 2 \text{ packages}
\end{aligned}
$$

where X^* refers to the break-even number of "packages." This means that the sale of 2 packages of 6 Regulars and 4 Deluxes per package, totaling 12 Regulars and 8 Deluxes, would contribute enough to break even.

Assume a Weighted-Average Contribution Margin

This approach also requires an assumed product mix, which we continue to assume is 60 percent Regulars and 40 percent Deluxes. The problem can be solved by using a weighted-average contribution margin per unit. When a company assumes a constant product mix, the contribution margin is the **weighted-average contribution margin** of all of its products.

Weighted-Average Contribution Margin The contribution margin of all of a company's products when a constant product mix is assumed.

For Dual Autos, the weighted-average contribution margin per unit could be computed by multiplying each product's proportion by its contribution margin:

$$
(.6 \times \$1,000) + (.4 \times \$3,000) = \underline{\$1,800}
$$

The multiple-product break-even for Dual Autos can be determined from the break-even formula:

$$
\begin{aligned}
\pi &= (\$1,800X) - \$36,000 \\
\text{If } \pi &= \$0 \\
\$0 &= (\$1,800X) - \$36,000 \\
\$1,800X &= \$36,000 \\
X &= \frac{\$36,000}{\$1,800} \\
&= \underline{20 \text{ cars}}
\end{aligned}
$$

where X refers to the break-even quantity. The product mix assumption means Dual Autos must sell 12 $(.6 \times 20)$ Regular models and 8 $(.4 \times 20)$ Deluxe models to break even.

Finding the Break-Even Volume in Dollars

Companies often measure volume in dollars rather than units when the CVP analysis deals with multiple products. When dollars are used, volume is no longer defined as X in the CVP model. Instead, volume is PX, where P is the unit price. Thus, we multiply both sides of the original break-even formula by P as follows:

Original formula for units:

$$X = \frac{F}{P - V}$$

Modified formula for dollars:

$$PX = \left(\frac{F}{P - V}\right)P$$

Since dividing the denominator by P is the same as multiplying the entire term by P, we obtain:

$$PX = \frac{F}{\dfrac{(P - V)}{P}}$$

Contribution Margin Ratio
Contribution margin as a percentage of sales revenue.

The term $\dfrac{P - V}{P}$ is known as the **contribution margin ratio**. The result can be derived directly from the break-even formula:

$$
\begin{aligned}
PX &= \frac{F}{1 - \dfrac{V}{P}} \\[2mm]
&= \frac{\$30,000}{1 - \dfrac{\$13,000}{\$15,000}} = \frac{\$30,000}{1 - .8667} \\[2mm]
&= \$225,000
\end{aligned}
$$

We can check this result by recalling that the break-even volume in units was 15 cars per month. If sold at a price of $15,000 each, the break-even volume measured in sales dollars is $225,000 (15 cars × $15,000).

Finding Target Sales Dollars
To consider a different example, suppose we want to find the break-even sales dollars for a management education course at a university. The tuition that 80 percent of the students pay is $1,000 each; 20 percent of the students receive a discount and pay $800 each. The variable cost is $240 per student, and the fixed cost of the course is $10,000. What is the break-even point in tuition dollars?

$$
\begin{aligned}
PX &= \frac{F}{1 - \dfrac{V}{P}} \\[2mm]
&= \frac{\$10,000}{1 - \left[\dfrac{240}{(.8 \times \$1,000) + (.2 \times \$800)}\right]} \\[2mm]
&= \frac{\$10,000}{1 - \left(\dfrac{\$240}{\$960}\right)} \\[2mm]
&= \frac{\$10,000}{.75} \\[2mm]
&= \underline{\underline{\$13,333}}
\end{aligned}
$$

The course breaks even if tuition receipts amount to $13,333. Note that the variable cost ratio in this case is a *weighted average* based on the assumed product mix of 80/20 (20 percent of the students receive a discount). If the product mix were to change, the variable cost ratio would change and the break-even sales dollars would change.

Finding Target Profit

Next, assume that the university has a target operating profit of $10,000 plus 10 percent of sales dollars for the management education course. From the original formula,

$$\pi = \left(1 - \frac{V}{P}\right) PX - F,$$

we incorporate these profit goals as follows:

$$\$10,000 + .10PX = \left(1 - \frac{V}{P}\right) PX - F$$

Combining terms and solving for PX gives:

$$
\begin{aligned}
\$10,000 + .10PX &= (1 - .25)PX - \$10,000 \\
.10PX &= .75PX - \$20,000 \\
.10PX - .75PX &= -\$20,000 \\
.65PX &= \$20,000 \\
PX &= \frac{\$20,000}{.65} \\
&= \underline{\$30,769}
\end{aligned}
$$

Results:

Revenues	$30,769
Less variable costs (.25 × $30,769)	7,692
Fixed costs	10,000
Operating profits	$13,077

To check, $13,077 = $10,000 + (.10 × $30,769).

Common Fixed Costs in CVP Analysis

Suppose that Dual Autos' total fixed costs of $36,000 can be attributed to the two products as follows:

Direct fixed costs:	
Regular model	$ 9,000
Deluxe model	9,000
Common fixed costs	18,000
Total fixed costs	$36,000

What is the break-even quantity for each product and for the company as a whole?

We compute the break-even volume for the Regular model:

$$X_r = \frac{F}{P - V} = \frac{\$9,000}{\$1,000} = \underline{\underline{9 \text{ cars}}}$$

and break-even volume for the Deluxe model:

$$X_d = \frac{F}{P - V} = \frac{\$9,000}{\$3,000} = \underline{\underline{3 \text{ cars}}}$$

If each product line just breaks even, the operating profit or loss for the company as a whole is:

$$\begin{aligned}
\pi &= (\$1,000X_r) + (\$3,000X_d) - \$36,000 \\
&= (\$1,000 \times 9) + (\$3,000 \times 3) - \$36,000 \\
&= \$18,000 - \$36,000 \\
&= - \underline{\underline{\$18,000}}
\end{aligned}$$

Although the sale of nine Regular models and three Deluxe models would make each product appear to break even, the company would lose $18,000.

This demonstrates a common problem in applying CVP analysis. The volume required for a specific product to break even will not cover unassigned common costs.

One way of dealing with the problem is to allocate the common costs to the products. This permits a CVP analysis for each product. Of course, the results depend on the allocation method. In such cases, it is wise to perform sensitivity analysis with various allocation methods to discover any that might affect management decisions.

For example, Illustration 11–9 presents CVP analyses for Dual Autos, first assuming that the $18,000 in common fixed costs are allocated evenly to the two products, and then assuming that two thirds of the common fixed costs are allocated to the Deluxe model and one third to the Regular model. As you can see, changing the allocation of fixed costs changes the product mix required to break even or to achieve a target level of operating profits for the company as a whole.

The break-even volumes shown in Illustration 11–9 are only two of many possible combinations. Allocating common fixed costs to products does not dispense with the product mix problem. Nonetheless, it makes product-line CVP analysis possible, and it ensures that common fixed costs are not ignored. Because the allocation of common fixed costs is often arbitrary, we recommend performing sensitivity analysis on the allocation method before using the information for decision making.

THE ECONOMIST'S PROFIT-MAXIMIZATION MODEL

The classical economist's profit-maximization model provides the foundation for CVP analysis. It assumes that management's goal is profit maximization, where profits are the difference between total revenues and total costs. Management's job is to determine and take the most profitable actions possible.

In general, accountants accept the classical economist's model, but they make two simplifying assumptions:

Illustration 11-9   **Impact of Common Fixed Cost Allocation Method on Break-Even Volume, Dual Autos**

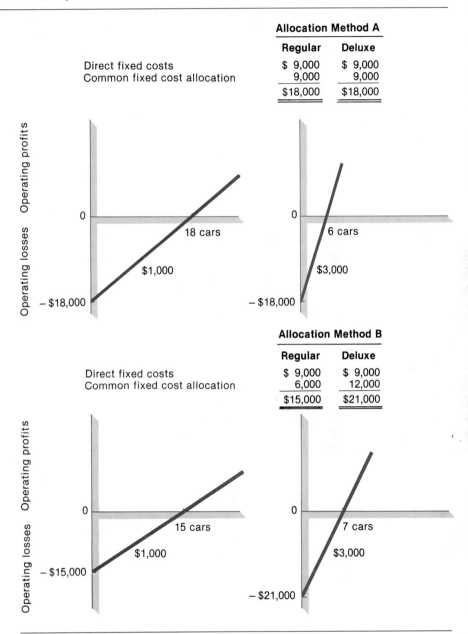

	Allocation Method A	
	Regular	Deluxe
Direct fixed costs	$ 9,000	$ 9,000
Common fixed cost allocation	9,000	9,000
	$18,000	$18,000

	Allocation Method B	
	Regular	Deluxe
Direct fixed costs	$ 9,000	$ 9,000
Common fixed cost allocation	6,000	12,000
	$15,000	$21,000

1. In economics, *total revenue and total cost curves* are usually assumed to be nonlinear. The linearity simplifications are usually considered valid within some appropriate range of volume, termed the *relevant range*.

2. The opportunity cost of invested equity capital is usually excluded in the accountant's cost measures, while it is included in the economist's

model. Thus, in economic terms, the accountant's measurement of total costs is understated.

A comparison of accountants' and economists' assumptions about the behavior of costs and revenue is shown in Illustration 11–10. The solid lines represent accountants' assumptions about cost and revenue behavior, while the dashed lines designate economists' assumptions. Note the difference in assumptions about linearity as well as the systematically higher economists' costs because accounting costs do not include the opportunity cost of capital.

Simplifying Assumptions about Cost and Revenue Behavior

Strictly speaking, neither model is "correct," because both economists and accountants have made simplifying assumptions about cost and revenue behavior. The actual curves would be disjointed and would take into account inconsistencies such as sales discounts for certain customers, costs that are neither strictly fixed nor strictly variable, and so forth. However, a cost-benefit analysis of more "accurate" data about cost and revenue behavior may yield little additional benefit to decision makers.

Limitations and Assumptions

Like any other tool, CVP analysis has limitations that make it more applicable to some decisions than to others. Some of these limitations and the impact they can have on the results of CVP analysis follow. As with any

Illustration 11–10   **Comparison of Economists' and Accountants' Assumed Cost and Revenue Behavior**

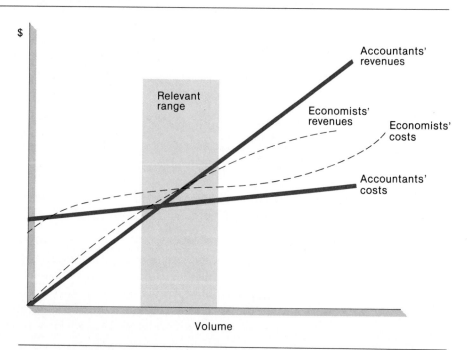

management information, the system is judged in terms of a cost-benefit test. Overcoming some of the listed limitations may not be cost justified.

Assumed and Actual Cost Behavior

A linear CVP analysis assumes that:

1. Revenues change proportionately with volume.
2. Total variable costs change proportionately with volume.
3. Fixed costs do not change at all with volume.

One useful feature of CVP analysis is its simplicity in showing the impact of sales prices, costs, and volume on operating profits (or cash flows). But the cost of this simplicity is often a lack of realism. Some costs cannot be easily classified. Costs seldom behave in a neat linear fashion. CVP analysis is based on the assumption that within a specific range of activity, the linear expression approximates reality closely enough that the results will not be badly distorted.

Assumed linear relationships are more likely to be valid for short time periods (one year or less) and small changes in volume than for long periods and large changes in volume. Most fixed costs are only fixed in the short run. Over time, management may make decisions that change fixed costs. For example, during a recent downturn in the economy, a steel company announced the closing of two of the four blast furnaces in one of its plants. Many costs that were fixed while all four blast furnaces were operating (for example, supervisory salaries, product inspection costs, some maintenance and utilities costs) were temporarily eliminated.

Also, many nonvolume factors that would affect prices and costs (for example, limited capacity, technological changes, and input factor prices) are more likely to be constant over short time periods.

Assuming a Constant Product Mix

As we saw earlier in the chapter with multiple products, a change in product mix can affect operating profits. Holding the product mix constant allows the analyst to focus on the impact of prices, costs, and volume on operating profits.

Recording Costs as Expenses

If the costs used in CVP analysis are not the same ones expensed in the financial statements, the resultant operating profit will not be the same. Discrepancies are usually caused by timing differences in the recognition of expenses.

The most common source of difference is the treatment of fixed manufacturing costs when production volume is not equal to sales volume. As discussed in Chapter 9, generally accepted accounting principles (GAAP) and income tax regulations require use of *full-absorption costing*. For financial statements, fixed manufacturing costs must be treated as product costs and expensed when the goods are sold. However, CVP analysis is like variable costing—*all* fixed costs, including fixed manufacturing costs, are treated as if they will be expensed during the period. Thus, while fixed manufacturing costs are treated as product costs for external financial reporting, they are treated as period costs for CVP analysis.

SUMMARY

CVP analysis examines the impact of prices, costs, and volume on operating profits, as summarized in the profit equation:

$$\pi = (P - V)X - F$$

where

π = Operating profits
P = Average unit selling price
V = Average unit variable costs
X = Quantity of output
F = Total fixed costs

CVP analysis is both a management tool for determining the impact of selling prices, costs, and volume on profits and a conceptual tool, or way of thinking, about managing a company. It helps management focus on the objective of obtaining the best possible combination of prices, volume, variable costs, and fixed costs.

An advantage of the CVP model is its simplicity. However, the price of such simplicity is a set of limiting assumptions that result in some loss of realism. When multiple products are analyzed, a constant product mix must be assumed or common costs must be allocated. Whenever assumptions are made, it is advisable to perform sensitivity analysis to determine whether (and how) the assumption affects decisions.

TERMS AND CONCEPTS

The following terms and concepts should be familiar to you after reading this chapter:

Break-Even Point   **Product Mix**
Contribution Margin   **Profit Equation**
Contribution Margin Ratio   **Profit-Volume Analysis**
Cost-Volume-Profit (CVP) Analysis   **Weighted-Average Contribution**
Isoprofit Lines   **Margin**
Margin of Safety

SUPPLEMENTARY READINGS

Camp, Roger A. "Multidimensional Break-Even Analysis." *Journal of Accountancy,* January 1987, pp. 132–3.

Chan, Ken. "Break-Even Analysis: A Unit Cost Model." *CGA Magazine,* March 1985, pp. 19–20, 31 (published in Canada).

Chastain, Clark E. "Streamlining: Necessary Strategy for Licking a Profit Crunch." *Business Horizons,* March–April 1984, pp. 69–76.

Cheatam, Carole. "Profit and Productivity Analysis Revisited." *Journal of Accountancy,* July 1987, p. 123.

Chow, Chee W.; Howard R. Toole; and Adrian Wong-Boren. "Make Better Decisions: Divide and Conquer." *Management Accounting,* August 1986, pp. 41–45.

Govindarajan, Vijayaraghavan. "Use of Accounting Data in Product Pricing." *Corporate Accounting,* Spring 1984, pp. 38–44.

Greer, Willis R., and Shu S. Liao. "Weapons Pricing Models for Defense Acquisition Policy." *Journal of Accounting and Public Policy,* Winter 1987, pp. 271–84.

Haka, Susan; Lauren Friedman; and Virginia Jones. "Functional Fixation and Interference Theory: A Theoretical and Empirical Investigation." *Accounting Review,* July 1986, pp. 455–74.

Koch, Bruce S. "Evaluating Offshore Energy Leases Using Cost-Volume-Profit Analysis." *Journal of Petroleum Accounting,* Summer 1986, pp. 35–42.

Lauderman, Mark L. "Practical Approach to Break-Even Analysis." *Journal of Commercial Bank Lending,* January 1987, pp. 41–48.

Lere, John C. "Product Pricing Based on Accounting Costs." *Accounting Review,* April 1986, pp. 318–24.

Martin, Howard. "Breaking through the Breakeven Barriers." *Management Accounting,* May 1985, pp. 31–34.

Mazhin, Reza. "CVP Analysis with an Electronic Spreadsheet." *Journal of Accountancy,* January 1987, pp. 110, 112, 114, 116.

Shashua, Laon, and Yaaqov Goldschmidt. "Break Even Analysis under Inflation." *Engineering Economist,* Winter 1987, pp. 79–88.

SELF-STUDY PROBLEM NO. 1: LEONARD COMPANY

Given the following information for Leonard Company for April:

Sales	$180,000
Fixed manufacturing costs	22,000
Fixed marketing and administrative costs	14,000
Total fixed costs	36,000
Total variable costs	120,000
Unit price	$9
Unit variable manufacturing cost	5
Unit variable marketing cost	1

Required:

Compute the following:

a. Operating profit when sales are $180,000 (as above).

b. Break-even quantity.

c. Quantity that would produce an operating profit of $30,000.

d. Quantity that would produce an operating profit of 20 percent of sales dollars.

e. Break-even sales quantity if unit variable costs are reduced by 10 percent per product unit, assuming no changes in total fixed costs.

f. Sales dollars required to generate an operating profit of $20,000.

g. Number of units sold in April.

SOLUTION TO SELF-STUDY PROBLEM NO. 1

a.

$$\pi = PX - VX - F$$
$$= \$180,000 - \$120,000 - \$36,000$$
$$= \underline{\underline{\$24,000}}$$

b. Break-even

$$X = \frac{F}{P - V}$$
$$= \frac{\$36,000}{\$9 - \$6}$$
$$= \underline{\underline{12,000 \text{ units}}}$$

c.

$$X = \frac{F + \text{Target } \pi}{P - V}$$
$$= \frac{\$36,000 + \$30,000}{\$9 - \$6}$$
$$= \underline{\underline{22,000 \text{ units}}}$$

d. Target

$$\pi = .2PX$$
$$\pi = PX - VX - F$$
$$.2PX = PX - VX - F$$
$$.8PX - VX = F$$
$$(.8P - V)X = F$$
$$X = \frac{F}{(.8P - V)}$$
$$= \frac{\$36,000}{[(.8)(\$9) - \$6]}$$
$$= \frac{\$36,000}{\$1.20}$$
$$= \underline{\underline{30,000 \text{ units}}}$$

e.

$$X = \frac{F}{P - V}$$
$$= \frac{\$36,000}{[\$9 - (.9)(\$6)]}$$
$$= \frac{\$36,000}{\$3.60}$$
$$= \underline{\underline{10,000 \text{ units}}}$$

f.

$$PX = \frac{F + \text{Target } \pi}{1 - \dfrac{V}{P}} = \frac{F + \text{Target } \pi}{\dfrac{P - V}{P}}$$
$$= \frac{\$36,000 + 20,000}{1 - \dfrac{\$6}{\$9}} = \frac{\$36,000 + 20,000}{\dfrac{\$9 - \$6}{\$9}}$$
$$= \frac{\$56,000}{\dfrac{\$3}{\$9}}$$
$$= \underline{\underline{\$168,000}}$$

g. Units sold in April:

$$X = \frac{\$180,000}{\$9}$$
$$= \underline{\underline{20,000 \text{ units}}}$$

SELF-STUDY PROBLEM NO. 2: MULTIPRODUCT COMPANY

Multiproduct Company produces these products with the following characteristics:

	Product I	Product II	Product III
Price per unit	$5	$6	$7
Variable cost per unit	3	2	4
Expected sales (units)	100,000	150,000	250,000

Total fixed costs for the company are $1,240,000.

Required:

Assuming the product mix would be the same at the break-even point, compute the break-even point in:

a. Units (total and by product line).

b. Sales dollars (total and by product line).

SOLUTION TO SELF-STUDY PROBLEM NO. 2

a. Compute weighted-average contribution margin:

	I	II	III	Total
	100,000 units	150,000	250,000	500,000
Product mix	20%	30%	50%	100%

Weighted-average contribution margin ($P^* - V^*$):

$$.20(\$2) + .30(\$4) + .50(\$3) = \underline{\$3.10}$$

Or

$$\frac{(100,000 \text{ units})(\$2) + (150,000 \text{ units})(\$4) + (250,000 \text{ units})(\$3)}{500,000} = \$3.10$$

$$X = \frac{\$1,240,000}{\$3.10} = \underline{400,000 \text{ units}}$$

b. To compute break-even sales dollars, find weighted-average price and variable costs:

$$P^* = (.20)(\$5) + (.30)(\$6) + (.50)(\$7)$$
$$= \$6.30$$
$$V^* = (.20)(\$3) + (.30)(\$2) + (.50)(\$4)$$
$$= \underline{\$3.20}$$

$$\text{Break-even } PX = \frac{\$1,240,000}{1 - \dfrac{\$3.20}{\$6.30}} = \frac{\$1,240,000}{\dfrac{\$3.10}{\$6.30}}$$

$$= \frac{\$1,240,000}{.492 \text{ (rounded)}}$$

$$= \underline{\$2,520,000} \text{ (rounded to nearest \$1,000)}$$

(Check: 400,000 units × $6.30 = $2,520,000.)

Product-line amounts:

	Total (100%)	Product I (20%)	II (30%)	III (50%)
Units	400,000	80,000	120,000	200,000
Units price	$6.30	$5	$6	$7
Sales dollars	$2,520,000	$400,000	$720,000	$1,400,000

QUESTIONS

11-1. Define the profit equation.

11-2. What are the components of total costs in the profit equation?

11-3. What is the meaning of the term *contribution margin*?

11-4. How does the total *contribution margin* differ from the *gross margin* that is often shown on companies' financial statements?

11-5. Compare cost-volume-profit (CVP) analysis with profit-volume analysis. How do they differ?

11-6. Is a company really breaking even if it produces and sells at the "break-even" point? What costs might not be covered?

11-7. What is usually the difference between CVP analysis on a cash basis and that on an accounting accrual basis? For a company having depreciable assets, would you expect the accrual break-even point to be higher, lower, or the same as the cash break-even point?

11-8. How is the profit equation expanded when multiproduct CVP analysis is used?

11-9. Is it possible to have many break-even points and many alternative ways to achieve a target operating profit when a company has multiple products?

11-10. Why is a constant product mix often assumed in multiproduct CVP analysis?

11-11. Define the contribution margin when a constant product mix is assumed in multiproduct CVP analyses.

11-12. When would the sum of the break-even quantities for each of a company's products not be the break-even point for the company as a whole?

11-13. What is the difference between economic "profit" and accounting "net income" or "operating profit"?

11-14. How can CVP analysis be used for planning and performance evaluation?

11-15. Name three common assumptions of linear CVP analysis.

11-16. Why might there be a difference between the operating profit calculated by CVP analysis and the net income reported in financial statements for external reporting?

11-17. Fixed costs are often defined as "fixed over the short run." Does this mean they are not fixed over the long run? Why or why not?

11-18. Why does the accountant use a linear representation of cost and revenue behavior in CVP analysis? How can this use be justified?

11-19. The following graph implies that profits increase continually as volume increases:

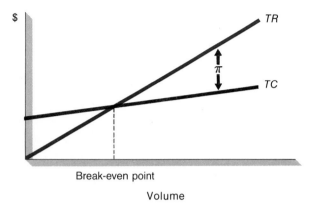

Break-even point

Volume

What are some of the factors that might prevent the increasing profits that are indicated when linear CVP analysis is employed?

11-20. Why would fixed costs tend not to be relevant for a typical CVP analysis? Under what circumstances might the fixed costs be relevant in CVP analyses?

11-21. CVP analysis is an oversimplification of the real-world environment. For this reason, it has little to offer a decision maker. Comment.

EXERCISES

11-22. Profit Equation—Components
(L.O.1)

Identify each of the following on the graph that follows.

a. The total cost line.

b. The total revenue line.

c. The total variable costs area.

d. Variable cost per unit.

e. The fixed costs area.

f. The break-even point.

g. The profit area (or volume).

h. The loss area (or volume).

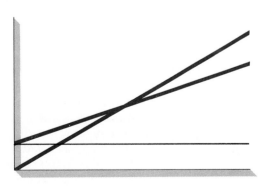

**11–23. Profit Equation—
Components**
(L.O.1)

Identify the places on the profit-volume graph indicated by the letters below:

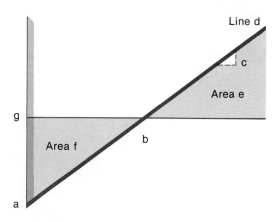

**11–24. CVP Analysis—
Planning and Decision Making**
(L.O.2)

The Magic Movies Company has the following costs and revenues for the year for movie ticket sales:

Total revenues	$5,000,000
Total fixed costs	1,000,000
Total variable costs	3,000,000
Total quantity	1,000,000 tickets

Required:

a. What is the average selling price per unit?

b. What is the average variable cost per unit?

c. What is the average contribution margin per unit?

d. What is the break-even point?

e. What quantity of movie ticket sales is required for Magic Movies Company to make an operating profit of $2 million for the year on ticket sales?

**11–25. CVP Analysis—
Planning and Decision Making**
(L.O.2)

Choose the *best* answer for each of the following questions:

a. If a firm has a negative contribution margin, to reach break-even:
  (1) Sales volume must be increased.
  (2) Sales volume must be decreased.
  (3) Fixed cost must be decreased.
  (4) Fixed cost must be increased.
  (5) None of the above.

b. If total contribution margin is decreased by a given amount, operating profit would:
  (1) Decrease by the same amount.
  (2) Decrease by more than the given amount.
  (3) Increase by the same amount.
  (4) Remain unchanged.
  (5) None of the above.

c. The break-even point would be increased by:
  (1) A decrease in fixed costs.
  (2) An increase in contribution margin ratio.
  (3) An increase in variable costs.

(4) A decrease in variable costs.

(5) None of the above.

(CPA adapted)

**11–26. CVP Analysis—
Planning and Decision Making**
(L.O.2)

ElectroSol Systems, Inc., has been organized to sell and install solar energy systems in the Southwest. The marketing consultants for the company estimate that at a selling price of $3,000 per unit, the company should be able to sell 10,000 units per year. However, the company's financial advisor believes sales will be 7,000 units per year at the same sales price.

The company's controller estimates annual fixed costs will equal $12 million and that the variable cost on each unit will be $1,600.

Required:

a. Determine the profit or loss at the 7,000-unit and 10,000-unit activity levels.

b. What is the break-even point?

**11–27. CVP Analysis—
Planning and Decision Making**
(L.O.2)

Alto Music Store, Inc., is considering introduction of a new product with the following price and cost characteristics:

Sales price	$	100 each
Variable costs		60 each
Fixed costs		200,000 per year

Required:

a. What quantity is required for Alto, Inc., to break even?

b. What quantity is required for Alto, Inc., to make an operating profit of $100,000 for the year?

**11–28. CVP Analysis—
Planning and Decision Making**
(L.O.2)

Refer to the data for Alto Music Store, Inc., exercise 11–27. Assume the projected quantity for the year is 8,000 units for each of the following situations:

1. What will the operating profit be for 8,000 units?

2. What would be the impact on operating profit if the sales price decreases by 10 percent? Increases by 20 percent?

3. What would be the impact on operating profit if variable costs per unit decrease by 10 percent? Increase by 20 percent?

4. Suppose fixed costs for the year are 10 percent lower than projected, while variable costs per unit are 10 percent higher than projected. What impact would these cost changes have on operating profit for the year? (Would profit go up? Down? By how much?)

**11–29. CVP Analysis—
Planning and Decision Making**
(L.O.2)

a. Given the following formulas, which one represents the break-even sales level in units? P = Selling price per unit; F = Total fixed costs; V = Variable cost per unit.

(1) $\dfrac{F}{P - V}$.

(2) $\dfrac{P}{F \div V}$.

(3) $\dfrac{F}{V \div P}$.

(4) $\dfrac{V}{P - F}$.

(5) $\dfrac{P}{F - V}$.

b. Which of the following assumptions is *not* made in break-even analysis?
  (1) Volume is the only factor affecting cost.
  (2) No change between beginning and ending inventory.
  (3) The sales mix is maintained as volume changes.
  (4) All of the above are assumptions sometimes required in break-even analysis.

c. A company increased the selling price for its products from $1 to $1.10 a unit when total fixed cost increased from $400,000 to $480,000 and variable cost per unit remained the same. How would these changes affect the break-even point?
  (1) The break-even point in units would be increased.
  (2) The break-even point in units would be decreased.
  (3) The break-even point in units would remain unchanged.
  (4) The effect cannot be determined from the given information.

(CPA adapted)

11–30. Extensions of the Basic Model—Semifixed (Step) Costs
(L.O.3)

Shift Manufacturing Company manufactures and sells one product. The sales price of $10 remains constant per unit regardless of volume, as does the variable cost of $6 per unit. The company can choose to operate at one of the following three levels of monthly operations:

	Volume Range (Production and Sales)	Total Fixed Costs
Level 1	0–16,000	$40,000
Level 2	16,001–28,000	72,000
Level 3	28,001–38,000	94,000

Required:

a. Calculate the break-even point(s).

b. If the company can sell everything it makes, should it operate at level 1, level 2, or level 3? Support your answer.

11–31. Extensions of the Basic Model—Taxes
(L.O.3)

The Wheelright bicycle shop is considering adding a type of helmet to its merchandise products. These helmets have the following prices and costs:

Selling price per helmet	$ 25.00
Variable cost per helmet	19.80
Fixed costs per year associated with these helmets	468,000.00
Income tax rate	40%

Required:

a. Wheelright's break-even point in units is:
  (1) 76,667.
  (2) 90,000.
  (3) 130,000.
  (4) 72,000.
  (5) Some other amount.

b. How many units would Wheelright have to sell in order to earn $156,000 after taxes?
  (1) 120,000 units.
  (2) 165,000 units.
  (3) 140,000 units.

(4) 148,889 units.

(5) Some other amount.

11–32. Extensions of the Basic Model—Taxes

(L.O.3)

Required:

Mary J. Sales Corporation is contemplating introducing a new line of cosmetic kits for skin care. The kits would sell for $12 each. The variable costs associated with each kit amount to $3. If the kits are to be introduced nationwide, the company will have to obtain acceptable profits on a test market basis. The fixed costs associated with test marketing amount to $260,000 per year.

a. Compute the break-even point in units for test market sales.

b. If the desired profit level is $80,000 before tax, compute the sales level in units required to attain that profit level.

c. Assuming the tax rate is 45 percent and the desired profit level is $80,000 after tax, compute the required unit sales level.

11–33. Multiple Products— Using CVP Analysis to Measure Volume

(L.O.4)

Required:

Giovanni's Restaurant estimates its fixed costs to be $300,000 per month.

a. Determine the break-even point in sales dollars if the variable cost ratio is 2:3.

b. Determine the break-even point in sales dollars if fixed costs remained at $300,000 per month but the contribution margin ratio was 4:10.

11–34. CVP Analysis— Multiple Products

(L.O.4)

Pete's Pizza produces two products, 12-inch pizzas and 16-inch pizzas, with the following characteristics:

	12-Inch Pizza	16-Inch Pizza
Selling price per unit	$5	$6
Variable cost per unit	$3	$2
Expected sales (units)	100,000	150,000

The total fixed costs for the company are $700,000.

Required:

a. What is the anticipated level of profits for the expected sales volumes?

b. Assuming that the product mix would be the same at the break-even point, compute the break-even point in terms of each of the products.

c. If the product sales mix were to change to four 12-inch pizzas for each 16-inch pizza, what would be the new break-even volume for each of the products?

11–35. CVP Analysis— Multiple Products

(L.O.4)

The Bay Street Submarine Shop sells three types of sandwiches with the following prices and costs:

	Selling Price per Sandwich	Variable Cost per Sandwich	Fixed Cost per Month
Sub. #1	$3	$2	—
Sub. #2	5	3	—
Sub. #3	8	5	—
Entire company	—	—	$48,000

The sales mix is: 50 percent Sub #1, 33⅓ percent Sub #2, and 16⅔ percent Sub #3.

Required: *a.* At what sales revenue does the company break even?

b. Draw a cost-volume-profit graph for the company.

PROBLEMS

11–36. Sensitivity Analysis

Peterson Publishing Corporation is currently selling a line of executive education courses at a price of $90 per course. The company maintains office and publishing facilities at an annual fixed cost of $800,000 for office and administration and $720,000 for publishing operations. The variable costs of each course unit include $15 for promotion, $6 for administration, and $12 for the published materials. At the present time, the company distributes 25,000 course units per year. Management is dissatisfied with the profitability of current operations and wishes to investigate the profit effects of several alternatives. The following questions have been raised by members of management in an attempt to evaluate the alternatives (each alternative should be considered independently).

Required: *a.* What is the break-even level in terms of unit sales?

b. The company can hire an educational representative to sell the course material independently of current sales activity. Current sales would remain the same, but the representative should be able to sell an additional 10,000 units at the $90 price. Promotion costs would amount to $20 per unit, and the representative would receive a commission of 25 percent of the sales price of each course unit. All other costs would remain unchanged. What is the profit effect of hiring the representative?

c. A publishing company has offered to produce the course materials at a price of $40 per course unit regardless of the number of course units. If this alternative is chosen, the fixed and variable costs of the current publishing operation would be eliminated. What is the profit effect of this alternative if sales remain at 25,000 units? If sales increase to 40,000 units?

11–37. CVP Analysis and Price Changes

Denton Manufacturing Company is concerned about the possible effects of inflation on its operations. Presently, the company sells 200,000 units at a unit price of $15. The variable costs of production are $8, and fixed costs amount to $1,120,000. The present profit level is $280,000. Production engineers have advised management that unit labor costs are expected to rise by 10 percent in the coming year and unit materials costs are expected to rise by 15 percent. Of the variable costs, 25 percent are from labor and 50 percent are materials. All other variable costs are expected to increase by 5 percent. Sales prices cannot increase more than 8 percent. It is also expected that fixed costs will rise by 2 percent as a result of increased taxes and other miscellaneous fixed charges.

The company wishes to maintain the same level of profits in real-dollar terms. It is expected that to accomplish this objective, profits will have to increase by 6 percent during the year.

Required: *a.* Compute the volume of sales and the dollar sales level necessary to maintain the present profit level in normal terms, assuming the maximum price increase is implemented.

b. Compute the volume of sales and the dollar sales level necessary to attain the same profit level in real-dollar terms, assuming the maximum price increase is implemented.

c. If the volume of sales were to remain at 200,000 units, what price increase would be required to attain the same profit level in real-dollar terms?

11-38. CVP Analysis

Sunspot Company manufactures and sells sunglasses. Price and cost data are as follows:

Selling price per pair of sunglasses	$25.00
Variable costs per pair of sunglasses:	
Raw materials	$11.00
Direct labor	5.00
Manufacturing overhead	2.50
Selling expenses	1.30
Total variable costs per unit	$19.80
Annual fixed costs:	
Manufacturing overhead	$192,000
Selling and administrative	276,000
Total fixed costs	$468,000
Forecasted annual sales volume (120,000 pairs)	$3,000,000
Income tax rate	40%

Required:

a. Sunspot Company estimates that its direct labor costs will increase 8 percent next year. How many units will Sunspot have to sell next year to reach break-even?
  (1) 97,500 units.
  (2) 101,740 units.
  (3) 83,572 units.
  (4) 86,250 units.
  (5) Some other amount.

b. If Sunspot Company's direct labor costs do increase 8 percent, what selling price per unit of product must it charge to maintain the same contribution margin ratio?
  (1) $25.51.
  (2) $27.00.
  (3) $25.40.
  (4) $26.64.
  (5) Some other amount.

11-39. CVP Analysis with Changes in Cost Structure

Stockton Picket Fence Company manufactures prefabricated fence sections that sell at $6 per unit. The present facilities use an older model of semiautomated equipment. Variable costs are $4.50 per unit, and fixed costs total $300,000 per year.

An alternate semiautomated fence machine can be rented. This alternate machine would increase fixed costs to $550,000 per year, but variable costs would be reduced to $3.25 per unit.

Another fence machine supplier offers a fully automatic machine that would result in annual fixed costs of $800,000. However, the fully automatic machine would reduce the variable costs to $2 per unit.

There are no other costs or cash flows affected by the choice among these three alternatives.

Management is concerned about the break-even point for operations using each of these machines. Moreover, the sales volume for fence sections is quite erratic. Management is interested in the profit or losses that would occur with each type of equipment if the sales volume were 175,000 units and if the sales volume were 250,000 units.

Required:

Prepare a schedule showing the break-even point and the profit or loss obtainable for each equipment alternative at sales volumes of 175,000 and 250,000 units.

11–40. CVP Analysis for Fare Pricing: Trans Western Airlines[2]

Trans Western Airlines is preparing to submit a proposal to its board of directors for air service between Phoenix, Arizona, and Las Vegas, Nevada. The route would be designed primarily to serve the recreation and tourist travelers who frequently travel between the two cities. By offering low-cost tourist fares, the airline hopes to persuade persons who now travel by other modes of transportation to switch and fly Trans Western on this route.

In addition, the airline expects to attract business travelers during the hours of 7 A.M. to 6 P.M. on Mondays through Fridays. The fare price schedule or tariff would be designed to charge a higher fare during business travel hours so that tourist demand would be reduced during those hours. The company believes that a business fare of $40 one way during business hours and a fare of $30 for all other hours would result in an equal number of passengers on each flight.

To operate the route, the airline would need two 120-passenger jet aircraft. The aircraft would be leased at an annual cost of $2,800,000 each. Other fixed costs attributable to the Phoenix–Las Vegas route would amount to $1,940,000 per year. These fixed costs would not change regardless of the number of flights.

Operation of each aircraft requires a flight crew whose salaries are based primarily on the hours of flying time. The cost of the flight crew is approximately $600 per hour of flying time.

Aircraft maintenance and fuel costs are also a function of flying time. These costs are estimated at $210 per hour of flying time. Flying time between Phoenix and Las Vegas is estimated at 45 minutes each way.

The costs associated with processing each passenger for each flight amount to $7. This includes ticket processing and variable costs of baggage handling. Food and beverage service is expected to break even through the charges levied for alcoholic beverages.

Required:

a. If 5 business flights and 3 tourist flights are offered each way each weekday, and 10 tourist flights are offered each way every Saturday and Sunday, what number of passengers must be carried per flight on average to break even? Assume the product mix for the route is 50 percent business and 50 percent tourist.

b. The board of directors requires an estimate of the load factor (or percentage of available seats occupied on a route) required to break even on a given route. What is the break-even load factor for this proposed route?

c. If Trans Western Airlines decides to operate the Phoenix–Las Vegas route, its aircraft on that route will be idle between midnight and 6 A.M. The airline is considering offering a daily "Red Die" special that would leave Phoenix at midnight and would return by 6 A.M. The marketing division estimates that if the one-way fare were no more than $35, at least 60 new passengers could be attracted to each one-way Red Die flight. Operating costs would be at the same rate for this flight, but additional advertising costs of $2,400 per week would be required for promotion of the service. Management wishes to know the minimum fare that would be required to break even on the Red Die special, assuming the marketing division's passenger estimates are correct.

11–41. CVP Analysis with Semifixed Costs: Discovery Day Care Center[3]

Beverly Miller, director and owner of the Discovery Day Care Center, has a master's degree in elementary education. In the seven years she has been running the Discovery Center, her salary has ranged from nothing to $10,000 per year. "The second year," she says, "I made 62 cents an hour."

Her salary is what's left over after all other expenses are met.

---

[2] © 1989 by CIPT Co., all rights reserved.
[3] © Michael W. Maher, 1988.

Could she run a more profitable center? She thinks perhaps she could if she increased the student-teacher ratio, which is currently five students to one teacher. (Government standards for a center like this set a maximum of 10 students per teacher.) However, she refuses to increase the ratio to more than six to one. "If you increase the ratio to more than 6:1, the children don't get enough attention. In addition, the demands on the teacher are far too great." She does not hire part-time teachers.

Beverly rents the space for her center in the basement of a church for $450 per month, including utilities. She estimates that supplies, snacks, and other nonpersonnel costs are $40 per student per month. She charges $190 per month per student. Teachers are paid $600 per month, including fringe benefits. There are no other operating costs. At present, there are 30 students and 6 teachers in addition to Ms. Miller, who is not considered a teacher for this analysis.

Required:

a. What is the present operating profit per month of the Discovery Day Care Center before Ms. Miller's salary?

b. What is (are) the break-even point(s) assuming a student-teacher ratio of 6:1?

c. What would be the break-even point(s) if the student-teacher ratio was allowed to increase to 10:1?

d. Ms. Miller has an opportunity to increase the student body by six students. She must take all six or none. Should she accept the six students if she wants to maintain a maximum student-teacher ratio of 6:1?

e. [Continuation of part *(d)*.] Suppose Ms. Miller accepts the six children. Now she has the opportunity to accept one more. What would happen to profit if she did, assuming she has to hire one more teacher?

11–42. Profit Targets: R. A. Ro & Company

R. A. Ro & Company, maker of quality handmade pipes, has experienced a steady growth in sales for the past five years. However, increased competition has led Mr. Ro, the president, to believe that an aggressive advertising campaign will be necessary next year to maintain the company's present growth.

To prepare for next year's advertising campaign, the company's accountant has prepared and presented Mr. Ro with the following data for this year (Year 1):

Cost Schedule

Variable costs:	
Direct labor	$ 8.00 per pipe
Direct materials	3.25 per pipe
Variable overhead	2.50 per pipe
Total variable costs	$13.75 per pipe
Fixed costs:	
Manufacturing	$ 25,000
Selling	40,000
Administrative	70,000
Total fixed costs	$135,000
Selling price per pipe	$25.00
Expected sales this year (Year 1) (20,000 units)	$500,000 20,000 units
Tax rate: 40%	

Mr. Ro has set the sales target for next year (Year 2) at a level of $550,000 (or 22,000 pipes).

Required:

a. What is the projected after-tax operating profit for this year (Year 1)?

b. What is the break-even point in units for Year 1?

c. Mr. Ro believes an additional selling expense of $11,250 for advertising in Year 2, with all other costs remaining constant, will be necessary to attain the sales target. What will be the after-tax net income for Year 2 if the additional $11,250 is spent?

d. What will be the break-even point in dollar sales for Year 2 if the additional $11,250 is spent for advertising?

e. If the additional $11,250 is spent for advertising in Year 2, what is the required sales level in dollars to equal Year 1 after-tax operating profit?

f. At a sales level of 22,000 units, what is the maximum amount that can be spent on advertising in Year 2 if an after-tax operating profit of $60,000 is desired?

(CMA adapted)

11–43. CVP Analysis with Semifixed Costs and Changing Unit Variable Costs

Torous Company manufactures and sells one product. The sales price, $50 per unit, remains constant regardless of volume. Last year's sales were 12,000 units, and operating profits were − $20,000 (i.e., a loss). "Fixed" costs depended on production levels, as shown below. Variable costs per unit are 20 percent *higher* in level 2 (night shift) than in level 1 (day shift) because of additional labor costs due primarily to higher wages required to employ workers for the night shift.

	Annual Production Range (in units)	Annual Total Fixed Costs
Level 1 (day shift)	0–15,000	$200,000
Level 2 (night shift)	15,001–25,000	264,000

Last year's cost structure and selling price are not expected to change this year. Maximum plant capacity is 25,000 units. The company sells everything it produces.

Required:

a. Compute the contribution margin per unit for last year for each of the two production levels.

b. Compute the break-even points for last year for each of the two production levels.

c. Compute the volume in units that will maximize operating profits. Defend your choice.

INTEGRATIVE CASES

11–44. Converting Full-Absorption Costing Income Statements to CVP Analysis

Pralina Products Company is a regional firm that has three major product lines—cereals, breakfast bars, and dog food. The income statement for the year ended April 30, Year 4, is shown below; the statement was prepared by product line using full-absorption costing. Explanatory data related to the items presented in the income statement follow.

PRALINA PRODUCTS COMPANY
Income Statement
For the Year Ended April 30, Year 4
(in thousands)

	Cereals	Breakfast Bars	Dog Food	Total
Sales in pounds	2,000	500	500	3,000
Revenue from sales	$1,000	$400	$200	$1,600
Cost of sales:				
Direct materials	330	160	100	590
Direct labor	90	40	20	150
Factory overhead	108	48	24	180
Total cost of sales	528	248	144	920
Gross margin	472	152	56	680
Operating costs:				
Selling costs:				
Advertising	50	30	20	100
Commissions	50	40	20	110
Salaries and related benefits	30	20	10	60
Total selling expenses	130	90	50	270
General and administrative costs:				
Licenses	50	20	15	85
Salaries and related benefits	60	25	15	100
Total general and administrative costs	110	45	30	185
Total operating costs	240	135	80	455
Operating profit before taxes	$ 232	$ 17	$(24)	$ 225

Other data:

1. *Costs of sales.* The company's inventories of direct materials and finished products do not vary significantly from year to year. The inventories at April 30, Year 4, were essentially identical to those at April 30, Year 3.

    Factory overhead was applied to products at 120 percent of direct labor-dollars. The factory overhead costs for the Year 4 fiscal year were as follows:

Variable indirect labor and supplies	$ 15,000
Variable employee benefits on factory labor	30,000
Supervisory salaries and related benefits	35,000
Plant occupancy costs	100,000
	$180,000

[handwritten annotations: 45000, (fixed), fixed]

There was no overapplied or underapplied overhead at year-end.

2. *Advertising.* The company has been unable to determine any direct causal relationship between the level of sales volume and the level of advertising expenditures. However, because management believes advertising is necessary, an annual advertising program is implemented for each product line. Each product line is advertised independent of the others.

3. *Commissions*. Sales commissions are paid to the sales force at the rates of 5 percent on the cereals and 10 percent on the breakfast bars and dog food.

4. *Licenses*. Various licenses are required for each product line. These are renewed annually for each product line.

5. *Salaries and related benefits*. Sales, and general and administrative personnel devote time and effort to all product lines. Their salaries and wages are allocated on the basis of management's estimates of time spent on each product line.

Required:

a. The controller of Pralina Products Company has recommended that the company do a CVP analysis of its operations. As a first step, the controller has requested that you prepare a revised income statement for Pralina Products Company that employs a product contribution margin format that will be useful in CVP analysis. The statement should show the profit contribution for each product line and the operating profit before taxes for the company as a whole.

b. The controller of Pralina Products Company is going to prepare a report, which he will present to the other members of top management, explaining CVP analysis. Identify and explain the following points that the controller should include in the report.

(1) The advantages that CVP analysis can provide to a company.

(2) The difficulties Pralina Products Company could experience in the calculations involved in CVP analysis.

(3) The dangers that Pralina Products Company should be aware of in using the information derived from the CVP analysis.

(CMA adapted)

11–45. Bill French[4]

Bill French picked up the phone and called his boss, Wes Davidson, controller of Duo-Products Corporation. "Say, Wes, I'm all set for the meeting this afternoon. I've put together a set of break-even statements that should really make people sit up and take notice—and I think they'll be able to understand them, too." After a brief conversation about other matters, the call was concluded, and French turned to his charts for one last check-out before the meeting.

French had been hired six months earlier as a staff accountant. He was directly responsible to Davidson and, up to the time of this case, had been doing routine types of analysis work. French was an alumnus of a graduate business school and was considered by his associates to be quite capable and unusually conscientious. It was this latter characteristic that had apparently caused him to "rub some of the working guys the wrong way," as one of his co-workers put it. French was well aware of his capabilities and took advantage of every opportunity that arose to try to educate those around him. Wes Davidson's invitation for French to attend an informal manager's meeting had come as some surprise to others in the accounting group. However, when French requested permission to make a presentation of some break-even data, Davidson acquiesced. The Duo-Products Corporation had not been making use of this type of analysis in its planning or review procedures.

Basically, what French had done was to determine the level at which the company must operate in order to break even. As he phrased it:

> The company must be able at least to sell a sufficient volume of goods so that it will cover all the variable costs of producing and selling the goods; further, it will

---

[4] Copyright © 1959 by the President and Fellows of Harvard College. This case was prepared by R. C. Hill, under the direction of Neil E. Harlan, as a basis for class discussion rather than to illustrate either effective or ineffective handling of an administrative situation. Reprinted by permission of the Harvard Business School.

not make a profit unless it covers the fixed, or nonvariable, costs as well. The level of operation at which total costs (that is, variable plus nonvariable) are just covered is the break-even volume. This should be the lower limit in all our planning.

The accounting records had provided the following information that French used in constructing his chart:

Plant capacity—2 million units.

Past year's level of operations—1.5 million units.

Average unit selling price—$1.20.

Total fixed costs—$520,000.

Average variable unit cost—$.75.

From this information, French observed that each unit contributed $.45 to fixed costs after covering the variable costs. Given total fixed costs of $520,000, he calculated that 1,155,556 units must be sold in order to break even. He verified this conclusion by calculating the dollar sales volume that was required to break even. Since the variable costs per unit were 62.5 percent of the selling price, French reasoned that 37.5 percent of every sales dollar was left available to cover fixed costs. Thus, fixed costs of $520,000 require sales of $1,386,667 in order to break even.

When he constructed a break-even chart to present the information graphically, his conclusions were further verified. The chart also made it clear that the firm was operating at a fair margin over the break-even requirements and that the pretax profits accruing (at the rate of 37.5 percent of every sales dollar over break-even) increased rapidly as volume increased (see Exhibit A).

Exhibit A (11–45)   **Break-Even Chart—Total Business**

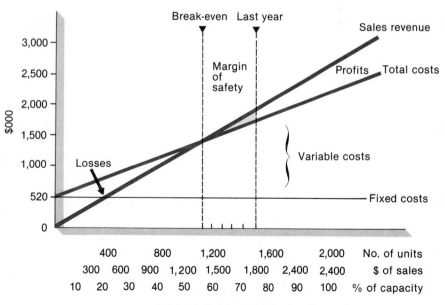

Sales performance in thousands
Break-even volume = 1,156,000 units or $1,387,000

Shortly after lunch, French and Davidson left for the meeting. Several representatives of the manufacturing departments were present, as well as the general sales manager, two assistant sales managers, the purchasing officer, and two people from the product engineering office. Davidson introduced French to the few people he had not already met, and then the meeting got under way. French's presentation was the last item on Davidson's agenda, and in due time, the controller introduced French, explaining his interest in cost control and analysis.

French had prepared enough copies of his chart and supporting calculations for everyone at the meeting. He described carefully what he had done and explained how the chart pointed to a profitable year, dependent on meeting the volume of sales activity that had been maintained in the past. It soon became apparent that some of the participants had known in advance what French planned to discuss; they had come prepared to challenge him and soon had taken control of the meeting. The following exchange ensued (see Exhibit B for a checklist of participants with their titles):

Cooper [production control]: You know, Bill, I'm really concerned that you haven't allowed for our planned changes in volume next year. It seems to me that you should have allowed for the sales department's guess that we'll boost sales by 20 percent unitwise. We'll be pushing 90 percent of what we call capacity then. It sure seems that this would make quite a difference in your figuring

French: That might be true, but as you can see, all you have to do is read the cost and profit relationship right off the chart for the new volume. Let's see—at a million-eight units we'd . . .

Williams [manufacturing]: Wait a minute, now!!! If you're going to talk in terms of 90 percent of capacity, and it looks like that's what it will be, you had better note that we'll be shelling out some more for the plant. We've already got okays on investment money that will boost your fixed costs by $10,000 a month, easy. And that may not be all. We may call it 90 percent of plant capacity but there are a lot of places where we're just full up and can't pull things up any tighter.

Cooper: See, Bill? Fred is right, but I'm not finished on this bit about volume changes. According to the information that I've got here—and it came from your office—I'm not sure that your break-even chart can really be used even if there were to be no changes next year. Looks to me like you've got average figures that don't allow for the fact that we're dealing with three basic products. Your report here [see Exhibit C] on costs, according to product lines, for last year makes it pretty clear that the "average" is way out of line. How would the break-even point look if we took this on an individual product basis?

French: Well, I'm not sure. Seems to me that there is only one break-even point for the firm. Whether we take it product by product or in total, we've got to hit that point. I'll be glad to check for you if you want, but. . . .

Bradshaw [assistant sales manager]: Guess I may as well get in on this one, Bill. If you're going to do anything with individual products, you ought to know that we're looking for a big swing in our product mix. Might even start before we get into the new season. The "A" line is really losing out and I imagine that we'll be lucky to hold two thirds of the volume there next year. Wouldn't you buy that, Arnie? [Agreement from the general sales manager.] That's not too bad, though, because we expect that we should pick up the 200,000 that we lose, and about a quarter million units more, over in "C" production. We don't see anything that shows much of a change in "B". That's been solid for years and shouldn't change much now.

Exhibit B (11–45)   **List of Participants in the Meeting**

Bill French	Staff accountant
Wes Davidson	Controller
John Cooper	Production control
Fred Williams	Manufacturing
Ray Bradshaw	Assistant sales manager
Arnie Winetki	General sales manager
Anne Fraser	Administrative assistant to president

Exhibit C (11–45)   **Product Class Cost Analysis (normal year)**

	Aggregate	"A"	"B"	"C"
Sales at full capacity (units)	2,000,000			
Actual sales volume (units)	1,500,000	600,000	400,000	500,000
Unit sales price	$ 1.20	$ 1.67	$ 1.50	$ .40
Total sales revenue	1,800,000	1,000,000	600,000	200,000
Variable cost per unit	.75	1.25	0.625	.25
Total variable cost	1,125,000	750,000	250,000	125,000
Fixed costs + (20,	520,000	170,000	275,000	75,000
Profit	155,000	80,000	75,000	–0–
Ratios:				
Variable cost to sales	.63	.75	.42	.63
Marginal income to sales	.37	.25	.58	.37
Utilization of capacity*	75.0%	30.0%	20.0%	25.0%

* Note: Each product requires the same amount of production capacity per unit.

Winetki [general sales manager]: Bradshaw's called it about as we figure it, but there's something else here too. We've talked about our pricing on "C" enough, and now I'm really going to push our side of it. Ray's estimate of maybe half a million—450,000 I guess it was—up on "C" for next year is on the basis of doubling the price with no change in cost. We've been priced so low on this item that it's been a crime—we've got to raise, but good, for two reasons. First, for our reputation; the price is out of line classwise and is completely inconsistent with our quality reputation. Second, if we don't raise the price, we'll be swamped and we can't handle it. You heard what Williams said about capacity. The way the whole "C" field is exploding, we'll have to answer to another half-million units in unsatisifed orders if we don't jack the price up. We can't afford to expand that much for this product.

At this point, Anne Fraser (administrative assistant to the president) walked up toward the front of the room from where she had been standing near the rear door. The discussion broke for a minute, and she took advantage of the lull to interject a few comments.

Fraser: This has certainly been enlightening. You clearly have a valuable familiarity with our operations. As long as you're going to try to get all the things together that you ought to pin down for next year, let's see what I can add to help you:

Number One: Let's remember that everything that shows in the profit area here on Bill's chart is divided just about evenly between the government and us. Now, for last year we can read a profit of about $150,000. Well, that's right. But we were left with half of that, and then paid out dividends of $50,000 to the stockholders. Since we've got an anniversary year coming up, we'd like to put out a special dividend of about 50 percent extra. We ought to retain $25,000 in the business, too. This means that we'd like to hit $100,000 profit *after* taxes.

Number Two: From where I sit, it looks as if we're going to have negotiations with the union again, and this time it's liable to cost us. All the indications are—and this isn't public—that we may have to meet demands that will boost our production costs—what do you call them here, Bill—variable costs—by 10 percent across the board. This may kill the bonus-dividend plans, but we've got to hold the line on past profits. This means that we can give that much to the union only if we can make it in added revenues. I guess you'd say that raises your break-even point, Bill—and for that one I'd consider the company's profit to be a fixed cost.

Number Three: Maybe this is the time to think about switching our product emphasis. Arnie may know better than I which of the products is more profitable. You check me out on this, Arnie—and it might be a good idea for you and Bill to get together on this one, too. These figures that I have [Exhibit C] make it look like the percentage contribution on line "A" is the lowest of the bunch. If we're losing volume there as rapidly as you sales folks say, and if we're as hard pressed for space as Fred has indicated, maybe we'd be better off grabbing some of that big demand for "C" by shifting some of the facilities over there from "A."

Davidson: Thanks, Anne, I sort of figured that we'd wind up here as soon as Bill brought out his charts. This is an approach that we've barely touched upon, but as you can see, you've all got ideas that have got to be made to fit here somewhere. Let me suggest this: Bill, you rework your chart and try to bring into it some of the points that were made here today. I'll see if I can summarize what everyone seems to be looking for.

First of all, I have the idea that your presentation is based on a rather important series of assumptions. Most of the questions that were raised were really about those assumptions; it might help us all if you try to set the assumptions down in black and white so that we can see just how they influence the analysis.

Then, I think that John would like to see the unit sales increase taken up, and he'd also like to see whether there's any difference if you base the calculations on an analysis of individual product lines. Also, as Ray suggested, since the product mix is bound to change, why not see how things look if the shift materializes as he has forecast? Arnie would like to see the influence of a price increase in the "C" line; Fred looks toward an increase in fixed manufacturing costs of $10,000 a month, and Anne has suggested that we should consider taxes, dividends, expected union demands, and the question of product emphasis.

I think that ties it all together. Let's hold off on your next meeting, fellows, until Bill has time to work this all into shape.

With that, the participants broke off into small groups and the meeting disbanded. French and Davidson headed back to their offices, and French, in a tone of concern, asked Davidson, "Why didn't you warn me about the hornet's nest I was walking into?"

"Bill, you didn't ask!"

 a. What are the assumptions implicit in Bill French's determination of his company's break-even point?

 b. On the basis of French's revised information, what does next year look like:

  (1) What is the break-even point?

(2) What level of operations must be achieved to meet both dividends and expected union requirements?

c. Assume that A's volume will drop to 400,000 units, B's volume remains unchanged, and C's volume increases by 450,000 units. Can the break-even analysis help the company decide whether to alter the existing product emphasis?

d. Calculate *each* of the three products' break-even points, using the data in Exhibit C. Why is the sum of these three volumes not equal to the 1,155,556 units aggregate break-even volume?

e. Evaluate Bill French's approach in developing and presenting his analysis.

DIFFERENTIAL COST ANALYSIS

LEARNING OBJECTIVES

1. Understanding the concept of differential cost analysis.

2. Knowing how to use cost analysis for pricing decisions.

3. Being able to prepare a cost analysis for make-or-buy decisions.

4. Seeing how cost data are used when planning to add or drop product lines.

In this chapter, we discuss the use of cost analysis in making such short-run operating decisions as pricing, whether to make or buy products, and whether to drop or add a product line. Each decision requires the comparison of one or more proposed alternatives with the status quo. The task is to determine how costs in particular and profits in general will be affected if one alternative is chosen over another. This process is called differential analysis. Although decision makers are usually interested in *all* differences between alternatives, including financial and nonfinancial ones, we focus our attention on financial decisions that involve costs and revenues.

Differential Analysis Process of estimating the consequences of the alternative actions that decision makers can take.

Differential analysis is the process of estimating the consequences of alternative actions that decision makers can take. Differential analysis is used for both short-run decisions, like the ones we discuss in this chapter and the next, and for long-run decisions, like those discussed in Chapters 15 and 16. Generally, the term **short run** is applied to decision horizons over which capacity will be unchanged—one year is usually used for convenience.

Short Run The period of time over which capacity will be unchanged.

There is an important distinction between short-run and long-run decisions. Short-run decisions affect cash flow for such a short period of time that the time value of money is immaterial and hence ignored. Thus, the *amount* of cash flows is important for short-run analysis, but their *timing* is assumed to be unimportant. If an action affects cash flows over a longer period of time (usually more than one year), the time value of money is taken into account, as discussed in Chapters 15 and 16.

DIFFERENTIAL COSTS VERSUS VARIABLE COSTS

Differential costs are costs that change in response to alternative courses of action. Both variable costs and fixed costs may be differential costs. Variable costs are differential costs when a decision involves possible changes in volume. For example, a decision to close a plant would usually reduce variable costs and some fixed costs. All of the affected costs would be termed *differential costs*. On the other hand, if a machine replacement does not affect either the volume of output or the variable cost per unit, variable costs would not be differential costs.

Differential Costs Costs that change in response to a particular course of action.

As the illustrations in this chapter are presented, you will find that differential analysis requires an examination of the facts for each option that is relevant to the decision to determine which costs will be affected. Differential and variable costs have independent meanings and applications and should not be considered interchangeable.

ARE HISTORICAL COSTS RELEVANT FOR DECISION MAKING?[1]

You have probably seen retailers advertise their products for sale at prices below invoice cost. And you may have wondered how they could stay in business if they sold their products below cost. Of course, they could not stay in business if they consistently sold below cost. Retailers recognize,

---

[1] Many of the concepts presented in this chapter were developed by J. M. Clark in his classic work, *Studies in the Economics of Overhead Costs* (Chicago: University of Chicago Press, 1923). Clark developed the notion that costs that are relevant for one purpose are not necessarily relevant for another. If the term *sacrifice* is used to summarize the various meanings of cost, then it becomes clear that the sacrifices (costs) for one set of actions are not necessarily the same as those for another set of actions.

however, that the original cost of their merchandise is a sunk cost—a cost that has already been incurred and is *not differential* when it comes to holding versus selling merchandise.

For example, suppose that a clothing shop has 15 pairs of slacks that each cost the retailer $20. No slacks have been sold at the established price of $39.95, and the retailer believes they can only be sold if the price is reduced. In repricing, the retailer should disregard the original $20 per pair cost. A number of marketing and inventory control issues might be considered, but the historical cost is irrelevant.

REAL WORLD APPLICATION

The Great Gretzky Deal: A Good Business Decision

When the Los Angeles Kings acquired Wayne Gretzky from the Edmonton Oilers for $15 million and other considerations, many hockey executives and analysts said it was a good deal for both sides. This was true because of the different business climates of the two teams and their effects on the differential cost analyses.

The Edmonton Oilers were an established NHL powerhouse, with a captive sports audience. They were the only game in town. While the initial uproar over the trade of a national hero was, as expected, loud and rancorous, it did not translate to a great loss in attendance.

The benefits for the Oilers were substantial. In addition to the $15 million windfall, the Oilers were able to lay the foundation for the future by acquiring a young star (Jimmy Carson) and three No. 1 draft picks over the next five years. If the competition for the Edmonton sports dollar became more intense, the Oilers would be able to maintain their fan loyalty by fielding a consistently outstanding team. Finally, the Oilers would be reducing their payroll by the amount of Gretzky's salary. For the Oilers, differential revenues clearly were greater than differential costs.

The differential analysis for the Los Angeles Kings was slightly more complicated. The Kings needed a big draw to compete in a sports market that included two professional football teams (the Rams and the Raiders), two major college football teams (UCLA and USC), two professional basketball teams

(the Lakers and the Clippers), and two major college basketball teams (UCLA and USC). The Kings management hoped that Gretzky would provide star quality to a faceless franchise and also be the foundation for a winning team.

Before making the deal, the Kings concluded that they could recoup their investment in three years. They consulted with the people who contracted for concessions and TV rights and estimated yearly differential revenues. They also estimated additional revenues from ticket sales.

Differential Analysis (dollars in millions)[a]

Increase in revenue:	
Season ticket sales	$ 4.5
Single-game ticket sales	2.0
Sale of cable television rights	1.0
Play-off game	2.0
Concessions	1.0
Total increase in yearly revenues	$10.5
Increase in costs:	
One-time payment to the Oilers	$15.0
Interest on borrowed funds per year	1.5
Payroll increase per year	2.0
Total increase in annual costs	$ 3.5
Three-year analysis:	
Total differential revenue (3 × $10.5)	$31.5
Total differential costs ($15.0 + (3 × $3.5))	25.5
Increase in profit	$ 6.0

[a] Based on Joshua Mills, "Gretzky: Deal with Dividends," *New York Times* August 20, 1988, pp. 17, 29.

Of course, if the slacks are sold for less than $20 per pair, the retailer's financial statement would show a loss. If the slacks were sold for $18 per pair, for example, the statement would be as follows:

Sale of slacks (15 pairs at $18)	$270
Cost of goods sold (15 pairs at $20)	300
Loss on sale	$ (30)

Decision makers are sometimes tempted to hold merchandise rather than sell it below cost in order to avoid showing a loss on their financial statements. In doing so, they may make a bad decision. If the merchandise is not sold immediately at a loss, it may be sold at a greater loss later, or it may have to be written off entirely if it cannot be sold at all. Under the circumstances, unless there is a possibility of a higher price later, the decision to sell now is the best.

The historical cost of an item is not always irrelevant, however. A decision to purchase an item for resale requires information about both its cost and its probable selling price. Nonetheless, once the merchandise *has been purchased,* the cash outlay (or promise to pay) has already occurred. The cost is *sunk,* and although it is relevant to income determination, it is irrelevant to subsequent marketing decisions.

DIFFERENTIAL ANALYSIS: AN OVERVIEW

Special Order An order that will not affect other sales and is usually a short-run occurrence.

Which costs are relevant depends on the decision under consideration. A framework for decision making, based on a company that receives a **special order**, is diagrammed in Illustration 12–1. First, each alternative is set forth as a branch of a decision tree. Second, the value of each alternative is determined. Third, the alternative with the highest value is chosen.

For example, Quick-Print uses a modern copy machine to make copies for walk-in customers. The machine is usually idle about two hours each day. On October 15, B. Onst, who is running for political office, asks Quick-Print to produce 10,000 copies of letters, speeches, memoranda, and other cam-

Illustration 12-1 **Framework for Decision Making**

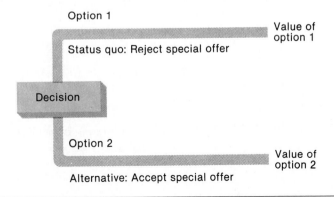

paign materials to be ready on October 22. Quick-Print has idle capacity adequate for this job. The candidate wants to pay only 8 cents per copy, even though the regular price is 10 cents per copy.

In deciding whether to accept the special order, the owner of Quick-Print estimates the following operating data for the week in question:

Sales (100,000 copies at 10¢)	$10,000
Variable costs, including paper, maintenance, and usage payment to machine owner (100,000 copies at 6¢)	6,000
Total contribution margin	4,000
Fixed costs (operators, plus allocated costs of the print shop)	2,500
Operating profit	$ 1,500

To make the decision, the owner identifies the alternatives, determines the value of each alternative to the company, and selects the alternative with the highest value to the company.

The values of the alternatives are shown in Illustration 12–2. The best economic decision is to accept the order because the company will gain $200 from it. Fixed costs are not affected by the decision because they are not differential in this situation. Therefore, they are not relevant to the decision.

Differential Costs versus Total Costs

Although the chapter focuses on differential costs, the information presented to management can show either the detailed costs which were included for making a decision or it can show just the differences between alternatives. For example, the first two columns in the Quick-Print example in Illustration 12–2 show the total operating profit under the status quo as well as under the special order alternative. This part of the presentation is referred to as the *total format*. The third column shows just the differences.

Illustration 12-2 **Analysis of Special Order, Quick-Print**

a. **Comparison of Totals**

	Status Quo: Reject Special Order	Alternative: Accept Special Order	Difference
Sales revenue	$10,000	$10,800	$800
Variable costs	(6,000)	(6,600)	(600)
Total contribution	4,000	4,200	200
Fixed costs	(2,500)	(2,500)	–0–
Operating profit	$ 1,500	$ 1,700	$200

b. **Alternative Presentation: Differential Analysis**

Differential sales, 10,000 at 8¢	$800
Less differential costs, 10,000 at 6¢	600
Differential operating profit (before taxes)	$200

This presentation is called the *differential format*. Some managers prefer the total format because it enables them to see what their total revenues, costs, and profits will be under each alternative. Others prefer the differential format because it highlights the costs and revenues that are affected by the decision and enables them to focus on those items alone. We have found that in practice, managers will ask for a report that shows both total differential costs similar to the formats used in Illustration 12–2. Mangers tell us that the costs of presenting both formats is relatively low. In addition, in complex organizations, decisions must often be approved by more than one person. By including both formats with a recommendation, one need not worry whether every person that must sign off on the report is going to want a total cost or a differential cost format.

The Full-Cost Fallacy

Full Cost The sum of the fixed and variable costs of manufacturing and selling a unit.

The terms **full cost** or *full product cost* are used to describe a product's cost that includes both (1) the variable costs of producing and selling the product and (2) a share of the organization's fixed costs. Sometimes decision makers use these full costs, mistakenly thinking they are variable costs.

For example, D. Facto, a Quick-Print employee, claims that accepting B. Onst's special order would be a mistake. "Since our variable costs are $6,000 and our fixed costs are $2,500, our total costs for the week without the special order are $8,500 for 100,000 copies. That works out to 8½ cents per copy, which is more than 8 cents per copy offered by Onst. We'd be losing a half cent per copy!"

Full-Cost Fallacy The assumption that fixed costs will vary with production.

By considering fixed costs in the analysis, D. Facto is including irrelevant information. The fixed costs will be incurred whether the special order is accepted or rejected, so they should not bear on the decision. This is known as the **full-cost fallacy** because it is incorrect to assume that *all* costs are relevant to every decision. This is a common mistake in short-run decisions, in part because full product costs are emphasized and readily available in accounting records. However, even though all costs must be covered in the long run or the company will fail, in the short run, it would be profitable to accept the order. While full product costs serve a wide variety of important purposes, they are not relevant to the kind of short-run operating decision described in the example above.

Differential Fixed Costs

In many short-run operating decisions, fixed costs remain unchanged because they are the costs of providing production capacity and capacity does not change in the short run. When short-run operating decisions do not involve a change in capacity, fixed costs remain unchanged and are therefore not differential.

In long-run decisions, however, fixed costs may be differential costs. For example, the addition of a new plant and new machines often involves differential fixed costs. Therefore, like variable costs, fixed costs must be carefully examined to determine if they are differential.

COST ANALYSIS FOR PRICING

The price-volume trade-off is derived from the market demand for a product. By definition, variable costs change with volume. If a change in price results in a change in volume, variable costs change too. Therefore:

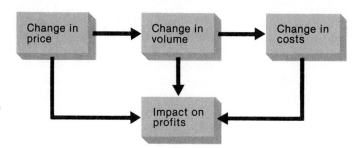

Thus, price-volume changes automatically involve changes in variable costs. The critical consideration for management is whether the joint effect of cost, price, and volume results in an increase or decrease in operating profits.

Cost-Plus Pricing. Some products are so unique, or their market price is unknowable, that costs plus a specified allowance for profits provide a basis for pricing. For construction jobs, defense contracts, most custom orders, and many new products, the cost of the product plays a significant role in determining its price.

An estimate of specific job costs is also an important guide for bidding on a job. If a bid price is too low compared to costs, the contract may be obtained, but the job will be performed at a loss. If a bid is considerably higher than costs, the contract will probably be lost.

Short-Run and Long-Run Differential Costs for Pricing

Sometimes the only way to sell a product is to cut its price. In such a case, the *minimum price is the differential cost that must be incurred to produce and/or sell the product.*

For example, Advent Manufacturing has a supply of products *on hand* that cost $4 each to manufacture. Selling them would require an additional $2 variable cost per unit. What is the *minimum* price Advent can charge? A quick answer might be $6 (manufacturing costs of $4 plus selling costs of $2). Actually, Advent can drop the price to $2, which is the differential cost to sell the products, and be no worse off than if it held the products unsold. Of course, the $2 is a *minimum* price; Advent's managers would prefer a higher price.

We observe theaters charging lower prices for matinee performances or airlines charging lower prices for certain kinds of passengers. These are examples of price discrimination to sell a product. **Price discrimination** exists when a product or service is sold at two or more prices that do not reflect proportional differences in marginal costs. If a seat would otherwise go unsold, airlines and theaters should be willing to sell it at a lower price, as long as the price exceeds the variable cost of filling the seat and does not decrease normal sales.

Price Discrimination Sale of product or service at different prices which do not reflect differences in marginal costs.

When used in pricing decisions, the differential costs required to sell and/or produce a product provide a floor. In the short-run, differential costs may be very low, as when selling one more seat on an already scheduled airline flight or allowing one more student into an already scheduled course in college.

In the long-run, however, differential costs are much higher. Returning to the airline example, long-run differential costs include the costs of buying and maintaining the aircraft, salaries for the crew, landing fees, and so forth. In the long run, these costs must be covered. To simplify this kind of analysis, the *full product costs* of making and/or selling a product are often used to estimate long-run differential costs. Hence, a common saying in business is: "I can drop my prices to just cover variable costs in the short run, but in the long run, my prices have to cover full product costs."

Use of Costs to Determine Legality of Pricing Practices

The Clayton and Sherman Anti-Trust Acts, the Robinson-Patman Act, and many state and local laws forbid certain pricing practices unless they are cost justified.[2] For example, predatory pricing to prevent or eliminate competition is illegal. A price that is below differential cost may be considered predatory. Certain kinds of price discrimination among customers are also illegal unless the discrimination is justified by actual differences in the costs of serving the different customers. While this is only a brief overview of the highly complex legal issues involved, it serves as a reminder of the necessity to maintain cost records to justify pricing practices.

COST ANALYSIS FOR MAKE-OR-BUY DECISIONS

Make-or-Buy Decision A decision whether to acquire needed goods internally or purchase them from outside sources.

A **make-or-buy decision** is any decision in which a company decides whether to meet its needs internally or acquire goods or services from external sources. A restaurant that uses its own ingredients in preparing meals "makes," while one that serves meals from frozen entrees "buys." A steel company that mines its own iron ore and coal and processes the ore into pig iron "makes," while one that purchases pig iron for further processing "buys."

The make-or-buy decision is often part of a company's long-run strategy. Some companies choose to integrate vertically to control the activities that lead up to the final product. Other companies prefer to rely on outsiders for some inputs and specialize in only certain steps of the total manufacturing process.

Whether to rely on outsiders for a substantial quantity of materials depends on both differential cost comparisons and other factors that are not easily quantified, such as suppliers' dependability and quality control. Although make-or-buy decisions sometimes appear to be simple one-time choices, they are frequently part of a more strategic analysis in which top management makes a policy decision to move the company toward more or less vertical integration.

For example, the Better Homes Construction Company currently does its own site preparation and foundation work on the houses it builds. This work costs Better Homes $15,000 per house for labor, materials, and variable overhead. Should Better Homes consider buying site preparation and foundation work from an outside supplier? If satisfactory quality work could be subcontracted at anything below $15,000, Better Homes could save some of the money it now spends. The decision to buy would then provide a differential cost saving.

---

[2] See F. M. Sherer, *Industrial Market Structure and Economic Performance* (Boston: Houghton-Mifflin, 1980); and H. F. Taggart, *Cost Justification* (Ann Arbor: Michigan Business School, Division of Research, 1959).

Make-or-Buy Decisions Involving Differential Fixed Costs

Net Minder Manufacturing produces tennis rackets. At the present time, it makes a cover for each racket at the following cost:

	Per Unit	10,000 Units
Costs that can be directly assigned to the product:		
Direct materials	$2.00	$20,000
Direct labor	1.00	10,000
Variable manufacturing overhead	.75	7,500
Fixed manufacturing overhead		2,500
Common costs allocated to this product line		15,000
		$55,000

This year's expected production is 10,000 units, so the full product cost is $5.50 ($55,000 ÷ 10,000 units).

Net Minder has received an offer from an outside supplier to supply any desired volume of covers at a price of $4.10 each. Here is the differential cost analysis that the accounting department prepared for management:

1. Differential costs are materials, labor, and variable overhead. These costs will definitely be saved if the covers are bought.

2. The direct fixed manufacturing overhead is the cost of leasing the machine for producing the covers. Although the machine cost is fixed for levels of production ranging from one unit to 20,000 units, it can be eliminated if we stop producing covers. Thus, although the machine cost is a fixed cost of producing covers, it is a *differential* cost if we eliminate the product.

3. No other costs would be affected.

The accounting department also prepared cost analyses at volume levels of 5,000 and 10,000 units per year, as shown in Illustration 12–3. At the volume of 10,000 units, it is less costly for Net Minder to make the racket covers. But if the volume of racket covers needed drops to 5,000, Net Minder would save money by buying the racket covers.

This decision is sensitive to volume. To see why, consider only the costs that are affected by the make-or-buy decision: direct materials, direct labor, variable overhead, and fixed overhead. By setting the costs of making equal to the costs of buying, we find there is a unique volume at which Net Minder is indifferent (in terms of costs) between making and buying as shown below:

Make		Buy
Direct Fixed Manufacturing Overhead	**Variable Manufacturing Costs**	**Costs to Purchase Covers**
$2,500 +	$3.75X =	$4.10X

where X = the quantity of racket covers.

Illustration 12-3   **Make-or-Buy Analysis, Net Minder Manufacturing**

	Status Quo: Make Product	Alternative: Buy Product	Difference
a. 10,000 Units			
Direct costs:			
Direct materials	$20,000	$41,000[a]	$21,000 higher
Labor	10,000	-0-	10,000 lower
Variable overhead	7,500	-0-	7,500 lower
Fixed overhead	2,500	-0-	2,500 lower
Common costs	15,000[d]	15,000[d]	-0-
Total costs	$55,000	$56,000	$ 1,000 higher

Differential costs *increase* by $1,000, so *reject* alternative to *buy.*

	Status Quo: Make Product	Alternative: Buy Product	Difference
b. 5,000 Units			
Direct costs:			
Direct materials	$10,000[b]	$20,500[c]	$10,500 higher
Labor	5,000[b]	-0-	5,000 lower
Variable overhead	3,750[b]	-0-	3,750 lower
Fixed overhead	2,500	-0-	2,500 lower
Common costs	15,000[d]	15,000[d]	-0-
Total costs	$36,250	$35,500	750 lower

Differential costs *decrease* by $750, so *accept* alternative to *buy.*

[a] 10,000 units purchased at $4.10 = $41,000.

[b] Total variable costs reduced by half because volume was reduced by half.

[c] 5,000 units purchased at $4.10 = $20,500.

[d] These common costs remain unchanged for these volumes. Since they do not change, they could be omitted from the analysis.

Solving for X:

$$\$2,500 + \$3.75X = \$4.10X$$
$$\$2,500 = \$.35X$$
$$\frac{\$2,500}{\$.35} = X$$
$$X = \underline{7,143}$$

The result is shown graphically in Illustration 12–4. At a volume greater than 7,143, the preferred alternative is to make; at a volume less than 7,143, the preferred alternative is to buy.

Note the importance of separating fixed and variable costs for this analysis. Although determining which costs are differential usually requires a special analysis, the work can be made simpler if costs have been routinely separated into fixed and variable components in the accounting system. The previous analysis would not have been possible for Net Minder if overhead costs had not been separated into fixed and variable components.

Opportunity Cost

Suppose Net Minder's volume is projected to be 10,000 covers. If volume is expected to be greater than 7,143 covers, the preceding analysis indicates that Net Minder should continue to produce the covers. However, that

Illustration 12-4   **Graphical Illustration of Make-or-Buy Analysis**

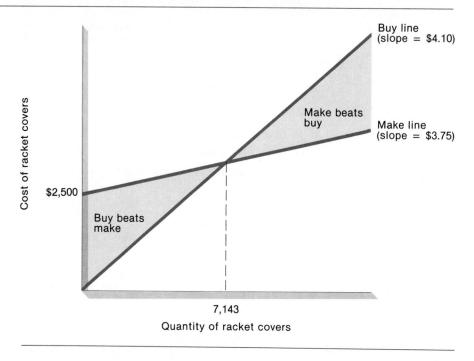

analysis has not considered the opportunity cost of the facilities being used to make racket covers. **Opportunity costs** are the foregone returns from not employing a resource in its best alternative use. Theoretically, determining opportunity cost requires consideration of every possible use of the resource in question. If Net Minder has no alternative beneficial use for its facilities, the opportunity cost is zero, in which case the previous analysis would stand.

Opportunity Cost The lost return that could have been realized from the best foregone alternative use of a resource.

But suppose that the facilities where covers are made could be used to assemble a cheaper version of the racket Net Minder presently produces. This cheaper version would provide a differential contribution of $4,000. If making rackets is the best alternative use of the facility, the opportunity cost of using the facility to make covers is $4,000. In that case, Net Minder would be better off buying the covers and using the facilities to make rackets, as shown by the two alternative ways to analyze the problem in Illustration 12–5.

Almost without exception, determining opportunity cost is very difficult and involves considerable subjectivity. Opportunity costs are not routinely collected with other accounting cost data because they are not the result of completed transactions. They are possibilities only and must be estimated for each individual decision.

Some opportunity costs may be estimated in monetary terms, like the possible wages from the best job foregone; others may not be so readily quantified, like the status that accompanies certain occupations. Further-

Illustration 12-5   **Make-or-Buy Analysis with Opportunity Cost of Facilities, Net Minder Manufacturing**

	Status Quo: Make Product	Alternative: Buy Product	Difference
a. Method 1:			
Total costs of covers from Illustration 12–3	$55,000	$56,000	$1,000 higher[a]
Opportunity cost of using facilities to make covers	4,000	–0–	4,000 lower[a]
Total costs, including opportunity cost	$59,000	$56,000	$3,000 lower[a]

Differential costs *decrease* by $3,000, so *accept* alternative to *buy*.

	Status Quo: Make Product	Alternative: Buy Product, Use Facility to Make Rackets	Difference
b. Method 2:			
Total costs of covers from Illustration 12–3	$55,000	$56,000	$1,000 higher[a]
Less margin from use of facilities for making rackets	–0–	−4,000	4,000 lower[a]
Net cost	$55,000	$52,000	$3,000 lower[a]

Although the presentation is different, the result is still a $3,000 cost *decrease* if the alternative is accepted.

[a] These indicate whether the alternative is higher or lower than the status quo.

more, if a benefit is foregone—and therefore never concretely existed—it is difficult to attach a realistic value to it.

Because they are so nebulous, opportunity costs are often omitted from decision-making analysis. It is easy to neglect them because they are not paid for and recorded in the accounts. Consequently, it is an accountant's responsibility to assist decision makers by reminding them that such costs exist. In general, opportunity costs occur whenever a scarce resource has multiple uses. Plants, equipment, money, time, and managerial talent all usually have opportunity costs. When a resource is not scarce or when a scarce resource can only be used in one way, opportunity costs are zero. Whether such costs should be measured precisely or only approximately depends on the costs and benefits of the resulting information.

ADDING AND DROPPING PRODUCT LINES

Campus Bookstore hired a new general manager, a recent business school graduate, to improve its profit performance. As could be expected, the new manager asked to see the store's financial statements for the past year. The statements were prepared by product line for each of the store's three product categories: books, supplies, and general merchandise.

The statement that the manager received is presented in Illustration 12–6. It shows that the general merchandise department lost money during the

Illustration 12-6

CAMPUS BOOKSTORE
Third-Quarter Product Line Financial Statement
(in thousands)

	Total	Books	Supplies	General Merchandise
Sales revenue	$400	$200	$80	$120
Cost of goods sold (all variable)	300	160	45	95
Gross margin	100	40	35	25
Less fixed costs:				
Rent ~~SGA~~	18	6	6	6
Salaries	40	16	10	14
Marketing and administrative ~Rent~	36	12	12	12
Operating profit (loss)	$ 6	$ 6	$ 7	$ (7)

third quarter of last year. "We could have increased operating profits from $6,000 to $13,000 for the quarter if we had dropped general merchandise," claimed the manager of the supplies department. "That department sold $120,000 worth of merchandise but cost us $127,000 to operate."

Although the economics of dropping the general merchandise line appeared favorable, the new manager asked an accountant to investigate which costs would be differential (that is, avoidable in this case) if that product line were dropped. According to the accountant:

1. *All* variable costs of goods sold for that line could be avoided.
2. *All* salaries presently charged to general merchandise, $14,000, could be avoided.
3. *None* of the rent could be avoided.
4. Marketing and administrative costs of $6,000 could be saved.

The accountant prepared the differential cost and revenue analysis shown in Illustration 12–7 and observed the following:

1. Assuming the sales of the other product lines would be unaffected, sales would decrease by $120,000 from dropping the general merchandise line.
2. Variable cost of goods sold of $95,000 would be saved by dropping the product line.
3. Fixed costs of $20,000 ($14,000 in salaries and $6,000 in marketing and administrative expenses) would be saved.
4. In total, the lost revenue of $120,000 exceeds the total differential cost saving by $5,000. Thus, Campus Bookstore's net income for the third quarter would have been $5,000 *lower* if general merchandise had been dropped.

The discrepancy between the supplies manager's claim that operating profits would have *increased* by $7,000 and the accountant's finding that operating profits would have *decreased* by $5,000 stems from their basic

Illustration 12-7

CAMPUS BOOKSTORE
Differential Analysis
(in thousands)

	Status Quo: Keep General Merchandise	Alternative: Drop General Merchandise	Differential: Increase (or Decrease) in Operating Profits
1. Sales revenue	$400	$280	$120 decrease
2. Cost of goods sold (all variable)	300	205	95 decrease
Contribution margin	100	75	25 decrease
3. Less fixed costs:			
Rent	18	18	-0-
Salaries	40	26	14 decrease
Marketing and administrative	36	30	6 decrease
4. Operating profits	$ 6	$ 1	$ 5 decrease

assumptions. The supplies manager assumed that the entire $32,000 in fixed costs allocated to general merchandise were differential and would be saved if the product line were dropped. The accountant's closer examination revealed that only $20,000 of the fixed costs would be saved—thus, the $12,000 discrepancy.

This example demonstrates the fallacy of assuming that all costs presented on financial statements are differential. The financial statement presented in Illustration 12–6 was designed to calculate department profits, not to identify the differential costs for this decision. Thus, using operating profit calculated after all cost allocations, including some that were not differential to this decision, incorrectly indicated the product line should be dropped. General purpose financial statements do not routinely provide differential cost information. Differential cost estimates depend on unique information that usually requires separate analysis. The bookstore statement, which was prepared on a contribution margin basis, clearly reveals the revenues and variable costs that are differential to this decision. But a separate analysis was required to determine which fixed costs are differential. It is, of course, possible to prepare division reports that reflect the division's contribution to companywide costs and profits. This *segment margin* would include division revenues less all direct costs of the division. Allocated costs would be excluded. These issues are addressed more fully in Chapter 22, "Decentralization and Performance Evaluation."

The Opportunity Cost of a Product Line

Keeping the general merchandise department may have an opportunity cost that we have not yet considered. Assume that the shelf space currently occupied by general merchandise could be used to increase the sale of books. The opportunity cost of retaining general merchandise is then measured by the probable foregone differential profits from the increased book sales. The accountant estimated the following figures to describe the substitution of increased book sales for general merchandise:

Drop general merchandise (from Illustration 12–7):	
Lost revenue	$120,000
Cost savings	115,000
Differential lost profit	$ 5,000
Add additional book sales:	
Additional book sales	$155,000
Less additional cost of books sold (all variable)	120,000
Contribution margin	35,000
Less additional fixed costs:	
Salaries	14,000
Marketing and administrative	4,000
Profit gained from additional book sales	$ 17,000

The analysis presented in Illustration 12–7 indicated that Campus Bookstore would lose $5,000 by eliminating general merchandise. However, given this additional information, an opportunity loss of $17,000 is incurred if the bookstore retains general merchandise and forgoes the opportunity to increase book sales. Based on these facts, Campus Bookstore is $12,000 ($17,000 gained from additional book sales − $5,000 lost from dropping general merchandise) better off to drop the general merchandise department and increase book sales. Illustration 12–8 presents a summary analysis for all three options: status quo, eliminate general merchandise, and eliminate general merchandise and increase book sales.

Illustration 12–8

CAMPUS BOOKSTORE
Comparison of Three Alternatives
(in thousands)

	Status Quo: Keep General Merchandise[a]	Alternative 1: Drop General Merchandise[a]	Alternative 2: Drop General Merchandise, Increase Book Sales
Sales revenue	$400	$280	$435 (280 + 155[b])
Cost of goods sold (all variable)	300	205	325 ($205 + 120[b])
Contribution margin	100	75	110
Less fixed costs:			
Rent	18	18	18
Salaries	40	26	40 ($26 + 14[b])
Marketing and administrative	36	30	34 ($30 + 4[b])
Operating profit	$ 6	$ 1	$ 18
		Worst	Best

[a] These columns are taken directly from Illustration 12–7.

[b] These amounts are the increase in revenue and costs taken from the discussion in the text.

SUMMARY

This chapter discusses *differential analysis*. Differential analysis determines *what* would differ and by *how much* if alternative actions are taken. Differential analysis is performed by comparing alternatives to the *status quo,* using the following model:

Status Quo	Alternative	Difference
Revenue	Revenue	Change in revenue
less	less	less
Variable costs	Variable costs	Change in variable costs
equals	equals	equals
Total contribution	Total contribution	Change in total contribution
less	less	less
Fixed costs	Fixed costs	Change in fixed costs
equals	equals	equals
Status quo's profit	Alternative's profit	Change in profits

This chapter has focused on identifying and measuring differential costs, which are the costs that are different under different alternatives. Costs that are different under alternative actions are also known as relevant costs. Costs that do *not* differ are not relevant for determining the financial consequences of alternatives.

TERMS AND CONCEPTS

The following terms and concepts should be familiar to you after reading this chapter:

Differential Analysis

Differential Costs

Full Cost

Full-Cost Fallacy

Make-or-Buy Decision

Opportunity Costs

Price Discrimination

Relevant Costs

Short Run

Special Order

Sunk Cost

SUPPLEMENTARY READINGS

Coulthurst, Nigel, and John Piper. "Framework for Analysis of Decision-Relevant Costs and Benefits." *Management Accounting,* June 1986, pp. 40–42 (published in Great Britain).

Dillon, R. D., and J. F. Nash. "The True Relevance of Relevant Costs." *The Accounting Review,* January 1978.

Hilton, Ronald W.; Robert J. Swieringa; and Martha J. Turner. "Product Pricing, Accounting Costs and the Use of Product-Costing Systems." *The Accounting Review,* April 1988, pp. 195–218.

Lee, John Y. "Developing a Pricing System for Small Business." *Management Accounting,* March 1987, pp. 50–53.

Penno, Mark. "Asymmetry of Pre-Decision Information and Managerial Accounting." *Journal of Accounting Research,* Spring 1984, pp. 177–91.

Plinke, Wulff. "Cost-Based Pricing: Behavioral Aspects of Price Decisions for Capital Goods." *Journal of Business Research,* October 1988, pp. 447–61.

Powers, Thomas L. "Breakeven Analysis with Semifixed Costs." *Industrial Marketing Management,* February 1987, pp. 35–42.

Sias, Randall G. "Pricing Bank Services." *Management Accounting,* July 1985, pp. 48–50.

Wichmann, Henry. "Cost-Volume-Profit Analysis for Small Business Retailers and Service Businesses." *Cost and Management,* May–June 1984, pp. 31–35.

SELF-STUDY PROBLEM NO. 1

The following is a true story. An executive joins a tennis club and pays a $300 yearly membership fee. After two weeks of playing, the executive develops a "tennis elbow" but continues to play (in pain), saying, "I don't want to waste the $300!" Comment.

SOLUTION TO SELF-STUDY PROBLEM NO. 1

The $300 is a sunk cost and should be irrelevant to the executive. The executive should consider only the advantages and disadvantages of playing henceforth, including the pain, but the $300 should be ignored. (The executive later quit playing until his tennis elbow healed.)

SELF-STUDY PROBLEM NO. 2

Vista Enterprises, Inc., has an annual plant capacity to produce 2,500 units. Its predicted operations for the year are:

Sales revenue (2,000 units at $40 each)	$80,000
Manufacturing costs:	
Variable	$24 per unit
Fixed	$17,000
Selling and administrative costs:	
Variable (commissions on sales)	$2.50 per unit
Fixed	$2,500

Should the company accept a special order for 400 units at a selling price of $32 each, which is subject to half the usual sales commission rate per unit? Assume no effect on regular sales at regular prices. What is the effect of the decision on the company's operating profit?

SOLUTION TO SELF-STUDY PROBLEM NO. 2

The special order should be accepted, as shown by the following two alternative analyses:

	Status Quo	Alternative	Difference
Sales revenues	$80,000	$92,800	$12,800
Variable costs	(53,000)	(63,100)	(10,100)
Contribution	27,000	29,700	2,700
Fixed costs	(19,500)	(19,500)	–0–
Operating profit	$ 7,500	$10,200	$ 2,700

Special-order sales (400 × $32)		$12,800
Less variable costs:		
Manufacturing (400 × $24)	$ 9,600	
Sales commission (400 × $1.25)	500	10,100
Addition to company profit		$ 2,700

SELF-STUDY PROBLEM NO. 3

Electronics, Inc., produces an electronic part used in guidance and navigation systems. Major customers are aircraft manufacturers.

The cost of an electronic part at the company's normal volume of 4,000 units per month is shown in Exhibit A.

The following questions refer only to the data given in Exhibit A. Unless otherwise stated, assume there is no connection between the situations described in the questions; each is to be treated independently. Unless otherwise stated, a regular selling price of $940 per unit should be assumed. Ignore income taxes and other costs that are not mentioned in Exhibit A or in a question itself.

a. *Price-volume analysis.* Market research estimates that volume would decrease to 3,500 units if the price were increased from $940 to $1,050 per unit. Assuming the cost behavior patterns implied by the data in Exhibit A are correct, would you recommend that this action be taken? What would be the impact on monthly sales, costs, and profits?

b. *Special order with opportunity costs.* On March 1, a contract offer is made to Electronics, Inc., by the federal government to supply 1,000 units to the Air

Exhibit A (SSP 12–3)

Unit manufacturing costs:		
Variable materials	$200	
Variable labor	150	
Variable overhead	50	
Fixed overhead	120	
Total unit manufacturing costs		$520
Unit nonmanufacturing costs:		
Variable	150	
Fixed	140	
Total unit nonmanufacturing costs		290
Total unit costs		$810

Force for delivery by March 31. Because of an unusually large number of rush orders from their regular customers, Electronics, Inc., plans to produce and sell 5,000 units during March, which will use all available capacity. If the government order is accepted, 1,000 units normally sold to their regular customers would be lost to a competitor for this month only. The contract given by the government would reimburse the government's share of March variable manufacturing costs, plus pay a fixed fee of $140,000. There would be no variable nonmanufacturing costs incurred on the government's units. What impact would accepting the government contract have on March profits?

c. *Special order without opportunity costs.* How would your answers to *(b)* change if Electronics, Inc., had planned to produce and sell only 3,000 units in March; hence, they would not have lost sales to a competitor?

d. *Make or buy.* A proposal is received from an outside contractor who will make and ship 1,000 units per month directly to Electronics, Inc.'s customers as orders are received from Electronics, Inc.'s sales force. Electronics, Inc.'s fixed non-manufacturing costs would be unaffected, but its variable nonmanufacturing costs would be cut by 20 percent for those 1,000 units produced by the contractor. Electronics, Inc.'s plant would operate at three fourths of its normal level, and total fixed manufacturing costs per month would be cut by 10 percent. Should the proposal be accepted for a payment to the contractor of $400 per unit? At what per-unit cost to the contractor would Electronics, Inc., be indifferent between making the product and buying from a contractor?

SOLUTION TO SELF-STUDY PROBLEM NO. 3

a. Raising this price would increase profits by $190,000.

	Status Quo	Alternative	Difference
Price	$ 940	$ 1,050	—
Volume	4,000	3,500	—
Sales revenue	$3,760,000	$3,675,000	$ 85,000 lower
Variable costs	2,200,000	1,925,000	275,000 lower
Contribution	1,560,000	1,750,000	190,000 higher
Fixed costs	1,040,000	1,040,000	–0–
Profit	$ 520,000	$ 710,000	$190,000 higher

b. Accepting the special order would reduce profits by $250,000.

	Status Quo	Alternative Regular	Government	Total	Difference
Volume	5,000 regular	4,000	1,000	5,000	
Sales revenue	$4,700,000	$3,760,000	$540,000	$4,300,000	$400,000 lower
Variable costs	2,750,000	2,200,000	400,000	2,600,000	150,000 lower
Contribution	1,950,000	1,560,000	140,000	1,700,000	250,000 lower
Fixed costs	1,040,000			1,040,000	–0–
Profit	$ 910,000			$ 660,000	$250,000 lower

c. Accepting the order would increase profits by $140,000—the amount of the fee.

d. Using the outside contractor at a cost of $400 per unit would increase profits by $78,000 ($478,000 increase in profit shown below − $400,000 paid to contractor).

	Status Quo	Alternative	Difference
Sales revenue	$3,760,000	$3,760,000	$ –0–
Variable cost ignoring payment to contractor	2,200,000	1,770,000[a]	430,000 lower
Contribution	1,560,000	1,990,000	430,000 higher
Fixed costs	1,040,000	992,000[b]	48,000 lower
Profit	$ 520,000	$ 998,000	$478,000 higher

[a] $1,770,000 = (1,000 units × $120) + (3,000 units × $550).

[b] $992,000 = $560,000 nonmanufacturing costs
+ (.90 × $480,000) manufacturing costs
= $560,000 + 432,000.

Electronics, Inc., would be indifferent between making and buying if the contractor charged $478 per unit, calculated as follows:

Set status quo profit equal to the alternative's profit
$$\$520,000 = \$998,000 - \text{Payment to contractor}$$
$$\text{Payment to contractor} = \$998,000 - \$520,000$$
$$= \underline{\$478,000} \text{ for 1,000 units, or \$478 per unit}$$

SELF-STUDY PROBLEM NO. 4: DIFFERENTIAL ANALYSIS, JUSTA CORPORATION

Justa Corporation produces and sells three products. The three products, A, B, and C, are sold in a local market and in a regional market. At the end of the first quarter of the current year, the following income statement has been prepared:

	Total	Local	Regional
Sales revenue	$1,300,000	$1,000,000	$300,000
Cost of goods sold	1,010,000	775,000	235,000
Gross margin	290,000	225,000	65,000
Marketing costs	105,000	60,000	45,000
Administrative costs	52,000	40,000	12,000
Total marketing and administrative	157,000	100,000	57,000
Operating profits	$ 133,000	$ 125,000	$ 8,000

Management has expressed special concern with the regional market because of the extremely poor return on sales. This market was entered a year ago because of excess capacity. It was originally believed that the return on sales would improve with time, but after a year, no noticeable improvement can be seen from the results as reported in the above quarterly statement.

In attempting to decide whether to eliminate the regional market, the following information has been gathered:

	Products		
	A	**B**	**C**
Sales revenue	$500,000	$400,000	$400,000
Variable manufacturing costs as a percentage of sales revenue	60%	70%	60%
Variable marketing costs as a percentage of sales revenue	3	2	2

	Sales by Markets	
Product	**Local**	**Regional**
A	$400,000	$100,000
B	300,000	100,000
C	300,000	100,000

All administrative costs and fixed manufacturing costs are common to the three products and the two markets and are fixed for the period. Remaining marketing costs are fixed for the period and separable by market. All fixed costs are based upon a prorated yearly amount.

Required:

a. Assuming there are no alternative uses for the Justa Corporation's present capacity, would you recommend dropping the regional market? Why or why not?

b. Prepare the quarterly income statement showing contribution margins by products.

c. It is believed that a new product can be ready for sale next year if the Justa Corporation decides to go ahead with continued research. The new product can be produced by simply converting equipment presently used in producing product C. This conversion will increase fixed costs by $10,000 per quarter. What must be the minimum contribution margin per quarter for the new product to make the changeover financially feasible?

(CMA adapted)

SOLUTION TO SELF-STUDY PROBLEM NO. 4

a. The regional market should not be dropped as this market not only covers all the variable costs and separable fixed costs but also gives net market contribution of $65,000 toward the common fixed costs.

$$\text{Sales} = \$300,000$$
$$\text{Variable manufacturing costs} = (.6 \times \$100,000) + (.7 \times \$100,000)$$
$$+ (.6 \times \$100,000)$$
$$= \$190,000$$
$$\text{Marketing costs} = \$45,000$$
$$\text{Net market contribution} = \underline{\$65,000} \ (\$300,000 - \$190,000 - \$45,000)$$

b. Quarterly income statement (in thousands):

	Product A	Product B	Product C	Total
Sales revenue	$500	$400	$400	$1,300
Less variable costs:				
Manufacturing	300	280	240	820
Marketing	15	8	8	31
Total variable cost	315	288	248	851
Contribution margin	185	112	152	449
Less fixed costs:				
Manufacturing ($1,010 − $820)				190
Marketing ($105 − $31)				74
Administrative				52
Total fixed costs				316
Operating profit				$ 133

c. The new product must contribute at least $162,000 ($152,000 + $10,000) per quarter so as not to leave the company worse off when product C is replaced.

QUESTIONS

12–1. One of your acquaintances notes: "This whole subject of differential costing is easy—variable costs are the only costs that are relevant." How would you respond?

12–2. When, if ever, are fixed costs differential?

12–3. What is the difference between a sunk cost and a differential cost?

12–4. Are sunk costs ever differential costs?

12–5. A manager in your organization just received a special order at a price that is "below cost." The manager points to the document and says: "These are the kinds of orders that will get you in trouble. Every sale must bear its share of the full costs of running the business. If we sell below our full cost, we'll be out of business in no time." Respond to this remark.

12–6. What factors should a company consider when deciding whether to close a division that shows an operating loss?

12–7. Why are opportunity costs often excluded from differential cost analyses?

12–8. Should opportunity costs be excluded from differential cost analyses? Why or why not?

12–9. If you are considering driving to a weekend resort for a quick break from school, what are the differential costs of operating your car for that drive?

12–10. If you are considering buying a second car, what are the differential costs of that decision? Are the differential costs in this question the same as in question 12–9? Why or why not?

12–11. Multiple-choice. Choose the best answer.
    a. In a make-or-buy decision:
        (1) Only direct materials costs are relevant.
        (2) Fixed costs that can be avoided in the future are relevant to the decision.

(3) Fixed costs that will not change regardless of the decision are relevant.

(4) Only conversion costs are relevant.

b. In deciding whether to manufacture a part or buy it from an outside vendor, a cost that is irrelevant to the short-run decision is:

(1) Direct labor.

(2) Variable overhead.

(3) Fixed overhead that will be avoided if the part is bought from an outside vendor.

(4) Fixed overhead that will continue even if the part is bought from an outside vendor.

c. Production of a special order will increase operating profit when the additional revenue from the special order is greater than:

(1) The conversion costs incurred in producing the order.

(2) The direct material costs in producing the order.

(3) The fixed costs incurred in producing the order.

(4) The indirect costs of producing the order.

(5) The differential costs of producing the order.

d. In considering a special-order situation that will enable a company to make use of presently idle capacity, which of the following costs would probably not be differential?

(1) Materials.

(2) Depreciation of buildings.

(3) Direct labor.

(4) Variable overhead.

(CPA adapted)

EXERCISES

Note: Income taxes should be ignored unless explicitly required in the exercise, problem or case.

12–12. Using Differential Analysis
(L.O.1)

Memory Corporation has 1,000 obsolete 4 meg DRAMS, which are carried in inventory at a cost of $20,000. If the DRAMS are remachined for $5,000, they could be sold for $9,000. If the DRAMS are scrapped, they could be sold for $1,000.

Required:

What is the optimal alternative? What costs are differential?

(CPA adapted)

12–13. Using Differential Analysis.
(L.O.1)

Bounce Company makes basketballs. Data from the forecasted income statement for the year before any special orders are as follows:

	Amount	Per Unit
Sales revenue	$4,000,000	$10.00
Manufacturing costs	3,200,000	8.00
Gross profit	800,000	2.00
Marketing costs	300,000	.75
Operating profit	$ 500,000	$ 1.25

Fixed costs included in the above forecasted income statement are $1,200,000 in manufacturing costs and $100,000 in marketing costs. These costs would not be affected by the order.

A special order offering to buy 50,000 basketballs for $7.50 each was made to Bounce. Bounce has enough idle capacity to process this order.

Required:

What impact would acceptance of the special order have on operating profit?

(CPA adapted)

12–14. Using Differential Analysis
(L.O.1)

Nubo Manufacturing, Inc., is presently operating at 50 percent of practical capacity and producing about 50,000 units annually of a patented electronic component. Nubo recently received an offer from a company in Yokohama, Japan, to purchase 30,000 components at $6 per unit. No other orders are foreseen. Nubo has not previously sold components in Japan. Budgeted production costs for 50,000 and 80,000 units of output follow:

Units	50,000	80,000
Costs:		
Direct materials	$ 75,000	$120,000
Direct labor	75,000	120,000
Factory overhead	200,000	260,000
Total costs	$350,000	$500,000
Cost per unit	$7.00	$6.25

The sales manager thinks the order should be accepted, even if it results in a loss, because she feels the sales may build up future markets. The production manager does not wish to have the order accepted, primarily because the order would show a loss of $.25 per unit when computed on the new average unit cost.

Required:

a. Explain what caused the drop in cost from $7 per unit to $6.25 per unit when budgeted production increased from 50,000 to 80,000 units. Show supporting computations.

b. Should the order from the company in Yokohama be accepted?

(CPA adapted)

12–15. Cost Analysis for Pricing Decisions
(L.O.2)

The following data relate to a year's budgeted activity for Patsy Corporation, a single-product company:

	Per Unit
Selling price	$5.00
Variable manufacturing costs	1.00
Variable marketing costs	2.00
Fixed manufacturing costs (based on 100,000 units)	.25
Fixed marketing costs (based on 100,000 units)	.65

Total fixed costs remain unchanged between 25,000 units and total capacity of 160,000 units.

An order is received to purchase 10,000 units to be used in an unrelated market. The sale would require production of 10,000 extra units.

Required:

What price per unit should be charged on the special order to increase operating profit by $9,000?

(CPA adapted)

12–16. Cost Analysis for Pricing
(L.O.2)

Icies sells ice cream for $3.00 per quart. The cost of each quart is as follows:

Materials	$1.00
Labor	.50
Variable overhead	.25
Fixed overhead ($50,000 per month, 50,000 quarts per month)	1.00
Total cost per quart	$2.75

One of Icies' regular customers asked the company to fill a special order of 500 quarts at a selling price of $2.25 per quart for a special picnic. The order could be filled with Icies' capacity without affecting total fixed costs for the month.

Icies' general manager was concerned about selling ice cream below the cost of $2.75 per quart and has asked for your advice.

Required:

a. Prepare a schedule to show the impact on Icies' profits of providing 500 quarts of ice cream in addition to the regular production and sales of 50,000 quarts per month.

b. Based solely on the data given, what is the lowest price per quart at which the ice cream could be sold without reducing Icies' profits?

12–17. Cost Analysis for Pricing
(L.O.2)

F. B. Floyd, Inc., has operated a violin case manufacturing business since 1920. The regular price of violin cases is $40 each. Floyd's controller has prepared cost data on these cases based on a normal selling volume of 20,000 cases per year:

Direct materials	$ 7.50
Direct labor	8.00
Overhead	6.00 (75% fixed)
Marketing and administrative	4.00 (all fixed)
Total cost	$25.50

This week, the Ness Corporation moved into Floyd's market area. Ness instituted a media campaign designed to lure Floyd's customers away. Indeed, Ness offered violin cases at one half of Floyd's selling price.

Floyd estimates that if he meets the Ness Corporation price, his volume will increase to 25,000 cases because people who previously were buying elsewhere would be induced to buy locally. However, if he does not meet Ness's price, Floyd's volume will fall to 4,000 cases per year.

Required:

a. Prepare a schedule to show the differential costs of the decision.

b. What should Floyd do?

12–18. Cost Analysis for Make-or-Buy Decision
(L.O.3)

Bikemakers makes bicycles. For years it has made the rear wheel assembly for its bicycles. Recently, Weeler Company offered to sell these rear wheel assemblies to Bikemakers. If Bikemakers makes the assembly, its cost per rear wheel assembly is as follows:

Direct materials	$ 6
Direct labor	30
Variable overhead	12
Fixed overhead applied	16
	$64

These costs are based on annual production of 20,000 units.

Weeler offered to sell the assembly to Bikemakers for $60 each. The total order would amount to 20,000 rear wheel assemblies per year. Bikemakers's management will buy these assemblies instead of making them if Bikemakers can save at least $25,000 per year. If Bikemakers accepts Weeler's offer, annual fixed overhead of $180,000 would be eliminated.

Required:

Should Bikemakers make rear wheel assemblies or buy them from Weeler? Prepare a schedule that shows the differential costs per rear wheel assembly.

12–19. Cost Analysis for Make-or-Buy Decision
(L.O.3)

Golden, Inc., has been manufacturing 5,000 units per month of part 10541, which is used in the manufacture of one of its products. At this level of production, the cost per unit of manufacturing part 10541 is as follows:

Direct materials	$ 2
Direct labor	8
Variable overhead	4
Fixed overhead applied	6
Total	$20

Brown Company has offered to sell Golden 5,000 units of part 10541 for $17 a unit. Golden has determined that it could use the facilities presently used to manufacture part 10541 to manufacture product RAC and generate an additional contribution margin per month of $8,000. Golden has also determined that one third of the fixed overhead applied will be saved even if part 10541 is purchased from Brown and product RAC is made.

Required:

Prepare a schedule to show the effect of purchasing part 10541 from Brown at $17 a unit. Assume Golden would take the opportunity to make product RAC.

(CPA adapted)

12–20. Cost Analysis for Make-or-Buy Decision
(L.O.3)

Cardinal Company needs 20,000 units of a certain part to use in its production cycle. Cardinal estimates the costs to make the part as follows:

Direct materials	$ 4
Direct labor	16
Variable overhead	8
Fixed overhead applied	10
Total	$38

The cost to buy the part from the Oriole Company is $36. Sixty percent of the fixed overhead applied to this product will continue regardless of what decision is made. What are the differential costs of the make-or-buy decision?

(CPA adapted)

12–21. Cost Analysis for Make-or-Buy Decision
(L.O.3)

Sailsport purchases sails and produces sailboats. It currently produces 1,000 sail-boats a year, operating at 70 percent of capacity. Currently, Sailsport purchases sails for $280 each, but the company is considering making sails instead. Sailsport can manufacture sails for $100 per sail for materials, $80 per sail for direct labor, and $120 per sail for overhead. Sails could be made without increasing Sailsport's capacity.

Sam Sport, the president of Sailsport, has come to you for advice. "It would cost me $300 to make the sails," he said, "but only $280 to buy. Should I continue buying them?" He added, "Materials and labor are variable costs, but variable overhead would be only $40 per sail." (Sam uses one sail per boat.)

Required:

What should Sam do? Prepare a schedule to show the differential costs.

12–22. Cost Analysis—Make or Buy with Opportunity Costs
(L.O.3)

Refer to the facts in exercise 12–21. If Sam suddenly finds an opportunity to rent out the unused capacity of his factory for $80,000 per year, would your answer in exercise 12–21 change? Why or why not?

12–23. Dropping Product Lines
(L.O.4)

Refer to the data for Campus Bookstores that appears in Illustration 12–8. Assume that all facts are the same as presented in Illustration 12–8 except the following:

1. Salaries listed under fixed costs are $40,000 under all three alternatives (that is, there is no reduction in fixed cost salaries under alternative 1).

2. Under alternative 2, rent increases to $32,000.

Required:

Prepare a new comparison of the three choices; namely, status quo, alternative 1, and alternative 2.

12–24. Dropping Product Lines
(L.O.4)

New England Ski Company is presently operating at 75 percent of capacity. Worried about the company's performance, the president is considering dropping the company's line of cross-country skis. If the cross-country skis are dropped, the revenue associated with cross-country skis would be lost and the related variable costs would be saved. In addition, fixed costs for the company would be reduced by 20 percent of the total fixed costs.

Segmented income statements appear as follows:

	Product		
	Downhill Racing Skis	Cross-Country Skis	Regular Downhill Skis
Sales	$32,600	$42,800	$51,200
Variable costs	22,000	38,000	40,100
Contribution margin	10,600	4,800	11,100
Fixed costs allocated to each product line	4,700	5,600	7,100
Operating profit (loss)	$ 5,900	$ (800)	$ 4,000

Required:

Prepare a differential cost schedule like the one in Illustration 12–7 to indicate whether New England Ski Company should drop the cross-country ski product line.

12–25. Dropping Product Lines
(L.O.4)

Anderhouse & Watersen is a public accounting firm that offers three types of services: audit, tax, and consulting. The firm is concerned about the profitability of its consulting business and is considering dropping that line. If the consulting business is dropped, more tax work would be done. If consulting is dropped, all consulting revenues would be lost, all of the variable costs associated with consulting would be saved, and 60 percent of the fixed costs associated with consulting would be saved. Tax revenues are expected to increase by 40 percent, the variable costs associated with tax would increase by 40 percent, and the fixed costs associated with tax would increase by 10 percent. Revenues and costs associated with auditing would not be affected.

Segmented income statements for these three product lines appear as follows:

	Product		
	Consulting	Tax	Auditing
Revenue	$300,000	$400,000	$500,000
Variable costs	250,000	300,000	350,000
Contribution margin	50,000	100,000	150,000
Fixed costs	50,000	60,000	80,000
Operating profit	$ -0-	$ 40,000	$ 70,000

Required:

Prepare a differential cost schedule like the one in Illustration 12–8 to indicate whether Anderhouse & Watersen should drop the consulting line.

PROBLEMS

12–26. Special-Order Costs

Brike Company, which manufactures robes, has enough idle capacity available to accept a special order of 10,000 robes at $8 a robe. A predicted income statement for the year without this special order is as follows:

	Per Unit	Total
Sales revenue	$12.50	$1,250,000
Manufacturing costs:		
Variable	6.25	625,000
Fixed	1.75	175,000
Total manufacturing costs	8.00	800,000
Gross profit	4.50	450,000
Marketing costs:		
Variable	1.80	180,000
Fixed	1.45	145,000
Total marketing costs	3.25	325,000
Operating profit	$ 1.25	$ 125,000

If the order is accepted, variable marketing costs on the special order would be reduced by 25 percent because all of the robes would be packed and shipped in one lot. However, if the offer is accepted, management estimates that it will lose the sale of 2,000 robes at regular prices.

Required:

What is the net gain or loss from the special order?

(CPA adapted)

12–27. New Product Introduction—CVP Considerations

Servo Gimmicks, Ltd., produces and sells new and unusual household products. The company recently received a proposal to manufacture a left-handed bottle opener. The product engineering department estimates variable manufacturing costs for each unit of:

Materials	$ .25
Labor	.50
Overhead	.30
Total	$1.05

Variable selling costs include $.55 for packaging and shipping. In addition, Servo allocates $.10 of common fixed costs to each unit sold. If Servo decides to sell the product, they will launch a media campaign on late-night television. The media campaign will cost $450,000. Of course, Servo has a number of products, and if they don't produce the left-handed bottle opener, they will manufacture some other item. Servo estimates that any product they sell must contribute at least $500,000 to after-tax profits.

The marketing department estimates that the optimal selling price for the product is $3.99.

Required:

If Servo's tax rate is 45 percent, how many left-handed bottle openers must be sold to meet the profit target? Show computations in good form.

12–28. Pricing Based on Costs—Multiple-Choice

E. Berg and Sons build custom-made pleasure boats, which range in price from $10,000 to $250,000. For the past 30 years, Mr. Berg, Sr., has determined the selling price of each boat by estimating the costs of material, labor, a prorated portion of overhead, and adding 20 percent to these estimated costs.

For example, a recent price quotation for boat A was determined as follows:

Direct materials	$ 5,000
Direct labor	8,000
Overhead	2,000
	$15,000
Plus 20 percent	3,000
Selling price	$18,000

The overhead figure was determined by estimating total overhead costs for the year and allocating them at 25 percent of direct labor costs.

If a customer rejected the price and business was slack, Mr. Berg, Sr., would often be willing to reduce his markup to as little as 5 percent over estimated costs. Thus, average markup for the year is estimated at 15 percent.

Mr. Ed Berg, Jr., has just completed a course on pricing and believes the firm could use some of the techniques discussed in the course. The course emphasized the contribution margin approach to pricing, and Mr. Berg, Jr., feels such an approach would be helpful in determining the selling prices of their custom-made boats.

Total manufacturing overhead for the year has been estimated at $150,000, of which $90,000 is fixed and the remainder varies in direct proportion to direct labor.

Required:

a. What is the proportion of variable overhead to total overhead used by E. Berg and Sons?

    (1) 60 percent.
    (2) 40 percent.
    (3) 25 percent.
    (4) 30 percent.

b. What is the variable overhead rate as a percent of direct-labor dollars?
    (1) 25 percent.
    (2) 30 percent.
    (3) 10 percent.
    (4) 15 percent.

c. If E. Berg and Sons accepts a customer's offer of $15,000 for boat A, how much profit (loss) will occur?
    (1) ($8,000).
    (2) $1,200.
    (3) $800.
    (4) ($1,500).

d. What is the minimum price that E. Berg and Sons should accept for boat A if they use full costing, that is, allocate fixed costs to each project?
    (1) $18,000.
    (2) $15,750.
    (3) $15,000.
    (4) $13,800.

(CMA adapted)

12–29. Special Order

George Jackson operates a small machine shop. He manufactures one standard product, which is available from many other similar businesses, and he also manufactures products to customer order. His accountant prepared the annual income statement shown below:

	Custom Sales	Standard Sales	Total
Sales revenue	$50,000	$25,000	$75,000
Materials	10,000	8,000	18,000
Labor	20,000	9,000	29,000
Depreciation	6,300	3,600	9,900
Power	700	400	1,100
Rent	6,000	1,000	7,000
Heat and light	600	100	700
Other	400	900	1,300
Total costs	44,000	23,000	67,000
Operating profit	$ 6,000	$ 2,000	$ 8,000

    The depreciation charges are for machines (based on time) used in the respective product lines. The power charge is apportioned on the estimate of power consumed. The rent is for the building space, which has been leased for 10 years at $7,000 per year. The rent and heat and light are apportioned to the product lines based on amount of floor space occupied. All other costs are current expenses identified with the product line causing them.

    A valued custom parts customer has asked Mr. Jackson if he would manufacture 5,000 special units for him. Mr. Jackson is working at capacity and would have to give up some other business in order to take this business. He can't renege on custom orders already agreed to, but he could reduce the output of his standard product by about one half for one year while producing the specially requested custom part. The customer is willing to pay $7 for each part. The material cost will be about $2 per unit, and the labor will be $3.60 per unit. Mr. Jackson will have to spend $2,000 for a special device, which will be discarded when the job is done.

Required:

Should Mr. Jackson take the order? Explain your answer.

(CMA adapted)

12–30. Comprehensive Differential Costing Problem

Hospital Supply, Inc., produced hydraulic hoists that were used by hospitals to move bedridden patients. The costs of manufacturing and marketing hydraulic hoists at the company's normal volume of 3,000 units per month are shown in Exhibit A.

Required:

Unless otherwise stated, assume there is no connection between the situations described in the questions; each is to be treated independently. Unless otherwise stated, a regular selling price of $740 per unit should be assumed. Ignore income taxes and other costs that are not mentioned in Exhibit A or in a question itself.

a. What is the break-even volume in units? In sales-dollars?

b. Market research estimates that volume could be increased to 3,500 units, which is well within hoist production capacity limitations, if the price were cut from $740 to $650 per unit. Assuming the cost behavior patterns implied by the data in Exhibit A are correct, would you recommend that this action be taken? What would be the impact on monthly sales, costs, and income?

c. On March 1, a contract offer is made to Hospital Supply by the federal government to supply 500 units to Veterans Administration hospitals for delivery by March 31. Because of an unusually large number of rush orders from their regular customers, Hospital Supply plans to produce 4,000 units during March, which will use all available capacity. If the government order is accepted, 500 units normally sold to regular customers would be lost to a competitor. The contract given by the government would reimburse the government's share of March manufacturing costs, plus pay a fixed fee (profit) of $50,000. (There would be no variable marketing costs incurred on the government's units.) What impact would accepting the government contract have on March income?

d. Hospital Supply has an opportunity to enter a foreign market in which price competition is keen. An attraction of the foreign market is that demand there is greatest when demand in the domestic market is quite low; thus idle production facilities could be used without affecting domestic business.

An order for 1,000 units is being sought at a below-normal price in order to enter this market. Shipping costs for this order will amount to $75 per unit, while total costs of obtaining the contract (marketing costs) will be $4,000. No other

Exhibit A (12–30)   **Costs per Unit for Hydraulic Hoists**

Unit manufacturing costs:		
Variable materials	$100	
Variable labor	150	
Variable overhead	50	
Fixed overhead	120	
Total unit manufacturing costs		$420
Unit marketing costs:		
Variable	50	
Fixed	140	
Total unit marketing costs		190
Total unit costs		$610

variable marketing costs would be required on this order. Domestic business would be unaffected by this order. What is the minimum unit price Hospital Supply should consider for this order of 1,000 units?

e. An inventory of 230 units of an obsolete model of the hoist remains in the stockroom. These must be sold through regular channels (thus incurring variable marketing costs) at reduced prices, or the inventory will soon be valueless. What is the minimum price that would be acceptable in selling these units?

f. A proposal is received from an outside contractor who will make and ship 1,000 hydraulic hoist units per month directly to Hospital Supply's customers as orders are received from Hospital Supply's sales force. Hospital Supply's fixed marketing costs would be unaffected, but its variable marketing costs would be cut by 20 percent for these 1,000 units produced by the contractor. Hospital Supply's plant would operate at two thirds of its normal level, and total fixed manufacturing costs would be cut by 30 percent. What in-house unit cost should be used to compare with the quotation received from the supplier? Should the proposal be accepted for a price (that is, payment to the contractor) of $425 per unit?

g. Assume the same facts as above in requirement (f) except that the idle facilities would be used to produce 800 modified hydraulic hoists per month for use in hospital operating rooms. These modified hoists could be sold for $900 each, while the costs of production would be $550 per unit variable manufacturing expense. Variable marketing costs would be $100 per unit. Fixed marketing and manufacturing costs would be unchanged whether the original 3,000 regular hoists were manufactured or the mix of 2,000 regular hoists plus 800 modified hoists were produced. What is the maximum purchase price per unit that Hospital Supply should be willing to pay the outside contractor? Should the proposal be accepted for a price of $425 per unit to the contractor?

12–31. Analyze Alternative Products

Ocean Company manufactures and sells three different products: Ex, Why, and Zee. Projected income statements by product line for the year are presented below:

	Ex	Why	Zee	Total
Unit sales	10,000	500,000	125,000	635,000
Sales revenue	$925,000	$1,000,000	$575,000	$2,500,000
Variable cost of units sold	285,000	350,000	150,000	785,000
Fixed cost of units sold	304,200	289,000	166,800	760,000
Gross margin	335,800	361,000	258,200	955,000
Variable nonmanufacturing costs	270,000	200,000	80,000	550,000
Fixed nonmanufacturing costs	125,800	136,000	78,200	340,000
Operating profit	$(60,000)	$ 25,000	$100,000	$ 65,000

Production costs are similar for all three products. Fixed nonmanufacturing costs are allocated to products in proportion to revenues. The fixed cost of units sold is allocated to products by various allocation bases, such as square feet for factory rent, machine-hours for repairs, and so forth.

Ocean management is concerned about the loss on product Ex and is considering two alternative courses of corrective action.

Alternative A. Ocean would purchase some new machinery for the production of product Ex. This new machinery would involve an immediate cash outlay of $650,000. Management expects that the new machinery would reduce variable production costs so that total variable costs (cost of units sold and nonmanufacturing costs) for product Ex would be 52 percent of product Ex revenues. The new machinery would increase total fixed costs allocated to product Ex to $480,000 per year. No additional fixed costs would be allocated to products Why or Zee.

Alternative B. Ocean would discontinue the manufacture of product Ex. Selling prices of products Why and Zee would remain constant. Management expects that product Zee production and revenues would increase by 50 percent. The machinery devoted to product Ex could be sold at scrap value that equals its removal costs. Removal of this machinery would reduce fixed costs allocated to product Ex by $30,000 per year. The remaining fixed costs allocated to product Ex include $155,000 of rent expense per year. The space previously used for product Ex can be rented to an outside organization for $157,500 per year.

Required:

Prepare a schedule analyzing the effect of alternative A and alternative B on projected total operating profit.

(CPA adapted)

12–32. Differential Costs of Alternative Marketing Strategies

Calco Corporation has been a major producer and distributor of plastic products for industrial use. The product engineering department has recently presented a proposal to produce a new product designed for the consumer market. The product was very well suited for the company's manufacturing process. No modification of machinery or molds would be required nor would operations in the assembly department have to be changed in any way. In addition, there was an adequate amount of manufacturing capacity available.

Management is considering two alternatives for marketing the product. The first is to add this responsibility to Calco's current marketing department. The other alternative is to acquire a small, new company named Jasco, Inc. Jasco was started by some former employees of a firm that specialized in marketing plastic products for the consumer market when they lost their jobs as a result of a merger. The only requirements of the Jasco people are that Calco hire the Jasco employees and take over a lease for office space.

The product would be manufactured by Calco, and the manufacturing costs would be the same for either marketing alternative. The product engineering department has prepared the following estimates of the unit manufacturing costs for the new product:

Direct materials	$14.00
Direct labor	3.50
Manufacturing overhead	10.00
Total	$27.50

Twenty-five percent of the total overhead rate is for variable costs like supplies, employee benefits, power, and so forth; and 75 percent for fixed costs like supervision, depreciation, insurance, and taxes.

Calco's marketing department has developed a proposal for the distribution of the new consumer product. The marketing department's forecast of the annual financial results for its proposal to market the new product is as follows:

Sales revenue (100,000 units at $45)	$4,500,000
Costs:	
Cost of units sold (100,000 units at $27.50)	2,750,000
Marketing costs:	
Additional people hired	600,000
Sales commission (5% of sales)	225,000
Advertising program	400,000
Promotion program	200,000
Share of current marketing department's management costs	100,000
Total costs	4,275,000
Operating profit	$ 225,000

The Jasco people also prepared a forecast of the annual financial results. The forecast presented below was based on the assumption that Jasco would become part of Calco and be responsible for marketing the new product in the consumer market.

Sales revenue (120,000 units at $50)	$6,000,000
Costs:	
Cost of units sold (120,000 units at $27.50)	3,300,000
Marketing costs:	
Personnel—sales	660,000
Personnel—sales management	200,000
Commissions (10%)	600,000
Advertising program	800,000
Promotion program	200,000
Office rental (the annual rental of a long-term lease already signed by Jasco)	50,000
Total costs	5,810,000
Operating profit	$ 190,000

Calco's management believes profits will be $35,000 higher ($225,000 − $190,000) if the marketing is done by Calco's marketing department, but they have turned to you for help.

Required:

Prepare a schedule of differential costs and revenues to assist management in deciding whether to enter the consumer market.

(CMA adapted)

12-33. Analyze Auto Rental versus Reimbursement Policy

G & H Real Estate Agency requires all of its agents to travel throughout the entire area to list and sell property. The company has a reimbursement policy of $.25 per mile for all business-connected travel. The agents are responsible for all costs associated with the operation of their own automobiles. Last year, the average mileage claimed by an agent was 50,000 miles. G & H offices are open 300 days a year.

Jack Golden, the president, senses that some of the agents may have been claiming excess miles during the year. Golden is convinced that the annual mileage use would drop to 42,000 miles per year if the agents were not using their own cars. Therefore, he is considering providing automobiles to the agents.

Golden asked both International Car Rental and a local automobile dealer, Aron Motor, to present proposals. The proposals are described below.

International Car Rental's Proposal

International presented a lease arrangement with the following requirements:
1. G & H would rent 20 automobiles for an entire year at $66 per week per automobile and $.14 per mile.
2. When one of the 20 automobiles is in for service, International would provide a replacement at $7 per day and $.20 per mile. International would absorb all repair and maintenance costs. Normally, an automobile would be out of service only one day at a time, and each automobile can be expected to be out of service 12 days per year.
3. Cost of insurance is included in the weekly rental rate.
4. G & H would be required to purchase the gasoline for the automobiles at an average cost of $1.50 per gallon. International estimates that G & H should expect to get 21 miles per gallon.

Aron Motor's Proposal

Aron offered a purchase-buy-back arrangement with the following requirements:
1. G & H would buy 20 automobiles at $12,000 each. Aron would buy the automobiles back after one year at $7,000 each.
2. G & H would have to bring each automobile in once every two months for preventive maintenance and service. The cost to G & H for each visit would be $50. Aron would provide a loaner automobile at no additional cost. Aron would accept responsibility for any additional repair and maintenance charges.
3. G & H would have to purchase insurance at an annual cost of $200 for each automobile.
4. G & H would purchase one new set of tires each year at $125 per set.
5. G & H would be responsible for the purchase of gasoline at an average cost of $1.50 per gallon. The automobiles will average 28 miles per gallon.

Golden has asked your help in comparing the alternatives.

Required:

Calculate an annual before-tax cost to G & H for:

a. The current reimbursement practice.

b. The proposal of International Car Rental.

c. The proposal of Aron Motor.

Based on these data, which alternative would you recommend that Golden accept?

(CMA adapted)

INTEGRATIVE CASES

12–34. Analyze Alternative Actions

Auer Company had received an order for a piece of special machinery from Jay Company. Just as Auer Company completed the machine, Jay Company declared bankruptcy, defaulted on the order, and forfeited the 10 percent deposit paid on the selling price of $72,500.

Auer's manufacturing manager identified the costs already incurred in the production of the special machinery for Jay as follows:

Direct materials used		$16,600
Direct labor incurred		21,400
Overhead applied:		
Manufacturing:		
Variable	$10,700	
Fixed	5,350	16,050
Nonmanufacturing:		5,405
Total cost		$59,455

Another company, Kaytell Corporation, would be interested in buying the special machinery if it is reworked to Kaytell's specifications. Auer offered to sell the reworked special machinery to Kaytell as a special order for a net price of $68,400. Kaytell has agreed to pay the net price when it takes delivery in two months. The additional identifiable costs to rework the machinery to the specifications of Kaytell are as follows:

Direct materials	$ 6,200
Direct labor	4,200
	$10,400

A second alternative available to Auer is to convert the special machinery to the standard model. The standard model lists for $62,500. The additional identifiable costs to convert the special machinery to the standard model are:

Direct materials	$2,850
Direct labor	3,300
	$6,150

A third alternative for the Auer Company is to sell, as a special order, the machine as is (that is, without modification) for a net price of $52,000. However, the potential buyer of the unmodified machine does not want it for 60 days. The buyer offers a $7,000 down payment, with final payment upon delivery.

The following additional information is available regarding Auer's operations:

1. Sales commission rate on sales of standard models is 2 percent, while sales commission rate on special orders is 3 percent. All sales commissions are calculated on net sales price (that is, list price less cash discount, if any).

2. Normal credit terms for sales of standard models are 2/10, net/30, Customers take the discounts except in rare instances. Credit terms for special orders are negotiated with the customer.

3. The application rates for manufacturing overhead and the nonmanufacturing costs are as follows:

Manufacturing:	
Variable	50% of direct labor cost
Fixed	25% of direct labor cost

(continued)

	Nonmanufacturing:
Fixed	10% of the total of direct material, direct labor, and manufacturing overhead costs

4. Normal time required for rework is one month.

Auer does not consider the time value of money in analysis of special orders and projects when the time period is less than one year because the effect is not significant.

Required:

a. Determine the dollar contribution that each of the three alternatives will add to the Auer Company's before-tax profits.

b. If Kaytell makes Auer a counter offer, what is the lowest price Auer Company should accept for the reworked machinery from Kaytell? Explain your answer.

(CMA adapted)

12–35. Discontinuing Product Lines

The Scio Division of Georgetown, Inc., manufactures and sells four related product lines. Each product is produced at one or more of the three manufacturing plants of the division. The product-line profitability statement for this year shows a loss for the baseball equipment line. A similar loss is projected for next year.

The baseball equipment is manufactured in the Evanston plant. Some football equipment and all miscellaneous sports items also are processed through this plant. A few of the miscellaneous items are manufactured, and the remainder are purchased for resale. The item purchased for resale is recorded as materials in the records. A separate production line is used for each product line.

SCIO DIVISION
Product-Line Profitability
(in thousands)

	Football Equipment	Baseball Equipment	Hockey Equipment	Miscellaneous Sports Items	Total
Sales revenue	$2,200	$1,000	$1,500	$500	$5,200
Cost of goods sold:					
Materials	400	175	300	90	965
Labor and variable overhead	800	400	600	60	1,860
Fixed overhead	350	275	100	50	775
Total	1,550	850	1,000	200	3,600
Gross profit	650	150	500	300	1,600
Marketing costs:					
Variable	440	200	300	100	1,040
Fixed	100	50	100	50	300
Corporate administration costs	48	24	36	12	120
Total	588	274	436	162	1,460
Operating profit	$ 62	$ (124)	$ 64	$138	$ 140

The cost schedule presents the costs incurred at the Evanston plant. Inventories at the end of the year were substantially identical to those at the beginning of the year.

Management of Georgetown, Inc., requested a profitability study of the baseball equipment line to determine if the line should be discontinued. The marketing department of the Scio Division and the accounting department at the plant have developed the following additional data to be used in the study:

1. If the baseball equipment line is discontinued, the company will lose approximately 10 percent of its sales in each of the other lines.

2. Equipment now used in the manufacture of baseball equipment cannot be used elsewhere in the company. It has a book value of $105,000 and a remaining useful life of five years. If sold today, it would have no salvage value.

3. The plant space now occupied by the baseball equipment line could be closed off from the rest of the plant and rented for $175,000 per year.

4. If the line is discontinued, the supervisor of the baseball equipment line will be released. In keeping with company policy, he would receive a one-time severance payment of $5,000.

EVANSTON PLANT
Cost Schedule
(in thousands)

	Football Equipment	Baseball Equipment	Misellaneous Sports Items	Total
Materials	$100	$175	$ 90	$ 365
Labor	100	200	30	330
Variable overhead:				
Supplies	85	60	12	157
Power	50	110	7	167
Other	15	30	11	56
Subtotal	150	200	30	380
Fixed overhead:				
Supervision[a]	25	30	21	76
Depreciation[b]	40	115	14	169
Plant rentals[c]	35	105	10	150
Other[d]	20	25	5	50
Subtotal	120	275	50	445
Total costs	$470	$850	$200	$1,520

[a] The supervision costs represent salary and benefit costs of the supervisors in charge of each product line.

[b] Depreciation cost for machinery and equipment is charged to the product line on which the machinery is used.

[c] The plant is leased. The lease rentals are charged to the product lines on the basis of square feet occupied.

[d] Other fixed overhead costs are the cost of plant administration and are allocated arbitrarily by management decision.

Required:

Should Georgetown, Inc., discontinue the baseball equipment line? Support your answer with appropriate calculations and qualitative arguments.

(CMA adapted)

12–36. Sell or Process Further

The management of Bay Company is considering a proposal to install a third production department within its existing factory building. With the company's present production setup, 200,000 pounds per year of direct materials are passed through Department I to produce Materials A and B in equal proportions. Material A is then passed through Department II to yield 100,000 pounds of Product C. One hundred thousand pounds of Material B is presently being sold "as is" at a price of $20.25 per pound.

The costs for the Bay Company are as follows:

	Department I (Materials A and B)[a]	Department II (Product C)[a]	(Material B)[a]
Prior department costs	$ —	$33.25	$33.25
Direct materials	20.00	—	—
Direct labor	7.00	12.00	—
Variable overhead	3.00	5.00	—
Fixed overhead:			
Direct (Total = $675,000)	2.25	2.25	—
Allocated (⅔, ⅓)	1.00	1.00	—
	$33.25	$53.50	$33.25

[a] Cost per pound.

The fixed costs were developed by using the production volume of 200,000 pounds of direct materials as the volume. Common fixed overhead costs of $300,000 are allocated to the two producing departments on the basis of the space used by the departments.

The proposed Department III would process Material B into Product D. One pound of Material B yields one pound of Product D. Any quantity of Product D can be sold for $30 per pound. Costs under this proposal are as follows:

	Department I (Materials A and B)	Department II (Product C)	Department III (Product D)
Prior department costs	$ —	$33.00	$33.00
Direct materials	20.00	—	—
Direct labor	7.00	12.00	5.50
Variable overhead	3.00	5.00	2.00
Fixed overhead:			
Direct (Total = $850,000)	2.25	2.25	1.75
Allocated (½, ¼, ¼)	.75	.75	.75
	$33.00	$53.00	$43.00

Required:

If sales and production levels are expected to remain constant in the foreseeable future, these cost estimates are expected to be true, and there are no foreseeable alternative uses for the available factory space, should Bay Company produce Product D? Show calculations to support your answer.

(CMA adapted)

12–37. Differential Costs and CVP Analysis

You have been asked to assist the management of Arcadia Corporation in arriving at certain decisions. Arcadia has its home office in Ohio and leases factory buildings in Texas, Montana, and Maine, all of which produce the same product. The management of Arcadia provided you with a projection of operations for next year, as follows:

	Total	Texas	Montana	Maine
Sales revenue	$4,400,000	$2,200,000	$1,400,000	$800,000
Fixed costs:				
Factory	1,100,000	560,000	280,000	260,000
Administration	350,000	210,000	110,000	30,000
Variable costs	1,450,000	665,000	425,000	360,000
Allocated home office costs	500,000	225,000	175,000	100,000
Total	3,400,000	1,660,000	990,000	750,000
Operating profit	$1,000,000	$ 540,000	$ 410,000	$ 50,000

The sales price per unit is $25.

Due to the marginal results of operations of the factory in Maine, Arcadia has decided to cease operations and sell that factory's machinery and equipment by the end of this year. Arcadia expects that the proceeds from the sale of these assets would be greater than their book value and would cover all termination costs.

Arcadia, however, would like to continue serving its customers in that area if it is economically feasible and is considering one of the following three alternatives:

1. Expand the operations of the Montana factory by using space presently idle. This move would result in the following changes in that factory's operations:

	Increase over Factory's Current Operations
Sales revenue	50%
Fixed costs:	
Factory	20
Administration	10

Under this proposal, variable costs would be $8 per unit sold.

2. Enter into a long-term contract with a competitor who will serve that area's customers. This competitor would pay Arcadia a royalty of $4 per unit based on an estimate of 30,000 units being sold.

3. Close the Maine factory and not expand the operations of the Montana factory.

Total home office costs of $500,000 will remain the same under each situation.

Required:

To assist the management of Arcadia Corporation, prepare a schedule computing Arcadia's estimated operating profit from each of the following options:

a. Expansion of the Montana factory
b. Negotiation of long-term contract on a royalty basis.
c. Shutdown of Maine operations with no expansion at other locations.

(CPA adapted)

MULTIPLE PRODUCT DECISIONS

LEARNING OBJECTIVES

1. Seeing how to use accounting data to make decisions about multiple products.

2. Knowing how to use linear programming for cost-based decisions.

3. Understanding the sensitivity of linear programming solutions to the cost data entered into the program.

This chapter continues the discussion of differential cost analysis by explaining how differential costing is used to choose among multiple products.

PRODUCT-CHOICE DECISIONS

Choosing which products to manufacture and sell is a common managerial decision. Most companies are capable of producing a great variety of goods and services but are limited by capacity. Campus Bookstore, in Chapter 12, had to decide whether to use its limited space to sell general merchandise or to increase book sales. Due to a shortage of personnel, a small CPA firm may have to choose between performing work for client A or for client B. Students have to choose how to allocate their study time among their courses. An automobile manufacturer with limited production facilities must decide whether to produce compacts, full-size sedans, or some other model.

We usually think of product choices as short-run decisions because we have adopted the definition that in the short run, capacity is fixed, while in the long run, capacity can be changed. Thus, the aircraft manufacturer may be able to produce both jumbo and narrow-body models in the *long run* by increasing capacity, and the CPA firm may be able to serve both client A and client B in the *long run* by hiring more professional staff. Nonetheless, in the short run, capacity limitations require choices.

For example, Glover Manufacturing makes two kinds of baseballs—hardballs and softballs. For now, assume that the company can sell all the baseballs it produces. Glover's cost and revenue information is presented in Illustration 13–1.

The profit-volume relationship for Glover's products is shown in Illustration 13–2. For instance, Glover Manufacturing can sell 250,000 hardballs or 250,000 softballs or any combination of hardballs and softballs totaling 250,000 to break even. The contribution margin of each product is the same, so the profit-volume relationship is the same regardless of the mix of products produced and sold.

PRODUCT CONTRIBUTION MARGIN WITH A SINGLE CONSTRAINED RESOURCE

Recall that Glover Manufacturing can sell all of the baseballs it can produce. Glover's objective is to maximize the contribution from its sales of hardballs and softballs. But should it produce hardballs or softballs? Without knowing either Glover's maximum production capacity or the amount of that capacity that is used by producing one product or the other, we might say that it doesn't matter because both products are equally profitable. But because

Illustration 13–1 **Revenue and Cost Information, Glover Manufacturing**

	Hardballs	Softballs
Sales revenue per unit	$10.00	$9.00
Less variable costs per unit:		
Materials	4.00	2.50
Labor	1.50	2.00
Variable overhead	.50	.50
Contribution margin per unit	$ 4.00	$4.00

Fixed manufacturing costs: $800,000 per month.
Marketing and administrative costs (all fixed): $200,000 per month.

Illustration 13-2   **Profit-Volume Relationship Assuming Hardballs and Softballs Use Equal Scarce Resources, Glover Manufacturing**

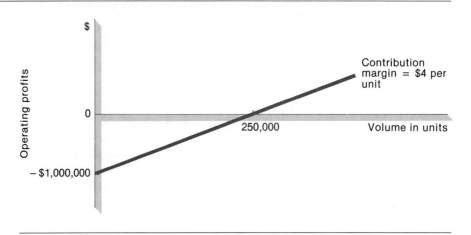

Constraints Activities,
resources, or policies that limit
or bound the attainment of an
objective.

**Contribution Margin per Unit of
Scarce Resource** Contribution
margin per unit of a particular
input with limited availability.

capacity is limited, that answer would be incorrect if Glover uses up its capacity at a different rate for each product.

Suppose that Glover's capacity is limited to 7,200 machine-hours per month. This limitation is known as a **constraint.** Further, assume that machines may be used to produce either 30 hardballs per machine-hour or 50 softballs per machine-hour.

With a single constrained resource, the important measure of profitability is the **contribution margin per unit of scarce resource** used, *not* contribution margin per unit of product. In this case, softballs are more profitable than hardballs because softballs contribute $200 per machine-hour ($4 per softball × 50 softballs per hour), while hardballs contribute only $120 per machine-hour ($4 per hardball × 30 hardballs per machine-hour). The hours required to produce one ball times the contribution per hour equals the contribution per ball.

For the month, Glover could produce 360,000 softballs (50 per hour × 7,200 hours) or 216,000 hardballs (30 per hour × 7,200 hours). If only softballs are produced, Glover's operating profit would be $440,000 (360,000 softballs times a contribution margin of $4 each minus fixed costs of $1 million). If only hardballs are produced, Glover's net *loss* would be $136,000 (216,000 hardballs times a contribution margin of $4 each minus $1 million). By concentrating on the product that yields the greater contribution per unit of scarce resource, Glover can maximize its profit.

**Mathematical
Representation of
the Problem**

The relationship between the usage of machine-hours to produce hardballs and softballs may be expressed as:

$$\left(\frac{1}{30}\right) H + \left(\frac{1}{50}\right) S \leq 7,200 \text{ machine-hours}$$

(To be precise, there are two more constraints that prevent negative production of either product. These are $H \geq 0$ and $S \geq 0$, but these are ignored in our discussion because negative production is not possible.)

The first term in the production expression reflects the fact that a hardball uses 1/30 hour of machine time. The second term indicates that each softball uses 1/50 hour of machine time. The third term or right-hand side constrains production time to 7,200 hours or less. Although it is possible to use fewer than 7,200 hours, that would indicate idle capacity. Hence, Glover is better off to use as many hours as possible. This point may also be shown mathematically, but we leave that to the operations researchers.

In short, the relationship between the product contribution margins and the constraints for Glover would be written as follows:

Objective function:

Maximize $\$4H + \$4S$

Constraints:

Subject to: $\left(\dfrac{1}{30}\right) H + \left(\dfrac{1}{50}\right)S \leq 7{,}200$ hours

The objective function states that the objective is to select the product mix that maximizes total contribution, given the unit contribution of hardballs is $4 and of softballs is $4. The constraint states that each hardball uses 1/30 of a machine-hour, each softball uses 1/50 of a machine-hour, and in total, no more than 7,200 hours are available.

Graphic Solution

Feasible Production Region
The area in a graph of production opportunities bounded by the limits of production.

Corner Point A corner of the feasible production region in linear programming.

Illustration 13–3 shows that relationship between production of each product and the amount of the scarce resources available. Glover Manufacturing can produce at any point along the line labeled "machine capacity constraint," or at any interior point in the **feasible production region**. The feasible production region is the area in the graph bounded by the constraints on operating activities. In this case, production is bounded by zero on the low side and by 7,200 machine-hours on the high side.

Because Glover can sell all it produces at a positive contribution margin for each product, it would prefer to produce as much as possible, which is at some point on the machine capacity line. Analysis of each **corner point** (that is, each corner of the feasible region) shows that it is optimal for Glover to produce and sell 360,000 softballs and no hardballs at corner point 3.

Why Will the Optimal Solution Always Be at a Corner Point?
If point 3 is better than point 2, then it must also be better than any place on the *straight line* between points 2 and 3.[1] By knowing that there can be no solution better than the solution at the optimal corner enables us to limit our search for the maximum profit combination to the corner points in the feasible region. The following example shows what happens if we move from corner point 3.

Glover's total contribution, and therefore total operating profit, is reduced if it moves toward corner point 2 from corner point 3. For example, the total contribution with production of 360,000 softballs is $1,440,000.

---

[1] Of course, if two corner points have the same total contribution, any point on a straight line between those two corners would have the same total contribution as either corner point.

Moving from corner point 3 towards corner point 2 by producing one hardball requires giving up 5/3 softballs, calculated as follows:

1. Start with the following constraint:

$$\left(\frac{1}{30}\right) H + \left(\frac{1}{50}\right)S \leq 7{,}200 \text{ machine-hours}$$

2. The choice requires no change in total machine-hours; 7,200 machine-hours are still used. There is only a substitution of hardballs for softballs, so set $(1/30)H + (1/50)S = 0$.

3. Now, find the number of softballs given up for each hardball produced (the symbol Δ refers to "change"):

$$\left(\frac{1}{50}\right)\Delta S = -\left(\frac{1}{30}\right)\Delta H$$

$$\Delta S = -\frac{\left(\frac{1}{30}\right)}{\left(\frac{1}{50}\right)} \Delta H = -\frac{.03333}{.02000}\Delta H$$

$$\Delta S = -\left(\frac{5}{3}\right) \Delta H$$

Illustration 13-3   **Single Constraint, Glover Manufacturing**

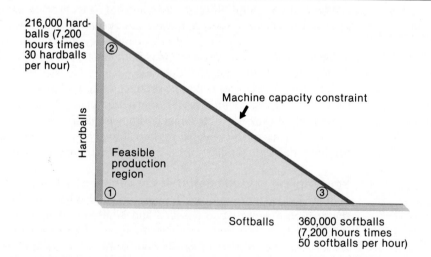

216,000 hardballs (7,200 hours times 30 hardballs per hour)

Hardballs

Machine capacity constraint

Feasible production region

Softballs   360,000 softballs (7,200 hours times 50 softballs per hour)

| Corner Point | Produce and Sell | | Total Contribution Margin | Fixed Costs | Operating Profits (loss) |
	Hardballs	Softballs			
1	-0-	-0-	-0-	$1,000,000	$(1,000,000)
2	216,000	-0-	216,000 × $4 = $864,000	1,000,000	(136,000)
3	-0-	360,000	360,000 × $4 = $1,440,000	1,000,000	440,000

4. If you substitute 1 for ΔH, then $\Delta S = -5/3$. Thus, every hardball produced requires giving up 5/3 softballs

5. The net effect on total contribution is:

Contribution gained (one hardball $\times$ $4)	$4.00
Contribution lost (5/3 softballs $\times$ $4)	6.67
Net contribution lost per hardball produced	$2.67

This loss occurs as we move from corner point 3 toward corner point 2. Moving from corner point 3 toward corner point 1 is obviously inferior to producing at corner point 3 because we give up production of some softballs as we move toward corner point 1.

What Is Really Sold?

In working with production constraints, it is often useful to think in terms of selling the service of the productive resources rather than selling units of product. For example, we can think of Glover as selling machine-hours, with each machine-hour contributing $200 if used to make softballs, $120 if used to make hardballs, and $0 if not used at all.

CONTRIBUTION MARGIN VERSUS GROSS MARGINS

Notice that Glover Manufacturing's costs were divided into fixed and variable portions. By definition, the variable costs are differential with volume changes. In some companies, variable costs are not separated from fixed costs. This can lead to serious product mix errors if fixed costs allocated to each unit of product are included when comparing the profitability of products. This error would result from treating fixed costs as differential costs.

For example, suppose that before any attempt was made to determine the optimal product mix for Glover Manufacturing, the accounting department had prepared the report in Illustration 13–4. As you can see, fixed and variable overhead costs are not separated. By applying overhead at 200 percent of labor, overhead *appears to vary with labor,* whereas we know that a substantial amount of the overhead is fixed. Based on this presenta-

Illustration 13–4   **Full Costs of the Product, Glover Manufacturing**

	Hardballs	Softballs
Sales revenue per unit	$10.00	$9.00
Less full manufacturing costs per unit:		
Materials	4.00	2.50
Labor	1.50	2.00
Overhead (applied at a rate of 200% of labor)[a]	3.00	4.00
Gross margin per unit	$ 1.50	$ .50

Marketing and administrative costs (all fixed): $200,000 per month.

[a] Any under- or overapplied overhead is written off as an expense of the period.

Illustration 13-5   **Comparison of Product Mix Analyses, Glover Manufacturing**

	Gross Margin Method Wrong Decision: Produce All Hardballs	Contribution Margin Method Right Decision: Produce All Softballs
Sales revenue:		
Hardballs (216,000 × $10)	$2,160,000	
Softballs (360,000 × $9)		$3,240,000
Less variable manufacturing costs:		
Hardballs (216,000 × $6)	1,296,000	
Softballs (360,000 × $5)		1,800,000
Total contribution margin	864,000	1,440,000
Less fixed costs:		
Manufacturing	800,000	800,000
Marketing and administrative	200,000	200,000
Operating profit (loss)	$ (136,000)	$ 440,000

tion, hardballs *appear* to be more profitable per unit of scarce resource than softballs, but in fact, the opposite is true.

Accounting information is sometimes sent to personnel in operations and engineering who are unaware of the important but subtle distinction between *gross margin* and *contribution margin* that we have emphasized in this book. For example, suppose that the gross margin per unit from Illustration 13–4 is used instead of the contribution margin per unit from Illustration 13–1. Illustration 13–3 shows that there are two extreme production possibilities: 216,000 hardballs or 360,000 softballs. Using the gross margins from Illustration 13–4, production of 216,000 hardballs at $1.50 (Total gross margin = $324,000) *appears* economically superior to production of 360,000 softballs at $.50 (Total gross margin = $180,000).

Of course, we know that is wrong. As shown in Illustration 13–5, producing 216,000 hardballs and no softballs would result in a net loss of $136,000, while the correct product mix of 360,000 softballs and no hardballs provides operating profit of $440,000.

Thus, a common mistake in product mix decisions stems from the failure to recognize which costs are differential. Fixed costs for different product mixes often do not differ in the short run. For purposes of valuing inventory for external reporting, however, fixed manufacturing overhead is assigned to units produced, thereby making fixed costs appear variable to the unsophisticated user of cost information. As in the other differential cost problems we have seen, it is important to determine which costs are *really differential* for decision making.

This is another example of a common problem in accounting. Costs that were assigned to units for one purpose (inventory valuation, in this case) could be inappropriately used for another purpose (product mix decisions, in this case).

OPPORTUNITY COST OF RESOURCES

In the multiproduct setting, machine capacity, or any other constraint, may have an **opportunity cost**. Computing the opportunity cost is facilitated with the type of analysis presented in this chapter. For example, what is the opportunity cost to Glover Manufacturing of not having one more hour of machine capacity? First, assume that the increase in machine time would change neither fixed manufacturing nor fixed selling costs. With one more hour of machine time, Glover could produce 50 more softballs, as shown below:

Before: $(1/30) H + (1/50) S \leq 7,200$ machine-hours. If only softballs are produced:

$$\left(\frac{1}{50}\right) S = 7,200$$

$$S = \frac{7,200}{\left(\frac{1}{50}\right)}$$

$$= \underline{\underline{360,000 \text{ softballs}}}$$

With one additional machine-hour and producing only softballs:

$$\left(\frac{1}{50}\right) S = 7,201$$

$$S = \frac{7,201}{\left(\frac{1}{50}\right)}$$

$$= \underline{\underline{360,050 \text{ softballs}}}$$

Shadow Price Opportunity cost of an additional unit.

With a unit contribution margin of $4, production of 50 more softballs would add $200 to profits. Thus, the opportunity cost of one hour of machine time is $200. This opportunity cost is also known as a **shadow price**

With this information, Glover's management can decide whether it is worth-while to add machine time. If additional machine time can be leased for any amount less than $200 per hour, for example, doing so would increase operating profits.

MULTIPLE CONSTRAINTS

With one constraint, it is easy to see that Glover could maximize contribution by producing only softballs. But the situation becomes more complex when there are multiple constraints. Suppose that the sale of softballs is temporarily restricted so that only 200,000 can be sold during the next production period. Further, suppose that Glover cannot hold baseballs in inventory so everything produced must be sold in the same period. Now the constraints are:

(1) $\left(\frac{1}{30}\right)H + \left(\frac{1}{50}\right)S \leq 7,200$ machine hours

(2) $S \leq 200,000$

These relationships are shown graphically in Illustration 13-6. Now, to determine the optimal product mix, we find the monthly operating profit at each of the four corner points labeled. The solution for corner point 3 is found by simultaneously solving for the machine and sales constraints. The calculations are as follows:

Illustration 13-6   **Product Choice with Multiple Constraints, Glover Manufacturing**

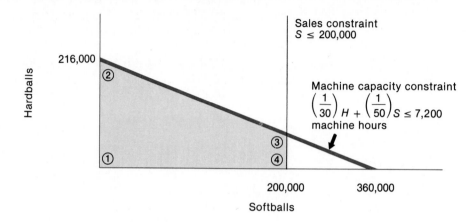

Corner Point	Produce and Sell		Total Contribution Margin	Fixed Costs	Operating Profit (loss)
	Hardballs	**Softballs**			
1	-0-	-0-	-0-	$1,000,000	$(1,000,000)
2	216,000	-0-	216,000 × $4 = $864,000	1,000,000	(136,000)
3	96,000	200,000	(96,000 × $4) + (200,000 × $4) = $1,184,000	1,000,000	184,000
4	-0-	200,000	200,000 × $4 = $800,000	1,000,000	(200,000)

$$\left(\frac{1}{30}\right)H + \left(\frac{1}{50}\right)S = 7{,}200 \text{ machine-hours}$$
$$S = \underline{200{,}000}$$

$$\text{so } \left(\frac{1}{30}\right)H + \left(\frac{1}{50}\right)(200{,}000) = 7{,}200$$

$$\left(\frac{1}{30}\right)H + 4{,}000 = 7{,}200$$

$$\left(\frac{1}{30}\right)H = 3{,}200$$

$$H = \underline{96{,}000}$$

This optimal solution is to produce as many softballs as can be sold, 200,000, and use the remaining capacity to produce 96,000 hardballs.

As more constraints and products are added, solving for product mixes becomes more complex. Although it is possible to solve these problems by hand, they are typically solved by computer (see the following section).

LINEAR PROGRAMMING

The product choice problem is often much more complex than the two-product, two-constraint problems just presented for Glover Manufacturing. Companies often have many constraints and many choices. The method we used to find the optimal product mix for Glover Manufacturing is called the

Illustration 13–7   **Hixon Company Facts**

	Armchairs per Unit	Bookshelves per Unit	Cabinets per Unit
Selling price	$14.00	$18.00	$24.00
Direct labor cost	6.00	7.20	10.80
Direct material cost	.80	1.40	2.00
Variable overhead	1.52	2.00	2.96
Contribution margins	5.68	7.40	8.24
Fixed manufacturing overhead	5.00	5.00	5.00
Gross margins	$ .68	$ 2.40	$ 3.24
Material requirements in board-feet per unit of output	4	7	10
Labor requirements in hours per unit of output:			
Cutting department	.30	.30	.40
Assembly and finishing department	.20	.30	.50

Graphic Method Graphic solution of a linear programming problem by selecting the best corner solution visually.

Simplex Method Solution of a linear programming problem using a mathematical technique.

graphic method. The graphic method is a useful way to see how linear programming works, but it is impractical for complex problems with many choices and constraints.

A mathematical technique, known as the **simplex method,** has been developed for solving complex product mix problems. This technique solves for corner solutions much as we did earlier in this chapter using graphs. Many computer software packages include the simplex method, or a variation of it, for solving product mix problems.

For the rest of this chapter, we assume product mix decisions are solved on the computer. Our focus will be on setting up the problems so they can be entered into the computer and on interpreting the output, not on the mathematical procedures used to derive solutions.[2]

COMPREHENSIVE LINEAR PROGRAMMING EXAMPLE

This section presents an example that we solved using the computer. We discuss how to set up the problem to enter it into the computer and how to interpret the results.

Assume that Hixon Company manufactures and sells three wood products—armchairs, labeled A; bookshelves, labeled B; and cabinets, labeled C. Each product must be processed through two departments—Cutting, and Assembly and Finishing—before it is sold.

Illustration 13–7 presents data about product selling prices, costs, and the rate at which each product uses scarce resources. In addition to the information provided in Illustration 13–7, we learn that only 2,000 board-feet of direct material can be obtained per week. The Cutting Department has 180 hours of labor available each week, and the Assembly and finishing Department has 240 hours of labor available each week. No overtime is allowed.

---

[2] More details on the mathematics of linear programming are available from books on operations research and quantitative methods. For example, see H. Bierman, C. Bonini, and W. Hausman, *Quantitative Analysis for Business Decisions,* 7th ed. (Homewood, Ill.: Richard D. Irwin, 1986).

Hixon Company's contract commitments require it to make at least 100 armchairs per week. Also, due to keen competition, no more than 100 bookshelves can be sold each week.

Fixed manufacturing overhead costs are estimated to be $1,500 per week. They are arbitrarily allocated to each unit at the rate of $5 per unit. Fixed manufacturing costs are unaffected by the product mix. Nonmanufacturing costs of $1,000 per week are fixed and unaffected by the product mix decision.

Problem Formulation

Hixon Company's product mix decision problem can be solved using linear programming. The constrained optimization problem is formulated as follows:

ⓐ Maximize total contribution margin:

$$\$5.68A + \$7.40B + \$8.24C$$

ⓑSubject to the following constraints:

$$
\begin{array}{rrrlll}
4A + & 7B + & 10C \leq & 2,000 & \text{board-feet} & \text{Direct material} \\
.30A + & .30B + & .40C \leq & 180 & \text{labor-hours} & \text{Cutting} \\
.20A + & .30B + & .50C \leq & 240 & \text{labor-hours} & \text{Assembly and finishing} \\
A & & \geq & 100 & \text{units sold} & \text{Product A's sales} \\
& B & \leq & 100 & \text{units sold} & \text{Product B's sales}
\end{array}
$$

Using a linear programming computer package, we can obtain a solution for the above model. Illustration 13–8 shows how this problem was entered into the computer using a particular software package. The circled letters are there to help you trace the steps in the computer input back to the formulation above.

The initial table in Illustration 13–8 is from the printout of the linear programming problem formulation. Illustration 13–9 shows the output. Most software packages present the output like that in Illustration 13–9.

Solution

The *Summary of Problem* in Illustration 13–9 lists the linear programming (LP) solution to the optimization problem. The total contribution margin is maximized if Hixon Company produces 500 armchairs and no bookshelves or cabinets. The maximum total contribution obtainable under the present resource constraints is approximately (see ©) $2,840. Hence the operating profit realized from this production mix is $340 ($2,840 − $1,500 fixed manufacturing costs − $1,000 fixed nonmanufacturing costs).

Opportunity Costs

Of the five constraints, only the direct material constraint has an opportunity cost attached to it. This opportunity cost figure, which is reflected on the output as a shadow price, shows us how total contribution margin changes as a result of a per unit change in the constraint. Thus, if we increase the direct material constraint from 2,000 board-feet to 2,001 board-feet, Hixon's

Illustration 13-8   **Linear Programming Input,[a] Hixon Company**

```
              :
(a & b)       MAX $5.68A + $7.40B + $8.24C
              ?
              SUBJECT TO
              ?
              (DIRECT MATERIAL) 4A + 7B + 10C < 2000
              ?
              (CUTTING) .3A + .3B + .4C < 180
              ?
              (ASSEMBLY AND FINISHING) .2A + .3B + .5C < 240
              ?
              (PROD A SALES) A > 100
              ?
              (PROD B SALES) B < 100
              ?
              END
```

A = Armchairs
B = Bookshelves
C = Cabinets

[a] Based on the linear programming package called LINDO.

Note: Circled letters cross-reference to the problem formulation in the text.

Illustration 13-9   **Linear Programming Output, Hixon Company**

Summary of Problem:

OBJECTIVE FUNCTION VALUE $2,840 ©

VARIABLE	VALUE	REDUCED VALUE
Armchairs	500.00	0.0
Bookshelves	0.0	2.54
Cabinets	0.0	5.96

CONSTRAINTS	TYPE	VALUE	SHADOW PRICE
Direct material	Slack	0.0	ⓓ $1.42
Cutting	Slack	30.00	0.0
Assembly and finishing	Slack	140.00	0.0
Armchair sales	Surplus	400.00	0.0
Bookshelf sales	Slack	100.00	0.0

Objective Function Coefficient Ranges

VARIABLE	CURRENT COEF	ALLOWABLE INCREASE	ALLOWABLE DECREASE
Armchairs	5.68	Infinity	1.45
Bookshelves	7.40	2.54	Infinity
Cabinets	8.24	5.96	Infinity

Right-Hand-Side Ranges

CONSTRAINTS	CURRENT RHS	ALLOWABLE INCREASE	ALLOWABLE DECREASE
Direct material	2000.00	400.00	1600.00
Cutting	180.00	Infinity	30.00
Assembly and finishing	240.00	Infinity	140.00
Armchair sales	100.00	400.00	Infinity
Bookshelf sales	100.00	Infinity	100.00

contribution margin will increase by approximately $1.42 (see ⓓ in Illustration 13–9).

Effects of Forcing Nonsolution Products into the Solution

The optimal solution *excludes* bookshelves and cabinets. What happens if we *force* one bookshelf or cabinet into the solution? That is, we require there to be one unit produced that would not be produced with the optimal solution. You would predict that the value of the optimal solution (the $2,840 in Illustration 13–9) would go down—but, by how much?

The column in Illustration 13–9 that is titled *Reduced Value* answers the following question: How much will the value of the solution (that is, Hixon's contribution margin) go down if Hixon produces one unit of a product that is not produced in the optimal solution? Bookshelves and cabinets have values of $2.54 and $5.96, respectively, as shown in Illustration 13–9. This means, if we force Hixon to produce one bookshelf, for example, total contribution margin to the firm will be reduced by $2.54. This is because some production of the more profitable armchairs will have to be given up to produce a bookshelf. Similarly, the production of an additional cabinet would lower the contribution margin by $5.96.

Nonbinding Constraints

Four of the constraints each have a nonzero value. This means that these constraints are not binding. The amounts shown under the heading *Value* in Illustration 13–9 are the amounts of the scarce resources, or constraints, still available. For example, 30 labor-hours are still available in the Cutting Department; only 150 hours of the available 180 labor-hours were used. This unused scarce resource is sometimes known as *slack*. In the Assembly and finishing Department, 140 labor-hours are still available. For bookshelf *sales,* an additional 100 units could be produced and sold before the market constraint becomes binding. (Recall that no more than 100 bookshelves could be sold per week. The optimal solution is to sell no bookshelves.) Finally, for armchairs, the solution value shows that optimal production of armchairs exceeds the specified minimum by 400 units; that is, there is a "surplus" over the specified minimum.

Whereas binding constraints have an opportunity cost (for example, $1.42 per unit for direct materials), no shadow price, or opportunity cost, is shown in the solution for the constraints that are not binding. For example, there is no shadow price for labor-hours in the Cutting Department because there is no value for having one additional hour, nor a loss for having one less hour.

Sensitivity Analysis

The parameters specified in this linear programming (LP) model are subject to some degree of estimation error. Decision makers need to know how much error can be tolerated before making a difference in the decision.

Under the heading, *Objective Function Coefficient Ranges* in Illustration 13–9, we are given the ranges within which the contribution margins of each product can change without changing the optimal mix of products, all other things equal. For example, the contribution margin of an armchair is

$5.68. This contribution margin could increase by an infinite amount without changing the fact that the optimal product mix includes 500 armchairs.

Bookshelves presently have a value of zero in the optimal solution. If their contribution margin was increased (by raising the selling price, for example) by more than $2.54 from its present level of $7.40, then bookshelves would become part of the optimal solution with a value greater than zero. In general, the optimal solution for Hixon Company is to produce 500 armchairs and none of the other two products within the objective function ranges shown, all other things equal.

The bottom panel in Illustration 13–9 has the heading *Right-Hand-Side Ranges*. These ranges give the allowable increase or decrease for values of the constraints before a binding constraint becomes nonbinding, or a nonbinding constraint becomes binding, all other things equal.

For example, the direct material constraint, which is presently a binding constraint, could increase by 400 or decrease by 1,600 board-feet before it would become nonbinding, all other things held constant. Suppose the number of board-feet dropped by more than 1,600 to less than 400 available (that is, current level of 2,000 minus 1,600 leaves 400 board-feet). Then the company could not satisfy its constraint to make at least 100 armchairs because each armchair requires 4 board feet.

Labor hours in the Cutting Department is not binding in the solution in Illustration 13–9. In fact, there are 30 available hours for this constraint. The *Right-Hand-Side Ranges* tells us that this constraint could decrease as much as 30 hours before it becomes binding.

Misspecifying the Objective Function

Suppose Hixon Company incorrectly specified its objective function—using gross margins in the objective function instead of contribution margins. Based on the gross margins given in Illustration 13–7, this would result in the following formulation of the problem:

Maximize total gross margin:

$$\$.68A + \$2.40B + \$3.24C$$

Subject to the following constraints:

Material	$4A + 7B + 10C \leq 2,000$	board-feet
Cutting	$.30A + .30B + .40C \leq$ 180	hours
Finishing and assembly	$.20A + .30B + .50C \leq$ 240	hours
Armchairs	$A \geq$ 100	units
Bookshelves	$B \leq$ 100	units

The constraints are the same as those previously formulated.

The computer solution to this LP problem is given in Illustration 13–10. It is interesting to note that as a result of misspecifying the values of the objective function, Hixon Company will make a suboptimal production decision of manufacturing 100 armchairs, 100 bookshelves, and 90 cabinets. Now, we compare this solution with the prior optimal solution in which contribution margins were used in the objective function.

	Gross Margin Method: Wrong Decision		Contribution Margin Method: Right Decision	
	Number of Units	Unit Contribution Margin	Number of Units	Unit Contribution Margin
Total contribution:				
Armchairs	100 ×	$5.68 = $ 568.00	500 ×	$5.68 = $2,840
Bookshelves	100 ×	7.40 = 740.00		–0–
Cabinets	90 ×	8.24 = 741.60		–0–
Total		$2,049.60		$2,840
Less fixed costs:				
Manufacturing		1,500.00		1,500
Nonmanufacturing		1,000.00		1,000
Operating profit (loss)		$ (450.40)		$ 340

The optimal value of the solution reported in the output of Illustration 13–10, $599.60, is an incorrect number because the analysis incorrectly treats fixed manufacturing costs as variable costs. If you compare this solution in Illustration 13–10 with the correct solution in Illustration 13–9, you will find numerous errors in Illustration 13–10. This demonstrates the importance of using contribution margins, not gross margins, in linear programming problems.

Illustration 13–10   **Linear Programming Output Incorrectly Using Gross Margins instead of Contribution Margins, Hixon Company**

Linear Programming Input

MAX $0.68 A + $2.4 B + $3.24 C
SUBJECT TO

Direct material	$4 A + 7 B + 10 C \leq 2000$
Cutting	$0.3 A + 0.3 B + 0.4 C \leq 180$
Assembly and Finishing	$0.2 A + 0.3 B + 0.5 C \leq 240$
Armchair sales	$A \geq 100$
Bookshelf sales	$B \leq 100$

Summary of Problem

OBJECTIVE FUNCTION VALUE $599.60[a]

VARIABLE	VALUE	REDUCED VALUE
Armchairs	100.00	0.0
Bookshelves	100.00	0.0
Cabinets	90.00	0.0

CONSTRAINT	TYPE	VALUE	SHADOW PRICE
Direct material	Slack	0.0	0.32
Cutting	Slack	84.00	0.0
Assembly and finishing	Slack	145.00	0.0
Armchair sales	Surplus	– 0.0	– 0.62
Bookshelf sales	Slack	0.0	0.13

[a] This is not the correct contribution because of the data errors noted in the text.

Removing a Binding Constraint

Suppose Hixon Company has access to an unlimited supply of direct material. The optimal production mix for Hixon can be found using the LP formulation in Illustration 13–11. Without a materials constraint, the solution to the production decision problem is to produce 100 armchairs, 100 bookshelves, and 300 cabinets. Armchairs, which use the least amount of material, are not as attractive as they were before because the supply of material is no longer a binding constraint.

This new optimum production point has a total contribution margin of $3,780. This is $940 ($3,780 − 2,840) greater than the optimum obtained in Illustration 13–9 where availability of direct material was a binding constraint. The constraints that are now binding are the availability of labor in the Cutting Department, the size of the market for bookshelves, and the minimum required sales for armchairs.

Note that the opportunity costs associated with the binding constraints on this new optimum are different from those presented in Illustration 13–9. The Cutting Department, which had an excess of 30 labor-hours before, now has an opportunity cost of $20.60 per unit of the scarce resource, labor-hours.

Introducing an Additional Constraint

Now, suppose that Hixon's contract commitments also require it to produce a minimum of 100 cabinets each week. Assume also that Hixon is once again facing a limited availability of direct material. The effect of an additional constraint on Hixon's optimal production decision can be seen in Illustration 13–12.

Illustration 13–11

Removal of a Binding Constraint, Problem Formulation, Hixon Company

Linear Programming Input

MAX $5.68A + $7.40B + $8.24C
SUBJECT TO

Cutting	.30A +	.30B +	.40C	≤	180
Assembly and finishing	.20A +	.30B +	.50C	≤	240
Armchair sales	A			≥	100
Bookshelf sales		B		≤	100

Summary of Problem

OBJECTIVE FUNCTION VALUE $3,780

VARIABLE	VALUE	REDUCED VALUE
Armchairs	100.00	0.0
Bookshelves	100.00	0.0
Cabinets	300.00	0.0

CONSTRAINT	TYPE	VALUE	SHADOW PRICE
Cutting	Slack	0.0	$20.60
Assembly and finishing	Slack	40.00	0.0
Armchair sales	Surplus	0.0	1.22
Bookshelf sales	Slack	0.0	0.50

Illustration 13–12   **Introducing an Additional Constraint, Problem Formulation, Hixon Company**

Linear Programming Input

MAX $5.68A + $7.40B + $8.24C
SUBJECT TO

Direct material	$4 A + 7 B + 10 C \leq$	2000
Cutting	$0.3 A + 0.3 B + 0.4 C \leq$	180
Assembly and Finishing	$0.2 A + 0.3 B + 0.5 C \leq$	240
Armchair sales	$A \geq$	100
Bookshelf sales	$B \leq$	100
Cabinet sales	$C \geq$	100

Summary of Problem

OBJECTIVE FUNCTION VALUE $2,244

VARIABLE	VALUE	REDUCED VALUE
Armchairs	250.00	0.0
Bookshelves	0.0	$2.54
Cabinets	100.00	0.0

CONSTRAINTS	TYPE	VALUE	SHADOW PRICE
Direct material	Slack	0.0	$1.42
Cutting	Slack	65.00	0.0
Assembly and finishing	Slack	140.00	0.0
Armchair sales	Surplus	150.00	0.0
Bookshelf sales	Slack	0.0	5.96

The *Summary of Problem* shows that Hixon's optimal product decision is to produce 250 armchairs and 100 cabinets. The total contribution margin now drops from $2,840 to $2,244.

One of the benefits of linear programming is to examine the effects of introducing additional constraints. Is the optimal solution affected? Does the solution value change when additional constraints are added? Managers frequently do not know the answers to these questions without using linear programming. For example, managers frequently ask "what if" questions like: What if at least 40 percent of the material in our hot dogs is beef (or chicken or turkey)? What if class enrollments are limited to 50 students per class? Linear programming can often be used to help answer questions like these, making it a useful short-run planning tool.

SUMMARY

This chapter presents the use of differential costing and linear programming models in making product choice decisions. The problem arises when there are limited amounts of resources that are being fully used and must be assigned to multiple products. The problem is to choose the optimal product mix within the constraints of limited resources.

The objective of product choice decisions is to maximize the contribution margin per unit of scarce resource used. For example, if the scarce resource is the limited number of hours a machine can operate per month and the machine can make either of two products, the objective is to maximize the contribution per hour (or other unit of time) that each of the two products makes, and then produce the product with the higher contribution margin per hour of machine time used.

Short-run product choice decisions assume fixed costs do not change regardless of product mix. It is important that product margins being optimized assume only variable costs change. Hence, product choice decisions use contribution margins, not gross margins.

Computerized linear programming models are widely used to derive the optimal product mix. Data are input to these models using objective functions that specify the contribution margin of each product and constraints that indicate the amount of scarce resource each product uses. Provided the right data have been entered, the linear programming model then computes the contribution margin per unit of scarce resource for all products and all constraints (that is, scarce resources). The output indicates the mix of products and the quantity of each product to produce and sell that maximizes total contribution.

TERMS AND CONCEPTS

Constraints

Contribution Margin per Unit of Scarce Resource

Corner Point

Feasible Production Region

Graphic Method

Objective Function

Opportunity Cost

Product-Choice Decisions

Shadow Price

Simplex Method

SUPPLEMENTARY READINGS

Adelberg, Arthur H. "Model for Determining Productive Capacity." *Cost and Management,* July–August 1985, pp. 41–77 (published in Canada).

Briggs, Frank R., and James E. Hosking. "Hospitals Eye Excess Capacity and Plan to Improve Productivity." *Modern Healthcare,* February 1, 1984, pp. 114, 116, 119.

Chen, Chou-Hong J., and Michael Engquist. "Primal Simplex Approach to Pure Processing Networks." *Management Science,* December 1986, pp. 1582–98.

Clarke, Peter J. "Optimal Solution? Try the Linear Programming Way." *Accountancy,* December 1984, pp. 119–20, 22 (published in Great Britain).

Harper, Robert M. "Linear Programming in Managerial Accounting: Misinterpretation of Shadow Prices." *Journal of Accounting Education,* Fall 1986, pp. 123–30.

Heard, W. J. "Linear Programming without Tears, Part 4." *Management Accounting,* May 1984, pp. 58–60 (published in Great Britain).

————. "Linear Programming without Tears, Part 5." *Management Accounting,* February 1985, pp. 72–74 (published in Great Britain).

Manes, Rene P.; K. C. W. Chen; and R. Greenberg. "Economies of Scope and Cost-Volume-Profit Analysis for the Multiproduct Firm." *Journal of Accounting Literature,* Spring 1985, pp. 77–111.

Saraf, S. K., and A. L. Soyster. "Capacity Planning to Maximize the Value of the Regulated Firm." *Engineering Economist,* Summer 1984, pp. 251–72.

Shamir, Ron. "Efficiency of the Simplex Method: A Survey." *Management Science,* March 1987, pp. 301–34.

SELF-STUDY PROBLEM NO. 1

Pacperson, Inc., manufactures two series of computer hardware: Twopack and Threepack. Data concerning selling prices and costs for each unit are as follows:

	Twopack	Threepack
Selling price	$1,000	$1,700
Materials	350	370
Direct labor	210	230
Overhead (80% fixed)	150	200
Gross margin	290	900
Marketing costs (variable)	80	240
Administrative costs (fixed)	60	80
Profit	$ 150	$ 580

Management decided that at least 500 units of Twopack must be manufactured and sold each month. Likewise, at least 150 Threepack models must be manufactured and sold each month.

The company's production facilities are limited by machine capacity in the assembly control section. Each Twopack model requires one fourth of an hour in the assembly control section. Each Threepack model, however, requires three fourths of an hour in the assembly area. There is a total of 250 available hours per month in the assembly control section. There are no other relevant constraints on production.

Required:

a. What is the appropriate objective function for these two products if management's objective is to maximize profits?

b. What equations would represent the constraints on the profitability from these two products?

c. Given the information in the problem, which product would management prefer to produce to maximize profits?

d. Graph the profit-maximization problem and identify the feasible production region and corner points.

e. What is the optimal production schedule and the optimal contribution margin at that schedule?

f. What is the maximum price management would be willing to pay for one more hour of assembly control section capacity?

SOLUTION TO SELF-STUDY PROBLEM NO. 1

a. Determine the contributions for each product:

	Twopack	Threepack
Selling price	$1,000	$1,700
Variable costs:		
Materials	350	370
Direct labor	210	230
Variable overhead (20%)	30	40
Variable marketing	80	240
Total variable costs	670	880
Contribution margin	$ 330	$ 820

Maximize profit = $330 (Twopack) + $820 (Threepack)

b. Constraints:

$$\text{Twopack} \geq 500$$
$$\text{Threepack} \geq 150$$
$$\tfrac{1}{4}\,(\text{Twopack}) + \tfrac{3}{4}\,(\text{Threepack}) \leq 250$$

c. Contribution per assembly control hour:

$$\text{Twopack } \$330/.25 = \$1,320$$
$$\text{Threepack } \$820/.75 = \$1,093$$

The Twopack is preferred because it gives a greater contribution per assembly control hour.

d.

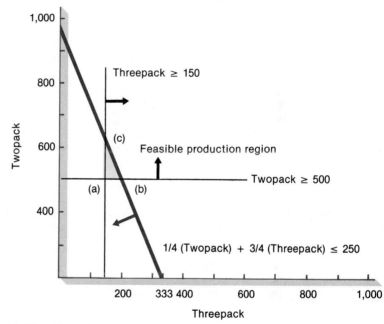

Note: (a), (b), and (c) are the *corner points.*

e.

	Produce and Sell		
Points	Twopacks	Threepacks	Total Contribution Margin
a	500	150	$330(500) + $820(150) = $288,000
b	500	167[a]	$330(500) + $820(167) = 301,940
c	550[b]	150	$330(550) + $820(150) = $304,500

[a] $\tfrac{1}{4}(500) + \tfrac{3}{4}$ Threepack $= 250$, from assembly control constraint

$$\text{Threepack} = \frac{250 - \tfrac{1}{4}(500)}{\tfrac{3}{4}}$$
$$= \underline{\underline{167}}$$

[b] $\tfrac{1}{4}$ Twopack $+ \tfrac{3}{4}(150) = 250$, from assembly control constraint

$$\text{Twopack} = \frac{250 - \tfrac{3}{4}(150)}{\tfrac{1}{4}}$$
$$= \underline{\underline{550}}$$

f. $1,320 plus the cost of assembly control time included in the objective function.

**SELF-STUDY
PROBLEM NO. 2:
YAKIMA, INC.**[3]

Yakima, Inc., a rapidly expanding company, manufactures three lines of skis—Economy, Standard, and Deluxe. Currently faced with labor and machine capacity constraints, the company wants to select the optimal product mix in order to maximize operating profits. The following linear programming model of the problem was formulated and run on the computer:

Maximize:

$$\text{Total contribution margin} = 30X_1 + 23X_2 + 29X_3$$

Subject to:

$$\text{Labor-hours} = 12X_1 + 10X_2 + 6X_3 \leq 40,000$$
$$\text{Machine-hours} = 8X_1 + 4X_2 + 10X_3 \leq 10,000$$

where

X_1 = Deluxe model
X_2 = Economy model
X_3 = Standard model

Required:

Using the computer output in Exhibit A, answer the questions below. Assume that all things are held constant in each case.

Exhibit A (SSP 13–2)   **Solution, Yakima, Inc.**

Summary of Problem

OBJECTIVE FUNCTION VALUE $57,500

VARIABLE	VALUE	REDUCED VALUE
Deluxe	0.0	$16.0
Economy	2,500.00	0.0
Standard	0.0	28.50

CONSTRAINTS	TYPE	VALUE	SHADOW PRICE
Labor-hours	Slack	15,000	$0.0
Machine-hours	Slack	0.0	5.75

Objective Function Coefficient Ranges

VARIABLE	CURRENT COEF	ALLOWABLE INCREASE	ALLOWABLE DECREASE
Deluxe	$30	$16.00	Infinity
Economy	23	Infinity	$8.00
Standard	29	28.50	Infinity

Right-Hand-Side Ranges

	CURRENT RHS	ALLOWABLE INCREASE	ALLOWABLE DECREASE
Labor-hours	40,000	Infinity	15,000
Machine-hours	10,000	6,000	10,000

---

[3] Prepared by Jean M. Lim under the supervision of Michael W. Maher.

a. What is the optimal production level of the Economy model? The Standard model? The Deluxe model?

b. What would happen to the optimal value if the available capacity of the labor constraint was decreased to 30,000 hours? If the machine-hours constraint was increased to 15,000 hours?

c. How much of the labor-hours resource is unused? How much of the machine-hours resource is unused?

d. The Standard model shows a *reduced value* of $28.50. Explain the meaning of this value.

e. Show how the optimal value of $57,500 was computed. Show how the *shadow price* of $5.75 for the machine-hours constraint was computed.

f. Suppose an error in the data exists and $23 is not the correct contribution margin of the Economy model. What is the optimal production level of the Economy model if the correct unit contribution margin is $18? If it is $12? (Indicate if "unknown," given the available information.)

SOLUTION TO SELF-STUDY PROBLEM NO. 2

a. Optimal production level for:
(1) Economy model = 2,500 units
(2) Standard model = zero units.
(3) Deluxe model = zero units.

b. *Labor constraint:* Total contribution remains the same since only 25,000 labor-hours are currently used.
Machine constraint: Total contribution increases by:

$$\$28,750 = \$5.75 \ (15,000 - 10,000)$$

c. Fifteen thousand labor-hours unused. Zero machine-hours unused.

d. If a decision to produce one unit of the Standard model is made, total contribution margin will decrease by $28.50. Producing a unit of the Standard model means that 2½ units of the Economy model is foregone (see the relation between the Economy and Standard models for the machine constraint, which is binding).

e. $57,500 = $23 × 2,500 units of the Economy model. Each additional machine-hour allows production of .25 (¼) units of the Economy model. Since the Economy model has a unit contribution margin of $23, the value of one more unit of the scarce machine-hour resource is $5.75.

f. If the contribution margin drops by $5 to $18, then 2,500 units of the Economy model will be produced, since the objective function coefficient is still within the range of allowable increase or decrease according to the objective function coefficient ranges. If the contribution margin drops by $11 to $12, the optimal production level of the Economy model will be unknown, since the value of the objective function coefficient lies outside the allowable range of decrease.

SELF-STUDY PROBLEM NO. 3[4]

This is a cost-minimization problem.

Feeding livestock in the most economical manner possible is an important and continuous problem. In the livestock business, the animals have to receive certain nutrients which are available in varying quantities in the commodities used.

Suppose the minimum nutrient requirement per day for each animal is two pounds

---

[4] Adapted from a problem by P. Marshall.

of protein, eight pounds of carbohydrates, and six pounds of roughage. Further suppose that there are four commodities available to feed: oats, corn, alfalfa, and linseed oil meal. The current prices and nutrient content for each commodity are:

	Price per Pound	Amount of Protein per Pound	Amount of Roughage per Pound	Amount of Carbohydrate per Pound
Oats	$.015	–0–	.2	.1
Corn	.02	.2	.1	.3
Alfalfa	.01	.1	.4	.2
Linseed oil meal	.05	.5	.1	–0–

Required:

Your objective is to feed the animals at the lowest cost. However, your choice is subject to the constraints of providing at least the minimum amount of nutrients.

SOLUTION TO SELF-STUDY PROBLEM NO. 3

The problem is formulated as follows:

	Choices				
	Oats	Linseed Oil Meal	Corn	Alfalfa	Amount of Resources
Protein	–0–	.5	.2	.1	≥ 2.0 pounds
Roughage	.2	.1	.1	.4	≥ 6.0 pounds
Carbohydrate	.1	–0–	.3	.2	≥ 8.0 pounds
	$.015	$.05	$.02	$.01	Minimize cost of commodities

In this problem it has been possible to specify: the choices (the amount of each commodity to feed), the constraints (the minimum pounds of each nutrient required), and the objective (minimize the cost of feeding). It has also been possible to state the rates as constant over the entire range of choices; for example, every pound of oats has the same amount of protein and costs the same as every other pound of oats.

The computer solution to this minimization problem is given in Exhibit A. As can be seen from the Summary of Problem, the optimal solution will be to feed the livestock only alfalfa. In this case, the optimal amount is 40 pounds of alfalfa a day. All the other possible alternatives—oats, linseed oil meal, or corn—have opportunity costs attached to their use. Linseed oil meal, by far the most expensive choice, will cost the farmer 5 cents for every additional pound used.

In the case of food requirement constraints, we find that only the carbohydrate constraint is binding. Forty pounds of alfalfa will provide the minimum eight pounds of carbohydrates needed per day. The 5-cent opportunity cost attached to the carbohydrate constraint means that every additional pound of carbohydrate needed will cost the farmer an additional 5 cents. The daily feed contains 2 pounds more protein and 10 pounds more roughage than the minimum required.

Exhibit A (SSP 13-3)

Linear Programming Input

Min: $.015 Oats + $.05 Linseed + $.02 Corn + $.01 Alfalfa
Subject To:

Protein	.00 Oats + .50 Linseed + .20 Corn + .10 Alfalfa $\geq$ 2.00
Roughage	.20 Oats + .10 Linseed + .10 Corn + .40 Alfalfa $\geq$ 6.00
Carbohydrate	.10 Oats + .00 Linseed + .30 Corn + .20 Alfalfa $\geq$ 8.00

Summary of Problem

OBJECTIVE FUNCTION VALUE $.40

VARIABLE	VALUE	REDUCED VALUE
Oats	0.0	$0.010
Linseed	0.0	0.050
Corn	0.0	0.005
Alfalfa	40.00	0.0

CONSTRAINTS	TYPE	VALUE	SHADOW PRICE
Protein	Surplus	2.00	$0.0
Roughage	Surplus	10.00	0.0
Carbohydrate	Surplus	0.0	0.05

Objective Function Coefficient Ranges

VARIABLE	CURRENT COEF	ALLOWABLE INCREASE	ALLOWABLE DECREASE
Oats	$0.015	Infinity	$0.010
Linseed	0.050	Infinity	0.050
Corn	0.020	Infinity	0.005
Alfalfa	0.010	$0.003	0.010

Right-Hand-Side Ranges

CONSTRAINT	CURRENT RHS	ALLOWABLE INCREASE	ALLOWABLE DECREASE
Protein	2	2	Infinity
Roughage	6	10	Infinity
Carbohydrate	8	Infinity	4

QUESTIONS

13-1. If we want to maximize profit, why do we use unit contribution margins in our analysis instead of unit gross margins?

13-2. Management notes that the contribution from one product is greater than the contribution from a second product. Hence, they conclude that the company should concentrate on production of the first product. Under what, if any, conditions will this approach result in maximum profits?

13-3. A company has learned that a particular input product required for its production is in limited supply. What approach should management take to maximize profits in the presence of this constraint?

13-4. What is the feasible production region?

13–5. Why are corner points on the feasible production region important for profitability analysis?

13–6. What do we mean by the opportunity cost of a constraint?

13–7. Under what circumstances would fixed costs be relevant when management is making decisions in a multiproduct setting?

13–8. Describe how to compute the maximum price that a company would be willing to pay to obtain additional capacity for a scarce resource.

13–9. At what point does the opportunity cost of a constraint change?

13–10. What is the role of the accountant in the management decision process that uses linear programming models (or other mathematical programming techniques)?

EXERCISES

13–11. The Role of Accounting Data

(L.O.1)

Thunderbird Productions, Inc., manufactures three products labeled A, B, and C. Data concerning the three products are as follows:

	A	B	C
Selling price	$40	$35	$50
Manufacturing costs:			
Materials	7	6	7
Direct labor	7	7	11
Overhead:			
Variable	3	3	6
Fixed	2	2	4
Total manufacturing	19	18	28
Gross profit	$21	$17	$22

Variable marketing costs equal 15 percent of the sales price of each product. Variable administrative costs are estimated at $1 per unit of product. Fixed administrative costs are allocated to each unit produced as follows: product A, $3; product B, $4; and product C, $5.

Required:

What is the equation representing the objective function for the product-mix decision?

13–12. The Role of Accounting Data

(L.O.1)

Management of TutTut Jewelry Corporation has been reviewing its profitability and attempting to improve performance through better planning. The company manufactures three products in its jewelry line: necklaces, bracelets, and rings. Selected data on these items are:

	Necklaces	Bracelets	Rings
Selling price	$80	$60	$40
Contribution margin	35	25	20
Machining time required	.5 hour	.25 hour	.30 hour

The machining time is limited to 120 hours per month. Demand for each product far exceeds the company's ability to meet the demand. There are no other relevant production constraints.

At the present time, management produces equal quantities of each product. The production vice president has urged the company to concentrate on necklace production because that has the greatest margin. No bracelets or rings would be produced if this recommendation were followed.

Required:

a. If fixed costs are $5,000 per month, what profit will be obtained by following the production vice president's recommendation?

b. What is the maximum profit obtainable and what product or product combination must be sold to obtain that maximum?

13–13. The Role of Accounting Data
(L.O.1)

Beldive Ltd. has formulated the following profit function:

$$\text{Profit} = \$12R + \$19S - \$20,000$$

where R and S are products and the $20,000 is the fixed costs for the company.

Production is limited by capacity in the quality control section. The constraint for that section is formulated as:

$$2R + 3S \leq 2,500$$

At present, each quality control unit as represented by the 2,500-unit constraint has a cost of $4. A subcontractor has offered to perform additional quality control services at a cost of $7 per quality control unit.

Required:

Should the company utilize the services of the subcontractor? Show supporting calculations.

13–14. Linear Programming
(L.O.2)

Milligan Company manufactures two models—small and large. Each model is processed as follows:

	Machining	Polishing
Small (S)	2 hours	1 hour
Large (L)	4 hours	3 hours

The time available for processing the two models is 100 hours per week in machining and 90 hours per week in polishing. The contribution margin is $5 for the small model and $7 for the large model.

Formulate the equations necessary to solve this product mix problem.

(CPA adapted)

13–15. Linear Programming
(L.O.2)

The Random Company manufactures two products, Zeta and Beta. Each product must pass through two processing operations. All materials are introduced at the start of process no. 1. There are no work in process inventories. Random may produce either one product exclusively or various combinations of both products subject to the following constraints:

	Process Number 1	Process Number 2	Contribution Margin per Unit
Hours required to produce one unit of:			
Zeta	1 hour	1 hour	$4.00
Beta	2 hours	3 hour	5.25
Total capacity in hours per day	1,000 hours	1,275 hours	

A shortage of technical labor has limited Beta production to 400 units per day. There are *no* constraints on the production of Zeta other than the hour constraints in the above schedule. Assume that all relationships between capacity and production are linear.

a. Given the objective to maximize total contribution margin, what is the production constraint for process no. 1?
   (1) Zeta + Beta ≤ 1,000.
   (2) Zeta + 2Beta ≤ 1,000.
   (3) Zeta + Beta ≥ 1,000.
   (4) Zeta + 2Beta ≥ 1,000.

b. Given the objective to maximize total contribution margin, what is the labor constraint for production of Beta?
   (1) Beta ≤ 400.
   (2) Beta ≥ 400.
   (3) Beta ≤ 425.
   (4) Beta ≥ 425.

c. What is the objective function of the data presented?
   (1) Zeta + 2Beta = $9.25.
   (2) $4.00 Zeta + 3($5.25) Beta = Total contribution margin.
   (3) $4.00 Zeta + $5.25 Beta = Total contribution margin.
   (4) 2($4.00) Zeta + 3($5.25) Beta = Total contribution margin.

(CPA adapted)

13–16. Linear Programming
(L.O.2)

Jabba, Inc., manufactures two products, X and Y. Each product must be processed in each of two departments: assembling and finishing. The hours needed to produce one unit of product per department and the maximum possible hours per department follow:

Department	Production Hours per Unit		Maximum Capacity in Hours
	X	Y	
Assembling	2	2	500
Finishing	2	3	600
Other restrictions:			
X ≥ 50			
Y ≥ 50			

The estimated gross margin on each product is $7 for *X* and $5 for *Y*. These gross margins include estimated fixed costs of $3 per unit. The total fixed costs are estimated at $320.

What is the optimal mix of output and what is the profit that would be obtained if the optimal mix were produced and sold?

13–17. Applying Linear Programming Techniques: The Graphic Method
(L.O.2)

The Hale Company manufactures product A and product B, each of which requires two processes, polishing and grinding. The contribution margin is $3 for product A and $4 for product B. The graph shows the maximum number of units of each product that may be processed in the two departments.

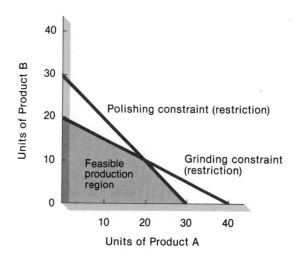

Required: Considering the constraints on processing, which combination of product A and product B maximizes the total contribution?

(CPA adapted)

13–18. Sensitivity of Data   Use the data in exercise 13–17 to answer each of the independent questions that
(L.O.3)   follow.

Required: *a.* How much contribution is given up if a minimum production of 25 units of A is required?

b. How much contribution is given up if a minimum production of 15 units of B is required?

c. What would be the increased contribution margin from relaxing the polishing constraint to allow production of 40 units of A, or 40 units of B, or some combination along a straight line that would connect those two production points?

d. What would be the increased contribution from relaxing the grinding constraint so that the company could produce 50 units of A or 25 units of B or some combination along a straight line that would connect those two production points?

13–19. Sensitivity of Cost Data   Tower Company produces two types of gloves, G1 and G2. The cost and production
(L.O.3)   data concerning these two products are as follows:

	G1	G2
Selling price	$12.00	$14.00
Manufacturing costs:		
Materials	4.00	1.50
Labor	3.00	6.00
Fixed Overhead	2.50	5.00
Gross margin per unit	$ 2.50	$ 1.50
Required production time/unit	2 hours	2 hours

Total production time available is 2,500 hours per month. Since production time is limited and gross margin per unit for G1 is higher than for G2, Tower Company management decided to produce and sell G1 exclusively.

Required: Did Tower Company management make the correct decision?

PROBLEMS

13-20. Product Mix—Graphic Analysis

The graph shows the constraints of a chair manufacturing company. Each kitchen chair contributes $8 per chair; each office chair contributes $5 per chair. Only 3,000 kitchen chairs can be produced.

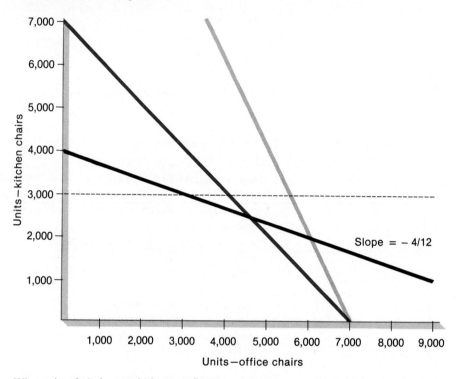

Required: What mix of chairs maximizes profits?

13-21. Determining Optimum Product Mix

Farside Enterprises makes and sells three types of stuffed toys. Management is trying to determine the most profitable mix. Sales prices, demand, and use of manufacturing inputs are as follows:

	Bears	**Cows**	**Dogs**
Sales price	$15	$32	$95
Annual demand	20,000 units	10,000 units	30,000 units
Input requirements per unit:			
Direct material	.5 yards	.3 yards	.6 yards
Direct labor	.7 hours	2 hours	7 hours
Costs:			
Variable costs:			
Materials	$10 per yard		
Direct labor	8 per hour		
Factory overhead	2 per direct labor-hour		
Marketing	10 % of sales price		
Fixed costs:[a]			
Manufacturing	$18,000 per year		
Marketing	4,000 per year		
Administration	15,000 per year		

[a] Fixed costs are allocated using direct labor-hours.

Not only does the company face limits on the volume of stuffed toys that it can sell, the layout of the plant is such that the company cannot have more than 30,000 direct labor-hours per year during normal shift hours.

Required:

Show supporting data in good form.

a. How much operating profit could the company earn if it were able to sell all of the bears, cows, and dogs that the market would buy?

b. Which of the three product lines makes the most profitable use of the constrained resource, direct labor?

c. Given the information in the problem so far, what product mix do you recommend?

d. What amount of operating profit should your recommended product mix generate?

e. Suppose the company could expand its labor capacity by running an extra shift. The extra shift could provide up to 10,000 more hours, but the cost would increase from $8 per hour to $9.50 per hour. What additional product(s) would Farside manufacture and what additional profit would be expected with the use of the added shift?

13-22. Analyze Constraints

Use the information for the Random Company in exercise 13-15 and assume that the present process 1 cost for each unit of Zeta is $2.35.

Required:

What is the maximum price that Random would be willing to pay for an additional hour of process 1 time?

13-23. Analyze Limits on Constraints

Use the information for the Random Company in exercise 13-15 and problem 13-22.

Required:

Assume Random could obtain additional process 1 hours at the price indicated by your solution to problem 13-22. How many additional units of Zeta would Random be willing to produce with the process 1 hours that it would obtain?

13–24. Interpreting Computer Output—One Constraint

Computer output for problem 13–24 is as follows:

Summary of Problem

Objective Function Value: $30,000

Variable	Value	Reduced Value
Product X	600.00	0.0
Product Y	0.0	$1.67
Product Z	0.0	0.0

CONSTRAINT	TYPE	VALUE	SHADOW PRICE
Machining time	Slack	0.0	$166.67

Objective Function Coefficient Ranges:

Variable	Current Coefficient	Allowable Increase	Allowable Decrease
Product X	$50.00	Infinity	$0.0
Product Y	40.00	$1.67	Infinity
Product Z	25.00	0.0	Infinity

Right-Hand-Side Ranges

	Current RHS	Allowable Increase	Allowable Decrease
Machining time	180.00	Infinity	180.00

Required:

Interpret the computer output for this problem by answering the following questions:

a. Formulate the objective function for this problem.

b. What is the optimal production level of product X?

c. What is the total contribution at the optimal production level? How was it computed?

d. How much would the company be willing to pay for an additional hour of machining capacity?

e. Product Y shows a reduced value of $1.67. Explain the meaning of this value.

f. Suppose that an error was made in figuring out the contribution margin for product Y. The contribution margin for product Y is supposed to be $41 instead of $40. What is the optimal production level for Y?

13–25. Interpreting Computer Output—Multiple Constraints

Computer output for problem 13–25 is as follows:

Linear Programming Input

MAX   41.5 P1 + 35.5 P2

SUBJECT TO:

Machining	2 P1 + 1.5 P2 ≤ 2000
Assembly	3 P1 + 3 P2 ≤ 3000
Demand for P2	P2 ≥ 500

Summary of Problem
Objective Function Value: $38,500

Variable	Value	Reduced Value
P1	500.00	0.0
P2	500.00	0.0

CONSTRAINT	TYPE	VALUE	SHADOW PRICE
Machining	Slack	250.00	0.0
Assembly	Slack	0.0	13.83
Demand for P2	Surplus	0.0	−6.00

Required:

Answer the following questions using the computer output.

a. What is the optimal production level for P1? For P2?

b. What is the total contribution margin obtained at the optimal production level and how was it computed?

c. How much of the machine-hours resource is unused? How much of the assembly-hours resource is unused?

d. How much would the company be willing to pay for an additional hour of machining time? For an additional hour of assembly time?

3–26. Product Mix Choice

Leastan Company manufactures a line of carpeting that includes a commercial carpet and a residential carpet. Two grades of fiber—heavy-duty and regular—are used in manufacturing both types of carpeting. The mix of the two grades of fiber differs in each type of carpeting, with the commercial grade using a greater amount of heavy-duty fiber.

Leastan will introduce a new line of carpeting in two months to replace the current line. The present fiber in stock will not be used in the new line. Management wants to exhaust the present stock of regular and heavy-duty fiber during the last month of production.

Data regarding the current line of commercial and residential carpeting are as follows:

	Commercial	Residential
Selling price per roll	$1,000	$800
Production specifications per roll of carpet:		
Heavy-duty fiber	80 pounds	40 pounds
Regular fiber	20 pounds	40 pounds
Direct labor-hours	15 hours	15 hours
Standard cost per roll of carpet:		
Heavy-duty fiber ($3 per lb.)	$240	$120
Regular fiber ($2 per lb.)	40	80
Direct labor ($10 per DLH)	150	150
Variable manufacturing overhead (60% of direct labor cost)	90	90
Fixed manufacturing overhead (120% of direct labor cost)	180	180
Total standard cost per roll	$700	$620

Lestan has 42,000 pounds of heavy-duty fiber and 24,000 pounds of regular fiber in stock. All fiber not used in the manufacture of the present types of carpeting during the last month of production can be sold as scrap at $.25 a pound.

There are a maximum of 10,500 direct labor-hours available during the month. The labor force can work on either type of carpeting.

Sufficient demand exists for the present line of carpeting so that all quantities produced can be sold.

Required:

a. Calculate the number of rolls of commercial carpet and residential carpet Leastan Company must manufacture during the last month of production to exhaust completely the heavy-duty and regular fiber still in stock.

b. Can Leastan Company manufacture these quantities of commercial and residential carpeting during the last month of production? Explain your answer.

(CMA adapted)

13–27. Product Mix Choice

Excelsion Corporation manufactures and sells two kinds of containers—paperboard and plastic. The company produced and sold 100,000 paperboard containers and 75,000 plastic containers during the month of April. A total of 4,000 and 6,000 direct labor-hours were used in producing the paperboard and plastic containers, respectively.

The company has not been able to maintain an inventory of either product due to the high demand; this situation is expected to continue in the future. Workers can be shifted from the production of paperboard to plastic containers and vice versa, but additional labor is not available in the community. In addition, there will be a shortage of plastic material used in the manufacture of the plastic container in the coming months due to a labor strike at the facilities of a key supplier. Management has estimated there will be only enough direct material to produce 60,000 plastic containers during June.

The income statement for Excelsion Corporation for the month of April is shown below. The costs presented in the statement are representative of prior periods and are expected to continue at the same rates or levels in the future.

EXCELSION CORPORATION
Income Statement
For the Month Ended April 30

	Paperboard Containers	Plastic Containers
Sales revenue	$220,800	$222,900
Less:		
Returns and allowances	6,360	7,200
Discounts	2,440	3,450
Total	8,800	10,650
Net sales	212,000	212,250
Cost of sales:		
Direct material cost	123,000	120,750
Direct labor	26,000	28,500
Indirect labor (variable with direct labor-hours)	4,000	4,500
Depreciation—machinery	14,000	12,250
Depreciation—building	10,000	10,000
Cost of sales	177,000	176,000
Gross profit	35,000	36,250
Nonmanufacturing expenses:		
Variable	8,000	7,500
Fixed	1,000	1,000
Commissions—variable	11,000	15,750
Total operating expenses	20,000	24,250
Income before tax	15,000	12,000
Income taxes (40%)	6,000	4,800
Net income	$ 9,000	$ 7,200

Required:

What is the optimal product mix, given the constraints in the problem?

(CMA adapted)

13-28. Multiple Products—Continue Operations

Stac Industries is a multiproduct company with several manufacturing plants. The Clinton Plant manufactures and distributes two household cleaning and polishing compounds—regular and heavy-duty—under the Cleen-Brite label. The forecasted operating results for the first six months of Year 1, when 100,000 cases of each compound are expected to be manufactured and sold, are presented in the following statement.

CLINTON PLANT
Cleen-Brite Compounds
Forecasted Results of Operations
For the Six-Month Period Ending June 30, Year 1
(in thousands)

	Regular	Heavy-Duty	Total
Sales revenue	$2,000	$3,000	$5,000
Cost of sales	1,600	1,900	3,500
Gross profit	400	1,100	1,500
Nonmanufacturing costs:			
Variable	400	700	1,100
Fixed[a]	240	360	600
Total nonmanufacturing costs	640	1,060	1,700
Income (loss) before taxes	$ (240)	$ 40	$ (200)

[a] The fixed nonmanufacturing costs are allocated between the two products on the basis of dollar sales volume on the internal reports.

The regular compound sold for $20 a case and the heavy-duty sold for $30 a case during the first six months of Year 1. The manufacturing costs by case of product are presented in the following schedule. Each product is manufactured on a separate production line. Annual normal manufacturing capacity is 200,000 cases of each product. However, the plant is capable of producing 250,000 cases of regular compound and 350,000 cases of heavy-duty compound annually.

	Cost per Case	
	Regular	Heavy-Duty
Direct materials	$ 7.00	$ 8.00
Direct labor	4.00	4.00
Variable manufacturing overhead	1.00	2.00
Fixed manufacturing overhead[a]	4.00	5.00
Total manufacturing cost	$16.00	$19.00
Variable nonmanufacturing costs	$ 4.00	$ 7.00

[a] Depreciation charges are 50 percent of the fixed manufacturing overhead of each line.

The schedule below reflects the consensus of top management regarding the price-volume alternatives for the Cleen-Brite products for the last six months of Year 1. These are essentially the same alternatives management had during the first six months of Year 1.

Regular Compound		Heavy-Duty Compound	
Alternative Prices (per case)	**Sales Volume (in cases)**	**Alternative Prices (per case)**	**Sales Volume (in cases)**
$18	120,000	$25	175,000
20	100,000	27	140,000
21	90,000	30	100,000
22	80,000	32	55,000
23	50,000	35	35,000

Top management believes the loss for the first six months reflects a tight profit margin caused by intense competition. Management also believes that many companies will be forced out of this market by Year 2, and profits should improve after that.

Required:

a. What unit selling price should Stac Industries select for each of the Cleen-Brite compounds (regular and heavy-duty) for the remaining six months of Year 1? Support your selection with appropriate calculations.

b. Without prejudice to your answer to requirement (a), assume the optimum price-volume alternatives for the last six months were a selling price of $23 and volume level of 50,000 cases for the regular compound and a selling price of $35 and volume of 35,000 cases for the heavy-duty compound.

   (1) Should Stac Industries consider temporarily closing down its operations until Year 2 in order to minimize its losses? Support your answer with appropriate calculations. (Stac could save none of its fixed costs by temporarily closing.)

   (2) Identify and discuss the qualitative factors that should be considered in deciding whether the Clinton Plant should be closed down during the last six months of Year 1.

(CMA adapted)

13–29. Multiple-Choice

A company markets two products, Alpha and Gamma. The contribution margins per gallon are $5 for Alpha and $4 for Gamma. Both products consist of two ingredients, D and K. Alpha contains 80 percent D and 20 percent K, while the proportions of the same ingredients in Gamma are 40 percent and 60 percent, respectively. The current inventory is 16,000 gallons of D and 6,000 gallons of K. The only company producing D and K is on strike and will neither deliver nor produce them in the foreseeable future. The company wishes to know the numbers of gallons of Alpha and Gamma that it should produce with its present stock of raw materials in order to maximize its total profit. Let X_1 refer to Alpha and X_2 refer to Gamma.

Required:

a. The objective function for this problem could be expressed as:
   (1) Max $0X_1 + 0X_2$.
   (2) Min $5X_1 + 4X_2$.
   (3) Max $5X_1 + 4X_2$.
   (4) Max $X_1 + X_2$.
   (5) Max $4X_1 + 5X_2$.

b. The constraint imposed by the quantity of D on hand could be expressed as:
   (1) $X_1 + X_2 \geq 16,000$.
   (2) $X_1 + X_2 \leq 16,000$.
   (3) $.4X_1 + .6X_2 \leq 16,000$.
   (4) $.8X_1 + .4X_2 \geq 16,000$.
   (5) $.8X_1 + .4X_2 \leq 16,000$.

c. The constraint imposed by the quantity of K on hand could be expressed as:
   (1) $X_1 + X_2 \geq 6,000$.
   (2) $X_1 + X_2 \leq 6,000$.
   (3) $.8X_1 + .2X_2 \leq 6,000$.
   (4) $.8X_1 + .2X_2 \geq 6,000$.
   (5) $.2X_1 + .6X_2 \leq 6,000$.

d. To maximize total profit, the company should produce and market:
   (1) 106,000 gallons of Alpha only.
   (2) 90,000 gallons of Alpha and 16,000 gallons of Gamma.
   (3) 16,000 gallons of Alpha and 90,000 gallons of Gamma.
   (4) 18,000 gallons of Alpha and 4,000 gallons of Gamma.
   (5) 4,000 gallons of Alpha and 18,000 gallons of Gamma.

e. Assuming that the marginal contributions per gallon are $7 for Alpha and $9 for Gamma, the company should produce and market:
   (1) 106,000 gallons of Alpha only.
   (2) 90,000 gallons of Alpha and 16,000 gallons of Gamma.
   (3) 16,000 gallons of Alpha and 90,000 gallons of Gamma.
   (4) 18,000 gallons of Alpha and 4,000 gallons of Gamma.
   (5) 4,000 gallons of Alpha and 18,000 gallons of Gamma.

(CPA adapted)

13–30. Formulate Objective Function and Constraints

The Witchell Corporation manufactures and sells three grades, A, B, and C, of a single wood product. Each grade must be processed through three phases—cutting, fitting, and finishing—before they are sold.

The following unit information is provided:

	A	B	C
Selling price	$10.00	$15.00	$20.00
Direct labor	5.00	6.00	9.00
Direct material	.70	.70	1.00
Variable overhead	1.00	1.20	1.80
Fixed overhead	.60	.72	1.08
Materials requirements in board-feet	7	7	10
Labor requirements in hours:			
Cutting	3/6	3/6	4/6
Fitting	1/6	1/6	2/6
Finishing	1/6	2/6	3/6

Only 5,000 board-feet per week can be obtained.

The cutting department has 180 hours of labor available each week. The fitting and finishing departments each have 120 hours of labor available each week. No overtime is allowed.

Contract commitments require the company to make 100 units of A per week. In addition, company policy is to produce at least 50 units of B and 50 units of C each week. Product C is constrained to a maximum of 130 units per week.

Required:

Formulate the objective function and constraints.

13–31. Analyze Costs in a Multiproduct Setting

Bright Tubes, Inc., manufactures projection devices for large television screens. The devices come in two models, 48X and 60X, designed for screens with diagonal measurements of 48 and 60 inches, respectively. Data on sales prices and costs for each model are:

	48X	60X
Selling price	$140	$220
Variable costs:		
Materials	45	60
Other	40	45
Allocated fixed costs	20	50
Profit per unit	$ 35	$ 65

Allocated fixed costs are based on total monthly fixed costs of $140,000.

The only production limitation is on the availability of titanium oxide extruders (abbreviated TOEs), which are required for each projection tube. The 48X model requires one TOE, while the 60X model requires two TOEs. There are 4,000 TOEs available per month. Management has decided that it must sell at least 1,000 of each model per month to maintain a full product line.

Last month the company used a linear programming package with the profit function:

$$\text{Maximize profit} = \$35X + \$65Y$$

where X represented the 48-inch model and Y represented the 60-inch model. Product outputs, unit revenues and unit variable costs, and total fixed costs were exactly as planned.

Nonetheless, profit performance for last month was disappointing. You have been called in to help management analyze the cause for the poor performance last month and to help improve performance in the future.

Required:

a. What profit was earned last month?

b. What product mix would you recommend this month, and what profit would be expected with your recommended product mix? Show supporting calculations.

13–32. Analyze Alternative Actions with Multiple Products

Rienz Corporation manufactures two models: Average and Deluxe. The following data are derived from company accounting records for the two products for the past month:

	Average	Deluxe
Sales volume	1,000 units	800 units
Sales revenue	$135,000	$160,000
Manufacturing costs:		
Variable	25,000	40,000
Fixed	45,000	50,000
Marketing costs (all variable)	27,000	32,000
Administrative costs (all fixed)	20,000	25,000
Total costs	117,000	147,000
Division profit	$ 18,000	$ 13,000

Production is constrained by the availability of certain materials. Each Average model takes 10 kg of these materials, while each Deluxe model uses 15 kg. There are 22,000 kg of materials available each month. Marketing constraints limit the number of Average models to 1,800 per month. Deluxe models are similarly limited to 1,200 per month.

The fixed manufacturing costs for each product would be eliminated if the product was no longer manufactured. However, administrative costs will not change with the elimination of either product.

Required:

What is the optimal product mix and what is the profit that would be earned at that product mix? Show computations.

13–33. Analyze Alternative Products with Differential Fixed Costs

Siberian Ski Company recently expanded its manufacturing capacity, which will allow it to produce up to 15,000 pairs of cross-country skis of the Mountaineering model or the Touring model. The sales department assures management that it can sell between 9,000 and 13,000 of either product this year. Because the models are very similar, Siberian Ski will produce only one of the two models. The following information was compiled by the accounting department.

	Model	
	Mountaineering	**Touring**
Selling price per unit	$88.00	$80.00
Variable costs per unit	52.80	52.80

Fixed costs will total $369,600 if the Mountaineering model is produced but will be only $316,800 if the Touring model is produced.

Required:

a. If Siberian could be assured of selling 12,000 of either model, which model would it sell? How much operating profit would be earned with sales of that product?

b. At what sales level, in units, would Siberian be indifferent regardless of the model it chooses to produce?

c. If Siberian faces a limitation on labor so that a maximum of 6,000 Mountaineering models or a maximum of 12,000 Touring models or some combination of models that would fall along that constraint can be produced, what is the optimal production schedule?

(CMA adapted)

13–34. Formulate and Solve Linear Program

The Elon Company manufactures two industrial products—X-10, which sells for $90 a unit, and Y-12, which sells for $85 a unit. Each product is processed through both of the company's manufacturing departments. The limited availability of labor, material, and equipment capacity has restricted the ability of the firm to meet the demand for its products. The production department believes that linear programming can be used to routinize the production schedule for the two products.

The following data are available to the production department:

	Amount Required per Unit	
	X-10	**Y-12**
Direct material: Weekly supply is limited to 1,800 pounds at $12 per pound	4 pounds	2 pounds
Direct labor: Department 1—weekly supply limited to 10 people at 40 hours each at an hourly cost of $6	⅔ hour	1 hour

	Amount Required per Unit	
	X-10	**Y-12**
Direct labor: Department 2—weekly supply limited to 15 people at 40 hours each at an hourly rate of $8	1¼ hours	1 hour
Machine time: Department 1—weekly capacity limited to 250 hours	½ hour	½ hour
Department 2—weekly capacity limited to 300 hours	0 hours	1 hour

The overhead costs for Elon are accumulated on a plantwide basis. The overhead is assigned to products on the basis of the number of direct labor-hours required to manufacture the product. This base is appropriate for overhead assignment because most of the variable overhead costs vary as a function of labor time. The estimated overhead cost per direct labor-hour is:

Variable overhead cost	$ 6
Fixed overhead cost	6
Total overhead cost per direct labor-hour	$12

The production department formulated the following equations for the linear programming statement of the problem.

$$A = \text{Number of units of X-10 to be produced}$$
$$B = \text{Number of units of Y-12 to be produced}$$

Objective function to minimize costs:

$$\text{Minimize } 85A + 62B$$

Constraints:
Material:

$$4A + 2B \le 1{,}800 \text{ pounds}$$

Department 1 labor:

$$\tfrac{2}{3}A + 1B \le 400 \text{ hours}$$

Department 2 labor:

$$1\tfrac{1}{4}A + 1B \le 600 \text{ hours}$$

Nonnegativity:

$$A \ge O, B \ge 0$$

Required:

a. The formulation of the linear programming equations as prepared by Elon Company's production department is incorrect. Explain what errors have been made in the formulation prepared by the production department.

b. Formulate and label the proper equations for the linear programming statement of Elon Company's production problem.

c. (Computer required.) Solve the linear program and determine the increase in the price of direct materials that would be required to change the product mix from that obtained in the optimal solution.

(CMA adapted)

13–35. Multiple Product Choice

Girth, Inc., makes two kinds of men's suede leather belts. Belt A is a high-quality belt, while belt B is of somewhat lower quality. The company earns a contribution margin of $7 for each unit of belt A that is sold and $2 for each unit sold of belt B. Each unit (belt) of type A requires twice as much manufacturing time as is required for a unit of type B. Further, if only belt B is made, Girth has the capacity to manufacture 1,000 units per day. Suede leather is purchased by Girth under a long-term contract that makes available to Girth enough leather to make 800 belts per day (A and B combined). Each belt uses the same amount of suede leather. Belt A requires a fancy buckle, of which only 400 per day are available. Belt B requires a different (plain) buckle, of which 700 per day are available. The demand for the suede leather belts (A or B) is such that Girth can sell all that it produces.

Required:

a. Construct a graph to determine how many units of belt A and belt B should be produced to maximize daily profits.

b. Assume the same facts as above except that the sole supplier of buckles for belt A informs Girth, Inc., that it will be unable to supply more than 100 fancy buckles per day. How many units of each of the two belts should be produced each day to maximize profits?

c. Assume the same facts as in requirement (b) except that Texas Buckles, Inc., could supply Girth, Inc., with the additional fancy buckles it needs. The price would be $3.50 more than Girth, Inc., is paying for such buckles. How many, if any, fancy buckles should Girth, Inc., buy from Texas Buckles, Inc.? Explain how you determined your answer.

(CMA adapted)

INTEGRATIVE CASES

13–36. Solve linear Programming Problem

(Computer required.) Golden Company management wants to maximize profits on its three products. Ooh, Ahh, and Wow. The following information is available from the company accounting records:

	Ooh	Ahh	Wow
Sales price	$9	$8	$12
Manufacturing costs:			
Direct materials	2	1	3
Direct labor	3	2	2
Overhead	2	3	3
Selling and administrative costs	1	1	1
Profit per unit	$1	$1	$ 3

Analysis of selling and administrative costs indicates that 50 percent of those costs vary with sales. The remaining amount is fixed at $90,000.

Manufacturing overhead costs are based on machine-hours. A regression equation was computed based on the past 30 months of cost data. The equation was:

$$OVH = \$285,000 + \$.35 \ MHR$$

where

OVH = Overhead
MHR = Machine-hours

The regression equation had an overall R-square of .85. Each Ooh requires .8 machine-hours. Each Ahh and Wow requires 1.2 machine-hours.

Each product requires usage of limited facilities. These time requirements in hours for each unit are:

	Ooh	Ahh	Wow
Preparation	.2	.1	.4
Molding	.1	.3	.5
Finishing	.3	.2	.1

There are 125,000 hours available in preparation; 85,000 hours available in molding; and 70,000 hours available in finishing.

Required:

a. Formulate the above as a linear programming problem.

b. Solve the problem and compute the profit at the optimal product mix.

13–37. Product Choices, Differential Costs of Inputs, Overhead Applications

Jenco, Inc., manufactures a combination fertilizer/weed-killer under the name Fertikil. This is the only product Jenco produces at the present time. Fertikil is sold through normal marketing channels to retail nurseries and garden stores.

Taylor Nursery plans to sell a similar fertilizer/weed-killer compound through its regional nursery chain under its own private label. Taylor has asked Jenco to submit a bid for a 25,000-pound order of the private brand compound. While the chemical composition of the Taylor compound differs from Fertikil, the manufacturing process is very similar.

The Taylor compound would be produced in 1,000-pound lots. Each lot would require 60 direct labor-hours and the following chemicals.

Chemicals	Quantity in Pounds
CW-3	400
JX-6	300
MZ-8	200
BE-7	100

The first three chemicals (CW-3, JX-6, MZ-8) are all used in the production of Fertikil. BE-7 was used in a compound that Jenco has discontinued. This chemical was not sold or discarded because it does not deteriorate and there have been adequate storage facilities. Jenco could sell BE-7 at the prevailing market price less $.10 per pound selling/handling expenses.

Jenco also has on hand a chemical called CN-5, which was manufactured for use in another product that is no longer produced. CN-5, which cannot be used in Fertikil, can be substituted for CW-3 on a one-for-one basis without affecting the quality of the Taylor compound. The quantity of CN-5 in inventory has a salvage value of $500.

Inventory and cost data for the chemicals are as follows:

Direct Materials	Pounds in Inventory	Actual Price per Pound When Purchased	Current Market Price per Pound
CW-3	22,000	$ .80	$ .90
JX-6	5,000	.55	.60
MZ-8	8,000	1.40	1.60
BE-7	4,000	.60	.65
CN-5	5,500	.75	(salvage)

The current direct labor rate is $7 per hour. The manufacturing overhead rate is established at the beginning of the year and is applied consistently throughout the year using direct labor-hours as the base. The predetermined overhead rate for the current year, based on a two-shift capacity of 400,000 total direct labor-hours (DLH) with no overtime, is as follows:

Variable manufacturing overhead	$2.25 per DLH
Fixed manufacturing overhead	3.75 per DLH
Combined rate	$6.00 per DLH

Jenco's production manager reports that the present equipment and facilities are adequate to manufacture the Taylor compound. However, Jenco is within 800 hours of its two-shift capacity this month before it must schedule overtime. If need be, the Taylor compound could be produced on regular time by shifting a portion of Fertikil production to overtime. Jenco's rate for overtime hours is one and one half the regular pay rate, or $10.50 per hour. There is no allowance for any overtime premium in the manufacturing overhead rate.

Jenco's standard markup policy for new products is 25 percent of full manufacturing cost.

Required:

a. Assume Jenco, Inc., has decided to submit a bid for a 25,000-pound order of Taylor's new compound. The order must be delivered by the end of the current month. Taylor has indicated that this is a one-time order that will not be repeated. Calculate the lowest price Jenco should bid for the order and not reduce its operating profit.

b. Without prejudice to your answer to requirement *(a),* assume that Taylor Nursery plans to place regular orders for 25,000-pound lots of the new compound during the coming year. Jenco expects the demand for Fertikil to remain strong again in the coming year. Therefore, the recurring orders from Taylor will put Jenco over its two-shift capacity. However, production can be scheduled so that 60 percent of each Taylor order can be completed during regular hours, or Fertikil production could be shifted temporarily to overtime so that the Taylor orders could be produced on regular time. Jenco's production manager has estimated that the prices of all chemicals will stabilize at the current market rates for the coming year and that all other manufacturing costs are expected to be maintained at the same rates or amounts.

Calculate the price Jenco, Inc., should quote Taylor Nursery for each 25,000-pound lot of the new compound, assuming that there will be recurring orders during the coming year.

(CMA adapted)

13–38. Selecting Appropriate Data for Product Mix Decisions

The Fiske Corporation manufactures and sells two products, A and B. The demand for both products exceeds current production capacity. The corporation has been unable to maintain an inventory of either product or of product B's primary direct material, which presently is in short supply. Labor also is in short supply, but the existing force can be used for production of either of the two products. Data are available on the number of units of each product sold (net of returns) and on the number of direct labor-hours expended on each product. Machinery life is directly related to the number of units of each of the products manufactured.

The company utilizes a standard costing system and has determined that the standard unit cost of these products is as shown below:

	Product A	Product B
Direct materials	$1.000	$1.953
Direct labor	.375	.781
Factory overhead	.975	1.344
	$2.350	$4.078

Overhead shown on the standard cost sheets is obtained from the flexible budget shown below. This budget is based on an assumption that 8,000 units of product A and 6,400 units of product B are being produced.

Outside consultants have been engaged to determine an optimal product mix, and they currently are developing a linear programming model to determine how many units of each product to manufacture in order to maximize profit.

FISKE CORPORATION
Overhead Budget

	Fixed	Variable[a]	Total	Allocation to Product A	Allocation to Product B	Basis for Allocation to Product
Factory overhead:						
Indirect labor	$ 500		$ 500	$ 200	$ 300	Direct labor-hours
Depreciation:						
Machinery	5,000		5,000	2,000	3,000	Direct labor-hours
Building	7,200		7,200	4,000	3,200	Estimated number of units sold
Insurance—property and plant	800		800	300	500	Per unit sales price
Payroll taxes	95	$ 1,505	1,600	600	1,000	Per unit sales price
Utilities	500		500	200	300	Direct labor-hours
Supplies	800		800	500	300	Traced to product
Total factory overhead	14,895	1,505	16,400	7,800	8,600	
Administrative:						
Product A	429	2,500	2,929	2,929		
Product B	571	4,000	4,571		4,571	
Total administrative	1,000	6,500	7,500	2,929	4,571	
Marketing:						
Commissions		8,820	8,820	2,970	5,850	
Advertising	1,000		1,000	1,000		
Bad debts	500		500	300	200	
Total marketing	1,500	8,820	10,320	4,270	6,050	
Total overhead	$17,395	$16,825	$34,220	$14,999	$19,221	

[a] Based upon a projected production and sales volume of 8,000 units of product A and 6,400 units of product B.

The following pro forma statement (in thousands) has been prepared for the month of April:

	Product A	Product B
Sales:		
A—8,000 units	$30.5	
B—6,400 units		$40.8
Gross sales	30.5	40.8
Less:		
Returns and allowances	.3	1.0
Discounts	.5	.8
Net sales	29.7	39.0
Cost of sales:		
Direct materials	8.0	12.5
Direct labor	3.0	5.0
Factory overhead	7.8	8.6
Total cost of sales	18.8	26.1
Gross margin	10.9	12.9
Operating expense:		
Administrative	2.9	4.6
Marketing	4.3	6.1
Total operating expense	7.2	10.7
Income from operations	3.7	2.2
Other:		
Interest revenue	.8	.5
Interest expense	(1.0)	(.8)
Total other	(.2)	(.3)
Operating profit before taxes	$ 3.5	$ 1.9

Required:

For each of the numbered items below select the lettered answer that best indicates in what way the preceding financial data should be used in the determination of the optimal product mix. Assume that variable revenues and expenses are completely variable.

Answer choices:

a. This aggregate dollar amount for the month divided by the aggregate number of units sold during the month should be used.

b. This aggregate dollar amount should be used.

c. This cost or revenue item should not be used.

d. This cost or revenue item should be included, but amounts inappropriate for financial accounting purposes should be used.

e. The information given is insufficient to determine whether or not the item should be used.

Items to be answered:

1. Sales.
2. Sales returns and allowances.
3. Sales discounts.
4. Direct materials.

5. Direct labor.
6. Indirect labor (fixed).
7. Depreciation—building.
8. Variable payroll taxes.
9. Utilities.
10. Supplies.
11. General and administrative expenses—variable.
12. General and administrative expenses—fixed.
13. Commissions on sales.
14. Advertising.
15. Bad debts expense.

(CPA adapted)

13–39. Bayview Manufacturing Company (Linear Programming and Cost Estimation)[5]

(Computer required.) In November 1984, the Bayview Manufacturing Company was in the process of preparing its budget for 1985. As the first step, it prepared a pro forma income statement for 1984 based on the first 10 months' operations and revised plans for the last two months. This income statement, in condensed form, was as follows:

Sales revenue		$3,000,000
Materials	$1,182,000	
Labor	310,000	
Factory overhead	775,000	
Selling and administrative	450,000	2,717,000
Net income before taxes		$ 283,000

These results were better than expected and operations were close to capacity, but Bayview's management was not convinced that demand would remain at present levels and hence had not planned any increase in plant capacity. Its equipment was specialized and made to its order; over a year's lead time was necessary on all plant additions.

Bayview produces three products; sales have been broken down by product, as follows:

100,000 of product A at $20		$2,000,000
40,000 of product B at $10		400,000
20,000 of product C at $30		600,000
		$3,000,000

Management has ordered a profit analysis for each product and has available the following information:

---

[5] Based on "Report of the Committee on the Measurement Methods Content of the Accounting Curriculum," *Supplement to Volume XLVI of The Accounting Review* (1971), pp. 229–36. The original version of this problem was developed by Professor Carl Nelson.

This case is a continuation of case 10–38 from Chapter 10.

	A	B	C
Material	$ 7.00	$ 3.75	$16.60
Labor	2.00	1.00	3.50
Factory overhead	5.00	2.50	8.75
Selling and administrative costs	3.00	1.50	4.50
Total costs	17.00	8.75	33.35
Selling price	20.00	10.00	30.00
Profit	$ 3.00	$ 1.25	$ (3.35)

Factory overhead has been applied on the basis of direct labor costs at a rate of 250 percent, and management asserts that approximately 20 percent of the overhead is variable and does vary with labor costs. Selling and administrative costs have been allocated on the basis of sales at the rate of 15 percent; approximately one half of this is variable and does vary with sales in dollars. All of the labor expense is considered to be variable.

As the first step in the planning process, the sales department has been asked to make estimates of what it could sell; these estimates have been reviewed by the firm's consulting economist and by top management. They are as follows:

A	130,000 units
B	50,000 units
C	50,000 units

Production of these quantities was immediately recognized as being impossible. Estimated cost data for the three products, each of which requires activity of both departments, were based on the following production rates:

	Product		
	A	B	C
Department 1 (molding)	2 per hour	4 per hour	3 per hour
Department 2 (finishing)	4 per hour	8 per hour	4/3 per hour

Practical capacity in department 1 is 67,000 hours and in department 2, 63,000 hours; and the industrial engineering department has concluded that this cannot be increased without the purchase of additional equipment. Thus, while last year department 1 operated at 99 percent of its capacity and department 2 at 71 percent of capacity, anticipated sales would require operating both departments 1 and 2 at more than 100 percent capacity.

These solutions to the limited production problem have been rejected: (1) subcontracting the production out to other firms is considered to be unprofitable because of problems of maintaining quality, (2) operating a second shift is impossible because of a shortage of labor, and (3) operating overtime would create problems because a large number of employees are "moonlighting" and would therefore refuse to work more than the normal 40-hour week. Price increases have been rejected; although they would result in higher profits this year, the long-run competitive position of the firm would be weakened, resulting in lower profits in the future.

The treasurer then suggested that product C has been carried at a loss too long and that now was the time to eliminate it from the product line. If all facilities are used to produce A and B, profits would increase.

The sales manager objected to this solution because of the need to carry a full line. In addition, he maintains that there is a group of loyal customers whose needs must be met. He provided a list of these customers and their estimated purchases (in units), which total as follows:

A	80,000
B	32,000
C	12,000

These contentions appeared to be reasonable and served to narrow the bounds of the problem, so the president concurred.

The treasurer reluctantly acquiesced but maintained that the remaining capacity should be used to produce A and B. Because A produced 2.4 times as much profit as B, he suggested that the production of A (in excess of the 80,000 minimum set by the sales manager) be 2.4 times that of B (in excess of the 32,000 minimum set by the sales manager).

The production manager made some quick calculations and said the budgeted production and sales would be about:

A	104,828
B	42,344
C	12,000

The treasurer then made a calculation of profits as follows:

A	104,828 at $3.00	$314,484
B	42,344 at $1.25	52,930
C	12,000 at ($3.25)	(40,200)
		$327,214

As this would represent an increase of almost 15 percent over the current year, there was a general feeling of self-satisfaction. Before final approval was given, however, the president said that he would like to have his new assistant check over the figures. Somewhat piqued, the treasurer agreed, and at that point the group adjourned.

The next day the above information was submitted to you as your first assignment in your new job as the president's assistant.

Required: Prepare an analysis showing the president what he should do.

Exhibits A and B contain information that you are able to obtain from the accounting system, which may help you to estimate an overhead cost breakdown into fixed and variable components different from that given in the case. (This breakdown was required for case 10–38 in Chapter 10.)

Exhibit A (13-39)

Year	Direct Labor Cost (in thousands) Department 1	2	Total	Overhead Cost (in thousands) Department 1	2	Total
1984	$140	$170	$310	$341	$434	$775
1983	135	150	285	340	421	761
1982	140	160	300	342	428	770
1981	130	150	280	339	422	761
1980	130	155	285	338	425	763
1979	125	140	265	337	414	751
1978	120	150	270	335	420	755
1977	115	140	255	334	413	747
1976	120	140	260	336	414	750
1975	115	135	250	335	410	745

Exhibit B (13-39)

Year	Sales (in thousands) Product A	Product B	Product C	Total	Marketing and Administrative Costs (in thousands)
1984	$2,000	$400	$600	$3,000	$450
1983	1,940	430	610	2,980	445
1982	1,950	380	630	2,960	445
1981	1,860	460	620	2,940	438
1980	1,820	390	640	2,850	433
1979	1,860	440	580	2,880	437
1978	1,880	420	570	2,870	438
1977	1,850	380	580	2,810	434
1976	1,810	390	580	2,780	430
1975	1,770	290	610	2,670	425

INVENTORY MANAGEMENT COSTS

LEARNING OBJECTIVES

1. To derive the economic order quantity (EOQ) for purchasing and production.

2. To apply the EOQ model to cases having order size restrictions or quantity discounts.

3. To find the optimal safety stock of inventory.

4. To identify the differential costs of a particular inventory policy.

5. To understand how to account for costs in a just-in-time (JIT) inventory setting.

In this chapter we discuss how cost data are used in inventory management. Inventory *management* costs should be distinguished from the cost of *producing* inventory. The cost of manufacturing products is made up of the materials, labor, and manufacturing overhead required to make the product. The inventory management costs discussed in this chapter are costs of keeping products in inventory.

Inventory management techniques are applicable in all types of organizations that have inventories, even those in which the only inventory is an inventory of office supplies. Merchandise organizations are particularly concerned about inventory management. Too much inventory results in unnecessary costs of carrying inventory. Too little inventory results in lost sales if customers buy the product elsewhere.

Most companies use complex computer models to manage their inventories. But these models are all based on the fundamental models we introduce here. We present the classical economic order quantity (EOQ) model and the costs it should include. We examine the problem of stockouts and how to use cost data to determine the optimal safety-stock policy. Balancing statement costs and costs to carry inventory loss become a major consideration in today's business environment. Finally, we discuss recent innovations, such as *just-in-time* inventory methods and *flexible manufacturing*, which are having an exciting impact on inventory management.

INVENTORY MANAGEMENT

Inventory management activities can range from ensuring that there is an adequate selection of different sizes of clothing available in a retail store to stocking necessary replacement parts for commercial aircraft. The underlying principles are similar in both situations. The primary objective is to minimize the total costs of maintaining inventory.

Inventory-related costs include the costs of carrying inventory, the costs of replenishing goods that have been sold or used, and the costs of running out of inventory. As we shall see, inventory management involves finding the minimum annual total of these three kinds of cost.

Inventory control models have been in use for some time. Operations research techniques and the advancement of computer systems resulted in the development of highly sophisticated inventory models. These models can monitor demand, forecast usage, calculate the most economic quantity to order, indicate when to order, and determine the optimal levels of inventory to keep on hand.[1]

Engineers and operations research specialists depend upon accountants for information about the costs that are relevant for use in these models. In cost accounting, we discuss issues in formulating the cost data necessary to use these techniques.

---

[1] These models and their mathematical derivation are presented in operations research texts such as Thomas E. Vollman, William Barry, and D. Clay Whybark, *Manufacturing, Planning and Control* (Homewood, Ill.: Richard D. Irwin, 1984).

INVENTORY MANAGEMENT COSTS

Carrying Costs   Those costs that increase with the number of units of inventory.

Ordering Costs   Costs that increase with the number of orders placed for inventory.

The goal in controlling inventory costs is to minimize total costs while maintaining the quantities of inventories needed for smooth operation. As already noted, some costs increase with the quantities of inventory on hand, while other costs decrease.

Carrying costs increase with the quantity of inventory on hand. There are two classes of carrying costs: (1) *out-of-pocket costs* and (2) *cost of capital*. Out-of-pocket costs include such items as insurance on the value of the inventory, inventory taxes, annual inspections, obsolescence, and the like. The *cost of capital* is the opportunity cost of having funds in inventory rather than in other earning assets.

Ordering costs decrease with the quantity of inventory on hand. For example, given a constant usage rate, the greater the inventory on hand, the less frequently one must order, thus, the lower the ordering costs. An optimal inventory policy minimizes the sum of these two types of costs.

Inventory costs can be represented graphically as in Illustration 14-1.

THE ECONOMIC ORDER QUANTITY (EOQ) MODEL

For analytical purposes, we divide inventory into two categories: (1) **working inventory**, which represents the units that are used in the normal course of operations, and (2) **safety stock**, which is the units that are kept on hand to protect against running out of inventory due to late deliveries, a speed-up in production rates, and other similar factors.

Working Inventory Management

The cost-management problems for working inventory are determining the optimal quantity to order and deciding when to place an order. These two decisions should be based on the carrying cost of the inventory and the cost to place an order. The inventory manager wants to know the point at which the total of these costs is minimized. We will see next how these costs are represented in the basic inventory models.

Carrying Costs and Ordering Costs

Carrying costs are usually expressed in terms of the average number of units in the inventory. That is, in a given year, one would expect to incur carrying costs of:

$$\frac{Q}{2} \times S$$

where S is the cost to carry one unit in the inventory for one year and is composed of out-of-pocket costs as well as cost of capital. The average inventory is presumed to be the average of the Q units that arrive at the start of the inventory cycle and the zero units that are left at the end. That is, $(Q + 0)/2 = Q/2$.

Ordering costs are expressed as the product of the number of orders placed in a year times the cost to place one order. This function is:

$$\frac{A}{Q} \times P$$

Illustration 14-1   **Economic Lot Size Cost Behavior**

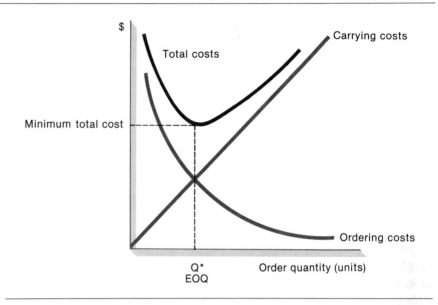

where A is the annual usage of the inventory item, and P is the cost of placing one order. The term A/Q is the number of orders placed per year. This cost function decreases as Q increases.

The total inventory carrying and ordering cost is:

$$TC = \frac{QS}{2} + \frac{AP}{Q}$$

This may be shown graphically, as in Illustration 14-1.

Note from the graph that the minimum total cost occurs at the point where the two cost functions are equal. This coincidence occurs in the most basic EOQ problem but may not be generalized to more complex problems. For this problem, the optimal Q (labeled Q^*) is referred to as the **economic order quantity (EOQ)**. It may be found by the equation:

$$Q^* = \sqrt{\frac{2AP}{S}}$$

REAL WORLD APPLICATION

Inventory control methods have been around for a long time. Incentives to use them have increased in recent years, however, because companies have begun to recognize how costly it is to carry excess inventory. For example, Firestone Tire & Rubber Company overhauled its entire inventory control system when it found excess inventory of $300 million.* With inventory carrying costs ranging from 20 to 40 percent of the cost of inventory in most companies, this excess inventory could have been costing Firestone as much as $120 million per year.

* "Business Aims for Stricter Controls as Slump Exposes Inventory Bulge," *The Wall Street Journal,* August 15, 1980, p. 15.

If Q^* units are ordered each time and inventory usage and costs continue as planned, the inventory carrying and ordering costs will be at a minimum. Note how carrying costs increase with the quantity of inventory on hand, while ordering costs decrease with the quantity on hand. Inventory management seeks to minimize total costs and to identify the point Q^*. The total cost to maintain a given inventory level decreases in the range of zero to Q^* and then increases from Q^* to the maximum possible inventory level. To find Q^*, it is necessary both to construct the mathematical relationship for the cost functions and to identify the elements of cost that should be included in each function. The first task is handled by operations research specialists; the second is the responsibility of cost accountants.

For example, Tri-Ply Company uses 25,000 units of material Z per year in the manufacture of a specialty line of plywood laminates. Out-of-pocket costs for carrying material Z are $2.50 per unit. Each unit costs $80, and the company's cost of capital is 25 percent. Thus, carrying costs are $22.50 per unit (= $2.50 + ($80 \times 25\%)$). The cost to place an order for material Z is $648. What is the optimal order size?

In this example, $A = 25,000$ units; $P = \$648$; and $S = \$2.50 + (\$80 \times 25\%) = \$22.50$. The optimal order size is:

$$Q^* = \sqrt{\frac{2 \times 25,000 \times \$648}{\$22.50}}$$
$$= \sqrt{1,440,000}$$
$$= \underline{1,200 \text{ units}}$$

Now, if Tri-Ply management follows the policy and orders 1,200 units each time, the annual costs of the inventory policy will be:

Carrying costs:

$$\frac{QS}{2} = \frac{1,200 \times \$22.50}{2} = \underline{\$13,500}$$

Ordering costs:

$$\frac{AP}{Q} = \frac{25,000 \times \$648}{1,200} = \underline{\$13,500}$$

so that costs amounted to $27,000 (that is, the $13,500 carrying costs plus $13,500 ordering costs). This is the minimum cost. In this case, the total carrying costs equal total ordering costs, which is consistent with Illustration 14–1.

Applications

The EOQ model can also be used to compute the optimal (least-cost) length of a production run. The costs to set up a production run are analogous to the ordering costs in the basic EOQ model. Carrying costs are the same as for a basic model.

For example, if the differential cost of setting up a production line to produce a specific type of item is $2,500, the demand for the item is 720,000 per year and the cost to carry each item in inventory is $1, then the **economic production run** size is:

$$Q* = \sqrt{\frac{2 \times 720,000 \times \$2,500}{\$1}}$$

which equals 60,000 units.

While the EOQ model discussed here sets forth the principles for inventory-management models, actual applications are usually much more complex. Quite often the demand (or usage) variable changes from one order period to the next. In addition, rarely does a company order only one product from a given supplier. When multiple products are procured from one supplier, it may be possible to obtain ordering cost savings by ordering several items at one time. Inventory-management models are so complex that they are almost always computerized. A computer model can simultaneously consider the various products ordered from a vendor and estimate the optimal time to place an order for one or more of them.

Although more complex models will be encountered, the basic model contains the elements that a cost accountant must consider in developing an optimal inventory policy.

EXTENSIONS OF THE BASIC EOQ MODEL

The classical EOQ model may be extended to include other costs and considerations. The following examples show how inventory-management costs may be incorporated in some more complex settings.

Orders in Round Lots

Many companies will accept orders only for round lots such as even dozens, hundreds, tons, and the like. These restrictions are often related to assembly-line or packaging requirements. When there are restrictions on order size, computation of $Q*$ using the basic EOQ model will not necessarily provide an acceptable order quantity. If $Q*$ is not equal to one of the allowed order quantities, it is necessary to determine the total annual cost of ordering the two allowed quantities on either side of $Q*$. In such cases, the optimal order size will be either $Q*$, if allowed, or the allowed quantity closest to $Q*$, whether greater than or less. Drawing lines on a cost graph to show order size restrictions as shown in Illustration 14–2 demonstrates why the optimal alternative is limited to the choices mentioned.

For example, suppose that the supplier of material Z accepts orders only in round lots of 500 units. An order for 1,200 units would not be acceptable, but Tri-Ply could order 500, 1,000, or 1,500 units. The two order sizes, 1,000 units and 1,500 units, comprise the set from which the optimal order size is obtained. To determine which order size is optimal, the total annual costs for each alternative are examined.

If 1,000 units are ordered, then the annual inventory costs are $27,450. This is the sum of the carrying costs computed as:

$$\frac{QS}{2} = \frac{1,000 \times \$22.50}{2} = \$11,250$$

and the ordering costs:

$$\frac{AP}{Q} = \frac{25,000 \times \$648}{1,000} = \underline{\$16,200}$$

$$\text{Total} \qquad \qquad \underline{\underline{\$27,450}}$$

Illustration 14–2   **EOQ with Order Size Restrictions**

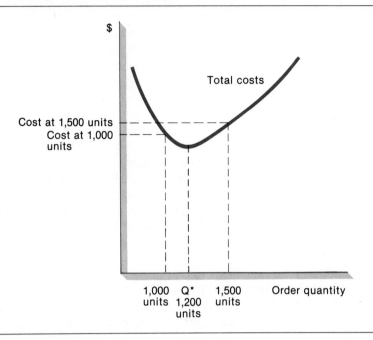

Illustration 14–3   **EOQ with Order Size Constraints**

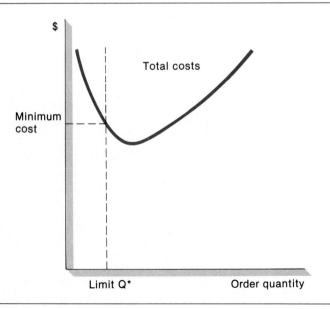

If 1,500 units are ordered at a time, then the annual costs are $27,675, which is the sum of the carrying costs:

$$\frac{QS}{2} = \frac{1,500 \times \$22.50}{2} = \$16,875$$

and the ordering costs:

$$\frac{AP}{Q} = \frac{25,000 \times \$648}{1,500} = \underline{\$10,800}$$

Total $\underline{\underline{\$27,675}}$

Therefore, the optimal policy, given the restrictions on order size, is to order 1,000 units each time.

Note that the difference in total costs between the two order sizes is relatively small ($225). If the actual order quantity is significantly different, however, the cost changes can be substantial. For example, at an order size of 500 units, the total costs increase to $38,025. (Carrying costs of $22.50 per unit times 250 units = $5,625, and ordering costs for 50 orders (25,000/500) at $648 = $32,400.) This computation highlights how the total costs change at different activity levels. Typically, they change very little for values close to Q^*; but as order size decreases, the total inventory-management costs increase rather rapidly. However, we highlight the point that the optimal inventory quantity will be at one of the two feasible order quantities adjacent to the initial Q^*.

Order Size Constraints

In today's "just-in-time" business environment, inventory levels are kept deliberately low. Maximum order sizes may be established by management to avoid obsolescence or to keep carrying costs low.

If there are order size constraints on the maximum number of units that may be stored and the computed value of Q^* is greater than the constraint, then the appropriate order size is the value of the constraint. This may be confirmed by inspecting the cost function graph in Illustration 14–1 and drawing a constraint line anywhere between zero and Q^*. The minimum total cost is at the constraint. This may be seen from Illustration 14–3, which shows the constraint imposed on the inventory cost function.

When there are storage constraints, management may ask whether it is economically justifiable to relax the constraint. Suppose that Tri-Ply has a capacity constraint of 750 units. It could obtain additional warehouse space for $6,000 per year that would enable it to store the additional 450 units indicated by the economic lot size model. Should the company obtain the additional space?

To decide, they must look at the differential cost of the alternatives. If 750 units were ordered at a time (since this is the best that can be done with the constraint), the costs are:

Carrying costs:

$$\frac{QS}{2} = \frac{750 \times \$22.50}{2} = \$ 8,437.50$$

Ordering costs:

$$\frac{AP}{Q} = \frac{25{,}000 \times \$648}{750} = \underline{\$21{,}600.00}$$

Total $\underline{\$30{,}037.50}$

From the initial example, we know that the optimal inventory costs without the constraint are \$27,000. The expected savings from the additional warehouse space are \$3,037.50 (the difference between \$30,037.50 and \$27,000). Since the rental cost exceeds the expected savings, it is better to forego the rental and order in lots of 750 units.

This may also be formulated in the same manner as other differential cost problems. A comparison of the costs under the alternatives "Maintain Present Storage" and "Rent Space" appears as:

Cost Item	Maintain Present Storage	Rent Space	Differential Costs
Carrying costs (excluding space rental)	\$ 8,437.50	\$13,500.00	\$5,062.50 higher
Ordering costs	21,600.00	13,500.00	8,100.00 lower
Space rental	–0–	6,000.00	6,000.00 higher
Total costs	\$30,037.50	\$33,000.00	\$2,962.50 higher

This analysis yields the same results, namely, that the differential costs of renting exceed the savings.

Quantity Discounts

Quantity Discounts Price reductions offered for bulk purchases.

Suppliers often offer **quantity discounts** on purchases of materials, or shipping charges may be lower for bulk shipments. In such situations, the savings from ordering in large lots may more than offset the incremental carrying costs. As a general rule, when quantity price breaks are available, the minimum EOQ will be the amount determined by the computation of Q^* without regard to price-break considerations. It may, however, be less costly to order a large quantity to obtain the price break.

Assume the supplier of material Z offers the following price breaks:

Number Ordered	Discount
0–999	None
1,000–1,999	\$1.00 per unit
2,000–4,999	1.50
5,000–9,999	1.75
10,000 and over	1.80

The optimal order quantity for Tri-Ply would either be 1,200 units—the optimal quantity ignoring the price breaks—or 2,000, 5,000, or 10,000 units. No other quantity is more economic than one of those four.

Tri-Ply management can analyze which of the four quantities is least costly if the price breaks are considered as *opportunity costs*. Forgoing the maximum available discount results in an opportunity cost equal to the difference between that maximum and the discount that Tri-Ply could obtain with its selected order policy. For example, if Tri-Ply orders in lots of 1,200 units, they obtain a discount of $1 per unit but forgo the opportunity to obtain a $1.80 discount. If they order 1,200 units at a time, there is a **foregone discount cost** of $.80 on each unit ordered. Over the year, discounts of $20,000 would be lost. That is based on the 25,000 units ordered per year times the $.80 in lost discounts per unit.

In addition, the dollar cost of capital per unit of inventory is reduced if they obtain a discount. The greater the discount, the greater the reduction. The reduction in cost equals the percent cost of capital times the dollar amount of discount. For example, if Tri-Ply orders 1,200 units, the discount is $1.00 per unit. If its cost of capital is 25 percent, then the reduction in cost of capital per unit is $.25 (25 percent × $1.00).

One way to analyze the EOQ when price breaks are available is to consider the total carrying cost, ordering cost, and foregone discount for the initial $Q*$ and the minimum quantities required to earn each additional price break. Such an analysis for Tri-Ply's purchases of material Z is presented in Illustration 14-4.

Illustration 14-4   **Optimal Order Quantity with Price Breaks**

Order Size	Carrying Costs	Ordering Costs	Foregone Discount	Total Costs
1,200	$ 13,500[a]	$13,500[b]	$20,000[c]	$ 47,000
2,000	$ 22,375[d]	$ 8,100[e]	$ 7,500[f]	$ 37,975 (optimal)
5,000	$ 55,781[g]	$ 3,240[h]	$ 1,250[i]	$ 60,271
10,000	$111,500[j]	$ 1,620[k]	–0–	$113,120

Computations:

[a] $13,500 = $\dfrac{1,200 \times (\$2.50 + 25\% \times \$80.00)}{2}$, assuming the $80 price is net of the discount at this level. (Recall that $2.50 = out-of-pocket carrying costs and 25% is the cost of capital expressed as a percent.)

[b] $13,500 = $\dfrac{25,000}{1,200}$ × $648. (Recall that the annual quantity ordered equals 25,000 and the cost to place an order is $648.)

[c] $20,000 = 25,000 × ($1.80 − $1.00), where $1.80 is the maximum price break available.

[d] $22,375 = $\dfrac{2,000 \times (\$2.50 + 25\% \times \$79.50)}{2}$, where $79.50 is $80 less the incremental $.50 discount.

[e] $8,100 = $\dfrac{25,000}{2,000}$ × $648.

[f] $7,500 = 25,000 × ($1.80 − $1.50).

[g] $55,781 (rounded) = $\dfrac{5,000 \times (\$2.50 + 25\% \times \$79.25)}{2}$, where $79.25 = $80.00 less the $.75 incremental discount.

[h] $3,240 = $\dfrac{25,000}{5,000}$ × $648.

[i] $1,250 = 25,000 × ($1.80 − $1.75).

[j] $111,500 = $\dfrac{10,000 \times (\$2.50 + 25\% \times \$79.20)}{2}$, where $79.20 is $80 less the $.80 incremental discount.

[k] $1,620 = $\dfrac{25,000}{10,000}$ × $648.

The optimal order quantity, then, is the one with the lowest total cost, in this case, 2,000 units. Note the behavior of the carrying costs and ordering costs with changes in quantities, and compare them to the patterns in Illustration 14–1.

INVENTORY MANAGEMENT UNDER UNCERTAIN CONDITIONS

Lead Time   The time between order placement and order arrival.

Stockout   Running out of inventory.

So far we have considered only working inventory in our cost analyses. If usage rates and **lead time** (the time between order placement and order arrival) are known for certain, inventory management is simplified. Usage rates may vary due to unforeseen circumstances, and lead times may vary due to events beyond management's control. If an inventory item is used faster than anticipated or if lead time is longer than expected, a **stockout** may occur.

Using just-in-time methods where inventory replenishment is expected just as needed for production or sale, stockouts are expected. Analyzing these costs may help minimize the costs of a just-in-time system.

Two kinds of stockouts are diagrammed in Illustration 14–5. In case A, an order was placed at time *T,* but the rate of use increased. As a result, the inventory on hand was used up before the new shipment arrived. In case B, the usage rate remained constant, but the new shipment did not arrive on time.

Illustration 14-5   **Inventory Flows under Uncertainty**

Case A: Change in Usage Rate

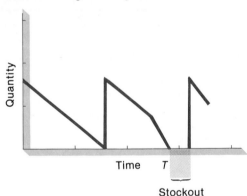

Case B: Change in Time of Arrival for New Shipment

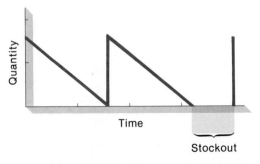

Stockouts Can Be Costly

Depending on the nature of the product, a stockout may require a special trip to pick up extra materials, or the shutting down of operations until new materials can be obtained, resulting in lost sales and customer ill will. Such added costs can be minimized by obtaining an optimal amount of *safety stock*. Had the company in the previous example maintained sufficient safety stock, then no stockout would have occurred.

By contrast, the costs to carry additional inventory may be so great that it is economical to incur stockouts. The situations from Illustration 14–5 are reproduced in Illustration 14–6 with the addition of safety stock. Now, in case A, the increased usage is satisfied from the safety stock, and the new order replenishes both the safety stock and the working inventory. In case B, the safety stock is used while awaiting the delayed arrival of the inventory order. Safety stock is replenished with subsequent orders.

Illustration 14-6   **Inventory Flows with Safety Stock**

Case A: Change in Usage Rate

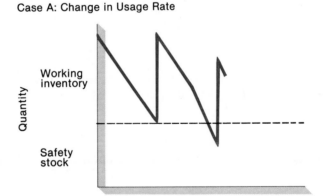

Case B: Change in Time of Arrival for New Shipment

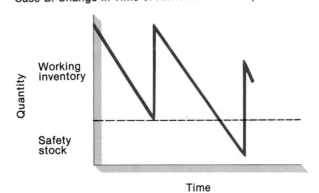

Cost Considerations for Safety Stock

Two costs must be considered in establishing an optimal safety-stock policy: (1) the *cost to carry safety stock* and (2) the *cost of a stockout*.

The cost of carrying safety stock is the same as the cost of carrying working inventory. The full quantity of safety stock is the same as the average inventory of safety stock. Because the safety stock on hand at the start of the period should equal the safety stock on hand at the end of the period, the average of these two numbers is the full quantity of safety stock. Although safety stock may decrease from time to time as events require its use, these decreases are usually ignored.

Stockout costs require separate consideration. In the first place, the cost of one stockout is usually expressed in terms of the costs of alternative sources of supply, loss of customers or goodwill, and shutting down of operations over the stockout period. These opportunity costs are estimated from many data sources. Second, the number of stockouts is an expected value. The **expected annual stockout cost** is the product of the cost of one stockout times the number of orders placed per year times the probability of a stockout on any one order.

Returning to the original example for Tri-Ply Company's inventory of material Z, let us consider that the company has a choice of alternative safety-stock levels, each of which will yield a different probability of a stockout. The staff determined that there is a .5 probability of a stockout if no safety stock is maintained. A safety stock of 100 units would reduce the stockout probability to .3. If the safety stock is maintained at 250 units of material Z, then there is a .05 probability of a stockout. Finally, a .01 probability of a stockout would be expected if the safety-stock level were 500 units. If the costs of one stockout are estimated at $3,200, the best choice of these four safety stocks is 250 units, as shown by the analysis in Illustration 14–7. (Recall the annual usage is 25,000 and the optimal order size is 1,200.)

Even with the optimal safety-stock level, there is a .05 probability of a stockout. Given that the company orders about 21 times a year (25,000 ÷ 1,200 ≈ 20.8), Tri-Ply can expect one stockout a year for material Z (21 × .05 ≈ 1). But it is more economical to incur this stockout cost than to maintain the additional safety stock. Inventory management seeks to find the least-cost policy with respect to safety-stock levels and stockouts.

Similar cost analyses can be prepared if, for example, there are different stockout costs depending on the size of the stockout. The shortage of a few items that can be obtained by alternative transportation may result in incurring only the cost of the incremental transport charges, but one that involves several hundred large items may not be so easily, or inexpensively, resolved.

Stockout Costs as Ordering Costs

Expected annual stockout costs vary directly with the number of orders placed in a year, so stockout costs are an ordering cost. The problem in including these costs in the EOQ and safety-stock models is that the two models are interdependent. The cost per order used in the EOQ model

Illustration 14-7 **Cost Analysis of Safety-Stock Policies**

Safety Stock	Carrying Costs	Expected Stockout Costs	Total Costs
0	0 × $22.50	$\frac{25,000^a}{1,200}$ × .5 × $3,200	
	= $0	= $33,333	$33,333
100	100 × $22.50	$\frac{25,000}{1,200}$ × .3 × $3,200	
	= $2,250	= $20,000	22,250
250	250 × $22.50	$\frac{25,000}{1,200}$ × .05 × $3,200	
	= $5,625	= $3,333	8,958 (optimal)
500	500 × $22.50	$\frac{25,000}{1,200}$ × .01 × $3,200	
	= $11,250	= $667	11,917

a The ratio 25,000/1,200 is the number of orders per year, and therefore the number of possible stockouts.

depends on the optimal stockout probability. Discussion of some of the more complex problems in inventory management such as the joint solution to this problem is beyond the scope of this text. Our intention is to familiarize you with the nature of the problem and its implications for cost accounting.

Reorder Point

Goods should be reordered when the quantity of inventory on hand has fallen to the sum of the usage over the lead time plus the safety stock. If an order is placed when the inventory has reached that level, the new shipment is expected to arrive when the total number of units on hand is equal to the safety stock—that is, the working inventory has fallen to zero.

For example, a safety stock of 250 has been chosen for material Z. The lead time is six working days, and the annual usage is 25,000 units. Assuming 220 working days per year, the **reorder point** for material Z is 932 units. This is computed as:

$$\left[\frac{25,000}{220 \text{ days}} \times 6\right] + 250 = (113.64 \times 6) + 250$$
$$= 682 + 250 = 932$$

When inventory falls to 932 units, an order should be placed for the optimal number of units (Q^* in the unconstrained problem or other cost-effective Q values in the presence of constraints). During the six days between order placement and order arrival, units are used at the rate of 113.64 per day. After six days, if all goes as planned, there will be approximately 250 units in inventory (the 932 units at reorder time less the 6 × 113.64 used during the lead time) when the new shipment of Q units arrives. This is diagrammed in Illustration 14–8. The reorder point is noted R. If an order is placed at that point in time, then 682 units will be used between the reorder time and the time when the new order arrives.

Illustration 14–8   **Reorder Point**

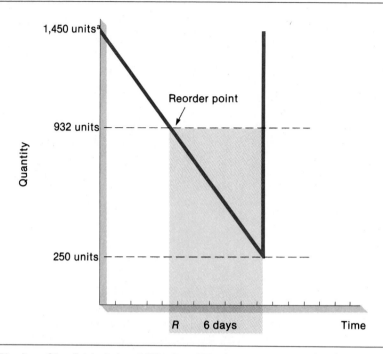

^{a} 1,450 units = Q^* + Safety stock = 1,200 units + 250 units.

DIFFERENTIAL COSTS OF INVENTORY POLICY

Selecting the costs that are relevant to the EOQ is an application of *differential costing*. When preparing cost data for inventory models, we look at each cost and ask whether it will change with the number of:

1. Units carried in inventory.
2. Units purchased.
3. Orders placed in a year.

For example, let's consider the costs obtained from Tri-Ply Company's records on a different inventory item. These costs are related to a specific inventory item:

Purchase price	$ 6.50 per unit
Transportation-in per unit	.50
Telephone call for order	11.00
Cost to unload a shipment	25.00 + $.15 per unit
Inventory taxes	.60 per unit per year
Costs to arrange for shipment of the material to the company	125.00
Salary of receiving dock supervisor (per month)	1,800.00
Insurance on inventory	.10 per unit per year
Warehouse rental	12,000.00 per month
Average spoilage costs	1.30 per unit per year
Cost of capital	20% per year
Orders handled per month	600

Which of these items should be included in the EOQ computation? Using the three costs categories mentioned earlier, let's classify each item.

1. Costs that vary with the average number of units carried in inventory:

Inventory taxes	$ .60 per unit
Insurance on inventory	.10
Average spoilage costs	1.30
Total	$2.00

2. Costs that vary with the number of units purchased:

Purchase price	$6.50 per unit
Transportation-in	.50
Costs to unload	.15
Total	$7.15

Total annual *carrying costs per unit* is the sum of the carrying costs from category 1, above, plus the cost of capital rate times the investment cost in category 2:

$$\$.60 + \$.10 + \$1.30 + (20\% \times \$7.15) = \$2.00 + (20\% \times \$7.15)$$
$$= \$3.43$$

3. Costs to place an order:

Costs of placing the order	$ 11.00 per order
Unloading the shipment	25.00
Arranging for the shipment	125.00
	$161.00

The total *ordering cost* is $161 per order.

The other costs (warehouse rental and supervisor's salary) usually do not vary with the number of units in inventory, the number of units purchased, or the number of orders during the inventory planning horizon. Those costs are, therefore, irrelevant for this decision (although they may be important for long-range decision making).

JUST-IN-TIME INVENTORY

Just-in-Time Inventory An inventory system designed to obtain goods just in time for production (in manufacturing) or sale (in merchandising).

Recent innovations in inventory management and manufacturing methods have the potential to revolutionize both inventory management and the way accounting is done in manufacturing companies. One of these is the **just-in-time inventory** philosophy. The objective of just-in-time (JIT) inventory is to obtain materials just in time for production and to provide finished goods just in time for sale and other inventory items just when needed. This reduces, or potentially eliminates, inventory carrying costs. It also has been found to have other, more subtle, benefits. For example, just-in-time inventory requires that processes or people making defective units be corrected immediately because there is no inventory where defective units can be sent to await reworking or scrapping. Manufacturing managers find that eliminating inventories can prevent production problems from being hidden. The principle feature of a just-in-time (JIT) inventory system is that production does not begin on an item until an order is received. Upon receipt of an order, raw materials are ordered and the production cycle begins. As soon as the order is filled, production ends.

In theory, a JIT system eliminates the needs for inventories because no production takes place until it is known that the item will be sold. As a practical matter, companies using this system will normally have a backlog of orders so they can keep their production operations going. The benefits of the JIT system would be lost if a company had to shut down its operations for lengthy periods of time while awaiting receipt of a new order.

Users of this system claim that it minimizes the need to carry inventories. Moreover, by producing only enough to fill orders, better control is initiated over goods lost or spoiled in production. This occurs because the entire production line is set up to produce just enough units to fill the order received. If there are spoiled or lost units, a supplemental order is required. Initiation of the supplemental order serves to notify management of the spoilage or lost goods.

Since JIT system production is made in response to the receipt of an order for goods, a JIT accounting system will normally charge all costs directly to cost of goods sold and bypass the usual inventory accounts. When it is necessary to report inventories in the financial statements, the inventory amounts are "backed out" of the cost of goods sold account.

For example, Denton Biotechnics Corp., which uses the JIT system, sells diagnostic kits for medical use. The kits are processed through two work in

---

REAL WORLD APPLICATION

When a Hewlett-Packard division introduced just-in-time inventory, the accountants found their traditional methods of cost accounting were no longer applicable.* By reducing the level of work in process and finished goods inventories, the accountants no longer needed to keep detailed records for inventory valuation.

Lowering inventories to immaterial levels for financial reporting purposes could reduce the amount of accounting time required to make journal entries to transfer costs between inventory accounts. The Hewlett-Packard plant saved an estimated 100,000 journal entries per month by simplifying the accounting for work in process inventories.

This did not eliminate the need for product costing. Managers wanted to know how much products cost for decision making, planning, and performance evaluation. By simplifying inventory accounting, however, the accountants at the Hewlett-Packard plant could turn their attention to providing better information for managers in a form managers could understand and use. The accountants found their new role in helping managers plan and control production to be exciting and challenging. Now they are part of the management team that plans and controls production activities.

* Based on an article by R. Hunt, L. Garrett, and C. M. Merz, "Direct Labor Cost Not Always Relevant at H-P," *Management Accounting,* February 1985, pp. 58-62.

process departments: (1) Culturing and (2) Packaging. Direct materials cost $1.50 per kit and other manufacturing costs are estimated at $.75 for culturing and $.30 for packaging. The company received an order for 10,000 kits. Materials costs of $15,000 were incurred as were other manufacturing costs of $11,000. For simplicity, assume that $4,000 of these other costs are wages and the remaining $7,000 were costs paid on account. The journal entries to record these events are:

Cost of Goods Sold	15,000	
Accounts Payable		15,000
To record the use of materials.		
Cost of Goods Sold	11,000	
Wages Payable		4,000
Accounts Payable		7,000
To record the incurrence of other manufacturing costs.		

All of the manufacturing costs are charged directly to cost of goods sold. There is no need to separate direct labor from other conversion costs in these systems because there is no allocation of costs based on direct labor.

Assume there are 1,000 units left in the culturing operation and 500 units left in process in packaging when financial reports are prepared. These units are complete within each operation but have not yet been transferred to the next operation. The 1,000 units in culturing are backed out of cost of goods sold based on a unit cost of $2.25, which is $1.50 for materials and $.75 for other manufacturing costs, for a total of $2,250 (1,000 units × $2.25). The 500 units in packaging are backed out using a unit price of $2.55, which is the $2.25 estimated cost after leaving culturing plus the $.30 unit cost added in packaging, for a total of $1,275 (500 units × $2.55). The journal entry to back out the inventory cost of goods sold is as follows:

Work in Process—Culturing	2,250	
Work in Process—Packaging	1,275	
Cost of Goods Sold		3,525
To record inventories.		

If the costs of these kits were charged into production using traditional costing methods, it would be necessary to debit the materials costs to a direct materials account. As the materials were used, their costs would be transferred to the culturing or packaging work in process accounts as appropriate. Other manufacturing costs would be charged to each work in process account using the cost accounting method in place in the organization. As goods were transferred out of each operation, their costs would be transferred out of the respective work in process account into the next one and, finally into cost of goods sold. The balances in each work in process account would be the ending inventory. Diagrams of the cost flows are compared in Illustration 14–9.

Comparing the cost flows, it becomes evident that the accounting system under the JIT system is simplified. The amount of time saved can be substantial given the large volume of accounting entries required in complex operations.

Although JIT systems are advertised as offering significant cost savings, some caveats are necessary. Use of a JIT system means that goods will not be produced to stockpile in inventory. With seasonal products, it is neces-

Illustration 14–9   **Just-in-Time Cost Flows**

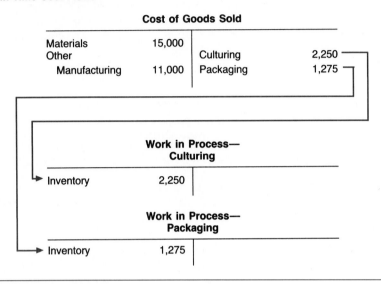

Just-in-Time Cost Flows

Cost of Goods Sold			
Materials	15,000		
Other		Culturing	2,250
Manufacturing	11,000	Packaging	1,275

Work in Process— Culturing	
Inventory	2,250

Work in Process— Packaging	
Inventory	1,275

sary to build inventories in preparation for the heavy sales period making a JIT system difficult. A company needs to have a backlog of orders and reliable suppliers so that it can keep the production line moving with a JIT system. If there is no backlog, production would stop when an order has been filled and remain idle until a new order is received. This could create chaos in the factory. Finally, materials must be readily obtained from suppliers; otherwise, production would not begin upon receipt of an order but would be delayed until goods were received. This could create customer dissatisfaction if the delay were long.

Many manufacturing companies have found that JIT can be used to varying degrees depending on the nature of a specific operation. If replacement goods could be obtained rapidly from reliable suppliers and their product was subject to rapid obsolescence, inventory levels of one week's supply or less could be optimal. On the other hand, replacement materials that were difficult to obtain (for example, goods imported from overseas) required substantially greater inventory levels. Analyzing EOQ costs and stockout cost studies enable companies to maintain appropriate inventory levels for all materials and products.

REDUCING SETUP TIME IN MULTIPRODUCT OPERATIONS

Companies that make several types of a product in a single operation are experimenting with ways of reducing *both inventory levels and the cost of setups*. Consider an automobile manufacturer that makes fenders for several models of cars using one manufacturing operation. When it's time to make left-side fenders instead of right-side fenders, or when it's time to stop making fenders for car model A and start making them for car model B, the

Illustration 14-9 (concluded)

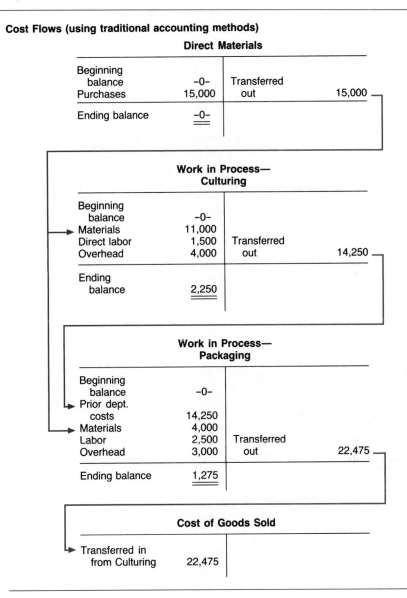

Cost Flows (using traditional accounting methods)

Direct Materials

Beginning balance	–0–	Transferred out	
Purchases	15,000		15,000
Ending balance	–0–		

Work in Process— Culturing

Beginning balance	–0–		
Materials	11,000		
Direct labor	1,500	Transferred out	
Overhead	4,000		14,250
Ending balance	2,250		

Work in Process— Packaging

Beginning balance	–0–		
Prior dept. costs	14,250		
Materials	4,000		
Labor	2,500	Transferred out	
Overhead	3,000		22,475
Ending balance	1,275		

Cost of Goods Sold

Transferred in from Culturing	22,475	

production line is stopped while workers change the machines to make the new fenders. It traditionally took from 4 to 16 hours to make this changeover and start producing new fenders without defects.

Companies are finding ways to reduce the length of these changeovers. This reduces the costs of setups because workers are not spending as much time making these changeovers and the company has less idle production time. Some companies are experimenting with flexible manufacturing techniques that allow them to make very quick changeovers using automated equipment and sophisticated computer software. These methods enable the companies to make products just in time for use because of the flexibility in changing from making one product to another. These methods may enable companies *both to maintain low inventories and to have low setup costs.*

These methods provide an opportunity for exciting advances in the way products are made and for reducing inventory-management costs. These methods are still at an experimental stage in many companies, however, so their advantages and disadvantages remain to be learned. It is important for accountants to be involved in the development of these production methods because it affects an important cost: that of managing inventory. Also, it affects accountants' jobs, as experienced by the accountants at the Hewlett-Packard plant noted above. Future cost accountants may spend relatively little time determining inventory costs and more time helping managers plan and control production activities.

SUMMARY

Adopting an inventory-management policy can be a source of significant cost savings to many organizations. The models are designed to determine the most economic order quantity (EOQ) under both constrained and unconstrained situations, the optimal level of safety stock, and the reorder point. Computer software packages have been developed to monitor inventories. These models rely on a significant amount of data from the accountant in order to find the minimum cost of alternative inventory-management decisions. The costs that are relevant for these inventory-management decisions are those costs that will change with the decision. Thus, for example, in an EOQ decision, the accountant estimates the costs that will change with the number of units ordered. These include ordering costs and carrying costs. In a decision concerning safety-stock levels, the differential costs include the costs to carry the safety stock and the stockout costs. The accountant performs a significant role in these decisions.

TERMS AND CONCEPTS

The following terms and concepts should be familiar to you after reading this chapter:

Carrying Costs	Ordering Costs
Economic Order Quantity (EOQ)	Quantity Discounts
Economic Production Run	Reorder Point
Expected Annual Stockout Cost	Safety Stock
Foregone Discount Cost	Stockout
Just-in-Time Inventory	Working Inventory
Lead Time	

SUPPLEMENTARY READINGS

Biddle, Gary C., and R. Kipp Martin. "Inflation, Taxes, and Optimal Inventory Policies." *Journal of Accounting Research,* Spring 1985, pp. 57–83.
Biggs, Joseph R., and Ellen J. Long. "Gaining the Competitive Edge with MRP/MRP II." *Management Accounting,* May 1988, pp. 27–32.

Foster, George, and Charles T. Horngren. "JIT: Cost Accounting and Cost Management Issues." *Management Accounting,* June 1987, pp. 19–25.

Jaouen, Pauline R. "Variance Analysis, Kanban, and JIT: A Further Study." *Journal of Accountancy,* June 1987, pp. 164–66, 168, 170–73.

Karmarkar, Uday S. "Lot Sizes, Lead Times, and Work in Process Inventories." *Management Science,* March 1987, pp. 409–18.

McIlhatten, Robert D. "How Cost Management Systems Can Support the JIT Philosophy." *Management Accounting,* September 1987, pp. 20–26.

Miller, Jeffrey G., and Thomas E. Vollmann. "Hidden Factory." *Harvard Business Review,* September–October 1985, pp. 142–50.

Neumann, Bruce R., and Pauline R. Jaouen. "Kanban, ZIPS, and Cost Accounting: A Case Study." *Journal of Accountancy,* August 1986, pp. 132, 134–38, 140–41.

Roth, Harold. "New Rules for Inventory Costing." *Management Accounting,* March 1987, pp. 32–36, 45.

Sadhwani, A. T. "Impact of Just-in-Time Inventory Systems on Small Businesses." *Journal of Accountancy,* January 1987, pp. 118, 120–22.

Swann, Don M. "Where Did the Inventory Go?" *Management Accounting,* May 1986, pp. 27–29.

Tatikonda, Lakshmi. "Production Managers Need a Course in Cost Accounting." *Management Accounting,* June 1987, pp. 26–29.

Williams, Jan. "Just-in-Time Ideally Suited to Smaller Manufacturing Operations." *CPA Journal,* March 1985, pp. 81–83.

SELF-STUDY PROBLEM

Margolis Manufacturing Company is a customer of your bank. The president of the company was in your office earlier in the day to apply for an additional line of credit. Trying to help your client, you note that there is a substantial sum of money tied up in inventory. When you pointed this out to the company president, the response was:

"We can't afford to run out of stock. Therefore, our policy is to order as infrequently as possible and to keep as much safety stock on hand as can be stored in our warehouse. We order 5,000 units at a time just to make sure we don't run out."

As part of your analysis of the company's loan requirements, you call up the controller of the company for some further information. From the conversation, it appears that the company has a substantial quantity of one particular part in its warehouse. The controller relates the following information on this part:

Invoice cost	$ 120.00
Shipping charges	2.50 per unit + $175 per shipment
Inventory insurance	1.00 per unit per year
Annual costs to audit and inspect inventory	2.60 per unit + $5,000 per year
Warehouse utilities	980.00 per month
Warehouse rental	1,500.00 per month
Unloading costs for units received (paid to shipper)	.80 per unit
Receiving supervisor salary	1,760.00 per month
Processing invoices and other purchase documents	16.00 per order
Allowable order quantity: 250 or multiples thereof.	

The company policy is to keep a safety stock of 3,000 units. Annual demand for the part is 45,000 units. The lead time for an order is 10 working days, and there are 250 working days per year for the plant. The controller indicated that if there is a stockout, it would be necessary to obtain the parts by special air courier at an additional cost of $8,100 per stockout. The probabilities of a stockout with various safety-stock levels are given as follows:

Safety Stock	Probability of Stockout
500	.25
1,000	.08
1,500	.02
2,000	.01

You estimate that the company's cost of capital is approximately 30 percent. You also know that the state has an inventory tax equal to 1 percent of the cost of items in inventory, which the state defines as the sum of the invoice price, shipping cost per unit, and the unloading costs. You assume for analysis purposes that a stockout probability of .02 would be reasonable for order cost determination in an optimal inventory policy.

Required:

a. What is the annual cost of the company's present inventory policy?
b. How many units should the company order at a time?
c. What is the optimal safety-stock level?
d. What is the annual cost of the optimal inventory policy identified in (b) and (c)?
e. What is the reorder point?

SOLUTION TO SELF-STUDY PROBLEM

a.

1. Investment costs:

Invoice cost	$120.00
Shipping cost	2.50
Unloading	.80
Total investment costs	$123.30

2. Carrying costs:

Cost of capital	$ 36.99 ($123.30 × 30%)
Insurance	1.00
Inventory tax	1.23 (1% × $123.30)
Audit and inspection	2.60
Total carrying costs	$ 41.82

Carrying costs per year:

Working inventory	5,000 units × ½ × $41.82 =	$104,550
Safety stock	3,000 units × $41.82 =	125,460
Total carrying costs		$230,010

Order costs:

Shipping	$175
Record processing	16
Total	$191

Annual order costs:

$$\frac{45,000}{5,000 \text{ per order}} \times \$191 = \underline{\$1,719}$$

Total annual costs of the present inventory policy:
$231,729, which is $230,010 + $1,719.

b. Economic order quantity (EOQ):

First determine Q^*, ignoring the order size restrictions:

Carrying costs *(S)*, \$41.82 (per requirement [a]).

Order costs *(P)*, \$353.00 (\$191 + .02 × \$8,100).

$$Q^* = \sqrt{\frac{2 \times 45,000 \times \$353}{\$41.82}}$$

$$= \sqrt{759,684.36}$$

$$= \underline{\underline{872 \text{ units}}}$$

Next, determine the annual costs at the next higher and lower allowable order quantity:

Quantity	Carrying Costs	Order Costs	Total Costs
750	$\frac{750}{2}$ × \$41.82 = \$15,682.50	$\frac{45,000}{750}$ × \$353.00 = \$21,180.00	\$36,862.50
1,000	$\frac{1,000}{2}$ × \$41.82 = \$20,910.00	$\frac{45,000}{1,000}$ × \$353.00 = \$15,885.00	\$36,795.00

so that the optimal order quantity given the restrictions on order size is 1,000 units.

c. Optimal safety-stock level:

Prepare a schedule showing the expected annual costs of each alternative safety-stock quantity:

Safety-Stock Quantity	Carrying Costs	Expected Stockout Costs	Total Costs
500	500 × \$41.82 = \$20,910	$\frac{45,000}{1,000}$ × \$8,100 × .25 = \$91,125	\$112,035
1,000	1,000 × \$41.82 = \$41,820	$\frac{45,000}{1,000}$ × \$8,100 × .08 = \$29,160	\$ 70,980
1,500	1,500 × \$41.82 = \$62,730	$\frac{45,000}{1,000}$ × \$8,100 × .02 = \$7,290	\$ 70,020 (Optimal)
2,000	2,000 × \$41.82 = \$83,640	$\frac{45,000}{1,000}$ × \$8,100 × .01 = \$3,645	\$ 87,285

Therefore, the most economic safety-stock level would be 1,500 units with a total expected stockout and carrying cost of \$70,020.

d. The total annual cost of the optimal inventory policy is computed as follows:

Costs of working inventory (per requirement [*b*])	$36,795
Carrying costs of safety stock	62,730
	$99,525

This is a substantial savings over the present costs of $231,729 in requirement *(a)* to this problem.

e. The reorder point is:

$$\text{Usage over lead time + Safety stock} = \left(\frac{45,000}{250} \times 10 \right) + 1,500$$
$$= 1,800 + 1,500$$
$$= \underline{\underline{3,300 \text{ units}}}$$

QUESTIONS

14–1. Since the operations research specialists develop and maintain inventory models, why does the accountant become concerned with inventory policy decisions?

14–2. Why is the cost of capital included as a carrying cost of inventory?

14–3. In determining economic order quantities, the carrying cost per unit is divided by two. Why?

14–4. A staff accountant for Percolators, Inc., noted that the annual carrying cost for a specific inventory item is estimated at $28,500, while the annual order cost is estimated at $14,150. Does this information tell you anything about the relationship of the actual order quantity to the optimal order quantity? Explain.

14–5. In terms of the specifics of the costs associated with inventory policy, how does the concept of differential costs apply to the problem of inventory policy?

14–6. For each of the following costs, indicate whether the cost would be an out-of-pocket carrying cost *(C)* or a cost of placing an order *(P)*. If the item does not qualify for either of these categories, note it as none of the above *(N)*. Assume that wages vary with the level of work while salaries are fixed for a monthly or longer time period.
a. Hourly fee for inventory audit.
b. Salary of purchasing supervisor.
c. Costs to audit purchase orders and invoices on a per-order basis.
d. Taxes on inventory.
e. Stockout costs.
f. Storage costs charged per unit in inventory.
g. Fire insurance on inventory.
h. Fire insurance on warehouse.
i. Obsolescence costs on inventory.
j. Shipping costs per shipment.

14–7. When constraints appear in an inventory problem, why is the optimal decision either Q^* *or* one of the alternatives adjacent to Q^*?

14–8. Supply labels for the lettered items in the following diagram of the quantities of an inventory item on hand over a recent time period:

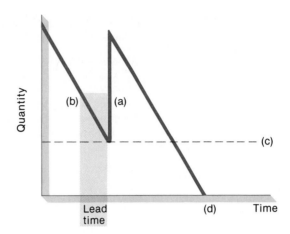

14-9. A company estimates that the lead time for a particular material is five days but that the demand over lead time is uncertain. The distribution of demand over lead time is best approximated by the normal distribution (that is, a symmetric, bell-shaped curve). If there is a great number of possible values for the demand over lead time and if no safety stock is maintained, how frequently would a stockout be expected?

14-10. "Our company orders 5,000 units at a time just to make sure we don't experience a stockout." Comment on this statement.

14-11. Phenerome Corporation is a diversified company that has acquired a number of subsidiaries through mergers. The company is instituting an inventory control system that would incorporate economic inventory policy considerations. One of the company officers has noted that some subsidiaries use last-in, first-out (LIFO) for financial reporting and others use first-in, first-out (FIFO). The officer asks you: "These different inventory methods make it very difficult for us to prepare the corporate financials and our tax return. How will they affect operation of an inventory system since the inventory costs will be different for the same item in a different subsidiary?"

14-12. Elimination of inventories through a JIT system is believed to result in a number of different types of cost savings. Itemize the types of savings from a JIT system.

14-13. What is the difference between accounting for costs under a JIT system and under a traditional process costing system?

14-14. What operating conditions are necessary for a company to make use of a JIT system?

EXERCISES

14-15. Compute EOQ
(L.O.1)

Required:

One of the inventory items at a company has a purchase price of $40. The annual demand for the item is 32,500 units. It costs $240 to place an order for the material, and out-of-pocket storage costs amount to $4.80 per unit. The company cost of capital is 25 percent.

Determine the EOQ.

14–16. Compute EOQ
(L.O.1)

Black Hills Co. uses 120,000 cartons of computer disks each year. Order costs amount to $480 each time an order is placed. Carrying costs are $125 per carton.

Required:

Compute the economic order quantity.

14–17. Find Missing Data for EOQ
(L.O.1)

Goliard Company manufactures Errantos, a consumer product, in optimal production runs of 3,500 units 20 times per year. It is estimated that the setup costs (including nonproductive labor) amount to $717.50 for each batch. The company's cost of capital is 20 percent, and the out-of-pocket cost to store an Erranto for one year is $1.60.

Required:

Solve for the unknown inventory cost of an Erranto.

14–18. EOQ—Multiple-Choice
(L.O.1)

a. The following information relates to the Henry Company:

Units required per year	60,000
Cost of placing an order	$400
Unit carrying cost per year	$300

Assuming that the units will be required evenly throughout the year, what is the EOQ?
(1) 200.
(2) 300.
(3) 400.
(4) 500.

b. Pierce Incorporated has to manufacture 30,000 blades for its electric lawn mower division. The blades will be used evenly throughout the year. The setup cost every time a production run is made is $60, and the cost to carry a blade in inventory for the year is $.40. Pierce's objective is to produce the blades at the lowest cost possible. Assuming that each production run will be for the same number of blades, how many production runs should Pierce make?
(1) 12.
(2) 10.
(3) 8.
(4) 4.

c. The Aron Company requires 40,000 units of product Q for the year. The units will be required evenly throughout the year. It costs $60 to place an order. It costs $120 to carry a unit in inventory for the year. What is the EOQ?
(1) 200.
(2) 400.
(3) 600.
(4) 1,600.

(CPA adapted)

14–19. Orders in Round Lots
(L.O.2)

Percona Corporation uses a direct material, Zelda, in its production processes. The company uses 99,000 units of Zelda a year. The carrying costs of Zelda amount to $28.50 per unit, while order costs are $325 per order. The manufacturer of Zelda will only accept orders in lots of even thousands.

Required:

What is the optimal order quantity and the annual inventory costs, given the restriction on order sizes?

14–20. Impact of Quantity Discounts on Order Quantity

(L.O.2)

Prescience Company uses 1,560 tankloads a year of a specific input material. The tankloads are delivered by rail to a siding on the company property. The supplier is offering a special discount for buyers of large quantities. The schedule is as follows:

Quantity Ordered (tankloads)	Discount
1–19	-0-
20–79	2%
80–149	5
150 and over	6

Ordering costs amount to $400, and carrying costs are $450 per unit and are not affected by the discounts. Each tankload costs $1,500.

Required:

Compute the optimal order quantity. (Round to the nearest whole number.)

14–21. Impact of Constraints on Optimal Order Quantity with Price Breaks

(L.O.2)

Considering the situation in exercise 14–20, suppose that the maximum storage capacity for the company is 100 tankloads.

Required:

What would the optimal order be? Demonstrate why.

14–22. Evaluate Safety-Stock Policy

(L.O.3)

Forest Products Corporation manufactures Maquis as one of its agriculture items. The manufacturing process requires several inputs including a nitrogen fixer, NFX. The company uses 39,000 units of NFX per year and makes 15 orders per year in economic lot sizes of 2,600 units. The cost to carry a unit of NFX is $24.40. If there is a stockout, a carload of NFX must be purchased at retail from a local supplier. The retail price is $1,650 per order greater than the price from the regular supplier.

Looking at the past order records, it appears that certain safety-stock levels would result in stockouts according to the following schedule:

Safety-Stock Quantity	Probability of Stockout
0	.60
150	.20
175	.06
250	.02

Required:

What level of safety stock would result in the least cost to the company?

14–23. Safety-Stock— Multiple-Choice

(L.O.3)

a. Hancock Company wishes to determine the amount of safety stock that they should maintain for product no. 135 that will result in the lowest cost. Each stockout will cost $75, and the carrying cost of each unit of safety stock will be $1. Product no. 135 will be ordered five times a year. Which of the following will produce the lowest cost?

(1) A safety stock of 10 units that is associated with a 40 percent probability of running out of stock during an order period.

(2) A safety stock of 20 units that is associated with a 20 percent probability of running out of stock during an order period.

(3)   A safety stock of 40 units that is associated with a 10 percent probability of running out of stock during an order period.

(4)   A safety stock of 80 units that is associated with a 5 percent probability of running out of stock during an order period.

b. Polly Company wishes to determine the amount of safety stock that it should maintain for product D that will result in the lowest costs.

The following information is available:

Stockout cost	$80 per occurrence
Carrying cost of safety stock	$2 per unit
Number of purchase orders	5 per year

The options available to Polly are as follows:

Units of Safety Stock	Probability of Running out of Safety Stock
10	50%
20	40
30	30
40	20
50	10
55	5

The number of units of safety stock that will result in the lowest cost is:

(1)   20.

(2)   40.

(3)   50.

(4)   55.

(CPA adapted)

14–24. Differential Costs of Inventory Policy
(L.O.4)

A review of the inventories of a company indicates the following cost data for a given item:

Invoice price	$102.25 per unit
Cost to arrange for the shipment	21.45 per order
Permit fees for shipping	201.65 per truckload
Inventory tax	2% of the invoice price
Insurance on shipments	$ 1.50 per unit
Insurance on inventory	2.80 per unit
Warehouse rental	985.00 per month
Stockout costs	122.00 per order
Cost of capital	25%
Unloading—per order	$ 80.20 per order

Required:

Show the differential costs that would be included in an EOQ model.

14–25. Differential Costs of Inventory Policy
(L.O.4)

A company uses 2,700 units of Zeron per year. Each unit has an invoice cost of $222, including shipping costs. Because of the volatile nature of Zeron, it costs $860 for liability insurance on each shipment. The costs of carrying the inventory amount to

$75 per item per year exclusive of a 20 percent cost of capital. Other order costs amount to $18 per order.

At present, the company orders 250 units at a time.

Required:

a. What is the annual cost of the company's current order policy?

b. What is the annual cost of the optimal economic order policy?

14–26. JIT Inventory Accounting
(L.O.5)

Cambridge Peripherals, Inc., manufactures networking devices for personal computer systems. The company uses a JIT system. An order for 600 devices was received. To fill this order, materials costing $7,000 were purchased on account. Manufacturing costs of $24,000 were incurred, of which $9,000 were paid in cash, $5,000 was for wages, and the balance was on account.

While production was in progress, it was necessary to compute an inventory value for financial statement purposes. The company has only one production division. The inventory cost was estimated at $1,240.

Required:

Prepare journal entries for these transactions.

14–27. JIT Inventory Accounting
(L.O.5)

Houston Biotech, Inc., manufactures surgical tools. An order was received for 500 autoclaves. Materials costing $12,500 were ordered on account. Additional manufacturing costs were $46,000, of which $25,000 was an account payable and the balance was wages payable. At the end of the accounting period, $3,700 of goods were not yet completed and were in the company's sole processing area.

Required:

Prepare the journal entries to show the flow of costs under a JIT system.

PROBLEMS

14–28. Determine Optimal Safety-Stock Levels

Wildridge Products, Inc., has expressed concern over the erratic delivery times for a critical product, Westovers. The company orders 3,000 at a time and has maintained a safety stock of 200 Westovers but has been experiencing frequent stockouts and production delays. The plant operates 270 days per year. The company estimates that the lead time for Westovers is five days, over which time 500 units will be used in production. The cost of storing a unit is $22 per year including capital costs. A stockout is estimated to cost $4,200 for each day that the company must wait for shipment. Any time a stockout occurs, the company must wait until its sole supplier delivers these units.

Over the past several years, the lead times have been as follows:

Lead Time (days)	Probability of Lead Time
9	.05
8	.15
6	.20
5	.40
4	.20

Other lead times have not occurred and may be ignored.

Required:

Determine the most economic safety-stock level.

14–29. Inventory Policy Cost Evaluation

Astatic, Inc., is a wholesaler of Protoxid for industrial clients. Demand for Protoxid is stable at 350,000 units per year. Astatic orders the product from its supplier four times a year. An order is placed when the total Protoxid on hand amounts to 25,000 units. This represents a nine-day working supply plus safety stock. The company works 300 days per year. Recently, management of Astatic has expressed concern over the costs of carrying inventory and is seeking to evaluate the present inventory order and safety-stock policies.

As a part of the study, the following costs were identified with respect to Protoxid:

Invoice price	$ 32.92
Weight per unit	1.5 kg
Shipping charges	$ 1.05 per unit + $640 per truck + $.40 per kg.
Tax on each unit	1.80
Special packaging	3.65 ($1 is refunded on return of the shipping container).
Insurance on shipment	1.76 per unit—casualty insurance
	415.00 per shipment—liability bond
Processing order documents	183.00
Unloading operations	.82 per unit + $1,800 per week
Inspect and count for annual inventory	2.63 per unit
Rental of unloading equipment (1-day minimum rental— 200,000-unit daily capacity)	222.00 per day
Estimated obsolescence costs	1.35 per unit
Inventory record maintenance	.92 per unit + $2,200 per week
Inventory tax	3% of invoice price
Inventory insurance	15% of invoice price + $4,100 per month

The company estimates its cost of capital is 22 percent. In addition, a study was conducted on the costs of a stockout. The average stockout costs $5,400 due to the need to request special shipments from alternate suppliers. With various safety-stock levels, the probabilities of a stockout decrease as follows:

Safety Stock	Probability of Stockout
0	.5
7,000	.1
14,000	.02
21,000	.01

For determining order quantity, a stockout probability per order of .02 may be assumed. Order sizes are restricted to round lots of 5,000. The company has the capacity to store 90,000 units.

Required:

a. What are the differential costs for inventory policy making?

b. What are the annual costs under the present order and safety-stock system?

c. What are the annual costs under the optimal order and safety-stock system?

d. What is the reorder point under the optimal order and safety-stock system?

14–30. Sensitivity of EOQ Computations to Changes in Cost Estimates

Retem & Company is instituting an economic order policy for its inventory. The following data are presented for one item in the inventory:

Annual usage	160,000 units
Storage costs	$7 per unit (out of pocket)
Cost of capital	30% of $275 purchase price per unit
Order costs	$808

Required:

a. What is the EOQ, given these data?

b. What is the annual cost of following the order policy in requirement (a) if the cost of capital were 15 percent?

c. What is the EOQ and total annual costs if the cost of capital were 20 percent?

14–31. Inventory Cycle Analysis—Multiple-Choice

Thoran Electronics Company began producing pacemakers last year. At that time, the company forecasted the need for 10,000 integrated circuits annually. During the first year, the company placed orders when the inventory dropped to 600 units so that it would have enough to produce pacemakers continuously during a three-week lead time. Unfortunately, the company ran out of this component on several occasions, causing costly production delays. Careful study of last year's experience resulted in the following expectations for the coming year:

Weekly Usage	Related Probability of Usage	Lead Time	Related Probability of Lead Time
280 units	.2	3 weeks	.1
180 units	.8	2 weeks	.9
	1.0		1.0

The study also suggested that usage during a given week was statistically independent of usage during any other week, and usage was also statistically independent of lead time.

Required:

a. The expected average usage during a regular production week is:
    (1) 180 units.
    (2) 200 units.
    (3) 280 units.
    (4) 460 units.
    (5) Some usage other than those given above.

b. The expected usage during lead time is:
    (1) 840 units.
    (2) 400 units.
    (3) 360 units.
    (4) 420 units.
    (5) Some usage other than those given above.

(CMA adapted)

14–32. Alternative Order Policy Costs

The Committee for Human Improvement (CHI) is planning a fund-raising benefit. As part of the publicity and as a means of raising money, the committee plans to sell T-shirts with the CHI logo and a design commemorating the benefit event. However, since the committee has never held one of these benefits previously, there is no experience about the quantity of T-shirts to order.

You've been asked to volunteer your knowledge of cost accounting and provide the committee with some information on the cost of alternatives. The committee expects it can sell 500 shirts at a minimum, but it will probably sell five times that amount. However, these numbers are very "soft." Since the committee is operating with limited funds, there is a desire to avoid undue risk in this T-shirt adventure.

After contacting several T-shirt manufacturers, you conclude that the best price structure is as follows:

Design logo and shirt	$75.00
Setup each production run	50.00
Cost per shirt:	
Order of 1–99	5.00
100–499	3.00
500–749	2.50
750–999	2.25
1,000–1,999	2.00
2,000–2,999	1.90
3,000 and over	1.80

The shirts are expected to sell for $5 each. There are no costs to store the shirts since one of the committee members has volunteered storage space. However, unsold shirts are valueless.

Required:

Prepare an analysis of the costs of alternative T-shirt order policies for the committee. Since the sales volume is unknown, your report will have to focus on possible volumes. Use those suggested by the committee. Indicate to the committee the costs of each alternative and the differential or opportunity cost of selecting a less risky order size.

14–33. Estimate Costs for Optimal Order Policy

Mariposa Recreational Products Company produces roller skates for street use. The company has been so involved responding to the increased demand (now at 200,000 units per year) for its product that an adequate cost control system has not been installed. Recently, however, management has been directing its attention to this problem. A question has arisen concerning the EOQ for the sets of unassembled skate parts that are the company's direct materials.

The set of parts comes from one supplier and costs $16 per set. There is a charge of $1 per set for shipping from the manufacturer. When the parts arrive, they must be checked to make certain that each set is complete and that defective units are identified and returned to the manufacturer. The checking requires one fourth hour per unit, and the labor rate for this activity is $6 per hour including variable fringe benefits. The same class of labor is required to check the inventory once a year as a part of the company's inventory management system. The checking requires an average of one-eighth hour per unit in inventory.

There is an inventory tax of $.62 per set of parts in inventory on February 28 each year. Insurance on the inventory amounts to $1.50 per unit. When placing an order, the company incurs out-of-pocket costs of $40 for bookkeeping and arranging transportation for the parts.

When the shipment arrives, a supervisor must review the documentation and determine the number of units in the shipment. This activity requires an incremental $35.00 of supervisory-related costs. A dockworker is also present to assist in unloading the shipment. This dockworker spends about 1⅔ hours in this activity and is paid at the $6 labor rate. The parts manufacturer will only accept orders in lots of even hundreds.

The company estimates its cost of capital is 16 percent.

Required:

Determine the EOQ for sets of skate parts.

14–34. Sensitivity of Economic Order Size Models

After presenting the analysis for the Mariposa Recreational Products Company (problem 14–33), you learn that the cost of supervision of unloading operations is not differential but is part of the supervisor's salary and a fixed cost.

Required:

Demonstrate the effect that this discovery would have on the optimal order policy.

14–35. Determine Optimal Safety-Stock Levels

The Starr Company manufactures several products. One of its main products requires an electric motor. The management of Starr Company uses the EOQ model to determine the optimum number of motors to order. Management now wants to determine how much safety stock to keep on hand.

The company uses 30,000 motors annually at the rate of 100 per working day. The motors regularly cost $60 each. The lead time for an order is five days. The cost to carry a motor in stock is $10. The cost to place an order is $1500. If a stockout occurs, management must purchase motors at retail from an alternate supplier. The alternate supplier charges $80 per motor.

Starr Company has analyzed the usage during the past reorder periods by examining inventory records. The records indicate the following usage patterns during past reorder periods:

Usage during Lead Time	Number of Times Quantity Was Used
440	6
460	12
480	16
500	130
520	20
540	10
560	6
	200

Required:

Determine the least-cost safety-stock level and the total differential costs at that level, ignoring the cost of capital. (The optimal order size must also be derived.)

(CMA adapted)

14–36. Determine Optimal Order Quantity with Price Breaks and Constraints

Weldone Supply offers discounts for quantity orders according to the following schedule:

Quantity	Discount
1–999	None
1,000–1,999	$1.00
2,000–4,999	1.50
5,000–9,999	2.00
10,000–19,999	4.00
20,000 and over	6.50

To decide whether to take advantage of the price-break system, you review your records and find that the order cost for this product is $400 and the carrying costs are $4. Usage amounts to 20,000 units per year. Your company has space to store up to 15,000 units. The cost of capital effect of the discount may be ignored.

Required: Prepare a schedule showing the optimal order quantity.

14–37. JIT Accounting

Quad Cities Precision Instruments produces sensitive heat measurement devices. The units are produced in three manufacturing stages: (1) meter assembly, (2) case assembly, and (3) testing. The company has a large backlog of orders and had no beginning inventories because all units in production last year were sold by the end of the year. At the start of this year, an order was received for 4,000 meters. The company purchased $260,000 of materials on account. The meter assembly division used $210,000 of the materials in production. The case assembly division used $40,000, and the testing division used $10,000.

Direct labor costs of $640,000 were incurred. These costs were assigned as follows: meter assembly, $200,000; case assembly, $350,000; testing, $90,000. Overhead costs of $1,040,000 were incurred and charged to departments based on materials used.

Ninety percent of the costs charged to meter assembly were transferred to case assembly during the period. Ninety-five percent of the costs charged to case assembly (including the costs transferred in from meter assembly) were transferred to testing. All of the costs charged to testing were transferred to finished goods, and all of the finished units were delivered to the buyer. There were no manufacturing cost variances.

Required:

a. Use T-accounts to show the flow of costs under a traditional costing system.

b. Use T-accounts to show the flow of costs using a JIT system.

INTEGRATIVE CASE

14–38. Overhead Application and Inventory Management Costs

Pointer Furniture Company manufactures and sells several brands of office furniture. The manufacturing operation is organized by the item produced rather than by the furniture line. Thus, the desks for all brands are manufactured on the same production line. The desks are manufactured in batches. For example, 10 high-quality desks might be manufactured during the first two weeks in October and 50 units of a lower-quality desk during the last two weeks. Because each model has its own unique manufacturing requirement, the change from one model to another requires the factory's equipment to be adjusted.

Management of Pointer wants to determine the most economical production run for each of the items in its product lines. One of the costs that must be estimated is the setup cost incurred when there is a change to a different furniture model. The accounting department has been asked to determine the setup cost for the desk model JE 40 as an example.

The equipment maintenance department is responsible for all of the changeover adjustments on production lines in addition to the preventive and regular maintenance of all the production equipment. The equipment maintenance staff has a 40-hour workweek; the size of the staff is changed only if there is a change in the workload that is expected to persist for an extended period of time. The equipment maintenance department had 10 employees last year, and they each averaged 2,000 hours for the year. They are paid $9 an hour, and employee benefits average 20 percent of wage costs. The other departmental costs, which include such items as supervision, depreciation, insurance, and so forth, total $50,000 per year.

Two workers from the equipment maintenance department are required to make the change on the desk line for model JE 40. They spend an estimated five hours in setting up the equipment. The desk production line on which model JE 40 is manufactured is operated by five workers. During the changeover, these workers assist the maintenance workers when needed and operate the line during the one-hour test run. However, they are idle for approximately 40 percent of the time required for the changeover.

The production workers are paid a basic wage rate of $7.50 an hour. Two overhead bases are used to apply the overhead costs of this production line because some of the costs vary in proportion to direct labor-hours while others vary with machine-hours. The overhead rates applicable for the current year are as follows:

	Based on Direct Labor-Hours	Based on Machine-Hours
Variable	$2.75	$ 5.00
Fixed	2.25	15.00
	$5.00	$20.00

These department overhead rates are based on an expected activity of 10,000 direct labor-hours and 1,500 machine-hours for the current year. This department is not scheduled to operate at full capacity because production capability currently exceeds sales potential at this time.

The estimated cost of the direct materials used in the test run totals $200. Salvage material from the test run should total $50. Pointer's cost of capital is 20 percent.

Required:

a. Prepare an estimate of Pointer Furniture Company's setup cost for desk model JE 40 for use in the economic production run model. For each cost item identified in the problem, justify the amount and the reason for including the cost item in your estimate. Explain the reason for excluding any cost item from your estimate.

b. Identify the cost items that would be included in an estimate of Pointer Furniture Company's cost of carrying the desks in inventory.

(CMA adapted)

CAPITAL INVESTMENT
CASH FLOWS

LEARNING OBJECTIVES

1. Understanding how to estimate the present value of cash flows for investment decisions.

2. To see the effect of taxes on investment decisions.

3. Estimating the effects of inflation on cash flows.

4. Understanding capital investment analysis in nonprofit organizations.

The acquisition of long-term assets is a very important decision for a company. Investment in long-term assets usually involves substantial sums of money and leaves funds at risk for long periods of time. While the final decision about asset acquisition is the responsibility of management, capital investment models have been developed by accountants, economists, and other financial experts to help managers make those decisions.

Accountants have the particularly important role of estimating the *amount* and *timing* of the cash flows used in capital investment decision models.

In this chapter, we discuss the process of estimating future cash flows from capital investment projects. In Chapter 16, we discuss alternative models used to evaluate the cash flows.

ANALYZING CASH FLOWS

Time Value of Money The concept that cash received earlier is worth more than cash received later.

Capital investment models are based on the future cash flows expected from a particular asset investment opportunity. The amount and timing of the cash flows from an investment project determines the economic value of capital investment projects. The timing of those flows is important because cash received earlier in time has greater economic value than cash received later. As soon as cash is received, it can be reinvested in an alternative profit-making opportunity. Thus, there is an opportunity cost for cash committed to any particular investment project. Because the horizon of capital investment decisions extends over many years, the **time value of money** is often a significant factor.

To recognize the time value of money, the future cash flows associated with a project are adjusted to their **present value** using a predetermined discount rate. Summing the discounted values of the future cash flows and subtracting the initial investment yields the **net present value** of a project. This net present value represents the economic value of the project to the company at a given point in time. The decision models used for capital investments attempt to optimize the economic value to the firm by optimizing the net present value of future cash flows.

For example, suppose an investor must choose between two very similar projects. Each project requires an immediate cash outlay of $10,000. Project 1 will return $14,000 at the end of two years, while Project 2 will return $14,000 at the end of three years. Clearly, the investor would prefer Project 1 over Project 2 because Project 1 will return the $14,000 one year earlier, and that amount would be available for reinvestment. Consequently, Project I has a higher net present value than Project 2.

Of course, the net present value alone does not indicate whether either project is worth the investment. The final decision involves a number of other factors.

Will either project fit within the present organization? Will the project help the firm keep up with changing markets and technology? Does management have the expertise to operate the new business? What are the social and legal implications of the project? Is the project risk acceptable? While all of these questions are important, to simplify our examples, we assume that the projects we are comparing all meet these criteria equally. This allows us to focus on the analysis of cash flows from projects and how that analysis affects net present values and decision making.

Hurdle Rate The discount rate required by the company before it will invest in a project.

Discount Rate An interest rate used to compute net present values.

Returning to the question of whether to invest in Project 1 or Project 2, we must determine if the net present value of the project is positive. If the net present value is positive, the project will earn a rate of return greater than its discount rate. This rate is often referred to as the **hurdle rate.** If the project can earn its **discount rate,** it has passed the hurdle of the net present value criterion for investment decisions. Projects that do not meet the hurdle rate are rejected because the funds that would be invested in them can earn a higher rate in some other investment.

Distinguishing between Revenues, Costs, and Cash Flows

Sometimes there is a *timing difference* between revenue recognition and cash inflow, on the one hand, and the incurrence of a cost and the related cash outflow, on the other hand. When this occurs, it is important to distinguish cash flows from revenues and costs and to note that capital investment analysis uses *cash flows, not revenues and costs*. For example, sometimes revenue from a sale is recognized on one date but not collected until a year later. In such cases, the cash is not available for other investment or consumption purposes until collected.

NET PRESENT VALUE

Present Value The amounts of future cash flows discounted to their equivalent worth today.

The **present value** of cash flows is the amount of future cash flows discounted to their equivalent worth today. The *net present value* of a project can be computed by using the equation:

$$NPV = \sum_{n=0}^{N} C_n \times (1 + d)^{-n}$$

where

$C_n =$ The cash to be received or disbursed at the end of time period n.
$d \ =$ The appropriate *discount rate* for the future cash flows.
$n \ =$ The time period when the cash flow occurs.
$N \ =$ The life of the investment, in years.

Use of the equation with a calculator or computer spreadsheet is the most efficient approach to computing net present values. Tables of present value factors are in Appendix B to this chapter and may also be used to find present values. We use the equation in all chapter illustrations, computations, and discussions and round all printed factors to three decimals. Therefore, if we want to discount $20,000 for two years at 10 percent, we find the value of $(1.10)^{-2}$ by a power function in the calculator. In the calculator, the result of this computation is .826446281. Multiplying this amount by $20,000 yields the present value of $16,529. In this chapter, we show our computations as:

$$\$20,000 \times (1 + .10)^{-2} = \$20,000 \times .826$$
$$= \underline{\$16,529}$$

We abbreviate the present value factor because it is simply an intermediate result. If you use the abbreviated factor or the factors from the present value tables, your answer will differ due to rounding. This should not cause alarm.

Applying Present Value Analysis

Now, let's look at how present value analysis is used for capital investment decisions. As an example, consider the two projects mentioned earlier in the chapter. If the appropriate discount rate is 15 percent, then the net present value of each project may be computed as follows:

Project 1:

Cash inflow	$14,000 \times (1 + .15)^{-2}$	
	$= \$14,000 \times .756$	$= \$10,586$
Cash outflow		$= -10,000$
Net present value		$\$\quad 586$

Project 2:

Cash inflow	$14,000 \times (1 + .15)^{-3}$	
	$= \$14,000 \times .658$	$= \$\;9,205$
Cash outflow		$= -10,000$
Net present value		$\$\quad(795)$

The starting time for capital investment projects is assumed to be Time 0. Therefore, any cash outlays required at the start of the project are not discounted. We enter them at their full amount.

At a discount rate of 15 percent, Project 1 is acceptable and Project 2 is not. Project 1 will earn more than the required 15 percent return, while Project 2 will earn less.

You should check for yourself to see that at a 20 percent discount rate, the present values of both projects are negative. Therefore, if our required rate were 20 percent, neither project would meet the investment criterion. Alternatively, at 10 percent, both projects have positive net present values and would be acceptable.

Of course, the cash flows in most business investment opportunities are considerably more complex than our simplified examples, but the method for computing net present values remains the same.

Consider, for example, the cash flow pattern in Illustration 15–1. The cash flows can be either positive or negative in any year. This cash flow

Illustration 15-1   **Example of Net Present Value Calculations**

Period	Net Cash Inflow or (Outflow)	PV Factor $(1 + d)^{-n}$ $d = 20$ Percent	Present Value[a]
0	$(80,000)	1.000	$(80,000)
1	(9,000)	.833	(7,500)
2	31,200	.694	21,667
3	14,800	.579	8,565
4	(42,100)	.482	(20,303)
5	76,800	.402	30,864
6	79,600	.335	26,658
7	74,500	.279	20,792
8	61,100	.233	14,210
9	43,600	.194	8,450
10	(39,700)	.162	(6,412)
Net present value			$ 16,991

[a] Cash flow times factor may not equal net present value because factor is rounded to three places.

pattern is characteristic of a project that will begin with a pilot operation. If the pilot operation proves successful, full-scale facilities will be installed in Year 4. Operations will continue until Year 10, at which time costs will be incurred to dismantle the operation. Once the cash flows are determined, computation of the present value is a mechanical operation. The critical problem for the accountant, however, is to estimate the amount and timing of the expected future cash flows.

CATEGORIES OF PROJECT CASH FLOWS

This section of the chapter outlines a method for estimating cash flows for investment projects. This is an important part of the accountant's job in making investment decisions. We start by setting up four major categories of cash flows for a project:

1. Investment flows.
2. Periodic operating flows.
3. Depreciation tax shield.
4. Disinvestment flows.

Each category of cash flows requires a separate treatment.

Investment Flows

There are three types of investment flows:

1. Asset acquisition, which includes:
   a. New equipment costs, including installation (outflow).
   b. Proceeds of existing assets sold, net of taxes (inflow).
   c. Tax effects arising from a loss or gain (inflow or outflow).
2. Working capital commitments.
3. Investment tax credit.

Asset Acquisition

Asset Acquisition Costs involved in the purchase and installation of an investment or inventory. May involve the disposal of obsolete equipment, including a gain or loss.

Asset acquisition includes not only the cost of purchasing and installing new assets but also the cash inflows that may result from the proceeds, net of taxes, of selling replaced equipment. Additionally, there may be a loss or gain to consider, arising from the difference between the sale proceeds and the tax basis of the equipment being replaced.

The primary outflow for most capital investments is the acquisition cost of the asset. Acquisition costs may be incurred in Time 0 and in later years. In some cases, they are incurred over periods of 10 to 20 years. All acquisition costs are listed as cash outflows in the years in which they occur. Installation costs are considered a cash outflow.

If the depreciation tax basis of the replaced equipment is not equal to the proceeds received from the sale of the replaced equipment, a gain or loss will occur and will affect the tax payment. It will be considered as a cash inflow (for a loss) or a cash outflow (with a gain).

For example, Kwik Press, a publishing company, commissioned a team of business students to conduct a customer satisfaction survey. The results of the survey showed the number one complaint by customers was the time it took Kwik Press to complete desktop publishing jobs. Kwik Press was working at capacity and losing customers to the local competition. Management decided to consider replacing slower copy machines with fast, state-of-the-art machines.

The new machines would cost $280,000 in two payments: $130,000 at Time 0 and $150,000 in Year 1. The depreciation that would be allowed for tax purposes would be $80,000 in Years 1 and 2, and $40,000 in Years 3–5. A tax rate of 40 percent is used.

The existing machines had been purchased several years ago. The tax basis of the existing machines is $52,500, and they would have been depreciated for tax purposes at the rate of $26,250 in Year 1 and $26,250 in Year 2. The estimated current salvage value is $45,000 which is the cash inflow from the sale of the existing machines. The difference between the tax basis of $52,500 and the salvage value of $45,000 results in a tax loss of $7,500. These cash flows for asset acquisition appear in Illustration 15–2.

Working Capital Commitments

Working Capital Cash, accounts receivable, and other short-term assets required to maintain an activity.

In addition to the cash for purchase of long-term assets, many projects require additional funds for **working capital** needs; for example, a retail establishment needs to acquire inventory which it maintains throughout its operations. The working capital committed to the project normally remains constant over the life of the project, although it is sometimes increased because of inflation. Kwik Press plans to commit $50,000 in working capital, Time 0, in order to maintain an average idle cash balance in a bank account to cover future cash transactions. Outlays for working capital items are shown when those outflows occur. The projected investment flows of Kwik Press are summarized in Illustration 15–2.

Investment Tax Credit (ITC)

Investment Tax Credit A reduction in federal income taxes arising from the purchase of certain assets.

The **investment tax credit** allows a credit against the federal income tax liability based on the cost of an acquired asset. This credit effectively reduces the cost of making investments by giving companies a credit against their corporate income taxes equal to, say, 10 percent of the purchase price. The investment tax credit has been in effect at various times since the early 1960s. As this book goes to press, the tax investment credit is limited to very few assets. Our examples in the text and the exercises and problems will tell you if the investment tax credit is to be considered.

Illustration 15–2   **Scheduling Investment Flows, Kwik Press**

	Time 0	Year 1
Investment flows:		
New equipment and installation	($130,000)	($150,000)
Proceeds, existing equipment	45,000	
Tax benefit from loss		
on equipment	3,000	
Working capital	(50,000)	
Total cash flows:	($132,000)	($150,000)

Tax benefit from loss on existing equipment:
($52,500 tax basis − $45,000 salvage value) × 40% tax rate
= $7,500 loss for tax purposes × 40% tax rate
= $3,000 tax benefit from loss.

For example, we assume Kwik Press would not receive an investment tax credit under current tax laws. If the tax laws were to change to allow a ten percent ITC, then Kwik Press would receive a tax credit of $13,000 (.10 × $130,000) in Year 1 and $15,000 (.10 × $150,000) in Year 2. These amounts would be considered cash inflows in the present value analysis in each of Years 1 and 2.

Periodic Operating Flows

The primary reason for acquiring long-term assets is usually to generate positive *periodic operating cash flows*. These positive flows may result from such *revenue-generating* activities as new products, or they may stem from *cost-saving* programs. In either case, actual cash inflows and outflows from operating the asset are usually determinable in a straightforward manner. The most important concept is to identify and measure the cash flows that will differ because of the investment. *If the revenues and costs are differential cash items, then they are relevant for the capital investment decision.*

Periodic operating flows include:

1. Period cash inflows (+) and outflows (−) before taxes.
2. Income tax effects of inflows (−) and outflows (+).

Kwik Press has determined that the revenues and costs will differ because of the investment and should therefore be included as differential cash flow items. The differential revenues, net of taxes, would be cash inflows. The differential costs, net of taxes, would be considered cash outflows. The projected differential costs and revenues are presented in Illustration 15–3 and explained below.

The schedule in Illustration 15–3 has been divided into two columns to separate all accounting costs that will arise due to the project from the differential cash flows that would be considered for purposes of the present value analysis. The left column shows all costs that would be allocated to the project if the investment were made, including depreciation for financial accounting purposes and other costs, such as reallocated fixed costs that would be allocated to the new project. We show the two separate columns to emphasize that all periodic costs allocated to a project are not necessarily differential cash flows that would be considered in the analysis.

The operating revenues and costs that represent differential cash flows are included in the differential cash flow column. Costs that do not involve cash (depreciation, depletion, and amortization) are excluded from the differential cash flow column. (For example, see line 6 in Illustration 15–3.)

If there are cash costs in other departments that change as a result of the project, then those other department costs should be included in the differential cash flow schedule. For this reason, $1,500 of allocated service department costs are included in the differential cash flow column. For example, assume that $3,500 of service department costs (repairs and maintenance) would be allocated to this project if the investment is made; however, only $1,500 of that amount would actually increase *because* of the project. (That is, only $1,500 are differential costs.) The remaining $2,000 ($3,500 − $1,500) would merely be reallocated from other parts of the company. In this case, only the $1,500 would be shown as a *differential cash*

Illustration 15-3   **Schedule of Project Revenues and Costs (Years 1-5), Kwik Press**

Differential Flows		Amount	Differential Cash Flow	Remarks
(1)	Project revenues	$210,285	$210,285	All cash
(2)	Direct materials and direct labor	(62,342)	(62,342)	All cash
	Manufacturing overhead:			
(3)	Indirect labor	(1,800)	(1,800)	All cash
(4)	Supplies	(6,500)	(6,500)	All cash
(5)	Allocated service department costs	(3,500)	(1,500)	2,000 is an allocation of costs that would not change with this decision
(6)	Accounting depreciation	(70,000)	0	Depreciation is not a cash flow
(7)	Other overhead	(6,076)	(6,076)	All cash
(8)	Selling commissions	(1,985)	(1,985)	All cash
	Administration:			
(9)	Direct	(3,700)	(3,700)	All cash
(10)	Indirect	(2,500)	0	Allocation of fixed costs
(11)	Tax and insurance on equipment and inventory	(18,200)	(18,200)	All cash
	Subtotals	$ 33,682	108,182	
(12)	Income tax on differential cash flows		43,273	Based on analysis of tax regulations
	Net operating cash flows for Years 1-5		$ 64,909	

cost. (See line 5 in Illustration 15–3.) Just because costs are allocated to a project does not mean they are necessarily differential costs.

For another example of allocated costs that are not differential, note that indirect administrative costs of $2,500 have been allocated to the project but are not differential (line 10). *Total indirect administrative costs* for the company are not affected in this example; they would just be allocated differently if the investment were made.

Financing costs such as interest costs on loans, principal repayments, and payments under financing leases are typically excluded under the assumption that the financing decision is separate from the asset-acquisition decision. Under this assumption, the decision to acquire the asset is made first. If the asset-acquisition decision is favorable, then a decision will be made to select the best financing.

For purposes of analysis, asset acquisitions are typically recorded in the full amount when the cash purchase payments are made, regardless of how that cash was acquired.

Tax Effects of Periodic Cash Flows

The income tax effects of the periodic cash flows from the project are also computed and considered in the present value analysis. (For this example, we assume the marginal tax rate to be applied to these cash flows is 40 percent.) Note that for purposes of calculating the net present value, only the tax effects related to differential project cash flows are considered. It is the *differential effect on our tax liability* we include in the present value analysis.

The income tax effect of depreciation is different than the depreciation used for financial or internal reporting purposes, which is not considered a differential cash flow. Therefore, any reductions in tax payments arising frrom depreciation of these assets are considered differential cash flows and treated separately.

The steps carried out to compute the net operating cash flows for the project are repeated for each year in the project life. In some cases, the computations can be simplified, by use of an annuity factor, if the project is expected to yield identical cash flows for more than one year.

Depreciation Tax Shield

Tax Shield The reduction in tax payment because of depreciation deducted for tax purposes.

To measure the income of an organization or one of its subunits, depreciation is used to allocate the cost of long-term assets over their useful lives. These depreciation charges are not cash costs and thus do not directly affect the net present values of capital investments. However, tax regulations permit depreciation write-offs that reduce the required tax payment. The reduction in the tax payment is referred to as a **tax shield.** *The depreciation deduction computed for this tax shield is not necessarily the same amount as the depreciation computed for financial reporting purposes.* The predominant depreciation method for financial reporting has been the *straight-line method*. With this method, the cost of the asset, less any salvage value, is allocated equally to each year of the expected life of the asset. For income tax purposes, faster depreciation write-offs are allowed.

The tax allowance for depreciation is one of the primary incentives used by tax policy makers to promote investment in long-term assets. The faster an asset's cost can be written off for tax purposes, the sooner the tax reductions are realized and, hence, the greater the net present value of the tax shield. In recent years, tax depreciation has been accelerated to allow write-offs over very short time periods regardless of an asset's expected life. To maximize present value, it is usually best to claim depreciation as rapidly as possible.

There are two effects of the depreciation tax shield:

1. Depreciation tax shield on assets acquired.
2. Forgone depreciation tax shield on assets disposed.

Consider the tax depreciation schedule of the new machines Kwik Press is considering. The machines have a depreciation tax basis of $280,000 over five years. The annual depreciation tax shield and the present value of the tax shield are computed in columns 2–5 in Illustration 15–4, using the 40 percent tax rate and a 15 percent discount rate. (All amounts given in this problem are for illustrative purposes only. They do not necessarily reflect the amount of depreciation allowed by the tax regulations). No salvage value has been assumed. Present value factors appear in Appendix B to this chapter.

Kwik Press also forgoes depreciation of $26,250 in each of Years 1 and 2 because it would dispose of assets having a depreciable tax base. The forgone depreciation and forgone tax shield, assuming a 40 percent tax rate,

rate, appear in Illustration 15–5. The amounts in column 3 of Illustration 15–4 and column 3 of Illustration 15–5 will then be transferred to the cash flow schedule, as seen later in Illustration 15–6.

To review the basic relationships, a portion of the $280,000 is deducted each year on the tax return as shown in column 2 of Illustration 15–4. The tax shield in column 3 is the tax rate times the depreciation deduction. This is the cash flow resulting from a reduction in the annual tax liability, which is generated by the tax shield.

Disinvestment Flows

The end of a project's life will usually result in some or all of the following cash flows:

1. Cash freed from working capital commitments (now as cash inflow).
2. Salvage of the long-term assets (usually a cash inflow, unless there are disposal costs).
3. Tax consequences for differences between salvage proceeds and the remaining depreciation tax basis of the property.
4. Other cash flows, such as employee severance payments and restoration costs.

Disinvestment Flows Cash flows that take place at the termination of a capital project.

The cash flows at the end of the life of the project are referred to as **disinvestment flows.**

Illustration 15-4

Present Value of Depreciation Tax Shield—Kwik Press

Tax rate: 40%   Depreciation basis: $280,000

(1) Year	(2) Depreciation Deducted on the Tax Return	(3) Tax Shield (40% × Depreciation Deduction)	(4) PV Factor (15%)	(5) Present Value (Tax Shield × PV Factor)
1	$ 80,000	$ 32,000	.870	$27,826
2	80,000	32,000	.756	24,197
3	40,000	16,000	.658	10,520
4	40,000	16,000	.572	9,148
5	40,000	16,000	.497	7,955
Totals	$280,000	$112,000		$79,646

Illustration 15-5

Foregone Depreciation Tax Shield—Kwik Press

Tax rate: 40%   Depreciation basis: $52,500

(1) Year	(2) Foregone Depreciation	(3) Foregone Tax Shield (40% × Column 2)
1	$26,250	$10,500
2	26,250	10,500
Totals	$52,500	$21,000

Return of Working Capital

When a project ends, there are usually some leftover inventory, cash and other working capital items that were used to support operations. These working capital items are then freed for use elsewhere or liquidated for cash. Therefore, at the end of a project's life, the return of these working capital items is shown as a cash inflow.

It is important not to double-count these items. Suppose that cash collected from a customer was already recorded as a cash inflow to the company, but it was left in the project's bank account until the end of the project's life. It should not be counted again as a cash inflow at the end of the project.

The return of working capital is recorded as an inflow whenever it is freed for use in other organizational activities. If that does not occur until the end of the project's life, the cash inflow is included as part of disinvestment flows.

Salvage of Long-Term Assets

Ending a project will usually require disposal of its assets. These are usually sold in secondhand markets. In some cases, more money is spent in disassembling the assets and disposing of them than is gained from their sale. Any net outflows from disposal of a project's assets become tax deductions in the year of disposal. The *net salvage value* (sometimes negative) of an asset is listed as a cash inflow or outflow at the time it is expected to be realized (or incurred), regardless of the book value or **tax basis** of the asset. The difference between the book value (tax basis) and the net salvage value may result in a taxable gain or loss.

Tax Basis Remaining tax-depreciable ''book value'' of an asset for tax purposes.

Tax Consequences of Disposal

Any difference between the tax basis of a project's assets (generally, the undepreciated balance) and the amount realized from project disposal results in a tax gain or loss. Therefore, a company's tax liability will be affected in the year of disposal. Tax laws on asset dispositions are complex, so tax advice should be sought well in advance of the proposed disposal date. In this chapter, we assume that any gains or losses on disposal are treated as ordinary taxable income or losses.

Suppose that an asset is carried in the financial accounting records at a net book value of $70,000 and is salvaged for $30,000 cash. The tax basis of the asset is $10,000, and the tax rate is 40 percent. What are the cash flows from disposal of this asset?

First, the company receives the $30,000 as a cash inflow. They report a taxable gain of $20,000, which is the difference between the $30,000 proceeds and the $10,000 tax basis. This $20,000 gain is taxed at 40 percent, which results in a cash outflow of $8,000. The cash inflow on disposal is $22,000, the net of the $30,000 inflow and the $8,000 cash outflow.

Consider the tax consequences of the new machines at Kwik Press upon disposal in Year 5. The machines will have a remaining net book value in the accounting records of $70,000, which is irrelevant for the present value analysis. The assets will have been fully depreciated for tax purposes and are salvaged for $105,000 cash. The tax rate is 40 percent. What are the cash flows from disposal of this asset?

First, the company receives the $105,000 as a cash inflow. They report a taxable gain of $105,000, since the asset is fully depreciated for tax purposes. This $105,000 gain is taxed at 40 percent, which results in a cash outflow of $42,000, which is Kwik Press's additional tax liability arising from the gain. The net cash inflow on disposal of the machines is $63,000 which equals $105,000 from the sale minus 40 percent times the $105,000 gain or $105,000 − $42,000.

Other Disinvestment Flows

The end of project operations may result in a number of costs that are not directly related to the sale of assets. It may be necessary to make severance payments to employees. Sometimes payments are required to restore the project area to its original condition. Some projects may incur regulatory costs when they are closed down. A cost analyst must inquire about the consequences of disposal to determine the costs that should be included in the disinvestment flows for a project.

PREPARING THE NET PRESENT VALUE ANALYSIS

Once the cash flow data have been gathered, they are assembled into a schedule that shows the cash flows for each year of the project's life. These flows may be classified into the four categories we just discussed:

1. Investment flows
2. Periodic operating flows.
3. Depreciation tax shield.
4. Disinvestment flows.

A summary schedule that shows the total of the annual cash flows and the net present value of the project is prepared. This summary may be supported by as much detail as management deems necessary for making the investment decision.

For example, consider the data collected thus far and summarized in Illustration 15–6 for the investment proposal for Kwik Press. The project is expected to earn higher than the 15 percent used to discount the cash flows because the net present value of the project is greater than zero. (If the net present value of the project had been less than zero, the project would have been expected to earn less than the 15 percent used to discount the cash flows.)

Depreciation is deducted for tax purposes as follows: Year 1, $80,000; Year 2, $80,000; and $40,000 per year in each of Years 3–5. Project costs include the equipment outlays in Time 0 and Year 1. The working capital requirements are shown as outflows in Time 0.

Annual cash flows are computed using the schedule of revenues and costs shown in footnote b of Illustration 15–6 and adjusting for the costs that are not differential (allocated service department costs and allocated administrative costs) or that are not cash costs (depreciation). The net cash inflow of $108,182 is then reduced by the tax liability that is expected to arise from taxing this inflow at the 40 percent marginal tax rate. The after-tax cash inflow of $64,909 is shown for each year of the project's life.

In the last year of the project, the disinvestment flows are given. These include the return of working capital and the proceeds from disposal of the

Illustration 15-6   **Cash Flow Schedule with Present Value Computations, Kwik Press**

	Time 0	Year 1	2	3	4	5
Investment flows:						
Equipment cost and installation	($130,000)	($150,000)				
Proceeds of assets sold, net of tax	45,000					
Tax benefit on loss[a]	3,000					
Working capital	(50,000)					
Periodic operating flows, net of tax[b]		64,909	$64,909	$64,909	$64,909	$64,909
Depreciation tax shield:						
Tax shield from depreciation[c]		32,000	32,000	16,000	16,000	16,000
Foregone tax shield[d]		(10,500)	(10,500)			
Disinvestment flows:						
Return of working capital						50,000
Proceeds on disposal						105,000
Tax on gain[e]						(42,000)
Total cash flows:	(132,000)	(63,591)	86,409	80,909	80,909	193,909
PV factor at 15%	1.000	.870	.756	.658	.572	.497
Present values[f]	($132,000)	($ 55,296)	$65,338	$53,199	$46,260	$ 96,407

Net present value of project $73,908

Computations:

[a] $3,000 = 52,500 − 45,000 × 40%.

[b] Net operating cash flow (after tax):

Revenues		$210,285
Differential cash outflows:		
Direct materials and direct labor	($62,342)	
Taxes and insurance on equipment and inventory	(18,200)	
Manufacturing overhead	(15,876)	
Selling Commission	(1,985)	
Direct administrative costs	(3,700)	(102,103)
Revenues net of differential cash costs (before tax)		108,182
Income taxes on differential net cash flows (40%)		43,273
Differential cash flows (after taxes)		$ 64,909

[c] Depreciation computations:

Year	Depreciation	Tax Shield (at 40%)
1	$ 80,000	$ 32,000
2	80,000	32,000
3	40,000	16,000
4	40,000	16,000
5	40,000	16,000
Totals	$280,000	$112,000

[d] Foregone Depreciation:

Year	Foregone Depreciation	Foregone Tax Shield
1	$26,250	$10,500
2	26,250	10,500

[e] Gain is equal to salvage since the asset is fully depreciated for tax purposes. The tax is 40% of the gain, or 40% × $105,000 = $42,000.

[f] PV factor shown is rounded to three places. Present values are derived from unrounded PV computations. Present value factors are shown in Appendix B to this chapter.

asset. In addition, the tax consequences from selling the equipment for more than the zero tax basis are considered, and the related $42,000 tax liability is included in the cash flow computations.

The net present value of the project is computed as the sum of the present values of each year's cash flow. The positive net present value of $73,908 indicates that the project is expected to earn better than the 15 percent used to discount the cash flows.

The schedule shown in Illustration 15–6 indicates the net cash flows in each year, thus assisting management in preparing its cash budgets for the life of the project. The net present value of each year's cash flow is presented for computational purposes and may not be required for management.

INFLATION CONSIDERATIONS IN CAPITAL BUDGETING

When prices and costs are expected to change significantly over a project's life, it is important to consider the effects of those changes on project cash flows. In many cases, the cash flows will not change uniformly over the life of the project. Therefore, a careful analysis of each cost item may be necessary. Cash flows that will be received in the future will have a different real value than dollars received today due to changes in the purchasing power of those dollars. The actual dollars to be received are called **nominal dollars**.

Nominal Dollars Actual numerical count of money exchanged.

The schedule of project cash flows can be adjusted to consider the nominal cash flows. The resulting nominal net cash flows are then discounted at a rate that recognizes inflation. This is the **nominal discount rate.** These adjustments compensate the company for the effects of inflation as well as for a return on capital.

Nominal Discount Rate A rate of interest that includes compensation or inflation.

Adjusting the Discount Rate

It is commonly accepted that the interest rate that the market demands includes elements of a return on capital as well as an adjustment for the effects of inflation. The discounting equation can be expanded to include the inflation element as a specific component:

$$[(1 + r)(1 + i)]^{-n}$$

where

r = The real return on capital required from now to period n.
i = The expected inflation rate between now and period n.
n = The number of the period in the future when the cash is to be received.

Real Return Return on capital after adjustment for the effects of inflation.

The **real return** is the return on capital after adjustment for the effects of inflation. This equation may be used with a constant value for i, or the value of i may be changed from one period to the next. In general, though, a constant inflation rate is assumed.

The terms within the brackets may be multiplied before the exponentiation operation. Subtracting 1 from the result of this multiplication gives the nominal discount rate for the project:

$$\text{Nominal rate} = (1 + r)(1 + i) - 1$$

In practice, the nominal discount rate implicitly considers the need to compensate for inflation. The schedule of cash flows is discounted using the nominal discount rate just as the value r was used earlier.

For example, a company has concluded that its projects should earn a real return of 15 percent and that the expected inflation rate over the project's life will be 6 percent per year. To find the nominal discount rate for present value, the following calculation is performed:

$$(1 + r)(1 + i) - 1 = (1.15)(1.06) - 1$$
$$= .219 \text{ or } 21.9\%$$

Management will discount the future cash flows using a 21.9 percent rate in the discounting equation:

$$(1 + d)^{-n} = (1.219)^{-n}$$

Adjusting Future Cash Flows

The effects of inflation may be considered in the same four categories as the cash flows for capital investment projects. When considering inflation, the future cash flows are also adjusted for inflation by the factor $(1 + i)^n$.

Investment Outflows

Cash requirements for the initial investment may need to be adjusted if costs are likely to change over the investment period. This is particularly common with projects that require several years to construct.

REAL WORLD APPLICATION

Investing in Improved Technology

Investments in improved technology frequently do not show a positive net present value when investment analysis is performed. Technological innovations usually have a high investment outlay and a long time period before cash flows are returned from the project. It is not unusual for an investment in automated equipment to take two or three years (or more) before it is fully operational. In companies with high discount rates, cash flows received, or cash savings, several years in the future have low present values. Furthermore, technological improvements frequently provide benefits that are not easily quantified, so they are often omitted from the analysis.

We observed the capital-budgeting process at work for technological improvements in one of the largest U.S. manufacturing companies. This company was considering investing in new equipment that would make the manufacturing operation more flexible. With this equipment, the company could change quickly from making one part to another, reduce setup costs, inventory levels, and production downtime, and introduce other potential savings. In addition to these cost savings, the engineers and production managers who supported this project saw it as a way of learning more about flexible manufacturing, which *could* provide major benefits to the company in the future. These benefits were not quantifiable, however, so no *explicit* weight was given to them in the discounted cash flow analysis.

Using a high discount rate (after-tax rate greater than 25 percent), the company initially rejected the project. The president of the company was subsequently convinced that the project had additional benefits beyond those explicitly considered in the discounted cash flow analysis. These additional benefits, which included learning about improved production methods that could have a major impact on the way the company does business, were believed to justify the project. The project was then accepted, and the investment was made.

Working capital requirements often increase with the increased volume of nominal dollars. That is, more dollars are required to support the same level of activity. The investment in inventory generally will not change. The initial costs were incurred to procure a given quanity of inventory. Inventory may cost more to replace, but the replacement costs are included in period cash outflows.

For initial investment outlays, then, the inflation adjustment simply requires revising any outlays that are expected to change as a result of increasing costs. Any increases in working capital levels (other than inventory) are scheduled when they are required.

For example, consider the cash flows for Kwik Copy in Illustration 15–6. Those flows ignored the effects of inflation. Now, let's consider the impact of inflation on these flows. Suppose the equipment costs that were originally $130,000 in Time 0 and $150,000 in Year 1 are not expected to increase with inflation. The $50,000 in working capital requirements must increase with the rate of inflation. How will an inflation rate of 6 percent per year affect the investment cash outflows?

1. Equipment cost: The Time 0 cost of $130,000 is unaffected. The Year 1 cost of $150,000 is not changed in this example but could increase with inflation in other cases.

2. The initial cash outflow for working capital remains $50,000 in Time 0. However, in Year 1, working capital must be increased to $53,000 to keep up with the effects of inflation on nominal dollars ($50,000 $\times$ 1.06). Therefore, in Year 1 there will be an additional $3,000 cash outflow to working capital to account for inflation.

In Year 2, an additional $3,180 will be added to working capital to bring the balance to $56,180 (that is, $53,000 $\times$ 1.06 $=$ $56,180). In Year 3, working capital will need to be increased by an additional $3,371; and in Year 4, the increase will be $3,573, for a total balance of $63,124. There is no increase in Year 5 because that is the end of the project's life, and the working capital for noninventory items is returned at that time.

Periodic Operating Flows

The operating cash flows for each year are adjusted by multiplying the original amounts by $(1 + i)^n$. This restates the original cash inflow to the nominal dollar amount to be received in Year n. In this case, the adjusted amounts are $64,909 $\times$ 1.06 $=$ $68,804 for Year 1; $64,909 $\times$ $(1.06)^2 =$ $72,932 for Year 2, and so forth. (We assume that Year 1 operating flows increase by 6 percent over Time 0.)

These net nominal cash flows are entered into the appropriate columns of the cash flow schedule in Illustration 15–7 in place of the original unadjusted cash flows.

Tax Shield

Depreciation is based on the original cost of an asset. Hence, the tax shield from depreciation is only changed if the original investment costs change. Under inflation, the real value of the tax shield from depreciation declines relative to the other cash flows from the project. Note that the discount rate recognizes inflation, but the tax shield does not increase with inflation.

Consequently, the higher the inflation rate, the lower the net present value of the depreciation tax shield.

Disinvestment Flows

Under conditions of inflation, disinvestment flows become more complex. The return of working capital will include all nominal cash and accounts receivable committed to the project. Therefore, the periodic cash outflows for working capital are summed and the total listed as a recovery at the end of the project's life.

The working capital returned in Year 5 includes the $50,000 initial outlay plus the outlays in Years 1 through 4 for a total return of $63,124 (which is $50,000 + $3,000 + $3,180 + $3,371 + $3,573).

The proceeds from disposal of the long-term assets and their tax impact are also included in the disinvestment computation. Any difference between the proceeds on disposal as adjusted for inflation and the tax basis of the property is taxed.

For Kwik Press, we assume that the market for used equipment similar to that used in the project is increasing at the rate of 7 percent per year. As a result, the proceeds from disposal are estimated as:

$$\$105,000 \times (1.07)^5 = \underline{\$147,268}$$

Since the asset has been fully depreciated for tax purposes, this entire amount is a gain, taxable at ordinary rates. The tax liability from the gain is:

$$40\% \times \$147,268 = \underline{\$58,907}$$

This amount is shown as an outflow in Year 5.

REAL WORLD APPLICATION

The Use of Inflation Adjustments in Capital Budgeting

Do managers adjust their present value calculations to consider inflation? A survey of top financial officers in 193 of the largest U.S. companies (all were Fortune 500 companies) indicates that many do. "Ninety-seven firms (50 percent of the 193 respondents) said that they specifically adjust estimated cash flows for anticipated inflation."[*]

The firms that make these inflation adjustments tend to have large capital budgets and use sophisticated techniques in evaluating investments. Firms in the petroleum industry were found to be the most likely to adjust cash flows for inflation, apparently because of the large size and long lives of their investments, and because price variations are large in this industry.

[*] J. A. Hendricks, "Capital-Budgeting Practices Including Inflation Adjustments: A Survey," *Managerial Planning*. January–February, 1983, p. 26.

Summarizing the Cash Flows.

The adjusted cash flows for Kwik Press under inflation are summarized in the cash flow schedule in Illustration 15–7 as they were in Illustration 15–6 with no inflation considered. That is, all cash flows are scheduled and summed for each year of the project's life. In this case, however, yearly cash flows represent the amounts expected to be realized under certain inflation conditions.

The cash flows for the project are discounted using the 21.9 percent rate computed earlier, and the present values are shown for each year of the project's life. The net present value of the project is then computed. For this project, the net present value is $64,863.

Capital investment analyses sometimes incorrectly ignore the effect of inflation on cash flows but increase their discount rate to reflect the changes in market rates of interest. These interest rates include inflationary expectations. On some projects, discounting the unadjusted cash flows with an inflation-adjusted interest rate can yield the opposite answer from what is optimal.

Taking explicit account of inflation in both the cash flow analysis and the discount rate directly recognizes the effects of inflation on each project. In

Illustration 15–7   **Cash Flow Schedule Adjusted for Inflation with Present Value Computations**

	Time 0	Year 1	Year 2	Year 3	Year 4	Year 5
Investment outflows:						
Equipment cost	($130,000)	($150,000)				
Proceeds of assets sold, net of tax	45,000					
Tax benefit on loss	3,000					
Working capital	(50,000)	(3,000)	($ 3,180)	($ 3,371)	($ 3,573)	
Periodic operating flows, net of tax:[a]		68,804	72,932	77,308	81,946	$86,863
Depreciation tax shield:						
Tax shield from depreciation		32,000	32,000	16,000	16,000	16,000
Foregone tax shield		(10,500)	(10,500)			
Disinvestment flows:						
Return of working capital[b]						63,124
Proceeds on disposal						147,268
Tax on gain						(58,907)
Total cash flows	(132,000)	(62,696)	91,252	89,937	94,373	254,348
PV factor at 21.9%	1.000	.820	.673	.552	.453	.372
Present values[c]	($132,000)	($51,432)	$61,409	$49,651	$42,740	$94,495
Net present value of project	$64,863					

Nominal rate = 1.15 × 1.06 − 1 = .219 = 21.9%

[a] Operating cash flows = $64,909 $(1.06)^n$, $n = 1, \ldots, 5$.

[b] $63,124 = Sum of cash released from working capital requirements = $50,000 + $3,000 + $3,180 + $3,371 + $3,573.

[c] Cash flow times PV factor does not equal present values because these PV factors are rounded.

addition to the direct effect of inflation on cash flows from revenues and operating costs, the tax shield is worth less under inflation because it is based on the uninflated original cost of the asset.[1] Additional working capital requirements are needed to support the increased transaction flow in nominal dollars. Finally, in many real applications, the inflation rates for a specific project differ from general rates.

CAPITAL BUDGETING IN NONPROFIT ORGANIZATIONS

Not-for-profit organizations, including governmental agencies, are subject to limitations on the availability of capital for investment purposes. They, too, make use of capital investment analysis to allocate cash efficiently. Normally, these organizations invest in equipment that will provide cost savings rather than generate revenue. In addition, since not-for-profit organizations are exempt from income taxation, there are no tax effects on the operating cash flows nor on disinvestment flows. Likewise, there is no tax shield from depreciation. These features result in a somewhat simplified analysis.

For example, assume that the U.S. Postal Service is considering purchase of advanced automated sorting equipment for its Urbana station. The equipment will cost $600,000 and has a useful life of five years. Salvage value is estimated at $10,000. Installation of the equipment will cost $8,000. The old equipment can be shipped to a post office that is using semiautomated equipment. It is assumed that the costs to dismantle and ship the old equipment will exactly offset the benefits received at the other post office.

Use of the new equipment will reduce power costs by $40,000 per year. One operator will be able to handle the volume of letters that five operators handled in the past. The average pay for each operator is $30,000 including

Illustration 15-8   **Capital Budgeting in Nonprofit Organizations**

Item	Time 0	Year 1	Year 2	Year 3	Year 4	Year 5
Investment flows:						
New equipment	($600,000)					
Other investment costs	(8,000)					
Annual operating flows		$160,000[a]	$160,000	$160,000	$160,000	$160,000
Disinvestment flows:						
Salvage value						10,000
Total cash flows	(608,000)	160,000	160,000	160,000	160,000	170,000
Discount factor	1.000	0.909	0.826	0.751	0.683	0.621
Present value	($608,000)	$145,455	$132,231	$120,210	$109,282	$105,557
Net present value	$4,735					

[a] $160,000 = $40,000 + $30,000 × 4.

---

[1] The failure to index the depreciation tax shield to inflation has been criticized as creating disincentives to invest. For a summary of the issues, see M. Maher and T. Nantell, "The Tax Effects of Inflation: Depreciation, Debt, and Miller's Equilibrium Tax Rates," *Journal of Accounting Research*, vol. 21, no. 1. (Spring 1983).

fringe benefits. The Postal Service uses a discount rate of 10 percent. What are the cash flows from the project and the net present value?

The results are shown in Illustration 15–8. As you may note, this is very similar to Illustration 15–6, which was used for a taxable organization.

POST-AUDIT OF CAPITAL INVESTMENT PROJECTS

Because capital investment projects are so important, companies commonly compare the cash flows that are actually realized from a project with the estimated flows in the original capital investment proposal. In that way, they hope to learn if the estimation process can be improved.

Some projects may improve reported accounting profits in the short run but result in suboptimal net present values. When this occurs, it is necessary to identify the reasons for choosing a project that improves accounting profits rather than net present value. There may be rational explanations for such decisions, but management should critically evaluate those reasons.

A capital investment control program must consider more than initial project estimates. It must also determine if the capital investment decision-making process is operating well.

SUMMARY

Capital investment planning involves a number of managerial and financial considerations. The accountant's role is to determine the amount and timing of relevant cash flows from the project. These cash flows are discounted back to the present to determine if the proposed project meets the established hurdle rate.

The net present value of a project is computed using the following equation:

$$\text{NPV} = \sum_{n=0}^{N} C_n \times (1 + d)^{-n}$$

where

C_n = Cash flows at the end of time period n.
d = Discount rate.
n = Time period when the cash flow occurs.
N = Total number of time periods in the project's life.

The accountant's primary task is to estimate cash flows used in the net present value equation. These cash flows and their effects are:

1. Investment
   a. Acquisition cost $(-)$.
   b. Investment tax credit $(+)$.
   c. Working capital commitments $(-)$.
   d. Proceeds of assets sold $(+)$.
   e. Tax effects from a loss or gain on sale of old assets $(+/-)$.
2. Periodic operating flows, including:
   a. Period cash inflows $(+)$ and outflows $(-)$ before taxes.
   b. Income tax effects of inflows $(-)$ and outflows $(+)$.

3. Depreciation tax shield:
   a. Tax shield benefits ($+$).
   b. Forgone tax shield benefits ($-$).
4. Disinvestment flows:
   a. Cash freed from working capital commitments ($+$).
   b. Salvage value of long-term assets (usually $+$ unless there are disposal costs).
   c. Tax consequences of gain or loss on disposal ($-$ or $+$, respectively).
   d. Other cash flows, such as severance or relocation payments to employees, restoration costs, and similar costs (usually $-$).

Income taxes are an extremely important consideration, particularly due to regulations designed to encourage investment. The accountant may be the only analyst on the management team who understands the income tax effects. Improper treatment of tax effects may lead to suboptimal decisions.

Under conditions of inflation, the discount rate is usually adjusted to compensate for changes in price levels. The changes in cash flows that stem from inflation may also be included explicitly in the cash flow analysis.

TERMS AND CONCEPTS

The following terms and concepts should be familiar to you after reading this chapter:

Asset Acquisition

Discount Rate

Disinvestment Flows

Hurdle Rate

Investment Tax Credit

Net Present Value

Nominal Discount Rate

Nominal Dollars

Present Value

Real Return

Tax Basis

Tax Shield

Time Value of Money

Working Capital

SUPPLEMENTARY READINGS

Bierman, H., Jr., and S. Smidt. *The Capital Budgeting Decision.* New York: Macmillan, 1980.

Casler, George L.; Bruce L. Anderson; and Richard D. Aplin. *Capital Investment Analysis: Using Discounted Cash Flows.* 3rd ed. New York: John Wiley, 1984.

Farragher, Edward J. "Capital Budgeting Practices of Non-Industrial Firms." *Engineering Economist,* Summer 1986, pp. 293–302.

Friedman, L. A., and B. R. Neuman. "The Effects of Opportunity Costs on Project Investment Decisions: A Replication and Extension." *Journal of Accounting Research,* Autumn 1980, pp. 407–19.

Howell, Robert A., and Stephen R. Soucy. "Capital Investment Analysis in the New Manufacturing Environment." *Management Accounting,* November 1987, pp. 26–32.

Kaufman, Mike, ed. *Capital Budgeting Handbook.* Homewood, Ill.: Dow Jones-Irwin, 1986.

Larcker, D. F. "The Perceived Importance of Selected Information Characteristics for Strategic Capital Budgeting Decisions." *Accounting Review,* July 1981, pp. 519–38.

Maher, M., and T. Nantell. "The Tax Effects of Inflation: Depreciation, Debt, and Miller's Equilibrium Tax Rates. *Journal of Accounting Research,* Spring 1983.

McCabe, George M., and George N. Sanderson. "Abandonment Value in Capital Budgeting: Another View." *Management Accounting,* January 1984, pp. 32–6.

Nance, Jon R. "Capital Budgeting with Continuous Cash Flows: An Application of Calculus to Managerial Accounting." *Journal of Accounting Education,* Spring 1988, pp. 67–81.

Pruitt, Stephen W., and Lawrence J. Gitman. "Capital Budgeting Forecast Biases: Evidence from the Fortune 500." *Financial Management,* Spring 1987, pp. 46–51.

Sundem, G. L. "Evaluating Simplified Capital Budgeting Models Using a Time-State Preference Metric." *Accounting Review,* April 1974, pp. 306–20.

Yagil, Joseph; Ben Amoako-Adu; and Jeffrey Kantor. "Capital Cost Allowance (Depreciation) and Capital Budgeting in Canada." *International Journal of Accounting Education and Research,* Spring 1986, pp. 47–54.

SELF-STUDY PROBLEM

Melwood Corporation is considering the purchase of a small computer to automate its accounting and word processing systems. Management has been considering several alternative systems including a model labeled the P–25. The supplier of the P–25 has submitted a quote to the company of $7,500 for the equipment plus $8,400 for software. Assume the equipment can be depreciated for tax over three years as follows: Year 1, $2,500; Year 2, $2,500; Year 3, $2,500. The software may be written off immediately for tax purposes. The company expects to use the new machine for four years and to use straight-line depreciation for financial reporting purposes. The market for used computer systems is such that Melwood would realize $1,000 for the equipment at the end of the four years. The software would have no salvage value at that time.

Melwood management believes that introduction of the computer system will enable the company to dispose of its existing accounting equipment. The existing equipment is fully depreciated for tax purposes and can be sold for an estimated $100.

Although the new system will not enable Melwood to reduce its work force, management believes that it will realize improvements in operations and benefits from the computer system that will be worth $8,000 per year before taxes.

Melwood uses a 15 percent discount rate for this investment and has a marginal income tax rate of 45 percent after considering both state and federal taxes.

Required:

a. Prepare the schedule showing the relevant cash flows for the project.

b. Indicate whether the equipment purchase meets Melwood's hurdle rate.

SOLUTION TO SELF-STUDY PROBLEM

a.

MELWOOD CORPORATION

	Time 0	Year 1	Year 2	Year 3	Year 4
Investment:					
Equipment	$ (7,500)				
Software ($8,400 × 55%)	(4,620)				
Old equipment ($100 × 55%)	55				
Annual operating flows:					
($8,000 × 55%)		$4,400	$4,400	$4,400	$4,400
Tax shield[a]		1,125	1,125	1,125	
Disinvestment ($1,000 × 55%)					550
Cash flows	(12,065)	5,525	5,525	5,525	4,950
Discount factors at 15%		.870	.756	.658	.572
Present values	$(12,065)	$4,804	$4,178	$3,633	$2,830
Net present value	$ 3,380				

Additional computations:
[a] Tax shield:

Year	Depreciation	Tax Shield
1	$2,500	$1,125
2	2,500	1,125
3	2,500	1,125
	$7,500	$3,375

b. With a positive net present cash flow of $3,380, the equipment meets the hurdle rate. The cost savings justify purchase of the equipment.

**APPENDIX A
Computing Net
Present Values
for Annuities**

When periodic cash flows are expected to be equal over a period of time, a short-cut method may be used to compute the net present value of those cash flows. A series of level periodic payments is referred to as an *annuity*. The *present value of an annuity* may be obtained using the equation:

$$\text{Present value} = C_n \times \frac{1 - (1 + d)^{-n}}{d}$$

where

  d = Discount rate.
  n = Number of periods over which the periodic payment (C) will be
     received.

For example, the present value of a series of six payments of $40,000 each at a discount rate of 25 percent is:

$$PV = \$40,000 \times \frac{1 - (1 + .25)^{-6}}{.25}$$
$$= \$40,000 \times 2.951424$$
$$= \$118,057$$

This amount may also be computed the long way by taking the present value of each year's cash flow as follows:

Year	Cash Flow	PV Factor	Present Value
1	$40,000	.800	$ 32,000
2	40,000	.640	25,600
3	40,000	.512	20,480
4	40,000	.410	16,384
5	40,000	.328	13,107
6	40,000	.262	10,486
		2.952	$118,057

The sum of the present value factors for the six periods is the same with rounding as the computed factor for the six-year annuity. The present values computed under either method are the same. As with other present value calculations, the use of a calculator will be more efficient and will give more accurate answers than will use of the tables. A set of tables is given in Appendix B to this chapter.

APPENDIX B
Present Value Tables

The present value of $1 shown in Illustration 15–9 gives the present value of an amount received n periods in the future. It is computed using the equation $(1 + d)^{-n}$ as discussed in the chapter.

For example, to find the present value of $20,000 received 11 years from now at a discount of 16 percent, look over the 11-year row to the 16 percent column and find the relevant factor, .195. Multiply the $20,000 by this factor to obtain the present value of $3,900.

If you perform this same computation with a calculator, you will obtain the somewhat more precise answer of $3,908. The difference is due to rounding.

The present value of an annuity is the value of a series of equal periodic payments discounted at a stated rate. Illustration 15–10 gives a set of factors for present values of an annuity.

For example, to find the present value of a series of nine annual payments of $5,000 each at a discount rate of 18 percent, look across the nine-year row to the 18 percent column and find the factor, 4.303. Multiply the $5,000 by the 4.303 to obtain the present value of those future payments, $21,515.

Illustration 15–11 provides the net present values for the text problems that are based on the recognition of inflation in the cash flow analysis.

Illustration 15-9   **Present Value of $1**

Year	8%	10%	12%	14%	15%	16%	18%	20%	22%	24%
1	.926	.909	.893	.877	.870	.862	.847	.833	.820	.806
2	.857	.826	.797	.769	.756	.743	.718	.694	.672	.650
3	.794	.751	.712	.675	.658	.641	.609	.579	.551	.524
4	.735	.683	.636	.592	.572	.552	.516	.482	.451	.423
5	.681	.621	.567	.519	.497	.476	.437	.402	.370	.341
6	.630	.564	.507	.456	.432	.410	.370	.335	.303	.275
7	.583	.513	.452	.400	.376	.354	.314	.279	.249	.222
8	.540	.467	.404	.351	.327	.305	.266	.233	.204	.179
9	.500	.424	.361	.308	.284	.263	.225	.194	.167	.144
10	.463	.386	.322	.270	.247	.227	.191	.162	.137	.116
11	.429	.350	.287	.237	.215	.195	.162	.135	.112	.094
12	.397	.319	.257	.208	.187	.168	.137	.112	.092	.076
13	.368	.290	.229	.182	.163	.145	.116	.093	.075	.061
14	.340	.263	.205	.160	.141	.125	.099	.078	.062	.049
15	.315	.239	.183	.140	.123	.108	.084	.065	.051	.040

Year	25%	26%	28%	30%	32%	34%	35%	36%	38%	40%
1	.800	.794	.781	.769	.758	.746	.741	.735	.725	.714
2	.640	.630	.610	.592	.574	.557	.549	.541	.525	.510
3	.512	.500	.477	.455	.435	.416	.406	.398	.381	.364
4	.410	.397	.373	.350	.329	.310	.301	.292	.276	.260
5	.328	.315	.291	.269	.250	.231	.223	.215	.200	.186
6	.262	.250	.227	.207	.189	.173	.165	.158	.145	.133
7	.210	.198	.178	.159	.143	.129	.122	.116	.105	.095
8	.168	.157	.139	.123	.108	.096	.091	.085	.076	.068
9	.134	.125	.108	.094	.082	.072	.067	.063	.055	.048
10	.107	.099	.085	.073	.062	.054	.050	.046	.040	.035
11	.086	.079	.066	.056	.047	.040	.037	.034	.029	.025
12	.069	.062	.052	.043	.036	.030	.027	.025	.021	.018
13	.055	.050	.040	.033	.027	.022	.020	.018	.015	.013
14	.044	.039	.032	.025	.021	.017	.015	.014	.011	.009
15	.035	.031	.025	.020	.016	.012	.011	.010	.008	.007

Illustration 15-10   **Present Value of an Annuity**

Year	8%	10%	12%	14%	15%	16%	18%	20%	22%	24%
1	.926	.909	.893	.877	.870	.862	.847	.833	.820	.806
2	1.783	1.736	1.690	1.647	1.626	1.605	1.566	1.528	1.492	1.457
3	2.577	2.487	2.402	2.322	2.283	2.246	2.174	2.106	2.042	1.981
4	3.312	3.170	3.037	2.914	2.855	2.798	2.690	2.589	2.494	2.404
5	3.993	3.791	3.605	3.433	3.352	3.274	3.127	2.991	2.864	2.745
6	4.623	4.355	4.111	3.889	3.784	3.685	3.498	3.326	3.167	3.020
7	5.206	4.868	4.564	4.288	4.160	4.039	3.812	3.605	3.416	3.242
8	5.747	5.335	4.968	4.639	4.487	4.344	4.078	3.837	3.619	3.421
9	6.247	5.759	5.328	4.946	4.772	4.607	4.303	4.031	3.786	3.566
10	6.710	6.145	5.650	5.216	5.019	4.833	4.494	4.192	3.923	3.682
11	7.139	6.495	5.938	5.453	5.234	5.029	4.656	4.327	4.035	3.776
12	7.536	6.814	6.194	5.660	5.421	5.197	4.793	4.439	4.127	3.851
13	7.904	7.103	6.424	5.842	5.583	5.342	4.910	4.533	4.203	3.912
14	8.244	7.367	6.628	6.002	5.724	5.468	5.008	4.611	4.265	3.962
15	8.559	7.606	6.811	6.142	5.847	5.575	5.092	4.675	4.315	4.001

Year	25%	26%	28%	30%	32%	34%	35%	36%	38%	40%
1	.800	.794	.781	.769	.758	.746	.741	.735	.725	.714
2	1.440	1.424	1.392	1.361	1.331	1.303	1.289	1.276	1.250	1.224
3	1.952	1.923	1.868	1.816	1.766	1.719	1.696	1.673	1.630	1.589
4	2.362	2.320	2.241	2.166	2.096	2.029	1.997	1.966	1.906	1.849
5	2.689	2.635	2.532	2.436	2.345	2.260	2.220	2.181	2.106	2.035
6	2.951	2.885	2.759	2.643	2.534	2.433	2.385	2.339	2.251	2.168
7	3.161	3.083	2.937	2.802	2.677	2.562	2.508	2.455	2.355	2.263
8	3.329	3.241	3.076	2.925	2.786	2.658	2.598	2.540	2.432	2.331
9	3.463	3.366	3.184	3.019	2.868	2.730	2.665	2.603	2.487	2.379
10	3.571	3.465	3.269	3.092	2.930	2.784	2.715	2.649	2.527	2.414
11	3.656	3.543	3.335	3.147	2.978	2.824	2.752	2.683	2.555	2.438
12	3.725	3.606	3.387	3.190	3.013	2.853	2.779	2.708	2.576	2,456
13	3.780	3.656	3.427	3.223	3.040	2.876	2.799	2.727	2.592	2.469
14	3.824	3.695	3.459	3.249	3.061	2.892	2.814	2.740	2.603	2.478
15	3.859	3.726	3.483	3.268	3.076	2.905	2.825	2.750	2.611	2.484

Illustration 15-11   **Present Value Tables for Inflation Problems**

YEAR	18.80%	20.96%	21.90%	23.20%	26.50%	28.80%	31.76%	39.08%
1	.842	.827	.820	.812	.791	.776	.759	.719
2	.709	.683	.673	.659	.625	.603	.576	.517
3	.596	.565	.552	.535	.494	.468	.437	.372
4	.502	.467	.453	.434	.391	.363	.332	.267
5	.423	.386	.372	.352	.309	.282	.252	.192
6	.356	.319	.305	.286	.244	.219	.191	.138
7	.299	.264	.250	.232	.193	.170	.145	.099
8	.252	.218	.205	.188	.153	.132	.110	.071
9	.212	.180	.168	.153	.121	.103	.084	.051
10	.179	.149	.138	.124	.095	.080	.063	.037
11	.150	.123	.113	.101	.075	.062	.048	.027
12	.127	.102	.093	.082	.060	.048	.037	.019
13	.107	.084	.076	.066	.047	.037	.028	.014
14	.090	.070	.062	.054	.037	.029	.021	.010
15	.075	.058	.051	.044	.029	.022	.016	.008

QUESTIONS

15-1. What are the two most important factors the accountant must estimate in the capital investment decision?

15-2. What is meant by the *time value of money?*

15-3. Given two projects with equal cash flows but different timings, how can we determine which (if either) project should be selected for investment.

15-4. What are the four types of cash flows related to a capital investment and why do we consider them separately?

15-5. For computing the depreciation tax shield, you conclude that either a five- or seven-year life for the asset is appropriate. Which life should you use for the computations? Why?

15-6. Fatigue Corporation has a division operating at a $200,000 cash loss per year. The company cannot dispose of the division due to certain contractual arrangements it has made that require continued operation of the division. However, Fatigue has just received a proposal to invest in some new equipment with an estimated operating life of 10 years for the division at a cost of $150,000. If the equipment is purchased, the division will operate at a $40,000 cash loss per year. Should Fatigue Corp. consider acquisition of the equipment? Why or why not?

15-7. How do tax policies provide an incentive for capital investment?

15-8. Is depreciation included in the computation of net present value? Explain.

15-9. "Every project should bear its fair share of all of the costs of the company. To do otherwise would make present operations subsidize new projects." Comment.

15-10. Regardless of depreciation methods used, the total tax deduction for depreciation is the same. Why then would one be concerned about the depreciation method for capital investment analysis?

15-11. How can we express the relationship of the desired real return to capital (r) and the inflation rate (i) that is used to discount nominal project cash flows under conditions of inflation?

15-12. Why might inflation be a disincentive to investment? What impact might inflation have on the present value of future cash flows and the future tax shield from the original investment?

15-13. Why could the investment in working capital increase over a project's life under conditions of inflation while inventory values (under LIFO) would not?

EXERCISES

15-14. Present Value of Cash Flows[2]

(L.O.1)

A city government is considering investing in street reconstruction that will require outlays as follows:

Year	Item	Amount
0	Engineering studies	$ 50,000
1	Project initiation	175,000
2	Project construction	850,000

---

[2] Refer to Appendix B of this chapter for present value tables.

Required:

Compute the net present value of these cash outlays if the appropriate discount rate is 10 percent.

15–15. Present Value of Cash Flows
(L.O.1)

Vale University is considering investment in an addition to the campus bookstore that is expected to return the following cash flows:

Year	Net Cash Flow
1	$35,000
2	32,000
3	40,000
4	40,000
5	50,000

This schedule includes all cash flows from the project. The project will require an immediate cash outlay of $130,000. The university is tax exempt, therefore no taxes need be considered.

Required:

a. What is the net present value of the project if the appropriate discount rate is 20 percent?

b. What is the net present value of the project if the appropriate discount rate is 12 percent?

15–16. Effects of Inflation
(L.O.3)

Refer to the data in exercise 15–15.

a. What is the net present value of the project if the inflation rate is 10 percent and the discount rate under no inflation is 12 percent? (Hint: Inflation affects both cash flows and the nominal rate of interest.)

b. Compare your answer in (*a*) to the result you got in part (*b*) of exercise 15–15. Explain why these two answers are the same (or different).

15–17. Present Value of Cash Flows
(L.O.1)

KPIV Television is considering investment in a new show that is expected to return the following cash flows from syndication:

Year	Net Cash Flow ($000 omitted)
1	$1,500
2	1,700
3	2,400
4	2,000
5	1,200

This schedule includes all cash flows from the project. The project will require an immediate cash outlay at Time 0 of $5 million. KPIV is tax exempt.

Required:

a. Complete the following schedule to determine the net present value of the project if the appropriate discount rate is 25 percent.

	Time 0	Year 1	2	3	4	5
Investment flows: Investment						
Operating flows: Net cash flows						
Total cash flows PV factor: 25%	1.000	.800	.640	.512	.410	.328
Present values						
Net PV of project:						

b. Complete the following net present value schedule for the project if the appropriate discount rate is 20 percent.

	Time 0	Year 1	2	3	4	5
Investment flows: Investment						
Operating flows: Net cash flows						
Total cash flows PV factor: 20%						
Present values						
Net PV of project:						

15–18. Effects of Inflation on Cash Flows
(L.O.3)

Refer to the cash flow data in exercise 15–17 and adjust as indicated below. Complete the following schedule to determine the net present value of the project if the inflation rate is 6 percent and the *no-inflation* discount rate is 15 percent. (Hint: Inflation affects both cash flows and the nominal rate of interest.)

KPIV Television

	Time 0	Year 1	2	3	4	5
Investment flows: Investment						
Operating flows: Net cash flows						
Total cash flows PV factor						
Present values						
Net PV of project:						

Calculations:

Nominal rate =

15–19. Effects of Inflation on Cash Flows
(L.O.3)

Refer to exercise 15–18. Would your answer be different if you had used real (no-inflation) cash flows and discount rate instead of the nominal amounts in 15–18?

Illustration 15–12

Schedule for Depreciation Tax Shield Calculations (for exercises 15-20 to 15-24)

Year	Depreciation	Tax Shield at __%	Present Value Factor	Present Value
1				
2				
3				
4				
5	_____	_____		_____
Totals	======	======		======

Net present value of tax shield: _____

Refer to Illustration 15–12 above to compute the present value of depreciation tax shields.

15–20. Compute Present Value of Tax Shield
(L.O.2)

The Financial Press Co. plans to acquire desktop publishing equipment at a cost of $200,000 that will be depreciated for tax purposes as follows: Year 1, $40,000; Year 2, $70,000; and $30,000 per year in each of Years 3–5. A 22 percent discount rate is appropriate for this asset, and the company's tax rate is 40 percent.

Required:

a. Compute the present value of the tax shield resulting from depreciation. Refer to Illustration 15–12 for format.

b. Compute the present value of the tax shield from depreciation assuming straight-time depreciation ($40,000 per year). Refer to Illustration 15–12 for format.

15–21. Present Value of Depreciation Tax Shield under Inflation
(L.O.2, L.O.3)

Refer to the data in exercise 15–20.

Required:

a. Using the accelerated tax depreciation deductions in exercise 15–20, what is the present value of the tax shield if the inflation rate is 8 percent and the no-inflation discount rate is 22 percent?

b. What is the present value of the tax shield if the inflation rate is 14 percent and the no-inflation discount rate is 22 percent?

c. What happens to the net present value of the tax shield as the inflation rate increases?

15–22. Present Value of Tax Shield
(L.O.2)

A company plans to acquire an asset at a cost of $750,000 that will be depreciated for tax purposes as follows: Year 1, $210,000; Year 2, $300,000; and $80,000 per year in each of Years 3–5. A 15 percent discount rate is appropriate for this asset, and the company's tax rate is 35 percent.

Required:

Compute the present value of the tax shield. Refer to Illustration 15–12 for format.

15–23. Present Value of Tax Shield
(L.O.2)

Refer to the data in exercise 15–22. Compute the present value of the tax shield from depreciation assuming the asset qualifies for straight-line depreciation ($150,000 per year). Refer to Illustration 15–12 for format.

15–24. Present Value of Tax Shield under Inflation
(L.O.2, L.O.3)

Refer to the data in exercise 15–22. The no-inflation discount rate is 15 percent. Using the tax depreciation deductions in exercise 15–22, what is the present value of the tax shield if the inflation rate is 6 percent. Refer to Illustration 15–12 for format.

15–25. Present Value of Cash Flows under Inflation
(L.O.3)

A company has concluded that its cost of capital is 8 percent in real terms. The company is considering an investment in a project having annual cash flows (before taxes and inflation) of $36,000 per year for five years. At disinvestment, the costs of disposal will equal any liquidation value of the project. No additional working capital is required for the project. The project costs $120,000 and will be depreciated for tax purposes over five years as follows: Year 1, 15 percent of the cost; Year 2, 22 percent; and 21 percent per year in each of Years 3–5. The company's marginal tax rate is 40 percent.

Required:

a. Assuming no inflation, complete the table below to compute the net present value of this project.

	Time 0	Year 1	Year 2	Year 3	Year 4	Year 5
Investment flows:						
New equipment	(a.)					
Operating flows:						
Cash flows		b.	b.	b.	b.	b.
Tax shield:						
Depreciation		c.	d.	e.	e.	e.
Total cash flows						
PV factor (8%)						
Present values						
Net PV of project:						

b. If inflation is expected to be 12 percent, what is the present value of the project? Refer to Illustration 15–11 for present value tables under inflation. (Hint: Inflation affects both cash flows and the nominal rate of interest.)

15–26. Present Value Analysis in Nonprofit Organizations
(L.O.4)

The Oakland Naval Shipyard bought machine 1 on March 5, Year 1, for $5,000 cash. The estimated salvage was $200, and the estimated life was 11 years. On March 5, Year 2, the company learned that it could purchase a different machine for $8,000 cash. The new machine would save the company an estimated $250 per year compared to machine 1. The new machine would have no estimated salvage value and an estimated life of 10 years. The company could get $3,000 for machine 1 on March 5, Year 2. As a government agency, the shipyard pays no taxes.

Required:

a. Which of the following calculations would best assist the company in deciding whether to purchase the new machine?
   (1) Present value of $250 savings per year + $3,000 − $8,000.
   (2) Present value of $250 savings per year − $8,000.
   (3) Present value of $250 savings per year + $3,000 − $8,000 − $5,000.
   (4) Present value of $250 savings per year + $3,000 − $8,000 − $4,750.

b. Calculate the net present value of the purchase of the new machine using differential costs. Assume a 12 percent discount rate. (Refer to Illustration 15–10, Appendix B, for annuity factors.)

c. Should the Oakland Naval Shipyard invest in the new machine?

15–27. Present Value Analysis in Nonprofit Organizations
(L.O.4)

The Complete Cure Hospital is considering buying laboratory equipment with an estimated life of seven years, so they will not have to use outsiders' laboratories for certain types of laboratory work. All of the cash flows affected by the decision are listed below. (The hospital is a nonprofit organization that does not pay taxes.)

Investment outflows at Time 0	$2,000,000
Periodic operating flows:	
Annual cash savings because outside laboratories are not used	800,000
Additional cash outflow for people and supplies to operate the equipment	100,000
Disinvestment flows:	
Salvage value after seven years, which is the estimated life of this project	200,000
Discount rate:	10%

Required:

Calculate the net present value of this decision using the following schedule. Should the hospital buy the equipment?

	Time 0	Year 1	2	. . . 7
Investment flows				
Periodic operating flows:				
Annual cash savings				
Additional cash outflow				
Disinvestment flows	_____	_____	_____	. . . _____
Net annual cash flow				
Present value factor (10%)	_____	_____	_____	. . . _____
Present values	_____	_____	_____	. . . _____
Net present value	=====			

15–28. Impact of Inflation on Net Present Value in Nonprofit Organizations
(L.O.3, L.O.4)

Refer to the data in exercise 15–27. Complete the following schedule to calculate the net present value if the real interest rate is 10 percent and inflation is expected to be 8 percent per year. Refer to Illustration 15–11 for present value tables under inflation. (Hint: Inflation affects both cash flows and the nominal rate of interest.)

	Time 0	Year 1	2	. . . 7
Net annual cash flow				
Present value factor	_____	_____	_____	. . . _____
Present values	_____	_____	_____	. . . _____
Net present value	=====			

PROBLEMS

15–29. Compute Present Values

You are considering the purchase of a truck. If you purchase a truck with a standard gasoline engine, you expect an average of 20 miles per gallon. If you purchase a diesel engine, you expect an average of 30 miles per gallon. You expect to drive 20,000 miles per year and keep the truck for four years. Gasoline costs $1.20 per gallon, and diesel fuel costs $1.25 per gallon. The diesel engine will cost $800 more than the standard gasoline engine. However, when you trade the truck in at the end of four years, it will be worth $150 more if it is equipped with a diesel engine. You estimate that maintenance costs would be $400 per year for both engines. Your before-tax cost of capital is 14 percent. (Ignore taxes.)

Required:

Which model would you purchase, the truck with the diesel or gasoline engine? Why? (Show supporting computations using differential cash flows.)

15–30. Sensitivity Analysis

Refer to the data in problem 15–29.

Required:

Would your answer change for the following situations?

a. The number of miles driven will be 10,000 miles per year. (All other data are the same.)

b. The number of miles driven will be 30,000 miles per year. (All other data are the same.)

15–31. Estimating Cash Flows in a Nonprofit Organization

Edmonton Machine Shop, a government vehicle repair shop, purchased a special purpose machine on January 1, Year 0. On December 31, Year 0, the company can purchase a more modern machine for $800,000. The new machine would be able to increase production by 25,000 service units per year. Shop management estimates the additional 25,000 service units can be utilized and will *not* affect the current charge of $8 per service unit. Edmonton pays no taxes. Other information related to the two machines is as follows:

	Old Machine	New Machine
Remaining useful life	5 years	5 years
Book value on December 31, Year 0	$250,000	$800,000
Salvage value on December 31, Year 0	200,000	n.a.
Salvage value on December 31, Year 5	–0–	100,000
Annual straight-line depreciation	50,000	140,000
Revenue per service unit	8.00	8.00
Variable cost per unit	4.00	4.75
Fixed cost per year (does not include depreciation on machine)	70,000	70,000
Cost to install new machine		8,000
Expected service units performed per year	75,000	100,000

Required:

a. Complete the following schedule of differential costs associated with the potential purchase of the new machine.

	Year					
	0	**1**	**2**	**3**	**4**	**5**
Investment:						
New equipment	(a.)					
Installation costs	(b.)					
Old equipment salvage	c.					
Periodic operating flows:						
Differential contribution from additional units		d.	d.	d.	d.	d.
Differential costs from existing units		(e.)	(e.)	(e.)	(e.)	(e.)
Disinvestment flows:						
New equipment salvage						f.
Total cash flows:	(g.)	h.	h.	h.	h.	i.
PV factor at 20%	1.000	.833	.694	.579	.482	.402
Present values	(j.)	k.	l.	m.	n.	o.
Net present value of project:	p.					
Calculations:						
Differential contribution from additional units:						
Differential costs from existing units:						

b. Based on a discount rate of 20 percent, recommend whether or not to purchase the new machine.

15–32. Compute Net Present Value

Essen Manufacturing Company is evaluating a proposal to purchase a new drill press as a replacement for a less efficient machine presently in use. The cost of the new equipment in Time 0 including delivery and installation, is $200,000. If the equipment is purchased, Essen will incur costs of $5,000 to remove the present equipment and revamp its facilities.

Depreciation for tax purposes will be allowed as follows: Year 1, $40,000; Year 2, $70,000; and $30,000 per year in each of Years 3–5. The existing equipment has a book and tax value of $100,000 and a remaining useful life of 10 years. However, the present equipment could be sold for only $40,000. The old equipment is being depreciated for book and tax purposes using the straight-line method over its actual life.

Management has provided you with the following comparative manufacturing cost data:

	Present Equipment	New Equipment
Annual capacity	400,000 units	400,000 units
Annual costs:		
Labor	$30,000	$25,000
Depreciation	10,000	14,000
Other (all cash)	48,000	20,000
Total annual costs	$88,000	$59,000

The existing equipment is expected to have no salvage value. The new equipment is expected to have a salvage value of $60,000 at the end of 10 years, which will be taxable. No changes in working capital are required with the purchase of the new equipment. The sales force does not expect any changes in volume of sales over the next 10 years. The company's cost of capital is 15 percent, and its tax rate is 45 percent.

Required:

a. Calculate the equipment removal costs net of tax effects.

b. Complete a depreciation schedule like the one in Illustration 15–12.

c. Compute the foregone tax benefits of the old equipment.

d. Calculate the cash inflow, net of taxes, from the sale of the new equipment in Year 10.

e. Calculate the tax benefit arising from the loss on the old equipment.

f. Compute the annual differential cash flows arising from the investment in Years 1–10.

g. Complete the following schedule and compute the net present value of the project.

	Time 0	Year 1	Year 2	. . . 9	10
Investment flows:					
Equipment					
Removal					
Salvage of old equipment					
Tax benefit of loss on old equipment					
Periodic operating flows					
Tax shield:					
New equipment					
Year 1: 40,000 × .45					
Year 2: 70,000 × .45					
Years 3, 4, 5: 30,000 × .45					
Old equipment (foregone when salvaged)					
Disinvestment:					
Proceeds of disposal					
Tax on gain					
Cash flows					
15% PV factor		.870	.756	284	.247
Present values				. . .	
Net present value					

15–33. Impact of Inflation on Net Present Value

Management of Essen Manufacturing Company (problem 15–32) received your report on the estimated net present value of the new equipment. (All numbers in 15–32 assumed no inflation.) However, management is disturbed about their economist's report, which indicates an expected inflation rate of 6 percent over the next 10 years.

Required:

a. Calculate the new nominal interest rate.

b. Prepare a schedule showing how inflation would affect annual operating flows.

c. Prepare a report indicating how this expectation would affect your computed net present values. Show supporting computations in good form.

15–34. Assess Net Present Value of Training Costs

MacDonald & Company operates a diversified company with several operating divisions. Division M has consistently shown losses. Management is considering a proposal to obtain training for division M employees that is designed to reduce labor and other operating costs.

The latest division income statement appears as follows (all dollar amounts in this problem have 000 omitted):

Revenues		$ 4,500
Costs:		
Direct materials	$1,250	
Direct labor	1,400	
Factory overhead:		
Indirect materials	200	
Indirect labor	350	
Utilities, taxes, etc.	600	
Depreciation	890	
Miscellaneous	120	
Division selling costs	450	
Division administrative costs	380	
Total costs		5,640
Division contribution		$(1,140)

The costs are expected to continue in the future unless the training is obtained.

With the training, direct labor is expected to be reduced by 55 percent, and other costs are expected to be reduced by $275 per year. These cost savings will continue for 10 years. The training will cost $5,000 and can be deducted for tax purposes in the year it is obtained. Working capital can be reduced by $110 if the new training is purchased.

Required:

If the company's cost of capital is 12 percent and its marginal tax rate is 40 percent, determine whether the new training should be purchased. Show supporting computations.

15–35. Make-or-Buy Decision

Company Z has contracted to supply a governmental agency with 50,000 units of a product each year for the next five years. A certain component of this product can either be manufactured by Company Z or purchased from X Corporation, which will enter into a subcontract for 50,000 units of the component each year for five years at a price of $1.50 per unit. These alternative methods of procurement are regarded as equally desirable, except for costs.

If Company Z decides to manufacture the component, it expects the following to occur: (No tax rate is needed to solve this problem because all cash flows are subject to the same tax rate.)

1. A special-purpose machine costing $30,000 per year for five years will be rented. No other equipment or working capital will be required. (These payments are deducted in the year paid, for tax purposes.)

2. The manufacturing operation will require 1,000 square feet of productive floor space. This space is available in a building owned by Company Z and will not be needed for any other purpose in the foreseeable future. The costs of maintaining this building (including repairs, utilities, taxes, and depreciation) amount to $2 per square foot of productive floor space per year.

3. Variable manufacturing costs—materials, direct labor, and so forth—are estimated to be 50 cents a unit.

4. Fixed factory costs other than those mentioned in 1 and 2—such as supervision and so forth—are estimated at $20,000 a year.

5. Company Z uses an after-tax discount rate of 20 percent.

Required:

Should Company Z make the component or buy it from X Corporation? (Ignore taxes because all cash flows are subject to the same rate.)

15–36. Estimate Relevant Cash Flows

Mariposa Recreational Products Corporation produces skateboards for street use. As a result of recent promotion of the sport, the company is considering expanding its facilities to increase production and sales by 35,000 units per year. The expansion will require an immediate outlay of $740,000 for the specialized equipment required for skateboard assembly. The company estimates the useful life of the project will be seven years. The company uses straight-line depreciation for book purposes but will depreciate for tax purposes as follows: Year 1, $140,000; Year 2, $240,000; and Years 3–5, $120,000 per year. Once the equipment is installed, it has no salvage value.

The project requires an estimated cash and accounts receivable balance of $10,000. The project will also require $17,000 in working inventory. All $27,000 working capital will be liquidated at the end of the last year of the project life.

The assembled skateboards sell for $29 wholesale each. The cost of materials for unassembled skateboards is $17 per kit, including shipping. In addition to the $17 cost of the unassembled parts, there is a cost of $6.50 per kit for assembly labor, power, and other variable overhead. All variable overhead is included in the $6.50 charge, and all such variable overhead requires current cash outlays.

The existing fixed overhead of the factory and equipment amounts to $162,857, including the book depreciation, for financial reporting purposes, on the new equipment. Except for the equipment depreciation, all of these fixed overhead items require current cash outlays. All fixed overhead is included in this amount.

A 12 percent rate is applicable for investment evaluation purposes. The tax rate applicable to the project income is 40 percent.

Required:

Prepare a schedule showing the net present value for the project with supporting details.

15–37. Estimate Relevant Cash Flows

Wyle Company is considering a proposal to acquire new manufacturing equipment. The new equipment has the same capacity as the current equipment but will provide operating efficiencies in direct and indirect labor, direct material usage, indirect supplies, and power. Consequently, the savings in operating costs are estimated at $150,000 annually. Only 60 percent of the estimated annual savings can be obtained in the first year.

The new equipment will cost $300,000. Wyle will incur a one-time cost of $30,000 to transfer the production activities from the old equipment to the new equipment. These costs will be deductible for tax purposes in Year 1.

The current equipment has been fully depreciated for book and tax purposes. Wyle Company could receive $5,000 net of removal costs if it elected to buy the new equipment and dispose of its current equipment at this time.

Wyle currently leases its manufacturing plant. The annual lease payments are $60,000. The lease, which will have five years remaining when the equipment installation would begin, is not renewable. Wyle Company would be required to remove any equipment in the plant at the end of the lease. The cost of equipment removal is expected to equal the salvage value of either the old or new equipment at the time of removal.

The asset must be depreciated for tax purposes as follows: Year 1, $60,000; Year 2, $120,000; Years 3–5, $40,000 per year. Any gain or loss on disposal is taxed at ordinary income tax rates.

The company is subject to a 40 percent income tax rate and requires an after-tax return of at least 12 percent on any investment.

Required:

a. Calculate the differential after-tax cash flows for Wyle Company's proposal to acquire the new manufacturing equipment.

b. Calculate the net present value of Wyle Company's proposal to acquire the new manufacturing equipment.

(CMA adapted)

15–38. Compute After-Tax Net Present Value

World of Chocolate, Inc., is considering the purchase of a newer, more efficient cookie-making machine. If purchased, the new machine would be acquired on January 2, Year 1. World of Chocolate expects to sell 300,000 dozen cookies in each of the next five years. The selling price of the cookies is expected to average $0.50 per dozen.

World of Chocolate, Inc., has two options: (1) continue to operate the old machine purchased two years ago or (2) sell the old machine and purchase the new machine. The following information has been assembled to help decide which option is more desirable.

	Old Machine	New Machine
Original cost of machine at acquisition	$80,000	$120,000
Useful life from date of acquisition	7 years	5 years
Expected annual cash operating expenses:		
Variable cost per dozen	$0.20	$0.14
Total fixed costs	15,000	14,000

Depreciation:

Age of Equipment	Tax Depreciation (Percent)
1	15%
2	25
3	20
4	20
5	20

Estimated cash value of machines:		
January 2, Year 1	40,000	120,000
December 31, Year 5	7,000	20,000

World of Chocolates, Inc., is subject to an income tax rate of 40 percent on all income.

Required:

Use the net present value method to determine whether World of Chocolate, Inc., should retain the old machine or acquire the new machine. World of Chocolate, Inc., requires an after-tax return of 16%.

15–39. Capital Investment Analysis under Inflation

Management of Excello Retail Corporation is considering the purchase of energy-saving equipment costing $250,000.

The equipment has an expected useful life of seven years, at which time it will have no salvage value. The equipment will be depreciated for tax purposes over five years as follows: Year 1, $50,000; Year 2, $80,000; Years 3–5, $40,000 per year.

Present energy costs for the activities related to this equipment are $120,000 per year before taxes. The equipment will save 60 percent of these costs.

Working capital will be reduced by an estimated 5 percent of the initial year's after-tax cash energy cost savings. The working capital reduction will be an additional 5 percent each year with inflation in future years until Year 7, when it is assumed that the company will have to restore the entire working capital savings.

The expected inflation rate is 5 percent per year. The company's marginal tax rate is 40 percent, and its nominal cost of capital is 18.80 percent, after considering expected inflation of 5 percent per year.

Required:

Compute the net present value of the project.

15–40. Capital Investment Analysis under Inflation with Investment Tax Credit

Each division of Catix Company has the authority to make capital expenditures up to $200,000 without approval of the corporate headquarters. The corporate controller has determined that the cost of capital for Catix Corporation is 12 percent. This rate does not include an allowance for inflation, which is expected to occur at an average rate of 8 percent each year. Catix pays income taxes at the rate of 40 percent.

The Electronic Division of Catix is considering the purchase of automated machinery for manufacture of its printed circuit boards. The divisional controller estimates that if the machine is purchased, two positions will be eliminated, yielding a cost savings for wages and employee benefits. However, the machine would require additional supplies and more power. The cost savings and additional costs in beginning of Year 1 prices are as follows:

Wages and employee benefits of the two positions eliminated ($25,000 each)	$50,000
Cost of additional supplies	3,000
Cost of additional power	10,000

The new machine would be purchased and installed at the beginning of Year 1 at a net cost of $80,000. If purchased, the machine would be depreciated for tax purposes as follows: Year 1, $16,000; Year 2, $28,000; Years 3–5, $12,000 each year. It would qualify for an investment tax credit of $8,000 in Year 1. The machine will become technologically obsolete in eight years and will have no salvage value at that time.

The Electronics Division compensates for inflation in capital expenditure analyses by adjusting the above cash flows for inflation, starting with end of Year 1 cash flows. The adjusted after-tax cash flows are then discounted using the appropriate discount rate. No changes are expected in working capital.

Required:

Prepare a schedule showing the expected future cash flows in nominal dollars. Also show the net present value of the project. (See Illustration 15–11 for present value factors under inflation.)

(CMA adapted)

15–41. Capital Investment Cash Flows with Research Credits

Microhard Development Corp. is working on a new spreadsheet program that can take a manager's ideas and convert them into cash flow analyses without the need to enter numerical data. The initial development costs of the project are estimated at $2.5 million. Marketing costs are estimated at $3.2 million. Ten percent of all development costs are subject to a research and development tax credit which is an immediate reduction in a company's income taxes.

Microhard expects that the project will return cash flows of $2.5 million in each of Years 1 and 2; $1.5 million in Year 3; $900,000 in Year 4; $700,000 in Year 5; and, $200,000 in Year 6.

Microhard can forestall the decline in cash flows by developing an enhancement to the program. Development costs of the enhancement would be $900,000 in each of Years 1 through 3. Marketing costs of $2 million would be required in Year 3 to promote the enhancement. If Microhard develops the enhancement, cash flows in

Years 1 and 2 would be the same. Year 3 cash flows would decline to $1.1 million because customers would wait for the enhancement. Cash flows in Years 4 and 5 would be $2.7 million each year, and $1,650,000 would be obtained in Year 6.

Microhard's marginal tax rate is 39 percent, and it uses a 20 percent hurdle rate. Development costs and marketing expenses are deductible when incurred.

Required:

Would the net present value of the spreadsheet program be greater with the enhancement?

15–42. Evaluate Capital Investment Cash Flows

Hammond Industries is a toy manufacturer that will have excess capacity at its single plant. Hammond's management is currently studying two alternative proposals that would utilize this excess capacity.

Proposal 1

Hammond has been approached by GloriToys, one of its competitors, to manufacture a partially completed doll. GloriToys, owner of the distribution rights for the doll, would finish the dolls in its plant and then market the dolls. The GloriToy doll would not compete directly with any of Hammond's products.

GloriToys would contract to purchase 5,000 unfinished dolls each month at a price of $7.50 each for Years 1 through 4. Hammond's estimated incremental cash outlays to manufacture the doll would be $250,000 per year during the four-year contract period. In addition, this alternative would require a $400,000 investment in manufacturing equipment in Time 0. The equipment would have no salvage value at the end of its useful life.

Proposal 2

Hammond is considering the production of a new stuffed toy to be added to its own product line. The new stuffed toy would be sold at $15 per unit, and the expected annual sales over the estimated six-year product life (19X4–19X9) for the toy is as follows:

Year	Annual Unit Sales
19X4	65,000
19X5	90,000
19X6	90,000
19X7	65,000
19X8	50,000
19X9	50,000

The variable unit manufacturing and selling costs are estimated to be $6 and $1, respectively, over this six-year period. The estimated annual incremental cash outlay for fixed costs would be $300,000. The manufacture and sale of the new stuffed toy would require a $700,000 investment in new manufacturing equipment. This equipment would have a salvage value of $50,000 at the end of the six-year period.

Additional information relative to a decision between the two proposals follows.

▼ Manufacturing equipment for either proposal would be placed in service during December 19X3, Time 0. Depreciation on the equipment would be recognized starting in 19X4. The allowable tax deduction for depreciation is:

Year 1	25%
Year 2	38
Year 3	37

▼ Hammond Industries is subject to a 30 percent income tax rate on all income.

▼ Hammond's management assumes that annual cash flows occur at the end of the year for evaluating capital investment proposals. Hammond uses a 15 percent after-tax discount rate.

Required:

Calculate the net present value at December 31, 19X3, of the estimated after-tax cash flows of Hammond Industries' proposal of:

a. Manufacturing unfinished dolls for GloriToys.

b. Manufacturing and selling a new stuffed toy to be added to its own product line.

15–43. Estimate Capital Investment Cash Flows with Investment Tax Credit

Beloit Company manufactures motorized utility equipment and trucks. Beloit's assembly department employs about 200 workers who are covered by a labor contract that will expire on December 31, 19X1. During negotiations with Beloit for a new contract, the union has presented a proposal covering the next four years (19X2–19X5). This proposal calls for an increase in wage rates of 15 percent over the life of the contract—an increase of $1 per hour at the beginning of 19X2 and an additional $0.50 per hour at the beginning of 19X4. Employee benefits will be 40 percent of regular wages (total wages exclusive of any overtime premium) under the terms of the union proposal. Management is concerned that the increase in labor costs will eliminate most or all of its profits.

In response to the union proposal, management wants to examine the possibility of automating the existing assembly department. Management is confident that the equipment could be acquired and installed in late 19X1 to be operational in January 19X2. It would operate for four years.

You have been asked to provide an economic analysis of the proposal to automate the existing assembly department based on the labor costs included in the union proposal. The controller has accumulated the following data for you:

▼ Sales revenues for the next four years are expected to be relatively stable.

▼ Production volume is uniform throughout the year. Currently, a total of 40,000 labor-hours are worked annually in the assembly department, of which 3,000 labor-hours are subject to an overtime premium of 50 percent of the wage rate.

▼ The wage rate under the current labor contract is $10 per hour, and employee benefits are 35 percent of regular hourly wages.

▼ The new equipment will be purchased and installed in the assembly department in December 19X1 at a cost of $1,500,000. The company will claim a 4 percent investment tax credit in the year the equipment is placed in service. For financial reporting, the equipment will be depreciated using the straight-line method over the four-year life. For tax purposes, this is three-year equipment and will be depreciated using the tax shield rates presented below:

Year 1	25%
Year 2	38
Year 3	37

▼ The labor-hours worked in the assembly department will be reduced to 15,000 annually with the new equipment. Overtime will be eliminated.

▼ Annual maintenance costs will increase by $6,000 with the new equipment.

▼ The existing facility can be sold for $800,000 at December 31, 19X5. However, if the assembly department is automated, the plant can then be sold for $1 million. The basis for tax purposes of the existing facility on December 31, 19X5, exclusive of the new equipment, will be $700,000, whether or not the assembly department is automated.

▼ Beloit Company is subject to a 40 percent income tax rate on all income.

▼ Management assumes annual cash flows occur at the end of the year for evaluating capital investment proposals. The company uses a 15 percent after-tax discount rate.

Required:

Based on the labor costs included in the union proposal, calculate the net present value at December 31, 19X1, of Beloit Company's proposal to automate the assembly department.

INTEGRATIVE CASES

15–44. Equipment Purchase and Maximum Price Decision

Transcontinental Oil Company has some oil properties that are now at the point where further production is not worthwhile without better equipment. Even with the better equipment, the properties would be economically productive for only six more years.

If Transcontinental Oil Company decides to buy the equipment, it will enter into a contract at Time 0 to purchase the equipment. The supplier of the equipment has made an initial offer of a contract that calls for a payment of $2 million. The company's management believes it can reduce this price by negotiating with the supplier. For tax purposes, 40 percent of the cost of the equipment could be deducted at the end of Year 1. This is true whether the amount paid is $2 million or some other amount. The remaining 60 percent would be depreciated on a straight-line basis over five years (Years 2–6).

The equipment purchase contract also has a provision that calls for the manufacturer of the equipment to do additional work at the end of Year 2. The contract specifies a payment of $1 million to be made at that time for this service. All of this Year 2 payment would be deductible for tax purposes at the end of Year 2.

Production expectations, prices of crude oil per barrel, and variable costs of production are as follows:

| | Expected Production | Per Barrel | |
Year	(barrels)	Price	Variable Costs
1	40,000	$18	$3
2	70,000	18	3
3	60,000	18	3
4	50,000	18	3
5	40,000	18	3
6	30,000	18	3

Both the prices per barrel of crude oil and variable costs are based on Time 0 prices. It is expected that the value of the properties at the end of Year 6 will be zero. The tax rate for the company is 40 percent.

Required:

a. Ignoring the effects of inflation and assuming a desired after-tax rate of return of 15 percent, should Transcontinental buy the equipment for $2 million?

b. What is the amount that Transcontinental would be willing to pay for the equipment to make the NPV of the project equal to zero?

15–45. Equipment Purchase with Inflation

Refer to the data in case 15–44. Suppose the after-tax rate of return of 15 percent is to be in *real* terms and the expected inflation rate is 8 percent per year. What would be the net present value of the equipment purchase? What is the amount Transcontinental would pay to make the NPV equal to zero?

15–46. Make-or-Buy— Liquid Chemical Co.[3]

Liquid Chemical Company manufactures products that require careful packing. The company has a special patented container lining made from a material known as GHL, and the firm operates a department especially to maintain its containers in good condition and to make new ones as needed.

Mr. Walsh, the general manager, believed the firm might save money and get equal service by buying its containers from an outside source. He approached Packages, Inc., and asked for a quotation from it. He also asked Mr. Dyer, his chief accountant for a statement of the cost of operating the container department.

Packages, Inc.'s quotation specified it would supply 3,000 new containers for $1,250,000 a year, the contract to run for a guaranteed term of five years and renewable from year to year thereafter. If the required quantity increased, the contract price would be increased proportionally. Additionally, and irrespective of whether the above contract was concluded or not, Packages, Inc., offered to perform routine maintenance on containers for $375,000 a year, on the same contract terms.

Mr. Walsh compared these figures with Mr. Dyer's cost figures for one year's container department operations. Those figures are as follows:

Materials		$ 700,000
Labor:		
Supervisor		50,000
Workers		450,000
Department overheads:		
Manager's salary	$ 80,000	
Rent on container department	45,000	
Depreciation of machinery	150,000	
Maintenance of machinery	36,000	
Other expenses	157,500	
		468,500
		1,668,500
Proportion of general administrative overheads		225,000
Total cost of department for year		$1,893,500

Walsh concluded that closing the department and entering into the contract offered by Packages, Inc., was optimal. However, he gave the manager of the department, Mr. Duffy, an opportunity to question this conclusion before he acted on it. Even if his department were closed, Duffy's own position was not in jeopardy. There are no net cash consequences for the firm of transferring Duffy to another position.

Mr. Duffy thought the matter over. The next morning he spoke to Mr. Walsh and said he thought there were a number of factors to consider before his department was closed. "For instance," he said, "what will you do with the machinery? It cost $1,200,000 four years ago, but you'd be lucky if you got $200,000 for it now, even though it's good for another five years. And then there's the stock of GHL that cost us $1 million. At the rate we're using it now, it'll last us another four years. Dyer's figure of $700,000 for materials includes $200,000 for GHL. We bought it for $5,000 a

[3] Adapted from a case by Professor David Solomons, Wharton School, University of Pennsylvania.

ton. Today's purchase price is $6,000. But you wouldn't have more than $4,000 a ton left if you sold it because of handling expenses.''

Walsh called Dyer in and put Duffy's points to him. Dyer said, ''I think my figures are pretty conclusive. We're paying $85,000 a year in rent for a warehouse for other corporate purposes. If we closed Duffy's department, we'd have all the warehouse space we need without renting.''

That's a good point,'' said Walsh. ''Moreover, I don't think we can find room for any of the workers elsewhere in the firm. I'd feel bound to give two of them a pension—$15,000 a year each, say.''

Duffy added, ''What about this $225,000 for general administrative overheads? You surely don't expect to sack anyone in the general office if I'm closed, do you?''

''Probably not,'' said Dyer, ''but someone has to pay for these costs. We can't ignore them when we look at an individual department, because if we do that with each department in turn, we shall finish up by convincing ourselves that directors, accountants, typists, stationery, and the like don't have to be paid for.''

''Well, I think we've thrashed this out pretty fully,'' said Walsh, ''but I've been considering the possibility of perhaps keeping on the maintenance work ourselves. What are your views on that, Duffy?''

''I don't know,'' said Duffy, ''but it's worth looking into. We shouldn't need any machinery for that, and I could hand the supervision over to the current supervisor, who earns $50,000 a year. You'd only need about one fifth of the workers, but you could avoid the pension costs. You wouldn't save any space, so I suppose the rent would be the same. I shouldn't think the other expenses would be more than $65,000 a year.'' ''What about materials?'' asked Walsh.

''We use 10 percent of the total on maintenance,'' Duffy replied.

''Well, I've told Packages, Inc., that I'd let them know my decision within a week,'' said Walsh. ''I'll let you know what I decide to do before I write to them.''

Assume the company has an after-tax cost of capital of 10 percent per year and uses an income tax rate of 40 percent for decisions like these. Depreciation for book and tax purposes is straight-line over 8 years. The machinery has a tax basis of $600,000. Any gain on the sale of machinery or the loss on GHL sales is taxed at 40 percent. Any GHL needed for Year 5 is purchased in Year 5.

Required:

a. What are the four alternatives implied in the case?

b. What action should be taken? Support your conclusion with a new present value analysis of all the mutually exclusive alternatives (assume a five-year time horizon).

c. What, if any, additional information do you think is necessary for a sound decision? Why?

CAPITAL INVESTMENT MODELS

LEARNING OBJECTIVES

1. To see the effects of constraints on capital investment decisions.

2. To understand alternative methods for evaluating capital projects.

3. To understand the role of sensitivity analysis on capital investment decisions.

4. To analyze the differences between leasing and borrowing-to-buy (Appendix).

This chapter expands our discussion of capital budgeting to cover the following topics:

1. The effects of capital budget constraints, which show ways of ranking projects that all have positive net present values but cannot all be accepted.
2. How the effect of the project on company risk and accounting earnings plays a role in making investment decisions.
3. How companies evaluate investments in highly risky projects.
4. Comparison of leasing and borrow-to-buy financing alternatives (Appendix).
5. The alternatives to net present value that companies use in making investment decisions.

We now examine alternative ways that management uses to select the projects it will undertake. Let's consider a set of five investment projects with net cash flows as indicated in Illustration 16–1.

EFFECT OF CONSTRAINTS ON CAPITAL INVESTMENT DECISIONS

Using a 15 percent discount rate, each project has a positive net present value. Therefore, if funds were available and if investment in one project did not exclude the possibility of investing in another project, all five projects would be chosen. However, there are often constraints on management's choice of projects.

For example, suppose management wanted to invest no more than $450,000 in these projects because of a shortage of managerial people to manage more than $450,000 of these investments. Which projects, if any, would it select? Or suppose that if Project B is selected, then Project C cannot be selected. Which project should then be chosen?

Illustration 16-1

Cash Flow Schedules for Alternative Projects (In thousands)

Year	Project A	B	C	D	E
0	$(425)	$(135)	$ (80)	$(170)	$ (90)
1	25	0	0	60	10
2	50	90	0	60	20
3	75	80	0	60	40
4	100	70	0	60	40
5	150	50	0	60	40
6	300	20	200	60	30
7	380	10	100	60	20
Totals	$ 655	$ 185	$220	$ 250	$110
Net present value (at 15%)	$ 88	$ 63	$ 44	$ 80	$ 23

Additional computations:
$88 = -\$425 + (\$25 \times 1.15^{-1}) + (\$50 \times 1.15^{-2}) + (\$75 \times 1.15^{-3}) + (\$100 \times 1.15^{-4}) + (\$150 \times 1.15^{-5}) + (\$300 \times 1.15^{-6}) + (\$380 \times 1.15^{-7})$;
$63 = -\$135 + (\$90 \times 1.15^{-2}) + (\$80 \times 1.15^{-3}) + (\$70 \times 1.15^{-4}) + (\$50 \times 1.15^{-5}) + (\$20 \times 1.15^{-6}) + (\$10 \times 1.15^{-7})$; and so forth.

When the amount to be invested in capital investment projects is limited, management usually considers the total net present values of all selected investments rather than the net present value of each investment alone. Although all of these projects have positive net present values, they must be ranked to decide which is more desirable if there are constraints on the amount that can be invested.

Net Present Value Index Method

Net Present Value Index Ratio of the net present value of a project to the funds invested in the project.

The **net present value index** is often used for ranking purposes. This approach relates the net present value of a project to the dollars invested in it. The index is computed by dividing the net present value of a project by the initial investment. In equation form, we have:

$$\text{Net present value index} = \frac{\text{Project net present value}}{\text{Investment in project}}$$

So, for Project A in Illustration 16–1, the net present value index is:

$$\frac{\$88}{\$425} = \underline{\underline{.21}}$$

The net present value indexes for the other projects are:

$$
\begin{array}{l}
\text{Project B } .47 = \$63 \div \$135 \\
\text{Project C } .55 = \$44 \div \$80 \\
\text{Project D } .47 = \$80 \div \$170 \\
\text{Project E } .26 = \$23 \div \$90
\end{array}
$$

For investment choice purposes, projects are ranked by the amount of their net present value index. The greater the index amount, the more desirable the investment.

If it is possible to fund each project in part rather than acquire the entire project, such as through partnership or joint venture arrangements, then by taking the projects in rank order, the maximum net present value could be obtained. Partial investments are common in real estate and natural resource projects. They are less common in manufacturing or other projects. Hence, the possibility of a partial investment may depend on the nature of the project.

In the example, the $450,000 is apportioned first to Project C, which costs $80,000 and has the greatest net present value index. Next selected are Project D, costing $170,000, and Project B, costing $135,000.

After making these three investments, $65,000 (that is, $450,000 − $80,000 − $135,000 − $170,000) is left for other projects. If we can fund a partial investment, we will invest the remaining $65,000 in Project E and obtain a 72.22 percent (that is, $65,000/$90,000) share in that project.

With this investment strategy, the net present value of the $450,000 investment is $203,611, which is the sum of the present values on Projects B through D plus 72.22 percent of the present value of Project E. No alternative strategy yields a higher net present value.

As a counter example, suppose we were to invest $425,000 in Project A and use the remaining $25,000 to acquire a 31.25 percent (that is, $25,000/$80,000) investment in Project C. The net present value from this combination is:

	Percent Acquired	Net Present Value
Project A	100.00%	$ 88,000
Project C	31.25	13,750 (that is, 31.25% × $44,000)
Total net present value		$101,750

This alternative offers a lower net present value than the one obtained using the present value index ranking method.

Indivisible Investments

Of course, it may not be possible to acquire a partial interest in Project E. If the projects cannot be subdivided, their appropriate ranking becomes more complex. It may not be possible to invest the full $450,000. Any funds not invested in these projects would be expected to earn the cost of capital rate and, hence, have no positive net present value. The optimal solution to the project rank ordering could no longer be based entirely on the net present value index. Rather, we would have to consider the total present value of all selected projects, however chosen.[1]

For the data in Illustration 16–1, the optimal ranking is to select Projects B, C, and D, which cost a total of $385,000 (total of $135,000 + $80,000 + $170,000). These three projects provide a combined net present value of $187,000 (which is the sum of $63,000 + $44,000 + $80,000). The uninvested funds of $65,000 (the net of $450,000 − $385,000) will earn a net present value of zero because they are presumed to earn the cost of capital and no more. No other combination of projects costing an aggregate of $450,000 or less will provide a greater net present value for the company when partial investment in projects is not possible. In this example, the ranking is identical to the net present value index ranking, but this will not always be the case.

Mutually Exclusive A situation where selection of one project precludes the selection of another.

In many cases, projects are **mutually exclusive.** That is, selecting one project precludes selecting another project. When this occurs, the project with the highest net present value is usually chosen. This selection technique is based on the assumption that unlimited capital is available. When investment funds are limited, net present value cannot be the sole basis of choice because selection of one project reduces the capital available for investment in other projects. The opportunity cost of the mutually exclusive project is, in part, the return that could be earned on the excluded project rather than the cost of capital for the company as a whole.

For example, if Projects B and C from Illustration 16–1 are mutually exclusive and if investment funds are not limited, then the company prefers Project B. Investing in Project B results in a net present value of $63,000, whereas Project C yields a net present value of only $44,000. The critical assumption here is that the company has no better alternatives for the

---

[1] The use of integer programming for this problem has been suggested in Richard H. Pettway, "Integer Programming in Capital Budgeting: A Note on Computations Experience," *Journal of Financial and Quantitative Analysis*, September 1973, pp. 665–72.

differential funds required for Project B. A comparison of differential investment and differential net present values shows the following:

	Project C	Project B	Differential
Initial cost	$80,000	$135,000	$55,000
Net present value	$44,000	$ 63,000	$19,000

The differential investment in Project B yields a differential net present value of $19,000. Now, if the differential $55,000 could be invested in another project (for example, a new Project F) with a net present value greater than $19,000, the company would be better off selecting both Project C and the new Project F.

For example, if Project F costs $55,000 and has a net present value of $22,000, by investing in Projects C and F the company obtains a net present value of $66,000 (which is the $44,000 from Project C plus $22,000 from Project F). This net present value is greater than the $63,000 from Project B. The increased present value is obtained with the same $135,000 investment.

Thus, when a company has limited capital and is unable to fund partial projects, the optimal set of projects is determined by considering the total net present value of all projects selected rather than the individual project net present values.

OTHER EVALUATION CONSIDERATIONS

Management considers factors other than net present values when making capital investment decisions. These factors may override the results of a pure present value analysis. We mention differences in the *riskiness* of projects, how well the project fits with other company projects, and the impact of projects on accounting income because these factors are frequently encountered by accountants.

Differences in Project Risk

There is often a correlation between the amount of risk a project entails and the return that can be earned from that project. If management uses net present values without adjustment for risk, high-risk projects with high expected returns may be the most commonly accepted. This outcome may be contrary to management intentions. Indeed, if management continues to accept riskier projects, overall company risk may increase. Its cost of capital will then increase to compensate lenders and investors for the greater risks. This will result in an increased hurdle rate.

Risk Premium Additional interest or other compensation required for risks in investments.

To avoid this problem, management may require a higher rate of return from riskier projects. This risk premium is determined by analyzing the characteristics of a specific project and relating them to the company's other assets.[2] Management must be aware of the trade-offs between risk and return and select projects that meet predetermined objectives for overall company risk.

---

[2] See, for example, Stephen A. Ross and Randolph W. Westerfield, *Corporate Finance* (St. Louis: Times Mirror/Mosby College Publishing, 1988).

Portfolio Considerations   Investing in capital assets requires consideration of how they will fit with a company's existing *portfolio of assets*. New assets may be used to diversify away some risk for a company just as diversification of a securities portfolio may be used to reduce risk for an investor. For example, a company may acquire companies in other industries to avoid the business-cycle, technological, and political risks associated with its own industry. That is one reason why conglomerate mergers have become quite popular. On the other hand, companies have found problems managing businesses in industries that are unfamiliar to them.

The ways in which a specific investment can enhance a company's overall asset structure is another aspect of the capital investment decision. For example, in recent years companies that are significant energy users have acquired energy companies to assure themselves of a reliable energy supply. Brokerage firms have been merged with other kinds of financial institutions, such as credit card companies and retail stores, to diversify the services they can offer to their customers. These considerations extend beyond the accountant's domain, but they are significant for evaluating whether capital investment projects meet management's objectives.

Effects on Income   Management considers accounting measures of income to evaluate organization performance and to measure compliance with contracts. For example, restrictive covenants in a loan agreement may require that a company maintain certain levels of working capital and retained earnings. Management will rarely select projects that have such an adverse effect on the working capital or other accounting numbers if, by so doing, the company no longer complies with contractual arrangements.

REAL WORLD APPLICATION*

Even successful and sophisticated companies make investments that turn out to be undesirable. For example, in the late 1970s, major oil companies were receiving high levels of cash flows due to rapid escalation in oil prices. There were few investment opportunities for finding profitable oil or gas fields. Moreover, the industry is very cyclical. For these reasons, company management made several major investments to diversify their companies. Arco purchased Anaconda Copper Co.; Exxon acquired Reliance Electric, a manufacturer of motors; Exxon started an office equipment business; Sohio purchased Kennecott Copper Co.; and Mobil acquired Montgomery Ward.

Unfortunately, none of these investments turned out to be profitable for the buyers. By the 1990s, all of the companies had disposed of these new businesses or had written off the investment. As part of one of the disposition announcements, the CEO of one of these companies stated: "We are disposing of our nonenergy investments so we can concentrate on the business which we know best."

* Source: Annual reports and *The Wall Street Journal*.

Management may also prefer to see growth in the income reported in the financial statements. In such cases, they will prefer projects that provide long-term growth over projects that show declining or level income trends.

For example, in Illustration 16–1, Project C has no net cash inflows for the first five years of its life. When depreciation is deducted from this zero cash flow to obtain net income for financial reporting, Project C shows net losses for its first five years. Management may decide to exclude Project C from consideration on this basis alone. To extend this example, a schedule of accounting income from each project is shown in Illustration 16–2. These accounting income data would be developed from sources other than those discussed in this chapter. As expected, Project C shows losses for the first five years.

Management may decide to select Project C in spite of the accounting losses because it yields a positive net present value, as shown in Illustration 16–1. But management would be unlikely to place all of its capital investment funds in ventures like Project C unless the company had other sources of income, was particularly adventurous, or if management had incentives to maximize long-run payoffs instead of short-run accounting income. If the company had loan agreements or other contracts that required it to maintain certain net income levels, the early accounting losses from Project C could cause the company to default on its loan agreements and thus preclude it from staying in business long enough to earn the later rewards from Project C.

Externally required accounting income considerations for project investments may be considered a constraint by management on the company's investment program. In some cases, managers require that projects have both a positive net present value and increase earnings by a specified amount.

ALTERNATE CAPITAL INVESTMENT MODELS

Due to the complexity of the capital investment decision, one model of analysis is sometimes considered insufficient for evaluating investment proposals.[3] The most common models for assessing capital investment projects are:

1. Net present value.
2. Internal rate of return.
3. Payback.
4. Accounting rate of return.

We will discuss each of these alternative models in turn. Each model has its own advantages and may be encountered in certain decision settings. In a

---

[3] Surveys of the use of capital investment models include V. B. Bavishi, " Capital Budgeting Practices at Multinationals," *Management Accounting,* August 1981, pp. 32–35; and Michael C. Walker and Thomas P. Klammer, "The Continuing Increase in the Use of Sophisticated Capital Budgeting Techniques," *California Mangement Review,* Fall 1984, pp. 137–48.

Illustration 16-2 **Accounting Income from Projects A through E**

Year	A	B	C	D	E
			Project		
1	($65)	($10)	($10)	$ 20	$ 0
2	5	80	(10)	30	10
3	45	70	(10)	40	10
4	70	40	(10)	50	20
5	150	20	(10)	50	30
6	330	10	220	40	30
7	120	(25)	50	20	10
Totals	$655	$185	$220	$250	$110

complex capital investment decision, it is likely that several alternative measures will be employed by management.

Net Present Value

As noted in the previous chapter, a project's net present value is computed by discounting its future cash flows to their equivalent value today. A discount rate must be selected for this computation. Finance texts recommend the use of a **weighted-average cost of capital.** With rapid changes in the value of money, some adjustment to book values is needed for determining the appropriate rate. Quite often companies adjust the rate to reflect inflationary effects. As noted in Chapter 15, the cash flows should also be adjusted for the effects of price-level changes. Some companies vary the rate to account for the differences in risk characteristics of different projects. Other companies use a rate that is determined as management's judgment of what a capital investment should earn. Whatever method is used for determining the discount rate, the end result is directed toward the objective of making the net present value an estimate of the economic value of the asset to the company.

Since the details of net present value calculations have been presented in Chapter 15, we will not repeat them here. Other alternative methods that we will discuss in more detail include internal rate of return, payback, and accounting rate of return.

Internal Rate of Return

Internal Rate of Return (IRR) The interest rate that equates the inflows and outflows from an investment project.

The **internal rate of return** or **IRR** is the rate of interest that a project is expected to earn over its life. If the internal rate of return (also known as the *time-adjusted rate of return*) were used as the cost of capital for discounting project cash flows, the net present value of the project would be exactly equal to zero. Thus, the IRR is that rate that makes the present value of project cash outflows equal to the present value of project cash inflows. This contrasts with the net present value method, which employs a predetermined discount rate.

For example, consider Project A from Illustration 16–1. We know that the IRR from that project is in excess of 15 percent because the net present value is greater than zero. The IRR is the discount rate that equates the present value of Project A's cash inflows and outflows.

To compute the IRR, it is usually necessary to use a calculator, a computer program, or an iterative trial-and-error technique. For Project A, a computer program gives an IRR of 19.4 percent.[4]

Internal Rate of Return with Constant Cash Flows

When the cash flows from a project are constant, it is possible to use the tables for present value of an annuity (Appendix B to Chapter 15) to find the approximate rate of return. Dividing the required investment by the annual net cash flow gives the factor for a project with a life equal to that of the project and an interest rate equal to the internal rate of return. All we need do is look across the row for number of periods until we come to the factor closest to our computed factor. The interest rate for the column of the table related to that factor is the approximate internal rate of return.

For Project D in Illustration 16–1, the factor is:

$$\frac{\text{Required investment}}{\text{Annual net cash flow}} = \frac{\$170,000}{\$60,000} = \underline{\underline{2.83}}$$

which, for a seven-year project, is closest to the factor 2.802 in the column headed by an interest rate of 30 percent. Therefore, we estimate the IRR on this project to be 30 percent.

Some Questions with IRR

While the internal rate of return is widely used for project evaluations, it is sometimes considered inferior to net present value. Its primary disadvantage is its built-in assumption that net cash inflows are reinvested at the project's internal rate of return. By contrast, the net present value method assumes that the net cash inflows are invested at the cost of capital rate. If funds will be reinvested at the cost of capital, the IRR method will make a project whose rate of return is greater than the cost of capital appear more attractive than a similar project using the net present value approach.

In some cases, the differences between the assumptions in the IRR method and the present value method result in differences in the rankings of projects using each method. The present value index ranking may differ from the IRR ranking. The choice that management makes in such a situa-

---

[4] The IRR can also be found by trial and error. For Project A, we know the rate is greater than 15 percent. Is it 20 percent? To find out, we discount the Project A cash flows using a 20 percent discount rate. This results in a net present value of $(11,014). Since this value is negative, the internal rate of return must be less than 20 percent. We then interpolate between the two interest rates based on the spread between the net present values as follows:

$$\text{Lower} \atop \text{rate} \; + \; \left[\frac{\begin{array}{ccc}\text{Present value} & & \text{Actual} \\ \text{at lower} & - & \text{present} \\ \text{rate} & & \text{value}\end{array}}{\begin{array}{ccc}\text{Present value} & & \text{Present value} \\ \text{at lower} & - & \text{at higher} \\ \text{rate} & & \text{rate}\end{array}}\right] \times \left(\begin{array}{c}\text{Higher} \\ \text{rate}\end{array} - \begin{array}{c}\text{Lower} \\ \text{rate}\end{array}\right)$$

$$= 15\% + \left[\frac{\$88,166 - \$0}{\$88,166 - (\$11,014)}\right] \times (20\% - 15\%) = 15\% + \left[\frac{\$88,166}{\$99,180} \times 5\%\right]$$

$$= 15\% + 4.4\% = 19.4\%$$

tion will depend on management's objectives and evaluation of the assumptions underlying the two methods.

Multiple Rates of Return

An interesting problem arises in computing internal rate of return for cash flows that change sign more than once in the project life. This change in sign may occur if significant additional investment is required later in the life of the investment or if a significant cost is incurred when the project is abandoned. Such projects will have more than one internal rate of return. This problem is referred to as **multiple rates of return**

Payback

Payback One method of assessing capital investment projects using the rationale that there is a positive relationship between the speed of payback and the rate of return.

Payback Period The time required to recoup an investment from the cash flows from the project.

It is generally assumed that the longer a company's funds are tied up in an investment, the greater the risk to the company. In addition, there is a relationship between the speed of **payback** and the rate of return on a typical investment. For these reasons, companies often consider the length of time it takes to obtain a return of the investment in the project as a measure for project evaluation. The **payback period** is the number of years that will elapse before the original investment is repaid. As with most other capital investment models, cash flow data are used for this computation. With level annual cash flows, the payback formula is:

$$\frac{\text{Payback}}{\text{period}} = \frac{\text{Investment}}{\text{Annual cash flow}}$$

With different annual cash flows, the analysis is more complex. For example, using the data from Illustration 16–1, the payback period for Project B appears in Illustration 16–3. A running balance of the net cash flow for the investment is maintained until the balance turns positive. For this project, the balance turns positive during the third year. The fraction of that third year that was required before the investment achieved payback is usually estimated by dividing the absolute value of the last negative balance in the balance column by the total cash flow in the payback year:

$$\frac{\text{Balance, end of Year 2}}{\text{Net cash flow, Year 3}}$$

or

$$\frac{\$45,000}{\$80,000} = \underline{\underline{.5625}}$$

Project payback would then be stated as 2.5625 years, or approximately 2 years and 7 months. The fraction-of-a-year computation is based on the

Illustration 16–3 **Payback Method, Project B**

Year	Net Cash Flow	Cash Flow Balance
0	$(135,000)	$(135,000)
1	–0–	(135,000)
2	90,000	(45,000)
3	80,000	35,000

assumption that the cash flows are received evenly throughout the payback year.

Shortcut Payback Computation

If a project has level cash flows throughout its life, the payback computation is simplified. The payback period may be computed in this case by dividing the project cost by the annual cash flow. For Project D from Illustration 16–1, the payback period is:

$$\frac{\$170,000}{\$60,000} = \underline{\underline{2.83 \text{ years}}}$$

Payback Reciprocal

Payback Reciprocal One divided by the payback period in years.

When a project life is at least twice the payback period and the annual cash flows are approximately equal, the **payback reciprocal** may be used to estimate of the rate of return for the project.

Thus, for Project D from Illustration 16–1, the payback reciprocal is:

$$\frac{1}{2.83} = \underline{\underline{.35}}, \text{ or } \underline{\underline{35\%}}$$

Programmed functions in calculators and computers are generally used to compute the rate of return directly. Therefore, use of the payback reciprocal approach is simply a rough, first-cut approximation.

Discounted Payback

Discounted Payback Method A method of assessing investment projects that recognizes the time value of money in a payback context.

A method that recognizes the time value of money in a payback context is the **discounted payback method.** This method is used to compute the payback in terms of discounted cash flows received in the future. That is, the periodic cash flows are discounted using an appropriate cost of capital rate. The payback period is computed using the discounted cash flow values rather than the actual cash flows. If the discounted payback method was used for Project D from Illustration 16–1 and a 15 percent cost of capital rate was employed, the discounted payback period would be as shown in Illustration 16–4, which is a discounted payback period of four years.

Evaluation of Payback Methods

Payback approaches are generally easy to compute and, to the extent that risk and payback are correlated, give some measure of a company's risk exposure from a project. However, the payback period tells nothing about profitability. Thus, a project that returns the entire investment in Year 1 but results in no further cash flows appears better using the payback criterion than does a project that returns 50 percent of the investment cost per year for three years. With an investment of $100,000 and a cost of capital of 15 percent, a comparison of the net present value and payback period for these two projects is shown in Illustration 16–5. Clearly, Project 2 is the better choice when cash flows are considered. The payback method gives a misleading signal about the relative desirability of the two projects.

Thus, when using payback, it is important to consider what will happen after the payback period is over. Managers often use payback as a screening

Illustration 16–4

Discounted Payback Method, Project D (dollars in thousands)

Year	Cash Flow	Discount Factor*	Discounted Cash Flow	Balance
0	$(170)	—	$(170)	$(170)
1	60	.870	52	(118)
2	60	.756	45	(73)
3	60	.658	39	(34)
4	60	.572	34	–0–

* Discount factors rounded to three places.

Illustration 16–5

Comparison of Net Present Value and Payback Periods

	Project 1	Project 2
Investment cost	$100,000	$100,000
Annual cash flows:		
Year 1	$100,000	$ 50,000
Year 2	–0–	50,000
Year 3	–0–	50,000
Years 4 and after	–0–	–0–
Payback	1 year[a]	2 years[b]
Net present value at 15%	$ (13,043)[c]	$ 14,161[d]

Additional computations:
[a] One year = $100,000 investment/$100,000 annual cash flow.
[b] Two years = $100,000 investment/$50,000 annual cash flow.
[c] $-13,043 = \$-100,000 + \$100,000 \times 1.15^{-1}$.
[d] $\$14,161 = \$-100,000 + \$50,000 \times 1.15^{-1} + \$50,000 \times 1.15^{-2} + \$50,000 \times 1.15^{-3}$.

device because it is easy (and therefore inexpensive) to use. The choice of the investment analysis model should be based on their costs and benefits compared to the alternative models. If decisions are sensitive to the decision model, then more care and expense is warranted than when decisions are the same regardless of the model used.

Accounting Rate of Return

Accounting Rate of Return A measure of project returns using accounting concepts of income.

The **accounting rate of return** measures a project's rate of return in terms of accounting income, however defined by management, rather than in terms of cash flows. It relates the average accounting income from a project to the investment in the project and is computed using the following equation:

$$\text{Accounting rate of return} = \frac{\text{Average accounting income}}{\text{Investment}}$$

The accounting income for this computation is approximately equal to the sum of the average incremental cash flow from the project less the average book depreciation. Investment may be based either on the *initial investment* or on the *average investment*. Average investment is usually assumed to equal one half of the sum of initial investment and salvage value. Incremental cash flows are usually approximated using revenues minus costs other than depreciation.

For example, consider Project D in Illustration 16–1. The project has an annual cash flow of $60,000 and an initial cost of $170,000. Assume that $154,000 of the investment cost is depreciable using a straight-line rate over the seven-year project life. This basis was determined by management's internal accounting procedures. Book depreciation is $22,000 per year (computed as $154,000/7 years). Average investment in the project is $85,000, which is one half of the original investment cost of $170,000.

$$R = \frac{C - D}{\frac{1}{2} \times I}$$

or

$$\frac{\$60,000 - \$22,000}{\$85,000} = \underline{\underline{44.7\%}}$$

where

C = Average annual cash flow from the investment.
D = Accounting depreciation.
I = Initial investment.

The accounting rate of return may also be computed using the initial investment rather than the average investment. This estimate of the accounting rate of return is:

$$R = \frac{C - D}{I}$$

or

$$\frac{\$60,000 - \$22,000}{\$170,000} = \underline{\underline{22.4\%}}$$

REAL WORLD APPLICATION

Capital Budgeting Methods

In the 1950s, the payback method was the most popular method for capital investment analysis, according to surveys of practice. Since then, discounted cash flow techniques (net present value and internal rate of return) have been used by more and more companies.

Most companies appear to use more than one method of capital investment analyses. A recent survey of practice indicated that "Over 86 percent of the respondents use IRR or NPV or both, but only 16 percent use one or both without also using [payback] or [accounting rate or return]."*

Payback and accounting rate of return are apparently used as supplements to discounted cash flow methods in most companies because of their familiarity and ease of use.

* L. D. Schall, G. L. Sundem, and W. R. Geijabeck, Jr., "Survey and Analysis of Capital Budgeting Methods," *The Journal of Finance*, 33, no. 1, p. 282.

Since the accounting rate of return averages the cash flows to be received from a project and averages the depreciation, and since the accounting rate of return ignores the time value of money, the method is rarely suitable for investment decision-making purposes. Sometimes management will constrain the investment decision to include only those projects that exceed a particular accounting rate of return in order to maintain particular financial accounting ratios. However, this method is considered inferior to a net present value evaluation if the objective is to maximize the long-run wealth of the organization.

Comments on Alternative Methods

Capital investment decisions are among the most important decisions made by managers because they are long-run commitments. Consequently, managers typically use as much information as possible in making decisions. Although the net present value method discussed in Chapter 15 is the most theoretically defensible model, managers often use the alternative models discussed in this chapter as ways of getting a different picture of the project. If the information has already been collected to do a net present value analysis, then the additional cost to the company of using these additional models is typically low.

A summary of the four main models discussed in Chapters 15 and 16 is presented in Illustration 16–7 (in the chapter summary).

INVESTMENTS IN HIGH TECHNOLOGY AND HIGHLY UNCERTAIN PROJECTS

To maintain competitiveness, companies must continue to invest in new technology or projects with highly uncertain payoffs. Because estimation of cash flows from these projects is difficult, some have suggested that companies make these decisions without considering the usual capital investment criteria such as NPV. In practice, though, companies do consider potential cash flows and net present values from such projects. Sensitivity analysis is usually performed to examine the effect of the widely different possible outcomes from the investment. Management can then consider not just one net present value but a range of present values when making an

Illustration 16-6   **Alternative NPV and IRR Scenarios**

	Cash Flows		
Year	Best Case	Expected	Worst Case
0	($80)	($80)	($80)
1	0	0	0
2	0	0	0
3	0	0	0
4	0	0	0
5	0	0	0
6	400	200	50
7	300	100	25
Net present value @ 15%	$206	$ 44	($49)
Internal rate of return	40%	23%	(1%)

investment decision. Management then decides whether to invest in a given project based on a combination of the expected net present value and other performance measures as well as the range of the performance measures and the impact of the project on the future of the company.[5]

For example, Project C from Illustration 16–1 offers high cash returns late in the life of the investment. It is quite difficult to predict cash flows very far in the future. Management might, therefore, analyze the alternative possibilities for this project to obtain some idea of the risk of the investment. Let's assume that there is a chance that the project will only return 25 percent of the estimated cash flows in Years 6 and 7, but there is also the possibility that the cash flows could be $400,000 in Year 6 and $300,000 in Year 7. There are the "worst case" and "best case" scenarios. The cash flow schedule in Illustration 16–1 is the "expected" outcome. Net present value and IRR analyses would be conducted under all three outcomes. A summary of the alternatives in Illustration 16–6 could be presented to management for its evaluation.

SUMMARY

When capital investment opportunities with positive net present values exceed capital budget constraints, the net present value index may be used to rank the projects. This index is calculated as follows:

---

[5] See R. Kaplan, "Must CIM Be Justified on Faith Alone," *Harvard Business Review*, March–April, 1986, pp. 87–95.

REAL WORLD APPLICATION*

When exploring for oil on the North Slope of Alaska, oil companies invested $12 million in research on the oil field and in exploratory drilling. At that time, it was uncertain whether there was any recoverable oil in the ground. Moreover, if there was oil in the ground, it was unknown whether or how it could be transported to consuming markets. Many "what if" studies were conducted to analyze the combinations of possible discovery sizes, methods of transportation, and related costs as well as future price scenarios. The final project investment totaled over $22 billion. At the latest estimation period, net revenues from the project appear to be on the order of $140 billion, and the after-tax rate of return from the proj-ect is estimated at approximately 23 percent. Cash outlays occurred over a 10-year period prior to the start of production from the field. However, the major portion of the cash outlays did not occur until most of the questions concerning volumes of crude oil and costs of the transportation system had been settled. Studies of the net present value of the project were conducted at all stages of the project life. Clearly, at the start, this was a project with highly uncertain costs and returns. Nonetheless, cash flow and net present value analyses were used to monitor the investment decision through all stages of the project.

* Based on the authors' research.

$$\text{Net present value index} = \frac{\text{Project net present value}}{\text{Investment in the project}}$$

When partial investments are not possible, a ranking by net present value index may not indicate the optimal set of projects because there may be leftover, uninvested funds that have a positive net present value. Consequently, various combinations of projects must be evaluated to find the set of projects with the highest net present value.

Projects with high returns are not necessarily better than those with lower returns. If a high-return project entails greater risk, management will often use a higher discount rate. In addition, when investing in capital assets, management must consider how the new investment will fit with the company's portfolio of assets and its overall strategy. Sometimes projects with lower returns are accepted because they are more compatible with the company's long-range plans.

Management may use more than one evaluation method for assessing capital investment projects. Several alternatives are summarized in Illustration 16–7. Internal rate of return expresses a project's return as an interest rate rather than as a net present value. Payback indicates how long a project will take to earn back its initial investment. Discounted payback indicates how long it will take to earn back the initial investment after discounting the cash flows. Accounting rate of return shows a project's effect on accounting income. Each of these alternatives to net present value is frequently criticized as a primary means of investment analysis. But given the importance of capital investment decisions to most organizations, use of more than one method may provide additional useful insights.

When investments are made in a high-risk project, companies will often prepare a sensitivity analysis using several alternate cash flow scenarios.

Illustration 16-7　　　　**Summary of Alternative Capital Investment Models**

Net present value:	Find the net present value of a project using the following formula: $$\text{NPV} = \sum_{n=0}^{N} C_n \times (1 + d)^{-n}$$ See Chapter 15 for details.
Internal rate of return:	Find the project rate of return that makes the project net present value equal to zero. This rate is compared to a "hurdle rate." If it exceeds the hurdle rate, then the project is acceptable.
Payback:	Find the number of years it will take for the project to "pay back" the investment. The shorter the payback period, the better, according to this decision criterion. This method ignores the time value of money and gives no explicit weight to cash flows after the payback period.
Accounting rate of return:	The accounting rate of return for a project is computed as follows: $$\frac{\text{Average accounting income}}{\text{Investment}}$$ This method ignores the time value of money.

TERMS AND CONCEPTS

The following terms and concepts should be familiar to you after reading this chapter:

Accounting Rate of Return

Discounted Payback Method

Internal Rate of Return (IRR)

Lease versus Borrow-to-Buy (Appendix)

Multiple Rates of Return

Mutually Exclusive

Net Present Value Index

Payback

Payback Period

Payback Reciprocal

Risk Premium

Sensitivity Analysis

Weighted-Average Cost of Capital

SUPPLEMENTARY READINGS

Antle, Rick, and Gary D. Eppen. "Capital Rationing and Organizational Slack in Capital Budgeting." *Management Science,* February 1985, pp. 163–74.

Blocher, E., and C. Stickney. "Duration and Risk Assessments in Capital Budgeting." *Accounting Review,* January 1979, pp. 180–88.

Brick, Ivan E., and Daniel G. Weaver. "Comparison of Capital Budgeting Techniques in Identifying Profitable Investments." *Financial Management,* Winter 1984, pp. 29–39.

Cannaday, Roger E.; Peter F. Colwell; and Hiram Paley. "Relevant and Irrelevant Internal Rates of Return." *Engineering Economist,* Fall 1986, pp. 17–38.

Carroll, John J., and Gerald D. Newbould. "NPV vs. IRR: With Capital Budgeting, Which Do You Choose?" *Healthcare Financial Management,* November 1986, pp. 62–4, 66, 68.

Chen, I. Keong, and Michael G. Ferri. "Approaches to Capital Budgeting when Projects Differ by Risk." *Review of Business and Economic Research,* Fall 1983, pp. 67–74.

Haka, Susan F.; Lawrence A. Gordon; and George E. Pinches. "Sophisticated Capital Budgeting Selection Techniques and Firm Performance." *Accounting Review,* October 1985, pp. 651–69.

Horowitz, Ira. "Misuse of Accounting Rates of Return: Comment." *American Economic Review,* June 1984, pp. 492–93.

Kee, Robert, and Bruce Bublitz. "The Role of Payback in the Investment Process." *Accounting and Business Research,* Spring 1988, pp. 149–55.

Kim, Sang-Hoon, and Hussein H. Elsaio. "Safety Margin Allocation and Risk Assessment under the NPV Method." *Journal of Business Finance & Accounting,* Spring 1985, pp. 133–44 (published in Great Britain).

Kruschwitz, Lutz. "Role of Payback Period in the Theory and Application of Duration to Capital Budgeting: A Comment." *Journal of Business Finance & Accounting,* Spring 1985, pp. 165–67 (published in Great Britain).

Louderback, Joseph G., and Charles W. McNichols. "Note on Net Present Value and IRR Functions in Electronic Spreadsheets." *Journal of Accounting Education,* Fall 1986, pp. 113–16.

Miller, M., and C. Upton. "Leasing, Buying, and the Cost of Capital Services." *Journal of Finance,* June 1976.

Salamon, Gerald L. "Accounting Rates of Return." *American Economic Review,* June 1985, pp. 495–504.

Truitt, Jack. "Financial Theory of the Firm: Capital Budgeting and Divisional Evaluation." *Journal of Cost Analysis,* Spring 1986, pp. 25–31.

SELF-STUDY PROBLEM

Assume an investment of $11,615 at time 0 has after-tax cash inflows as follows: $5,525 per year in Years 1–3, and $4,950 in Year 4. Compute the following alternative evaluation measures:

a. Present value index.

b. Internal rate of return.

c. Payback.

d. Discounted payback, using the 15 percent cost of capital rate.

SOLUTION TO SELF-STUDY PROBLEM

a. Present value index:

$$\frac{\text{Net present value}}{\text{Initial investment}} = \frac{\$3,830}{\$11,615} = \underline{\underline{33\%}}$$

b. Internal rate of return:

Because the net present value is positive at the 15 percent discount rate, we know the IRR must be greater than 15 percent. Trying several rates, we obtain:

		Rates	
Year	Cash Flow	30 Percent	31 Percent
0	$(11,615)	$(11,615)	$(11,615)
1	5,525	4,250	4,218
2	5,525	3,269	3,220
3	5,525	2,515	2,458
4	4,950	1,733	1,681
		$ 152	$ (38)

So, the IRR is a little more than 30 percent.

c. Payback:

Year	Cash Flow
0	$(11,615)
1	5,525
2	5,525
3	5,525

$$\text{Pay back} = \frac{\$11,615}{\$5,525} = \underline{\underline{2.10 \text{ years}}}$$

d. Discounted payback:

Year	Cash Flow	Balance
0	($11,615)	($11,615)
1	4,804	(6,811)
2	4,178	(2,633)
3	3,633	—

$$2 + \frac{\$2,633}{\$3,633} \text{ years } = \underline{\underline{2.72 \text{ years}}}$$

APPENDIX
Lease versus
Borrow-to-Buy

Once a project has been evaluated and found to have met all of the criteria for investment, a decision must be made about how to finance it. There are numerous variations in project financing that are designed to meet the specific needs of both borrower and lender. As has been well established in the finance literature, investment and financing decisions are normally separated. Some special financing opportunities may be linked to a specific capital investment, however. One such example is leasing instead of borrowing and buying. This appendix provides a general guideline for evaluating **leases versus borrowing-to-buy,** a common financing alternative.

It is important to recognize that the type of leases we are discussing here are forms of debt financing. The literature in finance considers these leases to be perfect substitutes for debt. Consequently, decisions about leasing assets should not be made by simply computing the net present value of lease payments and the other cash flows associated with the investment. Instead, the analysis has two steps:

Step 1. First, determine whether the investment should be made if the asset was purchased. This analysis would be done like the other investment analyses discussed in Chapters 15 and 16. If the decision is made to reject the investment, then there is no reason to go on to step 2. (There is no reason to analyze financing alternatives if the investment is not going to be made.)

Step 2. Second, determine the best financing alternative. If the company has an opportunity to lease the asset, then an alternative is to borrow the money to buy the asset. This comparison is made by finding the lowest cost financing alternative. The following example demonstrates how this comparison can be made.

Uni-Queue Company has decided to acquire an asset. They can either lease the asset for $15,000 per year during its five-year life or pay $70,000 for the asset and take out a loan for that amount. The loan is repayable at the rate of $14,000 per year on principal plus interest at 20 percent on each year's beginning loan balance. Both the lease and the loan are linked to the asset acquisition.

Under the proposed lease agreement, Uni-Queue is simply a lessee. They would not obtain the benefits of the tax shield. At the end of the five years, the asset is returned to the lessor. On the other hand, if Uni-Queue Company purchases the asset, they obtain the benefit of the tax shield.

At the end of five years, management estimates that they could sell the asset for $15,000. All income taxes are at the company's ordinary tax rate of 40 percent. We assume the risk to the company is the same whether the asset is acquired through lease or buy-borrow. Should management lease or borrow-to-buy?

To analyze this problem, we prepare a schedule of the differential cash flows for each financing alternative. We assume the periodic operating cash inflows generated by the project are the same whether the asset is leased or acquired through buying and borrowing. Hence, we ignore the operating cash inflows under both alternatives. The lease requires an annual outlay of $15,000, which is deductible for tax purposes, thus resulting in an after-tax cash outflow of $9,000 (computed as the $15,000 times 60 percent).

The present value of this outflow is computed by taking the present value of the $9,000 per year for five years, using the *after-tax interest rate that the firm would pay on an equivalent loan,* which would (in this case) be 12 percent [20 percent before tax × (1 − .40)]. (Note that this is *not* the discount rate used for investment decisions.)

The present value of the lease payments may be found by using the shortcut equation for a series of equal payments:

$$C \times \frac{1 - (1 + d)^{-n}}{d}$$

or by using the present value of an annuity table in Appendix B at the end of Chapter 15. The computation is:

$$\$(9,000) \times \frac{1 - (1.12)^{-5}}{.12} = \$(9,000) \times 3.605 = \underline{\$(32,445)}$$

This present value of leasing cash outlays is compared to the present value from borrowing to buy the asset.

The present value from buying the asset and borrowing the purchase amount requires consideration of four types of differential cash flows:

1. Investment flows.
2. Periodic cash flows (only those related to financing in this case).
3. Tax shield.
4. Disinvestment flows.

These are the same four categories used to analyze cash flows when deciding whether to acquire the asset in the first place. The analysis for the data in this example is provided in Illustration 16–8. The investment flows include the $70,000 outlay for the asset less the $70,000 in proceeds from the bank loan for a net of zero. Depreciation for tax purposes is assumed to be as follows: Year 1, $15,000; Year 2, $25,000; Years 3–5, $10,000 per year.

The periodic cash flows represent the repayment of principal at $14,000 per year, based on $70,000 repaid equally over the five years. Interest is computed on the loan balance. Since interest is deductible for tax purposes, the amount shown for interest is equal to 60 percent (which is one minus the 40 percent tax rate) of the gross interest payment.

Illustration 16-8   **Cash Flow Analysis for Borrowing-to-Buy Schedule
of After-Tax Cash Flows**

	Year					
	0	**1**	**2**	**3**	**4**	**5**
Investment flows:						
Asset purchase	$(70,000)					
Loan	70,000					
Depreciation tax shield[a]		$ 6,000	$ 10,000	$ 4,000	$ 4,000	$ 4,000
Periodic flows:						
Loan repayment		(14,000)	(14,000)	(14,000)	(14,000)	(14,000)
Interest after tax[b]		(8,400)	(6,720)	(5,040)	(3,360)	(1,680)
Disinvestment flows:						
Salvage value						15,000
Tax on gain or loss on disposal[c]						(6,000)
Total cash flows	–0–	$(16,400)	$(10,720)	$(15,040)	$(13,360)	$(2,680)
Present value factor (12%)		.893	.797	.712	.636	.567
Present values[d]	$ –0–	$(14,643)	$(8,546)	$(10,705)	$(8,491)	$(1,521)
Net present value	$(43,906)					

Additional computations:

[a] Depreciation schedule:

Year	Depreciation	Tax Effect (40 percent)
1	$15,000	$ 6,000
2	25,000	10,000
3	10,000	4,000
4	10,000	4,000
5	10,000	4,000
Totals	$70,000	$28,000

[b] Interest calculation:

Year	Loan Balance	Interest at 20 Percent	After Tax (1 − .40)
1	$70,000	$14,000	$8,400
2	56,000	11,200	6,720
3	42,000	8,400	5,040
4	28,000	5,600	3,360
5	14,000	2,800	1,680

[c] Salvage value	$15,000
Tax rate for this gain	40%
Tax on gain	$ 6,000

[d] Cash flow times present value factor does not equal present value because the present value factors shown here have been rounded to three places, while the present value is computed using the formula $(1 + d)^{-n}$, $n = 1, \ldots 5$.

For Year 1, then, the net interest payment is:

$$\$70,000 \times 20\% \times 60\% = \underline{\$8,400}$$

For Year 2:

$$\$(70,000 - \$14,000) \times 20\% \times 60\% = \underline{\$6,720}$$

And so forth for Years 3 through 5. These calculations are detailed in Illustration 16–8.

The disinvestment flows include the $15,000 salvage value. The asset will be fully depreciated at the time of salvage, so there is a taxable gain on the full amount of the disposal proceeds. The tax on the gain is equal to the tax rate times the salvage value. This comes to $6,000, which is $15,000 times 40 percent.

The cash flows in each year are summed, and the net present value is computed by discounting the flows back to the present using the 12 percent after-tax borrowing rate. The result is a present value for borrowing of ($43,906). This amount indicates that the present value cost of borrowing is greater than the ($32,443) present value cost from leasing, so the preferred alternative is to lease. Of course, the net present value of the entire project must be greater than or equal to zero or no investment will take place. In this situation, we first assumed that the project has a positive net present value and then analyzed the financing alternatives. This two-step process is the one managers usually follow when financing and investment decisions are independent.

Leasing and financing arrangements arise because of differences in the financial, risk, and tax situations of companies and investors. Leases and loan agreements therefore differ. This example should be viewed as a general guide to the approach that can be taken to evaluate alternatives in terms of the impact on cash flows and, hence, on present values.

QUESTIONS

16–1. If there are no budget constraints, why would we invest in all projects with a positive net present value?

16–2. In the presence of budget constraints, what method is suggested for evaluating capital investment projects? Why?

16–3. When there are both budget constraints and investment indivisibilities, what method should be used for capital investment analysis? Why?

16–4. What is the appropriate method for choosing from among mutually exclusive projects? Why is the method appropriate?

16–5. There is a danger in relying entirely on net present value evaluations for projects. What is the danger?

16–6. Management must consider a number of factors in making a capital investment decision. What are some of the factors in addition to net present value?

16–7. Management often has a choice of financing alternatives for certain projects. How should the financing decision be handled?

16–8. What is the benefit of the use of payback for evaluating capital investment projects?

16–9. How can the payback method be improved to account for the effect of the time value of money?

16–10. Why would management use capital investment evaluation methods that are often criticized as inferior to net present value?

16–11. Some authors suggest that when investment outcomes are highly uncertain, more extensive capital investment analysis techniques are appropriate. Comment on this suggestion.

16–12. The Real World Application in this chapter about the Alaska North Slope oil field provided some information on a project with a long time between initial investment and project returns. What are some of the factors which may have made the use of capital investment techniques helpful for analyzing this project?

EXERCISES

16–13. Effect of Constraints on Investment Decisions

A company with limited investment funds and a cost of capital of 20 percent must choose from among three competing capital investment projects with the following cash flow patterns (in thousands):

	Project		
Year	A	B	C
0	$(200)	$(350)	$(400)
1	50	80	70
2	90	190	150
3	100	250	270
4	100	120	200

The company has $600,000 available for investment.

Required:

How can the company optimally invest its $600,000 among the three projects, assuming no other constraints on investment?

16–14. Effect of Constraints on Investment Decisions (L.O.1)

Use the same data as in exercise 16–13 and assume that the projects are indivisible (that is, you must buy 100 percent of any project or else none of that project). Determine the optimal investment policy for the company.

16–15. Effect of Constraints on Investment Decisions (L.O.1)

Use the same data as in exercise 16–13 and assume that Projects A and B are mutually exclusive and that the projects are indivisible.
Determine the optimal investment policy for the company.

16–16. Effect of Constraints on Investment Decisions (L.O.1)

Carbondale and Company, a medical partnership, has $1.5 million available for investment in venture capital projects. The cost of capital is 18 percent. As a partnership, Carbondale pays no income taxes. The following opportunity ventures are available. Each has an estimated seven-year life.

A. Software Designs, an innovative software development company, has requested $900,000. The firm estimates no returns until Year 5. Years 5 through 7 should return $1 million per year.

B. Sunset Mall, a new shopping center development, will cost Carbondale $550,000. The project will return $65,000 per year for each of Years 1–3 and $250,000 per year in Years 4–7.

C. Nutri-care, a health food chain, requires an investment of $650,000 to open a new store. This project will return $260,000 in each of Years 1–3 and $60,000 per year in Years 4–7.

D. Marvin Gardens, a housing development, would require $850,000 and return $250,000 in each of Years 1–7.

Required:

Complete the following schedule (dollars in thousands) to:

a. Calculate the net present value index for each investment *b.* Determine how the company can optimally invest its venture capital funds. Assume no other constraints on investment.

		Year				
Project	**0**	**1**	. . .	**6**	**7**
A: Amounts	($)	$		$	$
PV factor		0.847		0.370	.314
Present values	($)	$		$	$
Net present value					
Net present value index	% = $ /$				
.					
.					
.					
D: Amounts	($)	$		$	$
PV factor		0.847		0.370	.314
Present values	($)	$		$	$
Net present value	$				
Net present value index	% = $ /$				

16–17. Effect of Constraints on Capital Investment Decisions
(L.O.1)

Refer to the data in exercise 16–16. Assume that the projects available to Carbondale and Company are indivisible.

Required:

Determine the optimal investment policy for the partnership. Show supporting calculations.

16–18. Effect of Constraints on Capital Investment Decisions
(L.O.1)

If Carbondale and Company (exercise 16–16) can invest in either of Software Designs or the Sunset Mall, but not both, and the projects are indivisible, what is the optimal investment policy for the company? Show supporting calculations.

16–19. Effect of Constraints on Capital Investment Decisions
(L.O.1)

Lucitania Oil Company has limited investment funds. It has $1 million available for investment. The company must choose from among three competing capital investment projects with the following cash flow patterns (in thousands).

		Year			
Project	**0**	**1**	**2**	**3**	**4**
Alpha	$(400)	$100	$180	$200	$200
Beta	(200)	60	80	100	140
Charlie	(800)	140	300	540	400

Lucitania's cost of capital is 15 percent.

Required:

How can Lucitania optimally invest $1 million among the three projects, assuming no other constraints on investment?

16–20. Effect of Constraints on Capital Investment Decisions
(L.O.1)

Refer to the data in exercise 16–19 on Lucitania Oil Company. Assume the projects are indivisible (that is, you must buy 100 percent of any project or else none of that project).

Required:

Determine the optimal investment policy for the company.

16–21. Effect of Constraints on Capital Investment Decisions
(L.O.1)

Refer to the data in exercise 16–19 on Lucitania Oil Company. Assume Projects Beta and Charlie are mutually exclusive and that the projects are indivisible.

Required:

Determine the optimal investment policy for the company.

16–22. Alternative Project Evaluation Measures
(L.O.2)

Yogurt and You Company is considering whether to invest in a yogurt machine that costs $350,000 and will return $90,000 after tax for each of the next seven years. After that the asset will have no value.

Required:

Compute the following items for this project:

a. Payback.

b. Internal rate of return (using a calculator, computer, or trial and error and interpolation).

c. Internal rate of return if the life is 12 years rather than 7.

16–23. Alternative Project Evaluation Measures
(L.O.2)

Branding Irons, Inc., is a manufacturer of western hats. The company has an opportunity to expand production by purchasing a new automatic hat bander. The bander costs $200,000 and is fully depreciable for tax purposes using the straight-line method over a four-year life. The machine will have no salvage value. No additional working capital is required. The bander will result in cost savings of $80,000 per year. The company has a tax rate of 45 percent.

Required:

Compute the following investment evaluation measures for the bander:

a. Payback period.

b. Internal rate of return (using a calculator, computer, or trial and error and interpolation).

c. Accounting rate of return on the initial investment.

16–24. Alternative Project Evaluation Measures, No Discounting
(L.O.2)

Hazman Company plans to replace an old piece of equipment that has no book value for tax purposes and no salvage value. The replacement equipment will provide annual cash savings of $7,000 before income taxes. The equipment costs $18,000 and will have no salvage value at the end of its five-year life. Hazman uses straight-line depreciation for both book and tax purposes. The company incurs a 40 percent marginal tax rate, and its after-tax cost of capital is 14 percent.

Required:

Compute the following performance measures for Hazman's proposed investment:

a. Payback period.

b. Payback reciprocal.

c. Accounting rate of return on average investment.

(CMA adapted)

16–25. Alternative Project Evaluation Measures with Discounting

Using the data for Hazman Company in exercise 16–24, compute the following investment performance measures.

a. Net present value.

b. Present value index.

c. Internal rate of return (using a calculator, computer, or trial and error and interpolation).

d. Discounted payback.

16–26. Alternative Project Evaluation Measures
(L.O.2)

ABC Company is considering a capital investment proposal with an initial cost of $54,000. The asset is depreciated over a six-year period on the straight-line basis for both book and tax purposes. No salvage value is expected at the end of the asset life. The before-tax cash inflow for the project is $20,000 per year. The income tax rate is 40 percent, and the company's after-tax cost of capital is 15 percent.

Required:

Compute the following:

a. Accounting rate of return on average investment.

b. Payback reciprocal.

c. Internal rate of return (using a calculator, computer, or trial and error and interpolation).

Choose the best answer for each of the following separate cases. All analyses are before tax.

16–27. Alternative Project Evaluation Methods
(L.O.2)

Multiple-Choice:

a. Polar Company is planning to purchase a new machine for $30,000. The payback period is expected to be five years. The new machine is expected to produce cash flow from operations of $7,000 a year in each of the next three years and $5,500 in the fourth year. Book depreciation of $5,000 a year will be charged against revenue for each of the five years of the payback period. What is the amount of cash flow from operations that the new machine is expected to produce in the last (fifth) year of the payback period?
  (1) $1,000.
  (2) $3,500.
  (3) $5,000.
  (4) $8,500.

b. The Fudge Company is planning to purchase a new machine, which it will depreciate on a straight-line basis over a 10-year period with no salvage value and a full year's depreciation taken in the year of acquisition. The new machine is expected to produce cash flow from operations of $66,000 a year in each of the next 10 years. The accounting (book value) rate of return on the initial investment is expected to be 12 percent. How much will the new machine cost?
  (1) $300,000.
  (2) $550,000.
  (3) $660,000.
  (4) $792,000.

c. Heap Company invested in a two-year project with an internal rate of return of 10 percent. The present value of $1 for one period at 10 percent is .909, and the present value of $1 for two periods at 10 percent is .826. The project is expected to produce cash flow from operations of $40,000 in the first year and $50,000 in the second year. How much will the project cost? (Use these rounded PV factors.)
  (1) $74,340.
  (2) $77,660.
  (3) $81,810.
  (4) $90,000.

(CPA adapted)

16–28. Sensitivity Analysis in Capital Investment Decisions
(L.O.3)

Automated Manufacturing Corp. is considering investing in a robotics manufacturing line. If the line is installed, it will cost an estimated $1.5 million. This amount must be paid immediately even though construction will take three years to complete (Years 0, 1, and 2). Year 3 will be spent testing the production line and, hence, will not yield any positive cash flows. If the operation is very successful, the company expects after-tax cash savings of $1 million per year in each of Years 4 through 7. After reviewing the use of these systems with managements of other companies, the controller of Automated concluded that the operation will most probably result in annual savings of $700,000 per year for each of Years 4 through 7. Further, it was entirely possible that the savings could be as low as $300,000 per year for each of Years 4 through 7.

Required:

Complete the following schedule to determine the IRR and NPV at 15 percent under the three scenarios.

Year	Best Case	Expected	Worst Case
0	($)	($)	($)
1			
2			
3			
4			
5			
6			
7			
Net present value at 15 percent	$_____	$_____	$_____
Internal rate of return	_____%	_____%	_____%

16–29. Sensitivity Analysis in Capital Investment Decisions
(L.O.3)

Ames, Inc., is a large marketing company. Management is considering whether to expand operations by opening a new chain of specialty stores. If the company embarks on this program, cash outlays for inventories, lease rentals, working capital, and other costs are expected to amount to $3.5 million in Year 0. The company expects break-even cash flows in each of Years 1 and 2. Cash flows are expected to increase to $1 million in each of Years 3 and 4, $2 million in Year 5, and $3 million in each of Years 6 and 7.

Management is aware that this is a risky venture because the economy can change over the next few years and consumer tastes could also change. For these reasons, data were obtained on worst case and best case scenarios. In the worst case, cash flows in each of Years 1 and 2 will be minus $500,000. In each of Years 3 through 7, cash flows may only equal $1 million. By contrast, the best case scenario projects positive cash flows of $500,000 in Years 1 and 2, $1.5 million in each of Years 3 and 4, and $4 million in each of Years 5 through 7.

The company's after-tax cost of capital is 20 percent. All cash flows are net of tax.

Required:

Complete the following schedule to show the net present values and internal rates of return for this venture for the expected, worst case, and best case scenarios.

Year	Best Case	Expected	Worst Case
0	($)	($)	($)
1			( )
2			( )
3			
4			
5			
6			
7			
Net present value at 20 percent	$____	$____	$____
Internal rate of return	____%	____%	____%

16–30. Sensitivity Analysis in Capital Investment Decisions: Research Organization
(L.O.3)

Boise University is considering establishing a computer technology research center. The research center will require the university to invest $1 million in equipment and facilities. During each of the first two years of operations, the university will incur costs of $150,000 for faculty and staff support. During this period, institute staff will conduct some research and write grants to obtain financial support. If the institute is moderately successful, it will obtain sufficient grant monies to break even in Year 3. After that, the institute expects to operate in such a manner that its cash inflows from grants will exceed its costs by $500,000 per year for Years 4 through 8.

Operation of a research institute is quite risky. It is possible that the annual net cash outflows of $150,000 will continue through Year 5. If the institute gets off to this slow a start, it is likely that the positive cash flows will only equal $400,000 in each of Years 6 through 8. On the other hand, university administrators estimate that the institute could break even as early as Year 2 and could receive enough grant money so that cash inflows exceed outflows by $500,000 per year for Years 3 through 8.

The university considers that its opportunity cost of funds is 10 percent. As a tax-exempt organization, it incurs no income tax liability.

Required:

Complete the following schedule to show the net present values and internal rates of return for this venture for the expected, worst case, and best case scenarios.

Year	Best Case	Expected	Worst Case
0	($)	($)	($)
1	( )	( )	( )
2		( )	( )
3			( )
4			( )
5			( )
6			
7			
8			
Net present value at 10 percent	$____	$____	$____
Internal rate of return	____%	____%	$____%

16–31. Present Value of Lease versus Buy (Appendix)
(L.O.4)

The owner of Ruggles Company, a sole proprietorship, decided she should acquire some new labor-saving equipment. If the equipment is acquired, it may either be leased or a special nonrecourse loan obtained for the total amount of the equipment purchase.

The lease calls for payments of $13,000 per year for eight years, whereas the loan calls for eight annual principal payments of $10,000 each plus 20 percent interest on the balance outstanding at the start of each year. Under the lease, the lessor obtains all tax benefits from equipment ownership.

The equipment, which cost $80,000, is depreciable for tax purposes as follows: Year 1, $16,000; Year 2, $28,000; Years 3–5, $12,000 per year. The equipment will have no value at the end of the project life (eight years).

Ruggles has a tax rate of 40 percent and uses an after-tax borrowing rate of 12 percent to discount all cash flows.

Required:

Complete the schedule to determine whether Ruggles should lease or borrow and buy the asset. (Assume Ruggles has already decided to make the investment, but has not yet decided whether to lease or borrow.)

	Year				
Item	1	2	. . .	7	8
Buying:					
Periodic flows:					
Loan principal	$ _____	_____		_____	_____
Interest (after tax)					
Tax shield	_____	_____		_____	_____
Cash flows	_____	_____		_____	_____
Discount factor (12%)	_____	_____		_____	_____
Present value	$ _____	_____		_____	_____
Net present value	$ _____				
Leasing:					

Net present value = (Annuity factor) × (After-tax series of payments)
= $ _____

16–32. Effect of Tax Rates on the Lease-versus-Buy Decision (Appendix)
(L.O.4)

If the marginal tax rate for Ruggles (exercise 16–31) was 60 percent and the after-tax borrowing rate was 8 percent, would your decision in exercise 16–31 remain the same? Show supporting data.

16–33. Present Value of Lease versus Buy (Appendix)
(L.O.4)

Mush Paper Company placed an order to purchase a new paper roller. The cost of the equipment is $475,000. Mush Paper has two alternatives for financing this acquisition. Mush can take out a nonrecourse loan for $475,000 at an annual interest rate of 11 percent on the beginning-of-year balance. The loan would extend for seven years and require equal principal payments over that period.

The seller of the paper roller offered Mush a 15 percent discount on the purchase price if Mush leases the roller. The lease payments are $75,000 per year for six years. At the end of Year 7, Mush would make a payment of $175,000.

The equipment is depreciable as follows: Year 1, $95,000; Year 2, $140,000; Year 3, $140,000; Year 4, $50,000; Year 5, $50,000. The equipment has no value at the end of the seven years.

Mush Paper's tax rate is 35 percent, and the company uses an after-tax borrowing rate of 10 percent to discount all cash flows.

Required:

Complete the following schedule to show whether Mush Paper should lease the roller or borrow to buy.

		Year			
	1	**2**	. . .	**6**	**7**
Lease payments					
PV factor	_____	_____		_____	_____
Present values	$_____	$_____		$_____	$_____
Net present value	$_____				
Loan principal					
Interest					
Tax shield					
Annual cash outflow					
PV factor	_____	_____		_____	_____
Present values	$_____	$_____		$_____	$_____
Net present value	$_____				

16–34. Present Value of Lease versus Buy (Appendix)
(L.O.4)

Refer to the information for Mush Paper Company (exercise 16–33). If the relevant tax rate is 45 percent and the annual lease payments are $85,000 for Years 1–6 and $185,000 in Year 7, would your decision in exercise 16–33 remain the same? Show supporting data.

PROBLEMS

16–35. Choosing from Alternative Investment Possibilities

Oakla Realty Partners has $1.4 million available for investment in real estate ventures. The partnership's cost of capital is 18 percent. As a partnership, Oakla pays no income taxes. The company has the following ventures available to it, all of which have seven-year lives:

1. Tulsa Shopping Center which will cost $500,000. This project will return $50,000 per year for each of the first three years and $250,000 per year in each of the remaining four years.
2. Wichita Falls Mixed-Use Development which will cost $900,000. This project will return nothing in each of the first four years and $1 million in each of the last three years.
3. Baton Rouge Apartment Complex which will cost $800,000 and return $230,000 per year for each of the seven years.
4. Shreveport Technical Centre which will cost $600,000. This project will return $250,000 per year for each of the first three years and $50,000 per year for each of the remaining four years.

Required:

How can the company optimally invest its $1.4 million assuming no other constraints on investment? Show supporting data.

16–36. Effect of Constraints on Project Selection

Assume that the projects available to Oakla Realty Partners (problem 16–35) are indivisible. Determine the optimal investment policy for the partnership. Show supporting data.

16–37. Effect of Mutually Exclusive Projects

If Oakla Realty Partners (problem 16–35) can invest in either of the Wichita Falls Mixed-Use Development or the Tulsa Shopping Center but not both, and the other projects are divisible, what is the optimal investment policy for the company? Show supporting data.

16–38. Assess Impact of Tax Policy

Assume that a provision of the Federal Tax Code permits a taxpayer to write off 75 percent of the first $10,000 in outlays for new capital equipment. However, if the taxpayer chooses to take the immediate write-off, the taxpayer loses the depreciation tax shield on that amount.

Assume your company acquired $10,000 in new capital equipment and now must decide whether to take the immediate write-off or depreciate the asset over a five-year life as follows: Year 1, $1,200; Year 2, $2,500; Years 3–5, $2,100 per year. Your company has an after-tax cost of capital of 20 percent and a marginal tax rate of 40 percent.

Required:

Prepare an analysis to show the following items for each alternative:

a. Net present value.

b. Internal rate of return.

c. Payback period.

d. Optimal decision for the company.

16–39. Assess Asset Write-off versus Capitalization

HighPotential Corporation made a $5,000 investment in equipment that qualifies for a three-year straight-line tax depreciation write-off. The financial manager of High Potential indicated that there is a tax policy that allows the company to write off 90 percent of this investment against current period income rather than take the depreciation. Your recommendation will be followed by the company. The company has a marginal tax rate of 40 percent and an after-tax cost of capital of 20 percent.

Required:

a. Compute the internal rate of return for the write-off.

b. Make your recommendation and offer supporting comments.

16–40. Assess Capital Investment Project with Alternative Measures

Baxter Company manufactures toys and other short-lived products. The research and development department came up with a product that would be a good promotional gift for office equipment dealers. Efforts by Baxter's sales personnel resulted in commitments for this product for the next three years. It is expected that the product's value will be exhausted by that time.

To produce the quantity demanded, Baxter will need to buy additional machinery and rent additional space. About 25,000 square feet will be needed; 12,500 square feet of presently unused space is available now. Baxter's present lease with 10 years to run costs $3 a foot, including the 12,500 feet of unused space. There is another 12,500 square feet adjoining the Baxter facility which Baxter can rent for three years at $4 per square foot per year if it decides to make this product.

The equipment will be purchased for about $900,000. It will require $30,000 in modifications, $60,000 for installation, and $90,000 for testing. All of these activities will be done by a firm of engineers hired by Baxter. All of the expenditures will be paid for on January 1 of the first year of production of the item.

The equipment will have a salvage value of about $180,000 at the end of the third year.

The following estimates of differential revenues and differential costs for this product for the three years have been developed:

	Year 1	Year 2	Year 3
Sales	$1,000,000	$1,600,000	$800,000
Material, labor, and variable overhead	400,000	750,000	350,000
Allocated fixed general overhead[a]	40,000	75,000	35,000
Rent	87,500	87,500	87,500
Depreciation	450,000	300,000	150,000
	977,500	1,212,500	622,500
Income before tax	22,500	387,500	177,500
Income tax (40%)	9,000	155,000	71,000
	$ 13,500	$ 232,500	$106,500

[a] Total fixed overhead will not be affected by this product. Each product is allocated some general overhead, however.

Required:

a. Prepare a schedule to show the differential after-tax cash flows for this project. Assume equipment must be depreciated on a three-year, straight-line basis for tax purposes.

b. If the company requires a two-year payback period for its investment, would it undertake this project?

c. Calculate the after-tax accounting rate of return for the project.

d. If the company sets a required discount rate of 20 percent after taxes, will this project be accepted?

(CMA adapted)

16–41. Capital Investment Measures with Constraints

The Los Alamos Atoms have the option to purchase a contract of the leading national quarterback at a price of $4 million. The contract is good for five years. If the Atoms purchase the contract, they estimate that revenues from television franchises and from ticket sales will increase by the amounts shown in column 1 of Exhibit 16–41A.

Franchise and other fees will increase by 10 percent of the amount of the increases in gross revenues. (These are cash outflows.)

The Atoms also have an opportunity to purchase a contract for a world-class wide receiver. This contract also runs for five years and costs $2.5 million. The expected revenue increase for this person are shown in the second column of Exhibit 16–41A.

Finally, for $1 million the Atoms can pick up the rights to the "Rookie of the Year" under a five-year contract. The expected cash flows are shown in column 3 of Exhibit 16–41A.

Although the Atoms would like to take all three, their budget is limited to $4 million. The Atom's cost of capital is 10 percent. Ignore taxes.

Required:

a. Determine the NPV index for each player.

b. To maximize net present value, how should the Atoms allocate their resources among the available contracts?

Exhibit 16–41A   **Revenue Increase**

	(1) Quarterback	(2) Receiver	(3) Rookie
Year 1	$1,500,000	$1,000,000	$ 0
Year 2	1,500,000	1,000,000	100,000
Year 3	1,500,000	1,000,000	100,000
Year 4	1,000,000	600,000	300,000
Year 5	800,000	300,000	1,500,000

16–42. Sensitivity Analysis in Capital Budgeting

Management of Savannah Export Co. is considering whether to install warehouse and terminal facilities to expand its business. If it can obtain the appropriate licenses in all countries involved, the company can earn after-tax cash flows of $1 million per year for Years 2 through 10. However, the problem is the costs that will be incurred to obtain licenses and permits. The company engaged an engineering firm which estimated that the cost to build the warehouse facilities would be $2.2 million. These costs include $200,000 for domestic permits and licenses. Based on prior experience, Savannah management expects to incur an additional $1.8 million in international permit and license fees from other governmental agencies. In addition, the company expects a net cash outflow of $150,000 in Year 1 due to meeting various regulatory requirements.

Legal advisors indicated to Savannah's management that in their experience with a similar operation, total international licensing costs could run as high as $2.8 million in Year 0. Moreover, during the first year of operations, net cash outflows could be as high as $600,000. On the other hand, recent efforts to expand international trade suggest that international licensing and related costs could be as low as $300,000 in Year 0, and that the company could break even in Year 1.

The company's cost of capital is 15 percent after tax.

Required:

a. What is the net present value and internal rate of return under the three scenarios?

b. Should the company make this investment?

16–43. Lease versus Buy with Constraints (Appendix)

Provo Airport Authority has $45 million in its airport capital funds account which is available for the acquisition of capital equipment for the airport. The following projects, with the cost of each project, need to be constructed at the airport ($ in millions):

Project	Cost	Annual Lease
Neutron security scanners	$19	$6
Control tower radar	34	9
Doppler radar	15	4
New runway lighting system	11	3
Jetways for new wing	18	5

The total cost of these projects is $97 million. None of the projects is divisible. However, each of the projects can be leased by making the annual lease payment shown above for a period of seven years. At the end of the lease period, the project becomes the property of the airport. The airport authority determined that it must acquire all of these projects. Those that cannot be acquired with the funds in the capital account must be leased.

Analysis of alternative investment opportunities shows that there is an annual opportunity benefit of $.10 for each $1 unused in the capital funds account. For example, if the total cost of projects purchased from the capital funds account is $35 million, the opportunity benefit from the $10 million in idle funds is $1 million per year over the seven-year lease period. The authority uses a 7.5 percent discount rate and is tax exempt. This discount rate is used regardless of the opportunity benefit noted above.

Required:

Which project should Provo Airport Authority purchase with the $45 million in the capital funds account? Show computational support for your choices.

INTEGRATIVE CASE

16–44. Sell or Process Further; Cash Flow Evaluation; Internal Rate of Return

Algonquin River Products Corporation extracts ores from an open-pit mine. Each year, 400,000 tons of ore are extracted. If the products from the extraction process are sold immediately after removal of dirt, rocks, and other impurities, a price of $65 per ton of ore can be obtained. The company estimates that extraction costs are 75 percent of the net realizable value of the ore.

Rather than sell all of the ore at the $65 price, 20 percent of it could be processed further.

To perform the additional processing, the company would install equipment costing $1,300,000. This equipment would qualify for tax depreciation as follows: Year 1, $300,000; Year 2, $400,000; Years 3–5, $200,000 per year. At the end of the six-year project life, the equipment could be salvaged and the company would obtain $50,000 salvage proceeds.

Further processing would cost $6 per ton in addition to the first processing costs. The processed ore would yield two products in equal proportion: A and B. Product A would sell for $44 per one half ton, while Product B would sell for $34 per one half ton.

Average inventory required would increase by 5,000 tons of ore. In addition, a cash balance of $45,000 would be needed to operate the additional process.

The company plans to obtain a loan for the project at an interest cost of 16 percent. The loan would be for the entire cost of the project, including inventories and working capital. The company estimates its cost of capital at 20 percent and its marginal tax rate at 40 percent.

Required:

a. Prepare a schedule of the cash flows from the investment and indicate the net present value of the project?

b. What is the internal rate of return from the project?

PART III

COST DATA FOR PERFORMANCE EVALUATION

OUTLINE

THE MASTER BUDGET

LEARNING OBJECTIVES

1. To understand the role of budgets in overall organization plans.
2. To estimate sales and production levels.
3. To estimate cash flows.
4. To develop budgeted financial statements.

Budget A financial plan of the resources needed to carry out tasks and meet financial goals.

The use of budgeting in organizations was well stated by a controller who explained: "At our company, we view our master **budget** as a blueprint for operations, much like an architect's blueprint for the construction of a building. Like the architect's blueprint, our master budget helps us plan and coordinate activities, determine the means for achieving our goals, and establish some norms against which we can measure our performance. We consider our budget to be a comprehensive plan through which all levels of management formally indicate what they expect the future to hold. It expresses, in dollars, our plans for achieving company goals."

Master Budget The financial plan for the coming year or other planning period.

This chapter shows how a **master budget** is developed and how it fits into the overall plan for achieving organizational goals.

THE OVERALL PLAN

A master budget is part of an overall organizational plan made up of three components:

1. Organizational goals.
2. The strategic long-range profit plan.
3. The master budget (tactical short-range profit plan).[1]

Organizational Goals

Organizational Goals Set of broad objectives established by management that company employees work to achieve.

Organizational goals are the set of broad objectives established by management that company employees work to achieve. For example, the following quote is taken from internal documents of a manufacturing company in the paper industry: "Our organizational goal is to increase earnings steadily while maintaining our current share of market sales and maintain profitability within the top one third of our industry. We plan to achieve this goal while providing our customers with high-quality products and meeting our social responsibilities to our employees and the communities in which they live."

Such broad goals provide a philosophical statement that the company is expected to follow in its operations. Many companies include statements of their goals in published codes of conduct and annual reports to stockholders.

Strategic Long-Range Profit Plan

Strategic Long-Range Plan Statement detailing steps to be taken in achieving a company's organization goals.

While a statement of goals is necessary to guide an organization, it is important to detail the specific steps that will be taken to achieve them.[2] These steps are expressed in a **strategic long-range plan.** Because the long-range plans look into the intermediate and distant future, they are usually stated in rather broad terms. Strategic plans discuss the major capital investments required to maintain present facilities, increase capacity, diversify products and/or processes, and develop particular markets. For example, the previously mentioned paper company's strategies, as stated in their policy manual included:

---

[1] For a more detailed description of these phases, see Glenn A. Welsch, *Budgeting: Profit Planning and Control* (Englewood Cliffs, N.J.: Prentice-Hall, 1976).

[2] A classic discussion of organization goal setting is provided by James G. March and Herbert A. Simon in *Organizations* (New York: John Wiley & Sons, 1958).

1. *Cost control.* Optimize contribution from existing product lines by holding product cost increases to less than the general rate of inflation. This will involve acquiring new machinery proposed in the capital budget as well as replacing our five least efficient plants over the next five years.
2. *Market share.* Maintain our market share by providing a level of service and quality comparable to our top competitors. This requires improving our quality control so that customer complaints and returned merchandise are reduced from a current level of 4 percent to 1 percent within two years.

Each strategy statement was supported by projected activity levels (sales volumes, aggregate costs, and cash flow projections) for each of the next five years. At this stage, the plans were not laid out in too much detail, but they were well thought out. Hence, the plans provided a general framework for guiding management's operating decisions.

The Master Budget (Tactical Short-Range Profit Plan)

Profit Plan The income statement portion of the master budget.

Long-range plans are achieved in year-by-year steps. The guidance is more specific for the coming year than it is for more distant years. The plan for the coming year is called the master budget. The master budget is also known as the *static budget,* the *budget plan,* or the *planning budget.* The income statement portion of the master budget is often called the **profit plan.** The master budget indicates the sales levels, production and cost levels, income, and cash flows that are anticipated for the coming year. In addition, these budget data are used to construct a budgeted statement of financial position (balance sheet).

Budgeting is a dynamic process that ties together goals, plans, decision making and employee performance evaluation. The master budget and its relationship to other plans, accounting reports, and management decision-making processes is diagrammed in Illustration 17–1. On the left side are the organization goals, strategies, and objectives that set the long-term plan for the company. The master budget is derived from the long-range plan in consideration of conditions that are expected during the coming period. Such plans are subject to change as the events of the year unfold. Recently, the long-range plan for a U.S. automobile manufacturer called for development of several new product lines, but unfavorable short-run economic conditions required their postponement.

The Human Element in Budgeting

The conditions anticipated for the coming year are based in part on individual managers' near-term projections. The individual's relationship to the budget is diagrammed on the right side of Illustration 17–1. Managers' beliefs about the coming period are affected by a number of factors, including their personal goals and values. Although budgets are often viewed in purely quantitative, technical terms, the importance of this human factor cannot be overemphasized.

Budget preparation rests on human estimates of an unknown future. People's forecasts are likely to be greatly influenced by their experiences with various segments of the company. For example, district sales managers are in an excellent position to project customer orders over the next several

Illustration 17-1   **Organizational and Individual Interaction in Developing the Master Budget**

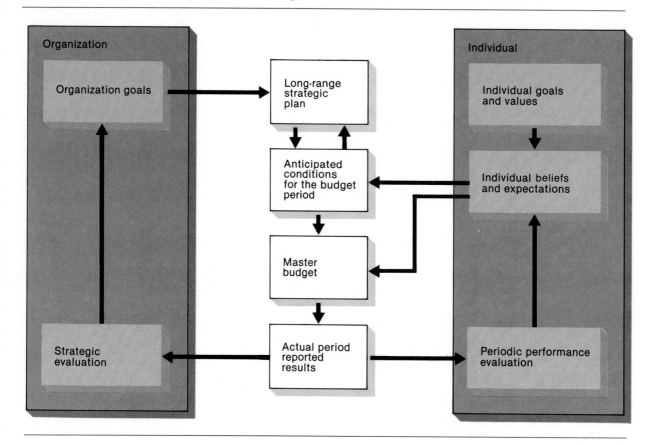

months, while market researchers are usually better able to identify long-run market trends and make macro forecasts of sales. One challenge of budgeting is to identify who in the organization is best able to provide the best information about particular topics.

Participative Budgeting

Participative Budgeting The use of input from lower- and middle-management employees, also called grass roots budgeting.

The use of input from lower- and middle-management employees is often called **participative budgeting** or *grass roots budgeting*. The use of lower and middle managers in budgeting has an obvious cost—it is time-consuming. But it also has some benefits. It enhances employee motivation and acceptance of goals, it provides information that enables employees to associate rewards and penalties with performance,[3] and it yields information that may not be otherwise obtainable.

---

[3] See S. W. Becker and D. O. Green, "Budgeting and Employee Behavior," *The Journal of Business,* October 1962. A more comprehensive discussion of the behavioral effects of individuals and budget plans is presented by Don T. DeCoster in "An Intuitive Framework for Empirical Research in Participative Budgeting." in *Accounting Research Convocation,* ed. Gary John Previts (University, Ala.: University of Alabama Press, 1976). General discussion of

A number of studies have shown that employees often provide inaccurate data when asked to give budget estimates. They may request more money than they need because they expect their request to be cut. And employees who believe the budget will be used as a norm for evaluating their performance may provide an estimate that will not be too hard to achieve.

Thus, managers usually view the technical steps required to construct a comprehensive tactical budget plan in the context of the effect that people have on the budget and the effect that the budget will have on people. Ideally, the budget will motivate people and facilitate their activities so that organizational goals can be achieved.

DEVELOPING THE MASTER BUDGET

While each organization is unique in the way it puts together its budget, all budgeting processes share some common elements. After organization goals, strategies, and long-range plans have been developed, work begins on the master budget. This is a detailed budget for the coming fiscal year, with some less-detailed figures for subsequent years. While budgeting is an on-going process in most companies, the bulk of the work is usually done in the six months immediately preceding the beginning of the coming fiscal year. Final budget approvals by the chief executive and board of directors are made a month to six weeks before the beginning of the fiscal year.

To envision the master budgeting process, picture the financial statements most commonly prepared by companies: the income statement, the balance sheet, and the funds flow statement. Then imagine preparing these statements *before* the fiscal period. One modification to the set of traditional financial statements, however, is that many companies prepare a *cash flow budget* rather than a funds flow budget due to the importance of this information for cash management. Either can be prepared, but we'll restrict our discussion to the cash flow budget. We begin at the top of the budgeted income statement with a forecast of revenues for the budget period.

Sales Forecasts

Forecasting sales is perhaps the most difficult aspect of budgeting because it involves considerable subjectivity. To reduce subjectivity and simultaneously gather as much information as possible, management often uses a number of different methods to obtain forecasts from a number of different sources.

Sales Staff

Salespeople are in the unique position of being close to the customers, and they may possess the best information in the company about customers' immediate and near-term needs. As previously indicated, however, they may be tempted to bias their sales forecasts if such forecasts are used as the norm for performance evaluation.

---

behavioral aspects of budgeting are available in Anthony Hopwood, *Accounting and Human Behavior* (Englewood Cliffs, N.J.: Prentice-Hall, 1974); R. J. Swieringa and R. H. Moncur, *Some Effects of Participative Budgeting on Managerial Behavior* (New York: National Association of Accountants, 1975); and G. Hofstede, *The Game of Budget Control* (New York: Van Nostrand Reinhold, 1967).

For example, Peter Jones is a district sales manager for Shasta Design, Inc., which manufactures mountaineering tents. For the coming budget year, he expects his district's sales to be $1 million, although they could drop as low as $800,000 or run as high as $1.2 million. His bonus at the end of next year will be 1 percent of the excess of actual sales over the sales budget. So, if the budget is $1 million and actual sales are also $1 million, he will receive no bonus.

However, if Peter provides a sales forecast that is too low, he will not be able to justify retaining his current number of employees. Further, if his sales forecasts are consistently much below the actual sales results or below what management thinks his district should be doing, he will lose credibility. Thus, Peter decides on a conservative but reasonable sales forecast of $900,000, which, he believes, will give him a high probability of getting a bonus and a low risk of losing his other objectives.

Of course, if Peter's performance were compared against a different set of norms, he would have different incentive. If, for instance, his bonus was a fixed percent of sales, he would have incentive to maximize sales. Then he would be motivated to make an optimistic sales forecast to justify obtaining a larger sales staff. Also, the high sales forecast would be used to estimate the amount of production capacity needed, thus ensuring that adequate inventory would be available to satisfy any and all customer needs. Of course, the managers and staff who receive forecasts usually recognize the subjectivity of the situation. As Peter's superior put it, "We've received sales forecasts from him for several years, and they're always a bit conservative. We don't ask him to revise his estimates. We simply take his conservatism into account when we put together the overall sales forecast."

Market Research

To provide a check on forecasts from local sales personnel, management often turns to market researchers. This group probably does not have the same incentives that sales personnel have to bias the budget. Furthermore, researchers have a different perspective on the market. While they may know little about customers' immediate needs, they can predict long-term trends in attitudes and the effects of social and economic changes on the company's sales, potential markets, and products.

The Delphi Technique

Delphi Technique Forecasting method where individual forecasts of group members are submitted anonymously and evaluated by the group as a whole.

The Delphi technique is another method that is employed to enhance forecasting and reduce bias in estimates. With this method, members of the forecasting group prepare individual forecasts and submit them anonymously. Each group member obtains a copy of all forecasts but is unaware of their sources. The group then discusses the results. In this way, differences between individual forecasts can be addressed and reconciled without involving the personality or position of individual forecasters. After the differences are discussed, each group member prepares a new forecast and distributes it anonymously to the others. These forecasts are then discussed in the same manner as before. The process is repeated until the forecasts converge on a single best estimate of the coming year's sales level.

Trend Analysis Method of forecasting which ranges from simple visual extrapolation of points on a graph to highly sophisticated computerized time series analysis.

Trend Analysis

Trend analysis, which can range from a simple visual extrapolation of points on a graph to a highly sophisticated computerized time series analysis, may also be helpful in preparing sales forecasts.

Time series techniques use only past observations of the data series to be forecasted. No other data are included. This methodology is justified on the grounds that since all factors that affect the data series are reflected in the actual past observations, the past data are the best reflection of available information. This approach is also relatively economical because only a list of past sales figures is needed. No other data have to be gathered.

Forecasting techniques based on trend analysis often require long series of past data to derive a suitable solution. For example, the class of forecasting techniques called Box-Jenkins models requires approximately 50 past observations to be used successfully.[4] Generally, when these models are used in accounting applications, monthly data are required so that an adequate number of observations can be obtained.

Econometric Models

Another forecasting approach is to enter past sales data into a regression model to obtain a statistical estimate of the projected sales, much like we used regression models to estimate costs in Chapter 10. These models often use observations from past data series, but the sales forecast is usually associated with relevant independent variables. For example, the predicted sales for the coming period may be related to such predictor variables as economic indicators, consumer-confidence indexes, back-order volume, and other internal and external factors that the company deems relevant. Advocates of these **econometric models** contend that many relevant predictors can be included and that by manipulating the assumed values of the predictors, it is possible to examine a variety of hypothetical conditions and relate them to the sales forecast. This is particularly useful for performing sensitivity analysis, which we discuss later in this chapter.

Econometric Models Statistical method of forecasting economic data using regression models.

Sophisticated analytical models for forecasting are now widely available. Most companies' computers have software packages that allow economical use of these models. Nonetheless, it is important to remember that no model removes the uncertainty surrounding sales forecasts. Management has often found that the intuition of local sales personnel is a better predictor than sophisticated analysis and models. As in any management decision, cost-benefit tests should be used to determine which methods are most appropriate.

Comprehensive Illustration

To make our discussion of the budgeting process more concrete, we'll develop the budget for Shasta Design, Inc. We use a manufacturing example

---

[4] See G. E. P. Box and G. M. Jenkins, *Time Series Analysis: Forecasting and Control* (San Francisco: Holden Day, 1970); and D. Z. Williams, W. B. DeMoville, and L. D. Franklin, "Costs and Forecasting," in *The Managerial and Cost Accountant's Handbook*, ed. H. A. Black and J. D. Edwards (Homewood, Ill.: Dow Jones-Irwin, 1979).

because it is the most comprehensive. The methods we discuss are also applicable to nonmanufacturing organizations.

Assume that Shasta Design's management went through the steps discussed above and arrived at the following sales budget for the next budget year:

	Units	Price per Unit	Total Sales Revenues
Estimated sales	6,400	$800	$5,120,000

The Production Budget

Production Budget Production plan of resources needed to meet current sales demand and ensure inventory levels are sufficient for activity levels expected.

The **production budget** plans the resources needed to meet current sales demand and ensure that inventory levels are sufficient for expected activity levels. It is necessary, therefore, to determine the required inventory level for the beginning and end of the budget period. The production level may be computed from the basic cost flow equation (also known as the basic inventory formula):

Beginning balance + Transfers-in = Transfers-out + Ending balance
BB + TI = TO + EB

Adapting that equation to inventories, production, and sales, we have:

Units in   Required   Budgeted sales   Units in
beginning + production =   units   +   ending
inventory   units   for the period   inventory

Rearranging terms to solve for *required productions:*

Required   Budgeted sales   Units in   Units in
production =   units   +   ending   − beginning
units   for the period   inventory   inventory

This equation states that production is equal to the sales demand plus or minus an inventory adjustment. Production and inventory are assumed to be stated in equivalent finished units.

From the sales budget above, Shasta Design, Inc., has projected sales of 6,400 units. Management estimates that there will be 900 units in the beginning inventory of finished goods. Based on management's analysis, the required ending inventory is estimated to be 1,000 units. We assume for simplicity that there is no beginning or ending work in process inventory. With this information, the budgeted level of production is computed as follows:

Required   = 6,400 units +   1,000 units   −   900 units
production   (sales)   (ending inventory)   (beginning inventory)

= 6,500 units

The production budget is then reviewed with management of the production facilities to ascertain whether the budgeted levels of production can be reached with the capacity available. If not, management may revise the sales forecast or consider ways of increasing capacity. If it appears that production capacity will exceed requirements, management may want to consider other opportunities for the use of the capacity.

One benefit of the budgeting process is that it facilitates the coordination of activities. It is far better to learn about discrepancies between the sales forecast and production capacity in advance so that remedial action can be taken. Lost sales opportunities due to inadequate production capacity or unnecessary idle capacity can thus be avoided.

Budgeted Cost of Goods Manufactured and Sold

Once the sales and production budgets have been developed and the efforts of the sales and production groups are coordinated, the budgeted cost of goods manufactured and sold can be prepared. The primary job is to estimate costs of direct materials, direct labor, and manufacturing overhead at budgeted levels of production.

Direct Materials

Direct materials purchases needed for the budget period are derived from the basic cost flow equation:

$$\begin{array}{c}\text{Units in beginning} \\ \text{materials inventory}\end{array} + \begin{array}{c}\text{Required} \\ \text{material} \\ \text{purchases}\end{array} = \begin{array}{c}\text{Materials to} \\ \text{be used in} \\ \text{production}\end{array} + \begin{array}{c}\text{Ending} \\ \text{materials} \\ \text{inventory}\end{array}$$

The beginning and ending levels of materials inventory for the budget period are estimated, often with the help of an inventory control model, while the materials to be used in production are based on production requirements. Once these are known, the required material purchases can be found by rearranging the terms in the above equation to:

$$\begin{array}{c}\text{Required} \\ \text{material} \\ \text{purchases}\end{array} = \begin{array}{c}\text{Materials to} \\ \text{be used in} \\ \text{production}\end{array} + \begin{array}{c}\text{Estimated} \\ \text{ending} \\ \text{materials} \\ \text{inventory}\end{array} - \begin{array}{c}\text{Estimated} \\ \text{beginning} \\ \text{materials} \\ \text{inventory}\end{array}$$

Production at Shasta Design, Inc., for the coming period will require two kinds of materials: material R and material S. For each unit of output, three units of R and five units of S are required. The beginning materials inventory is estimated to consist of 2,200 units of R and 4,000 units of S. The estimated ending inventory has been determined to equal 1,300 units of R and 4,600 units of S. The estimated cost for each unit of R is $10, and the estimated cost of each unit of S is $30. These costs are expected to remain constant during the coming budget period. Required production for the production budget is 6,500 units.

Computation of the required materials purchases in units of each material would be as follows:

$$\begin{array}{c}\text{Required} \\ \text{material} \\ \text{purchases}\end{array} = \begin{array}{c}\text{Materials to} \\ \text{be used in} \\ \text{production}\end{array} + \begin{array}{c}\text{Estimated} \\ \text{ending} \\ \text{materials} \\ \text{inventory}\end{array} - \begin{array}{c}\text{Estimated} \\ \text{beginning} \\ \text{materials} \\ \text{inventory}\end{array}$$

Illustration 17-2

SHASTA DESIGN, INC.
Budgeted Statement of Cost of Goods Manufactured and Sold
For the Budget Year Ended December 31

Beginning work in process inventory			–0–
Manufacturing costs:			
Direct materials:			
Beginning inventory (2,200 R @ $10 + 4,000 S @ $30)	$ 142,000		
Purchases (18,600 R @ $10 + 33,100 S @ $30)	1,179,000		
Materials available for manufacturing	1,321,000		
Less: Ending inventory (1,300 R @ $10 + 4,600 S @ $30)	(151,000)		
Total direct materials costs		$1,170,000	
Direct labor		949,000	
Manufacturing overhead[a]		1,131,000	
Total manufacturing costs			$3,250,000
Deduct: Ending work in process inventory			–0–
Cost of goods manufactured			3,250,000
Add: Beginning finished goods inventory (900 units)[b]			450,000
Deduct: Ending finished goods inventory (1,000 units)[b]			(500,000)
Cost of goods sold			$3,200,000

[a] This figure is supported by the schedule of budgeted manufacturing overhead that is detailed in Illustration 17–3.

[b] Finished goods are valued at $500 per unit $\left(\frac{\$3,250,000}{6,500 \text{ units produced}}\right)$ assuming FIFO. Hence, beginning finished goods inventory is estimated to be $450,000 (900 units × $500), and ending finished goods inventory is estimated to be $500,000 (1,000 units × $500).

$$R = (6,500 \times 3) + 1,300 - 2,200$$
$$= \underline{\underline{18,600 \text{ units}}}$$

$$S = (6,500 \times 5) + 4,600 - 4,000$$
$$= \underline{\underline{33,100 \text{ units}}}$$

In dollar terms, this would amount to estimated purchases of $186,000 for R (18,600 input units × $10) and $993,000 for S (33,100 input units × $30).

These data are then assembled into a budgeted statement of cost of goods manufactured and sold. This statement is shown in Illustration 17–2.

Direct Labor

Estimates of direct labor costs are often obtained from engineering and production management. For Shasta Design, Inc., the direct labor costs are estimated at $146 per output unit produced. Thus, for the budget year, the budgeted direct labor cost of production is 6,500 units × $146 = $949,000, which is also shown in Illustration 17–2.

Overhead

Unlike direct materials and direct labor, which can often be determined from an engineer's specifications for a product, overhead is composed of many different kinds of costs with varying cost behaviors. Some overhead costs vary in direct proportion to production (variable overhead); some costs vary with production, but in a step fashion (for example, supervisory labor); and

Illustration 17-3

SHASTA DESIGN, INC.
Schedule of Budgeted Manufacturing Overhead
For the Budget Year Ended December 31

Variable overhead needed to produce 6,500 units:		
Indirect materials and supplies	$ 38,000	
Materials handling	59,000	
Other indirect labor	33,000	$ 130,000
Fixed manufacturing overhead:		
Supervisor labor	175,000	
Maintenance and repairs	85,000	
Plant administration	173,000	
Utilities	87,000	
Depreciation	280,000	
Insurance	43,000	
Property taxes	117,000	
Other	41,000	1,001,000
Total manufacturing overhead		$1,131,000

other costs are fixed and will remain the same unless capacity or long-range policies are changed. Other costs do not necessarily vary with production, but they may be changed at management's discretion (some maintenance costs may be in this category).

Budgeting overhead requires an estimate based on production levels, management discretion, long-range capacity and other corporate policies, and external factors such as increases in property taxes. Due to the complexity and diversity of overhead costs, cost-estimation such as those described in Chapter 10 are frequently used. To simplify the budgeting process, costs are usually divided into fixed and variable components, with discretionary and semifixed costs treated as fixed costs within the relevant range.

The schedule of budgeted manufacturing overhead for Shasta Design, Inc., is presented in Illustration 17-3. For convenience, after consultation with department management, the budget staff has divided all overhead into fixed and variable costs. Shasta Design can now determine the budgeted total manufacturing costs by adding the three components—materials, labor, and overhead. This total is $3,250,000, as shown in Illustration 17-2.

Completing the Budgeted Costs of Goods Manufactured and Sold

We need only to include the estimated beginning and ending work in process and finished goods inventories to determine the required number of units produced—6,500. As previously indicated, there are no work in process inventories.[5] Finished goods inventories are as follows, assuming the cost per unit is estimated to be $500 in both beginning and ending inventory:

---

[5] If the company has beginning and ending work in process inventories, units are usually expressed as equivalent finished units, as discussed in Chapter 8 on process costing, and treated the way we have treated finished goods inventories. In most companies, estimates of work in process inventories are omitted from the budget because they have a minimal impact on the budget.

	Units	Dollars
Beginning finished goods inventory	900	$450,000
Ending finished goods inventory	1,000	500,000

Adding the estimated beginning finished goods inventory to the estimated cost of goods manufactured, then deducting the ending finished goods inventory yields a cost of goods manufactured and sold of $3,200,000, as shown in Illustration 17–2.

This completes the second major step in the budgeting process: determining budgeted production requirements and the cost of goods manufactured and sold. Obviously, this part of the budgeting effort can be extremely complex in manufacturing companies. It can be very difficult to coordinate production schedules among numerous plants, some using other plants' products as their direct materials. It is also difficult to coordinate production schedules with sales forecasts. New estimates of material availability, labor shortages, strikes, availability of energy, and production capacity often require reworking the entire budget.

Revising the Initial Budget

At this point in the budget cycle, a first-draft budget has been prepared. There is usually a good deal of coordinating and revising before the budget is considered final. For example, projected production figures may call for revised estimates of direct materials purchases and direct labor costs. Bottlenecks may be discovered in production that will hamper the company's ability to deliver a particular product and thus affect the sales forecast. The revision process may be repeated several times until a coordinated, feasible master budget evolves. No part of the budget is really formally adopted until the master budget is finally approved by the board of directors.

Marketing and Administrative Budget

Determining the appropriate budget for marketing and administrative costs is very difficult because managers have a lot of discretion about how much money is spent and the timing of expenditures. For example, a company hired a new marketing executive who was famous for cost-cutting skills. The executive ordered an immediate 50 percent cut in the company's advertising budget, a freeze on hiring, and a 50 percent cut in the travel budget. The result—costs fell, and there was little immediate impact on sales. A year later, looking for new challenges, the executive moved on to another company. Soon afterward, the executive's former employers noticed that sales were down because the company had lost market share to some aggressive competitors. Were the marketing executive's cost-cutting actions really in the best interest of the company? To this day, nobody can give a documented answer to that question because it is difficult to prove a causal link between the cost cutting and the subsequent decrease in sales.

In another case, a company's president was the only one who used the corporate jet—and he used it only rarely. So the internal audit staff recommended selling it. The company president rejected the idea, saying, "One of the reasons I put up with the pressures and responsibilities of this job is because I enjoy some of its perquisites, including the corporate jet. "Some costs that appear unnecessary, especially perquisites, are really part of the total compensation package and may, therefore, be necessary costs.

The budgeting objective here is to estimate the amount of marketing and administrative costs required to operate the company at its projected level of sales and production and to achieve long-term company goals. For example, the budgeted sales figures may be based on a new product promotion campaign. If production and sales are projected to increase, it is likely that an increase in support services—data processing, accounting, personnel, and so forth—will be needed to operate the company at the higher projected levels.

An easy way to deal with the problem is to start with a previous period's actual or budgeted amounts and make adjustments for inflation, changes in operations, and similar changes between periods. This method has been criticized and may be viewed as very simplistic, but it does have one advantage—it is relatively easy and inexpensive. As always, the benefits of improving budgeting methods must justify their increased costs.

At Shasta Design, each level of management submits a budget request for marketing and administrative costs to the next higher level, which reviews it and, usually after some adjustments, approves it. The budget is passed up through the ranks until it reaches top management. As shown in Illustration 17–4, the schedule of marketing and administrative costs is divided into variable and fixed components. In this case, variable marketing costs are those that vary with *sales* (not production). Fixed marketing costs are usually those that can be changed at management's discretion—for example, advertising.

Illustration 17–4

SHASTA DESIGN, INC.
Schedule of Budgeted Marketing and Administrative Costs
For the Budget Year Ended December 31

Variable marketing costs:		
Sales commissions	$260,000	
Other marketing	104,000	
Total variable marketing costs		$ 364,000
Fixed marketing costs:		
Sales salaries	100,000	
Advertising	193,000	
Other	78,000	
Total fixed marketing costs		371,000
Total marketing costs		735,000
Administrative costs (all fixed):		
Administrative salaries	254,000	
Legal and accounting staff	141,000	
Data processing services	103,000	
Outside professional services	39,000	
Depreciation—building, furniture, and equipment	94,000	
Other, including interest	26,000	
Taxes—other than income	160,000	
Total administrative costs		817,000
Total budgeted marketing and administrative costs		$1,552,000

Budgeted Income Statement

According to the controller at Shasta Design, "At this point, we're able to put together the entire budgeted income statement for the period (Illustration 17–5), so we can determine our projected operating profits. By making whatever adjustments are required to satisfy generally accepted accounting principles (GAAP) for external reporting, we can project net income after income taxes and earnings per share. If we don't like the results, we go back to the budgeted income statement and, starting at the top, go through each step to see if we can increase sales revenues or cut costs. We usually find some plant overhead, marketing, or administrative costs that can be cut or postponed without doing too much damage to the company's operations."

Shasta Design's board of directors approved the sales, production, and marketing and administrative budgets and budgeted income statement as submitted. Note that the budgeted income statement also includes estimated federal and other income taxes, which were obtained from the tax staff. We will not detail the tax-estimation process because it is a highly technical area separate from cost accounting.

Cash Budget

Although the budgeted income statement is an important tool for planning operations, a company also requires cash to operate. Cash budgeting is important to assure company solvency, maximize interest earned on cash balances, and determine whether the company is generating enough cash for present and future operations.

Cash Budget A statement of cash on hand at the start, expected cash receipts, expected cash disbursements, and the resulting cash balance at the end of the budget period.

Preparing a **cash budget** requires that all revenues, costs, and other transactions be examined in terms of their effects on cash. The budgeted cash receipts are computed from the collections from accounts receivable, cash sales, sale of assets, borrowing, issuing stock, and other cash-generating activities. Disbursements are computed by counting the cash required to pay for materials purchases, manufacturing and other operations, federal income taxes, and stockholder dividends. In addition, the cash disbursements necessary to repay debt and acquire new assets must also be incorporated in the cash budget.

Illustration 17-5

SHASTA DESIGN, INC.
Budgeted Income Statement
For the Budget Year Ended December 31

Budgeted revenues:		
Sales (6,400 units at $800)		$5,120,000
Costs:		
Cost of goods manufactured and sold (Illustration 17–2)	$3,200,000	
Marketing and administrative costs (Illustration 17–4)	1,552,000	
Total budgeted costs		4,752,000
Operating profit		368,000
Federal and other income taxes[a]		128,000
Operating profit after taxes		$ 240,000

[a] Computed by the company's tax staff.

Shasta Design's cash budget is shown in Illustration 17–6. The source of each item is indicated.

Key Relationships: The Sales Cycle

Assembling the master budget demonstrates some key relations among sales, accounts receivable, and cash flows in the sales cycle. Advantages of understanding these relationships include the ability to solve for amounts that are unknown and to audit the master budget to ensure that the basic accounting equation has been correctly applied.

At Shasta Design, for example, the relationships among budgeted sales, accounts receivable, and cash receipts were as follows:

Sales	Accounts Receivable	Cash (Illustration 17–6)	
	BB 220,000	BB 150,000	
Illustrations 17–5 and 17–7	Illustrations 17–6 and 17–7		
5,120,000 ⟶ 5,120,000	5,185,000 ⟶ 5,185,000		
		25,000	5,217,000
	EB 155,000	EB 143,000	

Illustration 17–6

SHASTA DESIGN, INC.
Cash Budget
For the Budget Year Ended December 31

Cash balance beginning of period[a]		$ 150,000
Receipts:		
Collections on accounts[a]	$5,185,000	
Sales of assets[a]	25,000	
Total receipts		5,210,000
Less disbursements:		
Payments for accounts payable[a]	1,164,000	
Direct labor (Illustration 17–2)	949,000	
Manufacturing overhead requiring cash less noncash depreciation charges (Illustration 17–3)	851,000	
Marketing and administrative costs less noncash charges (Illustration 17–4)	1,458,000	
Payments for federal income taxes (per discussion with the tax staff)	252,000	
Dividends[a]	140,000	
Reduction in long-term debt[a]	83,000	
Acquisition of new assets[b]	320,000	
Total disbursements		5,217,000
Budgeted ending cash balance (ties to Illustration 17–7)[c]		$ 143,000

[a] Estimated by the treasurer's office.

[b] Estimated by the treasurer's office, per the capital budget.

[c] Solved from the basic cost flow equation:

$$BB + TI = TO + EB$$
$$\$150,000 + \$5,210,000 = \$5,217,000 + EB$$
$$EB = \$143,000$$

Sales are assumed to be on account. Note that the cash account and the cash budget in Illustration 17–6 are identical.

If an amount in the sales cycle is unknown, the basic accounting equation can be used to find the unknown amount. For example, suppose all of the amounts in the above diagram are known except ending cash balance and sales. Using the basic cost flow equation,

$$BB + TI = TO + EB$$

find sales from the Accounts Receivable account:

$$\$220,000 + TI \text{ (sales)} = \$5,185,000 + \$155,000$$
$$TI = \$5,185,000 + \$155,000 - \$220,000$$
$$= \underline{\$5,120,000}$$

Find ending cash balance from the Cash account:

$$\$150,000 + (\$5,185,000 + \$25,000) = \$5,217,000 + EB$$
$$\$150,000 + \$5,185,000 + \$25,000 - \$5,217,000 = EB$$
$$EB = \underline{\$143,000}$$

Budgeted Balance Sheets

Budgeted balance sheets, or statements of financial position, combine an estimate of financial position at the beginning of the budget period with the estimated results of operations for the period (from the income statements) and estimated changes in assets and liabilities. The latter results from management's decisions about optimal levels of capital investment in long-term assets (the capital budget), investment in working capital, and financing decisions. Decision making in these areas is, for the most part, the treasurer's function. We shall assume these decisions have been made and incorporate their results in the budgeted balance sheets. Illustration 17–7 presents Shasta Design's budgeted balance sheets at the beginning and end of the budget year.

Master Budget Development in Review

We have completed the development of a comprehensive budget for Shasta Design. A model of the budgeting process is presented in Illustration 17–8. Although we have simplified the presentation, you can still see that assembling a master budget is a complex process that requires careful coordination of many different organization segments.

More Detailed Cash Flow Analysis

Cash flows are often analyzed in more detail than shown in the Shasta Design example. For example, assume the Near-Cash Wholesale Co. has the following information available about its monthly collection experience for sales or credit:

Cash collected from current month's sales	24%
Cash collected from last month's sales	70
Cash discounts taken (percent of gross sales)	4
Written off as a bad debt	2
	100%

Illustration 17-7

SHASTA DESIGN, INC.
Budgeted Balance Sheets
For the Budget Year Ended December 31
(in thousands)

	Balance (January 1)	Budget Year Additions	Budget Year Subtractions	Balance (December 31)
Assets				
Current assets:				
Cash	$ 150[a]	$ 5,210[a]	$ 5,217[a]	$ 143[a]
Accounts receivable	220*	5,120[b]	5,185[a]	155*
Inventories	592[c]	3,259[d]	3,200[e]	651[f]
Other current assets	23*	100*	100*	23*
Total current assets	985	13,689	13,702	972
Long-term assets:				
Property, plant, and equipment	2,475*	320[a]	300*	2,495*
Less: Accumulated depreciation	(850)*	(374)[g]	(275)*	(949)*
Total assets	$2,610	$13,635	$13,727	$2,518
Equities				
Current liabilities:				
Accounts payable	$ 140*	$ 1,179[h]	$ 1,164[a]	$ 155*
Taxes payable	156*	128[b]	252[a]	32*
Current portion of long-term debt	83*	0*	83[a]	0*
Total current liabilities	379	1,307	1,499	187
Long-term liabilities	576*	0*	0*	576*
Total liabilities	955	1,307	1,499	763
Shareholders' equity:				
Common stock	350*	0*	0*	350*
Retained earnings	1,305*	240[i]	140[a]	1,405*
Total shareholders' equity	1,655	240	140	1,755
Total equities	$2,610	$ 1,547	$ 1,639	$2,518

* Estimated by personnel in the company's accounting department.

[a] From cash budget (Illustration 17-6).

[b] From budgeted income statement (Illustration 17-5). Assumes all sales are on account.

[c] From budgeted statement of cost of goods manufactured and sold (Illustration 17-2), sum of beginning direct materials, work in process, and finished goods inventories ($142 + 0 + 450 = $592).

[d] From budgeted statement of costs of goods manufactured and sold (Illustration 17-2), sum of material purchases, direct labor, and manufacturing overhead ($1,179 + 949 + 1,131 = $3,259).

[e] From budgeted statement of cost of goods manufactured and sold (Illustration 17-2).

[f] From budgeted statement of cost of goods manufactured and sold (Illustration 17-2), sum of ending direct materials, work in process, and finished goods inventories ($151 + 0 + 500 = $651).

[g] Depreciation of $280 from schedule of budgeted manufacturing overhead (Illustration 17-3) plus depreciation of $94 from the schedule of budgeted marketing and administrative costs (Illustration 17-4) equals $374 increase in accumulated depreciation.

[h] From budgeted statement of cost of goods manufactured and sold (Illustration 17-2). Accounts payable increases are assumed to be for materials purchases only.

[i] From budgeted income statement (Illustration 17-5), operating profit after taxes.

This means that if July's sales on credit are $1 million, then $240,000 are expected to be collected in July; $700,000 are expected to be collected in August; $40,000 are expected not to be collected because the customers paid early enough to get a discount; and $20,000 are expected not to be collected because these accounts will be written off as bad debts.

Illustration 17-8   **Assembling the Master Budget: Manufacturing Organization**

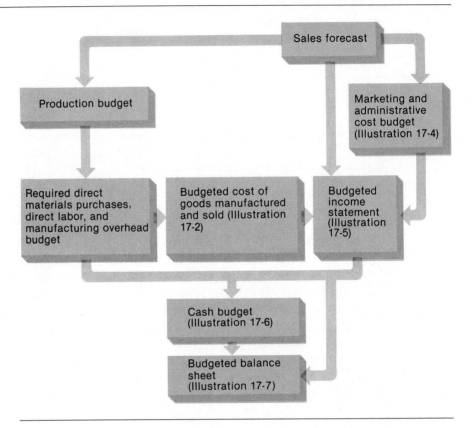

If sales on credit are expected to be $900,000 in June, $1 million in July, and $1.2 million in August, what are the expected cash collections in July and August?

Answers:

July: $870,000 [= (.24 × $1,000,000) + (.70 × $900,000)]
August: $988,000 [= (.24 × $1,200,000) + (.70 × $1,000,000)]

BUDGETING IN MERCHANDISING OPERATIONS

While a manufacturing operation provides a good comprehensive example, budgeting is extensively used in other environments as well, as discussed in this and the following sections.

As in manufacturing, the sales budget in merchandising drives the operating budget. The major difference is that a merchandiser has no production budget. Instead, there is a merchandise purchases budget, which is much like the direct materials purchases budget in manufacturing. For example, at Stores, Inc., the purchases budget for a line of women's suits was determined as follows:

	Units	Dollars
Estimated sales	100	$20,000
Add estimated ending inventory	10	2,000
Deduct estimated beginning inventory	(15)	(3,000)
Required purchases	95	$19,000

As you can see, this budget requires extensive coordination between the managers responsible for sales and those in charge of buying. Because of the critical importance of timing and seasonality in merchandising, special attention is usually given to short-term budgets (for example, spring, summer, Christmas season budgets). The budget helps formalize an ongoing process of coordinating buying and selling. This coordination is critical to the success of merchandising enterprises.

BUDGETING IN SERVICE ENTERPRISES

A key difference in the master budget of a service enterprise is the absence of product or material inventories. Consequently, there is no need for a production budget, as in manufacturing, or a merchandise purchases budget, as in merchandising. Instead, service businesses need to carefully coordinate sales (that is, services rendered) with the necessary labor. Managers must ensure that personnel with the right skills are available at the right times.

The budget at David & Sons Company, a regional accounting firm, is developed around the three major services offered: audit, tax, and consulting. Projections of revenue are based on estimates of the number and kinds of clients the firm would service in the budget year and the amount of services requested. The forecasts stem primarily from services provided in previous years with adjustments for new clients, new services to existing clients, loss of clients, and changes in the rates charged for services.

Once the quantity of services (expressed in labor-hours) is forecast, the firm develops its budget for personnel. Staffing to meet client needs is a very important part of the budgeting process. As a partner of the firm put it, "If we overestimate the amount of services we'll provide, we may lose money because we have overstaffed. Our labor costs will be too high compared to our revenues. If we underestimate, we may lose business because we can't provide the services our clients need."

BUDGETING IN NONPROFIT ORGANIZATIONS

The master budget has added importance in nonprofit organizations because it is usually a document used as a basis for authorizing the expenditure of funds. In many governmental units, *the approved budget is a legal authorization for expenditure,* and the penalties for exceeding the authorized expenditures in the budget could be severe. This partially explains why a balanced budget takes on added importance in nonprofit organizations.[6]

---

[6] For a further discussion of budgeting in government and other nonprofit organizations, see K. V. Ramanathan, *Management Control in Nonprofit Organizations* (New York: John Wiley & Sons, 1982); R. N. Anthony and D. W. Young, *Management Control in Nonprofit Organizations* (Homewood, Ill.: R. D. Irwin, 1984); and E. S. Lynn and R. J. Freeman, *Fund Accounting* (Englewood Cliffs, N.J.: Prentice-Hall, 1983).

BUDGETING UNDER UNCERTAINTY

Sensitivity Analysis The study of the effect of changes in assumptions on the results of a decision model.

Any projection of the future is uncertain. Recognizing this, managers often perform sensitivity analysis on their projections. This analysis is based on hypothetical questions, such as: What if labor costs are 10 percent higher (or lower) than projected? What if new health and safety regulations are passed that increase our costs of operations? What if our major supplier of direct materials goes bankrupt? By asking and answering such questions during the planning phase, management can discover the riskiness of various phases of its operations and can develop contingency plans.

As part of the budget plan at Shasta Design, for example, local managers were asked to provide three forecasts: their best estimate, an optimistic estimate (defined as "a 10 percent or less chance that conditions would be better than the optimistic estimate"), and a pessimistic estimate (defined as the situation where there is "a 10 percent or less chance that conditions would be worse"). The optimistic and pessimistic forecasts were not nearly so detailed as the best estimates, but they did highlight some potential problems and risks. From this analysis, top management learned that a major supplier of a distant plant was on the verge of bankruptcy. As a result, management developed relationships with other suppliers, increased the stockpiles of direct materials in the plant, and worked with the supplier to improve its financial position.

REAL WORLD APPLICATION

Participative Budgeting in a Hospital

Participative budgeting is used in a variety of organizations. For example, the University Community Hospital in Tampa, Florida, found that participative budgeting helped provide accurate forecasts and a strong sense of commitment to the organization.* Most of the work in the hospital is done by small work teams, so the best source of information for the budget is from those work teams. The budget process is carried out in the following steps:

1. The board of directors and the top administrators prepare general guidelines for the operation of the hospital.

2. The budget process is formally started with a "statement of conditions," which identifies conditions expected to affect the hospital's operations. Then they project monthly admissions, emergency room visits, average number of patients in the hospital, and similar statistical data.

3. Each department manager is given this information to convert into budgeted costs or revenues in

a revenue-generating department. For example, the emergency room director will use the estimated emergency room visits to estimate staffing needs, additional equipment required, supplies, and other items needed to operate the emergency room at the projected activity level.

4. These departmental budgets go up through various reviews until they are finally approved by the top administrators of the hospital and the board of directors.

The division of duties that occurs is interesting. The top administrative people provide general information about trends in demand for the hospital's services, but they do not tell department managers how much money they can spend. Instead, department managers convert the general information into specific cost projections because they have a comparative advantage over top administrators in doing so. Of course, the top administrators must still approve those departmental budgets.

*Based on M. A. Feldbush, "Participative Budgeting in a Hospital Setting," *Management Accounting*, September 1981, pp. 43–46.

Illustration 17–9   **Sensitivity Analysis and Contingency Planning**

Sensitivity analysis "What if?"	Contingency planning "If, then"
	Status quo
Optimistic (Economic conditions	Increase discretionary costs
and sales better than expected)	Increase production
Expected sales	Status quo
	Status quo
Pessimistic (Economic conditions	Reduce discretionary costs
and sales worse than expected)	Curtail production

Top management at Shasta Design also learned that if all costs were as expected and the pessimistic forecast of sales came true, the company would suffer an operating loss. The primary reason for this would be a worsening of general economic conditions that would decrease demand for the company's products. This was important information to consider in making financial analyses. Further, management put an "early warning" system in place in which it carefully monitored such key economic variables as unemployment, consumer spending, gross national product, and the like. If these indicators signaled a downturn in the economy, management's contingency plan was to reduce production gradually so excess inventories would not build up and to reduce discretionary spending on overhead, marketing, and administrative costs.

Illustration 17–9 provides an overview of sensitivity analysis and contingency planning. For each hypothesis in the sensitivity analysis, there is a choice of steps that can be taken. The procedure can be as simple as a diagram and a few notes on a piece of paper or as complex as a mathematical model incorporated into computerized formal planning models.[7] Of course, decisions about these models' degree of sophistication should be subject to cost-benefit analysis.

The incorporation of uncertainty into budget estimates can be quite useful. A major benefit of formal planning models is to explore many alternatives and options in the planning process. While it is beyond the scope of this book to go into details of formal corporate planning models, we think you can see how the budget plan can be integrated with formal planning models that set forth mathematical relationships among the operating and financial activities of an organization. The use of computer-based simulation models facilitates the asking of numerous "what if" questions, which become too difficult to deal with by hand as their number grows.

---

[7] Chapter 24 discusses the use of mathematical models to deal with uncertainty.

SUMMARY

This chapter has discussed and illustrated the budget process. The budget is part of the overall plan for achieving an organization's objectives. The master budget is a one-year (usually) plan that encompasses budgeted sales and production, budgeted income statement, balance sheet, and cash flow statement, as well as supporting schedules.

The key to the budget is a good sales forecast because so many other parts of the budget depend on the sales forecast. The sales forecast is usually derived from multiple sources of data, including data provided by sales personnel, market researchers, and from statistical analyses. Illustration 17–8 shows how the rest of the master budget relates to the sales forecast.

Merchandising budgets are similar to manufacturing, except they have no production budget. Service organizations are similar, except they have no inventories. The budget is not only a planning tool but also a legal authorization for expenditure in governmental units.

Budgeting under uncertainty involves making many forecasts, each representing a different possible set of circumstances. Sensitivity analysis ("what if") and contingency planning ("if, then") are used to derive a set of plans for each possible set of circumstances.

TERMS AND CONCEPTS

The following terms and concepts should be familiar to you after reading this chapter.

Budget
Budgeted Balance Sheets
Budgeting under Uncertainty
Cash Budget
Delphi Technique
Econometric Models
Master Budget
Organizational Goals

Participative Budgeting
Production Budget
Profit Plan
Sales Forecasts
Sensitivity Analysis
Strategic Long-Range Plan
Trend Analysis

SUPPLEMENTARY READINGS

Baber, William R. "Budget-Based Compensation and Discretionary Spending." *Accounting Review,* January 1985, pp. 1–9.

Brownell, P. "Participation in Budgeting, Locus of Control, and Organizational Effectiveness." *Accounting Review,* October 1981, pp. 844–60.

————. "Participation in the Budgeting Process—When It Works and When It Doesn't." *Journal of Accounting Literature,* Spring 1982.

Bruns, W. J., and J. Waterhouse. "Budgetary Control and Organization Structure." *Journal of Accounting Research,* Autumn 1975, pp. 177–203.

Burns, T. J., ed. *The Behavioral Aspects of Accounting Data for Performance Evaluation.* Columbus: College of Administrative Science, The Ohio State University, 1970.

Chow, Chee W.; Jean C. Cooper; and William S. Waller. "Participative Budgeting: Effects of Truth-Inducing Pay Scheme and Information Asymmetry on Slack and Performance." *Accounting Review,* January 1988, pp. 111–22.

Collins, Frank; Paul Munter; and Don W. Finn. "Budgeting Games People Play." *Accounting Review*, January 1987, pp. 29-49.

Covaleski, M. A., and M. W. Dirsmith. "The Use of Budgetary Symbols in the Political Arena: An Historically Informed Field Study." *Accounting, Organizations, and Society* 13, no. 1 (1988), pp. 1–24.

Demski, J. S., and G. A. Feltham. "Economic Incentives in Budgetary Control Systems." *Accounting Review*, April 1978, pp. 336–59.

Doost, Roger K. "Public vs. Private Budgeting: A Comparative Study." *Government Accountants Journal*, Fall 1984, pp. 47–52.

Gordon, Lawrence A., and Fred E. Sellers. "Accounting and Budgeting Systems: The Issue of Congruency." *Journal of Accounting & Public Policy*, Winter 1984, pp. 259–92.

Holstrum, G. L. "The Effect of Budget Adaptiveness and Tightness on Managerial Decision Behavior." *Journal of Accounting Research*, Autumn 1971, pp. 268–77.

Koehler, Kenneth G. "Link Budget to Overall Plan." *CMA*, May–June 1987, p. 17 (published in Canada).

Licata, Michael P.; Robert H. Strawser; and Robert B. Welker. "A Note on Participation in Budgeting and Locus of Control." *Accounting Review*, January 1986, pp. 112–17.

Lin, W. T. "Multiple Objective Budgeting Models: A Simulation." *Accounting Review*, January 1978, pp. 61–76.

Ranck, Harold, Jr. "Avoiding the Pitfalls in Sales Forecasting." *Management Accounting*, September 1986, pp. 51–55.

Rockness, H. O. "Expectancy Theory in a Budgeting Setting: An Experimental Examination." *Accounting Review*, October 1977, pp. 893–903.

Samuelson, Lars A. "Discrepancies between the Roles of Budgeting." *Accounting, Organizations, and Society* 11, no. 1 (1986), pp. 35–45.

Viscione, Jerry A. "Small Company Budgets: Targets Are Key." *Harvard Business Review*, May–June 1984, pp. 42–44, 48, 50, 52.

Welsch, G. A. *Budgeting: Profit Planning and Control*. Englewood Cliffs, N.J.: Prentice-Hall, 1978.

Young, Mark. "Participative Budgeting: The Effects of Risk Aversion and Asymmetric Information on Budgetary Slack." *Journal of Accounting Research*, Autumn 1985, pp. 829–42.

SELF-STUDY PROBLEM

Refer to the problem for Shasta Design, Inc., in the chapter example. Assume the sales forecast was increased to 7,000 units with no change in price. The new target ending inventories are:

Finished goods	1,200 units
Material R	1,500
Material S	4,900

Payments for income taxes and income tax expense are proportional to operating profit before tax. Accounts receivable will increase by another $40,000 at this new sales level. Accounts payable will increase by an additional $2,000 at the new production level.

Required:

Prepare a budgeted income statement, cost of goods manufactured and sold statement, administrative and selling cost budget, and cash budget for the coming year with this new data.

SHASTA DESIGN, INC.
Budgeted Statement of Cost of Goods Manufactured and Sold
For the Budget Year Ended December 31
(compare to Illustration 17–2)

Beginning work in process inventory			–0–
Manufacturing costs:			
Direct materials:			
Beginning inventory (Illustration 17–2)	$ 142,000		
Purchases[a] (21,200 R @ $10 + 37,400 S @ $30)	1,334,000		
Materials available for manufacturing	1,476,000		
Less: Ending inventory (1,500 R @ $10 + 4,900 S @ $30)	(162,000)		
Total direct materials costs		$1,314,000	
Direct labor $\left(\$949,000 \times \dfrac{7,300}{6,500}\right)$		1,065,800	
Manufacturing overhead (Exhibit B)		1,147,000	
Total manufacturing costs			$3,526,800
Deduct: Ending work in process inventory			–0–
Cost of goods manufactured			3,526,800
Add: Beginning finished goods inventory			450,000
Deduct: Ending finished goods inventory[a]			(579,748)
Cost of goods sold			$3,397,052

[a] Additional computations:

Required production:

$$\begin{array}{rll} \text{BB} & + \text{Production} & = \text{Sales} + \text{EB} \\ 900 + & \text{P} & = 7,000 + 1,200 \\ & \text{P} & = 7,300 \end{array}$$

Material requirements:

$$\begin{array}{rrll} \text{R:} & \text{BB} & + \text{Purchases} & = \text{Production} + \text{EB} \\ & 2,200 + & \text{P} & = (7,300 \times 3) + 1,500 \\ & & \text{P} & = 21,200 \end{array}$$

$$\begin{array}{rrll} \text{S:} & \text{BB} & + \text{Purchases} & = \text{Production} + \text{EB} \\ & 4,000 + & \text{P} & = (7,300 \times 5) + 4,900 \\ & & \text{P} & = 37,400 \end{array}$$

Ending finished goods inventory (assuming FIFO):

$$\frac{\text{Ending units}}{\text{Units produced}} \times \text{Cost of goods manufactured} = \frac{1,200}{7,300} \times \$3,526,800$$
$$= \$579,748$$

Exhibit B (SSP)

SHASTA DESIGN, INC.
Schedule of Budgeted Manufacturing Overhead
For the Budget Year Ended December 31
(compare to Illustration 17–3)

Variable (based on production of 7,300 units)[a]		
Indirect materials and supplies	$ 42,677	
Materials handling	66,261.5	
Other indirect labor	37,061.5	$ 146,000
Fixed (same as for production of 6,500 units):		
Supervisor labor	175,000	
Maintenance and repairs	85,000	
Plant administration	173,000	
Utilities	87,000	
Depreciation	280,000	
Insurance	43,000	
Property taxes	117,000	
Other	41,000	1,001,000
Total manufacturing overhead		$1,147,000

[a] Additional computations:

$$\text{Indirect materials:} \quad \$38,000 \times \frac{7,300}{6,500} = \$42,677$$

$$\text{Materials handling:} \quad \$59,000 \times \frac{7,300}{6,500} = \$66,261.5$$

$$\text{Other indirect labor:} \quad \$33,000 \times \frac{7,300}{6,500} = \$37,061.5$$

Exhibit C (SSP)

SHASTA DESIGN, INC.
Schedule of Budgeted Marketing and Administrative Costs
For the Budget Year Ended December 31
(compare to Illustration 17–4)

Variable marketing costs:[a]		
Sales commissions	$284,375	
Other marketing	113,750	
Total variable marketing costs		$ 398,125
Fixed marketing costs:		
Sales salaries	100,000	
Advertising	193,000	
Other	78,000	
Total fixed marketing costs		371,000
Total marketing costs		769,125
Administrative costs (all fixed):		
Administrative salaries	254,000	
Legal and accounting staff	141,000	
Data processing services	103,000	
Outside professional services	39,000	
Depreciation—building, furniture, and equipment	94,000	
Insurance	26,000	
Taxes—other than income	160,000	
Total administrative costs		817,000
Total budgeted marketing and administrative costs		$1,586,125

[a] Additional computations:

$$\text{Sales commissions: } \$284,375 = \$260,000 \times \frac{7,000 \text{ units}}{6,400 \text{ units}}$$

$$\text{Other marketing: } \quad \$113,750 = \$104,000 \times \frac{7,000 \text{ units}}{6,400 \text{ units}}$$

Exhibit D (SSP)

SHASTA DESIGN, INC.
Budgeted Income Statement
For the Budget Year Ended December 31
(compare to Illustration 17–5)

Budgeted revenues:		
Sales (7,000 units at $800)		$5,600,000
Budgeted expenses:		
Cost of goods manufactured and sold (Exhibit A)	$3,397,052	
Marketing and administrative costs (Exhibit C)	1,586,125	
Total budgeted costs		4,983,177
Budgeted operating profits		616,823
Federal and other income taxes[a]		214,547
Budgeted operating profits after taxes		$ 402,276

[a] Assumed proportional to operating profit:

$$\$128,000 \times \frac{\$616,823}{\$368,000} = \$214,547$$

Exhibit E (SSP)

SHASTA DESIGN, INC.
Cash Budget
For the Budget Year Ended December 31
(compare with Illustration 17–6)

Cash balance beginning of period		$ 150,000
Receipts:		
Collections on accounts[a]	$5,625,000	
Sales of assets (per management)	25,000	
Total receipts		5,650,000
Less disbursements:		
Payments for accounts payable[a]	1,317,000	
Direct labor (Exhibit A)	1,065,800	
Manufacturing overhead requiring cash less noncash depreciation charges (Exhibit B)	867,000	
Marketing and administrative costs less noncash charges (Exhibit C)	1,492,125	
Required payments for federal income taxes[c] (per discussion with the staff)	422,390	
Dividends and other distributions to shareholders (per Management)	140,000	
Reduction in long-term debt	83,000	
Acquisition of new assets	320,000	
Total disbursements		5,707,315
Budgeted ending cash balance		$ 92,685

Additional computations:

[a] Collections on account per Illustration 17–6	$5,185,000
Additional sales ($5,600,000 − $5,120,000) (from Exhibit D and Illustration 17–5)	480,000
Less increase in receivables	(40,000)
	$5,625,000
[b] Payments on account per Illustration 17–6	$1,164,000
Additional materials purchases—per Exhibit A and Illustration 17–2 ($1,334,000 − $1,179,000)	155,000
Less increase in payables	(2,000)
	$1,317,000

[c] Payments on federal taxes are assumed to increase proportionately with the increase in budgeted operating profits from the text example to this one.

$$\left[\frac{\text{Budgeting operating profits in Exhibit D}}{\text{Budgeted operating profits in Illustration 17–5}}\right] \times \left[\begin{array}{l}\text{Budgeted tax} \\ \text{payments in} \\ \text{Illustration 17–6}\end{array}\right] = \frac{\$616,823}{368,000} \times \$252,000 = \$422,390$$

QUESTIONS

17–1. Explain the difference between strategic plans and the budget plan.

17–2. Why would more detail be included in a budget for the coming period than appears in a longer range forecast?

17–3. The chief executive officer of Rigid Plastics Corporation remarked to a colleague, "I don't understand why other companies waste so much time in the budgeting process. I set our company goals, and everyone strives to meet them. What's wrong with that approach?" Comment on the executive's remarks.

17–4. If a company prepares budgeted income statements and balance sheets, why is there a need to prepare a cash budget?

17–5. List four methods used to estimate sales for budgeting purposes.

17–6. How would the use of a just-in-time inventory system affect a company's budget plans?

17–7. For governmental agencies, a budget is also a legal limitation on expenditures. If governmental employees are asked about their agencies' needs for the coming fiscal period, what types of biases are they likely to incorporate in their estimates? Why?

17–8. What are the relationships between organization goals, strategic plans, and a master budget for the coming period?

17–9. What is the danger in relying entirely on middle-management estimates of sales, costs, and other data used in budget planning?

17–10. Multigoal Corporation has established a bonus plan for its employees. An employee receives a bonus if the employee's subunit meets the cost levels specified in the annual budget plan. If the subunit's costs exceed the budget, no bonus is earned by employees of that subunit. What problems might arise with this bonus plan?

17–11. Why is it important to estimate inventory levels when estimating the production level required for a given sales forecast?

17–12. How can budgeting aid in the coordination of corporate activities?

17–13. Surveying the accounts payable records, a clerk in the controller's office noted that expenses appeared to rise significantly within a month of the close of the budget period. The organization did not have a seasonal product or service to explain this behavior. Do you have a suggested explanation?

17–14. Budgets in not-for-profit organizations have an additional purpose beyond that in for-profit organizations. What is that purpose?

17–15. Which of the following budgets is most important from management's perspective: the budgeted balance sheet or the budgeted income statement? Why?

EXERCISES

17–16. Estimate Sales Revenues

(L.O.2)

Drexel, Burned, Limbear is a large securities dealer. Last year, the company made 55,000 trades with an average commission of $225 per trade. Smaller investors are abandoning the market, which is expected to reduce marketwide volume by 12 percent for the coming year. Drexel expects that its volume generally changes with the market. However, in addition to market factors, Drexel expects an additional 10 percent decline in the number of trades due to unfavorable publicity.

Offsetting these factors is the observation that the average commission per trade is likely to increase by 26 percent because trades are expected to be larger in the coming year.

Required:

Estimate the commission revenues from the coming year.

17–17. Estimate Sales Revenues

(L.O.2)

Espera of America (EOA) is a banking organization. EOA has $40 million in commercial loans with an average interest rate of 11.5 percent. The bank also has $30 million in consumer loans with an average interest rate of 15 percent. Finally, the bank owns $8 million in securities with an average rate of 9 percent.

EOA estimates that next year its commercial loan portfolio will fall to $36 million, and the rate will fall to 11 percent. Its consumer loans will expand to $33 million with an average interest rate of 16 percent, and its government securities portfolio will increase to $9 million with an average rate of 8 percent.

Required:

Prepare an estimate of Espera of America's revenues for the coming year.

17–18. Estimate Sales Revenues

(L.O.2)

Welcome Company manufactures large balloons. Last year, the company sold 500,000 type A balloons at a price of $2 per unit. The company estimates that this volume represents a 20 percent share of the current type A balloons market. The market is expected to increase by 5 percent. Marketing specialists have determined that as a result of a new advertising campaign and packaging, the company will increase its share of this larger market to 24 percent. Due to changes in prices, the new price for the type A balloons will be $2.15 per unit. This new price is expected to be in line with the competition and have no effect on the volume estimates.

Required:

Estimate the sales revenues for the coming year.

17–19. Estimate Production Levels

(L.O.2)

XiPhi, Inc., has just made its sales forecast for the coming period. The marketing department estimates that the company will sell 480,000 units during the coming year. In the past, management has found that inventories of finished goods should be maintained at approximately three months' sales. The inventory at the start of the budget period is 27,000 units. Sales take place evenly throughout the year.

Required:

Estimate the production level required for the coming year to meet these objectives.

17–20. Estimate Production and Materials Requirements

(L.O.2)

Vivid Colors Corporation manufactures a special line of graphic tubing items. For each of the next two coming years, the company estimates it will sell 150,000 units of this item. The beginning finished goods inventory contains 40,000 units. The target for each year's ending inventory is 20,000 units.

Each unit requires five feet of plastic tubing. The tubing inventory currently includes 100,000 feet of the required tubing. Materials on hand are targeted to equal three months' production. Any shortage in materials will be made up by the immediate purchase of materials. Sales take place evenly throughout the year.

Required:

Compute the production target and the materials requirements for the coming year.

17–21. Estimate Purchases and Cash Disbursements

(L.O.3)

The Balloon Lady buys plain mylar balloons and prints different designs on them for various occasions. The plain balloons are imported from Taiwan, so a stock equal to the balloons needed for two months' sales should be kept on hand at all times. Plain balloons cost $1.35 each and must be paid for in cash. There are 14,000 plain balloons in the company's stock. Sales estimates, based on contracts received, are as follows for the next six months:

January	5,500
February	8,900
March	6,600
April	7,100
May	4,500
June	3,600

Required:

a. Estimate purchases (in units) for January, February, and March.

b. Estimate cash required to make purchases in January, February, and March.

17–22. Estimate Purchases and Cash Disbursements

(L.O.3)

Milkem Merchandising wishes to purchase goods in one month for sale in the next. On March 31, the company has 4,000 digital tape players in stock, although sales for the next month (April) are estimated to total 4,300 players. Sales for May are expected to equal 3,500 players, and June sales are expected to total 4,200 players.

Tape players are purchased at a wholesale price of $430. The supplier has a financing arrangement whereby Milkem pays 60 percent of the purchase price in the month when the players are delivered and 40 percent in the following month. Five thousand players were delivered in March.

Required:

a. Estimate purchases (in units) for April and May.

b. Estimate cash required to make purchases in April and May.

17–23. Estimate Cash Disbursements
(L.O.3)

Terry Company is preparing its cash budget for the month of April. The following information is available concerning its inventories:

Inventories at beginning of April	$ 90,000
Estimated purchases for April	440,000
Estimated cost of goods sold for April	450,000
Estimated payments in April for purchases in March	75,000
Estimated payments in April for purchases prior to March	20,000
Estimated payments in April for purchases in April	75%

Required:

What are the estimated cash disbursements for inventories in April?

17–24. Estimate Cash Collections
(L.O.3)

Fresh Company is preparing its cash budget for the month of May. The following information is available concerning its accounts receivable:

Estimated credit sales for May	$200,000
Actual credit sales for April	150,000
Estimated collections in May for credit sales in May	20%
Estimated collections in May for credit sales in April	70%
Estimated collections in May for credit sales prior to April	$ 12,000
Estimated write-offs in May for uncollectible credit sales	8,000
Estimated provision for bad debts in May for credit sales in May	7,000

Required:

What are the estimated cash receipts from accounts receivable collections in May?

a. $142,000.

b. $149,000.

c. $150,000.

d. $157,000.

(CPA adapted)

17–25. Estimate Cash Collections
(L.O.3)

Varsity Company is preparing a cash budget for the month of May. The following information on accounts receivable collections is available from Varsity's past collection experience:

Percent of current month's sales collected this month	12%
Percent of prior month's sales collected this month	75
Percent of sales two months prior to current month collected this month	6
Percent of sales three months prior to current month collected this month	4
The remaining 3 percent are not collected and are written off as bad debts.	

Credit sales to date are as follows:

May—estimated	$100,000
April	90,000
March	80,000
February	95,000

Required:

What are the estimated accounts receivable collections for May?

a. $85,100.

b. $87,100.

c. $88,100.

d. $90,100.

(CPA adapted)

17–26. Estimate Cash Disbursements
(L.O.3)

Serven Corporation, a merchandising company, has estimated its activity for next June. Selected data from these estimates are as follows:

Sales	$700,000
Cost of goods sold	490,000
Increase in trade accounts receivable during month	20,000
Change in accounts payable during month	–0–
Increase in inventory during month	10,000

Variable selling and administrative costs include a charge for uncollectible accounts of 1 percent of sales and are paid in the month of sale. Total selling and administrative costs are $71,000 per month plus 15 percent of sales. Depreciation expense of $40,000 per month are included in fixed selling and administrative costs. All of the rest of selling and administrative costs are paid in cash.

Required:

On the basis of the above data, what are the estimated cash disbursements from operations for June?

(CPA adapted)

17–27. Estimate Cash Receipts
(L.O.3)

Kathy's Bridal Designs is a custom clothing shop that specializes in wedding attire. The average price of each of Kathy's wedding ensembles is $3,200. For each wedding, Kathy's receives a 20 percent deposit two months before the wedding, 50 percent the month before, and the remainder on the day when the goods are delivered. Based on information at hand, Kathy's expects to prepare outfits for the following number of weddings during the coming months:

January	8
February	6
March	3
April	8
May	10
June	25

Required:

a. What are the expected revenues for Kathy's Bridal Designs for each month, January through April?

b. What are the expected cash receipts for each month, January through April?

17–28. Estimate Cash Receipts
(L.O.3)

Green Lawn Service manages neighborhood lawns in Iowa City. The company attempts to make service calls at least once a month to all homes that subscribe to Green Lawn's service. More frequent calls are made during the growing season. The number of subscribers also varies with the season. The following table shows the number of subscribers and the average number of calls to each subscriber for the months of interest here:

	Subscribers	Service Calls
March	50	.5
April	60	1.0
May	130	1.8
June	150	2.2
July	150	2.0
August	140	1.7

The average price charged for a service call is $40. 20 percent of the service calls are paid in the month when the service is rendered; 60 percent in the month after the service is rendered; and 15 percent in the second month after. The remaining 5 percent are uncollectible.

Required:

What are Green Lawn's expected cash receipts for May, June, July, and August?

17–29. Prepare Budgeted Financial Statements
(L.O.4)

Refer to the data in exercise 17–28.

Green Lawn estimates the number of subscribers in September should fall 10 percent below August levels, and the number of service calls should decrease by an estimated 5 percent. The following information is available for costs incurred in August. All costs except depreciation are paid in cash.

Manufacturing costs:	
Variable costs	$2,360
Maintenance and repair	2,100
Depreciation (fixed)	1,100
Total	5,560
Marketing and administrative costs:	
Marketing (variable)	1,250
Administrative (fixed)	1,150
Total	2,400
Total costs	$7,960

Variable cash costs and variable marketing costs will change with volume. Fixed depreciation will remain the same, while fixed administrative costs will increase by 5 percent beginning September 1. Maintenance and repair is provided by contract, which calls for an 18 percent increase over the next year (1.5 percent per month).

Required:

Prepare a budgeted income statement for September.

17–30. Prepare Budgeted Financial Statements
(L.O.4)

Audiodisc, Inc., is a fast growing start-up firm that manufactures compact disc players. The following income statement is available for Year 1.

Revenues (100 units @ $250/unit)	$25,000
Less:	
Manufacturing costs:	
Materials	1,450
Variable costs	1,228
Fixed costs	2,285
Depreciation (fixed)	8,590
Total manufacturing costs	13,553
Gross profit margin	11,447
Less:	
Marketing:	
Variable costs	3,640
Depreciation (fixed)	1,289
Administrative:	
Fixed costs (cash)	4,390
Depreciation (fixed)	649
Total marketing and administrative	9,968
Operating profits	$ 1,479

Sales volume is expected to increase by 25 percent in Year 2, while the sales price is expected to fall 10 percent. Materials prices are expected to increase 4 percent. Variable manufacturing costs are expected to increase by 3 percent in Year 2. Fixed manufacturing costs are expected to increase 5 percent.

Variable marketing costs will change with sales volume. Administrative costs are expected to increase by 10 percent.

Audiodisc operates on a cash basis and maintains inventories close to zero. Depreciation is fixed and should remain unchanged over the next three years.

Required:

Prepare a budgeted income statement for Year 2.

PROBLEMS

17–31. Prepare Budgeted Financial Statements

The following information is available for Year 1 for Digital Electronics:

Revenues (100,000 units)	$725,000
Manufacturing costs:	
Materials	42,000
Variable cash costs	35,600
Fixed cash costs	81,900
Depreciation (fixed)	249,750
Marketing and administrative costs:	
Marketing (variable, cash)	105,600
Marketing depreciation	37,400
Administrative (fixed, cash)	127,300
Administrative depreciation	18,700
Total costs	698,250
Operating profits	$ 26,750

Depreciation charges are all fixed and are expected to remain the same for Year 2. Sales volume is expected to increase by 18 percent, but prices are expected to fall by 5 percent. Materials costs are expected to decrease by 8 percent. Variable manufacturing costs are expected to decrease by 2 percent. Fixed manufacturing costs are expected to increase by 5 percent.

Variable marketing costs will change with volume. Administrative costs are expected to increase by 10 percent. Inventories are kept at close to zero.

Required: Prepare a budgeted income statement for Year 2.

17-32. Estimate Cash Receipts

Refer to the data in problem 17–31. Estimate the cash from operations expected in Year 2.

17-33. Prepare Budgeted Financial Statements

Monumental Designs has the following data from Year 1 operations, which are to be used for developing Year 2 budget estimates:

Revenues (100,000)	$746,000
Manufacturing costs:	
Materials	133,000
Variable cash costs	180,900
Fixed cash costs	72,000
Depreciation (fixed)	89,000
Marketing and administrative costs:	
Marketing (variable, cash)	95,000
Marketing depreciation	22,600
Administrative (fixed, cash)	90,110
Administrative depreciation	8,400
Total costs	691,010
Operating profits	$ 54,990

Depreciation charges are all fixed. Old manufacturing equipment with an annual depreciation charge of $9,700 will be replaced in Year 2 with new equipment that will incur an annual depreciation charge of $14,000. Sales volume is expected to increase by 12 percent, and prices are expected to increase by 6 percent. Materials costs are expected to increase by 10 percent for each unit produced. Variable manufacturing costs are expected to decrease by 4 percent on a per unit basis. Fixed manufacturing costs are expected to decrease by 7 percent.

Variable marketing costs will change with volume. Administrative costs are expected to increase by 8 percent. Inventories are kept at close to zero.

Required: Prepare a budgeted income statement for Year 2.

17-34. Estimate Cash Receipts

Refer to the data in problem 17–33. Estimate the cash from operations expected in Year 2.

17-35. Prepare a Production Budget

Eastern Forest Products Corporation manufactures floral containers. The controller is preparing a budget for the coming year and asked for your assistance. The following costs and other data apply to container production:

Direct materials per container:	
1 pound Z-A styrene at $.40 per pound	
2 pounds Vasa finish at $.80 per pound	
Direct labor per container:	
¼ hour at $8.60 per hour	
Overhead per container:	
Indirect labor	$.12
Indirect materials	.03
Power	.07
Equipment costs	.36
Building occupancy	.19
Total overhead per unit	$.77

You learn that equipment costs and building occupancy are fixed costs; these unit costs are based on a normal production of 20,000 units per year. Other overhead costs are variable. Plant capacity is sufficient to produce 25,000 units per year.

Labor costs are not expected to change during the year. However, the supplier of the Vasa finish has informed the company that a 10 percent price increase will be imposed at the start of the coming budget period. No other costs are expected to change.

During the coming budget period, the company expects to sell 18,000 units. Finished goods inventory is targeted to increase from 4,000 units to 7,000 units to get ready for an expected sales increase the year after next. Production will take place evenly throughout the year. Inventory levels for Vasa finish and Z-A styrene are expected to remain unchanged throughout the year. There is no work in process inventory.

Required:

Prepare a production budget for the coming year.

17–36. Estimate Administrative and Selling Budget

Compuware Corporation has just received its selling expense report for January. The report is reproduced below.

Item	Amount
Sales commissions	$135,000
Sales staff salaries	32,000
Telephone and mailing	16,200
Building lease payment	20,000
Heat, light, and water	4,100
Packaging and delivery	27,400
Depreciation	12,500
Marketing consultants	19,700

You have been asked to develop budgeted cost estimates for the coming year. Since this month is typical, you decide to prepare an estimated budget for a "typical month" in the coming year.

You uncover the following additional data:

1. Sales volume is expected to increase by 5 percent.
2. Sales prices are expected to increase by 10 percent.
3. Commissions are based on a percentage of selling price.

4. Sales staff salaries are scheduled to increase 4 percent next year.

5. Building rent is based on a five-year lease that expires in three years.

6. Telephone and mailing expenses are scheduled to increase by 8 percent even with no change in sales volume. However, these costs are variable with the number of units sold, as are packaging and delivery costs.

7. Heat, light, and water are scheduled to increase by 12 percent regardless of sales volume.

8. Depreciation includes furniture and fixtures used by the sales staff. The company has just acquired an additional $19,000 in furniture that will be received at the start of next year and will be depreciated over a 10-year life using the straight-line method.

9. Marketing consultant expenses were for a special advertising campaign. The company runs these campaigns from time to time. During the coming year, the costs are expected to average $35,000 per month.

Required:

Prepare a budget for selling expenses for a typical month in the coming year.

17–37. Budgeted Purchases and Cash Flows—Multiple-Choice

D. Tomlinson Retail seeks your assistance to develop cash and other budget information for May, June, and July. At April 30, the company had cash of $5,500; accounts receivable of $437,000; inventories of $309,400; and accounts payable of $133,055. The budget is to be based on the following assumptions:

Sales:
Each month's sales are billed on the last day of the month.
Customers are allowed a 3 percent discount if payment is made within 10 days after the billing date. Receivables are recorded in the accounts at their gross amounts (*not* net of discounts).
Sixty percent of the billings are collected within the discount period; 25 percent are collected by the end of the month; 9 percent are collected by the end of the second month; and 6 percent turn out to be uncollectible.

Purchases:
Fifty-four percent of all purchases of material and selling, general, and administrative expenses are paid in the month purchased and the remainder in the following month.
The number of units in each month's ending inventory is equal to 130 percent of the next month's units of sales.
The cost of each unit of inventory is $20.
Selling, general, and administrative expenses, of which $2,000 is depreciated, are equal to 15 percent of the current month's sales.

Actual and projected sales are as shown below:

	Dollars	**Units**
March	$354,000	11,800
April	363,000	12,100
May	357,000	11,900
June	342,000	11,400
July	360,000	12,000
August	366,000	12,200

Required:

Choose the best answer or indicate "none of the above."

a. Budgeted purchases in dollars for May are:
   (1) $244,800.
   (2) $225,000.
   (3) $238,000.
   (4) $357,000.

b. Budgeted purchases in dollars for June are:
   (1) $243,600.
   (2) $228,000.
   (3) $292,000.
   (4) $242,000.

c. Budgeted cash collections during the month of May are:
   (1) $333,876.
   (2) $355,116.
   (3) $340,410.
   (4) $355,656.

d. Budgeted cash disbursements during the month of June are:
   (1) $292,900.
   (2) $287,379.
   (3) $294,900.
   (4) $285,379.

e. The budgeted number of units of inventory to be purchased during July is:
   (1) 15,860.
   (2) 12,260.
   (3) 12,000.
   (4) 15,600.

(CPA adapted)

17–38. Comprehensive Budget Plan

C. L. Corporation appeared to be experiencing a good year. Sales in the first quarter were one third ahead of last year, and the sales department predicted that this rate would continue throughout the entire year. Ruth Keenan, assistant controller, was asked to prepare a new forecast for the year and to analyze the differences from last year's results. The forecast was to be based on actual results obtained in the first quarter plus the expected costs of programs to be carried out in the remainder of the year. She worked with various department heads (production, sales, and so on) to get the necessary information. The results of these efforts are presented below.

C. L. CORPORATION
Expected Account Balances for December 31, This Year
(in thousands)

Cash	$ 1,200	
Accounts Receivable	80,000	
Inventory (January 1, next year)	48,000	
Plant and Equipment	130,000	
Accumulated Depreciation		$ 41,000
Accounts Payable		45,000
Notes Payable (due within one year)		50,000
Accrued Payables		23,250
Common Stock		70,000
Retained Earnings		108,200
Sales		600,000
Other Income		9,000
Manufacturing costs:		
Materials	213,000	
Direct Labor	218,000	
Variable Overhead	130,000	
Depreciation	5,000	
Other Fixed Overhead	7,750	
Marketing:		
Commissions	20,000	
Salaries	16,000	
Promotion and Advertising	45,000	
Administrative:		
Salaries	16,000	
Travel	2,500	
Office Costs	9,000	
Income Taxes	—	
Dividends	5,000	
	$946,450	$946,450

Adjustments for the change in inventory and for income taxes have not been made. The scheduled production for this year is 450 million units, and planned sales volume is 400 million units. Sales and production volume was 300 million units last year. A full-absorption cost, FIFO inventory system is used. The company is subject to a 40 percent income tax rate. The actual income statement for last year is presented below:

C. L. CORPORATION
Statement of Income and Retained Earnings
for the Year Ended December 31, Last Year
(in thousands)

Revenue:			
Sales		$450,000	
Other income		15,000	$465,000
Expenses:			
Cost of goods manufactured and sold:			
Materials	$132,000		
Direct labor	135,000		
Variable overhead	81,000		
Fixed overhead	12,000		
	360,000		
Beginning inventory	48,000		
	408,000		
Ending inventory	48,000	360,000	
Selling:			
Salaries	13,500		
Commissions	15,000		
Promotion and advertising	31,500	60,000	
General and administrative:			
Salaries	14,000		
Travel	2,000		
Office costs	8,000	24,000	
Income taxes		8,400	452,400
Operating profit			12,600
Beginning retained earnings			100,600
Subtotal			113,200
Less: Dividends			5,000
Ending retained earnings			$108,200

Required:

Prepare a budgeted income statement and balance sheet.

(CMA adapted)

17–39. Prepare Budgeted Profit Plans for Alternative Market Shares

Barr Food Manufacturing Company produces a variety of consumer food and specialty products. Current-year data were prepared as shown below for the salad dressing product line, using five months of actual expenses and a seven-month projection. These data were prepared for a preliminary budget meeting for next year between the Specialty Products Division president, marketing vice president, production vice president, and the controller. The current-year projection was accepted as being accurate, but it was agreed that the operating profit of $2,450,000 was not high enough.

BARR FOOD MANUFACTURING COMPANY
Projected Income Statement
For Current Year Ended December 31
(5 months actual, 7 months projected)
(in thousands)

Volume in gallons	5,000
Gross sales	$30,000
Transportation, allowances, discounts	3,000
Net sales	27,000
Less manufacturing costs:	
Variable	13,500
Fixed	2,100
Depreciation	700
Total manufacturing costs	16,300
Gross profit	10,700
Less costs:	
Marketing	4,000
Brokerage	1,650
Administrative	2,100
Research and development	500
Total costs	8,250
Operating profit	$ 2,450

The division president wants a minimum 15 percent increase in gross sales-dollars and a before-tax profit for next year of at least 10 percent of gross sales. He also stated that he would be responsible for a $200,000 reduction in administrative costs to help achieve the profit goal.

Both the vice president—marketing and the vice president—production believe the president's objectives will be difficult to achieve. However, they offered the following suggestions to reach the objectives:

1. *Sales volume.* The current share of the salad dressing market is 15 percent, and the total salad dressing market is expected to grow 5 percent next year. Barr's current market share can be maintained by a marketing expenditure of $4.2 million. The two vice presidents estimate that the market share could be increased by additional expenditures for advertising and sales promotion. For an additional expenditure of $525,000, the market share can be raised by 1 percentage point until the market share reaches 17 percent. To get further market penetration, an additional $875,000 must be spent for each percentage point until the market share reaches 20 percent. Any advertising and promotion expenditures beyond this level are not likely to increase the market share to more than 20 percent.

2. *Selling price.* The selling price will remain at $6 per gallon. The selling price is closely related to ingredients' costs, which are not expected to change from last year.

3. *Variable manufacturing costs.* Variable manufacturing costs are projected at 50 percent of net sales (gross sales less transportation, allowances, and discounts).

4. *Fixed manufacturing costs.* An increase of $100,000 is projected for next year.

5. *Depreciation.* A projected increase in equipment will increase depreciation by $25,000 in the next year.

6. *Transportation, allowances, and discounts.* The current rate of 10 percent of gross sales-dollars is expected to remain unchanged.

7. *Commission.* A rate of 5 percent of gross sales-dollars is projected.

8. *Administrative costs.* A $200,000 decrease in administrative costs from the current year is projected for next year; this is consistent with the president's commitment.

9. *Research and development costs.* A 5 percent increase from the current year will be necessary to meet divisional research targets.

Required:

The controller must put together a preliminary budget from the facts given. Can the president's objectives be achieved? If so, present the budget that best achieves them. If not, present the budget that most nearly meets the president's objectives.

(CMA adapted)

17–40. Prepare Cash Budget for Nonprofit Organization

United Business Education, Inc. (UBE), is a nonprofit organization that sponsors a wide variety of management seminars throughout the United States. In addition, it researches improved methods of educating and motivating business executives. The seminar activity is largely supported by fees, and the research program from member dues.

UBE operates on a calendar-year basis and is in the process of finalizing the budget for next year. The following information has been taken from approved plans that are still tentative at this time:

Seminar program:

Revenue. The scheduled number of programs should produce $12 million of revenue for the year. Each program is budgeted to produce the same amount of revenue. The revenue is collected during the month the program is offered. The programs are scheduled so that 12 percent of the revenue is collected in each of the first five months of the year. The remaining programs, accounting for the remaining 40 percent of the revenue, are distributed evenly through the months of September, October, and November. No programs are offered in the other four months of the year.

Direct seminar costs are made up of three segments:

1. Instructor's fees, which are 70 percent of the seminar revenue, are paid in cash in the month following the seminar. The instructors are considered independent contractors and are not eligible for UBE employee benefits.

2. Facilities fees total $5.6 million for the year. They are the same for each program and are paid in the month the program is given.

3. Annual promotional costs of $1 million are spent equally in all months except June and July, when there is no promotional effort.

The research program requires total grant expense of $3 million for next year, which is expected to be paid out at the rate of $500,000 per month during the first six months of the year (that is, January through June).

Salaries and other UBE costs:

Office lease. Annual amount of $240,000 paid monthly at the beginning of each month.

General administrative costs (telephone, supplies, postage, and so forth). $1.5 million annually or $125,000 a month.

Depreciation expense. $240,000 a year.

General UBE promotion. Annual cost of $600,000, paid monthly.

Salaries and benefits:

Number of Employees	Annual Salary per Employee	Total Annual Salaries
1	$50,000	$ 50,000
3	40,000	120,000
4	30,000	120,000
15	25,000	375,000
5	15,000	75,000
22	10,000	220,000
50		$960,000

Employee benefits amount to $240,000 or 25 percent of annual salaries. Except for the pension contribution, the benefits are paid as salaries are paid. The annual pension payment of $24,000, based on 2.5 percent of salaries (included in the total benefits and 25 percent rate), is due by April 15 of next year.

Other information:

Membership income.   UBE has 100,000 members, each of whom pays an annual fee of $100. The fee for the calendar year is invoiced in late June. The collection schedule is as follows.

July	60%
August	30
September	5
October	5
	100%

Capital expenditures.   The capital expenditures program calls for $510,000 in cash payments to be spread evenly over the first five months of next year (that is, January through May).

Cash and temporary investments on January 1 of next year are expected to be $750,000.

Required:

a. Prepare a budget of the annual cash receipts and disbursements for UBE, Inc., for next year.

b. Prepare a cash budget for UBE, Inc., for January of next year.

c. Using the information you developed in requirements (a) and (b), identify two important operating problems of UBE, Inc.

(CMA adapted)

INTEGRATIVE CASES

17–41. Prepare Cash Budget for Service Organization

The Triple-F Health Club (Family, Fitness, and Fun) is a nonprofit health club. The club's board of directors is developing plans to acquire more equipment and expand club facilities. The board plans to purchase about $25,000 of new equipment each year and wants to begin a fund to purchase an adjoining property in four or five years when the expansion will need the space. The adjoining property has a market value of about $300,000.

The club manager is concerned that the board has unrealistic goals in light of its recent financial performance. She sought the help of a club member with an accounting background to assist her in preparing the club's records, including the cash basis income statements presented below. The review and discussions with the manager disclosed the additional information that follows the statement.

TRIPLE-F HEALTH CLUB
Statement of Income (Cash Basis)
For the Year Ended October 31
(in thousands)

	19X7	19X6
Cash revenues:		
Annual membership fees	$355.0	$300.0
Lesson and class fees	234.0	180.0
Miscellaneous	2.0	1.5
Total cash received	591.0	481.5
Cash costs:		
Manager's salary and benefits	36.0	36.0
Regular employees' wages and benefits	190.0	190.0
Lesson and class employee wages and benefits	195.0	150.0
Towels and supplies	16.0	15.5
Utilities (heat and light)	22.0	15.0
Mortgage interest	35.1	37.8
Miscellaneous	2.0	1.5
Total cash costs	496.1	445.8
Cash income	$ 94.9	$ 35.7

Additional information:

1. Other financial information as of October 31, 19X7:
    a. Cash in checking account, $7,000.
    b. Petty cash, $300.
    c. Outstanding mortgage balance, $360,000.
    d. Accounts payable for supplies and utilities that are unpaid as of October 31, 19X7, and due in November 19X7, $2,500.
2. The club purchased $25,000 worth of exercise equipment during the current fiscal year. Cash of $10,000 was paid on delivery, and the balance was due on October 1 but has not yet been paid as of October 31, 19X7.
3. The club began operations in 19X1 in rental quarters. In October 19X3, it purchased its current property (land and building) for $600,000, paying $120,000 down and agreeing to pay $30,000 plus 9 percent interest annually on the unpaid loan balance each November 1, starting November 1, 19X4.
4. Membership rose 3 percent during 19X7. This is approximately the same annual rate of increase the club has experienced since it opened and is expected to continue in the future.
5. Membership fees were increased by 15 percent in 19X7. The board has tentative plans to increase the fees by 10 percent in 19X8.
6. Lesson and class fees have not been increased for three years. The board policy is to encourage classes and lessons by keeping the fees low. The members have

taken advantage of this policy and the number of classes and lessons have grown significantly each year. The club expects the percentage growth experienced in 19X7 to be repeated in 19X8.

7. Miscellaneous revenues are expected to grow in 19X8 (over 19X7) at the same percentage as experienced in 19X7 (over 19X6).

8. Lesson and class employees' wages and benefits will increase to $291,525. The wages and benefits of regular employees and the manager will increase 15 percent. Towels and supplies, utilities, and miscellaneous expenses are expected to increase 25 percent.

Required:

a. Construct a cash budget for 19X8 for the Triple-F Health Club.

b. Identify any operating problem(s) that this budget discloses for the Triple-F Health Club. Explain your answer.

c. Is the manager's concern that the board's goals are unrealistic justified? Explain your answer.

(CMA adapted)

17–42. Estimate Cash Receipts Using Statistical Forecasting Model

Early in March, the Jackson City administrator presented a budget to the city council. This is four months prior to the start of the new fiscal year, which begins July 1. Most of the important amounts are estimated because the final budget data (1) will not be available until much closer to the end of the year or (2) are based upon estimates of events that occur in the next year.

City revenues are a good example of the data requirement problem. The city obtains its cash revenues from four sources: property taxes, city income tax, parking fees and fines, and other revenues. Property taxes are based on the assessed valuation of all the property in the city. The final assessment values for the fiscal year are not available until late May. Income tax receipts depend upon the income earned next year by the residents of the city. The parking fees and fines depend, to a large extent, on the size of the population.

The city administrator added an estimate of monthly cash receipts and disbursements for next year to the budget material he presented to the council. Cash receipts were estimated using a cash forecasting model developed in the controller's department. The model was the result of statistical analysis of prior years' results and is presented below:

$$C_i = mr_i A_t + \frac{(1 + I)T_{t-1}}{12} + \frac{(1 + G)P_{t-1}}{12} + \frac{(1 + G)R_{t-1}}{12}$$

where

C_i = Cash collected for the ith month (July = 1).
m = Property tax rate per $1,000 of assessed valuation.
r_i = Percent of property tax collected in the ith month (July = 1).
A_t = Assessed valuation of property in year t (t = budget year) in thousands of dollars.
I = Inflation rate (decimal).
T = Income taxes withheld from taxpayers.
G = Population growth (decimal).
P = Parking fees and fines collections.
R = Other revenues collections.

The assessed valuation in thousands of dollars, A_t, was estimated from the regression equation:

$$A_t = \$50,000 + 1.05A_{t-1} + \$3S$$

where

S = Thousands of square feet of new construction since the last assessment.

The numerical data shown below was available at the end of February when the budget for this fiscal year was constructed. The data for last fiscal year represents either actual figures or data projected for the entire year based on the first eight months of last fiscal year. The data for the new fiscal year represent either rates or amounts that were actually experienced or estimates of what is expected to be experienced.

Fiscal Year		
Last	Population (actual)	100,000 people
New	Population growth rate (estimated)	8%
Last	Assessed valuation (actual)	$600,000,000
Last	Square feet of new construction since last assessment (projected)	30,000,000 sq. ft.
New	Property tax rate per $1,000 of assessed valuation (actual)	$25
Last	Income taxes withheld (projected)	4,000,000
Last	Collections of parking fees and fines (projected)	1,000,000
Last	Other revenues collections (projected)	500,000
New	Inflation rate (estimated)	11% per year

The collection pattern for property taxes that has been experienced the past three years is shown below. City officials expected this pattern to persist in this fiscal year.

July	20%	January	1%
August	60	February	1
September	10	March	1
October	5	April	—
November	1	May	—
December	1	June	—

Required:

Estimate the cash receipts for the month of August that the Jackson City administrator included in the budget material presented to the city council in March. Use the cash forecasting model developed by the controller's department and the data available in February.

(CMA adapted)

USING THE BUDGET FOR PERFORMANCE EVALUATION AND CONTROL

LEARNING OBJECTIVES

1. To develop and use flexible budgets.

2. To compute the sales activity variance.

3. To prepare and use the profit variance analysis.

In Chapter 17, we described the development of the master budget as a first step in the budgetary planning and control cycle. This chapter carries the process a step further to examine the use of the budget as a tool for performance evaluation and control. The master budget can be thought of as a blueprint for achieving the company's goals. The control process assures that the blueprint is followed or, if changes are required, that the best alternative is chosen.

Operating Budgets Refers to the budgeted income statement, the production budget, the budgeted cost of goods sold, and supporting budgets.

Financial Budget Refers to the budget of financial resources; for example, the cash budget and the budgeted balance sheet.

Variances Differences between planned results and actual outcomes.

The master budget includes **operating budgets** (for example, the budgeted income statement, the production budget, the budgeted cost of goods sold) and **financial budgets** (for example, the cash budget, the budgeted balance sheet). When management uses the master budget for control purposes, it focuses on the key items that must be controlled to ensure company success. Most such items are in the operating budgets, although some also appear in the financial budgets. In this chapter, we focus on the income statement because it is the most important financial statement used by managers to control operations.

When reported income statements are compared to budgeted income statements, there are nearly always **variances** or differences between the budgeted and reported amounts. Managers spend considerable time and effort understanding causes of these variances, interpreting them, and taking corrective action. Later chapters discuss these variances in detail; this chapter presents the "big-picture" comparison of budgeted to reported profits. Understanding this "big-picture" helps understand where the details discussed in later chapters fit.

FLEXIBLE BUDGETING

Static Budget A budget for a single activity level—usually the master budget.

Flexible Budget A budget that indicates revenues, costs, and profits for different levels of activity.

Flexible Budget Line The expected monthly costs at different levels of output.

A master budget presents a comprehensive view of anticipated operations. Such a budget is typically a **static budget;** that is, it is developed in detail for one level of anticipated activity. A **flexible budget,** by contrast, indicates budgeted revenues, costs, and profits for virtually all feasible levels of activities. Since variable costs and revenues change with changes in activity levels, these amounts are budgeted to be different at each activity level in the flexible budget.

For example, studies of past cost behavior of labor costs of the surgical nurses in the operating rooms of Sierra Memorial Outpatient Center indicate that the department expects to incur fixed costs of $500,000 per year and variable costs of $50 per operating room hour. This cost function is graphed in Illustration 18-1. This is the same type of cost line that is used for cost-volume-profit (CVP) analysis as discussed in Chapter 11. The expected activity level for the period is budgeted at 100,000 hours. From the **flexible budget line** in Illustration 18-1, we find the budgeted costs at a planned activity of 100,000 operating room hours to be $5.5 million [$500,000 + ($50 × 100,000 hours)].

Suppose that actual costs are only $5 million. At first glance, one might assume that a good job of cost control was done because costs were $500,000 lower than the budget plan. But in fact, only 80,000 operating room hours were actually incurred instead of the 100,000 hours originally planned. According to the flexible budget concept, the master budget must be adjusted for this change in activity. The adjusted budgeted costs for control and performance evaluation purposes would be $4.5 million [$500,000 +

($50 × 80,000 hours)]. Now it is clear that while costs are lower than planned, they are $500,000 higher than they should be after *taking into account the level of activity in the department.*

The estimated cost-volume line in Illustration 18–1 is known as the flexible budget line because it shows the budgeted costs allowed for each level of activity. For example, if activity would increase to 120,000 operating room hours, budgeted costs would be $6.5 million [$500,000 + ($50 × 120,000 hours)]. If activity drops to 50,000 operating room hours, budgeted costs would drop to $3 million [$500,000 + ($50 × 50,000 operating room hours)]. Whatever level of activity occurred during the period is entered into the flexible budget equation:

$$TC = F + VX$$

where

TC = Total budgeted costs for the period.
F = Fixed costs for the period.
V = Variable costs per unit.
X = Activity expressed as quantity of units.

For the surgical nursing department at Sierra Memorial Outpatient Center:

$$TC = \$500,000 + \$50X$$

Illustration 18–1   **Comparison of Master and Flexible Budget, Surgical Nursing Department, Sierra Memorial Outpatient Center**

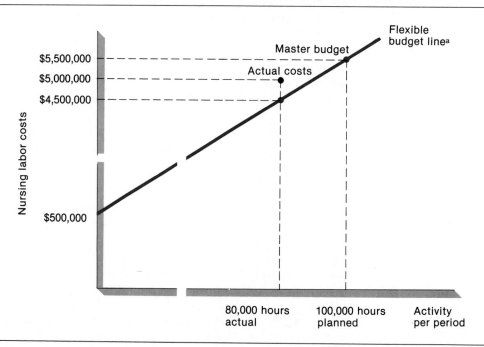

^a This is the cost line from cost-volume-profit analysis.

You can compare the master budget with the flexible budget by thinking of the master budget as an ex ante (before-the-fact) prediction of X (activity), while the flexible budget is based on ex post facto (after-the-fact) knowledge of the actual X.

COMPARING BUDGETS AND RESULTS

A comparison of the master budget with the flexible budget and with actual results forms the basis for analyzing differences between plans and actual performance. The following example is used in this and subsequent chapters to illustrate the comparison of plans with actual performance.

The Evergreen Company makes wooden crates for shipping fruit. Its master budget income statement is presented in Illustration 18–2. The format is consistent with variable costing, not full-absorption costing. We use this variable costing format for analyzing differences between actual and planned results because it separates fixed and variable costs. This separation is important for managerial estimates of cost behavior and profits.

The flexible budget, presented in Illustration 18–3, is based on *actual* activity. In May, 10,000 crates were actually produced and sold. The difference between operating profits in the master budget and operating profits in the flexible budget is called an **activity variance.** It is due to the 2,000-unit difference between actual sales and planned sales. The $22,000 variance results from the 2,000-unit difference times the $11 *budgeted* contribution margin per unit ($20 *budgeted* price − $9 *budgeted* variable costs). This difference can also be seen on the flexible budget profit-volume line in Illustration 18–4.

Activity Variance Variance due to changes in volume of sales or production.

Illustration 18-2   **Master Budget, Evergreen Company**

	Master Budget (based on 8,000 units)
Sales revenue (8,000 units at $20)	$160,000
Less:	
Variable manufacturing costs	64,000[a]
Variable marketing and administrative costs	8,000[b]
Contribution margin	88,000
Less:	
Fixed manufacturing costs	36,000
Fixed marketing and administrative costs	40,000
Operating profit	$ 12,000

The following estimates are used by Evergreen Company to prepare the master budget:

Sales price	$ 20 per crate
Sales volume	8,000 crates
Production volume	8,000 crates
Variable manufacturing costs	$ 8 per crate
Variable marketing and administrative costs	1 per crate
Fixed manufacturing costs	36,000
Fixed marketing and administrative costs	40,000

[a] 8,000 budgeted units at $8 per unit.
[b] 8,000 budgeted units at $1 per unit.

**Favorable versus
Unfavorable Variances**

Favorable Variances Variances
that, taken alone, result in an
addition to operating profit.

Unfavorable Variance
Variances that, taken alone,
reduce operating profit.

Note the use of F for favorable and U for unfavorable beside each of the variances in Illustration 18–3. These terms describe the impact of the variance on the budgeted operating profits. A *favorable variance increases* operating profits, holding all other things constant. An *unfavorable variance decreases* operating profits, holding all other things constant. These terms are not intended to be used in a normative sense; thus, a **favorable variance** is *not necessarily good,* and an **unfavorable variance** is *not necessarily bad.*

An excellent case in point is the sales activity or volume variance in Illustration 18–3. Holding everything else constant, the 2,000-unit increase in sales creates a favorable variance. Is this really good? Perhaps not. Economic conditions may have been better than planned, which increased the volume demanded by the market. Hence, perhaps, the 2,000-unit increase in sales volume should have been even greater taking everything into account.

Note that the variable cost variances are both labeled unfavorable. But this doesn't mean that they are bad for the company. Variable costs are expected to increase when volume is greater than planned.

Illustration 18–3

Flexible and Master Budget, Evergreen Company (May)

	Flexible Budget[b] (based on actual activity of 10,000 units)	Sales Activity Variance (based on variance in sales volume)	Master Budget (based on 8,000 units sold)
Sales revenue	$200,000	$40,000 F	$160,000
Less:			
Variable manufacturing costs[a] (at $8 per unit)	80,000	16,000 U	64,000
Variable marketing and administrative costs (at $1 per unit)	10,000	2,000 U	8,000
Contribution margin	110,000	22,000 F	88,000
Less:			
Fixed manufacturing costs	36,000	—	36,000
Fixed marketing and administrative costs	40,000	—	40,000
Operating profits	$ 34,000	$22,000 F	$ 12,000

[a] This can be thought of as "variable cost of goods sold."
U = "Unfavorable" variance.
F = "Favorable" variance.
[b] Calculations for flexible budget:
  $200,000 = 10,000/8,000 × $160,000
  $ 80,000 = 10,000/8,000 × $ 64,000
  $ 10,000 = 10,000/8,000 × $ 8,000.
  Fixed costs are not expected
   to change between 8,000 and
   10,000 units.

Sales Activity (Volume) Variance

Sales Activity Variance
Difference between operating profit in master budget and operating profit in flexible budget. Variance arises because the actual quantity of units sold is different than the budgeted quantity.

The information in Illustration 18–3 has a number of uses. First, it isolates the increase in operating profits caused by the increase in activity from the master budget. Further, the resulting flexible budget shows budgeted sales, costs, and operating profits *after* taking into account the activity increase but *before* considering differences in *unit* selling prices, variable costs, and fixed costs from the master budget.

In general, we refer to this change from the master budget plan as an activity variance. When the change from the master budget to the flexible budget is due to changes in sales volume, the activity variance is known as the sales activity variance

Some writers suggest that variance analysis is unnecessary when there are differences between planned and actual activity levels. Rather, they suggest that tabulating the difference in volume alone is sufficient. For example, rather than point out that Evergreen Company had a favorable sales activity variance of $22,000, they would report that Evergreen Company sold 2,000 more units than planned. In practice, managers prefer variance data because it provides information about the impact of differences between plans and actual results on profit amounts.

Illustration 18-4 **Flexible Budget Line, Evergreen Company**

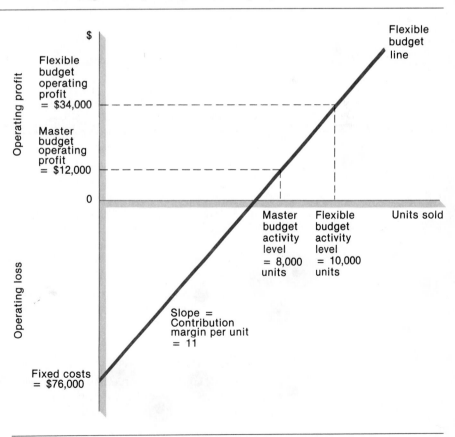

Note the makeup of the $22,000 sales activity variance in Illustration 18–3. First, the difference between the master budget sales of $160,000 and the flexible budget sales of $200,000 (which is the estimated $20 unit sales price times the 10,000 units actually sold) is $40,000. This is based on the 2,000–unit increase in sales volume times the estimated $20 unit sales price. We use the *estimated* unit sales price instead of the *actual* price because we want to isolate the impact of the activity increase from changes in the sales price. We want to focus on the effects of volume alone. Thus, the sales amount in the flexible budget is *not the actual revenue* (actual price times actual volume) but the *estimated unit sales price times the actual number of units sold*. This permits us to isolate the effects of the difference between actual and expected sales volume. Second, variable costs are expected to increase by $18,000, giving a favorable contribution margin of $22,000 ($40,000 − 18,000), which is the favorable sales activity variance.

Comparing Actual to the Flexible Budget

Assume the actual results for May are shown in the following table.

	Actual
Sales price	$ 21 per crate
Sales volume	10,000 crates
Variable manufacturing costs	$85,440
Variable marketing and administrative costs	11,000
Fixed manufacturing costs	37,000 for May
Fixed manufacturing and administrative costs	44,000 for May

Profit Variance Analysis
Analysis of the causes of differences between budgeted profits and the actual profits earned.

The **profit variance analysis** shows the cause of differences between the budgeted profits and the actual profits earned. Now the actual results can be compared with both the flexible budget and the master budget in a profit variance analysis, as shown in Illustration 18–5. Columns 5, 6, and 7 are carried forward from Illustration 18–3.

Column 1 is the reported income statement based on the facts presented above. Column 2 summarizes manufacturing variances (which are discussed in more detail in Chapter 19), and column 3 shows marketing and administrative variances (which are discussed in more detail in Chapter 21). Costs have been divided into fixed and variable portions here and would be presented in more detail to the managers of centers having responsibility for them.

Cost variances result from deviations in costs and efficiencies in operating the company. They are important for measuring productivity and helping to control costs.

Sales Price Variance

The sales price variance, column 4, is derived from the *difference between the actual and budgeted selling price times the actual number of units sold* ($10,000 = [$21 − $20] × 10,000 units).

Illustration 18-5 Profit Variance Analysis, Evergreen Company (May)

	(1) Actual (based on actual activity of 10,000 units sold)	(2) Manufacturing Variances	(3) Marketing and Administrative Variances	(4) Sales Price Variance	(5) Flexible Budget (based on actual activity of 10,000 units sold)	(6) Sales Activity (volume) Variance	(7) Master Budget (based on a prediction of 8,000 units sold)
Sales revenue	$210,000	—	—	$10,000 F	$200,000	$40,000 F	$160,000
Less:							
Variable manufacturing costs	85,440	$5,440 U [a]	—	—	80,000	16,000 U	64,000
Variable marketing and administrative costs	11,000	—	$1,000 U	—	10,000	2,000 U	8,000
Contribution margin	113,560	5,440 U	1,000 U	10,000 F	110,000	22,000 F	88,000
Less:							
Fixed manufacturing costs	37,000	1,000 U	—	—	36,000	—	36,000
Fixed marketing and administrative costs	44,000	—	4,000 U	—	40,000	—	40,000
Operating profits	$ 32,560	$6,440 U	$5,000 U	$10,000 F	$ 34,000	$22,000 F	$ 12,000

→ Total variance from flexible budget = $1,440 U

→ Total variance from master budget = $20,560 F

[a] Highlighted to make this amount easier for reference throughout this chapter and in Chapter 19.

Variable Manufacturing Cost Variances

Be careful (in Illustration 18–5) to distinguish the variable cost variances in columns 2 and 3, which are input variances, from the variable cost variances in column 6, which are part of the sales activity variance. Management *expects* the latter costs to be higher in this case because the sales volume is higher than planned.

Looking at column 5, we see that variable manufacturing costs *should have been* $80,000 for a production and sales volume of 10,000 units, not $64,000 as expressed in the master budget in column 7. We see from column 1 that the actual variable manufacturing costs *were* $85,440, some $21,440 higher than the master budget, but only $5,440 higher than the flexible budget. Which number should be used to evaluate manufacturing cost control—the $21,440 variance from the master budget or the $5,440 variance from the flexible budget?

The number that should be used to evaluate manufacturing performance is the $5,440 variance from the flexible budget. This points out a benefit of flexible budgeting. A superficial comparison of the master budget plan with the actual results would have indicated the variance to be $21,440. But, in fact, manufacturing is responsible for only $5,440, which is caused by deviation from production norms. We discuss the source of this $5,440 in more detail in Chapter 19.

Fixed Manufacturing Cost Variance

The fixed manufacturing cost variance is simply the difference between actual and budgeted costs. Fixed costs are treated as period costs; they are not expected to be affected by activity levels within a relevant range. Hence, the flexible budget fixed costs equal the master budget fixed costs.

Marketing and Administrative Costs

Marketing and administrative costs are treated like manufacturing costs. Variable costs are expected to change as activity changes; hence, variable costs were expected to increase by $2,000 between the flexible and master budgets, as shown in Illustration 18–5, because volume increased by 2,000 units. Comparing actual with the flexible budget reveals $1,000 U variance for marketing and administrative costs. Fixed marketing and administrative costs do not change as volume changes; hence, the flexible and master budget amounts are the same.

Units Produced versus Units Sold

In the previous example, production volume and sales volume were equal. But the analysis becomes more complicated when the units sold are not equal to the units produced.

Suppose that 12,000 units were produced in May, but only 10,000 units were sold. Also, assume there was no beginning inventory. This has no effect on the sales activity variance because the master budget and flexible budget are based on *sales* volume. Thus, columns 5, 6, and 7 of Illustration 18–5 remain unchanged. In addition, the sales price variance is based on units sold, so column 4 remains the same. Generally, marketing and administrative costs are not affected by *producing* 12,000 instead of 10,000 units, so we assume they do not change. This allows us to focus on columns 1 and 2, which would change.

Assume that actual variable manufacturing costs are $8.544 *per unit* and fixed manufacturing costs are $37,000 *for the period*. This leaves the fixed manufacturing cost variance of $1,000 U unchanged. However, the variable manufacturing cost variance changes. In the month units are produced, the following variable manufacturing cost variances are computed:

Units produced $\times$
$$\text{(Actual variable cost} - \text{Estimated variable cost)} = \text{Variance}$$

Previous example for *10,000 units produced* (Illustration 18–5):

$$10,000 \times (\$8.544 - \$8.00) = \$5,440 \text{ U}$$

Present example for *12,000 units produced* (Illustration 18–6):

$$12,000 \times (\$8.544 - \$8.00) = \$6,528 \text{ U}$$

The variable manufacturing cost variance for units *produced* in May is $6,528. This amount may be treated as a period cost and expensed in May, or it may be prorated to units sold and to units still in inventory. If prorated, $\frac{2}{12} \times \$6,528$ would be charged to inventory in this case because 2,000 of the 12,000 units produced in May are still in inventory at the end of May. In most companies, the $6,528 variance due to May's production is written off as a period expense in May and shown as a variance, as shown in Illustration 18–6.

Note that the actual variable manufacturing costs of $86,528 in Illustration 18-6 are really a hybrid—$80,000 in flexible budget costs (based on 10,000 units sold this period times $8 estimated cost per unit) plus the $6,528 variable manufacturing cost variance from the 12,000 units produced this period.

Reconciling Costs Incurred with Costs Expensed

The reconciliation between manufacturing costs incurred to produce goods and those expensed on the income statement can be made easier by using the following simple relationship:

$$\begin{array}{c} \text{Costs} \\ \text{incurred} \end{array} + \begin{array}{c} \text{Costs} \\ \text{from} \\ \text{inventory} \\ \text{decrease} \end{array} - \begin{array}{c} \text{Costs to} \\ \text{inventory} \\ \text{increase} \end{array} = \begin{array}{c} \text{Costs} \\ \text{expensed} \\ \text{on the} \\ \text{income} \\ \text{statement} \end{array}$$

For example, assume a company uses first-in, first-out inventory flows and has the following costs:

Production costs	$1,000,000
Beginning inventory	200,000
Ending inventory	300,000

Illustration 18–6 **Profit Variance Analysis when Units Produced Do Not Equal Units Sold, Evergreen Company (May)**

	(1) Actual (based on 10,000 units)[a]	(2) Manufacturing Variances	(3) Marketing and Administrative Variances	(4) Sales Price Variance	(5) Flexible Budget (based on 10,000 units)	(6) Sales Activity (volume) Variance	(7) Master Budget based on 8,000 units
Sales revenue	$210,000	—	—	$10,000 F	$200,000	$40,000 F	$160,000
Less:							
Variable manufacturing costs	86,528	$6,528 U	—		80,000	16,000 U	64,000
Variable marketing and administrative costs	11,000	—	$1,000 U	—	10,000	2,000 U	8,000
Contribution margin	112,472	6,528 U	1,000 U	10,000 F	110,000	22,000 F	88,000
Less:							
Fixed manufacturing costs	37,000	1,000 U	—	—	36,000	—	36,000
Fixed marketing and administrative costs	44,000	—	4,000 U	—	40,000	—	40,000
Operating profits	$ 31,472	$7,528 U	$5,000 U	$10,000 F	$ 34,000	$22,000 F	$ 12,000

→ Total variance from flexible budget = $2,528 U

→ Total variance from master budget = $19,472 F

[a] Based on 10,000 units sold and 12,000 units produced.

The reconciliation of production cost flows and costs expensed on the income statement would be:

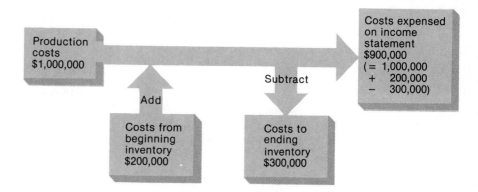

Returning to our example for Evergreen Company, the amount of costs that are expensed if 12,000 units are produced and 10,000 are sold is:

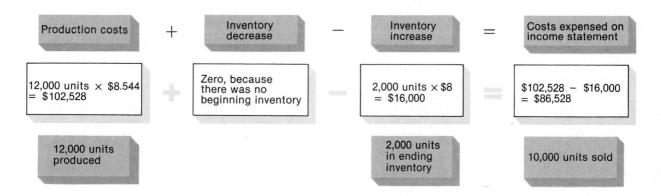

Reconciling Full-Absorption and Variable Costing

Assume that Evergreen Company produced 12,000 units and sold 10,000 units in May. There was no beginning inventory on May 1, so the ending inventory on May 31 was 2,000 units. Using variable costing, the entire *fixed manufacturing cost* of $37,000 would be expensed, as shown in Illustrations 18–3 through 18–6. Such would not be the case, however, when full-absorption costing is used and production and sales volume are not the same.

Using full-absorption costing, a portion of the fixed manufacturing costs would be allocated to the 2,000 units in ending inventory:

$$\frac{2{,}000 \text{ units}}{12{,}000 \text{ units}} \times \$37{,}000 = \underline{\$6{,}167}$$

Or, $\dfrac{\$37{,}000}{12{,}000 \text{ units}} = \$3.08\frac{1}{3}$ fixed manufacturing cost per unit. 2,000 units are in ending inventory from current period production, so $6,167 (2,000 units × $3.08⅓) fixed manufacturing costs are allocated to ending inventory.

Thus only $30,833 ($37,000 − $6,167) of the actual fixed manufacturing costs are expensed in May using full-absorption costing. In this case, full-

Illustration 18-7

Reconciling Actual Income Using Full-Absorption Costing and Variable Costing (columns 2-7 are the same as in Illustration 18-6)

	(1a) Actual Using Full Absorption	(1b) (Inventory Adjustment) Fixed Manufacturing Costs Going into Inventory Using Full Absorption	(1c) Actual Using Variable Costing
Sales revenue	$210,000		$210,000
Less:			
Variable manufacturing costs	86,528		86,528
Variable marketing and administrative costs	11,000		11,000
Contribution margin	112,472		112,472
Less:			
Fixed manufacturing costs	30,833	$6,167[a]	37,000
Fixed marketing and administrative costs	44,000		44,000
Operating profits	$ 37,639	$6,167	$ 31,472

[a] 2,000 units put into inventory times $3.08⅓ $\left(\dfrac{\$37,000}{12,000\ \text{units}}\right)$ fixed manufacturing cost per unit.

absorption operating profit would be $37,639 in May, or $6,167 higher than variable costing operating profit.[1] This $6,167 difference in profits is due to the accounting system and not to managerial efficiencies. Care should be taken to identify the cause of such profit differences so those due to accounting method are not misinterpreted as being caused by operating activities.

The budget planning and control methods presented in this book are based on the variable costing approach to product costing unless otherwise stated. Illustration 18–7 shows how the reported income statement under full-absorption would be reconciled with that using variable costing. The comparison of budget to actual results presented in Illustration 18–6 would still be used; however, additional columns (1a and 1b) would be added to reconcile actual results using variable costing to those using full-absorption costing.

SERVICE AND MERCHANDISING ACTIVITIES

The comparison of the master budget, the flexible budget, and actual results can also be used in service and merchandising organizations. The basic framework in Illustration 18–5 would be retained. Output would usually be

---

[1] Of course, as discussed in Chapter 9, if units sold exceed units produced, we expect the reverse to be true; that is, full-absorption operating profit would be lower than variable costing operating profit.

defined as sales units in merchandising, but other measures are used in service organizations. For example:

Organization	Units of Activity
Public accounting, legal, and consulting firms	Professional staff hours
Laundry	Weight or pieces of clothing
Hospital	Patient-days

Merchandising and service organizations focus on marketing and administrative costs to measure efficiency and to control costs. The key items to control are labor costs, particularly in service organizations, and occupancy costs per sales-dollar, particularly in merchandising organizations.

BEHAVIORAL ISSUES IN BUDGETING

"You should hold employees responsible for those things they can control" is sometimes claimed to be an important behavioral factor in designing accounting systems. This appeals to a sense of fairness that "the manager of the assembly department should not be charged with inefficiencies caused by the cutting department." Perhaps of more significance in an economic sense, is the idea that holding employees responsible for the things they can control focuses managers' attention on the things they can influence and reduces their risk. A well-established concept from the study of financial markets is that higher risk requires higher returns. In a similar fashion, risk-averse workers will demand a higher wage to assume greater risk, all other things equal. Flexible budgets can reduce risk to a worker, as demonstrated by the following example.

Assume that the manager of the repairs department has a budget of $100,000 for December. It turns out that machine time is low in December, and repairs can be easily scheduled without overtime. As a result, the manager spends only $90,000 of the budget. However, suppose production increases during the month of January, and department personnel are working overtime to make the necessary repairs. Expenditures for the repairs department are $110,000 in January.

The manager of the repairs department believes performance is evaluated according to the budget and that his bonus, raises, promotions, and job could depend on meeting the budget. A risk-averse manager will prefer a system that adjusts the budget down to $90,000 in December and up to $110,000 in January to reflect the changing levels of production, even though the average results for the two months are the same.

The idea that "employees should be held accountable for what they control" does not mean factors outside of their control should be ignored in evaluating performance. For example, information about an employee's peers may be useful in evaluating how well the employee is performing. This is analogous to "grading on the curve," where knowing how well a student did relative to the rest of the class is usually more informative about student exam performance than just knowing the student's own exam score. Few employers will ignore information about factors outside an employee's control that nevertheless affect the employee's performance.[2]

RESPONSIBILITY CENTERS

Budgets for performance evaluation and cost control are typically organized around **responsibility centers.** Responsibility centers are organizational units for which someone has responsibility. For example, a business school within a university is often a responsibility center. The dean of the business school has a budgeted level of resources to work with and is responsible to university officials for the way those resources are used to achieve the university's goals. Other examples are:

Responsibility Center	Person in Charge	Responsible for
Company	Chief executive officer	All assets, equities, revenues, and costs of the company
Division	Division vice president	Divisional assets, equities, revenues, and costs
Plant	Plant manager	Plant production and costs
Department store	Store manager	Store's revenues and costs
Secretarial pool	Secretarial pool supervisor	Costs and secretarial production

For example, the budget breakdown for Electronics, Inc., is shown in Illustration 18–8. Each of the three vice presidents—administrative, production, and marketing—is responsible for part of it. Based on accounting allocations, the marketing and administrative costs were divided equally between the marketing vice president and the administrative vice president. The administrative budget is subdivided into departments (data processing, accounting, personnel). The production budget is further divided among plant managers, who assign the budget to department heads (assembly, processing, quality control, warehousing). The marketing vice president assigned the marketing budget to the district sales managers.

Note that the production and marketing budgets both involve activity in units—units produced or units sold—while the administrative budget does not. This is one of the major difficulties in controlling marketing and administrative costs. It is difficult to relate these costs directly to changes in a company's sales and production. If the number of units sold increases 20 percent, should marketing and administrative cost increase by the same

---

[2] Extensive literature has been developed in recent years that deals with issues of risk sharing and incentives in organizations. While the work so far has been done in simplified analytical settings and the results are difficult to generalize to organizations, some fundamental principles for incentive and control systems have been developed. For a review, see S. Baiman, "Agency Research in Managerial Accounting: A Survey," *Journal of Accounting Literature,* 1982.

Illustration 18–8   **Budget Assigned to Responsibility Centers, Electronics, Inc.**

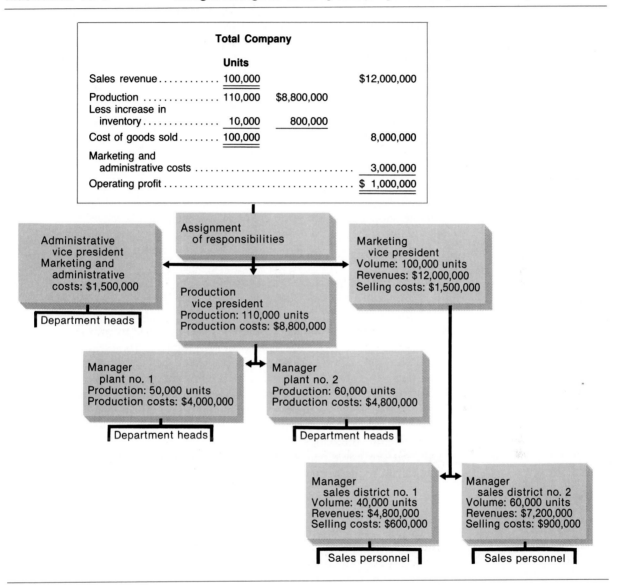

amount? This is not an easy question to answer. Many companies, governmental units, and not-for-profit organizations have responded to this problem by trying to measure marketing and administrative activity. (We discuss some of these methods in Chapter 21.)

BEHAVIORAL ISSUES IN SETTING BUDGET LEVELS

Many people in organizations are evaluated based on budgets, so they have an interest in how difficult or easy the budgets are to attain. These people often also have some input into setting budgets. In fact, operating personnel are likely to be the best sources of information about appropriate budgets in the company. But since the budgets will be used to judge their performance, they have incentives to make the budgets easily attainable.

As a manager of an assembly department put it, "The supervisor asked me how much time it will take to assemble product 102x, and I told him two labor-hours per unit based on ideal conditions. Then he used that against me when it actually took two and one half hours per unit. Now, when I am asked by a supervisor, I add about 30 percent to the time I think it will take. That gives us some slack and a chance to show a favorable variance."

Whether or not operating personnel actually bias the data they provide for establishing budgets, top management and the accounting staff recognize that operating personnel have *incentives* to do so. Thus, other sources of information, such as industry standards and estimates from similar departments in the company, are often used for comparison. Operational auditors (people who audit the efficiency and/or effectiveness of operations) and outside consultants are often called in to check the reasonableness of standards. Information from one source provides a check on information from another source.

How "Tight" Should Budget Levels Be?

Research indicates that budgets that are very difficult to achieve or those that are easily achievable may not lead to the best employee performance.[3] The motivational problems of employees are similar to those of students. For example, if it is virtually impossible to improve your grade by studying hard for a test, you may not be as motivated to study as hard as you would if you believed there was a good chance that studying would improve your grade. On the other hand, if you believe that you will get a good grade with minimal studying, you may not be inclined to study beyond that minimal level.

In general, the budget levels that seem to motivate best are moderately tight yet are perceived by employees as reasonable and attainable. This generalization may vary from situation to situation, of course.

ZERO-BASED BUDGETING

Zero-Base Budgeting A system of establishing financial plans beginning with an assumption of no activity and justifying each program or activity level.

Many organizations have attempted to manage discretionary costs through a budgeting method called **zero-base budgeting**.[4] Numerous companies (including Texas Instruments, Xerox, and Control Data) and governmental units (including some agencies of the federal government) have implemented zero-base budgeting at one time or another. One reason the approach has attracted considerable popularity in public sector organizations is that it is seen as a means of managing expenditures in a setting where the benefits of

---

[3] See Andrew C. Stedry, *Budget Control and Cost Behavior* (Englewood Cliffs, N.J.: Prentice Hall, 1960); and Gary L. Holstrum, "The Effect of Budget Adaptiveness and Tightness on Managerial Decision Behavior," *Journal of Accounting Research,* Autumn 1971, pp. 268–77.

[4] For more detailed information about zero-base budgeting, see P. Phyrr, *Zero-Base Budgeting* (New York: John Wiley & Sons, 1972); and J. Patillo, *Zero-Base Budgeting* (New York: National Association of Accountants, 1977). Also see R. Anthony and R. Herzlinger, *Management Control in Nonprofit Organizations* (Homewood, Ill.: Richard D. Irwin, 1980).

the expenditures cannot be traced to the costs as easily as they can in manufacturing.

The novel part of zero-base budgeting is the requirement that the budgeting process start at zero, with all expenditures completely justified. This contrasts with the usual approach, in which a certain level of expenditures is allowed as a starting point, and the budgeting process focuses on requests for incremental expenditures. However, a strict zero-base approach has been found to be generally impracticable because of the massive amount of time required for implementation. Thus, many organizations that use zero-base budgeting in fact allow a floor that does not have to be justified in as much detail. In many organizations, this has been set at around 80 percent of the current level of expenditures. This floor is the lowest amount of money that would enable a responsibility center to continue its operations at a minimal level. Proposed increments of activity above this level are evaluated one by one in terms of costs and benefits.

SUMMARY

This chapter discussed and illustrated the use of the budgeted income statement for performance evaluation and control. The master budget income statement was compared with actual results. Differences, or variances, between actual results and the master budget were analyzed to determine why budgeted results did not occur.

The master budget is typically static; that is, it is developed in detail for one level of activity. A flexible budget recognizes that variable costs and revenues are expected to differ from the budget if the actual activity (for example, actual sales volume) differs from what was budgeted. A flexible budget can be thought of as the costs and revenues that would have been budgeted if the activity level had been correctly estimated in the master budget. The general relationship between the actual, the flexible budget, and the master budget is shown below:

Actual	Flexible Budget	Master Budget
Actual costs and revenues based on actual activity	Costs and revenues that would have been budgeted if actual activity had been budgeted	Budgeted costs and revenues based on budgeted activity

Differences or variances between actual results and the flexible budget are differences between actual results and the budget that would have been prepared if activity had been accurately estimated. These variances include the sales price variance, manufacturing cost variances, and nonmanufacturing cost variances. Differences between the flexible and master budget results are due to the impact on revenues and costs of the difference between actual and budgeted volume.

When units produced and sold are not the same, a decision has to be made whether to prorate variances to units sold and those in inventory or to write off the variance as a period cost.

TERMS AND CONCEPTS

The following terms and concepts should be familiar to you after reading this chapter:

Activity Variance
Favorable Variances
Financial Budgets
Flexible Budget
Flexible Budget Line
Operating Budgets
Profit Variance Analysis

Responsibility Centers
Sales Activity (Volume) Variance
Static Budget
Unfavorable Variances
Variances
Zero-Base Budgeting

SUPPLEMENTARY READINGS

Ansari, S. L. "Behavioral Factors in Variance Control: Report on a Laboratory Experiment." *Journal of Accounting Research,* Autumn 1976, pp. 189–211.

Brownell, Peter, and Morris McInnes. "Budgetary Participation, Motivation, and Managerial Performance." *Accounting Review,* October 1986, pp. 587-600.

Butler, Stephen A., and Michael W. Maher. *Management Incentive Compensation Plans.* Montvale, N.J.: National Association of Accountants, 1986.

Cress, William P., and James B. Pettijohn. "A Survey of Budget-Related Planning and Control Policies and Procedures." *Journal of Accounting Education,* Fall 1985, pp. 61–78.

Dietemann, Gerard J. "Measuring Productivity in a Service Company." *Management Accounting,* February 1988, pp. 48-54.

Kelliher, Mathew E. "Managing Productivity, Performance, and the Cost of Services." *Healthcare Financial Management,* September 1985, pp. 22–28.

Maher, Michael W. "The Use of Relative Performance Evaluation in Organizations." In *Accounting and Management: Field Study Perspectives,* ed. William J. Bruns, Jr., and Robert S. Kaplan. Boston: Harvard Business School Press, 1987.

Merchant, K. A. "The Design of the Corporate Budgeting System: Influences on Managerial Behavior and Performance." *Accounting Review,* October 1981, pp. 813–29.

Mock, T. J. "The Value of Budget Information." *Accounting Review,* July 1973, pp. 520–34.

Owens, R. W. "Cash Flow Variance Analysis." *Accounting Review,* January 1980, pp. 111–16.

Shank, J., and N. Churchill. "Variance Analysis: A Management-Oriented Approach." *Accounting Review,* October 1977.

Siegel, Joel G., and Mathew S. Rubin. "Corporate Planning and Control through Variance Analysis." *Managerial Planning,* September–October 1984, pp. 35–39, 49–50.

Sorensen, J. E., and H. D. Grove. "Cost-Outcome and Cost-Effectiveness Analysis: Emerging Nonprofit Performance Evaluation Techniques." *Accounting Review,* July 1977, pp. 658–75.

Steedle, Lamont F., and James J. Darazsdi. "Measuring Productivity in an Integrated Poultry Operation." *Journal of Accountancy,* June 1986, pp. 142–48.

Suver, J. D., and Helmer, F. T. "Developing Budgeting Models for Greater Hospital Efficiency." *Management Accounting,* July 1979.

SELF-STUDY PROBLEM: CONTAINERS, INC.

In August, Containers, Inc., produced and sold 50,000 plastic minicomputer cases at a sales price of $10 each. Budgeted sales were 45,000 units at $10.15.

Budget:		
Standard variable costs per unit (that is, per case)	$ 4.00	
Fixed manufacturing overhead cost:		
Monthly budget	80,000	
Marketing and administrative:		
Variable		1.00 per case
Fixed	100,000	
Actual:		
Actual manufacturing costs:		
Variable costs per unit	4.88	
Fixed overhead	83,000	
Actual marketing and administrative:		
Variable (50,000 @ $1.04)	52,000	
Fixed	96,000	

Required:

Using variable costing, prepare a report comparing actual results with the flexible and master budgets for August. Include variances.

SOLUTION TO SELF-STUDY PROBLEM

The solution is shown on the next page.

QUESTIONS

18-1. What is a responsibility center?

18-2. Could some responsibility centers differ in the types of budget items they are accountable for? That is, might some responsibility centers be responsible only for costs, some only for revenues, and some for both? Give examples.

18-3. Does a line worker avoid responsibility because he or she is not included formally in the responsibility reporting system? How can management keep control of the line worker's activities in the absence of formal budget control?

18-4. Budgets for governmental units are usually prepared one year in advance of the budget period. Expenditures are limited to the budgeted amount. At the end of the period, performance is evaluated by comparing budget authorizations with actual receipts and outlays. What management control problems are likely to arise from such a system?

18-5. "I don't understand why you accountants want to prepare a budget for a period that is already over. We know the actual results by then—all that flexible budget does is increase the controller's staff and add to our overhead." Comment on this remark.

18-6. Why is a variable costing format more useful for performance evaluation purposes than an absorption costing format?

Profit Variance Analysis, Containers, Inc. (August)

	Actual (based on 50,000 units)	Manufacturing Variances	Marketing and Administrative Variances	Sales Price Variances	Flexible Budget (based on 50,000 units)	Sales Activity (Volume) Variance	Master Budget (based on 45,000 units)
Sales revenue	$500,000	—	—	$7,500 U	$507,500	$50,750 F	$456,750
Less:							
Variable manufacturing costs	244,000	$44,000 U	—	—	200,000	20,000 U	180,000
Variable marketing and administrative costs	52,000	—	$2,000[a] U	—	50,000	5,000 U	45,000
Contribution margins	204,000	44,000 U	2,000 U	7,500 U	257,500	25,750 F	231,750
Less:							
Fixed manufacturing costs	83,000	3,000 U	—	—	80,000	—	80,000
Fixed marketing and administrative costs	96,000	—	4,000 F	—	100,000	—	100,000
Operating profits	$ 25,000	$47,000 U	$2,000 F	$7,500 U	$ 77,500	$25,750 F	$ 51,750

Total variance from flexible budget = $52,500 U

Total variance from master budget = $26,750 U

[a] $2,000 = $.04 × 50,000 = ($1.04 − $1.00) 50,000 units.

18-7. "All costs 'flex' with activity." True or false? Why or why not?

18-8. How will the performance measurement system differ when a company is using the LIFO inventory system from when a company is using the FIFO system?

18-9. What is zero-base budgeting, and how does it differ from other budgeting practices?

18-10. Flexible budgets:

    a. The basic difference between a master budget and a flexible budget is that:

        (1) A flexible budget considers only variable costs, but a master budget considers all costs.

        (2) A flexible budget allows management latitude in meeting goals, whereas a master budget is based on a fixed standard.

        (3) A master budget is for an entire production facility, but a flexible budget is applicable to single departments only.

        (4) A master budget is based on a predicted level of activity, and a flexible budget is based on the actual level of activity.

    b. A flexible budget is:

        (1) Appropriate for control of factory overhead but not for control of direct materials and direct labor.

        (2) Appropriate for control of direct materials and direct labor but not for control of factory overhead.

        (3) Not appropriate when costs and expenses are affected by fluctuations in volume.

        (4) Appropriate for any level of activity.

(CPA adapted)

EXERCISES

18-11. Flexible Budgeting
(L.O.1)

PerkUp, Ltd., prepared a budget last period that called for sales of 7,000 units at a price of $12 each. The costs were estimated to be $5 variable per unit and $21,000 fixed. During the period, actual production and actual sales were 7,100 units. The selling price was $12.15 per unit. Variable costs were $5.90 per unit. Actual fixed costs were $21,000.

Required:

Prepare a flexible budget for PerkUp, Ltd.

18-12. Sales Activity Variance
(L.O.2)

Refer to the data in exercise 18-11 for PerkUp, Ltd.

Required:

Prepare a sales activity variance analysis like the one in Illustration 18-3.

18-13. Profit Variance Analysis
(L.O.3)

Refer to the data in exercises 18-11 and 18-12.

Required:

Prepare a profit variance analysis like the one in Illustration 18-5.

18-14. Flexible Budgeting, Service Organization
(L.O.1)

Outslay & Wheeler (OW) is a CPA firm that gets a large portion of its revenue from tax services. Last year, OW's billable tax hours were higher than expected; but as shown by the following data, profits from the tax department were lower than anticipated.

	Reported Income Statement	Master Budget
Billable hours[a]	58,000 hours	50,000 hours
Revenue	$3,300,000	$3,000,000
Professional salaries (all variable)	1,850,000	1,500,000
Other variable costs (e.g., supplies, certain computer services)	470,000	400,000
Fixed costs	580,000	600,000
Tax department profit	$ 400,000	$ 500,000

[a] These are hours billed to clients. They are less than the hours worked because there is nonbillable time (e.g., slack periods, time in training sessions) and because some time worked for clients is not charged to them.

Required: Prepare a flexible budget for Outslay & Wheeler.

18–15. Sales Activity Variance, Service Organization
(L.O.2)

Refer to the data in exercise 18–14 for Outslay & Wheeler.

Required: Prepare a sales activity variance analysis like the one in Illustration 18–3.

18–16. Profit Variance Analysis, Service Organization
(L.O.3)

Refer to the data in exercise 18–14 for Outslay & Wheeler.

Required: Prepare a profit variance for analysis like the one in Illustration 18–5 for Outslay & Wheeler.

18–17. Flexible Budget
(L.O.1)

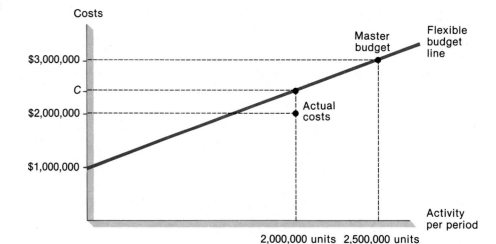

Required: Given the data shown in the graph, what are the following:

a. The budgeted fixed cost per period?

b. The budgeted variable cost per unit?

c. The value of c (that is, the flexible budget for an activity level of 2 million units)?

d. If the actual activity had been 4 million units, what would be the flexible budget cost amount?

18–18. Fill in Amounts on Flexible Budget Graph
(L.O.1)

Fill in the missing amounts for (a) and (b).

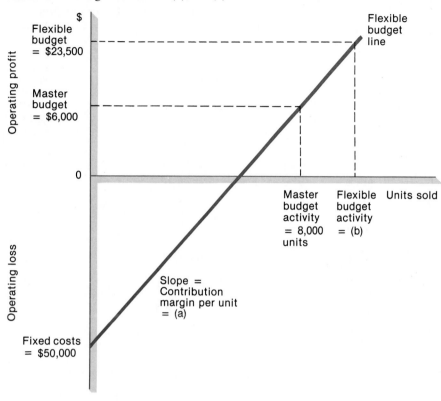

18–19. Flexible Budget
(L.O.1)

Label (a) and (b) in the graph and give the number of units sold for each.

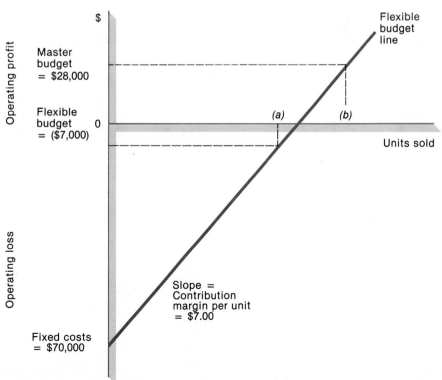

18–20. Prepare Flexible Budget
(L.O.1)

Full Moon Rising manufactures and sells compact disks for a variety of New Age groups. The company only produces when orders are received and, therefore, has no inventories. The following information is available for the current month:

	Actual (based on actual of 415,000 units)	Master Budget (based on budgeted 400,000 units)
Sales revenue	$1,930,000	$2,000,000
Less:		
Variable costs:		
Blank disks	600,000	600,000
Direct labor	165,000	140,000
Variable overhead	239,000	260,000
Variable marketing and administrative	205,000	200,000
Total variable costs:	1,209,000	1,200,000
Contribution margin	721,000	800,000
Less:		
Fixed costs:		
Manufacturing overhead	388,000	400,000
Marketing	120,000	120,000
Administrative	65,000	75,000
Total fixed costs	573,000	595,000
Operating profits	$ 148,000	$ 205,000

Required:

Prepare a flexible budget for Full Moon Rising.

18–21. Sales Activity Variance
(L.O.2)

Refer to the data in exercise 18–20 for Full Moon Rising.

Required:

Prepare a sales activity variance analysis like the one in Illustration 18–3.

18–22. Profit Variance Analysis
(L.O.3)

Use the information for Full Moon Rising (exercise 18–20).

Required:

Prepare a profit variance analysis like the one in Illustration 18–5.

PROBLEMS

18–23. Solve for Master Budget Given Actual Results

Oleander Enterprises lost the only copy of the master budget for this period. Management wants to evaluate this period's performance but needs the master budget to do so. Actual results for the period were:

Sales volume	120,000 units
Sales revenue	$672,000
Variable costs:	
Manufacturing	147,200
Marketing and administrative	61,400
Contribution margin	463,400
Fixed costs:	
Manufacturing	205,000
Marketing and administrative	113,200
Operating profit	$145,200

The company planned to produce and sell 108,000 units at a price of $5 each. At that volume, the contribution margin would have been $380,000. Variable marketing and administrative costs are budgeted at 10 percent of sales revenue. Manufacturing fixed costs are estimated at $2 per unit at the normal production level. Management notes: "We budget an operating profit of $1 per unit under normal production levels."

Required:

a. Construct the master budget for the period.

b. Prepare a profit variance analysis like the one in Illustration 18-5.

18–24. Find Missing Data for Profit Variance Analysis

	Reported Income Statement 750 Units	Manu- facturing Variances	Marketing and Administrative Variance	Sales Price Variance	Flexible Budget (a)	Sales Activity Variance	Master Budget 800 Units
Sales revenue	$1,950			(b)	$2,025	(c)	(d)
Variable manufacturing costs	(e)	$60 F			(f)	$38 F	(g)
Variable marketing and administrative costs	(h)		(i)		(j)	(k)	$240
Contribution margin	$1,240	(l)	(m)	(n)	(o)	(p)	(q)

Required:

Find the values of the missing items (*a*) through (*q*). Assume that the actual sales volume equals actual production volume. (There are no inventory level changes.)

18–25. Find Data for Profit Variance Analysis

Refer to the schedule positioned on the following page.

Required:

Find the values of the missing items (*a*) through (*x*). Assume that actual sales volume equals actual production volume. (There are no inventory level changes).

Table for Problem 18-25

	Reported Income Statement (based on actual sales volume)	Manufacturing Variance	Marketing and Administrative Variance	Sales Price Variances	Flexible Budget (based on actual sales volume)	Sales Activity (Volume) Variance	Master Budget (based on budgeted sales volume)
Units	(a)				(b)	$2,000 F	$ 10,000
Sales revenue	(g)			$18,000 F	(h)	(i)	150,000
Less:							
Variable manufacturing costs	(n)	(o)			$96,000	(j)	80,000
Variable marketing and administrative costs	$21,600		(p)		24,000	4,000 U	(c)
Contribution margin	(q)	$9,000 U	(s)	(x)	$60,000	(k)	$ 50,000
Less:							
Fixed manufacturing costs	(r)	2,000 F			(m)		(d)
Fixed marketing and administrative costs	18,000		(v)		15,000		(e)
Operating profits	(t)	(u)	(w)	$18,000 F	$20,000	(l)	(f)

18–26. Prepare Flexible Budget

The following information is provided concerning the operations of the 47th Street Company for the current period:

	Actual (based on actual of 90 units)	Master Budget (based on budgeted 100 units)
Sales revenue	$9,200	$10,000
Less:		
Manufacturing costs:		
Direct labor	1,420	1,500
Materials	1,200	1,400
Variable overhead	820	1,000
Marketing	530	600
Administrative	500	500
Total variable costs	4,470	5,000
Contribution margin	4,730	5,000
Less:		
Fixed costs:		
Manufacturing	485	500
Marketing	1,040	1,000
Administrative	995	1,000
Total fixed costs	2,520	2,500
Operating profits	$2,210	$ 2,500

There are no inventories.

Required: Prepare a flexible budget for the 47th Street Company.

18–27. Sales Activity Variance

Refer to the data in problem 18–26 for the 47th Street Company.

Required: Prepare a sales activity variance analysis like the one in Illustration 18–3.

18–28. Profit Variance Analysis

Use the information for the 47th Street Company in problem 18–26 to prepare a profit variance analysis like the one in Illustration 18–5.

18–29. Derive Amounts for Profit Variance Analysis

Orange Taxi Company operates a limousine and taxicab service. They want to compare this month's results with last month, which management felt was a typical "base period." The following information is provided:

	Last Month	This Month
Number of trips	14,000	16,100
Revenues	$151,000	$152,000
Variable costs	38,200	43,500
Contribution margin	$112,800	$108,500

Required: Compute the flexible budget, sales activity variance, and a profit variance analysis (like the one in Illustration 18–5) in as much detail as possible. (Hint: Use last month as the master budget and this month as the "actual.") What impact did the changes in number of trips and average revenues (i.e., sales price) have on Orange Taxi's contribution margin?

18–30. Flexible Budget—Multiple-Choice

The University of Burns operates a motor pool with 20 vehicles. The motor pool furnishes gasoline, oil, and other supplies for the cars and hires one mechanic who does routine maintenance and minor repairs. Major repairs are done at a nearby commercial garage. A supervisor manages the operations.

Each year, the supervisor prepares a master budget for the motor pool. Depreciation on the automobiles is recorded in the budget to determine the costs per mile.

The schedule below presents the master budget for the year and for the month of March.

The annual budget was based on the following assumptions:

1. 20 automobiles in the pool.
2. 30,000 miles per year per automobile.
3. 15 miles per gallon per automobile.
4. $0.90 per gallon of gas.
5. $0.006 per mile for oil, minor repairs, parts, and supplies.
6. $135 per automobile per year in outside repairs.

The supervisor is unhappy with the monthly report. He claims it unfairly presents his performance for March. His previous employer used flexible budgeting to compare actual costs to budgeted amounts.

UNIVERSITY MOTOR POOL
Budget Report for March

	Annual Master Budget	One-Month Master Budget	March Actual	Over or (Under)
Gasoline	$ 36,000	$ 3,000	$ 3,800	$800
Oil, minor repairs, parts, and supplies	3,600	300	380	80
Outside repairs	2,700	225	50	(175)
Insurance	6,000	500	525	25
Salaries and benefits	30,000	2,500	2,500	—
Depreciation	26,400	2,200	2,310	110
	$104,700	$ 8,725	$ 9,565	$840
Total miles	600,000	50,000	63,000	
Cost per mile	$0.1745	$0.1745	$0.1518	
Number of automobiles	20	20	21	

Required:

a. What is the gasoline monthly flexible budget and the resulting over or under budget? (Use miles as the activity base.)

	Flexible Budget	Over (Under) Budget
(1)	$3,000	$800
(2)	3,520	280
(3)	3,800	-0-
(4)	3,780	20

b. What is the oil, minor repairs, parts, and supplies monthly flexible budget and over or under budget? (Use miles as the activity base.)

	Flexible Budget	Over (Under) Budget
(1)	$400	$(20)
(2)	300	80
(3)	378	2
(4)	300	–0–

c. What is the salaries and benefits monthly flexible budget and the resulting over or under budget?

	Flexible Budget	Over (Under) Budget
(1)	$2,625	$125
(2)	2,500	(125)
(3)	2,625	–0–
(4)	2,500	–0–

d. What is the *major* reason for the cost per mile to decrease from $0.1745 budgeted to $0.1518 actual?
   (1) Decreased *unit* fixed costs.
   (2) Decreased *unit* variable costs.
   (3) Increased *unit* fixed cost and decreased *unit* variable cost.
   (4) Neither variable nor fixed *unit* costs decreased.

(CMA adapted)

18–31. Analyze Performance for a Restaurant

Persons Deli is planning to expand operations and, hence is concerned that its reporting system may need improvement. The master budget income statement for its Akron Persons Deli, which contains a delicatessen and restaurant operation, is (in thousands):

	Delicatessen	Restaurant	Total
Gross sales	$1,000	$2,500	$3,500
Purchases	600	1,000	1,600
Hourly wages	50	875	925
Franchise fee	30	75	105
Advertising	100	200	300
Utilities	70	125	195
Depreciation	50	75	125
Lease cost	30	50	80
Salaries	30	50	80
Total costs	960	2,450	3,410
Operating profit	$ 40	$ 50	$ 90

The performance report that the company uses for management evaluation is as follows:

PERSONS RESTAURANT-DELI
Akron, Ohio
Net Income for the Year
(in thousands)

	Actual Results				Over (Under) Budget
	Delicatessen	**Restaurant**	**Total**	**Budget**	
Gross sales	$1,200	$2,000	$3,200	$3,500	$(300)[a]
Purchases[b]	780	800	1,580	1,600	(20)
Hourly wages[b]	60	700	760	925	(165)
Franchise fee[b]	36	60	96	105	(9)
Advertising	100	200	300	300	—
Utilities[b]	76	100	176	195	(19)
Depreciation	50	75	125	125	—
Lease cost	30	50	80	80	—
Salaries	30	50	80	80	—
Total costs	1,162	2,035	3,197	3,410	(213)
Operating profit	$ 38	$ (35)	$ 3	$ 90	$ (87)

[a] There is no sales price variance.
[b] Variable costs. All other costs are fixed.

Required:

Prepare a profit variance analysis for the delicatessen segment. (Hint: Use gross sales as your measure of volume.)

(CMA adapted)

INTEGRATIVE CASES

18–32. Analyze Budget Planning Process: Behavioral Issues

RV Industries manufactures and sells recreation vehicles. The company has eight divisions strategically located near major markets. Each division has a sales force and two to four manufacturing plants. These divisions operate as autonomous profit centers responsible for purchasing, operations, and sales.

The corporate controller describes the divisional performance measurement system as follows: "We allow the divisions to control the entire operation from the purchase of direct materials to the sale of the product. We at corporate headquarters only get involved in strategic decisions such as developing new product lines. Each division is responsible for meeting its market needs by providing the right products at a low cost on a timely basis. Frankly, the divisions need to focus on cost control, delivery, and services to customers to become more profitable. However, being as close as they are to their markets, they are best qualified to do this.

"We give the divisions considerable autonomy, but we watch their monthly income statements very closely. Each month's actual performance is compared with the budget in considerable detail. If the actual sales or contribution margin is more than 4 or 5 percent below budget, we demand an immediate report from the division people. I might add that we don't have much trouble getting their attention. All of the management people at the plant and division level can add appreciably to their annual salaries with bonuses if actual net income is considerably greater than budget."

The budgeting process begins in August when division sales managers consult with their sales personnel to estimate sales for the next calendar year. These estimates are sent to plant managers, who use the sales forecasts to prepare production estimates. At the plants, production statistics, including direct material quantities, labor-hours, production schedules, and output quantities, are developed by operating personnel. Using the statistics prepared by the operating personnel, the plant accounting staff determines costs and estimates the plant's budgeted variable cost of goods sold and other plant expenses for each month of the coming calendar year.

In October, each division's accounting staff combines plant budgets with sales estimates and adds additional division expenses. "After the divisional management is satisfied with the budget," said Collins, "I visit each division to review their budget and make sure it is in line with corporate strategy and projections. I really emphasize sales forecasts because of the volatility in the demand for our product. For many years, we lost sales to our competitors because we projected production and sales too low and couldn't meet market demand. More recently, we were caught with large excess inventory when the bottom dropped out of the market for recreational vehicles.

"I generally visit all eight divisions during the first two weeks in November. After that the division budgets are combined and reconciled by my staff, and they are ready for approval by the board of directors in early December. The board seldom questions the budget.

"One complaint we've had from plant and division management is that they are penalized for circumstances beyond their control. For example, they failed to predict the recent sales decline. As a result, they didn't make their budget targets and, of cource, they received no bonuses. However, I point out that they are well rewarded when they exceed their budget. Furthermore, they provide most of the information for the budget, so it's their own fault if the budget is too optimistic. Indeed, they should have been the first to see the coming sales decline."

Required:

a. Identify and explain the biases the corporate management of RV Industries should expect in the communication of budget estimates by its division and plant personnel.

b. What sources of information can the top management of RV Industries use to monitor the budget estimates prepared by its divisions and plants?

c. What services could top management of RV Industries offer the divisions to help them in their budget development, without appearing to interfere with the division budget decisions?

d. The top management of RV Industries is attempting to decide whether it should get more involved in the budget process. Identify and explain what management needs to consider in reaching its decision.

(CMA adapted)

18–33. Adapt Budget Control Concepts to Research Organization

Argo Company has a well-organized research program. Each project is broken down into phases. Completion times and the cost of each phase are estimated. Project description and related estimates are used to develop the annual research department budget.

The schedule below presents the costs for the research activities budgeted for last year. Actual costs incurred by projects or overhead category are compared to estimates for each activity, and the variances are noted on this same schedule.

The director of research prepared a narrative statement of research performance for the year to accompany the schedule. The director's statement follows the schedule.

ARGO COMPANY
Profit Variance Analysis of Research Costs
(in thousands)

	Approved Activity for the Year	Actual Costs for the Year	(Over) Under Budget
Total research costs:			
Projects in progress:			
4–1	$ 23.2	$ 46.8	$(23.6)
5–3	464.0	514.8	(50.8)
New projects:			
8–1	348.0	351.0	(3.0)
8–2	232.0	257.4	(25.4)
8–3	92.8	—	92.8
Total research costs, including the indirect costs listed below	1,160.0	1,170.0	(10.0)
Indirect research costs (allocated to projects in proportion to their direct costs):			
Administration	50.0	52.0	(2.0)
Laboratory facilities	110.0	118.0	(8.0)
Total	$ 160.0	$ 170.0	$(10.0)

"The year has been most successful. The two projects, 4–1 and 8–1, scheduled for completion in this year were finished. Project 8–2 is progressing satisfactorily and should be completed next year as scheduled. The fourth phase of project 5–3, with estimated direct research costs of $100,000, and the first phase of project 8–3, both included in the approved activity for the year, could not be started because the principal researcher left our employment. They were resubmitted for approval in next year's activity plan."

Required:

From the information given, prepare an alternative schedule that will provide Argo Company management with better information to evaluate research cost performance for the year.

(CMA adapted)

18–34. Analyze Activity Variances—FIFO Process Costing

Fellite, Inc., manufactures foam padding for medical uses. The padding is produced in a continuous process. The company uses the FIFO process costing system for internal recordkeeping purposes. Since materials and conversion costs are added evenly throughout the process, it is not necessary to maintain separate accounts of materials and conversion costs for equivalent unit computations.

The master budget and actual results for the current period are reproduced as follows:

	Actual	Master Budget
Physical count of units:		
Beginning work in process inventory	1,000 (80% complete)	1,000 (50% complete)
Transferred to next department	2,500 units	3,200 units
Ending inventory	800 (⅝ complete)	600 (⅔ complete)
Current period costs:		
Direct materials	$30,000	$32,500
Direct labor	24,600	27,000
Manufacturing overhead:		
Variable	16,200	14,500
Fixed	24,100	26,000

Required:

a. Compute the equivalent units of production this period. (Note: Equivalent unit computations are discussed in Chapter 8.)

b. Prepare a profit variance analysis like the one in Illustration 18–5.

PRODUCTION COST VARIANCES

LEARNING OBJECTIVES

1. To compute and use variable cost variances.

2. To compute and use fixed cost variances.

3. To develop the comprehensive cost variance analysis.

4. To compare the two-way, three-way, and four-way analyses of overhead variances (Appendix).

Variances Differences between planned results and actual outcomes.

In management accounting, any deviation from a predetermined benchmark is a **variance.** In Chapter 17, we developed the master budget and, in Chapter 18, the flexible budget. We saw how the difference between the flexible budget and the master budget creates an activity variance and how differences between actual results and the flexible budget create a number of other variances. In this chapter, we examine in detail how a specific group of variances—cost variances—are developed, interpreted, and used.

Although we shall use a manufacturing company example in this chapter because it is the most comprehensive application we can find, the variances that we describe are also used in nonmanufacturing organizations. Service organizations in particular can use the labor and overhead variances to assess efficiency and control costs. Labor standards and variances are used in many financial institutions such as banks to assess transaction and check-processing efficiency. Labor standards are also used in fast-food restaurants to assess efficiency in preparing and serving food.

STANDARD COSTS

Standard Cost The anticipated cost of producing and/or selling a unit of output.

A *standard* is a benchmark or norm. There are, for example, standards for admittance to school, standards for passing a course, standards for product safety. In accounting, the term *standard* is used in a similar fashion. A **standard cost** is the anticipated cost of producing and/or selling a unit of output; it is a predetermined cost assigned to goods produced.

Some Clarifications

Standards versus Budgets

A standard cost is a *predetermined unit cost,* while a budget is a *financial plan.* Standard costs are often used to make up the financial plan. While in practice these terms are sometimes used interchangeably, standards usually refer to *per-unit amounts,* while budgets usually refer to *total amounts.*

In many companies, standards, like budgets, are developed and maintained "off the books." That is, they are not part of the formal accounting system. So, when we discuss standard costs in this chapter, we are referring to standards developed to facilitate control of personnel and operations. Whether they are entered into the records to value inventory is another issue.

Sources of Standard Costs

The following description of the way standard costs are set is based on an interview with a controller in a manufacturing company. It is representative of the standard-setting process in most companies.

Manufacturing Costs

Materials. A standard cost for every direct material used is computed by (1) examining current purchase prices and adjusting them for expected changes and (2) estimating the quantity of each direct material required to make each final product. The purchasing department helps us estimate how material prices will change. Our operations managers and industrial engineers help determine the quantities of materials needed to make our product.

Labor. Industrial engineers and operating managers estimate the number of direct labor-hours (or fractions of hours) required for each step of production by timing employees while they perform their duties. These hours are costed by accountants based on expected wage rates and fringe benefits during the period.

Variable overhead. Several years ago we began using regression analysis to estimate variable overhead rates. We ran actual variable overhead as the dependent variable and actual labor-hours as the independent variable for each production department. Each year we adjust the unit variable overhead rate based on feedback from production managers and accountants about changes in cost.

Budgeted fixed overhead. Production department managers and our accountants estimate the amount of fixed overhead that will be incurred in each production department, including service department costs (for example, maintenance) that have been allocated to the production department.

Review. All of these estimates are reviewed on a sample basis for reasonableness by our accounting staff and by our internal auditors. They are adjusted once a year to reflect changes.

Approvals. All standards are approved once a year by top management.

Despite the use of statistical techniques and industrial engineering methods for cost estimation, setting cost standards is more an art than a science.

SETTING STANDARDS: AN ILLUSTRATION

We will now illustrate how standard variable manufacturing cost variances are developed for the Evergreen Company example that was introduced in Chapter 18. The standard variable manufacturing cost, which we called the *estimated cost* in Chapter 18, was $8 per crate.

Direct Materials

Here is how the Evergreen Company determines the standard price of the lumber it uses to make crates. The standard price reflects the price of the product delivered to Evergreen Company, net of purchase discounts.

Direct Materials: Standard Price (per board-foot)

Purchase price of lumber	$ .23
Shipping costs	.04
Less purchase discounts	(.02)
Standard price per board-foot	$ .25

Note: A board-foot is a quantity measure equal to the volume in a piece of lumber 12 by 12 inches and 1 inch thick.

Direct materials are purchased by the board-foot, so the purchase price standard is expressed per *foot,* not per *crate*.

Direct material quantity standards are based on the quantity of direct material that should be used to make one unit under normal operating conditions. Each crate requires nine board-feet of lumber. One additional board-foot of lumber is the allowance for waste in cutting the lumber to the proper size and constructing the crate.

Direct Materials: Standard Quantity (board-feet)

Requirements per crate	9
Allowance for waste	1
Standard quantity per crate	10

The standard direct material cost per *crate* is then computed:

$.25 per board foot $\times$ 10 board-feet per crate = $2.50 per crate

Direct Labor

Direct labor standards are based on a standard labor rate for the work performed and the standard labor-hours required. The standard labor rate includes not only wages earned but also fringe benefits, such as medical insurance and pension plan contributions, and taxes paid by the employer (for example, unemployment taxes and the employer's share of an employee's social security taxes).

Direct Labor: Standard Rate (price per hour)

Wage rate	$ 8.00
Employer's payroll taxes and fringe benefits	2.00
Standard rate	$10.00

Most companies develop one standard rate for each category of labor. We assume Evergreen Company has only one category of labor.

Standard direct labor time is based on an estimate of the time required to perform each operation. For example, at Evergreen Company, the amount of time required to make each crate—to cut the lumber to size, to assemble the crate, and to finish and inspect it—is estimated by timing each step and adding some time for personal needs and breaks. Sometimes a crate is assembled but later rejected when inspected, so an allowance is made for time spent on crates that will later be rejected. These estimates for each crate are as follows:

Direct Labor: Standard Time (hours)

Cutting department:	
Cutting	.04
Personal time	.01
Allowance for rejects	.01
Total cutting department	.06
Assembly department:	
Assembly	.18
Personal time	.02
Total assembly department	.20
Finishing and inspection department:	
Finishing and inspection	.03
Personal time	.01
Total finishing and inspection department	.04
Standard time per good crate completed	.30

For each good crate that is completed, the standard labor cost is:

$10 per hour $\times$ .30 hours per crate = $\underline{\$3 \text{ per crate}}$

Variable Manufacturing Overhead

The first step in setting variable overhead standards is to find an activity measure that relates the cost to the product, that is, to determine x in the formula:

$$Y = a + bx$$

where

Y = Estimated total overhead (the dependent variable).
a = Estimated fixed overhead.
b = Estimated variable overhead rate per unit.
x = Independent variable(s) (an activity measure).

For example, Evergreen Company could develop a variable overhead rate per crate, which would be using crates as an activity measure, and apply that rate to each crate produced.

Selecting Activity Measures for Applying Overhead

Output Measures versus Input Measures of Activity

Output measures of activity (for example, number of crates produced at Evergreen Company or number of automobiles produced in an automobile factory) sometimes work well as a basis for applying overhead—especially when a single product is completely produced in a single work operation. However, it becomes difficult to measure departmental activity in terms of output when the department works on multiple products and only a portion of the product is completed in each department. Hence, most companies find input measures, like direct labor-hours or machine-hours, more practical.

If an input measure is used, its selection should consider the following issues:

1. *Causal relationship between the activity measure and variable overhead costs.* An increase in the activity measure should result in an increase in variable overhead costs. If an operation is labor-intensive, labor-hours would probably be causally related to variable overhead. On the other hand, for a capital-intensive operation, machine-hours could be the cause of variable overhead. As a product moves through several departments in a manufacturing operation, different activity bases may be used, as shown in the following diagram (the arrows refer to the movement of the product through various departments until it is finished):

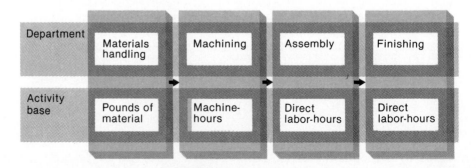

There is usually more than one cause of variable overhead, but to simplify matters, one independent variable is usually selected for a particular manufacturing department or work station.

2. *Physical units versus dollars.* Physical units are often used for the activity base instead of dollars. If labor-dollars are used, a contract settlement or other wage change could affect labor costs, but that does not necessarily mean that variable overhead costs would change.

3. *Cost-benefit constraints.* A model that specifies the relationship between variable overhead costs and their causes in so much detail that measures are precise could be quite costly. The benefits of such a complete model rarely justify its costs. Thus, a simplified model is usually preferred. For example, a simple regression model with one independent variable is often used in place of a multiple regression model, even though multiple regression may explain more variation in variable overhead. When examining variances between actual and standard costs, managers recognize that some variance is due purely to the infeasibility of setting perfect standards.

Evergreen Company uses a simple variable overhead basis, direct labor-hours, to determine its variable overhead standards. Management reviewed prior period activities and costs, estimated how costs will change in the future, and did a regression analysis in which overhead cost was the dependent variable and labor-hours the independent variable. After analyzing these estimates, the accountants decided to use $8.33⅓ per standard labor-hour as the variable manufacturing overhead rate for each department because variable overhead averaged about $8.33⅓ per standard direct labor-hour.

Illustration 19-1   **Summary of Costs, Evergreen Company**

	Standard Costs		
	(1) Standard Input Quantity	**(2)** Standard Input Price or Rate	**(1) × (2)** Standard Cost per Crate
Direct materials (all charged to cutting department)	10 feet	$ .25 per foot	$2.50
Direct labor	.30 hours	$10.00 per hour	3.00
Variable manufacturing overhead	.30 hours	$ 8.33⅓ per hour	2.50
Total standard variable cost per crate			$8.00

	Actual Costs		
	(1) Actual Input Quantity	**(2)** Actual Input Price or Rate	**(1) × (2)** Actual Cost per Crate
Direct materials (all charged to cutting department)	11 feet	$ .264 per foot	$2.904
Direct labor	.32 hours	$9.35 per hour	2.992
Variable manufacturing overhead	.32 hours	$8.275 per hour	2.648
Total actual variable cost per crate			$8.544

In practice, different departments may have different rates. *Activity-based costing*, as discussed in Chapter 2, acknowledges that different bases can be used to set standards. At times, different departments will have different rates, and multiple bases are used.

Variable manufacturing cost standards are summarized in a standard cost computer record or file. Illustration 19–1 presents the contents of such a file for Evergreen Company.

ANALYSIS OF COST VARIANCES

General Model

Cost Variance Analysis Comparison of actual input quantities and prices with standard input quantities and prices.

Price Variance Difference between actual costs and budgeted costs arising from changes in the cost of inputs to a production process or other activity.

Efficiency Variance Difference between budgeted and actual results arising from differences between the inputs that were budgeted per unit of output and the inputs actually used.

Total Variance Difference between total actual costs for the time period and the standard allowed per unit times the number of good units produced.

The conceptual **cost variance analysis** model compares actual input quantities and prices with standard input quantities and prices. *Both these actual and standard input quantities are for the actual output attained.* As shown in Illustration 19–2, a **price variance** and an **efficiency variance** can be computed for each variable manufacturing input. The actual costs incurred (column 1) for the time period are compared with the standard allowed per unit times the number of good units of output produced (column 3). This comparison provides the **total variance** for the cost or input.

In some companies, only the total variance is computed. In other companies, a more detailed breakdown into price and efficiency variances is made.

Managers who are responsible for price variances may not be responsible for efficiency variances and vice versa. For example, purchasing department managers are usually held responsible for direct materials price variances while manufacturing department managers are usually held responsible for using the direct materials efficiently.

This breakdown of the total variance into price and efficiency components is facilitated by the middle term, column 2, in Illustration 19–2. In going from column 1 to column 2, we go from *actual prices* (AP) times *actual quantity* (AQ) of input to *standard price* (SP) times *actual quantity* (AQ) of input. Thus, the price variance is calculated as:

$$\text{Price variance} = (AP \times AQ) - (SP \times AQ)$$
$$= (AP - SP)AQ$$

The efficiency variance is derived by comparing column 2, standard price times actual quantity of input, with column 3, standard price times standard quantity of input. Thus, the efficiency variance is calculated as:

$$\text{Efficiency variance} = (SP \times AQ) - (SP \times SQ)$$
$$= SP(AQ - SQ)$$

This general model may seem rather abstract at this point, but as we work examples, it will become more concrete and intuitive to you.

As the general model outlined in Illustration 19–2 is applied to each variable and fixed cost incurred, a more comprehensive cost variance analysis will result. The general model of the comprehensive cost variance analysis, as it appears in Illustration 19–3, will be applied to Evergreen Company's manufacturing costs. The comprehensive cost variance analysis

Illustration 19-2   **General Model for Cost Variance Analysis**

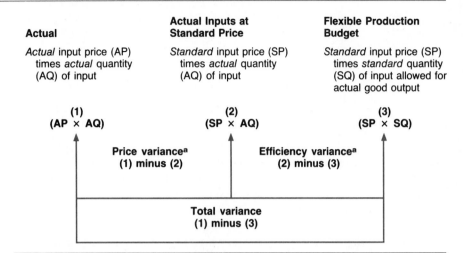

Actual	Actual Inputs at Standard Price	Flexible Production Budget
Actual input price (AP) times *actual* quantity (AQ) of input	*Standard* input price (SP) times *actual* quantity (AQ) of input	*Standard* input price (SP) times *standard* quantity (SQ) of input allowed for actual good output
(1) **(AP × AQ)**	**(2)** **(SP × AQ)**	**(3)** **(SP × SQ)**

Price variance[a]
(1) minus (2)

Efficiency variance[a]
(2) minus (3)

Total variance
(1) minus (3)

[a] The terms *price* and *efficiency* variances are general categories. While terminology varies from company to company, the following specific variance titles are frequently used:

Input	Price Variance Category	Efficiency Category
Direct materials	Price (or purchase price) variance	Usage or quantity variance
Direct labor	Rate variance	Efficiency variance
Variable overhead	Spending variance	Efficiency variance

We shall avoid unnecessary complications by simply referring to these variances as either a "price" or "efficiency" variance.

will ultimately explain, in detail, the unfavorable variable manufacturing variance of $5,440, as shown in Chapter 18, column 2 of Illustration 18–5.

As we proceed through the variance analysis for each manufacturing cost input—direct materials, direct labor, variable manufacturing overhead, and fixed manufacturing costs—you will notice some minor modifications from the general model presented in Illustration 19–2. It is important to recognize that these are *modifications of one general approach* rather than a number of independent approaches to variance analysis. In variance analysis, a few basic methods can be applied with minor modifications to numerous business and nonbusiness situations.

Direct Materials

Information about Evergreen Company's use of direct materials for the month of May is presented below:

Standard costs: 10 board-feet per crate @ $.25 per board-boot = $2.50 per crate
Crates produced in May: 10,000
Actual materials used: 110,000 board-feet @ $.264 per board-foot = $29,040

Illustration 19-3   **Detailed Computations of Price and Efficiency Variances**

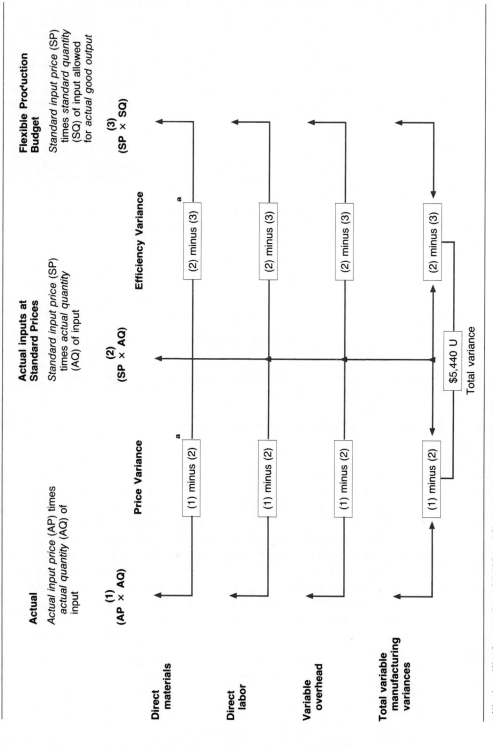

a (1) minus (2) refers to column (1) (AP × AQ) minus column (2) (SP × AQ).
  (2) minus (3) refers to column (2) (SP × AQ) minus column (3) (SP × SQ).

Illustration 19-4   **Direct Materials Variances, Evergreen Company (May)**
(10,000 crates)

	(1)	**(2)**	**(3)**
	Actual	**Actual Inputs at Standard Price**	**Flexible Production Budget**

<table>
<tr>
<td>

Actual materials price
(AP = $.264)
times *actual* quantity
(AQ = 110,000 feet)
of direct materials

</td>
<td>

Standard materials price
(SP = $.25)
times *actual* quantity
(AQ = 110,000 feet)
of direct materials

</td>
<td>

Standard materials price
(SP = $.25)
times *standard* quantity
(SQ = 10,000 crates
× 10 feet)
of direct materials
allowed for actual good
output

</td>
</tr>
<tr>
<td>

(AP × AQ)

$.264 × 110,000 feet
= $29,040

</td>
<td>

(SP × AQ)

$.25 × 110,000 feet
= $27,500

</td>
<td>

(SP × SQ)

$.25 × (10,000 crates ×
10 feet)
= $.25 × 100,000 feet
= $25,000

</td>
</tr>
</table>

Price variance:[a]
$29,040 − $27,500
= $1,540 U

Efficiency variance:[a]
$27,500 − $25,000
= $2,500 U

These relationships are shown graphically as:

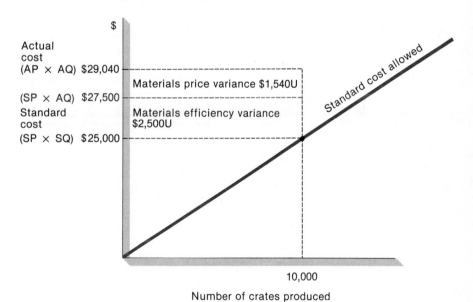

a Shortcut
Formulas: (AP × AQ) − (SP × AQ)   (SP × AQ) − (SP × SQ)
= (AP − SP) × AQ   = SP × (AQ − SQ)
= ($.264 − $.25) × 110,000   = $.25 × (110,000 − 100,000)
= $1,540 U   = $2,500 U

Total variance

= $4,040 U

Based on these data, the direct materials price and efficiency variances were calculated as shown in Illustration 19–4. Note that with a standard of 10 board-feet per crate and 10,000 crates actually produced in May, Evergreen Company expects to use 100,000 board-feet to produce the 10,000 crates. Since each board-foot has a standard cost of $.25, the standard materials cost allowed to make 10,000 crates is:

$$\text{Standard cost allowed to produce} = SP \times SQ$$
$$10,000 \text{ crates} = \$.25 \times (10 \text{ board-feet} \times 10,000 \text{ crates})$$
$$= \underline{\underline{\$25,000}}$$

Flexible Production Budget
Standard input price times standard quantity of input allowed for actual good output.

Note that column 3 of Illustration 19–4 is called the **flexible production budget.** The flexible budget concept can be applied to production as well as to sales. The flexible budget in Chapter 18 was based on actual *sales* volume (that is, crates *sold*). The flexible budget in Illustration 19–4 is based on actual production volume (that is, crates *produced*).

Responsibility for Direct Materials Variances

The direct materials price variance shows that in May the prices paid for direct materials exceeded the standards allowed, thus creating an unfavorable variance of $1,540. Responsibility for this variance is usually assigned to the purchasing department. Reports to management would include an explanation of the variance—for example, failure to take purchase discounts, transportation costs were higher than expected, different grade of direct material purchased, or changes in the market price of direct materials.

The explanation for the variance at Evergreen Company was that home construction in the economy has increased significantly, thus driving the price of lumber higher than expected. Further, prices were expected to continue climbing during the year. Based on this information, management began market research to determine if they should increase sales prices for their crates.

Direct materials efficiency variances are typically the responsiblity of production departments. In setting standards, an allowance is usually made for defects in direct materials, inexperienced workers, poor supervision, and the like. If actual materials usage is less than these standards, there is a favorable variance. If usage is in excess of standards, there is an unfavorable variance.

At Evergreen Company, the unfavorable materials efficiency variance was attributed to the recent hiring of some inexperienced laborers who, in an effort to keep up with the production schedule, improperly measured and cut lumber to the wrong lengths. The cutting department manager claimed this was a one-time occurrence and foresaw no similar problems in the future.

Direct Labor

To illustrate the computations of direct labor variances, assume for Evergreen Company:

Standard costs: .30 hours per crate @ $10 per hour = $3 per crate
Crates produced in May: 10,000
Actual direct labor costs: Actual hours worked were 3,200, while the total actual labor cost
was $29,920. Hence, the average cost per hour was $9.35 ($29,920 ÷ 3,200 hours).

The computation of the direct labor price and efficiency variances is shown
in Illustration 19–5.

Direct Labor Price Variance

The direct labor price variance is caused by the difference between actual
and standard labor costs per hour. Evergreen Company's direct labor costs
were less than the standard allowed, creating a favorable labor price variance of $2,080. The explanation given for Evergreen Company's favorable
labor price variance is that many inexperienced workers were hired in May.

Illustration 19-5 **Direct Labor Variances, Evergreen Company (May)**

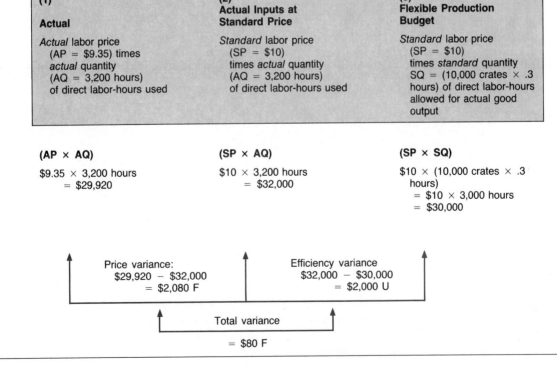

These inexperienced workers were paid a wage less than standard, thus reducing the *average* wage rate for all workers to $9.35.

In many companies, wage rates are set by union contract. If the wage rates used in setting standards are the same as those in the union contract, labor price variances will be nonexistent.

Labor Efficiency Variance

The labor efficiency variance is a measure of labor productivity. It is one of the most closely watched variances because it is usually controllable by production managers. A financial vice president of a manufacturing company told us: "Direct materials are 57 percent of our product cost, while direct labor is only 22 percent. We give direct materials price variances only a passing glance. But we carry out the labor efficiency variance to the penny; and we break it down by product line, by department, and sometimes by specific operation. Why? Because there's not much we can do about materials price changes, but there's a lot we can do to keep our labor efficiency in line."

Unfavorable labor efficiency variances have many causes. The workers themselves may be the cause. Poorly motivated or poorly trained workers will be less productive, whereas highly motivated and well-trained workers are more likely to generate favorable efficiency variances. Sometimes poor materials or faulty equipment can cause productivity problems. And poor supervision and scheduling can lead to unnecessary idle time.

Production department managers are usually responsible for direct labor efficiency variances. Scheduling problems may stem from other production departments that have delayed production. The personnel department may be responsible if the variance occurs because they provided the wrong kind of worker. The $2,000 unfavorable direct labor efficiency variance at Evergreen Company was attributed to the inexperienced workers previously mentioned. Note that one event, such as hiring inexperienced workers, can affect more than one variance.

Variable Manufacturing Overhead

To illustrate the computation of variable manufacturing overhead variances, assume for Evergreen Company:

Standard costs: .30 direct labor-hours per crate @ $8.33⅓ per hour
  (variable manufacturing overhead rate) = $2.50 per crate
Crates produced in May: 10,000
Actual variable overhead costs in May: $26,480

The computation of the variable manufacturing overhead price and efficiency variances is shown in Illustration 19–6.

Variable Manufacturing Overhead Price Variances

The variable overhead standard rate was derived from a two-stage estimation: (1) an estimate of costs at various levels of activity and (2) an estimate of the relationship between those estimated costs and the basis, which is direct labor-hours at Evergreen Company. The price variance could have

Illustration 19-6   **Variable Overhead Variances, Evergreen Company (May)**
                              (10,000 crates)

(1) **Actual** Sum of actual variable manufacturing overhead costs[a]	(2) **Actual Inputs at** **Standard Price** Standard variable overhead price (SP = $8.33⅓) (rate) times *actual* quantity (AQ = 3,200 hours) of the overhead base	(3) **Flexible Production** **Budget** Standard variable overhead price (SP = $8.33⅓) times *standard* quantity (SQ = 3,000 hours) of the overhead base (direct labor- hours in this example) allowed for actual good output
(AP − AQ) $26,480	**(SP − AQ)** $8.33⅓ × 3,200 hours = $26,667	**(SP − SQ)** $8.33⅓ × 3,000 hours = $25,000

Price variance:
$26,480 − $26,667
$187 F

Efficiency variance:
$26,667 − $25,000
$1,667 U

Total variance

= $1,480 U

---

[a] Total actual variable overhead costs also can be thought of as actual price (AP) times actual quantity (AQ). Divide the total actual variable overhead costs by the actual quantity of the variable overhead base:

$$AP = \$26,480 \div AQ$$
$$= \$26,480 \div 3,200 \text{ direct labor-hours}$$
$$= \$8.275$$

---

occurred because (1) actual costs—for example, machine power, materials handling, supplies, some direct labor—were different from those expected. Also, (2) the price variance could occur because the relationship between variable manufacturing overhead costs and direct labor-hours is not perfect.

The variable overhead price variance actually contains some efficiency items as well as price items. For example, suppose utilities costs are higher than expected. One reason could be that utility rates are higher than expected; but an additional reason could be that kilowatt-hours (kwhr.) per labor-hour are higher than expected (for example, if workers do not turn off power switches when machines are not being used). Both would be part of the price variance because jointly they cause utility costs to be higher than expected. In some companies, these components of the variable overhead price variance are separated. This is commonly done for energy costs in heavy manufacturing companies, for example.

At Evergreen Company, the unfavorable price variance for May was attributed to waste in using supplies and recent increases in rates charged for power to run the saws in the cutting department.

Variable Overhead Efficiency Variance
The variable overhead efficiency variance must be interpreted carefully. It is related to efficiency in using the base on which variable overhead is applied.

For example, at Evergreen Company, variable overhead is applied on the basis of direct labor-hours. Thus, if there is an unfavorable direct labor efficiency variance because actual direct labor-hours were greater than the standard allowed, there will be a corresponding unfavorable variable overhead efficiency variance. Evergreen Company used 200 direct labor-hours more than the standard allowed, resulting in the direct labor and variable overhead efficiency variances shown below:

Direct labor efficiency: $10 × 200 hours = $2,000 U (Illustration 19–5)
Variable overhead efficiency: $8.33⅓ × 200 hours = $1,667 U (Illustration 19–6)
Total direct labor and variable overhead efficiency variances: $18.33⅓ × 200 hours = $3,667 U

Variable overhead is assumed to vary directly with direct labor-hours, which is the base on which variable overhead is applied.

Thus, inefficiency in using the base (for example, direct labor-hours, machine-hours, units of output) is assumed to cause an increase in variable overhead. This emphasizes the importance of selecting the proper base for applying variable overhead. Managers who are responsible for controlling the base will probably be held responsible for the variable overhead efficiency variance as well. Whoever is responsible for the $2,000 unfavorable direct labor efficiency variance at Evergreen Company will probably be held responsible for the unfavorable variable overhead efficiency variance, too.

Summary of Variable Manufacturing Cost Variance

The variable manufacturing cost variances are summarized in Illustration 19–7. Note that the total variable manufacturing cost variance is the same as that derived in Chapter 18. The analysis of cost variances in this chapter is just a more detailed analysis of the variable manufacturing cost variance that was derived in Chapter 18. (See Illustration 18–5.)

A summary of this kind is useful for reporting variances to high-level managers. It provides both an overview of variances and their sources. When used for reporting, the computations shown at the right of Illustration 19–7 are usually replaced with a brief explanation of the cause of the variance.

Management may want more detailed information about some of the variances. This can be provided by extending each variance branch in Illustration 19–7 to show variances by product line, by department, or by other breakdowns.

FIXED MANUFACTURING COSTS—PRICE (SPENDING) VARIANCE

In variance analysis, fixed manufacturing costs are treated differently from variable manufacturing costs. For illustrative purposes, we assume these fixed manufacturing costs are all overhead. Other manufacturing costs also may be fixed; if so, they can be treated the same way that we treat fixed manufacturing overhead. It is usually assumed that fixed costs are unchanged when volume changes, so the amount budgeted for fixed overhead is the same in both the master and flexible budgets. This is consistent with the variable costing method of product costing.

Illustration 19-7   **Variable Manufacturing Cost Variance Summary, Evergreen Company (May)**

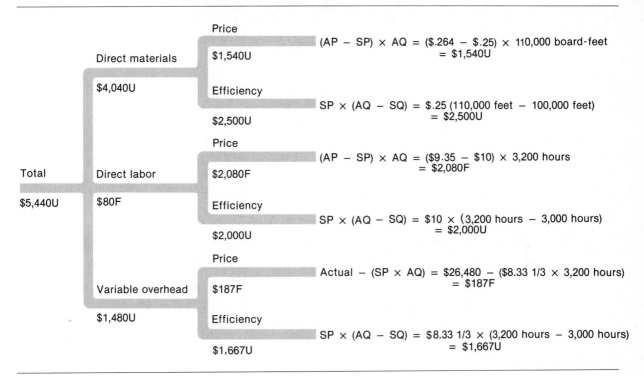

There are no input-output relationships for fixed overhead. Thus, there is no efficiency variance. The difference between the flexible budget and the actual fixed overhead is entirely due to changes in the costs that make up fixed overhead (for example, insurance premiums on the factory are higher than expected). Hence, the variance falls under the category of a price variance. (It is also called a **spending** or a **budget variance.**)

The fixed manufacturing overhead in both the flexible and master budgets in Chapter 18 was $36,000. Assume the actual cost is $37,000. The variance analysis is shown in Illustration 19–8. Note that there is no calculation of the efficiency with which inputs are used.

Spending Variance Price variance for fixed overhead.

Budget Variance A price variance for fixed overhead.

Comparison of Actual to Flexible Production Budget to Master Production Budget

Activity Variance Variance due to changes in volume of sales or production.

A comparison of actual results with the flexible and master budget was presented in Chapter 18 for *sales volume*. A similar comparison can be made for *production volume*, as shown in Illustration 19–9. This difference between the master production budget and the flexible production budget is the production **activity variance.**

Now that the actual production costs, flexible budget amounts, and variances have been presented (see columns 1, 2, 3, and 4 of Illustration 19–9), we can make the final comparison of budget to actual results. The master budget, which is shown in column 6, is based on a projected or budgeted production of 8,000 crates, based on the information given in Chapter 18.

Illustration 19-8   **Fixed Overhead Variances, Evergreen Company (May)**

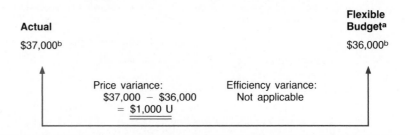

Actual
$37,000[b]

Flexible
Budget[a]
$36,000[b]

Price variance:
$37,000 − $36,000
= $1,000 U

Efficiency variance:
Not applicable

[a] For fixed costs, there is no difference between the flexible and master (or static) budget in Chapter 18.

[b] These amounts tie to Illustration 18–5, which presents an overview of the use of budgets for performance evaluation at Evergreen Company.

Illustration 19-9   **Profit Variance Analysis, Evergreen Company**

	(1) Actual (based on production of 10,000 crates)	(2) Price Variance	(3) Efficiency Variance	(4) Flexible Budget (based on actual production of 10,000 crates)	(5) Production Activity Variance	(6) Master Budget (based on estimated production of 8,000 crates)
Variable manufacturing costs:						
Direct materials	$29,040	$1,540 U	$2,500 U	$25,000	$ 5,000 U	$20,000
Direct labor	29,920	2,080 F	2,000 U	30,000	6,000 U	24,000
Variable overhead	26,480	187 F	1,667 U	25,000	5,000 U	20,000
Subtotal	$85,440[a]	$ 727 F	$6,167 U	$80,000[a]	$16,000 U	$64,000

Total = 5,440 U[a]

[a] Numbers tie to Illustration 18–5, Chapter 18.

The flexible production budget (column 4) tells us the standard variable costs allowed when the *actual production output* is 10,000 crates (Total = $80,000) and the budgeted fixed overhead is $36,000. The actual costs (column 1) tell us the actual amounts spent for each cost.

Comparing Illustration 19–9 with Illustration 18–5 (in Chapter 18) will help you to relate these detailed price and efficiency variances with the "big-picture" overview presented in Chapter 18. All we have done here is to break down the variable cost variances from Chapter 18 into more detail. Note that the $5,440 unfavorable variable cost variance from column 2 of Illustration 18–5 has been explained in more detail in Illustration 19–10 because of our analysis in this chapter.

This completes the basic variance analysis process. We next consider two extensions.

Illustration 19-10 **Comprehensive Cost Variance Analysis, Evergreen Company**

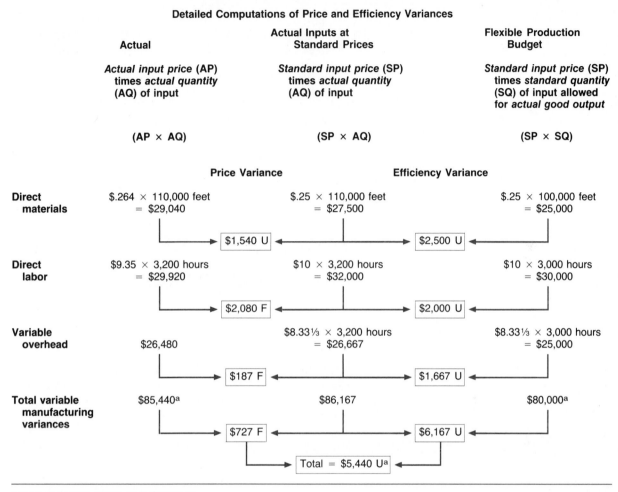

Detailed Computations of Price and Efficiency Variances

	Actual	Actual Inputs at Standard Prices	Flexible Production Budget
	Actual input price (AP) times *actual quantity* (AQ) of input	*Standard input price* (SP) times *actual quantity* (AQ) of input	*Standard input price* (SP) times *standard quantity* (SQ) of input allowed for *actual good output*
	(AP × AQ)	(SP × AQ)	(SP × SQ)

Price Variance | Efficiency Variance

Direct materials
$.264 × 110,000 feet = $29,040 → $1,540 U ← $.25 × 110,000 feet = $27,500 → $2,500 U ← $.25 × 100,000 feet = $25,000

Direct labor
$9.35 × 3,200 hours = $29,920 → $2,080 F ← $10 × 3,200 hours = $32,000 → $2,000 U ← $10 × 3,000 hours = $30,000

Variable overhead
$26,480 → $187 F ← $8.33⅓ × 3,200 hours = $26,667 → $1,667 U ← $8.33⅓ × 3,000 hours = $25,000

Total variable manufacturing variances
$85,440[a] → $727 F ← $86,167 → $6,167 U ← $80,000[a]

Total = $5,440 U[a]

[a] Numbers tie to Illustration 18–5, Chapter 18.

MATERIALS VARIANCES WHEN QUANTITY PURCHASED DOES NOT EQUAL QUANTITY USED

So far we have assumed that the amount of materials used equals the amount of materials purchased. Now we show how to calculate variances when the quantities purchased and used are not the same.

Recall the following facts from the Evergreen Company example:

> Standard costs: 10 board-feet per crate @ $.25 per board-foot = $2.50 per crate
> Crates produced in May: 10,000
> Actual materials used: 110,000 board-feet @ $.264 = $29,040

Now, let's assume that 250,000 board-feet were purchased in May at $.264 per board-foot, 110,000 board-feet were used, and there was no inventory on May 1.

Illustration 19-11 **Direct Materials Variances when Quantities Purchased and Used Are Not Equal, Evergreen Company (May)**

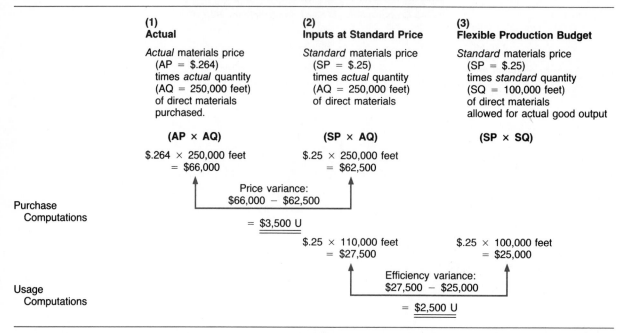

The variance calculations are shown in Illustration 19–11. Note that the **purchase price variance** is different from the earlier example in the chapter because *it is based on the materials purchased.* The efficiency variance is the same as in the previous example because it is based on materials used, which has not changed.

Purchase Price Variance The price variance based on the quantity of materials purchased.

FIXED MANUFACTURING COSTS— PRODUCTION VOLUME VARIANCE

So far, we have assumed that fixed manufacturing costs are treated as period costs, which is consistent with variable costing. If fixed manufacturing costs are unitized and treated as product costs, then another variance is computed. *This occurs when companies use full-absorption, standard costing.*

Developing the Standard Unit Cost for Fixed Manufacturing Costs

Like other standard costs, the fixed manufacturing standard cost is determined before the start of the production period. Unlike standard variable manufacturing costs, fixed costs are period costs by nature. To convert them to product costs requires an estimation of both the period cost and the production volume for the period. The formula is:

$$\text{Standard (or predetermined) fixed manufacturing overhead cost} = \frac{\text{Budgeted fixed manufacturing cost}}{\text{Budgeted activity level}}$$

Assume that the estimated annual fixed manufacturing overhead at Evergreen Company was $432,000 and the estimated annual production volume was estimated to be 96,000 crates (or 28,800 direct labor-hours at .30 hours per crate). Thus Evergreen Company would determine its standard fixed manufacturing cost per crate as follows:

$$\text{Standard cost} \over \text{per crate} = \frac{\$432,000 \text{ (budgeted fixed manufacturing cost)}}{96,000 \text{ crates (budgeted activity level for the year)}}$$

$$= \underline{\underline{\$4.50 \text{ per crate}}}$$

Or, the rate could be computed per direct labor-hour, as follows:

$$\text{Standard rate per} \over \text{direct labor-hour} = \frac{\$432,000}{28,800 \text{ hours}} = \underline{\underline{\$15 \text{ per direct labor-hour}}}$$

Each crate is expected to require .3 direct labor-hour $\left(\frac{28,800 \text{ hours}}{96,000 \text{ crates}}\right)$, so the standard cost per crate would still be \$4.50 (\$15 per hour × .3 hour per crate).

If 10,000 units are actually produced during the month, then \$45,000 of fixed overhead costs is applied to these units produced.

Production Volume Variance A variance that arises because the quantity of outputs used to apply overhead differs from the estimated quantity used to estimate fixed costs per unit of output.

The **production volume variance** is the difference between the \$45,000 applied fixed overhead and the \$36,000 budgeted fixed overhead. Hence, in this situation there would be a \$9,000 favorable production volume variance. The variance is favorable because more overhead was applied than was budgeted—production was greater than the average monthly estimate. This variance is a result of the full-absorption costing system; it does not occur in variable costing.

This \$45,000 applied equals \$4.50 per crate times 10,000 units *actually produced*. If the \$15.00 rate per direct labor-hour had been used, then the amount applied to the 10,000 units produced would still be \$45,000, computed as follows: \$15.00 per hour times .3 standard direct labor-hour per crate times 10,000 crates actually produced (\$15 × .3 × 10,000 = \$45,000).

If the number of units actually produced differs from the number of units used to estimate the fixed cost per unit, a variance will arise. This variance is commonly referred to as a production volume variance. (It is also called a *capacity variance,* an *idle capacity variance,* or a *denominator variance.*)

In our example, there is a production volume variance because the 10,000 crates actually produced during the month is not equal to the 8,000 $\left(\frac{96,000}{12 \text{ months}}\right)$ estimated for the month.

Consequently, production is charged with \$45,000 (10,000 crates × \$4.50 per crate) instead of \$36,000 (8,000 crates × \$4.50 per crate). The \$9,000 difference is the production volume variance because it is caused by a deviation in production volume level (number of crates produced) from that estimated to arrive at the standard cost.

If Evergreen Company had estimated 10,000 crates per month instead of 8,000 crates, then the standard cost would have been \$3.60 per crate $\left(\frac{\$36,000}{10,000 \text{ crates}}\right)$. Thus, \$36,000 (\$3.60 × 10,000 crates) would have been applied to units produced, and there would have been no production volume variance.

The production volume variance applies only to fixed costs and emerges because we are allocating a fixed period cost to units on a predetermined basis. It is unique to full-absorption costing. The benefits of calculating the variance for control purposes are questionable. While it signals a difference between expected and actual production levels, so does a simple production report of actual versus expected production quantities.

Illustration 19–12   **Fixed Overhead Variances**

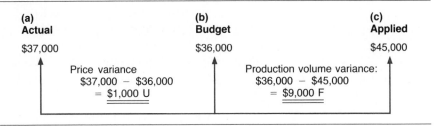

(a) Actual	(b) Budget	(c) Applied
$37,000	$36,000	$45,000

Price variance
$37,000 − $36,000
= $1,000 U

Production volume variance:
$36,000 − $45,000
= $9,000 F

Illustration 19–13   **Fixed Overhead Variances: Graphic Presentation**

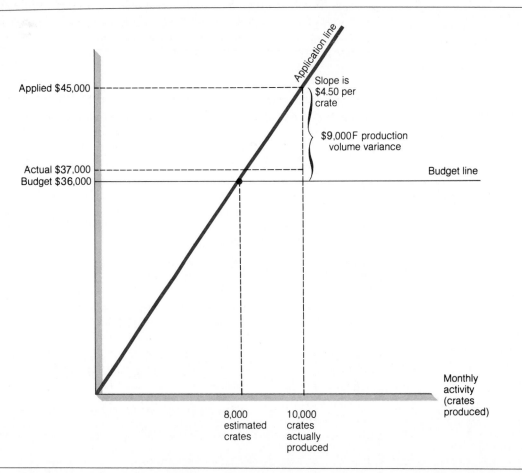

Compare with the Fixed Manufacturing Cost Price Variance

The fixed manufacturing cost price variance is the difference between actual and budgeted fixed manufacturing costs. Unlike the production volume variance, the price variance is commonly used for control purposes because it is a measure of differences between actual and budgeted period costs.

Illustrations 19–12 and 19–13 should help you see the relationship between *actual, budget,* and *applied* fixed manufacturing costs and to summarize the computation of the fixed manufacturing *price* (spending) and *production volume* variances.

SUMMARY OF OVERHEAD VARIANCES

Illustration 19–14 summarizes the four-way analysis of variable and fixed overhead variances, based on facts given in the chapter. Appendix A to this chapter shows two-way and three-way methods that are alternatives to the four-way method.

Key Points

There are several key points to keep in mind regarding overhead variances.

1. The variable overhead efficiency variance measures the efficiency in using the base (for example, direct labor-hours).
2. The production volume variance only occurs when fixed manufacturing cost is unitized (for example, when using full-absorption costing). Further, the budgeted fixed overhead is not the amount applied to units produced.

Illustration 19–14   **Summary of Overhead Variances: Four-Way Analysis**

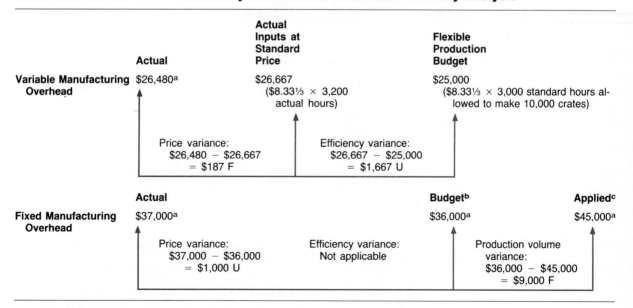

a Amount given in chapter.

b This amount appears in both the master budget and the flexible budget.

c This is the amount of fixed manufacturing overhead applied to units produced under full-absorption costing.

3. There is no efficiency variance for fixed manufacturing costs. (The production volume variance should not be confused with an efficiency variance.)

VARIANCE ANALYSIS IN NONMANUFAC- TURING SETTINGS

The analysis of price and efficiency variances in nonmanufacturing settings for nonmanufacturing costs is increasing. We find banks, fast-food outlets, hospitals, consulting firms, retail stores, and many others applying the variance analysis techniques discussed in this chapter to their labor and overhead costs.

Efficiency Measures

In some cases, an efficiency variance can be used to analyze variable nonmanufacturing costs. This efficiency computation requires a reliable measure of output activity. Ideally, this requires some quantitative input that can be linked to output.

For example, the personnel in the accounts receivable department of a retail merchandiser are expected to contact 10 delinquent customers per hour. The standard labor cost is $12 per hour including benefits. During July, 7,000 hours were worked, 65,000 contacts were made, and the average wage rate was $13 per hour. For 65,000 contacts, the standard labor-hours allowed was 6,500 (65,000 contacts ÷ 10 contacts per hour). Unfavorable price and efficiency variances were computed as shown below:

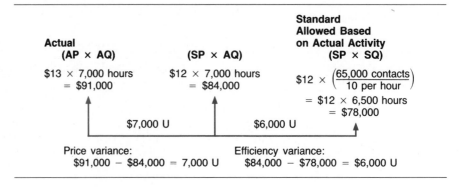

These calculations are similar to the ones used for labor variances in manufacturing.

Computing these efficiency variances requires some assumed relationship between input and output activity. Some examples are:

Department	Input	Output
Mailing	Labor-hours worked	Number of pieces mailed
Personnel	Labor-hours worked	Number of personnel changes processed
Food service	Hours worked	Number of meals served
Consulting	Billable hours worked	Customer revenues
Nursing	Labor-hours worked	Patients (of a particular care level) served
Check processing	Computer hours worked	Checks processed

In general, jobs with routine tasks lend themselves to efficiency measures, while jobs with nonroutine tasks—like most administrative positions—do not.

Attempts to measure efficiency sometimes leads to employee resentment. In other cases, the measurement results in both better performance and better morale. Often, employee participation in the measurement process helps improve morale, while a top-down imposed measurement system provokes employee resentment.

HOW MANY VARIANCES TO CALCULATE?

We noted at the beginning of this chapter that every organization has its own approach to variance analysis although virtually all are based on the fundamental model presented here. Because of the unique circumstances in each organization, we cannot generalize very much about which variances should be calculated. Managers and accountants in each organization should perform their own cost-benefit analysis to ascertain which calculations are justified.

In deciding how many variances to calculate, it is important to note the **impact** and **controllability** of each variance. When considering *impact,* we ask: "Does this variance matter? Is it so small that the best efforts to improve efficiency or control costs would have very little impact even if the efforts were successful?" If so, it's probably not worth the trouble to calculate and analyze. Hence, detailed variance calculations for small overhead items may not be worthwhile.

When considering the controllability of a variance, we ask: "Can we do something about it?" No matter how great the impact of the variance, if nothing can be done about the variance, then it is hard to justify spending resources to compute and analyze it. For example, materials purchase price variances are often high-impact items. They are hard to control, however, because materials prices fluctuate due to market conditions that are outside the control of managers.

In general, high-impact, highly controllable variances should get the most attention, while low-impact, uncontrollable variances should get the least attention, as shown below:

Impact The monetary effect that is likely from an activity (such as a variance).

Controllability The extent to which an item can be managed.

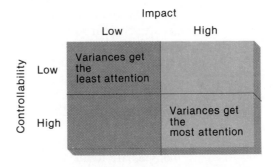

Labor and materials efficiency variances are often highly controllable. With sufficient attention to scheduling, quality of employees, motivation, and incentives, these variances can often be dealt with effectively. An example of a high-impact, but hard-to-control, item for many companies has been the cost of energy. Many organizations, from airlines to taxicab companies to steel mills, have been able to do little about rising energy costs in the short run. Over time, of course, actions could be taken to reduce energy usage through acquisition of energy-efficient equipment. In general, the longer the time interval, the greater the ability to control an item.

MANAGEMENT BY EXCEPTION AND VARIANCE INVESTIGATION

Management by Exception An approach to management requiring that reports emphasize the deviation from an accepted basing point, such as a standard, a budget, an industry average, or a prior-period experience.

After variances have been computed and the initial analysis made, managers and accountants must decide which variances should be investigated. Because a manager's time is a scarce resource, some priorities must be set. This can be done through cost-benefit analysis. Only the variances for which the benefits of correction exceed the costs of follow-up should be pursued. In general, this is consistent with the **management by exception** philosophy, which says, in effect, "Don't worry about what is going according to plan; worry about the exceptions."

But this is easier said than done. It may be almost impossible to predict either costs or benefits of investigating variances. So, while the principle is straightforward, it is difficult to apply. In this section, we identify some characteristics that are important for determining which variances to investigate. In Chapter 25, we discuss statistical models for investigating variances.

Some problems are easily corrected as soon as they are discovered. When a machine is improperly set or a worker needs minor instruction, the investigation cost is low and benefits are very likely to exceed costs. This is often a usage or efficiency variance and is reported frequently—often daily—so immediate corrective action can be taken.

Some variances are not controllable in the short run. Labor price variances due to changes in union contracts and overhead spending variances due to unplanned utility and property tax rate changes may require little or no follow-up in the short run. Such variances sometimes prompt long-run action, such as moving a plant to a locale with lower wage rates and lower utility and property tax rates. In such cases, the short-run benefits of variance investigation are low, but the long-run benefits may be higher.

Data and Timing Problems

Many variances occur because of errors in recording, bookkeeping adjustments, or timing problems. A variance-reporting system (and the accounting department) can lose credibility if it contains bookkeeping errors and adjustments. For this reason, the accounting staff must carefully check variance reports before sending them to operating managers.

UPDATING STANDARDS

Standards are estimates. As such, they may not reflect the conditions that actually occur. This is especially likely to happen when standards are not updated and revised to reflect current conditions. If prices and operating methods are frequently changed, standards may be constantly out of date.

In many companies, standards are revised once a year. Thus, variances will occur because conditions change during the year but standards don't. When conditions change, but are known to be temporary, some companies develop a **planned variance.** For example, an unexpected series of snowstorms curtailed activities much below normal in a steel plant in the Mid-

Planned Variance Variances that are expected to arise if certain conditions affect operations.

west. This affected the workers' productivity and created large unfavorable labor efficiency variances. In response, the accounting staff developed planned variances for a number of costs based on expected differences between actual costs and standard costs due to the snowstorms. For example, the January labor report for a particular department was as follows:

Item	Total Efficiency Variance	Planned Efficiency Variance	Unplanned Efficiency Variance
Direct labor—department xx	$11,242 U	$9,100 U	$2,142 U

The department manager was not held responsible for the entire $11,242 U variance, but only the $2,142 U unplanned efficiency variance.

SUMMARY

This chapter discusses the computation and analysis of manufacturing cost variances. A variance is the difference between a predetermined standard and an actual result.

The model used for calculating variable manufacturing cost variances is based on the following diagram, which divides the total variance between actual and standard into price and efficiency components.

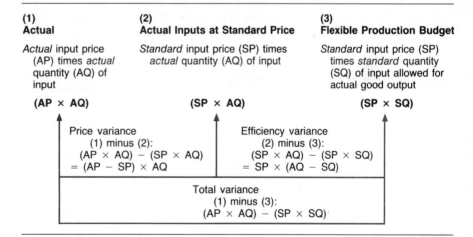

Fixed manufacturing costs have no efficiency variance. The price variance is the difference between actual fixed costs and the fixed costs in the flexible budget. If fixed costs are unitized and assigned to units produced, then a production volume variance can also arise. The production volume variance is the difference between the budgeted fixed costs and the amount applied to production.

A key managerial question is: How many variances should be calculated and investigated? The answer depends on the impact and controllability of variances. In general, the greater the impact of a variance on profits and the more controllable it is, the easier it is to justify analysis of the variance.

TERMS AND CONCEPTS

The following terms and concepts should be familiar to you after reading this chapter.

Activity Variance	Planned Variance
Budget Variance	Price Variance
Controllability	Production Volume Variance
Cost Variance Analysis	Purchase Price Variance
Efficiency Variance	Spending Variance
Flexible Production Budget	Standard Cost
Impact	Total Variance
Management by Exception	Variance

SUPPLEMENTARY READINGS

Baiman, S. and J. S. Demski. "Variance Analysis Procedures as Motivation Devices." *Management Science,* August 1980, pp. 840–48.

————. "Economically Optimal Performance Evaluation and Control Systems." *Journal of Accounting Research,* Supplement 1980, pp. 184–220.

Barlev, Benzion. "Total Factor Productivity and Cost Variances: Survey and Analysis." *Journal of Accounting Literature* vol. 5 (1986), pp. 35–56.

Chen, Kung H., and S. J. Lambert. "Impurity of Variable Factory Overhead Variances." *Journal of Accounting Education,* Spring 1985, pp. 189–96.

Dittman, D., and P. Prakash. "Cost Variance Investigation: Markovian Control versus Optimal Control." *Accounting Review,* April 1979, pp. 358–73.

Jaouen, P. R., and B. R. Neumann. "Variance Analysis, Kanban, and JIT: A Further Study." *Journal of Accountancy,* June 1987, pp. 164–66 +.

Lev, B. "An Information Theory Analysis of Budget Variances." *Accounting Review,* October 1969.

Marcinko, David, and Enrico Petri. "Use of the Production Function in Calculation of Standard Cost Variances—An Extension." *Accounting Review,* July 1984, pp. 488–95.

Ronen, J. "Nonaggregation versus Disaggregation of Variances." *Accounting Review,* January 1974.

Truitt, Jack. "Does the Joint Variance Make Economic Sense?" *Cost and Management,* May–June 1985, pp. 30–33.

SELF-STUDY PROBLEM NO. 1

Last month, the following events took place at Containers, Inc.:

1. Produced 50,000 plastic minicomputer cases.

2. Standard variable costs per unit (that is, per case):

Direct materials: 2 pounds at $1	$2.00
Direct labor: .10 hours at $15	1.50
Variable manufacturing overhead: .10 hours at $5	.50
	$4.00 per case

3. Fixed manufacturing overhead cost:

Monthly budget	$ 80,000

4. Actual production costs:

Direct materials purchased: 200,000 pounds at $1.20	$240,000
Direct materials used: 110,000 pounds at $1.20	132,000
Direct labor: 6,000 hours at $14	84,000
Variable overhead	28,000
Fixed overhead	83,000

Required:

a. Compute the direct materials, labor, and variable manufacturing price and efficiency variances.

b. Compute the fixed manufacturing overhead price variance. Compute the fixed manufacturing overhead production volume variance, assuming the *estimated* monthly production was 40,000 cases (or 4,000 standard labor-hours).

SOLUTION TO SELF-STUDY PROBLEM NO. 1

a. **Production variances:**

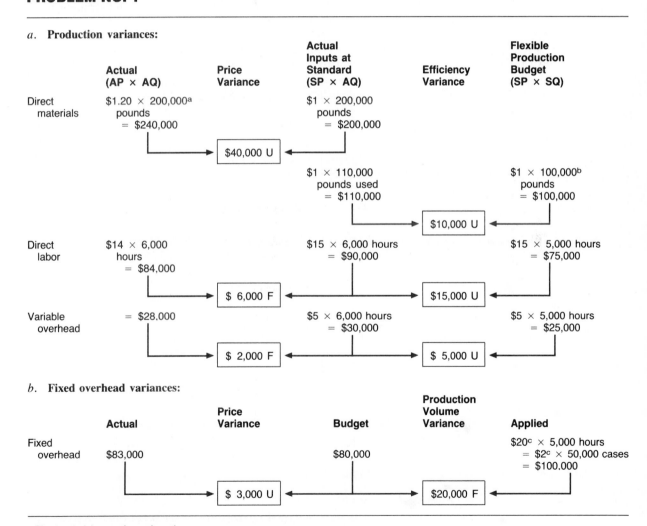

b. **Fixed overhead variances:**

---

[a] Direct materials pounds purchased.

[b] Standard direct materials pounds used in production per unit times units produced (2 pounds × 50,000 units).

[c] Fixed overhead rate $= \dfrac{\$80,000}{40,000 \text{ cases}} = \$2$ per case, or $\dfrac{\$80,000}{4,000 \text{ hours}} = \$20$ per standard labor hour.

APPENDIX A
Two-Way and Three-Way Analysis of Overhead Variance

The method of computing overhead variances described in this chapter is known as the four-way analysis of overhead variances because the following four variances are computed:

	Price	Efficiency	Production Volume
Variable	$ 187 F	$1,667 U	Not applicable
Fixed	1,000 U	Not applicable	$9,000 F

Companies also prepare alternative two-way or three-way analyses of manufacturing overhead variances.

Two-Way Analysis

The two-way analysis of overhead variances has just two variances: a *production volume variance,* computed like the production volume variance in the four-way analysis above, and a *spending,* or *budget variance,* which is the difference between the actual and budgeted overhead. (Think of the spending variance as including all three of the overhead variances computed in the four-way analysis besides the production volume variance.) If Evergreen Company does not break down its variances into fixed and variable components, then the actual overhead costs would be $63,480 ($26,480 variable plus $37,000 fixed, as shown in Illustration 19–14), and the budgeted overhead would total $61,000 ($25,000 variable plus $36,000 fixed, as shown in Illustration 19–14).

The following diagram shows how to compute the two overhead variances.

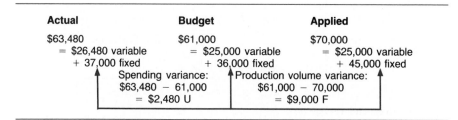

The amount of variable overhead applied to units produced ($25,000) is the standard allowed for the flexible production budget, so "applied equals budget" for variable overhead. This is not true for fixed overhead if there is a production volume variance.

Three-Way Analysis
The three-way analysis is like the four-way analysis except the two fixed and variable price variances are combined into one overhead price variance.

Illustration 19-15 **Alternative Ways of Computing Overhead Variances**

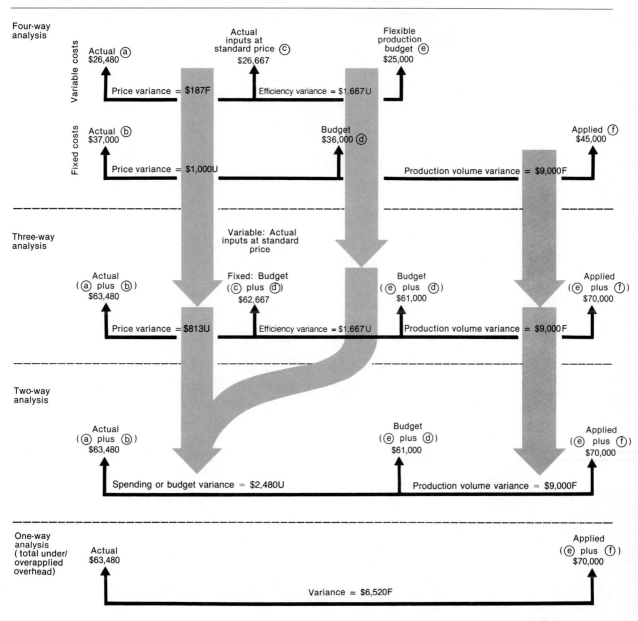

Consequently, the three variance computed in the three-way analysis are (1) the overhead price variance, (2) the variable overhead efficiency variance, and (3) the fixed overhead production volume variance. These are computed for Evergreen Company as follows:

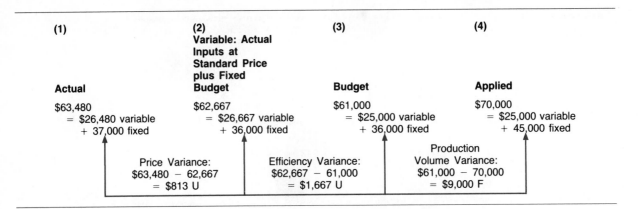

The new term in column (2) is made up of:

Variable:	$26,667	actual inputs at standard price (see illustration 19–14)
Fixed:	36,000	budgeted fixed overhead
Total	$62,667	

The budget (column 3) and applied (column 4) overhead for the three-way analysis are the same as for the two-way analysis.

In deciding whether to use two-way analysis or three-way analysis, managers should weigh the costs of computing and interpreting the variable overhead efficiency variance against the benefits of obtaining the data from that variance.

Illustration 19–15 summarizes the two-way, three-way, and four-way analyses of overhead variance. We start with the four-way analysis at the top and show how the numbers in the two-way and three-way analyses fit into the four-way analysis. Note that there could also be a "one-way analysis," which is the total under/overapplied overhead; that is, the $6,520 F difference between actual overhead ($63,480 in this example) and the amount applied to production ($70,000 in this example).

APPENDIX B
Alternative Division of Total Variance into Price and Efficiency Parts

In this chapter, we calculated each price variance based on actual quantity. That is:

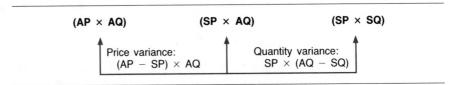

But suppose that the order was reversed so that the quantity variance was calculated first and based on actual prices:

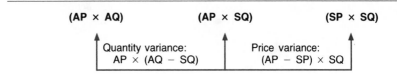

Note that the two end points are the same, but the middle point is different.

The effect on variance calculations can be seen from the following if the direct materials data from Evergreen Company are used:

> Standard costs: 10 board-feet @ $.25 per board-foot = $2.50 per crate
> Crates produced in May: 10,000
> Actual materials used: 110,000 board-feet @ $.264 per board-foot = $29,040

For this example, assume the quantity of board-feet purchased equals the quantity used.

The calculation in the chapter was as follows:

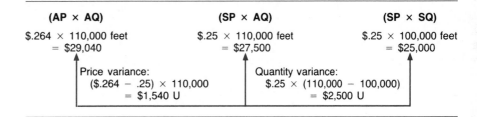

Illustration 19-16   **Graphic Analysis of Variance, Direct Materials, Evergreen Company**

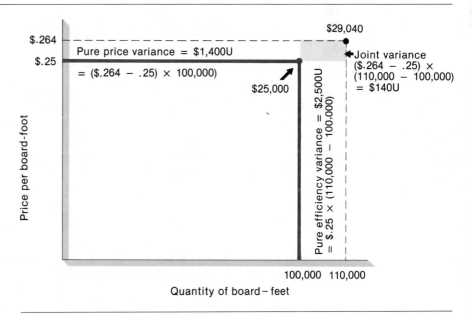

Note: The area inside the solid line represents the total standard costs allowed to make 10,000 crates. The area inside the dashed line represents the total actual costs incurred.

The alternative calculation is as follows:

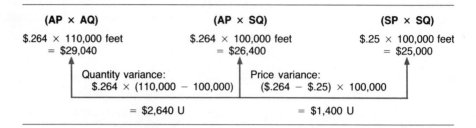

(AP × AQ)	**(AP × SQ)**	**(SP × SQ)**
$.264 × 110,000 feet = $29,040	$.264 × 100,000 feet = $26,400	$.25 × 100,000 feet = $25,000

Quantity variance:
$.264 × (110,000 − 100,000)
= $2,640 U

Price variance:
($.264 − $.25) × 100,000
= $1,400 U

Note that the *total* variance is the same in both cases—$4,040 U. However, the partition into price and efficiency variances is different. There are really three variances: a pure price variance ($1,400 in this case), a pure efficiency variance ($2,500), and a joint variance ($140 in this case). The joint variance is part of the price variance in the first calculation and part of the efficiency variance in the second. The graph in Illustration 19–16 shows these relationships.

QUESTIONS

19–1. Why should management want to divide manufacturing cost variances into price and efficiency variances?

19–2. What is the difference between a standard and a budget?

19–3. What is the difference between a flexible budget and inputs priced at standard?

19–4. The manager of the production division has just received a responsibility report that shows a substantial unfavorable variance for overtime premium. The manager objects to the inclusion of this variance because the overtime was due to the acceptance of a large rush order by the sales department. To whom should this variance be charged?

19–5. Many companies set wage rates through negotiations with unions. Under these circumstances, how would a labor price variance arise that would be the responsibility of a line manager?

19–6. One of the principles espoused by management is the idea that one should manage by exception. How can responsibility reporting systems and/or analysis of variances assist in that process?

19–7. What are the three primary sources of variances for variable costs?

19–8. Why are the variances for fixed costs different from the variances computed for variable costs?

19–9. Would the production volume variance represent a difference in the cash outflows for the company when compared to budgeted cash outflows?

19–10. Why might management decision making be enhanced if materials price variances are recognized at the time of purchase rather than at the time of use?

19–11. In a service environment where there are no inventories, would variance analysis be useful? Why or why not?

EXERCISES

19–12. Variable Cost Variances
(L.O.1)

The standard direct labor cost per reservation for the Omni Airline Reservation System is $1.30 ($13 per hour divided by 10 reservations per hour). Actual direct labor costs during the period totaled $89,000, 6,700 labor-hours were worked during the period, and 71,000 reservations were made.

Required:

Compute the direct labor price and efficiency variances for the period. (Refer to Illustration 19–5 for format.)

19–13. Variable Cost Variances
(L.O.1)

The standard direct labor cost per unit for a company was $16 ($8 per hour times two hours per unit). Actual direct labor costs during the period amounted to $33,780, 4,100 labor hours were worked during the period, and 1,900 units were produced.

Required:

Compute the direct labor price and efficiency variances for the period. (Refer to Illustration 19–5 for format.)

19–14. Variable Cost Variances
(L.O.1)

The data below reflect the current month's activity of Monterey Corporation:

Actual total direct labor	$43,400
Actual hours worked	14,000
Standard labor-hours allowed for actual output (flexible budget)	15,000
Direct labor price variance	$ 1,400 U
Actual variable overhead	22,100
Standard variable overhead rate per standard direct labor-hour	1.50

Required:

Compute the labor and variable overhead price and efficiency variances.

19–15. Variable Cost Variances
(L.O.1)

Information on Brooklyn Company's direct materials costs is as follows:

Actual quantities of direct materials used	20,000
Actual costs of direct materials used	$40,000
Standard price per unit of direct materials	2.10
Flexible budget for direct materials	41,000

Required:

What were Brooklyn Company's direct material price and efficiency variances?

19–16. Variable Cost Variances
(L.O.1)

Information on Fleishman Laboratories' direct materials costs is as follows:

Quantities of palladium purchased and used	1,200 ounces
Actual cost of palladium used	$223,000
Standard price per unit of palladium	160
Standard quantity of palladium allowed	1,100 ounces

Required:

What were Fleishman Laboratories' direct material price and efficiency variances?

19–17. Variable Cost Variances where Materials Purchased and Materials Used Are Not Equal
(L.O.1)

Baruch's Printers reported the following information concerning its direct materials:

Direct materials purchased (actual)	$406,852
Standard cost of materials purchased	407,391
Standard price times actual quantity of materials used	74,193
Actual production	28,000 units
Standard direct materials costs per unit produced	$2.68

Required:

Compute the direct materials cost variances. Prepare an analysis like the one in Illustration 19–11.

19–18. Fixed Cost Variances
(L.O.2)

Information on San Antonio Company's fixed overhead costs is as follows:

Overhead applied	$80,000
Actual overhead	86,000
Budgeted overhead	84,000

Required:

What are the fixed overhead price and production volume variances? (Refer to Illustration 19–12 for format.)

19–19. Fixed Cost Variances
(L.O.2)

Refer to the data in exercise 19–18. Prepare graphs like those shown in Illustration 19–13.

19–20. Fixed Cost Variances
(L.O.2)

Phoenix Rising, Inc., applies overhead at the rate of $4.35 per unit. Budgeted fixed overhead was $67,860, 16,000 units were produced this month, and actual overhead was $64,200.

Required:

What are the fixed overhead price and production volume variances for Phoenix Rising?

19–21. Comprehensive Cost Variance Analysis
(L.O.3)

Tough Tire, Inc., manufactures construction equipment and farm machinery tires. The following information is available for June, Year 1.

1. Tough Tire produced and sold 4,500 tires at a price of $1,000 each. Budgeted production was 5,000 tires.
2. Standard variable costs per tire were as follows:

Direct materials: 100 lbs. at $2.00	$200
Direct labor: 20 hours at $9.00	180
Variable manufacturing overhead:	
5 machine hrs. at $10.00 per hr.	50
Total variable costs	$430

3. Fixed manufacturing overhead costs:

Monthly budget	$1,900,000

4. Fixed overhead is applied at the rate of $380 per tire.

5. Actual production costs:

Direct materials purchased and used: 475,000 pounds at $1.80		$ 855,000
Direct labor: 88,000 hours at $9.10		800,800
Variable overhead: 21,600 machine hours at $10.20 per hr.		220,320
Fixed overhead		2,000,000

6. Machine hours: 21,600.

Required:

a. Prepare a comprehensive cost variance analysis for June for Tough Tire like the one in Illustration 19–10.

b. Prepare a fixed overhead cost variance analysis like the one in Illustration 19–12.

19–22. Comprehensive Cost Variance Analysis
(L.O.3)

Eagle Eye Optical is a fast growing chain of operations that specializes in optical care and contact lenses. The following data is available for last year's eye care exam services.

1. Eagle Eye performed 50,000 eye exams last year. Budgeted exams were 45,000 exams, averaging 50 minutes per exam.

2. Standard variable costs per exam were as follows:

Direct optometrist services: 50 minutes at $30.00 per hour	$25.00
Variable support staff and overhead: 1.1 labor-hours at $15.00 per hour	16.50

3. Fixed overhead costs:

Annual budget	$180,000

4. Fixed overhead is applied at the rate of $4 per exam.

5. Actual eye exam costs:

Direct optometrist services: 50,000 exams averaging 1 hour at $32.00	$1,600,000
Variable support staff and overhead: 1.2 labor-hours at $14.00 per hour × 50,000 exams	840,000
Fixed overhead	184,000

Required:

a. Prepare a cost variance analysis for last year like the one in Illustration 19–10.

b. Prepare a fixed overhead cost variance analysis like the one in Illustration 19–12.

19–23. Two-Way and Three-Way Overhead Variances (Appendix A)
(L.O.4)

Using the data in exercise 19–22, compute the following (assume full-absorption costing is used to apply overhead to units produced):

Required:

a. Total over/underapplied overhead, assuming full-absorption costing is used.

b. Two-way analysis of overhead variances.

c. Three-way analysis of overhead variances.

19–24. Overhead Variances
(L.O.1, L.O.2)

Hyperspace, Inc., shows the following overhead information for the current period:

Actual overhead incurred	$12,600, of which $3,500 is fixed and $9,100 is variable
Budgeted fixed overhead	3,300, $3,000 direct labor-hours budgeted
Standard variable overhead rate per direct labor-hour	3
Standard hours allowed for actual production	3,500 hours
Actual labor-hours used	3,200

Required:

What are the variable overhead price and efficiency variances and the fixed overhead price variance?

19–25. Two-Way and Three-Way Overhead Variances (Appendix A)
(L.O.4)

Using the data in exercise 19–24, compute the following (assume full-absorption costing is used to apply overhead to units produced).

Required:

a. Total over/underapplied overhead, assuming full-absorption costing is used.

b. Two-way analysis of overhead variances.

c. Three-way analysis of overhead variances.

19–26. Two-Way and Three-Way Overhead Variances (Appendix A)
(L.O.4)

UBC Inc. incurred total overhead costs of $178,360 during the month when 4,100 hours were worked. The normal workload for the company is 4,000 hours. The flexible budget for the output attained this period indicates that 4,300 hours were allowed.

Standard costs per hour are as follows:

Variable overhead	$13.60
Fixed overhead	27.70

Fixed overhead cost $2,170 more than budgeted.

Required:

a. Total over/underapplied overhead, assuming full absorption costing is used.

b. Two-way analysis of overhead variances.

c. Three-way analysis of overhead variances.

PROBLEMS:

19–27. Nonmanufacturing Cost Variances

Home Loan Company originates mortgage loans for residential housing. The company charges a service fee for processing loan applications. This fee is set twice a year based on the cost of processing a loan application. For the first half of this year, Home Loan estimated that it would process 75 loans. Correspondence, credit reports, supplies, and other materials that vary with each loan are estimated to cost $45 per loan. The company hires a loan processor at an estimated cost of $27,000 per year and an assistant at an estimated cost of $20,000 per year. The cost to lease office space and pay utilities and other related costs are estimated at $58,000 per year.

During the first six months of this year, Home Loan processed 79 loans. Use of cost of materials, credit reports, and other items related to loan processing was 8 percent greater than expected for the volume of loans processed. Actual cost of these items was $3,700.

The loan processor and her assistant cost $23,800 for the six months. Leasing and related office costs were $28,100.

Required:

Prepare an analysis of the variances, like the ones in Illustrations 19–10 and 19–12, for Home Loan Corp.

19–28. Nonmanufacturing Cost Variance Analysis

Black Forest Auto Repairs budgets $80,000 per year for fixed costs of its auto repair shop. Shop labor is estimated to cost $11 per hour, and the estimated annual workload is 18,000 labor-hours. Materials which are not charged to customers are estimated to cost an additional $2 per labor-hour. Each labor-hour is expected to result in one hour of time charged to customers.

During the past year, Black Forest spent $77,800 on fixed costs. Shop labor costs averaged $10.80 per hour for 18,700 labor-hours actually worked. A total of 18,300 hours time was charged to customers. The input price of materials was 5 percent greater than expected for the hours worked. Fixed overhead is applied based on hours charged to customers.

Required:

Prepare an analysis of variances, like the ones in Illustrations 19–10 and 19–12, for Black Forest including the production volume variance.

19–29. Direct Materials

Information about Pons Platinum Company's direct materials cost is as follows:

Standard price per materials ounce	$345
Actual quantity used	420 ounces
Standard quantity allowed for production	435 ounces
Price variance	$2,950 F

Required:

What was the actual purchase price per pound, rounded to the nearest cent?

19–30. Solve for Direct Labor-Hours

Santa Barbara Company reports the following direct labor information for Product CER for the month of October:

Standard rate	$7.00 per hour
Actual rate paid	7.20 per hour
Standard hours allowed for actual production	1,400 hours
Labor efficiency variance	$500 U

Required:

Based on these data, what were the actual hours worked and what was the labor price variance?

19–31. Overhead Variances

Space, Inc., shows the following overhead information for the current period:

Actual overhead incurred	$14,700, of which $9,800 is variable
Budgeted fixed overhead	4,320
Standard variable overhead rate per direct labor-hour	3
Standard hours allowed for actual production	3,500 hours
Actual labor-hours used	3,300

What are the variable overhead price and efficiency variances and fixed overhead price variance?

19–32. Manufacturing Variances

Hylab Company prepares its budgets on the basis of standard costs. A responsibility report is prepared monthly showing the differences between master budget and actual. Variances are analyzed and reported separately. Materials price variances are computed at the time of purchase.

The following information relates to the current period:

Standard costs (per unit of output):	
Direct materials, 1 kilogram @ $1 per kilogram	$ 1
Direct labor, 2 hours @ $4 per hour	8
Factory overhead:	
Variable (25% of direct labor cost)	2
Fixed (master budget 3,600 hours)	1 (based on direct labor-hours)
Total standard cost per unit	$12

Actual costs for the month:

Materials purchased	3,000 kilograms at $.90 per kilogram
Output	1,900 units using 2,100 kilograms of materials
Actual labor costs	3,200 hours at $5 per hour
Actual overhead:	
Variable	$4,500
Fixed	1,800

Required:

a. Prepare a comprehensive variable cost variance analysis like the one in Illustration 19–10.

19–33. Alternative Variance Calculations (Appendix B)

Refer to the labor and variable overhead data given in problem 19–32. Compute the labor and overhead variances using the method set forth in Appendix B.

19–34. Direct Labor and Variable Overhead Variance Relationships

A company applies variable overhead on the basis of 150 percent of its direct labor costs. This period, actual variable overhead was $11,420. There was a $900 favorable efficiency variable for variable overhead. There was a $725 unfavorable price variance for direct labor. During the period, 1,420 direct labor-hours were worked at a standard rate of $5 per hour.

Required:

Prepare a variable cost variance analysis for direct labor and variable overhead.

19–35. Overhead Cost and Variance Relationships

A company reported a $50 unfavorable price variance for variable overhead and a $500 unfavorable price variance for fixed overhead. The flexible budget had $32,100 variable overhead based on 10,700 direct labor-hours; only 10,600 hours were worked. Total actual overhead was $54,350. Estimated hours for computing the fixed overhead application rate were 11,000 hours.

Required:

a. Prepare a variable overhead analysis like the one in Illustration 19–6.

b. Prepare a fixed overhead analysis like the one in Illustration 19–12.

19–36. Comprehensive Variance Problem

Milner Manufacturing Company manufactures one product, with a standard cost detailed as follows:

Direct materials, 20 meters at $.90 per meter	$18
Direct labor, 4 hours at $6 per hour	24
Factory overhead applied at five sixths of direct labor (Variable costs = $15; Fixed costs = $5)	20
Variable selling and administrative	12
Fixed selling and administrative	7
Total unit costs	$81

Standards have been computed based on a master budget activity level of 2,400 direct labor-hours per month.

Actual activity for the past month was as follows:

Materials purchased	18,000 meters at $.92 per meter
Materials used	9,500 meters
Direct labor	2,100 hours at $6.10 per hour
Total factory overhead	$11,100
Production	500 units

Required:

Prepare comprehensive cost variance analyses like the ones in Illustrations 19–10 and 19–12. Indicate which variances cannot be computed.

(CPA adapted)

19–37. Find Actual and Budget Amounts from Variances

Columbus Company manufactures a new electronic game with the trademark "Beammo." The current standard costs per game are as follows:

Direct materials, 6 kilograms at $1 per kilogram	$ 6 per game
Direct labor, 1 hour at $4 per hour	4 per game
Overhead	3 per game
Total costs	$13 per game

The following data appeared in the Columbus Company records at the end of the past month:

Actual production	4,000 units
Actual sales	2,500
Purchases (26,000 kilograms)	$27,300
Materials price variance	1,300 U
Materials efficiency variance	1,000 U
Direct labor price variance	760 U
Direct labor efficiency variance	800 F
Underapplied overhead (total)	500 U

The materials price variance is computed at the time of purchase.

Required:

a. Prepare a schedule like Illustration 19–10 showing the flexible production budget, price and efficiency variances, and actual costs for direct materials and direct labor.

b. Assume that all manufacturing overhead is fixed, and the $500 underapplied is the only overhead variance that can be computed. What are the actual and applied overhead amounts?

(CPA adapted)

19–38. Variance Computations with Missing Data

The following information is provided to assist you in evaluating the performance of the manufacturing operations of the Madison Company:

Units produced (actual)	21,000
Master production budget:	
Direct materials	$165,000
Direct labor	140,000
Overhead	199,000
Standard costs per unit:	
Direct materials	$1.65 × 5 pounds per unit of output
Direct labor	$14 per hour × ½ hour per unit
Variable overhead	$11.90 per direct labor hour
Actual costs:	
Direct materials purchased and used	$188,700 (102,000 pounds)
Direct labor	140,000 (10,700 hours)
Overhead	204,000 (61% is variable)

Variable overhead is applied on the basis of direct labor-hours.

Required:

Prepare a table to show all variable manufacturing cost price and efficiency variances and fixed manufacturing cost price and production volume variances.

19–39. Comprehensive Variance Problem

Indianapolis Company manufactures two products. Florimene and Glyoxide, used in the plastics industry. The company prepares its master budget on the basis of standard costs. The following data are for the month of August.

	Florimene	Glyoxide
Standards:		
Direct materials	3 kilograms at $1 per kilogram	4 kilograms at $1.10 per kilogram
Direct labor	5 hours at $4 per hour	6 hours at $5 per hour
Variable overhead (per direct labor-hour)	$3.20	$3.50
Fixed overhead (per month)	$22,356	$26,520
Expected activity (direct labor-hours)	5,750	7,800
Actual data:		
Direct material	3,100 kilograms at $.90 per kilogram	4,700 kilograms at $1.15 per kilogram
Direct labor	4,900 hours at $4.05 per hour	7,400 hours at $5.10 per hour
Variable overhead	$16,170	$25,234
Fixed overhead	20,930	26,400
Units produced (actual)	1,000 units	1,200 units

Required:

a. Prepare a comprehensive cost variance analysis like the one in Illustration 19–10.

b. Prepare a fixed overhead variance analysis like the one in Illustration 19–12.

19–40. Two-Way, Three-Way, and Four-Way Overhead Variances (Appendix A)

Refer to the data in problem 19–39. Assume the fixed overhead costs are applied to units produced using the following standard rate per labor-hour:

$$\text{Florimene: } \$3.888 \text{ per hour} = \frac{\$22,356}{5,750 \text{ expected labor-hours}}$$

$$\text{Glyoxide: } \$3.40 \text{ per hour} = \frac{\$26,520}{7,800 \text{ expected labor-hours}}$$

Required:

Prepare two-way, three-way, and four-way analyses of overhead variances for each product.

19–41. Performance Evaluation in Service Industries

Rock City Insurance Company estimates that its overhead costs for policy administration should cost $72 for each new policy obtained and $2 per year for each $1,000 face amount of insurance outstanding. The company set a budget of selling 5,000 new policies during the coming period. In addition, the company estimated that the total face amount of insurance outstanding for the period would equal $10,800,000.

During the period, actual costs related to new policies amounted to $358,400. A total of 4,800 new policies were sold.

The cost of maintaining existing policies was $23,200. Had these costs been incurred at the same prices as were in effect when the budget was prepared, the costs would have been $22,900; however, some costs changed. Also, there was $12,100,000 in policies outstanding during the period.

Required:

Prepare a schedule to show the differences between master budget and actual costs for this operation.

19–42. Analyze Marketing Cost Variances

High Pressure Sales, Inc., uses telephone solicitation to sell products. The company has set standards that call for $450 of sales per hour of telephone time. Telephone solicitors receive a commission of 10 percent per dollar of sales. Other variable costs, including costs of sales in the operation, are budgeted at 45 percent of sales revenue. Fixed costs are budgeted at $411,500 per month. The number of sales-hours per month are determined based on the number of days in a month less an allowance for idle time, scheduling, and other inefficiencies. This month, the company expected 180 hours of telephone calling time for each of 40 callers.

During the month, $2,700,000 of revenues were earned. Actual calling hours amounted to 7,050. Marketing and administrative cost data for the period are provided below:

	Actual	Master Budget
Cost of sales	$810,000	$972,000
Telephone time charges	32,200	32,400
Delivery services	161,100	194,400
Uncollectible accounts	121,500	145,800
Other variable costs	112,700	113,400
Fixed costs	409,000	411,500

Required:

Using sales-dollars as a basis for analysis, compute the marketing cost variances for the period.

19–43. Efficiency Measures for Nonmanufacturing Costs

Refer to the data for High Pressure Sales, Inc., in problem 19–42. Measure the efficiency of marketing operations for the month. (Hint: Consider sales volume as an output measure and "calling hours" as an input.)

19–44. Comprehensive Review of Variances with Missing Data

Merriweather Company makes oil for whale oil lamps. One product, Interno, is manufactured as a blend of three chemicals: Alpha-28, Beta-32, and Gamma-07 (A, B, and G, for short). This solvent is very active and must be shipped in special containers, one container per unit of output. In addition to the materials, the blending process requires three direct labor-hours per liter of solvent. Factory overhead is applied at the rate of 150 percent of direct labor costs.

You have been working for Merriweather Company as a new management trainee in the controller's office. Today you had an opportunity to talk to the controller and advise him on the merits of your background and your education. The controller handed you some information on last month's production of industrial solvents and asked you to analyze the variances for the product Interno. Confident in your abilities, you carried the computer printout with you as you left the office. Unfortunately, on the way home a gust of wind blew some of your papers away. You were able to retrieve some of the information, but a good deal of it was torn or shredded.

At home, you have pieced together the following fragments from the computer printouts:

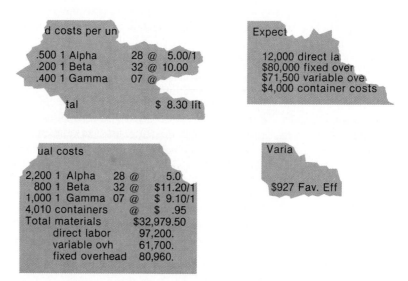

d costs per un

.500 1 Alpha   28 @   5.00/1
.200 1 Beta   32 @ 10.00
.400 1 Gamma   07 @

tal $ 8.30 lit

Expect

12,000 direct la
$80,000 fixed over
$71,500 variable ove
$4,000 container costs

ual costs

2,200 1 Alpha   28 @   5.0
  800 1 Beta   32 @ $11.20/1
1,000 1 Gamma 07 @ $ 9.10/1
4,010 containers   @ $ .95
Total materials $32,979.50
    direct labor   97,200.
    variable ovh   61,700.
    fixed overhead   80,960.

Varia

$927 Fav. Eff

You recall the $927 favorable efficiency variance applies to chemicals but not to containers. You also recall a discussion concerning the new direct labor rate of $9 per hour and how that rate had caused the production planning department to recommend a re-evaluation of the product line since certain products may not be profitable at this rate.

Required:

Defend your reputation with the controller and compute as many variances as possible. (Hint: Separating the chemical inputs from the containers will make the solution more manageable.) If any variances cannot be computed, state why.

INTEGRATIVE CASES

19–45. Process Costing Variances; Equivalent Units

Cherry Pink, Inc., produces a single product known as Apple Blossom White. Cherry Pink uses the FIFO process costing method.

To analyze production performance, actual results are compared to the flexible budget, and any variances are computed. The standard costs that form the basis for the budget are as follows:

Direct materials	1 kilogram at $10 per kilogram
Direct labor	2 hours at $4 per hour
Variable overhead	2 hours at $1.25 per hour

Data for the month are presented below:

1. Beginning inventory consisted of 2,500 units that were 100 percent complete with respect to direct materials and 40 percent complete with respect to conversion costs.
2. Ten thousand units were started during the month.
3. Ending inventory consisted of 2,000 units that were 100 percent complete with respect to direct materials and 40 percent complete with respect to conversion costs.
4. Costs applicable to the current period production are as follows:

	Actual Costs	Flexible Budget
Direct materials (11,000 kilograms)	$123,750	$100,000
Direct labor (25,000 hours)	105,575	82,400
Variable overhead	30,350	25,750

Required:

Compute variances. Materials are added at the beginning of the process; conversion costs are added evenly throughout.

19–46. Process Costing Variances

Alminex Mining Company uses a process costing system to account for the costs associated with ore benefication processes. Benefication is the process by which the valuable components are extracted or converted from raw ores. For one of these processes, standards call for a yield of 5 percent nickel from a given quantity of ore. For costing accounting purposes, equivalent units are expressed in terms of tons of nickel obtained from a particular quantity of ore.

Because yields vary from one batch of ore to another, it is necessary to monitor materials variances carefully. A FIFO costing system is required.

The following inventories were on hand at the start of the month:

	Raw Ore Quantities	Standard Cost
Unprocessed ore	2,100 raw ore tons	$23,100
Ore in process (i.e., work in process inventory): 100% complete for materials. (This ore had a nickel yield of 30T, which is exactly the 5% standard yield).	600 raw ore tons	6,600
		19,200

During the month, 14,000 tons of unprocessed ore were put into production. In this and subsequent months, the yield rate for this 14,000 tons of ore was 5.1 percent. During the month 680 tons of nickel were sent out of the processing plant. The ore on hand was 25 percent processed with respect to conversion costs at the end of the month, and 60 percent at the beginning of the month.

The unprocessed ore entered into production this month had an average actual cost of $11.20 per ton. During the month, there was a $10,814 favorable price variance for conversion costs. Actual conversion costs totaled $1,062,986.

Required: Determine the following:

a. Equivalent units of production for the month in terms of tons of nickel for
   materials and conversion costs.

b. A cost of production report showing the value of units transferred out and the
   value of ending inventory.

c. Price and efficiency variances for variable production costs.

19–47 Racketeer, Inc.[1]   "I just don't understand these financial statements at all!" exclaimed Mr. Elmo
(Comprehensive Overview of   Knapp. Mr. Knapp explained that he had turned over management of Racketeer,
Budgets and Variance)   Inc., a division of American Recreation Equipment, Inc., to his son, Otto, the
                                 previous month. Racketeer, Inc., manufactures tennis rackets.

Exhibit A (19–47)   **Profit Graph, Racketeer, Inc.**

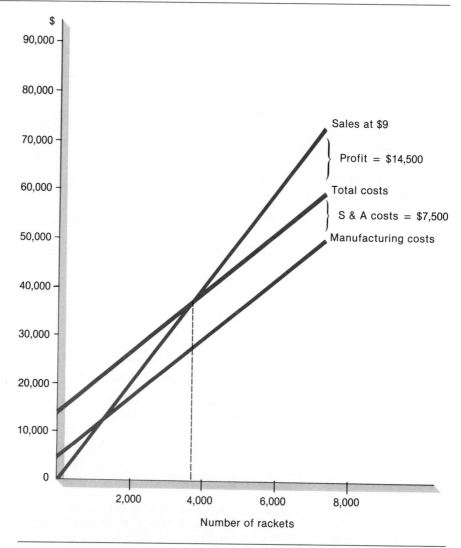

"I was really proud of Otto," he beamed. "He was showing us all the tricks he learned in business school, and if I say so myself, I think he was doing a rather good job for us. For example, he put together this budget for Racketeer, which makes it very easy to see how much profit we'll make at any sales volume (Exhibit A). As best as I can figure it, in March we expected to have a volume of 8,000 units and a profit of $14,500 on our rackets. But we did much better than that! We sold 10,000 rackets, so we should have made almost $21,000 on them."

"Another one of Otto's innovations is this standard cost system." said Mr. Knapp proudly. "He sat down with our production people and came up with a standard production cost per unit (see Exhibit B). He tells me this will tell us how well our production people are performing. Also, he claims it will cut down on our clerical work."

Mr. Knapp continued, "But one thing puzzles me. My calculations show that we should have earned profit of nearly $21,000 in March. However, our accountants

Exhibit B (19–47)   **Standard Costs,[a] Racketeer, Inc.**

	Per Racket
Raw material:	
Frame	$3.15
Stringing materials: 20 feet at 3¢ per foot	.60
Direct labor:	
Skilled: ⅛ hour at $9.60 per hour	1.20
Unskilled: ⅛ hour at $5.60 per hour	.70
Plant overhead:	
Indirect labor	.10
Power	.03
Supervision	.12[b]
Depreciation	.20[b]
Other	.15[b]
Total standard cost per frame	$6.25

[a] Standard costs are calculated for an estimated production volume of 8,000 units each month.
[b] Fixed costs.

Exhibit C (19–47)

RACKETEER, INC.
Income Statement for March
Actual

Sales:	
10,000 rackets at $9	$90,000
Standard cost of goods sold:	
10,000 rackets at $6.25	62,500
Gross profit after standard costs	27,500
Variances:	
Material variance	(490)
Labor variance	(392)
Overhead variance	(660)
Gross profit	25,958
Selling and administrative expense	7,200
Operating profit	$18,758

came up with less than $19,000 in the monthly income statement (Exhibit C). This bothers me a great deal. Now, I'm sure our accountants are doing their job properly. But still, it appears to me that they're about $2,200 short.''

"As you can probably guess," Mr. Knapp concluded, ''we are one big happy family around here. I just wish I knew what those accountants are up to . . . coming in with a low net income like that.''

Required:

Prepare a report for Mr. Elmo Knapp and Mr. Otto Knapp that reconciles the profit graph with the actual results for March (see Exhibit D). Show the source of each variance from the original plan (8,000 rackets) in as much detail as you can and evaluate Racketeer's performance in March. Recommend improvements in Racketeer's profit planning and control methods.

Exhibit D (19–47)   **Actual Production Data for March, Racketeer, Inc.**

Direct materials purchased and used:	
Stringing materials	175,000 feet at 2.5¢ per foot
Frames	7,100 at $3.15 per frame
Labor:	
Skilled: ($9.80 per hour)	900 hours
Unskilled ($5.80 per hour)	840 hours
Overhead:	
Indirect labor	$ 800
Power	250
Depreciation	1,600
Supervision	960
Other	1,250
Production	7,000 rackets

CHAPTER
20

STANDARD COSTING

LEARNING OBJECTIVES

1. Understanding how standard costs are incorporated into the accounting system.

2. Learning how to prorate variances at the end of an accounting period.

3. Seeing how standard costing systems work in an automated environment.

Virtually all companies use standards as a basis for evaluating performance. In some companies, standard costs replace actual costs in the accounting recordkeeping system. When this is done, products are costed at standard cost per unit of output instead of at actual cost. In this chapter, we discuss the characteristics of standard cost systems and demonstrate their flow of costs. The product costing emphasis of this chapter relates product costing concepts from Chapters 5 through 8 of this book to standard cost and variance concepts from Chapters 18 and 19.

ADVANTAGES OF STANDARD COSTING

Standard Costing A method of accounting whereby costs are assigned to cost objects at pre-determined amounts.

The use of standard costs instead of actual costs in the accounting records means that standard costs can be used for product costing as well as for performance evaluation. The use of standards instead of actual costs can greatly reduce the complexity of product costing for inventory valuation.

Under **standard costing**, the value of inventory is the number of units times the standard cost per unit. Cost flow assumptions such as FIFO and LIFO are unnecessary for all units that have the same standard costs. This reduces the clerical work needed to value inventories because records of the actual cost per unit are not kept. Every time a unit is produced, its standard cost is entered in the accounting records. At the end of the period, differences between the standard costs charged to production for all units and the actual costs of production are computed and analyzed.

For example, a sailboat manufacturer makes five models of small fiberglass sailboats. When the company used actual costs in the accounting system, recordkeeping was very detailed. According to the controller, "We kept track of the amount of direct materials and direct labor that went into each sailboat. Every worker had to keep track of the amount of time spent on *each sailboat*. We added a predetermined rate for variable and fixed overhead to give us the cost of each unit. We make about 50,000 sailboats each year, so you can imagine how much time was required by both operating people and accounting staff.

"We were already using standard manufacturing costs for budgeting and performance evaluation, so it was relatively easy to convert from an actual system to a standard system for product costing. Now we keep track of costs by department, by kind of input (direct material, direct labor, variable overhead, fixed overhead), and by product line. And we've saved a lot of time in keeping and checking records. We lost some data because we no longer know how much *each* sailboat costs. But we found that level of detail wasn't useful for management purposes and wasn't needed to value inventory."

The costs and benefits of using standard costing rather than actual costing varies from company to company. The benefits of standard costing increase with the amount of difficulty a company has in assigning costs to individual units of product. Thus, standard costing is often found in companies that use mass-production methods, particularly in conjunction with process costing. While standard costing may also be used in companies that make relatively large, heterogeneous units, it is relatively rare in that setting.

STANDARD COST FLOWS

When using standard costing, costs are transferred through the production process at their standard costs. This means the entry debiting Work in Process Inventory at standard cost could be made before actual costs are known. In process costing, units transferred between departments are valued at standard cost, while in job costing, standard costs are used to charge the job for its components. Actual costs are accumulated in accounts like Accounts Payable and Factory Payroll. Actual costs are compared with the *standard costs allowed for the output produced*. The difference between the actual costs assigned to a department and the standard cost of the work done is the variance for the department.

Use of standards in the accounting system can facilitate the recording and transfer of costs from one department to another. Standard costs can be transferred with the physical flow of product—there is no need to wait until the actual cost data about the particular units become known.

For example, automobile repair shops charge customers for services at a predetermined (standard) hourly rate. In addition, these shops often use standard times for each task included on a repair order. If a shop is using this standard cost system and you take your car in for a tune-up, you will be billed the standard hours for that task times the standard hourly rate. This happens regardless of the actual time it takes to perform the tune-up and the actual cost of the labor used.

A conceptual model of cost flows through T-accounts using a full-absorption standard costing system is shown in Illustration 20–1. This model will be helpful for future reference.

In the following sections, we discuss the flow of costs in a standard cost system, compare the actual and standard costs of work, and demonstrate how the variances are isolated in the accounting system. The variances are based on the calculations introduced in Chapter 19. Standard cost systems vary somewhat from company to company, so in reality, the method presented here may be modified a bit to meet a company's particular needs.

The example in this chapter continues the Evergreen Company example started in Chapter 18 and carried through Chapter 19. Illustration 20–2 summarizes the facts for Evergreen Company. The variances shown in the following entries were previously computed in Chapter 19 and are summarized in Illustration 20–2. (We use the example from Chapter 19 in which direct materials purchases do not equal usage.)

Direct Materials

Direct materials are purchased at their actual cost, but in a standard cost system they are often carried in direct materials inventory at the standard price per unit.[1] We assume that 250,000 feet are purchased and that 110,000 feet are used. The purchasing entry is:

---

[1] An alternative treatment is to carry materials at actual cost and then to charge materials into production at a standard price per unit.

Illustration 20-1   **Conceptual Model of Standard Cost Flows: Full-Absorption Costing**

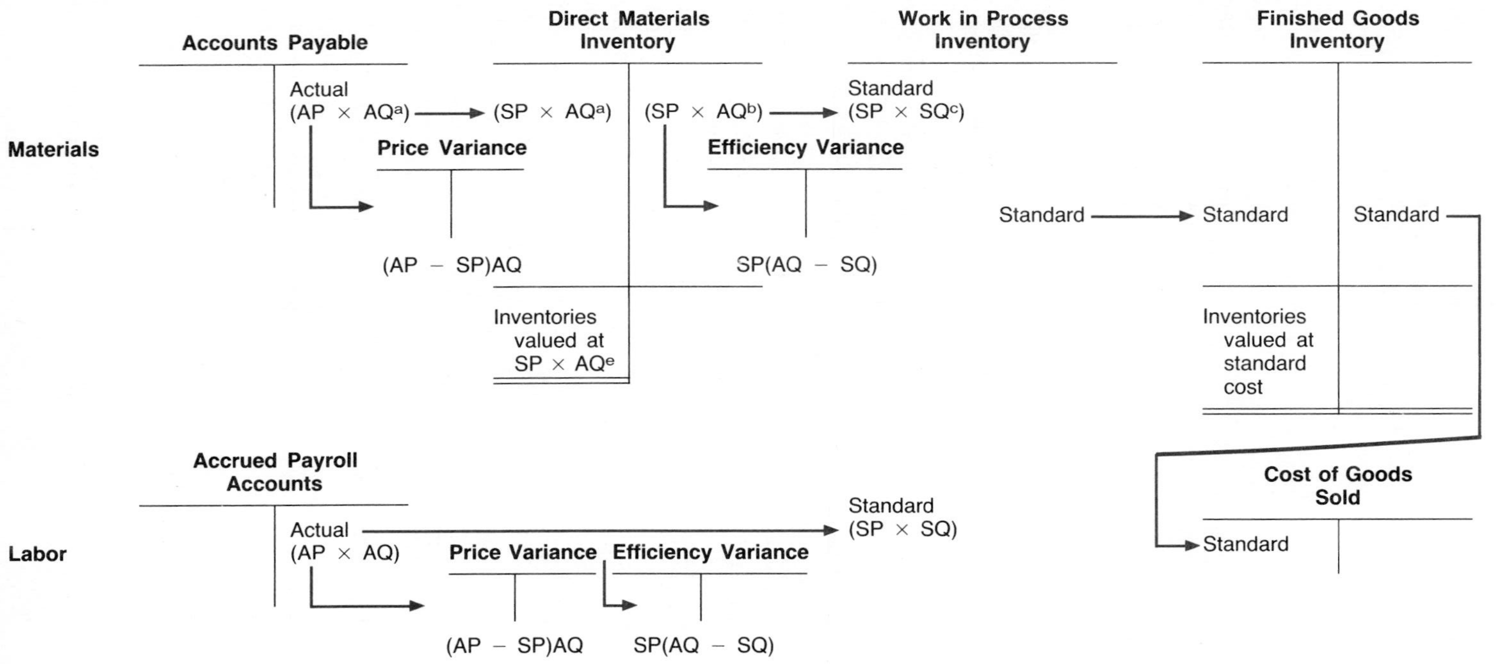

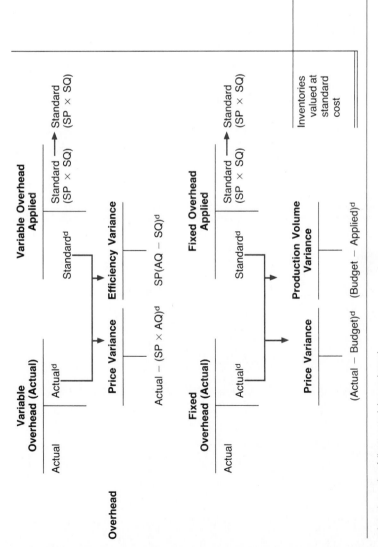

Overhead

Variable Overhead (Actual)

Actual   Actual[d]

Variable Overhead Applied

Standard[d]   Standard (SP × SQ)   →   Standard (SP × SQ)

Price Variance

Actual − (SP × AQ)[d]

Efficiency Variance

SP(AQ − SQ)[d]

Fixed Overhead (Actual)

Actual   Actual[d]

Fixed Overhead Applied

Standard[d]   Standard (SP × SQ)   →   Standard (SP × SQ)

Price Variance

(Actual − Budget)[d]

Production Volume Variance

(Budget − Applied)[d]

Inventories valued at standard cost

[a] Actual quantity of direct materials *purchased*.

[b] Actual quantity of direct materials *used*.

[c] Standard quantity of direct materials *used*.

[d] Closing entry.

[e] Actual quantity of direct materials in inventory.

AP = Actual input cost per input unit.

SP = Standard input unit price per input unit.

AQ = Actual input quantity.

SQ = Standard input quantity allowed for the actual good output produced.

Illustration 20-2 Cost Data, Evergreen Company (facts taken from example in Chapter 19)

Actual production output in May: 10,000 crates

Variable manufacturing cost data:

	Actuals	Variances		Standards
		Price	Efficiency	
Direct materials	250,000 board-feet purchased @ $.264 per board-foot = $66,000 110,000 board-feet used @ $.264 per board-foot = $29,040	250,000 feet × ($.264 − .25) = $3,500 U	(110,000 − 100,000 feet) × $.25 = $2,500 U	100,000 board-feet allowed @ $.25 per board-foot = $25,000
Direct labor	3,200 hours @ $9.35 = $29,920	3,200 hours × ($10.00 − 9.35) = $2,080 F	(3,200 − 3,000 hours) × $10.00 = $2,000 U	3,000 hours @ $10 per hour = $30,000
Variable manufacturing overhead (applied at $8.33⅓ per standard direct labor-hour	$26,480	$26,480 − ($8.33⅓ × 3,200 hours) = $187 F	3,200 − 3,000 hours × $8.33⅓ = $1,667 U	3,000 hours @ $8.33⅓ = $25,000

Fixed manufacturing cost data:

Actual	Price Variance	Budget	Production Volume Variance	Applied
$37,000	$37,000 − 36,000 = $1,000 U	$36,000	$36,000 − 45,000 = $9,000 F	$4.50 × 10,000 crates = $15.00 × 3,000 standard hours = $45,000

Direct Materials Inventory	62,500	
Materials Price Variance	3,500	
Accounts Payable		66,000

To record the purchase of 250,000 board-feet at the actual cost of 26.4 cents per foot, the transfer to Direct Materials Inventory at the standard cost per foot of 25 cents, and the materials purchase price variance for the difference.

We refer to the cost of direct materials inventory as a standard cost because 25 cents per foot is the standard allowed per unit of *input* (board-feet), *not* the standard cost per unit of *output* (crates).

When materials are placed in production, Work in Process Inventory is debited for the standard quantity of input used at the standard cost per unit. The cutting department is allowed a standard of 100,000 board-feet of lumber to make 10,000 crates at 25 cents per foot, but they actually used 110,000 board-feet. The entry charging production for the standard cost of direct materials is:

Work in Process Inventory	25,000	
Materials Efficiency Variance	2,500	
Direct Materials Inventory		27,500

To record the requisition of 110,000 actual board-feet at the standard cost per foot of 25 cents, the charge to Work in Process Inventory at $2.50 per crate times 10,000 crates (or 25 cents per foot times 100,000 board-feet allowed for 10,000 crates) and the materials efficiency variance for the difference.

The materials price variance is usually the responsibility of the purchasing department, whereas the efficiency variance is usually the responsibility of the production departments.

Direct Labor

Direct labor is credited to payroll liability accounts, such as Accrued Payroll or Payroll Payable, for the actual cost (including accruals for fringe benefits and payroll taxes) and charged to Work in Process Inventory at standard. The following entry is based on the facts about the standard costs allowed for Evergreen Company as described in Chapter 19 and in Illustration 20–2:

Work in Process Inventory	30,000	
Labor Efficiency Variance	2,000	
Labor Price Variance		2,080
Payroll Payable Accounts		29,920

To charge the production departments for the standard cost of direct labor at $10 per hour times 3,000 hours (10,000 crates times .30 hours allowed), to record the actual cost of $29,920, and to record the labor efficiency variance and the labor price variance.

This completes our presentation of standard cost journal entries for materials and labor. These journal entries are summarized in Illustration 20–3.

Variable Manufacturing Overhead

Standard overhead costs are charged to production based on standard direct labor-hours per unit of output produced at Evergreen Company. Overhead costs are often charged to production before the actual costs are known. This is demonstrated by the following sequence of entries:

1. Standard overhead costs are charged to production during the period. The credit entry is to an overhead applied account.

Illustration 20-3 **Standard Cost Flows—Materials and Labor (Evergreen Company)**

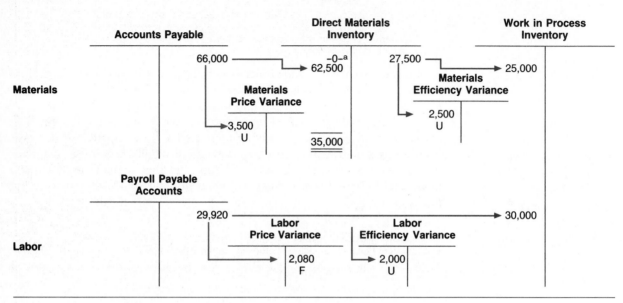

[a] Assume no beginning materials inventory balance.

2. Actual costs are recorded in various accounts and transferred to an overhead summary account. This accounting procedure is completed after the end of the period.

3. Variances are computed as the difference between the standard costs charged to production (overhead applied) and the actual costs.

This procedure is similar to that used to charge overhead to production using predetermined rates in normal costing.

Based on the data from Chapter 19 and Illustration 20–2, variable overhead is charged to production as follows:

Work in Process Inventory	25,000	
Variable Overhead Applied		25,000

Note that overhead is applied to Work in Process Inventory on the basis of standard labor-hours *allowed*. As we shall see shortly, over- or underapplied overhead will represent a combination of the variable overhead price and efficiency variances.

Actual variable overhead costs are recorded in various accounts and transferred to each department's variable manufacturing overhead account as follows:

Variable Overhead (Actual)	26,480	
Supplies inventory		
Accrued Payroll—Indirect Labor		
Accounts Payable—Power		26,480
Maintenance Department		
Etc. (other accounts and service departments)		

Variable overhead variances were computed in Chapter 19: price, $187 F, and efficiency, $1,667 U. These variable overhead variances are recorded by closing the applied and actual accounts as follows:

Variable Overhead Applied	25,000	
Variable Overhead Efficiency Variance	1,667	
Variable Overhead Price Variance		187
Variable Overhead (Actual)		26,480

These entries are shown in T-accounts in Illustration 20-4.

Fixed Manufacturing Overhead

For the purposes of this example, we assume Evergreen uses full-absorption costing because the amounts recorded will ultimately be used to prepare statements for external financial reporting. Fixed manufacturing costs are charged to units at $4.50 per crate ($15 per *standard* direct labor-hour) using full-absorption costing. The company produced 10,000 crates in May, for which 3,000 standard direct labor-hours are allowed at the rate of .3 hour per crate. Hence, the total fixed manufacturing overhead costs applied to production (that is, debited to Work in Process Inventory) amounted to $45,000 ($4.50 × 10,000 crates or $15 × 3,000 hours), as shown in the following entry.

Work in Process Inventory	45,000	
Fixed Overhead Applied		45,000

Actual fixed overhead costs are recorded in various accounts and transferred to each department's fixed overhead account as follows:

Fixed Overhead (Actual)	37,000	
Accumulated Depreciation—Building		
Accrued Payroll—Indirect Labor		
Accounts Payable—Heat		37,000
Plant Administration		
Etc. (other accounts and allocations from service departments)		

Recall that the price variance ($1,000 U) is the difference between actual ($37,000) and budgeted ($36,000) fixed manufacturing costs. The production volume variance ($9,000 F) is the difference between budgeted ($36,000) and applied ($45,000) fixed manufacturing costs. Fixed overhead variances are recorded by closing the applied overhead and actual overhead accounts as follows:

Fixed Overhead Applied	45,000	
Fixed Overhead Price Variance	1,000	
Fixed Overhead Production Volume Variance		9,000
Fixed Overhead (Actual)		37,000

These entries are summarized in Illustration 20–4.

Contrast with Variable Costing

Using variable costing, the entire *actual* fixed manufacturing overhead of $37,000 would be expensed in the period. Using full-absorption costing, fixed manufacturing overhead of $45,000 is applied to Work in Process Inventory, as shown in Illustration 20–4.

Illustration 20–4   **Standard Cost Flows—Overhead (Evergreen Company)**

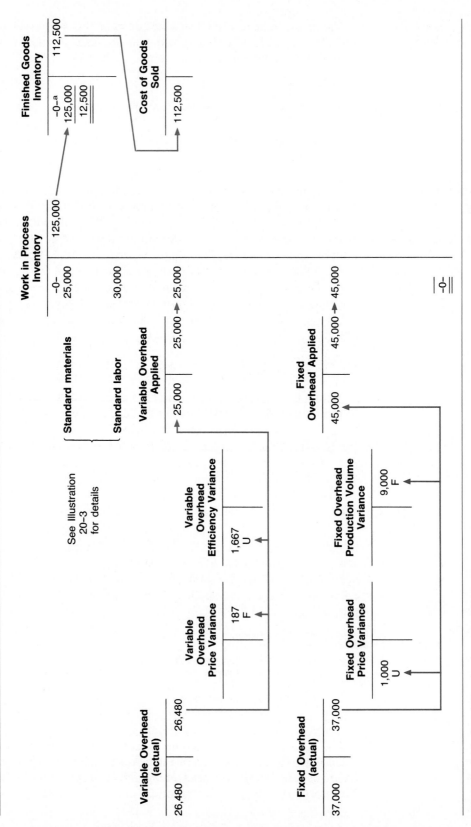

[a] Beginning finished goods inventory is assumed to be zero.

Transfer to Finished Goods Inventory and to Cost of Goods Sold

When all production work has been completed, units are transferred to Finished Goods Inventory and to Cost of Goods Sold at standard cost.

Finished Goods Inventory

This month 10,000 crates were finished and transferred to Finished Goods Inventory. After the crates have been finished and inspected, they are transferred to a finished goods storage area and recorded by the following entry (full-absorption, standard costing):

Finished Goods Inventory	125,000	
Work in Process Inventory		125,000

To record the transfer of 10,000 completed crates at $12.50 per unit ($8.00 variable plus $4.50 fixed) times 10,000 crates.

Cost of Goods Sold

For this example, assume the company sold 9,000 of the crates it produced for $21 per crate. This was recorded by the following entries:

Accounts Receivable	189,000	
Sales Revenue		189,000
Cost of Goods Sold	112,500	
Finished Goods Inventory		112,500

To record the sale of 9,000 crates at a price of $21 and a standard cost of $12.50 per crate.

PRORATING STANDARD COST VARIANCES

Prorating Variances Assigning portions of variances to the inventory and cost of goods sold accounts to which the variances are related.

Although inventory may be valued at standard cost for internal reporting purposes, sometimes the standard costs must be adjusted to actual costs for contract settlements, taxes, and financial reporting purposes. This will usually require **prorating the variances** to each account that has been debited or credited with the standard cost that is now being adjusted to actual. When proration is complete, the balances in the inventory accounts closely approximate actual costs, and the variance accounts have no balances.

To illustrate the proration of variances, we use the Evergreen Company example. The variances are prorated in the following sequence:

1. Materials price variance.
2. Materials efficiency variance.
3. Labor and overhead variances.

Materials Variance

Materials Price Variance

First, the materials price variance is prorated *to all accounts that contain standard materials costs purchased in the current period;* namely, Direct Materials Inventory, Materials Efficiency Variance, Work in Process Inventory, Finished Goods Inventory, and Cost of Goods Sold. Standard direct materials costs are 20 percent ($25,000 direct materials debit to Work in Process ÷ $125,000 total debit to Work in Process) of the total standard cost per crate. The amounts for direct materials at standard prices in each of these accounts are:

Ending Direct Materials Inventory (from Illustration 20–3)		Materials Efficiency Variance (from Illustration 20–3)		Ending Work in Process Inventory (see Illustration 20–4)		Ending Finished Goods Inventory (20% × $12,500 finished goods ending inventory is direct materials cost)		Cost of Goods Sold (20% of the $112,500 cost of goods sold is direct materials cost)		Total Materials Purchased This Period, at Standard Prices (see debit to Materials Inventory in Illustration 20–3)
$35,000	+	$2,500	+	$0	+	$2,500	+	$22,500	=	$62,500

These balances add up to the total materials costs purchased at standard prices. The materials price variance of $3,500 U is prorated to each account in proportion to the account balance's percentage of the total materials costs at standard prices. The proration of the $3,500 U appears in Illustration 20–5.

The journal entry to assign the prorated variance to accounts is as follows (amounts are from Illustration 20–5):

Direct Materials Inventory	1,960	
Materials Efficiency Variance	140	
Finished Goods Inventory	140	
Cost of Goods Sold	1,260	
Materials Price Variance		3,500

The variance account is closed when this journal entry is made.

Materials Efficiency Variance

Second, the materials efficiency variance to be prorated is now $2,640—that is, the original $2,500 (from Illustration 20–3) plus the $140 (from Illustration 20–5) that has been prorated from the Materials Price Variance account. The materials efficiency variance is prorated to the materials in ending Work in Process Inventory and Finished Goods Inventory and the materials in Cost of Goods Sold. These amounts are as follows, after adjusting for the proration of the materials price variance:

Illustration 20–5   **Prorating Materials Price Variance**

Account	(1) Materials at Standard Price in the Account	(2) Amount as a Percent of Total Materials Costs at Standard Price	Variance to Be Prorated (column 2 × $3,500)
Materials Inventory	$35,000	56%[a]	$1,960
Efficiency Variance	2,500	4	140
Work in Process Inventory	–0–	0	0
Finished Goods Inventory	2,500	4	140
Cost of Goods Sold	22,500	36	1,260
Total	$62,500	100%	$3,500

[a] 56.0% = $35,000 ÷ 62,500, etc.

Account	Materials in Account before Proration	Materials Price Variance Prorated in Illustration 20–5	Total
Work in Process Inventory	$ -0-	$ -0-	$ -0-
Finished Goods Inventory	2,500	140	2,640
Cost of Goods Sold	22,500	1,260	23,760

The materials efficiency variance is prorated, using the amounts computed above:

Account	(1) Materials Cost in the Account	(2) As a Percent of Total	Variance to Be Prorated (column 2 × $2,640)
Work in Process Inventory	$ -0-	0%	$ -0-
Finished Goods Inventory	2,640	10	264
Cost of Goods Sold	23,760	90	2,376
Total	$26,400	100%	$2,640

The journal entry to prorate the variance is:

Finished Goods Inventory	264	
Cost of Goods Sold	2,376	
Materials Efficiency Variance		2,640

Instead of using the materials costs in each account after prorating the price variance, we could obtain the same prorating of the materials efficiency variance if we used percentages [column (2) above] based on the original materials balances before prorating the materials price variance ($2,500 in Finished Goods Inventory and $22,500 in Cost of Goods Sold). This shortcut is often used in practice.

Labor and Overhead Variances

After prorating the materials price and efficiency variances, labor and overhead variances are prorated based on the standard cost of labor and overhead from the current period's production in ending Work in Process and Finished Goods Inventories and in Cost of Goods Sold.

To prorate these variances, first find the percent of labor and overhead in the current period's product cost by examining the debits to Work in Process Inventory this period. The calculation for Evergreen Company is as follows:

	(1) Debit to Work in Process Inventory for Each Cost (see Illustration 20–4)	(2) Total Debits to Work in Process Inventory This Period	(3) Percent of Cost in Total Product Cost (1) ÷ (2)
Labor	$30,000	$125,000	24%
Variable overhead	25,000	125,000	20
Fixed overhead	45,000	125,000	36

Next, find the amount of standard labor and overhead costs in Work In Process and Finished Goods Inventories, and in Cost of Goods Sold. Since there is no ending Work in Process Inventory, we need to deal only with Finished Goods and Cost of Goods Sold, as shown below:

	(1) Total Standard Cost in Account (see Illustration 20–4)	(2) Proportion (from calculation above)	(3) Particular Cost in Each Account (1) × (2)
Ending Finished Goods Inventory:			
Labor	$ 12,500	24%	$ 3,000
Variable overhead	12,500	20	2,500
Fixed overhead	12,500	36	4,500
Cost of Goods Sold:			
Labor	112,500	24	27,000
Variable overhead	112,500	20	22,500
Fixed overhead	112,500	36	40,500

Evergreen Company's labor and overhead variances for the period are:

Labor:		
Price	$2,080 F	
Efficiency	2,000 U	
Total		$ 80 F
Variable overhead:		
Price	187 F	
Efficiency	1,667 U	
Total		$1,480 U
Fixed overhead:		
Price	1,000 U	
Production volume	9,000 F	
Total		$8,000 F

Each of these variances is prorated to Finished Goods and Cost of Goods Sold based on the appropriate standard cost in each account. For example, 10 percent of the labor variance is allocated to Finished Goods Inventory because 10 percent of the standard labor cost for the period is in Finished Goods Inventory, as shown below:

	(1) Labor Cost in the Account	(2) As a Percent of Total	(3) Variance to Be Prorated (column 2 × $80 F)
Finished Goods Inventory	$ 3,000	10%	$ 8
Cost of Goods Sold	27,000	90	72
Total	$30,000	100%	$80

The journal entry to prorate the labor variance is:

Labor Price Variance:	2,080	
Labor Efficiency Variance		2,000
Finished Goods Inventory		8
Cost of Goods Sold		72

Overhead variances are allocated the same way:

	(1) Overhead Cost in the Account	(2) As a Percent of Total	(3) Variance to Be Prorated (column 2 × variance)
For variable overhead:			
Finished Goods Inventory	$ 2,500	10%	$ 148 (10% × $1,480)
Cost of Goods Sold	22,500	90	1,332
	$25,000	100%	$1,480
For fixed overhead:			
Finished Goods Inventory	$ 4,500	10%	$ 800 (10% × $8,000)
Cost of Goods Sold	40,500	90	7,200
	$45,000	100%	$8,000

Entries to close the variance accounts to Finished Goods Inventory and Cost of Goods Sold would be made like the labor variance entry.

The Finished Goods Inventory account and Cost of Goods Sold account now reflect an approximation of the actual cost of each inventory item. The variance accounts are closed.

Alternative Treatment for Variances

If the variances are relatively small, it may make little difference whether they are prorated or expensed as a period cost or as a write-off to Cost of Goods Sold. Under the alternative treatment, all variances are closed, and the net variance is debited or credited to Cost of Goods Sold or to a Summary of Variances Expense. For managerial purposes, we assume this is the method used, and variances are not prorated unless otherwise stated.

STANDARD COSTING IN A JUST-IN-TIME ENVIRONMENT

In just-in-time manufacturing settings with demand-pull of products through manufacturing, inventories are minimized. As a result, the accounting system is simplified because all costs are charged directly to Cost of Goods Sold. If there are inventories at the end of the period, then a portion of the current period costs originally charged to Cost of Goods Sold is credited to Cost of Goods Sold and debited to the respective inventory account as an end-of-period adjustment.

Standard costing is used in a demand-pull setting to keep track of differences between actual and expected costs. Costs are charged to Cost of Goods Sold at standard. Variances are charged to a separate account. If there are no inventories at the end of the period, the variance account is expensed or combined with cost of goods sold at standard. The latter result is cost of goods sold at actual.

If there are inventories at the end of the period and if the difference between the standard cost of inventories and actual cost is immaterial, the inventories may be stated at standard cost. In this situation, variances need not be prorated.

If, however, prorating variances would make a material difference in the financial statements or is required by contract, the variance is prorated *from* the Variance account *to* the respective inventory accounts based on the proportions of the current period costs in each of the Inventory and Cost of Goods Sold accounts, as described in the discussion on variance proration above. The results should be the same as if one had accounted for the variances in the traditional manner.

For example, if a company were using demand-pull accounting, assume the Cost of Goods Sold and related variance account would appear as follows before adjustment:

Cost of Goods Sold (Standard Costs)

Materials	60,000
Labor	30,000
Overhead	70,000

Standard Cost Variances

Materials price	3,500		
Materials efficiency	2,500		
		Labor and overhead	6,600

Debits to Cost of Goods Sold are Standard price (SP) × standard quantity of input per unit of output (SQ) times actual units produced. If inventories were minimal, the balance in the variance account would be expensed.

If the company has substantial ending inventories, the costs in Cost of Goods Sold are transferred to the inventory accounts in proportion to the current costs in each inventory account. Assume no beginning inventories. Assume that $42,000 of the $60,000 standard cost of materials is traced to the inventory accounts:

Materials Inventory	$35,000
Work in Process	5,000
Finished Goods	2,000
Total	$42,000

The total amount is credited to Standard Cost of Goods Sold with debits to each inventory account, as shown in Illustration 20–6.

A similar adjustment is made for labor and overhead. Assume that 20 percent of the labor and overhead amounts are still in Work in Process and 8 percent are in Finished Goods. The dollar amounts to be transferred from Cost of Goods Sold to the inventory accounts are as follows:

Illustration 20-6 **Allocation to Inventory in Demand-Pull Setting**

Materials Inventory	Work in Process	Finished Goods	Cost of Goods Sold (Standard Costs)
–0– 35,000	–0– Materials 5,000 Labor 6,000 Overhead 14,000 Balance 25,000	–0– Materials 2,000 Labor 2,400 Overhead 5,600 Balance 10,000	Materials 60,000 42,000 Labor 30,000 8,400 Overhead 70,000 19,600

	Labor	Overhead
Work in Process	$6,000	$14,000
Finished Goods	2,400	5,600
Total	$8,400	$19,600

The resulting inventory and Cost of Goods Sold accounts appear in Illustration 20-6 after adjustments.

COMPARISON OF PRODUCT (INVENTORY) VALUES UNDER ALTERNATIVE COSTING METHODS

We have now completed the discussion of six alternative methods of valuing products (and inventory) in this book. These six methods and the major chapters in which they were primarily discussed are as follows:

	Actual costing	Normal costing	Standard costing
Variable costing	Chapter 9	Chapter 9	Chapters 19 and 20
Full-absorption costing	Chapter 3	Chapter 7	Chapters 19 and 20

Illustration 20-7   **Product (Inventory) Values under Alternative Costing Methods**

	Actual Costing	Normal Costing	Standard Costing
Variable costing:			
Direct materials	Actual	Actual	Standard
Direct labor	Actual	Actual	Standard
Variable manufacturing overhead	Actual	Predetermined rate × actual inputs or output	Standard rate × standard inputs allowed for actual output
Fixed manufacturing overhead[a]	—	—	—
Full-absorption costing:			
Direct materials	Actual	Actual	Standard
Direct labor	Actual	Actual	Standard
Variable manufacturing overhead	Actual	Predetermined rate × actual inputs or output	Standard rate × standard inputs allowed for actual output
Fixed manufacturing overhead	Actual	Predetermined rate × actual inputs or output	Standard rate × standard inputs allowed for actual output

[a] Treated as a period cost in variable costing; not part of inventory.

Illustration 20-8 **Comparison of Product (Inventory) Values under Various Costing Systems, Evergreen Company (May)**

Facts:

1. Actual production costs:

Direct materials: 110,000 board-feet at $.264	$ 29,040
Direct labor: 3,200 hours at $9.35	29,920
Variable manufacturing overhead	26,480
Fixed manufacturing overhead	37,000
Total costs	$122,440

2. Predetermined overhead rates:

Variable overhead: $8.33⅓ per direct labor-hour

Fixed overhead rate per direct labor-hour

$$= \frac{\text{Estimated annual fixed manufacturing costs}}{\text{Estimated standard direct labor-hours worked based on estimated number of crates produced}}$$

$$= \frac{\$432,000}{28,800 \text{ hours}^a} = \$15.00 \text{ per direct labor-hour}$$

3. Standard variable manufacturing costs:

Direct materials: 10 board-feet per crate at $.25	$ 2.50 per crate
Direct labor: .3 hour per crate at $10	3.00
Variable manufacturing overhead: .3 hour at $8.33⅓	2.50
Total standard variable manufacturing costs	$ 8.00

4. Standard fixed manufacturing cost:

.3 hour per crate times $15 per hour = $4.50 per crate

Comparison of costing methods:

	Actual Costing (10,000 units)		Normal Costing (10,000 units)		Standard Costing (10,000 units)	
	Total[b]	Unit[c]	Total[b]	Unit[c]	Total[b]	Unit[c]
Variable costing:						
Direct materials	$ 29,040	$ 2.904	$ 29,040	$ 2.904	$ 25,000	$ 2.50
Direct labor	29,920	2.992	29,920	2.992	30,000	3.00
Variable manufacturing overhead	26,480	2.648	26,667[d]	2.667	25,000	2.50
Total	$ 85,440	$ 8.544	$ 85,627	$ 8.563	$ 80,000	$ 8.00
Full-absorption costing:						
Direct materials	$ 29,040	$ 2.904	$ 29,040	$ 2.904	$ 25,000	$ 2.50
Direct labor	29,920	2.992	29,920	2.992	30,000	3.00
Variable manufacturing overhead	26,480	2.648	26,667[d]	2.667	25,000	2.50
Fixed manufacturing overhead	37,000	3.700	48,000[e]	4.800	45,000	4.50
Total	$122,440	$12.244	$133,627	$13.363	$125,000	$12.50

[a] Assumes annual production of 96,000 crates:

96,000 crates × .3 standard direct labor-hours allowed per crate = 28,800 standard direct labor-hours

[b] Amount that would be charged to work in process in the month under each alternative costing method.

[c] Total divided by 10,000 crates produced in May.

[d] $8.33⅓ per direct labor-hour times 3,200 direct labor-hours actually worked.

[e] $15 × 3,200 direct labor-hours actually used.

The difference between variable and full-absorption costing is that full absorption includes a share of fixed manufacturing costs in the unit cost, while variable costing does not. The difference between actual and normal costing is in the treatment of overhead. **Normal costing** uses predetermined overhead rates times an actual base, while actual costing uses actual costs. Under standard costing, all manufacturing costs assigned to a unit are predetermined.

These differences are presented in Illustration 20–7. Illustration 20–8 presents a numerical comparison and contrast of these differences using data from the Evergreen Company illustration.

Normal Costing A system of accounting whereby direct materials and direct labor are charged to cost objects at actual, and manufacturing overhead is applied.

SUMMARY

This chapter describes cost flows using standard cost systems. In standard cost systems, the standard costs are part of the accounting system; they replace actual costs in recording transactions between work in process production departments and in recording transactions between Work in Process Inventory and Finished Goods Inventory.

A major advantage of a standard system is that it reduces recordkeeping. Records of actual cost per unit are not kept. Instead, unit costs are standard costs. Many companies that manufacture with processes (for example, chemicals and petroleum) use standard cost systems because there is little benefit and great cost to record actual cost of each unit produced.

An overview of the standard cost system model is presented in Illustration 20–1. The basic idea is that costs are accumulated at actual cost in Accounts Payable, Accrued Payroll, and similar accounts. Costs are debited to Work in Process Inventory at standard cost. Standard costs are used to reflect the transfer of units between work in process departments, and from Work in Process Inventory to Finished Goods Inventory, and from Finished Goods Inventory to Cost of Goods Sold.

Manufacturing cost variances for a period are sometimes prorated among inventories and Cost of Goods Sold. This has the effect of restating Cost of Goods Sold and ending inventories to actual cost.

A summary of the variance proration process is shown in Illustration 20–9.

We have presented the following six different methods of placing cost value on products in this text:

	Actual costing	Normal costing	Standard costing
Variable costing	X	X	X
Full-absorption costing	X	X	X

Illustration 20-9   **Summary of Variance Proration**

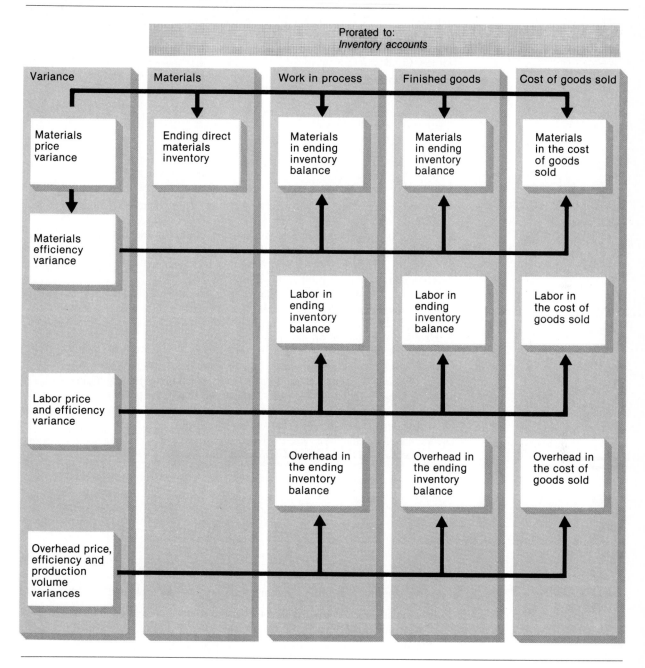

Prorated to:
Inventory accounts

Variance	Materials	Work in process	Finished goods	Cost of goods sold
Materials price variance	Ending direct materials inventory	Materials in ending inventory balance	Materials in ending inventory balance	Materials in the cost of goods sold
Materials efficiency variance				
		Labor in ending inventory balance	Labor in ending inventory balance	Labor in the cost of goods sold
Labor price and efficiency variance				
		Overhead in the ending inventory balance	Overhead in the ending inventory balance	Overhead in the cost of goods sold
Overhead price, efficiency and production volume variances				

TERMS AND CONCEPTS

The following terms and concepts should be familiar to you after reading this chapter:

Actual Costing
Normal Costing
Prorating Variances
Standard Costing

SUPPLEMENTARY READINGS

Atkinson, A. A. "Standard Setting in an Agency." *Management Science*, September 1978.

————. "Information Incentives in a Standard-Setting Model of Control." *Journal of Accounting Research*, Spring 1979, pp. 1–22.

Ball, D. M. "How Dutch Pantry Accounts for Standard Costs." *Management Accounting*, December 1982, pp. 32–35.

Barnes, J. L. "How to Tell if Standard Costs Are Really Standard." *Management Accounting*, June 1983, pp. 50–54.

Bennett, J. P. "Standard Cost Systems Lead to Efficiency and Profitability." *Healthcare Financial Management*, September 1985, pp. 46–54.

Calvasina, R. V., and E J. Calvasina. "Standard Costing Games that Managers Play." *Management Accounting*, March 1984, pp. 49–51, 77.

Foster, J., and A. Scott. "Standard Costing in a Manufacturing Environment." *Management Accounting*, April 1984, pp. 36–38 (Great Britain).

Galway, A. "Standard Costing and Control by Variance Analysis." *Management Accounting*, June 1985, pp. 58–61 (Great Britain).

Glendinning, R. "Standards Are the Nearest to Real Costs." *Management Accounting*, February 1986, pp. 44–45 (Great Britain).

Tait, G. "Truth about Standard Costing." *Management Accounting*, October 1985, pp. 36–38 (Great Britain).

SELF-STUDY PROBLEM

(This is a continuation of the Containers, Inc., self-study problem from Chapter 19.)

1. Containers, Inc., produced 50,000 and sold 40,000 plastic minicomputer cases at a sales price of $10 each. Budgeted sales were 45,000 units at $10.15.

2. Standard variable costs per unit (that is, per case):

Direct materials: 2 pounds at $1	$2.00
Direct labor: .10 hours at $15	1.50
Variable manufacturing overhead: .10 hours at $5	.50
	$4.00 per case

3. Fixed manufacturing overhead:

Monthly budget	$80,000
Estimated monthly production	40,000 cases or 4,000 hours
Fixed overhead application rate	?

4. Actual production costs:

Direct materials purchased: 200,000 pounds at $1.20	$240,000
Direct materials used: 110,000 pounds at $1.20	132,000
Direct labor: 6,000 hours at $14	84,000
Variable overhead	28,000
Fixed overhead	83,000

Required:

Use a full-absorption, standard costing system to—

a. Record the transactions using journal entries.

b. Trace the transactions through T-accounts.

c. Prorate the variances.

All inventory accounts have no beginning balances. Assume there is only one Work in Process Inventory account with no ending balance.

SOLUTION TO SELF-STUDY PROBLEM

a. (1)

Direct Materials Inventory	200,000	
Materials Price Variance	40,000	
Accounts Payable		240,000

To record the purchase of 200,000 pounds of materials at an actual cost of $1.20 per pound and to record the transfer to Direct Materials Inventory at the standard cost of $1 per pound.

(2)

Work in Process Inventory	100,000	
Materials Efficiency Variance	10,000	
Direct Materials Inventory		110,000

To record the requisition of 110,000 pounds of materials at the standard cost of $1 per pound and to charge Work in Process Inventory with the standard usage of 100,000 pounds of materials at the standard price.

(3)

Work In Process Inventory	75,000	
Labor Efficiency Variance	15,000	
Labor Price Variance		6,000
Accrued Payroll		84,000

To charge Work in Process Inventory for the standard cost of direct labor at $15 per hour times 5,000 standard hours allowed and to record the actual cost of $14 per hour times the 6,000 hours actually worked.

(4) Work in Process Inventory   25,000
         Variable Overhead Applied   25,000
     To apply overhead to production at $5 per standard di-
     rect labor-hour times the 5,000 hours allowed.

(5) Variable Overhead (Actual)   28,000
         Miscellaneous accounts (Cash, Accounts Payable,
             etc.)   28,000
     To record actual variable overhead.

(6) Variable Overhead Applied   25,000
     Variable Overhead Efficiency Variance   5,000
         Variable Overhead Price Variance   2,000
         Variable Overhead (Actual)   28,000
     To record variable overhead variances and to close the
     Variable Overhead Applied and Variable Overhead (Ac-
     tual) accounts.

(7) Work in Process Inventory   100,000
         Fixed Overhead Applied   100,000
     To record fixed overhead at a standard cost of $20 per
     direct labor-hour times 5,000 standard hours

     $\left(\dfrac{\$80{,}000}{4{,}000 \text{ hours}} = \$20 \text{ per hour}\right)$.

(8) Fixed Overhead (Actual)   83,000
         Miscellaneous accounts (Cash, Accounts Payable,
             etc.)   83,000
     To record actual fixed overhead.

(9) Fixed Overhead Applied   100,000
     Fixed Overhead Price Variance   3,000
         Fixed Overhead Production Volume Variance   20,000
         Fixed Overhead (Actual)   83,000
     To record fixed overhead variances and to close the
     Fixed Overhead accounts.

(10) Finished Goods Inventory   300,000
         Work in Process Inventory   300,000
     To record the transfer of 50,000 units of finished goods
     at the standard cost of $6 per unit.

(11) Cost of Good Sold   240,000
         Finished Goods Inventory   240,000
     To record the sale of 40,000 units at a standard cost of
     $6 per unit.

b. Cost flows through T-accounts:

Accounts Payable		Price Variance		Direct Materials Inventory		Efficiency Variance	
	240,000	40,000 U		200,000	110,000	10,000 U	

Accrued Payroll		Price Variance		Efficiency Variance		Work in Process Inventory	
	84,000		6,000 F	15,000 U		100,000	
							300,000

				Variable Overhead Applied			
				25,000	25,000	75,000	
						25,000	
						100,000	

Variable Overhead (Actual)		Price Variance		Efficiency Variance		Finished Goods	
28,000	28,000		2,000 F	5,000 U		300,000	240,000

Fixed Overhead (Actual)				Fixed Overhead Applied			
83,000	83,000			100,000	100,000		

		Price Variance		Production Volume Variance		Cost of Goods Sold	
		3,000 U			20,000 F	240,000	

c. **Prorate variances:**

Materials price variance:

Account	(1) Cost in Account	(2) Percent of Total Cost	Variance to Be Prorated (column 2 × $40,000)
Direct Materials inventory	$ 90,000	45	$18,000
Materials Efficiency Variance	10,000	5	2,000
Work in Process Inventory	–0–	—	—
Finished Goods Inventory	20,000	10	4,000
Cost of Goods Sold	80,000	40	16,000
	$200,000	100	$40,000

Materials efficiency variance:

Account	(1) Cost in Account	(2) Percent of Total Cost	Variance to Be Prorated (column 2 × $12,000[a])
Work in Process Inventory	-0-	—	-0-
Finished Goods Inventory	$ 24,000	20	$ 2,400
Cost of Goods Sold	96,000	80	9,600
	$120,000	100	$12,000

Labor and overhead variances:

Labor price variance	$ 6,000 F
Labor efficiency variance	15,000 U
Variable overhead price variance	2,000 F
Variable overhead efficiency variance	5,000 U
Fixed overhead price variance	3,000 U
Fixed overhead production volume variance	20,000 F
Net total	$ 5,000 F

Account	(1) Cost in Account	(2) Percent of Total Cost	Variance to Be Prorated (column 2 × $5,000)
Work in Process Inventory	-0-	-0-	-0-
Finished Goods Inventory	$ 15,000	20	$ 1,000
Cost of Goods Sold	60,000	80	4,000
	$ 75,000	100	$ 5,000

[a] $12,000 equals $10,000 variance before proration plus $2,000 materials price variance prorated to materials efficiency variance.

QUESTIONS

20–1. What are the advantages of a standard cost system?

20–2. How do you distinguish between a standard cost and an actual cost?

20–3. One manager was heard to remark, ''We don't believe in using artificial numbers in our accounting system. Standard costing systems just make the readers fool themselves. We use normal costing instead—that gives us the true costs.'' Is the manager right? Comment.

20–4. Standard costing eliminates the need to compute equivalent units since all costs are transferred out at a standard amount per completed unit. Do you agree? Why or why not?

20–5. What is the difference in the way labor and material costs are accounted for versus the way overhead costs are accounted for in a standard costing system?

20–6. How are variable overhead costs treated differently in a standard costing system from their treatment in a normal costing system?

20–7. How should variances be disposed of at the end of the year?

20–8. Why is it difficult to relate fixed costs to outputs from a production process?

20–9. ''Just like price and efficiency variances, the production volume variance indicates whether a company has spent more or less than called for in the budget.'' Comment on this quote.

20–10. How is the use of a standard cost system simplified in an automated environment?

EXERCISES²

**20–11. Standard Costing—
Journal Entries**
(L.O.1)

Elgin Company purchased 26,000 units of material A at a price of $1.25 per pound. The standard price of material A is $1.40 per pound. During the month, 14,000 units of material A were used, which was 2,500 pounds more than the standard allowed.

Required:

Prepare journal entries to record these transactions.

**20–12. Standard Costing—
T-Accounts**
(L.O.1)

Refer to the data in exercise 20–11.

Required:

Prepare T-accounts to show the flow of costs for these transactions.

**20–13. Standard Costing—
Service Organization**
(L.O.1)

Drawem & Bildem, P.A., is an architectural firm which uses standard cost analysis to help control the costs of its professional staff. On a recent project, Drawem & Bildem prepared the following estimates for Mega Towers using standard costs:

	Totals
Drafting: 450 hours @ $37.50	$16,875
Architectural: 120 hours @ $45.00	5,400
Engineering: 60 hours @ $130	7,800
	$30,075

When the job was complete, actual total costs were significantly greater than expected. The hours and total costs for each type of staff costs were as follows:

	Totals
Drafting: 420 hours	$15,200
Architectural: 200 hours	9,400
Engineering: 95 hours	13,300
	$37,900

Required:

Prepare journal entries for each cost category; namely, drawing, architectural, and engineering. Debit Work in Process for the standard costs, and credit Payroll Payable for actual costs.

20–14. Standard Labor Costs
(L.O.1)

Manor Lands, Inc., has a standard labor cost of $55 per unit of output. During the past month, 3,000 output units were manufactured. The total labor-hours allowed for this output were 22,000 hours. The actual labor costs were $161,280. Actual labor-hours were 22,600.

Required:

Prepare journal entries to record these transactions.

---

² Do *not* use the demand-pull method described in the section titled "Standard Costing in a Just-in-Time Environment" unless explicitly required.

20–15. T-Accounts for Standard Labor Costs
(L.O.1)

Refer to the data in exercise 20–14.

Required:

Prepare T-accounts to show the flow of costs through accounts.

20–16. Standard Overhead Costs
(L.O.1)

Standard Company developed standard overhead costs based on a monthly capacity of 90,000 machine-hours as follows:

Standard costs per unit:	
Variable portion: 1 hour at $6	$ 6
Fixed portion: 1 hour at $10	10
	$16

During April, 85,000 units were scheduled for production; however, only 80,000 units were actually produced. The following data relate to April:

1. Actual machine-hours totaled 82,500.
2. Actual overhead incurred totaled $1,378,000—$518,000 variable and $860,000 fixed.
3. There was no work in process inventory and no beginning finished goods inventory. All inventories are carried at standard cost.

Required:

Prepare journal entries to record these transactions and set up overhead variances.

20–17. T-Accounts for Standard Overhead Costs
(L.O.1)

Refer to the data in exercise 20–16. Show the flow of costs through T-accounts.

20–18. Prorate Variances
(L.O.2)

Refer to the variance calculations for exercise 20–16. Assume seventy-five percent of the units produced were sold. Prorate the variances to ending Finished Goods Inventory (25%) and Cost of Goods Sold (75%).

20–19. Standard Overhead Costs
(L.O.1)

Philadelphia Company uses a standard cost accounting system. The following overhead costs and production data are available for August:

Standard fixed overhead rate per direct labor-hour	$ 1.00
Standard variable overhead rate per direct labor-hour	4.00
Budgeted monthly direct labor-hours	40,000
Actual direct labor-hours worked	39,500
Standard direct labor-hours allowed for actual production	39,000
Overall overhead variance—favorable	$ 2,000
Actual variable overhead	159,500

Required:

Compute overhead variances, then prepare journal entries for these transactions.

(CPA adapted)

20–20. Standard Overhead Costs—T-Accounts
(L.O.1)

Use the data in exercise 20–19 to show the flow of these overhead costs in T-accounts.

20–21. Standard Overhead Costs
(L.O.1)

The following information appeared in the accounts of the Rapid Cities Corporation.

Actual manufacturing overhead:		$485,000
Fixed portion	$210,000	
Variable portion	275,000	
Overhead applied at standard:		465,836
Fixed portion	$215,900	
Variable portion	249,936	

Fixed overhead was applied at the rate of $4.25 per direct labor-hour, and 48,000 hours were budgeted for the period. The company uses a standard costing system. The 100,000 units produced during the period required 47,500 actual direct labor-hours.

Required:

Prepare journal entries for these transactions, including overhead variances. Units sold were 80,000. There were no beginning or ending work in process inventories, and no beginning finished goods inventory.

20–22. T-Accounts for Standard Overhead Costs
(L.O.1)

Use the data in exercise 20–21 to show the flow of costs through T-accounts.

20–23. Prorate Variances
(L.O.2)

Use the variance calculations in exercise 20–21. Prorate the variations to ending Finished Goods Inventory (20%) and Cost of Goods Sold (80%).

20–24. Standard Materials Costs
(L.O.1)

Armadillo Corporation acquired 50,000 units of direct materials for $70,000 last year. The standard price paid for the materials was $1.30 per unit. During last year, 40,000 units of materials were used in the production process. Materials are entered into production at the beginning of the process. The standard allowed was 42,000 units for the amount of output that was actually produced. Eighty percent of the units that used these materials were completed and transferred to Finished Goods Inventory. Seventy percent of these units that had been transferred to Finished Goods Inventory were sold this period. There were no beginning inventories.

Required:

Prepare journal entries and show the flow of costs through T-accounts.

20–25. Prorate Materials Variances
(L.O.2)

Refer to the variances calculated for exercise 20–24. Prorate the materials price variance to the materials efficiency variance, ending inventories and Cost of Goods Sold; and prorate the efficiency variance to ending inventories and the Cost of Goods Sold.

20–26. Standard Costing in a Demand-Pull Environment.
(L.O.3)

During the current period, Otter Co. paid $35,000 for 30,000 units of material. All of these materials were immediately put into process. During the period, 14,800 units of output were produced, and 14,500 units were sold. Three hundred units remain in Finished Goods Inventory. Each unit of output requires two units of material which has a standard cost of $1.25 per unit of material. Standard variable overhead is $69,600 for 15,000 units of production. The variable overhead efficiency variance was $1,800 U, and actual variable overhead was $68,412.

Fixed overhead, which includes all labor costs, is budgeted at $148,000. Actual fixed overhead for the period was $143,200. Fixed overhead is applied to production at $10 per unit of output. All variances are expensed.

Required:

a. Show the flow of these costs if the company initially charges all manufacturing costs to Cost of Goods Sold at standard.

b. Show the adjustment that would be made to reflect the ending inventory balances.

20–27. Standard Costing in a Demand-Pull Environment

(L.O.3)

Refer to the data for the Armadillo Corporation, exercise 20–24, above. If Armadillo Corp. were operating in a demand-pull environment and charging its standard costs directly to Standard Cost of Goods Sold, show the flow of costs through T-accounts that would be required to adjust the Standard Cost of Goods Sold account to reflect end-of-period inventories. Variances are expensed.

PROBLEMS

20–28. Standard Costs and Prorating Variances—Multiple-Choice

A Company used a traditional standard cost system in accounting for the cost of production of its only product, product A. The standards for the production of one unit of product A are as follows:

Direct materials: 10 feet of item 1 at $.75 per foot and 3 feet of item 2 at $1.00 per foot.
Direct labor: 4 hours at $15.00 per hour.
Manufacturing overhead: Applied at 150 percent of standard direct labor costs.

There were no inventories on hand on July 1. Following is a summary of costs and related data for the production of product A during the month ended July 31:

100,000 feet of items 1 were purchased at $.78 per foot.
30,000 feet of item 2 were purchased at $.90 per foot.
8,000 units of product A were produced, which required 78,000 feet of item 1, 26,000 feet of item 2, and 31,000 hours of direct labor at $16.00 per hour.
6,000 units of product A were sold.

On July 31, there are 22,000 feet of item 1; 4,000 feet of item 2; and 2,000 completed units of product A on hand. All direct materials purchases and transfers are debited at standard.

Required:

Choose the best answers (or indicate "none of the above"):

a. For the month ended July 31, the total debits to the Direct Materials Inventory account for the purchase of item 1 would be:
   (1) $75,000.
   (2) $78,000.
   (3) $58,500.
   (4) $60,000.

b. For the month ended July 31, the total debits to the Work in Process account for direct labor would be:
   (1) $496,000.
   (2) $465,000.
   (3) $480,000.
   (4) $512,000.

c. Before prorating variances, the balance in the Material Efficiency Variance account for item 2 was:

(1) $1,000 credit.
(2) $2,600 debit.
(3) $600 debit.
(4) $2,000 debit.

d. If all variances were prorated to Inventories and Cost of Goods Sold, the amount of material efficiency variance for item 2 to be prorated to Raw Materials Inventory would be:
(1) $0.
(2) $333 credit.
(3) $333 debit.
(4) $500 debit.

e. If all variances were prorated to Inventories and Cost of Goods Sold, the amount of material price variance for item 1 to be prorated to Raw Materials Inventory would be:
(1) $0.
(2) $647 debit.
(3) $600 debit.
(4) $660 debit.   (CPA adapted)

20–29. Standard Costs: Journal Entries and T-accounts

Armando Corporation manufactures a product with the following standard costs:

Direct materials: 20 yards at $1.35 per yard	$27
Direct labor: 4 hours at $9 per hour	36
Factory overhead—applied at five sixths of direct labor.	
Ratio of variable costs to fixed costs: 2 to 1	30
Total standard cost per unit of output	$93

Standards are based on normal monthly production involving 2,400 direct labor-hours (600 units of output).

Following are actual costs for the month of July:

Direct materials purchased: 18,000 yards at $1.38 per yard	$24,840
Direct materials used: 9,500 yards	
Direct labor: 2,100 hours at $9.15 per hour	19,215
Actual factory overhead	16,650

Five hundred units of the product were actually produced in July and transferred to Finished Goods Inventory.

Required:

a. Prepare journal entries to record the above transactions for a traditional standard cost system.

b. Show the flow of these costs using T-accounts.   (CPA adapted)

20–30. Compute Variances and Use T-Accounts to Show Standard Cost Flows

Juneau Company manufactures a line of clothing. At the beginning of the period, there were 1,000 units in stock at a variable cost of $400 per unit. The full-aborption cost of these units is $450 each.

Plans for the period call for the following standards and activity:

Units produced and sold	2,000
Standard cost per unit:	
Direct materials	$175
Direct labor	200
Overhead	100 (60% variable)
Total	$475

During the period, 2,200 units were produced and 1,800 were sold. The following costs were incurred:

Direct materials	$360,000
Direct labor	412,000
Overhead:	
Variable	135,000
Fixed	81,000

Direct materials price variances are recorded at the time of purchase. No materials were purchased this period. Actual direct labor costs were 5 percent less per hour of labor than the standard allowed. Overhead costs are applied to production as a percent of standard direct labor costs. A standard costing system is used.

Required:

a. Compute variable manufacturing cost price and efficiency variances. Compute fixed manufacturing cost, price, and production volume variances.

b. Use T-accounts to show the flow of costs through the system, assuming a traditional FIFO system.

20–31. Prorate Variances

Refer to the data for Juneau Company in problem 20–30.

Required:

Prorate variances for the Juneau Company. Show the proration with journal entries and T-accounts.

20–32. Comprehensive Standard Cost Problem

The following information is provided to assist you in evaluating the performance of the manufacturing operations at the Ashwood Company:

Units of output produced	21,000
Standard costs per unit:	
Direct materials: $1.65 × 5 pounds per unit of output	
Direct labor: $14.00 per labor-hour × .5 hour per unit	
Variable overhead: $11.90 per labor-hour × .5 hour per unit	
Actual costs:	
Direct materials purchased and used	$188,700 (102,000 pounds)
Direct labor	140,000 (10,700 hours)
Overhead	204,000 (61% is variable)

Variable overhead is applied on the basis of the direct labor-hours allowed. There were $440 F price and $4,000 F production volume variances for fixed overhead.

Required:

a. Prepare journal entries to show the transactions, using traditional standard, full-absorption costing in as much detail as possible.

b. Use T-accounts to show the flow of costs.

20–33. Comprehensive Prorating of Variances

Refer to the data for the Ashwood Company (problem 20–32).

Required:

Use T-accounts to show how the variances would be prorated at the end of the period. Assume 100 percent of the production had been transferred to Finished Goods Inventory, and 90 percent of the completed production had been sold.

20–34. Standard Costing in a Demand-Pull Environment.

Refer to the data for the Ashwood Company (problems 20–32 and 20–33, above). For this problem, assume that Ashwood charges all standard costs directly to Cost of Goods Sold and maintains a separate account for variances. At the end of the period, adjustments are made to reflect inventories and to prorate variances.

Required:

Use T-accounts to show the cost flows under this scenario.

20–35. Standard Costing in a Demand-Pull Environment

Ell-A Fear manufactures sport shoes. The company produces goods as orders are received. Hence, inventories are maintained at very low levels. An order was received for 5,000 pairs of the Shootout Running model. Standard costs for these shoes are:

Direct materials	$4.20
Direct labor (.25 hours)	1.35
Overhead (.5 machine hours)	6.46

Direct materials costs are based on expected usage of precut materials which are available in a complete package for each pair of shoes. That is, for each package of materials, expected good output is one pair of shoes.

While producing this order, Ell-A Fear had to purchase materials for $4.27. The extra cost was incurred to obtain the raw materials sooner than was expected. Due to an equipment malfunction, 50 packages of materials were destroyed. These 50 packages were replaced at a cost of $4.27 per package.

Direct labor costs were $7,200, and the rate was $5.20 per direct labor-hour. Actual overhead costs exceeded the planned rate by 8 cents per machine-hour. A total of 2,750 machine-hours was required. The extra machine-hours were primarily caused by the equipment malfunction.

Ell-A Fear charges all costs directly to Cost of Goods Sold at standard. Variances are identified and charged to a separate account: Manufacturing Variances Expensed.

Not all of the Shootout Running model shoes ordered had been shipped at the end of the period. Fifty pairs were still on hand in the shipping area at the end of the period.

Required:

Use T-accounts to show the cost flows for these events.

20–36. Prorate Variances

SmurfKind-Merc Pharmaceuticals purchased 80,000 grams of deuterial oxide at a cost of $124,000 and 40,000 grams of milaidium chloride at a cost of $89,600. Standard costs for this quantity of deuterial oxide is $120,000, and the milaidium chloride was expected to cost $92,000. These chemicals are the ingredients in its accounting knowledge booster pill: Mind-Warp. During the period, 280,000 Mind-Warp pills were manufactured, of which 30,000 remain in finished goods.

Production of 280,000 Mind-Warps is expected to require 70,000 grams of deuterial oxide and 30,000 grams of milaidium chloride. Actual use was 71,000 grams of deuterial oxide and 29,500 grams of milaidium chloride.

SmurfKind-Merc includes labor costs with its variable overhead for cost analysis purposes. The standard variable overhead cost for each Mind-Warp pill is 75 cents. During the period, actual variable overhead was $217,300. Variable overhead is applied to production based on machine-hours. The machine-hour standard for 280,000 pills is 3,500 hours. Actual machine-hour use during the month was 3,360 hours.

Fixed costs are charged to period expense as incurred. There is no Work in Process Inventory.

Required:

a. Show the standard costs for each inventory account and Cost of Goods Sold in T-accounts.

b. Prorate the variances to the appropriate accounts.

20–37. Prorate Variances

Thai Imports acquires clothing from Bangkok and completes the clothing in a *maquilladora* plant in Juarez. The company uses a traditional standard costing system so it can evaluate variances. During the fall season, Thai Imports received materials for 50,000 men's shirts at its Juarez plant. Forty-eight thousand unfinished shirts were started in production. Work was completed on 41,500 shirts, and 39,800 were sold. The shirts still in process were 50 percent complete at the end of the period. Certain information about standards and actual results are as follows:

	Standard (per shirt)	Actual (per shirt)
Unfinished shirts	$6.00	$6.10
Finishing materials	.75	.80
Total finishing overhead	.60	.73
Labor costs	.30	.34

The company expected to complete 50,000 shirts during the period and purchased sufficient finishing materials for the expected output. Labor is paid on a piecework basis. Overhead and labor costs are incurred equally throughout the finishing process so that the 6,500 shirts still in process at the end of the period are equivalent to 3,250 completed shirts for the purposes of evaluating standard costs for finishing materials, labor, and overhead. Overhead is applied based on the 44,750 (= 41,500 + 3,250) equivalent number of shirts produced.

Budgeted fixed overhead is equal to 30 percent of the total finishing overhead. Actual fixed overhead for the period, which is included in the 73 cent cost, above, was $4,400.

There were no beginning inventories.

Required:

Prepare the journal entries to prorate the variances for the period. A single entry may be used for all overhead variances.

20–38. Prorate Labor Variances

Nanron Company has a traditional process standard cost system for all its products. All inventories are carried at standard during the year. The inventories and cost of goods sold are adjusted for all variances considered material in amount for financial statement purposes. All products are considered to flow through the manufacturing process to finished goods and ultimate sale in a FIFO pattern.

The standard cost of one of Nanron's products manufactured in the Dixon Plant, unchanged from the prior year, is shown below.

Direct materials	$2
Direct labor (.5 direct labor-hour at $8)	4
Manufacturing overhead	3
Total standard cost	$9

There is no work in process inventory of this product due to the nature of the product and the manufacturing process.

The schedule below reports the manufacturing and sales activity measured at standard cost for the current fiscal year.

	Units	Dollars
Product manufactured	95,000	$855,000
Beginning finished goods inventory	15,000	135,000
Goods available for sale	110,000	990,000
Ending finished goods inventory	19,000	171,000
Cost of goods sold	91,000	$819,000

Manufacturing performance relative to standard costs both this year and last year was not good. The balance of the finished goods inventory, $140,800, reported on the balance sheet at the beginning of the year included a $5,800 proration adjustment for unfavorable variances from standard cost. The unfavorable standard cost variances for labor for the current fiscal year consisted of a wage rate variance of $32,000 and a labor efficiency variance of $20,000 (2,500 hours at $8). There were no other variances from standard cost for this year.

Required:

Adjust the inventories and cost of goods sold to reflect actual costs.

(CMA adapted)

20–39. Revisions of Standards

Lenco Company employs a traditional standard cost system as part of its cost control program. The standard cost per unit is established at the beginning of each year. Any revisions in standards are deferred until the beginning of the next fiscal year. However, to recognize changes in standards in the current year, the company includes "planned" variances in the monthly budgets prepared after such changes have been introduced.

The following labor standard was set for one of Lenco's products effective July 1, the beginning of the fiscal year.

Class I labor: 4 hours at $6	$24.00
Class II labor: 3 hours at $7.50	22.50
Class V labor: 1 hour at $11.50	11.50
Standard labor cost per 100 units	$58.00

The standard was based on the quality of material used in prior years and that expected for the current fiscal year. Labor activity is performed by a team consisting of four persons with Class I skills, three persons with Class II skills, and one person with Class V skills. This is the most economical combination.

Manufacturing operations occured as expected during the first five months of the year. However, the company received a significant increase in orders for delivery in the spring. There was an inadequate number of skilled workers available to meet the increased production. As a result, the production teams, beginning in January, were made up of more Class I labor and less Class II labor than the standard specified. The teams would consist of six Class I persons, two Class II persons, and one Class V person. This labor team is less efficient than the normal team. As a result, only 90 units are produced in the same time period that 100 units would normally be produced. No changes in direct materials used per unit of output will occur because of the change in the labor mix.

Lenco was notified by its materials supplier that a lower quality material would be supplied after January 1, however. One unit of direct material normally is required for each good unit produced. Lenco and its supplier estimate that 5 percent of the units manufactured would be rejected upon final inspection due to the lower quality material. Normally, no units are lost due to defective material.

Required:

a. How much of the lower quality material must be entered into production to produce 42,750 units of good production in January with the new labor teams? Show your calculations.

b. How many hours of each class of labor will be needed to produce 42,750 good units from the material input? Show your calculations.

c. What amount should be included in the January budget for the planned labor variance due to the labor team and material changes? What amount of this planned labor variance can be associated with the (1) material change and (2) the team change? Show your calculations.

(CMA adapted)

INTEGRATIVE CASES

20–40. Comprehensive Review of Variances and Standard Cost Flows with Proration

Longhorn Manufacturing Corporation produces only one product, Bevo, and accounts for the production of Bevo using a traditional standard cost system.

At the end of each year, Longhorn prorates all variances among the various inventories and cost of sales. Because Longhorn prices its inventories on the FIFO basis and all the beginning inventories are used during the year, the variances that had been allocated to the ending inventories are immediately charged to cost of sales at the beginning of the following year. This allows only the current year's variances to be recorded in the variance accounts in any given year.

Following are the standards for the production of one unit of Bevo: 3 units of item A at $1 per unit, 1 unit of item B at $.50 per unit, 4 units of item C at $.30 per unit, and 20 minutes of direct labor at $4.50 per hour. Separate variance accounts are maintained for each type of direct material and for direct labor. Direct materials are recorded at standard prices when purchased. Manufacturing overhead is applied at $9 per actual direct labor-hour and is not related to the standard cost system. There was no overapplied or underapplied manufacturing overhead at December 31, Year 1. After proration of the variances, the various inventories at December 31, Year 1, were costed as follows:

Direct materials:

Item	Number of Units	Unit Cost	Amount
A	15,000	$1.10	$16,500
B	4,000	.52	2,080
C	20,000	.32	6,400
			$24,980

Work in process:

Nine thousand units of Bevo were 100 percent complete as to items A and B, 50 percent complete as to item C, and 30 percent complete as to labor. The composition and cost of the inventory follows:

Item	Amount
A	$28,600
B	4,940
C	6,240
Direct labor	6,175
	45,955
Overhead	11,700
	$57,655

Finished goods:

Forty-eight hundred units of Bevo were costed as follows:

Item	Amount
A	$15,180
B	2,704
C	6,368
Direct labor	8,540
	32,792
Overhead	16,200
	$48,992

Following is a schedule of direct materials purchased and direct labor incurred for the year ended December 31, Year 2. Unit cost of each item of direct material and direct labor cost per hour remained constant throughout the year.

Purchases:

Item	Number of Units or Hours	Unit Cost	Amount
A	290,000	$1.15	$333,500
B	101,000	.55	55,550
C	367,000	.35	128,450
Direct labor	34,100	4.60	156,860

During the year ended December 31, Year 2, Longhorn sold 90,000 units of Bevo and had ending physical inventories as follows:

Direct materials:

Item	Number of Units
A	28,300
B	2,100
C	28,900

Work in process:

Seventy-five hundred units of Bevo were 100 percent complete as to items A and B, 50 percent complete as to item C, and 20 percent complete as to labor, as follows:

Item	Number of Units or Hours
A	22,900
B	8,300
C	15,800
Direct labor	800

Finished goods:

Fifty-one hundred units of Bevo, as follows:

Item	Number of Units or Hours
A	15,600
B	6,300
C	21,700
Direct labor	2,050

There was no overapplied or underapplied manufacturing overhead at December 31, Year 2.

a. Prepare a schedule showing all materials and direct labor variances arising from activity in Year 2.

b. Use T-accounts to show the flow of materials and direct labor costs under the standard costing system in use.

(CPA adapted)

20–41. Racketeer: Comprehensive Cost Flow Problem

Refer to the data presented in Racketeer, Chapter 19, problem 19–47. Using traditional standard, full-absorption costing for Racketeer, present the flow of costs through accounts, using journal entries and T-accounts.

20–42. Woodside Products, Inc.[3] (Profit Variance Analysis)

Phil Brooks, president of Woodside Products, Inc., called Marilyn Mynar into his office one morning in early July. Ms. Mynar was a business major in college and was employed by Woodside during her college summer vacation.

"Marilyn," Brooks began, "I've just received the preliminary financial statements for our current fiscal year, which ended June 30. Both our board of directors and our shareholders will want, and deserve, an explanation of why our pretax income was virtually unchanged even though revenues were up by more than $175,000. The accountant is tied up working with our outside CPA on the annual audit, so I thought you could do the necessary analysis. What I'd like is as much of a detailed explanation of the $1,950 profit increase as you can glean from these data (Exhibit A). Also, draft a statement for the next board meeting that explains the same $1,950 profit increase. Since the board of directors understands variable costing, I recommend that you convert everything to variable costing for the variance computations, then reconcile your variable costing numbers with the amounts shown in Exhibit A, if necessary."

---

[3] Copyright © Osceola Institute, 1979.

Exhibit A (20–42)

WOODSIDE PRODUCTS, INC.
Operating Results
For the Years Ended June 30

	Last Year	Current Year
Sales revenues	$3,525,000	$3,701,250
Cost of goods sold	2,115,000	2,310,450
Gross margin	1,410,000	1,390,800
Selling and administrative	902,400	881,250
Income before taxes	$ 507,600	$ 509,550

Other Data for Last Year

1. Sales = 88,125 units @ $40.
2. Cost of goods sold = 88,125 units @ $24.
3. Selling and administrative costs were $1.84 per unit
   variable selling cost plus $740,250 fixed S&A.
4. Production volume and sales volume were equal.
5. Production costs per unit were:

Materials	$ 9.60 (8 pounds at $1.20)
Direct labor	4.80 (75 hour at $6.40)
Variable overhead	1.60 (per unit)
Fixed overhead	8.00 (based on estimated production volume of 88,125 units)
	$24.00

Other Current Year Data

1. Sales = 78,750 units @ $47.
2. Cost of goods sold includes the current year's production
   cost variances.
3. Selling and administrative costs were $2 per unit variable
   selling cost plus $723,750 fixed S&A.
4. Actual production volume was 81,100 units; estimated
   volume was 88,125 units.
5. 626,200 pounds of material at $1.40 were consumed by
   production.
6. 64,860 direct labor-hours were worked at $6.90.
7. Actual variable overhead costs were $152,000.

Required:

Prepare the detailed analysis of the $1,950 profit increase from last fiscal year to the current fiscal year and draft an explanation for Woodside's board of directors, as requested by Phil Brooks. (Hint: Let last year's amounts be budgets or standards.) Assume that finished goods inventory was valued at $24 per unit (using full-absorption costing) at the end of this year.

MIX, YIELD, AND REVENUE VARIANCES

LEARNING OBJECTIVES

1. Understand the use of variances to evaluate marketing performance.
2. Know how to compute and use production mix and yield variances.

Variances Differences
between planned results
and actual outcomes.

In this chapter, we discuss variances for revenues and nonmanufacturing costs and how they are used to measure performance. The basic principles are the same as those presented in Chapters 18 through 20.

A **variance** is the difference between a predetermined norm and the actual results for a period. To illustrate the development of revenue and non-manufacturing cost variances, we continue the Evergreen Company example. The basic facts about the Evergreen Company example are reviewed in Illustration 21–1.

REPORTING ON MARKETING PERFORMANCE

Like manufacturing managers, marketing managers usually are evaluated on the basis of planned results versus actual outcomes. Marketing performance analysis looks at how well the company has done in terms of revenues and marketing costs compared to the plans that are reflected in the master budget.

Using Sales Price and Activity Variances to Evaluate Marketing Performance

Sales Price Variance Variance
arising from changes in the price
of goods sold.

Sales Activity Variance
Variance due to changes in
volume of sales.

The **sales price** and **sales activity variances** are often used to evaluate marketing performance. Sales price and activity variances would be computed as follows:

$$\text{Price variance} = (\text{Actual sales price} - \text{Budgeted sales price}) \times \text{Actual sales volume.}$$

For Evergreen Company:

$$\left(\begin{matrix}\text{Actual} \\ \text{price}\end{matrix} - \begin{matrix}\text{Budgeted} \\ \text{price}\end{matrix}\right) \times \begin{matrix}\text{Actual} \\ \text{sales} \\ \text{volume}\end{matrix}$$

$$(\ \$21\ -\ \$20\ ) \times 10{,}000 \text{ units} = \underline{\underline{\$10{,}000\text{F}}}$$

$$\text{Sales activity variance} = \text{Budgeted contribution margin} \times (\text{Actual sales volume} - \text{Master budget sales volume})$$

Illustration 21–1   **Evergreen Company**

	Actual	Master Budget
Sales price	$21 per crate	$20 per crate
Sales volume	10,000 crates	8,000 crates
Variable manufacturing costs	$8.544 per crate	$8 per crate
Variable marketing and administrative costs	1.10 per crate	1 per crate
Fixed manufacturing costs	37,000	36,000
Fixed marketing and administrative costs	44,000	40,000

For Evergreen Company:

$$
\begin{array}{c}
\begin{array}{c} \text{Budgeted} \\ \text{Contribution} \\ \text{Margin} \end{array} \times
\left(
\begin{array}{c} \text{Actual} \\ \text{Sales} \\ \text{Volume} \end{array} -
\begin{array}{c} \text{Master} \\ \text{Budget} \\ \text{Sales} \\ \text{Volume} \end{array}
\right)
\end{array}
$$

$$
\begin{aligned}
(\$20 - \$9) \times &\quad (10{,}000 - 8{,}000) \\
= \$11 \quad \times &\quad 2{,}000 \text{ crates} \\
= \underline{\$22{,}000} \text{ F}
\end{aligned}
$$

The budgeted contribution margin equals the budgeted unit sales price (SP) of $20 minus the budgeted (or standard) variable cost (SV) which is $9 (sum of $8 variable manufacturing and $1 variable marketing and administrative). Consequently, the *budgeted contribution margin per unit* is:

$$
\begin{aligned}
\$20 - (\$8 + \$1) &= \$20 - \$9 \\
&= \underline{\underline{\$11}}
\end{aligned}
$$

Illustration 21–2 presents a general model for computing these variances and applies it to the Evergreen Company example. Note that the method is similar to that used to compute cost variances in Chapter 19. To compare with the profit variance analysis in Chapter 18, we also show the actual contribution and the variable cost variances in Illustration 21–2. The actual variable cost (AV) equals $9.644 based on the data given for Evergreen Company in Chapter 18. (The $9.644 is the sum of the actual variable manufacturing cost and the variable marketing and administrative cost.)

Contribution Margin versus Gross Margin

Contribution Margin Variance
Variance from changes in revenues and variable costs.

When the contribution margin is used to compute the variances, the variances are called **contribution margin variances.** An alternative is to compute the variances using a budgeted gross margin instead of a budgeted contri-

---

Illustration 21-2   **Contribution Margin Variances, Evergreen Company**

Actual		**Flexible Sales Budget**	**Master Sales Budget**
[*Actual* sales price **(AP)** minus *actual* variable cost **(AV)**] times *actual* quantity **(AQ)**	[*Actual* sales price **(AP)** minus standard variable cost **(SV)**] times *actual* quantity **(AQ)**	[*Standard* sales price **(SP)** minus standard variable cost **(SV)**] times *actual* quantity **(AQ)**	[*Standard* sales price **(SP)** minus standard variable cost **(SV)**] times *standard* quantity **(SQ)** of units sold
(AP − AV) × AQ	**(AP − SV) × AQ**	**(SP − SV) × AQ**	**(SP − SV) × SQ**
($21 − 9.644) × 10,000 crates = $113,560	($21 − 9) × 10,000 crates = $120,000	($20 − 9) × 10,000 crates = $110,000	($20 − 9) × 8,000 crates = $88,000

Variable cost variances: $113,560 − $120,000	Price variance: $120,000 − $110,000	Activity variance: $110,000 − $88,000
= $6,440 U	= $10,000 F	= $22,000 F

Total sales variance = $32,000 F

Gross Margin Variance
Variance from changes in revenues and cost of goods sold.

bution margin. This method of computing the variances is known as the **gross margin variance.** The basic approach is the same as for contribution margin variances except that the calculation is based on a unit gross margin instead of a unit contribution margin.

Calculation of this contribution margin variance requires knowledge of which costs are fixed and which are variable. If this information is not available, the gross margin variance is sometimes calculated in place of the contribution margin variance. (Note that computation of the sales price variance is independent of the choice between the gross margin and contribution margin methods of computing sales activity variances.)

Incentive Effects of Commissions Based on Revenue versus Contribution Margins

Sales personnel are often given commissions or bonuses based on sales revenue. Suppose a salesperson has an opportunity to sell *one* of the following two products to a customer, *but not both:*

	Revenue	Standard Variable Cost	Contribution Margin
Product A:	$100,000	$90,000	$10,000
Product B:	50,000	30,000	20,000

If the salesperson's commission is 2 percent of sales, he or she would clearly prefer to sell product A, even though product B provides a greater contribution to profits.

An alternative incentive plan would give the salesperson a commission based on contribution margin. If the salesperson's commission were 10 percent of contribution margin, *both* the salesperson and the company would benefit from the sale of product B.

In general, it is best to tie employee incentives as closely to organizational goals as possible. If the organizational goal is to maximize current sales, a commission based on revenue makes sense. If the goal is current profit maximization, a commission based on contribution margins may be more appropriate.

Summary

If you recall from previous chapters, the "bottom line" objective in variance analysis is to compare the reported income statement amounts with the master budget. To keep in touch with the "big picture," we present the comparison of master budget to reported income statement that was first presented in Chapter 18. The sales price and activity variances, which are relevant for our discussion in this chapter, are shown in columns 4 and 6 of Illustration 21–3.

Illustration 21–3 shows that actual revenue exceeds budgeted revenue by $50,000 ($10,000 favorable price variance plus $40,000 difference between the flexible budget revenue and the master budget revenue). It would be incorrect to say that favorable sales results have increased profits by $50,000, however, because the favorable increase in sales volume is partly

Illustration 21-3   **Comparison of Actual to Master Budget, Evergreen Company**

	(1) Actual (based on actual activity of 10,000 units sold)	(2) Manufacturing Variances	(3) Marketing and Administrative Variances	(4) Sales Price Variances	(5) Flexible Budget (based on actual activity of 10,000 units sold)	(6) Sales Activity (volume) Variance	(7) Master Budget Plan (based on a prediction of 8,000 units sold)
Sales revenue	$210,000	—	—	$10,000 F	$200,000	$40,000 F	$160,000
Less:							
Variable manufacturing costs	85,440	$5,440 U	—	—	80,000	16,000 U	64,000
Variable marketing and administrative costs	11,000	—	$1,000 U	—	10,000	2,000 U	8,000
Contribution margin	113,560	5,440 U	1,000 U	10,000 F	110,000	22,000 F	88,000
Less:							
Fixed manufacturing costs	37,000	1,000 U	—	—	36,000	—	36,000
Fixed marketing and administrative costs	44,000	—	4,000 U	—	40,000	—	40,000
Operating profits	$ 32,560	$6,440 U	$5,000 U	$10,000 F	$ 34,000	$22,000 F	$ 12,000

Total variance from flexible budget = $1,440 U

Total variance from flexible budget = $20,560 F

offset by the variable costs of the additional 2,000 crates produced and sold. Therefore, we say the favorable sales results have increased profits by $32,000 ($10,000 F sales price variance + $22,000 F sales activity variance).

We next discuss further analysis of these sales variances.

Market Share Variance and Industry Volume Variance

Managers frequently wonder *whether the sales activity variance is due to general market conditions or to a change in the company's market share.* The cause may be significant because of promotional strategies and/or pricing policies. At Evergreen Company, for example, the marketing vice president wondered about the cause of the favorable activity variance of 2,000 units: "Our estimated share of the market was 20 percent. We projected industry sales of 40,000 crates, of which we would sell 8,000. We actually sold 10,000 crates. Was that because our share of the market went up from 20 percent to 25 percent (25% × 40,000 crates = 10,000 crates)? Or did we just hold our own at 20 percent, while the market increased to 50,000 crates (20% × 50,000 crates = 10,000 crates)?"

Numerous sources of data are available about industry volume (for example, trade journals, government census data). When these data are available, the activity variance could be divided into an industry volume variance and a market share variance. The **industry volume variance** tells how much of the sales activity variance is due to changes in industry volume. The **market share variance** tells how much of the activity variance is due to changes in market share. The market share variance is usually more controllable by the marketing department and is a measure of their performance.

The marketing vice president at Evergreen Company learned that the favorable sales activity resulted from an improvement in both industry volume and market share. Industry volume went up from 40,000 units to

Industry Volume Variance The portion of the sales activity variance due to changes in industry volume.

Market Share Variance The portion of the activity variance due to change in the company's proportion of sales in the markets in which the company operates.

Illustration 21-4   **Industry Volume and Market Share Variances**

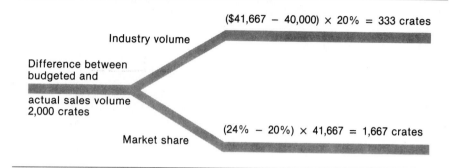

($41,667 − 40,000) × 20% = 333 crates

Industry volume

Difference between
budgeted and

actual sales volume
2,000 crates

Market share

(24% − 20%) × 41,667 = 1,667 crates

41,667, while market share went up from 20 percent to 24 percent. Hence, the 2,000-unit favorable activity variance can be broken down into an industry effect and a market share effect, as shown in Illustration 21-4. Of the 2,000-unit increase in company volume, 333 crates, which is 20 percent of 1,667 units, is due to the increase in industry volume (holding market share constant), while 1,667 crates, which is 4 percent of 41,667 units, is due to an increased share of the market. Multiplying each figure by the *standard contribution margin* gives the impact of these variances on operating profits (amounts are rounded):

Industry volume: ($20 − $9) ×   333 crates = $ 3,663 F
Market share: ($20 − $9) × 1,667 crates = $18,337 F
Total activity: ($20 − $9) × 2,000 crates = $22,000 F

Calculation of these variances is also shown in Illustration 21-5.

Use of the industry volume and market share variances enables management to separate that portion of the activity variance that coincides with changes in the overall industry from that which is specific to the company. Favorable market share variances indicate that the company is achieving better than industry average volume changes. This can be very important information to a company sensitive about its market share.

Sales Mix Variances

Sales Mix Variance   Variance arising from the relative proportion of different products sold.

When a company sells multiple products, a sales mix variance sometimes provides useful information. This is particularly so if the products are substitutes for each other. For example, an automobile dealer sells two kinds of cars: Super and Standard. For October, the estimated sales for the company were 1,000 cars: 500 Super models and 500 Standard models. The Super models were expected to have a contribution margin of $3,000 per car, while the Standard models were expected to have a contribution margin of $1,000 per car. Thus, the budgeted total contribution for October was:

Super: 500 at $3,000	$1,500,000
Standard: 500 at $1,000	500,000
Total contribution	$2,000,000

Illustration 21-5   **Breakdown of Sales Activity Variance into Industry Volume and Market Share Variances, Evergreen Company**

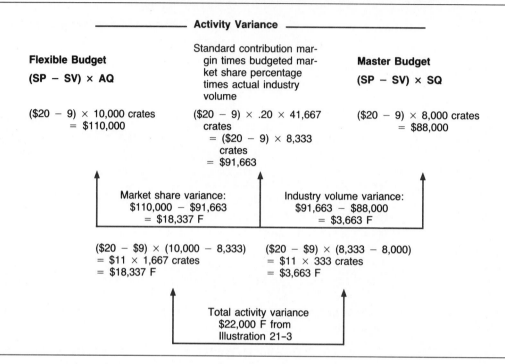

When the results for October were tabulated, the company had sold 1,000 cars, and each model had provided the predicted contribution margin per unit. But the total contribution was a disappointing $1,400,000 because instead of the predicted 50–50 mix of cars sold, the mix was 20 percent Super and 80 percent Standard, with the following results:

Super: 200 at $3,000	$ 600,000
Standard: 800 at $1,000	800,000
Total contribution	$1,400,000

The $600,000 decrease from the budgeted contribution margin is the *sales mix variance*. In this case, it occurred because 300 fewer Super models were sold (for a loss of 300 × $3,000 = $900,000), while 300 more Standard models were sold (for a gain of 300 × $1,000 = $300,000). The net effect is a loss of $2,000 in contribution margin for each Standard model that was sold instead of a Super model. (This emphasizes the importance of the substitutability assumption. If a store sells, among other things, jewelry and garden tractors, the mix variance would probably not be as useful as when comparing two products that are close substitutes.)

Illustration 21-6 **Contribution Margin Variances, Electron Company (First Quarter)**

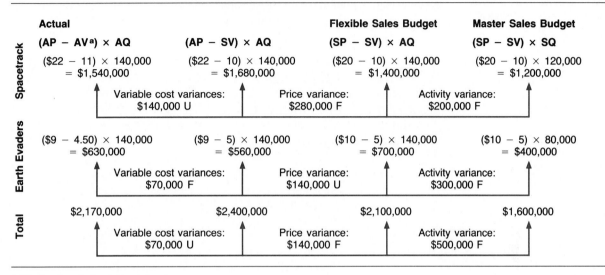

a AV refers to actual variable cost.

Computation of Sales Mix Variances

Assume Electron Company makes and sells two electronic games: Spacetrack and Earth Evaders. The estimated and actual results for the first quarter of the year were as follows:

	Spacetrack	Earth Evaders	Total
Standard sales price per unit	$20	$10	—
Actual sales price per unit	22	9	—
Standard variable cost per unit	10	5	—
Actual variable cost per unit	11	4.50	—
Estimated sales volume	120,000	80,000	200,000
Estimated sales activity percentage	60%	40%	100%
Actual sales volume	140,000	140,000	280,000
Actual sales activity percentage	50%	50%	100%

An analysis of contribution margin variances is shown in Illustration 21–6. This is the analysis that would be presented if the sales mix variance were ignored.

There are many ways to calculate sales mix variances. Each starts with the same total variance between actual and master budget but then breaks it down in a different manner.

Our computation of the sales mix variances allows us to break down the sales activity variance into two components: sales mix and sales quantity. The *sales mix variance measures the impact of substitution* (it appears Earth Evaders has been substituted for Spacetrack), while the **sales quantity vari-**

Sales Quantity Variance In multiproduct companies, a variance arising from the change in volume of sales, independent of any change in mix.

ance *measures the variance in sales quantity, holding the sales mix constant.*

Calculations for this example are presented in Illustration 21–7. The sales price variance is unaffected by our analysis, while the sales activity variance is broken down into the mix and quantity variances.

Source of the Sales Mix Variance

While we have calculated each product mix variance to show exact sources, the *total* mix variance ($140,000 U) is most frequently used. In this example, the unfavorable mix variance is caused by the substitution of the lower-contribution Earth Evaders for the higher-contribution Spacetrack. To be precise, the substitutions are:

Decrease in Spacetrack	28,000 @ $10 = $280,000 U
Increase in Earth Evaders	28,000 @ $ 5 = 140,000 F
Net effect in units	–0–
Net effect in dollars	$140,000 U

Illustration 21-7 **Sales Mix and Quantity Variances, Electron Company (First Quarter)**

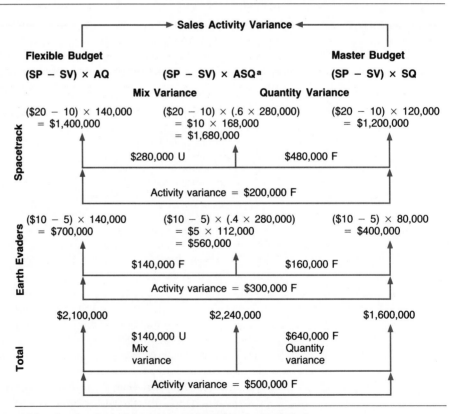

[a] ASQ = Quantity of units that would have been sold at the standard mix.

The quantity variance results from the sale of 80,000 more units than expected. More precisely:

Spacetrack:	(168,000 − 120,000) × $10 =	$480,000 F
Earth Evaders:	(112,000 − 80,000) × $ 5 =	160,000 F
Total quantity variance:	80,000 units	$640,000 F

By separating the activity variance into its mix and quantity components, we have isolated the pure mix effect by holding constant the quantity effects, and we have isolated the pure quantity effect by holding constant the mix effect.

PRODUCTION MIX AND YIELD VARIANCES

Our analysis of mix and quantity variances for sales can also be applied to production. Often a mix of inputs is used in production. Chemicals, steel, fabrics, plastics, and many other products require a mix of direct materials, some of which can be substituted for each other without greatly affecting product quality.

Mix and Yield Variances in Service Organizations

The same holds for labor. Consider a consulting firm that has bid a job for 1,000 hours—300 hours of partner time at a cost of $60 per hour and 700 hours of staff time at a cost of $20 per hour. Due to scheduling problems, the partner spends 500 hours and the staff member spends 500 hours. If the actual costs are $60 and $20 for partner and staff time, respectively, then there is no labor price variance. But even though the 1,000 hours time required was exactly what was bid, the job cost is $8,000 over budget, as shown below:

$$\text{Actual cost} = (500 \text{ hours} \times \$60) + (500 \text{ hours} \times \$20)$$
$$= \$30,000 + \$10,000$$
$$= \underline{\underline{\$40,000}}$$

$$\text{Budgeted cost} = (300 \text{ hours} \times \$60) + (700 \text{ hours} \times \$20)$$
$$= \$18,000 + \$14,000$$
$$= \underline{\underline{\$32,000}}$$

Production Mix Variance A variance that arises from a change in the relative proportion of inputs (a materials or labor mix variance).

The $8,000 over budget results from the substitution of 200 hours of partner time at $60 for 200 hours of staff time at $20. The **production mix variance** is the difference in labor costs per hour ($60 − $20 = $40) times the number of hours substituted (200): $40 × 200 hours = $8,000.

Two factors are important when considering mix variances. First, there is an assumed *substitutability of inputs,* just as there was an assumed substitutability of sales products to make the sales mix variance meaningful. While partner time may have been substitutable for staff time, the reverse may not have been true. Second, the input costs must be different for a mix variance to exist. If the hourly costs of both partners and staff were the same, the substitution of hours would have no effect on the total cost of the job.

Mix and Yield Variances in Manufacturing

With the general concept in mind, we proceed with another example, using direct materials, which is a common application of mix variances in a production setting.

The Clean Chemical Company makes a product—XZ—that is made up of two direct materials. The standard costs and quantities are:

Direct Material	Standard Price per Pound	Standard Number of Pounds per Unit of Finished Product
X	$4	5
Z	8	5
		10

The standard cost per unit of finished product is:

X: 5 pounds @ $4 =	$20
Z: 5 pounds @ $8 =	40
Total	$60

During June, Clean Chemical had the following results:

Units produced	1,000 units of finished product
Materials purchased and used:	
Material X	4,400 pounds at $5
Material Z	5,800 pounds at $8
	10,200 pounds

Our computation of the mix variance breaks down the direct materials efficiency variance into two components: mix and yield. The mix variance for costs is conceptually the same as the mix variance for sales, and the yield variance is conceptually the same as the sales quantity variance. The mix variance measures the impact of substitution (material Z appears to have been substituted for material X), while the **production yield variance** measures the input-output relationship holding the standard mix inputs constant. Standards called for 10,000 pounds of materials to produce 1,000 units of output; however, 10,200 pounds of input were actually used. The overuse of 200 pounds is a physical measure of the yield variance.

To derive mix and yield variances, we use the term *ASQ. ASQ is the actual amount of input used at the standard mix.*

Calculations for the three variances (price, mix, yield) for Clean Chemical are shown in Illustration 21–8. Note that the sum of the mix and yield variances equals the materials **efficiency variance**, which was discussed in Chapter 19. In examining these calculations, recall that the standard proportions (mix) of direct materials are X = 50 percent and Z = 50 percent, while 10,200 pounds were used in total. Thus, ASQ for each material is:

Production Yield Variance Differences between expected outputs from a given level of inputs and the actual outputs obtained from those inputs.

Efficiency Variance A difference between budgeted and actual results arising from differences between the inputs that were expected per unit of output and the inputs actually used.

X: .5 × 10,200 pounds = 5,100 pounds
Z: .5 × 10,200 pounds = 5,100
10,200

We have calculated the mix variance for each direct material to demonstrate its exact source. However, it is the *total* mix variance ($2,800 U) that

Illustration 21–8 **Mix and Yield Variances, Clean Chemical**

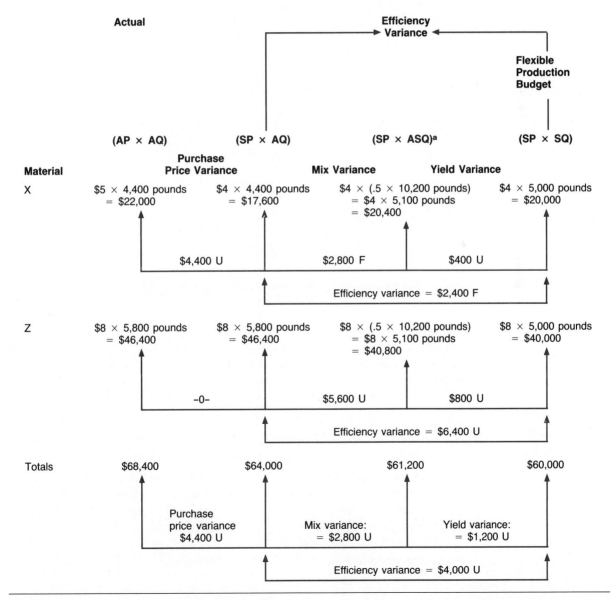

a ASQ = Actual amount of input used at the standard mix.

is frequently used. In this example, the unfavorable mix is caused by a substitution of the more expensive direct material Z for the less expensive direct material X. To be precise, the substitutions are:

Decrease in X:	700 pounds @ $4 =	$2,800 decrease
Increase in Z:	700 pounds @ $8 =	$5,600 increase
Net effect in pounds:	–0–	
Net effect in dollars:	$2,800 increase	

As previously indicated, the yield variance results from the overuse of 200 pounds. More precisely:

Material X:	100 pounds @ $4 =	$ 400 U
Material Z:	100 pounds @ $8 =	$ 800 U
Totals	200 pounds	$1,200 U

By separating the efficiency variance into its mix and yield components, we have isolated the pure mix effect by holding constant the yield effect, and we have isolated the pure yield effect by holding constant the mix effect.

SUMMARY

Contribution margin variances explain the impact of differences between budgeted and actual sales activity and price. Sales activity variances may be further analyzed as to the effects of changes in market share or industrywide volume factors. If several products are sold, the sales activity variance may be subdivided into quantity and sales mix variances.

Mix and yield variances can also be prepared for production costs where multiple inputs are used. In these cases, the efficiency variance is divided into mix and yield variances.

TERMS AND CONCEPTS

The following terms and concepts should be familiar to you after reading this chapter:

Sales Activity Variance

Contribution Margin Variance

Efficiency Variance

Gross Margin Variance

Industry Volume Variance

Market Share Variance

Production Mix Variance

Production Yield Variance

Sales Mix Variance

Sales Price Variance

Sales Quantity Variance

Standard Costs

Variance

SUPPLEMENTARY READINGS

Adelberg, A. "Improved Analysis of Production-Mix Variances." *Production and Inventory Management,* 4th Quarter 1984, pp. 35–41.

Bastable, C.W., and D. H. Bao. "The Fiction of Sales-Mix and Sales-Quality Variances." *Accounting Horizons,* June 1988, pp. 10–17.

Booth, John. "When Accountants Must Take a Role in Marketing Tasks." *Accountancy,* August 1985, pp. 80–81 (published in Great Britain).

Gonik, J. "Tie Salesmen's Bonuses to Their Forecasts." *Harvard Business Review,* May–June 1978.

Jackson, D., Jr.; L. Ostrom; and K. Evans. "Segmental and Performance Measures in Marketing." *Cost and Management,* July–August 1985, pp. 16–20 (published in Canada).

Peles, Y. C. "Notes on Yield Variance and Mix Variance." *Accounting Review,* April 1986, pp. 325–29.

Ramano, P. "NAA on Sales Forecasting Systems." *Management Accounting,* December 1985, p. 77.

Vangermeersch, R., and W. Brosnan. "Enhancing Revenues via Distribution Cost Control." *Management Account,* August 1985, pp. 56–60.

Wolk, H. I. and A. D. Hillman. "Materials Mix and Yield Variances." *Accounting Review,* July 1972, pp. 549–55.

SELF-STUDY PROBLEM NO. 1

Market Share and Industry Volume Variances

Required:

Insta-Pour Concrete, Inc., produces precast beams for highway and other bridge construction. The company's master budget called for sales of 20,000 beams, which would have been 16 percent of the market in their market area. The contribution margin on each beam is $215. During the year, 21,000 beams were sold. The company's market share had increased to 22 percent of the total market.

Compute the sales activity variances and break down the sales activity variance into industry volume and market share variances.

SOLUTION TO SELF-STUDY PROBLEM NO. 1

Standard Contribution Margin Times Budgeted Market Share

Flexible Budget	Industry Volume	Master Budget
	$215 \times (.16 \times 95,455^a)$	
$215 \times 21,000$	or $4,300,000 \times \left(\dfrac{95,455}{125,000}\right)^b$	$215 \times 20,000$
$= \$4,515,000$	$= \$3,283,652$	$= \$4,300,000$

$1,231,348 F
Market share variance

$1,016,348 U
Industry volume variance

Total sales activity variance
$= \$4,515,000 - 4,300,000$
$= \$215,000 F$

[a] $\dfrac{21,000}{.22} = 95,455$ actual size of market during the period.

[b] $\dfrac{20,000}{.16} = 125,000$ estimated size of market at master budget preparation time.

SELF-STUDY PROBLEM NO. 2

Sales Mix and Quantity Variances

Assume that the master budget has sales of 1,200 units of product A and 800 units of product B. Actual sales volumes were 1,320 of product A and 780 of product B. The expected contribution per unit of product A was $1 ($4 price − $3 standard variable cost), and the expected contribution of product B was $3.50.

Product A actually sold for 10 percent more than the expected price of $4 per unit. Product B sold for $6.688 per unit, while the expected price was $6.50.

Compute the sales activity variances and further break them down into sales mix and quantity components.

SOLUTION TO SELF-STUDY PROBLEM NO. 2

Activity Variance

	Flexible Budget (SP − SV) × AQ		(SP − SV) × ASQ		Master Budget (SP − SV) × SQ
		Mix variance		**Quantity variance**	
Product A	($4 − 3) × 1,320 = $1,320		($4 − 3) × (.6 × 2,100) = $1,260		($4 − 3) × 1,200 = $1,200

$60 F $60 F

Activity variance = $120 F

| **Product B** | ($6.50 − 3) × 780 = $2,730 | | ($6.50 − 3) × (.4 × 2,100) = $2,940 | | ($6.50 − 3) × 800 = $2,800 |

$210 U $140 F

Activity variance = $70 U

| **Total** | $4,050 | | $4,200 | | $4,000 |

$150 U $200 F
Mix variance   Quantity variance

Activity variance = $50 F

SELF-STUDY PROBLEM NO. 3

Mix and Yield Variances

Alexis Company makes a product, AL, from two materials: ST and EE. The standard prices and quantities are as follows:

	ST	EE
Price per pound	$2	$3
Pounds per unit of AL	10 pounds	5 pounds

In May, 7,000 units of AL were produced by Alexis Company, with the following actual prices and quantities of materials used:

	ST	EE
Price per pound	$1.90	$2.80
Pounds used	72,000	38,000

Required:

a. Compute materials price and efficiency variances.

b. Compute materials mix and yield variances.

SOLUTION TO SELF-STUDY PROBLEM NO. 3

a. Price and efficiency variance:

	Actual (AP × AQ)	Inputs at Standard Prices (SP × AQ)	Flexible Production Budget (SP × SQ)
ST	($1.90 × 72,000)	($2 × 72,000)	($2 × 70,000[a])
EE	+ ($2.80 × 38,000)	+ ($3 × 38,000)	+ ($3 × 35,000[b])
Total	= $243,200	= $258,000	= $245,000

Price Variance: $14,800 F   Efficiency variance: $13,000 U

b. Mix and yield variance:

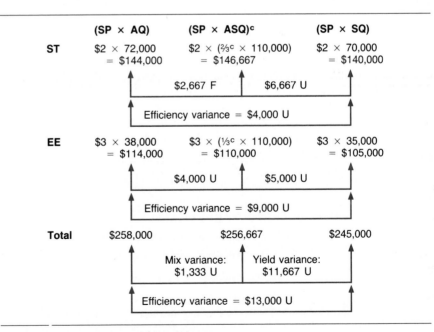

	(SP × AQ)	(SP × ASQ)[c]	(SP × SQ)
ST	$2 × 72,000 = $144,000	$2 × (⅔[c] × 110,000) = $146,667	$2 × 70,000 = $140,000

$2,667 F $6,667 U

Efficiency variance = $4,000 U

	(SP × AQ)	(SP × ASQ)	(SP × SQ)
EE	$3 × 38,000 = $114,000	$3 × (⅓[c] × 110,000) = $110,000	$3 × 35,000 = $105,000

$4,000 U $5,000 U

Efficiency variance = $9,000 U

Total	$258,000	$256,667	$245,000

Mix variance: $1,333 U   Yield variance: $11,667 U

Efficiency variance = $13,000 U

[a] 70,000 pounds = 7,000 units × 10 pounds per unit.

[b] 35,000 pounds = 7,000 units × 5 pounds per unit.

[c] Mix percentage ratio of ST pounds to total and EE pounds to total. For ST, $\frac{10}{10 + 5} = \frac{2}{3}$.
For EE, $\frac{5}{10 + 5} = \frac{1}{3}$.

ASQ = Actual amount of the input used at the standard mix.

QUESTIONS

21-1. We normally deduct standard costs from the actual revenues when analyzing revenue variances. Why not use actual costs and actual revenues?

21-2. Why is there no efficiency variance for revenues?

21-3. The marketing manager of a company noted: "We had a favorable revenue activity variance of $425,000, yet company profits only went up by $114,000. Some part of the organization has dropped the ball—let's find out where the problem is and straighten it out." Comment on this remark.

21-4. A production manager was debating with company management because production had been charged with a large unfavorable production volume variance. The production manager explained: "After all, if marketing had lined up sales for these units we would not have been forced to cut production. Marketing should be charged with the production volume variance, not production." Do you agree with the production manager? Why or why not?

21-5. What information does the computation of an industry volume variance provide?

21-6. If the activity variance is zero, could there be any reason to compute a mix variance?

21-7. How could a CPA firm use the mix variance to analyze its revenues?

21-8. How could a CPA firm use the mix variances to analyze salary costs regarding audit services?

21-9. A company has three products that must be purchased in a single package. Is there any benefit to computing a sales mix variance under these circumstances?

21-10. Give examples of companies that probably use materials mix and yield variances.

EXERCISES

21-11. Sales Price and Activity Variances
(L.O.1)

On-the-Road Picnic Supplies manufactures and sells picnic coolers. The business is very competitive. The master budget for the last year called for sales of 200,000 units at $9 each. However, as the summer season approached, management realized that they could not sell 200,000 units at the $9 price. Rather, they would have to offer price concessions. Budgeted variable cost is $3.65 per unit. Actual results showed sales of 185,000 units at an average price of $8.35 each.

Required:

Compute sales price and activity variances for On-the-Road Picnic Supplies.

21-12. Sales Price and Activity Variances
(L.O.1)

On-the-Road Picnic Supplies is trying to decide what to do in the coming year, given the events that transpired last year (see exercise 21-11). Management conducted a marketing survey, which indicated that the company had two sales alternatives:

1. Sell 220,000 units at $8 each.
2. Sell 185,000 units at $9.50 each.

The company has actual and standard variable costs of $3.85 per unit.

Required:

Compare the two alternatives and show the effect of activity and price differences between the two alternatives. Treat alternative 2 as "master budget" and the other as "actual."

21-13. Sales Price and Activity Variances
(L.O.1)

Season-All, Inc., makes bulk artificial seasonings for use in processed foods. A seasoning was budgeted to sell in 20-liter drums at a price of $48 per drum. The company expected to sell 150,000 drums. Budgeted variable costs are $10.05 per drum.

During the year, 120,000 drums were sold at a price of $47.50.

Required: Compute sales price and activity variances.

21–14. Industry Volume and Market Share Variances
(L.O.1)

Refer to the data in exercise 21–13. Assume that the budgeted sales volume was based on an expected 10 percent of a total market volume of 1.5 million drums, but the actual results were based on a 12 percent share of a total market of 1 million drums.

Required: Compute market share and industry volume variances.

21–15. Industry Volume and Market Share Variances
(L.O.1)

Bozeman Merchandising Company budgeted sales of 20,000 units of product B, assuming the company would have 20 percent of 100,000 units sold in a particular market. The actual results were 18,000 units, based on a 15 percent share of a total market of 120,000 units. The budgeted contribution margin is $2 per unit.

Required: Compute the sales activity variance and break it down into market share and industry volume.

21–16. Industry Volume and Market Share Variances— Missing Data
(L.O.1)

The following graph is like the one presented in Illustration 21–4 in the chapter. Actual sales volume for the firm exceeds its estimated sales volume.

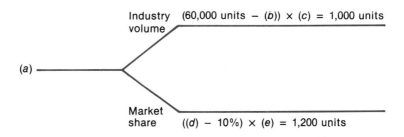

Industry volume $(60,000 \text{ units} - (b)) \times (c) = 1,000 \text{ units}$

(a)

Market share $((d) - 10\%) \times (e) = 1,200 \text{ units}$

Required: Find the missing amounts:

a. Budgeted minus actual sales volume.
b. Estimated industry volume.
c. Estimated market share percent.
d. Actual market share percent.
e. Actual industry volume.

21–17. Sales Price and Activity Variances
(L.O.1)

Gershwin, Rogers, Bach & Hammerstein operate an accounting firm with partners and staff members. Each billable hour of partner time has a budgeted price of $250 and budgeted variable cost of $130. Each billable hour of staff time has a budgeted price of $65 and budgeted variable cost of $35. This month, the partnership budget called for 8,500 billable partner-hours and 34,650 staff-hours. Actual results were as follows:

Partner revenue:	$2,150,000	9,000 hours
Staff revenue:	$2,225,000	34,000 hours

Required: Compute the sales price and activity variances for these data.

21–18. Sales Mix and Quantity Variances
(L.O.1)

Required:

Refer to the data in exercise 21–17.

Compute the sales mix and quantity variances.

21–19. Sales Mix and Quantity Variances
(L.O.1)

Personna, Inc., sells two models of personal hair care kits. The Basic model has a price of $10.35 per unit, while the Ultra model has a price of $24.60 per unit. The master budget called for sales of 400,000 Basics and 180,000 Ultras during the current year. Actual results showed sales of 300,000 Basics, with a price of $10.40 per unit, and 200,000 Ultras, with a price of $24.75 per unit. The standard variable cost is $5 per unit for a Basic and $10 per unit for Ultras.

Required:

a. Compute the activity variance for these data.

b. Break down the activity variance into mix and quantity parts.

21–20. Materials Mix and Yield Variances
(L.O.2)

Starship Steel Company had the following direct materials data for its product:

Standard costs for one unit of output: Material A, 10 units of input at $100 Material B, 20 units of input at $150

During August, the company had the following results:

Units of output produced	2,000 units
Materials purchased and used:	
Material A	22,000 units at $90
Material B	39,000 units at $152

Required:

a. Compute materials price and efficiency variances.

b. Compute materials mix and yield variances.

21–21. Labor Mix and Yield Variances
(L.O.2)

Quicki-Burgers has two categories of direct labor: unskilled, which costs $6.50 per hour, and skilled, which costs $10.30 per hour. Management has established standards per "equivalent meal," which has been defined as a typical meal consisting of a sandwich, a drink, and a side order. Standards have been set as follows:

Skilled labor:	4 minutes per equivalent meal
Unskilled labor:	10 minutes per equivalent meal

During May, Quicki-Burger sold 30,000 equivalent meals and incurred the following labor costs:

Skilled labor:	1,700 hours	$16,500
Unskilled labor:	4,200 hours	33,000

Required:

a. Compute labor price and efficiency variances.

b. Compute labor mix and yield variances.

PROBLEMS

21–22. Sales Price, Industry Volume, and Mix Variances

Oversea Airlines plans its budget and subsequently evaluates sales performance based on "passenger-miles." A passenger-mile is one paying passenger flying one mile. For this month, the company estimated its contribution margin would amount to 20 cents per passenger-mile and that 40 million passenger-miles would be flown.

As a result of improvement in the economy, 43 million passenger-miles were flown this month. The price per passenger-mile averaged 30.3 cents. The budgeted variable cost per mile was 10 cents. Subsequent analysis by management indicated that the industry flew 7 percent more passenger-miles this month than expected.

Required:

Compute the price, industry volume, and market share effects on company revenues for the month.

21–23. Revenue Analysis Using Industry Data and Multiple Product Lines

Arsco Company makes three grades of indoor-outdoor carpets. Sales volume for the annual budget is determined by estimating the total market volume for indoor-outdoor carpet and then applying the company's prior year market share, adjusted for planned changes due to company programs for the coming year. Volume is apportioned between the three grades based upon the prior year's product mix, again adjusted for planned changes due to company programs for the coming year.

Given below are the company budget and the results of operations for March.

Budget

	Grade 1	Grade 2	Grade 3	Total
Sales—units (000 omitted)	1,000 rolls	1,000 rolls	2,000 rolls	4,000 rolls
Sales—dollars (in thousands)	$1,000	$2,000	$3,000	$6,000
Variable costs	700	1,600	2,300	4,600
Contribution margin	300	400	700	1,400
Manufacturing fixed cost	200	200	300	700
Product margin	$ 100	$ 200	$ 400	700
Marketing and administrative costs (all fixed)				250
Operating profit				$ 450

Actual

	Grade 1	Grade 2	Grade 3	Total
Sales—units (000 omitted)	800 rolls	1,000 rolls	2,100 rolls	3,900 rolls
Sales—dollars (in thousands)	$ 810	$2,000	$3,000	$5,810
Variable costs	560	1,610	2,320	4,490
Contribution margin	250	390	680	1,320
Manufacturing fixed cost	210	220	315	745
Product margin	$ 40	$ 170	$ 365	575
Marketing and administrative costs (all fixed)				275
Operating profit				$ 300

Industry volume was estimated at 40,000 rolls for budgeting purposes. Actual industry volume for March was 38,000 rolls.

Required:

a. Prepare an analysis to show the effects of the sales price and sales activity variances.

b. Break down the sales activity variance into the parts caused by industry volume and market share.

(CMA adapted)

21-24. Sales Mix and Quantity Variances

Refer to the data for the Arsco Company (problem 21-23). Break down the total activity variance into sales mix and quantity parts.

21-25. Contribution Margin Variances

Markley Division of Rosette Industries manufactures and sells patio chairs. The chairs are manufactured in two versions—a metal model and a plastic model of a lower quality. The company uses its own marketing force to sell the chairs.

The chairs are manufactured on two different assembly lines located in adjoining buildings. Division management and the marketing department occupy the third building on the property. Division management includes a division controller responsible for divisional financial activities and preparation of variance reports. The controller structures these reports such that the marketing activities are distinguished from cost factors so that each can be analyzed separately.

The operating results and the related master budget for the first three months of the fiscal year follow. The budget for the current year assumes Markley Division will maintain its present market share of the estimated total patio chair market (plastic and metal combined). A status report was sent to corporate management toward the end of the second month indicating that divisional operating profit for the first quarter would probably be about 45 percent below budget; this estimate was just about on target. The division's operating income was below budget even though industry volume for patio chairs increased by 10 percent more than was expected when the budget was developed.

	Actual	Budget	Favorable (Unfavorable) Relative to the Budget
Sales in units:			
Plastic model	60,000	50,000	10,000
Metal model	20,000	25,000	(5,000)
Sales revenue:			
Plastic model	$630,000	$500,000	$130,000
Metal model	300,000	375,000	(75,000)
Total sales	930,000	875,000	55,000
Less variable costs:			
Manufacturing (at standard):			
Plastic model	480,000	400,000	(80,000)
Metal model	200,000	250,000	50,000
Marketing:			
Commissions	46,500	43,750	(2,750)
Bad debt allowance	9,300	8,750	(550)
Total variable costs (except variable manufacturing variances)	735,800	702,500	(33,300)
Contribution margin (except variable manufacturing variances)	194,200	172,500	21,700
Less other costs:			
Variable manufacturing cost variances from standards	49,600	—	(49,600)
Fixed manufacturing costs	49,200	48,000	(1,200)
Fixed marketing administrative costs	38,500	36,000	(2,500)
Corporation offices allocation	18,500	17,500	(1,000)
Total other costs	155,800	101,500	(54,300)
Divisional operating profit	$ 38,400	$ 71,000	$(32,600)

During the quarter, the company produced 55,000 plastic chairs and 22,500 metal chairs. The costs incurred by each manufacturing unit are presented below.

	Quantity	Price	Plastic Model	Metal Model
Direct materials (stated in equivalent finished chairs):				
Purchases:				
Plastic	60,000	$5.65	$339,000	
Metal	30,000	6.00		$180,000
Usage:				
Plastic	56,000	5.00	280,000	
Metal	23,000	6.00		138,000
Direct labor:				
9,300 hours at $6 per hour			55,800	
5,600 hours at $8 per hour				44,800
Manufacturing overhead:				
Variable:				
Supplies			43,000	18,000
Power			50,000	15,000
Employee benefits			19,000	12,000
Fixed:				
Supervision			14,000	11,000
Depreciation			12,000	9,000
Property taxes and other items			1,900	1,300

Standard variable manufacturing costs per unit and budgeted monthly fixed manufacturing costs for the current year are presented below.

	Plastic Model	Metal Model
Direct material	$ 5.00	$ 6.00
Direct labor:		
⅙ hour at $6 per direct labor-hour	1.00	
¼ hour at $8 per direct labor-hour		2.00
Variable overhead:		
⅙ hour at $12 per direct labor-hour	2.00	
¼ hour at $8 per direct labor-hour		2.00
Standard variable manufacturing cost per unit	$ 8.00	$10.00
Budgeted fixed costs per month:		
Supervision	$4,500	$3,500
Depreciation	4,000	3,000
Property taxes and other items	600	400
Total budgeted fixed costs for month	$9,100	$6,900

Variable marketing costs are budgeted to be 6 percent of sales-dollars.

Required:

Compute Markley Division's marketing price, mix, and quantity variances.

(CMA adapted)

21–26. Analyze Industry Effects on Contribution Margins

Refer to the data for the Markley Division (problem 21–25). Analyze the extent to which the activity variance can be explained in terms of industry and market share effects.

21–27. Sales Price, Mix, and Quantity Variances

The following information has been prepared by a member of the controller's staff of Duo, Inc.:

DUO, INC.
Income Statement
For the Year Ended December 31,
(in thousands)

	Product AR-10		Product ZR-7		Total	
	Budget	Actual	Budget	Actual	Budget	Actual
Unit sales	2,000	2,800	6,000	5,600	8,000	8,400
Sales	$6,000	$7,560	$12,000	$11,760	$18,000	$19,320
Variable costs	2,400	2,800	6,000	5,880	8,400	8,680
Fixed costs	1,800	1,900	2,400	2,400	4,200	4,300
Total costs	4,200	4,700	8,400	8,280	12,600	12,980
Operating profit	$1,800	$2,860	$ 3,600	$ 3,480	$ 5,400	$ 6,340

Required:

Analyze the above data to show the impact of price, quantity, and sales mix variances on operating profit.

(CMA adapted)

21–28. Materials Mix and Yield Variances

LAR Chemical Company manufactures a wide variety of chemical compounds and liquids for industrial uses. The standard mix for producing a single batch of 500 gallons of one liquid is as follows:

Liquid Chemical	Quantity (in gallons)	Cost (per gallon)	Total Cost
Maxan	100	$2.00	$200
Salex	300	.75	225
Cralyn	225	1.00	225
	625		$650

There is a 20 percent loss in liquid volume during processing due to evaporation. The finished liquid is put into 10-gallon bottles for sale. Thus, the standard material cost for a 10-gallon bottle is $13.

The actual quantities of direct materials and the cost of the materials placed in production during November were as follows (materials are purchased and used at the same time):

Liquid Chemical	Quantity (in gallons)	Total Cost
Maxan	8,480	$17,384
Salex	25,200	17,640
Cralyn	18,540	16,686
	52,220	$51,710

A total of 4,000 bottles (40,000 gallons) were produced during November.

Required:

Calculate the total direct material variance for the liquid product for the month of November and then further analyze the total variance into:

a. Materials price and efficiency variances.

b. Materials mix and yield variances.

21–29. Labor Mix and Yield Variances

Piece O' Rock Insurance Company compares actual results with a flexible budget. The standard direct labor rates used in the flexible budget are established each year at the time the annual plan is formulated and held constant for the entire year.

The standard direct labor rates in effect for the current fiscal year and the standard hours allowed for the actual output of insurance claims for the month of April in a claims department are shown in the schedule below:

	Standard Direct Labor Rate per Hour	Standard Direct Labor-Hours Allowed for Output
Labor class III	$8	500
Labor class II	7	500
Labor class I	5	500

The wage rates for each labor class increased under the terms of a new contract. The standard wage rates were not revised to reflect the new contract.

The actual direct labor-hours worked and the actual direct labor rates per hour experienced for the month of April were as follows:

	Actual Direct Labor Rate per Hour	Actual Direct Labor-Hours
Labor class III	$8.50	550
Labor class II	7.50	650
Labor class I	5.40	375

Required:

Calculate the dollar amount of the total direct labor variance for the month of April for Piece O' Rock Insurance Company and break down the total variance into the following components:

a. Direct labor price and efficiency variances.

b. Direct labor mix and yield variances.

(CMA adapted)

INTEGRATIVE CASES

21–30. Comprehensive Review of Variances, Mix Variances, Analysis of Differences between Budget and Actual

Sip-Fizz Bottling Company prepared a sales and production budget for the 48-ounce bottle, 12-ounce can, and 10-ounce bottle units that the company produces and sells. Unit variable costs per case of soda are calculated as follows:

	Per-Case Costs		
Ingredient	48 Ounce	12 Ounce	10 Ounce
Syrup	$1.45	$1.00	$ .80
CO_2 gas	.02	.01	.01
Crown	.04	—	.04
Bottle	1.40		.30
Can		1.64	
Label	.07		
Total manufacturing cost	2.98	2.65	1.15
Sales commission	.08	.14	.09
Advertising allowance	.08	.08	.08
Unit variable cost	$3.14	$2.87	$1.32

The advertising allowance is based on the number of cases sold. The selling price for the 48-ounce case is $5.40; for the 12-ounce case, $4.35; and for the 10-ounce case, $2.80. Sales for the month of November were forecasted at 70,000 cases of the 48-ounce bottles; 60,000 cases of 12-ounce cans; and 110,000 cases of 10-ounce bottles. Fixed costs were estimated at $175,000.

During November, actual sales amounted to 80,000 cases of 48-ounce bottles, 50,000 cases of 12-ounce cans, and 120,000 cases of 10-ounce bottles. Actual and budgeted selling prices were equal. Syrup costs were 10 percent greater than expected, but all other costs were at the same per-unit amount as indicated above. Total fixed costs, which are all other costs not explicitly identified above, amounted to $182,000.

The company uses variable costing for internal reporting purposes. There were no beginning and ending inventories.

Required:

a. Determine the budgeted and actual operating profits.

b. Explain the difference between the budgeted and actual net operating profits in as much detail as possible.

21–31. Dallas Consulting Group (Relate Activity Changes to Industry Effects)[1]

"I just don't understand why you're worried about analyzing our profit variance," said Dave Lundberg to his partner, Adam Dixon. Both Lundberg and Dixon were partners in the Dallas Consulting Group (DCG). "Look, we made $40,000 more profit than we expected (see Exhibit A). That's great as far as I am concerned," continued Lundberg. Adam Dixon agreed to come up with data that will help sort out the causes of DCG's $40,000 profit variance.

DCG was a professional services partnership of three established consultants who specialize in cost reduction through the use of time-motion studies and through the streamlining of production operations by optimizing physical layout, labor, and so on. In both of these areas, DCG consultants spend a great deal of time studying customers' operations.

The three partners each received fixed salaries that represented the largest portion of operating expenses. Each partner had an independent office and accounted for office costs separately. DCG itself had only a post office box. All other DCG employees were also paid fixed salaries. No other significant operating costs were incurred by the partnership.

Revenues consisted solely of professional fees charged to customers for the two different types of services. Charges were based on the number of hours actually

---

[1] Adapted from Robert Anthony, Glenn Welsch, and James S. Reece, *Fundamentals of Management Accounting*, 4th ed. (Homewood, Ill.: Richard D. Irwin, 1985).

Exhibit A (21–31)   **Budget and Actual Results**

	Budget	Actual	Variance
Sales revenues	$630,000	$670,000	$40,000
Expenses:			
Salaries	460,000	460,000	—
Income	$170,000	$210,000	$40,000

Exhibit B (21–31)   **Detail of Revenue Calculations**

Service[a]	Hours	Rate	Amount
Budget:			
A	6,000	$30	$180,000
B	9,000	50	450,000
	15,000		$630,000
Actual:			
A	2,000	$35	$ 70,000
B	12,000	50	600,000
	14,000		$670,000

[a] Service A = Time-motion studies. Service B = Consulting for production operations.

worked on a job. Thus, an increase in the actual number of hours worked on a job caused a corresponding increase in revenue. Since all salaries are fixed, however, DCG's total operating expenses do not change.

Following the conversation with Lundberg, Dixon gathered the data summarized in Exhibit B. He took the data with him to Lundberg's office and said, "I think I can identify several reasons for our increased profits. First of all, we raised the price for time-motion studies to $35 per hour. Also, if you remember, we originally estimated that the 10 consulting firms in the Dallas area would probably average about 15,000 hours of work each this year, so the total industry volume in Dallas would be 150,000 hours. However, a check with all of the local consulting firms indicates that the actual total consulting market must have been around 112,000 hours."

"This is indeed interesting, Adam," replied Lundberg. "These new data lead me to believe that there are several causes for our increased profits, some of which may have been negative. . . . Do you think you could quantify the effects of these factors in terms of dollars?"

Required: Use your knowledge of profit variance analysis to quantify this year's performance of DCG and explain the significance of each variance to Mr. Lundberg.

DECENTRALIZATION AND PERFORMANCE EVALUATION

LEARNING OBJECTIVES

1. Understand the role that accounting information plays in monitoring performance in complex organizations.

2. Learn the accounting-based methods used for evaluating performance of investment centers.

3. Know the impact of differences in the measurement of asset cost on accounting-based performance evaluation measures.

4. Analyze the differences between performance measures and capital investment criteria.

As organizations become large and complex, the manager's task grows increasingly difficult. A common rule of thumb is that one supervisor can usually manage about 10 subordinates. Consequently, managerial duties are delegated in all but very small organizations.

Accounting can play an important role in evaluating the performance of those who have been delegated organizational responsibility. The use of accounting for performance evaluation is often called **responsibility accounting.** Budgeting and variance analysis, as discussed in Chapters 17 through 21, are part of the responsibility accounting process. In this and the next chapter, we discuss the costs and benefits of decentralization, the structure of organizational units, and the accounting measures used to evaluate the performance of organizational units and their managers.

Responsibility Accounting A system of reporting tailored to an organizational structure so that costs and revenues are reported at the level having the related responsibility within the organization.

CONCEPTUAL FRAMEWORK

Principal-Agent Relationships The relationship between a superior, referred to as the principal, and a subordinate, called the agent.

When authority is decentralized, a superior, whom we call a *principal*, delegates duties to a subordinate, whom we call an *agent*. We find **principal-agent relationships** in many settings, including:

Principals	Agents
Stockholders	Top management
Corporate (top) managers	Divisional managers
Taxi company owner	Taxicab drivers
Retail store manager	Department managers

Many aspects of both financial and managerial accounting have been developed to help monitor agency relations. Accounting information enables principals to evaluate agents' performance and make decisions about their future employment prospects. In addition, accounting information is used in employment contracts. Employee commissions and bonuses are often based on accounting performance measures.

Thus, accounting information has a motivating effect. Agents who know that accounting information is used in their evaluation have incentives to make themselves "look good" on that basis. Sometimes, to make themselves look good, agents take actions that are not in the best interests of their company.

For example, a farm implement manufacturing company paid its sales managers commissions based on their sales to dealers. During an adverse economic period, the sales managers pressured dealers to make purchases with the provision that the company would take back any equipment not sold in six months. Sales rapidly rose, and production management increased output to meet the increased demand. The salespeople were paid substantial bonuses for improved performance. In the meantime, the equipment sat in the dealers' showrooms. At the end of the six-month period, the dealers returned substantial quantities of equipment to the manufacturer. The accounting performance measures—sales to dealers—did not represent the more significant performance measure of sales to final purchasers. Hence, the commissions were paid even though the equipment was never sold to a final buyer.

The key issue facing every principal is how to develop a cost-justified performance evaluation system that captures the relevant performance measure. If information was costless, principals would always prefer more information to less.[1] But information is not costless; there are costs to produce the information, and managers incur costs to process the information so they can use it. Indeed too much information can overwhelm a manager—leading to what is commonly referred to as **information overload.** So, principals must balance the cost of obtaining more information about an agent against the benefits of being better able to make decisions about the agent for future employment prospects and motivating the agent to take desired actions.

Information Overload A characteristic of too much data. The intended user is overwhelmed by the quantity of data supplied.

Goal Congruence

Goal Congruence When all members of a group hold a common set of objectives.

When all members of an organization have incentives to perform in the common interest, total **goal congruence** exists. This occurs when the group acts as a team in pursuit of a mutually agreed upon objective. Individual goal congruence occurs when an individual's personal goals are congruent with organizational goals.

While total congruence is uncommon, there are cases in which a strong team spirit suppresses individual desires to act differently. Examples include some military units and some athletic teams. Many companies attempt to achieve this espirit de corps. According to students of the Japanese management style, Japanese managers have created a strong team orientation among workers that has resulted in considerable goal congruence.

In most American business settings , however, personal goals and organizational goals differ. Employees and employers have different opinions of how much risk employees should take, how hard employees should work, and so forth. Performance evaluation and incentive systems are designed to encourage employees to *behave* as if their goals were congruent with organizational goals. This results in **behavioral congruence:** that is, an individual *behaves* in the best interests of the organization, regardless of his or her own goals.

Behavioral Congruence When individuals behave in the best interest of the organization regardless of their own goals.

Such behavioral congruence is also common in education. Examinations, homework, and the entire grading process are parts of a performance evaluation and incentive system that encourages students to behave in a certain manner. Sometimes the system appears to encourage the wrong kind of behavior, however. For example, if the goal of education is to encourage students to learn, they might be better off taking very difficult courses. But if students' grades suffer when they take difficult courses, they may have an incentive to take easier courses. As a result, some students take difficult courses and learn more, while others take easier courses in an attempt to maximize their grade-point averages.

Problems of this kind occur in all organizations whenever it is not in the employees' best interest to take actions that are also in the organization's best interest. Consider the case of a plant manager who believes that a promotion and bonus will result from high plant operating profits. Short-run

---

[1] See Steven Shavell, ''Risk Sharing and Incentives in the Principal and Agent Relationships,'' *The Bell Journal of Economics,* Spring 1979, pp 55–73.

profits will be lowered if the production line is closed for much-needed maintenance, but the company may be better off in the long run. The manager must decide between doing what makes the manager look good in the short run and doing what is in the best interest of the company.

Although such conflicts cannot be totally removed, if they are recognized, they can be minimized. To deal with the problem described above, some companies budget maintenance separately. Others encourage employees to take a long run interest in the company through stock-option and pension plans that are tied to long-run performance. Still others retain employees in a position long enough that any short-term counterproductive actions will catch up with them.

ORGANIZATIONAL STRUCTURE

Centralized   Refers to those organizations where decisions are made by a relatively few individuals in the high ranks of the organization.

Decentralized   Refers to those organizations where decisions are spread among relatively many divisional and departmental managers.

Some organizations are very **centralized:** decisions are handed down from the top, and subordinates carry them out. The military is a good example of centralized authority. At the other extreme are highly **decentralized** companies in which decisions are made at divisional and departmental levels. In many conglomerates, operating decisions are made in the field, while corporate headquarters is, in effect, a holding company.

The majority of companies fall between these two extremes. At General Motors, for example, operating units are decentralized, while the research and development and finance functions are centralized.

Many companies begin with a centralized structure but become more and more decentralized as they grow. Consider the following example of a fast-food franchise that started with one hamburger stand.[2]

> We had a counter and 10 stools when we started. When winter came, we had to take out two stools to put in a heating furnace and almost went broke from the loss of revenue! But during the following year, I obtained the statewide franchise for a nationally known barbecue chain, and I expanded my menu.
>
> At first, I did a little of everything—cooking, serving, bookkeeping, and advertising. I hired one full-time employee. There was little need for any formal management control system—I made all important decisions, and they were carried out. Soon we had eight outlets. I was still trying to manage everything personally. Decisions were delayed. A particular outlet would receive food shipments, but no one was authorized to accept delivery. If an outlet ran out of supplies or change, its employees had to wait until I arrived to authorize whatever needed to be done. With only one outlet, I was able to spend a reasonable amount of time on what I call high-level decision making—planning for expansion, arranging financing, developing new marketing strategies, and so forth. But with eight outlets, all of my time was consumed with day-to-day operating decisions.
>
> Finally, I realized that the company had grown too big for me to manage alone. So, I decentralized, setting up each outlet just like it was an independent operation. Now each outlet manager takes care of day-to-day operating decisions. Not only has this freed my time for more high-level decision making, but it also provides a better opportunity for the managers to learn about management, and it gives me a chance to evaluate their performance for promotion to higher management positions, which I intend to create soon.

---

[2] This example is based on an actual company for which one of the authors was a consultant.

Advantages of Decentralization

The larger and more complex an organization is, the greater the advantages of decentralization are. Some advantages of decentralization include:

1. *Faster response.* As described by the owner-manager of the fast food chain, local managers can react to a changing environment more quickly than can isolated top management. With centralized decision making, delays occur while information is transmitted to decision makers, and further delays occur while instructions are communicated to local managers.

2. *Wiser use of management's time.* The owner-manager of the fast-food chain complained that there was too little time for high-level decision making. Top management usually has a comparative advantage over middle management in this area. If their time is consumed by day-to-day operating decisions, they will be forced to ignore important strategic decisions. Furthermore, local managers may be able to make better operating decisions because of their technical expertise and knowledge about local conditions.

3. *Reduction of problems to manageable size.* There are limits to the complexity of problems that humans can solve.[3] Even with the aid of computers, some problems are too complex to be solved by central management. By dividing large problems into smaller, more manageable parts, decentralization reduces the complexity of problems.

4. *Training, evaluation, and motivation of local managers.* By decentralizing, managers receive on-the-job training in decision making. Top management can observe the outcome of local managers' decisions and evaluate their potential for advancement. By practicing with small decisions, managers learn how to make big decisions. Finally, ambitious managers are likely to be frustrated if they only implement the decisions of others and never have the satisfaction of making their own decisions and carrying them out. This satisfaction can be an important motivational reward for managers.

Disadvantages of Decentralization

While there are many advantages of decentralization, there are also disadvantages. The major disadvantage is that local managers may make decisions that are not congruent with the preferences of top management and constituents of the organization (such as stockholders). Thus, decentralized companies incur the cost of monitoring and controlling the activities of local managers. They incur the costs that result when local managers make decisions and take actions that are not in the best interest of the organization and are missed by the monitoring system.

A company must weigh the costs and benefits and decide on an economically optimal level of decentralization. One can assume that for organizations that are highly centralized, the disadvantages of decentralization outweigh the advantages, while the reverse is true for companies that are decentralized.

---

[3] This is often called bounded rationality. An excellent discussion is provided by Herbert A Simon, '' Rational Decision Making in Business Organizations,'' *The American Economic Review,* September 1979.

ORGANIZATION OF DECENTRALIZED UNITS

There are five basic kinds of decentralized units: cost centers, discretionary cost centers, revenue centers, profit centers, and investment centers. (A *center* is just a responsibility unit in an organization, such as a department in a store or a division of a company.)

Cost Centers

Cost Centers Organization subunits responsible only for costs.

In **cost centers,** managers are responsible for the cost of an activity for which there is a well-defined relationship between inputs and outputs. Cost centers are often found in manufacturing operations where inputs, such as direct materials and direct labor, can be specified for each output. The production departments of manufacturing plants are examples of cost centers. But the concept has been applied in nonmanufacturing settings too. In banks, for example, standards can be established for check processing, so check-processing departments might be cost centers. In hospitals, food services departments, laundries, and laboratories are often set up as cost centers.

Managers of cost centers are held responsible for the cost and volumes of inputs used to produce an output. Often these costs and volumes will be determined by someone other than the cost center manager, such as the marketplace, top management, or the marketing department. A plant manager is often given a production schedule to meet as efficiently as possible. If the plant is operated as a cost center, manufacturing cost variances like those discussed in Chapter 19 are typically used to help measure performance. (Illustration 22–1 shows how the cost center typically appears on the organization chart.)

Standard Cost Center An organization subunit where managers are held responsbible for costs and where the relationship between costs and output is well defined.

If the relationship between costs and outputs can be specified, the unit is called a **standard cost center.**

Discretionary Cost Centers

Discretionary Cost Center An organization unit where managers are held responsible for costs, but the relationship between costs and outputs is not well established.

The cost centers described above require a well-specified relationship between inputs and outputs for performance evaluation. When managers are held responsible for costs, but the input-output relationship is not well specified, a **discretionary cost center** is established. Legal, accounting, research and development, advertising, and many other administrative and marketing departments are usually discretionary cost centers (for example, see Illustration 22–1). Discretionary cost centers are also common in government and other nonprofit organizations where budgets are used as a ceiling on expenditures. Managers are usually evaluated on bases other than costs. However, there are usually penalties for exceeding the budget ceiling.

Revenue Centers

Revenue Center An organization subunit responsible for revenues and, typically, also for marketing costs.

Managers of **revenue centers** are typically responsible for marketing a product. Consequently, the manager is held responsible for revenue or contribution margin variances (see Chapters 18 and 21 for definitions of these variances). An example of a revenue center is the sportswear department of a large department store in which the manager is held responsible for merchandise sales.

Profit Centers

Managers of **profit centers** are held accountable for profits. They manage both revenues and costs (as shown in Illustration 22–1.) Managers of profit

Illustration 22-1   **Organization Structure and Responsibility Centers**

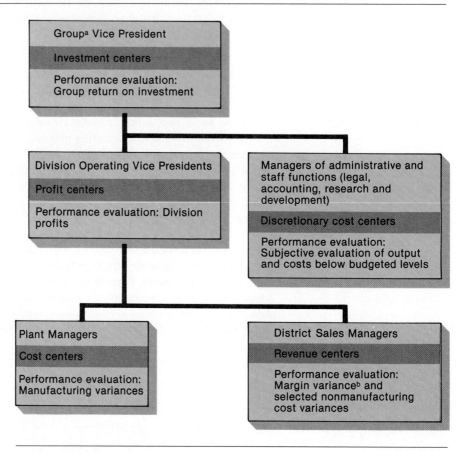

[a] "Group" refers to a group of divisions.

[b] Margin variances are based on the contribution margin (price minus variable cost) of the products sold.

Profit Center An organization subunit responsible for profits; usually responsible for revenues, costs, production, and sales volumes

centers have more autonomy than do managers of cost or revenue centers; thus, they sometimes have more status.

For example, a diversified company may organize its chemical manufacturing division as a cost center. However, if the company has its chemical operation organized so that chemical manufacturing and chemical marketing are both units within the chemical division, then the chemical division may be operated as a profit center. All revenues and costs of chemical division activities would be included in the performance evaluation basis. The manufacturing division would be a cost center. A profit center is evaluated based on a comparison of actual profits with planned profits. Profit variances are analyzed to support the evaluation decision.

Investment Centers

Managers of **investment centers** have responsibility for profits and investment in assets. These managers have relatively large amounts of money with which to make capital budgeting decisions. For instance, in one company, the manager of a cost center cannot acquire assets that cost more than

Investment Center
Organization sub-unit responsible for profits and for investment in assets.

$5,000 without approval from a superior, but an investment center manager can make acquisitions costing up to $500,000 without higher approval. Investment centers are evaluated using some measure of profits related to the invested assets in the center.

The Use of Responsibility Centers

A survey of the *Fortune* 1,000 largest industrial companies provided some interesting results about the use of responsibility centers.[4] Of the 620 companies that responded to the survey, 95.8 percent had profit centers or investment centers, and 74 percent had two or more investment centers. Investment centers were found in the majority of firms in all industries and for all sizes of companies with one exception: 56 percent of the companies in the smallest size category (sales less than $100 million) had no investment centers.

Responsibility Center A specific unit of an organization assigned to a manager who is held accountable for its operations and resources.

As depicted in Illustration 22–1, the form a **responsibility center** takes is closely related to its position in the organizational structure. For the company shown, plant managers run cost centers, and district sales managers operate revenue centers. Moving up the organizational chart, we find that division managers who are in charge of both plant managers and district sales managers have responsibility for profits.

Of course every company is organized uniquely (in some highly decentralized companies, manufacturing plants are profit centers, for example). However, it is generally true that a broader scope of authority and responsibility, hence profit or investment centers, is found at higher levels in an organization.

PERFORMANCE MEASUREMENT

We discussed performance measures for cost centers and revenue centers in Chapters 17 through 21. Here we examine performance measurement in discretionary cost centers, profit centers, and investment centers.

Performance Measurement in Discretionary Cost Centers

Discretionary costs, which may include research and development, accounting systems, and similar costs, are difficult to manage because their appropriate levels are difficult to determine. For the same reason, it is difficult to evaluate the performance of a discretionary cost center manager. Companies have tried numerous methods of determining appropriate relationships between discretionary costs and activity levels and comparison with other firms. But relating costs to activity levels remains primarily a matter of management judgment or discretion. Consequently, managers of **discretionary cost centers** are typically given a budget and instructed not to exceed it without higher-level authorization. In most governmental units, it is against the law to exceed the budget without obtaining authorization from a legislative body (Congress, the state legislature, the city council).

Discretionary Costs Costs that are difficult to relate to outputs.

Such a situation can invite suboptimal behavior. Managers have incentives to spend all of their budgets, even if some savings could be achieved, to support their request for the same or higher budgets in the following year.

---

[4] See James Reece and William Cool, "Measuring Investment Center Performance," *Harvard Business Review,* May–June 1978, pp. 28 ff.

Furthermore, there is often no well-specified relationship between the quality of services and costs. (Would the quality of research and development go down 10 percent with a 10 percent cut in funds? Would crime increase 10 percent if police department funds were cut 10 percent?)

Ideally, we want to measure performance in a well-specified way, as we do when comparing actual imputs to standard inputs in a cost center. But it is very difficult and costly to measure the performance of the manager and workers in a discretionary cost center. Thus, it is also hard to provide incentives for employees to perform at the levels that best achieve organizational goals.

Consequently, the budgets of discretionary cost centers are often based on negotiation and agreement between the cost center manager and top management. The budget then becomes a constraint on cost center operations. Cost center management is expected to perform as well as possible within the budget constraint. Top management often finds it pays to carefully pick discretionary cost center managers who are loyal to the organization and commited to helping achieve its objectives. These managers can be given considerable freedom with a high probability that they will not intentionally suboptimize.

Cost Cutting

Discretionary cost centers are prime targets for short-run cost cutting. It is easy to observe an immediate 10 percent cost savings, while the consequences may not be observed until the distant future, if ever. Therefore, when top management decides to cut costs, discretionary cost centers are often the first to be affected. On the other hand, when times are good, discretionary cost centers may receive a surplus of funds because of overoptimism about future prospects. As a result, managers of discretionary cost centers may try to build in some slack so that when funds are cut they can continue to provide at least minimal services. The manager of an accounting department put it this way: "When times are good, we spend a lot on employee training and recruiting, and we stock up on supplies and equipment. In tough times, we can cut out the frills and use up the excess supplies and equipment. This carries us through without drastically hurting our level of services." Whether this is the best way to manage remains an open question.[5]

Performance Measurement in Profit Centers

Decentralized organizations depend heavily on profit measures to evaluate the performance of decentralized units and their managers. Due to the difficulties of measuring profits, many companies have tried to use multiple measures of performance. In the early 1950s, General Electric proposed an extensive and innovative performance measurement system that evaluated market position, productivity, product leadership, personnel development, employee attitudes, public responsibility, and balance between short-range and long-range goals in addition to profitability. But even when a company

---

[5] See Michael Schiff and Arie Lewin, "The Impact of People on Budgets," *The Accounting Review*, April 1970, pp 259–69; and James March and Herbert Simon, *Organizations* (New York: John Wiley & Sons, 1958), Chaps. 5 and 6.

uses a broad range of performance measures, accounting results continue to play an important role in performance evaluation. A commonly heard adage is that "hard" measures of performance tend to drive out "soft" measures. Nevertheless, no accounting measure can fully measure the performance of an organizational unit or its manager.

In profit centers, we encounter the usual problems related to measuring profits for the company as a whole plus an important additional one: How are the company's revenues and costs allocated to each profit center? A profit center that is totally separate from all other parts of the company operates like an autonomous company. The profits of that kind of center can be uniquely identified with it.

But a completely independent profit center is a highly unusual case. Most profit centers have costs (and perhaps revenues) in common with other units. The profit center may share facilities with other units or use headquarters' staff services, for example. If so, the company faces a cost allocation problem (see Chapters 4 and 5).

A related problem involves the transfer of goods between a profit center and other parts of the organization. Such goods must be priced so that the profit center manager has incentives to trade with other units when it is in the best interests of the organization. Chapter 23 discusses this transfer pricing problem in more detail.

There are no easy ways to determine how to measure performance in a profit center. Much is left to managerial judgment. Whatever the process chosen, its objectives should be straightforward: measure employees' performance in ways that motivate them to work in the best interest of their employers and compare that performance to standards or budget plans.

Performance Measurement in Investment Centers

Return on Investment (ROI)
The ratio of profits to investment in the asset that generates those profits.

Managers of investment centers are responsible for profits and investment in assets. They are evaluated on their ability to generate a sufficiently high **return on investment (ROI)** to justify the investment in the division.

This return on investment (ROI) is computed as follows:

$$ROI = \frac{\text{Operating profits}}{\text{Investment center assets}}$$

It is often divided into *profit margin* and *asset turnover* parts, as follows:

$$ROI = \text{Profit margin} \times \text{Asset turnover}$$

$$= \frac{\text{Operating profit}}{\text{Sales}} \times \frac{\text{Sales}}{\text{Investment center assets}}$$

$$= \frac{\text{Operating profit}}{\text{Investment center assets}}$$

The profit margin is a measure of the investment center's ability to control its costs for a given level of revenues. The lower the costs required to generate a dollar of revenue, the higher the profit margin.

The asset turnover ratio is a measure of the investment center's ability to generate sales for each dollar of assets invested in the center.

Relating profits to capital investment is an intuitively appealing concept. Capital is a scarce resource. If one unit of a company shows a low return, the capital may be better employed in another unit where the return is higher, or invested elsewhere or paid to stockholders.

Relating profits to investment also provides a scale for measuring performance. For example, investment A generated $200,000 in operating profits, while investment B generated $2 million. But investment A required a capital investment of $500,000, while investment B required an investment of $20 million. As you can see from the following calculation, return on investment (ROI) provides a different picture from operating profits.

| | Investment | |
	A	B
1. Operating profits	$200,000	$ 2,000,000
2. Investment	500,000	20,000,000
3. Return on investment (1) ÷ (2)	40%	10%

Although ROI is a commonly used performance measure, it has its limitations. The many difficulties of measuring profits affect the numerator, while problems in measuring the investment base affect the denominator. Consequently, it is difficult to make precise comparisons among investment centers.

Measuring Investment Center Assets and Profits

Each company is likely to measure an investment center's operating profits and assets in somewhat different ways. For example, Reece and Cool found that 40 percent of the companies that had investment centers defined investment center profits consistently with the way net income is calculated for shareholder reporting. However, many companies did not assess income taxes, allocate corporate administrative costs, or allocate interest on corporate debt to investment centers.

Companies also differ in the assets that they assign to an investment center. Reece and Cool asked which assets were included in the calculation of an investment center's asset base and found the following assets were included by the indicated percentage of companies[6].

Asset	Percentage Included
Cash	63%
Receivables	94
Inventories	95
Land and buildings used solely by the investment center	94
Allocated share of corporate headquarter's assets	16

---

[6] Reece and Cool, op. cit.

Most companies define an asset base that is easily understandable and approximates the assets that the investment center manager is accountable for. Including assets in the base encourages managers to manage those assets.

Choice of Measure: ROI versus Residual Income

ROI evaluation is widely used in companies. However, the method has some drawbacks. Some contend that if managers are encouraged to maximize ROI, they may turn down investment opportunities that are above the minimum acceptable rate for the corporation but below the rate their center is currently earning. For example, suppose that a corporation has a cost of capital of 15 percent. A division has an opportunity to make an additional investment that will return $400,000 per year for a $2 million investment. The ROI for this project is 20 percent (which is $400,000 ÷ $2,000,000), so the project qualified at the corporate level in meeting ROI targets. Assuming the project meets all other corporate requirements, it should be accepted. However, the manager of the division in which the investment would take place may reject the investment if the division's ROI is greater than 20 percent. For example, suppose that the center currently earns:

$$\text{ROI} = \frac{\$1,000,000}{\$4,000,000} = 25 \text{ percent}$$

With the new investment, ROI would be:

$$\text{ROI} = \frac{\$1,000,000 + \$400,000}{\$4,000,000 + \$2,000,000} = 23.3 \text{ percent}$$

Because a comparison of the old and new returns would imply that performance had worsened, the center's manager might hesitate to make such an investment, even though the investment would have a positive benefit for the company as a whole.

An alternative is to measure **residual income (RI)**. Residual income is defined as:

Residual Income (RI) The excess of actual profit over the profit targeted for an organization subunit.

$$\text{Investment center operating profits} - (\text{Capital charge} \times \text{Investment center assets})$$

where the capital charge is the minimum acceptable rate of return.

Using the numbers from the previous example, we can see the impact of the investment in additional plant capacity on residual income. Before the investment:

$$
\begin{aligned}
\text{RI} &= \$1,000,000 - (.15 \times \$4,000,000) \\
&= \$1,000,000 - \$600,000 \\
&= \underline{\underline{\$400,000}}
\end{aligned}
$$

The residual income from the additional investment in plant capacity is:

$$
\begin{aligned}
\text{RI} &= \$400,000 - (.15 \times \$2,000,000) \\
&= \$400,000 - \$300,000 \\
&= \underline{\underline{\$100,000}}
\end{aligned}
$$

Hence, after the additional investment, the residual income of the division will increase to:

$$RI = (\$1,000,000 + \$400,000) - [.15 \times (\$4,000,000 + \$2,000,000)]$$
$$= \$1,400,000 - (.15 \times \$6,000,000)$$
$$= \$1,400,000 - \$900,000$$
$$= \underline{\underline{\$500,000}}$$

The additional investment in plant capacity *increases* residual income, appropriately improving the measure of performance.

Most managers recognize the weakness of ROI and take it into account when ROI is lowered by a new investment. This may partially explain why residual income does not dominate ROI as a performance measure. Moreover, residual income is not the net income reported to shareholders. Thus, it may be a less familiar concept for managers than operating profits or divisional net income. In addition, ROI is expressed as a percentage that can be compared with related percentages—like the cost of capital, the prime interest rate, and the Treasury bill rate. Most companies studied by Reece and Cool use ROI.[7] Only 2 percent used residual income alone, while 28 percent used both ROI and residual income.

For the remainder of this section, we use ROI for illustrative purposes, but the issues we discuss apply equally to ROI and residual income.

Measuring the Investment Base

Three issues are frequently raised in measuring investment bases: (1) Should *gross* book value be used? (2) Should investment in assets be valued at historical cost or current value? and (3) Should investment be measured at the beginning or at the end of the year? While no method is inherently right or wrong, some may have advantages over others. Further, it is important to understand how the measure of the investment base will affect ROI.

Gross Book versus Net Book Value

Suppose that a company uses straight-line depreciation for a physical asset with a 10-year life and no salvage value.

The cost of the asset does not change; it is the same in Year 3 as in Year 1. Illustration 22–2 compares ROI under net book value and gross book value for the first three years. For simplicity, all operating profits before depreciation in the computation are assumed to take place at the end of the year, and ROI is based on year-end value of the investment.

Note that the ROI increases each year under the net book value method even though no operating changes take place. This occurs because the numerator remains constant, while the denominator decreases each year as depreciation accumulates.

Critics contend that if these ROI numbers are used naively, investment center managers have incentives to postpone replacing assets longer than economically wise because their ROI will go down on replacement. In addition, the net book value method makes a center with old assets look

---

[7] Ibid.

Illustration 22-2

The Impact of Net Book versus Gross Book Value Methods on ROI (in thousands)

Facts: Operating profits before depreciation (all in cash flows at end of year):
Year 1, $100; Year 2, $100; and Year 3, $100.

Asset cost at *beginning* of Year 1, $500. The only asset is depreciable, with a 10-year life and no salvage value. Straight-line depreciation is used. The straight-line rate is 10% per year. The denominator in the ROI calculations is based on *end*-of-year asset values.

Year	Net Book Value	Gross Book Value
1	$ROI = \dfrac{\$100^a - (.1 \times \$500)^b}{\$500^c - (.1 \times \$500)^d}$	$ROI = \dfrac{\$50}{\$500}$
	$= \dfrac{\$50}{\$450} = \underline{\underline{11.1\%}}$	$= \underline{\underline{10\%}}$
2	$ROI = \dfrac{\$100 - (.1 \times \$500)}{\$450 - (.1 \times \$500)}$	$ROI = \dfrac{\$50}{\$500}$
	$= \dfrac{\$50}{\$400} = \underline{\underline{12.5\%}}$	$= \underline{\underline{10\%}}$
3	$ROI = \dfrac{\$100 - (.1 \times \$500)}{\$400 - (.1 \times \$500)}$	$ROI = \dfrac{\$50}{\$500}$
	$= \dfrac{\$50}{\$350} = \underline{\underline{14.3\%}}$	$= \underline{\underline{10\%}}$

[a] The first term in the numerator is the annual cash operating profit.

[b] The second term in the numerator is depreciation for the year.

[c] The first term in the denominator is the beginning-of-the-year value of the assets used in the investment base.

[d] The second term in the denominator reduces the beginning-of-year value of the asset by the amount of current year's depreciation.

[e] $50 = $100 − ($500 × .1). Companies sometimes use only cash flows in the numerator.

better than a comparable center with new assets. As one manager told us: "The secret is to get into a center just after assets have been bought and run until it's time to replace them. ROI is at a peak then because there is very little investment base. Then transfer to another center that has new assets. Of course, the poor fellow that follows you has to replace assets and watch ROI plummet." While such a strategy may work, we suspect the opportunities for such game playing are relatively few. Moreover, if top management is observant, a manager playing such a strategy should be detected after relatively few moves.

Historical Cost versus Current Cost

The previous example assumed no inflation. Working with the same facts, assume that the current replacement cost of the asset increases 20 percent per year, as do operating cash flows. Illustration 22–3 compares ROI under historical cost and **current cost.**

Current Cost   Cost to replace or rebuild an existing asset.

Note that ROI increases each year under the historical cost methods even though no operating changes take place. This occurs because the numerator is measured in current dollars to reflect current cash transactions, while the denominator and depreciation charges are based on historical cost. The current cost—gross book value method—reduces the effect by adjusting

Facts: Operating profits before depreciation (all in cash flows at end of year):
   Year 1, $100; Year 2, $120; and Year 3, $144.
   Annual rate of price changes is 20 percent.
   Asset cost at *beginning* of Year 1 is $500. The only asset is depreciable with a 10-year life and no salvage value. Straight-line depreciation is used; the straight line rate is 10 percent per year. The denominator in the ROI computation is based on *end*-of-year asset value.

Year	**Historical Cost Net Book Value** (1)	**Current Cost Net Book Value** (2)

Year 1:

$$\text{Historical: ROI} = \frac{\$100^a - (.1 \times \$500)^b}{\$500^c - (.1^f \times \$500)^d}$$

$$= \frac{\$50}{\$450} = 11.1\%$$

$$\text{Current: ROI} = \frac{\$100 - (.1 \times \boxed{1.2^e} \times \$500)}{\boxed{1.2^e} \times \$500 - (.1 \times \boxed{1.2^e} \times \boxed{\$500})}$$

$$= \frac{\$100 - 60}{\$600 - 60} = \frac{\$40}{\$540} = 7.4\%$$

Year 2:

$$\text{Historical: ROI} = \frac{\$120 - (.1 \times \$500)}{\$500 - (.2^f \times \$500)}$$

$$= \frac{\$70}{\$400} = 17.5\%$$

$$\text{Current: ROI} = \frac{\$120 - (.1 \times \boxed{1.2} \times \boxed{\$600})}{\boxed{1.2} \times \boxed{\$600} - (.2^f \times \boxed{1.2} \times \boxed{\$600})}$$

$$= \frac{\$120 - 72}{\$720 - 144} = \frac{\$48}{\$576} = 8.3\%$$

Year 3:

$$\text{Historical: ROI} = \frac{\$144 - (.1 \times \$500)}{\$500 - (.3^f \times \$500)}$$

$$= \frac{\$94}{\$350} = 26.9\%$$

$$\text{Current: ROI} = \frac{\$144 - (.1 \times \boxed{1.2} \times \boxed{\$720})}{\boxed{1.2} \times \boxed{\$720} - (.3^f \times 1.2 \times \boxed{\$720})}$$

$$= \frac{\$144 - 86.4}{\$864 - 259.2} = \frac{\$57.6}{\$604.8} = 9.5\%$$

Historical Cost Gross Book Value (3)	**Current Cost Gross Book Value** (4)

Year 1:

$$\text{Historical: ROI} = \frac{\$100 - 50}{\$500}$$

$$= \frac{\$50}{\$500} = 10\%$$

$$\text{Current: ROI} = \frac{\$100 - 60}{(\boxed{1.2} \times \$500)}$$

$$= \frac{\$40}{\$600} = 6.7\%$$

Year 2:

$$\text{Historical: ROI} = \frac{\$120 - 50}{\$500}$$

$$= \frac{\$70}{\$500} = 14\%$$

$$\text{Current: ROI} = \frac{\$120 - 72}{(\boxed{1.2} \times \boxed{\$600})}$$

$$= \frac{\$48}{\$720} = 6.7\%$$

Year 3:

$$\text{Historical: ROI} = \frac{\$144 - 50}{\$500}$$

$$= \frac{\$94}{\$500} = 18.8\%$$

$$\text{Current: ROI} = \frac{\$144 - 86.4}{(\boxed{1.2} \times \boxed{\$720})}$$

$$= \frac{\$57.6}{\$864} = 6.7\%$$

Note: Boxed amounts in the current cost computations are the cause of differences between current cost and historical cost methods.

[a] The first term in the numerator is the annual operating profit before depreciation.

[b] The second term in the numerator is depreciation for the year.

[c] The first term in the denominator is the beginning of the first year value of the assets used in the investment base.

[d] The second term in the denominator reduces the beginning-of-year value of the asset by the amount of accumulated depreciation.

[e] This term (1.2) adjusts the beginning-of-year asset value to the end-of-year value (current value).

[f] This term reduces the net book value of the asset. The replacement cost is reduced by 10 percent for depreciation at the end of Year 1, by 20 percent at the end of Year 2, and by 30 percent at the end of Year 3.

both the depreciation in the numerator and the investment base in the denominator to reflect price changes: Measuring current costs can be a difficult and expensive task, however, so there is a trade-off in the choice of performance measures.

We derived a level ROI in the current cost, gross book value method because the asset and all other prices increased at the same rate. If inflation affecting cash flows in the numerator increases faster than the current cost of the asset in the denominator, then ROI will increase over the years until asset replacement, under the current cost method. Of course, ROI will decrease over the years until asset replacement if the denominator increases faster than the numerator.

Although current cost may seem to be a superior measure of ROI, recall that there is no single right or wrong measure. In fact, Reece and Cool reported that 85 percent of the companies with investment centers used historical cost net book value.[8] In many cases, more than one half of the assets in the denominator are current assets which are not subject to these distortions.

In general, how a performance measure is used is more important than how it is calculated. All of the measures we have presented can offer useful information. As long as the measurement method is understood, it can enhance performance evaluation.

Beginning, Ending, or Average Balance

An additional problem arises in measuring the investment base for performance evaluation. Should the base be the beginning, ending or average balance? Using the beginning balance may encourage asset acquisitions early in the year to increase income for the entire year. Asset dispositions would be encouraged at the end of the year to reduce the investment base for next year. If end-of-year balances are used, similiar incentives exist to manipulate purchases and dispositions. Average investments would tend to minimize this problem although it may be more difficult to compute. In choosing an investment base, management must balance the costs of the additional computations required for average investment against the potential negative consequences of using the beginning or ending balances.

Comparing the Performance of Investment Centers

A company is often tempted to compare the performance of its investment centers and even to encourage competition among them. The problems inherent in ROI measurement complicate such comparisons. In addition, investment centers may be in very different businesses. It is very difficult to compare the performance of a manufacturing center with the performance of a center that provides consulting service and has a relatively small investment base. Differences in the riskiness of investment centers should also be taken into account. We recommend that when comparing the performance of investment centers these systematic differences should be considered.

---

[8] Ibid.

When there are diverse investment centers, management will frequently establish target ROIs for the individual investment centers. The investment center will be evaluated by comparing the actual ROI with the target ROI. Such a comparison procedure is similar to the budget versus actual comparisons that are made for cost centers, revenue centers, and profit centers. It sometimes makes more sense to compare the ROI of an investment center with a company in the same industry than to compare it with other investment centers in its company.

Evaluating Managers versus Evaluating Centers

The evaluation of a manager is not necessarily identical to the evaluation of the cost, profit, or investment center. As a general rule, managers are evaluated based on a comparison of actual results to targets. A manager who is asked to take over a marginal operation and turn it around may be given a minimal ROI target, consistent with the past performance of the division. If the manager meets or exceeds that target, the manager would be rewarded. However, it may be that even with the best management, a division cannot be turned around. Thus, it is entirely possible that the center would be disbanded even though the manager had received a highly positive evaluation. In addition, top management would like to reward the manager that performs well in an adverse situation but, conversely, should be willing to bail out of a bad operation if a better use can be made of company resources. Today, the **controllability concept** is widely used as a basis for managerial performance.

Controllability Concept The idea that managers should be held responsible for costs or profits over which they have decision-making authority.

An interesting problem arises in implementing this concept in an ongoing division. How does one evaluate the performance of a manager who takes over an existing division where the assets, operating structure, and markets are established prior to the manager's arrival at the helm? The new manager cannot control the fact that certain assets are on hand, nor can the new manager control the markets in which the division operates at the time the manager takes over. However, in time, the new manager can change all of these factors.

As a general rule, evaluating the manager on the basis of performance targets, as suggested earlier in this chapter, overcomes this problem. The new manager establishes a plan for operating the division and works with top management to set targets for the future. Those targets are compared to actual results as the plan is enacted, and the manager is evaluated based on those results. In short, the longer the manager is at the division, the more responsibility the manager takes for its success.

Performance Measures and Capital Investment Criteria

Neither return on investment nor residual income take into account the *timing* of the cash flows for a project. If two projects cost the same and yield the same cash flows, their ROI and RIs will be the same regardless of the time lag between the time of investment and start-up of the project. This problem is particularly acute in high-technology enterprises which often require substantial early investment and long time lags before operations commence.

Sixties Corp. has two divisions: Tie Division and Dye Division. The Tie Division invested $700 million in a pharmaceutical venture in 1984. This venture did not begin earning income until 1990. Cash flows were slightly less then expected. Cash flows (before-tax) are $165 million per year, and profits are $107 million per year. The profits are equal to the cash flows less depreciation of the initial investment. Depreciation is based on the straight-line method, 12-year life, and no salvage value, and equals $58 million per year. The cash flow and profit levels attained in 1990 are expected to continue for 12 years. Sixties Corp.'s before-tax cost of capital is 10 percent.

Scheduling the cash flows from this investment over the 12 years indicates that the net present value of the project is a negative $2 million. This is based on the method shown in Chapter 15.[9] Tie Division's ROI is equal to 15.29 percent, which is $107 million ÷ $700 million. Residual income for the division based on a 10 percent capital cost charge is $37 million, which equals $107 million less $700 million × .10.

Dye Division invested $1 billion in 1989 to acquire a developed and licensed pharmaceutical operation. The acquisition is expected to yield cash flows (before-tax) of $165 million per year for 12 years. When Dye Division management presented the investment proposal to Sixties Corp. management, they pointed out that the project would have a net present value of $124 million using the 10 percent discount rate. The $1 billion cost of the acquisition is fully depreciable over 12 years using the straight-line method. At the end of 1990, Sixties Corp. called Dye Division management in to find out why the project was not performing "up to snuff" according to Sixties Corp.'s performance evaluation criteria.

Since the Dye Division project has a higher net present value than the Tie Division project, what has gone amiss? Dye Division's profits are only $82 million per year, which is the $165 million cash flows minus $1 billion ÷ 12 years. ROI is only 8.2 percent which is $82 million ÷ $1 billion. Residual income is $82 million − $100 million or −$18 million.

The performance measures do not reflect the same criteria as used in the net present value calculations. Thus, even though Dye Division's project has a greater net present value, the ROI and residual income are lower because

---

[9] Present value calculations were performed using a spreadsheet program.

REAL WORLD APPLICATION

To encourage long-term growth, 3M Company requires that at least 25 percent of each division's sales come from products developed within the past five years. Adding this criterion to the performance profile of a division encourages managers to invest in longer term projects and take risks to invest in projects that may have an adverse impact on short-term performance indicators but will enable the company to stay competitive in the long run. 3M also provides incentives for innovation including allowing all employees to spend 15 percent of their time on innovative projects, encouraging employee feedback on any aspect of company performance, sharing of technology across divisions, and providing "seed" grants for employees to develop new products. 3M's program and corporate culture result in the company having a worldwide reputation for innovation. 3M's approach is being studied by other companies, and many of its programs have been implemented by these companies.

the project was acquired at a higher price. The timing of cash flows because Dye Division's project was acquired in 1989 whereas Tie Division's project was acquired in 1984 does not enter the ROI or RI calculations. In this case, the performance measures give different signals than the net present value calculations. Here the annual cash flows and life of the investment are identical. In actual applications, these factors differ, which makes the comparisons more difficult.

Nonfinancial Performance Measures

Financial performance measures such as return on investment and residual income are usually insufficient measures of performance when taken alone. Recent studies identified the short-term focus of management as a detrimental factor in the decline of the competitiveness of U.S. industry. ROI and RI are short-term performance measures. In addition, financial statistics do not tell the whole story about a division's operations. For these reasons, many companies have developed nonfinancial performance measures to encourage division managers to take actions consistent with other corporate goals.

In highly automated manufacturing environments, quality control is extremely important. Defective goods can generate costly damage to sensitive equipment as well as result in customer dissatisfaction. Incorporating rejection, rework, and defective goods rates into the performance profile tends to minimize the incidence of defects and serves to encourage managers to meet quality control requirements at the risk of lowering division returns in the short run.

A company can tailor a performance measurement system to include nonfinancial as well as financial measures into its profile of divisional activities. By covering all significant aspects of company goals into the performance system, a company can advance corporate goals beyond the short-term focus which ROI and RI measures encourage.

SUMMARY

Performance evaluation is usually based on a responsibility accounting system. The key factor in establishing a performance evaluation system is to encourage all segments of an organization to act to attain common organization goals. The evaluation system must be cost-effective. There is a great diversity in organization structures, ranging from highly centralized to highly decentralized organizations. We presume the degree of centralization is established to optimize the balance between the costs of decentralization and the benefits.

Organization subunits may be organized as cost centers, discretionary cost centers, revenue centers, profit centers, or investment centers. The basis for evaluation of each type of center is designed to capture the activities that are under the control of the center manager. Cost centers, revenue centers, and profit centers are usually evaluated based on a comparison of actual performance with budgeted goals. Investment centers are evaluated on the basis of the efficiency with which the assets employed in the center are used to generate profits. The usual form of measurement for investment centers is return on investment (ROI).

Managers are typically evaluated by comparing established performance targets with actual results. Centers are evaluated using an opportunity to cost approach. Hence, a manager can excel in the management of a mediocre center, and conversely, a manager could receive a poor evaluation in a highly profitable center. In general, top managers match the performance measurement system with the factors that are under the control of the center or of the manager of the center. This promotes evaluation based on the factors that the manager or center can use to impact results.

TERMS AND CONCEPTS

The following terms and concepts should be familiar to you after reading this chapter.

Behavioral Congruence	**Investment Center**
Centralized	**Principal-Agent Relationship**
Controllability Concept	**Profit Center**
Cost Centers	**Residual Income (RI)**
Current Cost	**Responsibility Accounting**
Decentralized	**Responsibility Center**
Discretionary Cost Centers	**Return on Investment (ROI)**
Discretionary Costs	**Revenue Center**
Goal Congruence	**Standard Cost Center**
Information Overload	

SUPPLEMENTARY READINGS

Dearden, John. "Measuring Profit Center Managers." *Harvard Business Review,* September–October 1987, pp 84–88

Demski, J. S. "Optimal Performance Measurement." *Journal of Accounting Research,* Autumn 1972, pp 243–58.

Edwards, James B. *Uses of Performance Measures.* Montvale, N.J.: National Association of Accountants, 1986.

Groves, T., And M. Loeb. "Incentives in Divisionalized Firms." *Management Science,* March 1979, pp 221–30.

Hopwood, A. G. "An Empirical Study of the Role of Accounting Data in Performance Evaluation." *Journal of Accounting Research,* Supplement 1972.

McGee, Robert W. "Measuring Divisional Performance . . . Three Companies . . . Three Approaches." *Controller's Quarterly,* 2, no. 1(1986), pp. 23–26.

McNair, C. J., and W. Mosconi. "Measuring Performance in an Advanced Manufacturing Environment." *Management Accounting,* July 1987, pp. 28–31.

Reece, J. S., and W. R. Cool. "Measuring Investment Center Performance." *Harvard Business Review,* May–June 1978.

Solomons, D. *Divisional Performance Measurement and Control.* Homewood, Ill: Richard D. Irwin, 1968.

Vancil, R. F. *Decentralization: Managerial Ambiguity by Design.* Homewood, Ill: Dow Jones-Irwin, 1979.

SELF-STUDY PROBLEM NO. 1

The Mars Division of Hyperspace Company has assets of $1.4 billion, operating profits of $.35 billion, and a cost of capital of 30 percent.

Required:

Compute ROI and residual income

SOLUTION TO SELF-STUDY PROBLEM NO. 1

$$\text{ROI} = \frac{\$.35 \text{ billion}}{\$1.4 \text{ billion}} = 25\%$$

$$\text{RI} = \$.35 \text{ billion} - (.30 \times \$1.4 \text{ billion})$$
$$= \$.35 \text{ billion} - .42 \text{ billion}$$
$$= -\$.07 \text{ billion (that is, a residual}$$
$$\text{``loss'' of \$70 million)}$$

SELF-STUDY PROBLEM NO. 2

Current Value versus Historical Cost

The E. Division of E. T. Enterprises acquired depreciable assets costing $2 million. The cash flows from these assets for three years were as follows:

Year	Cash Flow
1	$500,000
2	600,000
3	710,000

The current cost of these assets was expected to increase 25 percent per year. Depreciation of these assets for internal managerial purposes was 10 percent per year; the assets have no salvage value. The denominator in the ROI calculation is based on *end-of-year asset values*.

Required:

Compute the ROI for each year under each of the following methods:

a. Historical cost, net book value.

b. Historical cost, gross book value.

c. Current cost, net book value.

d. Current cost, gross book value.

SOLUTION TO SELF-STUDY PROBLEM NO. 2

(a) and *(b)* historical cost:

Year	Net Book Value	Gross Book Value
1	$\text{ROI} = \dfrac{\$500,000 - (.10 \times \$2,000,000)^a}{\$2,000,000 - (.10 \times \$2,000,000)}$	$\text{ROI} = \dfrac{\$300,000}{\$2,000,000}$
	$= \dfrac{\$300,000}{\$1,800,000} = 16.7\%$	$= 15\%$
2	$\text{ROI} = \dfrac{\$600,000 - (.10 \times \$2,000,000)}{\$1,800,000 - (.10 \times \$2,000,000)}$	$\text{ROI} = \dfrac{\$400,000}{\$2,000,000}$
	$= \dfrac{\$400,000}{\$1,600,000} = 25\%$	$= 20\%$
3	$\text{ROI} = \dfrac{\$710,000 - (.10 \times \$2,000,000)}{\$1,600,000 - (.10 \times \$2,000,000)}$	$\text{ROI} = \dfrac{\$510,000}{\$2,000,000}$
	$\dfrac{\$510,000}{\$1,400,000} = 36.4\%$	$= 25.5\%$

(c) and *(d)* current cost:

Year	Net Book Value	Gross Book Value
1	$\text{ROI} = \dfrac{\$500{,}000 - (.10 \times 1.25^b \times \$2{,}000{,}000)}{(1.25 \times \$2{,}000{,}000) - (.10^c \times 1.25 \times \$2{,}000{,}000)}$	$\dfrac{\$250{,}000}{\$2{,}500{,}000}$
	$= \dfrac{\$500{,}000 - \$250{,}000}{\$2{,}500{,}000 - \$250{,}000} = \underline{\underline{11.1\%}}$	$= \underline{\underline{10\%}}$
2	$\text{ROI} = \dfrac{\$600{,}000 - (.10 \times 1.25 \times \$2{,}500{,}000)}{(1.25 \times \$2{,}500{,}000) - (.20^c \times 1.25 \times \$2{,}500{,}000)}$	$\dfrac{\$287{,}500}{\$3{,}125{,}000}$
	$= \dfrac{\$600{,}000 - \$312{,}500}{\$3{,}125{,}000 - \$625{,}000} = \underline{\underline{11.5\%}}$	$= \underline{\underline{9.2\%}}$
3	$\text{ROI} = \dfrac{\$710{,}000 - (.10 \times 1.25 \times \$3{,}125{,}000)}{(1.25 \times \$3{,}125{,}000) - (.30^c \times 1.25 \times \$3{,}125{,}000)}$	$\dfrac{\$319{,}375}{\$3{,}906{,}250}$
	$= \dfrac{\$710{,}000 - \$390{,}625}{\$3{,}906{,}250 - \$1{,}171{,}875}$	$= \underline{\underline{8.2\%}}$
	$= \dfrac{\$319{,}375}{\$2{,}734{,}375} = \underline{\underline{11.7\%}}$	

[a] The first term in the numerator is annual cash flow; the second term in the numerator is annual depreciation; the first term in the denominator is the beginning-of-year net book value of the asset; the second term in the denominator reduces the beginning-of-year value by the amount of the current year's depreciation.

[b] This term increases asset value to replacement cost.

[c] This reduces the net book value of the asset by 10 percent after one year, by 20 percent after two years, and by 30 percent after three years.

QUESTIONS

22–1. Accounting is supposed to be a neutral, relevant, and objective measure of performance. Why would problems arise when applying accounting measures to performance evaluation contexts?

22–2. A company prepares the master budget by taking each division manager's estimate of revenues and costs for the coming period and entering the data into the budget without adjustment. At the end of the year, division managers are given a bonus if their division profit is greater than the budget. Do you see any problems with this system?

22–3. Is top management ever an agent in a principal-agency relationship as discussed in the chapter?

22–4. Is middle management ever a principal in a principal-agency relationship as discussed in the chapter?

22–5. Sales managers in a company were paid on an incentive system based on the number of units sold to ultimate buyers (that is, the units were not likely to be returned except if defective). How might that incentive system lead to dysfunctional consequences?

22–6. XYZ Division of Multitudenous Enterprises, Inc., produces and sells blank video disks. The division is evaluated based on income targets. The company uses the same measure of income for division performance evaluation as for external reporting. What problems, if any, can you envision in this performance evaluation system?

22–7. You overhear the comment, " This whole problem of measuring performance for segment managers using accounting numbers is so much hogwash. We pay our managers a good salary and expect them to do the best possible job. At least with our system there is no incentive to play with the account-ing data.'' Does the comment make sense?

22-8. What are the advantages of using an ROI-type measure rather than the absolute value of division profits as a performance evaluation technique?

22-9. Under what conditions would the use of ROI measures inhibit goal-con-gruent decision making by a division manager?

22-10. The chapter suggested there might be some problems in the use of residual income. Can you suggest what some of those problems might be?

22-11. Using historical costs of assets in the ROI denominator is a mismatch of current revenues and costs in the numerator with the denominator. This problem may be corrected by using current costs in the denominator. No changes need be made to the numerator. How do you feel about this suggestion?

22-12. Central management of Holdum, Inc., evaluated divisional performance using residual income measures. The division managers were ranked accord-ing to the residual income in each division. A bonus was paid to all division managers with residual income in the upper half of the ranking. The bonus amount was in proportion to the residual income amount. No bonus was paid to managers in the lower half of the ranking. What biases might arise in this system?

22-13. Parsed Phrases Corporation entered into a loan agreement that contained the provision that Parsed Phrases would be required to make additional interest payments if its net income fell below a certain dollar amount. Immediately after the agreement was signed, the FASB instituted a new accounting requirement that caused Parsed's income to fall below the requirements. Absent the accounting change, Parsed would have met the income require-ment.

(a) Should the pre-change or post-change income number be used to deter-mine if Parsed should pay the additional interest charge? Why or why not?

(b) Would your answer in (a) change if Parsed had entered into a manage-ment contract that provided that the new manager would be paid a bonus based on achieving certain income levels (but, after his taking office, the accounting rules changed so that the manager could never achieve those agreed-upon income levels)?

22-14. Management of division A is evaluated based on residual income measures. The division can either rent or buy a certain asset. Might the performance evaluation technique have an impact on the rent-or-buy decision? Why or why not?

22-15. What impact does the use of gross book value or net book value in the investment base have on the computation of ROI?

22-16. ''Every one of our company's divisions has a return on investment that is in excess of our cost of capital. Our company must be a blockbuster.'' Com-ment on this statement.

22-17. Bleak Prospects, Inc. found that its market share was slipping. Division managers were encouraged to maximize return on investment and made decisions consistent with that goal. Nonetheless, there were frequent cus-tomer complaints, with resulting loss of business. Moreover, Bleak de-pended on an established product line and was unable to find new products for expansion, while its competitors seemed to be able to generate new products almost yearly. What would you suggest Bleak Products' manage-ment do to improve its situation?

EXERCISES

22–18 Compute Residual Income and ROI
(L.O.2.)

Required:

22–19 ROI versus Residual Income
(L.O.2.)

Required:

22–20 Compare Alternative Measures of Division Performance
(L.O.2)

Required:

22–21 Impact of New Project on Performance Measures
(L.O.2)

Required:

22–22 Impact of Leasing on Performance Measures
(L.O.2)

Required:

22–23 Residual Income Measures and New Project Consideration
(L.O.2)

Required:

Des Moines Division of The Iowa Corporation has assets of $1.4 million. During the past year, the division had profits of $250,000. Iowa Corporation has a cost of capital of 14 percent.

a. Compute the division ROI.

b. Compute the division residual income.

A division is considering acquisition of a new asset. The asset will cost $160,000 and have a cash flow of $70,000 per year for each of the five years of its life. Depreciation is computed on a straight-line basis with no salvage value.

a. What is the ROI for each year of the asset's life if the division uses beginning-of-year asset balances, net book value for the computation?

b. What is the residual income each year if the cost of capital is 25 percent?

The following data are available for two divisions in your company:

	East Division	West Division
Division operating profit	$ 75,000	$ 500,000
Division investment	200,000	2,000,000

The cost of capital for the company is 20 percent.

a. Which division had the better performance? Why?

b. Would your evaluation change if the company's cost of capital was 25 percent?

A division manager is considering the acquisition of a new asset that will add to profit. The division is expected to earn $750,000 on other assets of $2.7 million. The company's cost of capital is 20 percent. The new investment has a cost of $450,000 and will have a yearly cash flow of $167,000. The asset will be depreciated using the straight-line method over a six-year life and is expected to have no salvage value. The new asset meets the company's discounted cash flow investment criteria. Division performance is measured using an investment base of the original cost of division assets.

a. What is the division ROI before acquisition of the new asset?

b. What is the division ROI after acquisition of the new asset?

The division manager in exercise 22–21 has the option of leasing the asset on a year-to-year lease. The lease payment would be $145,000 per year, and all depreciation and other tax benefits would accrue to the lessor.

What is the division ROI if the asset is leased?

Consider the investment project detailed in exercises 22–21 and 22–22.

a. What is the division's residual income before considering the project?

b. What is the division's residual income if the asset is purchased?

c. What is the division's residual income if the asset is leased?

22–24 Compare Historical Cost, Net Book Value to Gross Book Value
(L.O.3)

Raiders Division of Shark Company just started operations. It purchased depreciable assets costing $1 million and having an expected life of four years, after which the assets can be salvaged for $200,000. In addition, the division has $1 million in assets that are not depreciable. After four years, the division will have $1 million available from these nondepreciable assets. In short, the division has invested $2 million in assets that will last four years, after which it will salvage $1.2 million. Annual cash operating flows are $400,000. In computing ROI, this division uses *end-of-year* asset values in the denominator. Depreciation is computed on a straight-line basis, recognizing the salvage values noted above.

Required:

a. Compute ROI, using net book value.

b. Compute ROI, using gross book value.

22–25 Compute ROI Using Beginning-of-Year Asset Values
(L.O.3)

Assume the same data as in exercise 22–24, except the division uses *beginning-of-year* asset values in the denominator for computing ROI.

Required:

a. Compute ROI, using net book value.

b. Compute ROI, using gross book value.

c. If you worked exercise 22–24, compare these results with those from 22–24. How different is the ROI computed using end-of-year asset values, as in 22–24, from the ROI using beginning-of-year values, as in this exercise?

22–26 Compare Current Cost to Historical Cost
(L.O.3)

Assume the same data as in exercise 22–24, except all cash flows increase 10 percent at the end of the year. This has the following effect on the assets' replacement cost and annual cash flows:

End of Year	Replacement Cost	Annual Cash Flow
1	$2,000,000 × 1.1 = $2,200,000	$400,000 × 1.1 = $440,000
2	$2,200,000 × 1.1 = $2,420,000	$440,000 × 1.1 = $484,000
⋮	Etc.	Etc.

Required:

a. Compute ROI, using historical cost, gross book value.

b. Compute ROI, using historical cost, net book value.

c. Compute ROI, using current cost, gross book value.

d. Compute ROI, using current cost, net book value.

22–27 Effects of Current Cost on Performance Measurements
(L.O.3)

A division acquired an asset with a cost of $200,000 and a life of four years. The cash flows from the asset considering the effects of inflation were scheduled as:

Year	Cash Flow
1	$60,000
2	70,000
3	79,000
4	80,000

The current cost of the asset is expected to increase at a rate of 10 percent per year, compounded each year. Performance measures are based on gross values.

Required:

a. What is the ROI for each year of the asset's life, using a historical cost approach?

b. What is the ROI for each year of the asset's life if both the investment base and depreciation are based on the current cost of the asset at the start of each year?

22–28 ROI, Residual Income, and Net Present Value
(L.O.4)

Eighties Co. invested $1 billion in an asset in 1985 to develop a patented laser measurement process. Eighties Co. established its Yuppie Division to operate the laser operation. Delays caused by patent infringement litigation prevented the start-up of operations until the beginning of 1991. Before-tax cash flows that year equalled $550 million. This cash flow is expected to continue annually through the end of 1995. At the end of the project life, the asset will have no value. The $1 billion asset is depreciated using straight-line and a five year life starting in 1991.

In 1990, Eighties Co. established its Porcha Division. The Porcha Division was off to a fast start in a low-technology plastics operation. Porcha invested $1.5 billion in a plastics molding plant. Before-tax cash flows from the plant total $550 million per year and are expected to continue annually for each of the five years beginning in 1991. The $1.5 billion asset is depreciated using straight-line over five years starting in 1991. It will have no value at the end of five years.

Eighties Co. uses the straight-line method for depreciation. The company has a before-tax cost of capital of 15 percent and evaluates divisions based on return on investment and residual income. The company evaluates divisions on the basis of return on initial investment (that is, annual before-tax net income divided by $1 billion for Yuppie and by $1.5 billion for Porcha).

Required:

a. Which division's project has the greater net present value?

b. Which division has the greater ROI and RI?

c. If the rankings differ, how is this explained?

22–29 ROI, Residual Income, and Net Present Value
(L.O.4)

Sound Enterprises is a conglomerate located on the shore of the Gulf of Siam. Sound invested $800,000 in Container Shipping in 1984. Due to a glut in the availability of ships, Container Shipping had no positive cash flows until 1990. At that time, Container obtained a five-year charter for its entire fleet. The charter provides Container with annual before-tax cash flows of $400,000. Since Container believes that the ships will have no value after that date, Container is depreciating the $800,000 over the five years using the straight-line method and no salvage value starting in 1990.

Sound Enterprises became impatient with the problems at its shipping subsidiary. In 1988, it formed Herring Fisheries, S.A., and invested $1.2 million to acquire fishing rights and to charter ships. Herring Fisheries began operations in 1990. Cash flows are $450,000 per year and are expected to continue for five years. At the end of five years, the fishing rights and charters will expire. Hence, the investment cost of $1.2 million is being depreciated straight-line over a five-year period starting in 1990. The company evaluates divisions on the basis of return on initial investment. (that is, annual before-tax net income divided by $800,000 for Container Shipping and $1.2 million for Herring). The cost of capital (before-tax) is 15 percent.

Required:

a. Which subsidiary's project has the greater net present value?

b. Which subsidiary has the greater ROI and RI?

c. If the rankings differ, how is this explained?

PROBLEMS

22–30 Equipment Replacement and Performance Measures

You have been appointed manager of an operating division of HI-TECH, Inc., a manufacturer of products using the latest microprocessor technology. Your division has $800,000 in assets and manufactures a special chip assembly. On January 2 of the current year, you invested $1 million in automated equipment for chip assembly. At that time, your expected income statement was:

Sales revenue	$3,200,000
Operating costs:	
Variable	400,000
Fixed (all cash)	1,500,000
Depreciation:	
New equipment	300,000
Other	250,000
Division operating profit	$ 750,000

On October 25 you were approached by a sales representative from Mammoth Machine Company. Mammoth offers a new assembly machine at a cost of $1.3 million that offers significant improvements over the equipment you bought on January 2. The new equipment would expand department output by 10 percent while reducing cash fixed costs by 5 percent. The new equipment would be depreciated for accounting purposes over a three-year life. Depreciation would be net of the $100,000 salvage value of the new machine. The new equipment meets your company's 20 percent cost of capital criterion. If you purchase the new machine, it must be installed prior to the end of the year. For practical purposes, though, you can ignore depreciation on the new machine because it will not go into operation until the start of the next year.

The old machine must be disposed of to make room for the new machine. The old machine has no salvage value.

Your company has a performance evaluation and bonus plan based on ROI. The return includes any losses on disposals of equipment. Investment is computed based on the end-of-year balance of assets, net book value.

Required:

a. What is your division's ROI if the new machine is not acquired?

b. What is your division's ROI this year if the new machine is acquired?

c. If the new machine is required and operates according to specifications, what ROI would be expected for next year?

22–31 Evaluate Trade-offs in Return Measurement

As a division manager of HI-TECH, Inc. (problem 22–30), you are still assessing the problem of whether to acquire the Mammoth Machine Company's machine. You learn that the new machine could be acquired next year. However, if you wait until next year, the new machine will cost 15 percent more than this year's price. The salvage value would still be $100,000. Other costs or revenue estimates would be apportioned on a month-by-month basis for the time each machine is in use. Fractions of months may be ignored.

Required:

a. When would you want to purchase the new machine if you wait until next year?

b. What are the costs that must be considered in making this decision?

22–32 Analyze Performance Report for Decentralized Organization

Bio-grade Products manufactures animal feeds and feed supplements. The need for a widely based manufacturing and distribution system has led to a highly decentralized management structure. Each divisional manager is responsible for production and distribution of corporate products in one of eight geographical areas of the country.

Residual income is used to evaluate divisional managers. The residual income for each division equals each division's contribution to corporate profits before taxes less a 20 percent investment charge on a division's investment base. The investment base of each division is the sum of its year-end balances of accounts receivable, inventories, and net plant fixed assets (cost less accumulated deprection). Corporate policies dictate that divisions minimize their investments in receivables and inventories. Investments in plant fixed assets are a joint division/corporate decision based on proposals made by divisional plant managers, available corporate funds, and general corporate policy.

Alex Williams, divisional manager for the Southeastern Sector, prepared the Year 2 and preliminary Year 3 budgets for his division late in Year 1. Final approval of the Year 3 budget took place in late Year 2, after adjustments for trends and other information developed during Year 2. Preliminary work on the Year 4 budget also took place at that time. In early October of Year 3, Williams asked the divisional controller to prepare a report that presents performance for the first nine months of Year 3. The report is reproduced in Exhibit A below.

Required:

a. Evaluate the performance of Alex Williams for the nine months ending September Year 3. Support your evaluation with pertinent facts from the problem.

Exhibit A (22-32)

BIO-GRADE PRODUCTS—SOUTHEASTERN SECTOR
(in thousands)

	Year 3			Year 2	
	Annual Budget	**Nine-Month Budget**[a]	**Nine-Month Actual**	**Annual Budget**	**Actual Results**
Sales	$2,800	$2,100	$2,200	$2,500	$2,430
Divisional costs and expenses:					
Direct materials and labor	1,064	798	995	900	890
Supplies	44	33	35	35	43
Maintenance and repairs	200	150	60	175	160
Plant depreciation	120	90	90	110	110
Administration	120	90	90	90	100
Total divisional costs and expenses	1,548	1,161	1,270	1,310	1,303
Divisional margin	1,252	939	930	1,190	1,127
Allocated corporate fixed costs	360	270	240	340	320
Divisional profits	$ 892	$ 669	$ 690	$ 850	$ 807
	Budgeted Balance 12/31/Year 3	**Budgeted Balance 9/30/Year 3**	**Actual Balance 9/30/Year 3**	**Budgeted Balance 12/31/Year 2**	**Actual Balance 12/31/Year 2**
Divisional investment:					
Accounts receivable	$ 280	$ 290	$ 250	$ 250	$ 250
Inventories	500	500	650	450	475
Plant fixed assets (net)	1,320	1,350	1,100	1,150	1,100
Total	$2,100	$2,140	$2,000	$1,850	$1,825

[a] Bio-grade's sales occur uniformly throughout the year.

b. Identify the features of Bio-grade Products' divisional performance measurement reporting and evaluating system that need to be revised if it is to effectively reflect the responsibilities of the divisional managers.

(CMA adapted)

22-33 ROI and Management Behavior

Notewon Corporation is a highly diversified and decentralized company. Each division is responsible for its own sales, pricing, production, costs of operations, and the management of accounts receivable, inventories, accounts payable, and use of existing facilities. Cash is managed by corporate headquarters.

Divisional executives are responsible for presenting investment proposals to corporate management. Proposals are analyzed and documented at corporate headquarters. The final decision to commit funds for investment purposes rests with corporate management.

The corporation evaluates division executive performance by the ROI measure. The asset base is composed of fixed assets employed plus working capital exclusive of cash. The ROI performance of a division executive is the most important appraisal factor for salary changes. In addition, each executive's annual performance bonus is based on ROI results, with increases in ROI having a significant impact on the amount of the bonus.

Notewon Corporation adopted the ROI performance measure and related compensation procedures about 10 years ago. The corporation seems to have benefited from the program. The ROI for the corporation as a whole increased during the first years of the program. Although the ROI continued to grow in each division, corporate ROI has declined in recent years. The corporation has accumulated a sizable amount of short-term marketable securities in the past three years.

Corporate management is concerned about the increase in the short-term marketable securities. A recent article in a financial publication suggested that the use of ROI was overemphasized by some companies, with results similar to those experienced by Notewon.

Required:

a. Describe the specific actions division managers might have taken to cause the ROI to grow in each division but decline for the corporation. Illustrate your explanation with appropriate examples.

b. Explain, using the concepts of goal congruence and motivation of divisional executives, how Notewon Corporation's overemphasis on the use of the ROI measure might result in the recent decline in the corporation's return on investment and the increase in cash and short-term marketable securities.

c. What changes could be made in Notewon Corporation's compensation policy to avoid this problem? Explain your answer.

(CMA adapted)

22-34. Impact of Decisions to Capitalize or Expense on Performance Measurement

Oil and gas companies inevitably incur costs on exploration ventures that are unsuccessful. These ventures are called dry holes. There is a continuing debate over whether those costs should be written off as period expense or whether they should be capitalized as part of the full cost of finding profitable oil and gas ventures. PMX Drilling Company has been writing these costs off to expense as incurred. However, this year a new management team was hired to improve the profit picture of PMX's oil and gas exploration division. The new management team was hired with the provision that they would receive a bonus equal to 10 percent of any profits in excess of base-year profits of the division. However, no bonus would be paid if profits were less than 20 percent of end-of-year investment. The following information was included in the performance report for the division:

	This Year	Base Year	Increase over Base Year
Sales revenues	$4,100,000	$4,000,000	
Costs incurred:			
Dry holes	–0–	800,000	
Depreciation and other amortization	780,000	750,000	
Other costs	1,600,000	1,550,000	
Division profit	$1,720,000	$ 900,000	$820,000
End-of-year investment	$8,100,000*	$6,900,000	

*Includes other investments not at issue here.

During the year, the new team spent $1 million on exploratory activities, but $900,000 was spent on ventures that were unsuccessful. The new management team has included the $900,000 in the current end-of-year investment base because, they state, "You can't find the good ones without hitting a few bad ones."

Required:

a. What is the ROI for the base year and the current year?

b. What is the amount of the bonus that the new management team is likely to claim?

c. If you were on the board of directors of PMX, how would you respond to the new management's claim for the bonus?

22–35. Evaluate Performance Evaluation System: Behavioral Issues

ATCO Company purchased Dexter Company three years ago. Prior to the acquisition, Dexter manufactured and sold electronic products to third-party customers. Since becoming a division of ATCO, Dexter now manufactures electronic components only for products made by ATCO's Macon Division.

ATCO's corporate management gives the Dexter Division management considerable latitude in running the division's operations. However, corporate management retains authority for decisions regarding capital investments, product pricing, and production quantities.

ATCO has a formal performance evaluation program for all division managements. The evaluation program relies substantially on each division's return on investment. The income statement of Dexter Division provides the basis for the evaluation of Dexter's divisional management. (See income statement below.)

Division financial statements are prepared by the corporate accounting staff. Corporate general services costs are allocated on the basis of sales dollars, and the computer department's actual costs are apportioned among the divisions on the basis of use. The net division investment includes division fixed assets at net book value (cost less depreciation), division inventory, and corporate working capital apportioned to the divisions on the basis of sales-dollars.

ATCO COMPANY
Dexter Division
Income State ent
For the Year Ended October 31
(in thousands)

Sales revenue		$4,000
Costs and expenses:		
Product costs:		
Direct materials	$ 500	
Direct labor	1,100	
Factory overhead	1,300	
Total	2,900	
Less: Increase in inventory	350	2,550
Engineering and research		120
Shipping and receiving		240
Division administration:		
Manager's office	210	
Cost accounting	40	
Personnel	82	332
Corporate costs:		
General services	230	
Computer	48	278
Total costs and expenses		3,520
Divisional operating profit		$ 480
Net plant investment		$1,600
Return on investment		30%

Required:

a. Discuss the financial reporting and performance evaluation program of ATCO Company as it relates to the responsibilities of the Dexter Division.

b. Based on your response to requirement (a), recommend appropriate revisions of the financial information and reports used to evaluate the performance of Dexter's divisional management. If revisions are not necessary, explain why revisions are not needed.

(CMA adapted)

22–36. Divisional Performance Measurement: Behavioral Issues

Division managers of SIU Incorporated have been expressing growing dissatisfaction with SIU's methods used to measure divisional performance. Divisional operations are evaluated every quarter by comparison with the master budget prepared during the prior year. Division managers claim that many factors are completely out of their control but are included in this comparison. This results in an unfair and misleading performance evaluation.

The managers have been particularly critical of the process used to establish standards and budgets. The annual budget, stated by quarters, is prepared six months prior to the beginning of the operating year. Pressure by top management to reflect increased earnings has often caused divisional managers to overstate revenues and/ or understate expenses. In addition, once the budget is established, divisions must "live with the budget." Frequently, external factors such as the state of the economy, changes in consumer preferences, and actions of competitors have not been recognized in the budgets that top management supplied to the divisions. The credibility of the performance review is curtailed when the budget cannot be adjusted to incorporate these changes.

Top management, recognizing these problems, agreed to establish a committee to review the situation and to make recommendations for a new performance evaluation system. The committee consists of each division manager, the corporate controller, and the executive vice president. At the first meeting, one division manager outlined an Achievement of Objectives System (AOS). In this performance evaluation system, divisional managers are evaluated according to three criteria:

1. Doing better than last year. Various measures are compared to the same measures of the prior year.

2. Planning realistically. Actual performance for the current year is compared to realistic plans and/or goals.

3. Managing current assets. Various measures are used to evaluate the divisional management's achievements and reactions to changing business and economic conditions.

One division manager believed this system would overcome many of the inconsistencies of the current system because divisions could be evaluated from three different viewpoints. In addition, managers would have the opportunity to show how they would react and account for changes in uncontrollable external factors.

Another manager cautioned that the success of a new performance evaluation system would be limited unless it had the complete support of top management.

Required:

a. Explain whether the proposed AOS would be an improvement over the measure of divisional performance now used by SIU Incorporated.

b. Develop specific performance measures for each of the three criteria in the proposed AOS that could be used to evaluate divisional managers.

c. Discuss the motivational and behavioral aspects of the proposed performance system. Also, recommend specific programs that could be instituted to promote morale and give incentives to divisional management.

(CMA adapted)

22–37. ROI, Residual Income, Different Asset Bases

The manager of the Spears Department Store in Evanston is evaluated using return on investment. Spears headquarters requires that return on investment of 10 percent of assets employed. For the coming year, the manager estimates that revenues will equal $260,000. Cost of merchandise sold will equal $163,000. Operating expenses for this level of sales are expected to equal $26,000. Investment in the store assets is $187,500 before considering the following proposal.

The manager was approached by a representative of Sly Trading Company about carrying Sly's line of sporting goods. This line is expected to generate $75,000 in sales in the coming year at the Spears store with a merchandise cost of $57,000. Operating expenses for this additional line of merchandise are $8,500 per year. To carry the line of goods, an inventory investment of $55,000 is required. Sly is willing to floor plan the merchandise so that the Spears store will not have to invest in any inventory. The cost of floor planning would be $6,750 per year. Spears marginal cost of capital is 10 percent.

Required:

a. What is the Evanston Spears store's expected ROI for the coming year if the Sly sporting goods are not carried in the store?

b. What is the store's expected ROI if the manager invests in the Sly inventory and carries the sporting goods merchandise?

c. What would the store's expected ROI be if the manager elected to take the floor plan option?

d. Would the manager prefer *a.*, *b.*, or *c.*, above? Why?

INTEGRATIVE CASES

22–38. Evaluate Investment Choice and Its Impact on Performance Measures, with Joint Costs

Amberina, Inc., operates several different semiautonomous divisions. A problem arose with respect to two divisions that process and sell plastics products. The Plastics Blending Division obtains materials that it blends and, as a result of a joint process, splits into Phyrene and Extrene. The Plastics Blending Division processes the Phyrene further and sells the resulting product to the outside. The Extrene is sold to the Tools Division, where it is molded into tool handles and sold.

In a typical year, $240,000 of costs are incurred in the blending of the feedstock. Phyrene is processed further at a cost of $80,000 and is then sold to the outside at a price of $325,000. Extrene is sold to the Tools Division at "cost plus 20 percent," where cost is determined on the basis of net realizable value at the split-off point. The Tools Division incurs an additional cost of $60,000 to mold the plastic and sells the resulting tool handles for $175,000.

The company's cost of capital is 15 percent. The Plastics Blending Division has assets of $240,000, while the Tools Division has assets of $120,000.

The Tools Division learned that it could purchase the company that it is selling the handles to and, thus, obtain the ability to manufacture complete tools. The additional processing costs would amount to $61,000 per year, and revenues would amount to $360,000. In addition, depreciation expenses would be incurred based on the amount spent to purchase the tool manufacturing company. The manufacturing company is asking $265,000 for its assets. These assets would be depreciated on a straight-line basis for internal reporting purposes.

The assets are expected to last five years and have no salvage value. Tax depreciation would be as follows: Year 1, $35,000; Year 2, $80,000; Years 3–5, $50,000 per year. In addition, $50,000 in working capital would be required to operate the tool manufacturing plant. Income taxes are 40 percent of net income before taxes.

Required:

The head of the Tools Division wants your assessment of the feasibility of the investment in terms of (a) net present value of the project and (b) the impact of the project on the Tools Division return on investment. You may assume that if the tool manufacturing plant is acquired, there is no alternative market for the tool handles.

22–39. Capital Investment Analysis and Decentralized Performance Measurement[10]

The following exchange occurred just after a capital investment proposal was rejected at Diversified Electronics.

Ralph Browning (Product Development): I just don't understand why you rejected my proposal. This new investment is going to be a sure money maker for the Residential Products division. We can expect to make $230,000 on it annually before tax.

Sue Gold (Finance): I am sorry that you are upset with our decision, but this product proposal just does not meet our short-term ROI target of 15 percent after tax.

Ralph Browning: I'm not so sure about the ROI target, but it goes a long way toward increasing our earnings-per-share.

Phil Carlson (executive vice president): Ralph, you are right, of course, about the importance of earnings per share. However, we view our three divisions as investment centers. Proposals like yours must meet our ROI targets. It is not enough that you show an earnings-per-share increase.

Sue Gold: We believe that our company should increase its return on investment, especially given the interest rates we have had to pay recently. This is why we

---

[10] J. M. Lim, M. W. Maher, and J. S. Reece, copyright © 1991.

have targeted 15 percent as the appropriate minimum ROI for each division to earn next year.

Phil Carlson: If it were not for the high interest rates and poor current economic outlook, Ralph, we would not be taking such a conservative position in evaluating new projects. This past year has been particularly rough for our industry. Our two major competitors had ROIs of 10.8 and 12.3 percent. Though our ROI of 10.9 percent after tax was reasonable (see Exhibit C), performance varied from division to division. Professional Services did very well with 15 percent ROI, while the Residential Products Division managed just 11 percent. The performance of the Aerospace Products Division was especially dismal, with an ROI of only 7 percent. We expect divisions in the future to carry their share of the load.

Chris McGregor (Aerospace Products): My division would be showing much higher ROI if we had a lot of old equipment like the Residential Products or relied heavily on human labor like Professional Services.

Phil Carlson: I don't really see the point you are trying to make, Chris.

Diversified Electronics was a growing company in the electronics industry. (See Exhibits A, B, and C for financial data.) Diversified Electronics has three divisions—Residential Products, Aerospace Products, and Professional Services—each of which accounts for about one third of Diversified Electronics' sales. Residential Products, the oldest division, produces furnace thermostats and similar products. The Aerospace Products Division is a large "job shop" that builds electronic devices to customer specifications. A typical job or batch takes several months to complete. About one half of Aerospace Products' sales are to the U.S. Defense Department. The newest of the three divisions, Professional Services, provides consulting engineering services. This division has shown tremendous growth since its acquisition by Diversified Electronics four years ago.

Each division operates independently of the others and is treated essentially as a separate entity. Many of the operating decisions are made at the division level. Corporate management coordinates the activities of the various divisions, which includes review of all investment proposals over $400,000.

Exhibit A (22–39)

DIVERSIFIED ELECTRONICS
Statement of Operating Profits
For 19A and 19B
(in thousands)

	Year Ended December 31	
	19A	**19B**
Sales	$141,462	$148,220
Cost of goods sold	108,118	113,115
Gross margin	33,344	35,105
Selling and general	13,014	13,692
Profit before taxes and interest	20,330	21,413
Interest expense	1,190	1,952
Operating profit before taxes	19,140	19,461
Income tax expense	7,886	7,454
Operating profit after taxes	$ 11,254	$ 12,007

Exhibit B (22-39)

DIVERSIFIED ELECTRONICS
Balance Sheets
For 19A and 19B
(in thousands)

	December 31	
	19A	**19B**
Assets		
Cash and temporary investments	$ 1,404	$ 1,469
Accounts receivable	13,688	15,607
Inventories	42,162	45,467
Total current assets	57,254	62,543
Plant and equipment:		
Original cost	107,326	115,736
Accumulated depreciation	42,691	45,979
Net plant and equipment	64,635	69,757
Investments and other assets	3,143	3,119
Total assets	$125,032	$135,419
Liabilities and Owner's Equity		
Accounts payable	$ 10,720	$ 12,286
Taxes payable	1,210	1,045
Current portion of long-term debt	—	1,634
Total current liabilities	11,930	14,965
Deferred income taxes	559	985
Long-term debt	12,622	15,448
Total liabilities	25,111	31,398
Common stock	47,368	47,368
Retained earnings	52,553	56,653
Total owner's equity	99,921	104,021
Total liabilities and owner's equity	$125,032	$135,419

Exhibit C (22-39)

DIVERSIFIED ELECTRONICS
Ratio Analysis
For 19A and 19B

19A

$$\text{Average tax rate} = \frac{\$7,886}{\$19,140}$$
$$= .412$$

$$\text{ROI} = \frac{\$20,330 \ (1 - 0.412)}{\$12,622 + \$99,921}$$
$$= \frac{\$11,954}{\$112,543}$$
$$= 10.6 \text{ percent}$$

19B

$$\text{Average tax rate} = \frac{\$7,454}{\$19,461}$$
$$= .383$$

$$\text{ROI} = \frac{\$21,413 \ (1 - 0.383)}{\$1,634 + \$15,448 + \$104,021}$$
$$= \frac{\$13,212}{\$121,103}$$
$$= 10.9 \text{ percent}$$

Exhibit D (22–39)　　　　**Financial Data for New Product Proposal—Diversified Electronics**

1. Projected asset investment[a]
Cash	$200,000
Plant and equipment[b]	800,000
Total	$1,000,000

2. Cost data, before taxes (first year):
Variable cost per unit	$3.00
Differential fixed costs[c]	170,000

3. Price/market estimate (first year):
Unit price	$7.00
Sales	100,000 Units

4. Taxes: The company assumes a 40 percent tax rate for investment analyses. Assume that depreciation of plant and equipment for tax purposes will be taken as follows: Year 1, $100,000; Year 2, $300,000; Years 3–5: $200,000 per year. Taxes are paid for taxable income in Year 1 at the end of Year 1; taxes for Year 2, at the end of Year 2; and so on.

5. Inflation is assumed to be 10 percent per year and applies to revenues and all costs except depreciation. A 10 percent increase in cash investment is needed at the end of each year.

---

[a] Assumes sales of 100,000 units.

[b] Annual capacity of 120,000 units.

[c] Includes straight-line depreciation on new plant and equipment. Plant and equipment are expected to last eight years and to have no net salvage value at the end of eight years.

Diversified Electronic's measure of return on investment is defined as the division's operating profit before taxes and interest times one minus the income tax rate divided by investment. The investment is defined as interest-bearing debt plus owners' equity. (Calculations of ROI for the company are shown in Exhibit C.) Each division's expenses include a portion of corporate administrative expenses allocated on the basis of divisional revenues.

The details of Ralph Browning's rejected product proposal are shown in Exhibit D.

Required:

a. Why did corporate headquarters reject Ralph Browning's product proposal? Was their decision the right one? Would they have rejected the proposal if they had used the net present value (NPV) method? The company uses a 15 percent cost of capital (that is, hurdle rate) in evaluating projects such as these.

b. Evaluate the manner in which Diversified Electronics implemented the investment center concept. What pitfalls did they apparently not anticipate? What, if anything, should be done with regard to the investment center approach and the use of ROI as a measure of performance?

c. What conflicting incentives for managers can occur between the use of a yearly ROI performance measure and NPV for capital budgeting?

TRANSFER PRICING

LEARNING OBJECTIVES

1. Compute and use transfer prices in decentralized organizations.

2. Understand the behavioral issues and incentive effects of alternative transfer pricing systems.

3. Know economic consequences of transfer prices when third parties are affected by a transfer pricing system.

4. See how transfer prices are used in a financial reporting context.

When goods or services are transferred from one unit of an organization to another, the transaction is recorded in the accounting records. The value assigned to the transaction is called the *transfer price*. Considerable discretion can be used in putting a value on the transaction because this exchange takes place inside the organization. Transfer prices are widely used for decision making, product costing, and performance evaluation; hence, it is important to consider alternative transfer pricing methods and their advantages and disadvantages.

TRANSFER PRICING IN DECENTRALIZED ORGANIZATIONS

Transfer Price The price at which goods or services are traded between organization subunits.

Responsibility for decision making rests at lower levels of the organization in decentralized organizations. Relatively autonomous responsibility centers buy from, and sell to, each other. At General Motors, for example, it is common for one division to buy direct materials from a number of suppliers, including other divisions of General Motors. In effect, responsibility centers buy and sell from each other. The **transfer price** *is the price (or cost) assigned to the goods or services transferred.* It becomes a cost to the buyer and revenue to the seller division. If the divisions are evaluated based on some measure of profitability that includes these transfer-price-based costs and revenues, then setting the transfer price can have an impact on the reported performance measures and, hence, on the performance evaluation of each division. For example, the higher the transfer price, the more profitable the selling division (from higher revenues) and the less profitable the buying division, all other things equal.

Recording a Transfer

Division A of Shockless Power Company makes a motor that is purchased by division B, which manufactures refrigerators. When the motors are sold or transferred, their cost becomes a part of the cost of goods sold for division A. If they are sold to an outside buyer, the cash or receivable exchanged for the motors becomes revenue to division A. Likewise, if division A transfers motors to division B, some recognition of the transfer will be made on the books of division A. If the motors are transferred at cost, then division A would obtain no profit from the transfer. In a decentralized organization, the internal transfer is often priced at the market value of the goods transferred.

For example, let's assume that division A can sell the motors or transfer them to division B at a price of $50 per motor. The inventory cost of the motors is $40 each. This cost includes a variable manufacturing cost of $30 and allocated fixed manufacturing costs of $10 per motor. The transfer of 2,000 motors from division A to division B would be recorded on division A's books as:

Receivable from Division B	100,000	
Sales Revenue		100,000
Cost of Goods Sold	80,000	
Finished Goods Inventory		80,000

With this entry, division A would have a recorded gross margin of $20,000 from the transfer of motors to division B.

On division B's books, the receipt of the 2,000 motors from division A would be recorded as:

Direct Materials Inventory   100,000
    Payable to Division A   100,000

For evaluating the performance of each individual division, these costs and revenues would be used as the basis for profit measurement. However, for external financial reporting purposes, any interdivisional profits are eliminated to avoid double counting in the financial statements.

Recording the transfer of goods and services is a straightforward accounting procedure. The more difficult problem is determining the appropriate transfer price, as discussed next.

SETTING TRANSFER PRICES

The value placed on transferred goods and services is used *to make it possible to transfer goods and services between divisions while allowing them to retain their autonomy.*[1] The transfer price can be a device *to motivate managers to act in the best interest of the company.*

Aligning Division Managers' Incentives with Those of the Company

As might be expected, a conflict can arise between the company's interests and an individual manager's interests when transfer-price-based performance measures are used. The following example demonstrates such a conflict.

The production division of Ace Electronics Company was operating below capacity. The assembly division of the same company received a contract to assemble 10,000 units of a final product, XX-1. Each unit of XX-1 required one part, A-16, which was made by the production division. Both divisions are decentralized, autonomous investment centers and are evaluated based on operating profits and return on investment.

The vice president of the assembly division called the vice president of the production division and made a proposal:

Assembly VP: Look Joe, I know you're running below capacity out there in your department. I'd like to buy 10,000 units of A-16 at $30 per unit. That will enable you to keep up your production lines.

Production VP: Are you kidding, Meg? I happen to know that it would cost you a lot more if you had to buy A-16s from an outside supplier. We refuse to accept less than $40 per unit, which gives us our usual markup and covers our costs.

Assembly VP: Joe, we both know that your variable costs per unit are only $22. I realize I'd be getting a good deal at $30, but so would you. You should treat this as a special order. Anything over your differential costs on the order is pure profit. Look, Joe, if you can't do better than $40, I'll have to go elsewhere. I have to keep my costs down, too, you know.

Production VP: The $40 per unit is firm. Take it or leave it!

The assembly division subsequently sought bids on the part and was able to obtain its requirements from an outside supplier for $40 per unit. The

---

[1] The transfer pricing issue usually occurs at the division level, so we frequently refer to "divisions" or "division managers" instead of the longer "responsibility centers" or "responsibility center managers."

production division continued to operate below capacity. The actions of the two divisions cost the company $180,000. This amount is the difference between the price paid for the part from the outside supplier ($40) and the differential costs of producing in the assembly division ($22) times the 10,000 units in the order.

Although currently we cannot explain why the production VP would refuse such an order, we can surmise that competition between the two divisions for a share of bonus payments or other performance-based rewards may lead the production VP to expect a reduction in relative performance measures. This would occur if the assembly VP was to receive a windfall due to the bargain price paid for the transferred part. Research in this topic area is underway; perhaps when it is complete, we will have a better understanding of the reasons for such behavior.

How can a decentralized organization avoid this type of cost? Although there is no easy solution to this type of problem, there are three general approaches to the problem.

1. Direct intervention.
2. Centrally established transfer price policies.
3. Negotiated transfer prices.

Each of these approaches has advantages and disadvantages. Each may be appropriate under different circumstances. We discuss these alternatives in the next part of this section.

Direct Intervention

Ace Electronics' top management could have directly intervened in this pricing dispute and ordered the production division to produce the A-16s and transfer them to the assembly division at a management-specified transfer price. If this were an extraordinarily large order, or if internal product transfers were rare, direct intervention may be the best available solution to the problem. It would induce division managers to make the decision that maximizes company profits but at the same time allows managers to maintain their autonomy. The risk in direct intervention is that top management will become swamped with pricing disputes, and individual division managers will lose the flexibility and other advantages of autonomous decision making. Thus, direct intervention promotes short-run profits by minimizing the type of uneconomic behavior demonstrated in the Ace Electronics case, but the benefits from decentralization are reduced.

So long as the transfer pricing problems are infrequent, the benefits of direct intervention may outweigh the costs. However, if transfer transactions are common, direct intervention can be costly by requiring substantial top-management involvement in decisions that should be made at the divisional level. To avoid this problem, a company may establish a transfer pricing policy that encourages decentralized managers to make an economically optimal decision for the company without significantly reducing their autonomy.

Centrally Established Transfer Price Policies

A transfer pricing policy should allow divisional autonomy yet encourage managers to pursue corporate goals consistent with their own personal goals. Additionally, the use of transfer prices to determine the selling division's revenue and the buying division's cost should be compatible with the company's performance evaluation system. The two bases for transfer price policies are: (1) market prices and (2) cost. Although variations exist in both alternative bases, the two may be considered to encompass the most widely discussed approaches to establishing transfer pricing policies. We discuss these approaches and their advantages and disadvantages in the following sections.

Market Prices

Externally based market prices are generally considered the best basis for transfer pricing as when there is a competitive market for the product, there is little differentiation in the product, and market prices are readily available. Indeed, a number of economic analyses indicate the superiority of market prices in certain theoretical settings.[2] An advantage of market prices is that both the supplying and purchasing divisions can buy and sell as many units as they want at the market price. Managers of both supplying and purchasing divisions are indifferent between trading with each other or with outsiders. From the company's perspective, this is fine as long as the supplying unit is operating at capacity.

However, situations are rare in which such markets exist. Usually there are differences between products produced internally compared to those that can be purchased from outsiders, such as costs, quality, or product characteristics. The very existence of two divisions that trade with one another in one company tends to indicate that there may be advantages to not dealing with outside markets. For example, by trading within one company, it may be easier to assure quality control and reliability of delivery. Furthermore, costs of negotiating transactions can be reduced or eliminated when dealing internally. When such advantages exist, it is in the company's interest to create incentives for internal transfer. Top management may establish policies that direct two responsibility centers to trade internally unless they can show good reason why external trades are more advantageous. A variation on this approach may be an established policy that provides the buying division a discount for items purchased internally.

Establishing a Market Price Policy.

To encourage transfers that are in the interest of the company, management may set a transfer pricing policy based on the use of market prices for the intermediate product, such as part A-16. As a general rule, a **market-price-based transfer pricing** policy contains the following guidelines:

Market-Price-Based Transfer Pricing Transfer pricing policy where the transfer price is set at the market price or at a small discount from the market price.

1. The transfer price is usually set at a discount from the cost to acquire the item on the open market.

2. The selling division may elect to transfer or to continue to sell to the outside.

---

[2] A classic paper is J. Hirshleifer, "On the Economics of Transfer Pricing," *Journal of Business,* July 1956. Also see J. Ronen and G. McKinney, "Transfer Pricing for Divisional Autonomy," *Journal of Accounting Research,* Spring 1970; and R. Swieringa and J. Waterhouse, "Organizational Views of Transfer Pricing," *Accounting, Organizations and Society,* May 1982.

The first part of the policy induces the buying division to acquire from within the company. The discount is usually set so that the selling and buying divisions can share in the savings from avoiding the outside market transactions. With such a discount, the selling division and buying division would both be induced to transfer in normal circumstances.

For example, the typical solution to the Ace Electronics problem would have the production division sell to a wholesale market at the $40 price. The assembly division would probably be required to pay the wholesale price plus the wholesaler's markup. Let's say that the purchase price is $45. If management has established a transfer pricing policy that provides a 5 percent discount from the outside acquisition market price, then the transfer price would be $42.75, or 95 percent of $45. The assembly division would prefer to buy at that price due to the savings, and the production division would sell at that price because it exceeds the $40 they could obtain on the outside market. Under this policy, both divisions benefit from avoiding the wholesaler's markup in the outside market.

Imperfect Markets

Transfer pricing becomes more complex when selling and buying divisions cannot sell and buy all they want in perfectly competitive markets. In some cases, there may be no outside market at all. The transfer pricing problem can become quite complex when there are imperfect markets, and companies often find that not all transactions between divisions occur as top management would prefer. In extreme cases, the transfer pricing problem is so complex that the company is reorganized so that buying and selling divisions report to one manager who oversees the transfers. In effect, a manager is substituted for a transfer pricing policy.

General Rule: Differential Outlay Cost plus Opportunity Cost

There is a general **transfer pricing rule** for making transfers to maximize a company's profits in either perfect or imperfect markets. This rule is: *Transfer at the differential outlay cost to the selling division plus the opportunity cost to the company of making the internal transfers.*

This approach can be illustrated using the Ace Electronics example. Recall that the seller (the production division) could sell in outside markets for $40 and had a variable cost of $22, which we shall assume is its differential cost. (If the internal transfer requires *differential fixed costs*, then these would also be part of the differential costs.) Now consider two cases. (1) The seller (production division) operates below capacity, in which case there is probably no opportunity cost of the internal transfer because no outside sale is foregone. (2) The seller operates at capacity and would have to give up one unit of outside sales for every unit transferred internally. In case (2), the opportunity cost of transferring the product to a division inside the company is the forgone contribution of selling the unit in an outside market. Consequently, the optimal transfer price for Ace Electronics would be $22 for the below-capacity case or $40 for the at-capacity case, as shown in Illustration 23–1.

If the seller is operating at capacity, then the seller is indifferent between selling in the outside market for $40 or transferring internally at $40. Note that this is the same solution as the market price rule for competitive markets, (ignoring the wholesaler's markup) because sellers can sell every-

Illustration 23–1   **Application of General Transfer Pricing Rule—Ace Electronics**

	Differential Outlay Cost	**+**	**Opportunity cost of Transferring Internally**	**=**	**Transfer Price**
If the seller (that is, product division) has idle capacity	$22	+	-0- (probably)	=	$22
If the seller has no idle capacity	22	+	$18 (= $40 selling price − 22 variable cost)	=	40

thing they produce at the market price. Consequently, the "transfer at differential outlay cost plus opportunity cost" rule is consistent with the "transfer at market price in competitive markets" rule.

If the seller is operating below capacity, then the seller is indifferent between providing the product and receiving a transfer price equal to the seller's differential outlay cost or not providing the product at all. For example, if the production division received a price of $22 for the product, then it would be indifferent between selling it or not. In both the below-capacity and at-capacity cases, the selling division is no worse off if the internal transfer is made; however, the selling division does not earn a contribution on the transaction in the below-capacity case, and it earns only the same contribution for the internal transfer as it would for a sale to the outside market in the at-capacity case. The general rule stated above is optimal for the company but does not benefit the selling division for an internal transfer. (For practical purposes, we assume that the selling division will transfer internally if it is indifferent between an internal transfer and an external sale.)

Why is the "transfer at differential outlay cost plus opportunity cost" rule optimal for the company? Assume all divisions at Ace Electronics were operating below capacity; the assembly division has an opportunity to take part A-16 (for which the variable cost to the production division is $22), assemble it with other parts, and sell the final product. Assume that the variable costs of making and selling this product are $122, including the $22 variable cost of the production division and $100 for all other variable costs. (See Illustration 23–2.)

This $122 is the appropriate variable cost to the company of producing and selling this product. It is the cost that should be used to consider a special order for, say, a price of $130, and it is the variable cost that should be considered in other managerial decisions and flexible budgets. Suppose the selling division had received $40. Then, the total apparent variable cost to the company would have been incorrectly stated to be $140 ($40 to the production division plus $100 for all other variable costs). Note that the special order, which was acceptable at a price of $130 if the total variable cost was $122, would now be incorrectly rejected.

What if the production division had been operating at capacity (assume that all other divisions were operating below capacity)? In this case, the total variable cost of producing and selling the product *should be* $140, including

Illustration 23-2   **Compare Contributions from Alternative Sales—Ace Electronics**

	Production Division Sale of A-16 In the Inter- mediate Market	Assembly Division Special-Order Sale of Final Product
Variable outlay costs	$22	$100 + 22 production division variable outlay cost
		= $122
Outside market price	40	130
Contribution margin	18	8

the $18 ($40 − 22) lost contribution to the production division if part A-16 is transferred internally. At this cost of $140, the assembly division would reject the special order providing a price of $130. This is the correct decision because the company would prefer to receive a contribution of $18 on the sale of part A-16 by the production division in an intermediate market than to receive an $8 ($130 special-order price − $122 variable outlay cost) contribution from the special order sold by the assembly division.

To summarize, if the production division was operating below capacity, then both sales shown in Illustration 23–2 could be made. Setting the transfer price equal to the production division's variable outlay cost assures that the special order will be accepted. If the production division operates at capacity, then *only one alternative or the other* can be taken. Consequently, there is an opportunity cost of $18 of making the internal transfer. As long as the special-order price remains below $140, the company is better off taking the $18 contribution from the sale of A-16 in the intermediate market. If the special-order price increased above $140, then the contribution from the special order would exceed the contribution from the sale of A-16 in the intermediate market, and the company would prefer the special-order sale to the sale of A-16 in the intermediate market.

Alternative Cost Measures

Full-Absorption Cost-Based Transfers

Although the rule "transfer at differential outlay cost to the selling division plus the opportunity cost to the company of making the internal transfer" assumes the company has a measure of differential or variable cost, this is not always the case. Consequently, full-absorption costs are sometimes used in manufacturing firms.

If measures of market prices are not available, then it is impossible to compute the opportunity cost contribution margin required by the general rule. Consequently, companies will frequently use full-absorption costs, which are higher than variable costs but probably less than the market price.

The use of full-absorption costs will not necessarily lead to the profit-maximizing solution for the company; however, it has some advantages. First, these costs are available in the company's records. Second, they provide the selling division with a contribution equal to the excess of full-absorption costs over variable costs, which gives the selling division an incentive to transfer internally. Third, the full-absorption cost may sometimes be a better measure of the differential costs of transferring internally than the variable costs. For example, the transferred product may require engineering and design work that is buried in fixed overhead. In these cases, the full-absorption cost may be a reasonable measure of the differential costs, including the unknown engineering and design costs.

Cost-Plus Transfers

Cost-Plus Transfer Pricing Transfer pricing policy based on full costing or variable costing and actual cost or standard cost plus an allowance for profit.

We also find companies using **cost-plus transfer pricing** based on either variable costs or full-absorption costs. These methods generally apply a normal markup to costs as a surrogate for market prices when intermediate market prices are not available.

Standard Costs or Actual Costs

If actual costs are used as a basis for the transfer, any variances or inefficiencies in the selling division are passed along to the buying division. The problems of isolating the variances that have been transferred to subsequent buyer divisions becomes extremely complex. To promote responsibility in the selling division and to isolate variances within divisions, standard costs are usually used as a basis for transfer pricing in cost based systems.

For example, suppose Ace Electronics transferred based on variable costs for part A-16. The standard variable cost of producing the part is $22, but the actual cost of producing the part turns out to be $29 because of inefficiencies in the production division. Should this inefficiency be passed on to the buying division? The answer is usually "no" to give the production division incentives to be efficient. In these cases, companies will use standard costs for the transfer price. If standards are out of date or otherwise do not reflect reasonable estimates of costs, then the actual cost may be a better measure to use in the transfer price.

Other Motivational Aspects of Transfer Pricing Policies

When the transfer pricing rule does not give the supplier a profit on the transaction, motivational problems can arise. For example, if transfers are made at differential cost, the supplier earns no contribution toward profits on the transferred goods. Then, the transfer price policy does not motivate the supplier to transfer internally because there is no likely profit from internal transfers. This situation can be remedied in several ways.

A supplier whose transfers are almost all internal is usually organized as a cost center. The center manager is normally held responsible for costs, not for revenues. Hence, the transfer price does not affect the manager's performance measures. In companies where such a supplier is a profit center, the artificial nature of the transfer price should be taken into consideration when evaluating the results of that center's operations.

A supplying center that does business with both internal and external customers could be set up as a profit center for external business when the manager has price-setting power, and as a cost center for internal transfers when the manager does not have price-setting power. Performance on external business could be measured as if the center were a profit center, while performance on internal business could be measured as if the center were a cost center.

Dual Transfer Prices

A **dual transfer pricing** system could be installed to provide the selling division with a profit but charge the buying department with costs only. That is, the buyer could be charged the cost of the unit, however cost might be determined, and the selling division could be credited with cost plus some profit allowance. The difference could be accounted for by a special centralized account. This system would preserve cost data for subsequent buyer departments, and it would encourage internal transfers by providing a profit on such transfers for the selling divisions.

We have assumed that supplier center managers are rewarded on the basis of some profit measurement. However, other bases of reward are possible to encourage internal transfers. For example, many companies recognize internal transfers and incorporate them explicitly in their reward systems. Other companies base part of a supplying manager's bonus on the purchasing center's profits. There are ways of creating incentives for managers to transfer internally in organizational settings where profit-based transfer prices would be disadvantgeous. Management can choose from the cost-based pricing rules when such a policy would be cost beneficial.

Negotiated Prices

An alternative to a centrally administered transfer pricing policy is to permit managers to negotiate the price for internally transferred goods and services. Under this system, the managers involved act much the same as the managers of independent companies. Negotiation strategies may be similar to those employed when trading with outside markets. The major advantage to **negotiated transfer prices** is that they preserve the autonomy of the division managers. However, the two primary disadvantages are that a great deal of management effort may be consumed in the negotiating process, and the final price and its implications for performance measurement may depend more on the manager's ability to negotiate than on other factors.

For example, in the Ace Electronics case, the manager of the production division is at a distinct disadvantage in the negotiating process. There is idle capacity in the production division; hence, the manager is faced with a choice of zero profits or whatever he might be able to get from the assembly manager. The assembly manager has the upper hand here. The assembly manager could offer anything over $22, and it would improve the absolute value of the production manager's profit measure. If the assembly manager offered $23 per unit, the production manager's profits would increase by $1 per unit. However, the assembly manager would show an extra profit of $17 per unit over what she could make if she bought the units at $40 from an outside supplier. Depending on the compensation system, the production manager could realize a reduction in compensation because his relative profitability would fall if he makes the transfer.

CURRENT PRACTICES

In a survey of corporate practices, Vancil reported that nearly half of the 239 companies that reported their transfer pricing policies used a cost-based transfer pricing system. Thirty-one percent used a market-price-based system, and 22 percent used a negotiated system. The results of this survey are

Illustration 23-3   **Transfer Pricing Practices**

Method Used	Percent	Number
Cost based:		
Variable cost based	4.6%	11
Full cost based	25.5	61
Cost plus	16.7	40
Total cost based	46.8	112
Market based	31.0	74
Negotiated transfer prices	22.2	53
Total companies reporting their transfer pricing policy	100%	239

Source: Richard F. Vancil, *Decentralization, Managerial Ambiguity by Design* (Homewood, Ill.: Dow Jones-Irwin, 1979), p 180.

summarized in Ilustration 23–3. Generally, we find that when negotiated prices are used, the prices negotiated are between the market price at the upper limit and some measure of cost at the lower limit.[3]

Is there an optimal transfer pricing policy that dominates all others? The answer is no. An established policy will, most likely, be imperfect in the sense that it will not always work to induce the economically optimal outcome. However, as with other management decisions, the cost of any system must be weighed against the benefits of the system. Improving a transfer pricing policy beyond some point (say, to obtain better measures of variable costs and market prices) will result in the costs of the system exceeding the benefits. As a result, management tends to settle for a system that seems to work reasonably well rather than devise a "textbook" perfect system.

TRANSFER PRICING WITH THIRD-PARTY CONSEQUENCES

Transfer prices are used not only for internal recordkeeping and performance-evaluation purposes. There are several settings where transfer prices have direct cash consequences for a company. The most widely cited of these situations is in interstate and international transactions where transfer prices may affect tax liabilities, royalties, or other payments due to different governing jurisdictions. Since tax rates differ across jurisdictions, when transferring goods between jurisdictions, companies have an incentive to establish a transfer price which will increase the income in the lower tax jurisdiction and decrease income in the higher tax jurisdiction.

For example, assume the Nehru Jacket Corp. owns a manufacturing plant in India where its marginal tax rate is 60 percent of net income. These jackets are imported by Norway where the marginal tax rate is 75 percent of net income. For simplicity, assume that there are no currency controls and that tax regulations concerning the definition of taxable income are the same between the two jurisdictions. During the current year, the company in-

---

[3] See Ralph L. Benke and James Don Edwards, *Transfer Pricing: Techniques and Uses* (New York: National Association of Accountants, 1980).

curred production costs equivalent to $2 million in India. Costs incurred in Norway, aside from the cost of the jackets, amounted to an equivalent of $6 million. Sales revenues in Norway were $24 million. Similar goods imported by independent companies in Norway would have cost an equivalent of $3 million. However, Nehru Jacket Co. points out that because of its special control over its operations in India and the special approach it uses to manufacture its goods, the appropriate transfer price is $10 million. What would Nehru Jacket Co.'s total tax liability in both jurisdictions be if it used the $3 million transfer price? What would the liability be if it used the $10 million transfer price?

The solution to this is approached by determining the taxable income for each jurisdiction under the alternative transfer price scenarios. The resulting taxable income is multiplied by the tax rates in each jurisdiction to obtain the tax liabilities.

Assuming the $3 million transfer price, the tax liabilities are computed as follows:

	India	Norway
Revenues	$3,000,000	$24,000,000
Third-party costs	2,000,000	6,000,000
Transferred goods costs		3,000,000
Total costs	2,000,000	9,000,000
Taxable income	1,000,000	15,000,000
Tax rate	60%	75%
Tax liability	$ 600,000	$11,250,000
Total tax liability	$11,850,000	

Assuming the $10 million transfer price, the liabilities are computed as follows:

	India	Norway
Revenues	$10,000,000	$24,000,000
Third-party costs	2,000,000	6,000,000
Transferred goods costs		10,000,000
Total costs	2,000,000	16,000,000
Taxable income	8,000,000	8,000,000
Tax rate	60%	75%
Tax liability	$ 4,800,000	$ 6,000,000
Total tax liability	$10,800,000	

This tax liability of $10,800,000 is approximately 9 percent less than the liability that would be incurred if the transfer price was $3 million.

To say the least, international taxing authorities look closely at transfer prices when examining the tax returns of companies engaged in related-party transactions which cross jurisdictional lines. Companies must frequently have adequate support for the use of the transfer price which they have chosen for such a situation.

International related-party transfers are only one situation where transfer prices can have direct economic consequences. Frequently, there are transactions between related entities where the owner of one entity holds a different ownership percentage than he or she holds in another entity. It is generally in the best interest of this person to transfer income to the entity in which he or she holds the higher ownership percentage.

When transfer prices have direct economic consequences for an organization, the direct economic effects usually take precedence over the management performance evaluation aspects discussed earlier. In these situations, it is important to develop transfer prices in a manner that will meet third party scrutiny since taxing authorities may investigate transfer prices which affect cross-jurisdictional tax liabilities. Moreover, in situations where an individual acts on both sides of a related-party transaction, the possibility for litigation arises if transfer prices are not reasonable. Normally, a market pricing rule will work best when such a rule is available. However, the appropriate transfer price will depend on the facts related to a specific situation.

SEGMENT REPORTING

Companies engaged in different lines of business are required by the FASB to report certain information about segments which meet the FASB's technical requirements.[4] This reporting requirement is intended to provide a measure of the performance of those segments of a business which are significant to the company as a whole. Because the standard calls for

---

[4] The requirements, which are too detailed to cover here, are specified in FASB, *Statement of Financial Accounting Standards No. 14,* "Financial Reporting for Segments of a Business Enterprise" (Stamford, Conn. 1976).

REAL WORLD APPLICATION

Transfer Pricing and Third Parties*

United Bank, a local banking institution, was owned by one person who had 80 percent of the voting rights and a 20 percent interest in the earnings of the bank. The owner constructed a building in which he had a 100 percent interest. The bank leased four floors in this building at top local rates. Moreover, the square footage leased by the bank was so great that the bank had the largest number of square feet per dollar of deposits, loans, and equity of any bank in the region. After the bank failed, questions were raised concerning whether the lease was executed in the best interest of the bank or whether the lease was designed to benefit the owner of the building. In short, since the same person acted on behalf of both parties to the lease and since there was an economic benefit to be derived to the individual by designing the lease to favor the building owner, the transfer price for the leased space as well as other lease terms were subject to question.

* Based on the authors' research.

reporting of items which are a part of a larger organization, certain cost accounting principles come into play to separate segment activities.

The principal items which must be disclosed about each segment are:

1. Segment revenue.
2. Segment operating profits or loss.
3. Identifiable segment assets.
4. Depreciation and amortization.
5. Capital expenditures.
6. Certain specialized items.

In addition, if a company has significant foreign operations, it must disclose revenues, operating profits or losses, and identifiable assets by geographic region.

When computing segment operating profits, common corporate costs, interest, and income taxes are specifically excluded. Hence, the costs used to compute operating profit are limited to those that are either (*a*) directly related to the segment or (*b*) common costs that are indirectly attributable to the segment. The exclusion of general corporate overhead, interest, and income taxes greatly simplifies the calculations required for segment disclosures, although some companies do include these costs in the segment disclosures. When companies decide to allocate overhead to segments or when other costs are attributable to more than one segment, questions arise about the appropriate method of allocation.

Cost accounting concepts come into play in these disclosures in two major respects: (1) determining the transfer price for goods sold from one division of a company to another and (2) allocating the common costs for expenses or assets that are shared by two or more divisions. The second issue is handled under the general concepts of cost allocation discussed in Chapter 4. That is, the common cost is divided between segments based on the best measure of the cost/benefit or cause-and-effect relationship between the cost incurred and the segment to which the cost is assigned.

The transfer price for goods sold between divisions of a company is, however, a more complex matter. Negotiated transfer prices, which may be useful for internal purposes, are not generally acceptable for external segment reporting. In general, the accounting profession has indicated a preference for market-based transfer prices.[5] This preference arises because the purpose of the segment disclosure is to enable an investor to evaluate a company's divisions as though they were free-standing enterprises. Presumably, sales would be based on market transactions and not on the ability of managers to negotiate prices.

Although the conceptual basis for market-based transfer prices is sound in this setting, the practical application may be difficult. All of the questions raised earlier in this chapter about market-based transfer prices apply here. Frequently, the segments are really interdependent, so market prices may

---

[5] See, for example, FASB, *Statement of Financial Accounting Standards No. 69,* which specifies the use of market-based transfer prices when calculating the results of operations for an oil and gas exploration and production operation.

not really reflect the same risk in an intracompany sale that they do in third-party sales. In addition, in many situations, market prices are either not readily available, or they may exist for only some products. When these problems arise, management will usually attempt to estimate the market by obtaining market prices for similar goods and adjusting the price to reflect the characteristics of the goods transferred within the company. An alternative is to take the cost of the item transferred and add an allowance to represent the normal profit for the item. Either approach requires a number of assumptions. The problem that arises with the use of assumptions in this setting is that the computed price not only affects the segment revenues and operating profits of the selling segment but also determines the price charged to the buying segment. This, then, has an impact on the segment profits of the buying segment. Thus, care should be used when devising a transfer price for segment reporting purposes.

For example, Koala Kola Corp., a fictional company, has two segments for which separate reporting is required. The segments are a soft drink manufacturing and distribution operation and a chain of movie theaters. The movie theaters purchase substantial quantities of soft drinks from the soft drink segment. Data about the two segments are as follows (all dollars are in millions):

	Soft Drinks	Movie Theaters
Third-party sales	$425	$350
Operating costs other than goods transferred	320	260
Operating profits before transfers	$105	$ 90

During the past year, the goods transferred from the Soft Drinks segment had a retail price of $85 million. That is, if the goods could have been sold by Soft Drinks to third parties, based on the prices charged for goods actually sold, Soft Drinks would realize $85 million. However, the manager of the movie theaters segment noted that Soft Drinks was unable to expand its retail market. Therefore, the manager suggested that Soft Drinks should use a transfer price that better reflects Soft Drinks' ability to sell the goods externally. The movie theaters manager estimates that price to be $50 million because the Soft Drinks would be sold as generic products at a steep discount.

If the $85 million price were used, operating profits of the Soft Drinks segment would be $190 million ($105 + $85), and operating profits of the movie theaters would be $5 million ($90 − $85). At a $50 million transfer price, operating profits for Soft Drinks would be $155 million ($105 + $50) and for Movie Theaters, $40 million ($90 − $50).

Although we cannot answer which transfer price is correct, you can see that the choice of a price can have a significant impact on segment operating profits. Moreover, as this example illustrates, the market price basis may not be as objectively determined as some may think.

SUMMARY

When companies transfer goods or services between divisions, a price is assigned to that transaction. This transfer price becomes a part of the recorded revenues and costs in the divisions involved in the transfer. As a result, the dollar value assigned to the transfer can have significant implications in measuring divisional performance. Transfer pricing systems may be based on direct intervention, market values, costs, or through negotiation among the division managers. The appropriate method depends on the markets in which the company operates and management's goals. Top management usually tries to choose the appropriate method to promote corporate goals without destroying the autonomy of division managers.

TERMS AND CONCEPTS

The following terms and concepts should be familiar to you after reading this chapter:

Cost-Plus Transfer Pricing
Dual Transfer Pricing
Market-Price-Based Transfer Pricing
Negotiated Transfer Price
Transfer Price
Transfer Pricing Rule

SUPPLEMENTARY READINGS

Abdel-Khalik, A. R., and E. Lusk. "Transfer Pricing—A Synthesis." *Accounting Review,* January 1974.

Baxter, G. C., and R. A. Konopka. "Transfer Pricing across the Canada-U.S. Border." *CA Magazine,* June 1985, pp. 50–55 (published in Canada).

Beard, L. H. "Transfer Pricing Can Improve Sales and Credit Cooperation." *Management Accounting,* March 1984, pp. 60–65.

Benke, R., and J. Edwards. *Transfer Pricing: Techniques and Uses.* New York: National Association of Accountants, 1980.

Casey, M. P. "International Transfer Pricing." *Management Accounting,* October 1985, pp. 31–35.

Chan, K. H. "Transfer Pricing for Computer Services in Public Utilities." *Journal of Systems Management,* July 1986, pp. 23–29.

Kanodia, C. "Risk Sharing and Transfer Price Systems under Uncertainty." *Journal of Accounting Research,* Spring 1979.

Kelley, K. A. "Using Market Bidding to Regulate the Transfer Pricing of Utility Affiliate Coal." *Stanford Law Review,* May 1984, pp. 1215–41.

Rahman, M.Z., and R. W. Scarpens. "Transfer Pricing by Multinationals." *Journal of Business Finance and Accounting,* Autumn 1986, pp. 383–91 (published in Great Britain).

Spicer, B. H. "Towards an Organizational Theory of the Transfer Pricing Process." *Accounting, Organizations, and Society,* 13, no. 3 (1988), pp. 303–22.

Yunker, P. J. *Transfer Pricing and Performance Evaluation in Multinational Corporations: A Survey Study.* New York: Praeger Publishers, 1982.

SELF-STUDY PROBLEM NO. 1

The Peter Foote shoe company has two divisions: production and marketing. Production manufactures Peter Foote shoes, which it sells to both the marketing division and to other retailers (the latter under a different brand name). Marketing operates several small shoe stores in shopping centers. Marketing sells both Peter Foote and other brands.

Some relevant facts for production are as follows:

Production is operating far below its capacity	
Sales price to outsiders	$ 28.50[a] per pair
Variable cost to produce	19.00[a] per pair
Fixed costs	100,000 per month

[a] To keep the analysis from becoming unnecessarily complex, we assume Peter Foote makes one product line, and each pair of shoes has the same variable cost and price as each other pair.

The following data pertain to the sale of Peter Foote shoes by marketing:

Marketing is operating far below its capacity	
Sales price	$40 per pair
Variable marketing costs	5% of sales price

Marketing has decided to reduce the sales price of Peter Foote shoes. The company's variable manufacturing and marketing costs are differential to this decision, while *fixed* manufacturing and marketing costs are not.

Required:

a. What is the minimum price that can be charged by the marketing department for the shoes and still cover the company's differential manufacturing and marketing costs?

b. What is the appropriate transfer price for this decision?

c. If the transfer price was set at $28.50, what effect would this have on the minimum price set by the marketing manager?

SOLUTION TO SELF-STUDY PROBLEM NO. 1

a. From the company's perspective, the minimum price would be the variable cost of producing and marketing the goods. They would solve for this minimum price, P_C (the subscript C means this is the minimum price that is in the company's best interest), as follows:

$$P_C = \$19 + .05P_C$$
$$P_C - .05P_C = \$19$$
$$.95P_C = \$19$$
$$P_C = \underline{\underline{\$20}}$$

The minimum price the company should accept is $20. If the company was centralized, we would expect that this information would be conveyed to the manager of marketing, who would be instructed not to set a price below $20.

b. The transfer price that correctly informs the marketing manager about the differential costs of manufacturing is $19.

c. If the production manager set the price at $28.50, the marketing manager would solve for the minimum price (which we call P_M for marketing's solution):

$$P_M = \$28.50 + .05P_M$$
$$P_M - .05P_M = \$28.50$$
$$.95P_M = \$28.50$$
$$P_M = \underline{\underline{\$30}}$$

So, the marketing manager sets the price in excess of $30 per pair. In fact, prices of $28, $25, or anything greater than $20 would have generated a positive contribution margin from the production and sale of shoes.

SELF-STUDY PROBLEM NO. 2

How would your answer to self-study problem no. 1 change if the production division had been operating at full capacity?

SOLUTION TO SELF-STUDY PROBLEM NO. 2

If the production division had been operating at capacity, there would have been an implicit opportunity cost of internal transfers. Production would have foregone a sale in the wholesale market to make the internal transfer. The implicit opportunity cost to the company is the lost contribution margin ($28.50 − $19 = $9.50) from not selling in the wholesale market.

Thus, if production had sufficient sales in the wholesale market such that it would have had to forgo those sales to transfer internally, the transfer price should have been:

$$\begin{matrix} \text{Differential cost} \\ \text{of production} \end{matrix} + \begin{matrix} \text{Implicit opportunity cost} \\ \text{to company if goods are} \\ \text{transferred internally} \end{matrix} = \$19 + \$9.50$$
$$= \$28.50$$

Marketing would have appropriately treated the $28.50 as part of its differential cost of buying and selling the shoes. When production was operating below full capacity (hence, the implicit opportunity cost of transferring to marketing was zero), the minimum price for the shoes was derived as follows:

$$P_M = \$19 + .05P_M$$
$$.95P_M = \$19$$
$$P_M = \$20$$

However, if production is operating at full capacity, the minimum price is:

$$P_M = \$28.50 + .05P_M$$
$$.95P_M = \$28.50$$
$$P_M = \$30$$

QUESTIONS

23–1. What are some of the bases for establishing a transfer price?

23–2. Why do transfer prices exist even in highly centralized organizations?

23–3. What are some goals of a transfer pricing system in a decentralized organization?

23–4. Why are market-based transfer prices considered optimal under many circumstances?

23–5. What are the limitations to market-based transfer prices?

23–6. What are the advantages of a centrally administered transfer price (that is, direct intervention)? What are the disadvantages of such a transfer price?

23–7. Why do companies often use prices other than market prices for interdivisional transfers?

23–8. Division A has no external markets. It produces monofilament that is used by division B. Division B cannot purchase this particular type of monofilament from any other source. What transfer pricing system would you recommend for the interdivisional sale of monofilament? Why?

23–9. What is the basis for choosing between actual and standard costs for cost-based transfer pricing?

23–10. Some have suggested that managers should negotiate transfer prices. What are the disadvantages of a negotiated transfer price system?

23–11. Describe the economic basis for transfer pricing systems.

23–12. How does the choice of a transfer price affect the operating profits of both segments involved in an intracompany transfer?

23–13. Herman Karden owns 10 percent of the HK Partners Co., which sells laboratory furniture. However, he is the general partner of HK Partners and therefore has total decision-making authority for this company. He also owns 100 percent of HK Management Services Co., which supplies management advice to sales organizations. So far, the only client of HK Management Services Co. is HK Partners Co. What issues might arise with respect to the relationship between HK Management Services and HK Partners?

23–14. When setting a transfer price for goods which are sold across international boundaries, what factors should management take into account?

EXERCISES

23–15. Journal Entries for Transfer Pricing
(L.O.1)

Terra Firma Construction Company has two operating divisions. A precast concrete division manufactures building parts out of concrete. These parts are shipped to building sites and assembled on the site. The company also has a site construction division that constructs buildings from the precast concrete parts. The precast concrete division transferred units that cost $800,000 to a construction site operated by the site construction division. The units were transferred at a price of $950,000.

Required:

What journal entries would be required to record the transfer of the parts on the books of each division?

23–16. Journal Entries for Transfer Pricing
(L.O.1)

Mega Tower Realty owns and manages a high-rise building. The company leased one floor of the building for its Mega Realty Management division. The lease calls for a monthly rental of $75,000.

Required:

What journal entries are required to record the lease payments on the books of each division?

23–17. Compute Transfer Prices
(L.O.1)

Washington Enterprises is a real estate company with a leasing division that rents and manages properties for others and a maintenance division that performs services such as carpentry, painting, plumbing, and electrical work. The maintenance division has an estimated variable cost of $18 per labor-hour. The maintenance division works both for Washington Enterprises and for other companies. It could spend 100 percent of its time working for outsiders. The maintenance division charges $35 per hour for labor performed for outsiders. This rate is the same as the rates charged by other maintenance companies. The leasing division complained that it could hire its own maintenance staff at an estimated variable cost of $20 per hour.

Required:

a. What is the minimum transfer price that the maintenance division should obtain for its services, assuming it is operating at capacity?

b. What is the maximum price that the leasing division should pay?

c. Would your answers in a or b change if the maintenance division had idle capacity? If so, which answer would change, and what would the new amount be?

23–18. Evaluate Transfer Pricing System
(L.O.2)

Mar Company has two decentralized divisions, X and Y. Division X has always purchased certain units from division Y at $75 per unit. Because division Y plans to raise the price to $100 per unit, division X desires to purchase these units from outside suppliers for $75 per unit. Division Y's costs follow:

Y's variable costs per unit	$ 70
Y's annual fixed costs	15,000
Y's annual production of these units for X	1,000units

Required:

If division X buys from an outside supplier, the facilities division Y uses to manufacture these units would remain idle. What would be the result if Mar enforces a transfer price of $100 per unit between divisions X and Y?

(CPA adapted)

23–19. Evaluate Transfer Pricing System

(L.O.2)

A company permits its decentralized units to "lease" space to one another. Division X has leased some idle warehouse space to division Y at a price of $1 per square foot per month. Recently, division X obtained a new five-year contract, which will increase its production sufficiently so that the warehouse space would be more valuable to them. Division X has notified division Y that the new rental price will be $3.50 per square foot per month. Division Y can lease space at $2 per square foot in another warehouse from an outside company but prefers to stay in the shared facilities. Division Y's management states that it would prefer not to move. If division X cannot use the space now being leased to division Y, then division X will have to rent other space for $3 per square foot per month. (The difference in rental prices occurs because division X requires a more substantial warehouse building than division Y.)

Required:

Recommend a transfer price and explain your reasons for choosing that price.

23–20. Evaluate Transfer Pricing System

(L.O.2)

Selling division offers its product to outside markets at a price of $200. Selling incurs variable costs of $70 per unit and fixed costs of $50,000 per month based on monthly production of 1,000 units.

Buying division can acquire the product from an alternate supplier at a cost of $210 per unit. Buying division can also acquire the product from selling division for $200, but it must pay $15 per unit in transportation costs in addition to the transfer price charged by selling division.

Required:

a. What are the costs and benefits of the alternatives available to selling and buying divisions with respect to the transfer of the selling division's product? Assume that selling can market all that it can produce.

b. How would your answer change if selling had idle capacity sufficient to cover all of buying's needs?

23–21. Third-Party Transfer Prices

(L.O.3)

Vancouver Transit Ltd. (of Canada), operates a local mass transit system. The transit authority is a governmental agency and is related to the provincial government. Vancouver Transit has an agreement with the provincial government whereby it will provide rides to senior citizens at a fare of 10 cents per trip. The government will reimburse Vancouver Transit for the "cost" of each trip taken by a senior citizen.

The regular fare is $1.00 per trip. After conducting an analysis of its costs, Vancouver Transit figured that with its operating deficit, the full cost of each ride on the transit system is $2.50. Routes, capacity, and operating costs are unaffected by the number of senior citizens on any route.

Required:

a. What are the alternative prices that could be used for determining the governmental reimbursement to Vancouver Transit?

b. Which price would Vancouver Transit prefer? Why?

c. Which price would the provincial government prefer? Why?

d. If Vancouver Transit provides an average of 200,000 trips for senior citizens in a given month, what is the monthly value of the difference between the prices in *b*. and *c*., above?

23–22. Third-Party Transfer Prices
(L.O.3)

New Sweden Plant Perfections grows specimen plants for landscape contractors. The wholesale price of each plant is $40. During the past year, New Sweden Plant Perfections sold 5,000 specimen plants. New Sweden Plant Perfections is owned 60 percent by Mr. New and 40 percent by Ms. Sweden.

Of the plants sold last year, 1,000 were sold to Fayette Landscape Co. Mr. New has a 5 percent interest in Fayette Landscape Co., and Ms. Sweden has a 60 percent interest in Fayette Landscape Co. At the end of the year, Ms. Sweden noted that Fayette was the largest buyer of New Sweden plants. She suggested that the plant company give Fayette Landscape a 10 percent reduction in prices for the coming year in recognition of their position as a preferred customer.

Required:

Assuming that Fayette Landscape purchases the same number of plants at the same prices in the coming year, what effect would the price reduction have on the operating profits which accrue to Mr. New and to Ms. Sweden for the coming year?

23–23. International Transfer Prices
(L.O.3)

CanAm Corp. has two operating divisions. The company has a logging operation in Canada. The logs are milled and shipped to the United States where they are used by the company's building supplies division. Operating expenses in Canada amount to $5 million. Operating expenses in the United States amount to $11 million exclusive of the costs of any goods transferred from Canada. Revenues in the United States are $30 million.

If the lumber were purchased from one of the company's U.S. lumber divisions, the costs would be $6 million. However, if the lumber had been purchased from an independent Canadian supplier, the cost would be $8 million. The marginal income tax rate in Canada is 60 percent, while the U.S. tax rate is 40 percent.

Required:

What is the company's total tax liability to both jurisdictions for each of the two alternative transfer pricing scenarios ($6 million or $8 million)?

23–24. Segment Reporting
(L.O.4)

Ticky Tacky Home Builders, Inc., has a building division and a financing division. The building division oversees construction of single-family homes in "economically efficient" subdivisions. The financing division takes loan applications and packages mortgages into pools and sells them in the loan markets. The financing division also services the mortgages. Both divisions meet the requirements for segment disclosures under accounting rules.

The building division had $31 million in sales last year. Costs, other than costs charged by the finance division, totaled $26 million. The financing division obtained revenues of $6 million from servicing mortgages and incurred outside costs of $7 million. In addition, the financing division charged the building division $4 million for loan-related fees. The manager of the building division complained to the CEO of Ticky Tacky stating that the financing division was charging twice the commercial rate for loan-related fees and that the building division would be better off sending its buyers to an outside lender.

The financing division manager stated that although commercial rates might be lower, it was more difficult to sell Ticky Tacky houses, and therefore, the higher fees were justified.

Required:

a. What are the reported segment operating profits for each division ignoring income taxes, using the $4 million transfer price for the loan-related fees.

b. What are the reported segment operating profits for each division ignoring income taxes, using a $2 million commercial rate as the transfer price for the loan-related fees?

23–25. Segment Reporting
(L.O.4)

Louvre Glass Co. has two operating divisions: (1) an amusement park and (2) a hotel. The two divisions meet the requirements for segment disclosures. Before considering transactions between the two divisions, revenues and costs were as follows (dollars in thousands):

	Amusement Park	Hotel
Revenues	$6,500	$3,400
Costs	3,100	2,500

The amusement park and the hotel had a joint marketing arrangement whereby the hotel gave out free passes to the amusement park and the amusement park gave out discount coupons good for stays at the hotel. The value of the free passes to the amusement park redeemed during the past year totaled $800,000. The discount coupons redeemed at the hotel resulted in a decrease in hotel revenues of $300,000. As of the end of the year, all of the coupons for the current year have expired.

Required:

What are the operating profits for each division considering the effects of the costs arising from the joint marketing agreement?

PROBLEMS

23–26. Transfer Pricing with Imperfect Markets—ROI Evaluation, Normal Costing

Division S of S&T Enterprises has an investment base of $600,000. Division S produces and sells 90,000 units of a product at a market price of $10 per unit. Its variable costs total $3 per unit. The division also charges each unit with a share of fixed costs based on capacity production of 100,000 units per year. The fixed cost "burden" is computed at $5 per unit. Any production volume variance is written off to expense at the end of the period.

Division T wants to purchase 20,000 units from division S. However, division T is willing to pay only $6.20 per unit. The reason division T can pay only the lower amount is that division T has an opportunity to accept a special order at a reduced price. The order is economically justifiable only if division T can acquire the division S output at a reduced price.

Required:

a. What is the ROI for division S without the transfer to division T?

b. What is division S's ROI if it transfers 20,000 units to division T at $6.20 each?

c. What is the minimum transfer price for the 20,000-unit order that division S would accept if division S were willing to maintain the same ROI with the transfer as they would accept by selling their 90,000 units to the outside market?

23–27. Evaluate Profit Impact of Alternative Transfer Decisions

A. R. Oma, Inc. manufactures a line of men's colognes. The manufacturing process entails mixing and the addition of aromatic and coloring ingredients; the finished product is packaged in a company-produced glass bottle and packed in cases containing six bottles each.

Since sales volume is heavily influenced by the appearance of the bottle, the company developed unique bottle production processes.

All bottle production is used by the cologne manufacturing plant. Each division is considered a separate profit center and evaluated as such. As the new corporate controller, you are responsible for the definition of a proper transfer price to use for the bottles produced for the cologne division.

At your request, the bottle division general manager asked other bottle manufacturers to quote a price for the quantity and sizes demanded by the cologne division. These competitive prices are:

Volume	Total Price	Price per Case
2,000,000 eq. cases[a]	$ 4,000,000	$2.00
4,000,000	7,000,000	1.75
6,000,000	10,000,000	1.67

[a] An "equivalent case" represents six bottles.

A cost analysis of the bottle manufacture division indicates that they can produce bottles at these costs:

Volume	Total Price	Cost per Case
2,000,000 eq. cases	$3,200,000	$1.60
4,000,000	5,200,000	1.30
6,000,000	7,200,000	1.20

These costs include fixed costs of $1.2 million and variable costs of $1 per equivalent case. These data have caused considerable corporate discussion as to the proper price to use in the transfer of bottles to the cologne division. This interest is heightened because a significant portion of a division manager's income is an incentive bonus based on profit center results.

The cologne production division has the following costs in addition to the bottle costs:

Volume	Total Cost	Cost per Case
2,000,000 cases	$16,400,000	$8.20
4,000,000	32,400,000	8.10
6,000,000	48,400,000	8.07

The marketing department furnished the following price-demand relationship for the finished product:

Sales Volume	Total Sales Revenue	Sales Price per Case
2,000,000 cases	$25,000,000	$12.50
4,000,000	45,600,000	11.40
6,000,000	63,900,000	10.65

Required:

a. The A. R. Oma Company has used market price transfer prices in the past. Using the current market prices and costs, and assuming a volume of 6 million cases, calculate operating profits for:

(1) The bottle division.

(2) The cologne division.

(3) The corporation.

b. Is this production and sales level the most profitable volume for:

(1) The bottle division?

(2) The cologne division?

(3) The corporation?

Explain your answers.

(CMA adapted)

23–28. International Transfer Prices

Merchant Marine Corp. (MMC) operates a fleet of container ships in international trade between Great Britain and Thailand. All of the shipping income (that is, that related to MMC's ships) is deemed as earned in Great Britain. MMC also owns a dock facility in Thailand. This facility services MMC's fleet. Income from the dock facility is, however, deemed earned in Thailand. MMC income which is deemed attributable to Great Britain is taxed at a 75 percent rate. MMC income attributable to Thailand is taxed at a 20 percent rate. Last year, the dock facility in Thailand had operating revenues of $4 million, excluding services performed for MMC's ships. MMC's shipping revenues for last year were $26 million.

Operating costs of the dock facility were $5 million last year, and operating costs of the shipping operation, before deduction of dock facility costs, were $17 million. There are no similar dock facilities in Thailand which would be available to MMC.

However, there is a facility in Malaysia which would have charged MMC an estimated $3 million for the services which MMC's Thailand dock provided to MMC's ships. MMC management noted that if the services had been provided in Great Britain, the costs for the year would have totaled $8 million. MMC argued to the British tax officials that the appropriate transfer price is the price that would have been charged in Great Britain. British tax officials suggest that the Malaysian price is the appropriate one.

Required:

What is the difference in tax costs to MMC between the alternate transfer prices for dock services: price in Great Britain versus price in Malaysia?

23–29. Analyze Transfer Pricing Data

MultiProduct Enterprises, Inc., is a decentralized organization that evaluates division management based on measures of division contribution margin. Divisions A and B operate in similar product markets. Division A produces a solid state electronic assembly that may be sold to the outside market at a price of $16 per unit. The outside market can absorb up to 140,000 units per year. These units require two direct labor-hours each.

If A modifies the units with an additional one half hour of labor time, the units can be sold to division B at a price of $18 per unit. Division B will accept up to 120,000 of these units per year.

If division B does not obtain 120,000 units from A, then B will purchase the needed units for $18.50 from the outside. Division B incurs $8 of additional labor and other out-of-pocket costs to convert the assemblies into a home digital eletronic radio, calculator, telephone monitor, and clock unit. The unit can be sold to the outside market at a price of $45 each.

Division A estimates its total costs are $925,000 for fixed costs and $6 per direct labor-hour. Capacity in division A is limited to 400,000 direct labor-hours per year.

Required:

Determine the following:

a. Total contribution margin to A if it sells 140,000 units to the outside.

b. Total contribution margin to A if it sells 120,000 units to B.

c. The costs to be considered in determining the optimal company policy for sales by division A.

d. The annual contributions and costs for divisions A and B under the optimal policy.

23–30. Selecting a Transfer Price

Lorax Electric Company manufactures components for the electronics industry. The firm is organized into several divisions, with division managers given the authority to make virtually all operating decisions. Management control over divisional operations is maintained by a system of divisional profit and return-on-investment measures that are reviewed regularly by top management.

The devices division manufactures solid-state devices and is operating at capacity. The systems division asked the devices division to supply a large quantity of integrated circuit IC378. The devices division currently is selling this component to its regular customers at $40 per hundred.

The systems division, which is operating at about 60 percent capacity, wants this particular component for a digital clock system. It has an opportunity to supply large quantities of these digital clock systems to Centonic Electric which offered to pay $7.50 per clock system. Each clock requires five units of IC378.

The systems division prepared an analysis of the costs to produce the clock systems. The amount that could be paid to the devices division for the integrated circuits was determined by working backward from the selling price. The cost estimates employed by the division reflected the highest per unit cost the systems division could incur for each cost component and still leave a sufficient margin so that the division's income statement could show reasonable improvement. The cost estimates are:

Proposed selling price		$7.50
Costs excluding required integrated circuits (IC378):		
Components purchased from outside suppliers	$2.75	
Circuit board etching—labor and variable overhead	0.40	
Assembly, testing, packaging—labor and variable overhead	1.35	
Fixed overhead allocations	1.50	
Profit margin	0.50	6.50
Amount that can be paid for integrated circuits IC378 (5 @ $20 per hundred)		$1.00

As a result of this analysis, the systems division offered the devices division a price of $20 per hundred for the integrated circuit. This bid was refused by the manager of the devices division because he felt the systems division should at least meet the price of $40 per hundred that regular customers pay. When the systems division found that it could not obtain a comparable integrated circuit from outside vendors, the situation was brought to an arbitration committee that had been set up to review such problems.

The arbitration committee prepared an analysis that showed that 15 cents would cover variable costs of producing the integrated circuit, 28 cents would cover the full cost including fixed overhead, and 35 cents would provide a gross margin equal to the average gross margin on all of the products sold by the devices division. The manager of the systems division reacted by stating, ''They could sell us that integrated circuit for 20 cents and still earn a positive contribution toward profit. In fact, they should be required to sell at their variable cost—15 cents—and not be allowed to take advantage of us.''

The manager of Devices countered by stating, ''It doesn't make sense to sell to the systems division at $20 per hundred when we can get $40 per hundred outside on all we can produce. In fact, Systems could pay us more than $50 per hundred, and they would still have a positive contribution margin.''

The recommendation of the committee, to set the price at 35 cents per unit ($35 per hundred), so that devices could earn a fair gross margin, was rejected by both division managers. Consequently, the problem was brought to the attention of the vice president of operations.

Required:

a. What is the immediate economic effect on the Lorax Company as a whole if the devices division were required to supply IC378 to the systems division at 35 cents per unit—the price recommended by the arbitration committee? Explain your answer. Discuss the advisability of intervention by top management as a solution to transfer pricing disputes between division managers such as the one experienced by Lorax Electric Company.

b. Suppose that Lorax adopted a policy of requiring that the price to be paid in all internal transfers by the buying division be equal to the variable costs per unit of the selling division for that product and that the supplying division be required to sell if the buying division decided to buy the item. Discuss the consequences of adopting such a policy as a way of avoiding the need for the arbitration committee or for intervention by the vice president.

c. Suggest an alternative transfer price that would overcome some of the problems mentioned. Show how it would result in goal congruence.

(CMA adapted)

23–31. Transfer Pricing—Performance Evaluation Issues

The Ajax Division of Gunnco, operating at capacity, has been asked by the Defco Division of Gunnco Corporation to supply it with electrical fitting No. 1726. Ajax sells this part to its regular customers for $7.50 each. Defco, which is operating at 50 percent capacity, is willing to pay $5 each for the fitting. Defco will put the lifting into a brake unit that it is manufacturing on a cost-plus basis for a commercial airplane manufacturer.

Ajax has a variable cost of producing fitting No. 1726 of $4.25. The cost of the brake unit as built by Defco is as follows:

Purchased parts—outside vendors	$22.50
Ajax fitting—1726	5.00
Other variable costs	14.00
Fixed overhead and administration	8.00
	$49.50

Defco believes the price concession is necessary to get the job.

The company uses ROI and dollar profits in the measurement of division and division manager performance.

Required:

a. If you were the division controller of Ajax, would you recommend that Ajax supply fitting 1726 to Defco? (Ignore any income tax issues.) Why or why not?

b. Would it be to the short-run economic advantage of the Gunnco Corporation for the Ajax Division to supply the Defco Division with fitting 1726 at $5 each? (Ignore any income tax issues.) Explain your answer.

c. Discuss the organizational and manager behavior difficulties, if any, inherent in this situation. As the Gunnco controller, what would you advise the Gunnco Corporation president to do in this situation?

(CMA adapted)

23–32. Evaluate Transfer Price System

MBR, Inc., consists of three divisions: Boston Corporation, Raleigh Company, and Memphis Company. The three divisions operate as if they were independent companies. Each division has its own sales force and production facilities. Each division management is responsible for sales, cost of operations, acquisition and financing of divisional assets, and working capital management. MBR corporate management evaluates the performance of the divisions and division managements on the basis of ROI.

Memphis Division has just been awarded a contract for a product that uses a component manufactured by the Raleigh Division, which is operating well below capacity, as well as by outside suppliers. Memphis used a cost figure of $3.80 for the component manufactured by Raleigh in preparing its bid for the new product. This cost figure was supplied by Raleigh in response to Memphis's request for the average variable cost of the component and represents the standard variable manufacturing cost and variable marketing costs.

Raleigh's regular selling price for the component Memphis needs for the new product is $6.50. Raleigh management indicated that it could supply Memphis with the required quantities of the component at the regular selling price less variable selling and distribution expenses. Memphis management responded by offering to pay standard variable manufacturing cost plus 20 percent.

The two divisions have been unable to agree on a transfer price. Corporate management has never established a transfer price policy. The corporate vice president of finance suggested a price equal to the standard full manufacturing cost (that is, no selling and distribution expenses) plus a 15 percent markup. This price has been rejected by the two division managers because each considered it grossly unfair.

The unit cost structure for the Raleigh component and the suggested prices are shown below.

Costs:	
Standard variable manufacturing cost	$3.20
Standard fixed manufacturing cost	1.20
Variable selling and distribution expenses	.60
	$5.00
Prices:	
Regular selling price	$6.50
Regular selling price less variable selling and distribution expenses ($6.50 − .60)	$5.90
Variable manufacturing plus 20% ($3.20 × 1.20)	$3.84
Standard full manufacturing cost plus 15% ($4.40 × 1.15)	$5.06

Required:

a. Discuss the effect each of the proposed prices might have on the Raleigh Company management's attitude toward intracompany business.

b. Is the negotiation of a price between the Memphis and Raleigh divisions a satisfactory method to solve the transfer price problem? Explain your answer.

c. Should the corporate management of MBR, Inc., become involved in this transfer price controversy? Explain your answer.

(CMA adapted)

23–33. Transfer Prices and Tax Regulations

ExIm, Inc., has two operating divisions in a semiautonomous organization structure. Division Ex is located in the United States. It produces a part labeled XZ-1, which is an input to division Im, which is located in the south of France. Division Ex has idle capacity that it used to produce XZ-1. The market price of XZ-1 domestically is $60. The variable costs are $25 per unit. The company's U.S. tax rate is 40 percent of income.

After paying the transfer price for each XZ-1 received from division Ex, division Im also pays a shipping fee of $15 per unit. Part XZ-1 becomes a part of division Im's output product. The output product costs an additional $10 to produce and sells for an equivalent $115. Division Im could purchase part XZ-1 from a Paris supplier at a cost of $50 per unit. The company's French tax rate is 70 percent of income. Assume French tax laws permit transferring at either variable cost or market price. Assume the U.S. division's income is taxed at 40 percent.

Required:

What transfer price is economically optimal for ExIm, Inc.? Show computations.

23–34. Third-Party Transfer Prices

Peaches Ratliff owns a 20 percent interest in Global Tricycle Corp. Global Tricycle earns operating profits of $20 million per year before considering any of the transactions discussed in this problem. Global leases 500,000 square feet of office space from Peaches Building Corp., a leasing firm in which Peaches Ratliff holds an 80 percent interest. Rental payments averaged $15 per year per square foot. Costs associated with these rental payments average $8 per square foot.

Global Tricycle has a management agreement with Ratliff Management Corp., which is wholly owned by Peaches Ratliff. The management agreement requires Global Tricycle to pay Ratliff Management $250,000 per year plus 1 percent of Global's operating profits after rental payments. Ratliff Management incurs $120,000 in costs per year, which includes $30,000 in office rental paid to Peaches Building Corp. for 2,000 square feet of leased space. Costs of this leased space also average $8 per square foot.

The building has no other tenants, and the management company has no other clients.

Required:

a. What amount of operating profits from all of these activities accrues to Peaches Ratliff's share of the operating profits from each of these organizations.

b. By how much would Peaches Ratliff's operating profits increase or decrease if the rental charges for Peaches Building Corp. were increased to $16.50 per square foot per year?

23–35. Transfer Pricing— Third-Party Consequences

Arco owns a substantial interest in oil production in the northern part of Alaska. The North Alaska market for crude oil cannot absorb all of the production from the area. Hence, nearly all of the oil must be shipped through the Trans Alaska Pipeline System to the southern part of Alaska for delivery to tankers which then deliver the crude to the U.S. West Coast where all of Arco's Alaska crude oil is refined and marketed. The U.S. West Coast market faces an oversupply of crude oil. Some Alaska producers, therefore, ship their oil though the Panama Canal to the U.S. Gulf Coast where their crude oil is then refined and marketed. Arco's share of Alaska production is approximately 150 million barrels of crude oil per year. Production quantities are fixed by the capacity of the pipeline system to carry the crude oil across Alaska.

Oil production is subject to a severance tax due the state based on the value of the crude oil at the point of production and a royalty which is an amount paid to the landowner for the rights to produce. Severance taxes in Alaska equal 12 percent of the value of production. The royalty amount is effectively equal to 12.5 percent of the value of each barrel of oil produced. In the early 1980s, the federal government levied a windfall profit tax which, for our purposes, is equivalent to 15 percent of the value of oil and gas produced. These three cost items (severance taxes, royalty, windfall profit taxes) are based on a percentage of the value of production before the oil enters the pipeline system. However, value cannot be determined directly at that point because virtually no oil is sold at that point. It is necessary to determine a transfer price at the point where the crude oil leaves the producing field and enters the pipeline system. The greater the transfer price, the greater the royalty and taxes and vice versa. The transfer price is calculated by taking the ''market value'' of the crude oil where there is a market and deducting the costs to ship the crude oil through the pipeline system (known as a ''tariff'') and the costs of transporting the crude oil from the pipeline to the market. None of the pipeline operating costs are affected by the amount of the tariff. Other operating costs are estimated at $2.50 per barrel regardless of the method used for transfer pricing.

In recent years, the selling price for crude oil on the U.S. West Coast has been $19 per barrel. Costs to ship from the southern coast of Alaska to the U.S. West Coast approximate 75 cents per barrel. The selling price for crude oil on the U.S. Gulf Coast averages $20 per barrel. However, shipping costs from Alaska to the U.S. Gulf Coast average $3.70 per barrel. Arco argues that although it sells no oil on the U.S. Gulf Coast, that is the appropriate market because the U.S. West Coast is so flooded with Alaska crude oil that it is not an appropriate market for valuation purposes. Regardless of the basis for the transfer price, Arco will dispose of its crude oil on the U.S. West Coast and incur the costs to ship it to that destination.

Arco owns a proportional interest in the Trans Alaska Pipeline Company equivalent to its interest in production from northern Alaska. Unlike crude oil production, pipeline earnings are not subject to royalty, severance taxes, or windfall profit taxes. Arco argues that the cost to ship the crude oil through the pipeline system (the tariff) is $6 per barrel, based primarily on the assumption that the pipeline should be depreciated over one half of its useful life and that the cost of building the pipeline should be based on the assumption that Arco used 100 percent equity rather than leveraged the costs of pipeline construction. The state of Alaska and others argue that the pipeline shipping cost is closer to $3 per barrel based on straight-line depreciation over the expected useful life of the pipeline and based on recognition of the fact that 90 percent of the pipeline costs were financed with debt at less than prime lending rates. The value of the pipeline service cannot be determined through open market transactions because those who ship through the pipeline are the same companies as those who produce the crude oil.

Required:

a. What are the four possible combinations of valuation techniques for northern Alaska crude oil?

b. Prepare a schedule showing the annual severance taxes, royalty, windfall profit taxes, and operating profits to Arco from each of the four valuation methods.

c. Assuming there were no tax or royalty considerations, if you wanted to establish a market price for Arco's north Alaska crude oil, would you use the U.S. West Coast price or the U.S. Gulf Coast price as a starting point in the valuation exercise? Support the price you choose.

23–36. Third-Party Transfer Prices

Faster Electronics sells and services new computer systems. Faster has an arrangement with Swift Service Company whereby Swift Service performs warranty services on equipment sold by Faster as well as performs other repair work for

Faster. From time to time, Faster Electronics takes a computer system in trade as part payment for a new system. Used systems acquired through the trade-in arrangement are sold to Penny-Pincher Processing, a used computer dealer. Ken Hellums owns a 20 percent interest in Faster Electronics, a 100 percent interest in Swift Service, and a 50 percent interest in Penny-Pincher Processing.

In a recent transaction, Faster Electronics sold a computer system for $14,500. The system carried a one-year warranty. Faster Electronics paid Swift Service $2,000 for servicing this warranty. As part payment for the system, Mr. Hellums took an old system in trade and allowed $1,800 for the trade-in value. The old system was sold to Penny-Pincher Processing for $700. The difference between the trade-in value and the price to the wholesaler was deemed a discount on the sale price of the new system.

The majority stockholder in Faster Electronics reviewed the transaction. The stockholder suggested that instead of buying the $2,000 warranty, Faster should pay for warranty service if and when needed. Based on past experience, this service would cost $500. Moreover, the stockholder stated that a review of selling prices for the traded model indicated that the retail price of the model was $1,600 and that this amount should be used as the basis for the sale to Penny-Pincher Processing.

Required: What effect would the changes in the prices assigned to the trade-in and warranty service transaction have on the operating profits which accrue to Mr. Hellums from these three business interests?

23–37. Segment Reporting Allegiance Corp. has four operating divisions: (1) airline; (2) hotel; (3) auto rental; and, (4) travel services. Each division is a separate segment for financial-reporting purposes. Revenues and costs related to outside transactions were as follows for the past year (dollars in millions):

	Airline	Hotel	Auto Rental	Travel Services
Revenues	$245	$106	$89	$32
Costs	157	71	66	30

The airline participated in a frequent stayer program with the hotel chain. During the past year, the airline reported that it traded hotel award coupons for travel which had a retail value of $26 million, assuming that the travel was redeemed at full airline fares. The auto rental division offered 20 percent discounts to Allegiance's airline passengers and hotel guests. These discounts to airline passengers were estimated to have a retail value of $7 million. Allegiance hotel guests redeemed $3 million in auto rental discount coupons. Allegiance hotels provided rooms for flight crews on Allegiance's airline. The value of the rooms for the year was $13 million.

The travel services division booked flights on Allegiance's airline. This service was valued at $4 million for the year. This service for intracompany hotel bookings was valued at $2 million and for intracompany auto rentals at $1 million.

While preparing all of these data for financial statement presentation, the hotel division's controller stated that the value of the airline coupons should be based on the differential and opportunity costs of the travel awards, not on the full fare for the tickets issued. This argument was suppported because award travel is usually allocated to seats that would otherwise be empty or contains restrictions similar to those on discount tickets. If the differential and opportunity costs were used for this transfer price, the value would be $5 million instead of $26 million. The airline controller made a similar argument concerning the auto rental discount coupons. If the differential cost basis were used for the auto rental coupons, the transfer price would be $1 million instead of the $7 million above.

Allegiance reports assets in each segment as follows:

Airline	$955 million
Hotel	385 million
Car rental	321 million
Travel services	65 million

Required:

a. Using the retail values for transfer pricing for segment reporting purposes, what are the operating profits for each division of Allegiance Corp.?

b. What are the operating profits for each division of Allegiance Corp. using the differential cost basis for pricing transfers?

c. Rank each division by return on investment using the transfer pricing method in *a.*, above, as well as using the transfer pricing method in *b.*, above. What difference does the transfer pricing system have on the rankings?

INTEGRATIVE CASES

23–38. Analyze Transfer Pricing Policy

PortCo Products is a divisionalized furniture manufacturer. The divisions are autonomous segments, with each division being responsible for its own sales, costs of operations, working capital management, and equipment acquisition. Each division serves a different market in the furniture industry.

The commercial division plans to introduce a new line of counter and chair units for the restaurant industry. John Kline, the division manager, discussed the manufacturing of the new seat with Ruth Fiegel of the office division. They both believe a similar seat currently made by the office division could be modified for use on the new counter chair. Consequently, Kline asked Ruth Fiegel for a price for 100-unit lots of the office division seats. The following conversation took place about the price to be charged for the cushioned seats.

Fiegel: John, we can easily make the modifications to our seat. The direct materials used in your seat should cost about 10 percent more than those we use. Labor time should be the same. I would price the seat at our regular rate—standard full-absorption cost plus 30 percent markup.

Kline: That's higher than I expected, Ruth. I was thinking that a good price would be your variable manufacturing costs. After all, your fixed costs will not be affected by this job.

Fiegel: John, I'm at capacity. By making seats for you, I'll have to cut my own production. Of course, I can increase my production of economy office stools. The labor time freed by not having to fabricate the frame or assemble the deluxe stool can be shifted to the frame fabrication and assembly of the economy office stool. Fortunately, I can switch my labor force between these two models of stools without any loss of efficiency. I'd like to sell it to you at variable cost, but I have excess demand for both products. I don't mind changing my product mix to the economy model if I get a good return on the seats I make for you. Here are my standard costs for the two stools and a schedule of my manufacturing overhead. [See Exhibit A for standard costs, and see Exhibit B for the overhead budget.]

Kline: I guess I see your point, but I don't want to price myself out of the market. Maybe we should talk to corporate headquarters for guidance.

Exhibit A (23-38)   **Office Division, Standard Costs and Prices**

	Deluxe Office Stool		Economy Office Stool
Direct materials:			
Framing	$ 8.15		$ 9.76
Cushioned seat:			
Padding	2.40		—
Vinyl	4.00		—
Molded seat (purchased)	—		6.00
Direct labor:			
Frame fabrication (.5 × $7.50/DLH)	3.75	(.5 × $7.50/DLH)	3.75
Cushion fabrication (.5 × $7.50/DLH)	3.75		—
Assembly[a] (.5 × $7.50/DLH)	3.75	(.3 × $7.50/DLH)	2.25
Manufacturing:			
Overhead (1.5DLH × $12.80/DLH)	19.20	(.8DLH × $12.80/DLH)	10.24
Total standard cost	$45.00		$32.00
Selling price (30% markup)	$58.50		$41.60

[a] Attaching seats to frames and attaching rubber feet.

Exhibit B (23-38)   **Office Division, Manufacturing Overhead Budget**

Overhead Item	Nature	Amount
Supplies	Variable—at current market prices	$ 420,000
Indirect labor	Variable	375,000
Supervision	Nonvariable	250,000
Power	Use varies with activity; rates are fixed	180,000
Heat and light	Nonvariable—light is fixed regardless of production, while heat/air conditioning varies with fuel charges	140,000
Property taxes and insurance	Nonvariable—any change in amounts/ rates is independent of production	200,000
Depreciation	Fixed-dollar total	1,700,000
Employee benefits	20% of supervision, direct and indirect labor	575,000
Total overhead		$3,840,000
Capacity in direct labor-hours		300,000
Overhead rate/direct labor-hour		$12.80

Required:

John Kline and Ruth Fiegel asked PortCo corporate management for guidance on an appropriate transfer price. Corporate management suggested they consider using a transfer price based on variable manufacturing cost plus opportunity cost. Calculate a transfer price for the cushioned seat, using variable manufacturing cost plus opportunity cost.

(CMA adapted)

23-39. Differential Costing and Transfer Pricing Decisions

National Industries is a diversified corporation with separate operating divisions. Each division's performance is evaluated on the basis of total operating profits and return on division investment.

The WindAir division manufactures and sells air-conditioner units. Next year's budgeted income statement, based on a sales volume of 15,000 units, appears below.

WINDAIR DIVISION
Budgeted Income Statement
For Next Year

	Per Unit	Total (in thousands)
Sales revenue	$400	$6,000
Manufacturing costs:		
Compressor	70	1,050
Other direct materials	37	555
Direct labor	30	450
Variable overhead	45	675
Fixed overhead	32	480
Total manufacturing costs	214	3,210
Gross margin	186	2,790
Operating costs:		
Variable marketing	18	270
Fixed marketing	19	285
Fixed administrative	38	570
Total operating costs	75	1,125
Operating profit before taxes	$111	$1,665

WindAir's division manager believes sales can be increased if the unit selling price of the air conditioners is reduced. A market research study indicates that a 5 percent reduction in the selling price ($20) would increase sales volume 16 percent, or 2,400 units. WindAir has sufficient production capacity to manage this increased volume with no increase in fixed costs.

WindAir presently uses a compressor in its units that it purchases from an outside supplier at a cost of $70 per compressor. The division manager of WindAir approached the manager of the compressor division regarding the sale of a compressor unit to WindAir. The compressor division currently manufactures and sells a unit exclusively to outside firms that is similar to the unit used by WindAir. The specifications of the WindAir compressor are slightly different, which would reduce the compressor division's direct material cost by $1.50 per unit. The compressor division would not incur any variable selling costs in the units sold to WindAir. The manager of WindAir offered to pay $50 for each compressor unit purchased from the compressor division.

The compressor division has the capacity to produce 75,000 units. The coming year's budgeted income statement for the compressor division is shown below and is based on a sales volume of 64,000 units without considering WindAir's proposal.

COMPRESSOR DIVISION
Budgeted Income Statement
For Next Year

	Per Unit	Total (in thousands)
Sales revenue	$100	$6,400
Manufacturing costs:		
Direct materials	12	768
Direct labor	8	512
Variable overhead	10	640
Fixed overhead	11	704
Total manufacturing costs	41	2,624
Gross margin	59	3,776
Operating costs:		
Variable marketing	6	384
Fixed marketing	4	256
Fixed administrative	7	448
Total operating costs	17	1,088
Operating profit before taxes	$ 42	$2,688

Required:

a. Should WindAir division institute the 5 percent price reduction on its air-conditioner units even if it cannot acquire the compressors internally for $50 each? Support your conclusions with appropriate calculations.

b. Regardless of your answer to requirement a., assume WindAir needs 17,400 units. Should the compressor division be willing to supply the compressor units for $50 each? Support your conclusions with appropriate calculations.

c. Regardless of your answer to requirement a., assume WindAir needs 17,400 units. Would it be in the best interest of National Industries for the compressor division to supply the compressor units at $50 each to the WindAir division? Support your conclusions with appropriate calculations.

(CMA adapted)

23–40. Decentralization and Transfer Pricing: Calvin's Auto

Calvin's Auto was divided into three departments: new-car sales, used-car sales, and the service department. Department managers were told to run their departments as if they were independent businesses. To give department managers an incentive, most of their remuneration was to be calculated as a straight percentage of their department's operating profit.

A customer wanted to trade in his old car as part of the purchase price of a new one with a list price of $16,000. Before closing the sale, the new-car manager had to decide on the amount he would offer the customer for the trade-in value of the old car. He knew that if no trade-in were involved, he would deduct about 10 percent from the list price of this model new car to be competitive with other dealers in the area. He also wanted to make sure that he did not lose the sale by offering too low a trade-in allowance.

To establish the trade-in value of the car, the used-car manager accompanied the new-car manager and the customer out to the parking lot to examine the car. In the course of his appraisal, the used-car manager estimated that the car would require reconditioning work costing about $1,000, after which the car would retail for about $3,500. The used-car manager estimated that he could get about $2,100 for the car "as is" (that is, without any work being done to it) at a weekly auction at which dealers regularly buy and sell used cars.

The new-car department manager had the right to take any trade-in at any price he thought appropriate, but then it was his responsibility to dispose of the car. He had the alternative of either trying to persuade the used-car manager to take over the car and accepting the used-car manager's appraisal price, or he himself could sell the car at the auction.

The new-car manager decided he would allow $4,000 for the used car, provided the customer agreed to pay the list price of $16,000 for the new car. After some discussion, the $4,000 allowance and $16,000 list price were agreed upon.

The company's accountant set about recording the sale in the accounting records of the business. She saw the new car had been purchased from the manufacturer for $13,000; she was uncertain about the value she should place on the trade-in car. The new car's list price was $16,000 and it had cost $13,000, so she reasoned the gross margin on the new-car sale was $3,000. Yet the new-car manager had allowed $4,000 for the old car, which needed $1,000 in repairs, after which it could be sold retail for $3,500. Uncertain about the value she should place on the used car for inventory valuation purposes, the accountant decided that she would temporarily put down a value of $4,000, and await instructions from her superiors.

When the manager of the used-car department found out what the accountant had done, he went to the new-car deparment manager's office and stated forcefully that he would not accept $4,000 as the value of the used car. He stated:

> I never would have allowed the customer $4,000 for that car. My department has to make a profit too, you know. My own income is dependent on the profit I show on the sale of used cars, and I will not stand for having my income hurt because you are too generous.

The service manager arrived with Calvin Cline, the company president, and stated:

> There is something bothering me about this accounting system we've been using. I can't charge as much on an internal job as I would for the same job performed for an outside customer. If I did work costing $1,000 for an outside customer, I would be able to charge about $1,600 for the job. I figure that I should be able to make the same charge for repairing a trade-in as I would get for an outside repair job.

Required:

a. Suppose the new-car deal is consummated, with the repaired used car being retailed for $3,500 and the variable cost of the repairs being $1,000. Assume that all sales personnel are on salary (no commissions), and that department and company costs not explicitly mentioned in the case are fixed and not affected by this transaction. What is the dealership contribution on the total transaction (that is, new and repaired used cars sold)?

b. Assume each department (new, used, service) is treated as a profit center, as described in the case.
   (1) At what value should this trade-in (unrepaired) be transferred from the new-car department to the used-car department? Why?
   (2) How much should the service department be able to charge the used-car department for the repairs on this trade-in car if the service department operates below capacity? Why?
   (3) How much should the service department be able to charge if it operates at capacity? Why?

c. Given your responses to b., what will be each of the three departments' contributions on this transaction, assuming:
   (1) The service department is operating below capacity.
   (2) The service department is operating at capacity.

d. If the service department was operating at capacity, would the dealership be better off to repair and retail the used car or sell it "as is"?

e. Do you feel the three profit center approach is appropriate for the auto dealership? If so, explain why, including an explanation of how this is better than other specific alternatives. If not, propose a better alternative and explain why it is better than the three profit center approach and any other alternatives you have considered.

23–41. Birch Paper Company (Evaluate Transfer Pricing Policy and Use of Responsibility Centers)[6]

"If I were to price these boxes any lower than $480 a thousand," said James Brunner, manager of Birch Paper Company's Thompson Division, "I'd be countermanding my order for last month for our sales force to stop shaving their bids and to bid full-cost quotations. If I turn around now and accept this for something less than $480, I'll be tearing down my own orders. The division can't very well show a profit by putting in bids that don't even cover a fair share of overhead costs, let alone give us a profit."

Birch Paper Company was a medium-sized, partly integrated paper company, producing white and kraft papers and paperboard. A portion of its paperboard output was converted into corrugated boxes by the Thompson division, which also printed the outside surface of the boxes. Including Thompson, the company had four producing divisions and a timberland division, which supplied part of the company's pulp requirements.

For several years, each division had been judged independently on the basis of its profit and ROI. Top management had been working to gain effective results from a policy of decentralizing responsibility and authority for all decisions except those relating to overall company policy. The company's top officials felt that in the past few years the concept of decentralization had been successfully applied and that the company's profits and competitive position had definitely improved.

Early in the year, the Northern Division designed a special display box for one of its papers in conjunction with the Thompson Division, which was equipped to make the box. Thompson's package design and development staff spent several months perfecting the design, production methods, and materials that were to be used; because of the unusual color and shape, these were far from standard. According to an agreement between the two divisions, the Thompson Division was reimbursed by the Northern Division for the out-of-pocket cost of its design and development work.

When the specifications were all prepared, the Northern Division asked for bids on the box from the Thompson Division and from two outside companies, West Paper Company and Erie Papers, Inc. Each division manager normally was free to buy from whichever supplier he wished, and even on sales within the company, divisions were expected to meet the going market price if they wanted the business.

At this time, the profit margins of converters such as the Thompson Division were being squeezed. Thompson, as did many other similar converters, bought its board, liner, or paper; and its function was to print, cut, and shape it into boxes. Though it bought most of its materials from other Birch divisions, most of Thompson's sales were to outside customers. If Thompson got the order from Northern, it probably would buy its linerboard and corrugating medium from the Southern Division of Birch. The walls of a corrugated box consist of outside and inside sheets of linerboard sandwiching the corrugating medium.

About 70 percent of Thompson's variable cost of $400 a thousand for the order represented the cost of linerboard and corrugating medium. Though Southern Division had been running below capacity and had excess inventory, it quoted the market price, which had not noticeably weakened as a result of the oversupply. Its variable costs on liner and corrugating medium were about 60 percent of selling price.

The Northern Division received bids on the boxes of $480 a thousand from the Thompson Division, $430 a thousand from West Paper, and $432 a thousand from Erie Papers. Erie offered to buy from Birch the outside linerboard and corrugating medium. The outside liner would be supplied by the Southern Division at a price equivalent to $90 a thousand boxes and would be printed for $30 a thousand by the Thompson Division. Of the $30, about $25 would be variable costs.

Since this situation appeared to be a little unusual, William Kenton, manager of the Northern Division, discussed the wide discrepancy of bids with Birch's commercial vice president. He told the commercial vice president, "We sell in a very competitive market, where higher costs cannot be passed on. How can we be expected to show a decent profit and return on investment if we have to buy our supplies at more than 10 percent over the going market?"

Knowing that Brunner had on occasion in the past few months been unable to operate the Thompson Division at capacity, the commercial vice president thought it odd that Brunner would add the full 20 percent overhead and profit charge to his variable costs. When he asked Brunner about this over the telephone, his answer was the statement that appears at the beginning of the case. Brunner went on to say that having done the developmental work on the box, and having received no profit on that, he felt entitled to a normal markup on the production of the box itself.

The vice president explored further the costs of the various divisions. He remembered a comment the controller had made to the effect that costs that for one division were variable could be largely fixed for the company as a whole. He knew that in the absence of specific orders from top management, Kenton would accept the lowest bid; namely, that of West Paper for $430. However, it would be possible for top management to order the acceptance of another bid if the situation warranted such action. And though the volume represented by the transactions in question was less than 5 percent of the volume of any of the divisions involved, other transactions could conceivably raise similar problems later.

Required:

Does the system motivate Mr. Brunner in such a way that actions he takes in the best interests of the Thompson Division are also in the best interests of the Birch Paper Company? If your answer is no, give some specific instances related as closely as possible to the type of situation described in the case. Would the managers of other divisions be correctly motivated? What should the vice president do?

PART

IV

THE IMPACT OF UNCERTAINTY ON COST ANALYSIS

OUTLINE

DECISION MAKING UNDER UNCERTAINTY

LEARNING OBJECTIVES

1. Understand the quantitative approach to decision making in an uncertain environment.

2. Introduce alternate methods for analyzing the effects of uncertainty.

3. Apply decision analysis under uncertainty to the cost-volume-profit setting as an example of the more general setting.

In earlier chapters, the use of accounting data for decision making was based on the implicit assumption of certainty. The real world, however, is characterized by uncertainty. Decisions must be made and actions taken without definite knowledge of the results. For example, suppose that HyperMedical Engineering Company has developed a new device for modifying viral cells. Demand for the product exceeds the company's present manufacturing capacity. HyperMedical Engineering's management could build a new plant, in which case the capital budgeting techniques discussed in Chapters 15 and 16 would be employed.

But building a plant takes several years; moreover, competitors in the biomedical engineering field may develop a similar product and, hence, cut into HyperMedical's market. So, to meet the immediate demand, management is considering obtaining a new plant under a short-term lease. The fixed lease payments for a new plant will result in a step increase in costs similar to that diagrammed in Illustration 24–1. Point *A* on the volume axis represents the current level of activity, which is also the full capacity of the old plant. Management expects that volume will increase to the level represented by point *B*. If this happens, then the profits at *B* will be large enough to warrant leasing the new plant. However, the costs of operating the new plant result in a step increase in the fixed costs. If management is certain that the number of units represented by point *B* on the volume axis will be sold with the new plant, then the lease would be justified. Unfortunately, demand is rarely known with certainty.

Illustration 24–1 **Effect of Leased Plant on CVP Relationships**

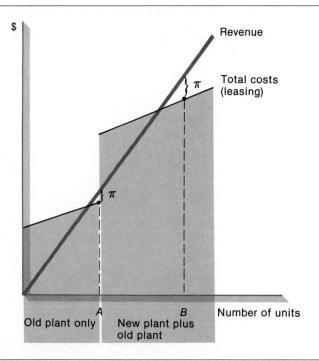

Note: *A* is also the capacity of the old plant.

Suppose management expected profit from a demand increase to point B and went ahead with the lease. Management would be unpleasantly surprised if actual demand was less than expected.

Knowledge of the extent of uncertainty and the impact of that uncertainty on decision outcomes is important information for decision making in an uncertain world. In this chapter, we introduce the concepts used to deal with uncertainty and illustrate how those concepts are applied to CVP analysis.

DEALING WITH UNCERTAINTY

We suggest that six steps be followed when dealing with decisions under uncertainty. These are:

1. Establish a set of mathematically quantified objectives.
2. Determine the set of actions that can be taken.
3. Estimate the various outcomes that are likely to occur after the decision.
4. Assign probabilities to those outcomes.
5. Compute the payoffs that are likely under each paired set of actions and outcomes.
6. Choose the action that is best in achieving objectives.

Use of this approach does not assure profitable operations, but it does provide a rational basis for decision making. In the long run, following this method can be expected to result in decisions that achieve established objectives.

Establishing Objectives

Objective Function
Mathematical statement of goals.

Company management usually establishes objectives. In addition to maximizing profit, management may seek to avoid excessive risk, attain certain market shares, or introduce new products. Once the qualitative objectives are determined, they must be expressed in mathematical terms. This mathematical statement of management goals is called an **objective function**. An example of an objective function is the expression:

Maximize profit (π), where

$$\pi = (P - V)X - F$$

This is the profit equation from Chapter 11. The term X represents the quantity sold per period, P is the price per unit, V represents the variable cost per unit, and F is the fixed costs per period.

Objective functions are stated based on all of the alternatives available to a company. For example, assume a company has capacity of 20,000 units, revenues of $9 per unit, variable costs of $6 per unit, and fixed costs of $16,000 per month. Further, the company can subcontract for units in excess of 20,000 by paying a variable cost of $8 per unit subcontracted. The objective function for this situation is:

$$\text{Max } \pi = [20{,}000 \times (\$9 - \$6)] + [X \times (\$9 - \$8)] - \$16{,}000$$

where X is the unit demand in excess of 20,000 units.

It is possible to formulate different objective functions for each decision alternative. In this analysis, the results suggest the objective function which has the greatest value as the one to be chosen for a specific decision.

If management wanted, they could extend this analysis to include more complex statements of objectives. For example, management may have different preferences for risk. A utility function that reflects management's attitude toward risk might be used instead of a profit equation. Management may face constraints in devising the profit plan. These constraints may also be incorporated in an uncertainty mode. We shall assume the profit equation above reflects management's objectives. More complex objective functions are discussed in the management science, statistics, and accounting literature.[1]

The role of cost data in an uncertain environment can be demonstrated using a linear profit function such as the CVP equation. Extensions to these more complex settings may be studied in operations research or statistics. No matter how complex the situation, the accountant's task is to provide the cost data relevant to the decision.

We can apply this approach to the problem faced by the management of HyperMedical Engineering. We will approach the problem in the suggested order and then discuss the results of the outcome of the analysis.

Determining the Action Set

Action Set The alternatives available to managers in a given decision setting.

Once objectives have been established, management must consider the alternative actions in the **action set** that may be taken to attain them. In our example, there may be several ways to meet the increased demand. As we noted, management might construct a new plant. Or it might subcontract for a certain amount of production. It might also purchase another company that is in the same business. Each action entails different amounts of profit and risk.

Management considers each alternative as a possible way to meet its established objectives. Other alternatives may also be considered. For example, management could ignore the increased demand and continue to produce at the same level as before. To simplify the discussion, we will assume that the only possibilities are to lease a new plant or to subcontract for the added demand.

Estimating Outcomes

Exogenous Factors Outside events that can influence an outcome.

Outcomes Possible results of a given action.

The outcome that will occur after the decision has been made is unknown and usually beyond the control of management. The external influences that affect the outcome are called **exogenous factors.** For example, in the Hyper-Medical example, management may expect that future demand for the product will continue to increase. But the level of future demand is affected by such factors as the state of the economy, competition, and technological change. When management makes its expansion decisions, it cannot know the exact level of future demand because it cannot perfectly predict these exogenous factors.

Nevertheless, management can estimate the possibilities of specific **outcomes.** While HyperMedical's management may expect future demand to

---

[1] For references in the accounting literature, see A. Charnes, W. Cooper, and Y. Ijiri, "Break-Even Budgeting and Programming to Goals," *Journal of Accounting Research,* Spring 1963; J. Hilliard and R. Leitch, "Cost-Volume-Profit Analysis under Uncertainty: A Log-Normal Approach," *The Accounting Review,* January 1975; J. Demski and G. Feltham, *Cost Determination: A Conceptual Approach* (Ames: Iowa State University Press, 1976); and J. Demski, *Information Analysis* (Reading, Mass.: Addison-Wesley Publishing, 1980).

increase by 5,000 units next year, they may estimate that demand could increase by as much as 40,000 units. The 5,000-unit increase is considered much more likely than the 40,000 increase, but both are possibilities.

A set of mutually exclusive and collectively exhaustive outcomes is constructed to represent the possible future outcomes. As a practical matter, a small representative set of possibilities is usually chosen or else we assume the outcomes will follow a continuous distribution, which may be analyzed through direct computation or some sampling method. In our example, the set of demand increases is 1,000, 2,000, 5,000, 10,000, and 40,000 units. In reality, demand increase *might* be 1,386 units or 61,903 units or any other number; but to avoid excessive computations, the limited set is usually sufficient.

Assigning Probabilities to Outcomes

Payoff The value of each outcome.

Probabilities Likelihoods that given outcomes will, in fact, occur.

Now that we have the set of five estimated future demand levels, the next task is to think about each outcome, estimate how likely it is to occur, and evaluate the payoffs. In the decision literature, the term **payoff** is used to indicate the value of each outcome.

The probability of each demand level's occurrence is estimated statistically or by other means. Marketing studies may be conducted to evaluate future demand levels and the related **probabilities** that those levels will, in fact, occur. Past trends may be extrapolated using time series analyses when there is a sufficient reason to believe the trends will continue in the future. Management may use its own judgment based on knowledge of contract negotiations with potential buyers or other factors. Assessing these probabilities is always a subjective process even though mathematical models may yield results that are precise to the last unit of production. Because the future is uncertain, probability statements about the future are also uncertain. Nonetheless, management uses such probability assessments when their benefits exceed the cost of obtaining them.

HyperMedical management may realize that a 5,000-unit increase is more likely than a 40,000-unit increase, but more precision is needed to evaluate risk. Based on quantified data about future demand levels, management assesses the future increases in demand and, based on experience and judgment, estimates the following set of probabilities, which are presented in a **payoff table.**[2]

Payoff Table A schedule showing the alternate outcomes from a decision together with the probability of their occurrence.

Increased Future Demand (units)	Probability
1,000	.10
2,000	.20
5,000	.50
10,000	.15
40,000	.05
Total	1.00

---

[2] See R. Libby, *Accounting and Human Information Processing* (Englewood Cliffs, N.J.: Prentice Hall, 1981), for a discussion of behavioral probability estimation and revision.

The set of probabilities may contain as few or as many demand levels as needed to obtain the desired degree of precision. The desired precision in the results will depend on the reliability of the data and the trade-off between the costs and benefits of gathering additional information. The probabilities must always sum to one, as they do here. It is assumed that the probabilities are independent of the decision. That is, whether HyperMedical leases a new plant or subcontracts, the set of probabilities for future demand levels will be the same.

Computing Payoffs

The accountant must often compute the payoffs for each alternative and for each outcome. To do this, the costs that are likely for each level of activity and for each alternative action choice must be considered. This is a direct application of the concepts of differential costing introduced earlier in this book. For example, assume that HyperMedical's management could subcontract any number of units at any time and obtain the profit function:

$$\pi = (\$8 - \$7)X_s$$

where

π = Operating profit from subcontracting.
X_s = Quantity subcontracted and sold.

This equation indicates a $1 net profit per unit.

Or management could lease a new plant capable of producing 10,000 units with a profit function of:

$$\pi' = (\$8 - \$2)X_p - \$20,000$$

where

π' = Operating profit from leasing.
X_p = Quantity produced and sold.
$20,000 is the fixed cost.

Management would want to lease only one plant.

The payoffs for each outcome under each alternative action are computed and shown in the following table:

Future Demand	Payoffs	
	Subcontract	Lease Plant
1,000	$ 1,000	$ -14,000[a]
2,000	2,000	-8,000
5,000	5,000	10,000
10,000	10,000	40,000
40,000	40,000	70,000[b]

Additional computations:
[a] $-14,000 = 1,000(\$8 - \$2) - \$20,000; \$-8,000 = 2,000(\$8 - \$2) - \$20,000$; etc.
[b] See following paragraph for computations at the 40,000-unit level.

At the 40,000-unit level, both manufacturing and subcontracting would be required since the plant can produce only 10,000 units. Manufacturing

10,000 at a profit of $40,000 plus subcontracting 30,000 (that is, 40,000 − 10,000) at a profit of $30,000 is necessary to obtain the $70,000 total.

To make its decision, HyperMedical's management computes the expected payoffs under each considered alternative action. The expected payoff for each action is the sum of the payoffs for each outcome times the probability associated with that outcome. For subcontracting, the expected payoff is:

Outcome	Probability		Payoff at This Level		Expected Payoff
1,000	.10	×	$ 1,000	=	$ 100
2,000	.20	×	2,000	=	400
5,000	.50	×	5,000	=	2,500
10,000	.15	×	10,000	=	1,500
40,000	.05	×	40,000	=	2,000
Expected payoff for subcontracting					$6,500

For the alternative to lease a new plant, the expected payoff is computed using the same method:

Outcome	Probability		Payoff at This Level		Expected Payoff
1,000	.10	×	$ −14,000	=	$ −1,400
2,000	.20	×	−8,000	=	−1,600
5,000	.50	×	10,000	=	5,000
10,000	.15	×	40,000	=	6,000
40,000	.05	×	70,000	=	3,500
Expected payoff for leasing					$ 11,500

Making the Decision

The expected payoff levels are compared, and the alternative with the higher expected payoff is selected under the decision criterion established in step 1. Since the expected payoff from leasing a new plant ($11,500) is greater than the expected payoff from subcontracting ($6,500), the data suggest that management should lease the new plant. This is only a suggestion. The decision is the responsibility of management, and management may elect to use other decision criteria. In the following section, we discuss some other decision criteria that managers use.

LOSS-MINIMIZATION CRITERIA

Risk The chance that the outcome that actually occurs from a given decision is less valuable than that which would be obtained from another decision.

Although leasing the new plant yields the highest expected payoff, Hyper-Medical runs the risk of a loss if this alternative is chosen and if demand is only 1,000 or 2,000 units. Adding the probabilities of these two demand levels suggests that there is a .3 probability of a loss. If management finds this loss exposure too great, they may seek a less risky alternative. Given the information in the example, there is no risk of accounting loss from subcontracting. However, if demand reaches 5,000 or more units, there is an opportunity loss from subcontracting—a greater payoff could have been earned if the plant had been leased.

Management may establish loss minimization as its objective in step 1. Risk minimization may be defined in terms of the probability of loss. Management may state its objectives in terms of loss minimization. For example, management may seek to minimize the maximum loss to which it would be exposed. This is called the **minimax** criterion. Or management may set some loss amount and a related expected value as a limit on risk. For example, the criterion could be: "Don't invest if there is more than a 30 percent probability of a loss."

Minimax   A criterion to minimize the maximum loss.

The appropriate decision would be to subcontract to minimize the risk of an accounting loss. By subcontracting, the risk of loss is reduced to zero, but with leasing there is a .3 probability of loss. Therefore, to minimize the probability of loss, management would probably prefer subcontracting.

Why would management give up the incremental expected payoff just to eliminate the possibility of a loss? Recent research suggests that management may be constrained by contracts (such as loan agreements) that call for severe penalties if particular profit levels are not maintained. Under such circumstances, the losses that would be incurred if demand did not permit profitable operation of the leased plant would trigger other costs. Indeed, loan terms may be renogtiated in favor of the lender, interest rates may be increased, or loans may be called. For these reasons, management may prefer risk minimization to payoff optimization for a specific proposal.

On the other hand, some managers would prefer the added risk because of the potential for greater profits should demand levels go higher than anticipated. Although we generally assume managers are risk averse, we realize that they differ in their risk preferences. Hence, a general rule for treating risky projects may not be applicable in a given circumstance.

Profit Variability and Risk

Another approach to comparing the risk of alternative projects is to measure the dispersion in returns from the alternatives. The **standard deviation** of the returns may be computed and used as a project risk measure.

The standard deviation for the payoff series is defined as:

Standard Deviation   A measure of risk based on the dispersion in a group of numbers.

$$s = \sqrt{\sum_{j=1}^{n} (I_j - \bar{I})^2 P_j}$$

where

n = Number of observations.
s = Standard deviation of the payoff series for each alternative.
I_j = Computed payoff or income at each demand level.
P_j = Probability of attaining that demand level.
$\bar{I}$ = Expected payoff level.

Illustration 24-2 shows the relationship of the standard deviation measure to the variability of outcomes. The distributions shown represent the probability distributions for the profits from each of two projects. Since Project A has a smaller standard deviation, it is considered less risky, all other things held constant.

Illustration 24-2   **Payoff Variability and Standard Deviation**

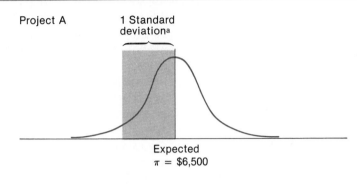

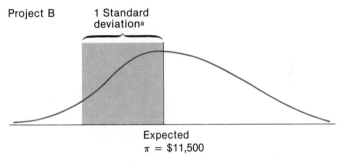

a Brackets indicate the relative standard deviations.

For HyperMedical, the standard deviation for subcontracting is:

$$s = \sqrt{\begin{array}{l}[(\$1,000 - \$6,500)^2(.10)] + [(\$2,000 - \$6,500)^2(.20)] + [(\$5,000 - \$6,500)^2(.50)] \\ + [(\$10,000 - \$6,500)^2(.15)] + [(\$40,000 - \$6,500)^2(.05)]\end{array}}$$

$$= \sqrt{\$3,025,000 + \$4,050,000 + \$1,125,000 + \$1,837,500 + \$56,112,500}$$

$$= \sqrt{\$66,150,000}$$

$$= \underline{\underline{\$8,133}}$$

If HyperMedical leases the plant, the standard deviation of the payoff is:

$$s = \sqrt{\begin{array}{l}[(\$-14,000 - \$11,500)^2(.10)] + [(\$-8,000 - \$11,500)^2(.20)] + [(\$10,000 - \$11,500)^2(.50) \\ + [(\$40,000 - \$11,500)^2(.15)] + [(\$70,000 - \$11,500)^2(.05)]\end{array}}$$

$$= \sqrt{\$65,025,000 + \$76,050,000 + \$1,125,000 + \$121,837,500 + \$171,112,500}$$

$$= \sqrt{\$435,150,000}$$

$$= \underline{\underline{\$20,860}}$$

Using this criterion, subcontracting results in a smaller standard deviation than leasing. Hence, subcontracting would be considered less risky if the standard deviation was used as the risk measure.

The standard deviation has some limitations as a risk measure. One disadvantage is that payoffs that exceed the expected value are treated the same as payoffs that are less than the expected value. Few would object to payoffs that exceed the mean. Yet in our example, the greatest contribution to the standard deviation comes from the payoffs in excess of the mean. This would indicate that the risk is unbalanced. Leasing is riskier, but the risk is likely to result in greater payoffs.

A second difficulty with the use of a single-project risk calculation such as standard deviation is that it ignores other company projects that may have offsetting effects. Portfolio theory has been developed in finance to consider the impact of a single project on a company's overall risk.

Coefficient of Variation The standard deviation of a project divided by the expected value of the project.

Finally, the standard deviation ignores the differences in the expected payoffs from projects. To compensate for this, the **coefficient of variation** (c.v.) may be computed. The c.v. is the *standard deviation of the project divided by the expected value of the project.* For the subcontracting alternative, the c.v. is:

$$\frac{s}{\bar{I}} = \frac{\$8,133}{\$6,500} = \underline{\underline{\$1.25}}$$

and for leasing the plant, the c.v. is:

$$\frac{s}{\bar{I}} = \frac{\$20,860}{\$11,500} = \underline{\underline{\$1.81}}$$

Scaling the standard deviation in this manner relates its value to the magnitude of the expected return. A lower c.v. may imply a lower level of relative risk. For the example, the c.v. is less for subcontracting. This suggests that subcontracting is less risky than leasing even when scaled for the difference in payoffs.

Risk Evaluation—An Indifference Approach

Another way to evaluate two alternatives is to consider the point at which the advantage switches from one alternative to the other. For example, at small increases in demand, it would pay to subcontract; but at some point, the advantage switches from subcontracting to leasing. The switch occurs at the point where the two payoff equations are equal. Illustration 24–3 indicates the conceptual basis for this assertion.

The diagram indicates that as long as the new demand is greater than 4,000 units, leasing will result in a greater profit than subcontracting. Management may consider the spread between expected demand (5,000 units) and the break-even quantity as a range of protection for its decision. Demand would have to be 1,000 units less than expected before management would have wished it had made the other decision. This indifference point is computed by finding the point where the two payoff functions are equal:

$$\pi = \pi^*$$
$$X(\$8 - \$7) = X(\$8 - \$2) - \$20,000$$
$$\$1X = \$6X - \$20,000$$
$$\$5X = \$20,000$$
$$X = \underline{\underline{4,000}} \text{ units}$$

Management can use this indifference approach to decide which alternative to use. If they are confident that the actual demand will exceed 4,000 by a substantial margin and by a significant probability, they will decide to lease the plant. But if the actual future demand is likely to be close to or less

Illustration 24-3   **Comparison of Subcontracting Profit with Profit from Leased Plant**

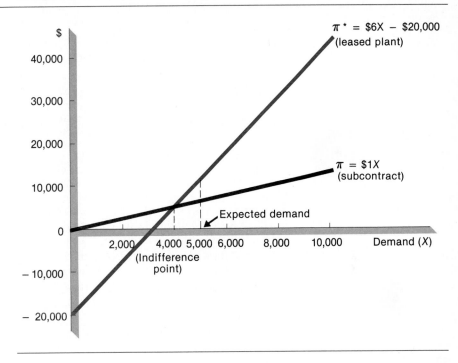

than 4,000 and management is risk averse, then they will probably sub-contract. If management is risk-seeking, they may choose to lease because of the greater potential reward. Later, as the actual demand becomes better known, the decision may be reviewed and changed if it is possible to do so.

CVP UNDER UNCERTAINTIES IN PRICES AND COSTS

Accountants also consider the impact of uncertainty on CVP analysis. Up to this point, we have assumed that the only uncertainty in CVP analysis was the **expected value** of X, the quantity of units produced and sold. But in reality, any of the inputs to the profit equation are uncertain. Indeed, the probability of obtaining profit numbers that are equal to plans is very small. When all the variables in the CVP equation are uncertain, the same approach that was used for uncertainties in X is extended to the other variables.

Since the number of computations rapidly increases as the number of uncertain variables increases, computer assistance is usually required. A technique known as **Monte Carlo** analysis is used to sample from the distributions of each variable and to compute the profit for each sampled combination of selling price, variable cost, unit volume, and fixed costs, labeled P, V, X, and F, respectively. The resulting expected profit and standard deviation can be used in exactly the same manner as when only X was uncertain.

Monte Carlo A method of sampling from an assumed distribution function to obtain simulated observations of costs or other variables.

To use Monte Carlo analysis, we must specify the distributions for each variable in the profit function. If we focus on the profit from leasing a new plant, we need to specify distributions for P, V, and F. The distribution for X that was obtained earlier will be used.

Let us assume the following distributions for the variables:

		Value	Probability
For P		$7	.3
		8	.4
		9	.3
For V		$1.50	.3
		1.75	.2
		2.00	.1
		2.50	.1
		3.00	.3
For F		$18,000	.4
		20,000	.2
		22,000	.4

These data are entered into a computer program that uses random numbers to sample from the distributions and compute an expected profit as well as the standard deviation for that profit. In addition, the program may be designed to plot the different outcomes and their frequencies.

The results of using such a program for 1,000 iterations indicated an expected profit of $21,020 and a standard deviation of $52,794. These data would be used for decision making the same way that the mean and standard deviation were used when only the quantity varied.

The plotted outcomes from this program are shown in Illustration 24–4. Note the concentration of outcomes at profit levels of $ - 15,000 to $15,000.

Illustration 24-4 **Monte Carlo Simulation Results for CVP Analysis (in thousands of dollars)**

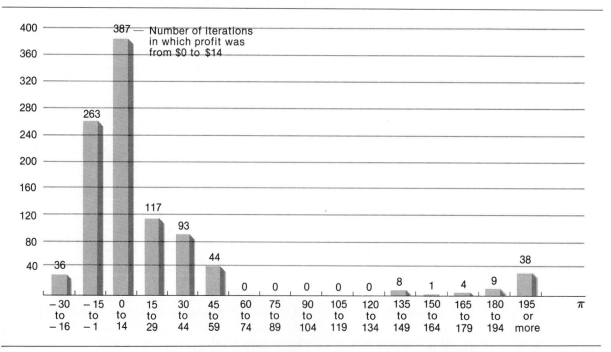

Simulation A method of studying problems whereby a model of a system or operational process is subjected to a series of assumptions and variations in an effort to find one or more acceptable solutions.

Overall, it appears that the probable outcome would be a modest profit in the range of zero to $45,000. The very high profits occur infrequently. Further analysis of these higher profits and their likelihood might be conducted if management were risk-seeking.

The advantage of using computer **simulation** is that the distribution of payoffs may be observed even with very complex interrelationships. Indeed, the Monte Carlo method could be extended to include prices, costs, and quantities for multiple products as well as interrelationships between the products. For example, if the price of one output increases more than 20 percent, consumers may switch to another alternative output. A computer simulation could be designed to include the switch when the specific round of the simulation indicated a 20 percent increase in price for the first output.

SUMMARY

In the uncertainty that characterizes the real world, decision makers must consider the possibility that the outcome they expect from a decision may not be the outcome that actually occurs. Because of the potential difference between actual results and expectations, there is a risk in decision making. Managers assess the extent of risk for decision alternatives. A six-step process is suggested for risk assessment. The role of the accountant is oriented primarily to evaluating the differential costs and revenues from the set of likely outcomes. The expected value of each alternative decision and a measure of the risk of loss or variability for each alternative can be used to help make decisions that conform to management's risk preferences. Monte Carlo simulations may be used to analyze more complex profit relationships.

TERMS AND CONCEPTS

The following terms and concepts should be familiar to you after reading this chapter.

Action Set	**Outcomes**
Coefficient of Variation (c.v.)	**Payoff**
Exogenous Factors	**Payoff Table**
Expected Value	**Probabilities**
Minimax	**Risk**
Monte Carlo	**Simulation**
Objective Function	**Standard Deviation**

SUPPLEMENTARY READINGS

Adar, Z.; A. Barnea; and B. Lev. "A Comprehensive Cost-Volume-Profit Analysis under Uncertainty." *Accounting Review*, January 1977.

Brockett, P., et al. "Chance Constrained Programming Approach to Cost-Volume-Profit Analysis." *Accounting Review*, July 1984, pp. 474–87.

Cheung, Joseph K. "Stochastic Dominance as an Approach to Uncertainty in Cost Accounting." *Journal of Accounting Education*, Fall 1985, pp. 91–102.

Clarke, Peter. "Bringing Uncertainty into the CVP Analysis." *CPA Journal*, November 1986, pp. 117–20.

Driscoll, Donna M.; W. Thomas Lin; and Paul R. Watkins. "Cost-Volume-Profit Analysis under Uncertainty: A Synthesis and Framework for Evaluation." *Journal of Accounting Literature,* Spring 1984, pp. 85–115.

Jaedicke, R. K., and A. A. Robichek. "Cost-Volume-Profit Analysis under Conditions of Uncertainty." *Accounting Review,* October 1964, pp. 917–26.

Johnson, G. L., and S. S. Simik. "Multiproduct C-V-P Analysis under Uncertainty." *Journal of Accounting Research,* Autumn 1971, pp. 278–86.

Kalish, Shlomo. "New Product Adoption Model with Price, Advertising, and Uncertainty." *Management Science,* December 1985, pp. 1569–85.

Shih, W. "A General Decision Model for Cost-Volume-Profit Analysis under Uncertainty." *Accounting Review,* October 1979, pp. 687–706.

Sinclair, Kenneth, and James A. Talbott. "Using Breakeven Analysis when Cost Behavior is Unknown." *Management Accounting,* July 1986, pp. 52–55.

Thakkar, Rashmi B.; David R. Finley; and Woody M. Liao. "Stochastic Demand CVP Model with Return on Investment Criteria." *Contemporary Accounting,* Fall 1984, pp. 77–86 (published in Canada).

SELF-STUDY PROBLEM

Thunder Manufacturing Company produces a volatile chemical, Vapo, that must be sold in the month produced or else discarded. Thunder can manufacture Vapo itself at a variable cost of $40 per unit, or they can purchase it from an outside supplier at a cost of $70 per unit. Thunder can sell Vapo at $80 per unit. Production levels must be set at the start of the period and cannot be changed during the period. The production process is such that at least 9,000 units must be produced during the period. Thunder management must decide whether to produce Vapo or whether to purchase it from the outside supplier.

The possible sales of Vapo and their probabilities are:

Demand (units)	Probability
4,000	.4
7,000	.5
11,000	.1

Required:

Determine the following:

a. Expected demand.

b. Expected profit from purchasing Vapo from an outside supplier and selling it.

c. Expected profit from manufacturing and selling.

d. Standard deviation of profits from purchasing and selling.

e. Standard deviation of profits from manufacturing and selling.

f. Coefficient of variation for each alternative.

SOLUTION TO SELF-STUDY PROBLEM

a. Expected demand is 6,200 units, computed as:

Demand (units)	Probability	Expected Demand (units)
4,000	.4	1,600
7,000	.5	3,500
11,000	.1	1,100
Expected demand		6,200

b. The expected profit from purchasing and selling would be equal to the unit contribution times the expected quantity or

$$(\$80 - \$70) \times 6{,}200 \text{ units} = \underline{\underline{\$62{,}000}}$$

c. Even though the production cost is stated as a variable cost, since a minimum of 9,000 units must be produced, the cost is really fixed up to that point because of minimum production constraints. Units produced in excess of the 9,000 minimum would carry the variable of $40 each. The expected profit from manufacturing is:

Demand (units)	Probability	Manufacturing Cost	Proft	Expected Profit
4,000	.4	$360,000	$ (40,000)	$ (16,000)
7,000	.5	360,000	200,000	100,000
11,000	.1	440,000	440,000	44,000
Expected profit				$128,000

d. The standard deviation from purchasing and selling is:

$(I - \bar{I})$	$(I - \bar{I})^2 p$ (millions)
(4,000 − 6,200) ($10)	$193.6
(7,000 − 6,200) ($10)	32.0
(11,000 − 6,200) ($10)	230.4
	$456.0

$$\underline{\underline{\$21{,}354}} = \sqrt{\$456.0 \text{ million}}$$

e. The standard deviation from manufacturing and selling is:

$(I - \bar{I})$	$(I - \bar{I})^2 p$ (millions)
$(−40.000 − 128,000)	$11,289.6
(200,000 − 128,000)	2,592.0
(440,000 − 128,000)	9,734.4
Total	$23,616.0

$$\underline{\underline{\$153{,}675}} = \sqrt{\$23{,}616.0 \text{ million}}$$

f. The coefficient of variation for purchasing and selling is:

$$\underline{\underline{.344}} = \frac{\$21,354}{\$62,000}$$

The coefficient of variation for manufacturing and selling is:

$$\underline{\underline{1.201}} = \frac{\$153,675}{\$128,000}$$

QUESTIONS

24–1. What are the steps in decision making under uncertainty?

24–2. What is the role of the accountant in decision making under uncertainty?

24–3. The comment, "Since we can't know the future, there's not much point in doing all this elaborate analysis," is frequently heard. Respond to this comment.

24–4. Why do we limit the possible outcomes to discrete numbers such as 3,000 units or $500,000 in revenues when the actual numbers might be 3,129 units, $486,313 in revenue, or some similar odd number?

24–5. Why would management give up a lucrative payoff in exchange for a project with a smaller payoff, but with little or no risk of loss?

24–6. What is the coefficient of variation, and why is it important?

24–7. Discuss the use of the standard deviation as a risk measure.

24–8. How can CVP analysis be used to assess project risk?

24–9. What are the problems in applying simulation analysis to the assessment of risk?

EXERCISES

24–10. Formulate Objective Function
(L.O.1)

Teasley Delivery Company provides courier services. The company can deliver packages with its own equipment or can subcontract. Revenues from any delivery average $10 per item regardless of how the package was delivered. The company's fixed costs are $20,000 per month, which gives them the capacity to deliver 15,000 packages. Variable costs are $1.70 per package delivered using the company's own equipment. If Teasley subcontracts, the costs to deliver a package total $6.80.

Required:

State, in mathematical form, Teasley Company's objective function.

24–11. Compute Expected Values
(L.O.1)

Paul Jones is considering two investment alternatives. He can buy Treasury bills, which have a guaranteed 10 percent return, or he can invest his money in a company stock with the following schedule of returns and probabilities.

Return on Stock	Probability
−4%	.05
2	.05
5	.10
10	.30
12	.15
15	.15
20	.10
25	.05
30	.05

Required:

What is the expected return on the company stock that he is considering buying? Does it have a higher expected return than the 10 percent expected on Treasury bills?

24–12. Estimate Risk Measures
(L.O.2)

Refer to the data for Paul Jones (exercise 24–11).

Required:

a. Estimate the standard deviation of the return on stock.

b. Estimate the probability of loss from buying the stock.

24–13. Compute Expected Values
(L.O.1)

Sound Company is considering a make-or-buy alternative. An outside supplier has agreed to sell the materials at a price of $40 per unit. If they produced the unit themselves, the costs of the materials would be as follows:

Cost per Unit	Probability
$30	.20
35	.25
40	.25
45	.20
50	.10

Required:

What is the expected cost per unit if they produce the unit themselves?

24–14. Compute Standard Deviation
(L.O.2)

Refer to the data for Sound Company (exercise 24–13). Estimate the standard deviation of the production alternative.

24–15. Compute Expected Values
(L.O.1)

Welcome Homes, Inc., is considering the alternatives of renovating a building and renting it or purchasing a new building and renting it. The new rental market in the area is fairly stable. An investor can purchase a $10 million building. Assuming a three-year holding period, the project will have a net present value of $2 million, after subtracting the $10 million cost.

Renovation property is riskier because the costs of the renovation are less certain than new construction. A typical renovation project may require the same $10 million cost. However, after completion of the renovation, the project may have a different present value than the new construction. Indeed, Welcome Homes' management has prepared the following schedule of net present values after subtracting the $10 million cost for the renovation project:

Net Present Value (millions)	Probability
$−2	.2
1	.2
4	.3
6	.2
9	.1

To simplify the analysis, assume there are no other possible outcomes from the renovation project.

Required:

What is the expected net present value of the renovation project?

24–16. Estimate Risk Measures
(L.O.2)
Required:

Refer to the data for Welcome Homes, Inc. (exercise 24–15).

Estimate:

a. The standard deviation of net present values for the renovation alternative.

b. The probability of a negative net present value from the renovation.

24–17. Assess Impact of Uncertainty
(L.O.2)

TimeDelay, Inc., has an opportunity to sell an asset for $15 million today. Alternatively, TimeDelay can use the asset in production for one month. If it is used, the expected profits and their probabilities are:

Profit	Probability
$ 8,000,000	.1
12,000,000	.2
15,000,000	.3
20,000,000	.4

The asset would be sold at the end of the month, and the present value of the sale is included in the profit computations.

Required:

Determine the following:

a. Expected value of the production alternative.

b. Standard deviation of the production alternative.

c. Coefficient of variation for the production alternative.

24–18. Assess the Impact of Uncertainty
(L.O.2)

Karen Jones has an opportunity to sell her house for $90,000 today, or she can rent her house for one year and then sell it. If it is rented, the present value of the rental profits plus the present value of the sale after one year and their probabilities are:

Present Value	Probability
$ 75,000	.15
85,000	.30
95,000	.45
105,000	.10

Required:

Determine the following:

a. Expected value of the renting and selling a year later alternative.

b. Standard deviation of the renting alternative.

c. Coefficient of variation for the renting alternative.

24–19. Assess the Impact of Uncertainty
(L.O.2)

Unusual Company has an opportunity to sell a group of machines for $25 million today. Alternatively, Unusual Company can use the machines in production for one more year. If used, the present value of the profits plus the present value of the sale one year from now and their probabilities are:

Present Value in Millions of Dollars	Probability
$15	.10
20	.15
25	.45
30	.20
35	.10

Required:

Determine the following:

a. Expected value of the production alternative.

b. Standard deviation of the production alternative.

c. Coefficient of variation for the production alternative.

24–20. Indifference Analysis under Uncertainty

(L.O.2)

Fanzole Corporation has a patent on a new medical device selling for $14 per unit. However, demand for the device is uncertain. The company can build its own manufacturing facilities and incur variable costs of $4 and fixed costs of $1.2 million per year.

On the other hand, the company could hire a subcontractor who would meet the demand for a variable cost of $12 per unit and no fixed costs.

Required:

Ignoring risk, at what demand level would management be indifferent between the alternatives?

24–21. Compute Expected Values—CVP

(L.O.2)

After further market analysis, Fanzole Corporation (exercise 24–20) obtained the following assessment of the demand levels and their probabilities.

Demand in Thousands of Units	Probability
50	.08
100	.25
150	.30
200	.27
250	.10

Required:

What is the expected sales volume?

24–22. Estimate Standard Deviation of Alternatives

(L.O.2)

Refer to the data for Fanzole Corporation (exercises 24–20 and 24–21). Estimate the standard deviation for manufacturing and for subcontracting.

24–23. Indifference Analysis under Uncertainty

(L.O.2)

Granduke Company has a patent on a new device that sells at a price of $75 per unit. They can build their own manufacturing facilities and incur variable costs of $30 per unit and fixed costs of $1.8 million per year. On the other hand, they could hire a subcontractor who would meet the demand at a cost of $60 per unit without any fixed costs. The problem is that demand for the device is uncertain.

Required:

Ignoring risk, at what demand level would management be indifferent between the alternatives?

24–24. Compute Expected Values—CVP

(L.O.3)

After further market analysis, Granduke Company (exercise 24–23) has obtained the following assessment of the demand levels and their probabilities:

Demand in Thousands of Units	Probability
40	.07
50	.20
60	.35
70	.18
80	.12
90	.08

The cost and revenue data are the same as in the previous exercise.

Required:

What is the expected value of Granduke Company's new device if they manufacture the product?

24–25. Estimate Standard Deviation of Alternatives
(L.O.2)

Refer to the data for Granduke Company (exercises 24–23 and 24–24). Estimate the standard deviation for manufacturing and for subcontracting.

24–26. Indifference Analysis under Uncertainty
(L.O.2)

Diamond Company is trying to decide whether to produce the new product they have recently been developing. Another alternative is to hire a subcontractor who would meet the demand at a cost of $65 per unit without any fixed costs. If they produce at their own plant, the variable cost per unit is $40 and a fixed costs are $1 million per year. However the demand for the product is uncertain. The product is going to be sold at a price of $80 per unit.

Required:

Ignoring risk, at what demand level would management be indifferent between the alternatives?

24–27. Compute Expected Values—CVP
(L.O.3)

After further market analysis, Diamond Company (exercise 24–26) has obtained the following assessment of the demand levels and their probabilities:

Demand in Thousands of Units	Probability
25	.15
35	.30
45	.45
55	.10

The cost and revenue data are the same as before. Assume there are no other possible demand outcomes.

Required:

What is the expected value of profits for Diamond Company's new product?

24–28. Estimate Standard Deviation of Alternatives
(L.O.2)

Refer to the data for Diamond Company (exercises 24–26 and 24–27). Estimate the standard deviation for manufacturing and for subcontracting.

PROBLEMS

24-29. Payoff Table

Jon Co. agreed to supply Arom Chemical, Inc. with a substance critical to Arom's manufacturing process. Due to the critical nature of the substance, Jon Co. has agreed to pay Arom $1,000 for any shipment that is not received by Arom on the day it is required.

Arom establishes a production schedule that enables it to notify Jon Co. of the necessary quantity 15 days in advance of the required date. Jon can produce the substance in five days. However, capacity is not always readily available, which means that Jon may not be able to produce the substance for several days. Therefore, there may be occasions when there are only one or two days available to deliver the substance. When the substance is completed by Jon Co.'s manufacturing department and released to its shipping department, the number of days remaining before Arom Chemical Inc. needs the substance will be known.

Jon Co. has undertaken a review of delivery reliability and costs of alternative shipping methods. The results are presented in the following table.

Shipping Method	Cost per Shipment	Probability that the shipment Will Take ___ Days					
		1	2	3	4	5	6
Motor freight	$100	—	—	.10	.20	.40	.30
Air freight	200	—	.30	.60	.10	—	—
Air express	400	.80	.20	—	—	—	—

Required:

Prepare a payoff table for Jon Co.'s shipping clerk to decide which shipping alternative to select if there is: (1) one day before delivery is required; (2) two days before delivery is required; and so forth, up to seven days before delivery is required.

(CMA adapted)

24-30. Expected Value of Sales

Jackson, Inc., manufactures and distributes a line of toys. The company neglected to keep its doll house line current. As a result, sales have decreased to approximately 10,000 units per year from a previous high of 50,000 units. The doll house was recently redesigned and is considered by company officials to be comparable to its competitors' models. Joan Blocke, the sales manager, is not sure how many units can be sold next year, but she is willing to place probabilities on her estimates. Blocke's estimates of the number of units that can be sold during the next year and the related probabilities are as follows:

Estimated Sales in Units	Probability
20,000	.10
30,000	.40
40,000	.30
50,000	.20

The units will sell for $20 each.

The entire year's sales must be manufactured in one production run. If demand is greater than the number of units manufactured, sales will be lost. If demand is below supply, the extra units cannot be carried over to the next season and must be discarded. Production and distribution cost estimates are listed below.

	Units Manufactured			
	20,000	**30,000**	**40,000**	**50,000**
Variable costs	$180,000	$270,000	$360,000	$450,000
Fixed (step) costs	140,000	140,000	160,000	160,000
Total costs	$320,000	$410,000	$520,000	$610,000

The company must decide on the optimal size of the production run.

Required:

Prepare a payoff table for the different sizes of production runs required to meet the four sales estimates prepared by Joan Blocke. If Jackson, Inc., relied solely on the expected monetary value approach to make decisions, what size of production run would be selected?

(CMA adapted)

24–31. Analyze Cost Alternatives under Uncertainty

The administrator for a large midwestern city continually seeks ways to reduce costs without cutting services. The administrator has asked all department heads to review their operations to determine if cost-saving procedures can be implemented.

The Gotham City Department of Streets is responsible for replacement of the 50,000 bulb units in the traffic lights. The department keeps detailed records regarding the failure rate of the bulb units. The pattern of bulb failures is as follows:

Failure Occurs within ___ Quarter of a Year of Replacement	Probability
First	.1
Second	.3
Third	.6

No bulbs last beyond the end of the third quarter.

The Department of Streets has been replacing the bulb units as they fail. The estimated cost to replace the bulb units using this procedure is $6.40 per unit.

The manager of the Department of Streets is considering replacing all of the bulb units at once (for example, at the beginning of every quarter) plus replacing bulbs as they fail. The manager estimates that the cost to replace all bulb units at once would be $2.40 per bulb unit. The cost to replace each unit as it failed would still be $6.40 per unit.

Required:

a. Assume all bulbs have just been replaced on January 1, Year 1. Calculate the bulb and replacement cost to the Department of Streets for Year 1 if the present policy of replacing the bulb units as they fail is continued.

b. Assume all bulbs have just been replaced on Janury 1, Year 1. Calculate the estimated bulb and replacement cost for Year 1 if all bulb units are replaced when they fail, plus all bulb units are replaced on a regular basis at the beginning of:
   (1) Every quarter (January 1, April 1, July 1, October 1).
   (2) Every second quarter (every January 1 and July 1).
   Show your calculations for both alternatives.

c. Why would there be such a large difference between the two estimated replacement costs per unit (replace as failure occurs, $6.40; replace all at once, $2.40)? Explain your answer.

(CMA adapted)

24–32. Computing Expected Values and Finding Probabilities

ANC Radio Company is trying to decide whether to introduce a new wrist "radio-watch" designed for shortwave reception of exact time as broadcast by the National Bureau of Standards. The "radiowatch" would be priced at $60, which is twice the variable cost per unit to manufacture and sell it. The differential fixed costs required to introduce this new product would be $240,000 per year. Estimates of the demand for the product are shown in the following probability distribution:

Annual Demand (units)	Probability
6,000	.2
8,000	.2
10,000	.2
12,000	.2
14,000	.1
16,000	.1

Required:

a. What is the expected value of the demand for the product?

b. What is the probability that the demand for the product will be below the break-even point?

(CMA adapted)

24–33. CVP Analysis under Uncertainty

Wing Manufacturing Corporation produces a chemical compound, product X, which deteriorates and must be discarded if it is not sold by the end of the month during which it is produced. The total variable cost of the manufactured compound, product X, is $50 per unit, and its selling price is $80 per unit. Wing can purchase the same compound from a competing company at $80 per unit plus $10 transportation per unit. Management estimates that failure to fill orders would result in the loss of 80 percent of customers placing orders for the compound. Wing has manufactured and sold product X for the past 20 months. Demand for the product has been irregular, with no consistent sales trend. During this period, monthly sales have been as follows:

Units Sold per Month	Probabilities
8,000	.25
9,000	.60
10,000	.15

To produce product X, Wing uses a primary ingredient, K-1, which it purchases for $24 per unit of compound. There is a 70 percent chance that the supplier of K-1 may be unable to deliver the ingredient for an indefinite period. A substitute ingredient, K-2, is available at $36 per unit of compound, but a firm purchase contract for either material must be made now for production next month. If an order was placed for K-1, but it was unavailable, then management would have to purchase product X from a competitor and sell it at a loss. (Otherwise, it would permanently lose important customers.) Assume that 9,000 units are to be manufactured and all sales orders are to be filled.

Required:

a. Compute the monthly contribution margin from sales of 8,000; 9,000; and 10,000 units if the substitute ingredient, K-2, is ordered. What is the expected contribution if K-2 is ordered?

b. Prepare a schedule computing the expected monthly contribution margin if the primary ingredient, K-1, is ordered, given the chance of nondelivery. For this requirement, assume that the expected average monthly contribution margin from manufacturing is $130,000 using K-1 and the expected average monthly loss from purchasing product X from the competitor is $45,000.

(CPA adapted)

24–34. CVP Analysis under Uncertainty

Commercial Products Corporation requested your assistance to estimate the potential loss on a purchase contract that will be in effect at the end of the year. The corporation produces a chemical compound (c) that deteriorates and must be discarded if it is not sold by the end of the month during which it is produced.

The total variable cost of the manufactured compound is $25 per unit, and it is sold for $40 per unit. The compound can be purchased from a competitor, company Z, at $40 per unit plus $5 transportation per unit. It is estimated that failure to fill orders would result in the complete loss of 8 out of 10 customers placing orders for the compound.

The cost of the primary ingredient (p) used to manufacture the compound is $12 per unit of compound c. It is estimated that there is a 60 percent chance that the primary ingredient supplier's plant may be shut down. A substitute ingredient (s) is available at $18 per unit of compound, but the corporation must contract immediately to purchase the substitute, or it will be unavailable when needed. A firm purchase contract for either the primary p or the substitute s ingredient must now be made with one of the suppliers for production next month. If an order was placed for the primary ingredient and the supplier shut down, management would purchase the manufactured compound c from its competitor, company Z.

The corporation has sold the compound for the past 30 months. Demand has been irregular, and there is no discernible sales trend. During this period, sales orders per month has been:

4,000 units per month in 6 of the 30 months
5,000 units per month in 15 of the 30 months
6,000 units per month in 9 of the 30 months

Required:

a. Prepare schedules of the following:
   (1) Probability of sales of 4,000, 5,000, or 6,000 units in any month.
   (2) Contribution to profit for the following combinations of sales and production levels in the same month assuming ingredient (p) is readily available:

	Production		
Sales Orders	4,000	5,000	6,000
4,000			
5,000			
6,000			

Assume there is no inventory and all sales orders must be filled in the month of the order. This means that if production is less than sales orders, only the amount produced is sold (for example, if sales orders are for 6,000 and production is 4,000, only 4,000 units are sold).

b. Should management order primary ingredient p or substitute ingredient s during the possible shutdown period? For this requirement, assume that 5,000 units will be produced, regardless of sales.

(CPA adapted)

24–35. Cost-Volume-Profit Analysis[3]

JR Company is considering introducing either of two new products. Each product requires an increase in annual fixed expenses of $800,000. The products have the same selling price ($20) and the same variable cost per unit ($16).

Management, after studying past experience with similar products, has prepared the following subjective probability distribution:

Outcomes (units demanded)	Probability— Product A	Probability— Product B
50,000	.0	.1
100,000	.1	.1
200,000	.2	.1
300,000	.4	.2
400,000	.2	.4
500,000	.1	.1
	1.0	1.0

Required:

a. What is the break-even point for each product?

b. Which product should be chosen? Why? Show computations.

c. Revise the data to assume management was absolutely certain that 300,000 units of product B would be sold. Which product should be chosen? Why? What benefits are available to management from the provision of the complete probability distribution instead of just a lone expected value?

24–36. Simulation When There Are Sales Constraints (Computer Required)

Excelsior Corporation has five products, A, B, C, D, and E. Relevant data for these products are as follows:

			Expected Value of:	
Product	Price	Variable Cost	Maximum Sales	Expected Sales
A	$15	$ 6	20,000 units	15,000 units
B	14	7	50,000	17,000
C	18	8	19,000	18,500
D	25	17	10,000	10,000
E	6	2	30,000	26,000

The standard deviation of each item in the list, except the sales limit, is equal to 25 percent of the expected value of the item. Aggregate sales of all products cannot exceed $1.5 million.

[3] This problem is adapted from Robert K. Jaedicke and Alexander A. Robichek, "Cost-Volume-Profit Analysis under Conditions of Uncertainty," *Accounting Review* 36, no. 4, pp. 917–26.

Required:

a. What is the expected profit from all products?

b. Use a simulation package on a computer to simulate the probabilistic behavior of each of the variables, assuming that they are normally distributed. Run the simulation for 100 iterations. What is the expected sales volume and profit for all products?

c. Expand the program to incorporate the maximum sales constraints. Using the same simulation data from requirement *b* show the expected sales volume and profits.

d. Comment on the differences in results for each of the three items listed above.

24–37. Discuss Simulation Analysis

Fred Adamson manages a large door-to-door selling organization. The pattern of weekly sales is seasonal but predictable. The typical annual pattern is shown below.

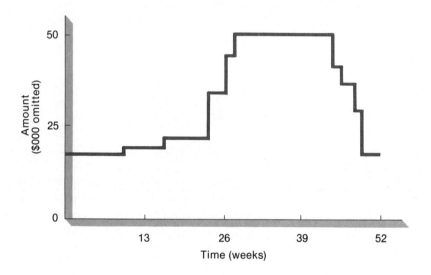

Adamson often experiences either a cash shortage or has idle cash balances. The cash outflows are not a problem because Adamson has a set payment schedule. The sales force is paid its 10 percent commission weekly, and Adamson's suppliers are paid five weeks after each sale.

The problem arises from Adamson's inability to accurately predict the cash collections from sales. All sales are made on account. Payment is due in four weeks. Six percent of the payments due are never received.

Adamson maintains collection experience records that have allowed him to specify a frequency distribution for the collection lag. This frequency distribution is presented in the following schedule:

Collection Lag (number of weeks from sale until actual collection)	Percentage of Accounts
1	2%
2	4
3	8
4	16
5	18
6	12
7	8
8	6
9	4
10	8
11	6
12	2
Uncollectible	6
	100%

Adamson has discussed his cash management problem with a business consultant, who suggested that Adamson consider using simulation analysis to estimate cash flows and balances.

Required:

a. Explain why simulation would be an appropriate analysis technique for Fred Adamson to use in an attempt to solve his cash management problem.

b. Explain the basic structure of a simulation model that would address Fred Adamson's cash management problem.

(CMA adapted)

VARIANCE
INVESTIGATION

LEARNING OBJECTIVES

1. Understand the costs and benefits from investigating variances.

2. Become familiar with the conceptual model which underlies the variance investigation decision.

3. Learn how statistical control techniques apply to the decision to investigate variances.

Variances represent differences between planned results and actual performance. A variance may be caused by a change in output activity, a change in the efficiency with which inputs are used, or a change in the unit cost of an input. Variance analysis is important for performance evaluation and control, as we discussed in Chapters 18 to 21. A substantial number of variances are usually included in any set of internal management reports, and managers don't have the time to investigate all of them. So, some method must be found to investigate only those variances that are expected to produce a benefit in excess of investigation costs. This methodology is generally referred to as **variance investigation.**

Variance Investigation The steps taken if managers judge that the expected benefits of correction exceed the costs of follow-up.

In this chapter, we discuss how to determine which variances should be investigated. We also examine the costs associated with the decision of whether to investigate a variance. The factors that affect these costs are identified. They include the reason for the variance, the costs of investigation and correction of a variance, and the costs of allowing a variance to continue uncorrected. The chapter also provides an overview of statistical quality control, an engineering approach to determining which variances should be investigated. The application of the concepts of these variance investigation models in a real world setting is also discussed.

THE INVESTIGATION SETTING

Imagine that you are managing the employee benefits section of the Great Plains Corporation and are responsible for its operations. The employee benefits section is a cost center in the company's organization. Your compensation and your future with the company will be evaluated on the basis of the cost center's performance. The monthly report on your cost center has just arrived. It appears as follows:

GREAT PLAINS CORPORATION
Employee Benefits Section
Responsibility Report
(in thousands)

Cost Item	Budget	Actual	Variance
Staff salaries	$155	$156	$ 1 U
Operator wages	137	151	14 U
Other wages	41	39	2 F
Communications	12	9	3 F
Utilities	39	48	9 U
Supplies	16	11	5 F
Maintenance and repairs	24	8	16 F
All other	80	85	5 U
Totals	$504	$507	$ 3 U

Net Present Value Difference between the discounted cash inflows and the discounted cash outflows.

How do you decide which variances to investigate? This decision is similar to other management decisions with the objective of minimizing the **net present value** of expected costs. To make the decision, consider the costs associated with your decision alternatives. These alternatives may be restricted to:

1. Investigate the variance.
2. Do not investigate.

Intermediate decisions may also be made. For example, you may wait until you receive next month's report before investigating. Or you might decide to conduct a very brief pilot study before deciding to carry on a full-fledged investigation. To minimize the complexity of our discussion, we will limit our consideration to the first two alternatives. Adding other choices makes the mathematics more complex, but the underlying approach is the same.

Essentially, you must consider the trade-offs between the costs of investigating and the costs of allowing the process to continue without investigation. You must determine the differential costs and a method for assessing the trade-offs.

If management needs to make a decision of whether to investigate a variance, it is necessary that there be costs associated with the investigation and that there be potential benefits received as a result of making an investigation. As with all other areas of cost-based decision making, the relevant costs are those that are differential with respect to the decision. All of the costs discussed here are differential.

Investigation Decision Costs

The costs that need to be considered are: (1) the costs to conduct an investigation, (2) the costs to correct an out-of-control process, and (3) the costs of allowing an out-of-control process to continue out of control. The first two costs can usually be specified based on the nature of the operation subject to the investigation. Some typical investigation costs include:

1. Opportunity costs of the time spent tracking down the cause of a variance.
2. Opportunity costs of the time spent in the investigation.
3. Costs to test equipment that may be out of adjustment.
4. Costs to shut down an operation while testing equipment.
5. Costs to restart or rearrange activities to increase efficiency.
6. Consulting fees of outside experts hired to examine operations.

For example, the costs to investigate the unfavorable variance in utilities costs may require an inspection tour of the operating area to check that lights and equipment are shut off when not in use. A more elaborate investigation might involve hiring a consulting firm to study utilities usage and suggest a conservation program.

It is important to note that some variances are so large that correction is indicated without conducting an investigation. For example, if your car normally obtains 20 miles per gallon and suddenly obtains only 5 miles per gallon, no investigation is necessary for you to take the car to the repair shop and have the problem fixed. In these situations, no investigation costs are incurred.

The costs of allowing a process to remain out of control depend on several factors. These costs are related to the inefficiencies caused by an out-of-control operation as well as the time before the operation is corrected. An operation may be self-correcting or may require intervention. It is generally agreed that the longer a process remains out of control, the greater the costs of allowing it to continue out of control. Sooner or later, however, out-of control processes are corrected.

Some examples of the costs of allowing a process to remain out of control include:

1. Costs of continued inefficient operations, including inefficient use of labor, materials, and energy.
2. Costs of improperly adjusted equipment, including failure to meet product specifications, damaged or defective goods, and hazardous operating conditions.

The utilities costs that might be incurred if no investigation was made include any energy costs from equipment that was left on when not in use, costs of heat loss through leakage in walls or insulation, and loss of lighting power through inefficient fixtures, dirty light covers, and the like.

The purpose of investigating a variance is to save future costs. But costs can be saved only if an investigation uncovers a factor that can be adjusted. This does not always occur. Sometimes, a variance is just a **random event.** If the variance is a random event, investigating it will yield no benefits to offset investigation costs. For example, there would be no benefit in discovering that a variance stemmed from an error in reading the utility meter that is offset in subsequent periods. If a variance is due to an increase in utility rates, then there is probably little management can do except adjust future budgets. Additional, but less direct, actions might include taking steps to reduce future energy use.

Random Event An occurrence that is beyond the control of the decision maker or manager.

Estimating the costs of an out-of-control process is illustrated by the following example.

Rosebud Industries runs an automated diode manufacturing operation. The diode manufacturing equipment is set to certain tolerances. With use, the machine settings can go out of control. The longer the machine is out of control, the greater the cost of allowing it to continue out of control. A corollary to this is that the greater the manufacturing costs, the higher the unfavorable variances, and the more likely management is to check the machines and correct the settings.

Assume the machines *are* out of control, but that management does not know this for certain. Costs related to the time that the machine is out of control and the related probabilities that the machine will be checked out and reset are presented in the following table:

Additional Time out of Control	Present Value of Out-of-Control Costs This Period	Probability of Investigation and Correction
1	$ 4,000	.10
2	9,000	.25
3	15,000	.60
4	30,000	.90
5	65,000	1.00

If the machine is out of control and remains out of control for just period 1, the expected cost is computed as follows:

$$\$4,000 \times (1 - .10) = \$3,600$$

If the machine is left out of control for period 1 and period 2, the expected cost is:

$$\$3,600 + [\$9,000 \times .9 \times (1 - .25)] = \$3,600 + \$6,075$$
$$= \$9,675$$

So for each period that the machine is out of control, the cost increases by the accumulated costs of leaving the machine out of control times the probability that the machine will be left out of control until that period times the probability that the machine will remain out of control that period. The out-of-control costs are a cumulative function of time. Thus, the expected costs through period 3 are:

$$\$9,675 + [\$15,000 \times .9 \times .75 \times (1 - .6)] = \$9,675 + \$4,050$$
$$= \$13,725$$

and the expected costs through period 4 are:

$$\$13,725 + \$30,000 \times [.9 \times .75 \times .4 \times (1 - .9)] = \$13,725 + \$810$$
$$= \$14,535$$

There are no costs for period 5 because the machine would be checked and reset that period.

Hence, if the variance is not investigated now, the expected costs are $14,535, which is the sum of the costs of being out of control for each period before correction is assured times the probability that the machine will remain out of control through that period. This is the basic approach to determining the cost of allowing a process to remain out of control.

CONCEPTUAL BASIS FOR INVESTIGATION DECISIONS

In deciding whether a variance investigation is likely to yield net benefits, a manager focuses on two important issues:

1. The importance or materiality of the variance.
2. The ability to control the causes of the variance.

Variances that are quite small are typically not investigated. Small cost variances usually do not indicate large benefits from investigating and correcting the cause of the variance.

Guidance about which types of variances are worth investigating comes from considering the sources of variances.

Causes of Variances

Just because a variance appears in a report does not necessarily mean that management can take action which will prevent the variance from recurring. The reason is that variances may be due to a number of different causes. These causes may be broken into three categories, each of which has its own implications for the managerial action that may be the optimal reaction to the variance.

Information system variances are those that arise because the data used either to establish standards or to report variances is in error. If budgets or standards are set in such a way that they do not reflect expectations, a variance will be reported. In this situation, management may be better off adjusting the standards or budget, since investigating the variance will not result in an improvement in operations. For example, if management had based its cost estimates for a trucking company on fuel costs that were out of date, a variance would probably be reported. However, there is nothing management can do in the short run about the costs of fuel, so the benefits from investigating such a variance would be zero.

The management reporting system may also contain errors as a result of incorrect data entry, coding, or other problems in the system. Investigating such variances will not change the underlying events. The benefits will arise though a more accurate report about operations, but operations themselves will not be affected.

Random variances are those that arise beyond the control of management. Machinery is normally subject to some changes in operating characteristics over time. Prices of goods and services acquired in open markets vary with market conditions. Although variance reports will capture differences between expected costs and those actually realized due to these random events, management usually cannot benefit from investigating these variances.

Controllable operating variances are the variances that arise from some change in operations that can be corrected by management action. Excessive use of materials due to equipment malfunctions, work delays due to scheduling errors, and high reject or rework rates due to labor or equipment failures are examples of controllable operating variances. Identifying and correcting the cause of these types of variances usually provide benefits to management.

The issue in this chapter is to consider some of the approaches to identifying which variances fall into the controllable operating variance class. This can be a complex task. Consider the situation of airline schedules. To keep an airline system operating smoothly, planes must depart and arrive relatively close to schedule. If planes are late, flights are delayed, connections missed, crew schedules upset, and other costs incurred. Similarly, if planes arrive too early, they usually must wait on the ground until gate space becomes available. This causes congestion on the ground and passenger irritation. At one point, for competitive reasons, airlines published schedules that shortened the reported time between destinations. This created havoc because planes were chronically late. The lateness caused by unrealistic schedules was an *information system variance*. However, weather can also delay flights. These delays are due to *random variance*. Finally, flights may be delayed due to mechanical problems and similar factors. These are *controllable operating variances* that management likes to focus on to improve operations. The issue for the airlines is: Given daily reports on thousands of flights, even if only 5 percent of them are not on schedule, how does an airline determine which schedule variances to investigate? The approach discussed here provides guidance in this effort.

Statistical Decision Models

Generally, managers will use subjective judgment about whether to investigate a variance. The statistical model illustrates the components of that judgment process. The statistical decision model for the variance investigation decision may be diagrammed as:

		Alternatives	
		Investigate	Do Not Investigate
State	In control	I	0
	Out of control	$C + I$	L

The two columns of the matrix represent the alternative management actions (Investigate, Do not investigate), and the two rows represent the unknown state of the process (In control, Out of control). Each cell represents a pairing of a decision alternative and a state of the process. The symbols in the cells represent the costs of each pairing.

For example, if we investigate the utilities cost variance, we incur an investigation cost (I) if the process is in control. Hence, the first cell in the matrix shows that I is the cost from the paired event "Investigate, In control." If the process is out of control and we investigate, our cost is the cost to correct (C) and the investigation cost (I). Thus, the cost in the first column of the second row of the matrix is $C + I$.

If we don't investigate and the process is in control, we incur zero costs. The zero is entered in the first row of the second column.

Finally, if we do not investigate and the process is out of control, we incur the cost (or loss) of letting the process stay out of control. This loss is labeled L and entered in the appropriate cell. Generally, variance investigation decisions are made on a periodic basis and are reviewed as each new report is issued. Therefore, if the process is out of control, subsequent variance reports will tend to signal this. The value of L, therefore, must be stated in terms of the costs that will be incurred until management intervenes and corrects the process. Some out-of-control processes may remain out of control only until the next report. Others can remain out of control for months or years. Computing L, then, involves considering these future management actions.

Since we don't know the state of the process until after we make the investigation decision, the costs of each alternative are conditional on the probability that the alternative reflects the actual situation. The cost of each alternative, then, is an expected value. The manager chooses the alternative whose cost has the lower expected value.

Suppose that the costs to investigate the variance in utilities expense is $500. The cost to correct an out-of-control process is $1,000, and the cost of allowing the utilities to remain out of control for another period is $4,000. (Assume this is a short-term problem. If this were a long-term problem, the procedure would be the same but the amounts would be present values of future costs.) We enter each cost in the appropriate place in the decision matrix and derive a cost for each paired alternative/state outcome. This yields the following matrix:

State		Alternatives	
		Investigate	Do Not Investigate
	In control	$ 500	$ 0
	Out of control	1,500	4,000

Role of Probabilities

In-Control Probability The likelihood that a process is operating within specifications.

Out-of-Control Probability The probability that a process is not operating according to specifications.

Once the costs of each state are known, we apply the probabilities that the state has occurred, to obtain an expected cost of each alternative decision (Investigate or Do Not Investigate). The important probabilities are (1) **in-control probability,** which is the likelihood that the process is functioning properly given the variance information received, and (2) **out-of-control probability,** which is the likelihood that the process is not operating properly given the variance information received. These probabilities are conditional upon receipt of a specific variance report. Presumably, the greater the variance, the higher the out-of-control probability. The probabilities can then be used to compute an expected cost of each alternative action.

If the out-of-control probability is .3, which is the less costly alternative for the utilities cost variance investigation decision? To answer the question, we must compute the expected value of each alternative. If we investigate, the probability is .3 that we will obtain the benefits of correcting the out-of-control process and .7 that we will find nothing wrong. The value .7 is the in-control probability. The expected cost of the investigation alternative is, therefore:

$$.7 \times \$500 + .3 \times \$1,500 = \$350 + \$450$$
$$= \underline{\underline{\$800}}$$

The expected value of the alternative "Do not investigate" is computed similarly. Since the cost of the pair "Do not investigate, In control" is zero, that term will equal zero and is ignored. The expected cost of not investigating is the product of the out-of-control probability times the cost of being out of control. For this example:

$$.3 \times \$4,000 = \underline{\underline{\$1,200}}$$

Since the expected cost of an investigation is less than the expected cost of not investigating, the model suggests that the variance should be investigated.

MANAGEMENT POLICY AND STATISTICAL THEORY

The cost and probability data are usually not readily available for the types of variance investigations encountered in typical monthly reporting settings. However, the statistical approach may be applied in principle; relating the statistical decision theory approach to the manager's decision, therefore, requires some additional steps.

Critical Probability *(p*)*   The probability of different outcomes that equalizes the value of the outcomes.

If we assume that the greater the variance, the greater the out-of-control probability, an investigation policy can be established that relates the variance amount to an out-of-control probability. At some probability, management is indifferent to whether an investigation is conducted. If the actual out-of-control probability (as indicated by the dollar amount of the variance) is greater than implied by our **critical probability** *(p*)*, it pays to investigate. Otherwise, the expected value of not investigating is greater. This critical probability is, in essence, a break-even point between two cost functions.

The expected costs of an out-of-control process *(L)* increase as the out-of-control probability increases. We can express the cost function for the out-of-control situation as *Lp,* where *p* is the out-of-control probability.

Likewise, the expected cost to correct an out-of-control process increases as the out-of-control probability increases. That is, if we investigate, as the value of *p* increases, so does the chance that we will discover and correct the out-of-control process. Hence, the cost of investigating is equal to *I* plus *Cp*.

If we diagram the relationship between the expected costs of investigating and not investigating, the point where the two cost functions are equal represents the value of *p**, the critical probability. This diagram is shown in Illustration 25–1.

To find *p**, we set the expected cost of investigating equal to the expected cost of not investigating and solve for the unknown *p**. We then must relate the variance data in the responsibility report to the out-of-control probability. If, as indicated by the variance report, that probability is greater than *p**, we initiate an investigation. Otherwise we do not.

The cost function for the decision to investigate may be obtained from the information used to compute the expected cost when the out-of-control

Illustration 25–1   **Cost Functions for Variance Investigation**

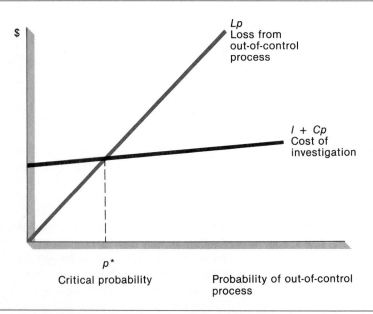

probability was .3. If we replace the given probabilities with $p*$, the cost of investigating is expressed:

$$(1 - p*)I + p*(I + C) = I - Ip* + Ip* + Cp*$$
$$= \underline{\underline{I + Cp*}}$$

The cost of not investigating is:

$$\underline{\underline{Lp*}}$$

Setting the cost functions equal to each other and solving for $p*$ gives:

$$I + Cp* = Lp*$$
$$I = Lp* - Cp*$$
$$I = (L - C)p*$$

$$\underline{\underline{p* = \frac{I}{(L - C)}}}$$

Using this formula for the data given for our utility cost investigation problem, we obtain a critical probability of:

$$p* = \frac{\$500}{\$4,000 - \$1,000}$$
$$= \underline{\underline{.16\tfrac{2}{3}}}$$

Therefore, as long as the out-of-control probability is greater than .16⅔, the expected investigation costs will be less than the expected costs of allowing the process to continue without investigation.

To check, should we investigate if the out-of-control probability is .15? By knowing the critical probability, we can immediately answer no. The following computations support this:

The expected cost of the investigation is:

$$(1 - .15) \times \$500 + .15 \times (\$1,000 + \$500) = \$425 + \$225$$
$$= \underline{\underline{\$650}}$$

The expected cost of not investigating is:

$$.15 \times \$4,000 = \underline{\underline{\$600}}$$

Hence, the model indicates that with an out-of-control probability of .15, the better alternative is not to investigate.

Relating Statistical Probabilities to Variances

Knowing $p*$, however, is only one basis for setting a variance investigation policy. Managers usually make a variance investigation decision based on the absolute monetary value of the variance itself. The additional steps to compute $p*$ are not carried out every time a manager receives a responsibility report. As a result, it is necessary to relate the magnitude of a variance to the out-of-control probability. Once this is accomplished, a policy may be set that states that a variance should be investigated if it exceeds the dollar value that is related to $p*$.

Relating the dollar value of a variance to the out-of-control probability is not an easy task. Some authors suggest that the out-of-control probability is equal to the complement of the in-control probability. That is, if the in-control probability is .75, the out-of-control probability is .25 (which is $1 -$ .75). This approach is computationally simple but incorrect in most circumstances. This is because when we observe a variance, we don't know the source of the variance. The cost function under uncertainty stated above was:

$$Y = a + bX + e$$

Observation of a variance may have come from a cost process represented by this equation. However, it may also have come from some other cost process represented by, say:

$$Y = a + b'X + e$$

which is an out-of-control process. The idea that the in-control probability may be computed as the complement of the out-of-control probability is conditioned on the assumption that e would be zero in the out-of-control equation above.

To illustrate, consider the diagram of the random process that generates variances for in-control and out-of-control processes presented in Illustration 25–2.

If the process is in control, variances are generated due to the random nature of the process. That is, spending or usage may differ from plans purely as a result of random factors. Such variances might follow a normal distribution, as in the top panel of Illustration 25–2. In such a case, the variance has an **expected value (or mean)** of $0. Nonetheless, some variances may be reported even though the process is in control.

The second panel of Illustration 25–2 shows the distribution of variances

Mean   The average of a series of data, sometimes referred to as the expected value.

Illustration 25–2   **Relationship between In-Control and Out-Of-Control Processes**

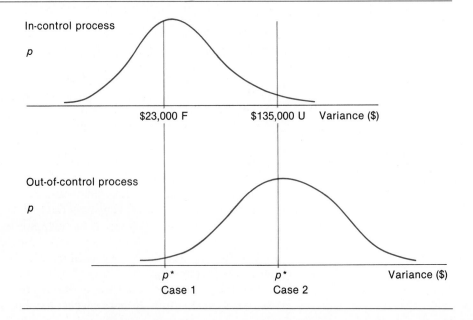

expected from an out-of-control process. If the process is out of control, we assume that there is a shift in costs to a higher level. The out-of-control process is also subject to random variation, as shown by the probability distribution.

Given a variance, we cannot know if the process is in or out of control. But we assess the out-of-control probability by referring to the two probability distributions. For example, case 1 in Illustration 25–2 shows a $23,000 favorable variance. Looking at the distribution of an out-of-control process, it appears that there is a very small probabililty that a process with that variance would be out of control.

By contrast, case 2 shows a variance of $135,000 U. The probability that this variance came from an in-control process is small, as shown by the location of that variance in the probability distribution in the first panel of Illustration 25–2. The probability that the $135,000 unfavorable variance came from an out-of-control process is higher, as shown in the second panel. The out-of-control probability is measured by looking at the relative probabilities of observing the variance from each of the two processes.

The out-of-control probability is not equal to the complement of the in-control probability. However, the lower the in-control probability, the greater the out-of-control probability. Therefore, if we find p^* on the out-of-control distribution, we can extend p^* to the distribution for the in-control process, just as was done in Illustration 25–2.

The mathematical process for computing exact values for p^* in terms of an in-control process (rather than the out-of-control process) requires knowledge of the probability distribution for the out-of-control process and the use of Bayesian statistics. Since we are presenting only a conceptual basis for the role of p^* in the establishment of a variance investigation policy, we will not discuss the mathematical details.

STATISTICAL QUALITY CONTROL CHARTS

Statistical Quality Control A method for evaluating a repetitive process to determine if the process is out of control.

Standard Deviation A measure of risk. It is computed as the square root of the sum of the squared differences between actual observations and the mean of the data series divided by one less than the number of observations.

In situations where there are a large number of units produced by some process, production engineering developed a method for sampling some of the units produced and comparing the samples to product specifications. If the sample fell within certain tolerances, the production process was considered in control and no further investigation was conducted. However, if the sample was beyond some tolerance limit, an investigation was conducted to see if the process was out of control. The procedure is referred to as **statistical quality control.**

A familiar example of this method is testing the weight of cereal in a box of cereal. To make certain that the machines that fill the boxes are operating properly, several filled cereal boxes are pulled from the production line and weighed. If the weight of the cereal in the box is within certain limits, it is assumed that the machines filling the boxes are operating properly.

It has been suggested that accounting data may be analyzed using statistical quality control methods to help management approach the variance investigation decision. With this method, the process that generates a cost variance is considered to have a mean of zero. If we know the **standard deviation** of the process that generates variances, we can set tolerance limits for variances. Those that fall within the tolerance limits are assumed to come from an in-control process; otherwise, the variance is investigated.

Although we have assumed a zero mean for the variance, it is possible to adapt the method to a broader set of values for the variance. However, estimating the standard deviation of an accounting cost is usually more of a problem. Sometimes the standard deviation can be obtained as a part of a regression-based cost estimate (see Chapter 10). In other cases, simulation techniques may be used to analyze the behavior of a process and the accounting data that would be generated from that process.

We usually assume that the in-control process is normally distributed, although other assumptions are possible. Assuming a zero mean, in the statistical quality control method, the variance is divided by the standard deviation for the variance. The result is a z-value. If the z-value is greater than 1.96, the probability that the variance came from an in-control process is less than .025. If the z-value is 2.56 or more, the probability that it came from an in-control process is no greater than .005.

For example, the variance in utilities costs for the employee benefits section of Great Plains was $9,000. If the standard deviation for that variance is $4,500, then the z-value is 2. That z-value is close enough to 1.96 for us to state that the probability of its coming from an in-control process is about .025.

When there are frequent observations of variances, it may be helpful to diagram the variances by their relationship to the in-control process. This may be done using statistical quality control charts. An example is reproduced in Illustration 25–3.

The chart is constructed by drawing a horizontal time line for the mean of the process. The vertical scale gives the values for the observations. For cereal weights, the scale would be grams. For accounting variances, the scale would be monetary amounts. The vertical scale could also be converted to z-values since any observed number when divided by its standard deviation gives a z-value. The specific scaling would be specified by the managers using the charts.

Upper Control Limit The maximum value of some observation that still indicates that a process is in control.

Lower Control Limit The minimum value of some observation that still indicates that the process is in control.

Sigma The number of standard deviations that a given observation is from the mean.

An **upper** and **lower control limit** is drawn on the chart at the observation values that are considered critical by management. An observation that falls within the control limits is considered acceptable; one that falls without is not. If the observation falls outside the control limits, the process is investigated. In the United States, the control limits are usually set at three standard deviations. Statisticians use the greek letter **sigma** (σ) for denoting the standard deviation of a population. Hence, control charts are frequently referred to as three-sigma or two-sigma control charts, depending on how many standard deviations are used to set the control limits.

Using the observations in Illustration 25–3, we note that observations 6 and 10 fall outside the control limits. These observations would be investigated.

Control Charts and Variance Investigation

The statistical quality control chart is based on engineering observations of repetitive processes. As a conceptual model, it is useful because if we can relate $p*$ to the in-control process; and if we set the upper and lower control limits in terms of $p*$, it is possible to construct control charts that illustrate observations that may need investigation. They provide a visual effect not possible from a numerical report. If we use the control chart to plot vari-

Illustration 25–3   **Statistical Quality Control Chart**

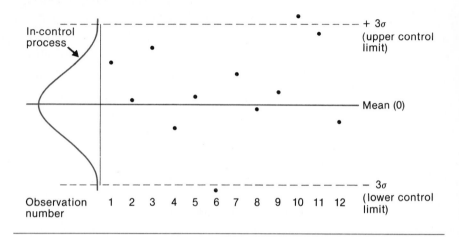

Illustration 25–4   **Highlighting Trends in Variances with a Statistical Quality Control Chart**

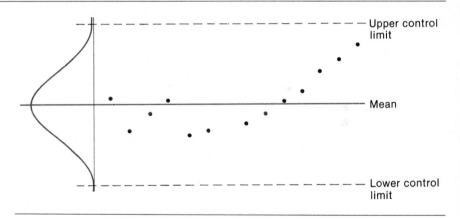

ances in a specific account over time, it may be possible to detect trends or other patterns in variances that would signal the need to investigate even if the control limits were not exceeded. For example, if a cost was relatively stable for several months and then began to show successively greater unfavorable variances, as in Illustration 25–4, a manager might decide to investigate the variance even though it falls within the control limits.

Management Investigation Policies

So far, we have assumed that a variance should be investigated only if the expected benefits from investigation outweigh the costs. This approach focuses on finding a critical probability of being out of control and relating the variance report data to that critical probability. As a practical matter, management usually sets an investigation policy based on some threshold dollar or percentage limitation for variances. For example, a policy may be established that says:

> Investigate all variances that exceed $7,000 or are greater than 20 percent of the flexible budget amount for the specific cost item.

Such a policy is easy to implement, does not require extensive statistical analysis every period, and can be cost-effective if its limits actually do approximate the amounts that would be obtained by a formal analysis of out-of-control probabilities.

If this policy was in effect for the employee benefits section of Great Plains, the following costs would be investigated based on the responsibility report earlier in the chapter:

Cost	Reason to Investigate
Operator wages	Exceeds $7,000
Communications	Exceeds 20%
Utilities	Exceeds both limits
Supplies	Exceeds 20%
Maintenance and repairs	Exceeds both limits

Assuming that the limits have been established to approximate the investigations that would be conducted using the $p*$-based minimum-cost approach, your investigations would be cost effective.

SUMMARY

The decision to investigate variances is an important management decision because the investigation requires the use of scarce management resources, while letting a process continue out of control may result in waste. *All* variances should rarely be investigated. Many are caused by random processes. Conceptually, a variance may be a signal that a process is out of control. If the signal indicates that the out-of-control probability exceeds the critical point where it is more cost-effective to investigate than not to investigate, management should conduct an investigation. It may be possible to compute this critical probability using statistical methods. An alternative approach is to use statistical quality control charts to monitor variances over time. However, managers usually establish an investigation rule based on the absolute amount of the variance or on the amount as a percentage of flexible budget. Such ad hoc rules are usually relatively easy to implement, and so long as they approximate the results that would occur with a more rigorous statistical analysis, they are probably cost-effective.

TERMS AND CONCEPTS

The following terms and concepts should be familiar to you after reading this chapter.

Critical Probability *(p*)*   **Lower Control Limit**

In-Control Probability   **Mean**

Net Present Value

Out-of-Control Probability

Random Event

Sigma (σ)

Standard Deviation

Statistical Quality Control

Upper Control Limit

Variance Investigation

SUPPLEMENTARY READINGS

Baiman, S., and J. Demski. "Variance Analysis Procedures as Motivational Devices." *Management Science,* August 1980, pp. 840–48.

Boer, G. "Solutions in Search of a Problem: The Case of Budget Variance Investigation Models." *Journal of Accounting Literature,* Spring 1984, pp. 47–69.

Brown, G. M. "Variance Analysis: Trend and Materiality." *Management Accounting,* June 1986, pp. 38–9 (published in Great Britain).

Demski, J. "Decision-Performance Control." *Accounting Review,* October 1969, pp. 669–79.

Dittman, D. A., and P. Prakash. "Cost Variance Investigation—Markovian Control of Markov Processes." *Journal of Accounting Research,* Spring 1978, pp. 14–25.

Jacobs, F. "When and How to Use Statistical Cost Variance Investigation Techniques." *Cost and Management,* January–February 1983, pp. 26–32.

Jacobs, F., and R. Marshall. "Note on the Choice Structure of Cost Variance Investigation Models." *Journal of Accounting Literature,* Spring 1984, pp. 71–83.

Kaplan, R. S. "Optimal Investigation Strategies with Imperfect Information." *Journal of Accounting Research,* Spring 1969, pp. 32–43.

————. "The Significance and Investigation of Cost Variances: Survey and Extensions." *Journal of Accounting Research,* Autumn 1975, pp. 311–37.

Lambert, R. "Variance Investigation in Agency Settings." *Journal of Accounting Research,* Autumn 1985, pp. 633–47.

SELF-STUDY PROBLEM

Wild and Crazy Lens Corporation has been experiencing problems in controlling costs. A recent responsibility report for one of the company's divisions indicated the following (in thousands):

Item	Budget	Actual	Variance
Direct materials	$ 45	$ 39	$6 F
Direct labor	40	48	8 U
Overhead			
Utilities	10	9	1 F
Property taxes	6	5	1 F
Supervision	8	6	2 F
Equipment repairs	7	10	3 U
Totals	$116	$117	$1 U

The division manager stated that there was no problem since the overall variance was less than 1 percent of total costs, and that was close enough.

As a member of the controller's staff, you learn that the cost to investigate each variance is $1,250. If the process is out of control, it costs an estimated $1,000 to correct. However, if the process is out of control and stays out of control, the variance in next month's report is expected to be the same as this month's variance. If the variance appears next month, the process will be investigated and controlled. Hence, the only loss of delay is one month's variance.

Required:

a. What is the critical probability for investigating the direct labor variance?

b. Given the stated costs from the problem, which other variances would you investigate and correct if they are out of control?

c. Can you suggest some possible causes for the variances that appear in this report?

SOLUTION TO SELF-STUDY PROBLEM

a. If L is equal to the $8,000 variance, then the cost functions may be set up as:

$$Lp = I + Cp$$
$$\$8,000p = \$1,250 + \$1,000p$$
$$\$7,000p = \$1,250$$
$$p = \underline{\underline{.179}}$$

which is the critical probability.

b. The only other costs that would be investigated are those with unfavorable variances greater than $2,250 ($1,250 cost to investigate + $1,000 cost to correct). The only cost meeting this criterion is equipment repairs.

c. It appears there is a significant drop in materials costs, which suggests the possibility that substandard materials may have been purchased. If so, this may explain why labor costs have such a high variance and why equipment repair costs are substantially greater than budget. This section of the problem is designed to illustrate how management judgment enters the variance investigation decision process. A review of the report and the given cost structure suggests that only unfavorable variances be investigated. However, it is likely that in this situation the unfavorable variances have a common cause. Management's experience would override any statistical analysis of the data.

QUESTIONS

25–1. Why doesn't management just investigate all unfavorable variances and forget about complex investigation rules?

25–2. What is the basic decision that management must make when considering whether to investigate a variance?

25–3. The larger a variance, the more likely management is to investigate it. What is the rationale for this?

25–4. Should favorable variances be investigated? Why or why not?

25–5. Nuts N' Bolts runs a highly automated process. the company monitors its equipment on a daily basis. Over each of the past three days, the company noted that the out-of-control probability for a boltmaker was .3, .45, and .7, respectively. The manager of the boltmaker operation suggested that the company initiate an investigation to determine whether the equipment was out of control. Past experience suggests that there is less than a .01 probability that an in-control process would show three consecutive increases in the out-of-control probability. The costs of leaving the process out of control are approximately twice the costs of an investigation. Would you recommend conducting an investigation? Why or why not? If you require additional information, specify the information needed.

25–6. If processes sooner or later go out of control, and if eventually it is so obvious that a process is out of control that management will repair the process without an investigation, why would one be interested in knowing investigation costs?

25–7. What is the role of the out-of-control probability in the variance investigation decision?

25–8. Under what conditions would statistical quality control charts be useful in a responsibility-reporting setting?

25–9. Management usually sets a variance investigation policy such as "Investigate all variances greater than $10,000 or 20 percent of the budgeted amount for the item." Why would management use such a rule when statistical rules give a more precise answer?

25–10. Why do we study statistical rules for variance investigation if they are not widely used by managers?

25–11. Alpha Corporation has implemented the use of statistical quality control charts for analyzing variances. The company has set upper and lower control limits equal to two standard deviations. Assuming there are no out-of-control situations anywhere in the company, what proportion of variances are expected to be outside the control limits?

EXERCISES

25–12. Costs of Variance Investigation

(L.O.1)

Greensward, Inc., observed an unfavorable variance of $25,000 in its direct materials usage. They estimate this variance indicates there is a .70 probability that the manufacturing process is out of control. To investigate this variance, an $8,000 cost of shutting down operations will be incurred. If the process is out of control, repairs will cost $15,000. In addition, the production line will stay closed during the repair process, which will cost an additional $26,000.

If the process is out of control and is left out of control, the company will use $45,000 in excess materials between now and the time when the next variance report comes out. At that time, the variance would indicate a 1.0 probability that the process was out of control.

Required:

a. What are the expected costs of:
   (1) Investigation?
   (2) Not investigating?

b. Should the variance be investigated?

25–13. Costs of Variance Investigation

(L.O.1)

A production manager of Sante Fe, Inc., notes there is an unfavorable direct labor efficiency variance of $30,000. He estimates that this variance indicates that there is a .60 probability that the manufacturing process is out of control. The cost to investigate this variance will be $7,500. If the process is found to be out of control, it will cost $40,000 to correct. If the process is not investigated and is out of control, the company expects that $55,000 in excess labor will be used until the next variance report, which would indicate a 1.0 probability that the process was out of control.

Required:

What are the expected costs of:

a. Investigating the variance?

b. Not investigating?

25–14. Determine Which Variances to Investigate

(L.O.2)

The manager of the sport shoe manufacturing division of Kansas City Products received the following report of variances in the manufacturing operation for the past month:

Item	Actual Cost	Variance	
Direct materials:			
Top fabric	$211,500	$14,029	F
Soles	141,620	6,315	U
Packing	37,980	1,855	U
Conversion costs:			
Labor	65,119	2,107	F
Machine rental	218,732	18	U
Property taxes	17,143	12	F
Insurance	10,422	279	U
Power utilities	18,309	1,153	U
Maintenance	31,596	1,478	F

Kansas City Products conducted a statistical evaluation of its costs and variances and determined that all variances which exceeded 5 percent of actual cost or $5,000 (whichever is less) should be investigated.

Required:

For each of the costs listed in the variance report, indicate which costs would be investigated under the company's rule. Also indicate why the cost should be investigated.

25–15. Estimate Critical Probabilities
(L.O.2)

The cost of an investigation is $4,000. If the process is out of control, it will cost $9,000 to correct. However, if the process stays out of control, the company expects it will cost $15,000 until the process is corrected.

Required:

What is the critical probability?

25–16. Estimate Critical Probabilities
(L.O.2)

At Life Company, the cost of an investigation is $10,000. If the process is out of control, it will cost $15,000 to correct. However, if the process stays out of control, the company will lose $35,000 until it is corrected.

Required:

What is the critical probability?

25–17. Estimate Critical Probabilities
(L.O.2)

At the Phoenix Corporation, the cost of an investigation is $5,000. If the process is out of control, it will cost $12,000 to correct. However, if the process stays out of control, the company will lose $20,000 until the process is corrected.

Required:

What is the critical probability?

25–18. Investigating a Process
(L.O.2)

A production manager of Robots, Inc., is trying to determine if a production process is in control. The cost of investigation is $6,000, and if the process is out of control, it will cost the company $14,000 to correct the error. By correcting the error, the present value of the cost savings until the next scheduled investigation will be $40,000. The in-control probability is .80, and the out-of-control probability is .20.

Required:

a. Should the process be investigated? Why or why not?

b. At what out-of-control probability level would the manager be indifferent about whether to investigate?

25–19. Investigating a Process
(L.O.2)

A production manager is considering whether to investigate a manufacturing process. The cost of investigation is $5,000, and if the process is out of control, the cost of correcting it will be $15,000. If they correct it, the present value of cost savings until the next scheduled inspection will be $50,000. The in-control probability is .75 and the out-of-control probability is .25.

Required:

a. Should the process be investigated? Why or why not?

b. At what out-of-control probability would the manager be indifferent about whether to investigate?

25–20. Investigating a Process
(L.O.2)

Manhatten Company's production manager is considering whether to investigate a production process. The cost of investigation is $7,000. If the process is found to be out of control, the cost of correcting it is $20,000. If the process is out of control and they correct it, they will have cost savings of $45,000 until the next scheduled investigation. The in-control probability is .65, and the out-of-control probability is .35.

Required:

a. Should the process be investigated? Why or why not?

b. At what out-of-control probability would the manager be indifferent about whether to investigate?

25–21. Investigating a Process
(L.O.2)

An unfavorable variance of $20,000 was reported for a manufacturing process. If no investigation is conducted and the process is out of control, the present value of avoidable excess production costs is $10,000. The cost of conducting an investigation is $2,000. If the process was actually out of control, the cost of correction would be an additional $1,000. There is a .20 probability that the $20,000 variance indicates the process is out of control.

Required:

a. Should the process be investigated?

b. At what out-of-control probability does the expected cost of investigating equal the expected cost of not investigating?

25–22. Statistical Quality Control
(L.O.3)

Eagle Feather Industries has a process with a standard deviation of $115 for each batch of feathers produced and an expected cost of $1,430 per batch. Six batches of feathers were produced in the current week. The costs for each batch are as follows:

Batch	Cost
A	$1,365
B	1,115
C	1,478
D	1,681
E	1,522
F	1,297

Eagle uses a two-standard deviation quality control limit.

Required:

Which of the six batches should be investigated? For each batch that should be investigated, state the reason for the investigation.

25–23. Statistical Quality Control
(L.O.3)

Refer to the information for Eagle Feather Industries in problem 25–22, above. Prepare a statistical quality control chart to reflect the upper and lower control limits as well as the costs for each of the six batches.

25–24. Statistical Quality Control
(L.O.3)

The expected cost to produce a batch of compact discs at Laser Audio is $17,200. The standard deviation for the cost is $450 per batch. Eight batches of compact discs were produced in the current week. The cost for each batch is as follows:

Batch	Cost
Rock	$16,218
Roll	17,918
Classical	16,444
Country	18,283
Oldies	17,391
Heavy metal	18,090
Punk	15,899
New age	18,004

Laser Audio uses a two-standard deviation quality control limit.

Required:

Which of the eight batches should be investigated? For each batch that should be investigated, state the reason for the investigation.

25–25. Statistical Quality Control
(L.O.3)

Refer to the information for Laser Audio in problem 25–24, above. Prepare a statistical quality control chart to reflect the upper and lower control limits as well as the costs for each of the eight batches.

PROBLEMS

25–26. Variance Investigation Costs and Benefits

Micro Parts, Inc., manufactures silicon wafers used in semiconductor chip assemblies. The company operates under a contract with Mega Mainframes. Part of the contract requires that the silicon wafers meet certain tolerances. If the silicon wafers do not meet these specifications, Micro Parts could lose its contract. Since Micro Parts operates a highly automated system, there is always a chance that its system will go out of control. If the system goes out of control for a short period of time, the costs of the out-of-control process are relatively low. However, if the process is out of control for a long enough period, the costs escalate rapidly. The following table shows the costs related to the time the silicon wafer process is out of control and the probability of investigation for each period:

Additional Time Out-of-Control	Out-of-Control Costs This Period	Probability of Investigation
1	$ 18,000	.20
2	49,000	.45
3	177,000	.85
4	350,000	.95
5	1,900,000	1.00

Required:

a. What is the expected cost of having the process remain out of control assuming that the process has just gone out of control?

b. What is the potential savings in costs of allowing its process to remain out of control if Micro Parts, Inc. were to change its investigation rules such that the probability of investigation in period 1 increased from .20 to .60 and the probability of investigation increased from .45 to .75 in period 2?

25–27. Variance Investigation Costs and Benefits

Hurst Cartoon Products Corp. manufactures T-shirts, buttons, stuffed toys, and other goods using the motif of cartoon characters. If a process is out of control, costs are relatively low since a lot of goods can be sold as "seconds" at a slight markdown from the regular price. The following table shows the costs related to the time the stuffed-toy process is out of control and the probability of investigation for each period:

Additional Time Out-of-Control	Out-of-Control Costs This Period	Probability of Investigation
1	$ 4,000	.10
2	7,000	.25
3	15,000	.35
4	37,000	.55
5	78,000	.70
6	122,000	1.00

Required:

a. What is the expected cost of having the stuffed-toy process remain out of control assuming that the process has just gone out of control?

b. What is the potential savings in costs of allowing its process to remain out of control if Hurst were to change its investigation rules such that the probability of investigation in period 1 increased from .10 to .20 and the probability of investigation in all other periods remained the same?

25–28. Analyze Costs and Variances

Clark Company has a contract with a labor union that guarantees a minimum wage of $500 per month to each direct labor employee having at least 12 years of service. One hundred employees currently qualify for coverage. All direct labor employees are paid $5 per hour.

The direct labor budget for this year was based on an annual usage of 400,000 hours of direct labor at $5, or a total of $2 million. Of this amount, $50,000 (100 employees × $500) per month (or $600,000 for the year) was regarded as fixed. Thus, the budget for any given month was determined by the formula $50,000 + $3.50 × direct labor-hours worked.

Data on performance for the first three months of this year follow:

	January	February	March
Direct labor-hours worked	22,000	32,000	42,000
Direct labor costs budgeted	$127,000	$162,000	$197,000
Direct labor costs incurred	110,000	160,000	210,000
Variance	17,000 F	2,000 F	13,000 U

The factory manager was perplexed by the results, which showed favorable variances when production was low and unfavorable variances when production was high, because he believed his control over costs was consistently good.

Required:

a. Why did the variances arise? Explain and illustrate, using amounts and diagrams as necessary.

b. Does this direct labor budget provide a basis for controlling direct labor cost? Explain, indicating changes that might be made to improve control over direct labor cost and to facilitate performance evaluation of direct labor employees.

(CPA adapted)

26–29. Costs of Investigation

Texas Oil Company currently sells three grades of gasoline: regular, unleaded, and unleaded plus, which is a mixture of unleaded and an octane enhancer. Unleaded plus is advertised as being "at least 10 percent higher octane than unleaded." Although any mixture containing 10 percent or more premium gas could be sold as unleaded plus, it is less costly to increase the octane by exactly 10 percent. The amount of octane enhancer in the mixture is determined by a valve in the blending machine. If the valve is properly adjusted, the machine provides a mixture that yields the 10 percent higher octane. If the valve is out of adjustment, the machine provides a mixture that yields 20 percent higher octane.

Once the machine is started, it must continue until 100,000 gallons of unleaded plus have been mixed.

Cost data available:	
Cost per gallon—unleaded	70¢
Cost per gallon—regular	65¢
Cost of checking the valve	$1,000
Cost of adjusting the valve	$ 500

The octane enhancer costs 5 cents per gallon to make unleaded plus at 10 percent higher octane than unleaded. If the 20 percent higher octane is produced, the octane enhancer costs 12¼ cents per gallon.

The probabilities of the valve's condition are estimated to be:

Event	Probability
In adjustment	.7
Out of adjustment	.3

Required:

a. Should Texas investigate the valve?

b. At what probability would Texas be indifferent about whether to investigate?

(CMA adapted)

25–30. Issues in Variance Investigation—Multiple Choice

The folding department supervisor must decide each week whether the department will operate normally the following week. Corrective action is ordered only if the folding department will operate inefficiently. The supervisor receives a weekly folding department efficiency variance report from the accounting department. A week in which the folding department operates inefficiently is usually preceded by a large efficiency variance. The graph below gives the probability that the folding department will operate normally in the following week as a function of the magnitude of the current week's variance reported to the supervisor:

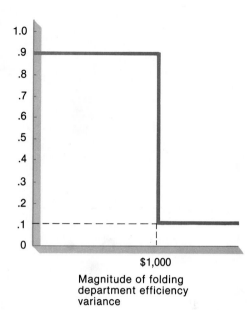

Probability of folding
department operating
normally next week

$1,000

Magnitude of folding
department efficiency
variance

Required:

a. An efficiency variance of $1,500 this week means the probability of operating normally the following week is:
  (1) 0 percent.
  (2) 10 percent.
  (3) 90 percent.
  (4) 100 percent.

b. What are the possible relationships between the current efficiency variance and next week's operations?
  (1) Large variance followed by normal operation, large variance followed by inefficient operation, small variance followed by normal operation, and small variance followed by inefficient operation.
  (2) Large variance followed by normal operation, small variance followed by inefficient operation, and small variance followed by normal operation.
  (3) Large variance followed by inefficient operation, small variance followed by normal operation, and small variance followed by inefficient operation.
  (4) Large variance followed by 90 percent of normal operation, small variance followed by 10 percent of normal operation, large variance followed by inefficient operation, and small variance followed by inefficient operation.

c. If the supervisor can determine for certain whether the folding department will operate normally next week, and the cost of corrective action is less than the extra cost of operating the folding department inefficiently, then the best decision rule for the supervisor to follow is:
  (1) If normal operations are predicted, do not take corrective action; if inefficient operations are predicted, take corrective action.
  (2) Regardless of the current variance, do not take corrective action.
  (3) If normal operations are predicted, take corrective action; if inefficient operations are predicted, do not take corrective action.
  (4) Regardless of the current variance, take corrective action.

d. The following cost information is relevant to the folding department supervisor in deciding whether corrective action is warranted:

$\ 500 =$ Cost of corrective action that will assure normal operation of folding department for the following week.

$\$3,000 =$ Excess cost of operating folding department inefficiently for one week.

The supervisor receives a report that the folding department efficiency variance is $600. The expected cost of not taking corrective action is:

(1) $0.
(2) $300.
(3) $2,700.
(4) $3,000.

(CPA adapted)

25–31. Control Charts

Jean Auel was recently appointed controller for a medium-sized manufacturing firm. Her first assignment is to investigate whether material usage within the plant is under control. She recalls studying statistical quality control techniques in a management education course and decided to apply it to her investigation. She took the following two samples:

Sample Number	Cost of Each Item			
1	$945	$876	$852	$941
2	822	943	949	782

Required:

The control limits specified are $880 ± $60.

a. Prepare a control chart using the designated control limits.

b. Comment on the results.

25–32. Control Charts

An engineer for Jordan Valley Tool Company specified that the diameter of a particular part should have tolerance limits of .352 and .356. An assistant to the controller asked production personnel to sample these parts. A random sample of 20 parts had the following diameters:

Exhibit A (25–32)

Number	Diameter
1	.351
2	.350
3	.353
4	.352
5	.359
6	.360
7	.362
8	.351
9	.353
10	.358
11	.355
12	.350
13	.353
14	.354
15	.353
16	.354
17	.355
18	.355
19	.356
20	.354

The mean and standard deviation of the diameter for this type of part has been established as .354 and .003, respectively. Jordan Valley Tool management established a policy that variances outside of the two-sigma limit should be investigated. By contrast, engineering and production personnel believe a process is in control as long as variances are within three standard deviations from the mean.

Required:

a. Construct a control chart and plot the sample on it.

b. Are the engineer's tolerance limits currently attainable? If not, what alternatives are open to the company?

25–33. Statistical Quality Control

Star Ferry Products, Ltd. manufactures a line of microcomputer motherboards. The company manufactures these boards in two divisions: Hong Kong Division and Kowloon Division. Company specifications indicate that each board should cost $460 and that for a day's production of boards at each division, the standard deviation for the average cost is $36. Exhibit B shows the average unit cost for production for the first 17 days of the month.

Exhibit B (25–33)

Day	Hong Kong Division Unit Cost	Kowloon Division Unit Cost
1	$445	$485
2	469	471
3	427	427
4	439	439
5	421	445
6	429	321
7	449	449
8	455	455
9	461	433
10	448	571
11	452	452
12	466	446
13	475	459
14	468	468
15	473	473
16	520	501
17	555	

The company uses a three-standard deviation control limit for variance investigation purposes.

Required:

a. Which variances would you investigate? Why?

b. Prepare a statistical quality control chart for each of the two divisions.

INFORMATION ECONOMICS

LEARNING OBJECTIVES

1. Present formal concepts of information benefits and costs.

2. Show why some accounting information has value and some does not.

3. Illustrate the principles for determining information value using Bayes' Theorem.

4. Demonstrate the costs from using the wrong information when making a decision.

Managers are employed to make and implement decisions. The outcome from such decisions is rarely known with certainty in advance. Hence, the decision may result in a profit or a loss. Information is used to assist the manager in making economic decisions. Cost accounting information is part of the manager's available information set. While managers can obtain a great deal of information to assist them in making a decision, at some point the information gathering must end and the decision must be made. Determining this point is a decision that results in incurring costs to, hopefully, obtain benefits. Hence, the decision to acquire information is an economic decision.

As providers of information, cost accountants need to understand the economics of the decision to acquire information. We assume in this chapter that routine information, such as that required for external reporting, will be gathered without an explicit economic analysis. Hence, in this chapter we focus on the economics of information used for special purposes such as for decision making.

Some examples of risky management decisions that require cost information include:

1. Setting a product price where the price must cover costs and provide an adequate profit.
2. Deciding whether to enter a new market.
3. Evaluating whether a new employee benefit would be cost-effective.
4. Deciding to explore for natural resources.
5. Determining whether to finance the company through debt or equity.

For each of these decisions, the net benefit to the company is affected by events beyond the control of the decision maker. Information is used to help management make more informed decisions.

Information Cost   Cost of obtaining information.

Value of Information   Value placed on information one could possibly obtain in a decision-making context.

However, decisions about how much information to acquire and the price to pay for such information are a part of management's process. This chapter focuses on these information-related aspects of management decision making. To decide whether to acquire information, management must evaluate the **information cost** and compare that to the **value of the information.**

COST DATA AND INFORMATION ECONOMICS

Information Economics   A formal system for evaluating whether the cost-benefit test has been met for information.

As discussed in earlier chapters, cost accounting differs from financial accounting in several ways. One major difference is that because the information is provided only to insiders, the user need not be limited by the rules for external reporting. Hence, the inside user can specify exactly the information to be provided for any given decision. The only limitation the user faces is that information, like any good, is costly. At some point, the cost of additional information will exceed the benefit that can be expected from it. The conceptual basis for determining how much information to request is found in the field of **information economics.**

Consider the decision-making problem of a manager of WowZow Audio Corporation who is about to introduce a miniature cassette player into the market. This cassette player will fit entirely in the ear, thus eliminating the need for earphones and a cumbersome playing device. The product will be called an EarHear. The EarHear requires an investment of $7 million in plant and equipment. Assume, for simplicity, that there are only two possible outcomes from this decision:

1. The product is well accepted, costs and revenues are equal to expected levels, and the future cash flows will be worth a net present value of $20 million.
2. The product is a failure, and the total investment will be lost.

If you were the manager, would you invest the $7 million with this information? This problem is similar to other decision-making problems under uncertainty. Similarities with the approach in Chapter 24 appear here also, except in this chapter we focus on the acquisition of information rather than on the production decision.

Outcomes Possible results of a given action.

Just knowing the possible **outcomes** is insufficient information on which to base this decision. The manager will seek information until the expected cost of that information exceeds its benefits.

Deciding whether the cost-benefit criterion has been met is usually a matter of personal judgment. Briefly, information is deemed to meet the cost-benefit test if the expected value of a decision (net of the costs of the information) increases as a result of obtaining additional information. That is, the expected value of the decision must increase by more than the cost of the information obtained. The value assigned to different outcomes from a decision is called a **payoff.** Payoffs may be positive or negative.

Payoff The value of an outcome from a decision.

The Expected Value Criterion

Just knowing all of the possible payoffs from a decision may not be very useful for decision making. Some way must be found to aggregate the different payoffs. The usual approach is to obtain the expected value of each decision alternative. The expected value is the sum of each possible outcome times the probability of its occurrence.

Let's return to our example. The manager faces a possible gain (or payoff) of $20 million from the investment. Against this he runs the risk of losing the $7 million investment. Before investing in such a risky project, he would at least want to assess the relative probabilities of making $20 million versus losing $7 million. If the probability of making the $20 million is equal to .60, we can compute the expected value of the project:

Payoff (millions)	Probability	Expected Value (millions)
$20	.60	$12.0
(7)	.40	(2.8)
Project expected value		$ 9.2

Expected Value The weighted average of all of the outcomes of a decision process.

The **expected value** is the sum of the product of each possible outcome times the probability of that outcome. It represents the expectation from the project, not the actual outcome. Indeed, in this example, the actual outcomes are limited to either a $20 million positive payment or a $7 million loss.

Since the expected value of the project is positive, we will assume that the project is acceptable to the manager from the standpoint of maximizing company values. However, the project is risky. If the manager accepts this project, there is a significant (.40) probability that the company will suffer a $7 million loss. Can the manager do anything about that loss?

THE OPPORTUNITY LOSS CONCEPT

Opportunity Loss Loss from an unfavorable outcome.

Perfect Information Information that predicts with complete accuracy the outcome that will occur from a decision.

By making a decision to accept the project, there is a .4 chance that a loss will be incurred. The $7 million loss from the unfavorable outcome is referred to as an **opportunity loss.** The loss may never actually be realized, but there is a .4 chance that it will occur.

Now, let's assume that the manager could acquire information that would make a perfect prediction of the project's success. Such information would be called **perfect information.** This information would provide the manager with perfect knowledge about the future. If the manager had such perfect knowledge, the project would be accepted only when the positive outcome was assured. This would occur with a .6 probability. Otherwise, the manager would avoid the project and, at least, avoid the loss. Hence, with perfect knowledge, the outcome with the highest payoff for each known state would be selected. The expected value of the project would be the sum of the expected values for each outcome and its related best action:

Outcome (millions)	Best Action	Probability	Expected Value (millions)
$20	Invest	.60	$12
–0–	Avoid	.40	–0–
Expected value of project with perfect information			$12

EXPECTED VALUE OF INFORMATION

With perfect knowledge about the future, the manager would be able to identify the 60 percent of the time when the new product would be successful. Under those circumstances, the manager would invest in the new product. The remaining 40 percent of the time, when the new product would fail, the manager would know not to invest. Hence, the manager could avoid the $7 million loss that 40 percent of the time when the loss would occur.

Expected Value of Perfect Information

The expected value of perfect information is the amount that could be saved with perfect knowledge about the future. That amount is also the difference between the $12 million expected value of the project with perfect information and the $9.2 million expected value of the project without perfect information. If the manager could obtain perfect information, the information would be worth up to $2.8 million. (Note that this value of perfect information equals .40 times the avoided opportunity loss of $7 million.) If the information cost is less than this, the manager's expected value would increase if the information were obtained.

Suppose a market research company can conduct a study of the product and its acceptance in a test market. The company will manufacture a sufficient quantity of the product for test-marketing purposes. As a result of this test, the manager will have perfect information about the outcome if the product is introduced to the general market. The total cost of the market research project is $1 million. This $1 million is an information cost. Should the manager pay for the market research and order the limited production run?

If the product will be successful, the market study will indicate this with absolute certainty. Therefore, with probability .6, WowZow Audio will obtain the $20 million payoff less the $1 million spent on the market study.

On the other hand, with probability .4, the market study will indicate that the product will not be successful. When this occurs, WowZow Audio will lose the $1 million cost of the market study, but no more.

The expected value of this decision with costly perfect information is:

Payoff (millions)	Probability	Expected Value (millions)
$19	.6	$11.4
(1)	.4	(.4)
Project expected value		$11.0

This is, of course, exactly $1 million less than the expected value of the project with costless perfect information.

Perfect versus Imperfect Information

So far we have discussed the value of information that provides a perfect prediction. But since information about the future will probably be imperfect, why then do we consider the value of perfect information?

First, the value of perfect information provides an upper limit on the costs that should be incurred to obtain information for decision making. Second, the framework used to estimate the value of perfect information can also be used to estimate the value of imperfect information.

Imperfect Information Information that is not 100 percent accurate, but may be used to revise the probabilities of certain decision outcomes.

Imperfect information does not allow certain prediction of the outcome that will occur, but it allows us to revise our probabilities about the outcomes of a decision. The value of imperfect information is the increase in the expected value of the decision that arises from the ability to revise the probabilities. The value of imperfect information can be estimated using the technique called *Bayesian statistics*.

Now, let's extend the example in the problem. We now assume that the marketing study and trial production run will provide imperfect information. The report can have two possible outcomes: a good report indicating that the product will be successful or a bad report showing that the product will fail. Since the study is an imperfect information source, a good report can occur even if the product will fail. Likewise, a bad report can occur even though the product would succeed. Nonetheless, use of the report may enable us to revise our initial probabilities and make a better decision. The initial probabilities are often referred to as **prior probabilities** or **priors**.

Prior Probabilities (Priors) Initial probability estimates.

Revising Prior Probabilities with Information

In deciding to conduct the market research, the relevant criterion is whether the expected value of the project will increase sufficiently to cover the cost of the study. To test this, WowZow management must know how reliable the report will be. That is, if they receive a good marketing report, what is the probability that the product will actually be successful?

The following discussion describes the process, which is summarized in Illustration 26–1. To conduct this analysis, some statistical notation is help-

---

Illustration 26-1   **Table of Probabilities**

Step 1: Set up the table and enter the prior probabilities of success (S) and failure (F) as the row totals.

	Report Good (G)	Report Bad (B)	Totals
Product Succeeds (S)			.60
Product Fails (F)			.40
Totals			1.00*

* Probabilities must sum to 1.0

Step 2: Compute the joint probabilities in each cell by multiplying the conditional probabilities [for example, p(G/S)] times the prior probabilities of success or failure (for example, p(S) = .60). Recall that p(G/S) = .85; p(B/S) = .15; p(G/F) = .20; and p(B/F) = .80.

	Report Good (G)	Report Bad (B)	Totals
Product Succeeds (S)	.85 × .60 = .51	.15 × .60 = .09	.60
Product Fails (F)	.20 × .40 = .08	.80 × .40 = .32	.40
Totals			1.00

Step 3: Compute the column totals, which are the probabilities of receiving a good report or a bad report.

	Report Good (G)	Report Bad (B)	Totals
Product Succeeds (S)	.51	.09	.60
Product Fails (F)	.08	.32	.40
Totals	.59	.41	1.00

ful. Using the symbol S to indicate a successful product and the symbol F to indicate a failure, we note that the prior probabilities are:

$$p(S) = .6$$
$$p(F) = .4$$

as discussed before and as entered in step 1 in Illustration 26–1.

The second step is to find out the probabilities of obtaining a good report (G) or a bad report (B) given that the product will be successful. These are called **conditional probabilities** because they depend on the actual, unknown outcome. This information must be obtained from other sources, perhaps from the market research company or from management's judgment about similar past projects. For the example, we assume these probabilities are:

$$p(G|S) = .85$$
$$p(B|S) = .15$$

This means that the probability of a good report given a successful product is .85, and so forth. From similar sources, we must also obtain the probabilities of each report given that the product will fail. We assume these are:

$$p(G|F) = .20$$
$$p(B|F) = .80$$

This information is used to compute the probabilities of getting a good or bad report before the report is ordered. If the probabilities of each report type are known, the expected value of the project with the imperfect information can be computed. This information is used to help decide whether to order the report. The difference in the value with the imperfect information and the value of the project without any information is the maximum price we would be willing to pay for the imperfect information, using the expected value criterion.

To obtain the probabilities of getting each kind of report, we add the probabilities of obtaining that report under each possible outcome. The probability of getting both a certain kind of report and a certain outcome is called a **joint probability.** (See step 2 in Illustration 26–1.) In the example, the probability of getting a good report is equal to the sum of the joint probability of a good report when the outcome is success plus the probability of a good report when the outcome is failure. Thus, we multiply the probability of success times the probability of getting a good report when the outcome will be success (.6 × .85 = .51). Then we multiply the probability of failure times the probability of getting a good report when the outcome will be failure (.4 × .2 = .08). Then we add the results of these two multiplications:

$$p(G) = [p(S) \times p(G|S)] + [p(F) \times p(G|F)]$$

which, for the example data, yields:

$$p(G) = (.6 \times .85) + (.4 \times .2)$$
$$= .51 + .08$$
$$= \underline{\underline{.59}}$$

We therefore have a .59 probability of getting a good report before contracting for the market study, as shown in step 3 of Illustration 26–1.

Conditional Probabilities Those likelihoods that depend on a specific result.

Joint Probability The probability of two or more events occurring.

The probability of getting a bad report is equal to $1 - .59$, or $.41$. This may be verified by computing the probabilities of a bad report conditioned on both possible outcomes just as was done for the good report. The calculations are:

$$p(B) = [p(S) \times p(B|S)] + [p(F) \times p(B|F)]$$
$$= (.6 \times .15) + (.4 \times .8)$$
$$= .09 + .32$$
$$= \underline{\underline{.41}}$$

These calculations are also shown in steps 2 and 3 in Illustration 26–1.

Now, before we incur the cost of acquiring the report, we know the probability that we will obtain a good report or a bad report. This information is important because if the report is to have any impact on our decision, the different type of report must result in a change in our decision. That is, in this limited situation, if the report is good, then the investment meets the expected value criterion. If the report is bad, then the investment would not meet the criterion and, presumably, would be avoided. If we will take one action or the other regardless of the type of report, then the report has no value. Why spend resources on information that has no potential to change a decision?

Regardless of which report we receive, the project can still succeed or fail. Hence, after receiving the report we must make a decision whether to embark on the project. At this point, it is helpful to diagram the possible outcomes. A decision tree is useful for this purpose, as shown in Illustration 26–2.

The first decision is whether to conduct the test. These are the two main branches of the decision tree. If we decide to conduct the test and, hence, acquire the report, we must make the investment decision after receipt of the report. The decision will be based on the expected payoff from each outcome. To make the decision, we must know the probabilities of success or failure after receiving each kind of report. These probabilities are called **posterior probabilities.** In this example, we ignore the possibility of investing in the project if the report is bad because the report outcome must affect our decision. We could extend the analysis to evaluate the expected payoff given a bad report. But, since receipt of a bad report would preclude us from investing in the project, we enter a zero payoff for that outcome.

Posterior Probabilities The probabilities obtained as a result of revising prior probabilities with additional conditional probability data.

Prior to receiving the report, we were given the probability of project success as $.6$ and the probability of failure as $.4$. The expected value of the project without the report is the second main branch in Illustration 26–2. Now we want to see if the expected value of the project is greater with the information in the report.

Revising Probabilities Using Bayes' Theorem

The objectives of this analysis is to find out how the report will revise the prior probabilities ($.6$ for success and $.4$ for failure). This process of revising probabilities requires knowledge of the probabilities of success and failure given each type of report. These probabilities, known as posterior probabilities, may be found using Bayes' Theorem. If the report is good (G), the probability of success (S) is estimated as:

Illustration 26-2   **Decision Tree for Information Evaluation**

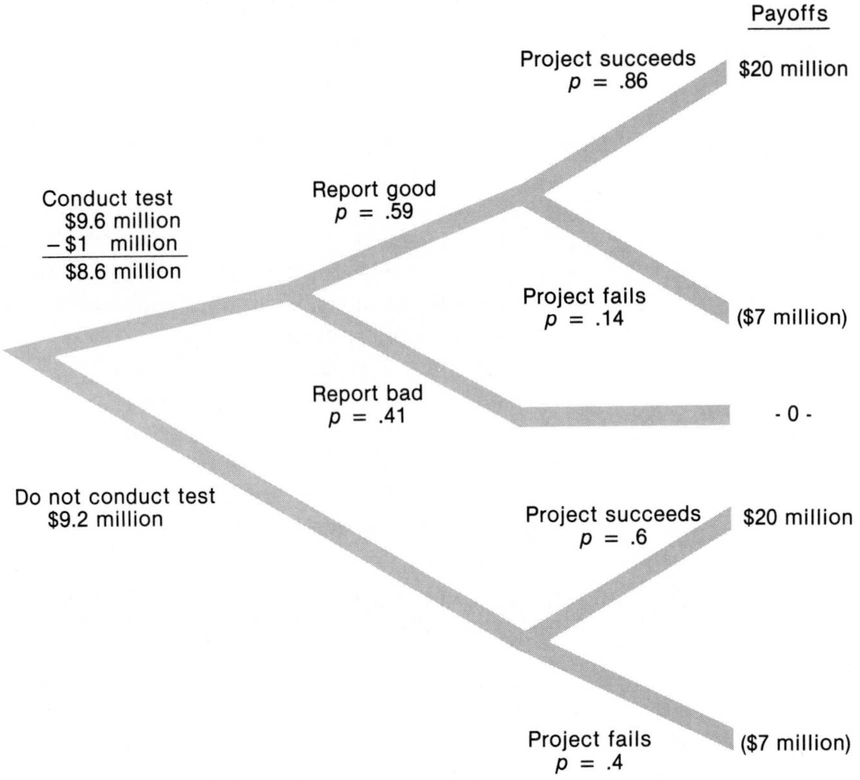

$$p(S|G) = \frac{p(G|S) \times p(S)}{p(G)}$$

$$= \frac{.85 \times .6}{.59} = \underline{\underline{.86}} \text{ (rounded)}$$

The posterior probability of failure *(F)* given a good report *(G)* is the complement of this amount, or .14, and is computed as follows:

$$p(F|G) = \frac{p(G|F) \times p(F)}{p(G)}$$

$$= \frac{.20 \times .40}{.59} = \underline{\underline{.14}} \text{ (rounded)}$$

The posterior probabilities when a bad report is received are computed in the same manner. For success, the probability is:

$$p(S|B) = \frac{p(B|S) \times p(S)}{p(B)}$$

$$= \frac{.15 \times .6}{.41} = \underline{\underline{.22}} \text{ (rounded)}$$

The probability of failure *(F)* given the bad report *(B)* is then .78, which is the complement of the probability of success.

These posterior probabilities have been entered on the decision tree in Illustration 26–2 and are used to compute the expected value of the project with imperfect information.

Computing the Value of Imperfect Information

The expected value of the decision to introduce the new product with imperfect information is obtained by computing the expected value of the project given each report. This is referred to as the conditional value of the decision given a certain report. That is, if we get a good report, we compute an expected value for the project conditioned on the good report. Multiplying that conditional value of the probability of obtaining that report gives us the expected value of the project after taking into account that a good report will only be received some fraction of the time. The expected value for the project is the sum of the expected values of each report outcome.

For the example, we have the following analysis to determine the expected value with a good report:

Outcome (millions)	Posterior Probability	Expected Value (millions)
$20	.86	$17.2
(7)	.14	(1.0)
Expected value given a good report		$16.2

If the report is good, WowZow Audio would invest in the EarHear because the expected $16.2 million payoff is positive. Before we order the test market study, we have a .59 probability that the report will be favorable. Therefore, before ordering the study, we expect that the value of the joint outcome of a good report and the decision to go ahead with the product introduction will be $9.6 million (.59 probability of a good report × $16.2 million).

Next, we find the expected value of going ahead with the product introduction in the face of a bad report:

Outcome (millions)	Posterior Probability	Expected Value (millions)
$20	.22	$ 4.4
(7)	.78	(5.5)
Expected value of product after a bad report		$(1.1)

Since the expected value of product introduction would be negative after receiving a bad report, management of WowZow Audio would not introduce the product if a bad report was received. This is as we anticipated. Hence, the expected payoff would be zero.

The value of the decision to introduce the project with imperfect information is, then, the sum of the values of the decision for each report outcome. That is, $9.6 million plus zero, or $9.6 million.

The value with imperfect information is compared to the value with no information. The increase represents the maximum that we would be willing to pay for the imperfect information. In this case, the difference is $.4 million ($9.6 million − $9.2 million).

If the cost of the market study and trial production run was $1 million, the decision would be not to commission the study. Its cost exceeds the $.4 million benefit that can be expected from it.

OTHER CONSIDERATIONS IN INFORMATION EVALUATION

Formal analysis of information needs provides a cost-minimizing approach to the obtaining of information. However, it has frequently been said that management lacks sufficient prior information to compute the expected value of imperfect information. Hence, formal analysis is not possible. In other cases, a decision can be made without formal analysis. Before analyzing information value, a manager will ask the following questions:

1. Will the information make a difference?
2. How costly would the error be if the action was taken without the information?

The first question asks if the information will possibly change the decision. The second asks about the cost of prediction error. Unless the information can be expected to make a difference and unless the value of the difference exceeds the cost of the information, the information should not be obtained.

Changing a Decision with Information

In the example, the imperfect market study and test production run had value because the decision involved a choice. If a bad report was received, management would avoid introducing the new product and, hence, avoid the related loss. But if the receipt of a bad report would not deter introduction of the new product, the test study would have no value in this context. That is, regardless of the outcome of the study, the decision would not change. In such a case, there would be no economic reason to conduct the study. We invest in the project, period. No formal analysis of information value is needed.

Why would management proceed with a project when the outcome of a test study is negative? Several possibilities exist. In some cases, management may be required to proceed with the project due to legal requirements, contract obligations, or other imperatives. In this situation, the set of outcomes has been misspecified—any outcome that is based on avoiding the project is not possible. In other cases, the information may be so unreliable that a bad report would not dissuade management from proceeding with the project.

Cost of Prediction Error

There is always the question of how much difference information makes in the decision-making process. We have seen that information enables a manager to avoid certain losses. This may be expanded into the concept of

Cost of Prediction Error   The difference between the actual cost incurred based on incorrect information and the cost that would have been incurred with correct information.

the **cost of prediction error.** The cost of prediction error is the difference between the actual cost incurred based on the incorrect information and the cost that would be incurred with the correct information.

To illustrate the cost of prediction error, let's consider an inventory management example. One problem in inventory management is to minimize the total annual inventory policy cost, which is the annual cost of ordering and carrying inventory. The total inventory policy cost may be represented by the equation:

$$TC = \frac{QS}{2} + \frac{AP}{Q}$$

where

Q = Quantity ordered at one time.
S = Cost to store one unit in inventory for a year.
A = Annual usage of the item.
P = Cost to place an order.

The basic economic order quantity (EOQ) model (described in Chapter 14) may be used to find the order quantity needed to minimize inventory policy cost. The minimum total cost is obtained when:

$$Q = \sqrt{\frac{2AP}{S}}$$

Suppose that we used values of:

$$A = 50,000$$
$$P = \$20$$
$$S = \$.50$$

and obtained an optimal Q of:

$$2,000 = \sqrt{\frac{2 \times 50,000 \times \$20}{\$.50}}$$

Total costs for the year would be estimated as:

$$TC = \frac{2,000 \times \$.50}{2} + \frac{50,000 \times \$20}{2,000}$$
$$= \underline{\underline{\$1,000}}$$

After adopting the policy of ordering 2,000 units at a time and using that policy for a year, it becomes evident that there was an error in estimating the storage costs per unit *(S)*. Instead of 50 cents, the actual storage costs were $1.50. What was the cost of prediction error?

First, we find the optimal cost that would have been incurred had we used the correct storage cost. The new EOQ given the new storage cost information is:

$$1,155 = \sqrt{\frac{2 \times 50,000 \times \$20}{\$1.50}}$$

If we had the good fortune to realize that this was the optimal order quantity instead of the 2,000 that we used during the year, our inventory policy costs would have been:

$$TC^* = \frac{1,155 \times \$1.50}{2} + \frac{50,000 \times \$20}{1,155}$$
$$= \underline{\underline{\$1,732}}$$

However, based on our incorrect data, we followed an order policy of 2,000 units per year. As a result, we incurred inventory policy costs of:

$$TC = \frac{2,000 \times \$1.50}{2} + \frac{50,000 \times \$20}{2,000}$$
$$= \underline{\underline{\$2,000}}$$

The difference between the costs incurred under the actual policy and the costs under the optimal (hindsight) policy is $268. This is the opportunity cost of having incorrect information at the start of the period and is the *cost of prediction error*. The amount reflects the most we could gain from the correct information, given that $1.50 was the actual storage cost per unit. Note that the expected $1,000 inventory policy cost is not relevant. It formed the basis for the initial budget and will probably be used in traditional variance analysis. However, because the input data were incorrect, the budgeted results could not be attained.

In general, the cost of prediction error ($2,000 − $1,732) could be used to evaluate the prediction procedure.

Cost of prediction error principles can be applied to other settings as well. The entire spectrum of differential cost decisions are subject to cost of prediction error analysis. The cost of prediction error is the opportunity cost from making an economically suboptimal decision based on information that later appeared to be in error. For example, assume that Mean Green Company receives a special order for a product. The special order price is $7.00 per unit; 5,000 units are ordered. Mean Green has excess capacity and estimates the unit costs for the product costs as follows:

Variable	$4.50
Fixed	5.00

Based on this estimate, Mean Green figures that operating profits will increase by $2.50 (the $7.00 price less the $4.50 variable cost) for each unit in the special order. After accepting the order, Mean Green learns that its unit costs are actually:

Variable	$7.50
Fixed	2.00

Mean Green lost $2,500 on the special order (5,000 units times $7.00 revenue less $7.50 variable costs). Assuming there was no other use for the capacity, the cost of prediction error is the $2,500 since the company would not have accepted the order if it had known that the order price was less than its variable costs.

Capital budgeting decisions are also subject to this type of analysis. In these situations, the cost of prediction error is usually considered as equal to the opportunity cost of capital invested in the project.[1]

For example, Peaches, Inc., has an after-tax cost of capital of 12 percent. Peaches invested $80,000 in a tricycle manufacturing project with the following expected cash inflows:

Year	Amount
1	$30,000
2	35,000
3	30,000
4	20,000
5	10,000

The net present value of the project was $12,880. The project did not turn out as well as expected. Actual cash inflows were as follows:

Year	Amount
1	$30,000
2	25,000
3	20,000
4	5,000
5	0

and the net present value was ($14,171). In this situation, the cost of prediction error is $14,171 since the company would not have invested in the project had the actual cash flows been known. The funds tied up in the project carried an opportunity cost of 12 percent. A project that earns exactly 12 percent would have a net present value of zero.

Cost of prediction error analysis should be limited to those situations where it is possible to improve a model or to obtain better data. If an event occurs that is totally unexpected, and that event results in a loss to the company, the costs of that loss should be assigned to the unexpected event, not to prediction error.

MANAGEMENT USES OF INFORMATION ECONOMICS

It is unlikely that management would routinely go through the formal analytical process described here to decide whether to gather information. Presumably this is because some of the probabilities are difficult to estimate (and, further, because managers may not be trained in the use of probability revision techniques). However, in general, informal consideration is given to the economic usefulness of information for any given decision setting. Otherwise, cost information would be demanded in unlimited quantities.

---

[1] Some consider that the appropriate cost is the income that could have been received from the most profitable project that was not invested in due to capital constraints. This method would be more complex than that presented here.

When very large investments are incurred and when there is sufficient information to permit specification of the probabilities, formal analysis may be carried out. Indeed, petroleum exploration companies make wide use of the techniques described here. In their operations, they gather information in a given location. The costs to drill and install production facilities are so high that the benefits of gathering information exceed the costs. Moreover, there have been so many deposits explored that a sufficient data base exists to estimate probabilities. Pharmaceutical manufacturers also evaluate information from drug trials to assess whether to go forward with development of a drug or whether to abandon the potential product.

It is generally believed that managers acquire information only when it is economically efficient to do so. In an information economics sense, managers will acquire information when the expected value of a decision with information, net of any information costs, exceeds the expected value of that decision without information. The Bayesian revision formulation provides a formal analysis that is reasonably descriptive of the manager's information evaluation process, although the exact terms of the manager's revision process may differ from the Bayesian specifications.

The cost accountant, consultant, or other supplier of information understands that the commodity supplied (information) will only be purchased if required or if the user perceives it is economical. Understanding the process by which information has value should enable the buyer of information to relate its price to its value. The mathematics of information economics

---

REAL WORLD APPLICATION

The airline industry has continually faced a problem of accepting reservations and holding seats for passengers only to have the passenger not show up for the flight. Frequently, the airline could have sold the seat to another paying passenger. When this occurs, the empty seat is an opportunity cost. To solve the problem, airlines routinely overbook by accepting more reservations than the number of seats available on the flight. The possibility exists, of course, that more passengers with reservations will appear for a flight than there are seats available. In these situations, airlines offer monetary incentives to passengers willing to give up their reservations and take another flight. The airlines balance the costs of non-showing passengers with the costs of overbooking.

To strike the optimal balance, airlines have a yield management function which gathers information about the relative number of no-shows on a given flight on a given day of the week. In addition, airlines found that passengers with nonrefundable tickets are more likely to show up for a flight than passengers with no-penalty tickets. Hence, the probability of a no-show is determined based on past history of the flight plus the number of passengers booked with various types of penalty and nonpenalty tickets. In addition, airlines ask their local employees to advise the yield management section about special events such as football games, spring break, and local festivals because that information affects no-show rate. When all of this information is entered into a computer model, an airline will know the optimal number of seats by which it can overbook a flight.

Gathering all of this information is costly, but the airlines have found that the benefits exceed the costs because they can minimize the sum of the opportunity costs from empty seats and the monetary incentives for passengers to voluntarily give up reserved seats.

becomes very complex when the number of choices increases and when the decision includes other factors characteristic of a real-world setting. However, the concepts are based on the information economics model presented here. Presumably, managerial accountants are hired because someone decides that managerial accounting information is economic in the sense discussed in this chapter.

SUMMARY

Information is a product that may have value just as any other commodity. Management must make decisions concerning whether to gather information for decision making and other purposes. Information economics is the field of study that established the concepts used to formalize management's decisions about gathering information. The analytic approach suggests that the difference in expected value of a decision that results from the acquisitions of information should be determined. If the information costs less than the difference in expected value, then it is economical to acquire the information. On a hindsight basis, it is sometimes possible to compare the profit that could have been attained with correct information and to compare that with the information actually used to set policy. The difference is referred to as the cost of prediction error. The concepts behind information economics models serve as general guidelines to management for decisions about the acquisition of information. After all, accountants are information producers and command a pecuniary reward for their services. If information had no value, what would become of accountants?

TERMS AND CONCEPTS

The following terms and concepts should be familiar to you after reading this chapter.

Conditional Probabilities	Opportunity Loss
Cost of Prediction Error	Outcomes
Expected Value	Payoff
Imperfect Information	Perfect Information
Information Cost	Posterior Probabilities
Information Economics	Prior Probabilities (Priors)
Joint Probability	Value of Information

SUPPLEMENTARY READINGS

Demski, Joel. *Information Analysis.* 2nd ed. Reading, Mass.: Addison-Wesley Publishing, 1980.

Feltham, G. A. "The Value of Information." *The Accounting Review,* October 1968.
_____. *Information Evaluation.* Sarasota, Fla.: AAA, 1972.

Hilton, R. W. "The Determinants of Cost Information Value: An Illustrative Analysis." *Journal of Accounting Research,* Autumn 1979.

Lobo, Gerald, and Michael Maher, eds. *Information Economics and Accounting Research: A Workshop Conducted by Joel S. Demski.* Ann Arbor: Graduate School of Business Administration, University of Michigan, 1980.

SELF-STUDY PROBLEM NO. 1: SOONG'S SOYBEAN PRODUCTS[2]

After several years of supplying tofu to several supermarket chains, the Soong family decided that it was time to diversify operations.

At a recent family conference, several members came up with new product ideas as possible alternatives to tofu. A dehydrated soybean protein was considered too low margin. Soybean jello, despite popularity within oriental communities, was rejected on the grounds that it was highly perishable and appealed only to a very small market segment.

Laura Soong, a recent biochemistry graduate, then suggested that they exploit the growing diet and health food market by introducing soybean ice cream. "I've perfected it in the lab," she said. "It is low in cholesterol and has only one quarter the calories of regular ice cream. But, more important, it tastes almost like the real thing!" She then provided her estimates of costs for the project.

Based on Laura's figures, David Soong, the family accountant, estimates that if sales are high, the total contribution margin from the product will be $300,000. If sales are low, the total contribution margin earned by the Soongs will be $50,000. Fixed costs for the project will be $150,000. David is uncertain as to what the probability distribution of sales would be. Hence, he attaches on a prior probability of .5 for high sales and .5 for low sales.

The Soong family can conduct a survey of various health food outlets to determine the true demand for the new product. The reliability of the survey is such that it will signal high sales 70 percent of the time when actual sales will be high, and signal low sales 90 percent of the time when actual sales will be low. The costs of such a survey are $20,000.

Required:

Assuming that the Soong family bases its decisions on expected value:

a. What action will they take without the survey?

b. Should the Soong family take the survey? What should their decision be?

c. How much will they be willing to pay for perfect information?

SOLUTION TO SELF-STUDY PROBLEM NO. 1

a.

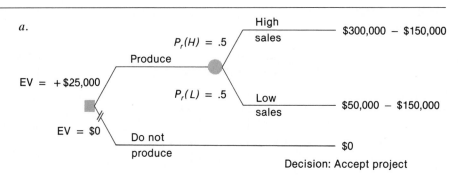

b. Let:
   H = Actual high-sales state.
   L = Actual low-sales state.
   Y_H = Survey signal for high-sales state.
   Y_L = Survey signal for low-sales state.
   Pr = Probability

$$Pr(Y_H|H) = .7$$
$$\therefore Pr(Y_L|H) = .3$$
$$Pr(Y_L|L) = .9$$
$$Pr(Y_H|L) = .1$$

[2] © Jean M. Lim and Michael W. Maher, 1990.

$$Pr(Y_H) = Pr(Y_H|L)Pr(L) + Pr(Y_H|H)Pr(H)$$
$$= .1(.5) + .7(.5)$$
$$= .4$$
$$Pr(Y_L) = Pr(Y_L|L)Pr(L) + Pr(Y_L|H)Pr(H)$$
$$= .9(.5) + .3(.5)$$
$$= .6$$
$$Pr(H|Y_H) = \frac{Pr(Y_H|H)Pr(H)}{Pr(Y_H)}$$
$$= \frac{.7(.5)}{.4}$$
$$= .875$$
$$\therefore Pr(L|Y_H) = .125$$
$$Pr(H|Y_L) = \frac{Pr(Y_L|H)Pr(H)}{Pr(Y_L)}$$
$$= \frac{.3(.5)}{.6}$$
$$= .25$$
$$\therefore Pr(L|Y_L) = .75$$

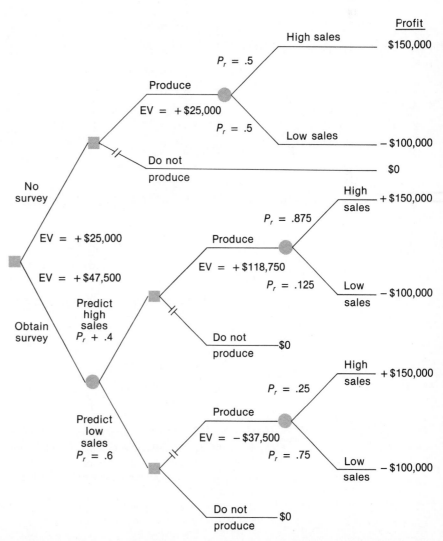

The Soong family should take the survey. The expected value of the project, less the cost of the survey, is:

$$\$47,500 - \$20,000 = \underline{\underline{\$27,500}}$$

Without the survey, the expected value of the project is:

$$\underline{\underline{\$25,000}}$$

c. Working through the Bayesian analysis in part *b.*, assuming perfect information, we get:

$$Pr(Y_H) = .5$$
$$Pr(Y_L) = .5$$
$$Pr(H|Y_H) = 1.0$$
$$Pr(L|Y_L) = 1.0$$

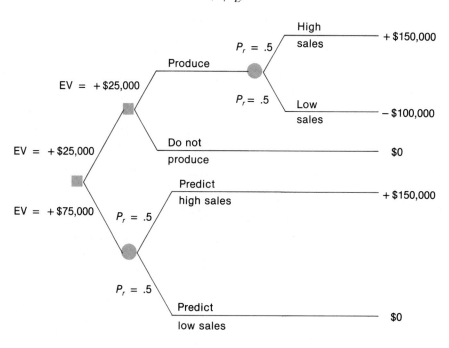

Expected value of perfect information = $75,000 − $25,000
$$= \underline{\underline{\$50,000}}$$

SELF-STUDY PROBLEM NO. 2: OPUS' DESIGNS

Opus' Designs imports formal wear and wholesales it to major retailing companies. Opus' Designs must order more suits than it expects to sell because a substantial number of ordered goods are defective and must be scrapped. When placing an order, Opus requests a total number of suits which, after eliminating the rejects, yields 1,000 good suits. If a given order does not yield 1,000 suits, the difference between 1,000 suits and the number of good suits received must be made up by purchasing from a local subcontractor at a price of $100 per suit, none of which will be defective.

The company had two alternative sources of supply for its most recent order. It could purchase suits from Afghanistan at a cost of $50 each (regardless of whether they were defective). Suits ordered from this source in Afghanistan have an expected reject rate of 25 percent, which means that Opus' Designs needs to order 1,333 suits. Alternatively, the suits could be ordered from South America at a cost of $65 each. The reject rate for South American source suits is expected to be 10 percent, so Opus needs to order 1,111 suits from South America. Based on this information, Opus decided to order from the source in Afghanistan at a total cost of $66,650 versus the cost of $72,215 for the suits from South America. After receiving the order, 40 percent of the suits were found to be defective.

Required:

What is the cost of the prediction error? (Round odd numbers of suits to the nearest whole number.)

SOLUTION TO SELF-STUDY PROBLEM NO. 2

For its $66,650, Opus' Designs received 800 good suits (1,333 ordered − 40% × 1,333 defective suits). Opus then had to purchase 200 suits to make up the shortfall. The price of the 200 suits was $20,000, which is 200 suits at $100 each. The total cost of the order from the source in Afghanistan is $86,650 ($66,650 + $20,000). The alternative cost was $72,215. The cost of prediction error is $14,435—the difference between the two costs.

QUESTIONS

26-1. A manager was overheard saying, "I want all the information before I make a decision. Get me all the information!" Comment on this quote.

26-2. Does information reduce the risk in a manager's decision?

26-3. Since no one can supply perfect information, why do we even consider the perfect information case?

26-4. "Imperfect information is worthless since it cannot predict the future with certainty." Comment on this quote.

26-5. Management has invested $8 million in a project. The payoffs from the project will either be zero or a present value of $20 million. Either event is equally likely. The original investment cost will be deducted in computing the profit from the project. Now management learns that it can obtain perfect information about the outcome from the project. What is the maximum value of that information for this investment project?

26-6. What are the limitations on the use of the information economics approach by management?

26-7. Management knows that if it purchases a report there is a good chance the results of the report will affect management's decision. Should management purchase the report or should they consider something in addition?

26-8. Miracle Pharmaceuticals has discovered a cure for heart disease. Miracle conducted tests which showed that its product completely eliminated heart disease in a sample of 1,000 people at high risk for the disease. The results were very impressive. Under the present economic circumstances, Miracle expects the project will have a positive net present value assuming a price of $200 per year for the product. Miracle's forecast assumes that the Food and Drug Administration will approve the product in one year. If approval is delayed five years, the project attains the same net present value as the one-year approval if the price is increased to $350 per year. Demand would be unaffected by the two prices considered. Miracle could invest $7 million in an expanded test which would assure approval in one year. *From a purely economic perspective,* should Miracle conduct the expanded test?

26–9. What is the difference between the value of information and the cost of prediction error?

26–10. When does a cost of prediction error arise?

26–11. Northern Airlines has a yield management model which determined that Northern could overbook Flight 1313 on June 20 by 30 seats, which it did. Southern Airlines, which competes with Northern on this route, went bankrupt without any preliminary warning on June 19. As a result, Northern had 24 more passengers show up for Flight 1313 than there were seats available. Northern had to give 24 passengers $500 each in compensation to get them to take a later flight. What was the cost of prediction error?

EXERCISES

26–12. Outcomes, Expected Values and Information Value
(L.O.1)

Strange Happenings, Inc., is considering producing a new horror movie. Production and distribution costs are estimated at $15 million. Strange estimates the following probabilities for cash inflows from the movie:

	Probability
$50 million	.3
$ 3 million	.7

Required:

a. What is the expected value of the movie?

b. What are the possible outcomes if Strange Happenings decides to produce and distribute the movie?

c. How much would Strange be willing to pay to find out for certain if the movie was going to be a blockbuster or a dud?

26–13. Outcomes, Expected Values and Information Value
(L.O.1)

Sue & Em Esquires, P.A., specializes in contract liability litigation. The firm believes that law is a matter of economics. The firm's motto is: "If the expected value of the verdict exceeds our fee, then SUE!" One of the firm's partners was presenting details of a case to Three Initial Corp. (TIC), a prospective client. The partner stated that the costs of the litigation would be $10 million. The partner stated that there was a 10 percent probability that the court would award a $200 million judgment in TIC's favor.

Required:

a. What is the expected value of the lawsuit?

b. What are the possible outcomes if TIC pursues the litigation?

c. How much would TIC be willing to pay to find out for certain if the court was going to award it the $200 million?

26–14. Information Value
(L.O.2)

Arch & Veronica Corp. is evaluating whether to obtain a franchise for a pocket telephone system. The costs of the franchise and other investments total $30 million. If the franchise is successful, Arch & Veronica will have a project with a present value of future cash flows of $250 million (that is, before deducting the initial investment cost). The probability of success is .4. If the franchise is not successful, the present value of the future cash inflows will be $35 million. Manny, Moe & Jack

Marketing Corp. offered to conduct a survey for Arch & Veronica which could inform them more precisely whether the franchise would be successful.

Manny, Moe & Jack provide the following probabilities for their reports:

$$Pr(G) = .5$$
$$Pr(S|G) = .7$$
$$Pr(S|B) = .1$$

where

G = Good report.
B = Bad report.
S = Successful franchise.

(Note: No probability revisions are required.)

Required:

a. What is the maximum price, if anything, Arch & Veronica would be willing to pay Manny, Moe & Jack to conduct the marketing study?

b. If the unsuccessful outcome were to have a negative present value of $50 million, which does include loss of the initial investment, what is the maximum price Arch & Veronica would be willing to pay Manny, Moe & Jack to conduct the marketing study?

c. If the answers to part a. and part b. differ, explain why.

26–15. Information Value
(L.O.2)

Calvin Hobbes, Inc., is evaluating whether to enter a contract to construct a fleet of space vehicles for personal travel. The costs of the franchise and other investments total $200 million. If the product is successful, Calvin Hobbes, Inc., will have a project with a present value of future cash flows of $400 million (that is, before deducting the initial investment cost). If the franchise is not successful, the present value of the future cash inflows will be $80 million. There is a .52 probability that the project will be successful. Tiger International Marketing Corp. offered to conduct a survey for Calvin Hobbes, Inc., which could inform them more precisely whether the franchise would be successful.

Tiger International provide the following probabilities for their reports:

$$Pr(G) = .6$$
$$Pr(S|G) = .8$$
$$Pr(S|B) = .1$$

where

G = Good report.
B = Bad report.
S = Successful franchise.

(Note: No probability revisions are required.)

Required:

a. What is the maximum price Calvin Hobbes Inc., would be willing to pay Tiger International to conduct the marketing study?

b. If the probability of a successful project given a good report is .6, what is the maximum price Calvin Hobbes Inc., would be willing to pay Tiger International to conduct the marketing study?

c. If the answers to part a. and part b. differ, explain why.

26–16. Value of Perfect Information
(L.O.2)

Suppose an oil driller is faced with the following options:

State of Nature	Probability	Payoff	
		Drill	Don't Drill
No oil	.7	− $100,000	–0–
Oil	.3	+ 150,000	–0–

The driller can obtain information from seismic tests that perfectly predict whether oil will be found if drilling commences.

Required:

a. What action would the driller take without any information?
b. What action would the driller take with the perfect information?
c. What is the value of the perfect information?

26–17. Value of Perfect Information

(L.O.2)

Suppose Buffalo Company is faced with the following situation for a new product:

State of Nature	Probability	Payoff
Success	.6	+ $350,000
Failure	.4	− 200,000

Assume Buffalo Company can obtain perfect information from a marketing research firm whether or not the product will be successful.

Required:

a. What action would Buffalo Company take without any information?
b. What action would they take with the perfect information?
c. What is the value of the perfect information?

26–18. Value of Perfect Information

(L.O.2)

A treasure hunter, who searches for treasure in sunken ships, is faced with the following options on a particular treasure hunt:

State of Nature	Probability	Payoff
No treasure	.95	− $ 100,000
Treasure	.05	+ 1,600,000

Assume the treasure hunter can obtain information from an old seaman who knows exactly where the ship was sunk.

Required:

a. What is the expected value of the action with no information?
b. What is the expected value of the action with the perfect information?
c. What is the value of the perfect information?

26–19. Value of Perfect Information

(L.O.2)

A manager is trying to decide whether to accept a special order. If the order is accepted, the increased revenue to the company will be $1 million. The costs of making the products for the special order are either $800,000 or $1.2 million, depending on how much time is needed for its manufacture. Hence, acceptance of the order would result in a net gain of $200,000 *or* a net loss of $200,000, while rejection will produce neither gain nor loss.

The manager regards the two production cost events as having the following probabilities: (1) there is a .6 probability that production costs will be low, hence, a

$200,000 profit would be made on the order; (2) there is a .4 probability that production costs will be high, hence, a $200,000 *loss* would be incurred if the order is accepted.

Before deciding whether to accept or reject the order, the manager can analyze a set of special orders already in production, thereby gaining information. The cost of setting up the records and analyzing the data is $50,000.

Required:

a. If the manager wants to maximize expected value, what is the best decision for the manager before considering the information?

b. Assuming the information is perfect, what is the value of that information to the manager? Should the information be obtained?

26–20. Value of Imperfect Information—Revising Probabilities Not Required

(L.O.2)

Refer to exercise 26–19. Suppose the information that the manager can obtain is not perfect. Past experience for similar information indicates that when the information predicts low production costs, production costs turn out to be low 80 percent of the time and high 20 percent of the time. When the information predicts high production costs, production costs turn out to be high 80 percent of the time and low 20 percent of the time. This relationship between high and low costs and the related information are summarized as follows:

$$P \ (low \ costs | \text{information } predicts \ low \ costs) = .80$$
$$P \ (high \ costs | \text{information } predicts \ low \ costs) = .20$$
$$P \ (low \ costs | \text{information } predicts \ high \ costs) = .20$$
$$P \ (high \ costs | \text{information } predicts \ high \ costs) = .80$$

Required:

Note that probabilities do not have to be revised using Bayes' Theorem.

a. What action would the manager take if the imperfect information was obtained?

b. What is the value of the imperfect information?

26–21. Improving the Accuracy of Information

(L.O.2)

Refer to exercise 26–20. Suppose the accuracy of the imperfect information could be improved. For an additional cost of $10,000, the accuracy of the information could be improved from 80 percent to 90 percent.

Required:

Is it worthwhile to obtain the more accurate information?

26–22. Revising Probabilities Using Bayes' Theorem

(L.O.3)

Refer to exercise 26–19. Suppose the manager receives information in the following form: P (information signal|event), which requires using Bayes' Theorem to revise probabilities. The manager believes that the information would correctly identify high costs 70 percent of the time and correctly identify low costs 30 percent of the time. The cost of this information is $40,000.

Required:

Should this information be obtained? What is its value?

26–23. Value of Imperfect Information—Applying Bayes' Theorem

(L.O.3)

Refer to exercise 26–17. Suppose that Buffalo Company could not obtain perfect information but could obtain imperfect information from the marketing research firm that was accurate 80 percent of the time (that is P(good report|success) = .8; P(good report|failure) = .2, etc.)

Required:

What is the value of the imperfect information? Should it be obtained?

26–24. Value of Imperfect Information—Applying Bayes' Theorem

(L.O.3)

Refer to exercise 26–18. Suppose that the treasure hunter could not obtain perfect information but could obtain imperfect information from the old seaman whose information is 60 percent accurate. (That is, P(good report|treasure) = .60; P(good report|no treasure) = .40; etc.)

Required:

What is the value of the imperfect information? Should it be obtained?

26–25. Cost of Prediction Error—Economic Order Quantity Model
(L.O.4)

Off The Rack, a clothing manufacturer, estimated the following components for determining economic order quantities for sweaters:

Annual demand	500,000
Storage cost per unit	$1.00
Cost to place an order	$650.00

Based on this information, the company ordered in lots of 25,495 units.

After reviewing the data for the year, management concluded that storage costs should have been increased to $8 per unit.

Required:

What is the cost of prediction error?

26–26. Cost of Prediction Error—Economic Order Quantity Model
(L.O.4)

Frozen Molecules, a manufacturer of biomedical tests, estimated the following components for determining economic order quantities for a certain monoclonal antibody test:

Annual demand	200,000
Storage cost per unit	$5.00
Cost to place an order	$3,900.00

Based on this information, the company ordered in lots of 17,664 units.

At the end of the year, Frozen Molecules' accountant reported that due to changes in regulations concerning the preparation of these tests, a special license costing $1,000 had to be obtained for each order of this component. The regulations were in place at the start of the year, but the cost of the license had not been included in the analysis.

Required:

What is the cost of prediction error?

26–27. Cost of Prediction Error—Capital Investments
(L.O.4)

NPV, Inc., determined that an investment of $250,000 in an automated ice-removal process would have a net present value of $290,000 using a 10 percent after-tax discount rate. Company management decided not to conduct further market testing and made the investment. Two years later, the company reevaluated the investment based on a two-year sales and production history. NPV management determined that the net present value of the investment should have been a negative $15,000. The manager who recommended the investment originally stated, "Although the project is not as profitable as we expected, we are receiving decent profits on the project and should not be concerned about the decline. All of you know that sometimes these projects do not turn out as well as we hope."

Required:

Is the manager's assessment of the situation correct? (Hint: Consider the cost of prediction error.)

26–28. Cost of Prediction Error—Capital Investments
(L.O.4)

Fun Fads, Inc., invests in high-technology, short useful life projects. Two years ago, the company evaluated a product with an investment cost of $1.5 million and expected cash flows of $1 million per year for three years. The company's cost of capital is 18 percent. The product did not perform as well as expected. The company knows that the cash flows in Years 1 and 2 were $700,000 and the expected cash flow in Year 3 is $400,000.

Required:

What is the cost of prediction error?

26–29. Cost of Prediction Error—Differential Costs
(L.O.4)

Lawrence Company estimates the following costs, prices, and volume for its single product:

Selling price	$ 200 per unit
Variable cost	150 per unit
Fixed costs	1,000,000 per period
Sales volume	40,000 units

The company then produced 40,000 units. Prices and costs were as expected, except sales were only 35,000 units. Due to the nature of the product, 5,000 units were scrapped for a net-of-salvage-cost revenue of $10,000.

Required:

Compute the cost of prediction error.

26–30. Cost of Prediction Error—Differential Costs
(L.O.4)

South Bend Company estimates the following costs, prices, and volume for its single product:

	Per Unit
Selling price	$ 450
Manufacturing costs:	
Material	75
Direct labor	135
Variable overhead	25
Fixed overhead	50
(allocated on basis of direct labor-hours)	
Sales volume	25,000 units

Based on this forecast, they produced 25,000 units. Prices and costs were as forecast, but the demand for the product turned out to be 30,000 units, which they could have produced without additional fixed costs. Assume that the excess demand was lost and cannot be met in subsequent periods.

Required:

Compute the cost of prediction error.

PROBLEMS

26–31. Value of Perfect Information

Vendo Company operated the concession stands at the university football stadium. Records of past sales indicate that there are basically four kinds of football weather, that sales of hot dogs depend on the weather, and that the percentage of football games played in each kind of weather is as follows:

Weather	Percentage of Game Days	Hot Dogs Sold
Snow	10%	10,000
Rain	20	20,000
Clear/warm	40	30,000
Clear/cold	30	40,000

Hot dogs cost Vendo Company 60 cents each and are sold for $1.00. Hot dogs unsold at the end of each game are worthless. Ignore income taxes.

Required:

a. Prepare a table with four rows and four columns showing the contribution margin from each of the four purchasing strategies of buying 10,000, 20,000, 30,000, or 40,000 hot dogs and the four weather conditions (snow, rain, clear/warm, and clear/cold).

b. Assuming that the chances of snow, rain, clear/warm, and clear/cold are 10 percent, 20 percent, 40 percent, and 30 percent, respectively, compute the expected contribution margin from each of the following purchasing strategies:
    (1) Buy 10,000 hot dogs.
    (2) Buy 20,000 hot dogs.
    (3) Buy 30,000 hot dogs.
    (4) Buy 40,000 hot dogs.

c. What is the optimal purchasing strategy in the absence of a weather forecast, and what is the expected contribution margin from following this strategy? (This answer will be the largest of the four expected payoffs computed in *b*.)

d. If Vendo had a perfect weather forecast for each game, it would buy 10,000 hot dogs when snow is predicted; 20,000 when rain is predicted; 30,000 when clear/warm is predicted; and 40,000 when clear/cold is predicted. What is the expected average contribution margin per football game, assuming the availability of a perfect weather forecast and that the four kinds of weather will occur in the frequencies 10, 20, 40, and 30 percent?

e. What is the expected dollar value to Vendo Company of a perfect weather forecast per football game? That is, what is the expected dollar value of the information from a perfect weather forecast?

(CMA adapted)

26–32. Value of Perfect Information

Jessica Company is searching for more formal ways to analyze its decisions. The expected value decision model was among those considered. To test the effectiveness of the expected value model, a one-year trial in a small department was authorized.

This department buys and resells a perishable product. A large purchase at the beginning of each month provides a lower cost than more frequent purchases and also assures that Jessica Company can buy all of the item it wants. Unfortunately, if too much is purchased, the product unsold at the end of the month is worthless and must be discarded.

If an inadequate quantity is purchased, additional quantities cannot be purchased. Hence, Jessica would lose potential sales if an inadequate quantity is ordered. The standard purchase arrangement is $50,000 plus 50 cents for each unit purchased for orders of 100,000 units or more. Jessica is paid $1.25 per unit by its customers.

The needs of Jessica's customers limit the possible sales volumes to only four quantities per month—100,000, 120,000, 140,000, or 180,000 units. However, the total quantity needed for a given month cannot be determined prior to the date Jessica must make its purchases. The sales managers are willing to place a probability estimate on each of the four possible sales volumes each month. They noted that the probabilities for the four sales volumes change from month to month because of the seasonal nature of the business. Their probability estimates for December sales units are 10 percent for 100,000, 30 percent for 120,000, 40 percent for 140,000, and 20 percent for 180,000.

The following schedule shows the quantity purchased each month based on the expected value decision model. The actual units sold and product discarded or sales lost are shown also.

	Quantity (in units)			Sales Units Lost
	Purchased	Sold	Discarded	
January	100,000	100,000	—	20,000
February	120,000	100,000	20,000	—
March	180,000	140,000	40,000	—
April	100,000	100,000	—	80,000
May	100,000	100,000	—	—
June	140,000	140,000	—	—
July	140,000	100,000	40,000	—
August	140,000	120,000	20,000	—
September	120,000	100,000	20,000	—
October	120,000	120,000	—	20,000
November	180,000	140,000	40,000	—

Required:

a. What quantity should be ordered for December if the expected value decision model is used?

b. Suppose Jessica could ascertain its customers' needs prior to placing its purchase order rather than relying on the expected value decision model. How much would it pay to obtain this information for December?

c. The model did not result in purchases equal to potential sales except during two months. Is the model unsuitable in this case, or is this a characteristic of the model? Explain your answer.

(CMA adapted)

26–33. Value of Imperfect Information

Rosetta Stone Exploration Co. has obtained information which suggests that an unusual formation of malachite might be found in the Sonora Desert. The deposit will cost $15 million for rights and permits and to develop. There is a 40 percent probability that the deposit will provide a present value of future cash inflows of $75 million before deducting the cost of the investment. On the other hand, there is a 60 percent probability that the deposit will provide no future cash inflows and that the company will have to pay an additional $2 million (present value) to restore the site to its original condition before it began its development project.

There are two approaches which can be taken to investigate this deposit further. Rosetta Stone can pay $3 million to conduct a detailed geologic study of the area. If Rosetta Stone decides to perform this study, past experience indicates that if the deposit will have a good outcome, the report will indicate that the deposit is valuable 90 percent of the time. If the deposit is not economically feasible, the report will indicate this 80 percent of the time.

The second approach is to conduct a reconnaissance survey at a cost of $500,000. These surveys are less accurate. If the deposit is valuable, the reconnaissance survey will provide a good report with a .7 probability. If the deposit is not valuable, the reconnaissance survey will provide a bad report with a .7 probability.

Required:

Which report, if either, should Rosetta Stone Corp. acquire to assist it in evaluating the malachite deposit? Prepare a decision tree for this information.

26–34. Value of Alternate Imperfect Information Sources

Laser Biomedical Corp. is developing a new drug for the treatment of high cholesterol. Based on the data gathered to date, Laser Biomedical estimates that there is a .65 probability that the drug is effective. To obtain approval to market the drug, the company needs to conduct a trial which will show that the product is effective. If the product is successful, the drug will have a net present value of $30 million before consideration of the testing costs.

The company can carry out two tests in its attempt to prove effectiveness of the drug. The final test requires the use of 1,500 patients. Half of the patients would receive a placebo (sugar pill), and the other half would receive the drug. A comparison of cholesterol levels between the two groups would indicate whether the drug was effective. This test will cost $2 million. If the drug is effective, this test will indicate effectiveness an estimated .7 of the time. If the drug is not effective, this test will indicate effectiveness an estimated .05 of the time. If this test does not indicate that the drug is effective, Laser Biomedical will repeat the test using 4,000 patients. The repeat will cost $6 million. If the drug is effective, the repeat test will indicate this with probability .95. If the drug is not effective, the repeat test will indicate this with probability 1.0. If the repeat test indicates that the product is not effective, all $6 million testing costs will be lost.

An alternative is to conduct the trials using 5,000 patients. This test will cost $3 million. If the drug is effective, this test will indicate effectiveness .9 of the time. If the drug is not effective, this test will never indicate that the drug is effective. If this test indicates that the drug is not effective, the project will be abandoned and the test costs will be lost.

Required:

Which drug trial should Laser Biomedical conduct? It is suggested that you draw a decision tree to show the alternatives and their respective payoffs.

26–35. Solving for the Value of Information

Albany Company is making decisions about the introduction of a new product. Consumer reports show that the probability of success of the new product is .75, while the probability of failure is .25. Since these surveys were made for a general product category, Albany consulted a consumer research firm to conduct tests about their particular product. The research firm said they will detect the success 75 percent of the time when the product will actually succeed (probability that tests says "success" given success equals .75) and signal "failure" 90 percent of the time when there will actually be failure. Albany would make a profit of $3 million if the product succeeded. They would lose $2 million if it failed.

Required:

What is the highest price Albany Company would be willing to pay the firm to conduct the survey?

26–36. The Cost of Prediction Error for Economic Order Quantity

Syracuse Company used the following formulas to determine the optimal order quantity and the total inventory policy cost:

$$Q = \sqrt{\frac{2AP}{S}}$$

$$TC = \frac{QS}{2} + \frac{AP}{Q}$$

where

Q = Quantity ordered at one time.
S = Cost to store one unit in inventory for a year.
A = Annual usage.
P = Cost to place an order.

Their predictions were:

A = 125,000 units
P = $150
S = $3.75

and Q was:

$$Q = \sqrt{\frac{2 \times 125,000 \times \$150}{\$3.75}}$$
$$= 3,162 \text{ units.}$$

After adopting the policy of ordering 3,162 units per order and using the policy for a year, they found out that actual storage cost was $3.00 per unit instead of $3.75.

Required:

a. What is the cost of prediction error?

b. Suppose that Syracuse Company found that its storage costs were such that 30 percent of any goods ordered in excess of 2,200 units would be spoiled and cost the company $7 per spoiled unit. This would be added to the company's storage cost of $3.75 per unit. What is the new optimal order quantity, and what is the cost of prediction error from ordering 3,162 units?

26–37. Cost of Prediction Error—Make-or-Buy Decision

Hersh Optical Corp. was considering whether to manufacture their own lenses or to purchase them from a subcontractor. Hersh Optical had an offer from a subcontractor to manufacture lenses at $14 each in lots of 5,000. Lenses received from a subcontractor would have to be inspected by Hersh Optical at a cost of 25 cents each. The subcontractor required a commitment from Hersh to purchase a minimum of 50,000 lenses per year.

Hersh considered the cost of manufacturing the lenses in its own facilities. The company prepared a cost estimate for a lot of 5,000 lenses with the following details:

Materials	$31,250
Labor	17,450
Equipment rental	13,150
Inspection costs	4,200
Other overhead	3,500

The equipment rental is based on an annual cost of $157,800. The equipment is leased on a year-to-year basis, with no requirement that the equipment lease be renewed for a subsequent year. All other costs vary with units produced. When preparing this cost data, the staff accountant estimated that the company would manufacture and sell 60,000 lenses per year. Hersh Optical made its decision whether to make or buy on the basis that 60,000 lenses would be required in a year. The lower-cost alternative was chosen.

Required:

a. Did Hersh make or buy? Show computations.

b. If actual demand was 50,000 units, what was the cost of prediction error?

26–38. Cost of Prediction Error—Capital Investment Analysis

Asahi Heavy Equipment Corp. was considering investing in a project with an initial investment cost of $70 million. After studying the market for the product, Asahi estimated that future cash flows would equal $20 million per year for five years. Using a 10 percent discount rate, Asahi concluded that the project met its net present value criteria and signed contracts under which it was committed to go forward with the project.

After spending $15 million, Asahi learned that government approvals would delay marketing the product for one full year. If marketing were delayed for a year, the future cash inflows would amount to $20 million per year for only four years instead of the planned five years.

If Asahi decides to complete the project, the company will spend the remaining $55 million in Year 0, but the cash inflows will not begin until Year 2. The contract has a clause which will permit Asahi to end the contract. In this case, Asahi will not be liable for any additional payments, but the contractor will obtain title to the project and Asahi will not be reimbursed for any part of the $15 million already spent.

Required:

a. What are the net present values of the alternatives available to Asahi at this time?

b. If Asahi had reason to believe it was possible that the project could have been delayed, what is the cost of prediction error?

c. Would the cost of prediction error be different if Asahi had spent $10 million on the project so far and had to spend the remaining $60 million in Year 0 to obtain the reduced cash flows? Why or why not?

CHOICES:
A Brief Introduction
to Ethics

As a professional accountant or businessperson, you will be facing ethical situations on an everyday basis. Therefore, it stands to reason that you, as students, should be provided with some preparation to face these upcoming predicaments. The following appendixes are meant to provide you with the exposure to prepare you for the decisions you will face.

Your personal ethical choices can affect not only your own self image, but others' perception of you. Ultimately, the ethical decisions you make directly influence the type of life you are likely to lead. You should confront ethical dilemmas bearing in mind the type of life that you would *like* to lead.

In an attempt to influence the accounting profession, many of its professional organizations such as the National Association of Accountants (NAA) and the American Institute of Certified Public Accountants (AICPA) have developed codes of ethics to which their members are expected to adhere. Similarly, businesses such as Johnson & Johnson generally use these codes as a public statement of their commitment to certain business practices with respect to their customers and also as a guide for their employees.

We have devoted two appendixes to the topic of ethics due to its increasingly important role in today's accounting profession. In Appendix A, we have cited Johnson & Johnson's *Credo;* Appendix B contains the NAA *Standards of Ethical Conduct for Management Accountants* and the AICPA *Code of Professional Conduct.*

These appendixes can be used as the basis of class discussion or as topics for independent assignments. Additional cases may be obtained by contacting organizations such as the National Association of Accountants or the American Accounting Association.

Regardless of how the material is used in the classroom setting, it is our hope that a code of ethics becomes an important part of your everyday decision-making in your profession.

Our Credo

We believe our first responsibility is to the doctors, nurses and patients,
to mothers and all others who use our products and services.
In meeting their needs everything we do must be of high quality.
We must constantly strive to reduce our costs
in order to maintain reasonable prices.
Customers' orders must be serviced promptly and accurately.
Our suppliers and distributors must have an opportunity
to make a fair profit.

We are responsible to our employees,
the men and women who work with us throughout the world.
Everyone must be considered as an individual.
We must respect their dignity and recognize their merit.
They must have a sense of security in their jobs.
Compensation must be fair and adequate,
and working conditions clean, orderly and safe.
Employees must feel free to make suggestions and complaints.
There must be equal opportunity for employment, development
and advancement for those qualified.
We must provide competent management,
and their actions must be just and ethical.

We are responsible to the communities in which we live and work
and to the world community as well.
We must be good citizens—support good works and charities
and bear our fair share of taxes.
We must encourage civic improvements and better health and education.
We must maintain in good order
the property we are privileged to use,
protecting the environment and natural resources.

Our final responsibility is to our stockholders.
Business must make a sound profit.
We must experiment with new ideas.
Research must be carried on, innovative programs developed
and mistakes paid for.
New equipment must be purchased, new facilities provided
and new products launched.
Reserves must be created to provide for adverse times.
When we operate according to these principles,
the stockholders should realize a fair return.

Appendix B
Codes of Conduct

National Association of Accountants
Standards of Ethical Conduct
for Management Accountants

Management accountants have an obligation to the organizations they serve, their profession, the public and themselves to maintain the highest standards of ethical conduct. In recognition of this obligation, the National Association of Accountants has promulgated the following standards of ethical conduct for management accountants. Adherence to these standards is integral to achieving the *Objectives of Management Accounting*[1] Management accountants shall not commit acts contrary to these standards nor shall they condone the commission of such acts by others within their organizations.

Competence

Management accountants have a responsibility to:

▼ Maintain an appropriate level of professional competence by ongoing development of their knowledge and skills.

▼ Perform their professional duties in accordance with relevant laws, regulations, and technical standards.

▼ Prepare complete and clear reports and recommendations after appropriate analyses of relevant and reliable information.

Confidentiality

Management accountants have a responsibility to:

▼ Refrain from disclosing confidential information acquired in the course of their work except when authorized, unless legally obligated to do so.

▼ Inform subordinates as appropriate regarding the confidentiality of information acquired in the course of their work and monitor their activities to assure the maintenance of that confidentiality.

▼ Refrain from using or appearing to use confidential information acquired in the course of their work for unethical or illegal advantage either personally or through third parties.

---

[1] National Association of Accountants, *Statements on Management Accounting: Objectives of Management Accounting*, Statement No. 1B, New York, N.Y., June 17, 1982.

Integrity

Management accountants have a responsibility to:

▼ Avoid actual or apparent conflicts of interest and advise all appropriate parties of any potential conflict.

▼ Refrain from engaging in any activity that would prejudice their ability to carry out their duties ethically.

▼ Refuse any gift, favor, or hospitality that would influence or would appear to influence their actions.

▼ Refrain from either actively or passively subverting the attainment of the organization's legitimate and ethical objectives.

▼ Recognize and communicate professional limitations or other constraints that would preclude responsible judgment or successful performance of an activity.

▼ Communicate unfavorable as well as favorable information and professional judgments or opinions.

▼ Refrain from engaging in or supporting any activity that would discredit the profession.

Objectivity

Management accountants have a responsibility to:

▼ Communicate information fairly and objectively.

▼ Disclose fully all relevant information that could reasonably be expected to influence an intended user's understanding of the reports, comments, and recommendations presented.

Resolution of Ethical Conflict

In applying the standards of ethical conduct, management accountants may encounter problems in identifying unethical behavior or in resolving an ethical conflict. When faced with significant ethical issues, management accountants should follow the established policies of the organization bearing on the resolution of such conflict. If these policies do not resolve the ethical conflict, management accountants should consider the following courses of action:

▼ Discuss such problems with the immediate superior except when it appears that the superior is involved, in which case the problem should be presented initially to the next higher managerial level. If satisfactory resolution cannot be achieved when the problem is initially presented, submit the issues to the next higher managerial level.

   If the immediate superior is the chief executive officer, or equivalent, the acceptable reviewing authority may be a group such as the audit committee, executive committee, board of directors, board of trustees, or owners. Contact with levels above the immediate superior should be initiated only with the superior's knowledge, assuming the superior is not involved.

▼ Clarify relevant concepts by confidential discussion with an objective advisor to obtain an understanding of possible courses of action.

▼ If the ethical conflict still exists after exhausting all levels of internal review, the management accountant may have no other recourse on significant matters than to resign from the organization and to submit an informative memorandum to an appropriate representative of the organization.

   Except where legally prescribed, communication of such problems to authorities or individuals not employed or engaged by the organization is not considered appropriate.

American Institute of Certified Public Accountants

Code of Professional Conduct

as adopted January 12, 1988

Composition, Applicability, and Compliance

The Code of Professional Conduct of the American Institute of Certified Public Accountants consists of two sections—(1) the Principles and (2) the Rules. The Principles provide the framework for the Rules, which govern the performance of professional services by members. The Council of the American Institute of Certified Public Accountants is authorized to designate bodies to promulgate technical standards under the Rules, and the bylaws require adherence to those Rules and standards.

The Code of Professional Conduct was adopted by the membership to provide guidance and rules to all members—those in public practice, in industry, in government, and in education—in the performance of their professional responsibilities.

Compliance with the Code of Professional Conduct, as with all standards in an open society, depends primarily on members' understanding and voluntary actions, secondarily on reinforcement by peers and public opinion, and ultimately on disciplinary proceedings, when necessary, against members who fail to comply with the Rules.

Section I—Principles

Preamble

Membership in the American Institute of Certified Public Accountants is voluntary. By accepting membership, a certified public accountant assumes an obligation of self-discipline above and beyond the requirement of laws and regulations.

These Principles of the Code of Professional Conduct of the American Institute of Certified Public Accountants express the profession's recognition of its responsibilities to the public, to clients, and to colleagues. They guide members in the performance of their professional responsibilities and express the basic tenets of ethical and professional conduct. The Principles call for an unswerving commitment to honorable behavior, even at the sacrifice of personal advantage.

Article I

Responsibilities

In carrying out their responsibilities as professionals, members should exercise sensitive professional and moral judgments in all their activities.

As professionals, certified public accountants perform an essential role in society. Consistent with that role, members of the American Institute of Certified Public Accountants have responsibilities to all those who use their professional services. Members also have a continuing responsibility to cooperate with each other to improve the art of accounting, maintain the public's confidence, and carry out the profession's special responsibilities for self-governance. The collective efforts of all members are required to maintain and enhance the traditions of the profession.

Article II

The Public Interest

Members should accept the obligation to act in a way that will serve the public interest, honor the public trust, and demonstrate commitment to professionalism.

A distinguishing mark of a profession is acceptance of its responsibility to the public. The accounting profession's public consists of clients, credit grantors, governments, employers, investors, the business and financial community, and others who rely on the objectivity and integrity of certified public accountants to maintain the orderly functioning of commerce. This reliance imposes a public interest responsibility on certified public accountants. The public interest is defined as the collective well-being of the community of people and institutions the profession serves.

In discharging their professional responsibilities, members may encounter conflicting pressures from among each of those groups. In resolving those conflicts, members should act with integrity, guided by the precept that when members fulfill their responsibility to the public, clients' and employers' interests are best served.

Those who rely on certified public accountants expect them to discharge their responsibilities with integrity, objectivity, due professional care, and a genuine interest in serving the public. They are expected to provide quality services, enter into fee arrangements, and offer a range of services—all in a manner that demonstrates a level of professionalism consistent with these Principles of the Code of Professional Conduct.

All who accept membership in the American Institute of Certified Public Accounts commit themselves to honor the public trust. In return for the faith that the public reposes in them, members should seek continually to demonstrate their dedication to professional excellence.

Article III

Integrity

To maintain and broaden public confidence, members should perform all professional responsibilities with the highest sense of integrity.

Integrity is an element of character fundamental to professional recognition. It is the quality from which the public trust derives and the benchmark against which a member must ultimately test all decisions.

Integrity requires a member to be, among other things, honest and candid within the constraints of client confidentiality. Service and the public trust should not be subordinated to personal gain and advantage. Integrity can accommodate the inadvertent error and the honest difference of opinion; it cannot accommodate deceit or subordination of principle.

Integrity is measured in terms of what is right and just. In the absence of specific rules, standards, or guidance, or in the face of conflicting opinions, a member should test decisions and deeds by asking: "Am I doing what a person of integrity would do? Have I retained my integrity?" Integrity requires a member to observe both the form and the spirit of technical and ethical standards; circumvention of those standards constitutes subordination of judgment.

Integrity also requires a member to observe the principles of objectivity and independence and of due care.

Article IV

Objectivity and Independence

A member should maintain objectivity and be free of conflicts of interest in discharging professional responsibilities. A member in public practice should be independent in fact and appearance when providing auditing and other attestation services.

Objectivity is a state of mind, a quality that lends value to a member's services. It is a distinguishing feature of the profession. The principle of objectivity imposes the obligation to be impartial, intellectually honest, and free of conflicts of interest. Independence precludes relationships that may appear to impair a member's objectivity in rendering attestation services.

Members often serve multiple interests in many different capacities and must demonstrate their objectivity in varying circumstances. Members in public practice render attest, tax, and management advisory services. Other members prepare financial statements in the employment of others, perform internal auditing services, and serve in financial and management capacities in industry, education, and government. They also educate and train those who aspire to admission into the profession. Regardless of service or capacity, members should protect the integrity of their work, maintain objectivity, and avoid any subordination of their judgment.

For a member in public practice, the maintenance of objectivity and independence requires a continuing assessment of client relationships and public responsibility. Such a member who provides auditing and other attestation services should be independent in fact and appearance. In providing all other services, a member should maintain objectivity and avoid conflicts of interest.

Although members not in public practice cannot maintain the appearance of independence, they nevertheless have the responsibility to maintain objectivity in rendering professional services. Members employed by others to prepare financial statements or to perform auditing, tax, or consulting services are charged with the same responsibility for objectivity as members in public practice and must be scrupulous in their application of generally accepted accounting principles and candid in all their dealings with members in public practice.

Article V

Due Care

A member should observe the profession's technical and ethical standards, strive continually to improve competence and the quality of services, and discharge professional responsibility to the best of the member's ability.

The quest for excellence is the essence of due care. Due care requires a member to discharge professional responsibilities with competence and diligence. It imposes the obligation to perform professional services to the best of a member's ability with concern for the best interest of those for whom the services are performed and consistent with the profession's responsibility to the public.

Competence is derived from a synthesis of education and experience. It begins with a mastery of the common body of knowledge required for designation as a certified public accountant. The maintenance of competence requires a commitment to learning and professional improvement that must continue throughout a member's professional life. It is a member's individual responsibility. In all engagements and in all responsibilities, each member should undertake to achieve a level of competence that will assure that the quality of the member's services meets the high level of professionalism required by these Principles.

Competence represents the attainment and maintenance of a level of understanding and knowledge that enables a member to render services with facility and acumen. It also establishes the limitations of a member's capacities by dictating that consultation or referral may be required when a professional engagement exceeds the personal competence of a member or a member's firm. Each member is responsible for assessing his or her own competence—of evaluating whether education, experience, and judgment are adequate for the responsibility to be assumed.

Members should be diligent in discharging responsibilities to clients, employers, and the public. Diligence imposes the responsibility to render services promptly and carefully, to be thorough, and to observe applicable technical and ethical standards.

Due care requires a member to plan and supervise adequately any professional activity for which he or she is responsible.

Article VI

Scope and Nature of Services

A member in public practice should observe the Principles of the Code of Professional Conduct in determining the scope and nature of services to be provided.

The public interest aspect of certified public accountants' services requires that such services be consistent with acceptable professional behavior for certified public accountants. Integrity requires that service and the public trust not be subordinated to personal gain and advantage. Objectivity and independence require that members be free from conflicts of interest in discharging professional responsibilities. Due care requires that services be provided with competence and diligence.

Each of these Principles should be considered by members in determining whether or not to provide specific services in individual circumstances. In some instances, they may represent an overall constraint on the nonaudit services that might be offered to a specific client. No hard-and-fast rules can be developed to help members reach these judgments, but they must be satisfied that they are meeting the spirit of the Principles in this regard.

In order to accomplish this, members should

▼ Practice in firms that have in place internal quality-control procedures to ensure that services are competently delivered and adequately supervised.

▼ Determine, in their individual judgments, whether the scope and nature of other services provided to an audit client would create a conflict of interest in the performance of the audit function for that client.

▼ Assess, in their individual judgments, whether an activity is consistent with their role as professionals (for example, Is such activity a reasonable extension or variation of existing services offered by the member or others in the profession?).

Section II—Rules

Applicability

The bylaws of the American Institute of Certified Public Accountants require that members adhere to the Rules of the Code of Professional Conduct. Members must be prepared to justify departures from these Rules.

Definitions

[Adoption of the revised Code of Professional Conduct will require modification of some of the definitions of terms used in the Principles and Rules. The Professional Ethics Executive Committee has this project under way. Until new definitions are adopted, the definitions of terms as they appeared prior to adoption of the new Rules on January 12, 1988, are presented for reference.]

Client. The person(s) or entity which retains a member or his firm, engaged in the practice of public accounting, for the performance of professional services.

Council. The Council of the American Institute of Certified Public Accountants.

Enterprise. Any person(s) or entity, whether organized for profit or not, for which a CPA provides services.

Financial statements. Statements and footnotes related thereto that purport to show financial position which relates to a point in time or changes in financial position which relate to a period of time, and statements which use a cash or other incomplete basis of accounting. Balance sheets, statements of income, statements of retained earnings, statements of changes in financial position, and statements of changes in owners' equity are financial statements.

Incidental financial data included in management advisory services reports to support recommendations to a client and tax returns and supporting schedules do not, for this purpose, constitute financial statements; and the statement, affidavit, or signature of preparers required on tax returns neither constitutes an opinion on financial statements nor requires a disclaimer of such opinion.

Firm. A proprietorship, partnership, or professional corporation or association engaged in the practice of public accounting, including individual partners or shareholders thereof.

Institute. The American Institute of Certified Public Accounting.

Interpretations of rules of conduct. Pronouncements issued by the division of professional ethics to provide guidelines concerning the scope and application of the rules of conduct.

Member. A member, associate member, or international associate of the American Institute of Certified Public Accountants.

Practice of public accounting. Holding out to be a CPA or public accountant and at the same time performing for a client one or more types of services rendered by public accountants. The term shall not be limited by a more restrictive definition which might be found in the accountancy law under which a member practices.

Professional services. One or more types of services performed in the practice of public accounting.

Rules

Rule 101   Independence
A member in public practice shall be independent in the performance of professional services as required by standards promulgated by bodies designated by Council.

Interpretation of Rule 101
Interpretation 101-1. Independence shall be considered to be impaired if, for

example, a member had any of the following transactions, interests, or relationships:

A. During the period of a professional engagement or at the time of expressing an opinion, a member or a member's firm
   1. Had or was committed to acquire any direct or material indirect financial interest in the enterprise.
   2. Was a trustee of any trust or executor or administrator of any estate if such trust or estate had or was committed to acquire any direct or material indirect financial interest in the enterprise.
   3. Had any joint, closely held business investment with the enterprise or with any officer, director, or principal stockholders thereof that was material in relation to the member's net worth or to the net worth of the member's firm.
   4. Had any loan to or from the enterprise or any officer, director, or principal stockholder of the enterprise. This proscription does not apply to the following loans from a financial institution when made under normal lending procedures, terms, and requirements.
      a. Loans obtained by a member or a member's firm that are not material in relation to the net worth of such borrower.
      b. Home mortgages.
      c. Other secured loans, except loans guaranteed by a member's firm which are otherwise unsecured.

B. During the period covered by the financial statements, during the period of the professional engagement, or at the time of expressing an opinion, a member or a member's firm
   1. Was connected with the enterprise as a promoter, underwriter or voting trustee, as a director or officer, or in any capacity equivalent to that of a member of management or of an employee.
   2. Was a trustee for any pension or profit-sharing trust of the enterprise.

The above examples are not intended to be all-inclusive.

Rule 102 Integrity and Objectivity
In the performance of any professional service, a member shall maintain objectivity and integrity, shall be free of conflicts of interest, and shall not knowingly misrepresent facts or subordinate his or her judgment to others.

Rule 201 General Standards
A member shall comply with the following standards and with any interpretations thereof by bodies designated by Council.

A. *Professional Competence.* Undertake only those professional services that the member or the member's firm can reasonably expect to be completed with professional competence.
B. *Due Professional Care.* Exercise due professional care in the performance of professional services.
C. *Planning and Supervision.* Adequately plan and supervise the performance of professional services.
D. *Sufficient Relevant Data.* Obtain sufficient relevant data to afford a reasonable basis for conclusions or recommendations in relation to any professional services performed.

Rule 202 Compliance With Standards

A member who performs auditing, review, compilation, management advisory, tax, or other professional services shall comply with standards promulgated by bodies designated by Council.

Rule 203 Accounting Principles

A member shall not (1) express an opinion or state affirmatively that the financial statements or other financial data of any entity are presented in conformity with generally accepted accounting principles or (2) state that he or she is not aware of any material modifications that should be made to such statements or data in order for them to be in conformity with generally accepted accounting principles, if such statements or data contain any departure from an accounting principle promulgated by bodies designated by Council to establish such principles that has a material effect on the statements or data taken as a whole. If, however, the statements or data contain such a departure and the member can demonstrate that due to unusual circumstances the financial statements or data would otherwise have been misleading, the member can comply with the rule by describing the departure, its approximate effects, if practicable, and the reasons why compliance with the principle would result in a misleading statement.

Rule 301 Confidential Client Information

A member in public practice shall not disclose any confidential client information without the specific consent of the client.

This rule shall not be construed (1) to relieve a member of his or her professional obligations under rules 202 and 203, (2) to affect in any way the member's obligation to comply with a validly issued and enforceable subpoena or summons, (3) to prohibit review of a member's professional practice under AICPA or state CPA society authorization, or (4) to preclude a member from initiating a complaint with or responding to any inquiry made by a recognized investigative or disciplinary body.

Members of a recognized investigative or disciplinary body and professional practice reviewers shall not use to their own advantage or disclose any member's confidential client information that comes to their attention in carrying out their official responsibilities. However, this prohibition shall not restrict the exchange of information with a recognized investigative or disciplinary body or affect, in any way, compliance with a validly issued and enforceable subpoena or summons.

Rule 302 Contingent Fees

Professional services shall not be offered or rendered under an arrangement whereby no fee will be charged unless a specified finding or result is attained, or where the fee is otherwise contingent upon the finding or results of such services. However, a member's fees may vary depending, for example, on the complexity of services rendered.

Fees are not regarded as being contingent if fixed by courts or other public authorities, or, in tax matters, if determined based on the results of judicial proceedings or the findings of governmental agencies.

Rule 401 [*There are currently no rules in the 400 series.*]

Rule 501 Acts Discreditable

A member shall not commit an act discreditable to the profession

Rule 502   Advertising and Other Forms of Solicitation

A member in public practice shall not seek to obtain clients by advertising or other forms of solicitation in a manner that is false, misleading, or deceptive. Solicitation by the use of coercion, over-reaching, or harassing conduct is prohibited.

Rule 503   Commissions

The acceptance by a member in public practice of a payment for the referral of products or services of others to a client is prohibited. Such action is considered to create a conflict of interest that results in a loss of objectivity and independence.

A member shall not make a payment to obtain a client. This rule shall not prohibit payments for the purchase of an accounting practice or retirement payments to individuals formerly engaged in the practice of public accounting or payments to their heirs or estates.

Rule 504   *[There is currently no rule 504.]*

Rule 505   Form of Practice and Name

A member may practice public accounting only in the form of a proprietorship, a partnership, or a professional corporation whose characteristics conform to resolutions of Council.

A member shall not practice public accounting under a firm name that is misleading. Names of one or more past partners or shareholders may be included in the firm name of a successor partnership or corporation. Also, a partner or shareholder surviving the death or withdrawal of all other partners or shareholders may continue to practice under such name which includes the name of past partners or shareholders for up to two years after becoming a sole practitioner.

A firm may not designate itself as "Members of the American Institute of Certified Public Accountants" unless all of its partners or shareholders are members of the Institute.

Source: Reprinted from "Standards of Ethical Conduct for Management Accountants," *Statements on Management Accounting*, No. 1C, June 1, 1983. Copyright by National Association of Accountants, Montvale, N.J.

GLOSSARY

The number in parentheses after each definition is the chapter(s) in which the term or concept is most extensively discussed.

Abnormal Spoilage Spoilage due to reasons other than the usual course of operations of a process. This may include goods spoiled as a result of error or as a result of casualty losses. (8)

Absorption Costing See *Full-Absorption Costing*.

Account Analysis The method of cost estimation that calls for a review of each account making up the total cost being analyzed. Each account is classified as fixed or variable based on the judgment of the classifier. (10)

Accounting Rate of Return A measure of project returns using accounting concepts of income. (16)

Acquisition Cost Costs to purchase an investment or inventory item and to get it in place and in condition for use. (15)

Action Set The alternatives available to managers in a given decision setting. (24)

Activity Variance Variance due to difference between budgeted and actual sales or production output. (18, 19, 21)

Activity-Based Costing A costing method that derives product cost as the sum of the cost of the activities that occur to make the product. (2)

Actual Costing A system of accounting whereby overhead is assigned to products based on actual overhead incurred. (5, 9, 20)

Actual Costs Amounts determined on the basis of actual (historical) costs incurred. (7)

Adjusted R-Square The correlation coefficient in regression squared and adjusted for the number of independent variables used to make the estimate. (10)

Administrative Costs Costs required to manage the organization and provide staff support for organization activities. (2)

Allocation Base A measure that can be directly related to two or more cost objects and is considered to approximate the proportion of a common cost shared by two or more cost objects. For example, direct labor-hours may be related to each unit produced. If direct labor-hours are used to assign manufacturing overhead costs to products, then the direct labor-hours are called the allocation base. (4)

Applied Overhead Overhead assigned to a job or other cost object using an estimated overhead rate. (7)

Autocorrelation See *Serial Correlation*.

Basic Cost Flow Equation (Also known as the basic inventory formula.) Beginning balance plus transfers-in equals transfers-out plus ending balance. (3)

Batch Orders consisting of identical units that go through the exact same production process. (7)

Batch Production   Manufacturing process characterized by the production of product groups that are varied enough to require frequent production line changes. (7)

Behavioral Congruence   When individuals behave in the best interest of the organization regardless of their own goals. (22)

Break-Even Point   The volume level where profits equal zero. (11)

Budget   A financial plan of the resources needed to carry out tasks and meet the financial goals. (17)

Budget Plan   Term for master budget. (17)

Budget Variance   A price variance for fixed overhead. (19, 20)

Budgeted Balance Sheets   Statements of financial position that combine estimates of financial position at the beginning and end of the budget period with the estimated results of operations for the period and estimated changes in assets and liabilities. (17)

Budgeting under Uncertainty   Making many forecasts, each representing a different possible set of circumstances. (17)

By-Products   Outputs of joint production processes that are relatively minor in quantity and/or value. (6)

Carrying Costs   Those costs that increase with the number of units in inventory. (14)

Cash Budget   A period-by-period statement of cash on hand at the start of a budget period; expected cash receipts classified by source; expected cash disbursements classified by function, responsibility, and form; and the resulting cash balance at the end of the budget period. (17)

Centralized   Refers to those organizations where decisions are made by a relatively few individuals at the high ranks of the organization. (22)

Certified Management Accounting   A program established to recognize educational achievement and professional competence in management accounting. (1)

CMA   Acronym for Certificate in Management Accounting. (1)

Coefficient of Variation   The standard deviation of a project divided by the expected value of the project. (24)

Common Costs   A synonym for indirect costs. Also costs of shared facilities, products, or services. (2, 4)

Conditional Probabilities   Those likelihoods that depend on a specific result. (26)

Constraints   Activities, resources, or policies that limit or bound the attainment of an objective. (13)

Continuous-Flow Processing   Systems that generally mass-produce a single, homogeneous output in a continuing process. (7)

Contribution Margin   The difference between revenues and variable costs. (2, 11)

Contribution Margin Format   The outline of a financial statement that shows the contribution margin as an intermediate step in the computation of operating profits or income (9, 11)

Contribution Margin per Unit of Scarce Resource   Contribution margin per unit of a particular input with limited availability. (13)

Contribution Margin Ratio   Contribution margin as a ratio of sales revenue. (11)

Contribution Margin Variance   Variance from changes in the differences between revenues and variable costs. (21)

Controllability Concept   The idea that managers should be held responsible for costs or profits over which they have decision-making authority. (22)

Controllability of Variance   One rationale used in deciding whether a variance should be calculated, analyzed, or investigated. (19)

Controllable Cost   A cost that can be affected by a manager in the short run. (2)

Controller   The chief accounting officer in most corporations. (1)

Conversion Costs   The sum of direct labor and manufacturing overhead. (2, 3, 8)

Corner Point   A corner of the feasible production region in linear programming. (13)

Correlation Coefficient   A measure of the linear relationship between two or more variables, such as cost and some activity measure. (10)

Cost   A sacrifice of resources. (1, 2)

Cost Accounting   The subfield of accounting that records, measures, and reports information about costs. (1)

Cost Accounting Standards Board   The federal governmental body set up to establish methods of accounting for costs by government defense contractors. (1)

Cost Accumulation   The process of adding costs to a cost object, such as a job, department, or inventory account. (3, 7, 8)

Cost Allocation   The process of assigning indirect costs to cost objects. (2, 4, 5, 6)

Cost-Benefit Requirements   The criterion that an alternative will be chosen if and only if the benefits from it exceed the costs. This criterion has been cited as a basis for evaluating cost data gathering and reporting systems. (1, 26)

Cost Centers   Organization subunits responsible only for costs. (22)

Cost Drivers   Activities or transactions that cause costs to occur. (2)

Cost Object   Any end to which a cost is assigned. Examples include a product, a department, or a product line. (2, 4)

Cost of Goods Finished   Cost of goods manufactured. (2, 3)

Cost of Goods Manufactured   The cost of goods completed and transferred to the finished goods storage area. (2, 3)

Cost of Goods Manufactured and Sold Statement   Statement that incorporates and summarizes the information from the direct materials costs schedule, the cost of goods manufactured schedule, and the cost of goods sold schedule. (2, 3, 7)

Cost of Goods Sold   The cost assigned to products sold during the period. (2, 3, 7, 8)

Cost of Prediction Error   The difference between the actual cost incurred based on incorrect information and the cost that would have been incurred with the correct information. (26)

Costs for Decision Making   Costs that are included in financial analysis by managers. See *Differential Costs*. (1)

Costs for Performance Evaluation   Costs that are used in planning and performance evaluation analysis by managers. (1)

Cost-Plus Transfer Pricing   Transfer pricing policy based on full costing or variable costing plus an allowance for profit. (23)

Cost Variance Analysis   Comparison of actual input quantities and prices with standard input quantities and prices. (19)

Cost-Volume-Profit (CVP) Analysis Study of the interrelationships among costs and volume and how they impact profit. (11)

Critical Probability The probability of different outcomes that equalizes the value of the outcomes. (25)

Cross-Department Monitoring A reason for allocating costs where it is hoped that managers of user departments have incentives to monitor the service department's costs. (5)

Current Costs Cost to replace or rebuild an existing asset. (22)

CVP Cost-volume-profit. (2, 11)

CVP under Uncertainty Consideration of the extent of uncertainty and the impact of that uncertainty on decision inputs and outcomes in cost-volume-profit decision analysis. (24)

Decentralized Refers to those organizations where decisions are spread out among relatively many divisional and departmental managers. (22)

Decremental Costs Costs that decrease with a particular course of action. (2, 12)

Delphi Technique Forecasting method where individual forecasts of group members are submitted anonymously and evaluated by the group as a whole. (17)

Denominator Reason Overhead variance caused by differences between actual activity and the activity used in the denominator of the formula used to compute the predetermined overhead rate See *Production Volume Variance.* (7, 20)

Departmental Rate The rate used to allocate overhead to an individual cost center within a firm. (5)

Dependent Variable In a cost-estimation context, the costs to be estimated from an equation. Also called the Y-term or the left-hand side (LHS) in regression. (10)

Differential Analysis Process of estimating the consequences of alternative actions that decision makers can take. (12)

Differential Costs Costs that change in response to a particular course of action. (1, 2, 12)

Direct Costing A synonym for variable costing. (9)

Direct Labor The cost of workers who transform the materials into a finished product at some stage of the production process. (2)

Direct Materials Those materials that can be feasibly identified with the product. (2)

Direct Method A method of cost allocation that charges costs of service departments to user departments and ignores any services used by other service departments. (5)

Discount Rate An interest rate used to compute net present values. (15)

Discounted Payback Method A method of assessing investment projects that recognizes the time value of money in a payback context. (16)

Discretionary Cost Center An organization unit where managers are held responsible for costs, but the relationship between costs and outputs is not well established. (22)

Discretionary Costs Costs that are difficult to relate to outputs. Examples include research and development, information systems, and some advertising. (22)

Disinvestment Flows Cash flows that take place at the termination of a capital project. (15)

Dual Rate Method A method of cost allocation that separates a common cost into fixed and variable components and then allocates each component using a different allocation base. (4)

Dual Transfer Pricing Transfer pricing system where the buying department is charged with costs only, and the selling department is credited with the cost plus some profit allowance. (23)

Econometric Models Statistical method of forecasting economic data using regression models. (10)

Economic Order Quantity (EOQ) The number of units to order at one time to minimize total expected annual costs of an inventory system. (14)

Economic Production Run The number of units per batch in a production line that will minimize the expected annual costs of setting up production runs and storing the units produced. (14)

Efficiency Variance Difference between budgeted and actual results arising from differences between the inputs that were expected per unit of output and the inputs that were actually used. (19, 20, 21)

Engineering Estimates Cost estimates based on measurement and pricing of the work involved in a task. (10)

EOQ Abbreviation for economic order quantity. (14)

Equivalent Units The amount of work actually performed on products with varying degrees of completion, translated to that work required to complete an equal number of whole units. (8)

Error Term The unexplained difference between predicted and actual outcomes. Sometimes called random error. (25)

Estimate A considered judgment about future events that takes into account past experience and probable changes in circumstances and conditions. (10)

Estimated Net Realizable Value Sales price of final product minus estimated additional processing costs from split-off point necessary to prepare a product for sale. (6)

Exogenous Factors Outside events that can influence an outcome. (24)

Expected Annual Stockout Cost The product of the cost of one stockout times the number of orders placed per year times the probability of a stockout in a year. A measure of the costs likely from running out of inventory at various times during the year. (14)

Expected Opportunity Loss A loss that may occur if certain unfavorable outcomes result after a decision has been implemented. (24)

Expected Value The weighted average of all of the outcomes of a decision process. (24)

Expense A cost that is charged against revenue in an accounting period. (2)

Factory Burden A synonym for manufacturing overhead. (2)

Factory Overhead A synonym for manufacturing overhead. (2)

Favorable Variances Variances that, taken alone, result in an addition to operating profit. (18)

Feasible Production Region The area in a graph of production opportunities bounded by the limits on production. (13)

Final Cost Center A cost center, such as a production or marketing department, from which costs are not allocated to another cost center. (5)

Financial Accounting The preparation of financial statements and data for outsiders, primarily stockholders and creditors. (1)

Financial Budget Refers to the budget of financial resources; for example, the cash budget and the budgeted balance sheet. (18)

Finished Goods Product that has been completed and is in inventory awaiting sale. (2)

First-in, First-out (FIFO) Costing The first-in, first-out inventory method whereby the first goods received are the first charged out when sold or transferred. (8)

Fixed Costs Costs that are unchanged as volume changes within the relevant range of activity. (2, 10, 11)

Flexible Budget A budget that indicates revenues, costs, and profits for different levels of activity. (18)

Flexible Budget Line The expected monthly costs at different levels of output. (11, 18)

Flexible Production Budget Standard input price times standard quantity of input allowed for actual output. (19)

Foregone Discount The opportunity cost of ordering in a smaller lot size than that which receives the maximum quantity discount. (14)

Freight-in An alternative term for transportation-in. (3)

Full-Absorption Costing A system of accounting for costs in which both fixed and variable manufacturing costs are considered product costs. (2, 9)

Full Cost The sum of the fixed and variable costs of manufacturing and selling a unit of product. (2, 12)

Full-Cost Fallacy The assumption that fixed costs will vary with production. (12)

Full Manufacturing Cost The cost used to compute a product's inventory value under generally accepted accounting principles. (2)

GAAP Acronym for generally accepted accounting principles. (2)

Generally Accepted Accounting Principles (GAAP) The rules, standards, and conventions that guide the preparation of financial accounting statements. (2)

Goal Congruence When all members of a group hold a common set of objectives. (22)

Good Output Units that are expected to be completed and suitable for further processing or for sale at the end of a production process. (8)

Graphic Method Graphic solution of a linear programming problem by selecting the best corner solution visually. (13)

Gross Margin The difference between sales revenues and manufacturing costs as an intermediate step in the computation of operating profits or net income (3)

Gross Margin Variance Variances from changes in revenues and cost of goods sold. (21)

Heteroscedasticity In regression analysis, the condition in which the errors are correlated with the magnitude of values of the independent variables. (10)

High-Low Cost Estimation A method of estimating costs based on two cost observations, usually costs at the highest activity level and costs at the lowest activity level. (10)

Hurdle Rate The discount rate required by a company before it will invest in a project. (15)

Hybrid   A costing system that incorporates both job and process costing concepts. (7)

Impact of a Variance   One rationale used in deciding whether a variance is important enough to compute, analyze, and investigate. (19)

Imperfect Information   Information that is not 100 percent accurate but may be used to revise the probabilities of certain decision outcomes. (26)

In-Control Probability   The likelihood that a process is operating within specifications. (25)

Incremental Costs   Costs that increase in response to a particular course of action. These are a subset of differential costs. (2, 12)

Independent Variables   The X-terms, or predictors, on the right-hand side of a regression equation. See *Predictors*. (10)

Industry Volume Variance   The portion of the sales activity variance that is due to changes in industry volume. (21)

Information Cost   Cost of obtaining information. (26)

Information Economics   A formal system for evaluating whether the cost-benefit test has been met for information. (26)

Information Overload   A characteristic of too much data. The intended user is overwhelmed by the quantity of data supplied.

Intercept   The point where a line crosses the vertical axis. In regression, this line is the regression line and the intercept is the constant term on the right-hand side of the equation. In cost estimation, the intercept is sometimes used as the fixed cost estimate. (10)

Intermediate Cost Center   A cost center whose costs are charged to other departments in the organization. Intermediate cost centers are frequently service departments. (5)

Internal Rate of Return (IRR)   The interest rate that equates the inflows and outflows from an investment project. (16)

Investment Centers   Organization subunits responsible for profits and for investment in assets. (22)

Investment Tax Credit   A reduction in federal income taxes arising from the purchase of long-term assets. Usually treated as a reduction in investment cost for analytical purposes. (15)

IRR   Abbreviation for internal rate of return. (16)

Isoprofit Lines   Family of constant profit lines where operating profits are the same for any combination of product volumes on each of those lines. (11)

Job Costing   An accounting system that traces costs to individual units for output or specific contracts, batches of goods, or jobs. (7)

Job Cost Record   The source document for entering costs under job costing. This is sometimes referred to as a job cost sheet, job cost file, or job card. (7)

Jobs   Units or batches of units that are easily distinguishable from other units or batches. (7)

Joint Cost   A cost of manufacturing process in which two or more outputs come from the process. (2, 6)

Joint Probability   The probability of two or more events occurring. (26)

Joint Products   Outputs from a common input and common production process. (6)

Just-in-Time   Method of production or purchasing such that each unit is purchased or produced just in time for its use. (1)

Last-in, First out (LIFO) Costing   The last-in, first-out inventory method whereby the last goods received are charged out first when transferred or sold. (3)

Lead Time   The time between order placement and order arrival. (14)

Learning Curve   The mathematical or graphic representation of the learning phenomenon. (10)

Learning Phenomenon   A systematic relationship between the amount of experience in performing a task and the time required to carry out the task. (10)

Lease versus Borrow-to-Buy   Choice of financing the investment in an asset through either a lease or a purchase using borrowed funds. (16)

Line   Officers and other corporate employees directly responsible for activities related to the main goals of the organization. (2)

Linear Programming—Graphic Method   Graphic solution of a linear programming problem by selecting the best corner solution. (13)

Linear Programming—Simplex Method   Solution of a linear programming problem using a mathematical technique. Used for solving complex product mix problems. (13)

Lost Units   Goods that evaporate or otherwise disappear during a production process. (8)

Lower Control Limit   The minimum value of some observation that still indicates that the process is in control. (25)

Make-or-Buy Decision   A decision whether to acquire needed goods internally or to purchase them from outside sources. (12)

Management by Exception   An approach to management requiring that reports emphasize the deviation from an accepted basing point, such as a standard, a budget, an industry average, or a prior-period experience. (18, 19)

Managerial Accounting   The preparation of cost and related data for managers to use in performance evaluation or decision making. (1)

Manufacturing   Term used to describe production departments in an organization that manufacture goods, such as an assembly department. (5)

Manufacturing Department   Production departments in organizations that produce goods. (3)

Manufacturing Organization   An organization characterized by the conversion of raw inputs into some other output products. (3)

Manufacturing Overhead   All production costs except direct materials and direct labor. (2)

Manufacturing Overhead Adjustment   The difference between applied and actual overhead. (7)

Margin of Safety   The excess of projected or actual sales over the break-even volume. (11)

Marginal Costs   The economist's analog to differential costs and/or variable costs. (2, 12)

Market-Based Transfer Pricing   Transfer pricing policy where the transfer price is set at the market price, or at a small discount from the market price. (23)

Marketing Costs   Costs to obtain customer orders and provide customers with the finished product. (2)

Market Share Variance   The portion of the sales activity variance due to change in the company's proportion of sales in the markets in which the company operates. (21)

Master Budget   The financial plan for the coming year or other planning period. (17)

Materials Requisition   A form used to obtain materials from a storeroom. It is the source document for recording the transfer of materials to production. (7)

Matrix Allocation   The simultaneous solution method of service department cost allocation. (5)

Mean   The average of a series of data; sometimes referred to as the expected value. (24)

Merchandise Inventory   In a merchandising organization, the cost of goods acquired but not yet sold. (3)

Merchandising Organization   An organization characterized by marketing goods or services rather than converting raw inputs into outputs. (3)

Minimax   The criterion to minimize the maximum loss from a decision. (24)

Mix Variance   A variance that arises from a change in the relative proportion of outputs (a sales mix variance) or inputs (a materials or labor mix variance). (21)

Mixed Cost   A cost that has both fixed and variable components. (2)

Monte Carlo   A method of sampling from the assumed distribution function to obtain simulated observations of costs or other variables. (24)

Multicollinearity   Correlation between two or more independent variables in a multiple regression equation. (10)

Multiple-Factor Formula   An allocation formula used as an allocation base when a cost is considered not reasonably assignable to just one base. (4)

Multiple Rates of Return   Problem arising when computing the internal rate of return for cash flows that change signs more than once in the project's life. It is possible, then, for such a project to have more than one internal rate of return. (16)

Mutually Exclusive   Term used in capital investment decisions to describe a situation where selection of one project precludes the selection of another. (16)

Negotiated Transfer Price   System whereby the transfer prices are arrived at through negotiation between managers of buying and selling departments. (23)

Net Income   Operating profit adjusted for interest, income taxes, extraordinary, and other items required to comply with GAAP and other regulations. (2)

Net Present Value   Difference between the discounted future cash flows from a project and the value of the discounted cash outflows to acquire the project. (15)

Net Present Value Index   Ratio of the net present value of a project to the funds invested in the project. (16)

Net Realizable Value Method   Joint cost allocation based on the proportional values of the joint products at the split-off point. (6)

Nominal Discount Rate   A rate of interest that includes compensation for inflation. (15)

Nominal Dollars   Actual numerical count of money exchanged without adjusting for inflation. (15)

Noncontrollable Cost A cost that cannot be changed or influenced by a given manager. (2)

Nonmanufacturing Costs Administrative and marketing costs. (2)

Normal Costing A system of accounting whereby direct materials and direct labor are charged to cost objects at actual, and manufacturing overhead is applied. (7, 9, 20)

Normal Costs Product cost amounts where actual direct materials and direct labor costs are assigned to products, but where manufacturing overhead is applied using a predetermined rate. (7)

Normal Spoilage Spoiled goods that are a result of the regular operation of the production process. (8)

Numerator Reason A difference between actual and applied overhead caused by differences between estimated overhead costs and actual overhead costs for the period. (7)

Objective Function Mathematical statement of an objective to be maximized or minimized in a linear programming model. (13)

Operating Budgets Refers to the budgeted income statement, the production budget, the budgeted cost of goods sold, and supporting budgets. (18)

Operating Profit The excess of operating revenues over the operating costs to generate those revenues. (2)

Operation A standardized method or technique that is repetitively performed. (7)

Operation Costing A hybrid costing system often used in manufacturing of goods that have some common characteristics plus some individual characteristics. (7)

Opportunity Cost The lost return an alternative course of action could provide. (2, 12, 13)

Opportunity Cost Approach Method of managerial performance evaluation based on a comparison of actual results to forgone alternatives.

Opportunity Loss Loss from an unfavorable outcome. (26)

Ordering Costs Costs that increase with the number of orders placed for inventory. (14)

Ordinary Least Squares Regression A regression method that minimizes the sum of the squared distances of each observation from the regression line. (10)

Organizational Goals Set of broad objectives established by management that company employees work to achieve. (17)

Outcomes Possible results of a given action. (24, 26)

Outlay Cost A past, present, or future cash outflow. (2)

Outliers Observations of costs of different activity levels (or similar phenomena) that are significantly different from other observations in the data series. (10)

Out-of-Control Probability The probability that a process is not operating according to specifications. (25)

Overapplied Overhead The excess of applied overhead over actual overhead incurred during a period. (7)

Overhead Usually refers to manufacturing overhead but is an ambiguous term when unmodified. (2)

Overhead Adjustment A debit or credit entry to change overapplied or underapplied overhead in total to cost of goods sold or to be prorated to goods in inventory and goods sold. (7)

Overhead Variance The difference between actual and applied overhead. (7)

Participative Budgeting The use of input from lower- and middle-management employees; also called grass roots budgeting. (17)

Payback One method of assessing capital investment projects using the rationale that there is a positive relationship between the speed of payback and the rate of return. (16)

Payback Period The time required to recoup an investment from the cash flows from the project. (16)

Payback Reciprocal One divided by the payback period in years. (16)

Payoff The value of an outcome from a decision. (24, 26)

Payoff Table A schedule showing the alternate outcomes from a decision together with the probability of occurrence. (24)

Perfect Information Information that predicts with complete accuracy the outcome that will occur from a decision. (26)

Period Costs Costs that can be more easily attributed to time intervals. (2, 9)

Periodic Inventory A method of inventory accounting whereby inventory balances are determined on specific dates (such as quarterly) by physical count rather than on a continuous basis. (3)

Perpetual Inventory A method of accounting whereby inventory records are maintained on a continuously updated basis. (3)

Physical Quantities Method Joint cost allocation based on measurement of the volume, weight, or other physical measure of the joint products at the split-off point. (6)

Planned Variance Variances that are expected to arise if certain conditions affect operations. (19)

Planning Budget Another term for master budget. (17, 18)

Plantwide Rate A single rate used to allocate overhead to all departments in the company. (5)

Posterior Probabilities The probabilities obtained as a result of revising prior probabilities with additional conditional probability data. (26)

Predetermined Overhead Rate An amount obtained by dividing total estimated overhead for the coming period by the total overhead allocation base for the coming period. It is used for applying overhead to cost objects in normal or standard cost systems. (7, 9)

Predictors The variables on the right-hand side of a regression equation (the X-terms) used to predict costs or a similar dependent variable. They are activities that are expected to affect costs. (10)

Present Value The amounts of future cash flows discounted to their equivalent worth today. (15)

Price Discrimination Sale of products or services at different prices when the different prices do not reflect differences in marginal costs. (12)

Price Variance Difference between actual costs and budgeted costs arising from changes in the cost of inputs to a production process or other activity. (19)

Prime Cost   The sum of direct materials and direct labor. (2)

Principal-Agent Relationships   The relationship between a superior, referred to as the principal, and a subordinate, called the agent. (22)

Prior Department Costs   Manufacturing costs incurred in some other department and charged to a subsequent department in the manufacturing process. These costs are related to goods transferred in from a department that is upstream in the manufacturing process. (8)

Prior Probabilities (Priors)   Initial probability estimates. (26)

Probabilities   Likelihoods that given outcomes will, in fact, occur. (24, 26)

Process Costing   An accounting system that is used when identical units are produced through an ongoing series of uniform production steps. Costs are allocated by department and then allocated to units produced. (8)

Product-Choice Decisions   The product-choice problem arises when there are limited amounts of resources that are being fully used and must be allocated to multiple products. The decision is to choose the optimal product mix. (13)

Product Costs   Those costs that can be attributed to products; costs that are part of inventory. For a manufacturer, they include direct materials, direct labor, and manufacturing overhead. The manufacturing overhead attributed to products differs under the variable costing and the full-absorption costing systems. (2, 9)

Product Mix   A combination of outputs to be produced within the resource constraints of an entity. (11, 13)

Production Budget   Production plan of resources needed to meet current sales demand and ensure inventory levels are sufficient for activity levels expected. (17)

Production-Cost Report   A report which summarizes production and cost results for a period. This report is generally used by managers to monitor production and cost flows. (8)

Production Departments   Departments in service, merchandising, or manufacturing organizations that generate goods or services that are ultimately sold to outsiders. (5)

Production Volume Variance   A fixed cost variance caused by a difference between actual and estimated volume. (7, 19, 20)

Profit Center   An organization subunit responsible for profits; usually responsible for revenues, costs, production, and sales volumes. (22)

Profit Equation   Operating profits equal total contribution margin less fixed costs. (11)

Profit Plan   The income statement portion of the master budget. (17)

Profit Variance Analysis   Analysis of the causes of differences between budgeted profits and the actual profits earned. (18)

Profit-Volume Analysis   A summary verson of CVP analysis where the cost and revenue lines are collapsed into a single profit line. See *Cost-Volume-Profit Analysis*. (11)

Project   A complex job that often takes months or years to complete and requires the work of many different departments, divisions, or subcontractors. (7)

Prorated Overhead Adjustment   Assigning portions of overapplied or underapplied manufacturing overhead to goods in inventory and goods sold. (7)

Prorating Variances   Assigning portions of variances to the inventory and cost of goods sold accounts to which the variances are related. (20)

Purchase Price Variance   The price variance based on the quantity of materials purchased. (19)

Quantity Discounts   Price reductions offered for bulk purchases. (14)

Random Event   An occurrence that is beyond the control of the decision maker or manager. (25)

Raw Materials   An alternative term for direct materials. (2)

Real Discount Rate   The discount rate that compensates only for the use of money, not for inflation. (15)

Real Dollars   Monetary measures that are adjusted for the effects of inflation so they have the same purchasing power over time. (15)

Real Return   Return on capital after adjustment for the effects of inflation. (15)

Reciprocal Allocation   An alternative term for the simultaneous solution method of service department cost allocation. (5)

Regression   Statistical procedure to determine the relationship between variables. (10)

Relative Sales Value Method   Joint cost allocation based on the proportional values of the joint products at the split-off point. The values may be based on actual market values of the joint product, or estimated from market values of a product generated with further processing of the joint product. (Also called net realizable method.) (6)

Relevant Costs   Costs that are different under alternative actions. (12)

Relevant Range   The activity levels within which a given fixed cost will be unchanged even though volume changes. (2)

Reorder Point   The quantity of inventory on hand that triggers the need to order another lot of materials. (14)

Repetitive Manufacturing   Production process characterized by long production runs, few products, and infrequent production line changes. (7)

Replacement Method   Joint cost allocation based on the change in cost arising from a change in the mix of outputs. (6)

Residual Income   The excess of investment center profit over the capital charge times investment center assets. (22)

Responsibility Accounting   A system of reporting tailored to an organizational structure so that costs and revenues are reported at the level having the related responsibility within the organization. (22)

Responsibility Center   A specific unit of an organization assigned to a manager who is held accountable for its operations and resources. (1, 18, 22)

Return on Investment (ROI)   The ratio of profits to investment in the assets that generate those profits. (22)

Revenue Center   An organization subunit responsible for revenues and, typically, also for marketing costs. (22)

Revenue Variances   Variances in prices and activity that affect sales or other revenues. (21)

Risk   The chance that the outcome, that actually occurs from a given decision, is less valuable than that which would be obtained from another decision. (24)

Risk Minimization   A managerial objective to reduce the probability of loss. (24)

Risk Premium   Additional interest of other compensation required for risks in investments. (16)

Safety Stock   Inventory carried to protect against delays in delivery, increased demand, or other similar factors. (14)

Sales Activity Variance   Variance due to difference between budgeted and actual volume of sales. (18, 21)

Sales Forecasts   Estimations of future sales. (17)

Sales Mix Variance   Variance arising from the relative proportion of different products sold. (21)

Sales Price Variance   Variance arising from changes in the price of goods sold.

Sales Quantity Variance   In multiproduct companies, a variance arising from the change in volume of sales, independent of any change in mix. (21)

Sales Volume Variance   See *Sales Activity Variance*.

Scattergraph   A plot of costs against past activity levels; sometimes used as a rough guide for cost estimation. (10)

Sensitivity Analysis   The study of the effect of changes in assumptions on the results of a decision model. (11, 17)

Serial Correlation   In regression, the condition of a systematic relationship between the residuals in the equation. Sometimes referred to as autocorrelation. (10)

Service Department   An organizational subunit whose main job is to provide services to other subunits in the organization. (4, 5)

Service Organizations   Organizations whose output product is a result of the performance of some activity rather than some physical product.

Shadow Price   Opportunity cost of an additional unity in a constrained multiple product setting. (13)

Short Run   Period of time over which capacity will be unchanged. (11, 12)

Sigma   The number of standard deviations that a given observation is from the mean. (25)

Simplex Method   Solution of a linear programming problem using a mathematical technique. (13)

Simulation   A method of studying problems whereby a model of a system or operational process is subjected to a series of assumptions and variations in an effort to find one or more acceptable solutions. (24)

Simultaneous Solution Method   The method of service department cost allocation that recognizes all services provided by any service department, including services provided to other service departments. (5)

Slope of Cost Line   The angle of a line to the horizontal axis. In cost estimation, the slope is usually considered the variable cost estimate. (10)

Source Document   A basic record in accounting that initiates the entry of an activity in the accounting system. (7)

Special Order   An order that will not affect other sales and is usually a short-run occurrence. (12)

Spending Variance   A variance caused by a difference between actual and estimated manufacturing costs. (7, 19)

Split-off Point   Stage of processing where two or more products are separated. (6)

Spoilage   Goods that are damaged, do not meet specifications, or are otherwise not suitable for further processing or sale as good output. (8)

Staff   A corporate group or employee with specialized technical skills, such as accounting or legal staff. (1)

Standard Cost   The anticipated cost of producing and/or selling a unit of output. (19)

Standard Cost Center   An organization subunit where managers are held responsible for costs and where the relationship between costs and output is well defined. (22)

Standard Cost System   An accounting system in which products are costed using standard costs instead of actual costs. (20)

Standard Costing   A method of accounting whereby costs are assigned to cost objects at predetermined amounts. (19, 20, 21)

Standard Deviation   A measure of risk based on the dispersion in a group of numbers. It is computed as the square root of the sum of the squared differences between actual observations and the mean of the data series divided by one less than the number of observations. (24, 25)

Static Budget   Another term for master budget. (17)

Statistical Quality Control   A method for evaluating a repetitive process to determine if the process is out of control. (25)

Step Method   The method of service department cost allocation that recognizes some interservice department services. (5)

Stockout   Running out of inventory. (14)

Strategic Long-Range Plan   Statement detailing specific steps to be taken in achieving a company's organizational goals. (17)

Sunk Cost   An expenditure made in the past that cannot be changed by present or future decisions. (2, 12)

Tax Basis   Remaining tax depreciable "book value" of an asset for tax purposes. (15)

Tax Credit Recapture   Recapture of investment tax credit taken on an asset if the asset is taken out of service before the time required to earn the investment tax credit.

Tax Shield   The reduction in tax payment because of depreciation deducted for tax purposes. (15, 16)

Time Value of Money   The concept that cash received earlier is worth more than cash received later. (15)

Total Manufacturing Costs   Total costs charged to work in process in a given period. (3)

Total Cost Variance   Difference between total actual costs for the time period and the standard allowed per unit times the number of good units produced. (19)

Transfer Price   The price at which goods or services are traded between organization subunits. (23)

Transferred-in Costs   An alternative term for prior department costs. (3)

Transportation-in Costs   The costs incurred by the buyer of goods to ship those goods from the place of sale to the place where the buyer can use the goods. (3)

Treasurer   The corporate officer responsible for cash management and financing corporate activities. (1)

Trend Analysis   Method of forecasting which ranges from simple visual extrapolation of points on a graph to highly sophisticated computerized time series analysis. (17)

Underapplied Overhead   The excess of actual overhead over applied overhead in a period. (7)

Unfavorable Variances   Variances that, taken alone, reduce the operating profit or net income. (18)

Upper Control Limit   The maximum value that may be observed and still assume that a process is in control. (25)

Usage Variance   An alternative term for efficiency variance, usually related to materials used. (19)

User Departments   Organization subunits that use the services of service departments. (4, 5)

Value of Information   Value placed on information one could possibly obtain in a decision-making context. (1, 26)

Variable Cost Ratio   Variable costs as a percentage of sales-dollars. (11)

Variable Costing   A system of accounting for cost that only assigns products with the variable cost of manufacturing. (2, 9)

Variable Costs   Costs that change with a change in volume of activity. (2, 9, 10, 11, 12, 18, 19)

Variance Investigation   The expected step taken if managers judge that the benefits of correction exceed the costs of follow-up. (19, 25)

Variances   Differences between planned results and actual outcomes. (18, 19, 20, 21)

Weighted-Average Contribution Margin   The contribution margin of all a company's products when a constant product mix is assumed. (11)

Weighted-Average Costing   The inventory method that combines costs and equivalent units of a period with the costs and equivalent units in beginning inventory for product-costing purposes. (8)

Working Capital   Cash, accounts receivable, and other short-term assets required to maintain an activity. (15)

Working Inventory   Units kept on hand in the normal course of operation. (14)

Work in Process   Uncompleted work on the production line. (2, 3)

X-Terms   The terms on the right-hand side of a regression equation, sometimes called the predictors of the independent variables. (10)

Y-Term   The dependent variable in a regression equation. In a cost context, it is the cost being estimated from the X-terms. (10)

Zero-Base Budgeting   A system of establishing financial plans beginning with an assumption of no activity and justifying each program or activity level. (18)

INDEX